EIGHTH EDITION

THE ORGANIZATIONAL BEHAVIOR READER

Edited by:

Joyce S. Osland

San Jose State University

Marlene E. Turner

San Jose State University

David A. Kolb

Case Western Reserve University

Irwin M. Rubin

Temenos, Inc.

Upper Saddle River, New Jersey 07458

Library of Congress Cataloging-in-Publication Data

The organizational behavior reader / edited by Joyce S. Osland, Marlene E. Turner.—8th ed.
p.cm.
Includes bibliographical references.
ISBN 0-13-144150-7 (alk. paper)
1. Psychology, Industrial. 2. Organizational behavior. I. Osland, Joyce. II. Turner, Marlene E.
HF5548.8.K552 2006
158.7—dc22

2005058689

Senior Acquisitions Editor: Jennifer Simon
VP/Editorial Director: Jeff Shelstad
Product Development Manager: Ashley Santora
Assistant Editor: Rich Gomes
Editorial Assistant: Denise Vaughn
Marketing Manager: Anke Braun
Managing Editor, Production: Renata Butera
Production Editor: Kelly Warsak
Permissions Coordinator: Charles Morris
Manufacturing Buyer: Diane Peirano
Manager, Multimedia Production/Design: Christy Mahon
Cover Design: Bruce Kenselaar
Cover Illustration: Getty Images
Composition: Integra Software Services, Inc.
Full-Service Project Management: Stefania Magaldi/Preparé, Inc.
Printer/Binder: Courier-Stoughton
Typeface: 10/12 Times

Credits and acknowledgments borrowed from other sources and reproduced, with permission, in this textbook appear on appropriate page within text.

Pearson Education LTD.
Pearson Education Singapore, Pte. Ltd
Pearson Education, Canada, Ltd
Pearson Education—Japan
Pearson Education Australia PTY, Limited
Pearson Education North Asia Ltd
Pearson Educación de Mexico, S.A. de C.V.
Pearson Education Malaysia, Pte. Ltd.

10 9
ISBN: 0-13-144150-7

CONTENTS

PREFACE

This book is a primer on human behavior in organizations for students of management at three different levels—undergraduate, graduate, and executive education. Our goal in this volume is to prepare employees and managers to diagnose and understand organizational issues so they can be more effective. The reader includes writings by both scholars and practitioners. It begins by setting the stage for global business, followed by topics that fall into four key areas of organizational behavior: "Understanding Yourself and Other People at Work," "Creating Effective Work Groups," "Leadership and Management," and "Managing Effective Organizations." This edition contains basic ideas and concepts, new research findings and practical applications, as well as emerging perspectives that suggest the future shape of the field. In contrast with previous editions, there is more emphasis on virtual and multicultural teams, trust, dealing with difficult people, ethics, mergers, and, in particular, the cultural issues that impact global business. There are three new chapters in this edition: Setting the Global Stage, Decoding Human Behavior, and Managing Creativity.

Our aim was to compile an exciting collection of significant, theoretical, and practical work that is both reader friendly and topical. We have read hundreds of articles to find "just the right ones," which can be classified in one or more of the following categories:

1. Classic, groundbreaking articles that, although written years ago, still provide the definitive treatment of a subject and deserve to be read in the scholar's original words.
2. Lucid overviews of research findings and theories on a particular topic.
3. Descriptions of cutting-edge research.
4. Practical guides for managers based on research findings.

Each chapter has a brief introduction to give readers some contextual background and provide a glimpse of what they can expect. This book is designed to be used with the textbook *Organizational Behavior: An Experiential Approach,* Eighth Edition, by Osland, Turner, Kolb, and Irwin. The articles contained herein form a complete package with the exercises and theory presented in the workbook, allowing the student to go through all the phases of the experiential learning process. Although designed as a companion volume, the Reader stands on its own and should be useful to teachers, managers, and consultants for the breadth of viewpoints and the wealth of data that it provides about the field of organizational behavior.

This is the first edition of the Reader that is co-edited with Marlene Turner. We are grateful for her able assistance on this project and delighted to have her on board.

When it comes to acknowledging contributions to this edition, we would like to first thank Pamela Wells, research assistant extraordinaire. Many colleagues gave us advice or help: Nancy Adler, Janet Bennett, Allan Bird, Richard Boyatzis, Barbara Deane, Bruce Drake, Carol Fox, Robert Hayles, Martin Gannon, Gary Oddou, Asbjorn Osland, Anthony Pratkanis, and Stephen Weiss. We owe a special debt of gratitude to the authors who responded to our pleas for tailor-made pieces for the book: Cristina Gibson, Roy Lubit, and Richard Neilsen. We are deeply grateful to Nicole Campbell, Prabha Chandrasekar, Alicia Escalante, Toby Matoush, Ethan Miller, Jodi Sanders, Barbara Somers, and especially Abdel El-Shaieb at San Jose State for their cheerful, unwavering support. The reviewers of the previous edition were extremely helpful and thorough: Anne Harper—Humber College, Cathleen McGrath—Loyola Marymount University, T. Roger Manley—Florida Institute of Technology, Thomas A. Timmerman—Tennessee Technological University, and Brenda Edwards—Wichita State University. Carol Henson set aside her own work to devote painstaking hours to proof galleys. It was a pleasure, as always, to work with the Prentice Hall crew—Richard Gomes, Jennifer Simon, Judy Leale, Anke Braun, Renata Butera, and Kelly Warsak—and with Stefania Magaldi at Preparé Inc.

An effort like this is never completed without numerous family sacrifices and favors for which no words of gratitude are ever adequate—our heartfelt thanks to Asbjorn, Jessica, Michael, Katrina, Ellie, Joe, Zoe, and Anna and to Anthony and Tony.

Joyce S. Osland
Marlene E. Turner

INTRODUCTION
SETTING THE GLOBAL STAGE

BROADENING THE DEBATE: THE PROS AND CONS OF GLOBALIZATION

Joyce S. Osland

CULTURAL CONSTRAINTS IN MANAGEMENT THEORIES

Geert Hofstede

Although some companies are slower than others to develop a global mind-set and adopt a global business strategy, we all operate, either passively or proactively, in a global economy. This necessitates a broader understanding of the world—in terms of macro issues like international trade and politics and in terms of micro issues such as the cultural differences we observe in an increasingly multicultural workplace.

The first article, "Broadening the Debate: The Pros and Cons of Globalization," takes a macro systems view of globalization. Joyce Osland, who specializes in international management and has worked overseas for 14 years, reviewed the empirical research on the globalization controversy to move beyond the ideological arguments that often cloud this issue. She found that much of the controversy stems from how broadly or narrowly the debate iself is framed. To help businesspeople and professors understand the context in which they work as well as the different views on globalization, Osland identifies the major "bones of contention" and the pros and cons that researchers have identified.

The second article has a more behavioral focus that also relates to global business. It is written by Geert Hofstede, an internationally famous scholar whose groundbreaking study of IBM employees has been a major influence on the field of international management since 1980. In "Cultural Constraints in Management Theories," Hofstede notes that *management* is conceptualized differently around the world. He warns that theories of management reflect cultural values and cannot, therefore, be applied in other countries. Most of the theories in this book have Western, or North American, roots. Therefore, Hostede's caveat is important to bear in mind, although some of the country comparisons in this classic article may seem outdated. We encourage readers to discuss whether the Reader articles seem infected or constrained by a cultural bias. Hofstede is best known for identifying five cultural dimensions that explain differences in national culture and business practices.

BROADENING THE DEBATE: THE PROS AND CONS OF GLOBALIZATION*

Joyce S. Osland

The roots of globalization began to take hold in the 15th century with voyages by intrepid explorers who were funded by European monarchs seeking new trade routes. It continued throughout the years of the imperial expansion of Europe and the colonization of other lands primarily for the purpose of trade. In the mercantilist era, trading companies (such as the Hudson Bay Company and the East India Tea Company) served as surrogate colonial governments, merging trade and government. Later, trading companies were privatized, and intercontinental railways and transoceanic steamships made it possible to open previously protected markets. The global markets present in the early 20th century were disrupted by both world wars. After World War II, the World Bank and the International Monetary Fund (IMF) were founded to aid development in war-ravaged countries and lesser developed countries (LDCs). The English term *globalization* first made its appearance around 1960 (Waters, 1995). In 1995, the World Trade Organization (WTO) was created as a successor to the General Agreement on Tariffs and Trade (GATT) "to help trade flow smoothly, freely, fairly and predictably" (World, 2003, p. 3).[1] In recent years, many nations have liberalized their trade policies—removing trade barriers and focusing on exports—which further stimulated globalization.

The level of global trade increased 14-fold in the period from 1950 to 1997 (World, 2003, p. 2). In addition to increased volume, beginning in the 1970s and 1980s, a shift to foreign direct investment and technology characterized globalization. Recent growth in globalization has been facilitated and driven by rapid improvements in international transportation, technology, and telecommunications (Wood, 1995). The Internet opened up service markets that were previously protected by geographical distance (Valaskakis, 1998). Today, cross-border capital flows are more important than trade flows, and some multinational enterprises (MNEs) now have budgets larger than the economies of many countries. Kobrin (1997), however, argued that foreign trade and investment are less important drivers of globalization than are increasing technological scale, interfirm alliances, and information flows.

Many businesspeople and, judging by the international business literature, many business scholars accept globalization as a fait accompli whose presence and benefits are largely unquestioned. In other circles, however, globalization has become a controversial topic, as first evidenced by labor protests in Korea and France, student riots in Indonesia, and the anti–World Trade Organization demonstrations in Seattle. A small but growing number of respected economists, sociologists, and political scientists criticize globalization and warn that protesters must be taken seriously to avoid dire consequences (Press, 2002, p. 12). Antiglobalization protests have become a familiar part of the social landscape, and there is little reason to suppose they will simply disappear. Furthermore, the issue is still fairly polarized with fervent free traders on one end of the continuum and radical protesters on the other. Polarization that prohibits room for dialogue seldom leads to lasting solutions, particularly in the case of complex issues. Therefore, this article

*Reprinted with permission from the *Journal of Management Inquiry*, 12(2), June 2003 (Thousand Oaks: Sage): 137–154. Special thanks to Kathy Dhanda and Kristi Yuthas.

is an attempt to help business practitioners, scholars, and students better understand the complexity of the issue and to challenge readers to think about win-win solutions benefiting more stakeholders.

The globalization debate continuum is anchored by these views: Proponents generally view globalization as an opportunity for economic growth and prosperity, whereas opponents perceive it as a threat to prosperity, political sovereignty, cultural integrity, and the environment. In developed countries, the primary concerns are the potential job loss for workers and the risk to contracting industries; developing countries worry about political sovereignty and losing control of their economies (Champlin and Olson, 1999). The burgeoning literature on globalization includes so many impassioned ideological arguments for or against it that a reader's first concern is to ascertain the potential bias of the author.[2] Many of these arguments lack empirical support. To complicate matters further, some of the existing economic research findings are highly contradictory. Much of the academic literature seems to fall primarily into pro and con categories. A recent review of the social science literature on globalization categorized it in terms of Hirschman's (1982) metaphor as either civilizing (positive), destructive (negative), or feeble (having no significant impact) and concluded that the feeble category was the least compelling (Guillén, 2001).

Disagreement over the definition of globalization impedes the debate. As Champlin and Olson (1999) noted, the debate cannot be resolved, not because we lack the definitive econometric analysis but because the debate is defined or framed in different ways. Is it simply an argument about the virtues of free markets and supply and demand, or does it include the broader sociocultural and environmental impact? Robert Reich described globalization as one of those concepts "that has passed from obscurity to meaninglessness without ever having an intervening period of coherence" (Duin, 2000, p. B-1). This meaninglessness can be traced to its usage as an "all-purpose catchword in public and scholarly debate" (Lechner and Boli, 2000, p. 1) with different connotations for different parties who support or oppose globalization.

Some definitions of globalization focus solely on cross-border trade—for example, globalization as the absence of borders and barriers to trade between nations (Ohmae, 1995). The International Monetary Fund describes globalization as "the growing economic interdependence of countries worldwide through the increasing volume and variety of cross-border transactions in goods and services and of international capital flows, and also through the more rapid and widespread diffusion of technology" (International, 1999, p. 45). Although these definitions convey a sense of dynamic change and boundarylessness, they portray the outcomes of globalization too narrowly. Brown (1992) and Renesch (1992) defined globalization as the interconnections between the overlapping interests of business and society, a definition that acknowledges the broader context in which globalization takes place. To ensure a systems view, globalization is defined here as a process leading to greater economic interdependence and networks and the economic, political, social, cultural, and environmental results of that process. There is plentiful, if sometimes contradictory, research on the financial and economic aspects of globalization; the broader impact of these phenomena, however, has received less attention by business scholars.

This article intends to make three contributions to the existing debate and literature: (a) expand the boundaries of the debate by examining the impact of globalization on other areas in the broader system; (b) provide a balanced, objective analysis of the benefits and liabilities of globalization based on scientific research rather than on rhetoric; and (c) offer a description of the more common stakeholder perspectives in the debate. The emprical data on the impact of globalization indicate that it is an uneven process yielding mixed results. Therefore, most of the findings in this article are presented in terms of trade-offs, highlighting both the positive and negative effects of globalization in the areas most affected: equality, labor, govenment, culture and community, and the environment.

THE IMPACT OF GLOBALIZATION ON EQUALITY

On the positive side of the ledger, globalization has resulted in increased access to more goods for consumers in many countries (Evenett, 1999), reduced prices due to competition with local monopolies, and increased food supply due to industrial agriculture in some countries (Mander and Goldsmith, 1996). Poor people in some countries have been able to buy cheaper imported goods rather than shoddy goods produced by local monopolies (Graham and Krugman, 1991). A recent study by the London-based Center for Economic Policy Research reports that globalization increased economic growth and improved the incomes of both rich and poor people. The researchers claim that the number of people living in poverty today would be even greater without globalization (Gaunt, 2002).

A look at the statistics on equality indicates that globalization has resulted in both winners and losers, which is supported by Lee's (1996) economic analysis of income levels. According to one expert estimate,[3] 30–40% of the world population has benefited from globalization, whereas the rest has not (Valaskakis, 1998). Globalization is blamed for increasing the chasm between new groups of haves and have-nots—between the well educated and the poorly educated, between the technologically skilled and the unskilled, and between those living in countries that compete successfully in the global economy and those who do not (Frank and Cook, 1995; Pritchett, 1997; United Nations Development, 1999). Globalization has resulted in more jobs in developing countries, creating another group of winners depending on the level of wages they receive. There have been examples of spectacular development, like the Asian Tigers (Singapore, Taiwan, Hong Kong, and South Korea), as well as examples of countries that are marginalized from the global economy, such as sub-Saharan Africa. Some developing countries have suffered job losses in local industries that could not compete with foreign multinationals once formerly protected markets were opened (Lee, 1996). Some critics believe that the structure of the global economy favors developed countries over lesser developed countries.

Amidst the occasionally contradictory economic findings, one piece of incontrovertible evidence stands out. There is more inequality among and within countries today than in the past. Between 1870 and 1990, the gap in per capita income between rich and developing countries has grown fivefold (Temple, 1999). The gap between the richest and poorest 20% of the world population has widened significantly since 1960, when the income ratio of the richest to the poorest was 30:1, to 82:1 in 1995 (United Nations Development, 1996). There are 1.2 billion people living on less than $1 a day (United Nations Development, 2001), a figure that is increasing rather than diminishing. The richest 20% of the world's population receives 86% of the world's

GDP, 82% of the export trade, and 68% of foreign direct investment; the lowest 20% receives only 1% of each (United Nations Development, 1999). A total of 358 people own as much wealth as 2.5 billion people own together—nearly half the world's population (United Nations Development, 1996). The global income of the poorest 20% of the world dropped from 2.3% to 1.4% of world GDP between 1989 and 1998 (Giddens, 2000). In virtually all developed countries, the gaps between skilled and unskilled workers in wages and/or unemployment rates have widened (Gottschalk and Smeeding, 1997; Murphy and Topel, 1997; Organization, 1997).

The notable exceptions—countries or commonwealths that have significantly reduced the gap since 1960—include South Korea, Taiwan, Singapore, Ireland, and Puerto Rico. In the East Asian economies, trade liberalization contributed to reduced wage inequality accompanied by rapid economic growth (Lee, 1996). In Latin America, however, wage inequality increased following liberalization, meaning that skilled workers benefited disproportionately (Berry, 1996; Robbins, 1995; see also United Nations Conference, 1997; Wood, 1997).

Given its egalitarian roots and the historic propensity of most U.S. citizens to consider themselves middle class, it is surprising to discover that nowhere is the inequality between the rich and the poor as great as in the United States (Longworth, 1999). The worth of the average hourly wage is 12% lower than it was in 1973 (Longworth, 1999), whereas the average pay for a U.S. CEO is 200 times higher, $7.4 million in 2002 (almost half the 2000 average) (Lavelle, Jespersen, Ante, and Kerstetter, 2003). The after-tax income of the richest 1% of U.S. households increased 72% from 1977 to 1994, whereas that of the poorest 20% of U.S. households decreased by 16% (Scott, Lee, and Schmidt, 1997). As in other countries, some parts of the United States have prospered from globalization, whereas other regions struggle to keep up.

The Silicon Valley, for example, benefited from globalization until the recent economic downturn; since 2001, employment has decreased 20% (Joint Venture, 2003). Previously, developed countries were concerned about losing blue-collar jobs, but the next wave of globalization is shifting white-collar jobs—highly trained knowledge workers and service jobs—off-shore to less expensive labor markets in Asia, Latin America, and Eastern Europe (Engardio, Bernstein, and Kripalani, 2003).

Researchers agree that the gap between rich and poor has widened; they disagree, however, on whether globalization has caused the gap by influencing wages. Although U.S. wages rose only 5.5% between 1979 and 1993, some economists claim that this is not the fault of globalization because international trade and investment have had little impact (Lawrence, 1995; Sachs and Schatz, 1994). Estimated shifts in product market demand, including the impact of imports, account for less than 10% of the increase in wage differential (Slaughter and Swagel, 2000). Other economists attribute labor inequalities to technological changes (Lawrence and Slaughter, 1993; Organization, 1997) rather than to globalization. Another contingent of scholars, however, points to globalization as the cause of inequality (Learner, 1998; Rodrik, 1997; Wood, 1994). More recent research by Wood (1998) indicated a causal relationship between globalization and the increased demand for skilled rather than unskilled workers in developed countries. Furthermore, Zhao's research (1998) found that foreign direct investments adversely affect union wages and employment. Baldwin and Martin (1999) summarized the empirical literature, writing that virtually all studies found some effect of trade on the labor market in both the

TABLE 1 The Impact of Globalization on Equality

Positive Effects	*Negative Effects*
Income increased globally for both rich and poor, decreasing poverty	Greater chasm between haves and have-nots on individual and country levels
Increased wages for the well educated	Some downward pressure on wages for the poorly educated
Increased wages for technologically skilled	Some downward pressure on wages for technologically unskilled
Improved economic conditions in countries and regions that successfully compete in the global economy	Worsened economic conditions in countries marginalized from the global economy and in certain regions of developed countries
Rich have become richer	Poor have become poorer
Increased access to more goods	
Reduced prices due to competition with local monopolies	
Increased food supply in some countries	

United States and Europe; the findings ranged, however, from almost 0% to 100% with a consensus range of perhaps 10–20% (p. 21).

Although globalization may not be the only factor involved in growing social inequality, it does seem safe to conclude that it has produced winners and losers on both the individual and country levels. The increasing gap between the haves and the have-nots raises the question of fairness. Intense debates over the fairness of the competitive advantages held by various countries are fought out at World Trade Organization meetings and trade negotiations. Increasingly, there are expressions of concern about the threat to political stability, because historically large, apparently insurmountable gaps between rich and poor have been a factor in revolutions (Marquand, 1998). In the opinion of Anthony Giddens (2000), sociologist and director of the London School of Economics, "Along with ecological risk, expanding inequality is the most serious problem facing world society" (p. 34).

The positive and negative effects that globalization has on equality and wages appear in Table 1.

THE IMPACT OF GLOBALIZATION ON LABOR CONDITIONS

Closely related to equality and wages, labor conditions is another area influenced by globalization. On the positive side, some workers in lesser developed countries have received more education and training from multinational companies due to globalization. Furthermore, there is some evidence that increased competition has resulted in upgrading educational systems to produce a more highly qualified workforce (Mander and Goldsmith, 1996; Schmidheiny, 1992).

The threat of job displacement is one of the most tangible concerns that critics have regarding globalization. Workers have more employment opportunities in some countries, but they have less in others where certain industries and firms (e.g., the import sector and small farmers) have been put out of business by global competition

(Mander and Goldsmith, 1996). Daly (1996) noted that some people have less choice about how they make their living as a result of globalization. Increasing imports from low-wage countries are perceived by some as a threat to manufacturing jobs in industrialized countries, particularly in labor-intensive sectors (Wood, 1994).

The labor movement and human rights advocates argue that globalization has had a negative effect on labor standards and that it threatens hard-won improvements in labor conditions. They warn about the *race to the bottom*, which assumes that competition will drive labor standards (and also environmental standards) to the lowest common denominator. Rodrik (1997) found evidence of negative impact on labor conditions, but Drezner (2000) insisted that the race to the bottom is merely a myth used as a scare tactic by both multinational enterprises and activists. For example, Drezner (2000) cited a 1996 Organization for Economic Cooperation and Development (OECD) study that found a positive correlation between "successfully sustained trade reforms" and improved core labor standards because multinationals tend to pay higher than average wages to attract better workers in developing countries (p. 65). Furthermore, the majority of global foreign direct investment (FDI) went to developed countries, which generally boast higher labor standards, during the 1990s (68.9% in 1992, 63.4% in 1995, and 71.5% in 1998), according to the United Nations Conference on Trade and Development (UNCTAD) (1992, 1995, 1998). There is no evidence that multinational enterprises choose to locate in countries where labor and environmental standards are absent or less stringent; other factors like stability, infrastructure, and the size of potential markets play stronger roles in strategic decisions.

Globalization critics, however, worry about the dynamics that occur when firms in developed nations with high wages transfer their manufacturing or processing operations to low-cost, lesser developed countries. Such transfers can be advantageous for the lesser developed countries, the recipients of new jobs, and the firms. When LDCs compete against one another to attract foreign employers to free trade zones or export processing zones (EPZs), however, critics fear this will degrade labor conditions.[4] Multinational enterprises are wooed with the lure of tax-free status for a set number of years, with facilities and infrastructure, and, in some countries, with exemptions from adhering to the national labor code. Five of the 11 nations examined in a U.S. Department of Labor study restricted their citizens' labor rights in export processing zones by allowing foreign firms to ignore national labor laws that were enforced elsewhere in the country (Charnovitz, 1992), which supports the race to the bottom argument. According to some sources, export processing zone workers are often temporary workers who are fired and rehired as needed to avoid having to provide them with benefits or career paths. When zone workers complain about working conditions, they may be fired (Klein, 2000).

The exploitative practices most commonly cited in export processing zones and outsourced factories are child labor, hazardous and unhealthy working conditions, absence of collective bargaining, repression of labor unions (Lawrence, Rodrik, and Whalley, 1996), and forced overtime (Klein, 2000). Labor union advocates and others fear that "exploitative practices in low-wage exporting countries artificially depress labor costs, leading to unfair competitive advantage in world markets and a downward pressure on labor standards in rich countries" (Lawrence et al., 1996, p. 12). There is some evidence that globalization has caused downward pressure on wages

(Lawrence, 1995) as well as on pensions and benefits (Krishnan, 1996; Sutherland, 1998) and has diminished the power of unions (Levi, 2000). Other economists argue that globalization has had very little negative impact on labor conditions and wages (Krugman, 1994).

The form of ownership and the transitory nature of many overseas factories have resulted in a different form of social contract between employer and employee. The reliance of some multinational enterprises on local subcontractors who run their factories means that workers do not "belong" to the company. This arm's-length relationship facilitates the closure of factories when labor costs rise prohibitively and another country becomes more attractive. In these cases, the social contract between employer and employee is limited to the simplest, most expedient transaction—pay for work, which is a stripped-down version of the social contract that exists in most developed countries (albeit with the exception of temporary workers). There have been instances of unscrupulous foreign factory operators in export processing zones who have closed down and fled the country without any warning or termination pay to employees.

Moving jobs offshore also affects the social contract that firms have with domestic employees. Boeing's engineers' union threatened to strike in December 2002 if the company didn't decrease the number of engineers working in the firm's Russian facility. The union's concerns were job loss and the potential danger of sharing technology; management's interests were significantly lower wages for engineers ($5,400 yearly) and entry into the Russian market (Holmes and Ostrovsky, 2003). Such disparate goals do not fit the preexisting social contract.

The onset of globalization served as a trigger event in some companies—a wake-up call that people must work more efficiently and more intelligently, which resulted in increased productivity (Evenett, 1999). The threat of globalization has, however, also been held over workers' heads. According to Longworth (1999),

> *The rhetoric is probably a more potent force than globalization itself. An employer doesn't have to move jobs to Asia to persuade those left behind to take pay cuts. The mere possibility that, in this global age, he can do it is enough. (p. 10)*

Interestingly, other aspects of globalization—worldwide telecommunications and the Internet—have contributed to calls for basic labor standards. The increased publicity and communications about poor working conditions in other countries, which is known as the *CNN effect*, has resulted in greater pressure from human rights groups and labor unions (Lawrence et al., 1996). The threat of Internet-driven international boycotts of goods made by offending multinationals exerts a counterbalancing force for better labor practices in some cases. Companies that engage in exploitative practices are subject to boycotts, negative publicity, and loss of both goodwill and revenue (Dohrs and Garfunkel, 1999). Widespread criticism from consumers and protesters induced some MNEs like Nike to demand that their subcontractors provide better working conditions in overseas factories. To avoid bad publicity, firms like Nike, Mattel, and Levi Strauss have established guidelines and invited monitors to inspect their operations.

In sum, there is both positive and negative evidence concerning the impact of globalization on labor conditions, as shown in Table 2.

TABLE 2 The Impact of Globalization on Labor Conditions

Positive Effects	*Negative Effects*
Increased job opportunities in some countries	Certain industries and companies were forced out of business
Upgraded educational system and more training in some countries	Job displacement affected some individuals
Increased labor standards or no change due to globalization*	Decreased labor standards*
Increased labor productivity	Caused downward pressure on benefits and pensions
CNN effect pressures firms to correct labor abuses	Decreased power of unions
Some firms taking proactive steps to avoid labor abuses	Child labor, unhealthy work conditions, and forced overtime in export processing zones (EPZs)
	Diminished social contract between employer and employee

*Contradictory findings

THE IMPACT OF GLOBALIZATION ON GOVERNMENTS

The key question regarding globalization and governments is whether or not globalization threatens national sovereignty. Historically, governments played a major role in promoting their country's economic development and managing its economy, albeit in quite varied forms. Today, however, some critics argue that government matters less and less in a global economy. Nation-states are simply other actors on the global stage rather than its directors. Aggressive global production systems and capital markets now occupy the "commanding heights" of global development, forcing governments on the defensive and pressuring them to deregulate, downsize, and privatize many of the social management functions they assumed during the past century (Yergin and Stanislaw, 2000). The political boundaries that define nation-states place them at a disadvantage when confronting the unique pressures of a boundaryless global economy. There is a "jurisdictional asymmetry" between an economic system composed of centrally controlled, transnational MNEs on one hand and a political system structured into geographically defined sovereign states on the other (Kobrin, 2001b). Yergin and Stanislaw (2000) argued:

> *Information technology—through computers—is creating a "woven world" by promoting communication, coordination, integration, and contact at a pace and scale of change that far outrun the ability of any government to manage. The accelerating connections make national borders increasingly porous—and, in terms of some forms of control, increasingly irrelevant. (p. 215)*

The growing power of globalized financial markets limits the scope of national policy (Lee, 1996). Because the world has become so interdependent and networked, nation-states are criticized if the "playing field" for business is not level, which limits the degree of freedom in their decision making. This brings us to the key question: "Who governs MNEs and a global economy?" "The market" is not a satisfactory answer for globalization critics and some governments, and the sense that globalization is out of control creates a feeling of powerlessness and resentment in protesters. Nation-states are not designed to govern MNEs, but the idea of yielding their power to international governing bodies is perceived by some countries as yet another threat to national sovereignty (Longworth, 1999).

On the positive side of the ledger, for some governments, globalization has resulted in expanded infrastructure, more jobs, and more economic development for their citizenry. Certain countries have benefited from the transfer of modern, more effective management techniques to their business sector. Furthermore, some observers believe that the increased interdependence of trading and investment partners will draw countries closer together and serve as a deterrent against war (Harris and Goodwin, 1995; Tyson, 1999).

On the negative side, MNEs have exerted pressure on governments in several ways. International competitiveness has influenced public policy in some countries by encouraging government officials to lower labor standards (Lee, 1997). Because governments may view themselves in competition with others in a race to the bottom to attract MNEs to their country, foreign firms can have the upper hand in negotiations unless governments have something unique to offer (such as rare natural resources, highly trained people, and a large consumer market). Singapore, for example, invested heavily in education, attracting high-tech and professional industry rather than limiting its population to employment in low-wage factories.

George Soros (2002) criticized globalization for making the provision of private goods more important than public goods such as peace, the eradication of poverty, the protection of human and labor rights, and the environment. Governments of developed countries with extensive entitlement programs—social security systems, health-care programs, and unemployment pay or welfare systems—are experiencing greater pressure to decrease such expenditures because they raise the rate of corporate taxation (Longworth, 1999). Nevertheless, Lee (1996) concluded that in spite of increasing globalization, national policies still determine levels of employment and labor standards. He warned, however, that there is a worldwide trend toward smaller government, which is evident in public expenditure reductions, lower taxes, less support for redistributive measures, and greater deregulation of markets, including the labor market. Thus, governments are less likely to compensate the losers from globalization at a time when globalization increases the demand for social insurance (Sutherland, 1998). A global economy allows companies (and the wealthiest citizens) to spread their tax liability to countries with the lowest rates and thereby decrease the taxes that national governments receive from formerly "local" companies. Capital mobility weakens the tax base, which means that there are less funds available for social insurance (Sutherland, 1998) in countries that previously received tax payments.

The blueprint for economic development promoted by the International Monetary Fund and World Bank decreased the role of government with calls for privatization, deregulation, and the reduction of corporate, trade, and capital gains taxes (United Nations Conference, 1999; United Nations Development, 1999). Not only did this make some government functions irrelevant, but it also left governments with less money in their coffers. Grunberg (1998) reported that governments have fewer funds available as a result of globalization. The proportion of coporate taxes has decreased as a percentage of the total revenues in the United States, and it has also decreased relative to the share of corporate profits in all of the Organization for Economic Cooperation and

Development countries (Kobrin, 2001a).[5] Hines (1999) found complex reasons for this phenomenon but also found evidence of aggressive tax avoidance behavior by MNEs and a race to the bottom by governments who reduced corporate tax rates to attract investment. Many EPZs grant tax-free status for the first years, but some MNEs shut down operations and leave as soon as the period is over, because they can take advantage of the same tax-free status elsewhere (Klein, 2000). Furthermore, MNEs sometimes influence local government policy and threaten to leave if their demands are not met. In this way, corporations externalize their costs to others.

Globalization makes it more difficult for governments to exercise their regulatory powers (Cox, 1996) and maintain their autonomy and independent decision making (Kobrin, 1997). In a literature review that examined whether globalization undermines the authority of nation-states, Guillén (2001) found mixed results. Some research concludes that MNEs have the upper hand with governments that now have less autonomy, whereas political scientists contend that the role of government has simply changed to include dealing with the problems of globalization. Kobrin (2001b) concluded that governments are not irrelevant, but they have been weakened as a result of globalization; they will continue to play a major role, but instead of exercising supreme authority, a nation may find that its sovereignty comes to mean simply being one of several prominent parties involved in international negotiations.

There is widespread agreement that governments are not designed or structured to deal with the problems of global business (Giddens, 2000), particularly problems like global warming and environmental degradation, that have accompanied economic development (Lechner and Boli, 2000). Partially to fill this gap, a growing number of nongovernmental organizations (NGOs) are trying to counterbalance the power of MNEs (Dohrs and Garfunkel, 1999). Nongovernmental organizations that focus on topics like human rights and environmental issues have organized themselves to exert pressure on MNEs, governments, and international organizations to ensure their agenda is heard. If one looks at globalization solely in terms of power, it has shifted from governments and organized labor to MNEs, markets, and international organizations (Kobrin, 2001a). This shift took place without a democratic vote—a silent coup that rankles protesters (Clarke, 2001). International organizations like the International Monetary Fund, World Bank, and World Trade Organization are not trusted by some factions of the antiglobalization protest movement because of the partiality these organizations show toward corporate interests and powerful governments. Stiglitz (2002), a former senior vice president and chief economist at the World Bank, claims that some of the protesters' complaints about the International Monetary Fund are based in fact—namely, that free-trade agreements primarily benefit the rich, that privatization has not proved successful in many countries, and that the IMF's vaunted structural adjustment programs have resulted in hardship for many.

UN Secretary-General Kofi Annan (1999) gave this warning at Davos:

> *The spread of markets outpaces the ability of societies and their political systems to adjust to them, let alone to guide the course they take. History teaches us that such an imbalance between the economic, social; and political worlds can never be sustained for very long.*

Table 3 summarizes the positive and negative impacts of globalization on governments.

TABLE 3 The Impact of Globalization on Government

Positive Effects	*Negative Effects*
Increased economic development benefits some governments	Power of multinational enterprises (MNEs) increased at the expense of government power, sovereignty, and ability to regulate business
Increased jobs and expanded infrastructure benefit some countries	MNEs externalize some of their costs to countries
Transfer of modern management techniques into business sector	Competition for factories and foreign direct investment (FDI) result in too many concessions to MNEs by some governments
Greater interdependence among trading and investment partners may deter war	Some MNEs influence local government policy and threaten to leave if their demands are not met
Proliferation of non-governmental organizations (NGOs) to counter-balance decreased governmental power	MNEs pay fewer taxes to governments and incorporate where the tax rate is lowest, depriving their own country of revenue
	Governments are pressured to reduce tax rates and decrease social benefits that may affect stability

THE IMPACT OF GLOBALIZATION ON CULTURE AND COMMUNITY

Globalization may be a positive force for greater cross-cultural understanding via more cross-cultural exposure and closer cross-border ties. As Tomlinson (1999) stated,

> *A world of complex connectivity (a global makert place, international fashion codes, an international division of labor, a shared ecosystem) thus links the myriad small everyday actions of millions with the fates of distant, unknown others and even with the possible fate of the planet. (p. 25)*

Tomlinson (1999) referred to the increased connectivity of the world as a double-edged sword that provides new and wider understanding at the same time that it takes away the securities of one's local world.

Critics claim that globalization is creating a monoculture that is rapidly spreading around the world. MTV culture, for instance, offends social conservatives in many countries. By this view, weakened cultural traditions combined with the importation of foreign media, stores, and goods encourage cultural homogenization. Multinational news outlets, like CNN and Rupert Murdoch's News Corporation, provoked the complaint that the "flow of information" (a term that includes both ideas and attitudes) is dominated by multinational entities based in the most powerful nations (MacBride and Roach, 2000, p. 286). Chains like Wal-Mart, with lower prices and extensive, standardized inventory, force uniquely local small stores out of business because consumers prefer the service and prices at Wal-Mart. Monbiot (1995) claimed that the use of

English as the language of business and in the media drives out and threatens minority languages. As transnational corporations grow and become more powerful, there is a concern that the culture of capitalism, which is heavily influenced by Western or U.S. culture and commoditization, will develop into a world monoculture. *Commoditization* is the process by which market capitalism transforms things that were previously not viewed as economic goods (such as human genes) into something with a price. In fact, many aspects of culture have been *commodified* as evidenced in the shopping opportunities incorporated into experiences in which they previously did not exist (Tomlinson, 1999) such as visits to natural wonders or religious ceremonies. Cultures have always influenced one another, often enriching each other in the process, but some observers conclude that cultural synchronization has been occurring at an unprecedented rate and that "never before has one particular cultural pattern been of such global dimensions and so comprehensive" (Hamelink, 1988).

Not all communication experts, however, share this opinion. Some maintain that the media have been decentralizing with the development of regional centers (e.g., Mexico for Spanish television, India for film, and Hong Kong for East Asian film and television) and indigenized programming. Thus, they argue that the homogenizing forces of the media, like satellite television, exist in tension with *heterogenization* (Sinclair, Jacka, and Cunningham, 1996). Tomlinson (1999) agreed with Hamelink that cultural synchronization is an unprecedented feature of global modernity but argued, "Movement between cultural/geographical areas always involves interpretation, translation, mutation, adaptation, and 'indigenisation' as the receiving culture brings its own cultural resources to bear, in dialectical fashion, upon 'cultural imports'" (p. 84). And as Howes (1996) noted,

> *No imported object, Coca-Cola included, is completely immune from creolization. Indeed, one finds that Coke is often attributed with meanings and uses within particular cultures that are different from those imagined by the manufacturer. These include that it can smooth wrinkles (Russia), that it can revive a person from the dead (Haiti), indigenised through being mixed with other drinks, such as rum in the Caribbean to make Cuba Libre or aguardiente in Bolivia to produce Ponche Negro. Finally, it seems that Coke is perceived as a "native product" in many different places—that you will often find people who believe the drink originated in their country not in the United States. (p. 6)*

Pressures for a global monoculture are counterbalanced by greater attention and efforts to maintain ethnic identity. Karliner (2000) argued that globalization may be responsible for the increasing popularity of indigenous movements to maintain ethnic identity. Although globalization was not the only cause of the Islamic revolution in Iran, it provided a target for rebellion and also forced the Muslims to "identify" themselves and determine how they wanted to live in a global society (Lechner and Boli, 2000). Anthropologist Clifford Geertz (1998) wrote that the world is "growing both more global and more divided, more thoroughly interconnected and more intricately partitioned at the same time" (p. 107). Although few social scientists support the creation of a monoculture (Guillén, 2001), this is a common fear among protesters.

Critics claim that globalization has irrevocably changed the social landscape of communities and constitutes a threat to national culture in various ways. For example, transnational agribusiness has replaced family farms in some areas, and cutting down

TABLE 4 The Impact of Globalization on Culture and Community

Positive Effects	*Negative Effects*
Increased cultural exposure, understanding, and ties	More mobility and disruption of rural life away from traditional safety nets
Encouraged proliferation of indigenous organizations and movements to preserve ethnic identity	Increased exposure to cultural homogenization
	Disintegration of some local communities

forests inhabited by indigenous people makes it difficult if not impossible for them to maintain their traditional way of life (Brown, Renner, and Flavin, 1998; Keck and Sikkink, 2000). The spread of newer cultures and technologies may result in the loss of knowledge about traditional practices and arts more compatible with natural systems. EPZs draw people from rural areas, moving them out of reach of their traditional safety nets. It is difficult to pinpoint how much of this migration from their traditional communities and ways of life can be attributed directly to globalization versus traditional economic development and a desire to better one's life. People, particularly men, have been forced to migrate to find work throughout history. In the case of the Mexican maquiladoras (a type of EPZ) along the U.S. border, however, the primary employees are young women, which has had a marked impact on the social structure.

Table 4 summarizes the positive and negative impacts of globalization on culture and community.

THE IMPACT OF GLOBALIZATION ON ENVIRONMENTAL SUSTAINABILITY

Sustainability is defined as meeting the needs of present generations without compromising the ability of future generations to meet their own needs. The moral basis for sustainability is the ethical position that destroying Earth's future capacity to support life is wrong. Global environmental issues such as global warming, deforestation, ozone depletion, reduction of biodiversity, degradation of ocean habitats (Lawrence et al., 1996), and pollution are the key areas affected by globalization.[6] Most of the empirical studies found in a literature review on globalization's impact on the environment, which are summarized below, focused on small pieces of the puzzle—they are "local" in nature due to the difficulty of studying the environment as a whole (Osland, Dhanda, and Yuthas, 2002).

On the positive side of the ledger, globalization has caused some countries to make a narrower range of products more efficiently; in other words, it has given them a comparative advantage. It has been responsible for creating and exporting technologies that use fewer natural resources and result in less waste and pollution.[7] Globalization has facilitated the dissemination of practices like improved energy efficiency, lowered carbon combustion, dematerialization (reducing overall use of materials), substitution of resources with reduced environmental impact, and metal recovery technologies (Allenby and Richards, 1994; Graedel and Allenby, 1995; Socolow, Andrews, Berkhout, and Thomas,

1994). The industrial ecology movement has sought to improve environmental responsiveness at the same time that it reduces the global cost of production for corporations.

On the negative side, because of globalization, harmful technologies and activities have also been exported. Although better technology is available, companies do not always use it because it can be highly capital intensive (Socolow et al., 1994).

Globalization is blamed as a source of pollution. For instance, industrial toxic effluents and pesticide runoffs from agribusiness have destroyed river fish (Khor, 1996). A recent study overseen by the UN Environment Program warns of the danger of the *Asian cloud*, which may be causing premature death, flooding, and drought. Not all of the two-mile-thick cloud is a direct result of increased industrialization and globalization; traditional practices and forest clearing are also responsible in addition to auto emission, factories, and waste incineration.[8] Since prevailing winds can carry pollution clouds around the world in a short period, they are becoming a global environmental problem (United Nations Environment, 2002).

The spread of factories around the world has made more infrastructure necessary, which requires extracted substances from the earth. Globalization promotes the transportation of raw materials and goods using nonrenewable resources. Increased travel by workers seeking jobs (Brown, Renner, and Flavin, 1998) and by MNE employees uses fossil fuel and contributes to global warming. Additionally, because MNEs have moved their operations to countries where environmental laws are absent or not enforced, greater environmental degradation has occurred. Some MNEs have taken advantage of lowered environmental protection to sell harmful products abroad that are banned in more developed countries.

Critics claim that countries are more likely to export more commodities that increase the exploitation of natural resources as a result of globalization (French, 1993). There are numerous examples of environmental degradation such as deforestation, threats to biodiversity, and depletion of fish stocks (French, 1993; Goldsmith, 1997; Wilkes, 1995). Some of these problems stem from inappropriate use or overuse, wheareas others involve inappropriate modern technologies such as modern trawl fishing that scrapes the bottom of the seabed and disturbs breeding grounds (Khor, 1996). Deforestation and technological innovations in agriculture have also resulted in habitat damage and extinction of species (Rackham, 1986).

Wackernagel and Rees (1996) popularized the concept of the *environmental footprint.* They demonstrated that developed countries require greater per capita material and energy flows, and therefore greater land surface, than do developing countries. The per capita effect on the earth's crust is greatest in the wealthiest countries that extract resources at a far greater rate than they can be replaced. The globalization of materially affluent lifestyles promulgated by the media and increased travel intensifies the demand for extracted materials (Duchin, 1996).

A conflict has arisen over the view of many developing countries that it is their turn to develop, as the more advanced developed countries did, without the constraints of environmental regulations. This dilemma pits the principle of equal capacity for economic development against the competing value of environmental sustainability.

The 1992 GATT annual report laid out the argument that increased trade will produce increased incomes, which will then result in more concern about the environment (Lawrence et al., 1996). Environmentalists, however, worry that globalization will encourage greater consumption as more goods are marketed to more people, creating artificial needs and using more natural resources (Mander and Goldsmith, 1996). Although globalization theoretically should result in greater efficiency in production, it has caused more surplus and scarcity (Brown, Renner, and Flavin, 1998), which points to a less than perfect use of resources.

It would be impossible to calculate the total impact of globalization on the environment, but there is a growing body of evidence documenting its harmful effects (Osland et al., 2002). Table 5 summarizes the positive and negative impacts of globalization on environmental sustainability.

TABLE 5 The Impact of Globalization on Environmental Sustainability

Positive Effects	*Negative Effects*
Countries make a narrower range of products more efficiently	Causes surplus and scarcity
Relative efficiency of energy use is improving	Development and increased affluence lead to larger demands for materials and energy as well as increased waste and energy-related pollution
More systematic dematerialization through manufacturing changes	Export of damaging extraction technologies continues despite existence of alternative technologies
Substitution of harmful materials by resources with reduced environmental impact	Spread of factories requires increased infrastructure that uses more extracted materials
Some firms do environmental impact studies of product's entire lifecycle	Increased travel of workers and multinational enterprise employees uses fossil fuel and contributes to global warming
Transfer of efficient technologies to assist developing countries to increase production	Some developing nations are exposed to toxic or dangerous products and technologies
Creation and transfer of more efficient technologies to some countries	Increased consumption uses more natural resources
Use of alternative energy sources decreases carbon combustion	Increased advertising creates artificial needs
Increased income may lead to concern for environmental protection	Increasing fossil fuel combustion emits gases and particles into the atmosphere
	Increased transportation of raw materials uses non-renewable resources
	Increased environmental degradation from factories in countries without enforced environmental protection laws
Modern trawl fishing maximizes the catch for maximum immediate revenue	Degradation due to agribusiness, logging, commercial fishing, and industrial waste
	Deforestation threatens species survival

CONCLUSIONS

The current debate raging on globalization and the explosion of publications on this topic reflect the importance this phenomenon has gained in recent years. When we expand the boundaries of the debate beyond the merits of free trade, a picture emerges of globalization as an uneven process that has resulted in both positive and negative consequences, both winners and losers. Thus, the quick answer to the question "What is the impact of globalization?" is "It's mixed." Globalization is neither a panacea nor an unmitigated plague. Given the complexity and scope of the topic, it is difficult to determine with precision whether some of the problems linked to globalization would exist independently and to what degree. We can conclude, however, that globalization in its current state often involves serious trade-offs such as economic development and jobs at the cost of environmental degradation and weakened labor protection. One important lesson is to include these trade-offs in the debate and in calculating the total cost of global business.

Where people stand with regard to these trade-offs often depends on their values and mind-sets—in particular their beliefs regarding free markets, government intervention, the importance of local versus global concerns, and individualist versus communitarian views about the common good (Gladwin, 2002). Understanding these differences in basic assumptions is the first step in creating a civil discourse on the topic. Although business-people may disagree with antiglobalization protesters' rhetoric or tactics, another key lesson is that some of their criticisms are valid and should be taken into consideration. In Kobrin's (2001a) description of the antiglobalization protest movement, he concluded that their protests may be "the canary in the mine"—the warning signal about globalization and the role of MNEs.

A third lesson is that businesspeople (and academics) should take a systems approach to globalization to avoid problems. Customers and protesters often see more linkages than some firms seem to consider, and many consumers do care about where their purchases come from. For example, the employees of a major company warned top executives about problems in overseas factories that could result in bad publicity. The person in charge ignored the warning, insisting, "These are just contract workers—they aren't really a part of our company." Years later, the company is still dealing with the PR fallout and targeting by protest groups. To the public, the distinction about whose employees they were was both legalistic and irrelevant. To avoid such problems, some MNEs are now entering into dialogue with all their various stakeholders, including non-governmental organizations.

The accounting systems used by governments and businesses discourage a systems perspective. As long as accounting systems fail to take into consideration the environmental and social costs of doing business, firms can "look good" while doing a fair amount of harm to the larger society. Social accounting is admittedly difficult, but its advantages may now outweigh its disadvantages (Sherman, Steingard, and Fitzgibbons, 2002).

As teachers, we need to make sure our students learn about the whole picture of globalization, including its unintended consequences. Yet my examination of international business textbooks yielded virtually no mention of the impact of globalization on the environment. Globalization is one of the most challenging and complex issues humans have ever faced. The way we teach it should reflect its requisite variety—a multidisciplinary focus including all stakeholders, understanding both the abstract as well as the human and environmental impact, teaching a thorough understanding of the pros and cons, and examining the solutions offered to counteract its problems.

Globalization is driven in large part by a mind-set—the belief in the sanctity of markets, which Soros (1998) called "market fundamentalism." Some obvious caveats come to mind, however. First, some economists question whether markets are really "free" (see Stiglitz, 2002, for an alternative view).

Second, once we broaden the globalization debate to include more than economic arguments, it seems obvious that free trade without any regulations or constraints has not been wholly successful (Giddens, 2000). The nations that have prospered under free trade have done so in part because they have laws and institutions that serve as checks and balances. In Giddens's (2000) view,

> *Trade always needs a framework of institutions, as do other forms of economic development. Markets cannot be created by purely economic means, and how far a given economy should be exposed to the world marketplace must depend upon a range of criteria. . . . Opening up a country or regions within it to free trade can undermine a local subsistence economy. An area that becomes dependent upon a few products sold on world markets is very vulnerable to shifts in prices as well as to technological change. (p. 35)*

Business scholars could help identify the criteria that Giddens mentioned and conceptualize globalization as occurring with a broader systemic context. Cookie-cutter approaches to economic development seldom work. Strategies have to fit the local context of each country with its unique institutions and historical, political, and social context.

Third, in addition to a framework of institutions, trade has to be embedded in a broader framework of shared social values that include at least some degree of concern for social justice and the common good.[9] Privatization has been successful in some countries but not where government officials or their cronies bought undervalued state assets and established monopolies. Either the rule of law or shared values is needed to prevent a winner-takes-all mentality. In their absence, perhaps MNEs have to accept that they too have social responsibilities and a broader role to play in society than maximizing shareholder wealth.[10] Concentration solely on economic growth no doubt made sense in an earlier time, but given what is known today about globalization and its impact, our focus should broaden to include a more balanced, integrated approach to economic development (United Nations Development, 2002).

If we needed further convincing that globalization demands a systems view, we might be persuaded by the backlash and counterbalancing forces it has provoked. The protest movements,[11] the growth of nongovernmental organizations, and the movements affirming ethnic identity are all reactions in part to globalization or perhaps an inherent part of globalization. It is more difficult to forecast how the nature of globalization might change in response to these forces. Some observers assume that the current state of globalization is akin to the robber baron era in the United States—a period of excess and abuse that eventually sparked a backlash resulting in policies and laws. Kell and Levin (2002) described globalization as an incomplete experiment in human history with systemic deficiencies that cause instability and social injustice. A consensus of sorts seems to be building around the need to somehow "tame" globalization, but there is no clarity yet about how this will occur, what form it will take, and who has the requisite authority to pull it off.[12]

One interesting response to globalization is the United Nations' Global Compact. This initiative, led by Secretary-General Kofi Annan, consists of a global network of companies, non-governmental organizations, major international labor federations, and several UN agencies. Its objective is to "create a more stable, equitable and inclusive global market by making its nine principles an integral part of business activities everywhere" (United Nations, 2002). These principles, which involve human rights, labor standards, and environmental practices, are an attempt to establish a universal standard.

Principle 1: Support and respect the protection of international human rights within their sphere of influence.
Principle 2: Make sure their own corporations are not complicit in human rights abuses.
Principle 3: Uphold freedom of association and the effective recognition of the right to collective bargaining.
Principle 4: Uphold the elimination of all forms of forced and compulsory labor.
Principle 5: Uphold the effective abolition of child labor.
Principle 6: Uphold the elimination of discrimination in respect of employment and occupation.
Principle 7: Support a precautionary approach to environmental challenges.
Principle 8: Undertake initiatives to promote greater environmental responsibility.
Principle 9: Encourage the development and diffusion of environmentally friendly technologies (United Nations, 2002).

The Global Compact is attempting to build shared values and create a forum for dialogue and institutional learning that will result in social change. In addition to recruiting companies who agree to integrate the nine principles into their business operations, the program's goals are to establish a learning bank that shares lessons on applying the principles, conducts issues dialogues, and generates partnership projects among the different stakeholders. Such partnerships could theoretically decrease the polarization among various groups. The architects of the Global Compact hope that it will be part of the solution to globalization's problems but do not view it as the definitive solution. To date, 700 companies have voluntarily joined the compact.

As stated in the introduction, much of the globalization literature has an ideological bent, which means there is a need for objective research on globalization's impact and for more questioning about the basic assumption of globalization itself. The U.S. acceptance of globalization as the status quo may reflect cultural and historical influences. In his Pulitzer Prize-winning book, *The Global Squeeze*, journalist Richard Longworth (1999) concluded:

> *The global economy is not an act of God, like a virus or a volcano, but the result of economic actions taken by human beings and thus responsive to human control. There is no need to say, as many American economists and businesspeople do, that the market knows best and must be obeyed. This cultural capitalism is confined mostly to the United States and the other English-speaking nations. Other nations, in Europe and in Asia, see the market as the source of both bountiful benefits and lethal damage and are determined to temper this force to their own priorities. (pp. 4–5)*

Given the ever-evolving history of economic development, trade, and international relations, there is little reason for scholars to assume that globalization as we know it today is the final version. Such an assumption is dangerous if it prevents us from seeing other possibilities and the systemic consequences of the current system. Business scholars have made good progress in describing this system and documenting what it takes to be profitable. Now it's time for us to consider what else we can contribute to the debate on globalization and whether we can take a stronger leadership role in influencing the way people think about and practice global business in the future.

Notes

1. The World Trade Organization's major functions are to administer trade agreements, serve as a forum for trade negotiations, settle trade disputes, review national trade policies, and assist developing nations in trade policy issues.
2. Having warned you about the potential biases of globalization writers, it's only fair to explain my own stance and my impetus for writing this article. At the behest of the Northwest Earth Institute, I joined a discussion group on the impact of globalization on the environment and commenced reading. I began with few preconceived notions and with no strong inclination either for or against globalization. If anything, I was positively disposed to creating jobs in lesser developed countries, since I had learned during a previous career in international development that providing employment goes a long way toward solving a variety of social ills for poor people. In the conclusion, I will explain my current position.
3. Simon Valaskakis is Canada's ambassador to the Organization for Economic Cooperation and Development (OECD) in Paris and a professor of economics at the University of Montreal.
4. As of 2002, there were more than 850 export processing zones in the world employing 27 million workers (Drezner, 2000). See International Labour Organization, *Labour and Social Issues Relating to Export Processing Zones* (1998), for information on conditions.
5. The Organization for Economic Cooperation and Development is an international organization that consists of 30 industrialized, market-economy countries. Their representatives meet "to exchange information and harmonize policy with a view to maximizing economic growth within Member countries and assisting non-Member countries develop more rapidly" (Organization, 2003). For more information, see http://www.oecdwash.org/ABOUT/aboutmain.htm.
6. Bioengineering is another controversial topic. Genetic engineering can preserve existing species and create new varieties, but the impact of the latter on biological systems is still unknown. There are also ethical concerns about the ability to patent genetically engineered species and human tissues, cells, and organs.
7. See the United Nations Conference on Environment and Development (1992) for information on the successful transfer of technological innovations. For a more complete analysis of the environmental impact of globalization, see J. Osland, K. Dhanda, and K. Yuthas (2002).
8. The Asian cloud is the result of traditional practices such as wood- and dung-burning stoves, cooking fires, and forest clearing as well as auto emissions, factories, and waste incineration.
9. See John Ruggie's (1982) description of embedded liberalism, which was originally conceptualized as a compromise of multilateral trade and domestic stability.
10. *BusinessWeek* devoted its cover story to "Global Capitalism: Can It Be Made to Work Better?" in its November 6, 2000 issue (Engardio and Belton, 2000). Its conclusions are similar to those found here and acknowledge the need for more social

responsibility on the part of multinationals and a more realistic view of the economic policy that has driven globalization.

11. For an interesting account of this movement, see Kobrin (2001a).

12. Articulating the suggested solutions lies outside the scope of this article, but one starting point is to look at the lessons learned from 50 years of tackling various global problems in Simmons and Oudraat (2001).

References

Allenby, B. R., and Richards, D. (1994). *Greening of Industrial Ecosystems.* Washington, DC: National Academy Press.

Annan, K. (1999, January 31). *Address to Davos World Economic Forum*, Davos, Switzerland.

Baldwin, R. E., and Martin, P. (1999). "*Two Waves of Globalization: Superficial Similarities, Fundamental Differences*" (NBER Working Paper Series 6904). Cambridge, MA: National Bureau of Economic Research.

Berry, A. (1996, January). Distributional Impact of Market-Oriented Reforms, Paper prepared at the Association for Comparative Economic Studies, San Francisco.

Brown, C. R., Renner, M., and Flavin, C. (1998). *Vital Signs.* New York: Norton.

Brown, J. (1992). "Corporation as community: A New Image for a New Era," in J. Renesch (Ed.), *New Traditions in Business* (123–139). San Francisco: Barrett-Kohler.

Champlin, D., and Olson, P. (1999). "The Impact of Globalization on U.S. Labor Markets: Redefining the Debate," *Journal of Economic Issues, 33*(2): 443–451.

Charnovitz, S. (1992, May). "Environmental and Labour Standards in Trade," *The World Economy, 15*(8): 343.

Clarke, T. (2001). "Silent Coup: Confronting the Big Business Takeover of Canada," Retrieved January 12, 2001, from www3.simpatico.ca/tryegrowth/MAI_can.htm

Cox, R. W. (1996). "A Perspective on Globalization," in J. H. Mittelman (Ed.), *Globalization: Critical Reflections* (21–30). Boulder, CO: Lynne Rienner.

Daly, H. (1996). *Beyond Growth.* Boston: Beacon.

Dohrs, L., and Garfunkel, J. (1999, February). *Time to Talk About Trade and Human Rights? Trade and Human Rights: A Pacific Rim Perspective, a Source Handbook.* Seattle, WA: Global Source Education.

Drezner, D. W. (2000, November/December). "Bottom Feeders," *Foreign Policy*: 64–70.

Duchin, F. (1996). "Population Change, Lifestyle, and Technology: How Much Difference Can They Make?" *Population and Development Review, 22*(2): 321–330.

Duin, S. (2000, December 3). "Reich Displays Designer Hips and a Deft Mind," *The Oregonian*: B-1.

Engardio, P., and Belton, C. (2000, November 6). "Global Capitalism: Can It Be Made to Work Better?" *BusinessWeek*: 72–76.

Engardio, P., Bernstein, A., and Kripalani, M. (2003, February 3). "Is Your Job Next?" *BusinessWeek*: 50–60.

Evenett, S. J. (1999). "The World Trading System: The Road Ahead," *Finance and Development, 36*(4): 22.

Frank, R. H., and Cook, P. J. (1995). *The Winner-Takes-All Society.* New York: Free Press.

French, H. (1993). *Costly Tradeoffs: Reconciling Trade and the Environment*, Washington, DC: World Watch Institute.

Gaunt, J. (2002, July 7). "Globalization Has Helped the Poor, Study Says," Reuters.

Geertz, C. (1998). "The World in Pieces: Culture and Politics at the End of the Century," *Focaal: Tigdschrift voor Antropologie, 32*: 91–117.

Giddens, A. (2000). *Runaway World: How Globalization Is Reshaping Our Lives.* New York: Routledge.

Gladwin, T. (2002, March). Keynote address presented at the Western Academy of Management, Santa Fe, New Mexico.

Goldsmith, E. (1997). "Can the Environment Survive the Global Economy?" *The Ecologist, 27*(6): 242–249.

Gottschalk, P., and Smeeding, T. (1997). "Cross-National Comparisons of Earnings and Income Inequality," *Journal of Economic Literature, 35*(2): 633–687.

Graedel, T. E., and Allenby, B. R. (1995). *Industrial Ecology.* New York: Prentice Hall.

Graham, E. M., and Krugman, P. R. (1991). *Foreign Direct Investment in the United States* (2nd ed.). Washington, DC: Institute for International Economics.

Grunberg, I. (1998). "Double Jeopardy: Globalization, Liberalization and the Fiscal Squeeze," *World Development, 26*(4): 591–605.

Guillen, M. F. (2001). "Is Globalization Civilizing, Destructive or Feeble? A Critique of Six Key Debates in the Social Science Literature," *Annual Review of Sociology, 27*: 235–260.

Hamelink, C. J. (1998). *Cultural Autonomy in Global Communications*, New York: Longman.

Harris, J. M., and Goodwin, N. R. (1995). *A Survey of Ecological Economics.* Washington, DC: Island Press.

Hirschman, A. O. (1982, December). "Rival Interpretations of Market Society: Civilizing, Destructive, or Feeble?" *Journal of Economic Literature, 20*, 1463–1484.

Holmes, S., and Ostrovsky, S. (2003, February 3). "The New Cold War at Boeing," *Business Week*: 58–59.

Howes, D. (Ed.). (1996). *Cross-Cultural Consumption: Global Markets, Local Realities.* London: Routledge.

International Labour Organization. (1998). *Labour and Social Issues Relating to Export Processing Zones.* Geneva: Author.

International Monetary Fund. (1999, May). *World Economic Outlook: A Survey by the Staff of the International Monetary Fund.* Washington, DC: Author.

Joint Venture. (2003). *Joint Venture's 2003 Index of Silicon Valley.* San Jose, CA: Author.

Karliner, J. (2000). Grassroots globalization: "Reclaiming the Blue Planet," in F. J. Lechner and J. Boli (Eds.), *The Globalization Reader* (34–38). Oxford: Blackwell.

Keck, M. E., and Sikkink, K. (2000). "Environmental Advocacy Networks," in F. J. Lechner and J. Boli (Eds.), *The Globalization Reader* (392–399). Oxford: Blackwell.

Kell, G., and Levin, D. (2002, August). "The Evolution of the Global Compact Network: An Historic Experiment in Learning and Action". Paper presented at the Academy of Management meeting, Denver, Colorado.

Khor, M. (1996). "Global Economy and the Third World," in J. Mander and J. Goldsmith (Eds.), *The Case Against the Global Economy and for a Turn Toward the Local* (47–59). San Francisco: Sierra Club.

Klein, N. (2000). *No Logo.* New York: Picador.

Kobrin, S. J. (1997). "The Architecture of Globalization: State Sovereignty in a Networked Global Economy," in J. H. Dunning (Ed.), *Governments, globalization, and international business* (146–171). New York: Oxford University Press.

Kobrin, S. J. (2001a, February). "Our resistance Is as Global as Your Oppression: Multinational Corporations, the Protest Movement and the Future of Global Governance". Paper presented at the meeting of the International Studies Association, Chicago.

Kobrin, S. J. (2001b). "Sovereignty @ bay: Globalization, multinational enterprise, and the international political system," in A. Rugman and T. Brewer (Eds.), *The Oxford Handbook of International Business* (181–205). New York: Oxford University Press.

Krishnan, R. (1996). "December 1995: The First Revolt Against Globalization," *Monthly Review, 48*(1): 1–23.

Krugman, P. (1994). "Does Third World Growth Hurt First World Prosperity?" *Harvard Business Review, 72*(4), 113–121.

Lavelle, L., Jespersen, F., Ante, S., and Kerstetter, J. (2003, April 21). "Executive Pay," *Business Week*: 86–90.

Lawrence, R. A. (1995, January). "U.S. wage Trends in the 1980s: The Role of International Factors," *Federal Reserve Bank of New York Economic Policy Review, 2*(1): 18–25.

Lawrence, R. Z., Rodrik, D., and Whalley, J. (1996). *Emerging Agenda for Global Trade: High Stakes for Developing Countries.* Washington, DC: Overseas Development Council.

Lawrence, R. Z., and Slaughter, M. (1993). "Trade and U.S. Wages in the 1980s: Giant Sucking Sound or Small Hiccup?" *Brookings Papers on Economic Activity: Microeconomics, 2:* 161–210.

Learner, E. (1998). "In Search of Stopler-Samuelson Linkages Between International Trade and Lower Wages," in S. Collins (Ed.),

Imports, Exports, and the American Worker (141–214). Washington, DC: Brookings Institution Press.

Lechner, F. J., and Boli, J. (Eds.). (2000). *The Globalization Reader.* Oxford: Blackwell.

Lee, E. (1996). "Globalization and Employment: Is Anxiety Justified?" *International Labour Review, 135*(5): 486–497.

Lee, E. (1997). "Globalization and Labour Standards: A Review of Issues". *International Labour Review, 136*(2): 173–189.

Levi, M. (2000, February). "Labor Unions and the WTO". Speech given at the University of Washington, Seattle.

Longworth, R. C. (1999). *The Global Squeeze.* Chicago: Contemporary Books.

MacBride, S., and Roach, C. (2000). "The New International Information Order," in F. J. Lechner and J. Boli (Eds.), *The Globalization Reader* (286–292). Oxford: Blackwell.

Mander, J., and Goldsmith, E. (Eds.). (1996). *The Case Against the Global Economy and for a Turn Toward the Local.* San Francisco: Sierra Club.

Marquand, D. (1998). *The New Reckoning.* Cambridge: Polity.

Monbiot, G. (1995, August 13). "Global Villagers Speak with Forked Tongues," *Guardian*: 24.

Murphy, K., and Topel, R. (1997). "Unemployment and Nonemployment," *American Economic Review, 87*(2): 295–300.

Ohmae, K. (1995). *The End of the Nation State.* New York: Free Press.

Organization for Economic Cooperation and Development (OECD) (1996). *Trade, Employment, and Labour Standards: A Study of Core Workers' Rights and International Trade.* Paris: Author.

Organization for Economic Cooperation and Development (OECD). (1997). "Trade, Earnings and Employment: Assessing the Impact of Trade with Emerging Economies on OECD Labour Markets," *OECD Employment Outlook*: 93–128.

Organization for Economic Cooperation and Development (OECD). (2003). "About the OECD." Retrieved on March 27, 2003, from http://www.oecdwash.org/ABOUT/aboutmain.htm

Osland, J. S., Dhanda, K., and Yuthas, K. (2002). "Globalization and environmental sustainability: An analysis of the impact of globalization using the Natural Step framework," in S. Sharma and M. Starik (Eds.), *Research in Corporate Sustainability: The Evolving Theory and Practice of Organizations in the Natural Environment* (31–60). Cheltenham, UK: Edward Elgar.

Press, E. (2002, June 10). "Rebel with a cause: The Re-education of Joseph Stiglitz," *The Nation*: 11–16.

Pritchett, I., (1997, 3rd trimester). "La distribution passee et future du revenu mondial". [The once (and future) distribution of world income.] *Economie Internationale, 0*(71): 19–42.

Rackham, O. (1986). *The History of the Countryside.* London: J. M. Dent and Sons.

Renesch, J. (Ed.). (1992). *New Traditions in Business.* San Francisco: Barrett-Kohler.

Robbins, D. J. (1995). "Trade, Trade Liberalization and Inequality in Latin America and East Asia: Synthesis of Seven Country Studies." Unpublished manuscript, Harvard University.

Rodrik, D. (1997). *Has Globalization Gone Too Far?* Washington, DC: Institute for International Economics.

Ruggie, J. (1982). "International regimes, transactions and change: Embedded liberalism in the postwar economic order," *International Organization, 36*(2), 379–415.

Sachs, J., and Schatz, H. (1994). *Trade and Jobs in US Manufacturing* (Brookings Papers on Economic Activity, 1: 1–84). Washington, DC: Brookings Institution.

Scmidheiny, S. (1992). *Changing Course.* Cambridge, MA: MIT Press.

Scott, R. E., Lee, T., and Schmitt, J. (1997). *Trading Away Good jobs: An Examination of Employment and Wages in the US 1979–94.* Washington, DC: Economic Policy Institute.

Sherman, R. W., Steingard, D. S., and Fitzgibbons, D. E. (2002). "Sustainable stakeholder accounting: Beyond complementarity and towards integration in environmental accounting," in S. Sharma and M. Starik (Eds.), *Research in Corporate Sustainability: The Evolving Theory and Practice of Organizations in the Natural Environment* (257–294). Cheltenham, UK: Edward Elgar.

Simmons, P. J., and de Jonge Oudraat, C. (Eds.). (2001). *Managing Global Issues: Lessons Learned.* Washington, DC: Carnegie Endowment.

Sinclair, J., Jacka, E., and Cunningham, S. (1996). *New Patterns in Global Television: Peripheral Vision.* Oxford: Oxford University Press.

Slaughter, M. J., and Swagel, P. (2000). "Does Globalization Lower Wages and Export Jobs?" in F. J. Lechner and J. Boli (Eds.), *The Globalization Reader* (177–180). Oxford: Blackwell.

Socolow, R., Andrews, C., Berkhout, F., and Thomas, V. (1994). *Industrial Ecology and Global Change.* New York: Cambridge University Press.

Soros, G. (1998). *The Crisis of Global Capitalism.* New York: Public Affairs.

Soros, G. (2002). *George Soros on Globalization.* New York: Public Affairs.

Stiglitz, J. (2002). *Globalization and Its Discontent.* New York: Norton.

Sutherland, P. D. *(1998, November 1).* "Sharing the bounty," *Banker, 148*(873).

Takashi, I. (1997). "Changing Japanese Labor and Employment System," *Journal of Japanese Trade and Industry, 16*(4), 20–24.

Temple, J. (1999). "The New Growth Evidence," *Journal of Economic Literature, 37*: 112–156.

Tisdell, C. (1997). "Local Communities, Conservation and Sustainability: Institutional Change, Altered Governance and Kant's Social Philosophy," *International Journal of Social Economics, 24*(12): 1361–1320.

Tomlinson, J. (1999). *Globalization and Culture.* Chicago: University of Chicago Press.

Tyson, D. L. (1999, May 31). "Why the US Should Welcome China to the WTO," *BusinessWeek, 30.*

United Nations. (2002). "Global Compact," Retrieved on August 29, 2002, from http://65.214.34.30/un/gc/unweb.nsf/webprintview/thenine.htm

United Nations Conference on Trade and Development (UNCTAD) (1992). *World Investment Report.* Geneva: Author.

United Nations Conference on Trade and Development (UNCTAD) (1995). *World Investment Report.* Geneva: Author

United Nations Conference on Trade and Development (UNCTAD) (1997).*Trade and Development Report.* Geneva: Author.

United Nations Conference on Trade and Development (UNCTAD) (1998). *World Investment Report.* Geneva: Author.

United Nations Conference on Trade and Development (UNCTAD) (1999). *North-South Trade, Employment and Inequality: The Social Responsibility of Transactional Corporations.* Geneva: Author.

United Nations Development Programme (UNDP). (1996). *Human Development Report 1996.* New York: Oxford University Press.

United Nations Development Programme (UNDP). (1999). *Human Development Report 1999.* New York: Oxford University Press.

United Nations Development Programme (UNDP). (2001). *Human Development Report 2001.* New York: Oxford University Press.

United Nations Development Programme (UNDP). (2002). "Human Development Reports—Fast Facts." Retrieved on September 9, 2002, from http://www/undp.org/dpa/publications

Valaskakis, K. (1998, Summer). "The Challenge of Strategic Governance: Can Globalization Be Managed?" *Optimum, 28*(2): 26–40.

Wackernagel, M., and Rees, W. (1996). *Our Ecological Footprint.* Gabriola Island, BC: New Society Publishers.

Waters, M. (1995). *Globalization.* New York: Routledge.

Wilkes, A. (1995). "Prawns, Profits and Protein: Aquaculture and Food Production," *Ecologist, 25*: 2–3.

Wood, A. (1994). *North-South Trade, Employment and Inequality: Changing Fortunes in a Skil-driven World.* Oxford: Clarendon.

Wood, A. (1995, Summer). "How Trade Hurt Unskilled Workers," *Journal of Economic Perspectives, 9*(3): 57–81.

Wood, A. (1997). Openness and Wage Inequality in Developing Countries: The Latin American Challenge to East Asian Conventional Wisdom. *World Bank Economic Review, 11*(1): 33–57.

Wood, A. (1998, September). "Globalization and the Rise in Labour Market Inequalities," *Economic Journal, 1998*(450), 1463–1483.

World Trade Organization (2003). Retrieved March 28, 2003, from http://www.wto.org

Yergin, D., and Stanislaw, J. (2000). "The Commanding Heights: The Battle Between Government and the Marketplace That is Remaking the Modern World," in F. J. Lechner and J. Boli (Eds.), *The Globalization Reader* (212–220). Oxford: Blackwell.

Zhao, L. (1998, April). "The Impact of Foreign Direct Investment on Wages and Employment," *Oxford Economic Papers, 50*(2): 284–302.

CULTURAL CONSTRAINTS IN MANAGEMENT THEORIES*

Geert Hofstede

Lewis Carroll's *Alice in Wonderland* contains the famous story of Alice's croquet game with the Queen of Hearts.

> *Alice thought she had never seen such a curious croquet-ground in all her life: it was all ridges and furrows; the balls were live hedgehogs, the mallets live flamingoes, and the soldiers had to double themselves up and to stand on their hands and feet, to make the arches.*

You probably know how the story goes: Alice's flamingo mallet turns its head whenever she wants to strike with it; her hedgehog ball runs away; and the doubled-up soldier arches walk around all the time. The only rule seems to be that the Queen of Hearts always wins.

Alice's croquet playing problems are good analogies to attempts to build culture-free theories of management. Concepts available for this purpose are themselves alive with culture, having been developed within a particular cultural context. They have a tendency to guide our thinking toward our desired conclusion.

As the same reasoning may also be applied to the arguments in this article, I better tell you my conclusion before I continue—so that the rules of my game are understood. In this article we take a trip around the world to demonstrate that there are no such things as universal management theories.

Diversity in management *practices* as we go around the world has been recognized in U.S. management literature for more than 30 years. The term *comparative management* has been used since the 1960s. However, it has taken much longer for the U.S. academic community to accept that not only practices but also the validity of *theories* may stop at national borders, and I wonder whether even today everybody would agree with this statement.

An article I published in *Organizational Dynamics* in 1980 entitled "Do American Theories Apply Abroad?" created more controversy than I expected. The article argued, with empirical support, that generally accepted U.S. theories like those of Maslow, Herzberg, McClelland, Vroom, McGregor, Likert, Blake, and Mouton may not or only very partly apply outside the borders of their country of origin—assuming they do apply within those borders. Among the requests for reprints, a larger number were from Canada than from the United States.

The issues explored here were presented by Dr. Hofstede, the Foundation for Administrative Research Distinguished International Scholar, at the 1992 Annual Meeting of the Academy of Management. Las Vegas, Nevada, August 11, 1992.

*Reprinted with permission from the *Academy of Management Executive* 7, no. 1 (1993): 81–93, via the Copyright Clearance Center.

MANAGEMENT THEORISTS ARE HUMAN

Employees and managers are human. Employees as humans was "discovered" in the 1930s, with the Human Relations school. Managers as humans was introduced in the late 1940s by Herbert Simon's "bounded rationality" and elaborated in Richard Cyert and James March's *Behavioral Theory of the Firm* (1963, and recently republished in a second edition). My argument is that management scientists, theorists, and writers are human too: They grew up in a particular society in a particular period, and their ideas cannot help but reflect the constraints of their environment.

The idea that the validity of a theory is constrained by national borders is more obvious in Europe, with all its borders, than in a huge borderless country like the United States. Already in the sixteenth century Michel de Montaigne, a Frenchman, wrote a statement which was made famous by Blaise Pascal about a century later "Vérite en-deça des Pyrenées, erreur au-delà"—There are truths on this side of the Pyrenées which are falsehoods on the other.

FROM DON ARMADO'S LOVE TO TAYLOR'S SCIENCE

According to the comprehensive 10-volume *Oxford English Dictionary* (1971), the words *manage*, *management*, and *manager* appeared in the English language in the sixteenth century. The oldest recorded use of the word *manager* is in Shakespeare's "Love's Labour's Lost," dating from 1588, in which Don Adriano de Armado, "a fantastical Spaniard," exclaims (Act I, scene ii, 188):

> *"Adieu, valour! rust, rapier! be still, drum! for your manager is in love; yea, he loveth."*

The linguistic origin of the word is from Latin *manus*, hand, via the Italian *maneggiare*, which is the training of horses in the *manege*; subsequently its meaning was extended to skillful handling in general, like of arms and musical instruments, as Don Armado illustrates. However, the word also became associated with the French *menage*, household, as an equivalent of *husbandry* in its sense of the art of running a household. The theatre of present-day management contains elements of both *manege* and *menage* and different managers and cultures may use different accents.

The founder of the science of economics, the Scot Adam Smith, in his 1776 book *The Wealth of Nations*, used *manage*, *management* (even *bad management*) and *manager* when dealing with the process and the persons involved in operating joint stock companies (Smith, V.i.e.). British economist John Stuart Mill (1806–1873) followed Smith in this use and clearly expressed his distrust of such hired people who were not driven by ownership. Since the 1880s the word *management* appeared occasionally in writings by American engineers, until it was canonized as a modern science by Frederick W. Taylor in *Shop Management* in 1903 and in *The Principles of Scientific Management* in 1911.

While Smith and Mill used *management* to describe a process and *managers* for the persons involved, *management* in the American sense—which has since been taken back by the British—refers not only to the process but also to the managers as a class of people. This class (1) does not own a business but sells its skills to act on behalf of the owners and (2) does not produce personally but is indispensable for making others produce, through motivation. Members of this class carry a high status and many American boys and girls aspire to the role. In the United States, the manager is a cultural hero.

Let us now turn to other parts of the world. We will look at management in its context in other successful modern economies: Germany, Japan, France, Holland, and among the Overseas Chinese. Then we will examine management in the much larger part of the world that is still poor, especially South-East Asia and Africa, and in the new political configurations of Eastern Europe, and Russia in particular. We will then return to the United States via mainland China.

Germany

The manager is not a cultural hero in Germany. If anybody, it is the engineer who fills the hero role. Frederick Taylor's *Scientific Management* was conceived in a society of immigrants—where large numbers of workers with diverse backgrounds and skills had to work together. In Germany this heterogeneity never existed.

Elements of the mediaeval guild system have survived in historical continuity in Germany until the present day. In particular, a very effective apprenticeship system exists both on the shop floor and in the office, which alternates practical work and classroom courses. At the end of the apprenticeship the worker receives a certificate, the *Facharbeiterbrief*, which is recognized throughout the country. About two thirds of the German worker population holds such a certificate and a corresponding occupational pride. In fact, quite a few German company presidents have worked their way up from the ranks through an apprenticeship. In comparison, two thirds of the worker population in Britain have no occupational qualification at all.

The highly skilled and responsible German workers do not necessarily need a manager, American-style, to "motivate" them. They expect their boss or *Meister* to assign their tasks and to be the expert in resolving technical problems. Comparisons of similar German, British, and French organizations show the Germans as having the highest rate of personnel in productive roles and the lowest both in leadership and staff roles.

Business schools are virtually unknown in Germany. Native German management theories concentrate on formal systems. The inapplicability of American concepts of management was quite apparent in 1973 when the U.S. consulting firm of Booz, Allen, and Hamilton, commissioned by the German Ministry of Economic Affairs, wrote a study of German management from an American viewpoint. The report is highly critical and writes among other things that "Germans simply do not have a very strong concept of management." Since 1973, from my personal experience, the situation has not changed much. However, during this period the German economy has performed in a superior fashion to the United States in virtually all respects, so a strong concept of management might have been a liability rather than an asset.

Japan

The American type of manager is also missing in Japan. In the United States, the core of the enterprise is the managerial class. The core of the Japanese enterprise is the permanent worker group; workers who for all practical purposes are tenured and who aspire at life-long employment. They are distinct from the non-permanent employees—most women and subcontracted teams led by gang bosses, to be laid off in slack periods. University graduates in Japan first join the permanent worker group and subsequently fill various positions, moving from line to staff as the need occurs while paid according to seniority rather than position. They take part in Japanese-style group consultation sessions for important decisions, which extend the decision-making period but guarantee fast implementation afterwards. Japanese are to a large extent controlled by their peer group rather than by their manager.

Three researchers from the East-West Center of the University of Hawaii, Joseph Tobin, David Wu, and Dana Danielson, did an observation study of typical preschools in three countries: China, Japan, and the United States. Their results have been published both as a book and as a video. In the Japanese preschool, one teacher handled 28 four-year-olds. The video shows one particularly obnoxious boy, Hiroki, who fights with other children and throws teaching materials down from the balcony. When a little girl tries to alarm the teacher, the latter answers, "What are you calling me for? Do something about it!" In the U.S. preschool, there is one adult for every nine children. This class has its problem child too, Glen, who refuses to clear away his toys. One of the teachers has a long talk with him and isolates him in a corner, until he changes his mind. It doesn't take much imagination to realize that managing Hiroki 30 years later will be a different process from managing Glen.

American theories of leadership are ill-suited for the Japanese group-controlled situation. During the past two decades, the Japanese have developed their own *PM* theory of leadership, in which *P* stands for *performance* and *M* for *maintenance*. The latter is less a concern for individual employees than for maintaining social stability. In view of the amazing success of the Japanese economy in the past 30 years, many Americans have sought the secrets of Japanese management hoping to copy them.

France

The manager, U.S. style, does not exist in France either. In a very enlightening book, unfortunately not yet translated into English, the French researcher Philippe d'Iribarne (1989) describes the results of in-depth observation and interview studies of management methods in three subsidiary plants of the same French multinational: in France, the United States, and Holland. He relates what he finds to information about the three societies in general. Where necessary, he goes back in history to trace the roots of the strikingly different behaviors in the completion of the same tasks. He identifies three kinds of basic principles (*logiques*) of management. In the United States, the principle is the *fair contract* between employer and employee, which gives the manager considerable prerogatives, but within its limits. This is really a labor *market* in which the worker sells his or her labor for a price. In France, the principle is the *honor* of each class in a society which has always been and remains extremely stratified, in which superiors behave as superior beings and subordinates accept and expect this, conscious of their own lower level in the national hierarchy but also of the honor of their own class. The French do not think in terms of managers versus non-managers but in terms of *cadres* versus *non-cadres*; one becomes cadre by attending the proper schools and one remains it forever, regardless of their actual task, cadres have the privileges of a higher social class, and it is very rare for a non-cadre to cross the ranks.

The conflict between French and American theories of management became apparent in the beginning of the twentieth century, in a criticism by the great French management pioneer Henri Fayol (1841–1925) on his U.S. colleague and contemporary Frederick W. Taylor (1856–1915). The difference in career paths of the two men is striking. Fayol was a French engineer whose career as a *cadre supérieur* culminated in the position of Président-Directeur-Général of a mining company. After his retirement he formulated his experiences in a pathbreaking text on organization: *Administration industrielle et générale*, in which he focused on the sources of authority. Taylor was an American engineer who started his career in industry as a worker and attained his academic qualifications through evening studies. From chief engineer in a steel company he became one of the first management consultants. Taylor was not really concerned with the issue of authority at all; his focus was on efficiency. He proposed to split the task of the first-line boss into eight specialisms, each exercised by a different person; an idea which eventually led to the idea of a matrix organization.

Taylor's work appeared in a French translation in 1913, and Fayol read it and showed himself generally impressed but shocked by Taylor's "denial of the principle of the Unity of Command" in the case of the eight-boss system.

Seventy years later André Laurent, another of Fayol's compatriots, found that French managers in a survey reacted very strongly against a suggestion that one employee could report to two different bosses, while U.S. managers in the same survey showed fewer misgivings. Matrix organization has never become popular in France as it has in the United States.

Holland

In my own country, Holland or as it is officially called, the Netherlands, the study by Philippe d'Iribarne found the management principle to be a need for *consensus* among all parties, neither predetermined by a contractual relationship nor by class distinctions, but based on an open-ended exchange of views and a balancing of interests. In terms of the different origins of the word *manager*, the organization in Holland is more *menage* (household) while in the United States it is more *menege* (horse drill).

At my university, the University of Limburg at Maastricht, every semester we receive a class of American business students who take a program in European Studies. We asked both the Americans and a matched group of Dutch students to describe their ideal job after graduation, using a list of 22 job characteristics. The Americans attached significantly more importance than the Dutch to earnings, advancement, benefits, a good working relationship with their boss, and security of employment. The Dutch attached more importance to freedom to adopt their own approach to the job, being consulted by their boss in his or her decisions, training opportunities, contributing to the success of their organization, fully using their skills and abilities, and helping others. This list confirms d'Iribarne's findings of a contractual employment relationship in the United States, based on earnings and career opportunities, against a consensual relationship in Holland. The latter has centuries-old roots; the Netherlands were the first republic in Western Europe (1609–1810), and a model for the American republic. The country has been and still is governed by a careful balancing of interests in a multi-party system.

In terms of management theories, both motivation and leadership in Holland are different from what they are in the United States. Leadership in Holland presupposes modesty, as opposed to assertiveness in the United States. No U.S. leadership theory has room for that. Working in Holland is not a constant feast, however. There is a built-in premium on mediocrity and jealousy, as well as time-consuming ritual consultations to maintain the appearance of consensus and the pretense of modesty. There is unfortunately another side to every coin.

The Overseas Chinese

Among the champions of economic development in the past 30 years we find three countries mainly populated by Chinese living outside the Chinese mainland: Taiwan, Hong Kong, and Singapore. Moreover, Overseas Chinese play a very important role in the economies of Indonesia, Malaysia, the Philippines, and Thailand, where they form an ethnic minority. If anything, the little dragons—Taiwan, Hong Kong, and Singapore—have been more economically successful than Japan, moving from rags to riches and now counted among the world's wealthy industrial countries. Yet very little attention has been paid to the way in which their enterprises have been managed. *The Spirit of Chinese Capitalism* by Gordon Redding (1990), the British dean of the Hong Kong Business School, is an excellent book about Chinese business. He bases his insights on personal acquaintance and in-depth discussions with a large number of Overseas Chinese businesspeople.

Overseas Chinese American enterprises lack almost all characteristics of modern management. They tend to be small, cooperating for essential functions with other small organizations through networks based on personal relations. They are family-owned, without the separation between ownership and management typical in the West, or even in Japan and Korea. They normally focus on one product or market, with growth by opportunistic diversification; in this, they are extremely flexible. Decision making is centralized in the hands of one dominant family member, but other family members may be given new ventures to try their skills on. They are low-profile and extremely cost-conscious, applying Confucian virtues of thrift and persistence. Their size is kept small by the assumed lack of loyalty of non-family employees, who, if they are any good, will just wait and save until they can start their own family business.

Overseas Chinese prefer economic activities in which great gains can be made with little manpower, like commodity trading and real estate. They employ few professional managers, except their sons and sometimes daughters who have been sent to prestigious business schools abroad, but who upon return continue to run the family business the Chinese way.

The origin of this system, or—in the Western view—this lack of system, is found in the history of Chinese society, in which there were no formal laws, only formal networks of powerful people guided by general principles of Confucian virtue. The favors of the authorities could change daily, so nobody could be trusted except one's kinfolk—of whom, fortunately, there used to be many, in an extended family structure. The Overseas Chinese way of doing business is also very well adapted to their position in the countries in which they form ethnic minorities, often envied and threatened by ethnic violence.

Overseas Chinese businesses following this unprofessional approach command a collective gross national product of some 200 to 300 billion U.S. dollars, exceeding the GNP of Australia. There is no denying that it works.

MANAGEMENT TRANSFER TO POOR COUNTRIES

Four-fifths of the world population live in countries that are not rich but poor. After World War II and decolonization, the stated purpose of the United Nations and the World Bank has been to promote the development of all the world's countries in a war on poverty. After 40 years it looks very much like we are losing this war.

If one thing has become clear, it is that the export of Western—mostly American—management practices and theories to poor countries has contributed little to nothing to their development. There has been no lack of effort and money spent for this purpose: students from poor countries have been trained in this country, and teachers and Peace Corps workers have been sent to the poor countries. If nothing else, the general lack of success in economic development of other countries should be sufficient argument to doubt the validity of Western management theories in non-Western environments.

If we examine different parts of the world, the development picture is not equally bleak, and history is often a better predictor than economic factors for what happens today. There is a broad regional pecking order with East Asia leading. The little dragons have passed into the camp of the wealthy; then follow South-East Asia (with its Overseas Chinese minorities), Latin American (in spite of the debt crisis), South Asia, and Africa always trails behind. Several African countries have only become poorer since decolonization.

Regions of the world with a history of large-scale political integration and civilization generally have done better than regions in which no large-scale political and cultural infrastructure existed, even if the old civilizations had decayed or been suppressed by colonizers. It has become painfully clear that development cannot be pressure-cooked; it presumes a cultural infrastructure that takes time to grow. Local management is part of this infrastructure; it cannot be imported in package form. Assuming that with so-called modern management techniques and theories outsiders can develop a country has proven a deplorable arrogance. At best, one can hope for a dialogue between equals with the locals, in which the Western partner acts as the expert in Western technology and the local partner as the expert in local culture, habits, and feelings.

Russia and China

The crumbling of the former Eastern bloc has left us with a scattering of states and would-be states of which the political and economic future is extremely uncertain. The best predictions are those based on a knowledge of history, because historical trends have taken revenge on the arrogance of the Soviet rulers who believed they could turn them around by brute power. One obvious fact is that the former bloc is extremely heterogeneous, including countries traditionally closely linked with the West by trade and travel, like Czechia, Hungary, Slovenia, and the Baltic states, as well as others with a Byzantine or Turkish past; some having been prosperous, others always extremely poor.

Let me limit myself to the Russian republic, a huge territory with some 140 million inhabitants, mainly Russians. We know quite a bit about the Russians as their country was a world power for several hundreds of years before communism, and in the

> The industrialized Western world and the World Bank seem committed to helping the ex-Eastern bloc countries develop, but with the same technocratic neglect for local cultural factors that proved so unsuccessful in the development assistance to other poor countries. Free market capitalism, introduced by Western-style management, is supposed to be the answer from Albania to Russia.

nineteenth century it has produced some of the greatest writers in world literature. If I want to understand the Russians—including how they could so long support the Soviet regime—I tend to re-read Lev Nikolayevich Tolstoy. In his most famous novel *Anna Karenina* (1876) one of the main characters, Levin, is a landowner whom Tolstoy uses to express his own views and convictions about his people. Russian peasants used to be serfs; serfdom had been abolished in 1861, but the peasants, now tenants, remained as passive as before. Levin wanted to break this passivity by dividing the land among his peasants in exchange for a share of the crops; but the peasants only let the land deteriorate further. Here follows a quote:

> *(Levin) read political economy and socialistic works . . . but, as he had expected, found nothing in them related to his undertaking. In the political economy books—in (John Stuart) Mill, for instance, whom he studied first and with great ardour, hoping every minute to find an answer to the questions that were engrossing him—he found only certain laws deduced from the state of agriculture in Europe; but he could not for the life of him see why these laws, which did not apply to Russia, should be considered universal. . . . Political economy told him that the laws by which Europe had developed and was developing her wealth were universal and absolute. Socialist teaching told him that development along those lines leads to ruin. And neither of them offered the smallest enlightenment as to what he, Levin, and all the Russian peasants and landowners were to do with their millions of hands and millions of acres, to make them as productive as possible for the common good.*

In the summer of 1991, the Russian lands yielded a record harvest, but a large share of it rotted in the fields because no people were to be found for harvesting. The passivity is still there, and not only among the peasants. And the heirs of John Stuart Mill (whom we met before as one of the early analysts of *management*) again present their universal recipes which simply do not apply.

Citing Tolstoy, I implicitly suggest that management theorists cannot neglect the great literature of the countries they want their ideas to apply to. The greatest novel in the Chinese literature is considered Cao Xueqin's *The Story of the Stone*, also known as *The Dream of the Red Chamber*, which appeared around 1760. It describes the rise and fall of two branches of an aristocratic family in Beijing, who live in adjacent plots in the capital. Their plots are joined by a magnificent garden with several pavillions in it, and the young, mostly female members of both families are allowed to live in them. One day the management of the garden is taken over by a young woman, Tan-Chun, who states:

> *I think we ought to pick out a few experienced trustworthy old women from among the ones who work in the Garden—women who know something about gardening already—and put the upkeep of the Garden into their hands. We needn't ask them to pay us rent; all we need ask them for is an annual share of the produce. There would be four advantages in this arrangement. In the first place, if we have people whose sole occupation is to look after trees and flowers and so on, the condition of the Garden will improve gradually year after year and there will be no more of those long periods of neglect followed*

by bursts of feverish activity when things have been allowed to get out of hand. Secondly there won't be the spoiling and wastage we get at present. Thirdly the women themselves will gain a little extra to add to their incomes which will compensate them for the hard work they put in throughout the year. And fourthly, there's no reason why we shouldn't use the money we should otherwise have spent on nurserymen, rockery specialists, horticultural cleaners and so on for other purposes.

As the story goes on, the capitalist privatization—because that is what it is—of the Garden is carried through, and it works. When in the 1980s Deng Xiaoping allowed privatization in the Chinese villages, it also worked. It worked so well that its effects started to be felt in politics and threatened the existing political order, hence the knockdown at Tienanmen Square of June 1989. But it seems that the forces of privatization are getting the upper hand again in China. If we remember what Chinese entrepreneurs are able to do once they have become Overseas Chinese, we shouldn't be too surprised. But what works in China—and worked two centuries ago—does not have to work in Russia, not in Tolstoy's days and not today. I am not offering a solution; I only protest against a naive universalism that knows only one recipe for development, the one supposed to have worked in the United States.

A THEORY OF CULTURE IN MANAGEMENT

Our trip around the world is over and we are back in the United States. What have we learned? There is something in all countries called *management*, but its meaning differs to a larger or smaller extent from one country to the other, and it takes considerable historical and cultural insight into local conditions to understand its processes, philosophies, and problems. If already the word may mean so many different things, how can we expect one country's theories of management to apply abroad? One should be extremely careful in making this assumption, and test it before considering it proven. Management is not a phenomenon that can be isolated from other processes taking place in a society. During our trip around the world we saw that it interacts with what happens in the family, at school, in politics, and government. It is obviously also related to religion and to beliefs about science. Theories of management always had to be interdisciplinary, but if we cross national borders they should become more interdisciplinary than ever.

Cultural differences between nations can be, to some extent, described using first four, and now five, bipolar *dimensions*. The position of a country on these dimensions allows us to make some predictions on the way their society operates, including their management processes and the kind of theories applicable to their management.

As the word *culture* plays such an important role in my theory, let me give you my definition, which differs from some other very respectable definitions. Culture to me is *the collective programming of the mind which distinguishes one group or category of people from another.* In the part of my work I am referring to now, the category of people is the nation.

Culture is a *construct*; that means it is "not directly accessible to observation but inferable from verbal statements and other behaviors and useful in predicting still other observable and measurable verbal and non-verbal behavior." It should not be reified; it is an auxiliary concept that should be used as long as it proves useful but bypassed where we can predict behaviors without it.

The same applies to the *dimensions* I introduced. They are constructs too that should not be reified. They do not "exist"; they are tools for analysis which may or may not clarify a situation. In my statistical analysis of empirical data the first four dimensions together explain 49 percent of the variance in the data. The other 51 percent remain specific to individual countries.

The first four dimensions were initially detected through a comparison of the values of similar people (employees and managers) in 64 national subsidiaries of the IBM Corporation. People working for the same multinational, but in different countries, represent very well-matched samples from the populations of their countries, similar in all respects except nationality.

The first dimension is labelled *Power Distance*, and it can be defined as the degree of inequality among people which the population of a country considers as normal: from relatively equal (that is, small power distance) to extremely unequal (large power distance). All societies are unequal, but some are more unequal than others.

The second dimension is labelled *Individualism*, and it is the degree to which people in a country prefer to act as individuals rather than as members of groups. The opposite of individualism can be called *Collectivism*, so collectivism is low individualism. The way I use the word it has no political connotations. In collectivist societies a child learns to respect the group to which it belongs, usually the family, and to differentiate between in-group members and out-group members (that is, all other people). When children grow up they remain members of their group, and they expect the group to protect them when they are in trouble. In return, they have to remain loyal to their group throughout life. In individualist societies, a child learns very early to think of itself as "I" instead of as part of "we." It expects one day to have to stand on its own feet and not to get protection from its group any more; and therefore it also does not feel a need for strong loyalty.

The third dimension is called *Masculinity* and its opposite pole *Femininity.* It is the degree to which tough values like assertiveness, performance, success, and competition, which in nearly all societies are associated with the role of men, prevail over tender values like the quality of life, maintaining warm personal relationships, service, care for the weak, and solidarity, which in nearly all societies are more associated with women's roles. Women's roles differ from men's roles in all countries; but in tough societies, the differences are larger than in tender ones.

The fourth dimension is labelled *Uncertainty Avoidance*, and it can be defined as the degree to which people in a country prefer structured over unstructured situations. Structured situations are those in which there are clear rules as to how one should behave. These rules can be written down, but they can also be unwritten and imposed by tradition. In countries which score high on uncertainty avoidance, people tend to show more nervous energy, while in countries which score low, people are more easygoing. A (national) society with strong uncertainty avoidance can be called rigid; one with weak uncertainty avoidance, flexible. In countries where uncertainty avoidance is strong a feeling prevails of "what is different, is dangerous." In weak uncertainty avoidance societies, the feeling would rather be "what is different, is curious."

The fifth dimension was added on the basis of a study of the values of students in 23 countries carried out by Michael Harris Bond, a Canadian working in Hong Kong. He and I had cooperated in another study of students' values which had yielded the same four dimensions as the IBM data. However, we wondered to what extent our common findings in two studies could be the effect of a Western bias introduced by the common Western background of the researchers: remember Alice's croquet game. Michael Bond resolved this dilemma by deliberately introducing an Eastern bias. He used a questionnaire prepared at his request by his Chinese colleagues, the *Chinese Value Survey* (CVS), which was translated from Chinese into different languages and answered by 50 male and 50 female students in each of 23 countries in all five continents. Analysis of the CVS data produced three dimensions significantly correlated with the three IBM dimensions of power distance, individualism, and masculinity. There was also a fourth dimension, but it did not resemble uncertainty avoidance. It was composed, both on the positive and on the negative side, from items that had not been included in the IBM studies but were present in the Chinese Value Survey because they were rooted in the teachings of Confucius. I labeled this dimension: *Long-term* versus *Short-term Orientation.* On the long-term side one finds values oriented towards the future, like thrift (saving) and persistence. On the short-term side one finds values rather oriented towards the past and present, like respect for tradition and fulfilling social obligations.

Table 1 lists the scores on all five dimensions for the United States and for the other countries we just discussed. The table shows that each country has its own configuration on the four dimensions. Some of the values in the table have been estimated based on imperfect replications or personal impressions. The different dimension scores do not "explain" all the differences in management I described earlier. To understand management in a country, one should have both knowledge of and empathy with the entire local scene. However, the scores should make us aware that people in other countries may think, feel, and act very differently from us when confronted with basic problems of society.

TABLE 1 Cultural Dimension Scores for Ten Countries

	PD	*ID*	*MA*	*UA*	*LT*
United States	40L	91H	62H	46L	29L
Germany	35L	67H	66H	65M	31M
Japan	54M	46M	95H	92H	80H
France	68H	71H	43M	86H	30*L
Netherlands	38L	80H	14L	53M	44M
Hong Kong	68H	25L	57H	29L	96H
Indonesia	78H	14L	46M	48L	25*L
West Africa	77H	20L	46M	54M	16L
Russia	95*H	50*M	40*L	90*H	10*L
China	80*H	20*L	50*M	60*M	118H

PD = Power Distance; ID = Individualism; MA = Masculinity; UA = Uncertainty Avoidance;
LT = Long-Term Orientation; H = top third; M = medium third; L = bottom third (among 53 countries and regions for the first four dimensions; among 23 countries for the fifth)
*estimated

IDIOSYNCRACIES OF AMERICAN MANAGEMENT THEORIES

In comparison to other countries, the U.S. culture profile presents itself as below average on power distance and uncertainty avoidance, highly individualistic, fairly masculine, and short-term oriented. The Germans show a stronger uncertainty avoidance and less extreme individualism; the Japanese are different on all dimensions, least on power distance; the French show larger power distance and uncertainty avoidance, but are less individualistic and somewhat feminine; the Dutch resemble the Americans on the first three dimensions, but score extremely feminine and relatively long-term oriented; Hong Kong Chinese combine large power distance with weak uncertainty avoidance, collectivism, and are very long-term oriented; and so on.

The American culture profile is reflected in American management theories. I will just mention three elements not necessarily present in other countries: the stress on market processes, the stress on the individual, and the focus on managers rather than on workers.

The Stress on Market Processes

During the 1970s and 1980s it has become fashionable in the United States to look at organizations from a "transaction costs" viewpoint. Economist Oliver Williamson has opposed "hierarchies" to "markets." The reasoning is that human social life consists of economic transactions between individuals. We found the same in d'Iribarne's description of the U.S. principle of the contract between employer and employee, the labor market in which the worker sells his or her labor for a price. These individuals will form hierarchical organizations when the cost of the economic transactions (such as getting information, finding out whom to trust etc.) is lower in a hierarchy than when all transactions would take place on a free market.

From a cultural perspective the important point is that the "market" is the point of departure or base model, and the organization is explained from market failure. A culture that produces such a theory is likely to prefer organizations that internally resemble markets to organizations that internally resemble more structured models, like those in Germany of France. The ideal principle of control in organizations in the market philosophy is competition between individuals. This philosophy fits a society that combines a not-too-large power distance with a not-too-strong uncertainty avoidance and individualism; besides the United States, it will fit all other Anglo countries.

The Stress on the Individual

I find this constantly in the design of research projects and hypotheses; also in the fact that in the United States, psychology is clearly a more respectable discipline in management circles than sociology. Culture, however, is a collective phenomenon. Although we may get our information about culture from individuals, we have to interpret it at the level of collectivities. There are snags here known as the "ecological fallacy" and the "reverse ecological fallacy." None of the U.S. college textbooks on methodology I know deals sufficiently with the problem of multilevel analysis.

A striking example is found in the otherwise excellent book *Organizational Culture and Leadership* by Edgar H. Schein (1985). On the basis of his consulting experience he compares two large companies, nicknamed "Action" and "Multi." He explains the differences in culture between these companies by the group dynamics in their respective boardrooms. Nowhere in the book are any conclusions drawn from the fact that the first company is an American-based computer firm, and the second a

Culture can be compared to a forest, while individuals are trees. A forest is not just a bunch of trees: It is a symbiosis of different trees, bushes, plants, insects, animals, and micro-organism, and we miss the essence of the forest if we only describe its most typical trees. In the same way, a culture cannot be satisfactorily described in terms of the characteristics of a typical individual. There is a tendency in the U.S. management literature to overlook the forest for the trees and to ascribe cultural differences to interactions among individuals.

Swiss-based pharmaceutics firm. This information is not even mentioned. A stress on interactions among individuals obviously fits a culture identified as the most individualistic in the world, but it will not be so well understood by the four-fifths of the world population for whom the group prevails over the individual.

One of the conclusions of my own multilevel research has been that culture at the national level and culture at the organizational level—corporate culture—are two very different phenomena and that the use of a common term for both is confusing. If we do use the common term, we should also pay attention to the occupational and the gender level of culture. National cultures differ primarily in the fundamental, invisible values held by a majority of their members, acquired in early childhood, whereas organizational cultures are a much more superficial phenomenon residing mainly in the visible practices of the organization, acquired by socialization of the new members who join as young adults. National cultures change only very slowly if at all; organizational cultures may be consciously changed, although this isn't necessarily easy. This difference between the two types of culture is the secret of the existence of multinational corporations that employ, as I showed in the IBM case, employees with extremely different national cultural values. What keeps them together is a corporate culture based on common practices.

The Stress on Managers Rather Than Workers

The core element of a work organization around the world is the people who do the work. All the rest is superstructure, and I hope to have demonstrated to you that it may take many different shapes. In the U.S. literature on work organization, however, the core element, if not explicitly then implicitly, is considered the manager. This may well be the result of the combination of extreme individualism with fairly strong masculinity, which has turned the manager into a culture hero of almost mythical proportions. For example, he—not really she—is supposed to make decisions all the time. Those of you who are or have been managers must know that this is a fable. Very few management decisions are just "made," as the myth suggests it. Managers are much more involved in maintaining networks; if anything, it is the rank-and-file worker who can really make decisions on his or her own, albeit on a relatively simple level.

An amusing effect of the U.S. focus on managers is that in at least 10 American books and articles on management I have been misquoted as having studied IBM managers in my research, whereas the book clearly describes that the answers were from IBM employees. My observation may be biased, but I get the impression that compared to 20 or 30 years ago less research in this country is done among employees and more on managers. But managers derive their raison d'être from the people managed: Culturally, they are the followers of the people they lead, and their effectiveness depends on the latter. In other parts of the world, this exclusive focus on the manager is less strong, with Japan as the supreme example.

CONCLUSION

This article started with *Alice in Wonderland.* In fact, the management theorist who ventures outside his or her own country into other parts of the world is like Alice in Wonderland. He or she will meet strange beings, customs, ways of organizing or disorganizing, and theories that are clearly stupid, old-fashioned or even immoral—yet they may work, or at least they may not fail more frequently than corresponding theories do at home. Then, after the first culture shock, the traveler to Wonderland will feel enlightened, and may be able to take his or her experiences home and use them advantageously. All great ideas in science, politics, and management have traveled from one country to another, and been enriched by foreign influences. The roots of American management theories are mainly in Europe: with Adam Smith, John Stuart Mill, Lev Tolstoy, Max Weber, Henri Fayol, Sigmund Freud, Kurt Lewin, and many others. These theories were replanted here and they developed and bore fruit. The same may happen again. The last thing we need is a Monroe Doctrine for management ideas.

PART I

UNDERSTANDING YOURSELF AND OTHER PEOPLE AT WORK

The goal of the first section is to help you become aware of your mental maps or models, as well as those of people with whom you work. Although the concept has existed since ancient times, the term *mental models* was coined by Kenneth Craik, a Scottish psychologist, in the 1940s. It refers to "the images, assumptions, and stories that we carry in our minds of ourselves, other people, institutions, and every aspect of the world. Like a pane of glass framing and subtly distorting our vision, mental models determine what we see and then how we act."* One way to understand our behavior is to make these usually tacit maps visible. In this section, you will have an opportunity to examine mental maps about psychological contracts, theories of management, learning styles, human behavior, ethics, and values. We hope you will finish the section with more self-knowledge and a greater appreciation for the differences you discover in other people.

---

*P. Senge, A. Kleiner, C. Roberts, R. Ross, and B. Smith, *The Fifth Discipline Fieldbook: Strategies and Tools for Building a Learning Organization* (New York: Currency, 1993): 235.

CHAPTER 1
THE PSYCHOLOGICAL CONTRACT

THE PSYCHOLOGICAL CONTRACT: VIOLATIONS AND MODIFICATIONS

Denise M. Rousseau

PUTTING PEOPLE FIRST FOR ORGANIZATIONAL SUCCESS

Jeffrey Pfeffer
John Veiga

The first mental map we are going to examine concerns the psychological contract, an individual's beliefs, shaped by the organization, regarding the terms and conditions of a reciprocal exchange agreement between individuals and their organization. People frame events at work, such as promises, expectations, and future payoffs for their contributions, according to their own mental model and past history. There are negative consequences when psychological contracts are violated; understanding this concept can prevent managers from making mistakes and harming their relationship with employees.

Denise Rousseau, an expert on psychological contracts, describes what happens when people fail to comply with the terms of a contract in "The Psychological Contract: Violations and Modifications." Rousseau identifies common sources of contract violation and typical responses. In a rapidly changing environment, it is sometimes impossible to avoid modifying psychological contracts. Rousseau explains how to change psychological contracts with the least possible disruption.

Psychological contracts are the link between the individual and the organization. In successful firms, that link is based on mutual expectations about what employees are capable of performing and how employees should be treated. In "Putting People First for Organizational Success," Jeffrey Pfeffer and John Veiga report on research conclusions on high-involvement management practices that result in increased economic performance. Despite the bottom-line proof that investing in employees pays off, many firms do just the opposite and, as a result, reduce employee commitment and performance just when they need it most to succeed in a highly competitive business environment. Pfeffer, organizational behavior professor and business speaker, and Veiga, management professor, identify and explain the seven key management practices linked to successful firms.

THE PSYCHOLOGICAL CONTRACT: VIOLATIONS AND MODIFICATIONS*

Denise M. Rousseau

> *"They promised me a job in marketing and here I am doing telephone sales."*
>
> *"The company promised that no one would be fired out of the training program—that all of us were 'safe' until placement. In return for this security, we accepted lower pay. The company subsequently fired four people from the training program."*
>
> *"Original representations of the company's financial and market strength (were) clearly fraudulent."*

The common thread found in these quotations from recently hired employees is a violation of the psychological contract, which is defined as individual beliefs, shaped by the organization, regarding terms of an exchange agreement between individuals and their organizations. A contract is a mental model that people use to frame events such as promises, acceptance, and reliance. The promises that make up contracts have no objective meaning. Promises ultimately are perceptions of what was sent and what was meant. Perceptions, however, are not simply passive interpretations of reality; people create their own meaning for many events. The close supervision one person sees as controlling may seem supportive and helpful to her co-worker. Yet reality is not constructed wholly in the minds of individuals. Groups sometimes do agree on events and their meaning. Investment bankers, for example, may share a belief that their firm rewards those who make profitable deals.

Contract violation erodes trust. It undermines the employment relationship, yielding both lower employee contributions (e.g., performance and attendance) and lower employer investments (e.g., retention and promotion) in employees. Therefore, it's important for managers to understand how to avoid violating psychological contracts unnecessarily and how to modify them without eroding trust when change is essential.

Psychological contract violation can run the gamut from subtle misperceptions to stark breaches of good faith. In organizations, violated contracts are at the heart of many lawsuits brought by customers and employees. Although potentially damaging to reputations, careers, and relationships, violations also appear to be both frequent and survivable.

The basic facts of contract violation are these:

- Contract violation is commonplace.
- Violated contracts lead to adverse reactions by the injured party.
- Failure to fulfill a contract need not be fatal to the relationship.

WHAT IS CONTRACT VIOLATION?

In the strictest sense, violation is a failure to comply with the terms of a contract. But, given the subjective nature of psychological contracts, how people interpret the circumstances of this failure determines whether they experience a violation. Violation

*Excerpted and reprinted with permission from D. M. Rousseau, *Psychological Contracts in Organizations* (Thousand Oaks, CA: Sage, 1995).

TABLE 1 Sources of Experienced Violation

Inadvertent	Able and willing (divergent interpretations made in good faith)
Disruption	Willing but unable (inability to fulfil a contract)
Breach of contract	Able but unwilling (reneging)

takes three forms (Table 1). *Inadvertent violation* occurs when both parties are able and willing to keep their bargain, but divergent interpretations lead one party to act in a manner at odds with the understanding and interests of the other. Two people who misunderstand the time of a meeting will inadvertently fail to honor their mutual commitment to attend. *Disruption* to the contract occurs when circumstances make it impossible for one or both parties to fulfill their end of the contract, despite the fact that they are willing to do so. A plant closing forced by a hurricane can prevent an employer from providing work. Similarly, a car accident can keep an employee from showing up to work on time. Reneging or *breach of contract* occurs when one side, otherwise capable of performing the contract, refuses to do so. A bank manager who wants to spend more time with his family leaves a high demand/high pay job with one bank for another with a smaller financial institution. The major attraction of the new bank for the manager is its low pressure environment, which is played up by the officers who recruit him. Within two weeks of taking the job, the manager learns that the smaller firm is starting an aggressive marketing campaign he is expected to head, which will keep him away from his family for even longer hours than before. Damages include increased stress and family conflict along with loss of reputation if he tries to change jobs again soon. The sense of betrayal and entrapment this manager feels exacerbates his personal costs from the organization's actions. Whether the victim understands the source of violation to be unwillingness or inability to comply has a tremendous impact on how violation is experienced and what victims do in response (Bies and Moag, 1986).

Although contracts can be violated in innumerable ways, there are a number of common forms (Table 2). Recruiters may overpromise a job's opportunity for challenge, growth, or development, while at the same time, eager job seekers may read into a promise what they want to hear. Managers, co-workers, or executives who say one thing and do another all can engender violation. A common cause of violation for many employees involves a change in superiors. When one's boss or mentor is promoted, terminated, or retired, old deals may be abrogated. Similarly, changes in human resource practices, even with constructive intent (e.g., to align with a new business strategy) can appear to break old commitments (e.g., introducing new results-based performance criteria among veteran employees used to a seniority system). Then there is the phenomenon of mixed messages, where different contract makers express divergent intentions. A mission statement can convey that the organization rewards based upon merit ("commitment to excellence") while the compensation system is based on seniority. Different contract sources may each convey mutually exclusive promises.

TABLE 2 Sources of Violation by Contract Makers and Systems

Sources	*Violations*
Contract Makers:	
recruiters	■ unfamiliar with actual job
	■ overpromise
managers	■ say one thing, do another
co-workers	■ failure to provide support
mentors	■ little follow-through
	■ few interactions
top management	■ mixed messages
Systems:	
compensation	■ changing criteria
	■ reward seniority, low job security
benefits	■ changing coverage
career paths	■ dependent on one's manager
	■ inconsistent application
performance review	■ not done on time
	■ little feedback
training	■ skills learned not tied to job
documentation	■ stated procedures at odds with actual practice

WHEN IS VIOLATION MOST LIKELY?

- When there is a history of conflict and low trust in the relationship.
- When social distance exists between the parties such that one does not understand the perspective of the other.
- When an external pattern of violations exists (e.g., an era of business retrenchment).
- When incentives to breach contracts are very high or when perpetrators perceive themselves to have no alternatives (e.g., organizational crises).
- When one party places little value in the relationship (e.g., alternative parties are relatively available and there are few sunk costs).

WHEN A CONTRACT IS VIOLATED

Responses to violation take many forms. Violated contracts promote mistrust, anger, and attrition and change the way people behave in subsequent interactions. The aftermath of contract violation can be seen in declining corporate loyalty and increased litigation. Managers decry the decline of employee loyalty, while at the same time, the workforce has been counselled to eschew reliance on job security and employee commitments, and to "pack its own parachute" instead. In both instances there is the suggestion of contract violation, and the implication that at least one party has failed to keep its side of the bargain.

TYPES OF RESPONSES

Whether organizations and individuals choose to end their relationship, resolve their dispute, sue, or suffer in silence is a function of both situational factors and the predispositions of the parties. Previous research on responses to the more general phenomenon of dissatisfaction has largely focused on four courses of action: exit, voice, loyalty, and destruction. Although studied in various combinations (e.g., Hirschman, 1970s *Exit, Voice, and Loyalty*) and labels (e.g., Farrell's, 1983, *Exit, Voice, Loyalty, and Neglect*), these courses of action reflect two essential dimensions: active-passive and constructive-destructive.

Personal characteristics predisposing the victim to believe that the relationship is valuable or can be saved should promote either relationship-building behaviors of voice or loyalty. Without this belief, behaviors that undermine the relationship, exit or destruction, are more likely. Research on individual reactions to inequitable situations suggests that people differ in terms of their willingness to tolerate unfair or inequitable exchanges (Berscheid and Walster, 1973). "Equity-sensitives" are people who tend to monitor their exchanges with others very carefully. "Beneficient" individuals are those who tend to be other-oriented, or comfortable when exchanges benefit others more than themselves. There is some evidence that men are more likely to be equity-sensitive and women more beneficient, although personality and other factors also enter in.

Situational factors promoting certain behaviors and inhibiting others also affect responses to violation. Social learning and the presence of behavioral role models tend to induce certain types of behaviors. Thus, employees in organizations where other victims have left might be inclined to leave themselves. Similarly, individuals who have observed others successfully complain about their treatment might themselves be inclined to complain (Robinson, 1992). It is likely that the culture of the organization shapes the type of violation responses people make. A very bureaucratic organization that stifles communication and deviant behavior probably engenders little voice and more neglect and disloyalty. An open, communal organization might foster more overt complaints, as well as attempting to repair the contract by communicating with superiors.

Exit is voluntary termination of the relationship. Employers can terminate workers whose performance does not meet standards (e.g., too frequently tardy, absent, or careless), while workers can quit an untrustworthy or unreliable employer (e.g., who fails to deliver promised training or promotions). Exit is most likely in employment with transactional terms, where its costs are relatively low. Transactional terms are exemplified by *a fair day's work for a fair day's pay*—focusing on short-term and monetizable exchanges. Employment agencies such as Manpower, Kelly, Nursetemps, and other temporary employment services offer organizations the opportunity to create purely transactional agreements with workers. Transactional contract terms include: specific economic conditions (e.g., wage rate) as the primary incentive, limited personal involvement in the job, closed-ended time frame (e.g., seasonal employment), commitments limited to well-specified conditions (e.g., union contract), unambiguous terms readily understood by outsiders, and the use of existing skills (no development).

Both active and destructive, exit terminates the relationship. The vast majority of people quitting jobs within the first two years of employment report that their employer had violated commitments it had made (Robinson and Rousseau, 1994).

Exit is most likely following violation when:

1. the contract is transactional;
2. many other potential jobs or potential employees are available;
3. the relationship is relatively brief;
4. other people are also exiting; and
5. attempts to remedy a violated contract have failed.

However, it should be pointed out that violations don't always lead to exit. Robinson and Rousseau (1994) found that although 79 percent of leavers reported violated contracts, so too did 52 percent of stayers. While enduring violation, stayers can manifest three forms of response: voice, loyalty, or neglect.

Voice refers to the actions victims take to remedy the violation. Any attempt to change the objectionable features in the situation, such as complaints to one's boss or to human resources, or the filing of a grievance, are efforts made to remedy or compensate for the violation while remaining in the relationship. As a means of expressing general dissatisfaction, voice has received wide study in terms of grievance filing (Allen and Keaveny, 1981), willingness to vote for unions (Getman, Goldberg, and Herman, 1976), and whistle-blowing (Near and Miceli, 1986). However, as a means of remediating a contract violation, voice has distinct features from reparations for dissatisfaction. Voice in contract violation focuses on (1) reducing losses and (2) restoring trust.

As a response to dissatisfaction, voice often has been associated with relationship-threatening alternatives, where members in effect burn their bridges (e.g., whistle-blowing). Voice in response to contract violation is an active, constructive effort and is manifest in a number of ways. In a study of MBA alumni, there were three major types of employee voice behaviors: talking with superiors, threats, and changes in behavior (Rousseau, Robinson, and Kraatz, 1992).

Talking with superiors was the most frequent type of voice:

I discussed my disappointment with my boss and also with my mentor. I was assured that, although I did not receive a bonus, my performance was above average. I was promoted and received a salary increase six months later.

Some complaints obtain some sort of substitution:

They said the situation was out of their hands and gave me a substantial salary increase.

Some complaints elicit no response:

My boss paid lip service to making changes, but nothing actually occurred.

Voice can take the form of a threat in a smaller number of cases:

I threatened to leave based on my work assignment, training, and development opportunities. I was given new assignments, more training, and was allowed to stretch for development . . . however, I believe that happened primarily because of my director; another director probably would have let me leave.

In a few instances, a change in the victim's behavior generates a response:

I was unhappy with the situation and my performance reflected it. The decision was made by (my) managers to reverse the situation. I now report to the marketing manager with a dotted line reporting relationship with the financial manager (a reversal of the previous situation).

Exit was the final resort for some:

First there was a confrontation on my part to bring the problem forth, then following further unkept promises, I left the company (giving over a month's notice).

Voice is most likely when:

1. A positive relationship and trust exist.
2. Voice channels exist.
3. Other people are using voice.
4. People believe that they can influence the other contract party.

Silence is a form of non-response. Manifest as loyalty or as avoidance, silence reflects a willingness to endure or accept unfavorable circumstances. Silence can imply pessimism, in terms of believing that one has no available alternatives. Or, silence can reflect loyalty—optimistically waiting for conditions to improve (Rusbult, Farrell, Rogers, and Mainous, 1988). As a passive, constructive response, silence serves to perpetuate the existing relationship:

I started spending more time with my family and worrying less about what was happening at work.

Silence is likely when:

1. there are no voice channels, or established ways of complaining or communicating violations, and
2. no available alternative opportunities exist elsewhere.

Neglect, which entails passive negligence or active destruction, is a complex form of response. It can involve neglect of one's duties to the detriment of the interests of the other party. Passive-aggressive employee behavior, as in work slowdowns or providing customers with poor service, is a form of neglect, as is an organization's failure to invest in certain employees while developing others. Even when passive, neglect reflects erosion of the relationship between the parties. Destruction involves more active examples of counterproductive behaviors, including vandalism, theft, and interpersonal aggression (e.g., violence at work).

VIOLATION ISN'T THE END OF THE CONTRACT

Exit is only one of many results of contract violation. The fact that so many people with violated contracts remain with their employer suggests although violation may be based on a discrete event (e.g., a willful breach of contract terms), a contract's fulfillment is more a matter of degree. When Robinson and Rousseau (1994) asked employees to indicate whether their contract had been violated using a yes/no format, a total of 59 percent indicated *Yes*. However, when respondents were asked if their contract had been ultimately fulfilled by their employer, a large proportion (73 percent) indicated that their employer had honored its commitments at least moderately well. Among those employees reporting a violation at some point in the first two years of employment, 48 percent indicated that their contract had been honored at least somewhat by their employer. The major difference was that for victims of violation, the model rating of fulfillment was 3 on a 5 point scale (mean=2.65) while for non-victims it was 4 (mean=3.93). Extent of contract keeping was affected by what benefits the employee received (e.g., if not the promotion as scheduled, then a later promotion) as well as whether the violation was an isolated incident or part of a larger pattern. These findings suggest that although violation is a discrete event, contract fulfillment is not. Rather, fulfillment is a continuum shaped by both the quality of the relationship and post-violation behavior of both the victim and perpetrator.

How people respond to violation is largely a function of attributions made regarding the violators' motives, the behavior of the violator, and the scope of losses incurred. To understand how events are experienced as violations, it is necessary to take into account the perspective of the victim and the behavior of the perpetrator. For the prospective victim, the experience of violation is heightened when:

- Losses seem greater; experienced violation is a matter of degree rather than a discrete event (all or nothing).
- The event occurs in a context where it poses a threat to the relationship between the parties (e.g., a history of previous breach or conflict).
- The violation event appears to be voluntary, as opposed to inadvertent, accidental, or due to forces beyond the violator's control.
- No evidence of good faith efforts to avoid violation (the appearance of irresponsibility or neglect) is perceived by the victim.

The strength and quality of the relationship affects not only the extent to which violation is tolerated or leads to dissolution of the contract, but also affects the ability of the parties to repair the relationship. How people are treated following violation can repair the relationship or exacerbate its problems.

The dynamics of psychological contract violation offer some lessons for both managers and workers. Perceptions are facts to the person who shares them and must be taken into account in a successful worker-manager relationship. When changes are introduced it is quite possible that workers will believe that new practices will violate old promises. Rather than merely accepting the inevitability of violation, a number of steps spell the difference between a well managed employment relationship and violation, anger, and mistrust.

Actively seek to understand what the people we work with interpret to be our and the organization's commitments to them. This understanding makes it easier to both honor existing commitments as well as to know how to effectively change a deal or create a new one.

Recognize that any departure from the status quo can involve losses, painful consequences for the people who have enjoyed its benefits. Managing these losses, first by recognizing what forms they might take, and then taking steps to offset or accommodate them, can spell the difference between successful management and a breach of trust.

Even when complaints and anger indicate a violation has been experienced, a sense of good faith can be restored when the issues are directly addressed through a joint problem-solving process. Such actions can make a so-so relationship far stronger by showing commitment to joint agreement and respect for the people involved.

References

R. Allen and T. Keaveny, "Correlates of Faculty Interests in Unionization: A Replication and Extension," *Journal of Applied Psychology 66* (1981): 582–588.

R. Bies and J. Moag, "Interactional Justice Communication Criteria of Fairness," M. Bazerman, R. Lewicki, and B. Shepard (Eds.) *Research on Negotiations in Organizations 1* (Greenwich, CT: JAI Press, 1986): 43–45.

D. Farrell. "Exit, Voice, Loyalty, and Neglect as Responses to Job Dissatisfaction: A Multidimensional Scaling Study," *Academy of Management Journal 26* (1983): 596–607.

J. Getman, S. Goldberg, and J. Herman, *Union Representation Elections: Law and Reality* (New York: Russell Sage, 1976).

A. O. Hirschman, *Exit, Voice, and Loyalty* (Cambridge, MA: Harvard University Press, 1970).

J. Near and M. Miceli, "Retaliation Against Whistleblowers: Predictors and Effects," *Journal of Applied Psychology 71* (1986): 137–145.

S. L. Robinson, *Responses to Dissatisfaction.* Unpublished dissertation, Northwestern University, Kellogg Graduate School of Management, 1992.

S. L. Robinson and D. M. Rousseau, "Violating the Psychological Contract: Not the Exception but the Norm," *Journal of Organizational Behavior 15* (1994): 245–259.

D. M. Rousseau, S. L. Robinson, and M. S. Kraatz, "Renegotiating the Psychological Contract" Paper presented at the Society for Industrial Organizational Psychology meetings, Montreal, May 1992.

C. Rusbult, D. Farrell, G. Rogers, and A. Mainous, "Impact of Exchange Variables on Exit, Voice, Loyalty, and Neglect: An Integrative Model of Response to Declining Job Satisfaction," *Academy of Management Journal 31* (1988): 599–627.

E. Walster, E. Bercheid, and G. Walster, "New Directions in Equity Research," *Journal of Personality and Social Psychology 25* (1973): 151–176.

PUTTING PEOPLE FIRST FOR ORGANIZATIONAL SUCCESS*

Jeffrey Pfeffer
John Veiga

Over the past decade or so, numerous rigorous studies conducted both within specific industries and in samples of organizations that cross industries have demonstrated the enormous economic returns obtained through the implementation of what are variously called high involvement, high performance, or high commitment management practices. Furthermore, much of this research serves to validate earlier writing on participative

*Reprinted with permission from the *Academy of Management Executive 13,* no. 2 (May 1999): 37–48, via the Copyright Clearance Center.

management and employee involvement. But even as these research results pile up, trends in actual management practice are, in many instances, moving in a direction exactly opposite to what this growing body of evidence prescribes. Moreover, this disjuncture between knowledge and management practice is occurring at the same time that organizations, confronted with a very competitive environment, are frantically looking for some magic elixir that will provide sustained success, at least over some reasonable period of time.

Rather than putting their people first, numerous firms have sought solutions to competitive challenges in places and means that have not been very productive treating their businesses as portfolios of assets to be bought and sold in an effort to find the right competitive niche, downsizing and outsourcing in a futile attempt to shrink or transact their way to profit, and doing a myriad of other things that weaken or destroy their organizational culture in efforts to minimize labor costs.

SHOW ME THE EVIDENCE

Though we could go on at length about a company like Apple as a case in point (see "The Apple Story"), executives frequently say, "Don't just give me anecdotes specifically selected to make some point. Show me the evidence!" Fortunately, there is a substantial and rapidly expanding body of evidence, some of it quite methodologically sophisticated, that speaks to the strong connection between how firms manage their people and the economic results achieved. This evidence is drawn from studies of the five-year survival rates of initial public offerings; studies of profitability and stock price in large samples of companies from multiple industries; and detailed research on the automobile, apparel, semiconductor, steel manufacturing, oil refining, and service industries. It shows that substantial gains, on the order of 40 percent, can be obtained by implementing high performance management practices.[1]

According to an award-winning study of the high performance work practices of 968 firms representing all major industries, "a one standard deviation increase in use of such practices is associated with a 7.05 percent decrease in turnover and, on a per-employee basis, $27,044 more in sales and $18,641 and $3,814 more in market value and profits, respectively."[2] Yes, you read those results correctly. That's an $18,000 increase in stock market value per *employee*! A subsequent study conducted on 702 firms in 1996 found even larger economic benefits: "A one standard deviation improvement in the human resources system was associated with an increase in shareholder wealth of $41,000 per employee"[3]—about a 14 percent market value premium.

Are these results unique to firms operating in the United States? No. Similar results were obtained in a study of more than 100 German companies operating in 10 industrial sectors. The study found "a strong link between investing in employees and stock market performance. Companies which place workers at the core of their strategies produce higher long-term returns to shareholders than their industry peers."[4]

One of the clearest demonstrations of the causal effect of management practices on performance comes from a study of the five-year survival rate of 136 non-financial companies that initiated their public offering in the U.S. stock market in 1988.[5]

THE APPLE STORY

Most accounts of Apple Computer's history have stressed either strategic mistakes, such as not licensing the Macintosh operating system, or leadership issues, such as the succession to CEO by John Sculley and others. However, the Apple story also illustrates rather poignantly the negative case of what happens when a firm whose success derives fundamentally from its people fails to put people first.

Apple was founded in 1976 by Stephen Wozniak and Stephen Jobs in Jobs's garage. Their vision was to bring the power of the computer to the individual user. The Macintosh operating system, introduced in 1984, was (and many would maintain, still is) a leading technology in terms of ease of use. Apple launched the desktop publishing movement, and the company's emphasis on networks and connectivity among machines was also ahead of its time.

Apple was a company largely built on a unique culture. The Macintosh design team worked in a separate building with a pirate flag flying over it. The company built a cult-like commitment among its employees. People were recruited to Apple with the idea that they would be helping to change the world. Apple was more than a company; it was a cause. Its strategy of being an innovator in designing user-friendly personal computers that would make people more productive required a highly talented, creative, and innovative workforce. When it took actions that resulted in the loss of that workforce, its ability to implement its business strategy and to regain market leadership was irreparably harmed.

Not all of Apple's problems can be traced to how it handled its people. Even though its competitive advantage lay in its operating system, employing a mouse and a graphical user interface, the company consistently failed to license the operating system to other manufacturers, thereby limiting its share of the personal computer market. Because its culture emphasized technological innovation, Apple would occasionally introduce products, such as the Newton personal digital assistant that were either far ahead of their time or had some remaining hardware or software bugs, or both, thus occasionally suffering commercial flops. But, a case can be made that its handling of its people made both its technical and market problems and its recovery from them much worse.

In the beginning, the *Apple Employee Handbook* espoused the importance of people to the firm's success and spelled out many of the company's cherished cultural traditions, such as management accessibility and open communication, mementos of significant company events, celebrations of important life events of employees, and bagels and cream cheese on Friday mornings. After John Sculley laid off 20 percent of its workforce to cut costs when sales did not meet expectations in 1985, Apple maintained that its responsibility to its employees was not to give them any security or a career with a progression of jobs, but rather simply to provide a series of challenging job assignments that would permit them to learn and develop so as to be readily employable. In a booming local job market, this encouraged people to develop talent and skills at Apple and then to use them elsewhere. Apple's shift in emphasis to an individualistic culture could also be seen in the language used to talk about employees, who were characterized as A, B, or C players. Apple wanted to attract and retain more As and get rid of the Cs.

In 1991, about 10 percent of the workforce was laid off. In 1993, Michael Spindler replaced Sculley and continued the cost cutting by laying off 2,500 people, about 14 percent of the workforce. In 1997, another round of layoffs affected almost a third of the remaining people. More damaging than the layoffs themselves was the way they occurred in waves over time, making people unsure of their futures and tempting the best people to leave. Salaries, which had been excellent to attract the best people, were cut, as were many of the amenities that had made working at the company special. Because they feared losing jobs when a project was over, many people slowed their progress substantially. The loss of key technical and marketing personnel made the firm's prospects even worse.

The pathologies of Apple Computer are all too common. A company initially having problems with its profits, costs, or share price, takes quick action to raise profits and lower costs. Since employee costs are typically the most quickly and easily changed, the following actions are common: training is curtailed; pay may be frozen or cut; promotions are held up; the use of part-time or temporary help increases; and people are laid off or forced to work reduced hours. These measures logically and inevitably reduce motivation, satisfaction, and loyalty to the company. Rather than focus on their jobs, employees spend time discussing rumors and sharing complaints with coworkers. Cutting training cuts skill and knowledge development and dissemination. Attention focused on unhappiness at work can create a climate in which accidents and poor customer service flourish. Poor service, high accident rates, and increased turnover and absenteeism adversely affect sales, profits, and costs. So the cycle continues.

In the short run, some firms may be able to cut costs and thereby increase profits. In some cases, cuts can be made in ways that do not damage the viability of the organization. And, of course, Apple's obituary has yet to be written. While employees admit that Apple was in a death spiral, the recent return of Stephen Jobs and Apple's introduction of the iMac suggest to some that a rebirth is possible.

Indeed, as Stephen Jobs told *Fortune,*[*] "Innovation has nothing to do with how many R&D dollars you have. . . . It's not about money. It's about the people you have, how you are led, and how much you get it."

[*]D. Kirkpatrick, "The Second Coming of Apple," *Fortune* (November 9, 1998): 90.

By 1993, some five years later, only 60 percent of these companies were still in existence. The empirical analysis demonstrated that with other factors such as size, industry, and even profits statistically controlled, both the value the firm placed on human resources—such as whether the company cited employees as a source of competitive advantage—and how the organization rewarded people—such as stock options for all employees and profit sharing—were significantly related to the probability of survival. Moreover, the results were substantively important. As shown in Figure 1, the difference in survival probability for firms one standard deviation above and one standard deviation below the mean (in the upper 16 percent and the lower 16 percent of all firms in the sample) on valuing human resource was almost 20 percent. The difference in survival depending on where the firm scored on rewards was even more dramatic, with a difference in five-year survival probability of 42 percent between firms in the upper and lower tails of the distribution.

How can such substantial benefits in profits, quality, and productivity occur? Essentially, these tremendous gains come about because high performance management practices provide a number of important sources for enhanced organizational performance. Simply put, people work harder because of the increased involvement and commitment that comes from having more control and say in their work; people work smarter because they are encouraged to build skills and competence; and people work more responsibly because more responsibility is placed in hands of employees farther down in the organization. These practices work not because of some mystical process, but because they are grounded in sound social science principles that have been shown to be effective by a great deal of evidence. And, they make sense.

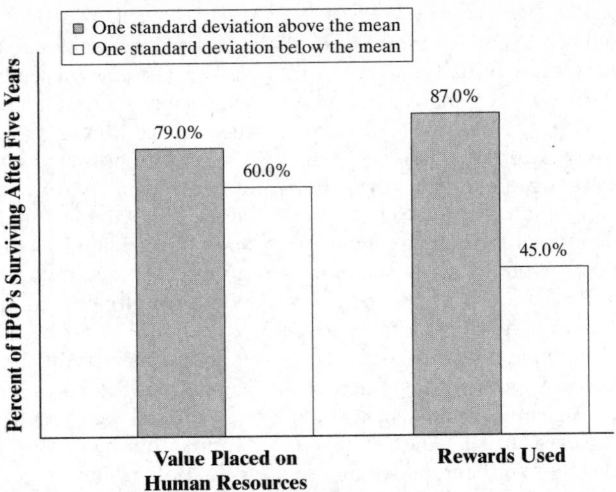

FIGURE 1 Probability of an Initial Public Offering Firm's Surviving Five Years

Source: Based on information from T. Welbourne and A. Andrews, "Predicting Performance of Initial Public Offering Firms: Should HRM Be in the Equation?" *Academy of Management Journal 39* (1996): 910–911.

SEVEN PRACTICES OF SUCCESSFUL ORGANIZATIONS

Based on these various studies, related literature, and personal observation and experience, a set of seven dimensions emerge that seem to characterize most, if not all, of the systems producing profits through people. Let's take a look at each one briefly.

EMPLOYMENT SECURITY

Most research on the effects of high performance management systems has incorporated employment security as an important dimension. Indeed, "one of the most widely accepted propositions . . . is that innovations in work practices or other forms of worker-management cooperation or productivity improvement are not likely to be sustained over time when workers fear that by increasing productivity they will work themselves out of their jobs."[6]

The idea of providing employment security in today's competitive world seems somehow anachronistic or impossible and very much at odds with what most firms seem to be doing. But employment security is fundamental to the implementation of most other high performance management practices. For example, when General Motors wanted to implement new work arrangements in its innovative Saturn plant in the 1990s, it guaranteed its people job security except in the most extreme circumstances. When New United Motors Manufacturing, Inc. (NUMMI) was formed to operate the Fremont automobile assembly plant, it offered its people job security. How else could it ask for flexibility and cooperation in becoming more efficient and productive?

Many additional benefits follow from employment assurances besides workers' free contribution of knowledge and their efforts to enhance productivity. One advantage to firms is the decreased likelihood that they will lay off employees during downturns. How is this a benefit to the firm? In the absence of some way of building commitment to retaining the workforce—either through pledges about employment security or through employment obligations contractually negotiated with a union—firms may lay off employees too quickly and too readily at the first sign of financial difficulty. This constitutes a cost for firms that have done a good job selecting, training, and developing their workforce because layoffs put important strategic assets on the street for the competition to employ. Herb Kelleher, the CEO of Southwest Airlines, summarized this argument best when he wrote:

> *Our most important tools for building employee partnership are job security and a stimulating work environment. . . . Certainly there were times when we could have made substantially more profits in the short-term if we had furloughed people, but we didn't. We were looking at our employees' and our company's longer-term interest. . . . [A]s it turns out, providing job security imposes additional discipline, because if your goal is to avoid layoffs, then you hire very sparingly. So our commitment to job security has actually helped us keep our labor force smaller and more productive than our competitors.'*[7]

SELECTIVE HIRING

Companies serious about obtaining profits through people will expend the effort needed to ensure that they recruit the right people in the first place. This requires several things. First, the organization needs to have a large applicant pool from which to select. In 1993, for example, Southwest Airlines received about 98,000 job applications, interviewed 16,000 people, and hired 2,700. In 1994, applications increased to more than 125,000 for 4,000 hires. Some organizations see processing this many job inquiries as an unnecessary expense. Southwest sees it as a necessary first step.

Second, the organization needs to be clear about what are the most critical skills and attributes needed in its applicant pool. At Southwest, applicants for flight attendant positions are evaluated on the basis of initiative, judgment, adaptability, and their ability to learn. These attributes are assessed in part from interview questions that evoke specific instances of these attributes. For instance, to assess adaptability, interviewers ask, "Give an example of working with a difficult co-worker. How did you handle it?"[8] To measure initiative, one question asks, "Describe a time when a co-worker failed to pull his or her weight and what you did about it."

Third, the skills and abilities sought need to be carefully considered and consistent with the particular job requirements and the organization's approach to its market. Enterprise Rent-A-Car is today the largest car rental company in the United States, and it has expanded at a rate of between 25 and 30 percent a year for the past 11 years. It has grown by pursuing a high customer service strategy and emphasizing sales of rental car services to repair garage customers. In a low-wage, often unionized, and seemingly low-employee-skill industry, virtually all of Enterprise's people are college graduates.

But these people are hired primarily for their sales skills and personality and for their willingness to provide good service, not for their academic performance. Brian O'Reilly interpolates Enterprise's reasoning:

> *The social directors make good sales people, able to chat up service managers and calm down someone who has just been in a car wreck. The Enterprise employees hired from the caboose end of the class have something else going for them . . . a chilling realization of how unforgiving the job market can be.*[9]

Fourth, organizations should screen primarily on important attributes that are difficult to change through training and should emphasize qualities that actually differentiate among those in the applicant pool. Southwest rejected a top pilot from another airline who did stunt work for movie studios because he was rude to a receptionist. Southwest believes that technical skills are easier to acquire than a teamwork and service attitude. Ironically, many firms select for specific, job-relevant skills that, while important, are easily acquired. Meanwhile, they fail to find people with the right attitudes, values, and cultural fit—attributes that are harder to train or change and that are quite predictive of turnover and performance.

One MBA job applicant reported that interviewers at PeopleSoft, a producer of human resource management software, asked very little about personal or academic background, except about learning experiences from school and work. Rather, the interviews focused mostly on whether she saw herself as team-oriented or as an individual achiever, what she liked to do outside school and work, and her philosophy on life. The specific question was, "Do you have a personal mission statement? If you don't, what would it be if you were to write it today?" Moreover, the people interviewing the applicant presented a consistent picture of the values that were shared among employees at PeopleSoft. Such a selection process is more likely to produce cultural fit. A great deal of research evidence shows that the degree of cultural fit and value congruence between job applicants and their organizations significantly predicts both subsequent turnover and job performance.[10]

SELF-MANAGED TEAMS AND DECENTRALIZATION AS BASIC ELEMENTS OF ORGANIZATIONAL DESIGN

Numerous articles and case examples, as well as rigorous, systematic studies, attest to the effectiveness of teams as a principle of organization design. For example, Honeywell's defense avionics plant credits improved on-time delivery—reaching 99 percent in the first quarter of 1996 as compared with below 40 percent in the late 1980s—to the implementation of teams.[11] Perhaps one of the greatest payoffs from team-based organizations is that teams substitute peer-based control for hierarchical control of work. Team-based organizations also are largely successful in having all of the people in the firm feel accountable and responsible for the operation and success of the enterprise, not just a few people in senior management positions. This increased sense of responsibility stimulates more initiative and effort on the part of everyone involved. In addition, and perhaps most importantly, by substituting peer for hierarchical control, teams permit removal of layers of hierarchy and absorption of administrative tasks previously performed by specialists, avoiding the enormous costs of having people whose sole job it is to watch people who watch other people do the work.

The tremendously successful natural foods grocery store chain, Whole Foods Markets, organized on the basis of teams, attributes much of its success to that arrangement. Between 1991 and 1996, the company enjoyed sales growth of 864 percent and net income growth of 438 percent as it expanded, in part through acquisitions as well as through internal growth, from 10 to 68 stores. In its 1995 annual report, the company's team-oriented philosophy is clearly stated.

> *Our growing information systems capability is fully aligned with our goal of creating a more intelligent organization—one which is less bureaucratic, elitist, hierarchical, and authoritarian and more communicative, participatory, and empowered. The ultimate goal is to have all team members contributing their full intelligence, creativity, and skills to continuously improving the company. Everyone who works at Whole Foods Market is a team member. This reflects our philosophy that we are all partners in the shared mission of giving our customers the very best in products and services. We invest in and believe in the collective wisdom of our team members. The stores are organized into self-managing work teams that are responsible and accountable for their own performance.*[12]

Teams also permit employees to pool their ideas to come up with better and more creative solutions to problems. Teams at Saturn and at the Chrysler Corporation's Jefferson North plant, for example, "provide a framework in which workers more readily help one another and more freely share their production knowledge—the innumerable 'tricks of the trade' that are vital in any manufacturing process."[13]

Team-based organizations are not simply a made-only-in-America phenomenon. Consider, for example, Vancom Zuid-Limburg, a joint venture in the Netherlands that operates a public bus company. This company has enjoyed very rapid growth in ridership and has been able to win transport concessions by offering more services at the same price as its competitors. The key to this success lies in its use of self-managed teams and the consequent savings in management overhead.

> *Vancom is able to [win transport contracts] mainly because of its very low overhead costs. . . . [O]ne manager supervises around 40 bus drivers. This management-driver ratio of 1 in 40 substantially differs from the norm in this sector. At best, competitors achieve a ratio of 1 in 8. Most of this difference can be attributed to the self-managed teams. Vancom . . . has two teams of around 20 drivers. Each team has its own bus lines and budgeting responsibilities. . . . Vancom also expects each individual driver to assume more responsibilities when on the road. This includes customer service (e.g., helping elderly persons board the bus), identifying problems (e.g., reporting damage to a bus stop), and active contributions (e.g., making suggestions for improvement of the services).*[14]

COMPARATIVELY HIGH COMPENSATION CONTINGENT ON ORGANIZATIONAL PERFORMANCE

It is often argued that high compensation is a consequence of organizational success, rather than its progenitor, and that high compensation (compared with the average) is possible only in certain industries that either face less competition or have particularly highly educated employees. But neither of these statements is correct.

Obviously, successful firms can afford to pay more, and frequently do so, but high pay can also produce economic success.

When John Whitney assumed the leadership of Pathmark, a large grocery store chain in the eastern United States in 1972, the company had about 90 days to live, according to its banks, and was in desperate financial shape. Whitney looked at the situation and discovered that 120 store managers in the chain were paid terribly. Many of them made less than the butchers, who were unionized. He decided that the store managers were vital to the chain's success and its ability to accomplish a turnaround. Consequently, he gave the store managers a substantial raise—about 40 to 50 percent. Whitney attributes the subsequent success of the chain to the store managers' focusing on improving performance instead of worrying and complaining about their pay.

The idea that only certain jobs or industries can or should pay high wages is belied by the example of many firms. Home Depot has been successful and profitable, and its stock price has shown exceptional returns. Even though the chain emphasizes everyday low pricing as an important part of its business strategy and operates in a highly competitive environment, it pays its staff comparatively well for the retail industry, hires more experienced people with building industry experience, and expects its sales associates to provide a higher level of individual customer service.

Contingent compensation also figures importantly in most high performance work systems. Such compensation can take a number of different forms, including gain sharing, profit sharing, stock ownership, pay for skill, or various forms of individual or team incentives. Wal-Mart, AES Corporation, Southwest Airlines, Whole Foods Markets, Microsoft, and many other successful organizations encourage share ownership. When employees are owners, they act and think like owners. However, little evidence suggests that employee ownership, by itself, affects organizational performance. Rather, employee ownership works best as part of a broader philosophy or culture that incorporates other practices. Merely putting in ownership schemes without providing training, information sharing, and delegation of responsibility will have little effect on performance. Even if people are more motivated by their share ownership, they don't necessarily have the skills, information, or power to do anything with that motivation.

EXTENSIVE TRAINING

Training is often seen as a frill in many U.S. organizations, something to be reduced to make profit goals in times of economic stringency. Studies of firms in the United States and the United Kingdom consistently provide evidence of inadequate levels of training and training focused on the wrong things: specialist skills rather than generalist competence and organizational culture. This is the case in a world in which we are constantly told that knowledge and intellectual capital are critical for success. Knowledge and skill *are* critical—and too few organizations act on this insight. Training is an essential component of high performance work systems because these systems rely on frontline employee skill and initiative to identify and resolve problems, to initiate changes in work methods, and to take responsibility for quality. All of this requires a skilled and motivated workforce that has the knowledge and capability to perform the requisite tasks.

Training can be a source of competitive advantage in numerous industries for firms with the wisdom to use it. The Men's Wearhouse, an off-price specialty retailer of men's tailored business attire and accessories, went public in 1991. Its 1995 annual report noted that it had achieved compounded annual growth rates in revenues and net earnings of 32 and 41 percent, respectively, and that the value of its stock had increased by approximately 400 percent. The company attributes its success to how it treats its people and particularly to the emphasis it has placed on training, an approach that separates it from many of its competitors. The company built a 35,000 square foot training center in Fremont, California, its headquarters. In 1994, some 600 "clothing consultants" went through Suits University, and that year the company added Suits High and Selling Accessories U.[15] During the winter, experienced store personnel come back to headquarters in groups of about 30 for a three- or four-day retraining program.

While training is an investment in the organization's staff, in the current business milieu it virtually begs for some sort of return-on-investment calculations. But such analyses are difficult, if not impossible, to carry out. Successful firms that emphasize training do so almost as a matter of faith and because of their belief in the connection between people and profits. Even Motorola does a poor job of measuring its return on training. Although the company has been mentioned as reporting a $3 return for every $1 invested in training, an official from Motorola's training group said that she did not know where these numbers came from and that the company is notoriously poor at evaluating its $170 million investment in training. The firm mandates 40 hours of training per employee per year, and believes that the effects of training are both difficult to measure and expensive to evaluate. Training is part and parcel of an overall management process and is evaluated in that light.

REDUCTION OF STATUS DIFFERENCES

The fundamental premise of high performance management systems is that organizations perform at a higher level when they are able to tap the ideas, skill, and effort of all of their people. In order to help make all organizational members feel important and committed, most high commitment management systems attempt to reduce the status distinctions that separate individuals and groups and cause some to feel less valued. This is accomplished in two principle ways—symbolically, through the use of language and labels, physical space, and dress, and substantively, in the reduction of the organization's degree of wage inequality, particularly across levels.

At NUMMI, everyone wears the same colored smock; executive dining rooms and reserved parking don't exist. At Kingston Technology, a private firm manufacturing add-on memory modules for personal computers, the two co-founders sit in open cubicles and do not have private secretaries.[16] Status differences are also reduced, and a sense of common fate developed, by limiting the difference in compensation between senior management and other employees. Herb Kelleher, who earns about $500,000 per year as the CEO of Southwest, including base and bonus, has been on the cover of *Fortune* magazine with the headline, "Is He America's Best CEO?" In 1995, when Southwest negotiated a five-year wage freeze with its pilots in exchange for stock options and occasional profitability bonuses, Kelleher agreed to freeze his base salary at $395,000 for four years. Sam Walton, the founder and chairman of Wal-Mart, was one of the most underpaid CEOs in the United States. Kelleher and Walton weren't poor; each owned stock in his company.

But stock ownership was also encouraged for their employees. Having an executive's fortune rise and fall together with those of the other employees differs dramatically from providing large bonuses and substantial salaries for executives even as the stock price languishes and people are being laid off.

SHARING INFORMATION

Information sharing is an essential component of high performance work systems. The sharing of information on such things as financial performance, strategy, and operational measures conveys to the organization's people that they are trusted. John Mackey, the chief executive of Whole Foods Markets, states, "If you're trying to create a high-trust organization . . . an organization where people are all-for-one and one-for-all, you can't have secrets."[17] Whole Foods shares detailed financial and performance information with every employee, including individual salary information. Every Whole Foods store has a book that lists the previous year's salary and bonus of all 6,500 employees.[18]

Even motivated and trained people cannot contribute to enhancing organizational performance if they don't have information on important dimensions of performance and training on how to use and interpret that information. The now famous case of Springfield ReManufacturing Corporation (SRC) illustrates this point. On February 1, 1983, SRC was created when the plant's management and employees purchased an old International Harvester plant in a financial transaction that consisted of about $100,000 in equity and $8.9 million in debt, an 89-1 debt-to-equity ratio that has to make this one of the most leveraged of all buy-outs. Jack Stack, the former plant manager and now chief executive, knew that if the plant was to succeed, all employees had to do their best, and had to share all their wisdom and ideas for enhancing the plant's performance. Stack came up with a system called "open-book management," that has become so popular that SRC now makes money by running seminars on it. When General Motors canceled an order in 1986 that represented about 40 percent of Springfield's business for the coming year, the firm averted a layoff by providing its people with information on what had happened and letting them figure out how to grow the company and achieve the productivity improvements that would obviate layoffs. SRC has since enjoyed tremendous financial success. In 1983, its first year of operation, sales were about $13 million. By 1992, sales had increased to $70 million and the number of employees had grown from 119 to 700. The original equity investment of $100,000 was worth more than $23 million by 1993. No one who knows the company, and certainly not Jack Stack or the other managers, believes this economic performance could have been achieved without a set of practices that enlisted the cooperation and ingenuity of all of the firm's people. The system and philosophy of open-book management took a failing International Harvester plant and transformed it into a highly successful, growing business.

IT ALL SEEMS SO EASY

How difficult can it be to increase the level of training, to share information and plans with people, to reorganize work into teams, to upgrade hiring practices, and to do all the other things described above? It is easy to form the ideas that are the foundation for people-centered management. But, if it were actually easy to implement those ideas, other airlines would have been able to copy Southwest, other grocery stores would be as successful as Whole Foods Markets, other power producers would be as profitable and efficient as AES, other retailers would have achieved the same record of growth and profitability as the Men's Wearhouse. Implementing these ideas in a systematic, consistent fashion remains rare enough to be an important source of competitive advantage for firms in a number of industries. Why is this so?

MANAGERS ARE ENSLAVED BY SHORT-TERM PRESSURES

Because achieving profits through people takes time to accomplish, an emphasis on short-term financial results will not be helpful in getting organizations to do the right thing. Short-term financial pressures and measurements abound. Many organizations provide raises and bonuses based on annual results. Ask senior managers how long it takes to change an organization's culture, and it's extremely unlikely that you will hear, "a year or less." But that is the time horizon of the evaluation process. Taking actions with payoffs that will occur beyond the time for which you will be measured on your performance is difficult and risky.

A second pressure occurs when organizations seek to create shareholder value by increasing stock price. The time horizon for evaluating stock market returns is again often quite short, often a year or less. Mutual fund and other institutional money managers are themselves frequently evaluated on a quarterly or at most an annual basis; they often invest in stocks for only a short time and have high portfolio turnover, so it is little surprise that they, in turn, put pressure on organizations for short-term, quick results.

A third pressure is that the immediate drives out the long-term. Today's pressing problems make it difficult to focus on actions aimed at building a better organization for the future. Managerial career processes contribute to this short-term pressure. When and where managers are hired for an indefinite period and careers are embedded in a single organization, it makes sense for those individuals to take a long-term view. But movements by managers across organizations have increased dramatically at nearly all organizational levels. Individuals trying to build a track record that will look good on the external labor market aren't likely to take a longer-term view of building organizational competence and capabilities. Stephen Smith has argued that the typical career system facing managers today encourages "managerial opportunism." He suggests that "managers are rewarded for appropriating the ideas of their subordinates or for improving the bottom line in the short run and then moving on to other positions before the long-term implications of the strategies they have adopted make themselves felt."[19]

ORGANIZATIONS TEND TO DESTROY COMPETENCE

Organizations often inadvertently destroy wisdom and competence or make it impossible for wisdom, knowledge, and experience to benefit the firm. Management practices that require programs and ideas to be explained and reviewed in groups are a major culprit.

That formal planning and evaluation, and particularly the use of financial criteria, destroy competence is consistent with the results of research on innovation. Experts on organizational management have acquired the ability to see and understand things that are not evident to novices. An expert advertising executive moves quickly and creatively to come up with a good advertising campaign; an expert in production management understands the dynamics of both the human and mechanical elements of the production system and can accurately and quickly diagnose problems and figure out appropriate action; an expert in management or leadership has a good grasp of the principles of human motivation, great intuition, and the ability to read people and situations. But in any domain of expertise, by definition, some portion of the expert's knowledge and competence must be tacit, not readily articulated or explainable, irreducible to a formula or recipe. If that were not the case, then the expert knowledge would be codified and novices could do about as well as experts at the task in question, given access to the same formulas or insights.

But if expert knowledge has a substantial component of tacit knowledge, it will be impossible for experts to present the real basis of their judgments and decisions. Experts are more likely to rely on those factors and evidence that are available and accessible to all. In so doing, they lose virtually all the benefits of their expertise. Forced to explain decisions to a wider audience, the experts will have to rely on the same data and decision processes as anyone else. Thus, the organization will have created a decision process in which its experts behave like novices, and will have lost the benefits of the experts' wisdom and competence.

Consider the following example. Bob Scott, associate director of the center for Advanced Study in the Behavioral Sciences at Stanford, had to give a talk about the center's management to an outside group interested in establishing an interdisciplinary, social-science research center. As he was giving the talk, he recalled thinking, "If we actually managed the center this way, it would be a disaster." It was not possible for him to articulate his expertise, to explain his tacit knowledge. Suppose that instead of a group of curious outsiders, his audience had been a governing board or oversight body that would hold Scott and his colleagues accountable for following and implementing the ideas he expressed? They might have been forced to manage in ways that could seriously degrade the organization's operations.

MANAGERS DON'T DELEGATE ENOUGH

Relying on the tacit knowledge and expertise of others requires trust and the willingness to let them do what they know how to do. Using self-managing teams as an organizing principle requires permitting the teams to actually manage themselves. At NUMMI, teams were given real responsibility and were listened to, while at the General Motors Van Nuys, California, plant, a culture of hierarchical control meant that team members were frequently told to be quiet and supervisors exercised the same control they had before the institution of teams.

Even though employee participation is associated with enhanced economic performance, organizations frequently fail to introduce it, and it remains fragile even when it is implemented. At least some of this resistance derives from two social psychological processes: first, belief in the efficacy of leadership, that is, the "faith in supervision" effect; and second, a self-enhancement bias. The faith in supervision effect means that observers tend to believe that the greater the degree of supervisor involvement and control, the better the work produced. In one study, for instance, identical company performance was evaluated more positively when the leadership factors accounting for the performance were made more apparent.[20] The self-enhancement bias is a pervasive social psychological phenomenon. Researchers have found that "one of the most widely documented effects in social psychology is the preference of most people to see themselves in a self-enhancing fashion. As a consequence, they regard themselves as more intelligent, skilled, ethical, honest, persistent, original, friendly, reliable, attractive, and fair-minded than their peers or the average person. . . . On the job, approximately 90 percent of managers and workers rate their performances as superior to their peers."[21] It is no wonder then that such a bias would lead supervisors to evaluate more positively the work they have been involved in creating.

Both of these processes contribute to the same prediction: work performed under more oversight and control will be perceived as better than the identical work performed with less oversight. This effect will be particularly strong for the person doing the supervision. In a real work setting, these social psychological processes would, of course, be counterbalanced by pressures to achieve results and by the knowledge that participation and empowerment may be helpful in improving performance. Nonetheless, these beliefs may be significant factors hindering the use of high performance work practices and the participation and delegation they imply.

PERVERSE NORMS ABOUT WHAT CONSTITUTES GOOD MANAGEMENT

Two norms about what constitutes good management are simultaneously growing in acceptance and are enormously perverse in their implications. The first is the idea that good managers are mean or tough, able to make such difficult choices as laying off thousands of people and acting decisively. The second is that good management is mostly a matter of good analysis, a confusion between math and management. The two views are actually related, since an emphasis on analysis takes one away from such issues as motivation, commitment, and morale, and makes it more likely that one can and will act in a tough fashion.

An article in *Newsweek* stated that "firing people has gotten to be trendy in corporate America. . . . Now you fire workers—especially white collar workers—to make your corporate bones. . . . Wall Street and Big Business have been in perfect harmony about how in-your-face capitalism is making America great."[22] *Fortune* magazine regularly runs an article entitled "America's Toughest Bosses." Does one want to appear on that list, especially since many of those on it do not last very long in their jobs, having been "fired—in part, for being too mean"?[23] Little evidence exists that being a mean or tough boss is necessarily associated with business success. "Financial results from these bosses' companies vary from superb to pathetic. The median return on shareholder's equity over the past five years for 7 of the 10 companies for which data are available ranged from 7.3 percent . . . to 18.1 percent. . . . That compares with the median for the *Fortune* 500 of 13.8 percent."[24] Nonetheless, *Fortune* predicts that "toughness . . . will probably become more prevalent. Most nominees for this list rose to prominence in industries shaken by rapid change. . . . As global competition heats up and turmoil rocks more industries, tough management should spread. So look for more bosses who are steely, super demanding, unrelenting, sometimes abusive, sometimes unreasonable, impatient, driven, stubborn, and combative."[25]

The belief that the good manager is a skilled analyst also has questionable merit and validity. The belief first arose after World War II with the emergence of Robert McNamara and systems analysis in the Defense Department. It spread to operations research and mathematical analysis in such business schools as Carnegie Mellon and such businesses as the Ford Motor Company. The emphasis on mathematical elegance and analysis as cornerstones for effective management implicitly derogates the importance of emotion, leadership, and building a vision. It represents an attempt to substitute data and analytical methods for judgment and common sense. Emphasizing analytical skills over interpersonal, negotiating, political, and leadership skills inevitably leads to errors in selection, development, and emphasis on what is important to an organization.

A ONE-IN-EIGHT CHANCE

Firms often attempt piecemeal innovations. It is difficult enough to change some aspect of the compensation system without having to also be concerned about training, recruitment and selection, and how work is organized. Implementing practices in isolation may not have much effect, however, and, can actually be counterproductive. Increasing the firm's commitment to training activities won't accomplish much unless changes in work organization permit these more skilled people to actually implement their knowledge. If wages are comparatively low and incentives are lacking, the better-trained people may simply depart for the competition. Employment security can be counterproductive unless the firm hires people who fit the culture and unless incentives reward outstanding performance. Implementing work teams will not accomplish much unless the teams receive training in specific technical skills and team processes, and are given financial and operating performance goals and information.

Implementing and seeing results from many of these practices takes time. It takes time to train and upgrade workers' skills and even more time to see the economic benefits of this training in reduced turnover and enhanced performance. It takes time to share operating and financial information with people, and to be sure that they understand and know how to use it. Even more time is needed before suggestions and insights can provide business results. It certainly requires time for employees to believe in employment security and for that belief to generate trust and produce higher levels of innovation and effort. Consequently, a long-term view of a company's development and growth is at least useful, if not absolutely essential, to implementation of high performance organizational arrangements.

One must bear in mind that one-half of organizations won't believe the connection between how they manage their people and the profits they earn. One-half of those who do see the connection will do what many organizations have done—try to make a single change to solve their problems, not realizing that the effective management of people requires a more comprehensive and systematic approach. Of the firms that make comprehensive changes, probably only about one-half will persist with their practices long enough to actually derive economic benefits. Since one-half times one-half times one-half equals one-eighth, at best 12 percent of organizations will actually do what is required to build profits by putting people first. Don't like these odds? Well, consider this: almost every other source of organizational success—technology, financial structure, competitive strategy—can be initiated in a short period of time. How many other sources of competitive advantage have a one-in-eight chance of success?

In the end, the key to managing people in ways that lead to profits, productivity, innovation, and real organizational learning ultimately lies in the manager's perspective. When managers look at their people, do they see costs to be reduced? Do they see recalcitrant employees prone to opportunism, shirking, and free riding, who can't be trusted and who need to be closely controlled through monitoring, rewards, and sanctions? Do they see people performing activities that can and should be contracted out to save on labor costs?

Or, do they see intelligent, motivated, trustworthy individuals—the most critical and valuable strategic assets their organizations can have? When they look at their people, do they see them as the fundamental resources on which their success rests and the primary means of differentiating themselves from the competition? With the right perspective, anything is possible. With the wrong one, change efforts and new programs become gimmicks, and no army of consultants, seminars, and slogans will help.

Endnotes

1. J. Pfeffer, *The Human Equation: Building Profits by Putting People First* (Boston, MA: Harvard Business School Press, 1998) Chapter 2.
2. M. A. Huselid, "The Impact of Human Resource Management Practices on Turnover, Productivity, and Corporate Financial Performance," *Academy of Management Journal 38* (1995): 647.
3. M. A. Huselid and B. E. Becker, "The Impact of High Performance Work Systems, Implementation Effectiveness, and Alignment with Strategy on Shareholder Wealth," Unpublished paper, Rutgers University, New Brunswick, NJ (1997): 18–19.
4. L. Blimes, K. Wetzker, and P. Xhonneux, "Value in Human Resources," *Financial Times,* February 1997, 10.
5. T. Welbourne and A. Andrews, "Predicting Performance of Initial Public Offering Firms: Should HRM Be in the Equation?" *Academy of Management Journal 39* (1996): 891–919.
6. R. M. Locke, "The Transformation of Industrial Relations: A Cross-National Review," *The Comparative Political Economy of Industrial Relations* eds. Kirsten S. Wever and Lowell Turner (Madison, WI: Industrial Relations Research Association, 1995) 18–19.
7. H. Kelleher, "A Culture of Commitment," *Leader to Leader 1* (1997): 23.
8. Southwest Airlines, *Case S-OB-28* (Palo Alto, CA: Graduate School of Business, Stanford University, 1994): 29.
9. B. O'Reilly, "The Rent-A-Car Jocks Who Made Enterprise #1," *Fortune,* 1996, 128.
10. See, for instance, C. A. O'Reilly, J. A. Chatman, and D. F. Caldwell, "People and Organizational Culture: A Profile Comparison Approach to Assessing Person-Organization Fit," *Academy of Management Journal 34* (1991): 487–516; and J. A. Chatman, "Managing People and Organizations: Selection and Socialization in Public Accounting Firms," *Administrative Science Quarterly 36* (1991): 459–484.
11. "Work Week," *Wall Street Journal,* May 28, 1996, Al.
12. Whole Foods Market, Inc., *1995 Annual Report,* Austin, TX: 3,17.
13. H. Shaiken, S. Lopez, and I. Mankita, "Two Routes to Team Production: Saturn and Chrysler Compared," *Industrial Relations 36* (1997): 31.
14. M. Van Beusekom, *Participation Pays! Cases of Successful Companies with Employee Participation* (The Hague: Netherlands Participation Institute, 1996): 7.
15. Men's Wearhouse, *1994 Annual Report,* Fremont, CA: 3.
16. "Doing the Right Thing," *The Economist 20* (1995): 64.
17. C. Fishman, "Whole Foods Teams," *Fast Company,* April/May 1996, 106.
18. Ibid., 105.
19. E. Appelbaum and R. Batt, *The New American Workplace* (Ithaca, NY: ILR Press, 1994): 147.
20. J. R. Meindl and S. B. Ehrlich, "The Romance of Leadership and the Evaluation of Organizational Performance," *Academy of Management Journal 30* (1987): 91–109.
21. Ibid.
22. A. Sloan, "The Hit Men," *Newsweek,* 1996, 44–45.
23. B. Dumaine, "America's Toughest Bosses," *Fortune,* 1993, 39.
24. S. Flax, "The Toughest Bosses in America," *Fortune,* 1989, 19.
25. P. Nulty, "America's Toughest Bosses," *Fortune,* 1989, 54.

CHAPTER 2
THEORIES OF MANAGING PEOPLE

THE MANAGER'S JOB

Henry Mintzberg

MASTERING COMPETING VALUES: AN INTEGRATED APPROACH TO MANAGEMENT

Robert E. Quinn

The second mental map we will examine has to do with theories of management. We all carry around models in our head about how managers should do their job or the best way to manage people. Sometimes these models are not made explicit or put into words until we run into managers who do not act like we think they should. Different people have different ideas about the role of managers.

Business scholars also have conflicting views on this topic. To settle this controversy, Henry Mintzberg carried out a classic, observational study of five chief executives at work, noting and timing everything they did. As a result, he was able to distinguish between the folklore and the facts surrounding managerial work. In an updated version of his original conclusions, "The Manager's Job," Mintzberg describes what managers actually do with their time as they manage action, people, and information.

Successful management involves a careful balancing act and the ability to manage paradox. The second article in this chapter, Robert Quinn's "Mastering Competing Values: An Integrated Approach to Management," captures the balancing act that occurs when mental maps for managing are based on competing values. Quinn, a business professor, developed a framework that includes four of the classic theories of management and explained how master managers and organizations should adapt to changing situations in their organizations. This is a practical treatment of the real challenges managers face in complex organizations.

THE MANAGER'S JOB*

Henry Mintzberg

SOME FOLKLORE AND FACTS ABOUT MANAGERIAL WORK

There are four myths about the manager's job that do not bear up under careful scrutiny of the facts.

Folklore: The manager is a reflective, systematic planner.

The evidence on this issue is overwhelming, but not a shred of it supports this statement.

Fact: Study after study has shown that managers work at an unrelenting pace, that their activities are characterized by brevity, variety, and discontinuity, and that they are strongly oriented to action and dislike reflective activities.

Consider this evidence:

- Half the activities engaged in by the five [American] chief executives [that I studied in my own research (Mintzberg, 1973a)] lasted less than nine minutes, and only 10 percent exceeded one hour. A study of 56 U.S. foremen found that they averaged 583 activities per eight-hour shift, an average of 1 every 48 seconds (Guest, 1956: 478). The work pace for both chief executives and foremen was unrelenting. The chief executives met a steady stream of callers and mail from the moment they arrived in the morning until they left in the evening. Coffee breaks and lunches were inevitably work related, and ever-present subordinates seemed to usurp any free moment.
- A diary study of 160 British middle and top managers found that they worked for a half hour or more without interruption only about once every two days (Stewart, 1967).
- Of the verbal contacts of the chief executives in my study, 93 percent were arranged on an ad hoc basis. Only 1 percent of the executives' time was spent in open-ended observational tours. Only 1 out of 368 verbal contacts was unrelated to a specific issue and could be called general planning.
- No study has found important patterns in the way managers schedule their time. They seem to jump from issue to issue, continually responding to the needs of the moment.

Is this the planner that the classical view describes? Hardly. The manager is simply responding to the pressures of the job. Clearly, these managers wanted to encourage the flow of current information. But more significantly, they seemed to be conditioned by their own work loads. They appreciated the opportunity cost of their own time, and they were continually aware of their ever-present obligations—mail to be answered, callers to attend to, and so on. It seems that no matter what he or she is doing, the manager is plagued by the possibilities of what he or she might do and must do.

---

*Adapted and reprinted with permission from *The Strategy Process: Concepts, Contexts, Cases* (Upper Saddle River, NJ: Prentice Hall, 1996): 19–34.

When the manager must plan, he or she seems to do so implicitly in the context of daily actions, not in some abstract process reserved for two weeks in the organization's mountain retreat. The plans of the chief executives I studied seemed to exist only in their heads—as flexible, but often specific, intentions. The traditional literature notwithstanding, the job of managing does not breed reflective planners; the manager is a real-time responder to stimuli, an individual who is conditioned by his or her job to prefer live to delayed action.

Folklore: The effective manager has no regular duties to perform.

Managers are constantly being told to spend more time planning and delegating, and less time on operating details. These are not, after all, the true tasks of the manager. To use the popular analogy, the good manager, like the good conductor, carefully orchestrates everything in advance, then sits back to enjoy the fruits of his or her labor, responding occasionally to an unforeseeable exception.

Fact: In addition to handling exceptions, managerial work involves performing a number of regular duties, including ritual and ceremony, negotiations, and processing of soft information that links the organization with its environment.

Consider some evidence from the early research studies:

- A study of the work of the presidents of small companies found that they engaged in routine activities because their companies could not afford staff specialists and were so thin on operating personnel that a single absence often required the president to substitute (Choran in Mintzberg, 1973a).
- One study of field sales managers and another of chief executives suggest that it is a natural part of both jobs to see important customers, assuming the managers wish to keep those customers (Davis, 1957; Copeman, 1963).
- Someone, only half in jest, once described the manager as that person who sees visitors so that everyone else can get his or her work done. In my study, I found that certain ceremonial duties—meeting visiting dignitaries, giving out gold watches, presiding at Christmas dinners—were an intrinsic part of the chief executive's job.
- Studies of managers' information flow suggest that managers play a key role in securing "soft" external information (much of it available only to them because of their status) and in passing it along to their subordinates.

Folklore: The senior manager needs aggregated information, which a formal management information system best provides.

But this never proved true at all. A look at how managers actually process information makes the reason quite clear. Managers have five media at their command—documents, telephone calls, scheduled and unscheduled meetings, and observational tours.

Fact: Managers strongly favor the verbal media—namely, telephone calls and meetings.

The evidence comes from every one of the early studies of managerial work. Consider the following:

- In two British studies, managers spent an average of 66 percent and 80 percent of their time in verbal (oral) communication (Stewart, 1967; Burns, 1954). In my study of five American chief executives, the figure was 78 percent.

- These five chief executives treated mail processing as a burden to be dispensed with. One came in Saturday morning to process 142 pieces of mail in just over three hours, to "get rid of all the stuff." This same manager looked at the first piece of "hard" mail he had received all week, a standard cost report, and put it aside with the comment, "I never look at this."
- These same five chief executives responded immediately to 2 of the 40 routine reports they received during the five weeks of my study and to four items in the 104 periodicals. In all, these chief executives of good-sized organizations initiated on their own—that is, not in response to something else—a grand total of 25 pieces of mail during the 25 days I observed them.

Consider another interesting finding. Managers seem to cherish "soft" information, especially gossip, hearsay, and speculation. Why? The reason is its timeliness; today's gossip may be tomorrow's fact. The manager who is not accessible for the telephone call informing him or her that the firm's biggest customer was seen golfing with its main competitor may read about a dramatic drop in sales in the next quarterly report. But then it's too late.

The manager's emphasis on the verbal media raises two important points:

First, verbal information is stored in the brains of people. Only when people write this information down can it be stored in the files of the organization—whether in metal cabinets or computer memory—and managers apparently do not write down much of what they hear. Thus the strategic data bank of the organization is not in the memory of its computers but in the minds of its managers.

Second, the managers' extensive use of verbal media helps to explain why they are reluctant to delegate tasks. When we note that most of the managers' important information comes in verbal form and is stored in their heads, we can well appreciate their reluctance. It is not as if they can hand a dossier over to someone; they must take the time to "dump memory"—to tell that someone all they know about the subject. But this could take so long that the managers find it easier to do the task themselves. Thus the managers are damned by their own information systems to a "dilemma of delegation"—to do too much themselves or to delegate to their subordinates with inadequate briefing.

Folklore: Management is, or at least is quickly becoming, a science and a profession.

By almost any definitions of science and profession, this statement is false. Brief observation of any manager will quickly lay to rest the notion that managers practice a science. A science involves the enaction of systematic, analytically determined procedures or programs. If we do not even know what procedures managers use, how can we prescribe them by scientific analysis? And how can we call management a profession if we cannot specify what managers are to learn?

Fact: The managers' programs—to schedule time, process information, make decisions, and so on—remain locked deep inside their brains.

I was struck during my study by the fact that the executives I was observing—all very competent by any standard—are fundamentally indistinguishable from their counterparts of a hundred years ago (or a thousand years ago, for that matter). The information they need differs, but they seek it in the same way—by word of mouth. Their decisions concern modern technology, but the procedures they use to make them are the same as the procedures of the nineteenth-century manager.

TOWARD A BASIC DESCRIPTION OF MANAGERIAL WORK

Now let us try to put some of the pieces of this puzzle together. The manager can be defined as that person in charge of an organization or one of its units. Besides chief executive officers, this definition would include vice presidents, head nurses, hockey coaches, and prime ministers. Our description takes the form of a model, building the image of the manager's job from the inside out, beginning at the center with the person and his or her frame and working out from there, layer by layer.

THE PERSON IN THE JOB

We begin at the center, with the person who comes to the job. Figure 1 shows that an individual comes to a managerial job with a set of *values*, by this stage in life probably rather firmly set, also a body of experience that, on the one hand, has forged a set of skills or *competencies*, perhaps honed by training, and, on the other, has provided a base of *knowledge*. That knowledge is, of course, used directly, but it is also converted into a set of *mental models*, key means by which managers interpret the world around them—for example, how the head nurse on a hospital ward perceives the behavior of the surgeons with whom she must work. Together, all these characteristics greatly determine how any manager approaches a given job—his or her *style* of managing. Style will come to life as we begin to see *how* a manager carries out *what* his or her job requires.

THE FRAME OF THE JOB

Embed the person depicted in a given managerial job and you get managerial work. At the core of it is some kind of *frame* for the job, the mental set the incumbent assumes to carry it out. Frame is strategy, to be sure, possibly even vision, but it is more than that. It is purpose, whether to create something in the first place, maintain something that has already been created or adapt it to changes, or else recreate something. Frame

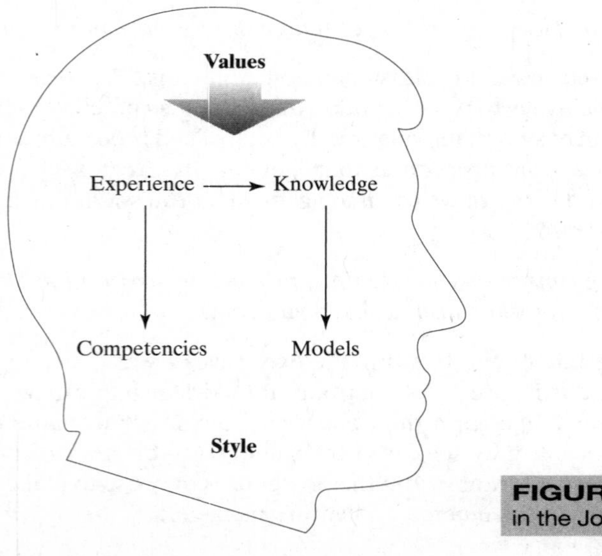

FIGURE 1 The Person in the Job

is also *perspective*—the broad view of the organization and its mission—and *positions*—concerning specific products, services, and markets.

THE AGENDA OF THE WORK

Given a person in a particular managerial job with a particular frame, the question arises of how this is manifested in the form of specific activities. That happens through the *agenda* to carry out the work, and the associated role of **scheduling**, which has received considerable mention in the literature of management. Agenda is considered in two respects here. First, the frame gets manifested as a set of current issues, in effect, whatever is of concern to the manager, broken down into manageable units—what Tom Peters likes to call "chunks." Ask any manager about his or her work, and the almost inevitable first reply will be about the "issues" of central concern, those things "on the plate," as the saying goes.

Second, the frame and the issues get manifested in the more tangible *schedule*, the specific allocations of managerial time on a day-to-day basis. Also included here, however implicitly, is the setting of priorities among the issues.

THE CORE IN CONTEXT

If we label the person in the job with a frame manifested by an agenda, the central core of the manager's job (shown by the concentric circles in Figure 2), then we turn next to the context in which this core is embedded, the milieu in which the work is practiced.

The context of the job is depicted in Figure 2 by the lines that surround the core. Context can be split into three areas, labeled Inside, Within, and Outside in Figure 2.

FIGURE 2 The Core in Context

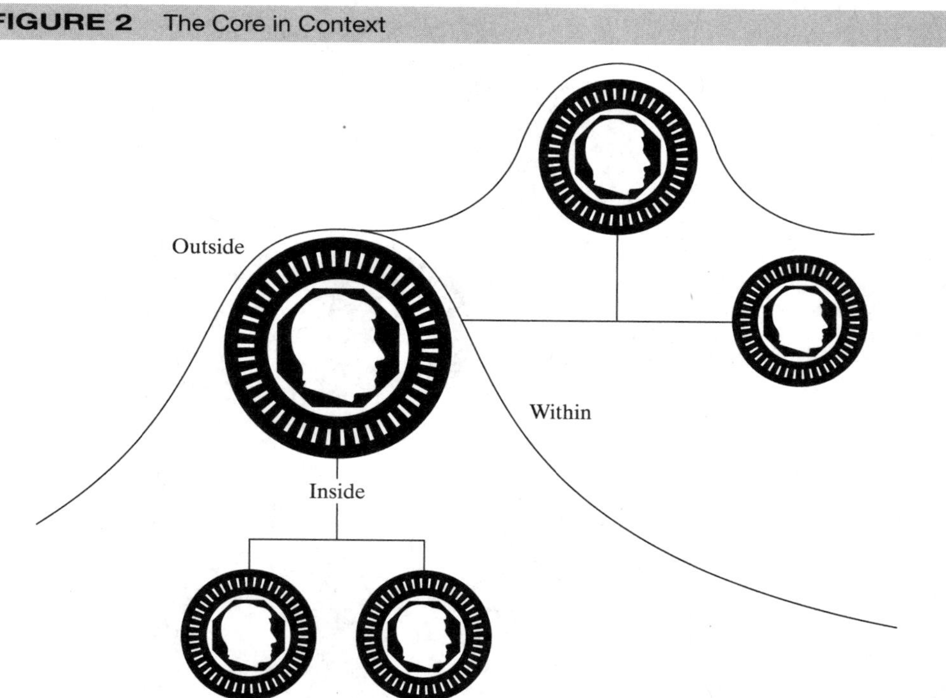

Inside refers to the unit being managed, shown below the manager to represent his or her formal authority over its people and activities—the hospital ward in the case of the head nurse, for example. *Within*, shown to the right, refers to the rest of the organization—other members and other units with which the manager must work but over which he or she has no formal authority, for example, the doctors, the kitchen, the physiotherapists in the rest of the hospital, to continue with the same example. And *outside* refers to the rest of the context not formally part of the organization with which the manager must work—in this example, patients' relatives, long-term care institutions to which some of the unit's patients are discharged, nursing associations, and so on. The importance of this distinction (for convenience, we shall mostly refer to inside versus outside) is that much of managerial work is clearly directed either to the unit itself, for which the manager has official responsibility, or at its various boundary contexts, through which the manager must act without that responsibility.

MANAGING ON THREE LEVELS

We are now ready to address the actual behaviors that managers engage in to do their jobs. The essence of the model, designed to enable us to "see" managerial work comprehensively, in one figure, is that these roles are carried out on three successive levels, each inside and outside the unit. This is depicted by concentric circles of increasing specificity, shown in Figure 3.

FIGURE 3 Three Levels of Evoking Action

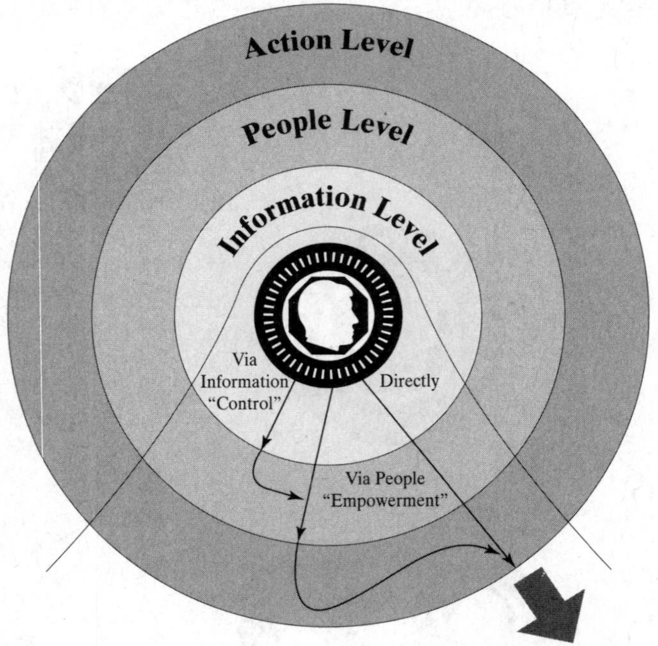

From the outside (or most tangible level) in, managers can manage *action* directly, they can manage *people* to encourage them to take the necessary actions, and they can manage *information* to influence the people in turn to take their necessary actions. In other words, the ultimate objective of managerial work, and of the functioning of any organizational unit, the taking of action, can be managed directly, indirectly through people, or even more indirectly by information through people. The manager can thus choose to intervene at any of the three levels, but once done, he or she must work through the remaining ones. Later we shall see that the level a given manager favors becomes an important determinant of his or her managerial style, especially distinguishing so-called "doers" who prefer direct action, "leaders" who prefer working through people, and "administrators" who prefer to work by information.

MANAGING BY INFORMATION

To manage by information is to sit two steps removed from the purpose of managerial work. The manager processes information to drive other people who, in turn, are supposed to ensure that necessary actions are taken. In other words, here the managers' own activities focus neither on people nor on actions per se, but rather on information as an indirect way to make things happen.

The manager's various informational behaviors may be grouped into two broad roles, here labeled communicating and controlling, shown in Figure 4. **Communicating** refers to the collection and dissemination of information. In Figure 4, communicating is shown by double arrows to indicate that managers devote a great deal of effort to the

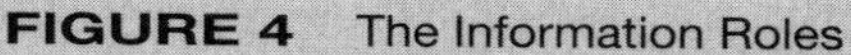

FIGURE 4 The Information Roles

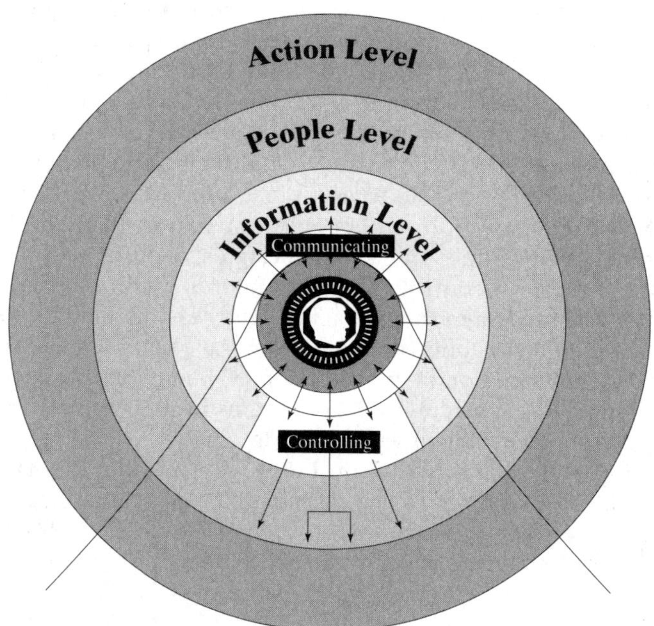

two-way flow of information with the people all around them—employees inside their own units, others in the rest of the organization, and especially, as the empirical evidence makes abundantly clear, a great number of outsiders with whom they maintain regular contact. Thus the head of one regional division of the national police force spent a good part of the day I observed him passing information back and forth between the central headquarters and the people on his staff.

Managers "scan" their environments, they monitor their own units, and they share with and disseminate to others considerable amounts of the information they pick up. Managers can be described as "nerve centers" of their units, who use their status of office to gain access to a wide variety of informational sources. Inside the unit, everyone else is a specialist who generally knows more about his or her specialty than the manager. But, because the manager is connected to all those specialists, he or she should have the broadest base of knowledge about the unit in general. This should apply to the head of a huge health care system, with regard to broad policy issues, no less than to the clinical director of one of its hospital units, with regard to the service rendered there. And externally, by virtue of their status, managers have access to other managers who are themselves nerve centers of their own units. And so they tend to be exposed to powerful sources of external information and thus emerge as external nerve centers as well.

The result of all this is that a considerable amount of the manager's information turns out to be privileged, especially when we consider how much of it is oral and nonverbal. Accordingly, to function effectively with the people around them, managers have to spend considerable time sharing their information, both with outsiders (in a kind of spokesperson role) and with insiders (in a kind of disseminator role).

I found in my initial study of chief executives that perhaps 40 percent of their time was devoted almost exclusively to the communicating role—just to gaining and sharing information—leaving aside the information processing aspects of all the other roles. In other words, the job of managing is fundamentally one of processing information, notably by talking and especially listening. Thus Figure 4 shows the inner core (the person in the job, conceiving and scheduling) connected to the outer rings (the more tangible roles of managing people and action) through what can be called the membrane of information processing all around the job.

What can be called the controlling role describes the managers' efforts, not just to gain and share information, but to use it in a directive way inside their units: to evoke or provoke general action by the people who report to them. They do this in three broad ways: they develop systems, they design structures, and they impose directives. Each of these seeks to control how other people work, especially with regard to the allocation of resources, and to what actions they are inclined to take.

First, developing systems is the most general of these three, and the closest to conceiving. It uses information to control peoples' behaviors. Managers often take charge of establishing and even running such systems in their units, including those of planning and performance control (such as budgeting).

Second, managers exercise control through designing the structures of their units. By establishing responsibilities and defining hierarchical authority, they again exercise control rather passively, through the processing of information. People are informed of their duties, which in turn is expected to drive them to carry out the appropriate actions.

Third is imposing directives, which is the most direct of the three, closest to the people and action, although still informational in nature. Managers pronounce: They make specific choices and give specific orders, usually in the process of "delegating" particular responsibilities and "authorizing" particular requests. In effect, managers manage by transmitting information to people so that they can act.

MANAGING THROUGH PEOPLE

To manage through people, instead of by information, is to move one step closer to action, but still to remain removed from it. That is because here the focus of managerial attention becomes affect instead of effect. Other people become the means to get things done, not the manager him or herself, or even the substance of the manager's thoughts.

Not until serious research on managerial work began did it become evident how important to managers were contacts with individuals outside their units. Virtually every single study of how all kinds of managers spent their time has indicated that outsiders, of an enormously wide variety, generally take as much of the managers' attention as so-called "subordinates." We shall thus describe two people roles here, shown in Figure 5, one internal, called *leading*, and one external, called *linking*.

The **leading** role has probably received more attention in the literature of management than all the other roles combined. And so we need not dwell on it here. But neither can we ignore it: managers certainly do much more than lead the people in their own units, and leading certainly infuses much else of what managers do (as, in fact, do all the roles, as we have already noted about communicating). But their work just as certainly cannot be understood without this dimension. We can describe the role of leading on three levels, as indicated in Figure 5.

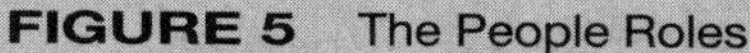
FIGURE 5 The People Roles

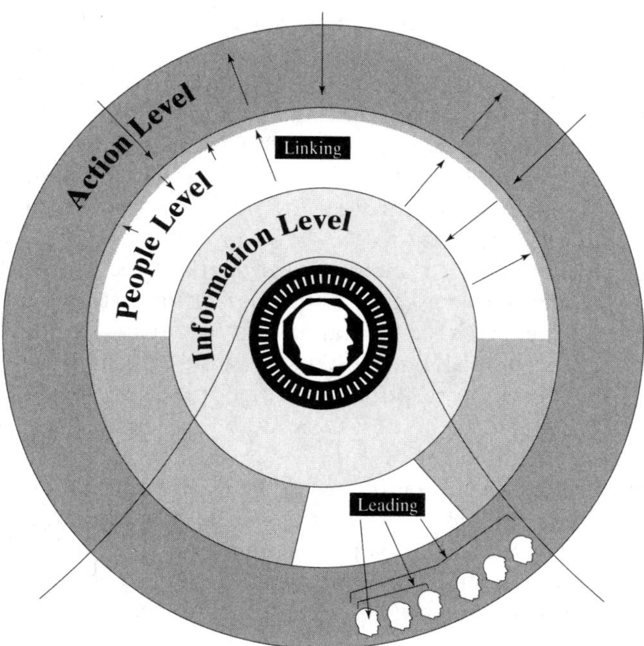

First, managers lead on the *individual* level, "one on one," as the expression goes. They encourage and drive the people of their units—motivate them, inspire them, coach them, nurture them, push them, mentor them, and so on. All the managers I observed, from the chief executive of a major police force to the front-country manager in a mountain park, stopped to chat with their people informally during the day to encourage them in their work. Second, managers lead on the *group* level, especially by building and managing teams, an effort that has received considerable attention in recent years. And third, they lead on the *unit* level, especially with regard to the creation and maintenance of culture, another subject of increasing attention in recent years (thanks especially to the Japanese). Managers, for example, engage in many acts of symbolic nature ("figurehead" duties) to sustain culture, as when the head of the national police force visited its officer training institute (as he did frequently) to imbue the force's norms and attitudes in its graduating class.

The excess attention to the role of leading has probably been matched by the inadequate attention to the role of **linking**. For, in their sheer allocation of time, managers have been shown to be external linkers as much as they are internal leaders, in study after study. Indeed, now more than ever, it must be understood, given the great growth of joint ventures and other collaborating and networking relationships between organizations, as well as the gradual reconception of the "captive" employee as an autonomous "agent" who supplies labor.

Figure 5 suggests a small model of the linking role. The arrows go in and out to indicate that the manager is both an advocate of its influence outside the unit and, in turn, a recipient of much of the influence exerted on it from the outside. In the middle are two parallel lines to represent the buffering aspect of this role—that managers must regulate the receipt of external influence to protect their units. To use a popular term, they are the *gate-keepers* of influence. Or, to add a metaphor, the manager acts as a kind of valve between the unit and its environment. Nowhere was this clearer than in my observation of three levels of management in a national park system—a regional director, the head of one mountain park, and the front-country manager of that park. They sit in an immensely complex array of forces—developers who want to enhance their business opportunities, environmentalists who want to preserve the natural habitat, tourists who want to enjoy the beauty, truckers who want to drive through the park unimpeded, politicians who want to avoid negative publicity, etc.

All managers appear to spend a great deal of time "networking"—building vast arrays of contacts and intricate coalitions of supporters beyond their own units, whether within the rest of the organization or outside, in the world at large. To all these contacts, the manager represents the unit externally, promotes its needs, and lobbies for its causes. In response, these people are expected to provide a steady inflow of information to the unit as well as various means of support and specific favors for it.

In turn, people intent on influencing the behavior of an organization or one of its sub-units will often exercise pressure directly on its manager, expecting that person to transmit the influence inside, as was most pointedly clear in the work of the parks manager. Here, then, the managerial job becomes one of delicate balance, a tricky act of mediation. Those managers who let external influence pass inside too freely—who act like sieves—are apt to drive their people crazy. (Of course, those who act like sponges and absorb all the influence personally are apt to drive themselves crazy!) And those who block out all influence—who act like lead to X-rays—are apt to detach their units from reality (and so dry up the sources of external support). Thus, what influence to pass on and how, bearing in mind the quid pro quo that influence exerted out is likely to be mirrored by influence coming back in, becomes another key aspect of managerial style, worthy of greatly increased attention in both the study of the job and the training of its occupants.

MANAGING ACTION

If managers manage passively by information and affectively through people, then they also manage actively and instrumentally by their own direct involvement in action. Indeed, this has been a long-established view of managerial work, although the excess attention in this century, first to controlling and then to leading and more recently to conceiving (of planned strategy), has obscured its importance.

I shall refer to this involvement as the **doing role**. But, in using this label, it is necessary to point out that managers, in fact, hardly ever "do" anything. Many barely even dial their own telephones! Watch a manager and you will see someone whose work consists almost exclusively of talking and listening, alongside, of course, watching and "feeling." (That, incidentally, is why I show the manager at the core of the model as a head and not a full body!)

What "doing" presumably means, therefore, is getting closer to the action, ultimately being just one step removed from it. Managers as doers manage the carrying out of action directly, instead of indirectly through managing people or by processing information. In the terms of decision making introduced earlier, here the manager diagnoses and designs as well as decides: he or she gets deeply and fully involved in the management of particular activities. Thus, in the day I spent with the head of the small retail chain, I saw a steady stream of all sorts of people coming and going, most involved with some aspect of store development or store operations, and there to get specific instructions on how to proceed next. He was not delegating or authorizing, but very clearly managing specific development projects step by step.

Just as they communicate all around the circle, so too do managers "do" all around it, as shown in Figure 6. *Doing inside* involves projects and problems. In other words, much "doing" has to do with changing the unit itself, both proactively and reactively. Managers champion change to exploit opportunities for their units, and they handle its problems and resolve its crises, often with "hands on" involvement. And the evidence, in fact, is that managers at all levels typically juggle many such projects concurrently, perhaps several dozen in the case of chief executives.

Some managers continue to do regular work after they have become managers as well. For example, a head nurse might see a patient, just as the Pope leads prayers, or a dean might teach a class. Done for its own sake, this might be considered separate from managerial work. But such things are often done for very managerial reasons as well. This may be an effective way of "keeping in touch" with the unit's work and finding out about its problems, in which case it falls under the role of communicating. Or it may be done to demonstrate involvement and commitment with others in the unit, in which case it falls under the role of culture building in the role of leading.

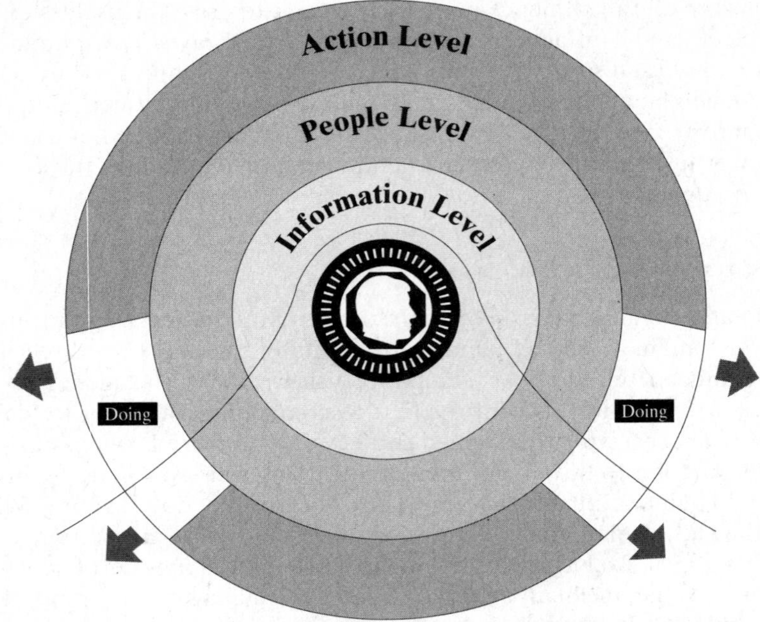

FIGURE 6 The Action Roles

Doing outside takes place in terms of deals and negotiations. Again, there is no shortage of evidence on the importance of negotiating as well as dealing in managerial work. Most evident in my observations was the managing director of the film company, who was working on one intricate deal after another. This was a small company, and making deals was a key part of her job. But even in larger organizations, senior managers have to spend considerable time on negotiations themselves, especially when critical moments arise. After all, they are the ones who have the authority to commit the resources of their unit, and it is they who are the nerve centers of its information as well as the energy centers of its activity, not to mention the conceptual centers of its strategy. All around the circles, therefore, action connects to people who connect to information, which connects to the frame.

THE WELL-ROUNDED JOB OF MANAGING

A final aspect of managerial style has to do with the interrelationships among the various components of managerial work. For example, an important distinction can be made between *deductive* and *inductive* approaches to managerial work. The former proceeds from the core out, as the conceived frame is implemented through scheduling that uses information to drive people to get action done. We can call this a *cerebral* style of managing—highly deliberate. But there is an alternate, emergent view of the management process as well, which proceeds inductively, from the outer surface to the inner core. We might label it an *insightful* style. As Karl Weick puts it, managers act in order to think. They try things to gain experience, retain what works, and then, by interpreting the results, gradually evolve their frames (Weick, 1979).

Clearly, there is an infinity of possible contexts within which management can be practiced. But just as clearly, perhaps, a model such as the one presented here can help to order them and so come to grips with the difficult requirements of designing managerial jobs, selecting the right people to fill them, and training people accordingly.

MASTERING COMPETING VALUES: AN INTEGRATED APPROACH TO MANAGEMENT*

Robert E. Quinn

It was awful. Everything was always changing and nothing ever seemed to happen. The people above me would sit around forever and talk about things. The technically right answer didn't matter. They were always making what I thought were wrong decisions, and when I insisted on doing what was right, they got pissed off and would ignore what I was saying. Everything was suddenly political. They would worry about what everyone was going to think about every issue. How you looked, attending cocktail parties—that stuff to me was unreal and unimportant.

I went through five and a half terrible years. I occasionally thought I had reached my level of incompetence, but I refused to give up. In the end, the frustration and pain turned out to be a positive thing because it forced me to consider some alternative perspectives. I eventually learned that there were other realities besides the technical reality.

I discovered perception and long time lines. At higher levels what matters is how people see the world, and everyone sees it a little differently. Technical facts are not as available or as important. Things are changing more rapidly at higher levels, you are no longer buffered from the outside world. Things are more complex, and it takes longer to get people on board. I decided I had to be a lot more receptive and a lot more patient. It was an enormous adjustment, but then things started to change. I think I became a heck of a lot better manager.

THE CONCEPT OF MASTERY

If there is such a thing as a master of management, what is it that differentiates the master from others? The answer has to do with how the master of management sees the world.

Most of us learn to think of the concept of organization in a very static way. Particularly at the lower levels, organizations seem to be characterized by relatively stable, predictable patterns of action. They appear to be, or at least we expect them to be, the product of rational-deductive thinking. We think of them as static mechanisms designed to accomplish some single purpose.

---

*Adapted from *Beyond Rational Management* (San Francisco: Jossey-Bass, Inc., 1988). With permission of author and publisher.

One of the most difficult things for most of us to understand is that organizations are dynamic. Particularly as one moves up the organizational ladder, matters become less tangible and less predictable. A primary characteristic of managing, particularly at higher levels, is the confrontation of change, ambiguity, and contradiction. Managers spend much of their time living in fields of perceived tensions. They are constantly forced to make tradeoffs, and they often find that there are no right answers. The higher one goes in an organization, the more exaggerated this phenomenon becomes. One-dimensional bromides (care for people, work harder, get control, be innovative) are simply half-truths representing single domains of action. What exists in reality are contradictory pressures, emanating from a variety of domains. This fact is important because much of the time the choice is not between good and bad, but between one good and another or between two unpleasant alternatives. In such cases the need is for complex, intuitive decisions, and many people fail to cope successfully with the resulting tension, stress, and uncertainty. This is well illustrated by the initial failure and frustration of the engineer who was quoted earlier.

The people who come to be masters of management do not see their work environment only in structured, analytic ways. Instead, they also have the capacity to see it as a complex, dynamic system that is constantly evolving. In order to interact effectively with it, they employ a variety of different perspectives or frames. As one set of conditions arises, they focus on certain cues that lead them to apply a very analytic and structured approach. As these cues fade, they focus on new cues of emerging importance and apply another frame, perhaps this time an intuitive and flexible one. At another time they may emphasize the overall task, and at still another they may focus on the welfare of a single individual.

Because of these shifts, masters of management may appear to act in paradoxical ways. They engage the contradictions of organizational life by using paradoxical frames. Viewed from a single point in time, their behaviors may seem illogical and contradictory. Yet these seeming contradictions come together in a fluid whole. Things work out well for these people.

The ability to see the world in a dynamic fashion does not come naturally. It requires a dramatic change in outlook, a redefinition of one's world view. It means transcending the rules of mechanistic logic used for solving well-defined problems and adopting a more comprehensive and flexible kind of logic. It is a logic that comes from experience rather than from textbooks. It requires a change not unlike a religious conversion.

THE EVOLUTION OF MASTERY

Dreyfus, Dreyfus, and Athanasion (1986) provide a five-stage model that describes the evolution from novice to expert.

In the novice stage people learn facts and rules. The rules are learned as absolutes that are never to be violated. For example, in playing chess people learn the names of the pieces, how they are moved, and their value. They are told to exchange pieces of lower value for pieces of higher value. In management, this might be the equivalent of the classroom education of an M.B.A.

In the advanced beginner stage, experience becomes critical. Performance improves somewhat as real situations are encountered. Understanding begins to exceed the stated facts and rules. Observation of certain basic patterns leads to the recognition of factors that were not set forth in the rules. A chess player, for example, begins to recognize certain basic board positions that should be pursued. The M.B.A. discovers the basic norms, values, and culture of the workplace on the first job.

The third stage is competence. Here the individual has begun to appreciate the complexity of the task and now recognizes a much larger set of cues. The person develops the ability to select and concentrate on the most important cues. With this ability competence grows. Here the reliance on absolute rules begins to disappear. People take calculated risks and engage in complex trade-offs. A chess player may, for example, weaken board position in order to attack the opposing king. This plan may or may not follow any rules that the person was ever taught. The M.B.A. may go beyond the technical analysis taught in graduate school as he or she experiments with an innovation of some sort. Flow or excellence may even be experienced in certain specific domains or subareas of management, as in the case of the engineer at the beginning of the article who displayed technical brilliance.

In the proficiency stage, calculation and rational analysis seem to disappear and unconscious, fluid, and effortless performance begins to emerge. Here no one plan is held sacred. The person learns to unconsciously "read" the evolving situation. Cues are noticed and responded to, and attention shifts to new cues as the importance of the old ones recedes. New plans are triggered as emerging patterns call to mind plans that worked previously. Here there is a holistic and intuitive grasp of the situation. Here we are talking, for example, about the top 1 percent of all chess players, the people with the ability to intuitively recognize and respond to change in board positions. Here the M.B.A. has become an effective, upper-level manager, capable of meeting a wide variety of demands and contradictions.

Experts, those at the fifth stage, do what comes naturally. They do not apply rules but use holistic recognition in a way that allows them to deeply understand the situation. They have maps of the territory programmed into their heads that the rest of us are not aware of. They see and know things intuitively that the rest of us do not know or see (many dimensions). They frame and reframe strategies as they read changing cues (action inquiry). Here the manager has fully transcended personal style. The master manager seems to meet the contradictions of organizational life effortlessly.

THE NEED FOR MORE COMPLEX THEORY

In their popular book, *In Search of Excellence* (1982), Peters and Waterman seek to discover what differentiates excellent companies from ordinary ones. Embedded in their work is an observation that is quite consistent with our observations. They conclude that managers in excellent companies have an unusual ability to resolve paradox, to translate conflicts and tensions into excitement, high commitment, and superior performance. In reviewing the book, Van de Ven (1983) applauds this insight and notes a grave inadequacy in the theories generated by administrative researchers. He argues that while the managers of excellent companies seem to have a capacity for dealing with paradox, administrative theories are not designed to take this phenomenon into account. In order to be internally consistent, theorists tend to eliminate contradiction. Hence, there is a need for a dynamic theory that can handle both stability and change, that can consider the tensions and conflicts inherent in human systems. Among other things, the theory would view people as complex actors in tension-filled social systems, constantly interacting with a "fast-paced, ever-changing array of forces" (Van de Ven, 1983, p. 624). The theory would center on transforming leadership that focuses on "the ethics and value judgments that are implied when leaders and followers raise one another to higher levels of motivation and morality" (Van de Ven, p. 624).

For most of us, discovering the contradictory nature of organizing is not easy. We have biases in how we process information, and we prefer to live in certain kinds of settings. Our biases are further influenced by our organizational experience at both the functional and cultural levels. At the functional level, for example, accountants and marketing people tend to develop very different assumptions about what is "good." At the cultural level, there is often a set of values that conveys "how we do things around here." Because these values tend to be so powerful, it is very difficult to see past them. It is difficult to recognize that there are weaknesses in our own perspective and advantages in opposing perspectives. It is particularly difficult to realize that these various perspectives must be understood, juxtaposed, and blended in a delicate, complex, and dynamic way. It is much more natural to see them as either/or positions in which one must triumph over the other.

A COMPETING VALUES MODEL

In the late seventies and early eighties, many of my colleagues and I became interested in the issue of organizational effectiveness. We were asking the question, What are the characteristics of effective organizations? Many studies were done in which people set out to measure the characteristics of organizations. These measures were then submitted to a technique called factor analysis. It produced lists of variables that characterized effective organizations. The problem was that these variables differed from one study to another. It seemed that the more we learned, the less we knew.

My colleague, John Rohrbaugh, and I therefore tried to reframe the question. Instead of asking what effective organizations looked like, we decided to ask how experts think about effective organizations. This would allow us to get to the assumptions behind the studies and perhaps make sense of what was causing the confusion. In a series of studies (Quinn and Rohrbaugh, 1983), we had organizational theorists and researchers make judgments regarding the similarity or dissimilarity between pairs of effectiveness criteria. The data were analyzed using a technique called multidimensional scaling. Results of the analyses suggested that organizational theorists and researchers share an implicit theoretical framework, or cognitive map (Figure 1).

Note that the two axes in the figure create four quadrants. The vertical axis ranges from flexibility to control, the horizontal axis ranges from an internal to an external focus. Each quadrant of the framework represents one of the four major models in organizational theory. The human relations model, for example, stresses criteria such as those in the upper-left quadrant: cohesion and morale, along with human resource development. The open systems model stresses criteria such as those in the upper-right quadrant. These include flexibility and readiness as well as growth, resource acquisition, and external support. The rational goal model stresses the kind of criteria found in the lower-right quadrant, including planning and goal setting and productivity and efficiency. The internal process model is represented in the lower-left quadrant. It stresses information management and communication, along with stability and control.

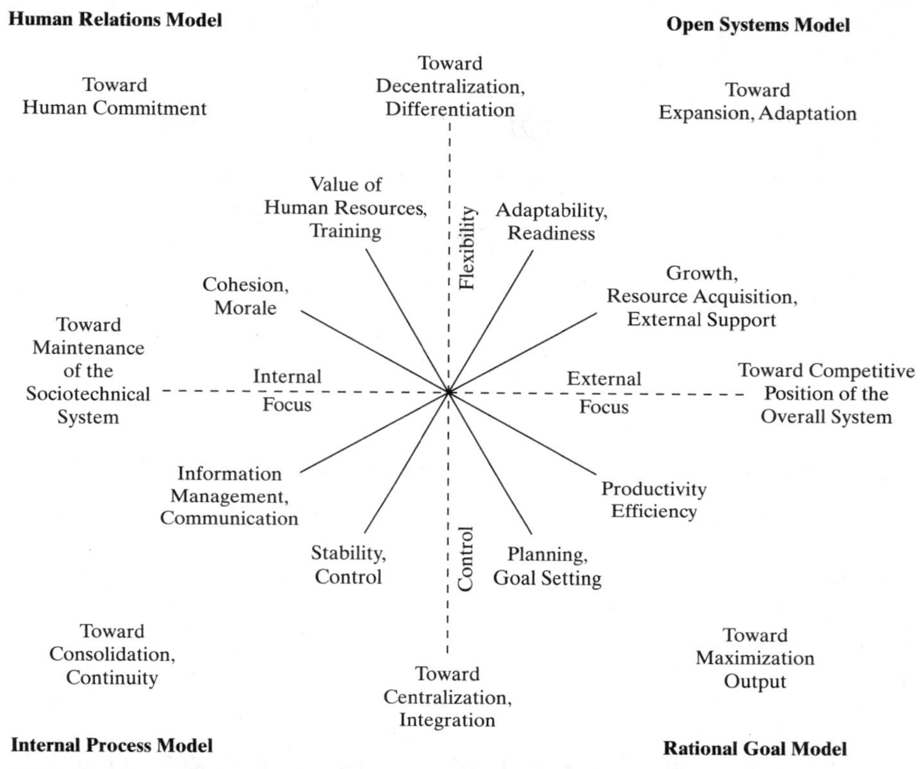

FIGURE 1 Competing Values Framework: Effectiveness

Each model has a polar opposite. The human relations model, which emphasizes flexibility and internal focus, stands in stark contrast to the rational goal model, which stresses control and external focus. The open systems model, which is characterized by flexibility and external focus, runs counter to the internal process model, which emphasizes control and internal focus. Parallels among the models are also important. The human relations and open systems models share an emphasis on flexibility. The open systems and rational goal models have an external focus (responding to outside change and producing in a competitive market). The rational goal and internal process models are rooted in the value of control. Finally, the internal process and human relations models share an internal focus (concern for the human and technical systems inside the organization).

Each model suggests a mode or type of organizing. The two sets of criteria in each quadrant also suggest an implicit means-ends theory that is associated with each mode. Thus, the rational goal model suggests that an organization is a rational economic firm. Here planning and goal setting are viewed as a means of achieving productivity and efficiency. In the open systems model we find the adhocracy, where adaptability and readiness are viewed as a means to growth, resource acquisition, and external support. In the internal process model is the hierarchy, where information management and communication are viewed as a means of arriving at stability and control. In the human relations quadrant we find the team. Here cohesion and morale are viewed as a means of increasing the value of human resources.

This scheme is called the competing values framework because the criteria seem to initially carry a conflictual message. We want our organizations to be adaptable and flexible, but we also want them to be stable and controlled. We want growth, resource acquisition, and external support, but we also want tight information management and formal communication. We want an emphasis on the value of human resources, but we also want an emphasis on planning and goal setting. The model does not suggest that these oppositions cannot mutually exist in a real system. It suggests, rather, that these criteria, values, and assumptions are oppositions in our minds. We tend to think that they are very different from one another, and we sometimes assume them to be mutually exclusive. In order to illustrate this point we will consider how values manifest themselves and, in so doing, consider some applied examples.

HOW VALUES MANIFEST THEMSELVES

In recent years much has been written about culture in organizations. When we think of the manifestation of values in organizations, it is their cultures that we are thinking of. Simply put, culture is the set of values and assumptions that underlie the statement, "This is how we do things around here." Culture at the organizational level, like information processing at the individual level, tends to take on moral overtones. While cultures tend to vary dramatically, they share the common characteristic of providing integration of effort in one direction while often sealing off the possibility of moving in another direction. An illustration may be helpful.

In October 1980 *Business Week* ran an article contrasting the cultures at JCPenney and PepsiCo. At Penney the culture focuses on the values of fairness and long-term loyalty. Indeed, a manager was once chewed out by the president of the company for making too much money! To do so was unfair to the customers, and at Penney one must never take advantage of the customer. Customers are free to return merchandise with which they are not satisfied. Suppliers know that they can establish stable, long-term relationships with Penney. Employees know that if their ability to perform a given job begins to deteriorate, they will not find themselves out on the street; rather, an appropriate alternative position will be found for them.

The core of the company's culture is captured in "The Penney Idea." Although it was adopted in 1913, it is a very modern-sounding statement, consisting of seven points:

> *To serve the public, as nearly as we can, to its complete satisfaction; to expect for the service we render a fair remuneration and not all the profit the traffic will bear; to do all in our power to pack the customer's dollar full of value, quality, and satisfaction; to continue to train ourselves and our associates so that the service we give will be more and more intelligently performed; to improve constantly the human factor in our business; to reward men and women in our organization through participation in what the business produces; to test our every policy, method, and act in this wise: "Does it square with what is right and just?"*

The culture at PepsiCo is in stark contrast to that at Penney's. After years as a sleepy company that took the back seat to Coca-Cola, PepsiCo underwent a major change by adopting a much more competitive culture. This new culture was manifest both externally and internally. On the outside PepsiCo directly confronted Coca-Cola. In bold ads customers were asked to taste and compare the products of the two companies. Internally, managers knew that their jobs were on the line and that they had to produce results. There was continuous pressure to show improvement in market share, product volume, and profits. Jobs were won or lost over a "tenth of a point" difference in these areas.

Staffs were kept small. Managers were constantly moved from job to job and expected to work long hours. The pressure never let up. During a blizzard, for example, the chief executive officer found a snowmobile and drove it to work. (This story is told regularly at PepsiCo.) Competitive team and individual sports are emphasized, and people are expected to stay in shape. The overall climate is reflected in the often repeated phrase, "We are the marines not the army."

The differences between these two companies could hardly be greater. Reading this account, you have probably concluded that one culture is more attractive than the other, and you would expect others to agree with your choice. But it is very likely that if you visited PepsiCo and spoke of "The Penney Idea," you would be laughed at. If you tried to press it upon PepsiCo employees, they would probably become incensed. Likewise, if you visited Penney's and described or tried to press upon them the values of PepsiCo, they would have the same reaction. You would be violating sacred assumptions.

Interestingly, the major problem at PepsiCo was seen as the absence of loyalty. Coca-Cola's response to the PepsiCo attack, for example, was to hire away some of PepsiCo's best "Tigers" and they were, because of the constant pressure, willing to go. (PepsiCo's rate of tenure is less than one-third of the rate at Penney.) And what, according to *Business Week*, was the major problem at Penney? Lack of competitiveness. Despite a reputation as one of the best places to work, and despite intense employee and customer loyalty, J. C. Penney had been rapidly losing market share to K-Mart. Some critics expressed doubt that Penney could respond to the challenge.

What is happening here? The surface conclusion is that two opposite cultures exist. Penney's reflects the human relations model in that the company seems to resemble a team, clan, or family. PepsiCo reflects the rational goal model in that it appears to be an instrumental firm. The strength of one is the weakness of the other. While this conclusion is true, there is a deeper insight to be gained. I will later return to this interesting contrast after considering the transformation of values.

INEFFECTIVENESS

The competing values framework consists of juxtaposed sets of organizational effectiveness criteria. Each of these "good" criteria can become overvalued by an individual and pursued in an unidimensional fashion. When this zealous pursuit of a single set of criteria takes place, a strange inversion can result. Good things can mysteriously become bad things. In Figure 2, I show how criteria of effectiveness, when pursued blindly, become criteria of ineffectiveness. These latter criteria are depicted in the negative zone on the outside of the diagram.

The structure of this model parallels the competing values framework of effectiveness. The axes, however, are negatively, rather than positively, labeled. Thus, the vertical

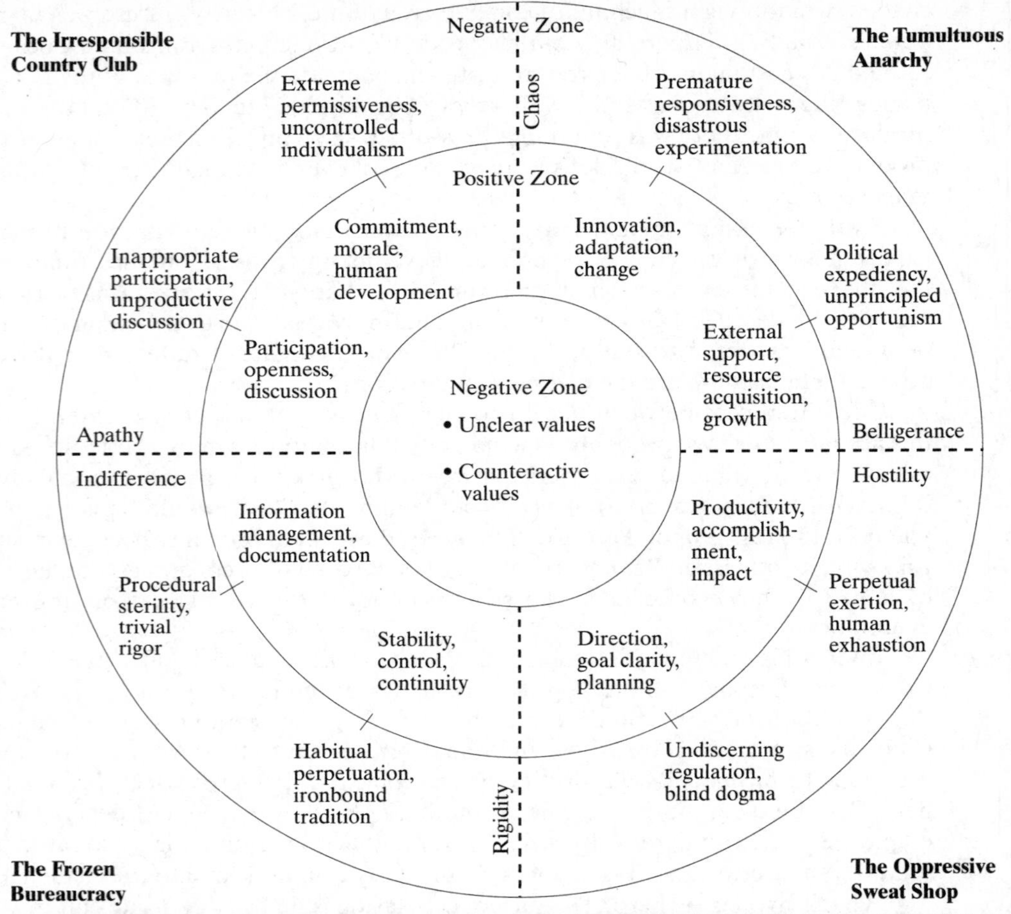

FIGURE 2 The Positive and Negative Zones

dimension ranges from chaos (too much flexibility and spontaneity) to rigidity (too much order and predictability). The horizontal dimension ranges from belligerence and hostility (too much external focus and too much emphasis on competition and engagement) to apathy and indifference (too much internal focus and too much emphasis on maintenance and coordination within the system). Each quadrant represents a negative culture with negative effectiveness criteria. Embedded within these quadrants are eight criteria of ineffectiveness.

In the upper-left quadrant is the irresponsible country club. In this quadrant, human relations criteria are emphasized to the point of encouraging laxity and negligence. Discussion and participation, good in themselves, are carried to inappropriate lengths. Commitment, morale, and human development turn into extreme permissiveness and uncontrolled individualism. Here, administrators are concerned only with employees, to the exclusion of the task.

In the upper-right quadrant is the tumultuous anarchy. In this quadrant, there is so much emphasis on the open systems criteria of effectiveness that disruption and discontinuity result. Emphasis on insight, innovation, and change turn into premature responsiveness and disastrous experimentation. Concern for external support, resource acquisition, and growth turn into political expediency and unprincipled opportunism. Here, administrators are concerned only with having a competitive advantage and show no interest in continuity and control of the work flow.

In the lower-right quadrant is the oppressive sweatshop. In this quadrant, there is too much emphasis on the criteria of effectiveness associated with the rational goal model. Effort, productivity, and emphasis on profit or impact of service turn into perpetual exertion and human exhaustion. Here, we see symptoms of burnout. Concern for goal clarification, authority, and decisiveness turn into an emphasis on strict regulation and blind dogma. There is no room for individual differences; the boss has the final say.

Finally, in the lower-left quadrant is the frozen bureaucracy. Here, there is too much concern with internal processes. The organization becomes atrophied as a result of excessive measurement and documentation; it becomes a system of red tape. Control measures, documentation, and computation turn into procedural sterility and trivial rigor. Everything is "by the book." The emphasis on stability, control, and continuity lead to the blind perpetuation of habits and traditions. Procedures are followed because "we've always done it this way"; there is no room for trying something new.

STRENGTH BECOMING WEAKNESS

Let us return to PepsiCo and JCPenney. Earlier I said that introducing the culture of one company into the other would be highly conflictual. Further, I pointed out that each culture had weaknesses. Now we can see that their very strengths put them at risk.

Because of the inability of the PepsiCo culture to tolerate the values in the human relations quadrant, the company is in danger of moving into the negative zone on the right side of Figure 2. Because of the inability of the JCPenney culture to more fully absorb the values on the right side of the figure, the company is in danger of moving into the negative zone on the left side of the figure. The more fully that each company pushes a particular set of positive values, without tending to the opposite positive values, the greater the danger to it.

The major point here is that everything in the two outer circles is related. The more that success is pursued around one set of positive values, the greater will be the pressure to take into account the opposite positive values. If these other values are ignored long enough, crisis and catastrophe will result.

STAYING IN THE POSITIVE ZONE: MASTERING PARADOX

Staying in the positive zone requires high levels of complex thought. Consider, for example, the stereotypical entrepreneur, like Steve Jobs of Apple Computer. Entrepreneurs are typically very creative and action oriented. They are usually not very sympathetic to the values in the hierarchy quadrant. When they build a new organization they often try to avoid hierarchy. Unfortunately, if their initial vision is successful, and their new company expands rapidly, the growth (an indicator of success) stimulates a need for hierarchical coordinating mechanisms (often seen as an indication of failure). This phenomenon is often called the formalization crisis. Many successful entrepreneurs are forced, like Steve Jobs at one point, to leave their company because they cannot comprehend the paradox or manage the competing values. For this reason, it is instructive to consider Bill Gates of Microsoft.

Microsoft is one of the largest software companies in the world. Run by Bill Gates, Microsoft had been best known for its widely used MS DOS system. But in 1987 Gates was successful in convincing IBM to adopt its newest product, called Windows, for use in IBM's new line of personal computers. Upon completion of the agreement analysts began to predict that within 12 months Microsoft would become the largest software company in the world.

In many ways, Gates is the stereotypical entrepreneur. He is a technical genius with a burning mission. He feels a drive to bring the power of computing to the masses. His company is marked by considerable flexibility and excitement. The median age of the workforce is 31. People work long days, with Gates himself setting the example with an early morning to midnight routine. There are frequent picnics, programmers set their own hours, dress is casual, and the turnover rate is less than 10 percent.

The company has grown rapidly. From 1980 to 1981, Gates watched his company go from 80 to 125 employees and saw profits double to $16 million. Given our earlier cases, all these indicators would lead us to worry about Gates and his ability to meet the demands for formalization.

In fact, however, Gates has already faced the formalization crisis and has come off well. What were the keys to this success? First, he made a very significant decision to bring in professional managers and to focus his own energies on technology. He seemed to grasp an important paradox that eludes most entrepreneurs: To have power means one must give up power. Maintaining a primary focus on technology, however, does not mean that he has abandoned the tasks of leadership. Instead, he has taken the time to learn the principles of law, marketing, distribution, and accounting and apply them to his work. He also has the paradoxical capacity of simultaneously caring and being tough. For example, dissatisfied with the performance of Microsoft's president, Gates removed him from office after only one year. But not long after, Gates was invited to be the best man at the wedding of the former president.

Perhaps the best summary of Gates and his abilities comes from one of his colleagues: "Bill Gates is very good at evaluating situations as they change." This, of course, is a key characteristic for staying in the positive zone.

Figure 2 has some important implications for management. It suggests that managers need to stay in the positive zone; that is, they need to pursue the seemingly "competing" positive values in the middle circle while also being careful to stay out of the external negative zone. They must maintain a dynamic, creative tension. Over time they must, like Bill Gates, be able to frame and reframe; that is, to move from one set of competing values to another.

SOME IMPLICATIONS FOR MANAGEMENT

The notions of mastery and competing values suggest a more complex and dynamic approach to management. The novice-like "rules" taught in the textbooks are misleading in that they usually represent only one of the competing perspectives or polarities embedded in organizational life. Theory X is not inherently better than theory Y. Change is not inherently better than the status quo. Productivity is not inherently better than cohesion and morale.

The challenge for experienced managers is threefold: the first is far more difficult than it sounds, to recognize and appreciate the positive (and the negative) aspects of all areas of the competing values framework; second, to assess and work on the roles and skills associated with each area; third, to analyze the present organizational moment, with all its dilemmas, and trust one's ability to integrate and employ the skills appropriate to that moment. Together these three steps are key points in the process of mastering management.

References

H. Dreyfus, S. Dreyfus, and T. Athanasion, *Mind Over Machine: The Power of Human Intuition and Expertise in the Era of the Computer* (New York: Free Press, 1986).

R. Quinn and J. Rohrbaugh, "A Spatial Model of Effectiveness Criteria: Towards a Competing Values Approach to Organizational Analysis," *Management Science 39*, no. 3 (1983): 363–377.

T. Peters and R. Waterman Jr., *In Search of Excellence* (New York: Harper & Row, 1982).

A. Van de Ven, "In Search of Excellence: Lessons from America's Best Run Companies," *Administrative Science Quarterly 28*, no. 4 (1993): 621–624.

CHAPTER 3
INDIVIDUAL AND ORGANIZATIONAL LEARNING

DEEP SMARTS

Dorothy Leonard
Walter Swap

THE LEADER'S NEW WORK: BUILDING LEARNING ORGANIZATIONS

Peter M. Senge

The ability to learn and to transfer that knowledge has become a key factor in organizational survival. Intellectual capital is a firm's most important asset in a knowledge economy and one that requires careful management. Individuals may have different learning styles and take different approaches to learning, but effective learning, mastery, and years of experience have the same end result—expert knowledge and cognition. Firms can help employees become experts by investing in their training and development, by hiring people who already possess expert knowledge, or by paying consultants for their knowledge. Regardless of the approach they use, many successful firms pay close attention to the learning needs of their employees and of the organization as a whole.

Dorothy Leonard and Walter Swap, professors of business and psychology, examine the development of "deep smarts"—explicit and tacit knowledge that extraordinarily competent people possess that allows them to both see the big picture and dive deep into the details of problems and decisions. Deep smarts, according to our first article, can be a difficult asset to manage because it resides in the heads of these experienced, competent employees, who may take those smarts with them if they retire or leave the organization. Leonard and Swap discuss how to develop deep smarts in individual employees and in the organization as a whole.

The ability to learn from experience, both on the individual and the organizational levels, is a key skill in a quickly changing business environment. The second article in this chapter, "The Leader's New Work: Building Learning Organizations" by Peter Senge, is a classic article on organizational learning. Senge, a former engineer who is the leading proponent of learning organizations, argues that companies have to surface and examine their mental maps—the assumptions on which decisions are based—in order to learn and survive. In addition to many practical suggestions about the skills and tools needed in learning organizations, Senge describes yet another aspect of the leader's job—the role of the leader in learning organizations.

DEEP SMARTS*

Dorothy Leonard
Walter Swap

When a person sizes up a complex situation and comes to a rapid decision that proves to be not just good but brilliant, you think, "That was smart." After you've watched him do this a few times, you realize you're in the presence of something special. It's not raw brainpower, though that helps. It's not emotional intelligence, either, though that, too, is often involved. It's deep smarts, the stuff that produces that mysterious quality, good judgment. Those who have deep smarts can see the whole picture and yet zoom in on a specific problem others haven't been able to diagnose. Almost intuitively, they can make the right decision, at the right level, with the right people. The manager who understands when and how to move into a new international market, the executive who knows just what kind of talk to give when her organization is in crisis, the technician who can track a product failure back to an interaction between independently produced elements—these are people whose knowledge would be hard to purchase on the open market. Their insight is based more on know-how than on facts; it comprises a system view as well as expertise in individual areas. Deep smarts are not philosophical—they're not "wisdom" in that sense—but they're as close to wisdom as business gets.

Throughout your organization, there are people with deep smarts. Their judgment and knowledge—both explicit and tacit—are stored in their heads and hands. Their knowledge is essential. The organization cannot progress without it. You will be a more effective manager if you understand what deep smarts are, how they are cultivated, and how they can be transferred from one person to another.

Very few organizations manage this asset well, perhaps because it's difficult to pin down and measure. Such neglect is risky. Individuals develop practical, often organization-specific expertise over the course of many years but can walk out the door in only a minute, taking their smarts with them. As the baby-boom-retirement tsunami approaches, lots of valuable employees and leaders will do precisely that. By 2006, for example, half of NASA's workforce will be eligible for retirement. It's not easy to harvest future retirees' knowledge, since much of it depends on context. Those with deep smarts know your business, your customers, and your product lines, both overall and in depth. And much of their insight is neither documented nor even articulated. You may not know you have lost it until you feel the cold breezes of ignorance blowing through the cracks in your product or service architecture.

---

*Reprinted with permission from *Harvard Business Review* (September 2004) 88–97.

Smaller-scale losses occur when employees with deep smarts are transferred to new locations, functions, or roles. A marketing director we know was promoted to a general management position, which encompassed new functions and required new skills. Her predecessor was scheduled to be on a plane to take a new position in Thailand within two days of the promotion, so she needed to learn about engineering, manufacturing, finance, and sales—fast. She couldn't possibly pick up the necessary skills in such a short time, but her superiors didn't even consider the costs of forcing her to muddle through on her own. Much of her predecessor's knowledge was lost.

When veterans leave, it is painful to lose strategic capabilities partly because growing them in the first place is extraordinarily challenging. Deep smarts are experience based. They can't be produced overmight or imported readily, as many companies pursuing a new strategy have discovered to their dismay. But with the right techniques, this sort of knowledge can be taught—if a company is willing to invest. Brad Anderson, the CEO of Best Buy, recently decided that the future success of his company depended on building an internal capability to innovate continuously. His employees were bright, hardworking, and terrific at delivering on set goals, but innovation had never been part of their job. Exhortation alone would not change the DNA of the organization. Anderson needed to have some deep smarts about the innovation process transferred into the company. He hired the consulting firm Strategos to coach a cohort of employees through a six-month innovation journey. He hoped participants would gain enough experience to start embedding innovative practices throughout the organization.

Best Buy's deliberate decision to build companywide expertise is unusual. In most organizations, deep smarts develop more by chance than by intent—and often in spite of management practices rather than because of them. Leaders toss people willy-nilly into new situations, incurring the costs of trial-and-error learning instead of those associated with more carefully planned transitions. But it is neither effective nor efficient to cultivate experience based know-how in such an ad hoc fashion or to rely on a company's existing processes for transferring knowledge. Most organizational practices are not grounded in a fundamental understanding of how people learn. Furthermore, most companies' training and development programs are designed to transfer explicit technical or managerial knowledge—but not deep smarts.

We learned to appreciate the importance of deep smarts when we studied how novices acquire complex managerial skills. Over two years, we conducted research at 35 start-up companies in the United States and Asia, looking most closely at how experienced coaches helped novice entrepreneurs. We also examined a number of mature organizations, including Jet Propulsion Laboratory in Pasadena, California, and Best Buy, in which managers were struggling with how to cultivate business wisdom. We interviewed more than 200 people (including each of the novice entrepreneurs and their coaches) twice, a year apart; sat in on dozens of meetings; shadowed one experienced leader as he made rounds to various protégés in India; and reviewed scores of videotapes made by people undergoing the intensive knowledge transfer effort at Best Buy. In the following pages, we draw on this field research to illustrate how organizations can develop and sustain profound institutional knowledge among their employees.

HOW DID HE *DO* THAT?

Let's look in particular at two examples of deep smarts—one technical and the other managerial.

In the 1980s, two companies were competing for a multibillion-dollar, decades-long government contract for tactical missiles. Neither had a performance advantage. The stalemate was broken by a scientist in one of the companies who was not a member of the project team. His reputation as a technical wizard (based on more than 20 years of experience developing missiles) was such that when he called a meeting of the primary project participants, they all came. For several hours, he enthralled them with a detailed proposal for design changes that he had worked out over a single week of dedicated effort. Without notes, he walked them through the redesign of an entire weapon. To put the extensive software, wiring, and hardware changes he suggested into production, as many as 400 people would have to work full time for up to a year and a half—but the expert's audience saw immediately that the modifications would create tremendous competitive advantage. His proposal precipitated a frenzy of activity, and his company won the contract. More than 20 years later, it is still reaping the harvest sown by this man with deep smarts.

Deep smarts are most easily recognized when, as in the previous example, they are based on technical knowledge. Managerial deep smarts are harder to identify, but we know that people who have them are compelling leaders. Take the case of a CEO who, in an unusual reversal of roles, had to talk his board of directors out of allowing the company to miss its earnings commitment. In early 1997, Intuit had just sold off its bill-paying operations. The board met to consider a new strategic direction. Because revenues were down, the sentiment around the boardroom table was that the company would have to miss its earnings commitments not only for that quarter but for the foreseeable future. Board members were further resigned to a drop in stock price when the earnings were announced.

CEO Bill Campbell argued passionately against this fatalistic viewpoint. Wall Street analysts, he said, had already discounted the slower growth and the resulting decline in the top line. Lower revenues would not hurt the stock price. But deliberately deciding midway through the quarter to miss earnings was contrary to good management practices. Perhaps even more important, Campbell pointed out, if the stock dropped, employee options would be worthless—and some critical individuals might well leave the company. Such defections could hurt Intuit even more than the financial blow per se. It was pure baloney that they could not make the bottom line! He knew how to cut costs—and where to start.

The board members were persuaded by Campbell, and the next few months proved him right. Managers cut expenses and hit their quarterly financial targets, and the stock stayed steady. The course set out in the board meeting was successful for Intuit, and Campbell's promise to employees that the stock would double within a year was fulfilled. What smarts did Campbell have that allowed him to make the right decision—and to sway his board? He knew, of course, the details of his company's operations well enough to pinpoint areas for potential cost cutting. But he also understood the big picture, the financial environment within which he operated; he knew how resilient Intuit could be and how to release the company's untapped energies.

He could foresee both Wall Street's reactions and those of his employees. And finally, he understood group dynamics and the personalities of his board members well enough to offer persuasive arguments.

Both the missile expert and Bill Campbell demonstrated an ability to do systems thinking *and* to dive into the details. The former, who redesigned a whole weapon by himself, knew a lot about each piece of software and hardware—but also about how they had to interact and which parts might need to be suboptimized in order to make the whole system perform better. Campbell could pull operational details about his company out of his head, but he also was emotionally intelligent about his organization as a collection of people and understood the larger financial milieu in which Intuit functioned.

THE SCIENCE BEHIND DEEP SMARTS

Experience is the obvious reason that such deeply knowledgeable individuals make swift, smart decisions. We would all rather fly with a pilot who has taken off, flown, and (especially) landed in all kinds of extreme weather than with one who has always enjoyed smooth conditions. Similarly, if we're about to go under anesthesia, we don't want to hear the surgeon exclaim. "Wow—never seen one of *these* before!" And when launching a new product, we would prefer a boss who understands design, marketing, and manufacturing over one who sees the world through only one lens. But what is it about experience that separates novices from experts?

Think about something you are really, really good at—chess or cooking or interviewing job candidates. Chances are, if you are not just competent, but truly expert, it took ten years or more to develop that expertise—in which time you've come across countless different situations. With so many of them under your belt, you have likely found some common ground and discovered a few rules of thumb that usually work: "Control the center of the board" in chess, for instance, or "Err on the side of letting people go early rather than late" in management. However, as an expert, you have the perspective to go beyond generalizations and respond to unusual situations. You know when facile rules don't apply, because you've seen so many exceptions. When confronted with a setback or a surprise, you can modify your course of action by combining elements from your menu of familiar options. In short, you can exploit an extensive *experience repertoire.*

Experts who encounter a wide variety of situations over many years accumulate a storehouse of knowledge and, with it, the ability to reason swiftly and without a lot of conscious effort. Those with keen managerial or technical intuition can rapidly determine whether current cases fit any patterns that have emerged in the past; they're also adept at coherently (though not always consciously) assembling disparate elements into a whole that makes sense. They can identify both trends and anomalies that would escape the notice of less-experienced individuals. When you ask your financial wizard how she decided so quickly that there was something wrong with the numbers on a page, she may not be able to tell you exactly how she homed in on the odd figure. In fact, when asked to explain a decision, experts often cannot re-create all the pathways their brains checked out and so cannot give a carefully reasoned answer. They chalk up to gut *feel* what is really a form of gut *knowledge.*

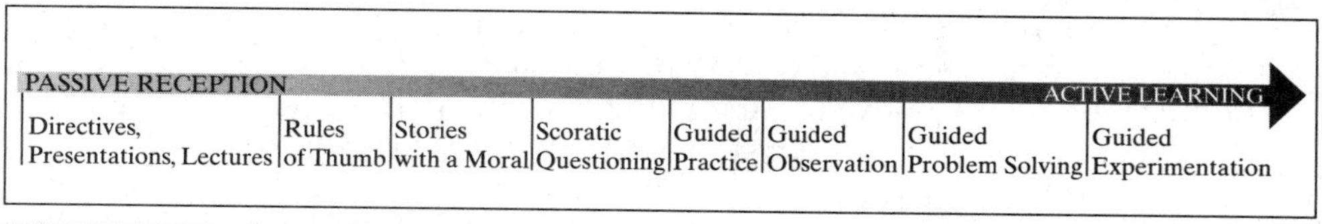

PASSIVE RECEPTION → ACTIVE LEARNING

Directives, Presentations, Lectures	Rules of Thumb	Stories with a Moral	Scoratic Questioning	Guided Practice	Guided Observation	Guided Problem Solving	Guided Experimentation

FIGURE 1 Moving Toward Deep Smarts

Of course, the experts aren't always right. Their confidence can lead to myopia or arrogance, blinding them to truly novel solutions or causing them to reject contributions from others. They can underestimate the extent to which knowledge is actually a set of beliefs and assumptions. When a physician confidently prescribes an acid suppressant for a woman who is in fact having a heart attack, not indigestion, he may be fitting her symptoms into a schema built on research about men. No chest pains—ergo, no heart attack. Only as research reveals that women's heart attack symptoms differ from men's, and as medicine builds enough knowledge to characterize these differences, will the physician be prepared to recognize the danger of his snap judgment.

MAKING SURE THE CATCHER IS READY BEFORE YOU PITCH

Many times in our lives, we need either to transfer our knowledge to someone else (a child, a junior colleague, a peer) or to access bits of wisdom accumulated in someone else's cranium. But before we can even begin to plan such a transfer, we must understand how our brains process incoming information.

What we already have in our heads determines how we assimilate new experiences. Without receptors—hooks on which to hang new information—we may not even perceive and process the information. It's like being sent boxes of documents but having no idea how they could or should be organized. Scientists who study specialized functions of the brain note that specific areas link our perceptions to long-term memory. For someone to capture complex, experience-based knowledge, his brain has to contain some frameworks, domain knowledge, or prior experiences to which current inputs can connect. Otherwise, the messages and information sent remain relatively meaningless suggestions. To a person who is unfamiliar with finance, the following advice is merely a string of words: "If you borrow money to buy back a lot of stock, you increase return on equity, but not in a way that those hawks at Moody's would approve of." Take a non-business example: "What three-dimensional avatar would you like to be in the next MUD you enter?" To many people, that question is almost unintelligible—but not to an online gamer who has represented herself in cyberspace as a three-dimensional object (an avatar) while playing in a multiuser domain (MUD). Even when the terms are explained, however, a non-gamer will not know what criteria to use in selecting an avatar. Someone who has not played such games lacks the receptors to process the query intelligently.

This cognitive limitation exists at an organizational level as well. When GE Healthcare sets up or transfers operations from one location to another, for instance, it appoints an experienced manager and team to be the "pitcher" and a team in the receiving plant to be the "catcher." These two teams work together, often over a period of years, first at the pitcher's location and then at the catcher's. To ensure a smooth transition, the pitcher team needs to be sensitive to the catcher team's level of experience and familiarity with GE Healthcare procedures. When a veteran operations manager arrived at a growing GE Healthcare plant in China, the local team was getting ready to move raw materials from the manufacturing facility into a warehouse. The operations manager could see numerous potential problems with the chosen site, but he knew that simply vetoing it would have transferred little knowledge. So he helped the team develop a list of critical-to-quality (CTQ) factors against which to evaluate potential sites. (Although this analytic process is standard operating procedure at GE, the Chinese plant hadn't adopted it yet.) The list included such factors as proximity to the manufacturing plant, easy access for large trucks, road conditions between facilities, and basic amenities for employees. List in hand, the catchers visited the selected site and could see that it met few of their criteria. They then understood the reasons for using the CTQ model for even apparently simple choices; they had a framework and some basic experience on which to build future decisions.

In many situations requiring the transfer of deep smarts, new people are thrown in to sink or swim. Sometimes they make it. They're often quick studies and have other adaptive skills. If they come into the job with few preconceptions about what does and doesn't work, they may suggest smart changes. So a deliberate decision *not* to transfer knowledge to the newcomer can have advantages. But usually, the sink-or-swim strategy is inefficient and—more important—ineffective. It is far better to deliberately create receptors by providing frameworks and tools or other types of mental structures to which experience can be tied.

TRANSFER TECHNIQUES

Receptors, of course, are not enough. The most valuable part of deep smarts is the tacit know-how (and often, know-who) that a person has built up over years of experience. This knowledge cannot be easily documented and handed over in a filing cabinet or on a CD. Managers are sophisticated; they recognize that documentation and software are inadequate to capture deep knowledge. Why, then, do they persist in relying on a thick deck of PowerPoint slides, a Web site of best practices, a repository of project reports, online training, or even in-person lectures for the transfer? Even the smartest people have difficulty gaining insight from such materials, because so much of the knowledge they need is tied to specific contexts and has tacit dimensions.

The central paradox in transferring deep smarts is that constantly reinventing the wheel is inefficient, but people learn only by doing. So what's the best way to get them up to speed? In our research, we identified a number of techniques used by what we call knowledge coaches—experts who were motivated to share some of their deep smarts with protégés. While some played the traditional mentor role of helping their protégés navigate organizations or providing personal advice, the coaches primarily served as teachers transmitting experience-based expertise.

TABLE 1 Guided Experience Versus Other Types of Learning

Guided experience—learning by doing with feedback from a knowledge coach—creates deep understanding. It is especially valuable when:

Situations	*Examples*
The skills to be learned involve interpersonal relations, so there is no set of absolute steps but rather an array of possible responses to the actions and emotions of others.	• working with a board of directors • negotiating a merger or acquisition • handling a talented prima donna
There are many tacit dimensions to the skills, so even an expert may not be able to make them all explicit.	• closing a sale • dissipating tension in a meeting • creating a new perfume or best-selling wine
The knowledge is context specific so it's appropriate to be adaptive rather than apply formulas.	• managing in a foreign culture • manufacturing with proprietary, plant-specific equipment • handling sexual harassment cases
The situation is new, so there is great uncertainty.	• launching a new service product in a new market • using a new mode of manufacturing

Rules create a mental scaffold on which to hang experience. They help people make sense of their experience but do not serve as a substitute for it. People with deep smarts will know exceptions to the rules in their domain and will feel comfortable augmenting them. But guidelines can be appropriate and helpful as a starting point especially when:

Situations	*Examples*
The skills to be learned are largely cognitive, generate little emotion, and are relatively independent of individual differences.	• accounting practices • statistical analysis of market segments
There are explicit, communicable ideas and models.	• strategic analysis using Michael Porter's "five forces" model • financial analysis of a business plan
The processes are unvarying and relatively independent of context.	• Six Sigma applications • the running of democratic meetings
The domain is well understood and expired, and there is little uncertainty about what works.	• high-volume assembly line manufacturing • product positioning on shelves

As the exhibit "Moving Toward Deep Smarts" suggests, approaches vary considerably—and predictably—in how effectively they address the deep-smarts paradox. Most of these modes are well understood. A number of books have been written about storytelling, for example, as a potent way to convey nuanced information. And Socratic questioning is pretty common. Queries such as "How do you know?" and "What would happen if . . . ?" stimulate reflection and active learning. However, the learning-by-doing methods are not as familiar to many readers. They require active engagement from both the teacher and the student, they take time, and they usually happen one-on-one.

Recall that deep smarts are based on an extensive experience repertoire. While it's true that merely describing experiences to people (or telling them what to do or giving them rules) may create some mental receptors upon which to hang experience, the

TABLE 2 Characteristics and Limitations of Deep Smarts

Sometimes an expert is the key actor in a managerial setting. Sometimes a novice is. Give them both a managerial task, and they'll approach it in characteristically different ways. And the experts aren't always right—they run risks, too.

Tasks	*Novice*	*Expert*	*Expert's Limitations*
Making decisions	Needs to review all facts and choose deliberately among alternatives	Makes decisions swiftly, efficiently without reviewing basic facts	Overconfidence; expert may ignore relevant data
Considering context	Relies on rules of thumb that minimize context	Takes context into account when solving problems	Difficulty transferring expert knowledge, because it is highly contextualized
Extrapolating information	Lacks receptors and thus has limited basis for extrapolation	Can extrapolate from a novel situation to find a solution	May base solution on inappropriate pattern
Exercising discrimination	Uses rules of thumb to obscure fine distinctions	Can make fine distinctions	May not communicate well to a novice who lacks receptors to understand distinctions
Being aware of knowledge gaps	Doesn't know what he doesn't know	Knows when rules don't apply	May assume expertise where none exists
Recognizing patterns	Has limited experience from which to draw patterns	Has large inventory of patterns drawn from experience	May be no better than novice when no patterns exist
Using tacit knowledge	Relies largely on explicit knowledge	Uses extensive tacit knowledge to drive decision making	May have a hard time articulating and thus transferring tacit knowledge

tacit dimensions of an expert's deep smarts have to be *re-created* to take hold. That is, the novice needs to discover the expert's know-how through practice, observation, problem solving, and experimentation—all under the direction of a knowledge coach. In the process, the smarts of both the expert and the novice are deepened.

Guided Practice

The old adage is right: Practice *does* make perfect—or at least better. But mindless repetition can hone the wrong skills. Better is mindful, reflective practice, in which outcomes are assessed and the method adjusted appropriately. But best of all is practice under the tutelage of someone who can guide the reflection and provide performance feedback. This is where an experienced coach comes in.

At SAIC, a consulting firm in San Diego that works primarily with the U.S. government, consultants learn their trade from a seasoned pro first by watching the expert help a client pick up a particular knowledge management process, next by leading a client session and receiving feedback from the coach, and then by teaching another consultant how to work with a client. This "see one, lead one, teach one" approach is one of SAIC's most useful knowledge transfer tools.

Guided Observation

Another powerful technique, guided observation, can be used for two very different purposes: to re-create deep smarts and to challenge ossified assumptions that may be based on outdated experience.

If your goal is to re-create deep smarts, you can have a "catcher" shadow an experienced, skilled colleague and arrange for the two to meet afterward to discuss what the catcher observed. A top consultant was once asked where and how he learned his skills in closing deals with clients. He explained that when he joined the company, an elder statesman in the firm asked him to sit in on client meetings. "You don't have to say a word," the older consultant told him. "Just listen and learn." The junior consultant rightly took that invitation as more than a suggestion and sat at the back of the room. After the meetings, he and the older consultant discussed what had occurred. "I learned more from those debriefs," he said, "than in four years at my prior company and two years of business school."

The combination of shadowing and feedback sessions works because, as we have said, deep smarts are based largely on pattern recognition and are highly contextual. Because there are so many tacit dimensions to this sort of insight, the individual possessing it will not always realize what she knows until a particular challenge calls her knowledge forth. This makes it difficult for her to give her protégé absolute, detailed directives to follow in general. She might not be able to tell a novice what the response should be to a particular situation, but she can show him.

What if the issue is not so much teaching new skills but convincing individuals to unlearn what they take for granted? We can't deepen our smarts without challenging our beliefs about our clients, our organizations, our services. Field trips—playing anthropologist for a few days to observe behaviors at other sites or companies—can help. Exposed to foreign ways of thinking and behaving, people not only extend their experience repertoire but are often shocked into questioning their own complacent understanding of the world.

When consultants from Strategos guided teams from Best Buy through the intricate steps of identifying, exploring, and prototyping new business opportunities, they first challenged the team members' assumptions about the company's uses of technology to attract typical Best Buy customers—young males who purchase powerful, feature-rich electronics. The consultants then sent team members on the road. Best Buy's Toby Nord took a trip with some colleagues to American Girl Place in Chicago that proved invaluable, though initially unsettling. American Girl specializes in a line of dolls representing historical eras. More of a destination than a retail outlet, the store features doll-centric activities: You can get a new hairdo for your doll, for example, or have tea and scones at the American Girl Cafe, where dolls sit at the table. Nord and his male colleagues were pushed out of their comfort zone. But Nord realized that the dolls at American Girl Place were a kind of platform for intergenerational socializing among grandmothers, mothers, and daughters. The store was entertaining, and its business focused tightly on a community built for a given demographic: women and girls.

The Best Buy team combined observations from this trip to Chicago and others to Mexico City, the Amish countryside in Indiana, and Seoul, South Korea, and began to see behavior patterns. All these visits stimulated thinking about social, communal behavior focused on a platform, product, or technology. The team began to generate ideas for products and services that would offer an experience or a social happening. Inspired by the groups of teens they saw in Seoul gathering to play video games, the Best Buy folks came up with a youth-centered entertainment concept: a "PCBang," where teenagers and people in their early twenties (a demographic group younger than Best Buy's typical consumers) will be able to play computer games together and socialize.

Guided Problem Solving

Guided problem solving serves different purposes and requires more active engagement from the protégé than does guided observation. A knowledge coach may or may not already know the answer to a problem. But either way, if he works on it with his protégé, the novice can learn how to approach the problem. That is, the knowledge coach transfers know-how more than know-what. During their residencies, newly minted physicians convert their book smarts into deeper, experience-based smarts as they work beside veteran doctors over a period of years.

Apprenticeships in business are less formalized—but they do occur in companies where managers are alert to the need for re-creating tacit knowledge. In an engineering company, a highly experienced design engineer was asked to train a younger colleague in the kind of systems thinking for which the older man was renowned. One of the senior engineer's most valued skills was the ability to bring multiple perspectives to any design—not just engineering knowledge about every component (software and hardware) in the complex systems the company manufactured, but also an understanding of how the systems were to be produced. He was famous for detecting and avoiding potential assembly problems and performance shortfalls. To transfer his understanding of the overall product architecture and his respect for manufacturing constraints, he had his protégé go down to the assembly line and work on problems with a test engineer for several months. The senior engineer joined many of these problem-solving sessions, adding information that the test technician lacked, such as historic customer biases and preferences. While the protégé gained specific knowledge about component parts, the more important know-how transferred was the ability to look at the whole system, see how the interfaces worked, and understand how different functional priorities led to specific design flaws. The protégé also got to know and respect the knowledge of people working on the assembly line. This experience enhanced his organizational know-who, altered his belief systems, and contributed to his technical expertise.

Guided problem solving combines many of the best features of the transfer techniques mentioned previously: focusing attention, sharpening process skills, giving feedback, providing an opportunity to mimic an expert, engaging the learner actively in developing her own deep smarts, and building an experience repertoire.

Guided Experimentation

In the first few years of their lives, children learn at a fantastic rate, partly because they are constantly experimenting. (Of course, that's what makes parents of toddlers so nervous.) Too often in organizations, we assume that experimentation is both a risky and an expensive way of learning. It doesn't have to be. The best entrepreneurial coaches in our study of 35 start-ups encouraged their charges to set up deliberate but modest experiments. This was the case with ActivePhoto, a company based on a software system that instantly downloads and catalogs digital photographs for use in a business process. In search of its best market, ActivePhoto initially considered three promising customer bases: public emergency services, insurance claims processing, and online auctioning. The tiny seven-person firm would ultimately have to choose one or two markets, but in its first few months of life it experimented with all three. Pilot studies, along with discussions with knowledge coaches, allowed the ActivePhoto people to evaluate the results of each experiment and quickly eliminate the first market.

Most retail companies use pilot markets to test new products—rolling them out in one area of the country before going national. When Whirlpool was considering custom-built appliances, the company was advised to find out whether customers were interested and whether customization would generate more market share or more profit. In a fairly simple and inexpensive experiment, Whirlpool selected two retail outlets in each of two cities (Dallas and Philadelphia) in which to set up tests for custom appliances. To draw crowds, the stores funded local advertising campaigns ("Come build your own Whirlpool refrigerator down at XYZ Appliances"). Computer kiosks in the stores allowed customers to choose from a variety of appliance features, and workers in the back busily assembled what people ordered. What did Whirlpool learn? As expected, customizing helped in the share game, at least for these four outlets. But the experiment also produced an unanticipated outcome: Customers ordered more features—approximately $70 more per refrigerator.

Coaches can offer good advice about where and how much to experiment—and more important, they can improve a team's attitude toward adding to deep smarts through experimentation. The Toyota Production System is admired for its efficient manufacturing and has attracted imitators worldwide. But researchers who have investigated the deep smarts underlying TPS have discovered that the explicit techniques so widely copied (kanban cards, andon cords, just-in-time inventory delivery) do not account for the true advantage that Toyota has. The real secret to Toyota's success is the mind-set of its employees: to constantly hypothesize about possible improvements and test those hypotheses in experiments. (See "Decoding the DNA of the Toyota Production System," by Steven Spear and H. Kent Bowen, in the September–October 1999 issue of HBR.) This sort of mind-set is possible in any industry, including service. At any given time, Bank of America's innovation and development teams are conducting more than two dozen experiments in operating branches, such as "virtual tellers," video monitors displaying financial and investment news, computer stations where customers can upload images of their canceled checks, and kiosks staffed by associates ready to open accounts or process loan applications.

BUT DOES IT COST TOO MUCH?

In our world of fast brain food, one might think that guided experience is passé at best—or at least too costly. We have heard an executive from a well-run *Fortune* 100 company say, "The days of apprenticeship are over. We don't have enough people to mentor newcomers." Many who share this view will nonetheless willingly spend millions of dollars and years of effort on data repositories and formal training. We certainly do not wish to suggest that all such investments are wasteful. But we're convinced that guided experience is the only way to cultivate deep smarts—and that managers need to be realistic about how much tacit, context-specific knowledge can be created or transferred through other means.

Fortunately, guided experience can deliver two benefits simultaneously and thus is not as costly as it might seem: first, a lasting asset in the form of transferred know-how, and second, delivery of a new business process, product idea, or capability. The learning happens on the job, so the business situations are real and relevant to today's problems. SAIC's training of U.S. Army personnel in the "peer assist" technique, for example, not only transfers process knowledge but does so in the context of a real problem—how to improve the performance of contract officers. Similarly, Strategos consultants were not only training Whirlpool and Best Buy employees to develop innovation processes; they were also showing these clients how to identify new business opportunities.

Guided experience increases value exponentially—it promotes dual-purpose learning and builds on all that we know about how people accumulate and retain knowledge. How can companies afford *not* to invest in it?

THE LEADER'S NEW WORK: BUILDING LEARNING ORGANIZATIONS*

Peter M. Senge

Human beings are designed for learning. No one has to teach an infant to walk, or talk, or master the spatial relationships needed to stack eight building blocks that don't topple. Children come fully equipped with an insatiable drive to explore and experiment. Unfortunately the primary institutions of our society are oriented predominately toward controlling rather than learning, rewarding individuals for performing for others rather than for cultivating their natural curiosity and impulse to learn. The young child entering school discovers quickly that the name of the game is getting the right answer and avoiding mistakes—a mandate no less compelling to the aspiring manager.

"Our prevailing system of management has destroyed our people," writes W. Edwards Deming, leader in the quality movement.[1] "People are born with intrinsic motivation, self-esteem, dignity, curiosity to learn, joy in learning. The forces of destruction begin with toddlers—a prize for the best Halloween costume, grades in school, gold stars, and up on through the university. On the job, people, teams, divisions are ranked—reward for the one at the top, punishment at the bottom. MBO, quotas, incentive pay, business plans, put together separately, division by division, cause further loss, unknown and unknowable."

Ironically, by focusing on performing for someone else's approval, corporations create the very conditions that predestine them to mediocre performance. Over the long run, superior performance depends on superior learning. A Shell study showed that, according to former planning director Arie de Geus, "a full one-third of the *Fortune* 500 industrials listed in 1970 have vanished by 1983."[2] Today, the average lifetime of the largest industrial enterprises is probably less than *half* the average lifetime of a person in an industrial society. On the other hand, de Geus and his colleagues at Shell also found a small number of companies that survived for seventy-five years or

*Reprinted from "The Leader's New Work," *Sloan Management Review* (Fall 1990) 7–23, by permission of publisher.

longer. Interestingly, the key to their survival was the ability to run "experiments in the margin," to continually explore new businesses and organizational opportunities that create potential new sources of growth.

If anything, the need for understanding how organizations learn and accelerating that learning is greater today than ever before. The old days when a Henry Ford, Alfred Sloan, or Tom Watson *learned for the organization* are gone. In an increasingly dynamic, interdependent, and unpredictable world, it is simply no longer possible for anyone to "figure it all out at the top." The old model, "the top thinks and the local acts," must now give way to integrating thinking and acting at all levels. While the challenge is great, so is the potential payoff. "The person who figures out how to harness the collective genius of the people in his or her organization," according to former Citibank CEO Walter Wriston, "is going to blow the competition away."

ADAPTIVE LEARNING AND GENERATIVE LEARNING

The prevailing view of learning organizations emphasizes increased adaptability. Given the accelerating pace of change, or so the standard view goes, "the most successful corporation of the 1990s," according to *Fortune*, "will be something called a learning organization, a consummately adaptive enterprise."[3] As the Shell study shows, examples of traditional authoritarian bureaucracies that responded too slowly to survive in changing business environments are legion.

But increasing adaptiveness is only the first stage in moving toward learning organizations. The impulse to learn in children goes deeper than desire to respond and adapt more effectively to environmental change. The impulse to learn, at its heart, is an impulse to be generative, to expand our capability. This is why leading corporations are focusing on *generative* learning, which is about creating, as well as *adaptive* learning, which is about coping.[4]

The total quality movement in Japan illustrates the evolution from adaptive to generative learning. With its emphasis on continuous experimentation and feedback, the total quality movement has been the first wave in building learning organizations. But Japanese firms' view of serving the customer has evolved. In the early years of total quality, the focus was on "fitness to standard," making a product reliably so that it would do what its designers intended it to do and what the firm told its customers it would do. Then came a focus on "fitness to need," understanding better what the customer wanted and then providing products that reliably *met* those needs. Today, leading edge firms seek to understand and meet the "latent need" of customers—what customers might truly value but have never experienced or would never think to ask for. As one Detroit executive commented recently, "You could never produce the Mazda Miata solely from market research. It required a leap of imagination to see what the customer *might* want."[5]

Generative learning, unlike adaptive learning, requires new ways of looking at the world, whether in understanding customers or in understanding how to better manage a business. For years, U.S. manufacturers sought competitive advantage in aggressive controls on inventories, incentive against overproduction, and rigid adherence to production forecasts. Despite these incentives, their performance was eventually eclipsed by Japanese firms who saw the challenges of manufacturing differently. They realized that eliminating delays in the production process was the key to reducing instability and improving cost, productivity, and service. They worked to build networks of relationships with trusted suppliers and to redesign physical production processes so as to reduce delays in materials procurement, production setup, and in-process inventory—a much higher-leverage approach to improving both cost and customer loyalty.

As Boston Consulting Group's George Stalk has observed, the Japanese saw the significance of delays because they see the process of order entry, production scheduling, materials procurement, production, and distribution *as an integrated system.* "What distorts the system so badly is time," observed Stalk—the multiple delays between events and responses. "These distortions reverberate throughout the system, producing disruptions, waste, and inefficiency."[6] Generative learning requires seeing the systems that control events. When we fail to grasp the systematic source of problems, we are left to "push on" symptoms rather than eliminate underlying causes. The best we can ever do is adaptive learning.

THE LEADERS' NEW WORK

"I talk with people all over the country about learning organizations, and the response is always very positive," says William O'Brien, CEO of the Hanover Insurance companies. "If this type of organization is so widely preferred, why don't people create such organizations? I think the answer is leadership. People have no real comprehension of the type of commitment it requires to build such an organization."[7]

Our traditional view of leaders—as special people who set the direction, make the key decisions, and energize the troops—is deeply rooted in an individualistic and nonsystemic worldview, especially in the West, leaders are *heroes*—great men (and occasionally women) who rise to the fore in times of crisis. So long as such myths prevail, they reinforce a focus on short-term events and charismatic heroes rather than on systematic forces and collective learning.

Leadership in learning organizations centers on subtler and ultimately more important work. In a learning organization, leaders' roles differ dramatically from that of the charismatic decision maker. Leaders are designers, teachers, stewards. These roles require new skills: the ability to build shared vision, to bring to the surface and challenge prevailing mental models, and to foster more systematic patterns of thinking. In short, leaders in learning organizations are responsible for *building organizations* where people are continually expanding their capabilities to shape their future—that is, leaders are responsible for learning.

CREATIVE TENSION: THE INTEGRATING PRINCIPLE

Leadership in a learning organization starts with the principle of creative tension.[8] Creative tension comes from seeing clearly where we want to be, our "vision," and telling the truth about where we are, our "current reality." The gap between the two generates a natural tension (See Figure 1.)

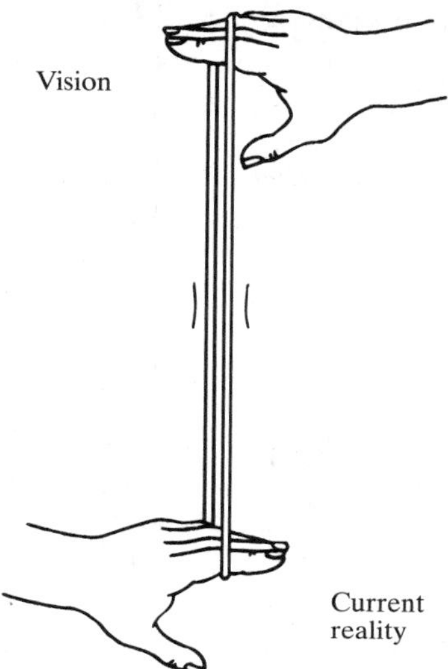

FIGURE 1 The Principle of Creative Tension

Creative tension can be resolved in two basic ways: by raising current reality toward the vision, or by lowering the vision toward current reality. Individuals, groups, and organizations who learn how to work with creative tension learn how to use the energy it generates to move reality more reliably toward their visions.

The principle of creative tension has long been recognized by leaders. Martin Luther King, Jr. once said, "Just as Socrates felt that it was necessary to create a tension in the mind, so that individuals could rise from the bondage of myths and half truths . . . so must we . . . create the kind of tension in society that will help men rise from the dark depths of prejudice and racism."[9]

Without vision there is no creative tension. Creative tension cannot be generated from current reality alone. All the analysis in the world will never generate a vision. Many who are otherwise qualified to lead fail to do so because they try to substitute analysis for vision. They believe that, if only people understood current reality, they would surely feel the motivation to change. They are then disappointed to discover that people "resist" the personal and organizational changes that must be made to alter reality. What they never grasp is that the natural energy for changing reality comes from holding a picture of what might be that is more important to people than what is.

But creative tension cannot be generated from vision alone; it demands an accurate picture of current reality as well. Just as King had a dream, so too did he continually strive to "dramatize the shameful conditions" of racism and prejudice so that they could no longer be ignored. Vision without an understanding of current reality will more likely foster cynicism than creativity. The principle of creative tension teaches that *an accurate picture of current reality is just as important as a compelling picture of a desired future.*

Leading through creative tension is different than solving problems. In problem solving, the energy for change comes from attempting to get away from an aspect of current reality that is undesirable. With creative tension the energy for change comes from the vision, from what we want to create, juxtaposed with current reality. While the distinction may seem small, the consequences are not. Many people and organizations find themselves motivated to change only when their problems are bad enough to cause them to change. This works for a while, but the change process runs out of steam as soon as the problems driving the change become less pressing. With problem solving, the motivation for change is extrinsic. With creative tension, the motivation is intrinsic. This distinction mirrors the distinction between adaptive and generative learning.

NEW ROLES

The traditional authoritarian image of the leader as "the boss calling the shots" has been recognized as oversimplified and inadequate for some time. According to Edgar Schein, "Leadership is intertwined with culture formation." Building an organization's culture and shaping its evolution is the "unique and essential function" of leadership.[10] In a learning organization, the critical roles of leadership-designer, teacher, and steward have antecedents in the ways leaders have contributed to building organizations in the past. But each role takes on a new meaning in the learning organizations and, as will be seen in the following sections, demands new skills and tools.

LEADER AS DESIGNER

Imagine that your organization is an ocean liner and that you are "the leader." What is your role?

I have asked this question of groups of managers many times. The most common answer, not surprisingly, is "the captain." Others say, "The navigator, setting the direction." Still others say, "The helmsman, actually controlling the direction," or, "The engineer down there stroking the fire, providing energy," or, "The social director, making sure everybody's enrolled, involved, and communicating." While these are legitimate leadership roles, there is another which, in many ways, eclipses them all in importance. Yet rarely does anyone mention it.

The neglected leadership role is the *designer* of the ship. No one has a more sweeping influence than the designer. What good does it do for the captain to say, "Turn starboard 30 degrees," when the designer has built a rudder that will only turn to port, or which takes six hours to turn to starboard? It's fruitless to be the leader in an organization that is poorly designed.

The functions of design, or what some have called "social architecture," are rarely visible; they take place behind the scenes. The consequences that appear today are the result of work done long in the past, and work today will show its benefits far in the future. Those who aspire to lead out of a desire to control, or gain fame, or simply to be at the center of the action, will find little to attract them to the quiet design work of leadership.

But what, specifically, is involved in organizational design? "Organizational design is widely misconstrued as moving around boxes and lines," says Hanover's O'Brien. "The first task of organization design concerns designing the governing ideas of purpose, vision, and core values by which people will live." Few acts of leadership have a more enduring impact on an organization than building a foundation of purpose and core values.

In 1982, Johnson & Johnson found itself facing a corporate nightmare when bottles of its bestselling Tylenol were tampered with, resulting in several deaths. The corporation's immediate response was to pull all Tylenol off the shelves of retail outlets. Thirty-one million capsules were destroyed, even though they were tested and found safe. Although the immediate cost was significant, no other action was possible given the firm's credo. Authored almost 40 years earlier by president Robert Wood Johnson, Johnson & Johnson's credo states that permanent success is possible only when modern industry realizes that:

- service to its customers comes first;
- service to its employees and management comes second;
- service to the community comes third; and
- service to its stockholders, last.

Such statements might seem like motherhood and apple pie to those who have not seen the way a clear sense of purpose and values can affect key business decisions. Johnson & Johnson's crisis management in this case was based on that credo. It was simple, it was right, and it worked.

If governing ideas constitute the first design task of leadership, the second design task involves the policies, strategies, and structures that translate guiding ideas into business decisions. Leadership theorist Philip Selznick calls policy and structure the "institutional embodiment of purpose."[11] "Policy making (the rules that guide decisions) ought to be separated from decision making," says Jay Forrester.[12] "Otherwise, short-term pressures will usurp time from policy creation."

Traditionally, writers like Selznick and Forrester have tended to see policy making and implementation as the work of a small number of senior managers. But that view is changing. Both the dynamic business environment and the mandate of the learning organization to engage people at all levels now make it clear that this second design task is more subtle. Henry Mintzberg has argued that strategy is less a rational plan arrived at in the abstract and implemented throughout the organization than an "emergent phenomenon." Successful organizations "craft strategy" according to Mintzberg, as they continually learn about shifting business conditions and balance what is desired and what is possible.[13] The key is not getting the right strategy but fostering strategic thinking. "The choice of individual action is only part of the policymaker's need," according to Mason and Mitroff.[14] "More important is the need to achieve insight into the nature of the complexity and to formulate concepts and world views for coping with it."

Behind appropriate policies, strategies, and structures are effective learning processes; their creation is the third key design responsibility in learning organizations. This does not absolve senior managers of their strategic responsibilities. Now, they are not only responsible for ensuring that an organization have well-developed strategies and policies, but also for ensuring that processes exist whereby these are continually improved.

In the early 1970s, Shell was the weakest of the big seven oil companies. Today, Shell and Exxon are arguably the strongest, both in size and financial health. Shell's ascendence began with frustration. Around 1971 members of Shell's "Group Planning" in London began to foresee dramatic change and unpredictability in world oil markets. However, it proved impossible to persuade managers that the stable world of steady growth in oil demand and supply they had known for 20 years was about to change. Despite brilliant analysis and artful presentation, Shell's planners realized, in the words of Pierre Wack, that they "had failed to change behavior in much of the Shell organization."[15] Progress would probably have ended there, had the frustration not given way to a radically new view of corporate planning.

As they pondered this failure, the planner's view of their basic task shifted: "We no longer saw our task as producing a documented view of the future business environment 5 or 10 years ahead. Our real target was the microcosm (the 'mental model') of our decision makers." Only when the planners reconceptualized their basic task as fostering learning rather than devising plans did their insights begin to have an impact. The initial tool used was "scenario analysis," through which planners encouraged operating managers to think through how they would manage in the future under different possible scenarios. It mattered not that the managers believed the planners' scenarios absolutely, only that they became engaged in ferreting out the implications. In this way, Shell's planners conditioned managers to be mentally prepared for a shift from low prices to high prices and from stability to instability. The results were significant. When OPEC became a reality, Shell quickly responded by increasing local operating company control (to enhance maneuverability in the new political environment), building buffer stocks, and accelerating development of non-OPEC sources—actions that its competitors took much more slowly or not at all.

Somewhat inadvertently, Shell planners had discovered the leverage of designing institutional learning processes, whereby, in the words of former planning director de Geus, "Management teams change their shared mental models of their company, their markets, and their competitors."[16] Since then, "planning as learning" has become a byword at Shell, and Group Planning has continually sought out new learning tools that can be integrated into the planning process. Some of these are described later.

LEADER AS TEACHER

"The first responsibility of a leader," writes retired Herman Miller CEO Max de Pree, "is to define reality."[17] Much of the leverage leaders can actually exert lies in helping people achieve more accurate, more insightful, and more *empowering* views of reality.

Leader as teacher does *not* mean leader as authoritarian expert whose job it is to teach people the correct" view of reality. Rather, it is about helping everyone in the organization, oneself included, to gain more insightful views of current reality. This is in line with a popular emerging view of leaders as coaches, guides, or facilitators.[18] In learning organizations, this teaching role is developed further by virtue of explicit attention to people's mental models and by the influence of the system's perspective.

The role of leader as teacher starts with bringing to the surface people's mental models of important issues. No one carries an organization, a market, or a state of technology in his or her head. What we carry in our heads are assumptions. These mental pictures of how the world works have a significant influence on how we perceive problems and opportunities, identify courses of action, and make choices.

One reason that mental models are so deeply entrenched is that they are largely tacit. Ian Mitroff, in his study of General Motors, argues that an assumption that prevailed for years was that, in the United States, "Cars are status symbols. Styling is therefore more important than quality."[19] The Detroit automakers didn't say, "We have a mental model that all people care about is styling." Few actual managers would even say publicly that all people care about is styling. So long as the view remained unexpressed, there was little possibility of challenging its validity or forming more accurate assumptions.

But working with mental models goes beyond revealing hidden assumptions. "Reality," as perceived by most people in most organizations, means pressures that must be borne, crises that must be reacted to, and limitations that must be accepted. Leaders as teachers help people restructure their views of reality to see beyond the superficial conditions and events into the underlying causes of problems—and therefore to see new possibilities for shaping the future.

Specifically, leaders can influence people to view reality at three distinct levels: events, patterns of behavior, and systemic structure.

Systemic Structure
(Generative)
↓
Patterns of Behavior
(Responsive)
↓
Events
(Reactive)

The key question becomes *where do leaders predominantly focus their own and their organization's attention*?

Contemporary society focuses predominantly on events. The media reinforces this perspective, with almost exclusive attention to short-term, dramatic events. This focus leads naturally to explaining what happens in terms of those events: "The Dow Jones average went up 16 points because high fourth-quarter profits were announced yesterday."

Pattern-of-behavior explanations are rarer, in contemporary culture, than event explanations, but they do occur. "Trend analysis" is an example of seeing patterns of behavior. A good editorial that interprets a set of current events in the context of long-term historical changes is another example. Systemic, structural explanations go even further by addressing the questions, "What causes the patterns of behavior?"

In some sense, all three levels of explanation are equally true. But their usefulness is quite different. Event explanations—who did what to whom—doom their holders to a reactive stance toward change. Pattern-of-behavior explanations focus on identifying long-term trends and assessing their implications. They at least suggest how, over time, we can respond to shifting conditions. Structural explanations are the most powerful. Only they address the underlying causes of behavior at a level such that patterns of behavior can be changed.

By and large, leaders of our current institutions focus their attention on events and patterns of behavior, and, under their influence, their organizations do likewise. That is why contemporary organizations are predominantly reactive, or at best responsive—rarely generative. On the other hand, leaders in learning organizations pay attention to all three levels, but focus especially on systemic structure; largely by example, they teach people throughout the organization to do likewise.

LEADER AS STEWARD

This is the subtlest role of leadership. Unlike the roles of designer and teacher, it is almost solely a matter of attitude. It is an attitude critical to learning organizations.

While stewardship has long been recognized as an aspect of leadership, its source is still not widely understood. I believe Robert Greenleaf came closest to explaining real stewardship, in his seminal book *Servant Leadership.*[20] There, Greenleaf argues that "the servant leader is servant *first.* . . . It begins with the natural feeling that one wants to serve, to serve *first.* This conscious choice brings one to aspire to lead. That person is sharply different from one who is leader *first,* perhaps because of the need to assuage an unusual power drive or to acquire material possessions."

Leaders' sense of stewardship operates on two levels: stewardship for the people they lead and stewardship for the larger purpose or mission that underlies the enterprise. The first type arises from a keen appreciation of the impact one's leadership can have on others. People can suffer economically, emotionally, and spiritually under inept leadership. If anything, people in a learning organization are more vulnerable because of their commitment and sense of shared ownership. Appreciating this naturally instills a sense of responsibility in leaders. The second type of stewardship arises from a leader's sense of personal purpose and commitment to the organization's larger mission. People's natural impulse to learn is unleashed when they are engaged in an endeavor they consider worthy of their fullest commitment. Or, as Lawrence Miller puts it, "Achieving return on equity does not, as a goal, mobilize the most noble forces of our soul."[21]

Leaders engaged in building learning organizations naturally feel part of a larger purpose that goes beyond their organization. They are part of changing the way businesses operate, not from a vague philanthropic urge, but from a conviction that their efforts will produce more productive organizations, capable of achieving higher levels of organizational success and personal satisfaction than more traditional organizations. Their sense of stewardship was succinctly captured by George Bernard Shaw when he said,

> *This is the true joy in life, the being used for a purpose you consider a mighty one, the being a force of nature rather than a feverish, selfish clod of ailments and grievances complaining that the world will not devote itself to making you happy.*

NEW SKILLS

New leadership roles require new leadership skills. These skills can only be developed, in my judgment, through a lifetime commitment. It is not enough for one or two individuals to develop these skills. They must be distributed widely throughout the organization. This is one reason that understanding the disciplines of a learning organization is so important. These disciplines embody the principles and practices that can widely foster leadership development.

Three critical areas of skills (disciplines) are building shared vision, surfacing and challenging mental models, and engaging in systems thinking.[22]

BUILDING SHARED VISION

How do individual visions come together to create shared visions? A useful metaphor is the hologram, the three-dimensional image created by interacting light sources.

If you cut a photograph in half, each half shows only part of the whole image. But if you divide a hologram, each part, no matter how small, shows the whole image intact. Likewise, when a group of people come to share a vision for an organization, each person sees an individual picture of the organization at its best. Each shares responsibility for the whole, not just for one piece. But the component pieces of the hologram are not identical. Each represents the whole image from a different point of view. It's something like poking holes in a window shade; each hole offers a unique angle for viewing the whole image. So, too is each individual's vision unique.

When you add up the pieces of a hologram, something interesting happens. The image becomes more intense, more lifelike. When more people come to share a vision, the vision becomes more real in the sense of a mental reality that people can truly imagine achieving. They now have partners, co-creators; the vision no longer rests on their shoulders alone. Early on, when they are nurturing an individual vision, people may say it is "my vision." But, as the shared vision develops, it becomes both "my vision" and "our vision."

The skills involved in building shared vision include the following:

- ***Encouraging Personal Vision.*** Shared visions emerge from personal visions. It is not that people only care about their own self-interest—in fact, people's values usually include dimensions that concern family, organization, community, and even the world. Rather, it is that people's capacity for caring is personal.
- ***Communicating and Asking for Support.*** Leaders must be willing to continually share their own vision, rather than being the official representative of the corporate vision. They also must be prepared to ask, "Is this the vision worthy of your commitment?" This can be difficult for a person used to setting goals and presuming compliance.
- ***Visioning as an Ongoing Process.*** Building shared vision is a never-ending process. At any one point there will be a particular image of the future that is predominant, but that image will evolve. Today, too many managers want to dispense with the "vision business" by going off and writing the Official Vision Statement. Such statements almost always lack the vitality, freshness, and excitement of a genuine vision that comes from people asking, "What do we really want to achieve?"
- ***Blending Extrinsic and Intrinsic Visions.*** Many energizing visions are extrinsic—that is, they focus on achieving something relative to an outsider, such as a competitor. But a goal that is limited to defeating an opponent can, once the vision is achieved, easily become a defensive posture. In contrast, intrinsic goals like creating a new type of product, taking an established product to a new level, or setting a new standard for customer satisfaction can call forth a new level of creativity and innovation. Intrinsic and extrinsic visions need to coexist; a vision solely predicated on defeating an adversary will eventually weaken an organization.
- ***Distinguishing Positive from Negative Visions.*** Many organizations only truly pull together when their survival is threatened. Similarly, most social movements aim at eliminating what people don't want: for example, anti-drugs, anti-smoking, or anti-nuclear arms movements. Negative visions carry a subtle message of powerlessness: People will only pull together when there is sufficient threat. Negative

visions also tend to be short term. Two fundamental sources of energy can motivate organizations: fear and aspiration. Fear, the energy source behind negative visions, can produce extraordinary changes in short periods, but aspiration endures as a continuing source of learning and growth.

SURFACING AND TESTING MENTAL MODELS

Many of the best ideas in organizations never get put into practice. One reason is that new insights and initiatives often conflict with established mental models. The leadership task of challenging assumptions without invoking defensiveness requires reflection and inquiry skills possessed by a few leaders in traditional controlling organizations.[23]

- ***Seeing Leaps of Abstraction.*** Our minds literally move at lightning speed. Ironically, this often slows our learning, because we leap to generalizations so quickly that we never think to test them. We then confuse our generalizations with the observable data upon which they are based, treating the generalizations as if they were data. The frustrated sales rep reports to the home office that "customers don't really care about quality, price is what matters," when what actually happened was that three consecutive large customers refused to place an order unless a larger discount was offered. The sales rep treats her generalization, "customers care only about price," as if it were absolute fact rather than an assumption (very likely an assumption reflecting her own views of customers and the market). This thwarts future learning because she starts to focus on how to offer attractive discounts rather than probing behind the customers' statements. For example, the customers may have been so disgruntled with the firm's delivery or customer service that they are unwilling to purchase again without larger discounts.
- ***Balancing Inquiry and Advocacy.*** Most managers are skilled at articulating their views and presenting them persuasively. While important, advocacy skills can become counterproductive as managers rise in responsibility and confront increasingly complex issues that require collaborative learning among different, equally knowledgeable people. Leaders in learning organizations need to have both inquiry and advocacy skills.[24]

  Specifically, when advocating a view, they need to be able to:
  - explain the reasoning and data that led to their view;
  - encourage others to test their view (e.g., Do you see gaps in my reasoning? Do you disagree with the data upon which my view is based?); and
  - encourage others to provide different views (e.g., Do you have either different data, different conclusions, or both?).

  When inquiring into another's views, they need to:
  - actively seek to understand the other's view, rather than simply restating their own view and how it differs from the other's view; and
  - make their attributions about the other's view explicit (e.g., Based on your statement that . . . ; I am assuming that you believe . . . ; Am I representing your views fairly?).

  If they reach an impasse (others no longer appear open to inquiry), they need to:
  - ask what data or logic might unfreeze the impasse, or if an experiment (or some other inquiry) might be designed to provide new information.

- ***Distinguishing Espoused Theory from Theory in Use.*** We all like to think that we hold certain views, but often our actions reveal deeper views. For example, I may proclaim that people are trustworthy, but never lend friends money and jealously guard my possessions. Obviously, my deeper mental model (my theory in use) differs from my espoused theory. Recognizing gaps between espoused views and theories in use (which often requires the help of others) can be pivotal to deeper learning.
- ***Recognizing and Defusing Defensive Routines.*** As one CEO in our research program puts it, "Nobody ever talks about an issue at the 8:00 business meeting exactly the same way they talk about it at home that evening or over drinks at the end of the day." The reason is what Chris Argyris calls "defensive routines," entrenched habits used to protect ourselves from the embarrassment and threat that come with exposing our thinking. For most of us, such defenses began to build early in life in response to pressures to have the right answers in school or at home. Organizations add new levels of performance anxiety and thereby amplify and exacerbate this defensiveness. Ironically, this makes it even more difficult to expose hidden mental models, and thereby lessens learning.

The first challenge is to recognize defensive routines, then to inquire into their operation. Those who are best at revealing and defusing defensive routines operate with a high degree of self-disclosure regarding their own defensiveness (e.g., I notice that I am feeling uneasy about how this conversation is going. Perhaps I don't understand it or it is threatening to me in ways I don't yet see. Can you help me see this better?).

SYSTEMS THINKING

We all know that leaders should help people see the big picture. But the actual skills whereby leaders are supposed to achieve this are not well understood. In my experience, successful leaders often are "systems thinkers" to a considerable extent. They focus less on day-to-day events and more on underlying trends and forces of change. But they do this almost completely intuitively. The consequence is that they are often unable to explain their intuitions to others and feel frustrated that others cannot see the world the way they do.

One of the most significant developments in management science today is the gradual coalescence of managerial systems thinking as a field of study and practice. This field suggests some key skills for future leaders:

- ***Seeing Interrelationships, Not Things, and Processes, Not Snapshots.*** Most of us have been conditioned throughout our lives to focus on things and to see the world in static images. This leads us to linear explanations of systemic phenomenon. For instance, in an arms race each party is convinced that the other is the cause of problems. They react to each new move as an isolated event, not as part of a process. So long as they fail to see the interrelationships of these actions, they are trapped.
- ***Moving Beyond Blame.*** We tend to blame each other or outside circumstances for our problems. But it is poorly designed systems, not incompetent or unmotivated individuals, that cause most organizational problems. System thinking shows us that there is no outside—that you and the cause of your problems are part of a single system.

- ***Distinguishing Detail Complexity from Dynamic Complexity.*** Some types of complexity are more important strategically than others. Detail complexity arises when there are many variables. Dynamic complexity arises when cause and effect are distant in time and space, and when the consequences over time of interventions are subtle and not obvious to many participants in the system. The leverage in most management situations lies in understanding dynamic complexity, not detail complexity.
- ***Focusing on Areas of Higher Leverage.*** Some have called systems thinking the "new dismal science" because it teaches that most obvious solutions don't work—at best, they improve matters in the short run, only to make things worse in the long run. But there is another side to the story. Systems thinking also shows that small, well-focused actions can produce significant, enduring improvements, if they are in the right place. Systems thinkers refer to this idea as the principle of "leverage." Tackling a difficult problem is often a matter of seeing where the high leverage lies, where a change—with a minimum of effort—would lead to lasting, significant improvement.
- ***Avoiding Symptomatic Solutions.*** The pressures to intervene in management systems that are going awry can be overwhelming. Unfortunately, given the linear thinking that predominates in most organizations, interventions usually focus on symptomatic fixes, not underlying causes. This results in only temporary relief, and it tends to create still more pressures later and for further, low leverage intervention. If leaders acquiesce to these pressures, they can be sucked into an endless spiral of increasing intervention. Sometimes the most difficult leadership acts are to refrain from intervening through popular quick fixes and to keep the pressure on everyone to identify more enduring solutions.

While leaders who can articulate systemic explanations are rare, those who can will leave their stamps on an organization. One person who had this gift was Bill Gore, the founder and longtime CEO of W.L. Gore and Associates (makers of Gore Tex and other synthetic fiber products). Bill Gore was adept at telling stories that showed how the organization's core values of freedom and individual responsibility required particular operating policies. He was proud of his egalitarian organization, in which there were (and still are) no "employees," only "associates," all of whom own shares in the company and participate in its management. At one talk, he explained the company's policy of controlled growth: "Our limitation is not financial resources. Our limitation is the rate at which we can bring in new associates. Our experience has been that if we try to bring in more than a 25 percent per year increase, we begin to bog down. Twenty-five percent per year growth is a real limitation; you can do much better than that with an authoritarian organization." As Gore tells the story, one of the associates, Esther Baum, went home after this talk and reported the limitation to her husband. As it happened, he was an astronomer and mathematician at Lowell Observatory. He said, "That's a very interesting figure." He took out his pencil and paper and calculated and said, "Do you realize that in only fifty-seven and a half years, everyone in the world will be working for Gore?"

Through the story, Gore explains the systemic rationale behind a key policy, limited growth rate—a policy that undoubtedly caused a lot of stress in the organization. He suggests that, at larger rates of growth, the adverse effects of attempting to integrate too many new people too rapidly would begin to dominate. (This is the "limits to growth" systems archetype explained later.) The story also reaffirms the organization's commitment to creating a unique environment for its associates and illustrates the types of sacrifices that the firm is prepared to make in order to remain true to its vision. The last part of the story shows that, despite the self-imposed limit, the company is still very much a growth company.

The consequences of leaders who lack systems thinking skills can be devastating. Many charismatic leaders manage almost exclusively at the level of events. They deal in visions and in crises, and little in between. Under the leadership, an organization hurtles from crisis to crisis. Eventually, the worldview of people in the organization becomes dominated by events and reactiveness. Many, especially those who are deeply committed, become burned out. Eventually, cynicism comes to pervade the organization. People have no control over their time, let alone their destiny.

Similar problems arise with the "visionary strategist," the leader with vision who sees both patterns of change and events. This leader is better prepared to manage change. She or he can explain strategies in terms of emerging trends, and thereby foster a climate that is less reactive. But such leaders still impart a responsive orientation rather than a generative one.

Many talented leaders have rich, highly systemic intuitions but cannot explain those intuitions to others. Ironically, they often end up being authoritarian leaders, even if they don't want to, because only they see the decisions that need to be made. They are unable to conceptualize their strategic insights so that these can become public knowledge, open to challenge and further improvement.

NEW TOOLS

Developing the skills described previously requires new tools—tools that will enhance leaders' conceptual abilities and foster communication and collaborative inquiry. What follows is a sampling of tools starting to find use in learning organizations.

SYSTEMS ARCHETYPES

One of the insights of the budding, managerial systems-thinking field is that certain types of systemic structures recur again and again. Countless systems grow for a period, then encounter problems and cease to grow (or even collapse) well before they have reached intrinsic limits to growth. Many other systems get locked in runaway vicious spirals where every actor has to run faster and faster to stay in the same place. Still others lure individual actors into doing what seems right locally, yet which eventually causes suffering for all.[25]

Some of the system archetypes that have the broadest relevance include:

- ***Balancing Process with Delay.*** In this archetype, decision makers fail to appreciate the time delays involved as they move toward a goal. As a result, they overshoot the goal and may even produce recurring cycles. Classic example: Real estate developers who keep starting new projects until the market has gone soft, by which time an eventual glut is guaranteed by the properties still under construction.
- ***Limits to Growth.*** A reinforcing cycle of growth grinds to a halt, and may even reverse itself, as limits are approached. The limits can be resource constraints,

or external or internal responses to growth. Classic examples: Product life cycles that peak prematurely due to poor quality or service, the growth and decline of communication in a management team, and the spread of a new movement.

- ***Shifting the Burden.*** A short-term "solution" is used to correct a problem, with seemingly happy immediate results. As this correction is used more and more, fundamental long-term corrective measures are used less. Over time, the mechanisms of the fundamental solution may atrophy or become disabled, leading to an even greater reliance on the symptomatic solution. Classic example: using corporate human resource staff to solve local personnel problems, thereby keeping managers from developing their own interpersonal skills.
- ***Eroding Goals.*** When all else fails, lower your standards. This is like "shifting the burden," except that the short-term solution involves letting a fundamental goal, such as quality standards or employee morale standards, atrophy. Classic example: A company that responds to delivery problems by continually upping its quoted delivery times.
- ***Escalation.*** Two people or two organizations, who each see their welfare as depending on a relative advantage over the other, continually react to the other's advances. Whenever one side gets ahead, the other is threatened, leading it to act more aggressively to reestablish its advantage, which threatens the first, and so on. Classic examples: Arms race, gang warfare, price wars.
- ***Tragedy of the Commons.***[26] Individuals keep intensifying their use of a commonly available but limited resource until all individuals start to experience severely diminishing returns. Classic examples: Sheepherders who keep increasing their flocks until they overgraze the common pasture; divisions in a firm that share a common salesforce and compete for the use of sales reps by upping their sales targets, until the salesforce burns out from overextension.
- ***Growth and Underinvestment.*** Rapid growth approaches a limit that could be eliminated or pushed into the future, but only by aggressive investment in physical and human capacity. Eroding goals or standards cause investment that is too weak, or too slow, and customers get increasingly unhappy, slowing demand growth and thereby making the needed investment (apparently) unnecessary or impossible. Classic example: Countless once-successful growth firms that allowed product or service quality to erode, and were unable to generate enough revenues to invest in remedies.

The Archetype Template is a specific tool that is helping managers identify archetypes operating in their own strategic areas (see Figure 2).[27] The template shows the basic structural form of the archetype but lets managers fill in the variables of their own situation. For example, the shifting the burden template involves two balancing processes ("B") that compete for control of a problem symptom. The upper, symptomatic solution provides a short-term fix that will make the problem symptom go away for a while. The lower, fundamental solution provides a more enduring solution. The side-effect feedback ("R") around the outside of the diagram identifies unintended exacerbating effects of the symptomatic solution, which, over time, make it more and more difficult to invoke the fundamental solution.

Several years ago, a team of managers from a leading consumer goods producer used the shifting the burden archetype in a revealing way. The problem they focused on

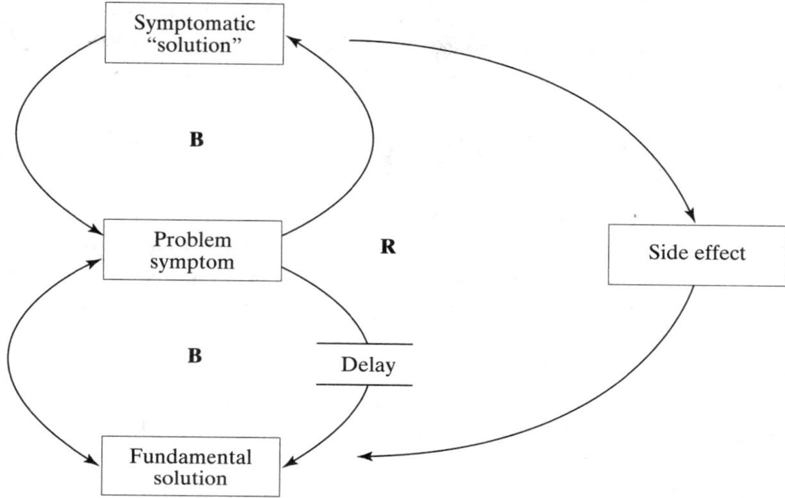

FIGURE 2 "Shifting the Burden" Archetype Template In the "shifting the burden" template, two balancing processes (B) compete for control of a problem symptom. Both solutions affect the symptom, but only the fundamental solution treats the cause. The symptomatic "solution" creates the additional side effect (R) of deferring the fundamental solution, making it harder and harder to achieve.

was financial stress, which could be dealt with in two different ways: by running marketing promotions (the symptomatic solution) or by product innovation (the fundamental solution). Marketing promotions were fast. The company was expert in their design and implementation. The results were highly predictable. Product innovation was slow and much less predictable, and the company had a history over the past ten years of product-innovation mismanagement. Yet only through innovation could they retain a leadership position in their industry, which had slid over the past ten to twenty years. What the managers saw clearly was that the more skillful they became at promotions, the more they shifted the burden away from product innovation. But what really struck home was when one member identified the unintended side effect: The last three CEOs had all come from advertising, which had become the politically dominant function in the corporation, thereby institutionalizing the symptomatic solution. Unless the political values shifted back toward product and process innovation, the managers realized, the firm's decline would accelerate—which is just the shift that had happened over the past several years.

CHARTING STRATEGIC DILEMMAS

Management teams typically come unglued when confronted with core dilemmas. A classic example was the way U.S. manufacturers faced the low cost–high quality choice. For years, most assumed that it was necessary to choose between the two. Not surprisingly, given the short-term pressures perceived by most managements, the prevailing choice was low cost. Firms that chose high quality usually perceived themselves as aiming exclusively for high quality, high price market niche. The consequences of this perceived either–or choice have been disastrous, even fatal, as U.S. manufacturers have encountered increasing international competition from firms that have chosen to consistently improve quality and cost.

In a recent book, Charles Hampden-Turner presented a variety of tools for helping management teams confront strategic dilemmas creatively.[28] He summarizes the process in seven steps:

- ***Eliciting the Dilemmas.*** Identifying the opposed values that form the "horns" of the dilemma, for example, cost as opposed to quality, or local initiative as opposed to central coordination and control. Hampden-Turner suggests that humor can be a distinct asset in this process since "the admission that dilemmas even exist tends to be difficult for some companies."
- ***Mapping.*** Locating the opposing values as two axes and helping managers identify where they see themselves, or their organization, along the axes.
- ***Processing.*** Getting rid of nouns to describe the axes of the dilemma. Present participles formed by adding "ing" convert rigid nouns into processes that imply movement. For example, central control versus local control becomes "strengthening national office" and "growing local initiatives." This loosens the bond of implied opposition between the two values. For example, it becomes possible to think of "strengthening national services" from which local branches can benefit.
- ***Framing/Contextualizing.*** Further softening the adversarial structure among different values by letting "each side in turn be the frame or context for the other." This shifting of the "figure–ground" relationship undermines any implicit attempts to hold one value as intrinsically superior to the other, and thereby to become mentally closed to creative strategies for continuous improvement of both.
- ***Sequencing.*** Breaking the hold of static thinking. Very often, values like low cost and high quality appear to be in opposition because we think in terms of a point in time, not in terms of an ongoing process. For example, a strategy of investing in a new process technology and developing a new production-floor culture of worker responsibility may take time and money in the near term, yet reap significant long-term financial rewards.
- ***Waving/Cycling.*** Sometimes the strategic path toward improving both values involves cycles where both values will get "worse" for a time. Yet, at a deeper level, learning is occurring that will cause the next cycle to be at a higher plateau for both values.
- ***Synergizing.*** Achieving synergy where significant improvement is occurring along all axes of all relevant dilemmas. (This is the ultimate goal, of course.) Synergy, as Hampden-Turner points out, is a uniquely systemic notion, coming from the Greek *Syn-ergo* or "work together."

"THE LEFT-HAND COLUMN": SURFACING MENTAL MODELS

The idea that the mental models can dominate business decisions and that these models are often tacit and even contradictory to what people espouse can be very threatening to managers who pride themselves on rationality and judicious decision making. It is important to have tools to help managers discover for themselves how their mental models operate to undermine their own intentions.

One tool that has worked consistently to help managers see their own mental models in action is the "left-hand column" exercise developed by Chris Argyris and his colleagues. This tool is especially helpful in showing how we leap from data to generalization without testing the validity of our generalizations.

When working with managers, I start this exercise by selecting a specific situation in which I am interacting with other people in a way that is not working, that is not producing the learning that is needed. I write out a sample of the exchange, with the script on the right-hand side of the page. On the left-hand side, I write what I am thinking but not saying at each stage in the exchange (see sidebar).

The left-hand column exercise not only brings hidden assumptions to the surface, it shows how they influence behavior. In the example, I make two key assumptions about Bill: he lacks confidence and he lacks initiative. Neither may be literally true, but both are evident in my internal dialogue, and both influence the way I handle the situation. Believing that he lacks confidence, I skirt the fact that I've heard the presentation was a bomb. I'm afraid that if I say it directly, he will lose what little confidence he has, or he will see me as unsupportive. So I bring up the subject of the presentation obliquely. When I ask Bill what we should do next, he gives no specific course of action. Believing he lacks initiative, I take this as evidence of his laziness; he is content to do nothing when action is definitely required. I conclude that I will have to manufacture some form of pressure to motivate him, or else I will simply have to take matters into my own hands.

THE LEFT-HAND COLUMN: AN EXERCISE

Imagine my exchange with a colleague, Bill, after he made a big presentation to our boss on a project we are doing together. I had to miss the presentation, but I've heard that it was poorly received.

ME: How did the presentation go?
BILL: Well, I don't know. It's really too early to say. Besides, we're breaking new ground here.
ME: Well, what do you think we should do? I believe that the issues you were raising were important.
BILL: I'm not so sure. Let's just wait and see what happens.
ME: You may be right, but I think we may need to do more than just wait.

Now, here is what the exchange looks like with my "left-hand column":

WHAT I'M THINKING	WHAT IS SAID
Everyone says the presentation was a bomb.	ME: How did the presentation go?
Does he really not know how bad it was? Or is he not willing to face up to it?	BILL: Well, I don't know. It's too early to say. Besides, we're breaking new ground here.
He really is afraid to see the truth. If he only had more confidence, he could probably learn from a situation like this.	ME: Well, what do you think we should do? I believe that the issues you were raising are important.
I can't believe he doesn't realize how disastrous that presentation was to our moving ahead.	BILL: I'm not so sure. Let's just wait and see what happens.
I've got to find some way to light a fire under the guy.	ME: You may be right, but I think we may need to do more than just wait.

The exercise reveals the elaborate webs of assumptions we weave, within which we become our own victims. Rather than dealing directly with my assumptions about Bill and the situation, we talk around the subject. The reasons for my avoidance are self-evident: I assume that if I raised my doubts, I would provoke a defensive reaction that would only make matters worse. But the price of avoiding the issue is high. Instead of determining how to move forward to resolve problems, we end our exchange with no clear course of action. My assumptions about Bill's limitations have been reinforced. I resort to a manipulative strategy to move things forward.

The exercise not only reveals the need for skills in surfacing assumptions, but that we are the ones most in need of help. There is no one right way to handle difficult situations like my exchange with Bill, but any productive strategy revolves around a high level of self-disclosure and willingness to have my views challenged. I need to recognize my own leaps of abstraction regarding Bill, share the events and reasoning that are leading to my concern over the project, and be open to Bill's views on both. The skills to carry on such conversations without invoking defensiveness take time to develop. But if both parties in a learning impasse start by doing their own left-hand column exercise and sharing them with each other, it is remarkable how quickly everyone recognizes their contribution to the impasse and progress starts to be made.

LEARNING LABORATORIES: PRACTICE FIELDS FOR MANAGEMENT TEAMS

One of the most promising new tools is the learning laboratory or "microworld": constructed microcosms of real-life settings in which management teams can learn how to learn together.

The rationale behind learning laboratories can be best explained by analogy. Although most management teams have great difficulty learning (enhancing their collective intelligence and capacity to create), in other domains team learning is the norm rather than the exception—team sports and the performing arts, for example. Great basketball teams do not start off great. They learn. But the process by which these teams learn is, by and large, absent from modern organizations. The process is a continual movement between practice and performance.

The vision guiding current research in management learning laboratories is to design and construct effective practice fields for management teams. Much remains to be done, but the broad outlines are emerging.

First, since team learning in organizations is an individual-to-individual and individual-to-system phenomenon, learning laboratories must combine meaningful business issues with meaningful interpersonal dynamics. Either alone is incomplete.

Second, the factors that thwart learning about complex business issues must be eliminated in the learning lab. Chief among these is the inability to experience the long-term, systemic consequences of key strategic decisions. We all learn best from experience, but we are unable to experience the consequences of many important organizational decisions. Learning laboratories remove this constraint through system dynamics simulation games that compress time and space.

Third, new learning skills must be developed. One constraint on learning is the inability of managers to reflect insightfully on their assumptions, and to inquire

LEARNING AT HANOVER INSURANCE

Hanover Insurance has gone from the bottom of the property and liability industry to a position among the top 25 percent of U.S. insurance companies over the past 20 years, largely through the efforts of CEO William O'Brien and his predecessor, Jack Adam. The following comments are excerpted from series of interviews Senge conducted with O'Brien as background for his book.

SENGE: Why do you think there is so much change occurring in management and organizations today? Is it primarily because of increased competitive pressures?

O'BRIEN: That's a factor, but not the most significant factor. The ferment in management will continue until we find models that are more congruent with human nature.

One of the great insights of modern psychology is the hierarchy of human needs. As Maslow expressed this idea, the most basic needs are food and shelter. Then comes belonging. Once these three basic needs are satisfied, people begin to aspire toward self-respect and esteem, and toward self-actualization—the fourth- and fifth-order needs.

Our traditional hierarchical organizations are designed to provide for the first three levels, but not the fourth and fifth. These first three levels are now widely available to members of industrial society, but our organizations do not offer people sufficient opportunities for growth.

SENGE: How would you assess Hanover's progress to date?

O'BRIEN: We have been on a long journey away from traditional hierarchical culture. The journey began with everyone understanding some guiding ideas about purpose, vision, and values as a basis for participative management. This is a better way to begin building a participative culture than by simply "letting people in on decision making." Before there can be meaningful participation, people must share certain values and pictures about where we are trying to go. We discovered that people have real need to feel that they're part of an ennobling mission. But developing shared visions and values is not the end, only the beginning.

Next we had to get beyond mechanical, linear thinking. The essence of our jobs as managers is to deal with "divergent" problems—problems that have no simple answer.

"Convergent" problems—problems that have a "right" answer-should be solved locally. Yet we are deeply conditioned to see the world in terms of convergent problems. Most managers try to force-fit simplistic solutions and undermine the potential for learning when divergent problems arise. Since everyone handles the linear issues fairly well, companies that learn how to handle divergent issues will have a great advantage.

The next basic stage in our progression was coming to understand inquiry and advocacy. We learned that real openness is rooted in people's ability to continually inquire into their own thinking. This requires exposing yourself to being wrong—not something that most managers are rewarded for. But learning is very difficult if you cannot look for errors or incompleteness in your own ideas.

What all this builds to is the capability throughout an organization to manage mental models. In a locally controlled organization, you have the fundamental challenge of learning how to help people make good decisions without coercing them into making particular decisions. By managing mental models, we create "self-concluding" decisions—decisions that people come to themselves—which will result in deeper conviction, better implementation, and the ability to make better adjustments when the situation changes.

SENGE: What concrete steps can top managers take to begin moving toward learning organizations?

O'BRIEN: Look at the signals you send through the organization. For example, one critical signal is how you spend your time. It's hard to build a learning organization if people are unable to take the time to think through important matters. I rarely set up an appointment for less than one hour. If the subject is not worth an hour, it shouldn't be on my calendar.

(*Continued*)

(Continued)

SENGE: Why is this so hard for so many managers?

O'BRIEN: It comes back to what you believe about the nature of your work. The authoritarian manager has a "chain gang" mental model: "The speed of the boss is the speed of the gang. I've got to keep things moving fast, because I've got to keep people working." In a learning organization, the manager shoulders an almost sacred responsibility: to create conditions that enable people to have happy and productive lives. If you understand the effects the ideas we are discussing can have on the lives of people in your organization, you will take the time.

effectively into each other's assumptions. Both skills can be enhanced in a learning laboratory, where people can practice surfacing assumptions in a low-risk setting. A note of caution: It is far easier to design an entertaining learning laboratory than it is to have an impact on real management practices and firm traditions outside the learning lab. Research on management simulations has shown that they often have greater entertainment value than the educational value. One of the reasons appears to be that many simulations do not offer deep insights into systemic structures causing business problems. Another reason is that they do not foster new learning skills. Also, there is no connection between experiments in the learning lab and real life experiments. These are significant problems that research on laboratory design is now addressing.

DEVELOPING LEADERS AND LEARNING ORGANIZATIONS

In a recently published retrospective on organization development in the 1980s, Marshall Sashkin and N. Warner Burke observe the return of an emphasis on developing leaders who can develop organizations.[29] They also note Schein's critique that most top executives are not qualified for the task of developing culture.[30] Learning organizations represent a potentially significant evolution of organizational culture. So it should come as no surprise that such organization will remain a distant vision until the leadership capabilities they demand are developed. "The 1990s may be the period," suggest Sashkin and Burke, "during which organization development and (a new sort) of management development are reconnected."

I believe that this new sort of management development will focus on the roles, skills, and tools for leadership in learning organizations. Undoubtedly, the ideas offered in this article are only a rough approximation of this new territory. The sooner we begin seriously exploring the territory, the sooner the initial map can be improved—and the sooner we will realize an age-old vision of leadership.

The wicked leader is he who the people despise.
The good leader is he who the people revere.
The great leader is he who the people say, "We did it ourselves."—Lao Tsu

References

1. P. Senge, *The Fifth Discipline: The Art and Practice of the Learning Organization* (New York: Doubleday/Currency, 1990).
2. A. P. de Geus, "Planning as Learning," *Harvard Business Review* (March-April 1988): 70–74.
3. B. Domain, *Fortune,* July 3, 1989, 48–62.
4. The distinction between adaptive and generative learning has its roots in the distinction between what Argyris and Schon have called their "single-loop" learning, in which individuals or groups adjust their behavior relative to fixed goals, norms, and assumptions, and "double-loop" learning, in which goals, norms, and assumptions, as well as behavior, are open to change (e.g., see C. Argyris and D. Schon, *Organizational Learning: A Theory-in-Action Perspective* [Reading, MA: Addison-Wesley, 1978]).
5. All unattributed quotes are from personal communications with the author.
6. G. Stalk, Jr., "Time: The Next Source of Competitive Advantage," *Harvard Business Review* (July-August 1988): 41–51.
7. Senge (1990).
8. The principle of creative tension comes from Robert Fritz's work on creativity. See R. Fritz, *The Path of Least Resistance* (New York: Ballantine, 1989) and *Creating* (New York: Ballantine, 1990).
9. M. L. King, Jr., "Letter from Birmingham Jail," *American Visions* (January-February 1986): 52–59.
10. E. Schein, *Organizational Culture and Leadership* (San Francisco: Jossey-Bass, 1985). Similar views have been expressed by many leadership theorists. For example, see: P. Selznick, *Leadership in Administration* (New York: Harper & Row, 1957); W. Bennis and B. Nanus, *Leaders* (New York: Harper & Row, 1985); and N. M. Tichy and M. A. Devanna, *The Transformational Leader* (New York: John Wiley & Sons, 1986).
11. Selznick (1957).
12. J. W. Forrester, "A New Corporate Design," *Sloan Management Review* (formerly *Industrial Management Review*) (Fall 1965): 5–17.
13. See, for example, H. Mintzberg, "Crafting Strategy," *Harvard Business Review* (July-August 1987): 66–75.
14. R. Mason and I. Mitroff, *Challenging Strategic Planning Assumptions* (New York: John Wiley & Sons, 1981): 16.
15. P. Wack, "Scenarios: Uncharted Waters Ahead," *Harvard Business Review* (September-October 1985): 73–89.
16. de Geus (1988).
17. M. de Pree, *Leadership Is an Art* (New York: Doubleday, 1989): 9.
18. For example, see T. Peters and N. Austin, *A Passion for Excellence* (New York: Random House, 1985); and J. M. Kouzes and B. Z. Posner, *The Leadership Challenge* (San Francisco: Jossey-Bass, 1987).
19. I. Mitroff, *Break-Away Thinking* (New York: John Wiley & Sons, 1988): 66–67.
20. R. K. Greenleaf, *Servant Leadership: A Journey into the Nature of Legitimate Power and Greatness* (New York: Paulist Press, 1977).
21. L. Miller, *American Spirit: Visions of a New Corporate Culture* (New York: William Morrow, 1984): 15.
22. These points are condensed from the practices of the five disciplines examined in Senge (1990).
23. The ideas below are based to a considerable extent on the work of Chris Argyris, Donald Schon, and their Action Science colleagues: C. Argyris and D. Schon, *Organizational Learning: A Theory-in-Action Perspective* (Reading, MA: Addison-Wesley, 1978); C. Argyris, R. Putnam, and D. Smith, *Action Science* (San Francisco: Jossey-Bass, 1985); C. Argyris, *Strategy Change and Defensive Routines* (Boston: Pitman, 1985); and C. Argyris, *Overcoming Organizational Defenses* (Upper Saddle River, NJ: Prentice Hall, 1990).
24. I am indebted to Diana Smith for the summary points that follow.
25. The system archetypes are one of several systems diagramming and communication tools. See D. H. Kim, "Toward Learning Organizations: Integrating Total Quality Control and Systems Thinking"

(Cambridge, MA: MIT Sloan School of Management, Working Paper No. 3037-89-BPS, June 1989).

26. This archetype is closely associated with the work of ecologist Garrett Hardin, who coined its label: G. Hardin, "The Tragedy of the Commons," *Science,* December 13, 1968.
27. These templates were originally developed by Jennifer Kemeny, Charles Kiefer, and Michael Goodman of Innovation Associates, Inc., Farmingham, Massachusetts.
28. C. Hampden-Turner, *Charting the Corporate Mind* (New York: The Free Press, 1990).
29. M. Sashkin and W. W. Burke, "Organization Development in the 1980s" and "An End-of-the-Eighties Retrospective," *Advances in Organization Development,* ed. F. Masarik (Norwood, NJ: Ablex, 1990).
30. E. Schein (1985).

CHAPTER 4
DECODING HUMAN BEHAVIOR

One of the major challenges people face lies in understanding why people, in particular people who are very different from oneself, behave the way they do. There are many reasons that explain behavior, such as personality, individual background and attitudes, group norms, and culture. The articles in this section were chosen to help you decode behavior and understand why people act as they do.

The first article, "The Tyranny of Toxic Managers," was written by Roy Lubit, a psychiatrist who does executive coaching to develop emotional intelligence in people with difficult personalities. Lubit's article provides a framework for understanding toxic behavior in the workplace and provides advice on how to deal with each personality type. The article emphasizes the importance of developing emotional intelligence and explains how it can be increased. He also identifies the major behavioral differences that people struggle to accept in others in the workplace. Understanding how we are different from others is often the first step in appreciating, tolerating, and leveraging the strengths of their behavior (and our own).

A new movement in research, Positive Psychology and Positive Organizational Behavior, focuses on the positive aspects of work and life, rather than the traditional concern with the negative. For example, Fred Luthans and his colleagues argue that personal characteristics like confidence, hope, optimism and resilience constitute an organization's positive psychological capital. These qualities, as well as happiness, the subject of the second article in this chapter, seldom made their way into research or textbooks in the past. Thomas Wright and Russell Cropanzano, both prolific scholars, shed new light for both scholars and practitioners in "The Role of Psychological Well-Being in Job Performance: A Fresh Look at an Age-Old Quest."

The third article, "Beyond Sophisticated Stereotyping: Cultural Sensemaking in Context," focuses on understanding behavior that is influenced by culture. This article sounds a cautionary warning about stereotyping people from different cultures using bipolar cultural dimensions, like those identified in Geert Hofstede's article in the Introduction. Joyce Osland and Allan Bird are business professors and consultants who spent many years working overseas. As a result, they became intrigued by the paradoxical aspects of culture and devised a sensemaking model that encourages people to consider the context when trying to decode cultural behavior. Since this article was written, their sensemaking model has been applied, not just to paradoxes, but to cultural behavior in general.

THE TYRANNY OF TOXIC MANAGERS: APPLYING EMOTIONAL INTELLIGENCE TO DEAL WITH DIFFICULT PERSONALITIES*

Roy Lubit

Toxic managers are a fact of life. Some managers are toxic most of the time; most managers are toxic some of the time. Knowing how to deal with people who are rigid, aggressive, or self-centered, or who exhibit other types of dysfunctional behavior can improve your own health and that of others in the workplace. This author describes the mechanisms for coping.

Toxic managers dot the landscape in most organizations, making them seem, at times, like war zones. These managers can complicate your work, drain your energy, compromise your sanity, derail your projects, and destroy your career. Your ability to deal with these corporate land mines will have a significant impact on your career. Those who are able to recognize toxic managers quickly and understand what makes them tick will be in the best position to protect themselves. Difficult managers are a fact of life and how they affect your life depends upon the skills you develop to deal with them.

The issue is not simply a matter of individual survival. Toxic managers divert people's energy from the real work of the organization, destroy morale, impair retention, and interfere with cooperation and information sharing. Their behavior, like a rock thrown into a pond, can cause ripples distorting the organization's culture and affecting people far beyond the point of impact. Senior management and HR can significantly improve an organization's culture and functioning by taking steps to find and contain those who are most destructive. Leadership can spare an organization serious damage by learning how to recognize problematic personality traits quickly,

*Written for the *Reader*, based on a similarly-titled article for *Ivey Business Journal Online*, March–April 2004, 68(4). Dr. Lubit can be contacted at the Executive Development Network, roylubit@rcn.com.

placing difficult managers in positions in which their behavior will do the least harm, arranging for coaching for those who are able to grow, and knowing which managers are time bombs that need to be let go.

This article will help you learn how to avoid becoming a scapegoat, to survive aggressive managers' assaults, and to give narcissistic and rigid managers the things they need to be satisfied with you. It will also help senior management and HR to recognize toxic managers before they do serious damage. *The basic theme of the article is that to deal effectively with toxic behavior you need to understand what lies underneath it, design an intervention to target those underlying factors, and have sufficient control of your own feelings and behavior so that you can do what is most effective, rather than let your own anger or anxiety get the best of you.* To do this, you need to develop your emotional intelligence (including your self-control) along with your understanding of how difficult people view the world and what motivates them.

TYPES OF DIFFICULT CO-WORKERS

Toxic managers can be divided into four categories: narcissistic, aggressive, rigid, and impaired. Underneath these difficult behaviors are either problematic personality traits, mood disorders, or impulsivity. By personality traits, we mean enduring patterns of perceiving, interpreting, and relating to the world and oneself. Problems of mood and concentration can often mimic personality problems. When people are stressed by anxiety, depression, trauma, Attention Deficit Hyperactivity Disorder, alcohol, drugs, or a difficult environment, any tendency they have for aggressive, rigid, or narcissistic behavior intensifies. Having a professional assess whether the problem is due primarily to personality problems or to a problem of mood and concentration is crucial, since problems of mood and concentration can often be ameliorated fairly quickly with appropriate treatment.

The four types of toxic managers are described below as are ways for coping with, and even changing, their behavior.

NARCISSISTIC MANAGERS

Preoccupied with their own importance, narcissistic managers are grandiose and arrogant. They devalue others, lack empathy for others and have little, if any, conscience. Feeling exempt from the normal rules of society, they exploit people without remorse. Narcissistic individuals are also very sensitive to anything that threatens their self-esteem. Challenges to their grandiose self-image can lead to narcissistic rage that sees them lose all judgment and attack in ways that are destructive to themselves and their victims.

Arrogant with peers and subordinates, they may suddenly become submissive in the presence of a superior. Once the superior has left, they may well disparage her. They generally deprecate and exploit others, including former idols. They may, however, idealize powerful individuals who support them, though only for a short time.

Under the surface, narcissistic managers struggle with fragile self-esteem. They also have a sense of emptiness arising from their lack of true self-love and inability to care about other people or about abstract values such as honesty and integrity. Their grandiose fantasies are attempts to fill the emptiness and reinforce their fragile self-esteem.

The classic narcissistic manager is grandiose. Grandiose managers are legends in their own minds. Preoccupied with their exaggerated accomplishments and grandiose expectations for the future, they expect others to hold them in awe. Constantly boasting, they resemble peacocks strutting around with their tail feathers unfurled.

Some narcissistic managers are not effusive about their abilities and accomplishments. What stands out about them is a willingness to exploit others, a willingness to break the law, or a desire to control and dominate others.

Narcissistic managers are less likely to make major changes in their behavior than are managers with other issues. They are also particularly likely to become outraged and vindictive if someone challenges their behavior. Therefore, when you are dealing with managers who are rigid or aggressive, it is important to know whether narcissism or other disorders lie underneath their destructive behaviour.

A milder variant of narcissistic managers are those with learned narcissism. They are not desperately trying to hide and shield fragile self-esteem arising from a troubled childhood. Rather, their success in some area has brought sufficient fame and fortune that they have been shielded from the normal consequences of behaving arrogantly and treating others poorly. Moreover, as people incessantly flatter them, they come to believe the glorifying compliments. Although somewhat grandiose and inconsiderate of others, these people have a conscience and can feel empathy for others; they simply do not realize the full impact of their behavior on others. People with learned narcissism are far more amenable to change than are those with narcissism resulting from problems early on in emotional development. Another variety of narcissist focuses on power more than adulation and becomes control freaks. Their micromanagement comes from both a desire to be in control in order to prove that they are superior, and from devaluation of others and the need to control things lest they fall apart.

The most prominent trait for the antisocial variety is the devaluation of others and the willingness to violate their rights. They take whatever they wish, whether it is credit for work done or more than their share. They play by a different set of rules: All is fair in love, war, and business.

Coping with narcissistic managers is very difficult for most people. You can't make it a fun experience, but there are things you can do to make yourself less vulnerable to them, as shown in Table 1.

AGGRESSIVE MANAGERS

There are a variety of factors that can lead to aggressive behavior. Frantic and irritable managers have enduring problems modulating the intensity of their feelings. They are often flooded by them, and then ignore the feelings and rights of others in desperate attempts to deal with their distress. They are often clueless about the impact of their behavior on others. Some aggressive individuals chronically view themselves as victims; what others view as aggression they see as self-defense or compensation for wrongs done to them in the past. The most problematic aggressive managers have underlying narcissistic personality traits. For example, ruthless managers lack empathy and concern for the well-being of others. Moreover, they perceive the world as a dog-eat-dog competition in which people are out to get you. In their eyes, if you are not a predator, you will become someone's prey. Bullies derive a perverse pleasure from intimidating others.

RIGID MANAGERS

Rigid managers insist on doing things their way. Underneath this insistence can be a variety of factors. Compulsive managers fear being wrong. They live in a world of "should" and "should have." Avoiding making mistakes dominates their decision making. Authoritarian managers believe that rigid hierarchies are the best way to run organizations. Oppositional

TABLE 1 Types of Narcissistic Managers

Varieties	*Primary Traits*	*Objective*	*Subordinate Survival Tactics*	*Superior's Actions For All Varieties*
Grandiose: Psychodynamic	Outward grandiose self-image; exploits others; devalues others; enraged if self-esteem threatened; limited conscience and capacity for empathy; desperately protects underlying fragile self-esteem	Be admired	General tactics: Avoid criticizing them; show admiration; outshine them; don't play down your accomplishments and ambition; document your work; build relationships with a mentor; keep your eyes open for other positions; do not take their behavior personally; consult with mentor or executive coach	Maintain close oversight to continually assess their treatment of others; do not automatically believe superiors over their subordinates; get 360° feedback on them; get coaching for them; place them where they cannot do serious harm; consider getting rid of them; don't ignore signs of trouble; consider possible presence of depression, anxiety, alcohol abuse
Grandiose: Learned	Grandiose self-image; exploits others out of carelessness; is inconsiderate in treatment of others due to not receiving negative feedback for behavior	Be admired	See general tactics above	
Control Freak	Micromanages; seeks absolute control of everything; inflated self-image and devaluation of others' abilities; fear of chaos	Control others	See general tactics plus: Avoid direct suggestions; let them think new ideas are their own	
Antisocial	Takes what he wants, lies to get ahead, hurts others if they are in his way; lacks both a conscience and capacity for empathy	Excitement of violating rules and abusing others	Avoid provoking them; transfer out before they destroy you; do not get dragged into their unethical/illegal activities; seek allies in co-workers and mentors; seek executive coach to help you cope	

TABLE 2 Types of Aggressive Managers

Varieties	*Primary Traits*	*Objective*	*Surviving Them*
Frantic	Always hyper and pressured	Avoid being in trouble; accomplishing a lot	Help them with their objectives; help them see that a frantic pace may be inefficient; evaluate for anxiety and depression
Irritable	Difficulty modulating their stress level; highly reactive to certain things	Varies	Find out what upsets them and avoid pushing their buttons; provide support; evaluate for depression and anxiety problems; gently let them know their behavior is destructive
Narcissistic	Underlying fragile self-esteem leads to eruptions of anger if the self-esteem is challenged	Maintain their self-esteem	Show deference; play down your accomplishments, avoid outshining them, never criticize them
Ruthless	Calmly goes after what he or she wants	Get what he wants	Watch your back
Bully	Seeks to intimidate for the pure excitement of it	Dominate and intimidate	Stay out of their way; don't let them see you are intimidated

and passive-aggressive individuals perpetually feel that their autonomy is constantly being threatened, and they must push back in order to defend themselves. They fail to see that in doing so they are stepping on the rights of others. Narcissistic managers who are rigid feel that their way is best and that there is no reason to listen to others' ideas.

TABLE 3 Types of Rigid Managers

Type	*Belief System*	*Underlying Dynamics*	*How to Deal With Them*
Compulsive	His way is the only way, since trying a new way would be very hard	Fears being wrong	Show them that many, many respected people do it a different way and that this way will work out in this particular situation; avoid arguing about what way is best
Authoritarian	The bosses' way is the way it should be done	Fears the world being out of control unless someone is rigidly in charge	Show them that an authority they respect does things differently
Oppositional	People are trying to dominate him and he must speak up	Feels that they are always being dominated and need to push back	Let them feel a part of the decision
Passive-Aggressive	People are trying to dominate him, and he can't speak up	Feels pushed around	Encourage their participation
Narcissistic	Feels he is remarkably skilled and knows better than anyone	Covering over fragile self-esteem by a rigid grandiose self-image	Feed their ego; don't criticize them; explain how your ideas fit into their plans

TABLE 4 Types of Impaired Managers

	Main Symptoms	*Dealing with Them*
ADHD	Easily distracted, disorganized, talks incessantly, interrupts others	Get them treatment
Anxiety	Fearful—generally or with a focus	Get them treatment
PTSD	Preoccupied, emotionally numb, withdrawn, jumpy, fearful, irritable	Get them treatment
Depression	Loss of interest and energy, pessimistic, tends to worry, sleep and appetite changes	Get them treatment
Burnout	Feels overwhelmed, loss of motivation and interest	Get them treatment
Alcohol Abuse	Declining performance, often late or absent	Get them treatment

IMPAIRED MANAGERS

Many managers, at one time or another, suffer from depression, an anxiety disorder, burnout, or alcohol abuse. Many have attention deficit disorder that has never been diagnosed. Each of these can significantly impair someone's performance and ability to work effectively with others. Failure to recognize and treat these common problems costs businesses billions of dollars a year in lost productivity.

Unfortunately, most of the time, the nature of the problem is not recognized. In addition to damaging productivity, these problems can markedly exacerbate, or even mimic, the various personality disorders discussed above. Most of these can be treated relatively quickly and yield a marked improvement in performance.

CASE STUDY: DEALING WITH A NARCISSISTIC VP

Bill was the vice president of a mid-sized company. His unit had grown rapidly and was profitable. He had special knowledge and skills that made him very valuable to the company. At the same time, the company's president was increasingly aware that the morale in Bill's unit was poor and that turnover was high. The president instructed Bill to obtain some coaching. He balked and the CEO relented. In time, however, things went from bad to worse. The CEO considered firing Bill. The cost of finding a replacement, and the inefficiencies suffered while the new person came up to speed, would be high. Nevertheless, he couldn't let the unit continue to bleed people. Faced with the possibility of being fired, Bill agreed to executive coaching.

Bill balked at 360° feedback but he agreed to let the coach speak with people and observe his ways of interacting. What people reported, and what the coach saw, was a driven person who lacked concern for others, focused on his own needs, was constantly snapping at people, rarely gave a pat on the back, and sometimes stole credit for others' work. He certainly fit the description of the narcissistic manager.

There was, however, another part of him. At times, he really seemed concerned about others. In individual discussions with the coach, Bill's insecurity and depression stood out more than his grandiosity. The coach determined that rather than having the core personality structure of a narcissistic individual,

Bill had been so successful that he had been able to get away with stepping on people and was relatively clueless about how others felt and how his behavior affected their performance.

A major factor in Bill's behavior was a mild chronic depression. He did not enjoy things that much and rarely smiled. A great deal of his irritability came from the mild depression. The coach convinced him to try an antidepressant. Bill's snapping at people declined in a few days. In a month he seemed like a different person. With his depression gone he not only felt much less irritable, but had the emotional energy to think about others' feelings and to begin to look at his own behavior more than he had before. He had many bad habits in how he related to people, but he was now able to begin to look at them and gradually make changes.

DESIGNING EFFECTIVE INTERVENTIONS

Effective interventions take into consideration what is driving difficult behavior, and not simply what appears on the surface. Interventions that would lead to a positive change in a manager with one underlying personality type could intensify the problematic behavior of someone with another personality type. For example, aggressive and rigid behavior can be driven by fear and insecurity, by cluelessness, or by a ruthless desire to dominate and control people. Managers whose aggression or rigidity arises from fear and insecurity are likely to improve if treated with tolerance and reassurance. Tolerance of toxic behavior arising from ruthlessness, however, is likely to exacerbate the situation. Similarly, while a strong negative response to aggressive or rigid behavior may deter someone who is ruthless, it could increase the anxiety and tension of someone who is driven by fear, and thereby worsen the problem. *The better you understand how other people view the world and what motivates them, the better you will be able to influence their behavior.*

Senior management and human resources professionals also need to understand why someone is doing poorly in order to know whether to work with the person to improve the troubling behavior or to let him or her go. You do not want to give too many chances to someone who rains chaos and problems on others. At the same time, you do not want to get rid of a potentially fine manager who is suffering from readily treatable anxiety, depression, or stress, or who could learn better social skills in a reasonable period of time.

DEVELOPING YOUR EMOTIONAL INTELLIGENCE

It is puzzling that we seek expert advice on improving our golf game but avoid professional advice on how we can deal with other people. We pay personal trainers remarkable fees one or more times a week to encourage us to exercise harder. We avoid, however, engaging an expert to help us learn more about ourselves and others—someone who could help us learn to deal with different types of difficult people. Somehow, we are supposed to be experts on dealing with other people and with our own emotions even though these issues were never formally addressed in our education and training.

You are unlikely to bring about wholesale personality change in someone, but you do not need to. Rounding off rough spots and bringing greater flexibility and responsiveness to situations is all that is needed to make a significant improvement in the quality of the work environment and work output. This is very doable if handled with skill and understanding of what is needed for change.

Enhancing your emotional intelligence is preventative medicine, a vaccine against the development of toxic relationships as well as a suit of armor limiting the damage that toxic managers can do. Emotional intelligence is the key to understanding others' perspectives and needs, resolving conflicts, and wielding influence. It also helps you to know who is dangerous before problems begin, enabling you to take steps to decrease your vulnerability. Emotional intelligence helps you deal with the rigid, aggressive, and grandiose behavior you may be subjected to. Emotional intelligence also enables leaders to spot, and then either coach or remove, managers who behave in ways that are toxic to others.

There are two major components of emotional intelligence, personal competence and social competence. Personal competence refers to the ability to understand your own feelings, strengths, and weaknesses (self-awareness), and the ability to manage those feelings effectively (self-management). For example, being able to contain your anger and anxiety and thereby think clearly in upsetting situations is crucial to making good decisions and influencing others.

Social competence refers to the ability to understand what others are feeling (social awareness) and having the skills to work effectively with others (relationship management). The ability to understand what people think and feel, and then to know how to persuade, motivate, and resolve conflicts with specific individuals is among the most important skills of successful leaders and managers.

COMPONENTS OF EMOTIONAL INTELLIGENCE

Personal Competence

Self-Awareness

- Aware of your emotions and their impact
- Aware of your strengths and weaknesses

Self-Management

- Emotional self-control
- Adaptability: flexibility in adapting to changing situations and obstacles
- Integrity, honesty, trustworthiness
- Drive to grow and achieve
    - Achievement oriented
    - Continuous learner
    - Willing to take initiative
    - Optimistic

Social Competence

Social Awareness

- Empathy and insight
    - Understanding others' perspectives and feelings
    - Appreciation of others' strengths and weaknesses
- Political awareness

Relationship Management

- Respect for others
- Conflict management skills
- Collaborative approach
- Sense of humor
- Persuasive: visionary, diplomatic
- Able to leverage diversity

People are born with varying levels of talent for understanding their own feelings and the feelings of others. Nevertheless, with conscious effort most people can make significant strides in improving their emotional intelligence.

The keys to developing your personal competence (self-awareness and self-management) are (1) paying attention to your emotional reactions to situations, (2) enhancing your understanding of why you react as you do, (3) thinking of alternate ways to interpret upsetting situations, and (4) finding constructive ways to deal with whatever emotional stress remains. The more time you invest in introspection and talking with confidants about how to understand your emotional reactions and behavior, the more your personal competence will grow.

Certain psychological issues can present an enormous barrier to developing emotional intelligence. Obstacles include a tendency to interpret situations in ways that lead to self-fulfilling prophecies, black-and-white thinking, having interpretations controlled by past painful memories, and holding attitudes that color your interpretation of experiences. These blinders can block learning. Executive coaching with someone trained as a therapist can remove the obstacles and enable you to learn.

Social competence involves understanding why people behave as they do and being able to select a course of action that will be most effective in dealing with them. The first part of this paper discussed why people may engage in various types of toxic behavior. If you understand the concepts presented and are now better able to assess why someone is engaging in toxic behavior, your social competence has grown.

In general, social competence grows through a process of (1) paying attention to the emotions and behavior of others, (2) seeking to understand others' behavior through reflection and discussions with third parties, (3) thinking of various ways to deal with situations, and (4) observing the effects of your actions. You do not have to be directly involved in situations to learn from them. You can enhance your social competence by observing others, thinking about why people are behaving and reacting as they do, and seeing what behavior seems helpful in which situations.

Whether or not they engage in toxic behavior, it is valuable to understand the personality types and work styles of people you work with. Any relationship can become toxic if the people do not understand each other and become locked in a disagreement. Having the tools to understand people is preventative medicine. The key to being a good manager lies in recognizing people's strengths and weaknesses, being able to place them in positions where their strengths will be utilized and their weaknesses will not interfere with the work, and knowing how to communicate with and work with people whose style differs from your own.

DECODING WORK STYLES

Everyone's style is unique and made up of innumerable factors. Nevertheless, there are certain key factors to look at when deciding on whether someone would be a good fit for a position. Familiarity with one or more models can help you to understand the people you work with by providing structure to your thoughts about them. Several typologies of personality styles have been developed including the "Five-Factor Model," Myers-Briggs Type Indicator, and Bolton's "People Styles at Work." I have created a "Work Styles Model" by integrating the insights from these three models (See *The Five-Factor Model of Personality* edited by J. S. Wiggins (Guilford Press, 1996); *Introduction to Type in Organizations* by Sandra K. Hirsh and Jean M. Kummerow (CPP, 1998); *Work It Out: Clues for Solving People Problems at Work* by Sandra Krebs Hirsh and Jane A. G. Kise (Davies-Black, 1996); *WorkTypes: Understanding Your Work Personality—How It Helps You and Holds You Back, and What You Can Do to Understand It* by Jean M. Kummerow, Nancy J. Barger, and Linda Kirby (Warner Books, 1997); *People Styles at Work: Making Bad Relationships Good and Good Relationships Better* by Robert Bolton and Dorothy Grover Bolton (Touchstone, 1986).

Work Styles Model

Introverts	Extroverts
Detail-Oriented	Big Picture
Task-Oriented	People-Oriented
Emotional Intelligence	Limited Social Skills
Planners	Spontaneous
Self-Centered	Group-Oriented
Conservative	Imaginative
Initiative	Followers
Conscientious	Unreliable
Strong Conscience and Moral Values	Machiavellian Attitude

Introverts vs. Extroverts

"Extroverts" are energized by external factors (being with people) while "introverts" rejuvenate themselves by spending time alone. Extroverts are outgoing and enjoy being with groups of people whenever possible. Introverts avoid loud parties preferring one-on-one interactions or doing something on their own. Introverts find their ideas and energy inside. Interacting with others, even if fun, absorbs energy rather than creates it.

Extroverts tend to speak before they have thought a matter through, while introverts tend to gather their thoughts before thinking. Because of their tendency to talk a lot, extreme extroverts often make it hard for others to be heard, particularly introverts. On the other hand, when people are unsure of what to do, extroverts can be very helpful in getting the discussion going.

Teams benefit from having a mix of introverts and extroverts. A team consisting only of introverts could sit and say little to each other and have a hard time getting a conversation going and getting the work done. A group of extroverts could slowly and progressively increase in tension since most of the people are used to speaking 30 to 50% of the time in groups and can't when they are facing other extroverts rather than introverts.

The key to dealing with these differences is first to understand them, second to respect the strengths and limitations of each, and then to have each do what he or she are good at. Introverts should not be assigned to positions in which rapid networking is crucial. Extroverts are likely to run into trouble when someone is needed who will listen more than speak.

Detail People vs. Big-Picture People

Detail people are invaluable when being meticulous is important, such as in planning and implementation. At the same time, they can miss the big picture. Overly focused on getting every detail correct, they may needlessly drive up costs and run behind schedule.

Big-picture people are the ones to create visions and to make sure that a team is going in the right direction. They generally have good intuition and can synthesize large amounts of material and come up with a plan and direction. Implementing is usually not their forte, however, and they can miss important details unless a detail person is backing them up.

Task-Oriented vs. People-Oriented

Some people are overwhelmingly focused on the tasks they have been assigned, ignoring the cost to people of accomplishing the task. They try to be unemotional and avoid letting feelings or the well-being of individuals get in the way of careful analyses of problems. They are all business at work and interact with people primarily when it is necessary to get the work done.

People-oriented individuals are much more concerned about their relationships. They want to have friends at work. They care as much about whom they work with as what they are doing. They spend time and energy talking around the water cooler because it is fun, and not simply because they need to exchange information.

While task-oriented individuals provide the direction and drive for action to overcome obstacles (including the needs and desires of some people), people-oriented individuals provide the glue that holds the office together and the support to keep people engaged and motivated. Both are needed.

Emotional Intelligence vs. Limited Social Skills

Being interested in people is not the same as having social skills. Some people like to talk and to have an audience more than they like to get to know other people and listen to other people. They don't really converse with people, they talk at them. They are so preoccupied with expressing what they are feeling and thinking that they have no energy to find out what you are thinking and feeling and wish. Some people fail to pick up on messages that someone has heard enough about a topic or that he or she is busy and does not want to be interrupted. Some people do not know how to make small talk and develop a relationship and trust before jumping into business. Having limited social skills will almost always interfere with someone's success. Whether it is a minor obstacle or a disaster waiting to happen depends upon the position and the situation. It is important that people with limited social skills be placed where their limitations will not severely undermine their success, and that they obtain some coaching to improve their skills.

Planners vs. Spontaneous

Planners like order and predictability. They like to plan carefully and then follow through. They want to know in advance that everything is set, and they seek to avoid surprises. Once decisions are made they don't want to revisit them.

Spontaneous people like spontaneity; they like to keep options open and don't want to be locked into old decisions. They will keep their eyes open to new opportunities, be flexible about timetables, and head off in new directions that seem promising.

Teams generally benefit from having a combination of planners and spontaneous people. You both want your team to get the job done and want someone to keep their eyes open to new opportunities.

Self-Centered vs. Group-Oriented

Some people have difficulty seeing beyond their own perspectives and wishes to such an extent that they label anyone who disagrees with them as unfair, unreasonable, or stupid. Other people are very concerned with the views and wishes of others and readily give up some of what they want in order to respect the wishes and needs of others. Group-oriented people are better team players and more trustworthy. Self-centered individuals, however, may be easier to motivate and convince to put in enormous hours in the pursuit of building their career and power.

Conservative vs. Imaginative

Some individuals strongly prefer to stay with standard ways of doing things while others want to try something new. A conservative style can come from being risk prone averse, from having difficulty learning new ways, or from difficulty imagining new ways of doing things. Imaginative individuals are able to think of new options, willing to consider taking risks, and able to learn new things. You want people with both traits on most teams, unless the task is very mundane, has been well assessed for potential new ways of doing things and no amount of imagination could improve current practices.

Initiative vs. Followers

Some individuals are self-starters. If given an opportunity they will find useful things to do and will deliver. Others are good at following directions, but they are likely to sit and do little if not given explicit directions. A follower does not necessarily need close supervision, but a follower needs clear directions.

Conscientious and Reliable vs. Unreliable

There are "can do" people you can go to with a very difficult task and feel confident that they will get it done somehow. Other people have marked difficulty with organizing themselves or figuring out how to do things if any glitches arise. It is important to know the reliability and resourcefulness of an individual when you select someone for a task that you will not be able to carefully supervise and support.

Strong Conscience and Morals vs. Machiavellian

Some people have a strong sense of right and wrong, while others are more Machiavellian and believe that the ends justify the means. Some believe that anything that serves their personal goals is acceptable. The latter leaves the gate open to unethical behavior. Positions that present opportunities for personal gain through unethical behavior should not be filled with Machiavellian individuals unless they are well monitored. This is particularly the case if such behavior could do the company great harm.

CONCLUSION

Toxic managers and subordinates are a fact of life in organizations. Some are toxic most of the time; most are toxic some of the time. Knowing how to deal with people when they are being rigid, aggressive, self-centered, or performing poorly separates the good from the great managers. Using your emotional intelligence and analytic skills to understand what motivates toxic behavior enables you to find an appropriate intervention to ameliorate the impact on the work environment, including making the right decision about retaining them or letting them go.

Even when individuals are not toxic, your interactions with them can become inefficient if you do not understand their styles and cannot adjust your style to effectively work with them. Moreover, you need to understand the skills and weaknesses of people to know what jobs to assign subordinates, how to combine people to make effective teams, and how to work effectively with your boss.

THE ROLE OF PSYCHOLOGICAL WELL-BEING IN JOB PERFORMANCE: A FRESH LOOK AT AN AGE-OLD QUEST*

Thomas A. Wright

Russell Cropanzano

The thirst after happiness is never extinguished in the heart of man.

—JEAN JACQUES ROUSSEAU,
Les Confessions [1781–1788], IX

Like social philosophers such as Rousseau, both business executives and organizational researchers have long been fascinated with the happy/productive worker thesis. There is a very strong practical basis for this interest. Most readers are familiar with the famous Hawthorne experiments undertaken during the 1920s and 1930s at the Western Electric Company in Cicero, Illinois. Initially undertaken to examine the role of such physical job factors as level of illumination on productivity, the studies evolved into much more, eventually securing a prominent spot in the folklore of modern management thought. In particular was the belief widely held by a number of Hawthorne researchers, including Elton Mayo and G.A. Pennock, suggesting that happiness (broadly defined) *should* produce better job performance. In addition, happiness provides a number of positive benefits for not only the happy individuals themselves, but also for those with whom they come in contact. Seen in this light, happiness is almost a responsibility to ourselves, to be sure, but also to our co-workers, who often rely on us to be steadfast and supportive in difficult times.

Prior research efforts to test the thesis have, unfortunately, often not matched this strong practical appeal. Simply stated, the results to date have been rather disappointing and, similar to the conclusions reached by Barry M. Staw and his colleagues in the mid-1980s, still remain a source of much controversy and confusion. Extending the seminal work of Staw, we suggest that the primary reason for these disappointing findings lies in

*Reprinted with permission of Elsevier from *Organizational Dynamics 33*, no. 4 (2004): 338–351.

how happiness has been operationalized. Traditionally, happiness has been considered as employee job satisfaction, with literally thousands of job satisfaction studies already published and hundreds more published every year. In the pages that follow, we will explore our ideas in greater detail. As we shall see, our central theme is that it is both reasonable and highly practical for both business executives and management scholars to understand that happiness is a valuable tool for maximizing both personal betterment and employee job performance.

But first, as proof positive of this trend toward the positive, consider the uplifting results from a study on the handwritten autobiographies of 180 Catholic nuns. The autobiographies, composed before the nuns took their final vows at a mean age of 22 years, were coded for both positive and emotional content. An example of positive emotional content is taken from one nun's autobiography: ". . . The past year which I have spent as a candidate studying at Notre Dame College has been a very happy one. Now I look forward with eager joy to receiving the Holy Habit of Our Lady and to a life of union with Love Divine." Providing solid testimony to the value of "thinking positively," positive emotional content was strongly associated with longevity six decades later. Happier, more productive nuns lived significantly longer (and healthier). Nuns in the highest quartile of reported positive emotion sentences taken from their autobiographies lived healthier and an average of 6.9 years longer, compared with those in the lowest quartile. The moral of the story: Being happy and positive in one's outlook on work and life has a number of tangible benefits, including living longer and healthier. As much as this may make intuitive sense to many of us, an emphasis on the positive has been a surprisingly neglected topic in organizational research.

ACCENTUATE THE NEGATIVE!

Historically, the organizational sciences have been preoccupied with negative aspects of work and life. This focus on the negative can be traced back over 100 years to the very beginnings of applied research in the latter part of the 19th/early part of the 20th centuries. The prevailing belief of early organizational research was that the most profitable business techniques were those that focused on the negative, as opposed to positive, aspects of human motivation. As a case in point, the following example, taken from a series of studies conducted in the 1920s and published in the *Journal of Applied Psychology*, clearly emphasizes this early, applied focus on the negative. In particular, and strongly influencing this accentuation on the negative, the first systematic applications of applied psychology to business problems involved how to generate increased sales dollars through "better" advertising. Essentially, increased sales were thought to result from advertisements all too often designed to frighten and scare potential customers into buying the product!

The research involved an ad test campaign for a proprietary medicine. Five advertisements were created and circulated in 15 eastern American cities of roughly equal size. The advertising appeals ranged from a highly positive one promoting the attainment of good health and its preservation, to a strongly negative one warning against the dire and costly consequences of ill health. The results speak volumes: Positive appeals to good health met with so little success (sales actually went down 10%) that they were, for the most part, discarded. Alternatively, negative appeals to the potential consequences of ill health from not purchasing the medicine met with tremendous success, with sales increasing 171%! Drawing on recent, fascinating work on human emotions, we provide a brief explanation for *why* this widespread focus on the negative, to the apparent neglect of the positive.

A key assertion made by many traditional models of emotion is that human emotions are associated with specific action tendencies. A leading positive psychologist, Barbara Fredrickson, defines a specific action tendency as "the outcome of a psychological process that narrows a person's momentary thought-action repertoire by calling to mind an urge to act in a particular way." In other words, a specific action tendency is what helps to get our attention. For example, anger leads to attacking behavior and fear leads to escape behavior. In a distinction that will become more relevant as our discussion unfolds, a number of prominent researchers on human emotions suggest that specific action tendencies better describe both the form and function of negative, as opposed to positive emotions.

To further illustrate this critical distinction, consider the primary role of negative emotion in our most basic decision to "fight or flee" in a given situation. In the fight or flight (flee) scenario, the negative emotion of fear is best viewed as an evolved adaptation that was highly instrumental in assisting our prehistoric ancestors' to survive various life-threatening situations. For instance, one of the authors currently lives at the base of the Sierra Nevada Mountains on the Nevada/California border. The mountain area is highly populated with such wild animals as mountain lions and bears. If, on one of his hikes in the mountains, the author happened upon a huge, ferocious bear, his initial response would most likely be to become frightened and then attempt to escape from this dangerous situation. In other words, the negative emotion of fear initiates the specific action tendency to flee from the fear-evoking stimulus of the man-eating bear. As our thoughts about various actions narrow to, and then focus on, these specific urges, the body's role becomes one of mobilizing optimal physiological resources to meet the life-threatening challenge. Our prehistoric survival instincts take over. This constricted or narrowed thought-action sequence can be highly adaptive in nature and helps foster quick, decisive and potentially life-saving action.

While potentially adaptive in nature, the focus on negative, to the neglect of positive emotions, can be [and has been] very problematic if overindulged in the business environment. An excellent example of this negative focus is the typical yearly performance evaluation procedure. Why so? The answer rests on the apparent need of many evaluators to primarily focus on various negative aspects of employee behavior. Your employee neglected to do this, or your employee failed to do that. This overemphasis on the negative by many evaluators has repeatedly been shown to have a detrimental effect on subsequent employee goal achievement. Is it any wonder that managers and employees alike widely report that the most stressful job-related task is to give/get performance evaluations?

How "successful" or widespread has this buy-in to the negative been in social science research? Well, a recent computer search of contemporary literature in psychology found approximately 375,000 articles on "negative" concepts (i.e., mental illness, depression, burnout, anxiety, fear and anger) and only about 1,000 articles on various positive concepts and capabilities of people. This constitutes a negative/positive ratio of approximately 375/1.

Once again, consider our advertising example. The primary purpose of the negative warnings against the dire and costly effects of ill health was to narrow the potential product buyer's thought–action response repertoire to focus on the detrimental consequences of not purchasing the product. The negative message was one intentionally framed to be perceived by the potential customer as distressing, fearful, or anxiety inducing. The intended message was that a failure to take this medicine would result in grave consequences. Similar to the bear scenario, in our advertising example, the effect is immediate and significant. Over the years, these and many similar results, covering a wide gamut of organizational topics, got the full attention of a business audience highly interested in maximizing short-term revenue.

This prevailing emphasis on the negative is especially ironic when one considers the increasing prominence of the Positive Psychology and Positive Organizational Behavior/Scholarship movements. We say ironic because Abraham Maslow first introduced the term "positive psychology" to us 50 years ago in his ground-breaking book, *Motivation and Personality.* In his last chapter titled "Toward a Positive Psychology," Maslow laid out a research agenda proposing investigation of such "new" and "central" concepts as growth, self-sacrifice, love, optimism, spontaneity, courage, acceptance, contentment, humility, kindness, and actualization of potential. Do these concepts sound familiar today? Given Maslow's earlier work, they should! However, Maslow was unsuccessful in bucking the prevailing viewpoint and, unfortunately, as a result, organizational research continues to focus on the negative. Adopting a "repair shop" perspective, and extending our advertising example, applied research has tended to unduly concentrate on identification of the pecuniary costs to the organization of distressed, dissatisfied, and unhappy employees. In addition, the cause of this employee dissatisfaction and unhappiness is typically seen from this negative-based or "repair shop" perspective as being deeply embedded in the emotional maladjustment of the employee, as opposed to aspects of the job itself. As a result, the "cure" for this malady usually involves some type of prevention-based employee therapy. Among others, the authors have previously referred to this approach as the disease model and suggest that while important, the disease approach is incomplete in scope. However, as we now demonstrate, the potential benefits of a positive, what we call a health approach, can also be very evident, especially over time, when considering the role of employee psychological well-being (PWB) in the happy/productive worker thesis.

BACK TO THE FUTURE: PSYCHOLOGICAL WELL-BEING AND HAPPINESS

"Happiness" is a lay construct, replete with personal meaning for each of us. In order to study the idea scientifically, we need a more precise definition that lends itself to systematic measurement. In this regard, scholars have tended to treat "happiness" as PWB, also referred to as emotional well-being or subjective well-being.

PWB is usually thought of in terms of the overall effectiveness of an employee's psychological functioning. Definitions of happiness/PWB have at least three characteristics. First, happiness is a subjective experience. People are happy to the extent that they believe themselves to be happy. Second, happiness includes both the relative presence of positive emotion and the relative absence of negative emotions. Third, happiness is a global judgment. It refers to one's life as a whole. PWB is not tied to any particular situation. Additionally, PWB has been shown to exhibit consistency over time.

How one feels today influences how one feels tomorrow, next week, next month, next year, even years in the future. Fortunately, this does not mean that PWB is immutable to change. PWB has been shown to be strongly influenced by any number of environmental events and is considered to be responsive to therapeutic interventions. In sum, it is generally accepted that happiness refers to a subjective and global judgment that one is experiencing a good deal of positive emotion and relatively little negative emotion. As we shall see, recent research has consistently demonstrated that high levels of PWB can boost performance on the job, while simultaneously increasing each individual's capacity to appreciate new opportunities and experiences.

JOB PERFORMANCE: THE ORGANIZATIONAL CONSEQUENCES OF HAPPINESS

In support of the happy/productive worker thesis, a growing body of empirical research has found significant links between various measures of employee PWB and measures of job-related performance. In one study involving M.B.A. students, participants high on well-being were shown to be superior decision makers, demonstrated better interpersonal behaviors, and received higher overall performance ratings. These results are important for two reasons. First, the study design used objective, quantifiable indices of performance (e.g., an "in-basket" measure). This argues against the possibility that correlations between well-being and job performance are simply misperceptions. Second, the experimental design of this research suggests a causal relation: that performance increases when PWB is high. In another study, employees high in well-being had superior performance evaluations and higher pay 18 months later. Considered together, these PWB studies clearly demonstrate that PWB is predictive of both a subjective measure of performance, supervisory performance evaluations, and a more objective indicator of performance, actual pay. In addition, the consistency of PWB over time is especially relevant for practitioners concerned with issues involving employee selection, training and development, and placement. Using a sample of experienced management personnel, our next example clearly demonstrates the magnitude of this stability.

Incorporating multiple measures of both PWB and performance, one of the present authors recently found that PWB significantly predicted not only contemporaneous employee performance, but also subsequent supervisory performance ratings several *years* in the future. In addition, PWB predicted subsequent employee performance even after controlling for their prior performance. In a series of studies involving well-paid management personnel from a variety of different organizations and occupations, the current authors have found that PWB remained significantly related to performance even after controlling for employee age, gender, ethnicity, job tenure, and educational attainment level.

These findings are important for at least three reasons. First, the use of longitudinal research designs supports the possibility that PWB is not only correlated with performance, but could also be a cause of job performance. Incorporating multiple measures of both performance and PWB, these research designs provide a measure of rigor not typically found in research conducted in actual organizational settings. Second, the fact that both subjective *and* objective quantifiable indices of performance have consistently been found to be related to PWB strongly argues against the possibility that the significant findings are the result of supervisory misperceptions, a consequence of what is typically referred to as the "halo" error.

Halo error is a potentially serious problem in performance evaluation. Halo error is defined as the tendency to evaluate an employee's overall job performance primarily based upon how well they perform, or are perceived to perform, on one salient performance dimension. In the present case, this salient performance dimension might be the employee's level of PWB and the possibility of halo error can be explained in the following manner. Employees who are more psychologically well may be seen by their supervisors as more likeable and fun to be around. Because people in general, and supervisors in particular, tend to be more tolerant of those they like, they may provide more positive performance evaluations for those subordinates considered to be more psychologically well. As a result, rather than being directly related to changes in performance, PWB could serve as a systematic source of halo in performance evaluations. If true, halo error could bias our ability to interpret these findings of a relationship between PWB and job performance.

Though one cannot totally rule out the halo alternative, drawing on previous research in the area, we offer three basic arguments minimizing the possibility of halo error. First, a number of the studies reported here have used longitudinal designs, affording the opportunity to measure the influence of PWB on incremental changes in job performance evaluations over time. A major strength of having multiple measures of performance over time is the ability to capture any halo contained in the prior measure(s) of job performance. Second, PWB has been related to job performance in a number of studies which have also examined a number of possible third variable explanations, including job satisfaction, positive employee affect, negative employee affect and employee burnout. If halo bias was accounting for the obtained relationship between PWB and job performance, then we can also expect significant relations between these other measures of employee affect/emotion and job performance. The results have consistently demonstrated that this is not the case. In fact, the available data point to a common conclusion: When employee happiness is operationalized as PWB, it is positively related to various measures of employee job performance.

Third, this line of research is important because significant correlations between PWB and job performance have typically been found in the .30–.50 range. Not only are these findings *statistically* significant, they are *practically* relevant. As a case in point, taking a correlation of .30 between PWB and job performance indicates that roughly 10% of the variance in job performance is associated with differences in PWB, while taking a correlation of .50 points to a substantial 25% of the variance in job performance being associated with differences in PWB.

The available data consistently point to a common, highly practical conclusion. Whether measured with subjective ratings or objective indices, whether examined in quasi-experimental, cross-sectional or longitudinal designs, even after controlling for the effects of a number of possible confounding variables, when happiness is measured as PWB, it is consistently and positively related to various measures of job performance. In the following sections, using current research and theory emanating from the Positive Psychology/Positive Organizational Behavior movements, we propose an expanded role of PWB for those interested in enhancing worker performance.

BROADEN-AND-BUILD: THE HUMAN CONSEQUENCES OF HAPPINESS

All things being equal, not many individuals would prefer to be unhappy when they could be happy. At least since the time of the famous utilitarian philosopher Jeremy Bentham (circa 1748–1832), many would agree that seeking pleasure and avoiding pain is fundamental to human motivation. Certainly many organizational reward systems are predicated on this assumption. Consistent with this hedonistic approach, positive emotions can be seen as providing the distinct value-added of making us feel good. In fact, the balance between positive and negative emotions contributes to how we view our life.

Of noteworthy relevance is Barbara Fredrickson's broaden-and-build model of positive emotions. According to the broaden-and-build model, a number of positive emotions, including the experience of employee PWB, all share the capacity to "broaden" an individual's momentary thought–action repertories through expanding the selection of potential thoughts and actions that come to mind. For example, the positive emotion, interest, fosters the desire to explore, assimilate new experiences, encounter new information, and grow. Likewise, the positive emotion, joy, creates the urge to play, to think outside the box and be creative. Positive emotions have the beneficial effect of potentially widening one's available arsenal of thoughts and actions by "enlarging" the available cognitive context. Properly implemented in the workplace environment, the manifestation of such positive employee emotions as joy and interest fosters employee perceptions of enhanced meaning from their work. As a result, those employees who see positive meaning in their work often come to view it as a Calling, not just as a Job or Career. Those with a Calling orientation work not only for the positive financial rewards (Job orientation) or personal achievement (Career orientation), but also for the personal fulfillment that doing one's job can bring. One practical consequence is that those who view their work as a Calling may well be more productive.

EXECUTIVE ILLUSTRATION

"Today's workers are not committed anymore" is a lament we hear expressed by an ever-increasing number of corporate executives. If accurate, and using the Job, Career, and Calling categories as our framework, more and more of today's employees view their work as merely a Job. When work is considered as a Job, the employee focuses on the material benefits derived from working. Work is simply the necessary means to a financial end. The fulfillment of personal happiness and contentment are sought during one's time off the job. On the other hand, those with a Career orientation work for the rewards that accompany their advancement, either organizational or professional in nature. Employees with a Career orientation are driven by the strong desire to obtain power and prestige through the increased pay and promotional opportunities that Career advancement brings. Alternatively, employees with a Calling orientation do not work primarily for either financial or promotional advancement opportunities. Instead, they work for the fulfillment that doing their work affords. Doing their work well is considered an end in and of itself. Considered together, employees with a Calling orientation report a much more rewarding relation with the work itself, spend more time on work-related activities, and appear to gain more enjoyment, fulfillment, and satisfaction from it. Those who are optimistic and conscientious appear to be more likely to report themselves as having a Calling orientation. Interestingly, and highly relevant when one considers possible intervention strategies, recent research indicates that many employees have the ability to accurately differentiate their work orientation among the Job, Career, and Calling categories.

Fascinating research has further confirmed that the enlarging effect of positive emotion has a physiological base and is linked to increases in brain dopamine levels. In addition, while negative emotions have been shown to adversely increase both heart rate and blood pressure, positive emotions can suppress or "undo" these lingering maladaptive effects! More specifically, compared to such negative emotions as anger and sadness, positive emotions have been shown to produce more rapid returns to the individuals's normal cardiovascular baseline levels. In other words, following the initial, evolutionary surge in heart and blood pressure rates which typically accompany our response to stressful situations, positive emotions help speed the body's recovery to its normal, pre-stress levels.

Based on Fredrickson's work, we also propose that these positive emotions assist in "building" the individual's enduring personal resources, ranging from physical, psychological, intellectual and social in nature. This capacity to experience the positive seems to be crucial to one's capacity to thrive, mentally flourish and psychologically grow. This sense of flourishing appears to make psychologically well or happy people more proactive, resilient to adverse situations, and less prone to stress symptoms. As a result, a continued focus on these positive feelings expands (broadens) and builds on these positive urges, creating a potentially moderating "upward spiral" effect, which can further enhance employee character development. This capacity to experience positive feelings is considered to be a fundamental human strength.

GOOD MORNING AMERICA CASE

Positive emotions help people to not only survive, but also to thrive when confronted with adverse situations. This capacity to overcome potential adversity was vividly demonstrated on a segment of the *Good Morning America* program. C. R. Snyder, one of the founding fathers of positive psychology and a psychology professor at the University of Kansas, gave a test of positive emotion to the *Good Morning America* regular cast. Not surprisingly for many regular viewers of the popular show, host Charles Gibson outscored everyone else by a wide margin. Then, testing the hypothesis that positive or happy people have developed the necessary psychological and physical resources for coping with adversity, Snyder had the members of the crew hold their hand in a bucket of ice before the live cameras and studio audience. Consistent with Snyder's prediction, everyone in the cast removed his or her hand before 90 seconds had elapsed—everyone, that is, except Charles Gibson! In fact, Gibson still had his hand in the ice bucket [while continuing to smile, not grimace] right up until the commercial break, well beyond the time endured by the rest of the program crew. Gibson's resilience to the pain and ability to cope with adversity was clearly attributable to his positive, optimistic personality.

Consider the positive emotion *interest*. Interest has both individual and organizational benefits. At the individual level, interest creates the urge to explore, take in new information and experiences, and expand oneself in the process. At the organizational level, interest, considered collectively, can facilitate meaningful interpersonal encounters. These meaningful interpersonal encounters result in enchanced social connections and team-building behavior. A beneficial organizational consequence is the creation of a better work climate and increased productivity.

This upward spiraling effect is in marked contrast to the effects of a number of negative emotions. Consider the case of depression. Distressingly, depression has reached epidemic proportions in the United States. Recent figures indicate that literally tens of millions of Americans have taken (or are currently taking) various forms of antidepression medications. Unlike the uplifting effect of positive emotion, negative feelings of depression or anger or fear tend to lead to narrowed, pessimistic thinking, which can produce a further downward spiral, leading to ever-worsening moods and feelings.

HOW HAPPINESS HELPS US TO GROW: A DEMONSTRATION OF THE BROADEN-AND-BUILD APPROACH TO MANAGEMENT

We have already seen that happiness, when defined as PWB, promotes higher levels of job performance. We have also learned that those high in PWB are in a better position to benefit from positive work experiences than are their counterparts who are lower in PWB. Through the impetus provided by high levels of PWB, happier or more psychologically well employees are more easily able to "broaden-and-build" themselves and become more creative, resilient, socially connected, physically and mentally healthy, and more productively effective. In addition, and of further benefit, these effects are seen as persisting over time and across situations.

As an illustration of this idea, consider a recent study by the present authors. In this study we found strong empirical support for the idea that those high in PWB can benefit more from a satisfying job than do those low in PWB. In other words, employee PWB moderated or influenced the job satisfaction to job performance relation. Specifically, the more positive the PWB of the employee, the stronger [more statistically robust] was the observed relation between job satisfaction and job performance. Considered together, PWB, job satisfaction and the PWB by job satisfaction interaction (the moderator effect) accounted for approximately 25% of the variance in employee job performance ratings. This finding strongly supports our premise of a distinct competitive advantage for those organizations able and willing to foster a psychologically well workforce and work environment.

To emphasize the potential pecuniary benefits of these findings, consider the following example. Suppose you manage 10 electrical engineers. Furthermore, each engineer is paid $1,250 per week, or $65,000 a year in salary. You know that, for a number of reasons—including their PWB—each engineer's productivity varies by as much as $500 a week, or roughly $25,000 a year. (This is consistent with national averages across occupations, which indicate your engineers are typically productive for only 4.8 hours for every 8 hours that you pay them!) Let us put this in the context of our reported results. PWB and job satisfaction account for roughly 25% of this $500 a week in performance variance for our engineers. This translates into $125 per week/per person in lost productivity! With 10 employees, this translates to $1,250 per week in performance variance, for 100 employees, the numbers are $12,500 per week or $650,000 per year. Of equal importance, as we will momentarily detail, various intervention strategies can be used to select psychologically well job applicants. Current employees can also be more effectively trained and placed based upon knowledge of their PWB. In our concluding sections, we provide suggestions for proactive business executives interested in developing progressive, employee-centered intervention strategies designed to serve the dual purpose of enhancing both PWB and employee performance.

HOW TO BUILD A HAPPY WORKFORCE

Employee-focused, positive psychological-based interventions at work can take three general forms: composition, training, and situational engineering. Composition emphasizes selecting and placing people into appropriate positions, training emphasizes assisting workers so that they "fit" their jobs more closely, and situational engineering emphasizes changing the work environment so that it more closely fits the needs of one's employees. Our "extended" happy/productive worker thesis has implications for each approach.

THE COMPOSITION (OR SELECTION) APPROACH TO PROMOTING HAPPINESS

Research has clearly established that PWB is stable over time. In fact, one of our studies has established substantial test-retest correlations of up to five years in duration. These findings give clear support to the notion that people who report being happy (or unhappy) at one point in time are likely to be happy (or unhappy) at another point in time, and provide evidence supportive of the notion of the heritability of happiness.

Interesting research on the possible heritability of happiness (and job satisfaction) has been reported by a number of scholars. While beyond the scope of the present discussion, the possibility of a genetic basis for various employee attitudes and emotions has been highly controversial in organizational research. Nevertheless, and very relevant from a management perspective, research supportive of a possible genetic basis does not necessarily imply that well-being stability is solely due to the personal characteristics of the individual. Employee PWB, and level of job satisfaction for that matter, may well be stable over time because one's life or job circumstances are stable as well. For example, an employee may remain at the same job or at a very similar one for any number of reasons. As a result, the "fact" of employee attitudinal stability should not solely be used to argue against the possibility of successful training and situational engineering-based interventions.

We should point out that selecting the happiest employees does raise the specter of some potentially serious ethical issues. The failure to select prospective employees on the basis of their level of PWB could depress these individuals further, which in turn could make these job candidates even more unemployable in the future. This can engender considerable human and societal costs. As a consequence, careful consideration of these and other related issues is of paramount importance for management personnel, employing organizations, and practicing consultants interested in using various measures of PWB to select happy workers.

TRAINING

Another option is to change employees by helping them learn to be happier. There is good evidence that various types of stress management training can have positive effects on worker happiness. A number of strategies exist where individual employees can proactively self-monitor or manage their personal perceptions to enhance positive, and discourage negative, displays of momentary mood and emotion. For example, constructive self-talk is a conscious effort to replace negative with more positive and reinforcing self-talk. There are a number of other cognitive restructuring techniques designed to be beneficial in temporarily altering an employee's current emotional state or providing more permanent or dispositionally-based changes in their behavior. One such trait is learned optimism. Learned optimism is viewed as a developed trait or style emphasizing positive thought patterns. As the name indicates, employees can be trained to better utilize "learned" optimism techniques, both within and outside the work environment. As one benefit, research has clearly demonstrated that optimistic employees perform more effectively on a wide range of jobs and occupations, especially those involving significant interactions with others.

METROPOLITAN LIFE CASE

As everyone knows, selling is not easy. It requires great persistence in the face of seemingly consistent rejection. The executives at Metropolitan Life learned this fact all too well. While they rigorously selected less than 1 in 10 sales agent applicants, half would quit in the first year. Equally disheartening, of those who stayed, most produced less and less the longer they remained with the company as sales agents. In any event, by the end of the fourth year, 80% were gone. As it turned out, employee optimism predicted level of sales. Sales agents ranked in the top half on an optimism scale sold 37% more insurance on average in their first 2 years than those agents who scored in the lower half of the scale and were more pessimistic. Even more impressive, agents who scored in the top 10% on optimism sold 88% more than those in the bottom 10%. As executives at Metropolitan Life discovered, the best news was that an optimistic approach is learnable.

SITUATIONAL ENGINEERING

The third approach to possible interventions involves changing the environment so that it promotes, or at least does not impair, worker PWB. Situational engineering would appear to be a promising technique, in that there is evidence that working conditions strongly affect employee PWB. As with the selection and training approaches, situational engineering provides a variety of options for organizations to create a happier, more satisfied, workforce. In fact, research has documented that something as simple as providing tangible social support can help reduce the negative impact of stressful jobs. More generally, employers can manipulate or reengineer any number of organizational factors (i.e., physical, role, task, and/or interpersonal demands) shown to be related to increased displays of employee emotion at work. For example, work-family conflict seems to diminish life satisfaction and increase negative displays of emotion. Alternatively, family-friendly policies, such as flextime and child-care programs, should increase employee PWB. Finally, we should not neglect the more obvious change strategies. Research has shown that equitable pay tends to promote high levels of PWB. In short, there are a number of available options for designing human resource techniques to enhance PWB and subsequent employee performance.

CONCLUDING THOUGHTS

Applied research's interest in employee happiness has long centered on the happy/productive worker thesis. However, the results have sometimes proved disappointing. Fortunately, recent work shows great promise. It seems that the generations of managers and business executives who believed that a happy worker is a productive worker are correct when considering employee happiness as PWB. Of noteworthy relevance in the "holy grail" pursuit of providing greater insight into the happy/productive worker thesis is the further development of such positive-based approaches as the broaden-and-build model. The broaden-and-build model provides the necessary framework to explain the possible interactive role of PWB on the job satisfaction/job performance relation. Considered individually, PWB has demonstrated statistically significant relations to employee performance. The psychological well-being/job performance correlation is consistently in the .30–.50 range. Furthermore, results were discussed here that clearly demonstrate that consideration of the interaction effects of PWB on the job satisfaction/job performance relation are significantly more statistically robust.

In addition to PWB, the broaden-and-build model supports the possible adaptive and interactive nature of a number of other positive-based employee emotions. Joy, exhilaration, optimism, and interest all share the potential ability to broaden an employee's momentary thought–action experiences and provide valuable assistance in helping to further build the employee's personal resource arsenal. This means that in addition to studies on happy/productive workers, we may eventually see [and we actively encourage] research on serene/thoughtful workers, caring/helpful workers, joyous/honest workers, and exhilarated/creative workers:

We close by emphasizing an important point. Employee PWB has both theoretical and applied relevance in today's society. Using the Positive Psychology/Positive Organizational Behavior (POB) framework, it seems evident that promoting employee PWB is an intrinsic good for which all should work. If this approach promotes better job performance, which the findings strongly suggest is the case, then so much the better. Regardless, the pursuit of employee PWB remains valuable for its own sake. In closing, roughly 2,500 years ago, Aristotle posed the question of what constitutes the good life. Similar to Aristotle, our response is that the pursuit of happiness (*eudaimonia* to Aristotle), properly defined, is a pivotal first step in any attempt to address this age-old question.

Selected Bibliography

For a further discussion of the happy/productive worker thesis and related topics, see E. Mayo, *The Problems of an Industrial Civilization* (New York: MacMillan, 1933); B. M. Staw, "Organizational Psychology and the Pursuit of the Happy/Productive Worker," *California Management Review* 28 (1986): 40–43; B. M. Staw and J. Ross, "Stability in the Midst of Change: A Dispositional Approach to Job Attitudes,"

Journal of Applied Psychology 70 (1985): 469–480; B. M. Staw, N. E. Bell, and J. A. Clausen, "The Dispositional Approach to Job Attitudes: A Lifetime Longitudinal Test," *Administrative Science Quarterly* 31 (1986): 56–77; R. Cropanzano and T. A. Wright, "When a 'Happy' Worker Is a 'Productive' Worker: A Review and Further Refinement of the Happy-Productive Worker Thesis," *Consulting Psychology Journal: Practice and Research* 53 (2001): 182–199; T. A. Wright, "The Role of 'Happiness' in Organizational Research: Past, Present, and Future Directions," in P. L. Perrewe and D. C. Ganster, eds., *Research in Occupational Stress and Well-Being*, Vol. 4 (Amsterdam: JAI Press, 2005).

For those interested in reading more about the nun study, see D. D. Danner, D. A. Snowden, and W. V. Friesen, "Positive Emotions in Early Life and Longevity Findings from the Nun Study," *Journal of Personality and Social Psychology* 80 (2001): 804–813.

For a fascinating look at early work on advertising, see the following work, all by D. B. Lucas and C. E. Benson, "The Relative Value of Positive and Negative Advertising Appeals as Measured by Coupons Returned," *Journal of Applied Psychology* 13 (1929): 274–300; "The Historical Trend of Negative Appeals in Advertising," *Journal of Applied Psychology* 13 (1929): 346–356; "The Recall Values of Positive and Negative Advertising Appeals," *Journal of Applied Psychology* 14 (1930): 218–238; "Some Sales Results for Positive and Negative Advertisements," *Journal of Applied Psychology* 14 (1930): 363–370.

Highly readable overviews of the broaden-and-build model of positive emotions are contained in B. L. Fredrickson, "What Good Are Positive Emotions?" *Review of General Psychology* 2 (1998): 300–319; B. L. Fredrickson, "The Role of Positive Emotions in Positive Psychology: The Broaden-and-Build Theory of Positive Emotions," *American Psychologist* 56 (2001): 219–226; B. L. Fredrickson, "Positive Emotions and Upward Spirals in Organizations," in K. S. Cameron, J. E. Dutton, and R. E. Quinn, eds., *Positive Organizational Scholarship: Foundations of a New Discipline* (San Francisco: Berrett-Koehler, 2003).

To read more about the positive psychology/positive organizational behavior movements, see F. Luthans, "Positive Organizational Behavior: Developing and Maintaining Psychological Strengths," *Academy of Management Executive* 16 (2002): 57–72; F. Luthans, "The Need for and Meaning of Positive Organizational Behavior," *Journal of Organizational Behavior* 23 (2002): 695–706; T. A. Wright, "Positive Organizational Behavior: An Idea Whose Time Has Truly Come," *Journal of Organizational Behavior* 24 (2003): 437–442.

For a further discussion of the "repair shop" perspective, see C. D. Ryff and B. Singer, "The Contours of Positive Human Health," *Psychological Inquiry* 9 (1998): 1–28; C. L. M. Keyes and J. Haidt, "Introduction: Human Flourishing—The Study of That Which Makes Life Worthwhile," in C. L. M. Keyes and J. Haidt, eds., *Flourishing: Positive Psychology and the Life Well-Lived* (Washington, D.C.: American Psychological Association, 2003).

For a good overview of what psychological well-being is and how it is defined, see E. Diener, E. M. Suh, R. E. Lucas, and H. L. Smith, "Subjective Well-Being: Three Decades of Progress," *Psychological Bulletin* 125 (1999): 276–302.

The following empirical work by Staw and his colleagues is highly supportive of the happy/productive worker thesis: B. M. Staw and S. G. Barsade, "Affect and Managerial Performance: A Test of the Sadder-but-Wiser vs. Happier-and-Smarter Hypotheses," *Administrative Science Quarterly* 38 (1993): 304–331; B. M. Staw, R. I. Sutton, and L. H. Pelled, "Employee Positive Emotion and Favorable Outcomes at the Workplace," *Organization Science* 5 (1994): 71–91; T. A. Wright and B. M. Staw, "Affect and Favorable Work Outcomes: Two Longitudinal Tests of the Happy-Productive

Worker Thesis," *Journal of Organizational Behavior* 20 (1999): 1–23.

The present authors have consistently demonstrated that PWB is related to various measures of job performance. For one of the first studies examining the relation between PWB and performance, see T. A. Wright, D. G. Bonett, and D. A. Sweeney, "Mental Health and Work Performance: Results of a Longitudinal Field Study," *Journal of Occupational and Organizational Psychology* 66 (1993): 277–284; T. A. Wright and R. Cropanzano, "Psychological Well-Being and Job Satisfaction as Predictors of Job Performance," *Journal of Occupational Health Psychology* 5 (2000): 84–94; T. A. Wright, R. Cropanzano, P. J. Denney, P. J., and G. L. Moline, "When a Happy Worker Is a Productive Worker: A Preliminary Examination of Three Models," *Canadian Journal of Behavioral Science* 34 (2002): 146–150.

For a further discussion on halo effects, see T. L. Robbins and A. S. DeNisi, "A Closer Look at Interpersonal Affect as a Distinct Influence on Cognitive Processing in Performance Evaluation," *Journal of Applied Psychology* 79 (1994): 341–353.

For work on the meaning of work, see A. Wrzesniewski, "Finding Positive Meaning in Work," in K. S. Cameron, J. E. Dutton, and R. E. Quinn, eds., *Positive Organizational Scholarship: Foundations of a New Discipline* (San Francisco: Berrett-Koehler, 2003); M. G. Pratt and B. E. Ashforth, "Fostering Meaningfulness in Working and at Work," in K. S. Cameron, J. E. Dutton, and R. E. Quinn, eds., *Positive Organizational Scholarship: Foundations of a New Discipline* (San Francisco: Berrett-Koehler, 2003).

For a fascinating look at the possible physiological basis for human emotions, see B. L. Fredrickson and R. W. Levenson, "Positive Emotions Speed Recovery from the Cardiovascular Sequalae of Negative Emotions," *Cognition and Emotion* 12 (1998): 191–220.

To read further on the possible moderating effect of psychological well-being on the job satisfaction to job performance relation, see T. A. Wright and R. Cropanzano, "The Role of Psychological Well-Being as a Moderator of the Relation Between Job Satisfaction and Job Performance," Paper presented at the 2003 meeting of the *Society for Industrial and Organizational Psychology*, Orlando, Florida.

For a further discussion of work intervention strategies, see D. R. Ilgen, "Teams Imbedded in Organizations: Some Implications," *American Psychologist* 54 (1999): 129–139; R. Cropanzano and T. A. Wright, "A Five-Year Study of Change in the Relationship Between Well-Being and Job Performance," *Consulting Psychology Journal: Practice and Research* 51 (1999): 252–265.

For some entertaining reading on the possible heritability of happiness (and job satisfaction), see R. D. Arvey, T. J. Bouchard, N. L. Segal, and L.M. Abraham, "Job Satisfaction: Environmental and Genetic Components," *Journal of Applied Psychology* 74 (1989): 187–192; T. J. Bouchard, D. T. Lykken, M. McGue, N. Segal, and A. Tellegen, "The Sources of Human Psychological Differences: The Minnesota Study of Twins Reared Apart," *Science* 250 (1990): 223–228. For an alternative interpretation to Arvey et al., see R. Cropanzano and K. James, "Some Methodological Considerations for the Behavioral Genetic Analysis of Work Attitudes," *Journal of Applied Psychology* 75 (1990): 433–439.

To learn more about the benefits of learned optimism, see M.E.P. Seligman, *Authentic Happiness* (New York: Free Press, 2002); M. E. P. Seligman, *Learned Optimism: How to Change Your Mind and Your Life* (New York: Pocket Books, 1998).

For a more comprehensive review of research on organizational reengineering, see J. C. Quick, J. D. Quick, D. L. Nelson, and L. L. Hurrell, *Preventive Stress Management in Organizations* (Washington, D.C.: American Psychological Association, 1997).

BEYOND SOPHISTICATED STEREOTYPING: CULTURAL SENSEMAKING IN CONTEXT*

Joyce S. Osland
Allan Bird

If U.S. Americans are so individualistic and believe so deeply in self-reliance, why do they have the highest percentage of charitable giving in the world and readily volunteer their help to community projects and emergencies?

In a 1991 survey, many Costa Rican customers preferred automatic tellers over human tellers because "at least the machines are programmed to say 'Good morning' and 'Thank you.' "[1] Why is it that so many Latin American cultures are noted for warm interpersonal relationships and a cultural script of simpatía (positive social behavior),[2] while simultaneously exhibiting seeming indifference as service workers in both the private and public sectors?

Based on Hofstede's[3] value dimension of Uncertainty Avoidance, the Japanese have a low tolerance for uncertainty while Americans have a high tolerance. Why then do the Japanese intentionally incorporate ambiguous clauses in their business contracts, which are unusually short, while Americans dot every *i*, cross every *t*, and painstakingly spell out every possible contingency?

Many people trained to work in these cultures found such situations to be paradoxical when they first encountered them. These examples often contradict and confound our attempts to neatly categorize cultures. They violate our conceptions of what we think particular cultures are like. Constrained, stereotypical thinking is not the only problem, however. The more exposure and understanding one gains about any culture, the more paradoxical it often becomes. For example, U.S. Americans are individualistic in some situations (e.g., "the most comprehensive of rights and the right most valued is the right to be left alone"[4]) and collectivist in others (e.g., school fundraising events).

Long-term sojourners and serious cultural scholars find it difficult to make useful generalizations since so many exceptions and qualifications to the stereotypes, on both a cultural and individual level, come to mind. These cultural paradoxes are defined as situations that exhibit an apparently contradictory nature.

Surprisingly, there is little mention of cultural paradoxes in the management literature.[5] Our long-term sojourns as expatriates (a combined total of 22 years), as well as our experience in teaching cross-cultural management, preparing expatriates to go overseas, and doing comparative research, has led us to feel increasingly frustrated with the accepted conceptualizations of culture. Thus, our purpose is to focus attention on cultural paradoxes, explain why they have been overlooked and why they exist, and present a framework for making sense of them. Our intent is to initiate a dialogue that will eventually provide teachers, researchers, and people who work across cultures with a more useful way to understand culture.

A look at the comparative literature reveals that cultures are described in somewhat limited terms.[6] There are 22 dimensions commonly used to compare cultures, typically presented in the form of bipolar continua, with midpoints in the

*Reprinted with permission from the *Academy of Management Executive 14*, no. 1 (2000): 65–77, via the Copyright Clearance Center.

TABLE 1 Common Cultural Dimensions

Subjugation to nature	Harmony	Mastery of nature
Past	Present	Future
Being	Containing and controlling	Doing
Hierarchical relationships	Group	Individualistic
Private space	Mixed	Public
Evil human nature	Neutral or mixed	Good
Human nature as changeable		Human nature as unchangeable
Monochronic time		Polychronic time
High-context language		Low-context language
Low uncertainty avoidance		High uncertainty avoidance
Low power distance		High power distance
Short-term orientation		Long-term orientation
Individualism		Collectivism
Masculinity		Femininity
Universalism		Particularism
Neutral		Emotional
Diffuse		Specific
Achievement		Ascription
Individualism		Organization
Inner-directed		Outer-directed
Individualism (competition)		Group-organization (collusion)
Analyzing (reductivist)		Synthesizing (larger, integrated wholes)

Sources: Kluckhohn and Strodtbeck (1961); Hall and Hall (1990); Hofstede (1980); Parsons and Shils (1951); Trompenaars and Hampden Turner (1993); Trompenaars (1994). The dimensions are bipolar continua, with the first six containing midpoints.

first examples, as shown in Table 1. These dimensions were developed to yield greater cultural understanding and allow for cross-cultural comparisons. An unanticipated consequence of using these dimensions, however, is the danger of stereotyping entire cultures.

SOPHISTICATED STEREOTYPING

In many parts of the world, one hears a generic stereotype for a disliked neighboring ethnic group—"The (fill in the blank) are lazy, dirty thieves, and their women are promiscuous." This is a low-level form of stereotyping, often based on lack of personal contact and an irrational dislike of people who are different from oneself. Professors and trainers work very hard to dispel such stereotypes. Rarely, however, do we stop to consider whether we are supplanting one form of stereotyping for another. For example, when we teach students and managers how to perceive the Israelis using Hofstede's[7] cultural dimensions, they may come to think of Israelis in terms of small power distance, strong uncertainty avoidance, moderate femininity, and moderate individualism. The result is to reduce a complex culture to a shorthand description they may be tempted to apply to all Israelis. We call this *sophisticated stereotyping*, because it is based on theoretical concepts and lacks the negative attributions often associated with its lower-level counterpart. Nevertheless, it is still limiting in the way it constrains individuals' perceptions of behavior in another culture.

Do we recommend against teaching the cultural dimensions shown in Table 1 so as to avoid sophisticated stereotyping? Not at all. These dimensions are useful tools in explaining cultural behavior. Indeed, cultural stereotypes can be helpful—provided we acknowledge their limitations. They are more beneficial, for example, in making comparisons between cultures than in understanding the wide variations of behavior within a single culture. Adler[8] encourages the use of "helpful stereotypes," which have the following limitations: They are consciously held, descriptive rather than evaluative, accurate in their description of a behavioral norm, the first best guess about a group prior to having direct information about the specific people involved, and modified based on further observations and experience. As teachers, researchers, and managers in cross-cultural contexts, we need to recognize that our original characterizations of other cultures are best guesses that we need to modify as we gain more experience.

For understandable, systemic reasons, business schools tend to teach culture in simple-minded terms, glossing over nuances and ignoring complexities. An examination of the latest crop of organizational behavior and international business textbooks revealed that most authors present only Hofstede's cultural dimensions, occasionally supplemented by Hall's theory of high- and low-context cultures.[9] Although these disciplines are not charged with the responsibility of teaching culture in great depth, these are the principal courses in many curricula where business students are exposed to cross-cultural concepts. Another handicap is that many business professors do not receive a thorough grounding in culture in their own disciplines and doctoral programs. One could further argue that we are joined in this conspiracy to give culture a quick-and-dirty treatment by practitioners and students who are looking for ways to simplify and make sense of the world.

The limitations of sophisticated stereotyping become most evident when we confront cultural paradoxes. This is the moment we realize our understanding is incomplete, misleading, and potentially dangerous. Perhaps because cultural paradoxes reveal the limitations in our thinking, they are often left unmentioned, even though virtually anyone with experience in another culture can usually identify one or two after only a moment's reflection.

WHY DON'T WE KNOW MORE ABOUT CULTURAL PARADOXES?

With one exception,[10] the cross-cultural literature contains no mention or explanation of cultural paradoxes. This absence can be explained by:

- homegrown perceptual schemas that result in cultural myopia;
- lack of cultural experience that leads to misinterpretation and failure to comprehend the entire picture;
- cultural learning that plateaus before complete understanding is achieved;
- Western dualism that generates theories with no room for paradox or holistic maps;
- features of cross-cultural research that encourage simplicity over complexity; and
- a between-culture research approach that is less likely to capture cultural paradoxes than a within-culture approach.

PERCEPTUAL SCHEMAS

When outsiders look at another culture, they inevitably interpret its institutions and customs using their own lenses and schemas; cultural myopia and lack of experience prevent them from seeing all the nuances of another culture.

In particular, a lack of experience with the new culture creates difficulties for new expatriates trying to make sense of what they encounter. The situation is analogous to putting together a jigsaw puzzle. Though one may have the picture on the puzzle box as a guide, making sense of each individual piece and understanding where and how it fits is exceedingly difficult. As more pieces are put into place, however, it is easier to see the bigger picture and understand how individual pieces mesh. Similarly, as one acquires more and varied experiences in the new culture, one can develop an appreciation for how certain attitudes and behaviors fit the puzzle and create an internal logic of the new culture.

The danger with sophisticated stereotyping is that it may lead individuals to think that the number of shapes that pieces may take is limited and that pieces fit together rather easily. As Barnlund notes: "Rarely do the descriptions of a political structure or religious faith explain precisely when and why certain topics are avoided or why specific gestures carry such radically different meanings according to the context in which they appear."[11]

Expatriates and researchers alike tend to focus first on cultural differences and make initial conclusions that are not always modified in light of subsequent evidence.[12] Proactive learning about another culture often stops once a survival threshold is attained, perhaps because of an instinctive inclination to simplify a complex world. This may lead us to seek black-and-white answers rather than tolerate the continued ambiguity that typifies a more complete understanding of another culture.

One of the best descriptions of the peeling away of layers that characterizes deeper cultural understanding is found in a fictionalized account of expatriate life written by an expatriate manager, Robert Collins.[13] He outlines ascending levels on a Westerner's perception scale of Japanese culture that alternate, in daisy-petal-plucking fashion, between seeing the Japanese as significantly different or not really that different at all:

> *The initial level on a Westerner's perception scale clearly indicates a "difference" of great significance. The Japanese speak a language unlike any other human tongue. . . . They write the language in symbols that reason alone cannot decipher. The airport customs officers all wear neckties, everyone is in a hurry, and there are long lines everywhere.*
>
> *Level Two is represented by the sudden awareness that the Japanese are not different at all. Not at all. They ride in elevators, have a dynamic industrial/trade/financial system, own great chunks of the United States, and serve cornflakes in the Hotel Okura.*
>
> *Level Three is the "Hey, wait a minute" stage. The Japanese come to all the meetings, smile politely, nod in agreement with everything said, but do the opposite of what's expected. And they do it all together. They really are different.*
>
> *But are they? Level Four understanding recognizes the strong group dynamics, common education and training, and the general sense of loyalty to the family—which in their case is Japan itself. That's not so unusual, things are just organized on a larger scale than any social unit in the West. Nothing is fundamentally different.*

Level Five can blow one's mind, however. Bank presidents skipping through streets dressed as dragons at festival time; single ladies placing garlands of flowers around huge, and remarkably graphic, stone phallic symbols; Ministry of Finance officials rearranging their bedrooms so as to sleep in a "lucky" direction; it is all somewhat odd. At least, by Western standards. There is something different in the air.

And so on. Some Westerners, the old Japan hands, have gotten as far as Levels 37 or 38.[14]

The point of Collins's description is that it takes time and experience to make sense of another culture. The various levels he describes reflect differing levels of awareness as more and more pieces of the puzzle are put into place. Time and experience are essential because culture is embedded in the context. Without context it makes little sense to talk about culture. Yet just as its lower-order counterpart does, sophisticated stereotyping tends to strip away or ignore context. Thus, cognitive schemas prevent sojourners and researchers from seeing and correctly interpreting paradoxical behavior outside their own cultures.

THEORETICAL LIMITATIONS

Another reason for the inattention to cultural paradoxes stems from the intersection between cognitive schemas and theory. Westerners have a tendency to perceive stimuli in terms of dichotomies and dualisms rather than paradoxes or holistic pictures.[15] The idea of paradox is a fairly recent wrinkle on the intellectual landscape of management theorists[16] and has not yet been incorporated into cultural theories in a managerial context.

Cross-cultural research is generally held to be more difficult than domestic studies. Hofstede's[17] work represented a major step forward and launched a deluge of studies utilizing his dimensions. Hundreds of studies have used one or more of Hofstede's dimensions to explore similarities and differences across cultures regarding numerous aspects of business and management. However, Hofstede himself warned against expecting too much of these dimensions and of using them incorrectly. For example, he defended the individualism-collectivism dimension as a useful construct, but then went on to say: "This does not mean, of course, that a country's Individual Index score tells all there is to be known about the backgrounds and structure of relationship patterns in that country. It is an abstraction that should not be extended beyond its limited area of usefulness."[18]

When we fail to specify under what conditions a culture measures low or high on any of the common cultural dimensions, or to take into consideration the impact of organizational culture, it misleads rather than increases our understanding of comparisons of culture and business practices. Such an approach prevents rather than opens up opportunities for learning and exploration.

A final explanation for the failure to address cultural paradoxes can be traced to the emic/etic distinction commonly used in the cultural literature. An emic perspective looks at a culture from within its boundaries, whereas an etic perspective stands outside and compares two or more cultures. To make between-culture differences more prominent, the etic approach minimizes the inconsistencies within a culture.

Most cultural approaches in management adopt a between-culture approach, playing down the within-culture differences that expatriates must understand in order to work successfully in the host country.

Anthropologist Claude Levi-Strauss warned that explanation does not consist of reducing the complex to the simple, but of substituting a more intelligible complexity for one that is less intelligible.[19] In failing to acknowledge cultural paradoxes or the complexity surrounding cultural dimensions, we may settle for simplistic, rather than intelligently complex, explanations.

SOURCES OF PARADOX IN CULTURAL BEHAVIOR

Behavior that looks paradoxical to an expatriate in the initial stages of cultural awareness may simply reflect the variance in behavioral norms for individuals, organizational cultures, subcultures, as well as generational differences and changing sections of the society. In addition, expatriates may also form microcultures[20] with specific members of the host culture. The cultural synergy of such microcultures may not be reflective of the national culture. These false paradoxes need to be discarded before more substantive paradoxes can be evaluated.

Based on an analysis of all the paradoxes we could find, we have identified six possible explanations for cultural behaviors that appear truly paradoxical. They are:

- the tendency for observers to confuse individual with group values;
- unresolved cultural issues;
- bipolar patterns;
- role differences;
- real versus espoused values; and
- value trumping, a recognition that in specific contexts certain sets of values take precedence over others.

Confusing individual with group values is exemplified by the personality dimension labeled allocentrism versus idiocentrism, which is the psychological, individual-level analog to the individualism–collectivism dimension at the level of culture.[21] Allocentric people, those who pay primary attention to the needs of a group, can be found in individualistic cultures, and idiocentric people, those who pay more attention to their own needs than to the needs of others, in collectivist cultures. What we perceive as cultural paradox may not reflect contradictions in cultural values, but instead may reveal the natural diversity within any culture that reflects individual personality and variation.

Unresolved cultural issues are rooted in the definition of culture as a learned response to problems. Some paradoxes come from problems for which there is no clear, happy solution. Cultures may manifest a split personality with regard to an unresolved problem.[22] As a result, they shuttle back and forth from one extreme to the other on a behavioral continuum. U.S. Americans, for example, have ambivalent views about sex, and, as one journalist recently noted: "Our society is a stew of prurience and prudery."[23] Censorship, fears about sex education, and sexual taboos coexist uncomfortably with increasingly graphic films and TV shows and women's magazines that never go to press without a feature article devoted to sex. This melange is more than a reflection of a diverse society that has both hedonists and fundamentalists with differing views of sex; both groups manifest inconsistent behaviors and attitudes about sex, signaling an enduring cultural inability to resolve this issue.

Bipolar patterns make cultural behavior appear paradoxical because cultural dimensions are often framed, perhaps inaccurately, as dualistic, either–or continua. Cultures frequently exhibit one of these paired dimensions more than the other, but it is probable that both ends of the dimensions are found in cultures—but only in particular contexts. For example, in Latin America, ascribed status, derived from class and family background, is more important than its polar opposite, achieved status, which is based on talent and hard work. When it comes to professional soccer, however, achieved status trumps class and ascription.

Often some groups and roles appear to deviate from cultural stereotypes. For example, in the United States, autocratic behavior is frequently tolerated in CEOs, even though the United States is characterized as an egalitarian culture. Such behavior may also be an example of a high power distance context in a low power distance culture: We accept that CEOs possess an unequal degree of power and that they will behave in a different manner than most U.S. Americans.

There is also a difference between real versus espoused values. All cultures express preferences for ideal behaviors—for what should be valued and how people should act. Nevertheless, people do not always act consistently with ideal behaviors and values. For example, U.S. Americans may simultaneously pay lip service to the importance of equality (an espoused value), while trying to acquire more power or influence for themselves (a real value).

A final possible explanation of cultural paradoxes derives from a holistic, contextual view of culture in which values co-exist as a constellation, but their salience differs depending on the situation. Using the Gestalt concept of figure-ground, at times a particular value becomes dominant (figure), while in other circumstances, this same value recedes into the background (ground).[24] In India, for example, collectivism is figural when individuals are expected to make sacrifices for their families or for the larger society—such as Hindu sons who postpone marriage until their sisters marry, or daughters who stay single to care for their parents. In other circumstances, however, collectivism fades into the background and individualism comes to the fore and is figural when Indians focus more upon self-realization—for example, elderly men who detach themselves from their family to seek salvation.[25] Taking the figure-ground analogy a step further, depending on the context, one cultural value might trump another, lessening the influence another value normally exerts.[26] For example, we find it useful to view culture as a series of card games in which cultural values or dimensions are individual cards. Depending on the game, previous play, and the hand one is dealt, players respond by choosing specific cards that seem most appropriate in a given situation. Sometimes a particular card trumps the others; in another round, it does not. In a given context, specific cultural values come into play and have more importance than other values. To a foreigner who does not understand enough about the cultural context to interpret why or when one value takes precedence over another, such behavior looks paradoxical. Members of the culture learn these nuances more or less automatically. For example, children learn in what context a socially acceptable white lie is more important than always telling the truth. A true understanding of the logic of another culture includes comprehending the interrelationships among values, or how values relate to one another in a given context.

A MODEL OF CULTURAL SENSEMAKING

To make sense of cultural paradoxes and convey a holistic understanding of culture, we propose a model of cultural sensemaking. The model shown in Figure 1 helps explain how culture is embedded in context.[27] Cultural sensemaking is a cycle of sequential events:

- ***Indexing Context.*** The process begins when an individual identifies a context and then engages in indexing behavior, which involves noticing or attending to stimuli that provide cues about the situation. For example, to index the context of a meeting with a subordinate, we consider characteristics such as prior events (recent extensive layoffs), the nature of the boss–subordinate relationship within and without work (golfing partner), the specific topic under discussion (employee morale), and the location of the interaction (boss's office).
- ***Making Attributions.*** The next step is attribution, a process in which contextual cues are analyzed in order to match the context with appropriate schema. The matching process is moderated or influenced by one's social identity (e.g., ethnic or religious background, gender, social class, organizational affiliation) and one's history (e.g., experiences and chronology). A senior U.S. American manager who fought against the Japanese in World War II will make different attributions about context and employ different schema when he meets with a Japanese manager than will a Japanese-American manager of his generation, or a junior U.S. manager whose personal experience with Japan is limited to automobiles, electronics, and sushi.
- ***Selecting Schema.*** Schemas are cultural scripts, "a pattern of social interaction that is characteristic of a particular cultural group."[28] They are accepted and appropriate ways of behaving, specifying certain patterns of interaction. From personal or vicarious experience, we learn how to select schema. By watching and working with bosses, for example, we develop scripts for how to act when we take on that role ourselves. We learn appropriate vocabulary and gestures, which then elicit a fairly predictable response from others.
- ***The Influence of Cultural Values.*** Schemas reflect an underlying hierarchy of cultural values. For example, people working for U.S. managers who have

FIGURE 1 Cultural Sensemaking Model

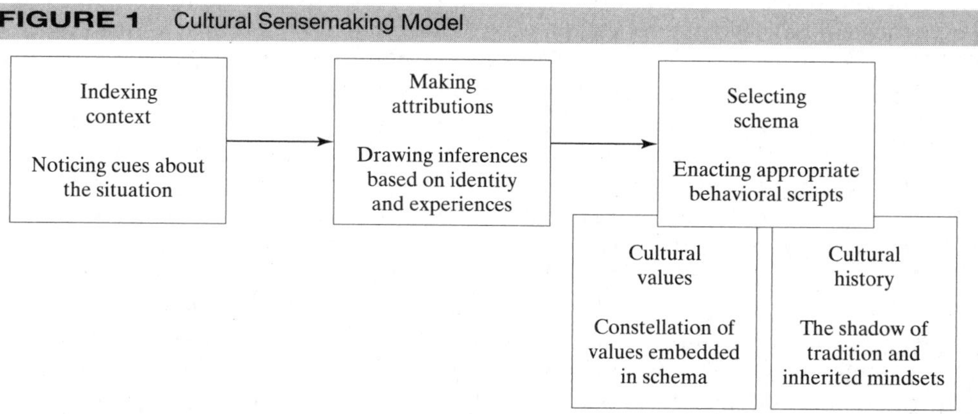

a relaxed and casual style and who openly share information and provide opportunities to make independent decisions will learn specific scripts for managing in this fashion. The configuration of values embedded in this management style consists of informality, honesty, equality, and individualism. At some point, however, these same managers may withhold information about a sensitive personnel situation because privacy, fairness, and legal concerns would trump honesty and equality in this context. This trumping action explains why the constellation of values related to specific schema is hierarchical.

- ***The Influence of Cultural History.*** When decoding schema, we may also find vestiges of cultural history and tradition. Mind-sets inherited from previous generations explain how history is remembered.[29] For example, perceptions about a colonial era may still have an impact on schemas, particularly those involving interactions with foreigners, even though a country gained its independence centuries ago.

SOME ILLUSTRATIONS OF SENSEMAKING

Sensemaking involves placing stimuli into a framework that enables people "to comprehend, understand, explain, attribute, extrapolate, and predict."[30] Let's analyze each of the cultural paradoxes presented in the introduction using the sensemaking model. In the United States, when a charity requests money, when deserving people are in need, or when disaster hits a community (indexing contexts), many U.S. Americans (e.g., religious, allocentric people making attributions) respond by donating their money, goods, or time (selecting schema). The values underlying this schema are humanitarian concern for others, altruism,[31] and collectivism (cultural values). Thus, individualism (a sophisticated stereotype) is moderated by a communal tradition that has its roots in religious and cultural origins (cultural history).

Fukuyama[32] writes that U.S. society has never been as individualistic as its citizens thought, because of the culture's relatively high level of trust and resultant social capital. The United States "has always possessed a rich network of voluntary associations and community structures to which individuals have subordinated their narrow interests."[33] Under normal conditions, one should take responsibility for oneself and not rely on others. However, some circumstances and tasks can overwhelm individual initiative and ingenuity. When that happens, people should help those in need, a lesson forged on the American frontier (cultural history). To further underscore the complexity of culture, in the same contexts noted above, the tax code and prestige associated with philanthropy (cultural history) may be the primary motivations for some citizens (e.g., idiocentric, upwardly ambitious people making attributions) to act charitably (selecting schema), but the value underlying the schema would be individualism.

The Costa Rican example is illustrated in Figure 2. When bank tellers interact with clients (indexing context) many of them (e.g., members of various in-groups, civil servants making attributions) do not greet customers and make eye contact, but concentrate solely on their paperwork (selecting schema). The values that underlie this schema are in-group out-group behavior[34] and power (cultural values). In collectivist cultures such as Costa Rica, members identify strongly with their in-group and treat members with warmth and cooperation. In stark contrast, out-group members

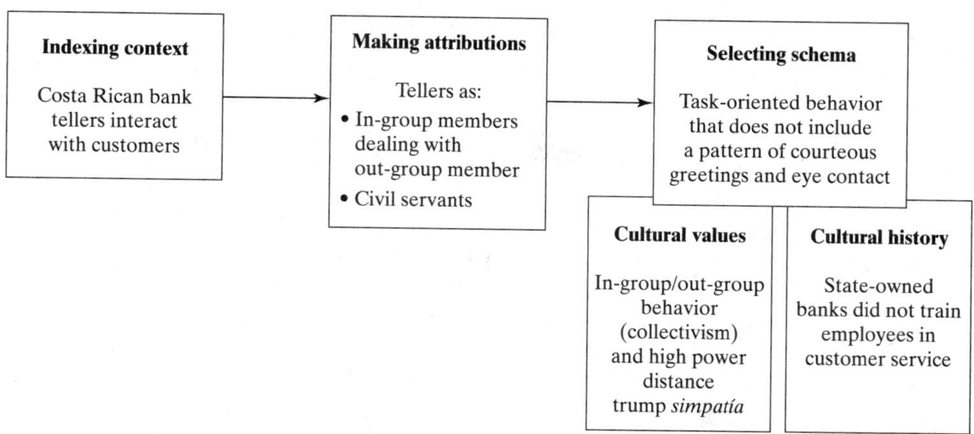

FIGURE 2 Making Sense of Paradoxical Behavior: Seemingly Indifferent Customer Service in a Culture Characterized by Positive, Warm Relations

are often treated with hostility, distrust, and a lack of cooperation. Customers are considered as strangers and out-group members who do not warrant the special treatment given to in-group members (family and friends). One of the few exceptions to simpatía and personal dignity in Costa Rica, and Latin America generally, is rudeness sometimes expressed by people in positions of power.[35] In this context, the cultural value of high power distance (the extent to which a society accepts the fact that power in institutions and organizations is distributed unequally)[36] trumps *simpatía*. Whereas simpatía lessens the distance between people, the opposite behavior increases the distance between the powerful and the powerless. Unlike many other contexts in Costa Rica, bank telling does not elicit a cultural script of simpatía, and state-owned banks did not have a history of training employees in friendly customer service (cultural history) at this time.

In the third cultural example, when Japanese business people make contracts (indexing context), they (e.g., business people making attributions) opt for ambiguous contracts (selecting schema). The dominant value underlying this schema is collectivism (cultural value). In this context, collectivism is manifested as a belief that those entering into agreement are joined together and share something in common; thus, they should rely on and trust one another. Collectivism trumps high uncertainty avoidance (sophisticated stereotype) in this context, but uncertainty avoidance is not completely absent. Some of the uncertainty surrounding the contract is dealt with upstream in the process by carefully choosing and getting to know business partners, and by using third parties. An additional consideration is that many Japanese like flexible contracts, because they have a greater recognition of the limits of contracts and the difficulties of foreseeing all contingencies (cultural history). Even though U.S. Americans are typically more tolerant of uncertainty (sophisticated stereotype), they value pragmatism and do not like to take unnecessary risks (cultural values). If a deal falls through, they rely on the legal system for a resolution (cultural history).

WORKING FROM A SENSEMAKING APPROACH

Sophisticated stereotypes are useful in the initial stages of making sense of complex behaviors within cultures. However, rather than stereotyping cultures somewhere along a continuum, we can advance understanding by thinking in terms of specific contexts that feature particular cultural values that then govern behavior. Geertz maintains that "culture is best seen not as complexes of concrete behavior patterns—customs, usages, traditions, habit clusters—as has by and large been the case up to now, but as a set of control mechanisms—plans, recipes, rules, instructions (what computer engineers call *programs*)—for the governing of behavior."[37]

Understanding the control mechanisms within a culture requires the acquisition of attributional knowledge, the awareness of contextually appropriate behavior.[38] This is in contrast to factual knowledge and conceptual knowledge. Factual knowledge consists of descriptions of behaviors and attitudes. For example, it is a fact that Japanese use small groups extensively in the workplace. Conceptual knowledge consists of a culture's views and values about central concerns. Sophisticated stereotyping operates in the realm of conceptual knowledge. This category of knowledge is an organizing tool, but it is not sufficient for true cultural understanding. Knowing that the Japanese are a communal society (conceptual knowledge) does not explain the non-communal activities that exist in Japanese organizations or when the Japanese will or will not be communal. For example, why are quality control circles used in some work settings and not in others? Factual and conceptual knowledge about Japanese culture cannot answer that question; only attributional knowledge can.

Managers can acquire attributional knowledge from personal experience, vicariously from others' experience, and from cultural mentoring. The personal experience method involves carefully observing how people from another culture act and react, and then formulating and reformulating hypotheses and cultural explanations for the observed behavior. When expatriates test their hypotheses and find them valid, they form schemas about specific events in the host culture.

One can learn vicariously by reading about other cultures, but the best form of vicarious learning is via cultural assimilator exercises.[39] These are critical incidents of cross-cultural encounters, accompanied by alternative explanations for the behavior of people from the foreign culture. After choosing what they perceive as the most likely answer, trainees then read expert opinions relating why each answer is adequate or inadequate. These opinions are validated by cross-cultural experts and include information about the relative importance of cultural dimensions or context-specific customs in the culture in question.

A cultural mentor can be viewed as a hybrid of vicarious and personal acquisition of attributional knowledge—a sort of live cultural assimilator. Cultural mentors are usually long-term expatriates or members of the foreign culture. The latter are often helpful souls who have lived abroad themselves and understand the challenge of mastering another culture or people not totally in step with their own culture.[40] "They interpret the local culture for expatriates and guide them through its shoals, as well as providing them with the necessary encouragement when it feels like the expatriates will never 'break the code' of another culture and fit in comfortably."[41] Reading an explanation from a book or working through a series of cultural assimilators is different from receiving an explanation of an experience the expatriate has personally lived through and now wishes to understand. Cultural mentors can correct inaccurate hypotheses about the local culture. Expatriates who had cultural mentors overseas have been found to fare better than those who did not have such mentors: They were more fluent in the foreign language; they perceived themselves as better adapted to their work and general living conditions abroad; they were more aware of the paradoxes of expatriate life, indicating a higher degree of acculturation and understanding of the other culture; and they received higher performance appraisal ratings from both their superiors and themselves.[42]

In spite of the benefits of mentoring, few multinationals formally assign a cultural mentor to their expatriates. Yet another way of developing an expatriate's attributional knowledge is to provide more training in the host country rather than relying solely an predeparture culture "inoculations."

Admittedly, there are trade-offs to developing attributional knowledge. The acquisition of cultural knowledge takes a good deal of time and energy, which is not available to all managers. Nor is it reasonable to expect employees who work with people from various cultures on a daily basis to master each culture. Nevertheless, organizing the knowledge they do acquire as context-specific schemas can speed up cultural learning and prevent confusion and errors in making sense of cultural paradoxes.

If we accept that cultures are paradoxical, then it follows that learning another culture occurs in a dialectical fashion—thesis, antithesis, and synthesis. Thesis entails a hypothesis involving a sophisticated stereotype; antithesis is the identification of an apparently oppositional cultural paradox. Synthesis involves making sense of contradictory behavior—understanding why certain values are more important in certain contexts. Behavior appears less paradoxical once the foreigner learns to index contexts and match them with the appropriate schemas in the same way that members of the host culture do. Collins's description of the Westerner's Perception Scale in comprehending Japanese culture[43] illustrates one form of dialectical culture learning, an upwardly spiraling cycle of cultural comprehension.

USING THE MODEL

Because this cultural sensemaking model provides a more complex way of understanding culture, it has clear implications for those who teach culture, for those who work across cultures, and for organizations that send expatriates overseas.

TEACHING ABOUT CULTURAL UNDERSTANDING

Sophisticated stereotyping should be the beginning of cultural learning, not the end, as is so often the case when teaching or learning about culture. Recognition of a more complex, holistic, sensemaking model of culture allows us to respond more effectively when students or trainees provide examples of paradoxes that seem to contradict cultural dimensions. The model also requires a somewhat different teaching approach. We have developed a sequential method that has been effective in our teaching:

- ***Help students understand the complexity of their own culture.*** To acquaint students with the vast challenge of comprehending culture, we begin with a thorough understanding of the internal logic of one's own culture and its socioeconomic, political, and historical roots. We add complexity by pointing out paradoxes as well as identifying regional, ethnic, religious, organizational, and individual variations in behavior. For example, when Thai students describe their culture as friendly, we ask the following series of questions: "Are all Thais friendly? Are Thais always friendly? Under what circumstances would Thais not exhibit friendly behavior? Why?"

- ***Give students cultural dimensions and values as well as sophisticated stereotypes as basic tools.*** These dimensions, including the values listed in Table 1, can then be used to explain contrasting behavior from two or more different cultures (e.g., what can sample obituaries from the United States and Mexico reveal about cultural values? What is the typical response of businesses in both countries when a member of an employee's family dies?). Students practice recognizing cultural dimensions in cross-cultural dialogues and cases and learn sophisticated stereotypes. This helps them gain conceptual knowledge about different cultures so they can make between-culture distinctions.
- ***Develop students' skills in cultural observation and behavioral flexibility.*** One of the difficulties expatriates confront in making sense of a new culture is the contradiction between the expected culture, the sophisticated stereotype taught in predeparture training or gleaned from others, and the manifest culture, the one actually enacted in a situation.[44] To help students become skilled at observing and decoding other cultures, teach them to think more like anthropologists and give them practice in honing observational and interpretive skills. To help students develop the behavioral flexibility needed to adapt to unanticipated situations, role-playing and videos of cross-cultural interactions can be used.
- ***Have students do an in-depth study or experience with one culture.*** To go beyond sophisticated stereotypes, students learn the internal logic and cultural history of a single culture. They acquire attributional knowledge from cultural mentors and/or cultural immersion, in addition to extensive research.
- ***Focus on learning context-appropriate behavior in other cultures and developing cultural hypotheses and explanations for paradoxical behavior.*** Once students have mastered the preceding steps, the emphasis changes to learning schemas for different contexts. For example, student teams are instructed to deliberately demonstrate incorrect behavior; they ask others to point out the mistakes and then replay the scene using correct behavior. To model the crucial behavior of asking for help in understanding cultural mysteries,[45] students use cultural mentors to explain situations they choose to learn about (e.g., "How do managers in ___ encourage employees to perform at high levels? Why does that work for them?") The variation in the mentors' answers ("Some managers are successful doing this while others . . . ") and the qualified answers ("This seems to work unless . . . ; it depends on . . . ") helps students develop more complex understandings of the other culture. To highlight the message of moving beyond cultural stereotypes, use language that focuses on forming and testing hypotheses about contextual behavior: "What are your hypotheses about why a French employee behaves this way in this situation? How can you find out if these hypotheses are correct?"

SENSEMAKING FOR INDIVIDUALS WORKING ACROSS CULTURES

After the training program, and once on assignment in a new culture, this cultural sensemaking approach has other practical implications.

- ***Approach learning another culture more like a scientist who holds conscious stereotypes and hypotheses in order to test them.*** One of the key differences between managers who were identified by their fellow MBA students as the "most internationally effective" and the "least internationally effective" is that the former changed their stereotypes of other nationalities as they interacted with them while the latter did not.[46]
- ***Seek out cultural mentors and people who possess attributional knowledge about cultures.*** Perhaps one of the basic lessons of cross-cultural interaction is that tolerance and effectiveness result from greater understanding of another culture. Making sense of a culture's internal logic and decoding cultural paradoxes is easiest with the aid of a willing and knowledgeable informant.
- ***Analyze disconfirming evidence and instances that defy cultural stereotypes.*** Even people with a great deal of experience in another culture can benefit from analyzing cultural paradoxes. For instance, the question "In what circumstances do Latin Americans fail to exhibit *simpatía*?" led to a more complex cultural understanding for one of the authors, who had already spent nine curious years in that region. Once expatriates can function reasonably well in another culture, it is easy for them to reach plateaus in their cultural understanding and mistakenly assume that they comprehend the entire puzzle. This presents a danger when expatriates inadvertently pass on inaccurate information about the local culture, or make faulty, and even expensive, business decisions based on partial understandings.
- ***Learn cultural schemas that will help you be effective.*** Knowing how to act appropriately in specific cross-cultural settings results in self-confidence and effectiveness. One cannot memorize all the rules in another culture, but understanding the values that underlie most schemas can often prevent us from making serious mistakes.

HOW MULTINATIONAL ORGANIZATIONS CAN USE THE SENSEMAKING MODEL

The cultural sensemaking model also has practical implications for multinational organizations.

- ***Use cognitive complexity as a selection criterion for expatriates and people in international positions.*** Avoid black-and-white thinkers in favor of people who exhibit cognitive complexity, which involves the ability to handle ambiguity and multiple viewpoints. This skill is better suited to a thesis–antithesis approach to understanding the paradoxical nature of culture.
- ***Provide in-country cultural training for expatriates that goes beyond factual and conceptual knowledge.*** Predeparture cultural training is complemented by on-site training, which has the advantage of good timing. In-country culture training takes place when expatriates are highly motivated to find answers to real cultural dilemmas and when they are ready for greater complexity.[47]
- ***Gauge the cultural knowledge possessed by expatriates within a country.*** The accuracy and depth of one's cultural understanding is not always linked to the time one has spent in another country; it depends on the degree of involvement with the other culture as well as cultural curiosity and desire to learn. Nevertheless, when

companies determine the optimum length of overseas assignments, they should consider how much time is generally necessary to function effectively in a particular culture. If a firm's expatriates stay abroad for only two years, it is less likely that a deep understanding of the culture will be shared among them than if they were to stay for longer periods. As long as the longer-term expatriates do not stop at a low-level plateau of cultural learning, mixing short-term (2–3 years) with. longer-term expatriates (6–7 years) with permanent expatriates could produce more shared organizational learning about the culture. It is also essential to recognize that expatriates working for the same organization may be at different levels of cultural understanding.

- ***Act like learning organizations with regard to cultural knowledge.*** Multinationals benefit from formal mechanisms to develop a more complex understanding of the cultures where they do business through such methods as cultural mentors and in-country cultural training. There should also be mechanisms for sharing cultural knowledge. For example, having returned expatriates give formal debriefing sessions in which they report what they learned in their assignment increases the company's collective cultural knowledge and eases the expatriates' transition home by helping them make sense of a highly significant experience.[48]

Endnotes

1. This was one of the findings of a class research project on the acceptance of ATMs by Dr. Osland's graduate students at INCAE's (Central American Institute of Business Administration) Banking Program in 1991.
2. J. C. Triandis, G. Marin, J. Lisansky, and H. Betancourt, "Simpatía as a Cultural Script of Hispanics," *Journal of Personality and Social Psychology 47*, no. 6 (1984): 1363–1375.
3. G. Hofstede, *Culture's Consequences: International Differences in Work-Related Values* (Beverly Hills: Sage, 1980).
4. *Olmstead v. United States*, 277 U.S. 438, 478 (1928) (J. Brandeis, dissenting).
5. The descriptions of cultural metaphors in *Understanding Global Cultures: Metaphorical Journeys Through 17 Countries* (Thousand Oaks, CA: Sage, 1994) by Martin Gannon and his associates contain passing references to paradoxes, but do not address the issue directly.
6. T. Parsons and E. Shils, *Toward a General Theory of Action* (Cambridge: Harvard University Press, 1951); F. Kluckhohn and F. L. Strodtbeck, *Variations in Value Orientations* (Evanston, IL: Row, Peterson, 1961); Hofstede; H. C. Triandis, "Dimensions of Cultural Variations as Parameters of Organizational Theories," *International Studies of Management and Organization 12,* no. 4 (1982): 139–169; S. Ronen and O. Shenkar, "Clustering Countries on Attitudinal Dimensions: A Review and Synthesis," *Academy of Management Review 10* (1985): 435–454; E. T. Hall and M. R. Hall, *Understanding Cultural Differences* (Yarmouth, ME: Intercultural Press, 1990); A. P. Fiske, "The Four Elementary Forms of Sociality: Framework for a Unified Theory of Social Relations," *Psychological Review 99*, no. 4 (1992): 689–723; S. Schwartz, "Universals in the Content and Structure of Values: Theoretical Advances and Empirical Tests in 20 Countries," *Advances in experimental Social Psychology,* ed. M. Zanna (New York, NY: Academic Press, 1992): 1–66. F. Trompenaars and C. Hampden Turner, *The Seven Cultures of Capitalism* (New York: Doubleday, 1993).
7. Hofstede.
8. N. Adler, *International Dimensions of Organizational Behavior,* 3rd ed. (Cincinnati: South-Western, 1997): 75–76.
9. Hall and Hall.

10. Gannon.
11. D. Barnlund, *Public and Private Self in Japan and the United States* (Yarmouth, ME: Intercultural Press, 1975): 6.
12. J. S. Osland, *The Adventure of Working Abroad: Hero Tales from the Global Frontier* (San Francisco: Jossey-Bass, 1995).
13. R. J. Collins, *Max Danger: The Adventures of an Expat in Tokyo* (Rutland, VT: Charles E. Tuttle Co., 1987).
14. Ibid., 14–15.
15. R. C. Tripathi, "Aligning Development to Values in India," *Social Values and Development: Asian Perspectives*, eds. H. S. Sinha and R. Kao (New Delhi: Sage, 1988): 315–333; J. Wilbur, *A Brief History of Everything* (New York: Shambala 1995).
16. R. Quinn and K. S. Cameron, eds., *Paradox and Transformation* (Cambridge, MA: Ballinger, 1988); K. K. Smith and D. N. Berg, *Paradoxes of Group Life* (San Francisco: Jossey-Bass, 1987).
17. Hofstede.
18. G. Hofstede, in U. Kim, H. S. Triandis, C. Kâgitçibasi, S. Choi, and G. Yoon, eds., *Individualism and Collectivism* (Thousand Oaks. CA: Sage, 1994): XI.
19. C. Levi-Strauss, *La Pensée Sauvage* (Paris: Adler's Foreign Books, Inc., 1962).
20. G. Fontaine, *Managing International Assignments: The Strategy for Success* (Upper Saddle River, NJ: Prentice Hall, 1989).
21. H. C. Triandis, R. Bontempo, M. J. Villareal, M. Asai, and N. Lucca, "Individualism and Collectivism: Cross-Cultural Perspectives on Self-Ingroup Relationships," *Journal of Personality and Social Psychology 54* (1998): 323–338.
22. G. Bateson, *Steps to an Ecology of Mind* (London: Paladin Books, 1973).
23. J. Haught, "What Does Sex Have to Do with It?" *Oregonian*, December 29, 1993, D7.
24. Tripathi, Marin, et al.
25. Ibid.
26. A. Bird, J. S. Osland, M. Mendenhall, and S. Schneider, "Adapting and Adjusting to Other Cultures: What We Know but Don't Always Tell," *Journal of Management Inquiry 8* (1999): 152–165.
27. Context is also embedded in culture, so one could argue that the entire model is situated within the broader culture. For simplicity's sake, however, we chose to focus only on the sensemaking that occurs in deciphering cultural paradoxes.
28. Triandis, Marin, et al.
29. G. Fisher, *Mindsets: The Role of Culture and Perception in International Relations* (Yarmouth, ME: Intercultural Press, 1997).
30. W. H. Starbuck and F. J. Milliken, "Executives' Personal Filters: What They Notice and How They Make Sense," *The Executive Effect: Concepts and Methods for Studying Top Managers*, ed. D. Hambrick (Greenwich, CT: JAI Press, 1988): 51.
31. Barnlund.
32. F. Fukuyama, *Trust* (New York: Penguin Books, 1996).
33. Ibid., 29.
34. Triandis, et al.
35. J. S. Osland, S. De Franco, and A. Osland, "Organizational Implications of Latin American Culture: Lessons for the Expatriate Manager," *Journal of Management Inquiry 8*, no. 2 (1999): 219–234.
36. Hofstede, *Culture's Consequences.*
37. C. Geertz, *The Interpretation of Cultures* (New York: HarperCollins Basic Books, 1973): 44.
38. A. Bird, S. Heinbuch, R. Dunbar, and M. McNulty, "A Conceptual Model of the Effects of Area Studies Training Programs and a Preliminary Investigation of the Model's Hypothesized Relationships," *International Journal of Intercultural Relations 17*, no. 4 (1993): 415–436.
39. The original cultural assimilators were developed by Harry Triandis at the University of Illinois. A recent collection is found in *Intercultural Interactions: A Practical Guide* by R. Brislin, K. Cushner, C. Cherrie, and M. Yong (Thousand Oaks, CA: Sage, 1986 and 1996—second edition).
40. Osland, *Working Abroad.*
41. Ibid., 68.
42. Ibid., 74.
43. Collins.
44. J. Schermerhorn Jr. and M. H. Bond, "Cross-Cultural Leadership Dynamics in

Collectivism and High Power Distance Settings," *Leadership and Organization Development Journal 18*, no. 4 (1997): 187–193.

45. On occasion we have heard frustrated cross-cultural trainers grumble that some expatriates view seeking out cultural explanations with the same disdain they reserve for stopping to ask for driving directions.
46. I. Ratiu, "Thinking Internationally: A Comparison of How International Students Learn," *International Studies of Management and Organization 13* (1983): 139–150.
47. Bird, Osland, et al.
48. Osland, *Working Abroad.*

CHAPTER 5
INDIVIDUAL AND ORGANIZATIONAL MOTIVATION

THAT URGE TO ACHIEVE

David C. McClelland

MOTIVATION: A DIAGNOSTIC APPROACH

David A. Nadler
Edward E. Lawler III

RECOGNIZE CONTRIBUTIONS

James M. Kouzes
Barry Z. Posner

Part of being a good manager is understanding what motivates employees and knowing how to design an organization that inspires people to work at their full potential. Once again, we find individual differences in motivation patterns, which can be viewed as yet another type of mental map.

There are many internal human needs that drive motivation. David McClelland devoted his academic career to studying three primary human needs—achievement, power, and affiliation. McClelland wrote the classic article "That Urge to Achieve" and answered the question that often plagues managers—why some employees are hard workers and others are not.

Internal needs, however, are only one piece of the motivation puzzle. Employees make decisions about how hard to work based on their expectations about the results and rewards of their effort. Expectancy theory, developed by Victor Vroom, shows the effect of the environment, in particular the actions taken by managers, on employee motivation. David Nadler and Edward Lawler, two famous business scholars with a practical bent, describe expectancy theory in a classic article entitled "Motivation: A Diagnostic Approach." Failure to understand this theory often results in demotivated employees (and students for that matter). Although managers cannot easily change the internal needs employees bring to work, they can place people in jobs that fit their needs, make sure they are capable of doing a good job, and then reward them appropriately.

James Kouzes and Barry Posner spell out how to use rewards in "Recognize Contributions," a chapter from one of their best-selling books on leadership. Kouzes and Posner asked people who had been named by others as outstanding leaders to describe their "personal best" leadership experience, a time when they had accomplished something extraordinary in their organizations. By analyzing these experiences, Kouzes and Posner pinpointed five practices of effective leadership: challenging the process, inspiring a shared vision, enabling others to act, modeling the way, and encouraging the heart. The last practice highlighted the importance of recognizing and rewarding people's contributions as a key aspect of motivation.

THAT URGE TO ACHIEVE*

David C. McClelland

Most people in this world, psychologically, can be divided into two broad groups. There is that minority which is challenged by opportunity and willing to work hard to achieve something, and the majority which really does not care all that much.

For nearly 20 years now, psychologists have tried to penetrate the mystery of this curious dichotomy. Is the need to achieve (or the absence of it) an accident, is it hereditary, or is it the result of environment? Is it a single, isolatable human motive, or a combination of motives—the desire to accumulate wealth, power, fame? Most important of all, is there some technique that could give this will to achieve to people, even whole societies, who do not now have it?

While we do not yet have complete answers for any of these questions, years of work have given us partial answers to most of them and insights into all of them. There is a distinct human motive, distinguishable from others. It can be found, in fact tested for, in any group.

Let me give you one example. Several years ago, a careful study was made of 450 workers who had been thrown out of work by a plant shutdown in Erie, Pennsylvania. Most of the unemployed workers stayed home for a while and then checked back with the U.S. Employment Service to see if their old jobs or similar ones were available. But a small minority among them behaved differently: the day they were laid off, they started job-hunting.

They checked both the United States and the Pennsylvania Employment Office: they studied the "Help Wanted" sections of the papers; they checked through their union, their church, and various fraternal organizations; they looked into training courses to learn a new skill; they even left town to look for work, while the majority when questioned said they would not under any circumstances move away from Erie to obtain a job. Obviously the members of that active minority were differently motivated. All the men were more or less in the same situation objectively: they needed work, money, food, shelter, job security. Yet only a minority showed initiative and enterprise in finding what they needed. Why? Psychologists, after years of research, now believe they can answer that question. They have demonstrated that

*Excerpted and reprinted with the author's permission from *THINK Magazine*, published by IBM, © 1966 by International Business Machines Corporation.

these men possessed in greater degree a specific type of human motivation. For the moment let us refer to this personality characteristic as "Motive A" and review some of the other characteristics of the persons who have more of the motive than other persons.

Suppose they are confronted by a work situation in which they can set their own goals as to how difficult a task they will undertake. In the psychological laboratory, such a situation is very simply created by asking them to throw rings over a peg from any distance they may choose. Most persons throw more or less randomly, standing now close, now far away, but those with Motive A seem to calculate carefully where they are most likely to get a sense of mastery. They stand nearly always at moderate distances, not so close as to make the task ridiculously easy, nor so far away as to make it impossible. They set moderately difficult, but potentially achievable goals for themselves, where they objectively have only about a one-in-three chance of succeeding. In other words, they are always setting challenges for themselves, tasks to make them stretch themselves a little.

But they behave like this only if *they* can influence the outcome by performing the work themselves. They prefer not to gamble at all. Say they are given a choice between rolling dice with one-in-three chances of winning and working on a problem with a one-in-three chance of solving in the time allotted, they choose to work on the problem even though rolling the dice is obviously less work and the odds of winning are the same. They prefer to work at a problem rather than leave the outcome to chance or to others.

Obviously they are concerned with personal achievement rather than with the rewards of success per se, since they stand just as much chance of getting those rewards by throwing the dice. This leads to another characteristic the Motive A persons show—namely, a strong preference for work situations in which they get concrete feedback on how well they are doing, as one does, say in playing golf, or in being a salesperson, but as one does not in teaching, or in personnel counseling. Golfers always know their score and can compare how well they are doing with par or with their own performance yesterday or last week. Teachers have no such concrete feedback on how well they are doing in "getting across" to their students.

THE *n*ACH PERSON

But why do certain persons behave like this? At one level the reply is simple: because they habitually spend their time thinking about doing things better. In fact, psychologists typically measure the strength of Motive A by taking samples of a person's spontaneous thoughts (such as making up a story about a picture they have been shown) and counting the frequency with which she mentions doing things better. The count is objective and can even be made these days with the help of a computer program for content analysis. It yields what is referred to technically as an individual's *n*Ach score (for "need for Achievement"). It is not difficult to understand why people who think constantly about "doing better" are more apt to do better at job-hunting, to set moderate achievable goals for themselves, to dislike gambling (because they get no achievement satisfaction from success), and to prefer work situations where they can tell easily whether they are improving or not. But why some people and not others come to think this way is another question. The evidence suggests it is not because they are born that way, but because of special training they get in the home from parents who set moderately high achievement goals but who are warm, encouraging, and non-authoritarian in helping their children reach these goals.

Such detailed knowledge about one motive helps correct a lot of common sense ideas about human motivation. For example, much public policy (and much business policy) is based on the simpleminded notion that people will work harder "if they have to." As a first approximation, the idea isn't totally wrong, but it is only a half-truth. The majority of unemployed workers in Erie "had to" find work as much as those with higher *n*Ach, but they certainly didn't work as hard at it. Or again, it is frequently assumed that any strong motive will lead to doing things better. Wouldn't it be fair to say that most of the Erie workers were just "unmotivated?" But our detailed knowledge of various human motives shows that each one leads a person to behave in *different ways.* The contrast is not between being "motivated" or "unmotivated" but between being motivated toward A or toward B or C, etc.

A simple experiment makes the point nicely: Subjects were told that they could choose as a working partner either a close friend or a stranger who was known to be an expert on the problem to be solved. Those with higher *n*Ach (more "need to achieve") chose the experts over their friends, whereas those with more *n*Aff (the "need to affiliate with others") chose friends over experts. The latter were not "unmotivated"; their desire to be with someone they liked was simply a stronger motive than their desire to excel at the task. Other such needs have been studied by psychologists. For instance, the need for Power is often confused with the need for Achievement because both may lead to "outstanding" activities. There is a distinct difference. People with a strong need for Power want to command attention, get recognition, and control others. They are more active in political life and tend to busy themselves primarily with controlling the channels of communication both up to the top and down to the people so that they are more "in charge." Those with high *n*Power are not as concerned with improving their work performance daily as those with high *n*Ach.

It follows, from what we have been able to learn, that not all "great achievers" score high in *n*Ach. Many generals, outstanding politicians, great research scientists do not, for instance, because their work requires other personality characteristics, other motives. A general or a politician must be more concerned with power relationships, a research scientist must be able to go for long periods without the immediate feedback the person with high *n*Ach requires, etc. On the other hand, business executives, particularly if they are in positions of real responsibility or if they are salespeople, tend to score high in *n*Ach. This is true even in a Communist country like Poland: apparently there, as well as in a private enterprise economy, a manager succeeds if he is concerned about improving all the time, setting moderate goals, keeping track of his or the company's performance, etc.

MOTIVATION AND HALF-TRUTHS

Since careful study has shown that common sense notions about motivation are at best half-truths, it also follows that you cannot trust what people tell you about their motives. After all, they often get their ideas about their own motives from common sense. Thus a general may say he is interested in achievement (because he has obviously achieved), or a businesswoman that she is interested only in making money (because she has made money), or one of the majority of unemployed in Erie that he desperately wants a job (because he knows he needs one); but a careful check of what each one thinks about and how each one spends his or her time may show that each is concerned about quite different things. It requires special measurement techniques to identify the presence of *n*Ach and other such motives. Thus what people say and believe is not very closely related to these "hidden" motives, which seem to affect people's "style of life" more than their political, religious, or social attitudes. Thus *n*Ach produces enterprising women and men among labor leaders or managers, Republicans or Democrats, Catholics or Protestants, capitalists or communists.

Wherever people begin to think often in *n*Ach terms, things begin to move. People with higher *n*Ach get more raises and are promoted more rapidly, because they keep actively seeking ways to do a better job. Companies with many such people grow faster. In one comparison of two firms in Mexico, it was discovered that all but one of the top executives of a fast-growing firm had higher *n*Ach scores than the highest scoring executive in an equally large but slow-growing firm. Countries with many such rapidly growing firms tend to show above-average rates of economic growth. This appears to be the reason why correlations have regularly been found between the *n*Ach content in popular literature (such as popular songs or stories in children's textbooks) and subsequent rates of national economic growth. A nation that is thinking about doing better all the time (as shown in its popular literature) actually does do better economically speaking. Careful quantitative studies have shown this to be true in Ancient Greece, in Spain in the Middle Ages, in England from 1400 to 1800, as well as among contemporary nations, whether capitalist or communist, developed or underdeveloped.

MOTIVATION: A DIAGNOSTIC APPROACH*

David A. Nadler

Edward E. Lawler III

- What makes some people work hard while others do as little as possible?
- How can I, as a manager, influence the performance of people who work for me?
- Why do people turn over, show up late to work, and miss work entirely?

These important questions about employees' behavior can only be answered by managers who have a grasp of what motivates people. Specifically, a good understanding of motivation can serve as a valuable tool for understanding the causes of behavior in organizations, for predicting the effects of any managerial action, and for directing behavior so that organizational and individual goals can be achieved.

EXISTING APPROACHES

During the past 20 years, managers have been bombarded with a number of different approaches to motivation. The terms associated with these approaches are well known—*human relations*, *scientific management*, *job enrichment*, *need hierarchy*,

*Reprinted with permission from *Perspectives on Behavior in Organizations* (New York: McGraw-Hill, 1977): 26–34.

self-actualization, etc. Each of these approaches has something to offer. On the other hand, each of these different approaches also has its problems in both theory and practice. Running through almost all of the approaches with which managers are familiar are a series of implicit but clearly erroneous assumptions.

Assumption 1: All employees are alike Different theories present different ways of looking at people, but each of them assumes that all employees are basically similar in their makeup. Employees all want economic gains, or all want a pleasant climate, or all aspire to be self-actualizing, etc.

Assumption 2: All situations are alike Most theories assume that all managerial situations are alike, and that the managerial course of action for motivation (for example, participation, job enlargement, etc.) is applicable in all situations.

Assumption 3: One best way Out of the other two assumptions there emerges a basic principle that there is "one best way" to motivate employees.

When these "one best way" approaches are tried in the "correct" situation they will work. However, all of them are bound to fail in some situations. They are therefore not adequate managerial tools.

A NEW APPROACH

During the past 10 years, a great deal of research has been done on a new approach to looking at motivation. This approach, frequently called *expectancy theory*, still needs further testing, refining, and extending. However, enough is known that many behavioral scientists have concluded that it represents the most comprehensive, valid, and useful approach to understanding motivation. Further, it is apparent that it is a very useful tool for understanding motivation in organizations.

The theory is based on a number of specific assumptions about the causes of behavior in organizations.

Assumption 1: Behavior is determined by a combination of forces in the individual and forces in the environment Neither the individual nor the environment alone determines behavior. Individuals come into organizations with certain "psychological baggage." They have past experiences and a developmental history, which has given them unique sets of needs, ways of looking at the world, and expectations about how organizations will treat them. These all influence how individuals respond to their work environment. The work environment provides structures (such as a pay system or a supervisor), which influence the behavior of people. Different environments tend to produce different behavior in similar people just as dissimilar people tend to behave differently in similar environments.

Assumption 2: People make decisions about their own behavior in organizations While there are many constraints on the behavior of individuals in organizations, most of the behavior that is observed is the result of individuals' conscious decisions. These decisions usually fall into two categories. First, individuals make decisions about *membership behavior*—coming to work, staying at work, and in other ways being a member of the organization. Second, individuals make decisions about the amount of *effort* they will direct towards performing their jobs. This includes decisions about how hard to work, how much to produce, at what quality, etc.

Assumption 3: Different people have different types of needs, desires, and goals Individuals differ on what kinds of outcomes (or rewards) they desire. These differences are not random; they can be examined systematically by an understanding of the differences in the strength of individuals' needs.

Assumption 4: People make decisions among alternative plans of behavior based on their perceptions (expectancies) of the degree to which a given behavior will lead to desired outcomes In simple terms, people tend to do those things which they see as leading to outcomes (which can also be called "rewards") they desire and avoid doing those things they see as leading to outcomes that are never desired.

In general, the approach used here views people as having their own needs and mental maps of what the world is like. They use these maps to make decisions about how they will behave, behaving in those ways that their mental maps indicate will lead to outcomes that will satisfy their needs. Therefore, they are inherently neither motivated nor unmotivated; motivation depends on the situation they are in, and how it fits their needs.

THE THEORY

Based on these general assumptions, expectancy theory states a number of propositions about the process by which people make decisions about their own behavior in organizational settings. While the theory is complex at first view, it is in fact made of a series of fairly straightforward observations about behavior. Three concepts serve as the key building blocks of the theory:

Performance-Outcome Expectancy

Every behavior has associated with it, in an individual's mind, certain outcomes (rewards or punishments). In other words, the individual believes or expects that if he or she behaves in a certain way, he or she will get certain things.

Examples of expectancies can easily be described. An individual may have an expectancy that if he produces 10 units he will receive his normal hourly rate while if he produces 15 units he will receive his hourly pay rate plus a bonus. Similarly an individual may believe that certain levels of performance will lead to approval or disapproval from members of her work group or from her supervisor. Each performance can be seen as leading to a number of different kinds of outcomes and outcomes can differ in their types.

Valence

Each outcome has a "valence" (value, worth, attractiveness) to a specific individual. Outcomes have different valences for different individuals. This comes about because valences result from individual needs and perceptions, which differ because they in turn reflect other factors in the individual's life.

For example, some individuals may value an opportunity for promotion or advancement because of their needs for achievement or power, while others may not want to be promoted and leave their current work group because of needs for affiliation with others. Similarly, a fringe benefit such as a pension plan may have great valence for an older worker but little valence for a young employee on his or her first job.

Effort-Performance Expectancy

Each behavior also has associated with it in the individual's mind a certain expectancy or probability of success. This expectancy represents the individual's perception of how hard it will be to achieve such behavior and the probability of his or her successful achievement of that behavior.

For example, you may have a strong expectancy that if you put forth the effort, you can produce 10 units an hour, but that you have only a fifty-fifty chance of producing 15 units an hour if you try.

Putting these concepts together, it is possible to make a basic statement about motivation. In general, the motivation to attempt to behave in a certain way is greatest when:

a. The individual believes that the behavior will lead to outcomes (performance outcome expectancy).
b. The individual believes that these outcomes have positive value for him or her (valence).
c. The individual believes that he or she is able to perform at the desired level (effort performance expectancy).

Given a number of alternative levels of behavior (10, 15, and 20 units of production per hour, for example) the individual will choose that level of performance which has the greatest motivational force associated with it, as indicated by the expectancies, outcomes, and valences.

In other words, when faced with choices about behavior, the individual goes through a process of considering questions such as, "Can I perform at that level if I try?" "If I perform at that level, what will happen?" "How do I feel about those things that will happen?" The individual then decides to behave in that way which seems to have the best chance of producing positive, desired outcomes.

A GENERAL MODEL

On the basis of these concepts, it is possible to construct a general model of behavior in organizational settings (see Figure 1). Working from left to right in the model, motivation is seen as the force on the individual to expend effort. Motivation leads to an observed level of effort by the individual. Effort, alone, however, is not enough. Performance results from a combination of the effort that an individual puts forth and the level of ability which he or she has (reflecting skills, training, information, etc.). Effort thus combines with ability to produce a given level of performance. As a result of performance, the individual attains certain outcomes. The model indicates this relationship in a dotted line, reflecting the fact that sometimes people perform but do not get desired outcomes. As this process of performance-reward occurs, time after time, the actual events serve to provide information which influences the individual's perceptions (particularly expectancies) and thus influences motivation in the future.

Outcomes, or rewards, fall into two major categories. First, the individual obtains outcomes from the environment. When an individual performs at a given level he or she can receive positive or negative outcomes from supervisors, co-workers, the organization's rewards systems, or other sources. These environmental rewards are thus one source of outcomes for the individual. A second source of outcomes is the individual.

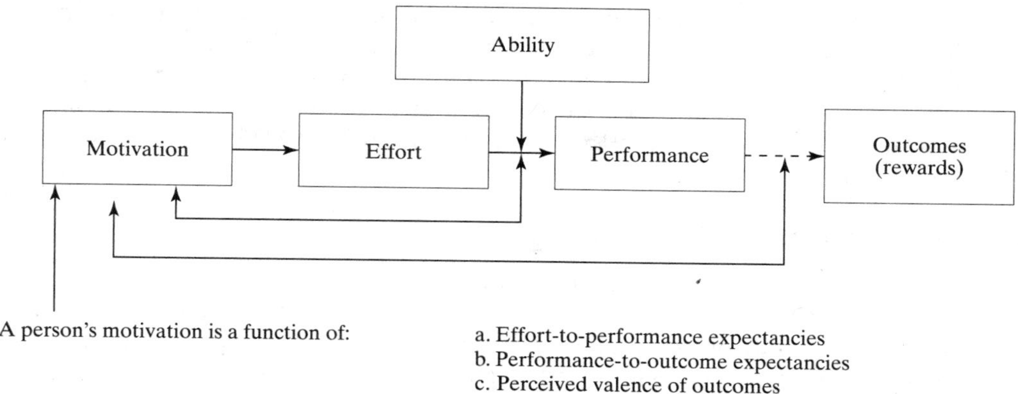

FIGURE 1 The Basic Motivation-Behavior Sequence

These include outcomes that occur purely from the performance of the task itself (feelings of accomplishment, personal worth, achievement, etc.). In a sense, the individual gives these rewards to himself or herself. The environment cannot give them or take them away directly; it can only make them possible.

SUPPORTING EVIDENCE

Over 50 studies have been done to test the validity of the expectancy-theory approach to predicting employee behavior.[1] Almost without exception, the studies have confirmed the predictions of the theory. As the theory predicts, the best performers in organizations tend to see a strong relationship between performing their jobs well and receiving rewards they value. In addition they have clear performance goals and feel they can perform well. Similarly, studies using the expectancy theory to predict how people choose jobs also show that individuals tend to interview for and actually take those jobs which they feel will provide the rewards they value. One study, for example, was able to correctly predict for 80 percent of the people studied which of several jobs they would take.[2] Finally, the theory correctly predicts that beliefs about the outcomes associated with performance (expectancies) will be better predictors of performance than will feelings of job satisfaction since expectancies are the critical causes of performance and satisfaction is not.

QUESTIONS ABOUT THE MODEL

Although the results so far have been encouraging, they also indicate some problems with the model. These problems do not critically affect the managerial implications of the model, but they should be noted. The model is based on the assumption that individuals make very rational decisions after a thorough exploration of all the available alternatives and on weighing the possible outcomes of all these alternatives. When we talk to or observe individuals, however, we find that their decision processes are frequently less thorough. People often stop considering alternative behavior plans when they find one that is at least moderately satisfying, even though more rewarding plans remain to be examined.

People are also limited in the amount of information they can handle at one time, and therefore the model may indicate a process that is much more complex than the one that actually takes place. On the other hand, the model does provide enough information and is consistent enough with reality to present some clear implications for managers who are concerned with the question of how to motivate the people who work for them.

IMPLICATIONS FOR MANAGERS

The first set of implications is directed toward the individual manager who has a group of people working for him or her and is concerned with how to motivate good performance. Since behavior is a result of forces both in the person and in the environment, you as manager need to look at and diagnose both the person and the environment. Specifically, you need to do the following:

Figure out what outcomes each employee values As a first step, it is important to determine what kinds of outcomes or rewards have valence for your employees. For each employee you need to determine "what turns him or her on." There are various ways of finding this out, including; (a) finding out employees' desires through some structured method of data collection, such as a questionnaire; (b) observing the employees' reactions to different situations or rewards; or (c) the fairly simple act of asking them what kinds of rewards they want, what kind of career goals they have, or "what's in it for them." It is important to stress here that it is very difficult to change what people want, but fairly easy to find out what they want. Thus, the skillful manager emphasizes diagnosis of needs, not changing the individuals themselves.

Determine what kinds of behavior you desire Managers frequently talk about "good performance" without really defining what good performance is. An important step in motivating is for you yourself to figure out what kinds of performances are required and what are adequate measures or indicators of performance (quantity, quality, etc.). There is also a need to be able to define those performances in fairly specific terms so that observable and measurable behavior can be defined and subordinates can understand what is desired of them (e.g., produce 10 products of a certain quality standard-rather than only produce at a high rate).

Make sure desired levels of performance are reachable The model states that motivation is determined not only by the performance-to-outcome expectancy, but also by the effort-to-performance expectancy. The implication of this is that the levels of performance that are set as the points at which individuals receive desired outcomes must be reachable or attainable by these individuals. If the employees feel that the level of performance required to get a reward is higher than they can reasonably achieve, then their motivation to perform well will be relatively low.

Link desired outcomes to desired performances The next step is to directly, clearly, and explicitly link those outcomes desired by employees to the specific performances you desire. If your employee values external rewards, then the emphasis should be on the rewards systems concerned with promotion, pay, and approval. While the linking of these rewards can be initiated through your making statements to your employees, it is extremely important that employees see a clear example of the reward process working in a fairly short period of time if the motivating "expectancies" are to be created in the employees' minds. The linking must be done by some concrete public acts, in addition to statements of intent.

If your employee values internal rewards (e.g., achievement), then you should concentrate on changing the nature of the person's job, for he or she is likely to respond well to such things as increased autonomy, feedback, and challenge, because these things will lead to a situation where good job performance is inherently rewarding. The best way to check on the adequacy of the internal and external reward system is to ask people what their perceptions of the situation are. Remember it is the perceptions of people that determine their motivation, not reality. It doesn't matter for example whether you feel a subordinate's pay is related to his or her motivation. Motivation will be present only if the subordinate sees the relationship. Many managers are misled about the behavior of their subordinates because they rely on their own perceptions of the situation and forget to find out what their subordinates feel. There is only one way to do this: Ask. Questionnaires can be used here, as can personal interviews.

Analyze the total situation for conflicting expectancies Having set up positive expectancies for employees, you then need to look at the entire situation to see if other factors (informal work groups, other managers, the organization's reward systems) have set up conflicting expectancies in the minds of the employees. Motivation will only be high when people see a number of rewards associated with good performance and few negative outcomes. Again, you can often gather this kind of information by asking your subordinates. If there are major conflicts, you need to make adjustments, either in your own performance and reward structure, or in the other sources of rewards or punishments in the environment.

Make sure changes in outcomes are large enough In examining the motivational system, it is important to make sure that changes in outcomes or rewards are large enough to motivate significant behavior. Trivial rewards will result in trivial amounts of effort and thus trivial improvements in performance. Rewards must be large enough to motivate individuals to put forth the effort required to bring about significant changes in performance.

Check the system for its equity The model is based on the idea that individuals are different and therefore different rewards will need to be used to motivate different individuals. On the other hand, for a motivational system to work it must be a fair one—one that has equity (not equality). Good performers should see that they get more desired rewards than do poor performers, and others in the system should see that also. Equity should not be confused with a system of equality where all are rewarded equally, with no regard to their performance. A system of equality is guaranteed to produce low motivation.

IMPLICATIONS FOR ORGANIZATIONS

Expectancy theory has some clear messages for those who run large organizations. It suggests how organizational structures can be designed so that they increase rather than decrease levels of motivation or organization members. While there are many different implications, a few of the major ones are as follows:

Implication 1: The design of pay and reward systems Organizations usually get what they reward, not what they want. This can be seen in many situations, and pay systems are a good example.[3] Frequently, organizations reward people for membership (through pay tied to seniority, for example) rather than for performance. Little wonder that what the organization gets is behavior oriented toward "safe," secure employment rather than effort directed at performing well. In addition, even where organizations do pay for performance as a motivational device, they frequently negate the motivational value of the system by keeping pay secret, therefore preventing people from observing the pay-to-performance relationship that would serve to create positive, clear, and strong performance-to-reward expectancies. The implication is that organizations should put more effort into rewarding people (through pay, promotion, better job opportunities, etc.) for the performances that are desired, and that to keep these rewards secret is clearly self-defeating. In addition, it underscores the importance of the frequently ignored performance evaluation or appraisal process and the need to evaluate people based on how they perform clearly defined specific behaviors, rather than on how they score on ratings of general traits such as "honesty," "cleanliness," and other, similar terms that frequently appear as part of the performance appraisal form.

Implication 2: The design of tasks, jobs, and roles One source of desired outcomes is the work itself. The expectancy-theory model supports much of the job enrichment literature, in saying that by designing jobs which enable people to get their needs fulfilled, organizations can bring about higher levels of motivation.[4] The major difference between the traditional approaches to job enlargement or enrichment and the expectancy-theory approach is the recognition by expectancy theory that different people have different needs and, therefore, some people may not want enlarged or enriched jobs. Thus, while the design of tasks that have more autonomy, variety, feedback, meaningfulness, etc., will lead to higher motivation in some, the organization needs to build in the opportunity for individuals to make choices about the kind of work they will do so that not everyone is forced to experience job enrichment.

Implication 3: The importance of group structures Groups, both formal and informal, are powerful and potent sources of desired outcomes for individuals. Groups can provide or withhold acceptance, approval, affection, skill training, needed information, assistance, etc. They are a powerful force in the total motivational environment of individuals. Several implications emerge from the importance of groups. First, organizations should consider the structuring of at least a portion of rewards around group performance rather than individual performance. This is particularly important where group members have to cooperate with each other to produce a group product or service, and where the individual's contribution is often hard to determine. Second, the organization needs to train managers to be aware of how groups can influence individual behavior and to be sensitive to the kinds of expectancies that informal groups set up and their conflict or consistency with the expectancies that the organization attempts to create.

Implication 4: The supervisor's role The immediate supervisor has an important role in creating, monitoring, and maintaining the expectancies and reward structures that will lead to good performance. The supervisor's role in the motivation process becomes one of defining clear goals, setting clear reward expectancies, and providing the right rewards for different people (which could include both organizational rewards and personal rewards, such as recognition, approval, or support from the supervisor). Thus, organizations need to provide supervisors with an awareness of the nature of motivation as well as the tools (control over organizational rewards, skill in administering those rewards) to create positive motivation.

Implication 5: Measuring motivation If things like expectancies, the nature of the job, supervisor-controlled outcomes, satisfaction, etc. are important in understanding how well people are being motivated, then organizations need to monitor employee perceptions along these lines. One relatively cheap and reliable method of doing this is through standardized employee questionnaires. A number of organizations already use such techniques, surveying employees' perceptions and attitudes at regular intervals (ranging from once a month to once every year-and-a-half) using either standardized surveys or surveys developed specifically for the organization. Such information is useful both to the individual manager and to top management in assessing the state of human resources and the effectiveness of the organization's motivational systems.[5]

Implication 6: Individualizing organizations Expectancy theory leads to a final general implication about a possible future direction for the design of organizations. Because different people have different needs and therefore have different valences, effective motivation must come through the recognition that not all employees are alike and that organizations need to be flexible in order to accommodate individual differences. This implies the "building in" of choice for employees in many areas, such as reward systems, fringe benefits, job assignments, etc., where employees previously have had little say. A successful example of the building in of such choice can be seen in the experiments at TRW and the Educational Testing Service with "cafeteria fringe-benefits plans," which allow employees to choose the fringe benefits they want, rather than taking the expensive and often unwanted benefits that the company frequently provides to everyone.[6]

SUMMARY

Expectancy theory provides a more complex model of humankind for managers to work with. At the same time, it is a model that holds promise for the more effective motivation of individuals and the more effective design of organizational systems. It implies, however, the need for more exacting and thorough diagnosis by the manager to determine (a) the relevant forces in the individual, and (b) the relevant forces in the environment, both of which combine to motivate different kinds of behavior. Following diagnosis, the model implies a need to act—to develop a system of pay, promotion, job assignments, group structures, supervision, etc.—to bring about effective motivation by providing different outcomes for different individuals.

Performance of individuals is a critical issue in making organizations work effectively. If a manager is to influence work behavior and performance, he or she must have an understanding of motivation and the factors that influence an individual's motivation to come to work, to work hard, and to work well. While simple models offer easy answers, it is the more complex models that seem to offer more promise. Managers can use models (such as expectancy theory) to understand the nature of behavior and build more effective organizations.

References

1. For reviews of the expectancy theory research see T. R. Mitchell, "Expectancy Models of Job Satisfaction, Occupational Preference and Effort: A Theoretical, Methodological, and Empirical Appraisal," *Psychological Bulletin 81* (1974): 1053–1077. For a more general discussion of expectancy theory and other approaches to motivation see E. E. Lawler, *Motivation in Work Organizations* (Belmont, CA: Brooks/Cole, 1973).
2. E. E. Lawler, W. J. Kuleck, J. G. Rhode, and J. F. Sorenson, "Job Choice and Postdecision Dissonance," *Organizational Behavior and Human Performance 13* (1975): 133–145.
3. For a detailed discussion of the implications of expectancy theory for pay and reward systems, see E. E. Lawler, *Pay and Organizational Effectiveness: A Psychological View* (New York: McGraw Hill, 1971).
4. A good discussion of job design with an expectancy theory perspective is in J. R. Hackman, G. R. Oldham, R. Janson, and K. Purdy, "A New Strategy for Job Enrichment," *California Management Review* (Summer 1975): 57.
5. The use of questionnaires for understanding and changing organizational behavior is discussed in D. A. Nadler, *Feedback and Organizational Development: Using Data Based Methods* (Reading, MA: Addison-Wesley, 1977).
6. The whole issue of individualizing organizations is examined in E. E. Lawler, "The Individualized Organization: Problems and Promise," *California Management Review 17* (2) (1974): 31–39.
7. For a more detailed statement of the model see E. E. Lawler, "Job Attitudes and Employee Motivation: Theory, Research and Practice," *Personnel Psychology 23* (1970): 223–237.

RECOGNIZE CONTRIBUTIONS*

James M. Kouzes

Barry Z. Posner

Would people value having a colleague say "Thank You" and "Good Job"? I thought about how I would feel—and I realized the incredible power of recognizing and appreciating others.

ANDRIS RAMANS, Intuitive Surgical

Never underrate the importance of visibly appreciating others and their efforts.

JOAN NICOLO, Computing Resources, Inc.

Almost midway through her career, Joan Nicolo found that the leadership skill of encouraging the heart remained particularly challenging. She was uncomfortable

*Adapted and reprinted with permission from *The Leadership Challenge*, 3rd edition (San Francisco: Jossey-Bass, 2002): 315–338, 349.

praising people in public and started asking herself what was holding her back. On the surface, it seemed such a simple task. So what was the big deal?

After considerable soul-searching, she came up with some theories. She was afraid that if she praised one person, others would think she was playing favorites. She also felt that praising and encouraging activities took too much time, time that—with her already burgeoning list of responsibilities—was in short supply. Recognition, she worried, was for warm-and-fuzzy types, not for serious and performance-oriented managers. And maybe providing recognition would play into stereotypes of women as "nurturing." The more she thought about it, however, the more she realized that her associates really did deserve to be recognized, and it was high time for her to give it a try.

Shortly thereafter, during a presentation, she made a special point of thanking people publicly for fostering a collaborative spirit in the project they were working on. It felt great—to her and to others! She said, "I found that my spirit was lifted. They felt appreciated, and I felt that they had received the credit they deserved." Joan knew beyond a shadow of a doubt that she'd established a human connection with her colleagues that hadn't been there before. Communication became more open, and she felt far less guarded. This was a real turning point for her.

In the weeks ahead she brought much more of herself to her work relationships, and people responded with a new level of enthusiasm for her leadership. Indeed, she began to see her co-workers in a different light. She could focus on getting the job done and enjoy a human a bond with everyone around her. Contrary to her worst fears, nobody got jealous when she praised one person or another, and the time it took to show her appreciation was well worth it. Coming to work in the morning, she felt more energetic than ever, and when she went home in the evening she increasingly felt deep satisfaction with what she'd accomplished. At first it wasn't clear how these changes were going to affect productivity. Would they translate into anything that would benefit the company? In a short time she saw that this new way of relating brought her group together as never before, fueling an esprit de corps that spurred everyone on to give their personal best whenever an extraordinary effort was required.

Joan, like other leaders we talked with, came to understand that recognition is about acknowledging good results and reinforcing positive performance. It's about shaping an environment in which everyone's contributions are noticed and appreciated.

Andy Pearson, as CEO of PepsiCo, was named one of the 10 toughest bosses in America. More than 20 years later, now at Tricon (the world's second-largest fast-food chain, a $22 billion retail operation with more than 30,000 restaurants and 725,000 employees), Andy has discovered, like Joan, that the human heart drives a company's success, and that this kind of success must be kindled through attention, awareness, recognition, and reward. Says Andy:

> *If the need for recognition and approval is a fundamental human drive, then the willingness to give it is not a sign of weakness. . . . Great leaders find a balance between getting results and how they get them. A lot of people make the mistake of thinking that getting results is all there is to the job. They go after results without building a team or without building an organization that has the capacity to change. Your real job is to get results and to do it in a way*

that makes your organization a great place to work—a place where people enjoy coming to work, instead of just taking orders and hitting this month's numbers.[1]

Andy is right in tune with what we found. In our personal-best case studies, people reported working very intensely and very long hours—and enjoying it. Yet to persist for months at such a pace, people need encouragement. Literally, they need the heart to continue with the journey. One important way that leaders give heart to others is by recognizing individual contributions. That praise is important, too—most people rate "having a caring boss" even higher than they value money or fringe benefits. In fact, how long employees stay at a company, and how productive they are there, is determined by the relationship they have with their immediate supervisor.[2]

Exemplary leaders understand this need to recognize contributions and are constantly engaged in these *essentials*:

- Focus on clear standards;
- Expect the best;
- Pay attention; and
- Personalize recognition.

By putting these four essentials into practice and recognizing contributions, leaders stimulate and motivate the internal drive within each individual.

FOCUS ON CLEAR STANDARDS

When you were a kid you might have read Lewis Carroll's *Alice in Wonderland.* Remember the croquet match? The flamingos were the mallets, the playing card soldiers were the wickets, and the hedgehogs were the balls. Everyone kept moving and the rules kept changing all the time. Poor Alice. There was no way of knowing how to play the game to win. Besides, it was all rigged in favor of the queen.

You needn't have gone down the rabbit hole to know how Alice felt: We've all been Alice at one time or another in our lives. We've all been at a place where we're not sure where we're supposed to be going, what the ground rules are that govern how we behave, or how we're doing along the way. And just when we think we get the hang of it, the organization comes along and changes everything. This is a recipe for maddening frustration and pitiful performance. Our hearts just aren't in it.

If leaders want us to give our all, to put our hearts into it, leaders must first focus on clear standards. Here we're using *standards* to mean both goals and values. They both have to do with what's expected. Goals connote something shorter-term than values (or principles), which connote something more enduring. Typically, values and principles serve as the basis for goals. They define the arena in which goals and metrics must be set.

STANDARDS CONCENTRATE US

Values set the stage for action. Goals release the energy. The ideal state—on the job, in sports, in other areas of life—is often called *flow.* "Flow experiences" are those times when we feel pure enjoyment and effortlessness in what we do.[3] To experience flow, it helps to have clear goals—because goals help us concentrate and avoid distractions. By having an intention to do something that is meaningful to us, by setting a goal, we take action, action with a purpose.

Goals help us keep our eye on the prize. Way back in the late 1990s, the average employee received 180 different messages a day.[4] Imagine what it is today! Voice mail, e-mail, fax, phone calls, internal memos, instant messages, pagers, shouts over the cubicle wall all disrupt our work constantly. How do we know what needs attention? How do we know how to respond? Goals and intentions keep us on track. They help us put the phone in do-not-disturb mode, shut out the noise, and schedule our time. Goal-setting affirms the person, and, whether we realize it or not, contributes to what people think about themselves.

Now is it better that individuals set their own goals, or should leaders set the goals for others? In the best of all worlds, people would set their own. Vast amounts of research show that people feel best about themselves and what they do when they voluntarily do something. People feel worst "when what they do is motivated by not having anything else to do."[5] The lesson for leaders is to make sure that whenever people engage in something they know why it's important and what end it's serving. This knowledge helps people feel more alive, more in charge, and more significant.

FEEDBACK KEEPS US ENGAGED

People need to know if they're making progress toward the goal or simply marking time. Standards help to serve that function. But standards and goals are not enough. People's motivation to increase their productivity on a task increases *only* when they have a challenging goal *and* receive feedback on their progress.[6] As shown in Figure 1, goals without feedback, and feedback without goals, have little effect on motivation.

So just announcing that the idea is to reach the summit is not enough to get people to put forth more effort. People will ask, "The summit? What summit? Why are you giving me feedback about that? I didn't know that was our goal!" We need to know if

FIGURE 1 How Goals and Feedback Affect Motivational (Performance) Levels

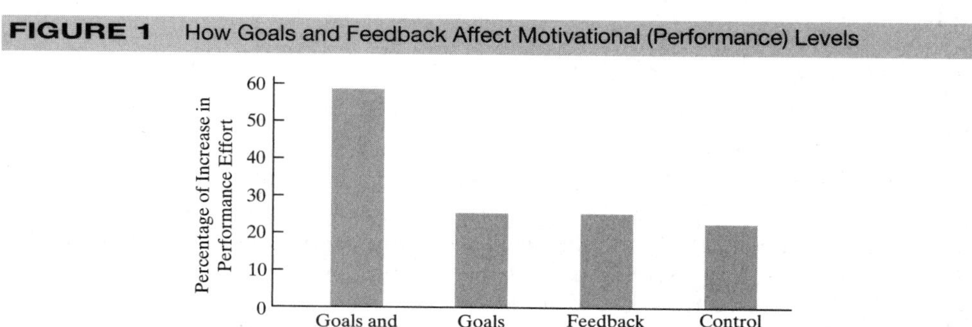

Source: A. Bandura and D. Cervone, "Self-Evaluative and Self-Efficacy Mechanisms Governing the Motivational Effects of Goal Systems," *Journal of Personality and Social Psychology 45* (1983): 1017–1028.

we're still climbing, or if we're sliding downhill. With clear goals and detailed feedback, people can become self-correcting and can more easily understand their place in the big picture. With feedback they can also determine what help they need from others and who might be able to benefit from their assistance. Under these conditions they will be willing to put forth more productive effort.

The importance of feedback was demonstrated in an empirical study involving soldiers who, after several weeks of intensive training, were competing for places in special units. The soldiers were divided into four groups, which were unable to communicate with one another. All the men marched twenty kilometers (about twelve-and-a-half miles) over the same terrain on the same day. The first group was told how far they were expected to go and were kept informed of their progress along the way. The second group was told only that "this is the long march you hear about." These soldiers never received any information about the total distance they were expected to travel, nor were they told how far they had marched. The third group was told to march 15 kilometers, but when they had gone 14 kilometers, they were told that they had to go 6 kilometers farther. The fourth group was told that they had to march 26 kilometers, but when they reached the 14-kilometer mark, they were told that they had only 6 more kilometers to go.

The groups were assessed as to which had the best performance and which endured the most stress. The results indicated that the soldiers who knew exactly how far they had to go and where they were during the march were much better off than the soldiers who didn't get this information. The next-best group was the soldiers who thought that they were marching only 15 kilometers. Third best was the group told to march a longer distance, then given the good news at the 14-kilometer mark. Those who performed worst were the soldiers who received no information about the goal (total distance) or the distance that they had already traveled (feedback).[7]

We can draw numerous conclusions from this and similar research. Certainly the type of leadership that even highly motivated, achievement-oriented people receive can make a difference in the level of stress and success they experience. When leaders provide a clear sense of direction and feedback along the way, they encourage people to reach inside and do their best. Information about goals and about progress toward those goals strongly influences our abilities to achieve—and influences how well and how long we live.[8] Talk about encouraging the heart!

ENCOURAGEMENT IS FEEDBACK

Encouragement is a form of feedback: wonderful, personal feedback. It's positive information that tells us that we're making progress, that we're on the right track, that we're living up to the standards. Giving encouragement requires us to get close to people and show that we care. And because it's more personal and positive than other forms of feedback, it's more likely to accomplish something that other forms cannot: strengthening trust between leaders and constituents.

In a study of the effects of feedback on self-confidence, MBA students were praised, criticized, or received no feedback on their performance in a simulation of creative problem solving. They had been told that their efforts would be compared with how well hundreds of others had done on the same task. Those who heard nothing about how well they did suffered as great a blow to their self-confidence as those who were criticized.[9] People hunger for feedback. They really do prefer to know how they are doing, and clearly no news has the same impact as bad news.

To ensure that people achieve their best, leaders have to take steps to bring forth the best from others. This begins with an expectation of high standards, which then becomes a self-fulfilling prophecy.

EXPECT THE BEST

Successful leaders have high expectations, both of themselves and of their constituents. These expectations are powerful because they are the frames into which people fit reality. People are much more likely to see what they expect to see even when it differs from what may be actually occurring. Social psychologists have referred to this as the "Pygmalion effect," based on the Greek myth about Pygmalion, a sculptor who carved a statue of a beautiful woman, fell in love with the statue, and brought it to life by the strength of his perceptions. Leaders play Pygmalion-like roles in developing people. Research on the phenomenon of self-fulfilling prophecies provides ample evidence that other people act in ways that are consistent with our expectations of them.[10] If we expect others to fail, they probably will. If we expect them to succeed, they probably will.

Our expectations also shape our own behavior. Much of this has to do with how we behave toward others. The high expectations that leaders have of others are based in large part on their expectations of themselves. This is one reason why leaders model the way. What gives their expectations for others credibility is their own record of achievement and dedication, and daily demonstrations of what and how things need to be done. What's more, leaders tend not to give up on people, because doing so means giving up on themselves, their judgment, and their ability to encourage others to accomplish their best.

One of the clearest and most often mentioned responses to the question "What is so special about leaders?" is that they bring out the best in us. Leaders recognize the impact of self-fulfilling prophecies. Leaders treat people in a way that bolsters their self-confidence, making it possible for them to achieve more than they may have initially believed possible of themselves. Feeling appreciated by others increases a person's sense of self-worth, which in turn, precipitates success at school, home, and work. Research and everyday experience confirms that men and women with high self-esteem, of all ages and levels of education and socioeconomic backgrounds, "feel unique, competent, secure, empowered, and connected to the people around them."[11] If we have someone in our life who believes in us, and who constantly reinforces that belief through their interactions with us, we are strongly influenced by that support. If the potential exists within us, it will come out when a leader takes the time to bring us along.

No right-thinking manager would do anything that would not help people to succeed, right? Surprisingly, European researchers' meticulous studies show "that bosses—albeit accidentally and usually with the best intentions—are often complicit in an employee's lack of success. How? By creating and reinforcing a dynamic that essentially sets up perceived under-performers to fail. If the Pygmalion effect describes the dynamic in which an individual lives up to great expectations, the set-up-to-fail syndrome explains the opposite."[12]

The set-up-to-fail syndrome may begin quite innocently. An employee seems to have a performance problem—a missed deadline, a lost account. Or it can even start when a manager is distant (figuratively or literally) from the direct report for personal reasons. This triggers an increase in the manager's supervision and control of the direct report, who then begins to believe that the manager lacks trust and confidence. Eventually, because of low expectations the direct report withdraws, stops making independent decisions or taking initiative—and the problem intensifies.

The leader's expectations have their strongest and most powerful influence in times of uncertainty and turbulence. When accepted ways of doing things are not working well enough, then a leader's strong expectations about the destination, the processes to follow, and the capabilities of the team serve to make dreams come true. There is no doubt, expectations—high or low—influence other people's performance. But only high expectations have a positive impact—on actions and on feelings about oneself. Only high expectations can encourage the heart.

HIGH EXPECTATIONS LEAD TO HIGH PERFORMANCE

The high expectations of leaders aren't just fluff that they hold in their minds to keep a positive outlook or to psych themselves up. Another person's belief in our abilities accomplishes much more than that. The expectations that successful leaders hold provide the framework into which people fit their own realities. Just as with Pygmalion, these frameworks play an important role in developing people. Maybe you can't turn a marble statue into a real person but you can draw out the highest potential of your constituents.

Nancy Tivol, executive director of Sunnyvale Community Service (SCS), demonstrates this principle in action. She believes strongly in her own ability and in the abilities of every staff member and volunteer at SCS. Before Nancy, administrators and paid staff had made certain assumptions about volunteers. They assumed that volunteers would not be motivated, skilled, or experienced enough to take on the responsibility of some of the tasks, including interactions with clients and corporate contacts. As a result, volunteers were given only minimal responsibilities and did not have opportunities to explore or demonstrate their own capacities beyond these menial tasks. In contrast, Nancy encouraged the same group of people to excel. She placed volunteers in responsible positions, gave them the training and direction they required, and encouraged them to do their best. And they did just that!

Today, SCS has over 200 volunteers year-round doing things that only staff members did previously; indeed, three major operations are run by volunteers, mostly over 65 years of age. Though programs have exploded in terms of clients served and amount of aid distributed, these volunteers' efforts and dedication have enabled SCS to reduce its pay-roll costs by over one-third.

Under Nancy's leadership, SCS became the county's only emergency assistance agency that doesn't turn people away for lack of funds. Over an eight-year period, SCA increased its funding for the prevention of evictions and utility disconnections and for paying for medical, prescription, and other critical services from $34,000 a year to $450,000—despite recessions and significantly reduced government and corporate contributions. During the same period the number of families served by its food program sky-rocketed, climbing by 80 each month to more than 650.

The SCS picture changed so radically because Nancy had very high *expectations* of her volunteers, and these higher expectations breathed new life into the people around her. She prophesied their success. Listen to what one of those volunteers, Carol Schweizer, has to say: "I think you always rise to expectations. If somebody thinks that you can't do something, then you can't do it. But when they ask me around here to do some things I've never done before . . . I think, gosh, I can try it. I bet I could do that. And I can."[13]

Our own research has shown that people are often anxious or nervous when they are encouraged by people in leadership positions to go out and deliver their personal best. Yet those same people marched in and did what was expected of them. They were all willing; they were all excited by the challenges they faced. Spurred on by their leaders' high expectations, they developed the self-confidence, courage, and volition to live up to their leaders' expectations.

POSITIVE IMAGES CREATE POSITIVE POSSIBILITIES

Positive expectations yield positive results. They also begin to create positive images in our minds and generate other positive possibilities. Positive futures for self and others are first constructed in our minds. "We see," say researchers, "what our imaginative horizon allows us to see."[14] Seeing is believing, and the results can be life-affirming and life-enhancing.

Athletes have known for a long time that stored mental pictures influence performance. Unless we can see ourselves as being successful, it is very difficult to produce the behavior that leads to success. Experiment after experiment shows that positive images make groups more effective, relieve symptoms of illness, and enhance achievement in school, the military, and business.[15]

One rather intriguing experiment demonstrates the power of positive images on performance. Divided into different groups, people were first instructed in effective bowling methods. Following these lessons, the bowlers practiced. Some of those who practiced were videotaped. One group of the videotaped bowlers saw only the positive things they did, and the other group saw only the negative. Those who saw only their positive moves improved significantly more than any of the other bowlers.[16]

Consider how this principle was put into practice by Kyle Von Raesfeld, a Santa Clara University freshman, who told us about coaching a football team at an elementary school while he was only in high school himself:

> *My first year there I was an assistant coach. The head coach knew a lot about football. He probably would have been a good coach for older kids, but he did not stay very positive with the kids, which is essential for any team, especially a younger team. He would always point out their mistakes, and very seldom point out their successes.*
>
> *It didn't take very long for the kids to start getting down on themselves. The coach seemed to be constantly shouting. Soon enough, attendance at practices started to drop. The kids had lost all of their desire to play the game, and they clearly were not having fun. When it came my turn to talk at the end of a game or practice, I would try to encourage them and lift their spirits, but they were already defeated by the coach's comments. Needless to say, we did not have a very successful season, not only in terms of win-loss record, but also in accomplishing the primary goal, providing a good time for the kids.*

The next year, I was the head coach with a friend from high school as an assistant. I had the same kids, we played the same teams, ran the same plays—and this year we went undefeated. Even better than that, each kid improved greatly and had a great time playing football. After we were a few weeks into the season I began to ponder why this team had basically done a 180° turnaround from the previous season. The first thing I noticed was that each kid had a big smile on his face as he came running out to practice. The kids were very enthusiastic about practice and always showed up. Why? I always made sure to keep a positive attitude. Where the previous coach would say, "Here's what you did wrong," I would say, "Here's what you guys did right," and then, "Here are two or three things you can improve upon." I also required the kids to stay positive with each other. I had the players tell each other when they did something good, and encourage each other when they make a mistake. Instead of hearing shouts of, "Why didn't you catch it? That was an easy catch," a player would be greeted by, "You'll get it next time." More often than not, he would catch the next pass!

Kyle had learned how high expectations lead to high performance. By focusing on positive images, he was able to noticeably change the way the kids felt about themselves and about others on the team. As he puts it, "If people feel like they've been defeated, whether it be from not receiving any praise, having a pessimistic leader, or comments from teammates, they will act and perform like they are defeated. But if you encourage and motivate them, more often than not, they will excel."

What do we learn from all this? Clearly, before we can lead, we have to believe in others, and we have to believe in ourselves. This has positive benefits for individual leaders, positive benefits for their constituents, and positive benefits for the organizations they serve. High expectations matter—and they matter a lot. To hold the belief that we and others can change and can develop new skills and abilities not only works its magic on the constituents but on the leader that holds this perception. Exemplary leaders know this and know how to purposefully hold in their minds high expectations for themselves and for other people.

With the attitude that people will live up to high expectations and with clear standards, leaders have to pay attention to what's happening around them so they can find those positive examples to recognize.

PAY ATTENTION

Leaders are out and about all the time. They're attending meetings, visiting customers, touring the plants or service centers, dropping in on the lab, making presentations at association gatherings, recruiting at local universities, holding roundtable discussions, speaking to analysts, or just dropping by employees' cubicles to say "Hello." Being mobile goes with the territory. In fact, at its root the word *lead* comes from an Old English word that means "go, travel, guide."

This is not purposeless wandering. Leaders are out there for a reason. One of the reasons, we would maintain, is to show that they care. One way of showing you care is to *pay attention* to people, to what they are doing, and to how they are feeling. And if you are clear about the standards you're looking for and you believe and expect that people will perform like winners, then you're going to notice lots of examples of people doing things right and doing the right things.

In contrast, what happens in organizations where managers are constantly on the lookout for problems? Three things: Managers get a distorted view of reality; over time, production declines; and the managers' personal credibility hits bottom. Wandering around with an eye for trouble is likely to get you just that. More trouble.

Put yourself in the situation. If you knew someone was coming around to check up on you, how would you behave? Conventional wisdom holds that as soon as we spot the boss coming we put on our best behavior. Wrong, We may put on different behavior, but it's not our best. In fact, it can be our worst because we get nervous and tense. Plus, when we know that people are coming around to look for problems, we're more likely to hide them than to reveal them. People who work for more controlling managers are more likely to keep information to themselves, not reveal the truth, not be honest about what is going on. They know that little good comes from telling the truth.

No surprise then, that controlling managers have low credibility. Highly controlling behaviors—inspecting, correcting, checking up—signal lack of trust. How do you respond to people who don't trust you? You don't trust them. And since trustworthiness is a key element of personal credibility, credibility diminishes. We are just much less likely to believe someone who does not exhibit trust in us.[17] So when we're walking around our organizations paying attention, we need to have on our Pygmalion glasses and fully expect to find the best.

RELEASE THE POSITIVE

It's human nature: when we're being watched by a person who is looking for our faults, we act very differently than we do in a supportive environment in which there's an opportunity to be rewarded for special achievements. When we know someone is looking for positive examples we'll make an effort to reveal them. Pygmalions don't so much carve a statue from the stone as release the beauty that's already in it.

When you see yourself as a caring leader, you act differently than you do when you see yourself as a controller. You begin to behave like a person who is genuinely interested in seeing others succeed, someone who is a cheerleader and coach much more than a militant authority figure out patrolling the neighborhood. People soon begin relating to you differently, they open up. They no longer dread seeing you coming down the hallway.

If people know there's a caring leader in their midst, in search of achievements to recognize, they'll want to show the best of themselves. That translates into increased productivity. This positive focus on behavior and performance, linked to goals and values, significantly improves morale as it moves the company toward higher levels of performance. In a supportive climate people are also much more likely to help each other succeed. They teach and coach each other. In this more open environment people are more likely to let you know when problems are brewing and to lend a hand in solving them before they escalate.

LISTEN WITH YOUR EYES AND YOUR HEART

Learning to understand and see things from another's perspective—to walk in that person's shoes—is absolutely crucial to building trusting relations and to career success.[18]

Comedian and actor Michael Pritchard told us a story that we'll never forget. He was making a presentation at a local elementary school (at the time he was a probation officer), and he got to talking with a third grader. When he asked her what she'd been learning, she responded that she'd been learning sign language. Michael was, as we were, intrigued. Sign language? Kids don't typically learn sign language in third grade. So he asked how she got started on that educational adventure.

The young girl explained that her best friend since first grade couldn't speak and couldn't hear. So she asked her mom if she could learn sign language to communicate with her friend. Her mom agreed. Now, the young girl said, "I listen with my eyes and my heart, not just my ears and my brain." All leaders can learn from this third grader. Listening with the eyes and the heart, not just the ears and the brain, requires a deeper level of paying attention and understanding. It requires that we hear the heart and see the soul.

Eyes-and-heart-listening can't be from a distance, reading reports or hearing things second hand. Our constituents want to know who we are, how we feel, and whether we really care. They want to see us in living color. Since proximity is the single best predictor of whether two people will talk to one another, you have to get close to people if you're going to communicate. It means regularly walking the halls and plant floors, meeting often with small groups, and hitting the road for frequent visits with associates, key suppliers, and customers. It may even mean learning another language if a large portion of your workforce or customer base speak it.

The third grader in Michael's story learned the language of another to strengthen their relationship. "Well," you might say, "she had to if she wanted to be her friend." Precisely! Learning another's language, literally or figuratively, is essential to leadership, and absolutely critical in this era of global leadership.[19] Unfortunately, listening is not well practiced. Research by the Hay Group, covering a million employees in over two thousand organizations, reveals that only about one in three people respond favorably when asked how well their company listens to them.[20] Yet it's only by learning what others value, what others enjoy, what others treasure, that we can expect to reach their hearts.

When you're out there paying attention to the positive, you're highly visible and you also make yourself known to others. While you're getting to know them, they're getting to know you. And who do you trust more, someone you know or someone you don't know? In general we're all much more likely to trust friends than strangers. Paying attention and actively appreciating others increases their trust in you. This kind of relationship is becoming more and more critical as we become increasingly global and diverse in our workforce. If others know we genuinely care about them, they're more likely to care about us. This is how we bridge cultural divides.

BE A FRIEND

As Daniela Maeder, of the Department of Economics and Labor, Switzerland, said to us: "Organizational diagrams don't matter at all. Be sure to treat employees as human beings and not as functional workers." Yet managerial myth says we shouldn't get too close to our associates, we can't be friends with people at work. Well, set this myth aside. Over a five-year period, researchers observed groups of friends and groups of acquaintances—people who knew each other only vaguely—performing motor skill and decision making tasks. The results were unequivocal. The groups composed of friends completed, on average, more than three times as many projects as the groups composed merely of acquaintances. In terms of decision-making assignments, groups of friends were over 20 percent more effective than groups of acquaintances were.[21]

There is an important caveat, however. Friends have to be strongly committed to the group's goals. If not, then friends may not do better. This is precisely why we said earlier that it is absolutely necessary for leaders to be clear about standards and to create a condition of shared goals and values. When it comes to performance, commitment to standards and good relations between people go together.

People are just more willing to follow someone they like and trust. To become fully trusted we must trust. And that means being open: open to others, open *with* others. An open door is a physical demonstration of a willingness to let others in. So is an open heart. This means disclosing things about yourself. We don't mean tabloid-style disclosures. We mean talking about your hopes and dreams, your family and friends, your interests and your pursuits. We mean telling others the same things you'd like to know about them.

When we're open we make ourselves vulnerable—and this vulnerability makes us more human and more trusted. If neither person in a relationship takes the risk of trusting, at least a little, the relationship remains stalled at a low level of caution and suspicion. If leaders want the higher levels of performance that come with trust and collaboration, then they must demonstrate their trust *in* others before asking for trust *from* others. When it comes to trust, leaders ante up first.

Certainly, disclosing information about ourselves can be risky. We can't be certain that other people will like us, will appreciate our candor, will agree with our aspirations, will buy into our plans, or will interpret our words and actions in the way we intend. But by demonstrating the willingness to take such risks, leaders encourage others to take a similar risk—and thereby take the first steps necessary to build mutual trust. Disclosing information about yourself is a start, as is asking for and encouraging feedback. When you're out there attending to what's happening, noticing the positive contributions people are making, stop and ask for feedback yourself. It's a demonstration that you appreciate your associates and a way to encourage people to provide more information.[22]

Often, on the basis of this information, leaders are able to learn more about other people, their colleagues as well as their constituents, and in this process better understand how to personalize their recognition. We can only genuinely honor others when we know who they are; what they like, and what they've done. We have to have the person in mind to make it special.

PERSONALIZE RECOGNITION

One of the more familiar complaints that we've heard about recognition is that it's too often highly predictable, routine, and impersonal. A one-size-fits-all approach to recognition feels disingenuous, forced, and thoughtless. Over time it can even increase cynicism and actually damage credibility. That's why it's so important for leaders to pay attention to the likes and dislikes of each and every individual. To make recognition personally meaningful, you first have to get to know your constituents. By personalizing recognition, leaders send the message that someone took the time to notice the achievement, seek out the responsible individual, and personally deliver praise in a timely manner.

Linda Lewis of Charles Schwab & Company understands that timeliness and personalization count. About a month after Linda arrived as senior vice president of learning and education, she initiated the Giraffe Award (given, naturally enough, for sticking your neck out, going above and beyond normal responsibilities and duties). Linda told the first person who received the award to select another deserving person and present the award at the next meeting.

The Giraffe Award is given monthly; everyone within Schwab is eligible. Winners receive custody of a stuffed giraffe, plus a colored poster to commemorate the event. Cute but maybe a bit predictable? Not so—and that's the beauty of it. Schwab University associates found a way to take the predictable and make it a surprise. They found a way to take something that might be impersonal and make it a personal, one-to-one experience. Somewhere along the way, Paul Oknaian decided he'd add a little something extra, and he put a lei around the stuffed giraffe's neck. Pretty soon the giraffe had a cowboy hat, some shoes, and a shoulder bag. Then came the navel piercing that Linda Chan gave the giraffe before she passed it on to Denise Green, who'd jumped in above and beyond the call to assist Chan in facilitating some classes.

Along with the stuffed giraffe, which gets passed from person to person each month, there's a small poster. The prior recipient personalizes the poster, which is then proudly displayed in each recipient's cubicle or office area for everyone to see. What Linda started was a process that enabled everyone to get involved and to make every recognition special. She created a climate of personalization; which, when you think about it, is one of things that Schwab values.

Ann Cessaris of Key Communication reminds us all of another reason why it's essential to personalize, or "culturalize," recognition. "I had a client," she reports, "who was born in Asia, came to this country at age 12, and was very well acclimated to life in the United States. However, when his boss rewarded him for exceptional contribution on a team project by giving him a delightful corner office, the client was horrified. He felt it destroyed the feeling of teamwork and his future relations with his team members."

"Culture values run deep," says Ann, and she's absolutely correct. Personalizing requires knowing what's appropriate individually and culturally. It's pretty arrogant for someone to assume that he or she naturally know what's right for others without even bothering to inquire or observe. Leaders know that uncomfortable or embarrassing as it may seem at first to recognize someone's efforts, it's really not difficult to do. And it's well worth the effort to make a connection with each person. Leaders learn from many small and often casual acts of appreciation what works for each of their constituents and how best to personalize recognition.

USE A VARIETY OF REWARDS

Leaders don't rely exclusively on the organization's formal reward system, which offers only a limited range of options. After all, promotions and raises are scarce resources. So don't make the mistake of assuming that individuals respond only to money. Although salary increases or bonuses are certainly appreciated, individual needs for and appreciation of rewards extend much further. Verbal recognition of performance in front of one's peers and visible awards, such as certificates, plaques, and other tangible gifts, are powerful indeed and almost unlimited.

Spontaneous and unexpected rewards are often more meaningful than the expected formal rewards. "The form of recognition that has the most positive influence on us, and that is used most often, is on-the-spot recognition," says HR manager Michelle Carlson.

"When something fantastic happens, I comment on it right away and to whomever may be close enough to hear. In a group setting, when one person really goes the extra mile to make sure the company delivers on its promises, we all really try to give that person public recognition."

In contrast, relying upon an organization's formal reward system typically requires considerable effort. For example, we found that the time lapse between performance and promotion is often more than six months.[23] So instead of relying only or even primarily on formal rewards, effective leaders make tremendous use of *intrinsic* rewards—rewards that are built into the work itself, including such factors as a sense of accomplishment, a chance to be creative, and the challenge of the work—immediate outcomes of an individual's effort. These rewards are far more important than salary and fringe benefits in improving job satisfaction, commitment, retention, and performance.[24] Often it's the simple, personal gestures that are the most powerful rewards. It's true that money may get people to do the job but it doesn't get them to do a *good* job.

Praise and coaching are significant forms of recognition. Not enough people make enough use of one powerful but inexpensive two-word reward—"thank you." Personal congratulations rank at the top of the most powerful nonfinancial motivators identified by employees.[25] There are few if any more basic needs than to be noticed, recognized, and appreciated for our efforts. And that's as true for volunteers, teachers, doctors, priests, and politicians as it is for the maintenance staff and those in the executive suite. There's little wonder, then, that a greater volume of thanks is reported in highly innovative companies than in low-innovation firms.[26] Extraordinary achievements do not come easily and seldom bloom in barren and unappreciative settings.

Leaders are constantly on the lookout for ways to spread the psychological benefits of making people feel like winners, because winners contribute in important ways to the success of their projects. Leaders often serve as a mirror for the team. They reflect back to others what a job well done looks like, make certain that the members of the team know that they have done well, and ensure that others in the organization are aware of the group's effort and contributions. To that end, when he was vice president of business development for Comerica Bank, Sam Bhaumik hung a large bell on the wall. Every time an associate booked a new deal or signed up a new client, that person got to ring the bell. The individual was instantly recognized, and others were stimulated to make a sale so that they, too, could ring the bell. Simple, but satisfying. That also describes something that Naomi Boyd did during her very first leadership experience, as the senior QA analyst for Visa International. Boyd explains:

> *Because I knew everyone was working hard and long hours, I would often bring in breakfast or dinner, depending on the shift. The team members viewed it as a sign that I appreciated the hard work and the sacrifices they were making working such long hours and not spending time with their families. Saying thank you and showing appreciation will get you a long way.*

Naomi understood that rewards—especially rewards that are made personal—do make a difference.

What happens when you provide both intrinsic and extrinsic rewards? The idea of an additive effect is intuitively appealing—but it does not always occur. In fact, there is some evidence that intrinsic and extrinsic rewards are negatively related and may actually work against one another. For example, in a situation that is already intrinsically rewarding, the addition of extrinsic rewards may reduce the effectiveness of the intrinsic rewards.[27] On the other hand, some studies show that while achievement-oriented people do find success rewarding in and of itself, money and fame are also important rewards, serving as symbols of that success.[28] One executive referred to this as the "fun being in playing the game down on the field, while the results are posted on the scoreboard." What we found among leaders was not so much an either-or mentality as a "both-and" type of thinking. Leaders are remarkably skillful in using these types of rewards in complementary ways.

The extent to which recognition and rewards are applied to each individual in a personal (rather than an impersonal) manner also explains a lot about how leaders and their organizations get a motivational bang for their buck (or not) from recognizing people's contributions. After all, leaders get the best from others not by building fires under people but by building the fire within them. As U.S. Postal Service district manager Mike Matuzek observes: "There is a fire that already burns inside of each person. My job is to simply stoke it." This explains Mike's own motivation in sending out *personally* addressed and *personally* signed birthday cards to all 13,567 postal employees in his district each year (that's 37 a day, 7 days a week!). This human touch and the few minutes it takes to establish some personal connection with each person in the organization is certainly a factor in why Mike's district is consistently at the top in the United States.

BE THOUGHTFUL

What personalized recognition comes down to is *thoughtfulness.* It means taking those observations you've made about an individual and asking: "What would really make this special and unique for this person? What could I do to make this a memorable experience so that he always remembers how important his contributions are?" This kind of thoughtfulness was evident in how Wayne Bennett gave personalized recognition—and did so in a manner that reinforced clear standards, acknowledged high expectations, and indicated that he had been paying attention. Wayne was the founder and president of Glenn Valley Homes, a unique company set up to build computer-designed, precision-crafted custom homes in a plant in Orland, California, a small town northeast of Sacramento.

As a start-up, the company was so successful that its new factory was faced with a backlog of home orders. When Wayne needed a highly skilled production manager to meet this extraordinary challenge, he selected Ray Freer, a veteran with 15 years in the industry. Ray was an eager and energetic worker whose talents and expertise had not been fully used in previous jobs. Wayne believed in Ray and entrusted him with full responsibility to lead the crew.

Wayne's confidence in Ray was well placed. After several six- and seven-day weeks, they were ready to begin regular production. The plant was state-of-the-art, the previously inexperienced crew well-trained, and Ray had personally built and installed additional buffer stations to augment production during unexpected delays. The first house was successfully cut, sized, and shipped within three days of the start of production.

Wayne wanted to acknowledge Ray's accomplishments, so—during a barbecue party he was holding for all the workers and their families—he called the group over to one side of the factory and asked Ray to show how one of the buffer stations worked. When Ray threw the lever to operate the skate-wheel conveyer that he had designed and constructed, an automotive radio antenna popped up, displaying a flag with an envelope attached. Ray looked inside the envelope, and found a $1,000 check and a personal letter from Wayne thanking him for his outstanding work. Wayne read the letter out loud to everyone else in the company (and their spouses and families) acknowledging the importance of Ray's innovativeness, dedication, and tireless work. Ray was clearly moved by Wayne's public display of appreciation, and the loud clapping and cheers of his co-workers and crew demonstrated their mutual support for his well-earned award.

Wayne obviously put some *thought* into this recognition. He closely observed what Ray had done to contribute to the success of the factory, and he used equipment that Ray had constructed as an integral part of the celebration. Wayne could have just handed a check to Ray in private without all the ceremony. Not Wayne. He knew that personalizing recognition was essential. He also knew that telling the story in public would create more meaning, go a long way toward thanking everyone for their hard work, and help build a strong sense of community. This is exactly what leaders do when they celebrate values and victories.

COMMITMENT NUMBER 9: RECOGNIZE CONTRIBUTIONS BY SHOWING APPRECIATION FOR INDIVIDUAL EXCELLENCE

Leaders have high expectations of themselves and of their constituents. Their standards are clear and help people focus on what needs to be done. Leaders provide clear directions, feedback, and encouragement. They expect the best of people and create self-fulfilling prophecies about how ordinary people can produce extraordinary actions and results. By paying attention, offering encouragement, personalizing appreciation, and maintaining a positive outlook leaders stimulate, rekindle, and focus people's energies and drive.

Leaders make people winners, and winning people like to up the ante, raise the standards, and explore uncharted territory. Leaders recognize and reward what individuals do to contribute to vision and values. And leaders express their appreciation far beyond the limits of the organization's formal performance appraisal system. Leaders enjoy being spontaneous and creative in saying thank you, whether by sending notes, handing out personalized prizes, listening without interrupting, or trying any of the myriad other forms of recognition. We provide a variety of strategies that you can adapt to your situation for help in using recognition as a leadership process and linking rewards with performance. (See Table 1.)

TABLE 1 Recognize Contributions by Showing Appreciation for Individual Excellence

- Be creative about rewards.
- Make recognition public.
- Provide feedback en route.
- Be a Pygmalion.
- Foster positive expectations.
- Make the recognition presentation meaningful.
- Find people who are doing things right.
- Don't be stingy about saying thank you.

Source: The Leadership Challenge by James M. Kouzes and Barry Z. Posner. Copyright © 2002.

Endnotes

1. D. Dorsey, "Andy Pearson Finds Love," *Fast Company* (August 2001): 78 ff.
2. A. Zipkin, "Management: The Wisdom of Thoughtfulness," *New York Times* (31 May 2000): C1.
3. For a discussion of "flow," see M. Csikszentmihalyi, *Finding Flow: The Psychology of Engagement with Everyday Life* (New York: Basic Books, 1997).
4. "Workers Drowning in Messages," *San Jose Mercury News* (20 May 1998): 7C.
5. Csikszentmihalyi, *Finding Flow*, 23.
6. See, for example, J. E. Sawyer, W. R. Latham, R. D. Pritchard, and W. R. Bennett Jr., "Analysis of Work Group Productivity in an Applied Setting: Application of a Time Series Panel Design," *Personnel Psychology* 52 (1999): 927–967; and A. Gostick and C. Elton, *Managing with Carrots: Using Recognition to Attract and Retain the Best People* (Layton, Utah: Gibbs Smith, 2001).
7. Blood tests taken during the march and again 24 hours later showed similar patterns. Blood levels of cortisol and prolactin (chemicals whose levels rise as stress increases) were, as expected, highest for the group that knew the least about the march and lowest for those soldiers who knew exactly where they were and how much farther they were expected to go. D. Eden and G. Ravid, "Pygmalion vs. Self-Expectancy: Effects of Instructor and Self-Expectancy on Trainee Performance," *Organizational Behavior and Human Performance* 30 (1982): 351–364; and D. Eden and A. B. Shani, "Pygmalion Goes to Boot Camp: Expectancy, Leadership, and Trainee Performance," *Journal of Applied Psychology* 67 (1982): 194–199.
8. See, for example, R. M. Ryan and E. L. Deci, "Self-Determination Theory and the Facilitation of Intrinsic Motivation, Social Development, and Well-Being," *American Psychologist* 55, no. 1 (2000): 68–78.
9. P. A. McCarty, "Effects of Feedback on the Self-Confidence of Men and Women," *Academy of Management Journal* 20 (1986): 840–847.
10. Hundreds of research studies have since been conducted to test this notion, and they all clearly demonstrate that people tend to act in ways that are consistent with the expectations they perceive. See, for example, D. Eden, *Pygmalion in Management: Productivity as a Self-Fulfilling Prophecy* (Lexington, Mass.: Lexington Books, 1990); D. Eden, "Leadership and Expectations: Pygmalion Effects and Other Self-Fulfilling Prophecies in Organizations," *Leadership Quarterly* 3, no. 4 (1992): 271–305; and A. Smith, L. Jussim, J. Eccles, M. Van Noy, S. Madon, and P. Palumbo, "Self-Fulfilling Prophecies, Perceptual Biases, and Accuracy at the Individual and Group Levels," *Journal of Experimental Social Psychology* 34, no. 6 (1998): 530–561.

11. R. J. Blitzer, C. Petersen, and L. Rogers, "How to Build Self-Esteem," *Training and Development Journal* (February 1993): 59.
12. J-F. Manzoni and J.-L. Barsoux, "The Set-Up-to-Fail Syndrome," *Harvard Business Review* 76, no. 2 (March–April 1998): 101–113, quote on p. 102.
13. CRM Learning (Producer), *Encouraging the Heart* (videotape featuring James M. Kouzes and Barry Z. Posner) (Carlsbad, Calif.: CRM Learning, 2000). Available from CRM Learning at http://www.crmlearning.com/ or call 1-800-421-0833.
14. D. L. Cooperrider, "Positive Image, Positive Action: The Affirmative Basis of Organizing," in S. Srivastva, D. L. Cooperrider, and Associates, *Appreciative Management and Leadership: The Power of Positive Thought and Action in Organizations* (San Francisco: Jossey-Bass, 1990), 103.
15. For a discussion of group effectiveness and positive images, see Srivastva, Cooperrider, and Associates, *Appreciative Management and Leadership*, 108, 115. Also see O. R. Lightsey, "Positive Thoughts Versus States of Mind Ratio as a Stress Moderator: Findings Across Four Studies," *Cognitive Therapy and Research* 23, no. 5 (1999): 469–482. For the original study on group images, see R. Schwartz, "The Internal Dialogue: On the Asymmetry Between Positive and Negative Coping Thoughts," *Cognitive Therapy and Research* 10 (1986): 591–605.
16. Cooperrider, "Positive Image, Positive Action," 114.
17. For a more in-depth discussion of personal credibility, see J. M. Kouzes and B. Z. Posner, *Credibility: How Leaders Gain and Lose It, Why People Demand It* (San Francisco: Jossey-Bass, 1993).
18. R. Fisher and S. Brown, *Getting Together* (Boston: Houghton Mifflin, 1988), and M. W. McCall, M. Lomdardo, and A. Morrison, *The Lessons of Experience* (Lexington, Mass.: Lexington Books, 1988).
19. R. Rosen and P. Dign, *Global Literacies: Lessons on Business Leadership and National Cultures* (New York: Simon & Schuster, 2000).
20. As quoted in F. Rice, "Champions of Communications," *Fortune* (3 June 1991): 111 ff.
21. J. A. Ross, "Does Friendship Improve Job Performance?" *Harvard Business Review* (March–April 1977): 8–9. See also K. A. Jehn and P. P. Shah, "Interpersonal Relationships and Task Performance: An Examination of Mediating Processes in Friendship and Acquaintance Groups," *Journal of Personality and Social Psychology* 72, no. 4 (1997): 775–790.
22. D. Jamieson and J. O'Mara, *Managing Workforce 2000: Gaining the Diversity Advantage* (San Francisco: Jossey-Bass, 1991).
23. J. L. Hall, B. Z. Posner, and J. W. Harder, "Performance Appraisal Systems: Matching Theory with Practice," *Group and Management Studies* 14, no. 1 (1989): 51–69.
24. J. T. Bond, E. Galinsky, and J. E. Swanberg, *The 1997 National Study of the Changing Workforce* (New York: Families and Work Institute, 1998).
25. B. Nelson, "The Power of Rewards and Recognition," presentation to the Consortium on Executive Education, Leavey School of Business, Santa Clara University, 20 September 1996.
26. R. M. Kanter, "The Change Masters," presentation to the Executive Seminar in Corporate Excellence, Leavey School of Business, Santa Clara University, 13 March 1984.
27. See, for example, E. L. Deci and R. Flaste, *Why We Do What We Do: Understanding Self-Motivation* (New York: Putnam, 1995); and E. L. Deci, R. Koestner, and R. M. Ryan, "A Meta-Analytic Review of Experiments Examining the Effects of Extrinsic Rewards on Intrinsic Motivation," *Psychological Bulletin* 125 (1999): 627–668. For an intelligent critique of incentive systems and the potentially detrimental effects of reliance on rewards on long-term performance, see A. Kohn, *Punished by Rewards* (Boston: Houghton Mifflin, 1993).
28. D. C. McClelland, *The Achieving Society* (New York: Van Nostrand Reinhold, 1961).

CHAPTER 6
ETHICS AND VALUES

MANAGING TO BE ETHICAL: DEBUNKING FIVE BUSINESS ETHICS MYTHS

Linda Klebe Treviño
Michael E. Brown

THINK MACRO, ACT MICRO: ETHICS ACTION METHODS AND INVESTOR CAPITALISM

Richard P. Nielsen

WHEN ETHICS TRAVEL: THE PROMISE AND PERIL OF GLOBAL BUSINESS ETHICS

Thomas Donaldson
Thomas W. Dunfee

Ethics and values are yet another type of mental map and another source of individual differences in the workplace. Ethical conflicts often arise from incompatible ideas and assumptions about right and wrong. Another source of ethical conflict is determined by how different groups define the issue—where is the boundary that determines which stakeholders' needs have to be considered? Some of the most blatant scandals in the twenty-first century grew from business decisions that did not take the best interests of employees or investors into consideration.

In "Managing to Be Ethical: Debunking Five Business Ethics Myths," Linda Treviño and Michael Brown, business ethicists, demolish common beliefs about business ethics. Building on theory, research, and examples, they contend that executives have to actively manage ethics and provide ethical leadership in order to create ethical organizations. Their description of Arthur Andersen's transition from an ethical to an unethical firm highlights the crucial role played by leadership and organizational culture.

In the second article, "Think Macro, Act Micro: Ethics Action Methods and Investor Capitalism," Richard Nielsen, a prolific scholar and advocate for ethical behavior in business and government, describes the systemic corruption found in the dominant form of capitalism in the United States—investor capitalism. Nielsen goes beyond identifying a large-scale, macro problem to contribute one of the best practical guides for people confronted with unethical behavior in the workplace and society. Nielsen lists six types of ethics interventions and reform methods and provides numerous examples of their use.

Ethical controversies are sometimes rooted in dissimilar value systems. Such value clashes are even more likely in cross-cultural interactions involving different sets of ethical customs. Thomas Donaldson and Thomas Dunfee, well-known business ethicists and consultants, portray some of the value differences that result in international ethics conflicts in "When Ethics Travel: The Promise and Peril of Global Business Ethics." They provide a model that managers can use to resolve ethical dilemmas in global settings.

MANAGING TO BE ETHICAL: DEBUNKING FIVE BUSINESS ETHICS MYTHS*

Linda Klebe Treviño
Michael E. Brown

The twenty-first century has brought corporate ethics scandals that have harmed millions of employees and investors, and sent shock waves throughout the business world. The scandals have produced "perp walks" and regulatory backlash, and business ethics is once again a hot topic. Academics and managers are asking: What caused the recent rash of corporate wrongdoing, and what can we do, if anything, to prevent similar transgressions in the future? Perhaps because everyone has opinions about ethics and personal reactions to the scandals, a number of pat answers have circulated that perpetuate a mythology of business ethics management. In this article, we identify several of these myths and respond to them based upon knowledge grounded in research and practice.

MYTH 1: IT'S EASY TO BE ETHICAL

A 2002 newspaper article was entitled "Corporate ethics is simple: If something stinks, don't do it." The article went on to suggest "the small test," or "If you don't want to tell your mom what you're really doing. . . or read about it in the press, don't do it."[1] The obvious suggestion is that being ethical in business is easy if one wants to be ethical. A further implication is that if it's easy, it doesn't need to be managed. But that suggestion disregards the complexity surrounding ethical decision making, especially in the context of business organizations.

ETHICAL DECISIONS ARE COMPLEX

First, ethical decisions aren't simple. They're complex by definition. As they have for centuries, philosophers argue about the best approaches to making the right ethical decision. Students of business ethics are taught to apply multiple normative

*Reprinted with permission from *Academy of Management Executive 18*, no. 2 (2004): 69–81, via the Copyright Clearance Center.

frameworks to tough dilemmas where values conflict. These include consequentialist frameworks that consider the benefits and harms to society of a potential decision or action, deontological frameworks that emphasize the application of ethical principles such as justice and rights, and virtue ethics with its emphasis on the integrity of the moral actor, among other approaches.[2] But, in the most challenging ethical dilemma situations, the solutions provided by these approaches conflict with each other, and the decision maker is left with little clear guidance. For example, multinational businesses with manufacturing facilities in developing countries struggle with employment practice issues. Most Americans believe that it is harmful and contrary to their rights to employ children. But children routinely contribute to family income in many cultures. If corporations simply refuse to hire them or fire those who are working, these children may resort to begging or even more dangerous employment such as prostitution. Or they and their families may risk starvation. What if respecting the rights of children in such situations produces the greater harm? Such business decisions are more complex than most media reports suggest, and deciding on the most ethical action is far from simple.

MORAL AWARENESS IS REQUIRED

Second, the notion that "it's easy to be ethical" assumes that individuals automatically know that they are facing an ethical dilemma and that they should simply choose to do the right thing. But decision makers may not always recognize that they are facing a moral issue. Rarely do decisions come with waving red flags that say, "Hey, I'm an ethical issue. Think about me in moral terms!"[3] Dennis Gioia was recall coordinator at Ford Motor Company in the early 1970s when the company decided not to recall the Pinto despite dangerous fires that were killing the occupants of vehicles involved in low-impact rear-end collisions. In his information-overloaded recall coordinator role, Gioia saw thousands of accident reports, and he followed a cognitive "script" that helped him decide which situations represented strong recall candidates and which did not. The incoming information about the Pinto fires did not penetrate a script designed to surface other issues, and it did not initially raise ethical concerns. He and his colleagues in the recall office didn't recognize the recall issue as an ethical issue. In other examples, students who download their favorite music from the Internet may not think about the ethical implications of "stealing" someone else's copyrighted work. Or a worker asked to sign a document for her boss may not recognize this as a request to "forge" legal documents.

Researchers have begun to study this phenomenon, and they refer to it as moral awareness, ethical recognition, or ethical sensitivity. The idea is that moral judgment processes are not initiated unless the decision maker recognizes the ethical nature of an issue. So, recognition of an issue as an "ethical" issue triggers the moral judgment process, and understanding this initial step is key to understanding ethical decision-making more generally.

T. M. Jones proposed that the moral intensity of an issue influences moral issue recognition,[4] and this relationship has been supported in research. Two dimensions of moral intensity—magnitude of consequences and social consensus—have been found in multiple studies to influence moral awareness.[5] An individual is more likely to identify an issue as an ethical issue to the extent that a particular decision or action is expected to produce harmful consequences and to the extent that relevant others in the social context view the issue as ethically problematic. Further, the use of moral language has been found to influence moral awareness.[6] For example, in the above cases, if the words "stealing" music (rather than downloading) or "forging" documents (rather than signing) were used, the individual would be more likely to think about these issues in ethical terms.

ETHICAL DECISION MAKING IS A COMPLEX, MULTI-STAGE PROCESS

Moral awareness represents just the first stage in a complex, multiple-stage decision-making process[7] that moves from moral awareness to moral judgment (deciding that a specific action is morally justifiable), to moral motivation (the commitment or intention to take the moral action), and finally to moral character (persistence or follow-through to take the action despite challenges).

The second stage, moral judgment, has been studied within and outside the management literature.[8] Lawrence Kohlberg's well-known theory of cognitive moral development has guided most of the empirical research in this area for the past 30 years.[9] Kohlberg found that people develop from childhood to adulthood through a sequential and hierarchical series of cognitive stages that characterize the way they think about ethical dilemmas. Moral reasoning processes become more complex and sophisticated with development. Higher stages rely upon cognitive operations that are not available to individuals at lower stages, and higher stages are thought to be "morally better" because they are consistent with philosophical theories of justice and rights.

At the lowest levels, termed "preconventional," individuals decide what is right based upon punishment avoidance (at stage 1) and getting a fair deal for oneself in exchange relationships (at stage 2). Next, the conventional level of cognitive moral development includes stages 3 and 4. At stage 3, the individual is concerned with conforming to the expectations of significant others, and at stage 4 the perspective broadens to include society's rules and laws as a key influence in deciding what's right. Finally, at the highest "principled" level, stage 5, individuals' ethical decisions are guided by principles of justice and rights.

Perhaps most important for our purposes is the fact that most adults in industrialized societies are at the "conventional" level of cognitive moral development, and less than 20 percent of adults ever reach the "principled" level, where thinking is more autonomous and principle-based. In practical terms, this means that most adults are looking outside themselves for guidance in ethical dilemma situations, either to significant others in the relevant environment (e.g., peers, leaders) or to society's rules and laws. It also means that most people need to be led when it comes to ethics.

THE ORGANIZATIONAL CONTEXT CREATES ADDITIONAL PRESSURES AND COMPLEXITY

Moral judgment focuses on deciding what's right—not necessarily *doing* what is right. Even when people make the right decision, they may find it difficult to follow through and do what is right because of pressures from the work environment.

Research has found that principled individuals are more likely to behave in a manner consistent with their moral judgments, and they are more likely to resist pressures to behave unethically.[10] However, most people never reach the principled level. So, the notion that being ethical is simple also ignores the pressures of the organizational context that influence the relationship between moral judgment and action.

Consider the following ethical-dilemma situation. You find yourself in the parking lot, having just dented the car next to you. The ethical decision is relatively simple. It's about you and your behavior. No one else is really involved. You have harmed someone else's property, you're responsible, and you or your insurance company should pay for the repairs. It's pretty clear that you should leave a note identifying yourself and your insurance company. Certainly, there may be negative consequences if you leave that note. Your insurance rates may go up. But doing the right thing in this situation is fairly straightforward.

Contrast that to business-context situations. It is much harder to "just say no" to a boss who demands making the numbers at all costs. Or to go above the boss's head to someone in senior management with suspicions that "managing earnings" has somehow morphed into "cooking the books." Or to walk away from millions of dollars in business because of concerns about crossing an ethical line. Or to tell colleagues that the way they do business seems to have crossed that line. In these situations, the individual is operating within the context of the organization's authority structure and culture—and would likely be concerned about the consequences of disobeying a boss's order, walking away from millions of dollars in business, or blowing the whistle on a peer or superior. What would peers think? How would the leadership react? Would management retaliate? Is one's job at risk?

It may seem curious that people often worry about whether others will think of them as too ethical. But all of us recognize that "snitches" rarely fit in, on the playground or in life, and whistle-blowers are frequently ostracized or worse.[11] The reasons for their ostracism are not fully understood, but they may have to do with humans' social nature and the importance of social group maintenance. Research suggests that people who take principled stands, such as those who are willing to report a peer for unethical behavior, are seen as highly ethical while, at the same time, they are thought to be highly unlikable.[12] Nearly a third of respondents to the 2003 National Business Ethics Survey[13] said "their co-workers condone questionable ethics practices by showing respect for those who achieve success using them." Further, about 40 percent of respondents said that they would not report misconduct they observed because of fear of retaliation from management. Almost a third said they would not report misconduct because they feared retaliation from co-workers.

If you think this applies only to the playground or the factory floor, ask yourself why we haven't seen more CEOs proclaiming how appalled they are at the behavior of some of their peers after recent ethics scandals. Yes, we heard from a few retired CEOs. But very few active senior executives have spoken up. Why not? They're probably uncomfortable passing moral judgment on others or holding themselves up as somehow ethically better than their peers. So, social context is important because people, including senior executives, look to others for approval of their thinking and behavior.

In sum, being ethical is not simple. Ethical decisions are ambiguous, and the ethical decision-making process involves multiple stages that are fraught with complications and contextual pressures. Individuals may not have the cognitive sophistication to make the right decision. And most people will be influenced by peers' and leaders' words and actions, and by concerns about the consequences of their behavior in the work environment.

MYTH 2: UNETHICAL BEHAVIOR IN BUSINESS IS SIMPLY THE RESULT OF "BAD APPLES"

A recent headline was "How to Spot Bad Apples in the Corporate Bushel."[14] The bad-apple theory is pervasive in the media and has been around a long time. In the 1980s, during a segment of the *McNeil Lehrer Report* on PBS television, the host was interviewing guests about insider trading scandals. The CEO of a major investment firm and a business school dean agreed that the problems with insider trading resulted from bad apples. They said that educational institutions and businesses could do little except to find and discard those bad apples after the fact. So, the first reaction to ethical problems in organizations is generally to look for a culprit who can be punished and removed. The idea is that if we rid the organization of one or more bad apples, all will be well because the organization will have been cleansed of the perpetrator.

Certainly there are bad actors who will hurt others or feather their own nests at others' expense—and they do need to be identified and removed. But, as suggested above, most people are the product of the context they find themselves in. They tend to "look up and look around," and they do what others around them do or expect them to do.[15] They look outside themselves for guidance when thinking about what is right. What that means is that most unethical behavior in business is supported by the context in which it occurs—either through direct reinforcement of unethical behavior or through benign neglect.

An example of how much people are influenced by those around them was in the newspaper in November 2002. Police in New Britain, Connecticut, confiscated a 50-ft. long pile of stolen items, the result of a scavenger hunt held by the "Canettes," New Britain High School's all-girl drill team. According to the *Hartford Courant*, police, parents, and school personnel were astonished that 42 normally law-abiding girls could steal so many items in a single evening. But the girls had a hard time believing that they had done anything wrong. One girl said: "I just thought it was a custom . . . kind of like a camaraderie thing, [and] if the seniors said it was okay and they were in charge, then it was OK!" In another incident in May 2003, suburban Chicago high school girls engaged in an aggressive and brutal "hazing ritual" that landed five girls in the hospital.[16] We might say that these are teenagers and adults are different. But many of these teenagers are about to start jobs, and there are only a few years between these high school students and young people graduating from college. Most adults are more like these teens than most of us think or would prefer to think. The influence of peers is powerful in both cases.

When asked why they engaged in unethical conduct, employees will often say, "I had no choice," or "My boss told me to do it." Stanley Milgram's obedience-to-authority experiments, probably the most famous social psychology experiments ever conducted, support the notion that people obey authority figures even if that means harming another person.[17] Milgram, a Yale psychologist, conducted his obedience-to-authority experiments in the Hartford community on normal adults. These experiments demonstrated that nearly two-thirds of normal adults will harm another human being (give them alleged electric shocks of increasing intensity) if asked to do so by an authority figure as part of what was billed as a learning experiment. Were these people bad apples? We don't think so. Most of them were not at all comfortable doing what they were being asked to do, and they expressed sincere concern for the victim's fate. But in the end most of them continued to harm the learner because the authority figure in a lab coat told them to do so.

How does this apply to work settings? Consider the junior member of an audit team who discovers something problematic when sampling a firm's financials and asks the senior person on the audit team for advice. When the leader suggests putting the problematic example back and picking another one, the young auditor is likely to do just that. The leader may add words such as the following: "You don't understand the big picture" or "Don't worry, this is my responsibility." In this auditing example, the harm being done is much less obvious than in the learning experiment and the junior auditor's responsibility even less clear, so the unethical conduct is probably easier to carry out and more likely to occur.

The bottom line here is that most people, including most adults, are followers when it comes to ethics. When asked or told to do something unethical, most will do so. This means that they must be led toward ethical behavior or be left to flounder. Bad behavior doesn't always result from flawed individuals. Instead, it may result from a system that encourages or supports flawed behavior.

A corollary of the bad-apples argument is that ethics can't be taught or even influenced in adults because adults are autonomous moral agents whose ethics are fully formed by the time they join work organizations, and they can't be changed. This is simply not true. We know from many empirical studies[18] that the large majority of adults are not fully formed when it comes to ethics, and they are not autonomous moral agents. They look outside themselves for guidance in ethical-dilemma situations, and they behave based to a large extent upon what those around them—leaders and peers—expect of them. So, we have to look at the very powerful signals that are being sent about what is expected. We also know that the development of moral reasoning continues into adulthood. Those who are challenged to wrestle with ethical dilemmas in their work will develop more sophisticated ways of thinking about such issues, and their behavior will change as a result.

MYTH 3: ETHICS CAN BE MANAGED THROUGH FORMAL ETHICS CODES AND PROGRAMS

If people in organizations need ethical guidance and structural support, how can organizations best provide it? Most large organizations now have formal ethics or legal compliance programs. In 1991 the U.S. Sentencing Commission created sentencing guidelines for organizations convicted of federal crimes (see www.ussc.gov for information). The guidelines removed judicial discretion and required convicted organizations to pay restitution and substantial fines depending upon whether the organization turns itself in, cooperates with authorities, and whether it has established a legal compliance program that meets seven requirements for due diligence and effectiveness. These formal programs generally include the following key elements: written standards of conduct that are communicated and disseminated to all employees, ethics training, ethics advice lines and offices, and systems for anonymous reporting of misconduct. The Sarbanes-Oxley law, passed during the summer of 2002, requires corporations to set up an anonymous system for employees to report fraud and other unethical activities. Therefore, companies that did not previously have such reporting systems are busy establishing them.

Research suggests that formal ethics and legal compliance programs can have a positive impact. For example, the Ethics Resource Center's National Business Ethics Survey[19] revealed that in organizations with all four program elements (standards, training, advice lines, and reporting systems) there was a greater likelihood (78 percent) that employees would report observed misconduct to management. The likelihood of reporting declined with fewer program elements. Only half as many people in organizations with no formal program said that they would report misconduct to management.

Yet, creating a formal program, by itself, does not guarantee effective ethics management. Recall that Enron had an ethics code, and the board voted to bypass its conflict-of-interest policy.[20] Not surprisingly, research suggests that actions speak louder than words. Employees must perceive that formal policies go beyond mere window dressing to represent the real ethical culture of the organization. For example, the National Business Ethics Survey reports that when executives and supervisors emphasize ethics, keep promises, and model ethical conduct, misconduct is much lower than when employees perceive that the "ethics walk" is not consistent with the "ethics talk."[21] In another study[22] formal program characteristics were found to be relatively unimportant compared with more informal cultural characteristics such as messages from leadership at both the executive and supervisory levels. In addition, perceived ethics program follow-through was found to be essential. Organizations demonstrate follow-through by working hard to detect rule violators, by following up on ethical concerns raised by employees, and by demonstrating consistency between ethics and compliance policies and actual organizational practices. Further, the perception that ethics is actually talked about in day-to-day organizational activities and incorporated into decision-making was found to be important.

So, for formal systems to influence behavior, they must be part of a larger, coordinated cultural system that supports ethical conduct every day. Ethical culture provides informal systems, along with formal systems, to support ethical conduct.[23] For example, the research cited above found that ethics-related outcomes (e.g., employee awareness of ethical issues, amount of observed misconduct, willingness to report misconduct) were much more positive to the extent that employees perceived that ethical conduct was rewarded and unethical conduct was punished in the organization. Further, a culture that demands unquestioning obedience to authority was found to be particularly harmful while a culture in which employees feel fairly treated was especially helpful.

THE FALL OF ARTHUR ANDERSEN

Barbara Toffler's book *Final Accounting: Ambition, Greed, and the Fall of Arthur Andersen*[24] can help us understand this notion of ethical (or unethical) organizational culture. Andersen transformed over a number of years from having a solid ethical culture to having a strong unethical culture. The company's complete demise is a rather dramatic example of the potential results of such a transformation.

In the mid-1990s, Arthur Andersen did not have a formal ethics office, but it did have formal ethical standards and ethics training. Ironically, it also established a consulting group whose practice was aimed at helping other businesses manage their ethics. Barbara Toffler was hired to run that practice in 1995 after spending time on the Harvard Business School faculty and in her own ethics consulting business. After joining Andersen, Toffler learned quickly that the firm's own ethical culture was slipping badly, and she chronicles that slippage in her book.

The book opens with the following statement: "The day Arthur Andersen loses the public's trust is the day we are out of business." Steve Samek, country managing partner, made that statement on a CD-ROM concerning the firm's Independence and Ethical Standards in 1999. It was reminiscent of the old Arthur Andersen. Andersen's traditional management approach had been a top-down, "one firm" concept. Arthur Andersen had built a strong ethical culture over the years where all of the pieces fit together into a seamless whole that supported ethical conduct. No matter where they were in the world, if customers were dealing with Andersen employees, they knew that they could count on the same high-quality work and the same integrity. Employees were trained in the "Andersen Way," and that way included strong ethics. Training at their St. Charles, Illinois, training facility was sacred. It created a cadre of professionals who spoke the same language and shared the same "Android" values.

Founders create culture, and Arthur Andersen was no exception. Toffler says that in the firm's early days, the messages from the top about ethical conduct were strong and clear. Andersen himself said, "My own mother told me, 'Think straight—talk straight.' . . . This challenge will never fail anyone in a time of trial and temptation." "Think straight, talk straight" became a mantra for decades at Arthur Andersen. Partners said with pride that integrity mattered more than fees. And stories about the founder's ethics became part of the firm's lore. At the young age of 28, Andersen faced down a railway executive who demanded that his books be approved—or else. Andersen said, "There's not enough money in the city of Chicago to induce me to change that report." Andersen lost the business, but later the railway company filed for bankruptcy, and Arthur Andersen became known as a firm one could trust. In the 1930s Andersen talked about the special responsibility of accountants to the public and the importance of their independence of judgment and action. Arthur Andersen died in 1947 but was followed by leaders with similar convictions who ran the firm in the 1950s and 1960s, and the ethical culture continued for many years. Pretty much through the 1980s, Andersen was considered a stable and prestigious place to work. People didn't expect to get rich, rather; they wanted "a good career at a firm with a good reputation."

But, the ethical culture eventually began to unravel, and Toffler attributes much of this to the fact that the firm's profits increasingly came from management consulting rather than auditing. The leadership's earlier commitment to ethics came to be drowned out by the firm's increasing laser-like focus on revenues. Auditing and consulting are very different, and the cultural standards that worked so well in auditing didn't fit the needs of the consulting side of the business. But this mismatch was never addressed, and the resulting mixed signals helped precipitate a downward spiral into unethical practices. Serving the client began to be defined as keeping the client happy and getting return business. And tradition became translated into unquestioning obedience to the partner, no matter what one was asked to do. For example, managers and partners were expected to pad their prices. Reasonable estimates for consulting work were simply doubled or more as consultants were told to back into the numbers.

The training also began falling apart when it came to hiring experienced people from outside the firm—something that happened more and more as consulting took over. New employees had always been required to attend a three-day session designed to indoctrinate them into the culture of the firm, but new consultants were told not to forego lucrative client work to attend. So, Toffler never made it to the training, and many other consultants didn't either.

By the time Toffler arrived at Andersen, the firm still had a huge maroon ethics binder, but no one bothered to refer to it. Ethics was never talked about. And, she says, "when I brought up the subject of internal ethics, I was looked at as if I had teleported in from another world." The assumption, left over from the old days in auditing, was that "we're ethical people; we recruit people who are screened for good judgment and values. We don't need to worry about this stuff." But, as we all learned, their failure to worry about ethics led to the demise of the firm.

Could a formal ethics office have helped Arthur Andersen? Probably not, unless that office addressed the shift toward consulting, identified the unique ethical issues faced in the consulting side of the business, developed ethical guidelines for consulting, and so on. It is easy for formal ethics offices and their programs to be marginalized if they don't have the complete support of the organization's leadership and if they are inconsistent with the broader culture. In fact, Andersen still had ethics policies and they still talked about ethics in formal documents. But the business had changed along with the culture that guided employee actions every day, while the approach to ethics management had not kept pace.

MYTH 4: ETHICAL LEADERSHIP IS MOSTLY ABOUT LEADER INTEGRITY

In our discussion of Arthur Andersen, we suggested the importance of leadership. But what is executive ethical leadership? The mythology of ethical leadership focuses attention narrowly on individual character and qualities such as integrity, honesty, and fairness. The *Wall Street Journal* recently ran a story on its website entitled "Plain Talk: CEOs Need to Restore Character in Companies." It said, "The chief problem affecting corporate America right now is not the regulatory environment or snoozing board directors. It's character."[25] But as Arthur Andersen demonstrated, leaders must be more than individuals of high character. They must "lead" others to behave ethically.

Recent research has found that certain individual characteristics are necessary but not sufficient for effective ethical leadership. Such leadership at the executive level is a reputational phenomenon. In most large organizations, employees have few face-to-face interactions with senior executives. So, most of what they know about a leader is gleaned from afar. In order to develop a reputation for ethical leadership, an executive must be perceived as both a "moral person" and a "moral manager."[26]

Being perceived as a "moral person" is related to good character. It depends upon employee perceptions of the leader's traits, behaviors, and decision-making processes. Ethical leaders are thought to be honest and trustworthy. They show concern for people and are open to employee input. Ethical leaders build relationships that are characterized by trust, respect and support for their employees. In terms of decision-making, ethical leaders are seen as fair. They take into account the ethical impact of their decisions, both short term and long term, on multiple stakeholders. They also make decisions based upon ethical values and decision rules, such as the golden rule.

But being perceived as a "moral person" is not enough. Being a "moral person" tells followers what the leader will do. It doesn't tell them what the leader expects *them* to do. Therefore, a reputation for ethical leadership also depends upon being perceived as a "moral manager," one who leads others on the ethical dimension, lets them know what is expected, and holds them accountable. Moral managers set ethical standards, communicate ethics messages, role model ethical conduct, and use rewards and punishments to guide ethical behavior in the organization.

Combining the "moral person" and "moral manager" dimensions creates a two-by-two matrix (see Figure 1). A leader who is strong on both dimensions is perceived to be an *ethical* leader. We can point to Arthur Andersen as an exemplar of ethical leadership. He was known as a strong ethical person who also clearly led his organization on ethics and values. People knew what they could expect of him, and they knew what he expected of them from an ethics perspective. Another example of ethical leadership is James Burke, CEO of Johnson & Johnson during the early 1980s Tylenol crisis (when Tylenol was laced with cyanide in the Chicago area). Burke handled that crisis masterfully, recalling all Tylenol at a huge financial cost to the firm. But his ethical leadership had begun much earlier when he first took the CEO helm. He focused the organization's attention on the company's long-standing credo and its values. He demanded that senior executives either subscribe to the credo or remove it from the wall. He didn't want to run a hypocritical organization. He also launched the credo survey, an annual survey that asks employees how the company is doing relative to each of the credo

FIGURE 1 Executive Ethical Leadership Reputation Matrix

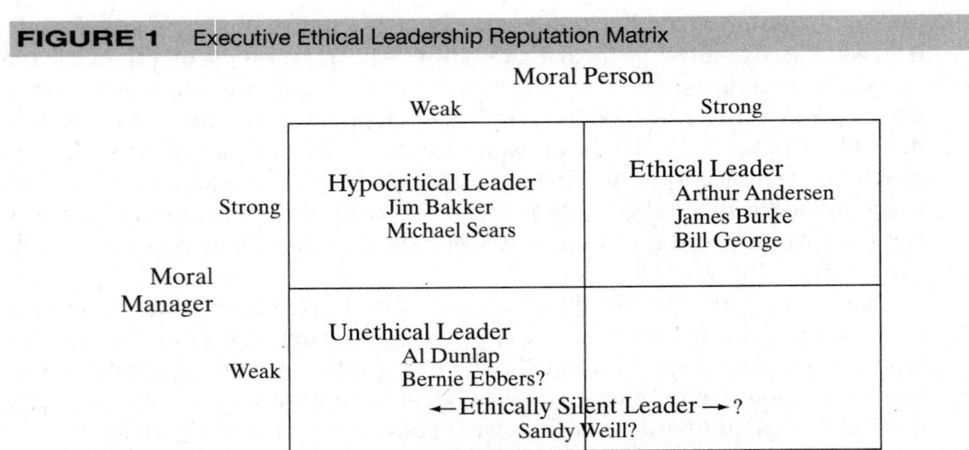

Figure adapted with permission from Treviño, L. K., Hartman, L. P., Brown, M. 2000. "Moral person and moral manager: How executives develop a reputation for ethical leadership" *California Management Review*, 42(4): 128–142.

values. Bill George, recently retired CEO of Medtronic, is a more current example of an ethical leader. In his book *Authentic Leadership,* George calls for responsible ethical leadership in corporate America while recounting his own struggles to stay true to the company's mission and to himself.[27]

A leader who is neither a moral person nor a moral manager is an *unethical leader.* In our research, Al Dunlap was frequently identified as an unethical leader. Subject of a book entitled *Chainsaw*,[28] Dunlap was known as an expert turnaround manager. But while at Sunbeam, he also became known for "emotional abuse" of employees. As a result of his demands to make the numbers at all costs, employees felt pressure to use questionable accounting and sales techniques, and they did. Dunlap also lied to Wall Street, assuring them that the firm would reach its financial projections. In the end, Dunlap could no longer cover up the sorry state of affairs, and he left a crippled company when the board fired him in 1998. In 2002, he paid a $500,000 fine for financial fraud and agreed never to serve as an officer or director of a public corporation. Unfortunately, there are many candidates for a more current example of unethical leadership: Dennis Kozlowski from Tyco, Bernie Ebbers from WorldCom, and Richard Scrushy from Health South are just a few executive names attached to recent business scandals.

Leaders who communicate a strong ethics/values message (who are moral managers), but who are not perceived to be ethical themselves (they are not moral persons) can be thought of as *hypocritical leaders*. Nothing makes people more cynical than a leader who talks incessantly about integrity, but then engages in unethical conduct himself and encourages others to do so, either explicitly or implicitly. Hypocritical leadership is all about ethical pretense. The problem is that by spotlighting integrity, the leader raises expectations and awareness of ethical issues. At the same time, employees realize that they can't trust the leader.

Jim Bakker, the founder of PTL Ministries, is our favorite example of a hypocritical leader. At its peak, his television ministry had 2000 employees and reached more than 10 million homes. Bakker preached about doing the Lord's work while raising funds for his Heritage USA Christian theme park. The problem was that he sold more memberships than could ever be honored. He tapped millions of dollars donated by his followers to support PTL operating expenses, including huge salaries and bonuses for his family and high ranking PTL officials. PTL filed for bankruptcy in 1987, and Bakker spent eight years in prison.[29]

Michael Sears, recently fired from Boeing for offering a job to an Air Force procurement specialist while she was overseeing negotiations with Boeing, represents a more recent example of a hypocritical leader. Sears had played a significant role at the Boeing Leadership Center which is known for its programs related to ethics. Also, shortly before his firing, Sears released advance copies of his book *Soaring Through Turbulence*, which included a section on maintaining high ethical standards.[30]

We call the final combination *ethically silent leadership*. It applies to executives who are neither strong ethical nor strong unethical leaders. They fall into what employees perceive to be an ethically neutral leadership zone. They may be ethical persons, but they don't provide leadership in the crucial area of ethics, and employees aren't sure where the leaders stand on ethics or if they care. The ethically silent leader is not perceived to be unethical but is seen as focusing intently on the bottom line without setting complementary ethical goals. There is little or no ethics message coming from the top.

But silence represents an important message. In the context of all the other messages being sent in a highly competitive business environment, employees are likely to interpret silence to mean that the top executive really doesn't care how business goals are met, only that they are met, so employees act on that message. Business leaders don't like to think that their employees perceive them as ethically silent. But given the current climate of cynicism, unless leaders make an effort to stand out and lead on ethics, they are likely to be viewed that way.

Sandy Weill, CEO of Citigroup, may fit the "ethically silent leader" category. The company has been playing defense with the media, responding to ugly headlines about ethics scandals, especially at its Smith Barney unit, where stock analysts were accused of essentially "selling" their stock recommendations for banking business. Weill's management style is to hire competent people to run Citigroup's units and to let them do their jobs. That may work well for other aspects of the business, but ethics must be managed from the top and center of the organization. According to *Fortune* magazine, Weill has now "gotten religion," if a bit late. Weill has "told his board that he feels his most important job from now on is to be sure that Citigroup operates at the highest level of ethics and with the utmost integrity." New procedures and business standards are being developed at corporate headquarters, and a new CEO was appointed at Smith Barney. However, *Fortune* also cites cynicism about this recent turnabout, noting that Weill is often "tone deaf" on ethical issues.[31]

So, developing a reputation for ethical leadership requires more than strong personal character. Employees must be "led" from the top on ethics just as they must be led on quality, competitiveness, and a host of other expected behaviors. In order to be effective ethical leaders, executives must demonstrate that they are ethical themselves, they must make their expectations of others' ethical conduct explicit, and they must hold all of their followers accountable for ethical conduct every day.

MYTH 5: PEOPLE ARE LESS ETHICAL THAN THEY USED TO BE

In the opening to this article, we said that business ethics has once again become a hot topic. The media have bombarded us with information about ethics scandals, feeding the perception that morals are declining in business and in society more generally.

According to a poll released by the PR Newswire in summer 2002, 68 percent of those surveyed believe that senior corporate executives are less honest and trustworthy today than they were a decade ago.[32] But unethical conduct has been with us as long as human beings have been on the earth, and business ethics scandals are as old as business itself. The Talmud, a 1500-year-old text, includes about 2 million words and 613 direct commandments designed to guide Jewish conduct and culture. More than 100 of these concern business and economics. Why? Because "transacting business, more than any other human activity, tests our moral mettle and reveals our character," and because "working, money, and commerce offer . . . the best opportunities to do good deeds such as . . . providing employment and building prosperity for our communities and the world."[33]

So unethical behavior is nothing new. It's difficult to find solid empirical evidence of changes over time. But studies of student cheating have found that the percentage of college students who admit to cheating has not changed much during the last 30 years.[34] Some types of cheating have increased (e.g., test cheating, collaboration on individual assignments). Other types of cheating have declined (e.g., plagiarism, turning in another student's work). Certainly, given new technologies and learning approaches, students have discovered some clever new ways to cheat, and professors have their work cut out for them keeping up with the new methods. But the amount of overall cheating hasn't increased that much. Further, when employees were asked about their own work organizations, the 2003 National Business Ethics Survey found that employee perceptions of ethics are generally quite positive. Interestingly, key indicators have actually improved since the last survey conducted in 2000.[35]

Alan Greenspan said it well on July 16, 2002: "It is not that humans have become any more greedy than in generations past. It is that the avenues to express greed [have] grown so enormously." So, unethical behavior is nothing new, and people are probably not less ethical than they used to be. But the environment has become quite complex and is rapidly changing, providing all sorts of ethical challenges and opportunities to express greed.

If ethical misconduct is an ongoing concern, then organizations must respond with lasting solutions that embed support for ethics into their cultures rather than short-term solutions that can easily be undone or dismissed as fads. The risk is that the current media focus on unethical conduct will result in "faddish" responses that offer overly simplistic solutions and that result inevitably in disillusionment and abandonment. Faddish solutions often result from external pressures to "do something" or at least look like you're doing something. The current focus on scandal certainly includes such pressures.[36] But the recognition that unethical conduct is a continuing organizational problem may help to convince managers that solutions should be designed that will outlast the current intense media focus.

WHAT EXECUTIVES CAN DO: GUIDELINES FOR EFFECTIVE ETHICS MANAGEMENT

Building upon what we have learned, we offer guidelines for effective ethics management. The overarching goal should be to create a strong ethical culture supported by strong ethical leadership. Why culture? Because we've seen that being ethical is not simple, and that people in organizations need ethical guidance and support for doing the right thing. Executive leaders must provide that structure and ethical guidance, and they can do that best by harnessing multiple formal and informal cultural systems.[37] People should respond positively to the kind of structure that aims to help them do the right thing. If management says, "We want you to do the right thing, the ethical thing, and we're going to try to create a culture that helps you to do that," employee response should be quite positive so long as employees believe that management is sincere and they observe consistency between words and actions.

FIRST: UNDERSTAND THE EXISTING ETHICAL CULTURE

Leaders are responsible for transmitting culture in their organizations, and the ethical dimension of organizational culture is no exception. According to Schein, the most powerful mechanisms for embedding and reinforcing culture are: (1) what leaders pay attention to, measure, and control; (2) leader reactions to critical incidents and organizational crises; deliberate role modeling, teaching, and coaching by leaders; (3) criteria for allocation of rewards and status; and (4) criteria for recruitment, selection, promotion, retirement, and excommunication.[38]

If leaders wish to create a strong ethical culture, the first step is to understand the current state: What are the key cultural messages being sent about ethics? It's a rare executive who really understands the ethical culture in an organization. And the higher you go in the organization, the rosier the perception of the ethical culture is likely to be.[39] Why? Because information often gets stuck at lower organizational levels, and executives are often insulated from "bad news," especially if employees perceive that the organization "shoots the messenger." Executives need anonymous surveys, focus groups, and reporting lines, and people need to believe that the senior leaders really want to know, if they are to report honestly on the current state of the ethical culture.

In surveys, ask for employee perceptions of supervisory and executive leadership and the messages they send by their communications and behavior. And listen to what employees say. Ask employees whether they perceive that they are treated fairly, and whether the company acts as if it cares about them, its customers, and other stakeholders. Find out what messages the reward system is sending. Do employees believe that ethical "good guys" are rewarded and unethical "bad guys" are punished in the organization? What do employees think is required in order to succeed or to be fired? Follow the kinds of calls coming in to ethics telephone lines. Learn whether employees are asking questions and reporting problems. Use this information to identify needs for training and other interventions. In focus groups, find out who the organizational heroes are. Is it the sales representative who steps on peers in order to get ahead or a manager who is known for the highest integrity? Ask what stories veterans would tell a new hire about ethics in your organization.

SECOND: COMMUNICATE THE IMPORTANCE OF ETHICAL STANDARDS

Employees need clear and consistent messages that ethics is essential to the business model, not just a poster or a website. Most businesses send countless messages about competition and financial performance, and these easily drown out other messages. In order to compete with this constant drumbeat about the short-term bottom line, the messages about ethical conduct must be just as strong or stronger and as frequent. Simply telling people to do the right thing, is not enough. They must be prepared for the types of issues that arise in their particular business and position, and they must know what to do when ethics and the bottom line appear to be in conflict. Executives should tie ethics to the long-term success of the business by providing examples from their own experience or the experiences of other successful employees.

Make sure that messages coming from executive and supervisory leaders are clear and consistent. Train employees to recognize the kinds of ethical issues that are likely to arise in their work. Demand discussion of ethics and values as part of routine business decision making. When making important decisions, ask, "Are we doing the 'right' (i.e., ethical) thing? Who could be hurt by this decision? How could this affect our relationships with stakeholders and our long-term reputation?" Share those deliberations with employees. Finally, be sure to let employees know about exemplary ethical conduct. For example, the famous story about Arthur Andersen losing the railway business because he refused to alter the books was recounted over and over again in the firm and made it absolutely clear that "think straight, talk straight" actually meant something in the firm.

THIRD: FOCUS ON THE REWARD SYSTEM

The reward system may be the single most important way to deliver a message about what behaviors are expected. B.F. Skinner knew what he was talking about. People do what's rewarded, and they avoid doing what's punished.[40] Let's look at the positive side first: Can we really reward ethical behavior? In the short term, we probably cannot. For the most part, ethical behavior is simply expected, and people don't expect or want to be rewarded for doing their jobs the right way.[41] But in the longer term, ethical behavior can be rewarded by promoting and compensating people who are not only good at what they do, but who have also developed a reputation with customers, peers, subordinates, and managers as being of the highest integrity. The best way to hold employees accountable for ethical conduct is to incorporate evaluation of it into 360° performance management systems and to make this evalution an explicit part of compensation and promotion decisions. The idea is that the bottom line and ethical performance both count; unless individuals have both, they should not advance in the organization.

Also, exemplary behavior can be rewarded. At Lockheed Martin's annual Chairman's meeting, a "Chairman's Award" goes to an employee who exhibited exemplary ethical conduct in the previous year. All senior corporate leaders are expected to expend effort each year to find examples of exemplary ethical conduct in their own business units and make nominations. The award ceremony, attended by all 250 senior executives, is exactly the kind of "ritual" that helps to create an ethical culture. Stories are shared, they become part of the organization's lore, the potential impact growing as the stories accumulate over time.[42]

Perhaps even more important than rewarding ethical conduct is taking care not to reward unethical conduct. That's what began to happen at Arthur Andersen as generating revenue became the only rewarded behavior, and it didn't matter how you did it. For example, consultants were rewarded for making a project last by finding reasons (legitimate or not) to stay on. Toffler says, "Like the famous Roach Motel, consultants were taught to check in, but never check out."[43] So, clients were overcharged, consulting jobs were dragged out, and colleagues were "screwed" along the way because the rewards supported such unethical conduct.

And what about discipline? Unethical conduct should be disciplined swiftly and fairly when it occurs at any level in the organization. The higher the level of the person disciplined, the stronger the message that management takes ethics seriously. That's what is behind the "perp walks" we have observed in the media. The public wants to see that fraudulent conduct among America's executives will not be tolerated. Similarly, inside organizations, employees want to see misconduct disciplined, and disciplined harshly.[44] Overall, employees must perceive that good guys get ahead and bad guys don't—they get punished. But, remember, it's often not enough to punish or remove a bad guy or a bad apple. The system should be checked to see if the existing reward system or other messages contributed to the bad behavior.

FOURTH: PROMOTE ETHICAL LEADERSHIP THROUGHOUT THE FIRM

Recall that being a "moral person" who is characterized by integrity and fairness, treats people well, and makes ethical decisions is important. But those elements deal only with the "ethical" part of ethical leadership. To be ethical leaders, executives have to think about the "leadership" part of the term. Providing ethical "leadership" means making ethical values visible—communicating about not just the bottom-line goals (the ends) but also the acceptable and unacceptable means of getting there (the means). Being an ethical leader also means asking very publicly how important decisions will affect multiple stakeholders—shareholders, employees, customers, society—and making transparent the struggles about how to balance competing interests. It means using the reward system to clearly communicate what is expected and what is accepted. That means rewarding ethical conduct and disciplining unethical conduct, even if the rule violator is a senior person or a top producer. Find a way to let employees know that the unethical conduct was taken seriously and the employee disciplined.

Ethical cultures and ethical leaders go hand in hand. Building an ethical culture can't be delegated. The CEO must be the Chief Ethics Officer of his or her organization.[45] Many CEOs may feel that they would rather pass on this challenge—that they don't really know how to do it—or they may prefer to believe that everyone in their organization is already ethical. But ethics is being "managed" in their organizations with or without their attention to it. Benign neglect of the ethical culture simply leads to employees reaching the conclusion, rightly or wrongly, that leaders don't care as much about ethics as they do about other things. Leaders develop a reputation in this arena. Chances are that if the leader hasn't thought much about this reputation or hasn't been very proactive about it, people in the organization will likely label him or her as an ethically neutral leader. That doesn't mean that the leader *is* ethically neutral or doesn't take ethics into account in decision making. It does mean that people aren't sure where the leader stands on the frequent conflicts between ethics and the bottom line. Without explicit guidance, they assume that the bottom-line messages are the most important.

As we've said, senior executives are extremely important. They set the tone at the top and oversee the ethical culture. But from an everyday implementation perspective, front-line supervisors are equally important because of their daily interactions with their direct reports. An ethical culture ultimately depends upon how supervisors treat employees, customers, and other stakeholders, and how they make decisions. Do they treat everyone honestly, fairly and with care? Do supervisors point out when their group is facing a decision with ethical overtones? Do they consider multiple stakeholder interests and the long-term reputation of the organization in decision making? Do they hold themselves and their people accountable for ethical conduct? Or, do they focus only on short-term bottom-line results?

ETHICS ISN'T EASY

Unethical conduct in business has been with us as long as business transactions have occurred. People are not necessarily more unethical today, but gray areas abound along with many opportunities to cross into unethical territory. Much unethical conduct is the result not just of bad apples but of neglectful leadership and organizational cultures that send mixed messages about what is important and what is expected. It isn't easy to be ethical. Employees must recognize ethical issues in their work, develop the cognitive tools to make the right choices, and then be supported in those choices by the organizational environment. Executives must manage the ethical conduct of their employees as proactively as they manage any important behavior. And the complexity of the management system should match the complexity of the behavior being managed.

The best way to manage ethical conduct is by aligning the multiple formal and informal cultural systems in support of doing the right thing. Cultural messages about the importance of trust and long-term relationships with multiple stakeholders must get at least as much attention as messages about the short-term bottom line, and employees must be held accountable for ethical conduct through performance management and reward systems.

Endnotes

1. St. Anthony, N. "Corporate Ethics Is Simple: If Something Stinks, Don't Do It," *Star Tribune (Minneapolis-Saint Paul) Newspaper of the Twin Cities*. 28 June 2002.
2. For a simple overview of these theories, see Treviño, L. K., & Nelson, K. *Managing Business Ethics: Straight Talk About How to Do It Right, 3rd ed.* New York: Wiley (2003).
3. Gioia, D. "Pinto fires and personal ethics: A script analysis of missed opportunities," *Journal of Business Ethics*, 11 (5,6) (1992): 379–389; Gioia, D. A. 2003. Personal reflections on the Pinto Fires case. In Treviño & Nelson.
4. Jones, T. M. 1991. "Ethical decision making by individuals in organizations: An issue-contingent model," *Academy of Management Review*, 16: 366–395.
5. May, D. R., & Pauli, K. P. 2000. "The role of moral intensity in ethical decision making: A review and investigation of moral recognition, evaluation, and intention." Manuscript presented at the meeting of the National Academy of Management, Toronto, August 2000.
6. Butterfield, K., Treviño, L. K., & Weaver, G. 2000. "Moral awareness in business organizations: Influences of issue-related and social context factors," *Human Relations*, 53(7): 981–1018.
7. Rest, M. 1986, *Moral Development: Advances in Research and Theory.* New Jersey: Praeger.
8. Weber, J. 1990. "Managers' moral reasoning: Assessing their responses to three moral dilemmas," *Human Relations* 43: 687–702; Weber, J., & Wasieleski, 2001. "Investigating influences on managers' moral reasoning: The impact of context, personal, and organizational factors," *Business and Society*, 40(1): 79–111; Treviño, L. K. 1986. "Ethical decision making in organizations: A person-situation interactionist model," *Academy of Management Review*, 11(3): 601–617; Treviño, L. K. 1992. "Moral reasoning and business ethics," *Journal of Business Ethics*, 11: 445–459.
9. Kohlberg, L. 1969. Stage and sequence: "The cognitive-developmental approach to socialization," In *Handbook of socialization theory and research.* D. A. Goslin, ed. Rand McNally, 347–380.
10. Thoma, S. J. 1994. "Moral judgment and moral action." In J. Rest and D. Narvaez (ed.). *Moral Development in the Professions: Psychology and Applied Ethics.* Hillsdale, NJ: Erlbaum: 199–211.
11. Miceli, M., & Near, J. 1992. *Blowing the Whistle.* New York: Lexington Books.
12. Treviño, L. K., & Victor, B. 2004. "Peer reporting of unethical behavior: A social context perspective," *Academy of Management Journal*, 353: 38–64.
13. Ethics Resource Center. 2003. *National Business Ethics Survey: How Employees View Ethics in Their Organizations.* Washington, DC.
14. PR Newswire. "How to spot bad apples in the corporate bushel." 13 January 2003. Ithaca, NY.
15. Treviño and Nelson; Jackall, R. 1988. *Moral Mazes: The World of Corporate Managers.* New York: Oxford University Press.

16. Drill team benched after scavenger incident, "Sleepover busted," *Hartford Courant*, 15 November 2002; Paulson. A. "Hazing case highlights girl violence," *Christian Science Monitor*, 9 May 2003.
17. Milgram, S. 1974. *Obedience to Authority: An Experimental View.* New York: Harper and Row.
18. Rest, J. S. (Ed.). 1986. *Moral Development: Advances in Research and Theory.* New York: Praeger. Rest, J. S., et al. 1999. *Postconventional Moral Thinking: A Neo-Kohlbergian Approach.* Mahwah, NJ: Erlbaum.
19. Ethics Resource Center, 2003. op. cit.
20. Schmitt, R. B. "Companies add ethics training: Will it work?," *Wall Street Journal* (Eastern edition), 4 November 2002: B1.
21. Ethics Resource Center, 2003. op. cit.
22. Treviño, L. K. et al. 1999. "Managing ethics and legal compliance: What works and what hurts," *California Management Review*, 41(2): 131–151.
23. Treviño and Nelson.
24. Toffler, B. L., with J. Reingold. 2003. *Final Accounting: Ambition, Greed, and the Fall of Arthur Andersen.* New York: Broadway Books. All of the following material on Toffler's experience at Arthur Andersen is from this source.
25. Kansas, D. "Plain talk: CEOs need to restore character in companies," WSJ.COM. Dow Jones and Company, Inc., 7 July 2002.
26. Treviño, L. K., Hartman, L. P., and Brown, M. 2000. "Moral person and moral manager: How executives develop a reputation for ethical leadership," *California Management Review*, 42(4): 128–142; Treviño, L. K., Brown, M., and Pincus-Hartman, 2003. "A qualitative investigation of perceived executive ethical leadership: Perceptions from inside and outside the executive suite," *Human Relations*, 56(1): 5–37.
27. George, B. 2003. *Authentic Leadership: Rediscovering the Secrets to Creating Lasting Value.* San Francisco: Jossey-Bass.
28. Byrne, J. 1999. *Chainsaw: The Notorious Career of Al Dunlap in the Era of Profit-at-Any-Price.* New York: HarperBusiness.
29. Tidwell, G. 1993. "Accounting for the PTL scandal," *Today's CPA.* July/August: 29–32.
30. Frieswick, K. Boing. *CFO Magazine*, 1 January 2004. www.cfo.com.
31. Treviño and Nelson; Loomis, C. "Whatever it takes," *Fortune*, 25 November 2002: 76.
32. PR Newswire. "Big majority believes tough new laws needed to address corporate fraud; modest majority at least somewhat confident that Bush will support such laws." 27 July 2002.
33. Kahaner, L. 2003. *Values, Prosperity and the Talmud: Business Lessons from the Ancient Rabbis.* New York: Wiley.
34. McCabe, D., and Treviño, L. K. 1996. "What we know about cheating in college," *Change: The Magazine of Higher Learning.* January/February: 28–33; McCabe, D. L., Treviño, L. K., and Butterfield, K. 2001. "Cheating in academic institutions: A decade of research," *Ethics and Behavior*, 11(3): 219–232.
35. Ethics Resource Center, 2003. op cit.
36. Abrahamson, E. 1991. "Managerial fads and fashions," *Academy of Management Review*, 16: 586–612; Carson, 1999; Gibson, J. W., and Tesone, D. V. 2001. Management fads: Emergence, evolution, and implications for managers. *The Academy of Management Executive*, 15: 122–133.
37. Treviño and Nelson, K.
38. Schein, E. H. 1985. *Organizational Culture and Leadership.* San Francisco, CA: Jossey-Bass.
39. Treviño, L. K., Weaver, G. A., and Brown, M. 2000. "Lovely at the top." Paper presented at the Academy of Management meeting, Toronto, August.
40. Skinner, B. F. 1972. *Beyond Freedom and Dignity.* New York: Bantam Books.
41. Treviño, L. K., and Youngblood, S. A. 1990. "Bad apples in bad barrels: A causal analysis of ethical decision-making behavior," *Journal of Applied Psychology*, 75: 376–385.
42. Treviño and Nelson.
43. Toffler, p. 123.
44. Treviño, L. K. 1992. "The social implications of punishment in organizations: A justice perspective," *Academy of Management Review*, 17: 647–676; Treviño, L. K., and Ball, G. A. 1992. "The social implications of punishing unethical behavior: Observers' cognitive and affective reactions," *Journal of Management*, 18: 751–768.
45. Treviño, Hartman, and Brown.

THINK MACRO, ACT MICRO: ETHICS ACTION METHODS AND INVESTOR CAPITALISM*

Richard P. Nielsen

Give us serenity to accept what cannot be changed, courage to change what should be changed, and wisdom to distinguish the one from the other.

REINHOLD NIEBUHR

THINK MACRO: INVESTOR CAPITALISM AND UNETHICAL BEHAVIOR

There are at least five types of capitalism: small family-owned business capitalism; large family-owned business capitalism; managerial capitalism; state-owned enterprise capitalism; and investor capitalism. Within managerial capitalism, there are at least three important forms: German-bank financed, Japanese network, and U.S.-British stock market-financed managerial capitalism (Chandler, 1977; Nielsen, 2003a; Nielsen, 2005; *The Economist*, 2004a; *Financial Times*, 2004a).

In small family-owned capitalism, control is exercised by the family that owns and manages the business. In large family-owned capitalism, the family still owns controlling shares of the company and family members occupy key managerial positions.

In managerial capitalism, family members withdraw from the business and sell most of the family shares. Families sell their ownership shares for family financial diversification reasons and for personal reasons—i.e., often, later generations of family members are not interested in managerial careers. Professional, non-family managers replace family members as the key managers who control the business. In this type of managerial capitalism, when outside investors are dissatisfied with the financial performance of the business, they sell their shares and buy shares of other companies.

In German-bank-financed managerial capitalism, most of a company's stock is owned by large banks. In Japanese-network managerial capitalism, most of a company's stock is owned by the suppliers and customers of the company. In U.S. and British stock market managerial capitalism, most of a company's stock is owned by individuals and families. This type of capitalism began to disappear in the U.S. as early as the mid-1970s (Drucker, 1980; Useem, 1996).

Today, the dominant form of capitalism and business organization in the United States is investor capitalism. It began around 1980 and grew to dominance by 2000. It is also spreading rapidly around the world (Useem, 1996; Tagliabue, 1998; Baker and Smith, 1999; *The Economist*, 2002a; Margolis and Walsh, 2003). What is investor capitalism? Useem (1996, pp. 1, 11) explains,

If the principles of family capitalism dominated industrialization at the turn of the century, and if the concepts of managerial capitalism rose to dominance by mid-century, the new rules of investor capitalism are coming

*This article is a generalized, condensed, and practitioner-oriented version of an academic theoretical article by the same author, "Systematic Corruption in Financial Services, Types of Capitalism, and Ethics Intervention Methods," *Business & Professional Ethics Journal 23*, nos. 1 and 2, 2004:1–31.

> *to prevail by century's end. . . . Managerial capitalism tolerated a host of company objectives besides shareholder value. Investor capitalism does not. . . . The developing relationships between investors and managers resemble neither markets nor organizations. Rather, they are emerging as enduring networks, a lattice of informal ties that come to guide a continuous two-way exchange of information and exercise of influence. . . . Now, when a large investor is dissatisfied with a company's top management, it often retains much of the holding but (along with other large investors) presses for improved performance. If results are not forthcoming, it lobbies the directors, votes against management, or even seeks new management—as the executives of the Bank of Boston, Kmart, Morrison Knudsen, Philip Morris, and W.R. Grace learned to their dismay.*

The same can also be said for the firing of the chief executive officers of General Motors and IBM in the 1980s (Nielsen, 2003a).

How are features of this form of capitalism linked to unethical organizational behavior? How do features of this type of capitalism put pressure on more or less normal and ethical employees to initiate and/or cooperate with unethical organizational behavior? An examination of some of the numbers may help explain the relationships (*The Economist*, 1999a; Krugman, 2002; Lublin, 2003; Roberts, 2004; Sapsford, 2004). For example, as Gretchen Morgenson (2004, p. 1), Business Section columnist for *The New York Times* explains, "At the heart of earnings management is—what else?—executive compensation. The greater the percentage of pay an executive receives in stock, the bigger the incentive to produce results that propel share prices."

In 1980, the average total compensation of the average employee of the S&P largest 100 companies was $37,000. The average CEO compensation was $3.7 million. In 2000, average employee compensation, wages and benefits, remained about the same at $37,000. However, the average compensation of CEOs had grown from $3.7 million to $37 million. During this same period, the average tenure of CEOs dropped from over 15 years to less than 7 years. Also, the form of compensation changed from primarily salary to primarily incentives in the form of stock options and stock bonuses tied to the price of the company's stock (Baker and George, 1999; Useem, 1996; Pollock, Fischer and Wade, 2002; Nielsen, 2003).

By the year 2000, the ownership and control structure of large, public U.S. corporations had also changed (Useem, 1996; Baker and George, 1999; Nielsen, 2003). Individuals and families no longer directly owned most of the stock of these corporations. Instead, institutional investors led by the investment bankers and private equity firms, but also including the large mutual fund companies, pension funds, private bankers, insurance companies, and hedge funds, controlled and voted more stocks than individuals and families. (Investment bankers help arrange new stock and bond offerings, mergers, and acquisitions, while private equity firms buy companies with funds arranged by the investment bankers, restructure the companies, and then re-sell the companies). By the year 2000, the institutional investors had financial control of most publicly traded U.S. corporations.

These institutional investors offered the following deal to corporate CEOs and top managers that was very difficult for these managers to refuse (Useem, 1996; Baker and

George, 1999; Nielsen, 2003; Margolis and Walsh, 2003). The managers were told to increase the price of the company's stock by some minimum percentage per year and sometimes even by every three months. If the managers were able to make their profitability and stock price targets on time, they would be richly rewarded. The total compensation, including stock bonuses and stock options, of the CEOs of the five largest integrated financial services institutions in the U.S. was more than $50 million per year, and former CEO Sanford Weill accumulated about $1 billion worth of Citigroup stock during a five year period (Sapsford, 2004). However, if the CEOs did not make their financial targets, they would be fired.

The optimization criterion became the price of the stock. As the years passed, it became more and more difficult to maintain the growth levels of profits and stock prices. Lowell (2003) estimates that real profits, as compared to misrepresented accounting profits, peaked in 1997.

Because the penalty for failing to make their numbers was so high (losing their job and millions of dollars), too many CEOs, top managers, and cooperating employees opted to misrepresent the accounting numbers so that it would look like they made their target numbers (Blakey and Roddy, 1996; Bryan-Low, 2002; *The Economist*, 2002d; Levitt, 2002).

This situation was compounded by large accounting firms in which most profits come not from auditing but from management consulting, technology consulting, and tax consulting. To avoid losing the lucrative consulting contracts and subsequent profits, compensation, and promotions, too many accounting firms and their partners and employees went along with the fraudulent numbers (Levitt, 2002; *The Economist*, 2002d; Lowell, 2003).

Similarly large parts of the compensation for research analysts, brokers, or mutual fund managers at firms like Citigroup, Merrill Lynch, Credit Suisse First Boston, Goldman Sacks, and J. P. Morgan Chase came directly or indirectly from cooperation with the investment banking side and/or private equity sides of the business (Dietz and Levy, 2004). If these employees reveal that a company's numbers are not what they appear to be and/or downgrade the company's stock, recommend against the stock to their brokerage clients, or sell the stock in the mutual fund that they manage, the investment banking and private equity sides of the corporation risk losing very profitable and very large investment banking fees from the corporation as well as appreciation in the value of the stocks that are owned by the private equity group. If they don't reveal the fraudulent numbers, don't downgrade the corporation's stock, do sell the stock to brokerage clients, and do buy the stock for the mutual fund that they manage, they are considered to be cooperative employees and good team players; this helps them receive increased bonuses, and the company keeps the investment banking business (Morgenson, 2002; Smith, 2002; Levitt, 2002; Doetz and Levy, 2004).

Features of investor capitalism are also entangled with features of the U.S. political campaign financing system. For example, congressmen may have conflicts of interests that are sometimes acted upon (Levitt, 2002; Cloud, Fields, Cummings, Markon, and Lucchetti, 2001; Hitt and Haburger, 2002). Individuals and groups of individuals who work for the corporations, accounting firms, and institutional investors make large contributions to the political campaigns of politicians of both parties. In order to get elected and re-elected, politicians need large amounts of money to run political campaigns. Appointing regulators, for example, to the Securities and Exchange Commission or the Food and Drug Administration, who are not too aggressive and offensive to the institutional investors, investment bankers, private equity groups, accounting firms, and corporations may result in large campaign contributions. Failure to cooperate puts candidates and their parties at risk of losing large amounts of campaign funds.

In the short run and even with fraudulent numbers, this system was a very profitable win-win setup for many of the key managers, employees, accountants, analysts, regulators, and politicians. As referred to above, the CEOs of the corporations received their average $37 million a year, the CEOs of the key financial institutions received their more than $50 million a year, and the institutional investors made billions on the appreciating stock values and new stock offerings. The brokers received large commissions from the sale of stocks, the research analysts were richly compensated from the investment banking sides of the business, the accounting firms received larger profits from consulting services than from auditing services. The politicians and political parties received large and increased campaign contributions. Meanwhile, individuals and families directly and indirectly through their reduced pension funds lost billions of dollars, and millions lost jobs in the subsequent bursting of the bubble, recession, and slower economic growth (Browning and Dugan, 2002; Fraser, 2001; Kelly, 2001; Krugman 2002; Levitt, 2002). Unfortunately, this system did not benefit everyone.

ACT MICRO: ETHICS ACTION AND INTERVENTION METHODS

What can managers and employees do about unethical behaviors that are stimulated by such features of organizational systems that put pressure on people to initiate and/or cooperate with unethical behaviors? There are at least six sets of ethics action and intervention methods that can help us to not just mind our own business and act ethically in our individual work lives, but also to act ethically as citizens of our organizational communities to effectively oppose unethical behaviors and build more ethical communities (Nielsen and Bartunek, 1996; Nielsen, 1996, 2003a; Trevino and Nelson, 2003).

The six types of methods are (1) win-lose forcing methods; (2) win-win methods; (3) dialogic methods; (4) internal due process methods; (5) alternative institution building; and (6) social movement methods. There are many more methods within these six categories. Determining which methods will be more appropriate and effective often depends on the different types of individual, organizational, and environmental obstacles that characterize the problem situation (Argyris, 1990; Nielsen, 1996). For example, some top executives of corporations have been unwilling and/or unable to engage in dialog about ethical issues (Brown, 2003). Ethical and effective managers and employees may need to understand and be able to practice a wide variety of ethics action-intervention methods, including such difficult methods as secret whistle-blowing, to realize our duties as professionals and citizens of organizations and communities.

WIN-LOSE FORCING METHODS

Win-lose forcing methods include top-down, compliance and punishment-based ethics codes, secret whistle-blowing, public whistle-blowing, and felony RICO prosecutions. Win-lose forcing methods try to establish ethical behaviors through threats of punishment, embarrassment, and exposure. Win-lose methods concentrate on changing behaviors, unlike some other types of methods that try to change both how people think and behave (Nielsen and Bartunek, 1996; Nielsen, 1996; Argyris, 2003).

Top-Down Ethics Codes

For the most part, ethics codes are rules and regulations written by top management and their lawyers to control the behavior of lower-level organizational members. Occasionally, codes are more dialogically and participatively developed by people from many layers and parts of an organization (Nielsen, 1996; Trevino and Nelson, 2003). There are rules that require behaviors and rules that prohibit behaviors. For example, there are rules that require employees to obtain open and multiple bidding from organizational vendors. There are rules that forbid employees from taking kickbacks from vendors. There are rules that require compliance with Generally Accepted Accounting Principles. There are rules that forbid misrepresentation of accounting numbers. There are rules that require that potential conflicts of interest be revealed, and rules that prohibit acting upon conflicts of interests.

The top-down, compliance codes include punishments for breaking the rules, such as firings, suspensions, demotions, fines, and even felony prosecutions. Organizations that use punishment-based compliance codes tend to be organizations that have been caught doing extensive unethical and illegal behaviors as well as authoritarian, older, larger, bureaucratic organizations.

The older, bureaucratic types of organizations are often characterized by a type of Theory X, win-lose, authoritarian type of management and leadership, where top management acts as if lower-level employees were lazy, irresponsible people who have to be closely supervised and controlled (McGregor, 1960). Examples of these types of organizations with very thick rule books are military organizations, government bureaucracies, and older industries such as mining, banking, insurance, and railroad companies.

Another type of organization that often uses ethics codes are organizations that have been caught doing extensive illegal and unethical behaviors. For example, part of the legal settlement with prosecutors in the investment banking, mutual fund, and insurance industry scandals of 2000–2004 is the establishment of compliance-based ethics codes. Similarly, this happened in the 1970s when many military and defense contractors were caught doing extensive corruption. The U.S. government "sentencing guidelines" for judges offered companies lighter sentences and penalties if they established ethics programs with compliance codes and ethics officers to administer the codes (Trevino and Nelson, 2003).

A strength of top-down, punishment-based compliance codes is that they clearly articulate that the unethical behaviors are unethical, are forbidden by the organization, and might be punished. A key limitation of such codes is that they can and have been selectively ignored by the top managers who have the discretion on whether and how to enforce the codes. For example, in the investment banking, mutual fund, and insurance industry scandals, almost all of the organizations had ethics codes, compliance officers, and ethics officers that did not appear to play any significant or effective role in preventing the unethical behaviors.

Similarly, the ethics codes and ethics officer programs established as a result of the 1970s' junk bond scandals in the financial services industries and the bid-rigging and bribery/extortion scandals in the defense industries appear to have played very little positive role in either exposing or preventing the financial scandals of 1990–2004.

Another problem with top-down, punishment-based compliance codes is that at least in some industries where there are rapid changes in industry practices, such as in financial services, pharmaceutical, and defense industries, the rules tend to prohibit yesterday's unethical behaviors. The belief can be common in such rapidly changing organizations that use compliance codes that if something is not forbidden by the rules, it is permitted, at least until there is another scandal.

For example, the rules that were developed out of the pharmaceutical product testing scandals of the 1960s and the rules against the fraudulent junk bond financial reporting of the 1970s did not cover or help much with the more recent scandals [e.g. the pain medicine and coronary artery stent scandals (Krasner, 2004), the fraudulent earnings predictions, earnings reporting, auditing, investment banking, mutual fund late trading, and New York Stock Exchange specialist companies that systematically engaged in front-running trading of their personal and firm investments ahead of buying and selling for customers (Nielsen, 2003a; Kelly and Craig, 2004)].

Publicly Blow the Whistle

Given the financial pressures managers and employees are under and the limitations of top-down, punishment-based compliance codes, it is often essential for organizational members to blow the whistle outside the organization when top management selectively ignores its own codes and/or suppresses information about code violations (Sender and Zuckerman, 2003).

After unsuccessfully trying to get the attention of top management at Enron, Sherron Watkins, an investment manager, testified before the United States Senate about Enron's deceptive accounting and energy investments (Watkins, 2003). Her testimony was very important in exposing and stopping the unethical and illegal behaviors at Enron and indirectly at the investment banks that supported the Enron frauds. Similarly, Peter Rost, a Vice-President of Marketing for Pfizer, publicly blew the whistle to the media that the big pharmaceutical companies were untruthful when they insisted that importing drugs from abroad is unsafe (Barry and Welch, 2004).

When top management ignores it own codes, internal action-intervention methods are often not politically possible. In such cases, external whistle-blowing that asks for outside help from the government, the courts, and/or the media may be necessary. Unfortunately, there is much evidence that public whistle-blowers suffer very effective retaliation (Alford, 2001; Harding, 2002)

Secretly Blow the Whistle Outside the Organization

Noreen Harrington, a veteran manager with experience as a managing director at Goldman Sacks, Stern Asset management, and Barclays Capital first tried to discuss the ethics of late trading in mutual funds, but top management would not pay serious attention and continued with the unethical practices. Finally, she secretly blew the whistle to New York State Attorney General Eliot Spitzer. This secret whistle-blowing resulted in exposure of the massive unethical practices in the mutual fund industry as well as several important reforms (Sender and Zuckerman, 2003). Harrington explains why she intervened and acted, "All of a sudden, I thought about this from a different vantage point. I saw one face—my sister's face—and then I saw the faces of everyone whose only asset was a 401(k) (pension). At that point I felt the need to try to make the regulators look into these abuses" (Chatzky, 2004, p. 156). Harrington later decided to reveal her identity to the *Wall Street Journal.* The key advantage of secretly blowing the whistle outside the organization is that the whistle-blower is for the most part protected from retaliation. The disadvantage of the method is that the organization is hurt by public exposure of the unethical behavior.

Secretly Blow the Whistle Inside the Organization

In 2003, a financial analyst secretly blew the whistle about fraudulent earnings in his division of a large financial services company to the Chairman of the Audit Committee of the Board of Directors (*Financial Analyst*, 2003). Subsequently, the audit committee reviewed the division's numbers and restated them. The misrepresentation was stopped and corrected. The key advantages of this method are that the unethical behavior is sometimes stopped, the secret whistle-blower is protected, and the organization is given the opportunity to solve the ethics problem before it becomes a public embarrassment to the organization. Disadvantages of the method are that the organization may ignore the warning and/or the organization might seek out and punish the internal whistle-blower.

RICO

If the Racketeer Influenced and Corrupt Organizations Act (Blakey and Roddy, 1996) could be applied in felony prosecutions of top managers, this might have a more important deterrence effect compared, for example, to organizations that pay relatively small fines and admit no guilt. The RICO Act permits judges to find top management guilty for the illegal behaviors of subordinates when there is systematic and pervasive corruption in their organizations. Such systematic and pervasive corruption appears to have been the case for several investment banking, mutual fund, and insurance industry companies in the 1990s. For example, Citigroup former CEO and current Chairman, Sanford Weill received total compensation over a five-year period of close to $1 billion, but Citigroup paid a fine of "only" $400 million and did not admit any guilt. To date judges have unfortunately not allowed prosecutors to use the RICO Act in this type of case (Bowe, 2004; DeBaise, 2004).

WIN-WIN METHODS

The intention of win-lose methods is to force change through, for example, the threats of punishments for violations of ethics codes and/or exposure through external whistle-blowing to the press or government about perpetrators and top managers who initiate and/or cooperate with unethical and illegal behaviors. Unlike these threat based methods, win-win methods try to offer incentives for ethical behavior and incentives for cessation of unethical behaviors (Nielsen, 1996). Two important types of win-win methods are mutual gain negotiating (Fisher and Ury, 1991) and reciprocal networking (Nielsen, 2003a). As with the win-lose forcing methods, the focus of these methods is behavior change rather than changes in how people think.

Win-Win Negotiation

Within financial services organizations there have been conflicts of interest that have been acted upon with respect to relationships between the investment banking and financial analysis sides of the business. For example, David Komansky, former CEO of Merrill Lynch, and Denis Kozlowski, former CEO of Tyco, discussed how to manipulate research coverage of Tyco by Merrill hiring an analyst that Tyco favored. According to an e-mail introduced at Koslowski's trial sent to Mr. Komansky by Samuel Chapin, Merrill's Vice-Chairman, "To demonstrate the impact this hire has on our relationship, Denis Kozlowski called me on Phua's (the analyst Tyco wanted Merrill to hire) first day of work to award us the lead management of a $2.1 billion bond offering." Instead of incentives like this for unethical behavior, a possible win-win incentive is to offer financial rewards or points toward promotion for ethical behavior.

Organizations can offer rewards to financial analysts who previously misrepresented their evaluations of stocks in cooperation with misrepresented investment banking deals. For example, the financial analyst who had misrepresented the prospects for a stock in exchange for a bonus from the investment banking unit might instead be offered a bonus for the accuracy of his predictions. However, for something like this to work, the relationship between the investment banking side and the analyst side of financial institutions would have to be separated. This has been done as part of the settlement that Citigroup, Goldman, J.P. Morgan Chase, Credit Swiss First Boston, and Merrill Lynch made with the Securities and Exchange Commission and New York Attorney General Elliot Spitzer.

Reciprocal Networking

Reciprocal networking operates as follows. Person A helps Person B. Person A asks Person B to help Person C. Person A asks Person B and Person C to help Person D, and so on. Person A can do this because Person A is an ethical person who wants to help others or for reasons of selfish self-interest. It works both ways. Through this method, Person A builds a network of reciprocal win-win relationships with Person A at the center of the win-win network. If Person A wants to intervene to stop an unethical behavior and/or increase an ethical behavior, Person A has the political allies to exercise organizational influence (Nielsen, 2003a).

Reciprocal networking is different than Mafia-type networking in two key areas. First, the network leader is trying to help people rather than exploit others. Second, the network is inclusive rather than exclusive.

A key strength of win-win methods relative to win-lose methods is that most people prefer to be rewarded for behavior change rather than being threatened into behavior change. A key limitation may be that the ethics change agent may not have anything to offer that is an adequate material incentive for stimulating ethical behavior and/or stopping unethical behavior. In the above Citigroup and Tyco-Merrill Lynch cases, the financial rewards from high-level corruption are often much greater than the material rewards ethics and corruption reformers can offer very highly compensated managers.

DIALOGIC METHODS

There are at least three sets of dialogic methods. There are the ethics arguments/criteria that can be used to discuss an issue. There are different methods for structuring conversations. There are different organizational structures for participating in organizational decision making.

Ethics Arguments/Reasons

Examples of ethics arguments/criteria include Aristotle's proportionality criterion where something is less right or wrong than too much or too little, Aristotle's common good criterion, Kant's (1797) "treat people as ends in themselves and not solely as means" criterion, Bentham's (1789) utilitarian cost–benefit criterion, Derrida's (1988) postmodern power bias criterion—i.e., the more powerful often write the rules and the histories to favor the more powerful at expense of the less powerful, etc. There are at least twenty different types or arguments/criteria that could be used in an ethics intervention conversation (Nielsen, 2003a).

For example, with respect to a safety issue, one could reason with Aristotle's proportionality argument that our incidence of accidents relative to the industry is too high. One could reason with Aristotle's common-good criterion that unnecessary worker injuries are not good for our organizational community. One could reason with Kant's "treat people as ends in themselves and not solely as means" criterion that avoidable accidents for the sake of profitability do not treat people as ends in themselves. One could consider with Bentham's cost benefit criteria whether the costs of accidents were greater than the benefits of improved safety. One could reason with Derrida's postmodern criterion that injuries may be occurring more frequently among the least powerful and most vulnerable organizational members.

Dialogic Conversation Structures

There are at least six different methods of structuring dialogic conversations (Nielsen, 1996). For example, one could use the Socratic method, where the interventionist asks questions without advocating positions. One could use Argyris's (1990, 2003) action-learning method where the interventionist combines inquiry with advocacy and experimentation. One could use Woolman's (Nielsen, 1996) method, where the interventionist inquires about organizational system/tradition forces that may be pressuring organizational members to behave in less ethical ways.

Dialogic Organizational Structures

There are many different types of organizational structures for organizing participative decision making (Heller, Pusic, Strauss, and Wilpert, 1998). For example, there are self-managed work teams. There are joint management–employee committees, there are quality circles, there are employee boards and mixed stakeholder group boards that combine internal and external organizational stakeholders in advisory discussions.

The key advantages of dialogic methods are that they can result in belief conversion toward the ethical as well as behavior change toward the ethical and that dialog can be more friendly and less adversarial. The key problems with dialogic methods are that the people engaging in the unethical activities may already understand that what they are doing is unethical and that they understand that they are choosing what they anticipate will be wealth and power rewards instead of ethics. In addition, powerful people who may be engaged in unethical activities can often choose not to engage in dialog. There is often not much political space in organizations to discuss ethics issues with top management.

INTERNAL DUE PROCESS SYSTEMS

There are at least four different types of internal due process systems: investigation and punishment, grievance and arbitration, mediation, and employee board systems (Nielsen, 2000d). Due process systems are very important because in the emotionality of a scandal and the rush to closure, sometimes top managements find scapegoats rather than fundamental reforms. Typically, lower- and middle-level employees take the blame for either actions or pressures that come from top management.

For example in the Citigroup case referred to above, while several middle- and lower-level managers lost their jobs, the Citigroup CEO and now Chairman Sanford Weill was not penalized but handsomely rewarded. There is a great deal of variation in the fairness, costs, and flexibility of due process systems.

Investigation and Punishment System

In an investigation and punishment system, management does an investigation about an unethical behavior and then announces a decision with punishments if the accused is found guilty by management. This type of system is very fast and relatively inexpensive but offers few protections to the accused. This is the type of system that is very popular in U.S. business but is illegal in the European Union since it offers so little protection to the accused employee.

Grievance and Arbitration System

In a grievance and arbitration system, several layers of management and employees discuss the case against the accused. If at progressive levels of management and employee representation, agreement can't be reached, a decision is made by an outside arbitrator. This type of system is common in unionized environments and government organizations. It offers a great deal of protection to the accused but is very time-consuming and expensive.

Mediation System

In a mediation system, typically a human resources manager tries to mediate and work out some type of win-win agreement between the parties to an ethics conflict. This type of system is very informal, inexpensive, and flexible. However, its fairness depends to a great extent on the individual character and skills of the mediator.

Employee Board System

In an employee board system, a jury of employees investigates a potential ethics violation and makes recommendations and decisions about the individual case and/or changes in an organization's policies and procedures that may have contributed to the ethics problem. This system is also very flexible and fair but is more expensive and time consuming than a mediator system. This is a relatively rare form of due process system in U.S. business since top managements are often reluctant to cede power to an employee board.

ALTERNATIVE INSTITUTION BUILDING

Sometimes it is not possible or it would take too long for organizational ethics efforts to work. In such a situation, it may be possible to build an alternative institution. For example, in several emerging market countries, the state-owned banking systems are so corrupt that it is not possible to reform them. Bankers are often hired and promoted on the basis of political connections. The administrators of the banks often make intentionally bad loans to friends, relatives, and political allies and collect kickbacks from bank purchases. Bank resources are spent on nonbank activities.

For many years, reformers both within and outside state banking systems in many emerging market countries tried to reform the systems, but it was not possible. Instead, the reformers got together to build alternative private banks. Bankers were hired and promoted on the basis of demonstrated abilities rather than political connections. Lower-level employees were hired on the basis of their achievements rather than their political connections. Customers were invited to apply for loans and other financial services based on their achievements and abilities rather than their political connections. In many emerging markets, the private banks are succeeding. Bankers who did excellent work were hired and promoted based on their achievements rather than their political connections. Excellent employees were recruited and promoted. Many of these banks have been growing at a rate of 15 percent a year for the last twenty years. There is little financial corruption in banking purchases and investments. In some cases, the state banks have begun to imitate some aspects of the ethical private banks.

A key strength of this method is that ethical institutions can be created when older corrupt organizations can't be changed. The U.S. Securities and Exchange Commission may be an example of an institution that can't be changed due to its links to political appointments and campaign contributions and may need to be replaced with an alternative institution (Levitt, 2002).

However, sometimes when the new ethical organization succeeds and gains prominence and market share, the older corrupt institutions decide to try to change in order to survive in the new competitive environment where before they were protected by their relative monopoly position.

Key limitations of this method are that it can take enormous resources to build an alternative institution and there is often very strong opposition to the new institution that is perceived by the old guard as a threat to their institutional position. Unfortunately, sometimes the reverse happens, and the private institutions that were founded to become corruption reform institutions become as corrupt as the public institutions that they were originally trying to reform.

SOCIAL MOVEMENT METHODS

Social movement methods are used when the problem is too big for one individual, group, or even organization to address. Examples of social movements include the U.S. civil rights movement, the Swedish Natural Step environmental movement, the Korean

People's Solidarity for Participatory Democracy corruption reform movement, and the worldwide auditing and corporate governance reform movement (Davis and Thompson, 1994; McAdam, 1982; Nielsen, 2000a; Kelly and Craig, 2004; Davis, 2004). Typically, social movement methods combine the resources and efforts of many individuals, groups, organizations, and even professional associations.

A common series of processes within a social movement includes the following (Nielsen, 2000a). An example from the auditing and corporate governance reform movement are described.

a. Dialog among friends about biases in traditions and systems that also discover political opportunities for reform. Many accounting firm partners, accounting professors, business journalists, and top managers from pension funds, mutual fund companies, and diversified financial services organizations have known about and talked about governance and auditing problems for many years. The investment banking, mutual fund, and insurance industry scandals as well as the worldwide decline of stock markets in the 2000–2002 period that was partially caused by these ethical scandals provided political opportunities for reform.
b. Dialog among friends about personal values among reformers and leaders of established, directly shared interest organizations that result in alliances between reformers and established organization leaders. Some individual leaders were able to mobilize support from their professional accounting associations, media organizations, investment officer associations, pension fund associations, mutual fund associations, etc. to formally back reforms in corporate governance, securities, and auditing legislation.
c. Reframing among the leaders of established organizations and members concerning the meaning of membership in terms of active support for reform of biases in traditions/systems. Some of the leaders of professional associations also asked the members of their associations to individually and collectively support the reforms.
d. Win-win development of specialized reform organizations. For example, the Public Company Accounting Oversight Board was established by the U.S. Congress in 2002 to focus on auditing and governance reforms. The Board has publicly asked practicing accounting auditors to blow the whistle to the Board about illegal and unethical activities of their firms and the clients of their auditing firms (Associated Press, 2004).
e. Selected win-lose actions against opponents to reform. For example, with the information provided by the secret whistle-blowers, the Oversight Board as well as prosecutors can require companies to release e-mails, documents, and other types of information that can then be used to prosecute individual and organizational violators.
f. Trailing, win-win development of support of the reform movement through instrumental alliances with external support groups. For example, after corporate governance successes, reformers ask current supporters for more help and ask potential new allies to support the movement.

A key strength of the social movement method is that it is able to help develop large social changes that would have been impossible for individuals, groups, organizations, and associations acting alone. In addition, very important friendships are developed in the long struggle for positive social change. A key limitation of social movement methods is that they require an enormous amount of time from key leaders who are often not compensated financially very much or at all. This requires an enormous personal commitment of a few key leaders, which typically takes a great deal of time away from family and normal career endeavors. In addition, social movements require an enormous amount of resources from key supporting organizations and individuals.

CONCLUSION

As illustrated above, there have been and probably still are various types of unethical behaviors that are at least partially caused by features of our organizational and political-economic systems. That is, the types of unethical business behaviors are linked to the types of capitalism, in the recent cases, to the "investor capitalist" type. Fortunately, there are many effective ethics action and intervention methods that we can use to resist unethical behaviors and build ethical organizational communities.

Unfortunately, as *The Economist* (2004b, p. 83) has observed, "Like the invest-bank settlement, this week's agreement (mutual fund industry) is less punitive than the seven-figure sum suggests. As with the Wall Street penalties, the mutual-fund fines are easily digestible. . . . As in the investment-bank case, no senior executives of the parent companies have been held liable." The government prosecutors in the investment banking, mutual fund, and insurance industry corruption scandals have allowed the CEOs of the largest financial institutions to keep and increase their massive compensation packages while having their organizations pay relatively small fines without admitting guilt for the massive corruption and unethical behaviors (Solomon, 2004).

Therefore, while we might prefer to use the dialogic and win-win methods, the win-lose forcing methods of asking for outside help through secret external whistle-blowing to the press and to prosecutors as well as aggressive application of felony RICO Act (Blakey and Roddy, 1996) prosecutions against CEOs and board chairmen of the largest corporations may also be necessary.

It is often not enough to "mind our own business" and act ethically in our individual work lives when there are serious unethical behaviors around us. We have an ethical obligation to act, to ask others inside and outside the organization for help if necessary, and to intervene to help others in resisting unethical and corrupt behaviors and in building ethical organizational communities.

Thinking globally at a macro level about how the larger political-economic systems may be at least in part causing unethical behaviors can help us understand the systematic nature of the problem. Acting locally at a micro level with application of ethics action-intervention methods can help solve the problems. As Aristotle observed, "The student of ethics *must* apply himself to politics." As the Irish political theorist Edmund Burke advocated, "When bad men combine, the good must associate; else they will fall one by one, an unpitied sacrifice in a contemptible struggle." And as Reinhold Niebuhr asks, "Grant us serenity to accept what cannot be changed, courage to change what should be changed, and wisdom to distinguish the one from the other." It is the conclusion of this paper that while there is much that cannot be changed with respect to the type of capitalism and political-economy that we may live within during any generation, at least in the short and medium term, there is also much that can be changed; and, with wisdom to know the difference and with practical ethics action and intervention methods, we can help make a positive and ethical difference.

References

Alford, C. Fred. 2001. *Whistleblowers: Broken Lives and Organizational Power.* Ithaca, N.Y.: Cornell University Press.

Argyris, C.R., Putnam, R., and Smith, D.M. 1985. *Action Science.* San Francisco: Jossey-Bass.

Argyris, C.R. 1990. *Overcoming Organizational Defenses.* Boston: Allyn and Bacon.

Argyris, C.R. 2003. "A Life Full of Learning," *Organization Studies*, 24:7: 1178–1192.

Associated Press. 2004. "Group Encourages Whistleblowing," *The Boston Globe*, August 24: 8.

Auletta, K. 1986. *Greed and Glory on Wall Street: The Fall of the House of Lehman.* New York: Random House.

Baker, George and Smith, George. 1999. *The New Financial Capitalists.* Cambridge: Cambridge University Press.

Barry, Patricia. 2004. "The Insiders," *AARP Bulletin*, November, p. 10.

Bauman, Zygmunt. 1993. *Postmodern Ethics.* Oxford: Blackwell Publishers.

Bentham, J. 1789, 1897. *An Introduction to the Principles of Morals and Legislation.* Oxford: Clarendon.

Blakey, G.R. and Roddy, K.P. 1996. "Reflections on Reves v. Ernst and Young: Its Meaning and Impact on Substantive, Accessory, Aiding, Abetting and Conspiracy Liability under RICO," *American Criminal Law Review*, 33, 5: 1345–1702.

Blasi, A. 1980. "Bridging Moral Cognition and Moral Action: A Critical Review of the Literature," *Psychological Bulletin*, 88: 1–45.

Bowe, Christopher. 2004. "Tyco Trial: Judge Drops 'Mafia' Charge," *Financial Times,* March 6: 9.

Bowe, Christopher and Silverman, Gary. 2004. "Merrill Rewarded After Hiring Analyst Tyco Favored," *Financial Times*, February 3: 1.

Bowie, Norman E. and Freeman, R. Edward. 1992. *Ethics and Agency Theory.* New York: Oxford University Press.

Bowie, N. E. 1999. *Business Ethics: A Kantian Perspective.* Oxford: Blackwell Publishers.

Brown, Ken. 2002. "When Enron Auditors Were on a Tear," *Wall Street Journal*, March 21: C1, C20.

Brown, Ken. 2003. "Wall Street Plays Numbers Game with Earnings, Despite Reforms," *Wall Street Journal*, July, 22: 1, 2.

Browning, E.S. and Dugan, Ianthe Jeanne. 2002. "Aftermath of a Market Mania: Memories of Euphoria, Despair." *The Wall Street Journal Online*, December 16: 1–13.

Bryan-Low, Cassell. 2002. "Accounting Firms Are Still Consulting." *Wall Street Journal*, September 23: C1 and C7.

Carter, Adrienne, Feldman, Amy, and Zweig, Jason. 2003. "The Greed Machine," *Money*, December: 130–136.

Chandler, Alfred D. 1977. *The Visible Hand: The Managerial Revolution in American Business.* Cambridge: Harvard University Press.

Chatzky, Jean. 2004. "Meet the Whistle-Blower," *Money*, February: 156.

Cloud, David S., Fields, Gary, Cummings, Jeanne, Markon, Jerry, and Lucchetti, Aaron. 2001. "Money and Connections Paved the Way Home for Fugitive Marc Rich," *Wall Street Journal*, January 29: 1, 6.

Craig, Susanne and Brown, Ken. 2004. *Wall Street Journal*, March 29: C1, C5.

Davis, G.F. and Thompson, T.A. 1994. "A Social Movement Perspective on Corporate Control," *Administrative Science Quarterly* 39: 141–173.

Davis, Ann. 2004. "Wall Street, Companies It Covers, Agree on Honesty Policy," *Wall Street Journal*, March 11: C1, C6.

DeBaise, Colleen. 2004. "Tyco Corruption Count Is Dropped," *Wall Street Journal*, March 8: C4.

Derrida, Jacques. 1988. *Limited INC.* Evanston, Ill.: Northwestern University Press.

Dietz, David and Levy, Adam. 2004. "Bank Funds: Draining Investors," *Bloomberg Markets*, November: 68–79.

Donaldson, Thomas and Werhane, Patricia. 1983. *Ethical Issues in Business.* Upper Saddle River, NJ: Prentice Hall.

The Economist, 1999a. "Cutting the Cookie, and the Rich Get Richer," September 11: 26.

The Economist. 2002a. "The End of Tycoons: A New Generation, a New Economy, and a New Capitalism Are Changing the Way in Which Business Is Done in East Asia," April 29: 67–69.

The Economist. 2002b. "Japanese Corporate Scandals," September 7: 57–58.

The Economist. 2002c. "Did Wall Street Firms Bribe Bosses with Shares?" September 7: 66.

The Economist. 2002d. "The Lessons from Enron: After the Energy Firm's Collapse, the Entire Auditing Regime Needs Radical Change," February 9: 9–10.

The Economist. 2003. "The Wall Street Settlement: Unclean Slate," January 4: 59.

The Economist. 2004a. "Capitalism's New Kings: How Private Equity Is Changing the Business World," November 27: 9–10.

The Economist. 2004b. "America's Mutual-Fund Scandal," March 20: 83.

Ewing, D. W. 1977. *Freedom Inside the Organization.* New York: McGraw Hill.

Ewing, D.W. 1983. *Do It My Way or You're Fired.* New York: John Wiley.

Ewing, D.W. 1989. *Justice on the Job.* Boston: Harvard Business School Press.

Financial Analyst. 2003. "The Financial Analyst Prefers to Remain Anonymous."

Financial Times. 2004. "Private Equity," November 30: 1–2.

Fisher, Roger and Ury, William. 1991. *Getting to Yes.* New York: Penguin.

Fraser, Jill Andresky. (2001). *White-Collar Sweatshop: The Deterioration of Work and Its Rewards in Corporate America.* New York: Norton.

Friedman, Milton. 1970. "The Social Responsibility of Business Is to Increase Its Profits," *New York Times Magazine*, September 13.

Gasparino, Charles. 2002. "Salomon Says It Sent Hot IPOs WorldCom's Way," *Wall Street Journal*, August 27: C1.

Harding, James. 2002. "Whistle While You Work (and Face the Consequences)," *Financial Times*, February 10: 9.

Hartman, Edwin M. 1996. *Organizational Ethics and the Good Life.* New York: Oxford University Press.

Heller, F., Pusic, E. Strauss, G. and Wilpert, B. 1998. *Organizational Participation: Myth and Reality.* Oxford: Oxford University Press.

Hitt, Greg and Hamburger, Tom. 2002. "New Campaign Law Restores PAC's Appeal," *Wall Street Journal*, July 29: A4.

Jensen, M.C. and Meckling, W.H. 1976. "Theory of the Firm: Managerial Behavior, Agency Costs and Ownership Structure." *Journal of Financial Economics*, 3: 305–360.

Kane, E. J., 1993. "What Lessons Should Japan Learn from the U.S. Deposit-Insurance Mess?" *Journal of the Japanese and International Economies*, 7: 329–355.

Kant, Immanuel. 1797, 1994. "The Metaphysical Principles of Virtue," in *Ethical Philosophy.* Indianapolis/Cambridge: Hackett Publishing: 52.

Kelly, Marjorie. 2001. *The Divine Right of Capital.* San Francisco: Barrett-Koehler.

Kelly, Kate and Craig, Susanne. 2004. "NYSE Traders Will Pay Fines of $240 million," *Wall Street Journal*: C1, C3.

Krasner, Jeffery. 2004. "Stents Sold Despite High Failure Rates," *The Boston Globe*, December 26: 1, A42.

Krugman, Paul. 2002. "For Richer: How the Permissive Capitalism of the Boom Destroyed American Equality," *The New York Times Magazine*, October 20: 62–67, 76–77, 141.

Levitt, Arthur. 2002. *Take on the Street: What Wall Street and Corporate America Don't Want You To Know.* New York: Pantheon Books.

Li, Stan X. and Berta, Whitney Blair. 2002. "The Ties That Bind: Strategic Actions and Status Structure in the U.S. Investment Banking Industry." *Organization Studies*, 23, 3: 339–368.

Lowell, James. 2003. "Market Monitor," *Fidelity Investor*, 6, 1: 4.

McAdam, D. 1982. *Political Process and the Development of Black Insurgency 1930–1970.* Chicago: University of Chicago Press.

McGregor, D. 1960. *The Human Side of Enterprise.* New York: McGraw-Hill.

Morgenson, Gretchen. 2002. "Analyze This: What Those Analysts Said in Private," *New York Times*, September 15, section 3: 1.

Morgenson, Gretchen. 2004. "Pennies That Aren't from Heaven," *New York Times*, November 7, section 3: 1, 8.

Nielsen, Richard P. and Bartunek, Jean M. 1996. "Opening Narrow, Routinized Schemata to Ethical Stakeholder Consciousness and Action," *Business and Society*, 35, 4: 483–519.

Nielsen, Richard P. 1996. *The Politics of Ethics: Methods for Acting, Learning and Sometimes Fighting, With Others in Addressing Ethics Problems in Organizational Life.* New York: Oxford University Press, the Ruffin Series in Business Ethics.

Nielsen, Richard P. 2003a. "Corruption Networks and Implications for Ethical Corruption Reform," *Journal of Business Ethics*, 42: 125–149.

Nielsen, Richard P. 2003b, "Ethics and Organizational Theory: Varieties and Dynamics of Constrained Optimization in Different Types of Capitalism," In Christian Knudsen and Haridimos Tsoukas (Eds.), *The Oxford Handbook of Organizational Theory: Meta-Theoretical Perspectives.* London: Oxford University Press: 476–501.

Nielsen, Richard P. 2000c. "Do Internal Due Process Systems Permit Adequate Political and Moral Space for Ethics Voice, Praxis, and Community?" *Journal of Business Ethics*, 24, 1: 1–27.

Nielsen, Richard P. 1998. "Can Ethical Character Be Stimulated and Enabled? An Action-Learning Approach to Teaching and Learning Organization Ethics," *Business Ethics Quarterly*, 8, 3, July: 581–604.

Noonan, J. T. 1984. *Bribes.* New York: Macmillan.

Orey, Michael. 2003. "WorldCom-Inspired 'Whistle-Blower' Law Has Weaknesses," *Wall Street Journal*, October 1: B1, B6.

Pollock, Timothy C., Fischer, Harald M., and Wade, James B. 2002. "The Role of Power and Politics in the Repricing of Executive Options." *Academy of Management Journal*, 45, 6: 1172–1182.

Ricoeur, Paul. 1991. *From Text to Action: Essays in Hermeneutics.* Evanston, Illinois: Northwestern University Press: 334.

Roberts, Dan. 2004. "Executive Bonuses Set to Match Boom Levels," *Financial Times*, March 22: 1.

Sapsford, Jathon. 2004. "Citigroup's Weill Received Bonus of $29 Million in Cash for 2003," *Wall Street Journal*, March 17: C3.

Sender, H. and Zuckerman, G. 2003. "Behind the Mutual Fund Probe: Three Informants Opened Up," *Wall Street Journal*, December 14: 1, 6.

Smith, Randall. 2002. "Regulators Set Accord with Securities Firms, but Some Issues Persist," *Wall Street Journal*, December 23: C1, C12.

Smith, Randall, Craig, Susanne and Solomon, Deborah. 2003. "Wall Street Firms to Pay $1.4 Billion to End Inquiry," *Wall Street Journal*, April 29: 1, 6.

Solomon, Deborah. 2004. "As Corporate Fines Grow, SEC Debates How Much Good They Do," *Wall Street Journal*, November 12: 1, A6.

Syre, Steven. 2002. "Beyond the Zeroes," *Boston Globe*, December 22: E2.

Trevino, Linda K. and Nelson, Katherine A. 2000. *Managing Business Ethics.* New York: John Wiley.

Tsoukas, Hardimos and Cummings, Stephen. 1997. "Marginalization and Recovery: The Emergence of Aristotelian Themes in Organization Studies," *Organization Studies*, 18, 4: 655–683.

Useem, Michael. 1996. *Investor Capitalism.* New York: Basic Books.

Velasquez, Manuel G. 1982. *Business Ethics.* Upper Saddle River, NJ: Prentice Hall.

Watkins, Sherron. 2003. "Former Enron Vice President Sherron Watkins on the Enron Collapse," *Academy of Management Executive*, 17, 4: 119–125.

WHEN ETHICS TRAVEL: THE PROMISE AND PERIL OF GLOBAL BUSINESS ETHICS*

Thomas Donaldson
Thomas W. Dunfee

Global managers often must navigate the perplexing gray zone that arises when two cultures—and two sets of ethics—meet. Suppose:

> *You are a manager of Ben & Jerry's in Russia. One day you discover that the most senior officer of your company's Russian joint venture has been "borrowing" equipment from the company and using it in his other business ventures. When you confront him, the Russian partner defends his actions. After all, as a part owner of both companies, isn't he entitled to share in the equipment?*[1]
>
> *Or, competing for a bid in a foreign country, you are introduced to a "consultant" who offers to help you in your client contacts. A brief conversation makes it clear that this person is well connected in local government and business circles and knows your customer extremely well. The consultant will help you prepare and submit your bid and negotiate with the customer . . . for a substantial fee. Your peers tell you that such arrangements are normal in this country—and that a large part of the consulting fee will go directly to staff people working for your customer. Those who have rejected such help in the past have seen contracts go to their less fussy competitors.*[2]

What should you do in such cases? Should you straighten out your Russian partner? How should you deal with the problem of bribery? Bribery is just like tipping, some people say. Whether you tip for service at dinner or bribe for the benefit of getting goods through customs, you pay for a service rendered. But while many of us balk at a conclusion that puts bribery on a par with tipping, we have difficulty articulating why.

Most Western companies' codes of ethics never dreamed of cross-cultural challenges like these. How can managers successfully maneuver the disturbing gray zones that lie at the intersections of different cultures? Issues such as these have tended to bedazzle many modern multinational corporations. Companies are finding—and stumbling over—ethics issues abroad as never before. Corporate ethics and values programs are in vogue; and many companies are asking whether they should take their ethics and values programs global. But confusion abounds.

---

*Reprinted by permission of Harvard Business School Press. Excerpt from "Ties That Bind: A Social Contracts Approach to Business Ethics" by T. Donaldson and T. W. Dunfee.

Some companies, recognizing cultural differences, simply accept whatever prevails in the host country. This is a mistake because it exposes the company (and its brand names) to corruption and public affairs disasters, and because it misses the opportunity to find the glue that cements morale and cooperative strategy. It neglects the important role for hypernorms.* It substitutes unmitigated relativism for good sense. Years ago, foreign companies operating in South Africa broke the South African apartheid law that required segregated washrooms for employees. Not to break that South African law, and to leave the washrooms segregated, would have been unethical. Consider a more recent example:

> *The* SS United States, *arguably the most luxurious ocean liner during the 1950s, was loaded with asbestos and would have cost about $100 million to be refurbished for luxury cruising. In 1992 it was towed to Turkey, where the cost of removing the asbestos was only $2 million. Turkish officials refused to allow the removal because of the danger of cancer. In October 1993 it was towed to the Black Sea port of Sebastopol where laws are lax. It will have more than one-half million square feet of carcinogenic asbestos removed for even less than $2 million, and in the context we can predict that the safety standards will be even lower.*[3]

Few would argue that exposing workers to hazardous asbestos is the ethically correct policy. A company must sometimes refuse to adopt host-country standards even when there is no law requiring it. Yet it is all too possible to make exactly the opposite mistake. Some companies attempt to export all home-country values to the host country. Wanting to duplicate successful ethics and values programs, these companies "photocopy" home-country ethics initiatives. Photocopying values is a mistake because it is disrespectful of other cultures. It neglects the important role of moral free space.

To create and succeed with a clear, consistent overseas policy, any company must face up to home-/host-country conflicts in ethics. It must develop responses and craft relevant policies. It must anticipate that sometimes the policies it discovers in other countries will appear to fall below its own standards. The Gordian knot of international business ethics is formed around the vexing question, "How should a company behave when the standards followed in the host country are lower than those followed in the home country?"

This article will show ways in which Integrative Social Contracts Theory (ISCT)** can provide a practical guide for corporations operating globally. In particular, it will demonstrate how cutting the Gordian knot of international business ethics means utilizing two key aspects of ISCT: hypernorms and microsocial contracts. First, it is important to make use of hypernorms, especially the structural hypernorm of

*Hypernorms are principles so fundamental that, by definition, they serve to evaluate lower-order norms, reaching to the root of what is ethical for humanity. They represent norms by which all others are to be judged.

**ISCT (an approach developed by the authors in their book) is "pluralism," not "relativism." It allows for tolerance without amoralism by combining two previously unconnected traditions of social contract thinking—the hypothetical or "macro" contract and the extant or "micro" contract. Under ISCT, business communities cannot claim that their set of ethical norms is necessarily universal: they must exercise tolerance of some approaches from different communities.

necessary social efficiency.* Second, many problems dissolve when relevant microsocial contracts are carefully identified and the proper priority is established among them. In order to illustrate the application of these and other concepts in ISCT, we will look once again at the issue of corruption. As we will see here, ISCT is capable of unraveling such problems, and it has obvious application to many other problems in international business, including those of intellectual property, host government relations, sourcing, and environmental policy.

MAPPING INTERNATIONAL BUSINESS ETHICS: IS THERE EVIDENCE OF MICROSOCIAL CONTRACTS AND MORAL FREE SPACE?

No one denies that cultural differences abound in global business activities. That much is indisputable. The real question is whether these differences add up to different microsocial contracts with different authentic, legitimate norms being affirmed by different cultures: in other words, attitudes and behaviors operating in true moral free space. Might it be the case, instead, that in every instance of cultural difference, one side is invariably more "right" than the other is? If so, the task of an international manager turns out to be simply one of discovering what the "right" norms are, and acting accordingly. ISCT's notion of the microsocial contract provides a tool for interpreting the significance of ethical differences, a tool we will use here.

Kluckhorn,[4] Hofstede,[5] Turner and Trompenaars,[6] and many other management theorists have shown the importance of cultural differences to business—but the further issue of the ethical implications of many of these differences remains unexplored. For example, researchers have documented the importance of understanding the time sensitivity of the Swiss in contrast to the time laxity of South Americans, or the group orientation of the Japanese in contrast to the individualism of the Americans. Not understanding such differences, most business managers now recognize, can trigger missteps and financial losses. But the importance of understanding ethical differences among cultures is much less well understood; this is a puzzling oversight, since ethical differences often take a volatile, sensitive form.

On a positive note, a clearer picture of the significance of cultural differences has slowly been emerging in the last decade, and a few of these have shed light on implicit ethical differences. In one study,[7] for example, thousands of international managers around the world responded to the following question:

> *While you are talking and sharing a bottle of beer with a friend who was officially on duty as a safety inspector in the company you both work for, an accident occurs, injuring a shift worker. The national safety commission launches an investigation and you are asked for your evidence. There are other witnesses. What right has your friend to expect you to protect him?*

*The hypernorm of "necessary social efficiency," or "efficiency" hypernorm, speaks to the need for institutions and coexistent duties designed to enable people to achieve basic or "necessary" social goods. These are goods desired by all rational people, such as health, education, housing, food, clothing, and social justice.

The choices offered as answers to the question were these:

1. *A definite right?*
2. *Some right?*
3. *No right?*

Here the explicit ethical notion of a "right" and the implicit notion of the duties of friendship come into play. The results of the questionnaire were striking, with cultural patterns perspicuous. To cite only one set of comparisons, approximately 94 percent of U.S. managers and 91 percent of Austrian managers answered "3" (i.e., "no right") whereas only 53 percent of French and 59 percent of Singaporean managers did.

Surveys of international managers also show striking differences among cultural attitudes towards profit. When asked whether they affirmed the view that "the only real goal of a company is making profit," 40 percent of U.S. managers, 33 percent of British managers, and 35 percent of Austrian managers affirmed the proposition, in contrast to only 11 percent of Singaporean managers, and only 8 percent of Japanese managers selected.[8]

Or, consider studies that show striking differences among ethical attitudes toward everyday business problems. One study revealed that Hong Kong managers rank taking credit for another's work at the top of a list of unethical activities, and, in contrast to their Western counterparts, they consider it more unethical than bribery or the gaining of competitor information. The same study showed that among Hong Kong respondents, 82 percent indicated that additional government regulation would improve ethical conduct in business, whereas only 27 percent of U.S. respondents believed it would.[9]

Not only individual, but group ethical attitudes vary. This clearly holds for corporations; different corporations can have strikingly different cultures and sets of beliefs. ISCT implies that companies as well as cultures vary in microsocial contract norms. But what is it that stamps a company's culture as unique from the vantage point of ethics? Theorists have recently begun distinguishing global companies in terms of their distinctive styles of ethical approach. George Enderle, for example, has identified four types of approach, each of which is analogous to a posture taken historically by nation-states.[10] These are:

- Foreign Country Type
- Empire Type
- Interconnection Type
- Global Type

The first, or Foreign Country, type does not apply its own, home-country concepts to host countries abroad. Instead, as the Swiss have historically done in Nigeria, it conforms to local customs, assuming that what prevails as morality in the host climate is an adequate guide. The second, or Empire type, resembles Great Britain in India and elsewhere before 1947. This type of company applies domestic concepts and theories without making any serious modifications. Empire-type companies export their values in a wholesale fashion—and often do so regardless of the consequences. Next, the Interconnection type of company is analogous to states engaging in commercial relations in the European Union, or NAFTA. Such companies regard the international sphere as differing significantly from the domestic sphere, and one in which the interconnectedness of companies transcends national identities. In this model, the entire notion of national interest is blurred. Companies don't see themselves as projecting or defending a national identity.

Finally, the Global type abstracts from all regional differences. Just as the phenomenon of global warming exhibits the dominance of the international sphere over that of the domestic, so the Global type views the domestic sphere as irrelevant. From this vantage point the citizens of all nations, whether they are corporate or individual citizens, must become more cosmopolitan. The nation-state is vanishing, and in turn, only global citizenry makes sense.

It is helpful to analyze these basic types of corporate approaches from the standpoint of ISCT's two key concepts (i.e., moral free space and hypernorms). Each type may be seen to have strengths and weaknesses explainable through these concepts. What is ethically dangerous about the Foreign Country type is that nothing limits the moral free space of the host-country culture. If a given culture accepts government corruption and environmental degradation, then so much the worse for honest people and environmental integrity. From the vantage point of the Foreign Country type, no rules of thumb restrain granting an automatic preference to host-country norms—whatever they are.

Both the Global and the Empire types succeed in avoiding the vicious relativism that characterizes the Foreign Country type, but manage to fall prey to exactly the opposite problem. Since each type acts from a fixed blueprint of right and wrong, each suffocates the host country's moral free space and leaves no room for legitimate local norms. The Empire type displays a version of moral imperialism. It is bedazzled, as it were, by its own larger-than-life goodness. Just as the nations of Western Europe have so often in the past colonized others in a smug, self-righteous manner, so too a company adopting the Empire posture sees itself as the bearer of moral truth. The Global type, too, suffocates the host country's moral free space, but for a different reason. Instead of imposing its home morality on a host culture, it imposes its interpretation of a global morality on a host culture. Because only global citizenry makes sense, the company can be numb to the moral differences that mark a culture's distinctiveness. The opportunity for host cultures to define their moral and economic identity is lost; it is dissolved by the powerful solvent of global Truth, administered by the all-knowing multinational.

The Interactive type alone satisfies ISCT by acknowledging both universal moral limits and the ability of communities to set moral standards of their own. It balances better than the other types a need to retain local identity with the acknowledgment of values that transcend individual communities. Its drawbacks are practical rather than moral. As noted earlier, the entire notion of national interest is blurred in this model, an ambiguity that may make it difficult to integrate the interests of any nation-state in the corporation's deliberations. Even so, it manages to balance moral principles with moral free space in a way that makes it more convincing than its three counterparts.

As intriguing as the differences in global ethical attitudes in business are, they leave nagging questions in their wake. Granted, differences in global ethical attitudes abound, and granted also that it may be possible to map and identify those differences. As Enderle suggests, even global companies may be seen to vary along ethical dimensions, and these differences, too, can be mapped. So far so good. But does it follow that those differences entail the existence of moral free space? It did not turn out to be true, as noted earlier, that in every instance of cultural difference, one side is simply more "right" than the other is. If such an explanation were true, then the task of an international manager would be simply to discover what the "right" norms were, and to act accordingly. Moral free space, and in turn, the need for corporations to attend to subtle differences among cultures, would vanish.

Evidence does exist to confirm the existence of different, legitimate norms in domestic contexts. For example, in the area of employee drug testing, Strong and Ringer have shown that microsocial contracts differ among employee and non-employee populations, with non-employees affirming significantly different norms for privacy in such testing than employees, even when the views of both populations appear authentic and legitimate.[11]

New evidence suggests global ethical differences exist that are not only quite subtle, but that represent beliefs treated as both legitimate and authentic by ISCT. They are beliefs, in other words, residing in what we have called "moral free space." Bigoness and Blakely used measures drawn from Milton Rokeach's Value Scale to investigate cross-national differences in managerial values.[12] A total of 567 managers from twelve nations participated. Their data indicated that different values not only existed, but also converged neatly in most instances on a national basis. The Rokeach value matrix contains values such as "responsible," "honest," "clean," and "broad-minded," none of which are likely to be over-turned by hypernorms. And yet groups differed significantly by national type. For example, analysis by means of Duncan multiple range tests showed that Japanese managers assigned a significantly higher priority than did managers from other nations to the value dimension that included the characteristics "clean, obedient, polite, responsible, and self-controlled."[13] The three other available value groupings were:

- forgiving, helpful, loving, and cheerful;
- broad-minded, capable, and courageous; and
- imaginative, independent, and intellectual.

Swedish and Brazilian managers, for their part, assigned much higher significance than their global peers to the category of "broad-minded, capable, and courageous."

DIFFERING ADVICE FROM ACADEMICS

Having seen evidence that business ethics vary from country to country, and that at least some of these constitute authentic, legitimate norms, the obvious question for a multinational manager is "What should I do?" How does a manager navigate these moving, complex currents of international values?

Many business writers lack clear solutions and give sharply differing advice. Some seem hopelessly callous, and others idealistically impractical. At one extreme, Boddewyn and Brewer have defended the view that managers should consider the host-country government on a par with any other competitive factor.[14] The government is seen merely as another factor of production, or set of "agents" that international firms can use in the management of their chain of economic value-adding activities in cross-border activity.[15] For his own part, Boddewyn has even argued that when companies seek competitive advantages, bribery, smuggling, and buying absolute market monopolies are not necessarily ruled out.[16]

At the other extreme, DeGeorge has postulated 10 guidelines for multinational corporations.[17] The second of these 10 guidelines specifies that every company must "produce more good than harm for the host country." This claim seems innocent enough until one realizes that it entails information and decision-making requirements possessed by few if any large multinational corporations. How is a company to know with confidence that on balance it is doing more good than harm? This is an enormously challenging requirement involving an all-things-considered assessment of, for example, pollution effects, wage labor effects, hypothetical alternatives (what would have happened if the MNC had not done business in the country), host-country government effects, and so on. It would at a minimum require a separate moral "accounting" process. That DeGeorge means for the evaluation to be intentionally undertaken is obvious, for in explaining the guideline he remarks, "If an American chemical company builds a chemical plant in a less developed country, it must ensure that its plant brings more good than harm to the country."[18] While the requirement is reasonable as a general principle, it imposes accounting requirements that may divert corporate resources in an inefficient manner. It exists in stark contrast to Boddewyn's blunt, self-seeking prescriptions, and reflects well-wishing idealism.

THE ISCT GLOBAL VALUES MAP

In the face of such conflicting and confusing advice, the application of ISCT categories to global problems is helpful. The broadest categories for sorting authentic global norms through ISCT may be displayed in a diagram. (See Figure 1.)

FIGURE 1 Categories of Authentic Global Norms under ISCT

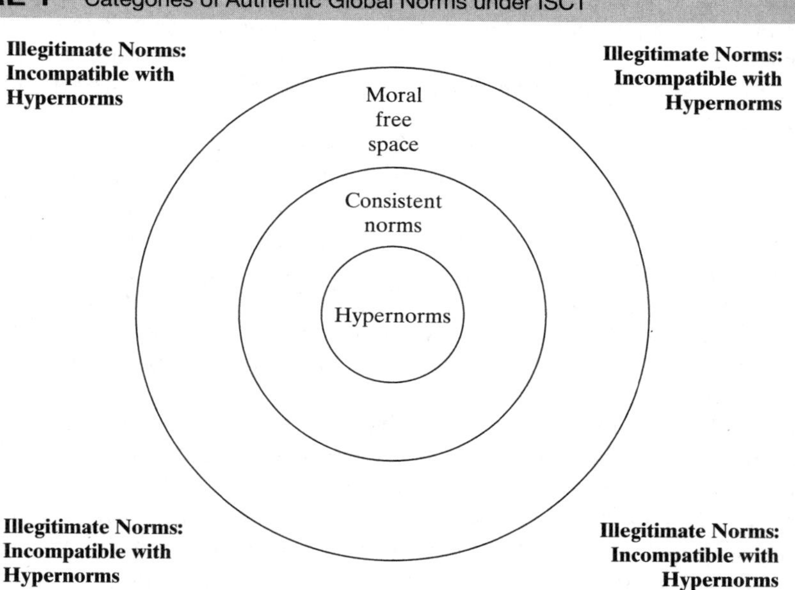

The concentric circles represent core norms held by particular corporations, industries, or economic cultures. Particular values of a corporation, as expressed through its actions and policies, may be plotted as points within the circles.

- ***Hypernorms.*** These include, for example, fundamental human rights or basic prescriptions common to most major religions. The values they represent are by definition acceptable to all cultures and all organizations.
- ***Consistent Norms.*** These values are more culturally specific than those at the center but are consistent both with hypernorms and other legitimate norms, including those of other economic cultures. Most corporations' ethical codes and vision-value statements would fall within this circle. Johnson & Johnson's famous "Credo" and AT&T's "Our Common Bond" are examples.
- ***Moral Free Space.*** As one moves away from the center of the circle to the circle signifying moral free space, one finds norms that are inconsistent with at least some other legitimate norms existing in other economic cultures. Such norms can be in mild tension with hypernorms, even as they are compatible with them. They often express unique, but strongly held, cultural beliefs.
- ***Illegitimate Norms.*** These are norms that are incompatible with hypernorms. When values or practices reach a point where they transgress permissible limits (as specified, say, by fundamental human rights), they fall outside the circle and into the "incompatible" zone. Exposing workers to unreasonable levels of carcinogens (asbestos), for example, is an expression of a value falling outside the circle.

NAVIGATING USING THE ISCT MAP: THE CASE OF BRIBERY AND SENSITIVE PAYMENTS

To gain an understanding of the implications of ISCT for international business, it helps to apply it to a single, concrete instance. Accordingly, we shall probe the issue of corruption—in particular, the question of bribery or "sensitive payments." Although a single example, it is one with ringing significance for contemporary global business. It is widely known that sensitive payments flourish in many parts of the globe. Once this illustrative application is complete, we will draw—later in the article—implications of ISCT for a much broader array of international cases.

Consider two typical instances of sensitive payments. First, there is the practice of low-level bribery of public officials in some developing nations. In some developing countries, for example, it is difficult for any company, foreign or national, to move goods through customs without paying low-level officials a few dollars. The payments are relatively small, uniformly assessed, and accepted as standard practice. But the salaries of such officials are sufficiently low that the officials require the additional income. One suspects the salary levels are set with the prevalence of bribery in mind.

Or consider a second kind of instance where a company is competing for a bid in a foreign country, and where in order to win the competition a payment must be made not to a government official, but to the employee of a private company. Nonetheless, it is clear that the employee, instead of passing on the money to the company, will pocket the payment. In a modified version of this scenario, the bribe may even appear one level deeper. For example, a company competing for a bid may be introduced to a "consultant" who offers to help to facilitate client contacts. (See the example that begins this article.)

It is not obvious where the norms and issues that arise from such cases should be situated on the ISCT map, if indeed they belong there at all. Are practices involving such payments examples of authentic norms, thus qualifying them to be located on the map? Are payments invariably direct violations of hypernorms and hence located outside the circles in the "illegitimate" arena? Or, instead, do some practices tolerating payments qualify as expressions of moral free space?

Ethical views about business vary around the globe. Bribery is no exception. Not only does the incidence of bribery vary, so does its perception as being unethical. In one study, for example, Greeks perceived the actions in some bribery scenarios as being less unethical than Americans.[19] In another, Hong Kong managers were shown to be somewhat less critical of bribery than their American counterparts.[20] Tsalikis showed that ethical reactions to bribery vary, with Nigerians perceiving some scenarios being less unethical than they seemed to Americans.[21]

From the vantage point of ISCT, then, are there ethical problems with bribery? The answer is *yes*, as the following list clarifies:

1. From the standpoint of the bribe recipient, the acceptance usually violates a microsocial contract specifying the duties of the agent (i.e., the bribe recipient, to the principal or the employing body, such as the government, a private company, etc.).

Perhaps the most obvious problem with bribery is that it typically involves the violation of a duty by the person accepting the bribe to the principal for whom he acts as an agent. Note that in both the illustrative cases above, the bribe recipient performs an action at odds with the policies established by his employer. In the case of the customs official, he accepts money for a service that he was supposed to provide anyway. In the case of the company competing for a bid, the employee pockets money in violation of company policy, and the company is shortchanged. In other words, if the money belongs to anyone, it belongs to the customer's company, not the individual employee. Such policies may or may not be written down. Often they are explicit, but even where they are not, they usually reflect well-understood, implicit agreements binding the employee as agent to the interests of his employer (the principal). In short, even when not formally specified, such duties flow from well-understood microsocial contracts existing within the relevant economic community.

But while this rationale shows one ethical problem with bribery, it is inconclusive. To begin with, it shows an ethical objection to accepting a bribe, but says nothing about offering a bribe. Has the person making the payment also committed an ethical error? Second, although violating a duty to an employer is one reason for considering an act unethical, it remains uncertain whether this reason could not be overridden by other, more pressing reasons. Perhaps other microsocial contracts in the culture firmly endorse the ethical correctness of bribe giving and bribe taking. Perhaps these microsocial contracts, along with an employee's legitimate interest in supporting his family, etc., override the prima facie obligation of the employee to follow the policies of his employer. It makes sense to explore the further implications of ISCT.

2. Bribery is typically not an authentic norm.

The mythology is that bribery is accepted wherever it flourishes. This image is badly distorted. Despite the data mentioned earlier that shows variance in the degree to which various people regard bribery as unethical in comparison with other unethical activity, there is a surprising amount of fundamental agreement that bribery is unethical.

All countries have laws against the practice. This is a striking fact often overlooked by individuals who have something to gain by the practice. "There is not a country in the world," writes Fritz Heimann, "where bribery is either legally or morally acceptable." That bribes have to be paid secretly everywhere, and that officials have to resign in disgrace if the bribe is disclosed, makes it clear that bribery violates the moral standards of the South and the East, just as it does in the West.[22]

Some countries, even ones where the practice has flourished, not only outlaw it, but prescribe draconian penalties. "In Malaysia, which is significantly influenced by the Moslem prescriptions against bribery, execution of executives for the offense of bribery is legal."[23] In China in 1994, the President of the Great Wall Machinery and Electronics High-Technology Industrial Group Corp., Mr. Shen Haifu, was executed by a bullet to the back of his neck for bribery and embezzlement offenses.

Many broad efforts are currently being made against bribery. The OECD is among the leading organizations mounting such efforts, in part due to U.S. pressure resulting from a provision in the amendment of the Foreign Corrupt Practices Act, which requires the President to take steps to bring about a level playing field of global competition. At a symposium held in Paris, France, in March 1994, the OECD launched a campaign aimed at reducing the incidence of bribery in trade transactions, especially in international contracts.[24] And in 1996 an OECD committee, with support from an international non-governmental organization (NGO) dedicated to eradicating bribery, Transparency International, passed a resolution requiring that all member countries pass laws prohibiting the tax-deductibility of bribery in foreign transactions undertaken by their domestic firms. The outcome of this last effort is unclear at the time of this writing; but the OECD is clearly ramping up its battle against bribery. Reflecting this same spirit, some academics have suggested the implementation of a worldwide code against bribery and the use of ethical impact statements by corporations.[25] Many leading accounting firms, among them KPMG, and Coopers & Lybrand, now offer services that enhance the ability of internal auditing functions to control the payment of bribes.

When one of the authors of this article (Donaldson) interviewed CEOs in India in 1993, he discovered that they were willing to acknowledge that their companies constantly engaged in bribery and payoffs. (They justify their actions on grounds of extortion—the practice began with the Indian government, and they were forced to bribe.) More surprising, however, was their disgust for the practice. They had no illusions about the propriety of bribery and were aware that its most pernicious aspect was its effect on efficiency. Under ISCT this implies that even among a community of bribe payers, bribery cannot necessarily be established as an authentic norm.

Philip Nichols cites specific references from each of the world's major religions condemning bribery. "Corruption is condemned and proscribed," he writes, "by each of the major religious and moral schools of thought. Buddhism, Christianity, Confucianism, Hinduism, Islam, Judaism, Sikhism, and Taoism each proscribe corruption. Adam Smith and David Ricardo condemned corruption, as did Karl Marx and Mao Tse Tung."[26]

In short, in many if not most instances, the necessary condition imposed by ISCT that the norm be authentic (i.e., that it is both acted upon and believed to be ethically correct by a substantial majority of the members of a community) cannot be met. To the extent that this is true, most instances of bribery would fail the ISCT test.

3. Bribery may violate the hypernorm supporting political participation as well as the efficiency hypernorm.

Even this last consideration, however, leaves a nagging doubt behind. In particular, is bribery only wrong because most people dislike it? Is there nothing more fundamentally wrong with bribery? Suppose, hypothetically, that the world came to change its mind about bribery over the next 30 years. Suppose that in some future state, a majority of people finds bribery morally acceptable. If so, would bribery be ethically correct? In such a world, would reformers who spoke out against bribery be speaking illogical nonsense?

The answer to this question turns on the further question of whether a hypernorm disallowing bribery exists. For if such a hypernorm existed, then no legitimate microsocial norm could support bribery, and, in turn, it would deserve moral condemnation even in a world whose majority opinion endorsed it.

At least two hypernorms may be invoked in seeking a more fundamental condemnation of bribery. The first is rather obvious. To the extent that one places a positive, transnational value on the right to political participation, large bribes of publicly elected officials damage that value. For example, when Prime Minister Tanaka of Japan bought planes from the American aircraft manufacturer Lockheed in the 1970s, after accepting tens of millions of dollars in bribes, people questioned whether he was discharging his duties as a public official correctly. In addition to the fact that his actions violated the law, the Japanese citizenry was justified in wondering whether their interests, or Tanaka's personal political interest, drove the decision. Implicit in much of the political philosophy written in the Western world in the last 300 years—in the writings of Rousseau, Mill, Locke, Jefferson, Kant, and Rawls—is the notion that some transcultural norm supports a public claim for the citizenry of a nation-state to participate in some way in the direction of political affairs. Many have discussed and articulated the implications of this right in current contexts.[27] If such a right exists, then it entails obligations on the part of politicians and prospective bribe givers to not violate it. In turn, large-scale bribery of high government officials of the sort that the Lockheed Corporation engaged in during the 1970s would be enjoined through the application of a hypernorm. It would thus be wrong regardless of whether a majority of the members of an economic community, or even the majority of the world's citizens, endorsed it.

This, then, is the first hypernorm that may affect an ISCT interpretation of bribery. But notice that it, too, leaves nagging questions unanswered. Suppose it is true that large-scale payoffs to public officials in democratic or quasi-democratic countries are proscribed by considerations of people's right to political participation. In such countries, bribery may defeat meaningful political rights. But many countries in which bribery is prevalent are not democratic. Bribery in countries such as Zaire, Nigeria, and China may not have a noticeable effect on political participation by ordinary citizens, since that participation is directly repressed by authoritarian governments.

Many other troubling questions may be raised. What about much smaller payoffs to public officials? And what about bribes not to public officials, but to employees of corporations? It seems difficult to argue that small, uniformly structured bribes to customs officials, or that bribes to purchasing agents of companies in host countries, seriously undermine people's right to political participation. These questions prompt the search for yet another hypernorm relevant to the issue of bribery.

The second hypernorm that appears relevant to the present context is the efficiency hypernorm, which requires that economic agents efficiently utilize resources in which their society has a stake. This hypernorm arises because all societies have an interest in husbanding public resources, developing strategies to promote aggregate economic welfare (Efficiency Strategies), and, in turn, developing economizing parameters to do so. Indeed, nations and NGOs that oppose bribery most commonly couch their opposition in terms of the damage bribery does to the economic efficiency of the nation-state.

Is bribery inefficient? It certainly appears to be. As the economist Kenneth Arrow noted years ago, "a great deal of economic life depends for its viability on a certain limited degree of ethical commitment."[28] To the extent that market participants bribe, they interfere with the market mechanism's rational allocation of resources, and their actions impose significant social costs. When people buy or sell on the basis of price and quality, with reasonable knowledge about all relevant factors, the market allocates resources efficiently. The best products relative to price, and, in turn, the best production mechanisms, are encouraged to develop. But when people buy or sell not on the basis of price and quality, but on the basis of how much money goes into their own pockets, the entire market mechanism is distorted. By misallocating resources, bribery damages economic efficiency. As economists Bliss and Di Tella note, "Corrupt agents exact money from firms."[29] Corruption affects, they observe, the number of firms in a free-entry equilibrium, and in turn increases costs relative to profits. In contrast, "the degree of deep competition in the economy increases with lower overhead costs relative to profits; and with a tendency towards similar cost structures."[30] Corruption can even be shown to take a toll on social efforts to improve economic welfare, including industrial policy initiatives,[31] and on predictability in economic arrangements.

A striking example of the effect of corruption on predictability occurred recently in Brazil. When a large U.S. company's crates were unloaded on the docks of Rio de Janeiro, handlers regularly pilfered them. The handlers would take about 10 percent of the contents of the crates. Not only did the company lose this portion of the contents, it also never knew which 10 percent would be taken. Finally, in desperation, the company began sending two crates for every one sent in the past. The first crate contained 90 percent of the merchandise normally sent; the second contained 10 percent. The handlers learned to take the second crate and to leave the first untouched. The company viewed this as an improvement. It still suffered a 10 percent loss—but it now knew which 10 percent it would lose![32]

Interviews with Indian CEOs in 1993 revealed that they were well aware that inefficiency metastasizes as decisions are made not on the basis of price and quality, but on the basis of how much money people are getting under the table. This they acknowledged as their principal reason for concern about the widespread phenomenon of Indian bribery. Again, the market is a remarkably efficient tool for allocating resources, but it only works if people buy based on price and quality—not clandestine payoffs. A trip to the streets of Calcutta in 1993 would have brought home the bitter fruits of corruption. The Indian economy in 1993 was one so inefficient that even dramatic redistribution of wealth would leave most of its inhabitants in dire poverty. The poverty is so stark that social activists have given up their attempt to enforce child labor laws and have turned instead to advocating better working conditions for children—better conditions, for example, for eight-year-old children in match factories. Most of the Indian executives interviewed believed that a great deal of India's economic inefficiency was driven by the presence of massive corruption.

NGOs and government bodies usually cite the negative impact of bribery on efficiency as their principal rationale for attempting to eliminate it. From 1993 to 1997, the OECD targeted bribery as one of its key concerns. Its rationale has focused almost exclusively on the way corrupt practices hamper development of international trade by "distorting competition, raising the cost of transactions and restricting the operation of free markets."[33]

As David Vogel notes, the conviction that bribery harms efficiency is especially pronounced in the United States, the only country to pass a comprehensive act against bribery that prohibits bribes to officials of non-U.S. countries (i.e., the Foreign Corrupt Practices Act). He writes, "The U.S. view that not only bribery but other forms of corruption are regarded as inefficient . . . [helps] account for the fact that during the 15-year period from 1977 to 1992, the United States fined or imprisoned more corporate officers and prominent businessmen than all other capitalist countries combined."[34]

The rejection of bribery through ISCT using an appeal to hypernorms, refutes the claim often heard that bribery is inevitably the product of primitive, non-universalistic perspectives. For example, the philosopher David Fisher once commented:

> *Bribery, as a practice, belongs to a pre-modern world in which inequality of persons is assumed, and in which moral obligation is based on (1) birth into gender and class, (2) birth order, and (3) personal relationships that define duties. The theoretical perspectives of modern ethics, such as those of Kant or Mill, have little to offer those who inhabit such worlds, because they construe moral identity in ways that deny the universalism implied by all forms of modern ethics.*[35]

This seems wrong-headed. Developing countries possess at least as many universalistic conceptions as developed ones. To think otherwise is to indulge in the kind of moral imperialism that brought well-educated scientists in the nineteenth century to regard all primitive people as "savages." Recent studies of the moral development of people in Belize, for example, found that they scored higher on Kohlberg-style moral development tests than did people in the United States. A comparative field study evaluated the moral reasoning used by U.S. and Belize business students in resolving business-related moral dilemmas. The Belize business students, inhabitants of a less-developed country, though with a Western heritage, resolved the dilemmas using higher stages of moral judgment than did the U.S. business students.[36]

Nonetheless, at the level most individual managers confront it, bribery has no satisfactory solution. Refusing to bribe is very often tantamount to losing business. Often sales and profits are lost to more unscrupulous companies, with the consequence that both the ethical company and the ethical individual are penalized. (Of course, companies help employees caught in the bribery trap by having clear policies and giving support to employees who follow them.) The answer, then, lies not at the level where individuals face bribery, but at the level of the host country's background institutions. A solution involves a broadly based combination of business pressure, legal enforcement, and political will. Companies, in turn, should make a point not only of speaking out against bribery, but of doing so in cooperation with other companies.

PRACTICAL IMPLICATIONS OF ISCT FOR GLOBAL COMPANIES

The principles of moral free space and adherence to hypernorms imply a balanced approach for companies attempting to navigate global international waters. The presence of hypernorms means that companies must never simply adopt a "do in Rome as the Romans do" philosophy. They must be alert to the transcultural value implications of their actions. Moral free space, in turn, implies the need to precede judgment with an attempt to understand.

HYPERNORMS

Hypernorms are more than abstractions. The research over the last 15 years shows that in business ethics we're more alike than we think. Practically speaking, hypernorms mean that sometimes there is no compromising in business ethics. In 1992 Levi-Strauss cited its "Business Partners Terms of Engagement" when it broke off business with the Tan family in the Mariana Islands, a U.S. territory. The Tan family reportedly "held 1,200 Chinese and Philippine women in guarded compounds, working them 74 hours a week."[37] Strauss's "Business Partners Terms of Engagement" deals with the selection of contractors and requires practices compatible with the company's values on issues such as working hours, child labor, prison labor, discrimination, and disciplinary practices. Yet hypernorms should be applied carefully in the international arena and without rigidity. Even when it comes to ethics, facts make a difference. Consider the issue of price gouging in controlled economies. Price gouging is more unethical in a closed market than an open one because free markets automatically restrain arbitrary pricing (if one seller gouges, then another will grab his customers). In a controlled market, however, sellers can exploit customers by manipulating prices. When polled, Soviet Enterprise Executives in the former Soviet Union once ranked price gouging as the worst ethical problem they confronted in business.[38] This is not because the Soviet executives were confused; rather, it was because the rules of the Soviet game were different. When the rules of the game are different, so are the ethics of playing it.

Complying with hypernorms often demands considerable managerial creativity. Consider another situation confronted by Levi-Strauss, this time involving the hypernorms connected with child labor. The company discovered in the early 1990s that two of its suppliers in Bangladesh were employing children under the age of 14—a practice that violated the company's principles but was tolerated in Bangladesh. Forcing the suppliers to fire the children would not have insured that the children received an education, and it would have caused serious hardship for the families depending on the children's wages. In a creative arrangement, the suppliers agreed to pay the children's regular wages while they attended school and to offer each child a job at age 14. Levi-Strauss, in turn, agreed to pay the children's tuition and provide books and uniforms. This approach allowed Levi-Strauss to uphold its principles and provide long-term benefits to its host country.[39]

MORAL FREE SPACE

Despite the importance of hypernorms, it is well to remember that ISCT implies the need for moral free space in global transactions. Here too, managerial creativity is often required. The most tempting and popular answer available for global companies is the "photocopy approach." Its simple advice is, "Do the same thing abroad you do at home." Falling into this trap, CEOs are often heard boasting that their companies act the same way ethically around the globe. Such claims are well-meaning, but eventually subvert the very ethics they intend to support. Saying "we pride ourselves on doing the same thing around the globe" is a bit like saying "I pride myself on saying the same thing to every one of my friends." Friends are different; cultures are different. And the demonstration of a company's ethics must be different as it recognizes cultural differences abroad.

Being true to one's own ethics often means not only sticking by one's own sense of right and wrong, but respecting the right of other cultures to shape their own cultural and economic values. Forgetting this can be a disaster. Consider the mess one well-intentioned effort created. In 1993, a large U.S. computer-products company insisted on using exactly the same sexual harassment exercises and lessons with Muslim managers halfway around the globe that it used with American employees in California. It did so in the name of "ethical consistency." The result was ludicrous. The managers were baffled by the instructors' presentation, and the instructors were oblivious of the intricate connections between Muslim religion and sexual manners.

The U.S. trainers needed to know that Muslim ethics are especially strict about male–female social interaction. By explaining sexual harassment in the same way to Muslims as to Westerners, the trainers offended the Muslim managers. To the Muslim managers, their remarks seemed odd and disrespectful. In turn, the underlying ethical message about avoiding coercion and sexual discrimination was lost. Clearly, sexual discrimination does occur in Muslim countries. But helping to eliminate it there means respecting—and understanding—Muslim differences.

Such cultural conflicts suggest that we should revise a common litmus test for ethics, the one that asks, "How would you react if your action were described on the front page of the *Wall Street Journal*?" Instead we should sometimes ask the additional question: "How would you react if your action were described on the front page of Bangkok's *Daily News*, Rome's *Corriere Della Sera*, or the *Buenos Aires Herald*?" For example, in Africa, a businessperson may be invited to a family banquet following business dealings—and in order to attend he is expected to pay. This invitation is likely not to be a bribe, but a genuine sign of friendship and a commitment to good-faith business dealings in the future.

Companies in India sometimes promise employees a job for one of their children when the child reaches the age of majority. Yet while such a policy may be in tension with Western notions of egalitarianism and anti-nepotism, it is clearly more in step with India's traditional values of clan and extended family. The ISCT framework we propose acknowledges that the Indian company's policy is in tension with the norms of other economic communities around the globe (hence placing it in the "moral free space" ring of the ISCT circle) while stopping short of declaring it ethically impermissible (a conclusion that would place it outside the circle). This third ring of the circle of the ISCT framework depicts an inevitable tension in values that any global manager must confront, and accept.

In short, ISCT suggests that international business ethics seldom come in black and white. On the one hand, managers must respect moral free space and cultural diversity. On the other, they must reject any form of relativism. Common humanity and market efficiency are part of the equation, but so too is a certain amount of moral tension. The lesson? Any manager unprepared to live with moral tension abroad should pack her bags and come home. Because ISCT is designed to help managers navigate the gray zones between ethical worlds, it pictures reality in more than black and white.

Endnotes

1. S. Puffer and D. J. McCarthy, "Finding the Common Ground in Russian and American Business Ethics," *California Management Review*, 37/2 (Winter 1995): 29–46.
2. Anonymous case study.
3. M. J. Satchell, "Deadly Trade in Toxics," *U.S. News and World Report*, March 7, 1994: 64.
4. C. Kluckhohn, "Ethical Relativity: Sic et Non," *Journal of Philosophy 52* (1955): 663–677.
5. G. Hofstede, *Culture's Consequences* (Beverly Hills, CA: Sage, 1980).
6. C. H. Turner and F. Trompenaars, *The Seven Cultures of Capitalism* (New York, NY: Doubleday, 1993).
7. Ibid.
8. Ibid.
9. G. M. MacDonald, "Ethical Perceptions of Hong Kong/Chinese Business Managers," *Journal of Business Ethics 7* (1988): 835–845.
10. G. Enderle, "What Is International? A Topology of International Spheres and Its Relevance for Business Ethics" Paper presented at the annual meeting of the International Association of Business and Society, Vienna, Austria, 1995.
11. K. C. Strong and R. C. Ringer, "An Empirical Test of Integrative Social Contracts Theory: Social Hypernorms and Authentic Community Norms in Corporate Drug Testing Programs" Proceedings of the International Association for Business and Society Annual Meeting, 1997.
12. W. J. Bigoness and G. L. Blakely, "A Cross-National Study of Managerial Values," *Journal of International Business Studies*, 27/4 (1996): 739–752.
13. Ibid., 747.
14. J. J. Boddewyn and T. L. Brewer, "International Business Political Behavior: New Theoretical Directions," *Academy of Management Review*, 19/1 (1994): 119–143.
15. Ibid., 126
16. J. J. Boddewyn, "International Political Strategy: A Fourth 'Generic' Strategy" Paper presented at the Annual Meeting of the American Academy of Management and at the Annual Meeting of the International Academy of Business, 1986.
17. R. T. DeGeorge, *Competing with Integrity in International Business* (Oxford: Oxford University Press, 1993).
18. Ibid.
19. J. Tsalikis and M. S. LaTour, "Bribery and Extortion in International Business: Ethical Perceptions of Greeks Compared to Americans," *Journal of Business Ethics 4* (1995): 249–265.
20. MacDonald, op. cit.
21. J. Tsalikis and O. Wachukwu, "A Comparison of Nigerian to American Views of Bribery and Extortion in International Commerce," *Journal of Business Ethics*, 10/2 (1991): 85–98.
22. F. F. Heimann, 1994. "Should Foreign Bribery Be a Crime?" cited in P. M. Nichols, "Outlawing Transnational Bribery through the World Trade Organization," *Law and Policy in International Business*, 28/2 (1997): 305–386, footnote 73.

23. S. J. Carroll and M. J. Gannon, *Ethical Dimensions of International Management* (Thousand Oaks, CA: Sage, 1997).
24. C. Yannaca-Small, "Battling International Bribery: The Globalization of the Economy," *OECD Observer* (1995): 16–18.
25. G. R. Laczniak, "International Marketing Ethics," *Bridges* (1990), 155–177.
26. P. M. Nichols, "Outlawing Transnational Bribery through the World Trade Organization," *Law and Policy in International Business*, 28/2 (1997): 321–322.
27. See, for example, H. Shue, *Basic Rights: Subsistence, Affluence, and U.S. Foreign Policy* (Princeton, NJ: Princeton University Press, 1980); T. Donaldson, *The Ethics of International Business* (New York, NY: Oxford University Press, 1989); *Universal Declaration of Human Rights*, 1948, reprinted in T. Donaldson and P. Werhane, eds., *Ethical Issues in Business* (Upper Saddle River, NJ: Prentice Hall, 1979), 252–255.
28. K. J. Arrow, "Social Responsibility and Economic Efficiency," *Public Policy*, 3/21 (1973): 300–317.
29. C. Bliss and R. Di Tella, "Does Competition Kill Corruption?" paper presented at the University of Pennsylvania, Philadelphia, 1997.
30. Ibid., 1.
31. A. Ades and A. Di Tella, "National Champions and Corruption: Some Unpleasant Interventionist Arithmetic," paper presented at the University of Pennsylvania, Philadelphia, 1997.
32. T. Donaldson, "Values in Tension: Ethics Away from Home," *Harvard Business Review*, 74/5 (1996): 48–56.
33. Yannaca-Small, op. cit.
34. D. Vogel, "The Globalization of Business Ethics: Why America Remains Distinctive," *California Management Review*, 35/1 (Fall 1992): 30–49.
35. D. Fisher, "A Comment on Bribery," e-mail communication, in LABS Listserver, April 16, 1996.
36. D. Worrell, B. Walters, and T. Coalter, "Moral Judgment and Values in a Developed and a Developing Nation: A Comparative Analysis," *Academy of Management Best Paper Proceedings*, 1995: 401–405.
37. Franklin Research and Development Corporation, "Human Rights: Investing for a Better World," Boston, MA, 1992.
38. J. M. Ivancevich, R. S. DeFrank, and P. R. Gregory "The Soviet Enterprise Director: An Important Resource Before and After the Coup," *Academy of Management Executive*, 6/1 (1992): 42–55.
39. J. Kline, "Corporate Social Responsibility and Transnational Corporations," *World Investment Report 1994: Transnational Corporations, Employment and the Workplace* (New York and Geneva: United Nations, 1994): 313–324.

CHAPTER 7
PERSONAL GROWTH AND WORK STRESS

ON THE REALIZATION OF HUMAN POTENTIAL: A PATH WITH A HEART

Herbert A. Shepard

THE BALANCING ACT—AT WORK AND AT HOME

Jonathan D. Quick
Amy B. Henley
James Campbell Quick

Given the job insecurity engendered by downsizing, restructuring, and mergers and acquisitions, employees are taking on more responsibility for managing their own careers. The burden lies on employees to continuously learn skills that are in demand to maintain their employability. Nevertheless, companies that want to develop and retain a workforce capable of implementing their strategic goals are well aware that training and career development are crucial issues. Both employees and employers, therefore, can profit from educating themselves on career issues and developing career management skills.

Career development begins with self-awareness, which facilitates the all-important fit between the job and the person. Herb Shepard, one of the earliest writers and practitioners of organization behavior and development, wrote a classic essay entitled, "On the Realization of Human Potential: A Path with a Heart." Shepard criticizes the societal institutions that prevent people from seeking their own road to fulfillment, a phenomenon that still occurs. We've included this article to encourage you to consider whether your own path is the right one for you.

Stress is an unavoidable topic when we look at current career issues. In our second article, physician Jonathan Quick, doctoral student Amy Henley, and professor James Campbell Quick take a compelling look at how work demands—including stress—can negatively impact employees' family life and nonwork activities. They argue that effectively balancing the mutual demands of both work and non-work roles is an essential component of managing today's workforce. They examine the sources of work–family conflict, including work demands, home demands, and self-imposed demands. They conclude with a discussion of effective balancing strategies that can be productively implemented by both employees and employers so that both work and nonwork roles can be successfully fulfilled.

ON THE REALIZATION OF HUMAN POTENTIAL: A PATH WITH A HEART*

Herbert A. Shepard

A VISION UNFULFILLED

The central issue is a life fully worth living. The test is how you feel each day as you anticipate that day's experience. The same test is the best predictor of health and longevity. It is simple.

If it's simple, why doesn't everyone know it? The answer to that question is simple, too. We have been brought up to live by rules that mostly have nothing to do with making our lives worth living; some of them in fact are guaranteed not to. Many of our institutions and traditions introduce cultural distortions into our vision, provide us with beliefs and definitions that don't work, distract us from the task of building lives that are fully worth living, and persuade us that other things are more important.

The human infant is a life-loving bundle of energy with a marvelous array of potentialities, and many vulnerabilities. It is readily molded. If it is given a supportive environment, it will flourish and continue to love its own life and the lives of others. It will grow to express its own gifts and uniqueness, and to find joy in the opportunity for doing so. It will extend these talents to the world and feel gratified from the genuine appreciation of others. In turn, it will appreciate the talents of others and encourage them, too, to realize their own potential and to express their separate uniqueness.

But if a child is starved of a supportive environment, it will spend the rest of its life trying to compensate for that starvation. It becomes hungry for what it has been denied, and compulsively seeks to satisfy perceived deficiencies. In turn, these perceived deficiencies become the basis for measuring and relating to others. As Maslow pointed out, such deficiency motivation does not end with childhood (Maslow, 1962; Maslow and Chang, 1969). Rather, the struggle makes a person continually dependent on and controllable by any source that promises to remove the deficiencies.

DEFICIENCY MOTIVATION IN OPERATION

Frequently we refer to deficiency motivation in terms of needs: needs for approval, recognition, power, control, status; needs to prove one's masculinity, or smartness, or successfulness in other's eyes—and in one's own eyes, which have been programmed to see the world in terms of one's deficiencies. An emphasis on such needs can lead to a denial of individual uniqueness and may make us vulnerable to exploitation. In either case, the outcome for the individual can be devastating, and the rich promise of human potential remains unfulfilled.

---

*Reprinted with the author's permission from *Working with Careers* by Michael B. Arthur, Lotte Bailyn, Daniel J. Levinson, and Herbert A. Shepard. Columbia University School of Business, 1984: 25–46.

Denial of Uniqueness

The way this process takes place can be illustrated by a fable, "The School for Animals":

> *Once upon a time the animals got together and decided to found a school. There would be a core curriculum of six subjects: swimming, crawling, running, jumping, climbing and flying. At first the duck was the best swimmer, but it wore out the webs of its feet in running class, and then couldn't swim as well as before. And at first the dog was the best runner, but it crash landed twice in flying class and injured a leg. The rabbit started out as the best jumper, but it fell in climbing class and hurt its back. At the end of the school year, the class valedictorian was an eel, who could do a little bit of everything, but nothing very well.*[1]

The school for animals, of course, is much like our schools for people. And the notion of a common, unindividualized curriculum has permeated the whole fabric of our society, bringing with it associated judgments about our worth as human beings. It is all too easy for uniqueness to go unrecognized, and to spend a lifetime trying to become an eel.

Exploitation of Uniqueness

A second, perhaps subtler way that deficiency motivation can operate is illustrated by the story of the cormorant. Dr. Ralph Siu, when asked what wisdom the ancient oriental philosophers could contribute to modern men in modern organizations on how to preserve their mental health, developed a list of "advices." One of them was as follows:

> *Observe the cormorant in the fishing fleet. You know how cormorants are used for fishing. The technique involves a man in a rowboat with about half a dozen or so cormorants, each with a ring around the neck. As the bird spots a fish, it will dive into the water and unerringly come up with it. Because of the ring, the larger fish are not swallowed but held in the throat. The fisherman picks up the bird and squeezes out the fish through the mouth. The bird then dives for another, and the cycle repeats itself.*
>
> *Observe the cormorant. . . . Why is it that of all the different vertebrates the cormorant has been chosen to slave away day and night for the fisherman? Were the bird not greedy for fish, or not efficient in catching it, or not readily trained, would society have created an industry to exploit the bird? Would the ingenious device of a ring around its neck, and the simple procedure of squeezing the bird's neck to force it to regurgitate the fish have been devised? Of course not. (Siu, 1971)*

The neo-Taoist alerts us to how the cormorant's uniqueness is exploited by the fisherman for his own selfish use. Similarly, human motives can get directed to making others prosper, but not always in a way that benefits the person providing the talent. Human life can too easily parallel that of the captive cormorant.

INSTITUTIONS AND DEFICIENCY MOTIVATION

Let us stay with Dr. Siu's cormorant story a little longer. His advice continues:

> *Greed, talent, and capacity for learning, then, are the basis of exploitation. The more you are able to moderate and/or hide them from society, the greater*

will be your chances of escaping the fate of the cormorant. . . . It is necessary to remember that the institutions of society are geared to making society prosper, not necessarily to minimize suffering on your part. It is for this reason, among others, that the schools tend to drum into your mind the high desirability of those characteristics that tend to make society prosper—namely, ambition, progress, and success. These in turn are valued in terms of society's objectives. All of them gradually but surely increase your greed and make a cormorant out of you (Siu, 1971).

The further point here is even more far-reaching: that the institutions and organizations in which we spend our lives collude with one another in causing denials, deflections, or distortions of human potential. In particular, three sets of institutions—parents, schools, and organizations—demand consideration.

Parents

First, parents, sincerely concerned for their children's ability to survive in the world, unwittingly ignore their individuality and measure their offspring's progress by a simple set of common standards. What parents are not delighted to be able to say that their children are ambitious, talented, and have a great capacity for learning? It is something to boast about, rather than something to hide. Outside confirmation of achievement earns love and recognition, its absence draws disapproval. Any evidence of "A" student behavior is immediately rewarded. Lesser performance calls for added effort so that deficiencies can be corrected. Much of this parental energy is targeted toward helping children qualify for an occupational future that will in no way reflect their true interests and abilities. The expression or suppression of talent is externally defined, and parents stand as the most immediate custodians of society's standards and its dogma.

Schools

In our schools, the ideal is the "Straight A" student. It is this student who is most sought after, either at the next stage of institutional learning, or by employers from the world of work. What "Straight A" means is that the student has learned to do a number of things at a marketable level of performance, regardless of whether the student has any interest in or innate talent for the activity, and regardless of whether it brings pain, joy, or boredom. The reward is in the grade, not the activity. On the one hand, schools collaborate with parents to reinforce this concern over grades as ends in themselves. On the other, as Dr. Siu points out, the school's objectives are to serve the needs of society, not necessarily those of the student. Once more, a person's uniqueness is not valued for its own sake. Schools are selective about the talents they identify, and represent outside interests in the talents that they choose to develop.

Organizations

Lastly, in organizations, the continued external denial or manipulation of talent has its direct career consequences. Organizations have implicit ways of teaching about careers, regardless of whether they have explicit career planning and development programs. Reward systems are geared to common deficiencies—needs for status, approval, power—and a career consists of doing the right things to move up the ladder. A vice president of one company counselled his subordinates: "The work day is for doing your job; your overtime is for your promotion."

In many companies the message about careers is very clear: not only is your career more important than the rest of your life, it is more important than your life. In one large corporation, great emphasis was placed on moving young professionals and managers through many company functions as their preparation for general management responsibility. The career plan was well understood: "When you're rotated, don't ask if it's up, down or sideways; the time to worry is when you stop rotating." In such companies, successful careers are based on working hard at any job you are given whether you like it or not, and on conforming to the organization's unwritten rules and to the expectations of your superiors in such matters as office manners, dress, presentation style, language, and prejudices.

Do these paths have "heart"? Do they provide for the expression of human potential and facilitate individual growth? For some, as much through good luck as good management, they do. But perhaps a greater number ultimately lose their way, and get labeled as suffering from "burnout" or "retiring on the job."

In one company that recruits only top graduates, devotes a great deal of managerial time to tracking their performance, and moves each one along at what is judged to be an appropriate pace into jobs that are judged to be suited to his or her talents and potentials, the amount of burnout observed in mid-career management ranks became a matter of concern. As a result, the company offered career planning workshops to mid-career managers, the main objective of which was, according to one executive: ". . . to revitalize them by reminding them that in an ultimate sense each of them is in business for themself!"

For deficiency-motivated people, moving up the hierarchy of management is likely to be such a compelling need that they may desert careers that did have some heart for them. In an informal survey of industrial research scientists conducted by the author some years ago, it was possible to identify the ones for whom their career path had a heart, by their response to the question: "What is your main goal over the next two or three years?" Some responded in such terms as, "Some equipment I've tried to get for three years has finally made it into this year's budget. With it, I can pursue some very promising leads." Others responded in such terms as, "I hope to become a department head." But the second group seemed to have lost its zest. Many of them enjoyed their work and had no real desire to leave it in order to direct the work of others. They were just singing the preferred organizational song.

Don Juan, in teaching Carlos Casteneda about careers, asserted that to have a path of knowledge, a path with a *heart*, made for a joyful journey and was the only conceivable way to live. But he emphasized the importance of thinking carefully about our paths before we set out on them. For by the time people discover that their path "has no heart," the path is ready to kill them. At that point, he cautions, very few people stop to deliberate, and leave that path (Castaneda, 1968).[2] For example, in a life/career planning workshop for the staff of a mid-west military research laboratory, a 29-year-old engineer confessed that he was bored to death with the laboratory work, but his eyes lit up at the prospect of teaching physical education and coaching athletic teams at the high school level. He emerged with a career plan to do just that, and to do it in his favorite part of the country, northern New England. He resolved to do it immediately upon retirement from his civil service job as an engineer, at age 65—a mere 36 years away!

Thus, all these institutions—parents, schools, and organizations—are suspect when they attempt to give career guidance. Suspect if, like the school for animals, they discourage uniqueness and enforce conformity. Suspect if, like the fisherman with his cormorant, they harness talent only to serve their vested interests. Suspect if they address only the development of a career, so that the rest of life becomes an unanticipated consequence of the career choice. Suspect if they stress only the how-to's of a career and not its meaning in your life. And suspect, too, if they describe a career as a way to make a living, and fail to point out that the wrong career choice may be fatal. In sum, suspect because they are not concerned with whether a life is fully worth living.

A FRAMEWORK FOR UNDERSTANDING HUMAN POTENTIAL

An outcome of people's experience with society and its institutions is that many adults cannot remember, if they ever knew, what their unique talents and interests were. They cannot remember what areas of learning and doing were fulfilling for them, what paths had heart. These have to be discovered and rediscovered.

For many, the relationship between formal schooling and subsequent occupation needs to be re-examined. In adult life/career planning workshops, the author has found that of the things participants actually enjoy doing, less than 5 percent are things they learned in school as part of formal classroom work. A related outcome is that adults distinguish between work and play. Work is something you have to be "compensated" for, because it robs you of living. Play is something you usually have to pay for, because your play is often someone else's work. Children have to be taught these distinctions carefully, for they make no sense to anyone whose life is fully worth living. As one philosopher put it:

> *A master in the art of living draws no sharp distinction between his work and his play, his labor and his leisure, his mind and his body, his education and his recreation. He scarcely knows which is which. He simply pursues his vision of excellence through whatever he is doing and leaves others to determine whether he is working or playing. To himself he always seems to be doing both.*[3]

But pursuing a vision of excellence is not always simple. What does "vision of excellence" mean? How do you acquire your own? We can be reasonably sure that it has little to do with getting A's, excelling against others in competition, or living up to someone else's standards. It is one's own unique vision. It will not emerge in school, if each person must be comparable to every other person so that grades and rank can be assigned. Such a system defines individuality as differences in degree, not in kind. Consider, too, the word "genius." To most of us it means a person with a high IQ. But differences in IQ are differences of degree, whereas the notion of "unique" makes it impossible to rank and compare.

In the search for your own unique vision, you need a different definition of *genius*, one closer to the dictionary definition as "the unique and identifying spirit of a person or place." By this definition, your genius consists of those of your talents that you love to develop and use. These are the things that you can now or potentially could do with excellence, which are fulfilling in the doing of them; so fulfilling that if you also get paid to do them, it feels not like compensation, but like a gift.

DISCOVERING GENIUS AND DEVELOPING AUTONOMY

Discovering your genius may be easy or difficult. At some level of your being you already know it; you are fortunate if it is in your conscious awareness. If not, there are several routes to discovery, and many sources of pertinent information.

The first source is *play*. Make a list of the things you enjoy doing and find the common themes. Observe what you do when you are not obliged to do anything. What activities are you likely to engage in? What catches your eye when you thumb through a magazine? When you are in an unfamiliar environment, what interests you, what catches your attention? What are the contents of your fantasies and daydreams? What do you wish you were doing? Your sleep-dreams are also important. Record them, for some of them contain important wishes that you may want to turn into plans.

The second source is your own *life history*. Record in some detail the times in your past when you were doing something very well and enjoying it very much. What themes or patterns of strength, skill, and activity pervade most of those times? What were the sources of satisfaction in them?

The third source is *feedback* from others. What do those who know you have to say about your strengths and talents? As they see it, what seems to excite you, give you pleasure, engage you? And if you can find people who knew you when you were a child, can they recall what used to capture your attention and curiosity, what activities you enjoyed, what special promise and talents you displayed?

The fourth source is *psychological instruments*, which provide a variety of ways of helping you to organize and interpret your experience. There are many such instruments that can provide you with clues to your interests, strengths, and sources of satisfaction. Perhaps the most valuable is the Myers-Briggs Type Indicator, which is based on the insights of the psychologist Carl Jung. A recent book, based on these ideas, identifies four basic temperaments, four quite different ways of approaching life (Keirsey and Bats, 1978). One of these is oriented to tradition and stability in the world, and devoted to making systems work and to the maintenance of order. The second type loves action, freedom, excitement, and the mastery of skills. The third type is oriented to the future and to mastery of the unknown. The fourth loves to work in the service of humanity and bring about a better world. One can learn to perform competently in activities that do not fit one's temperament, and to some extent one must, but it always feels like "work." In contrast, if the activities are in accord with one's temperament, it feels more like "play." It follows that your temperament is one of the important components of your genius.

As you take these four routes, you may find the same messages about yourself over and over again—and you may also find a few surprises and contradictions. In general, the truth strategy you employ is the one enunciated in *Alice in Wonderland*: "What I tell you three times is true." You may emerge from the search with some hunches to explore further; you may emerge with certainty about a new direction to take; or you may simply affirm what you already knew—confirming or disconfirming the life and career choices you have already made. This discovery or affirmation of your genius is a first step, but it needs also to be nourished and developed, and you need to learn how to create the conditions that will support you in practicing it. The second step then, is to acquire the resources you need in order to build a world for yourself that supports you in the pursuit and practice of your genius. The process of acquiring these resources can be called the *development of autonomy*—learning the skills needed to build that world.

Consider the following case:

> *Jerome Kirk, a well-known sculptor, discovered his genius through play, though not until his late twenties. Alone on an island off the Maine coast for a week, he amused himself by fashioning sculptures out of driftwood. It was a dazzling experience. But his education had prepared him for work in the field of personnel administration. For the following 20 years he developed his skill as a sculptor, "while earning a living" as a personnel administrator—and he was quite successful in this profession. After 20 years, his sculptures matched his own vision of excellence, he was a recognized artist, and the income from his art was sufficient to enable him to devote all his time to it. It was the realization of a dream. His comment: "I was good in the personnel field, but I never really enjoyed it. It wasn't me. And now I'm utterly convinced that if a person really loves something, and focuses his energy there, there's just no way he can fail to fulfill his 'vision of excellence.' "*[4]

The point of this story is not to idealize the creative arts. For others, discovery of genius would take them in a different direction, perhaps toward greater interaction with people rather than away from it. But the story does illustrate the qualities that get released when a person discovers his or her genius. Passion, energy, and focus all came as a natural by-product of Kirk's discovery. These were the qualities needed to develop the autonomy that ultimately allowed Kirk to realize his dream. They were inspired by the knowledge of his genius that he carried within him. The same qualities will be evident in any person who has discovered his or her genius, whether it is in sculpture or in the leadership of organizations. (Vaill, 1982)

LIVING OUT YOUR POTENTIAL

You began your life as a bundle of life-loving energy with a marvelous array of potentialities. As you grew up you learned to do many things and not to do other things. Some of these things were good for you, some bad for you, some good for others, some bad for others. Out of the things you learned, you fashioned an identity, a self-image. Thus, your self-image is a cultural product, and the distortion it contains may prevent you from recognizing yourself anymore as a bundle of life-loving energy with a marvelous array of potentialities. Acquiring a renewed identity, an identification with what is truly wonderful about yourself and therefore worth nourishing and loving, is not an easy task. It requires a lot of unlearning and letting go, as well as new learning and risk-taking.

How can you tell when you have achieved this goal? What can you feel from communion with others that confirms your own life as fully worth living? What should living out your potential mean in relationship to the outer world? Three qualities are critical indications that you have achieved a life fully worth living. They can be called tone, resonance, and perspective. Tone refers to feeling good about yourself, resonance to feeling good about your relationships, and perspective to feeling good about the choices in your life. To experience these qualities consistently is to know that you are living life well. Once again, though, our society interferes with and disguises the messages that we receive. Therefore, it is necessary not only to grasp the essence of these qualities, but also to recognize and to separate oneself from the distortions of them that our culture imposes.

Tone

Tone refers to your aliveness as an organism. When you think of good muscle tone, you think of a relaxed alertness, a readiness to respond. As used here, the term tone refers to your entire being, your mental and emotional life as well as your muscle and organ life. Hence anxiety is as much the enemy of tone as drugs or being overweight. Lowen expressed this idea as follows:

> *A person experiences the reality of the world only through his body. . . . If the body is relatively unalive, a person's impressions and responses are diminished. The more alive the body is, the more vividly does he perceive reality and the more actively does he respond to it. We have all experienced the fact that when we feel particularly good and alive, we perceive the world more sharply. . . . The aliveness of the body denotes its capacity for feeling. In the absence of feeling, the body goes "dead" insofar as its ability to be impressed by or respond to situations is concerned. . . . It is the body that melts with love, freezes with fear, trembles in anger, and reaches for warmth and contact. Apart from the body these words are poetic images. Experienced in the body, they have a reality that gives meaning to existence. (Lowen, 1967)*

But the self-images we forge on our journey through society's institutions often deprive us of our ability to maintain tone. We are no longer in touch with our bodies or with our genuine feelings, and our self-images have been distorted.

One of the most common distortions is to comprise your self-image out of some role or roles you play in society. Great actors and actresses use their capacity for total identification with another human being as a basis for a great performance, but their self-image is not that of a person portrayed. That costume is removed at the end of each performance. Cornelia Otis Skinner declared that the first law of the theater is to love your audience. She meant, of course, that the actor or actress, rather than the character portrayed, must love the audience. You cannot love the audience unless you love yourself, and yourself is not a role. Thus, it is vitally important to recognize your roles as costumes you wear for particular purposes, and not to let them get stuck to you. Your prospects at retirement from your profession or organization will otherwise be for a very short life.

A second common distortion is to make your head (your brain) your self-image, and the rest of you part of your environment. Cutting your body into two segments places enormous stress on it, and your tone will suffer severely. "You don't exist within your body. Your body is a person" (Lowen, 1967). A third distortion is to make your gender your self-image. The sexual-reproductive aspects of people are among their most wonderful potentialities, but to identify with your gender leads you to spend the first years of your life learning some bad habits that you spend the rest of your life trying to liberate yourself from.

Other common distortions include being the public relations representative of your family (often forced on boys and girls), being an underdog, a clown, or a representative of superior values. All such distortions will exact their price by robbing you of tone: by causing you to eat too much or drink too much or worry too much or keep your body in continuous stress, and miss the joy of being alive.

Resonance

The second quality for living out your genius is your capacity for resonance. This involves an enhanced, stimulated, and yet relaxed vitality that you can experience in interaction with particular others and particular environments. Discovering those others and those environments that are able to provide resonance can be one of the most fulfilling aspects of the journey through a life fully worth living. The word *resonance* is chosen rather than the word *love*, with which it has much in common, because the very meaning of love has become distorted in our society. It has become a commodity in short supply, a marketable item, a weapon used to control others; it is difficult to distinguish love from exploitation or imprisonment.

The term *resonance* is chosen for other reasons as well. It conveys the notion of being "in tune" with other people and environments; it suggests the synergy and expansion of tone when your energy has joined with the energy of others. It also implies harmony. Harmony is a beautiful arrangement of different sounds, in contrast to mere noise, which is an ugly arrangement. Resonance, as used here, implies people's capacity to use their differences in ways that are beautiful rather than ugly.

The world you build that supports you in the pursuit of your genius is not worth living in if it lacks resonance. But once again, your capacity to build and maintain resonant relationships, and to transform dead or noisy relationships into resonant ones, may have been damaged. To regain that capacity first requires that you become aware of the cultural forces that have damaged it, and robbed you of the potential resonance in your life.

Perhaps the greatest distortion to resonance that we face comes from our intensely adversarial society. Almost everything is perceived in competitive, win-lose, success-failure terms. "Winning isn't everything. It's the *only* thing!" We have been encouraged to believe that the world is our enemy. One must be either on the defensive or offensive, or both at once. One must conquer, control, exploit, or be conquered, controlled, exploited. One must fight or run away. As a result one experiences others and is experienced by them either as hostile, aggressive, aloof, or as frightened, shy, withdrawn. Under these circumstances, resonance is hard to come by and short-lived. For many people, win-lose competitiveness does not dominate all aspects of their lives, but is induced by particular kinds of situations—and destroys the potential resonance and synergy of those situations.

For example, many seminars and staff meetings bring in thoughts of winning or losing, succeeding or failing, proving oneself or making points. These displace the potential resonance and synergy that can evolve when a group works creatively together, building on one another's thoughts, stimulating each other's ideas, and mixing work and laughter.

Three further cultural themes that can cripple the capacity for resonance are materialism, sexism, and violence. Materialism is defined as the tendency to measure one's self-worth by the number and kinds of possessions one has, and the tendency to turn experiences into things so that they can be possessions. Collectibles are a way of "life." Sexism is defined as the tendency to turn sexual relationships and partners into materials, and to use sexual labels to sum oneself and others up—gay, macho, or liberated. Morality and fidelity have lost all but their sexual meanings. Lastly, "Violence is as American as apple pie."[6] We have more guns than people. Our folk heroes were violent men.

Various combinations of adversarial, materialistic, sexist, and violent themes are commonly destructive of resonance in intimate relationships, such as marriage. Jealousy, possessiveness, and feelings of being exploited can dominate the relationship and the partners become each other's prisoners and jailers. But if they are able to free themselves of these distortions, the relationship can be transformed and resonance restored. If you think of any intimate relationships as consisting of three creatures: yourself, the other person, and the couple, you can see that the phrase "a life fully worth living" applies to each. It follows that you would reserve for the couple only those things that are growthful and fulfilling for it. In pursuing the other aspects of your life, your partner can be a resource to you, and you a resource to your partner. Rather than being each other's jailers, you become the supporters of each other's freedom—and this will enhance your resonance. An application of this principle is not difficult for most parents to grasp: your delight in seeing your child leading a fulfilling life as a result of the support you provided. Cultural distortions make it more difficult to understand that the principle applies equally to intimate relationships among adults.

Perspective

The third important quality of a worthwhile life is the perspective necessary to guide choices and to inform experience. If you have only one way of looking at the situation you are in, you have no freedom of choice about what to do. And if you have only one framework for understanding your experience, all of your experiences will reinforce that framework. If your outlook is adversarial, you will interpret whatever happens as evidence that the world is hostile, and your choices will be limited to fighting or running away. If you fight, it will confirm your belief that the world is hostile. If you run away, you will know that you were wise to do so. If your perspective is differentiated—if you can see, for example, the potential of a new relationship to be either collaborative or adversarial—you enlarge your range of choices. Thus, if you are aware of "the multiple potential of the moment," you will usually be able to make a choice that will make the next moment better for you and for the others in the situation.

The cultural distortions that lock you into a limited undifferentiated perspective, which lead you to make self-destructive choices, are the same ones that interfere with your tone and self-image, or your capacity for resonance. The messages of adversarialism, materialism, and sexism seek to dictate to you how you should see the world. And your life roles, as defined by other people, are an all too convenient set of prescriptions for your behavior. Take heed of your own feelings, ask what may be causing them, and whether cultural forces are at work. That such distortions are blocking your access to a useful perspective is evidenced whenever you find yourself humorless. The essence of humor is a sudden shift in point of view. To be without humor is to be dying, and laughter is one of the most valuable sources of health and well-being on the journey called a life fully worth living (Cousins, 1979).

Thus tone, resonance, and perspective are the signs that you have discovered your genius and have developed the autonomy to live by it, rather than by society's dictates.

PROSPECTS FOR CHANGE

The foregoing pages have offered a framework for understanding human potential, parts of which may be familiar, parts of which may be new. In some ways the categories of genius, autonomy, tone, resonance, and perspective are arbitrary, and they should only be used when they fit your purposes. And, clearly, these aspects of life are not separable. The expression of genius needs autonomy. Poor tone, low resonance, and limited perspective almost always have a confirming effect upon one another, and serve to limit autonomy. The essential point is to work in a direction that will begin to free human potential, and to rid it of its cultural fetters.

A ROLE FOR INSTITUTIONS

The view presented here is critical of the way society's institutions impose cultural distortions on people, and prevent them from finding a path with a heart. Does this mean that, for the well-being of all of us, our institutions should refrain from showing any interest in careers? Does it mean that there can be no institution with a vested interest in people having a life that is fully worth living?

I believe the answer to both questions is no. Two concurrent forces are operating to change the culture quite rapidly. One of these is the dawning realization in many American organizations that the theories of management and organization on which our society has operated in the past have failed us, and will not serve us in the future. They have failed because they have regarded human beings as part of a social machine and have treated as irrelevant individual spirit and well-being. Nor have these theories capitalized on individuals' needs and capacities to work harmoniously with each other. This realization of past failure is bringing about a transformation in industrial organizations, and non-industrial organizations will eventually catch up. The second force for change is technological progress, especially the rapid development of electronic communications and computers. The more that routine operations are performed by machines, the more demand there is that the non-routine operations be performed with excellence. This kind of excellence in human performance can only be attained by persons who are fully alive and operating in the area of their genius. Only if the path has a heart will it sustain excellence.

When the aerospace industry was in its infancy, the technical challenge, and hence the need for creativity and teamwork, was immense. One of the most successful companies recognized this fully in its organizational structure and culture. It invented new organizational forms that were suited to its mission and the capacities of its members to work together creatively. In the process, it created most of the principles and processes that are in use today in what has come to be called organization development. Among other things, it offered its members Life and Career Planning workshops, to help them identify their talents and interests. The approach was somewhat different from the one outlined in this paper, but its intent was the same. The spirit of these workshops was summed up in the way the company introduced them: "What you do with your life and career is your responsibility. But because you are a member of this company, the company shares some of that responsibility with you. Perhaps it's 80 percent yours, 20 percent the company's. This workshop is the company's effort to contribute towards its 20 percent." In a similar spirit, another company offers workshops based on their version of Dalton and Thompson's career-stages model, to help employees identify their position on the path, understand their potential more clearly, and find ways of fulfilling it (Dalton, Thompson, and Price, 1977).

These companies have a vested interest in having their members rediscover their genius. Our hope for changing the order of things is that more and more organizations will follow their example. But we must insist that their interventions be explicitly on their members' behalf. And their processes must seek to liberate people from their cultural surroundings—including organizational cultures—rather than to reaffirm their dependencies. Then their example can be picked up by the schools, who can help others much earlier in their lives. Parents, in turn, will come to appreciate the freedom of spirit that they can encourage in their own children. The path with a heart is also the path to improving our institutions. Let our teaching about careers stand for nothing less.

Notes

1. The version here is that told by Leo Buscaglia (1982). However, an earlier version has been attributed to Casberg (1961), although no published source could be found.
2. Whether these sentiments really reflect Don Juan's thoughts, or only Castaneda's (see Harris, 1979: 322-323), is irrelevant to the present discussion, which emphasizes the content of what is being expressed.
3. Author unknown.
4. Personal communication.
5. Attributed to Vince Lombardi.
6. Attributed to H. Rap Brown.

References

Buscaglia, L., *Love* (New York: Random House, 1982).

Castaneda, C., *The Teaching of Don Juan, A Yaqui Way of Knowledge* (Berkeley: University of California Press, 1968).

Cousins, N., *The Anatomy of an Illness* (New York: Norton, 1979).

Dalton, G. W., Thompson, P. H., and Price, R. L., "The Four Stages of Professional Careers: A New Look at Performance by Professionals," *Organizational Dynamics,* Summer 1977: 19–42.

Harris, M. *Cultural Materialism: The Struggle for a Science of Culture* (New York: Random House, 1979).

Keirsey, D., and Bates, M., *Please Understand Me* (Del Mar, CA: Nemesis Books, 1978).

Lowen, A., *The Betrayal of the Body* (New York: Macmillan, 1967).

Maslow, A. H., *Toward a Psychology of Being* (New York: Van Nostrand, 1962).

Maslow, A. H., and Chang, H., *The Healthy Personality* (New York: Van Nostrand, 1969).

Siu, R., "Work and Serenity," *Journal of Occupational Mental Health*, 1971: 1,5.

Vail, P. "The Purposing of High Performance Systems," *Organizational Dynamics,* Fall 1982 23–29.

THE BALANCING ACT—AT WORK AND AT HOME*

Jonathan D. Quick
Amy B. Henley
James Campbell Quick

> Thomas and Caroline have been married for 30 years. Both are very successful in their careers: she has steadily climbed her way up to a division manager for a Fortune 500 organization, while he has built a strong private medical practice in their community. Along the way, there have been tradeoffs. Work interfered with their personal lives and family goals at times. There have been disagreements about how much work should be brought home, and feelings of neglect when one partner was preoccupied with thoughts of work instead of focusing on the family. He feels that she brings too much work home with her, and she feels that he spends too much time at the office. They both believe that they have too many social obligations and not enough free time. This couple does not agree about a significant decision that was made early in their marriage—whether or not to have children.

*Reprinted with permission of Elsevier from *Organizational Dynamics*, *33*(4) (2004): 426–438.

Caroline says that the decision not to have children was a choice they consciously made to focus on their respective careers and future success. However, Thomas disagrees and states that this path in their lives was not a chosen one. What would cause two individuals, in what appears to be a successful marriage, to have such differing viewpoints regarding a critical decision made in their marital lives?

This vignette illustrates the complexity of the interactions, intersections, and overlaps between the domains of work life and home life with the private domain of the self. We capture these three separate domains, their intersections, and their overlaps in Figure 1. An overlap does not necessarily lead to conflict. Alternatively, it may lead to balance and dynamic interaction. If, for example, work and home life are mutually reinforcing, then there is balance, not conflict. However, if they are not mutually reinforcing, then there is potential conflict. Or, if they are in dysfunctional competition for an individual's time or other resources, then there is active conflict. We plan to explore these issues of conflict and balance throughout the article.

WHAT'S AT STAKE?

Why should the happy, healthy, productive worker make it a priority to effectively balance the demands from his or her family and work? Quite simply, because so much is at stake when we fail to manage these often-competing demands. Conflict between a person's work responsibilities and family obligations can significantly impact all aspects of the individual's life. There are key consequences that accompany the failure to effectively balance the two domains for the employees themselves, their families and organizations. As a result, not only does the individual suffer from pressures associated with work–family conflict, but the impact extends to spouses, children, bosses, subordinates, etc.

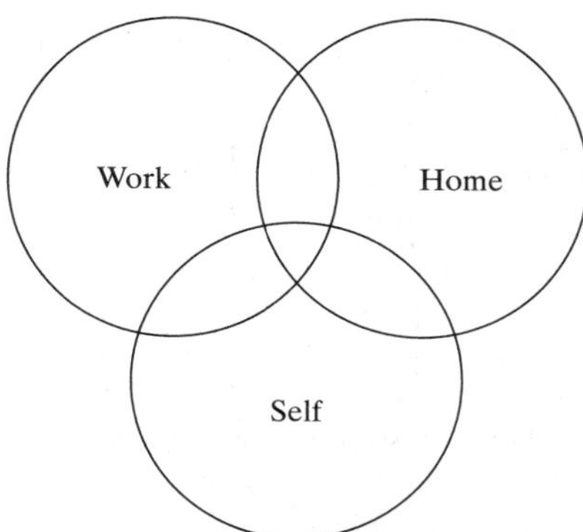

FIGURE 1 The Balancing Act—Work, Home, Self

Consider the following example: Robert works an average of 60 hours a week as a sales manager in a rapidly expanding technology firm. He's been married for 11 years and has one daughter, age 8, and a son, age 5. Robert sees that his high performance now at work could pay off in quick advancement up the corporate ladder. As a result, he puts the majority of his energy into his work life and often pushes family requests and obligations to the background. While his wife is understanding at first, over time she begins to put pressure on Robert to spend more time with her and the kids. As a result, Robert becomes tense and feels guilty when he stays late at work to meet with a client or finish a report. His work performance begins to slide, only putting more pressure on Robert. Eventually, Robert becomes so tense and frustrated that his ability to function effectively in either the family or work domain is hindered. His work suffers, and both his organization and his family are affected by the work–family spillover that occurs. Robert becomes trapped in seemingly endless cycle impacting all aspects of his life.

It is obvious that work–family conflict, or the failure to effectively balance work and family demands, has unique consequences for the individual employee or executive involved, his or her family, and the organization. These outcomes affect the employee in all aspects of life and are not isolated to the work domain. As the amount of work–family conflict that an individual is experiencing increases, his or her job satisfaction and life satisfaction fall. These individuals report lower levels of general happiness and subjective well-being than workers who do not experience work–family conflict. Research has also shown that their psychological distress levels increase, and negative health consequences often result. Failure to balance the demands between work and family has been linked with higher levels of depression and increased alcohol use. In regards to their work domain itself, workers tend to become less committed to an organization when they are experiencing work–family conflict. Individuals may see the organization as the cause of distress in their lives, thereby resulting in decreased levels of attachment to that organization. It should be no surprise that workers who are experiencing work–family conflict also report higher intentions to leave their current organizations as well as increased reports of actual turnover.

EFFECTS ON THE FAMILY AND ORGANIZATION

The effects of work–family conflict are not isolated to merely the individual employee, but extend to the family as well. Family performance often suffers as a result of the competing demands of work and family domains. In turn, work–family conflict has been associated with lower levels of marital satisfaction for both spouses and increased instances of divorce and family strife. The increasing number of dual-career couples also creates a unique dynamic in the balance of work and family, because research has shown that the amount of work–family conflict experienced by one partner directly affects the amount of work–family conflict experienced by the other partner. This spillover of conflict from one spouse to another makes balancing the competing demands of work and family all the more complex, in that now the focus is on managing the demands of two individuals, their respective careers, and their mutual family environment. Reported parental problems have been associated with higher levels of work–family conflict, as have instances of juvenile delinquency and violence. Increased stress levels and tension within the home that often accompany work–family conflict affect the day-to-day functionality of the family unit. This can be observed in seemingly minor details, such as the dad who rarely sees his kids in the morning before they go to school or the mom who consistently breaks her promises to attend key school events, which over time can create feelings of resentment and hurt in the family and affect the overall vitality of the family domain.

Organizations are also victims of the employee's inability to balance work and home demands. Work–family conflict directly affects the job satisfaction, career satisfaction, and performance of the worker, thereby indirectly influencing overall organizational performance. Absenteeism is often higher for individuals experiencing work–family conflict, resulting in increased labor costs for the organization. Because intentions to leave and actual turnover are greater for sufferers of work–family conflict, the organization must incur the costs of replacing these employees in the form of recruitment, selection, and training. Health-care costs for the organization can also rise as workers suffer from the negative health ramifications that often result from the distress associated with work–family conflict.

WHAT FORMS DOES IT TAKE?

Based upon the extensive ramifications associated with work–family conflict, it is obvious that the failure to balance work and family obligations should be of significant concern for both executives and their organizations. But how does work–family conflict occur? What forms does it take? Jeffrey Greenhaus and Nicholas Beutell have identified three distinct types of work–family conflict that can occur when work stressors, such as role overload, extensive pressure, lack of autonomy, and role ambiguity, limit the ability for workers to effectively manage their work and family lives. While they differ in terms of their nature, all three can result in the negative outcomes discussed above.

Time-based conflict occurs when the time devoted to work makes it difficult to fulfill the obligations and requirements of the family role and can impact the worker in either of two ways. One form of this conflict addresses the simple zero-sum nature of time management. In other words, any time spent by the worker in one domain makes it physically impossible for that worker to spend that same time in the other domain. To understand the effect of this type of work–family conflict, consider the executive who consistently stays late at the office and misses the family evening meal. Over time, this individual is left out of the communication within the family that takes place during this daily activity. As a result, he or she can become increasingly isolated from the family. Time-based conflict can also occur when the employee is physically present in the family domain, but mentally preoccupied with work concerns. So while this individual is trying to meet their family obligations in body, his or her mind is still at work. For example, the parent who attends a child's sporting event or birthday party but spends the majority of the time on a cell phone dealing with problems at the office is not truly committing his or her full self to this time in the family domain.

Strain-based conflict occurs when the pressures of the work role spill over and affect interactions within the family domain. Greenhaus and Beutell define this type of work–family conflict as "strain from participation in one role makes it difficult to fulfill requirements of another." In other words, the employee who has a particularly stressful day at work comes home in a bad mood and takes it out on his family. He may snap at his spouse for no particular reason or be so tired from the workday's events that he doesn't feel like playing baseball when his child asks. While these individuals are not directly preoccupied with office tasks as in time-based conflict, the negative effects of work stressors are manifested within the home environment as workers displace their negative emotions that stem from work experiences and express them within the family.

Behavior-based conflict is the third and final type of work–family conflict. This type of conflict occurs when behaviors that are acceptable, and even rewarded, in the work domain are incompatible with the behaviors that are desired in the home domain. Problems occur then when the employee fails to recognize the need to adjust her behaviors between the two domains. For example, an authoritative boss who must give clear direction to her employees at work in order to get the job done may find that her attempts to behave in the same manner at home with her children are not equally successful and can even result in hurt feelings and resentment. Likewise, the key executive who spends the majority of his day solving problems may encounter resistance when he comes home to a wife who wants him to simply listen attentively to her problems without necessarily instructing her on how to solve them. The key component in this type of work–family conflict involves the need to adjust the behavior between the work and family domains.

SOURCES OF WORK–FAMILY CONFLICT

Work–family conflict is a reality for those who live in families, and even for those executives who do not live in families—yet must catch the crossover effects of colleagues' or employees' conflicts as they spill into the workplace. One of the keys to conflict management is an understanding of the sources of work–family conflict. The core of the conflict comes from three separate, competing, and overlapping sets of demands which, respectively, originate in the home, the workplace, and within one's self. We address the demands of each of these sources of demands separately.

Much that has been written about work–family conflict focuses on conflicting time demands. We offer a different perspective. Rather than framing the conflict in terms of time, we suggest framing it in terms of energy, attention, and engagement. This perspective becomes important in both understanding the conflict and in managing the conflict. For example, if time is seen as the central issue, this then converts the conflict into a form of mathematical problem. If energy is seen as the central issue, then it becomes more of a human issue than a math problem, and each family, as we saw in the opening vignette, can work out their own balancing act for work–family.

HOME DEMANDS

Every home needs a wonderful wife, and it does not have to be the woman. As more and more women continue both a professional and a family life, home demands have changed. Now more pressure accrues to the male working spouse or a surrogate chosen by the husband and wife jointly, in the case of traditional family homes. Home demands fall into two broad categories, one physical or material and the other interpersonal. The physical or material demands concern framing and maintaining the home, which are especially substantive in large, elaborate homes. For families with financial resources to hire staff and delegate a range of tasks such as cooking, cleaning, and laundry, this frees both husband and wife to devote more energy to interpersonal aspects of home life. For families without such resources, the challenges are more complicated.

Children within the family add another dimension to the home demands. Because the American culture often assigns primary home responsibility to women, the stereotypic response to their struggle with work–family balance is unfairly written off as of their own making. Prior to becoming chairman and chief executive officer (CEO) of Hewlett-Packard Co., Lew Platt had a direct experience with the conflict in his own life after his first wife Susan died in 1981 and left him to raise two daughters. At the time of his wife's death, Mr. Platt was a general manager at HP with significant professional responsibilities, and no longer a spousal partner who took the primary lead at home and within the family. He quickly grasped the dilemma that many of HP's women managers were faced with on an ongoing basis.

What made Mr. Platt's loss particularly poignant was the critical ages of his daughters: nine and eleven. There are several critical ages in the development of children, and the developmental opportunity comes only once chronologically. Author and Focus on Family founder James Dobson made a conscious decision during the early years of his children's lives to devote more energy to his family and less energy to his career development. While Dr. Dobson's personal and family choice was his, and others may choose differently, it is important to be fully aware of the key developmental and personal issues at stake for one's spouse, children, and other family members as decisions are made. For example, the critically and terminally ill child in a family may call forth the need for extended family or faith community family members to supplement the energy and concern of the parents in the family.

WORK DEMANDS

We have described in detail elsewhere (see Annotated Bibliography) the wide array of task, role, physical, and interpersonal demands for people at work. These demands create either stress or challenge for the individual depending upon individual idiosyncrasy and vulnerability. The sources of work stress are independent of a person's home life and other considerations. However, from the standpoint of work–family conflict, the work demands that may be most problematic are role ambiguity and overload, career stage, and family stage. The work role may contribute to work–family conflict when the role expectations are unclear or the volume of work is greater than the time and energy available for that role. Thus, the confusion and volume overload can spill into the home in both unaware and unintended ways, with adverse impact.

Career stage is a second consideration relevant to work–family conflict. In recollecting at age 93 the early stages of his career and its effect on his family life, a distinguished physician and educator observed that he did not have to work as hard as he did at age 33 to be as successful as he was over his entire career. Of course, such retrospective observation is much easier when one has fulfilled a highly successful career. The physician-educator was fortunate that he did not lose his family in the process, and retrospective guilt can be unwarranted. One world renowned cancer researcher experienced some of the same reflective guilt as the physician educator and, upon engaging in a family process of reconciliation, discovered that his wife and children had, in fact, not felt shortchanged throughout their lives with him. Still, a young executive's or professional's striving to achieve in the early career stage may place unwitting pressure on the family.

In addition to the career stage being an important source of work demands creating conflict with the family, one's stage in family life can a source of overlapping conflict. Working parents with small and adolescent children often feel the conflict and tension of the competing role demands from work and home life. While family-friendly work environments may help ease the tension, individual preferences for separation or integration of these two major life domains are important considerations in this regard as well.

SELF-IMPOSED DEMANDS

Individuals often contribute to their own work–family conflicts by way of self-imposed demands. The most problematic self-imposed demands for work–family conflict center around over-achievement drive and workaholism. These self-imposed demands share some overlapping variance with Type A Behavior Pattern, often known as coronary-prone behavior and occasionally the Sisyphus Complex. Preoccupation with work was first suspected as a risk for cardiovascular disease by the Dutch cardiologist Von Dusch, who observed in the 1860s that an excessive involvement with work contributed to heart disease. Workaholism contributes to work–family conflict to the extent that it prevents one from strategic disengagement from work for alternative purposes in life. Table 1 contains a set of 20 self-assessment questions to help assess whether or not you are a workaholic.

TABLE 1 How Do You Know If You Are a Workaholic?

1. Do you get more excited about your work than about family or anything else?
2. Are there times when you can charge through your work and other times when you can't?
3. Do you take work with you to bed? on weekends? on vacation?
4. Is work the activity you like to do best and talk about most?
5. Do you work more than 40 hours a week?
6. Do you turn your hobbies into money-making ventures?
7. Do you take complete responsibility for the outcome of your work efforts?
8. Have your family or friends given up expecting you on time?
9. Do you take on extra work because you are concerned that it won't otherwise get done?
10. Do you underestimate how long a project will take and then rush to complete it?
11. Do you believe that it is okay to work long hours if you love what you are doing?
12. Do you get impatient with people who have other priorities besides work?
13. Are you afraid that if you don't work hard you will lose your job or be a failure?
14. Is the future a constant worry for you even when things are going very well?
15. Do you do things energetically and competitively, including play?
16. Do you get irritated when people ask you to stop doing your work in order to do something else?
17. Have your long hours hurt your family or other relationships?
18. Do you think about your work while driving, falling asleep, or when others are talking?
19. Do you work or read during meals?
20. Do you believe that more money will solve the other problems in your life?

Reprinted with permission from Workaholics Anonymous, World Service Organization (2002).

AMPLIFYING THE CONFLICT

In addition to the three sources of work–family conflict just discussed, there are a number of factors that can amplify or enflame the conflict beyond its natural origins. These factors may exacerbate work–family conflict, may be symptoms of work–family conflict, or may be immediate consequences of work–family conflict. The five factors are alcohol and other substances, sleep disturbances, business travel, toxic corporate cultures, and the e-mail paradox. These are not intended to be an exhaustive set of factors, and families may discover for themselves specific accelerants that ignite an otherwise routine work–family conflict into a full-blown wildfire. Identifying these factors within the family and then knowing the early warning signs of their pending activation can go a long way in early detection and prevention of specific conflicts for the family and the workplace.

ALCOHOL AND OTHER SUBSTANCES

Alcohol abuse is one of the most potential destructive forces in family life, and for those who have lived with an alcoholic, the personality-changing dynamics of the abuser are clear. For those in the workplace, the abuse of alcohol or other substances may be very difficult to detect. For example, a senior military documents security officer was widely known in Washington, DC to abstain from alcohol consumption, as was his wife. The couple never drank at any political, military, or diplomatic functions. However, after an investigation was triggered when a Top Secret document went missing, it was discovered that the couple were alcoholics who carefully concealed their abuse in the privacy of their home.

While this is a dramatic Jekyll-and-Hyde case of alcohol abuse, it reveals the insidious effects that alcohol or other substance abuse may have in terms of work–family conflict. The common characteristic of the home in which alcohol is abused is disorder and the experience of a lack of control. For families of abusers, this experience is both deeply disturbing and very disorienting. It may be akin to being in a funny house at the amusement park.

SLEEP DISTURBANCES

Stress is a known cause of sleep disturbances and insomnia, one early warning sign of change in an individual's life. However, sleep disturbances in turn may play a causal or inflammatory role in work–family conflict, depending upon the individual's response to the sleep disturbance. Not all sleep disturbances are problematic and, to the extent that they are short-term responses to peak workloads or changing work demands, they may simply be short-term symptoms of the mind–body adjustment to these changing conditions.

However, chronic and long-term sleep disturbances are of concern for the individual, the family, and the organization. For the individual, sleep deprivation can lead to attention deficits that may contribute to health problems and even accidents in the workplace. For the family, one member's sleep disturbance may become "contagious" with other family members. For the organization, sleep disturbances and deprivation may lead to loss of productivity. One senior municipal executive experienced a two-year period of rather severe insomnia for which medical treatment found little effect.

This senior executive's emotional reactivity was enhanced, leading to chronic interpersonal conflicts with members of his city council, which in turn had spillover effects into his marriage and home life.

TRAVEL . . . AND MORE TRAVEL

Travel can exacerbate work–family conflicts in at least two ways. The first way is due to the emotional separation caused by the physical distance of the traveling family member. If the family is a secure base of emotional operation for a husband or wife, travel serves to interrupt the periodic emotional reassurance and social support that intimate family relationships provide. The famous folk singers Peter, Paul, and Mary found during one year that they were on the road well over 200 days, significantly cutting into their individual family relationships. Strong family bonds can withstand reasoned periods of separation due to travel, but any fragility within the family bonds is strained by the separation.

The second way in which travel exacerbates work–family conflict is the additional burden which such travel places on the at home spouse. There are a variety of functional and mundane aspects of home life, such as taking out the garbage, which simply must be managed if the home is to be healthy for the family. Most families divide duties among parents and children, or contract with domestic help for childcare and other important home duties. Who assumes the traveling parent's duties in the absence of that parent?

TOXIC CORPORATE CULTURES

Peter Frost has brought our attention to the organizational problem of toxic emotions and pain that is often endemic to work life. William Cohen and his clinical psychologist wife further brought attention to the paranoid organization and other dysfunctional forms of corporate cultures. In some organizations, it does seem that it is necessary to be a little bit paranoid, or a little bit schizophrenic, or somewhat manic to succeed within that specific corporate culture. This in no way suggests neither that these corporate cultures are healthy, nor that they should be emulated by other executives or organizations. The problem from a healthy family standpoint is that unhealthy corporate cultures have unhealthy spillover effects into the family.

The "pressure cooker" corporate culture is particularly problematic for those seeking a healthy work–family balance. Organizations that are pressure cookers simply drive their employees, not allowing time for energy recovery nor strategic disengagement from production. The old joke in Schenectady, New York, was that you could tell a General Electric Company man by his blood pressure. There are peak work periods, however, when long hours may be appropriate. For example, when the Rotary International year comes to an end in June, Russell-Hampton President Bob Lyons joins other employees in manning the phones every day and in working 14-hour days in the office as thousands of Rotary Clubs around the world order the President's Awards recognitions.

THE E-MAIL PARADOX

An emergent factor that may amplify work–family conflict is the ever-present e-mail system, which creates a paradox. E-mail is a double-edged sword that may simplify and streamline, or become a 24-7 cowbell that strangles the family life out of the employee.

When an executive or employee allows e-mail to overwhelm his or her attention with expectations of rapid response, then this electronic aide intrudes upon family life in an adverse manner. This is the negative side of e-mail which can exacerbate work–family conflict.

On the positive side, e-mail can be a simplifying tool that allows an executive to send praise and positive reinforcement quickly, simply, and personally. For example, university president Jim Spaniolo has found that e-mail is a wonderful way to communicate positive feedback and to send personal, congratulatory notes to colleagues everywhere who are performing well. Spaniolo is always careful to reserve any difficult or potentially confusing communication to one-on-one, face-to-face contact that ensures the accuracy of such difficult communications. Used appropriately, e-mail can give executives and employees alike the discretionary control in their communication that enables them to accommodate work–family demands and reduce resultant conflicts.

BALANCING STRATEGIES: HOW CAN WE EFFECTIVELY BALANCE WORK AND FAMILY?

It is obvious that work–family conflict has serious ramifications for the individual employee, his or her family, and organization. While a large amount of research has documented the nature of work–family conflict and the negative outcomes often associated with it, less attention has been focused on the ways employees can effectively balance these often incompatible pressures from their work and family domains. However, many options exist for the worker who wishes to alleviate some of this conflict in her life. These management strategies occur at the individual level in terms of managing work responsibilities, family obligations, and self-imposed expectations.

WITHIN THE WORKPLACE

First, the employee must take an active role in the management of his work responsibilities. While some characteristics of the work environment may appear to be out of one's personal control, there are many active choices that executives and employees can make to help balance their work and personal lives. As discussed above, individuals experiencing work–family conflict are typically faced with irregular or inflexible work hours, extensive travel, and work overload. The first key to balancing such work demands involves time management: such as setting clear and reasonable goals for work tasks, negotiating travel demands and meeting obligations, and the delegation of assignments when feasible.

To help achieve effective time management, Boris A. Baltes and Heather A. Heydens-Gahir have suggested that a life-management strategy known as selection, optimization, and compensation (SOC) be applied to reduce work–family conflict. When using this strategy, employees first identify and set goals to give them clear direction in how to exert their energy—i.e., selection. In the second phase, optimization, individuals acquire, refine, and use the necessary means to achieve those goals set in the first stage of the process. This stage is often characterized by modeling personal behavior after others whom we find successful, learning new skills relevant to achieving our goals, and actively scheduling time and energy. In the final stage of SOC, individuals use additional resources to compensate for their lack of ability to fully meet those goals that were outlined in the first stage. For example, an executive may have to utilize live-in child-care options to help achieve her goal of providing a supportive environment for her children when work demands force her to be away from home. The key objective of this life-management strategy involves focusing on what the important goals are for a person and then directing resources, such as time, to fulfilling those goals.

Boundary management also represents a key coping strategy for balancing the demands between work and home. According to Ellen Kossek and Raymond Noe, this approach recognizes that individuals must play an active role in managing the "joint enactment" of both work and family roles. Therefore, this option seeks to achieve work–family synthesis while allowing an individual to remain in his or her current position. Such a synthesis is attempted through the concept of boundary management that organizes and separates role demands and expectations based on the boundaries set by the individual. Some individuals choose to set strong boundaries by making the domains mutually exclusive and allowing no interaction between them, while others choose to apply no boundaries at all and allow constant interaction and overlap between family and work life.

Christena Nippert-Eng identified two strategies for managing work–family conflict, based on their position along this continuum of boundary management. Segmentation describes the approach in which clear boundaries are laid between the two domains and overlap is rarely permitted. Individuals utilizing this strategy establish a high level of boundary separation and aim to keep their work and family roles completely distinct. These employees deal with work demands during the established work time and home concerns only during the established home hours. Conflict is reduced because individuals are focused on only one domain at a time, and, therefore, fulfilling only the demands associated with that particular role.

Integration, on the other hand, is utilized when few boundaries exist between domains and no clear distinctions are made regarding the appropriate time for enactment of either role. Individuals using this strategy to reduce work–family conflict will make themselves available to either domain at any time. Therefore, conflict is reduced because the domain with the most pressing need is always addressed, regardless of the time of day or the individual's physical location. For example, individuals applying integration to their domains will accept work calls at home on Saturday, but may also leave work on a Tuesday morning to run an errand with their children.

Finally, the personal management of work responsibilities can be achieved through choices made when structuring and choosing career paths and job assignments. Research shows that as employees receive more autonomy and flexibility in their positions, their level of work–family conflict significantly decreases. Therefore, individuals attempting to balance their work demands should seek avenues in their careers which allow greater flexibility and autonomy. These choices may be made when deciding whether to accept a promotion or position with a new organization or by simply communicating the need for greater control in their current positions. Employees should also actively understand themselves and their personal needs when making job choices and seek a degree of person-organization fit which complements the various priorities in their lives. Such active management of work responsibilities can significantly alleviate the amount of work–family conflict experienced.

WITHIN THE FAMILY

While executives and employees must manage their job responsibilities when negotiating between work and family lives, family obligations also play a significant role in the balancing act. Numerous pressures in the family environment—such as the presence of young children, the primary responsibility for caring for children, and the management of care for elder family members—can all stimulate conflict between the work and family domains. However, individuals can take steps to manage their family obligations while simultaneously fulfilling their responsibilities at work.

The design of the family structure itself can intensify the degree of work–family conflict experienced. Work–family conflict increases as families become larger and more complex, such as through dual-career families with increasing levels of obligation. However, research has shown that these factors can be mitigated by support within the family. Employees who report that their spouses provide career support, personal support, and help with the children experience less difficulty in balancing the two domains. Communication within the family plays a key role in fostering this social support. For example, simply letting your spouse know that this is a particularly stressful time at the office and you may have to work late the next few weeks can help everyone in the family adjust to changes in responsibility without feelings of abandonment or resentment.

When managing family obligations, it important to realize that the quantity of time is not always the key factor. Instead, quality of time spent in the family role may be even more important. The majority of the average waking workday is spent either in the work environment, commuting to and from work, or handling other work obligations, leaving little time in the day to accomplish home responsibilities. However, Jim Loehr and Tony Schwartz point out that managing energy, not time, is the key to higher performance and personal renewal. In other words, it may not be the amount of time spent with the family, but the nature of that time. Three hours of energetic, fully engaged, time spent with the family on a weeknight may not equal the amount of time spent at the office that day, but may be more rewarding in terms of the energy and fulfillment achieved. Also, the chosen time spent with the family may be equally important. For example, the average weeknight may not be very significant to the family, but the weeknight that a child has a piano recital or a spouse is receiving an award may be of considerable importance. In other words, while quality time is important, the right time may carry even greater significance.

SELF-MANAGEMENT

The final component that must be managed when balancing work and family responsibilities focuses on self-imposed expectations and reactions to role demands. Self-management is a central ingredient in high levels of emotional competence. Key individual difference factors influence the degree of work–family conflict experienced. Neuroticism, Type A tendencies, and negative affectivity have all been found to increase perceptions of work–family conflict. Additionally, predispositions to stress, such as a lack of personality hardiness, and differences in ability to cope with life stressors will further limit an individual's ability to effectively balance work and family demands. It is important that employees recognize the role that their individual personalities play in shaping their reactions to these life stressors. It is interesting to note that as workers age, they report less work–family conflict, thus reflecting the impact of learning experiences on the ability to recognize and manage work–family interactions.

Self-imposed expectations of one's performance in work and/or family roles can be directly related to the level of psychological involvement one feels toward that role. As work becomes more important to us in terms of how we define ourselves, the decisions we make and the direction toward which we expend our energy are affected. This concept is most clearly reflected when considering the classic workaholic mentioned previously. While lack of adequate attention to one's job can result in poor performance and dismissal, an intense obsession and preoccupation with one's job can pose a significant risk for one's health and family. It is difficult for executives—in that commitment, long hours, high performance, and job involvement are all characteristics common to success in today's organizations. However, when taken to the extreme, these behaviors can become destructive for both the individual and her family. Workaholics often suffer from chronic fatigue, obsessive worry, short temper, poor communication, insomnia, and mood fluctuations. In turn, their performance at work may suffer, leading to more pressure and extreme behaviors. All of these negative outcomes inevitably influence the family environment and the attempt to effectively balance the two domains.

The individual must play an active role in self-management in order to balance work and family lives. A key step in this process is the realization of the need to balance both of these aspects of their lives and the examination of self-expectations. It is important for employees to be aware of the demands that they place upon themselves in order to understand how to generate reasonable expectations that allow for a balance between the two domains. This self-knowledge must be gained in order to create the awareness that an individual needs to alter his or her perceptions, behaviors, and lifestyles. The resulting increased awareness will open the door for the individual to seek the support that helps reduce work–family conflict. Employees must be willing to ask for the support they need, whether from their partner or their organization, in order to benefit from this valuable source of strength. Communication of individual needs to all those affected by a poor work–family balance—for example, partners, children, supervisors, plays an important role in this process. The acceptance of support, when offered—is essential for managing these dual obligations.

While the failure to balance work and family lives effectively holds significant ramifications for individuals, their families, and their organizations, it is important for employees to realize that they have options available to help manage the amount of work–family conflict they experience. There are three key components which must all be addressed to achieve this desired balance: managing work responsibilities, managing family obligations, and managing self-imposed expectations. Each of these components represents a distinct aspect of the worker's life over which he must exhibit a degree of control to effectively manage all of the conflicting pressures often found in work and family domains. For the individual, it is important to realize that he plays an active role in determining the degree of work–family conflict he experiences.

A WORD TO THE WISE EXECUTIVE

Effectively balancing the mutual demands of both work and non-work lives is an essential component of managing today's workforce. While the demands between the alternative domains may create a conflict for some employees, we believe that each of these aspects of an individual's life can coexist successfully. In other words, conflict does not have to occur, and the alternative aspects of an individual's life can be complimentary, rather than competitive. The key consideration for employees, executives, and organizations is the active management of each role. Once that is achieved, the probability of engaging fully in all domains increases greatly.

It is obvious that many opportunities exist for conflict between an executive's work and non-work roles, due to time demands and the ever-present strain associated with demanding organizational positions. However, management strategies can enable the executive to find a balance in his or her life in which success in each of the life roles is attainable. We do not believe that success in the work role necessarily constitutes decreased functioning in the non-work role or vice versa. Instead, both roles, as well as self-expectations, can be managed, and even embraced, simultaneously. All of the contributing forces, such as self, family, and organizational demands, can co-exist without creating conflict. The key factor is that individuals are aware of the potential impact of each role on the other roles in their lives. Consequently, the active management of energy, as opposed to time, can enable executives to achieve in all areas. Therefore, the potential solution to work–family conflict is more complex than simply spending the same amount of quantitative hours in each domain. Instead, the understanding of which time, and the quality of that time, becomes much more important. As a result, executives may still spend a greater number of hours outside of the home domain, but the total hours spent enacting the family role may become less influential on life and family satisfaction than the nature of those hours.

Selected Bibliography

Insight into the development and types of work–family conflict can be achieved by reading Jeffrey Greenhaus and Nicholas Beutell's article entitled "Sources of Conflict Between Work and Family Roles," *Academy of Management Review*, 1985: 10, 76–88. A thorough explanation of the effects of work–family conflict, in terms of individual, family, and societal implications, can be found in Donna Wiley's 1987 article "The Relationship Between Work–Nonwork Role Conflict and Job-Related Outcomes: Some Unanticipated Findings," which appeared in the *Journal of Management*, as well as Linda Thomas and Daniel Ganster's article "Impact of Family-Supportive Work Variables on Work–Family Conflict and Strain: A Control Perspective," *Journal of Applied Psychology* 80: 6–15. Further evidence is documented in the article entitled "Compelling Evidence of the Need for Corporate Work/Life Balance Initiatives: Results from a National Survey of Stressful Life Events," by Charles Hobson, Linda Delunas, and Dawn Kesic from the *Journal of Employment Counseling* 38: 38–44. Other information on the issues of work/life balance can be gained from reading Joan Kofodimos's *Balancing Act* (San Francisco: Jossey-Bass, 1993) and the *Harvard Business Review*'s book on *Work and Life Balance* (Cambridge: Harvard Business School Press, 2000) and accessing web-based resources such as www.worklifebalance.com or www.worklifebalancecenter.org.

Additional in-depth readings on stress, the demands that more broadly cause it in addition to work–family conflict, its array of psychological, behavioral, and medical consequences, the various moderating variables in the stress process, and the range of individual and organizational interventions for healthy stress management are available in *Preventive Stress Management in Organizations* by James Campbell Quick, Jonathan D. Quick, Debra L. Nelson, and Joseph J. Hurrell, Jr. (Washington, DC: American Psychological Association, 1997), the *Handbook of Work Stress*, edited by Julian Barling, Kevin Kelloway, and Michael Frone (Thousand Oaks, CA: Sage Publications, 2005), and the *Handbook of Stress, Medicine, and Health*, Second Edition, edited by Cary L. Cooper (Boca Raton, FL: CRC Press, 2005).

To gain an understanding of the alternatives that individuals can use to simultaneously manage work, family, and self-expectations, interested readers should pick up Jim Loehr and Tony Schwartz's book entitled *The Power of Full Engagement* (New York: Free Press, 2003). These authors stress that managing energy, as opposed to time, is the key ingredient for successfully engaging in all areas of one's life. Additionally, Boris Baltes and Heather Heydens-Gahir have suggested that the life-management strategy of selection, optimization, and compensation (SOC) can be a useful tool for individuals seeking to find a work–family balance in their lives. Their suggestions can be found in the article "Reduction of Work–Family Conflict through the Use of Selection, Optimization, and Compensation Behaviors," which was printed in the *Journal of Applied Psychology*, 2003, 88: 1005–1018.

Finally, two key pieces illustrate the need for individuals to play an active role in managing the joint enactment of both work and family roles. Ellen Kossek and Raymond Noe suggest that boundary management is a key factor for individuals faced with conflicting role demands ("Work–Family Role Synthesis: Individual and Organizational Determinants," *International Journal of Conflict Management* 10: 102–129). They propose that individuals can achieve a work–family synthesis while continuing to meet the obligations of each life role. In a similar vein, Christena Nippert-Eng proposes in her book *Home and Work: Negotiating Boundaries through Everyday Life* (Chicago: University of Chicago Press, 1996) that an effective balance between work and family can be achieved along a continuum of boundary management. She presents two alternative approaches in which individuals either clearly segment their lives into work and family time, or integrate the two domains with each other. Each of these tools can help individuals, organizations, and families understand the role they play in balancing the competing demands in employees' lives.

PART II

CREATING EFFECTIVE WORK GROUPS

This section of the book is devoted to the key skills that employees and managers need to work well with others.

CHAPTER 8
INTERPERSONAL COMMUNICATION

Communication is the number one skill recruiters seek in candidates for business jobs. It is the basis for numerous tasks such as giving instructions that get obeyed, settling conflicts, and influencing others to follow your leadership, important and frequently used workplace skills. Communication extends beyond the actual words that are said to the symbolic meaning of one's actions as a manager.

Carl Rogers, a noted psychologist, is famous for his work on active listening. Rogers and Richard Farson wrote "Active Listening," the classic description of this crucial skill. They wrote this article long before the advent of gender-neutral language, so be prepared for a raft of masculine pronouns and see whether this type of writing has any effect on you personally.

In another classic communication article, "Defensive Communication," Jack Gibb expanded on Rogers's work. Gibb explains why it's important to avoid making other people defensive when you communicate with them and distinguishes between behaviors that result in defensive versus supportive communication climates.

There are many factors that influence the way we communicate, such as family and socioeconomic backgrounds, the region where people grew up, gender, education, and culture. Given the demands of global business and multicultural teams, many businesses are paying more attention to lessons from the field of intercultural communication. David Thomas and Joyce Osland, international management researchers with overseas experience, distill some of these lessons in "Mindful Communication." This selection is written as a basic primer for businesspeople who want to decode messages accurately and be more effective in global business interactions. Thomas and Osland describe the basic style differences to look for and provide practical advice for intercultural encounters. Becoming more mindful makes for better communicators, whether or not there are cultural barriers involved.

ACTIVE LISTENING*

Carl R. Rogers
Richard E. Farson

THE MEANING OF ACTIVE LISTENING

One basic responsibility of the supervisor or manager is the development, adjustment, and integration of individual employees. He tries to develop employee potential, delegate responsibility, and achieve cooperation. To do so, he must have, among other abilities, the ability to listen intelligently and carefully to those with whom he works.

There are, however, many kinds of listening skills. The lawyer, for example, when questioning a witness, listens for contradictions, irrelevancies, errors, and weaknesses. But this is not the kind of listening skill we are concerned with. The lawyer usually is not listening in order to help the witness adjust, cooperate, or produce. Our emphasis will be on listening skills of the supervisor or manager that will help employees gain a clearer understanding of their situations, take responsibility, and cooperate with each other.

TWO EXAMPLES

The kind of listening we have in mind is called "active listening." It is called "active" because the listener has a very definite responsibility. He does not passively absorb words which are spoken to him. He actively tries to grasp the facts and the feelings in what he hears, and he tries, by his listening, to help the speaker work out his own problems.

To get a clearer picture of what active listening means, let us consider two different approaches to the same work problem. The example is set in the printing industry, but the behavior of the men could surface in any organization.

Example no. 1

Foreman: Hey, Al, I don't get this rush order. We can't handle any 50,000 run today. What do they think we are?

Supervisor: But that's the order. So get it out as soon as you can. We're under terrific pressure this week.

F: Don't they know we're behind schedule already because of that press breakdown?

S: Look, Kelly, I don't decide what goes on upstairs. I just have to see that the work gets out and that's what I'm gonna do.

F: The guys aren't gonna like this.

S: That's something you'll have to work out with them, not me.

---

*Reprinted by special permission of the Industrial Relations Center of the University of Chicago and the authors.

Example no. 2

F: Hey, Ross, I don't get this rush order. We can't handle any run of 50,000 today. What do they think we are?
S: They're pushing you pretty hard, aren't they Kelly?
F: They sure are and I'm getting sore. We were just about back to schedule after the press breakdown. Now this comes along.
S: As if you didn't have enough work to do, huh?
F: Yeah. I don't know how I'm going to tell the pressman about this.
S: Hate to face him with a rush order now, is that it?
F: I really do. Joe is under a real strain today. Seems like everything we do around here is rush, rush, rush!
S: I guess you feel it's unfair to load anything more on him today.
F: Well, yeah. I know there must be plenty of pressure on everybody to get the work out, but—well, Joe doesn't deserve all the rush orders. But, if that's the way it is—I guess I'd better get the word to him and see how I can rearrange the work flow.

There are obviously many differences between these two examples. The main one, however, is that Ross, the supervisor in the second example, is using the active listening approach. He is listening and responding in a way that makes it clear that he appreciates both the meaning and the feeling behind what Kelly is saying.

Active listening does not necessarily mean long sessions spent listening to grievances, personal or otherwise. It is simply a way of approaching those problems which arise out of the usual day-to-day events of any job.

To be effective, active listening must be firmly grounded in the basic attitudes of the user. We cannot employ it as a technique if our fundamental attitudes are in conflict with its basic concepts. If we try, our behavior will be empty and sterile, and our associates will be quick to recognize such behavior. Until we can demonstrate a spirit which genuinely respects the potential worth of the individual, which considers his rights and trusts his capacity for self-direction, we cannot begin to be effective listeners.

WHAT WE ACHIEVE BY LISTENING

Active listening is an important way to bring about changes in people. Despite the popular notion that listening is a passive approach, clinical and research evidence clearly shows that sensitive listening is a most effective agent for individual personality change and group development. Listening brings about changes in people's attitudes toward themselves and others, and also brings about changes in their basic values and personal philosophy. People who have been listened to in this new and special way become more emotionally mature, more open to their experiences, less defensive, more democratic, and less authoritarian.

When people are listened to sensitively, they tend to listen to themselves with more care and make clear exactly what they are feeling and thinking. Group members tend to listen more to each other, become less argumentative, more ready to incorporate other points of view. Because listening reduces the threat of having one's ideas criticized, the person is better able to see them for what they are and is more likely to feel that his contributions are worthwhile.

Not the least important result of listening is the change that takes place within the listener himself. Besides the fact that listening provides more information about people than any other activity, it builds deep, positive relationships and tends to alter constructively the attitudes of the listener. Listening is a growth experience.

HOW TO LISTEN

The goal of active listening is to bring about changes in people. To achieve this end, it relies upon definite techniques—things to do and things to avoid doing. Before discussing these techniques, however, we should first understand why they are effective. To do so, we must understand how the individual personality develops.

THE GROWTH OF THE INDIVIDUAL

Through all of our lives, from early childhood on, we have learned to think of ourselves in certain, very definite ways. We have built up pictures of ourselves. Sometimes these self-pictures are pretty realistic but at other times they are not. For example, an average, overweight lady may fancy herself a youthful, ravishing siren, or an awkward teenager regard himself as a star athlete.

All of us have experiences which fit the way we need to think about ourselves. These we accept. But it is much harder to accept experiences which don't fit. And sometimes, if it is very important for us to hang on to this self-picture, we don't accept or admit these experiences at all.

These self-pictures are not necessarily attractive. A man, for example, may regard himself as incompetent and worthless. He may feel that he is doing his job poorly in spite of favorable appraisals by the organization. As long as he has these feelings about himself he must deny any experiences which would seem not to fit this self-picture, in this case any that might indicate to him that he is competent. It is so necessary for him to maintain this self-picture that he is threatened by anything which would tend to change it. Thus, when the organization raises his salary, it may seem to him only additional proof that he is a fraud. He must hold onto this self-picture, because, bad or good, it's the only thing he has by which he can identify himself.

This is why direct attempts to change this individual or change his self-picture are particularly threatening. He is forced to defend himself or to completely deny the experience. This denial of experience and defense of the self-picture tends to bring on rigidity of behavior and create difficulties in personal adjustment.

The active-listening approach, on the other hand, does not present a threat to the individual's self-picture. He does not have to defend it. He is able to explore it, see it for what it is, and make his own decision as to how realistic it is. He is then in a position to change.

If I want to help a man or woman reduce defensiveness and become more adaptive, I must try to remove the threat of myself as a potential changer. As long as the atmosphere is threatening, there can be no effective communication. So I must create a climate which is neither critical, evaluative, nor moralizing. The climate must foster equality and freedom, trust and understanding, acceptance and warmth. In this climate and in this climate only does the individual feel safe enough to incorporate new experiences and new values into his concept of himself. Active listening helps to create this climate.

WHAT TO AVOID

When we encounter a person with a problem, our usual response is to try to change his way of looking at things—to get him to see his situation the way we see it, or would like him to see it. We plead, reason, scold, encourage, insult, prod—anything to bring about a change in the desired direction—that is, in the direction we want him to travel. What we seldom realize, however, is that under these circumstances we are usually responding to *our own* needs to see the world in certain ways. It is always difficult for us to tolerate and understand actions which are different from the ways in which *we* believe *we* should act. If, however, we can free ourselves from the need to influence and direct others in our own paths, we enable ourselves to listen with understanding, and thereby employ the most potent available agent of change.

One problem the listener faces is that of responding to demands for decisions, judgments, and evaluations. He is constantly called upon to agree or disagree with someone or something. Yet, as he well knows, the question or challenge frequently is a masked expression of feelings or needs which the speaker is far more anxious to communicate than he is to have the surface questions answered. Because he cannot speak these feelings openly, the speaker must disguise them to himself and to others in an acceptable form. To illustrate, let us examine some typical questions and the type of answers that might best elicit the feeling beneath them.

These responses recognize the questions but leave the way open for the employee to say what is really bothering him. They allow the listener to participate in the problem or situation without shouldering all responsibility for decision-making or actions. This is a process of thinking *with* people instead of *for* or *about* them.

Passing judgment, whether critical or favorable, makes free expression difficult. Similarly, advice and information are almost always seen as efforts to change a person and thus serve as barriers to his self-expression and the development of a creative relationship. Moreover, advice is seldom taken and information hardly ever utilized. The eager young trainee probably will not become patient just because he is advised that, "The road to success is a long, difficult one, and you must be patient." And it is no more helpful for him to learn that "only one out of a hundred trainees reach top management positions."

Employee's Question	*Listener's Answer*
Just who is responsible for getting this job done?	Do you feel that you don't have enough authority?
Don't you think talent should count more than seniority in promotions?	What do you think are the reasons for your opinion?
What does the boss expect us to do about those broken-down machines?	You're tired of working with worn-out equipment, aren't you?
Don't you think my performance has improved since the last review?	Sounds as if you feel your work has picked up over these last few months.

Interestingly, it is a difficult lesson to learn that *positive evaluations* are sometimes as blocking as negative ones. It is almost as destructive to the freedom of a relationship to tell a person that he is good or capable or right, as to tell him otherwise. To evaluate him positively may make it more difficult for him to tell of the faults that distress him or the ways in which he believes he is not competent.

Encouragement also may be seen as an attempt to motivate the speaker in certain directions or hold him off rather than as support. "I'm sure everything will work out okay." is not a helpful response to the person who is deeply discouraged about a problem.

In other words, most of the techniques and devices common to human relationships are found to be of little use in establishing the type of relationship we are seeking here.

WHAT TO DO

Just what does active listening entail, then? Basically, it requires that we get inside the speaker, that we grasp, from his point of view, just what it is he is communicating to us. More than that, we must convey to the speaker that we are seeing things *from his point of view*. To listen actively, then, means that there are several things we must do.

Listen for Total Meaning

Any message a person tries to get across usually has two components: the content of the message and the *feeling* or attitude underlying this content. Both are important, both give the message *meaning*. It is this total *meaning* of the message that we must try to understand. For example, a secretary comes to her boss and says, "I've finished that report." This message has obvious factual content and perhaps calls upon the boss for another work assignment. Suppose, on the other hand, that the secretary says, "Well! I'm finally finished with your damn report!" The factual content is the same, but the total meaning of the message has changed—and changed in an important way for both supervisor and worker. Here sensitive listening can facilitate the work relationship in this office. If the boss were to respond by simply giving his secretary some letters to type, would the secretary feel that she had gotten her total message across? Would she feel free to talk to her boss about the difficulty of her work? Would she feel better about the job, more anxious to do good work on her next assignment?

Now, on the other hand, suppose the supervisor were to respond, "Glad to get that over with, huh?" or "That was a rough one, wasn't it?" or "Guess you don't want another one like that again," or anything that tells the worker that he heard and understands. It doesn't necessarily mean that her next work assignment need be changed or that he must spend an hour listening to the worker complain about the problems she encountered. He may do a number of things differently in the light of the new information he has from the worker—but not necessarily. It's just that extra sensitivity on the part of the supervisor that can transform an average working climate into a good one.

Respond to Feelings

In some instances the content is far less important than the feeling which underlies it. To catch the full flavor or meaning of the message one must respond particularly to the feeling component. If, for instance, our secretary had said, "I'd like to pile up all those carbons and make a bonfire out of them!" responding to content would be obviously absurd. But to respond to her disgust or anger in trying to work with the report recognizes the meaning of this message. There are various shadings of these components in the meaning of any message. Each time the listener must try to remain sensitive to the total meaning the message has to the speaker. What is she trying to tell me? What does this mean to her? How does she see this situation?

Note All Cues

Not all communication is verbal. The speaker's words alone don't tell us everything he is communicating. And, hence truly sensitive listening requires that we become aware of several kinds of communication besides verbal. The way in which a speaker hesitates in his speech can tell us much about his feelings. So too can the inflection of his voice. He may stress certain points loudly and clearly, and he may mumble others. We should also note such things as the person's facial expressions, body posture, hand movements, eye movements, and breathing. All of these help to convey his total message.

WHAT WE COMMUNICATE BY LISTENING

The first reaction of most people when they consider listening as a possible method for dealing with human beings is that listening cannot be sufficient in itself. Because it is passive, they feel, listening does not communicate anything to the speaker. Actually, nothing could be farther from the truth.

By consistently listening to a speaker you are conveying the idea that:

> *I'm interested in you as a person, and I think that what you feel is important. I respect your thoughts, and even if I don't agree with them, I know that they are valid for you. I feel sure that you have a contribution to make. I'm not trying to change you or evaluate you. I just want to understand you. I think you're worth listening to, and I want you to know that I'm the kind of person you can talk to.*

The subtle but most important aspect of this is that it is the *demonstration* of the message that works. Although it is most difficult to convince someone that you respect him by *telling* him so, you are much more likely to get this message across by really *behaving* that way—by actually *having* and *demonstrating* respect for this person. Listening does this most effectively.

Like other behavior, listening behavior is contagious. This has implications for all communications problems, whether between two people, or within a large organization. To insure good communication between associates up and down the line, one must first take the responsibility for setting a pattern of listening. Just as one learns that anger is usually met with anger, argument with argument, and deception with deception, one can learn that listening can be met with listening. Every person who feels responsibility in a situation can set the tone of the interaction, and the important lesson in this is that any behavior exhibited by one person will eventually be responded to with similar behavior in the other person.

It is far more difficult to stimulate constructive behavior in another person but far more valuable. Listening is one of these constructive behaviors, but if one's attitude is to "wait out" the speaker rather than really listen to him, it will fail. The one who consistently listens with understanding, however, is the one who eventually is most likely to be listened to. If you really want to be heard and understood by another, you can develop him as a potential listener, ready for new ideas, provided you can first develop yourself in these ways and sincerely listen with understanding and respect.

TESTING FOR UNDERSTANDING

Because understanding another person is actually far more difficult than it at first seems, it is important to test constantly your ability to see the world in the way the speaker sees it. You can do this by reflecting in your own words what the speaker seems to mean by his words and actions. His response to this will tell you whether or not he feels understood. A good rule of thumb is to assume that one never really understands until he can communicate this understanding to the other's satisfaction.

Here is an experiment to test your skill in listening. The next time you become involved in a lively or controversial discussion with another person, stop for a moment and suggest that you adopt this ground rule for continued discussion. Before either participant in the discussion can make a point or express an opinion of his own, he must first restate aloud the previous point or position of the other person. This restatement must be in his own words (merely parroting the words of another does not prove that one has understood, but only that he has heard the words). The restatement must be accurate enough to satisfy the speaker before the listener can be allowed to speak for himself.

You might find this procedure useful in a meeting where feelings run high and people express themselves on topics of emotional concern to the group. Before another member of the group expresses his own feelings and thought, he must rephrase the *meaning* expressed by the previous speaker to that person's satisfaction. All the members in the group should be alert to the changes in the emotional climate and the quality of the discussion when this approach is used.

PROBLEMS IN ACTIVE LISTENING

Active listening is not an easy skill to acquire, it demands practice. Perhaps more important, it may require changes in our own basic attitudes. These changes come slowly and sometimes with considerable difficulty. Let us look at some of the major problems in active listening and what can be done to overcome them.

THE PERSONAL RISK

To be effective in active listening, one must have a sincere interest in the speaker. We all live in glass houses as far as our attitudes are concerned. They always show through. And if we are only making a pretense of interest in the speaker, he will quickly pick this up, either consciously or subconsciously. And once he does, he will no longer express himself freely.

Active listening carries a strong element of personal risk. If we manage to accomplish what we are describing here—to sense the feelings of another person, to understand the meaning his experiences have for him, to see the world as he sees it, we risk being changed ourselves. For example, if we permit ourselves to listen our way into the life of a person we do not know or approve of—to get the meaning that life has for him, we risk coming to see the world as he sees it. We are threatened when we give up, even momentarily, what we believe and start thinking in someone else's terms. It takes a great deal of inner security and courage to be able to risk one's self in understanding another.

For the manager, the courage to take another's point of view generally means that he must see *himself* through another's eyes—he must be able to see himself as others see him. To do this may sometimes be unpleasant, but it is far more difficult than *unpleasant*. We are so accustomed to viewing ourselves in certain ways—to seeing and hearing only what we want to see and hear—that it is extremely difficult for a person to free himself from the need to see things his way.

Developing an attitude of sincere interest in the speaker is thus no easy task. It can be developed only by being willing to risk seeing the world from the speaker's point of view. If we have a number of such experiences, however, they will shape an attitude which will allow us to be truly genuine in our interest in the speaker.

HOSTILE EXPRESSIONS

The listener will often hear negative, hostile expressions directed at himself. Such expressions are always hard to listen to. No one likes to hear hostile words or be the target of hostility. And it is not easy to get to the point where one is strong enough to permit these attacks without finding it necessary to defend himself or retaliate.

Because we all fear that people will crumble under the attack of genuine negative feelings, we tend to perpetuate an attitude of pseudo-peace. It is as if we cannot tolerate conflict at all for fear of the damage it could do to us, to the situation, to the others involved. But of course the real damage is done by the denial and suppression of negative feelings.

OUT-OF-PLACE EXPRESSIONS

Expressions dealing with behavior that are not usually acceptable in our society also pose problems for the listener. These out-of-place expressions can take the extreme forms that psychotherapists hear—such as homicidal fantasies or expressions of sexual perversity. The listener often blocks out such expressions because of their obvious threatening quality. At less extreme levels, we all find unnatural or inappropriate behavior difficult to handle. Behavior that brings on a problem situation may be anything from telling an "off-color" story in mixed company to seeing a man cry.

In any face-to-face situation, we will find instances of this type which will momentarily, if not permanently, block any communication. In any organization, expressions of weakness or incompetency will generally be regarded as unacceptable and therefore will block good two-way communication. For example, it is difficult to listen to a manager tell of his feelings of failure in being able to "take charge" of a situation in his department because all administrators are supposed to be able to "take charge."

ACCEPTING POSITIVE FEELINGS

It is both interesting and perplexing to note that negative or hostile feelings or expressions are much easier to deal with in any face-to-face relationship than are positive feelings. This is especially true for the manager because the culture expects him to be independent, bold, clever, and aggressive and manifest no feelings of warmth, gentleness, and intimacy. He therefore comes to regard these feelings as soft and inappropriate. But no matter how they are regarded, they remain a human need. The denial of these feelings in himself and his associates does not get the manager out of a problem of dealing with them. The feelings simply become veiled and confused. If recognized they would work for the total effort; unrecognized, they work against it.

EMOTIONAL DANGER SIGNALS

The listener's own emotions are sometimes a barrier to active listening. When emotions are at their height, when listening is most necessary, it is most difficult to set aside one's own concerns and be understanding. Our emotions are often our own worst enemies when we try to become listeners. The more involved and invested we are in a particular situation or problem, the less we are likely to be willing or able to listen to the feelings and attitudes of others. That is, the more we find it necessary to respond to our own needs, the less we are able to respond to the needs of another. Let us look at some of the main danger signals that warn us that our emotions may be interfering with our listening.

Defensiveness

The points about which one is most vocal and dogmatic, the points which one is most anxious to impose on others—these are always the points one is trying to talk oneself into believing. So one danger signal becomes apparent when you find yourself stressing a point or trying to convince another. It is at these times that you are likely to be less secure and consequently less able to listen.

Resentment of Opposition

It is always easier to listen to an idea which is similar to one of your own than to an opposing view. Sometimes, in order to clear the air, it is helpful to pause for a moment when you feel your ideas and position being challenged, reflect on the situation, and express your concern to the speaker.

Clash of Personalities

Here again, our experience has consistently shown us that the genuine expression of feelings on the part of the listener will be more helpful in developing a sound relationship than the suppression of them. This is so whether the feelings be resentment, hostility, threat, or admiration. A basically honest relationship, whatever the nature of it, is the most productive of all. The other party becomes secure when he learns that the listener can express his feelings honestly and openly to him. We should keep this in mind when we begin to fear a clash of personalities in the listening relationship. Otherwise, fear of our own emotions will choke off full expression of feelings.

LISTENING TO OURSELVES

To listen to oneself is a prerequisite to listening to others. And it is often an effective means of dealing with the problems we have outlined above. When we are most aroused, excited, and demanding, we are least able to understand our own feelings and attitudes. Yet, in dealing with the problems of others, it becomes most important to be sure of one's own position, values, and needs.

The ability to recognize and understand the meaning which a particular episode has for you, with all the feelings which it stimulates in you, and the ability to express this meaning when you find it getting in the way of active listening, will clear the air and enable you once again to be free to listen. That is, if some person or situation touches off feelings within you which tend to block your attempts to listen with understanding, begin listening to yourself. It is much more helpful in developing effective relationships to avoid suppressing these feelings. Speak them out as clearly as you can, and try to enlist the other person as a listener to your feelings. A person's listening ability is limited by his ability to listen to himself.

ACTIVE LISTENING AND ORGANIZATION GOALS

"How can listening improve productivity?"
"We're in business, and it is a rugged, fast, competitive affair. How are we going to find time to counsel our employees?"
"We have to concern ourselves with organizational problems first."
"We can't afford to spend all day listening when there is work to do."
"What's morale got to do with service to the public?"
"Sometimes we have to sacrifice an individual for the good of the rest of the people in the organization."

Those of us who are trying to advance the listening approach in organizations hear these comments frequently. And because they are so honest and legitimate, they pose a real problem. Unfortunately, the answers are not so clear-cut as the questions.

INDIVIDUAL IMPORTANCE

One answer is based on an assumption that is central to the listening approach. That assumption is: The kind of behavior which helps the individual will eventually be the best thing that could be done for the work group. Or saying it another way: The things that are best for the individual are best for the organization. This is a conviction of ours, based on our experience in psychology and education. The research evidence from organizations is still coming in. We find that putting the group first, at the expense of the individual, besides being an uncomfortable individual experience, does not unify the group. In fact, it tends to make the group less a group. The members become anxious and suspicious.

We are not at all sure in just what ways the group does benefit from a concern demonstrated for an individual, but we have several strong leads. One is that the group feels more secure when an individual member is being listened to and provided for with concern and sensitivity. And we assume that a secure group will ultimately be a better group. When each individual feels that he need not fear exposing himself to the group, he is likely to contribute more freely and spontaneously. When the leader of a group responds to the individual, puts the individual first, the other members of the group will follow suit, and the group comes to act as a unit in recognizing and responding to the needs of a particular member. This positive, constructive action seems to be a much more satisfying experience for a group than the experience of dispensing with a member.

LISTENING AND PRODUCTIVITY

As to whether or not listening or any other activity designed to better human relations in an organization actually makes the organization more productive—whether morale has a definite relationship to performance is not known for sure. There are some who frankly hold that there is no relationship to be expected between morale and productivity—that productivity often depends upon the social misfit, the eccentric, or the isolate. And there are some who simply choose to work in a climate of cooperation and harmony, in a high-morale group, quite aside from the question of achievement or productivity.

A report from the Survey Research Center at the University of Michigan on research conducted at the Prudential Life Insurance Company lists seven findings related to production and morale. First-line supervisors in high-production work groups were found to differ from those in low-production groups in that they:

1. Are under less close supervision from their own supervisors.
2. Place less direct emphasis upon production as the goal.
3. Encourage employee participation in the making of decisions.
4. Are more employee-centered.
5. Spend more of their time in supervision and less in straight production work.
6. Have a greater feeling of confidence in their supervisory roles.
7. Feel that they know where they stand with the company.

After mentioning that other dimensions of morale, such as identification with the company, intrinsic job satisfaction, and satisfaction with job status, were not found significantly related to productivity, the report goes on to suggest the following psychological interpretation:

> *People are more effectively motivated when they are given some degree of freedom in the way in which they do their work than when every action is prescribed in advance. They do better when some degree of decision making about their jobs is possible than when all decisions are made for them. They respond more adequately when they are treated as personalities than as cogs in a machine. In short, if the ego motivation of self-determination, of self-expression, of a sense of personal worth can be tapped, the individual can be more effectively energized. The use of external sanctions, or pressuring for production may work to some degree, but not to the extent that the more internalized motives do. When the individual comes to identify himself with his job and with the work of his group, human resources are much more fully utilized in the production process.*

The Survey Research Center has also conducted studies among workers in other industries. In discussing the results of these studies, Robert L. Kahn writes:

> *In the studies of clerical workers, railroad workers, and workers in heavy industry, the supervisors with the better production records gave a larger proportion of their time to supervisory functions, especially to the interpersonal aspects of their jobs. The supervisors of the lower-producing sections were more likely to spend their time in tasks which the men themselves were performing, or in the paper-work aspects of their jobs.*

MAXIMUM CREATIVENESS

There may never be enough research evidence to satisfy everyone on this question. But speaking from an organizational point of view, in terms of the problem of developing resources for productivity, the maximum creativeness and productive effort of the human beings in the organization are the richest untapped source of power available. The difference between the maximum productive capacity of people and that output which the organization is now realizing is immense. We simply suggest that this maximum capacity might be closer to realization if we sought to release the motivation that already exists within people rather than try to stimulate them externally.

This releasing of the individual is made possible first of all by listening, with respect and understanding. Listening is a beginning toward making the individual feel himself worthy of making contributions, and this could result in a very dynamic and productive organization. Profit making organizations are never too rugged or too busy to take time to procure the most efficient technological advances or to develop rich sources of raw materials. But technology and materials are but paltry resources in comparison with the resources that are already within the people in the organization.

G. L. Clements, of Jewel Tea Co., Inc., in talking about the collaborative approach to management says:

> *We feel that this type of approach recognizes that there is a secret ballot going on at all times among the people in any business. They vote for or against their supervisors. A favorable vote for the supervisor shows up in the cooperation,*

teamwork, understanding, and production of the group. To win this secret ballot, each supervisor must share the problems of his group and work for them.

The decision to spend time listening to employees is a decision each supervisor or manager has to make for himself. Managers increasingly must deal with people and their relationships rather than turning out goods and services. The minute we take a man from work and make him a supervisor he is removed from the basic production of goods or services and now must begin relating to men and women instead of nuts and bolts. People are different from things and our supervisor is called upon for a different line of skills completely. These new tasks call for a special kind of person. The development of the supervisor as a listener is a first step in becoming this special person.

DEFENSIVE COMMUNICATION*

Jack R. Gibb

One way to understand communication is to view it as a people process rather than as a language process. If one is to make fundamental improvement in communication, he must make changes in interpersonal relationships. One possible type of alteration—and the one with which this paper is concerned—is that of reducing the degree of defensiveness.

DEFINITION AND SIGNIFICANCE

"Defensive behavior" is behavior which occurs when an individual perceives threat or anticipates threat in the group. The person who behaves defensively, even though he also gives some attention to the common task, devotes an appreciable portion of his energy to defending himself. Besides talking about the topic, he thinks about how he appears to others, how he may be seen more favorably, how he may win, dominate, impress or escape punishment, and/or how he may avoid or mitigate a perceived or anticipated attack.

Such inner feelings and outward acts tend to create similarly defensive postures in others; and, if unchecked, the ensuing circular response becomes increasingly destructive. Defensive behavior, in short, engenders defensive listening, and this in turn produces postural, facial, and verbal cues which raise the defense level of the original communicator.

Defensive arousal prevents the listener from concentrating upon the message. Not only do defensive communicators send off multiple value, motive, and affect cues, but also defensive recipients distort what they receive. As a person becomes more and more defensive, he becomes less and less able to perceive accurately the motives, the values, and the emotions of the sender. The writer's analysis of tape recorded discussions revealed that increases in defensive behavior were correlated positively with losses in efficiency in communication.[1] Specifically, distortions became greater when defensive states existed in the groups.

*Reprinted with permission from the *Journal of Communication 11*, no. 3 (September 1961): 141–48.

The converse also is true. The more "supportive" or defense reductive the climate the less the receiver reads into the communication distorted loadings which arise from projections of his own anxieties, motives, and concerns. As defenses are reduced, the receivers become better able to concentrate upon the structure, the content, and the cognitive meanings of the message.

CATEGORIES OF DEFENSIVE AND SUPPORTIVE COMMUNICATION

In working over an eight-year period with recordings of discussions occurring in varied settings, the writer developed the six pairs of defensive and supportive categories presented in Table 1. Behavior which listeners perceive as possessing any of the characteristics listed in the left-hand column arouses defensiveness, whereas that which they interpret as having any of the qualities designated as supportive reduces defensive feelings. The degree to which these reactions occur depend upon the personal level of defensiveness and upon the general climate in the group at the time.[2]

EVALUATION AND DESCRIPTION

Speech or other behavior which appears evaluative increases defensiveness. If by expression, manner of speech, tone of voice, or verbal content the sender seems to be evaluating or judging the listener, then the receiver goes on guard. Of course, other factors may inhibit the reaction. If the listener thinks that the speaker regards him as an equal and is being open and spontaneous, for example, the evaluativeness in a message will be neutralized and perhaps not even perceived. This same principle applies equally to the other five categories of potentially defense-producing climates. The six sets are interactive.

Because our attitudes toward other persons are frequently, and often necessarily, evaluative, expressions which the defensive person will regard as nonjudgmental are hard to frame. Even the simplest question usually conveys the answer that the sender wishes or implies the response that would fit into his value system. A mother, for example, immediately following an earth tremor that shook the house, sought for her small son with the question: "Bobby, where are you?" The timid and plaintive "Mommy, I didn't do it" indicated how Bobby's chronic mild defensiveness predisposed him to react with a projection of his own guilt and in the context of his chronic assumption that questions are full of accusation.

TABLE 1 Categories of Behavior Characteristic of Supportive and Defensive Climates in Small Groups

Defensive Climates	*Supportive Climates*
1. Evaluation	1. Description
2. Control	2. Problem orientation
3. Strategy	3. Spontaneity
4. Neutrality	4. Empathy
5. Superiority	5. Equality
6. Certainty	6. Provisionalism

Anyone who has attempted to train professionals to use information-seeking speech with neutral affect appreciates how difficult it is to teach a person to say even the simple "Who did that?" without being seen as accusing. Speech is so frequently judgmental that there is a reality base for the defensive interpretations which are so common.

When insecure, group members are particularly likely to place blame, to see others as fitting into categories of good or bad, to make moral judgments of their colleagues, and to question the value, motive, and affect loadings of the speech which they hear. Since value loadings imply a judgment of others, a belief that the standards of the speaker differ from his own causes the listener to become defensive.

Descriptive speech, in contrast to that which is evaluative, tends to arouse a minimum of uneasiness. Speech acts which the listener perceives as genuine requests for information or as material with neutral loadings is descriptive. Specifically, presentations of feelings, events, perceptions, or processes which do not ask or imply that the receiver change behavior or attitude are minimally defense-producing. The difficulty in avoiding overtone is illustrated by the problems of news reporters in writing stories about unions, Communists, Negroes, and religious activities without tipping off the "party" line of the newspaper. One can often tell from the opening words in a news article which side the newspaper's editorial policy favors.

CONTROL AND PROBLEM ORIENTATION

Speech which is used to control the listener evokes resistance. In most of our social intercourse someone is trying to do something to someone else—to change an attitude, to influence behavior, or to restrict the field of activity. The degree to which attempts to control produce defensiveness depends upon the openness of the effort, for a suspicion that hidden motives exist heightens resistance. For this reason attempts of non-directive therapists and progressive educators to refrain from imposing a set of values, a point of view, or a problem solution upon the receivers meet with many barriers. Since the norm is control, non-controllers must earn the perceptions that their efforts have no hidden motives. A bombardment of persuasive "messages" in the fields of politics, education, special causes, advertising, religion, medicine, industrial relations, and guidance has bred cynical and paranoidal responses in listeners.

Implicit in all attempts to alter another person is the assumption by the change agent that the person to be altered is inadequate. That the speaker secretly views the listener as ignorant, unable to make his own decisions, uninformed, immature, unwise, or possessed of wrong or inadequate attitudes is a subconscious perception which gives the latter a valid base for defensive reactions.

Methods of control are many and varied. Legalistic insistence on detail, restrictive regulations and policies, conformity norms, and all laws are among the methods. Gestures, facial expressions, other forms of non-verbal communication, and even such simple acts as holding a door open in a particular manner are means of imposing one's will upon another and hence are potential sources of resistance.

Problem orientation, on the other hand, is the antithesis of persuasion. When the sender communicates a desire to collaborate in defining a mutual problem and in seeking its solution, she tends to create the same problem orientation in the listener, and, of greater importance, she implies that she has no predetermined solution, attitude, or method to impose. Such behavior is permissive in that it allows the receiver to set his own goals, make his own decisions, and evaluate his own progress—or to share with the sender in doing so. The exact methods of attaining permissiveness are not known, but they must involve a constellation of cues, and they certainly go beyond mere verbal assurances that the communicator has no hidden desires to exercise control.

STRATEGY AND SPONTANEITY

When the sender is perceived as engaged in a stratagem involving ambiguous and multiple motivations, the receiver becomes defensive. No one wishes to be a guinea pig, a role player, or an impressed actor, and no one likes to be the victim of some hidden motivation. That which is concealed, also, may appear larger than it really is, with the degree of defensiveness of the listener determining the perceived size of the suppressed element. The intense reaction of the reading audience to the material in the *Hidden Persuaders* indicates the prevalence of defensive reactions to multiple motivations behind strategy. Group members who are seen as "taking a role, " as feigning emotion, as toying with their colleagues, as withholding information, or as having special sources of data are especially resented. One participant once complained that another was "using a listening technique" on him!

A large part of the adverse reaction to much of the so-called human relations training is a feeling against what are perceived as gimmicks and tricks to fool or to "involve" people, to make a person think he is making his own decision, or to make the listener feel that the sender is genuinely interested in him as a person. Particularly violent reactions occur when it appears that someone is trying to make a stratagem appear spontaneous. One person has reported a boss who incurred resentment by habitually using the gimmick of "spontaneously" looking at his watch and saying, "My gosh, look at the time—I must run to an appointment." The belief was that the boss would create less irritation by honestly asking to be excused.

Similarly, the deliberate assumption of guilelessness and natural simplicity is especially resented. Monitoring the tapes of feedback and evaluation sessions in training groups indicates the surprising extent to which members perceive the strategies of their colleagues. This perceptual clarity may be quite shocking to the strategist, who usually feels that he has cleverly hidden the motivational aura around the "gimmick."

This aversion to deceit may account for one's resistance to politicians who are suspected of behind-the-scenes planning to get his vote; to psychologists whose listening apparently is motivated by more than the manifest or content-level interest in his behavior, or to the sophisticated, smooth, or clever person whose "one-upmanship" is marked with guile. In training groups the role-flexible person frequently is resented because his changes in behavior are perceived as strategic maneuvers.

Conversely, behavior which appears to be spontaneous and free of deception is defense reductive. If the communicator is seen as having a clean id, as having uncomplicated motivations, as being straightforward and honest, and as behaving spontaneously in response to the situation, he is likely to arouse minimal defense.

NEUTRALITY AND EMPATHY

When neutrality in speech appears to the listener to indicate a lack of concern for his welfare, he becomes defensive. Group members usually desire to be perceived as valued persons, as individuals of special worth, and as objects of concern and affection. The clinical, detached, person-is-an-object-of-study attitude on the part of many psychologist-trainers is resented by group members. Speech with low affect that communicates little warmth or caring is in such contrast with the affect-laden speech in social situations that it sometimes communicates rejection.

Communication that conveys empathy for the feelings and respect for the worth of the listener, is particularly supportive and defense reductive. Reassurance results when a message indicates that the speaker identifies himself with the listener's problems, shares his feelings, and accepts his emotional reactions at face value. Abortive efforts to deny the legitimacy of the receiver's emotions by assuring the receiver that he need not feel bad, that he should not feel rejected, or that he is overly anxious, though often intended as support giving, may impress the listener as lack of acceptance. The combination of understanding and empathizing with the other person's emotions with no accompanying effort to change him apparently is supportive at a high level.

The importance of gestural behavior cues in communicating empathy should be mentioned. Apparently spontaneous facial and bodily evidences of concern are often interpreted as especially valid evidence of deep-level acceptance.

SUPERIORITY AND EQUALITY

When a person communicates to another that he feels superior in position, power, wealth, intellectual ability, physical characteristics, or other ways, he arouses defensiveness. Here, as with the other sources of disturbance, whatever arouses feelings of inadequacy causes the listener to center upon the affect loading of the statement rather than upon the cognitive elements. The receiver then reacts by not hearing the message, by forgetting it, by competing with the sender, or by becoming jealous of him.

The person who is perceived as feeling superior communicates that he is not willing to enter into a shared problem-solving relationship, that he probably does not desire feedback, that he does not require help, and/or that he will be likely to try to reduce the power, the status, or the worth of the receiver.

Many ways exist for creating the atmosphere that the sender feels himself equal to the listener. Defenses are reduced when one perceives the sender as being willing to enter into participative planning with mutual trust and respect. Differences in talent, ability, worth, appearance, status, and power often exist, but the low defense communicator seems to attach little importance to these distinctions.

CERTAINTY AND PROVISIONALISM

The effects of dogmatism in producing defensiveness are well known. Those who seem to know the answers, to require no additional data, and to regard themselves as teachers rather than as co-workers tend to put others on guard. Moreover, in the writer's experiment, listeners often perceived manifest expressions of certainty as connoting inward feelings of inferiority. They saw the dogmatic individual as needing to be right, as wanting to win an argument rather than solve a problem, and as seeing his ideas as truths to be defended. This kind of behavior often was associated with acts which others regarded as attempts to exercise control. People who were right seemed to have low tolerance for members who were "wrong" (i.e., who did not agree with the sender).

One reduces the defensiveness of the listener when he communicates that he is willing to experiment with his own behavior, attitudes, and ideas. The person who appears to be taking provisional attitudes, to be investigating issues rather than taking sides on them, to be problem solving rather than debating, and to be willing to experiment and explore tends to communicate that the listener may have some control over the shared quest or the investigation of the ideas. If a person is genuinely searching for information and data, he does not resent help or company along the way.

CONCLUSION

The implications of the above material for the parent, the teacher, the manager, the administrator, or the therapist are fairly obvious. Arousing defensiveness interferes with communication and thus makes it difficult—and sometimes impossible—for anyone to convey ideas clearly and to move effectively toward the solution of therapeutic, educational, or managerial problems.

Endnotes

1. J. R. Gibb, "Defense Level and Influence in Small Groups," *Leadership and Interpersonal Behavior*, eds. L. Petrullo and B. M. Bass (New York: Holt, Rinehart & Winston, 1961): 66–81.
2. J. R. Gibb, "Sociopsychological Processes of Group Instruction," *The Dynamics of Instructional Groups*, ed. N. B. Henry (Fifty-Ninth Yearbook of the National Society for the Study of Education, Part 11, 1960): 115–35.

MINDFUL COMMUNICATION*

David C. Thomas
Joyce S. Osland

Interpersonal skills are competencies that all people have to some degree. They have to do with how people understand the world. We think of them as interpersonal because they are related to how people exert influence over others on a one-to-one basis. In fact, exercising interpersonal influence over others requires a range of multidimensional and complex skills. We are focusing on two of the most critical global competencies, mindful communication and creating and building trust.

MINDFUL COMMUNICATION

Communication involves significantly more than speaking the same language. Communication is the act of transmitting messages to another person who interprets the message by giving it meaning. In order for such exchange of meaning to occur, the sender and receiver must share common understanding. We call this shared understanding *grounding*. Such grounding is updated constantly over the course of any communication.[1] When individuals have less shared understanding, they lack common information, which explains why the difficulty of communication increases.

---

*Adapted and reprinted with permission from *The Blackwell Handbook of Global Management: A Guide to Managing Complexity* (Oxford, UK: Blackwell Publishing, 2004): 94–108.

Todd works for an American company in Korea. Sometimes he wonders why he ever accepted a position overseas—there seems to be so much that he just doesn't understand. Todd's secretary, Chungmin, speaks English with him because he is not fluent in Korean. Nevertheless, one incident in particular occurred the previous Friday when Chungmin made a mistake and forgot to type a letter. Todd considered this a small error but made sure to mention it when he saw her during lunch in the company cafeteria. Ever since then, Chungmin has been acting rather strange and distant. When she walks out of his office, she closes the door more loudly than usual. She will not even look him in the eye, and she has been acting very moody. She even took a few days' sick leave, which she has not done in many years. Todd has no idea how to understand her behavior. Perhaps she really is ill or feels a bit overworked.

When Chungmin returned to work the following Wednesday, Todd called her into his office. "Is there a problem?" he asked. "Because if there is, we need to talk about it. It's affecting your performance. Is something wrong? Why don't you tell me? It's okay."

At this, Chungmin looked quite distressed. She admitted the problem had something to do with her mistake the previous Friday, and Todd explained that it was no big deal. "Forget it," he said, feeling satisfied with himself for working this out. "In the future, just make sure to tell me if something is wrong." But over the next few weeks, Chungmin took six more sick days and did not speak to Todd once.

Adapted from Cushner, K., & Brislin, R. W. *Cultural Interactions: A Practical Guide*, Thousand Oaks, CA: Sage, 1996.

The miscommunication in the opening vignette also illustrates the transactional nature of the communication process.[2] Both Todd and Chungmin were sending and receiving messages, adapting their communication based on what they thought the other person was communicating to them, escalating the problem. Both have mistaken assumptions about the extent of grounding they share and expect the other person to communicate according to their own cultural script.[3] As a result, both Todd and Chungmin are communicating in a "mindless" manner. They are simply reacting to the situation in a semiautomatic way based on their own cultural grounding without considering possible cultural differences. For example, what Todd saw as giving constructive feedback, Chungmin perceived as a very rude public reprimand, which she attributed to Todd's thoughtlessness. She responded, mindlessly, by using a Korean script for expressing her displeasure through subtle cues. Because Todd was a novice at intercultural interaction, he failed to perceive this message accurately (he lacked knowledge of Korean culture and grounding) and had difficulty figuring out and making an accurate attribution for Chungmin's behavior. He tried to solve the problem by having an open and frank discussion with Chungmin, another U. S. communication script that was not well received.

Once negative emotions were involved, Chungmin had even less motivation to decode Todd's communication accurately. She responded with more subtle cues to show her discomfort and began to stereotype Todd as an Ugly American. Like an airplane in an ever tightening spin, Todd and Chungmin's failure to correctly diagnose the situation and behave effectively resulted in a negative spiral that only an expert interculturalist could pull out of. The best way to recover from this type of situation is to avoid it in the first place, by learning to engage in mindful communication across cultures.

In this part of the chapter, we first explore what mindful communication is. The two most critical contributors to mindful communication are knowledge of the culture and communication skills, both of which we investigate. We then describe how to build competency in mindful communication and close with a brief summary.

WHAT *MINDFUL* COMMUNICATION IS

Mindfulness means attending to one's internal assumptions, cognitions, and emotions, and simultaneously attuning to the other's assumptions, cognitions, and emotions. It also involves learning to see behavior or information presented in the situation as novel or fresh: viewing a situation from several vantage points or perspectives; attending to the context and the person in which we are perceiving the behavior; and creating new categories through which this new behavior may be understood.[4] The antithesis of mindfulness, *mindlessness*, is exemplified in the following vignette.

MINDLESSNESS

Yesterday, my wife called me at work and asked me to pick up some groceries for dinner on my way home. I have a carefully selected route home that I have designed to minimize traffic, and I follow it every day. In order to stop at the grocery store, I would have to make a slight adjustment to the route. Only after I arrived home to be greeted with the question, "Where are the groceries?", did I realize that I had automatically driven my normal route straight home.

The act of driving an automobile is a complex behavior, but most of us do it this semiautomatic way. And in this case, even when we have been cued to break out of our script, we fall back into it. Much of our behavior, including communication behavior, occurs in this scripted, seemingly mindless manner, which is a semi-reflexive response to the situation. As shown in the opening vignette, the adverse results of mindless communication across cultures are all too apparent. Someone who does not share the same cultural grounding easily misunderstands semi-reflexive communication guided by cultural norms. Mindfulness, on the other hand, puts us in a stage of readiness to interact with people who are different from ourselves. As such, it is a mediating step in linking knowledge with skillful practice.

Mindful communication can be judged by the criteria of appropriateness, effectiveness, and satisfaction.[5] Appropriate communication matches the expectations of both sender and receiver and is perceived as proper. Effective communication achieves mutual shared meaning and the goals desired by the communicators. Finally, satisfaction occurs when a communicator's desired identity image is affirmed rather than disconfirmed during the interaction. Competence in intercultural communication involves (1) the heightened mindfulness described above, which builds on (2) the acquisition of in-depth knowledge, and the development of (3) communication skills. We address both knowledge and communication in the following sections.

KNOWLEDGE OF THE CULTURE

An in-depth knowledge of the culture of the other party in a cross-cultural communication is an important first step in negotiating shared meaning. Understanding cultural values is the foundation for comprehending and decoding the behavior of others and ourselves. Cultural values result in different communication norms that individuals use to guide behavior in certain settings. Knowledge of cultural identities, values, attitudes, and communication practices such as those described previously makes for greater predictability and more accurate attributions. This knowledge allows a better grasp on the internal logic and modal behavior of another culture, which can serve as a first best-guess[6] about behavior in another culture. For instance, individualists tend to express themselves in low-context, direct communication because they value efficiency and are asserting an independent self-identity.

Developing cultural knowledge and sensitivity, a process supported by a global mindset, helps global managers understand the habitual verbal and nonverbal messages and the interaction styles they observe in the multicultural workplace and overseas. Global managers need general knowledge they can extrapolate to incidents to form hypotheses about cultural behavior. Knowledge provides the basic lesson that not all cultures communicate in the same way. Therefore, special attention and caution are required before accurate interpretations can be made. Key elements of knowledge that are important to mindful intercultural communication include knowledge about the communication process itself and about the effects of language, communication style, and nonverbal communication.

THE COMMUNICATION PROCESS

Communication occurs within social systems, and each communicator has a personal context, a field of experience. These backgrounds cause people to encode and decode messages in a unique fashion, which makes it necessary to find a shared field of experience or common grounding. Like all behavior, much communication proceeds in a routine manner without much conscious thought and is consistent with the cultural field in which it is embedded. The communication process can be influenced, however, by "noise," anything that interferes with the intended communication, such as environmental, physiological, and emotional states.

The entire communication process is embedded in culture, which affects how messages are encoded (converted to symbolic form) and sent by some means (a channel) to the receiver, who then interprets (decodes) the message. In this chapter, we define mindful intercultural communication as *a symbolic exchange in which individuals interactively negotiate shared meanings*.[7] The effectiveness of this exchange is critical in a business environment characterized by an ever-increasing number of intercultural interactions. Mastering the intercultural communication process is a fundamental requirement of effective international management.

The basic model of intercultural interaction presented in this section provides a tool for examining the effects of culture on communication. As shown in Figure 1, we can envision intercultural communication as involving three related stages, all affected by culture.

The first stage concerns how messages are sent, perceived, diagnosed, and decoded. Then, individuals must identify how to respond, which involves making attributions about the meaning of the message they have received. Finally, individuals must choose

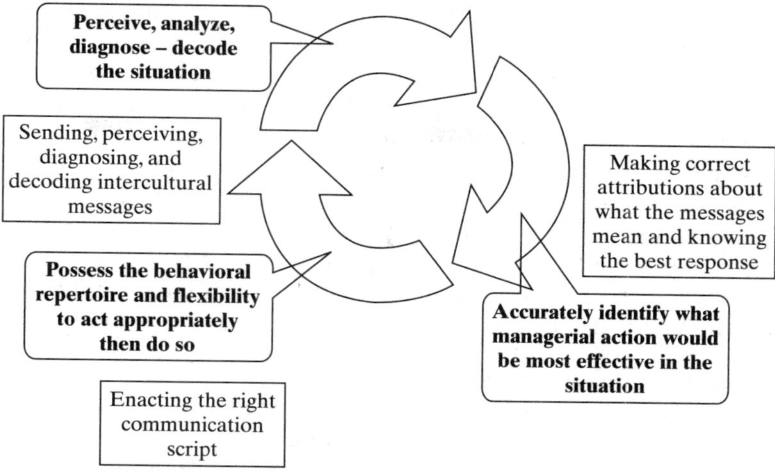

FIGURE 1 Effective Intercultural Communication

from their repertoire of possible responses and enact those that they think are most appropriate. This requires a degree of behavioral flexibility that often separates novices from experts. Expert intercultural communicators are better at diagnosing and decoding messages and more skilled at choosing and enacting effective scripts. The effectiveness of the communication depends on a lack of distortion, which can occur at any stage of the process. Common sources of distortion, explained in the following section, include language, communication style, non-verbal communication, social categorization and stereotyping, and the willingness to communicate.

LANGUAGE

An obvious consideration in intercultural communication is the language being used. Three aspects of language influence the ability to create shared meanings. These are language fluency, language accommodation, and second-language use.

Language Fluency

With reference to our basic model on intercultural interaction, fluency in a foreign language affects a global manager's ability to accurately perceive and diagnose the situation and limits the behavioral repertoire with which he or she can respond. However, the relationship between language fluency and effective communication is not so straightforward that we can simply say more fluency is always better. First, compared to a total lack of fluency, a small amount of language skill (knowing a few words) is beneficial to a manager. To reach a higher level of benefit in intercultural interactions, however, individuals need to develop a much more advanced degree of fluency that permits "conversational currency" (being able to make conversation about everyday things such as local sporting events, and so on).[8] Second, the willingness to communicate with others who are culturally different may be more important than fluency itself.[9] Finally, fluency in a foreign language creates certain perceptions among host-country nationals. Fluent foreign managers are perceived as having beliefs more closely aligned with the locals. Furthermore, host-country nationals may also assume that higher degrees of language fluency by a manager are linked to higher competency in other areas, such as knowledge of cultural norms. For example, cultural blunders by a foreign manager are more likely to be forgiven when people are less fluent; fluency sometimes brings higher expectations for culturally appropriate behavior.[10]

People often restrict their communication to those who speak their own language. For example, when large MNCs buy a local company in countries with a different language, they sometimes appoint as their liaison or local manager the host-country national who is most fluent in the language of the MNC. This person is not necessarily the most competent or best able to teach them about the local subsidiary and context; however, the transaction costs of communicating with them are the lowest.[11]

Language Accommodation

In our opening vignette, Chungmin accommodated to Todd's inability to speak Korean and spoke English. Language accommodation often relates to the behavioral flexibility stage of our model and identifying the behavior that is most appropriate to the particular situation. Determining who will accommodate can be complex and depends on the motives of the parties in the interaction, the identities of the parties, and the situation itself.[12] Japanese managers, for example, tend to believe that it is not possible for foreigners to be really fluent in the Japanese language and will automatically switch to the foreigner's language. The effort that one party puts into accommodating the other's language is often appreciated and reciprocated. In business situations, the default language is often English, but as we will see in the next section, expecting people to work in a second language may have drawbacks.

Second-Language Use

Most intercultural communication involves at least one of the parties switching to a second language. Often this means switching into English. Using a second or bridge language (second language for both parties) may be the most appropriate behavioral response, but the use of a second language has a number of implications for cross-cultural communication. First, working in a second language can create cognitive strain, requiring more effort on the part of second-language users and putting them at a disadvantage. Over long periods of time, second language use can be exhausting. Second, if the native language speaker is unable to recognize signals that indicate lack of understanding or does not work to create an environment where it is acceptable to check for understanding, the second-language speaker may pretend to understand in order to appear competent or avoid embarrassment. To avoid distortion, both participants must devote more attention to the communication process in order to achieve a negotiated meaning.

COMMUNICATION STYLE

Having a language in common does not ensure mutual understanding. Todd and Chungmin spoke the same language, but the differences in their communication styles distorted their communication. Communication style differences are logical extensions of the internalized values and norms of their respective cultures. They are often a barrier to effectively perceiving, analyzing, and decoding intercultural interactions. To avoid misinterpretations and false attributions, managers who work across cultures must learn the culturally based rules that govern the style, conventions, and practices of language use. Some of the most common style differences are high-context versus low-context communication, direct versus indirect communication, succinct versus elaborate communication, and self-enhancement versus self-effacement. We now review each of these style differences.

High- and Low-Context Styles[13]

Cultures vary in terms of the extent to which they use language itself to communicate the message. Low-context communication relies on explicit verbal messages to convey intention or meaning, whereas in high-context communication most of the information is either contained in the physical context or internalized in the person; very little is in the coded or explicit part of the message. In the opening vignette, Todd, in accordance with his low-context style, expected Chungmin to communicate in words, but given her high-context style, she expected him to read the meaning in her nonverbal communication and actions.

HIGH-CONTEXT COMMUNICATION

An Indonesian woman invited the mother of the young man who was courting her daughter to tea. The woman was not pleased with the possibility that her daughter might marry into a family that she viewed as having a lower socioeconomic status. During the visit she never mentioned the relationship of their children, but she served bananas with the tea, an unlikely combination. The message that her son did not belong with the woman's daughter any more than bananas go with tea was subtle and implicit; nonetheless, the young man's mother received the message loud and clear.

Source: Thomas, D., *Essentials of International Management: A Cross-Cultural Perspective*, Thousand Oaks, CA: Sage, 2000.

As shown in this example, high-context communication involves multilayered contexts (historical context, social norms, roles, situational and relational contexts), and the listener is expected to understand the nuances of the implicit messages. In contrast, in the low-context communication style, the onus lies on the sender to transmit a clear, explicit message that listeners can easily decode. High-context style is more likely in collectivist cultures such as Asia and Latin America and low-context style in individualist cultures such as Switzerland, Germany, and the United States.

Direct Versus Indirect Communication

Cultures also vary in the extent to which their language and tone of voice reveal or hide intent. Speakers who use a direct style specify their intentions in a forthright manner, whereas in the indirect style nuances in verbal statements hide the speaker's meaning. People from cultures using indirect styles (typically collectivists, such as Chungmin in the opening vignette) may perceive those with a direct style as blunt or insensitive. Conversely, Westerners (such as Todd), who prefer a direct style, often perceive the indirect style of Eastern cultures as insincere and untrustworthy. This is understandable, because in collectivist cultures being polite and avoiding embarrassment often takes precedence over *truth*, as truth is defined in individualist cultures. For collectivists, the social setting determines the degree of directness or truthfulness that is appropriate.

Succinct Versus Elaborate Communication

Communication styles also vary in terms of the quantity of talk (or silence) used to communicate. Styles range from succinct (low quantity of talk), to exacting (just the right amount of words), to elaborate (a high quantity of talk).[14] Failure to recognize these differences often results in misattributions that are barriers to negotiated shared meanings. People with a succinct style may discount elaborate speakers as illogical or inefficient and may even stop listening to them. Elaborate speakers may assume that succinct communicators have very little to say or contribute. The periods of silence used in Eastern cultures are often misunderstood by Westerners, who interpret them as a lack of understanding and then try to shorten them with further explanation or with moving on to the next point. In multicultural work groups, members of highly verbal cultures often fill in the silences and do not allow enough room for people with a more succinct style to talk.

Arab cultures have an elaborate style, involving detailed descriptions, repetition, verbal elaboration and exaggeration, and the use of metaphor, similes, and proverbs. In contrast, the exacting style, typical of England, Germany, Finland, and Sweden, emphasizes clarity and precise meanings. These cultures perceive the use of too many words as exaggeration, while the use of too few words is viewed as ambiguity. The succinct styles of China, Japan, Korea, and Thailand are characterized by understatements and meaningful pauses. To some extent, the succinct style of collectivist cultures employs silence as a way of controlling the communication interaction in the same way that individualists use talking.[15]

Self-Enhancement Versus Self-Effacement

The self-enhancement verbal style emphasizes the importance of boasting about one's accomplishments and abilities. The self-effacement verbal style, on the other hand, emphasizes the importance of humbling oneself via verbal restraints, hesitations, modest talk, and the use of self-deprecation concerning one's effort or performance.[16] Failures to establish shared meanings occur when people from self-enhancing cultures do not perceive the accomplishments and real worth of people from self-effacing cultures. Furthermore, employees from self-effacing cultures find "selling themselves" to gain promotion in self-enhancing cultures difficult and even repugnant. For example, when counseled to explain why he was the best person for a promotion, a Chinese engineer opted instead to quit one U.S. firm for another that was more cross-culturally sensitive and accustomed to working with Asians. Negative perceptions can also occur when the boastful mode of self-enhancers is not well received in self-effacing cultures. Collectivist Asian cultures are generally self-effacing, while Arab and African-American cultures are self-enhancing.

This style difference also relates to the use of praise—how frequently praise is used, what is praised, and the appropriate response to it. For example, Americans use praise frequently and are prone to praise people who are close to them, such as friends or family; they are also likely to praise physical appearance. Japanese are more likely to praise strangers, and Arabs are more likely to praise skill and work than physical characteristics. Response to praise also varies across cultures. In cultures like China, where modesty is a virtue, praise may cause embarrassment. The Hong Kong Chinese, for example, tend to deflect praise, whereas British people are more likely to politely accept it.[17]

NONVERBAL COMMUNICATION

Nonverbal communication (such as Chungmin slamming the door and avoiding eye contact) conveys important messages and is produced more automatically than words.

It includes body movements and gestures, facial expressions and facial gazing, tone of voice, and the emphasis of certain words. According to some researchers, as much as 70 percent of communication between people in the same language group is non-verbal.[18] It is possible that people rely even more heavily on the non-verbal component in cross-cultural communications.

Non-verbal communication helps to regulate intercultural interaction by providing information about our feelings and emotional state, adding meaning to our verbal messages, and governing the timing and sequencing of the interaction. Non-verbal behaviors serve the same functions across cultures. As with language, however, nonverbal systems of communication have a significant amount of variation around the world. Failures in establishing shared meanings occur because the same nonverbal behavior can have very different meanings across cultures, and because the same meaning is conveyed by different nonverbal cues in different cultures. For example, in Samoa people sit down to show respect, whereas in many cultures they stand up; showing the sole of one's shoe in a Moslem society is a sign of great disrespect; and, while in North America repeatedly crooking the index finger with the palm up beckons another person to come closer, this same gesture is obscene in some cultures.

As with all intercultural behavior, individuals often fall into the trap of using their own cultural lenses to interpret and explain non-verbal gestures. The challenge is to interpret nonverbal communication as intended by the senders, not as it would be perceived in our own culture.

Table 1 outlines some of the most common categories of non-verbal behaviors and their influence in intercultural communication.

TABLE 1 Categories of Non-verbal Behavior

Tone of voice	Pitch, volume, speed, tension, variation, enunciation, and a number of other voice qualities such as breathiness or creakiness convey different meaning based on cultural norms.
Proxemics[19]	People follow predictable patterns when establishing distance between themselves and others that are consistent with cultural norms. However, what is appropriate in one culture may seem unusual or even offensive in another.
Body position	The way people position their body conveys information in all cultures. People learn which body position is appropriate in a given situation in the same way that they internalize other aspects of culture. The vast array of possible body positions is difficult to categorize in any systematic way.
Gestures	Hand gestures are used both intentionally and unintentionally in communication. Those gestures that are used as a substitute for words are called emblems. Because the hand can be configured in numerous ways and with great precision, the number of possible hand gestures is quite extensive. To further complicate matters, the same hand gesture can have different meanings in different parts of the world.
Facial expression	Underlying emotional states seem to be closely linked to facial expression. The six basic emotions of anger, fear, sadness, disgust, happiness, and surprise are evident in facial expressions around the world from a very early age. However, individuals often

(*Continued*)

(Continued)	
	deliberately seek to override the link between their emotions and their facial expressions as a result of display rules appropriate to their culture.
Eye contact (gaze)	All cultures utilize eye contact (gaze) in non-verbal communication. Maintaining and avoiding eye contact communicate important messages. Cultural differences in gaze patterns seem to be fixed relatively early in life and persist regardless of subsequent cross-cultural experiences.

COMMUNICATION SKILLS

Intercultural communication skills are our ability to interact effectively in a given situation; they consist of mindful observation, mindful listening, identity confirmation, and collaborative dialogue.[20] They also include the willingness to communicate.

Mindful observation involves an analytical sequence of observing, describing, interpreting, and suspending evaluation when we encounter new behavior. Mindful observation and reliance on description of cultural behavior that is different from one's own is more effective than are reflexive and often evaluative attributions about this behavior. When a Samoan student visited one of the authors, he immediately seated himself without being invited to do so and averted his eyes. Instead of evaluating this behavior as casual and disrespectful, the mindful response would be to think "He sat down immediately upon entering the room and is not making eye contact with me. Perhaps this is appropriate behavior in Samoa, even though in my culture it is disrespectful. I need to check this out before making any judgments or reacting to this behavior." Investigation revealed that for Samoans to stare at or occupy a position physically above a person of higher status is exceedingly impolite. Mindful observation involves a reflective inner dialogue grounded in non-judgmental description and interpretation. It also requires self-awareness so people can monitor and control their reactions to the "different" behaviors and interactions.

Mindful listening refers to hearing more than just the words that are said. It also involves checking for accurate perception and paraphrasing the speaker's message into one's own words. Checking for mutual understanding and shared meanings is critical in order to overcome all the possible barriers in an intercultural interaction.

Identity confirmation means addressing people by their preferred titles, labels and identities, and using inclusive rather than exclusive language. This behavior indicates a sensitivity to and respect for the perceptions people have of themselves. For example, in Latin American cultures, people of a certain rank usually expect to be addressed with the formal verb tense (*Usted* rather than *tú*) until they signal otherwise, with the title that reflects their occupation (*Ingeniero* [Engineer] Gonzalez) or educational degree (*Licenciado* Martinez [college graduate]), or with a deferential term of respect (*Don* or *Doña*). Ignoring these communication rules disconfirms their sense of identity or the way they see themselves.

Collaborative dialogue means suspending one's assumptions about culturally different people and refraining from imposing one's views on them. Engaging in collaborative dialogue is analogous to what has been called an ethno-relative perspective.[21] In contrast to ethnocentrism (viewing one's own culture as superior), an ethno-relative approach involves greater recognition and acceptance of cultural differences. It assumes that behavior can be understood only within a cultural context rather than judged on a universal standard of right or wrong.

Willingness to communicate is involved in both perceiving and decoding the intercultural situation and identifying appropriate behavioral responses to that situation. This willingness to communicate is influenced both by the way we view other groups and how receptive we are to communication. When people categorize others and themselves as members of particular groups, such as a cultural group, they make assumptions that affect their beliefs, attitudes, and behaviors. They see people less as individuals and more as members of the group to which they belong. They assume group members are relatively more similar with regard to their beliefs and behavior, and the group is believed to be a more important cause of their behavior than individual characteristics.[22]

The in-group out-group boundary that results from social categorization has several implications for the way individuals select, structure, and process social information. First, this categorization invokes a comparison of one's own group with other cultural groups, resulting in intergroup bias. While it can be either positive or negative, inter-group bias most often favors one's own group. People are more likely to respond favorably to information from an in-group member. Novices to international work are often heard making such negative comparisons between host-country nationals and their own culture ("People are more reliable, ethical, trustworthy, and so on, in my country"). Expert interculturalists avoid comparisons and sweeping generalizations, and use stereotypes only when they are helpful as a first "best-guess" about how others might act. Second, in-group members sometimes develop their own brand of communication, especially the nonverbal component, which can be very difficult for an out-group member to interpret correctly. Finally, when people categorize others as out-group members, they tend to rely on stereotypes when interacting with them. Stereotyping means assigning identical characteristics to all members of a group, regardless of the actual variation among them.[23] Based on relatively little information, stereotypes are resistant to change even in light of new information, and are rarely accurately applied to specific individuals.[24]

Stereotypes affect the senders' ability to communicate their messages because they interfere with their ability to be "heard" and accurately judged. The senders' stereotype about receivers also determines how much and what type of information they will share with them. Stereotypes create expectations of how out-group members will behave. These expectations, in turn, influence the way in which we interpret incoming messages and the predictions we make about out-group member behavior.

Early research on stereotypes indicated that people could nurture intense stereotypes about other national cultures even though they had never met a person from that culture.[25] These cultural stereotypes, however, are often associated with other groups with which one's culture has had a long (often negative) history. National stereotypes may also be susceptible to what is called social dominance theory,[26] which involves a hierarchy of nationalities based on generally accepted status. High status may be attached to a particular nation because of economic dominance or other desirable characteristics. For example, some cultures give Canadians and Norwegians high status because of their generous foreign aid and peacemaking roles. According to this theory, the extent to which one's national group has high status will influence the attitude of others toward a communicator. Their message is more likely to be attended to by others.

The final factor with regard to the willingness of individuals to communicate is receptiveness. Receptiveness involves both cosmopolitanism and satisficing behavior. Cosmopolitanism refers to the willingness to engage with others who are different.[27] People with a cosmopolitan mindset are more likely to seek out and communicate with "strangers," even when doing so requires extra effort.

One's willingness to continue making an effort to communicate across cultures can be affected by satisficing. Satisficing in decision making refers to accepting a decision that is "good enough" because the costs of maximizing are too great.[28] In an intercultural context, we find satisficing in two areas, in the plateauing that occurs in both language acquisition and cultural understanding.[29] When these skills are good enough to get by, some people stop learning. There is no motivation to reach a higher level of cultural understanding or fluency unless an event occurs that initiates another round of cultural sensemaking or a return to the dictionary or language teacher.

DEVELOPING COMPETENCE IN MINDFUL COMMUNICATION

Communication competence is a strong predictor of job performance, psychological adjustment, overall intercultural effectiveness in living in the host culture, the extent of social interaction with host nationals, and transfer of technology.[30] We suggest the path to communication competence is through mindful communication. Experts in mindful intercultural communication possess these competencies: empathy, respect, interest in the local culture and people, flexibility, tolerance, nonjudgmental attitudes, initiative, open-mindedness, sociability, positive self-image, positive attitudes, and stress tolerance.[31] Kealey contends that effective intercultural communicators are characterized by adaptation skills, cross-cultural skills, and partnership skills,[32] all of which are necessary for global managers.

There is a large body of research indicating that cross-cultural training can be effective in sensitizing individuals to cultural issues, enhancing cultural self-awareness and empathy, decreasing the use of negative stereotypes, developing complex rather than oversimplified thinking about another culture, and facilitating cross-cultural interaction.[33] Such training significantly increases employee productivity, business skills, and commitment to the employer.[34] In today's diverse, virtual workplace, mindful communication has become essential even for people without a passport.

Endnotes

1. For a discussion of the concept of grounding, see Clark, H. H., and Brennan, S. E., "Grounding in Communication", in L. B. Resnick, J. M. Levine, and S. D. Teasley, eds., *Perspectives on Socially Shared Cognition* (Washington, D.C.: American Psychological Association, 1991).
2. J. T. Wood (1997) provides a good description of the transactional communication process in *Communication in Our Lives* (New York: Wadsworth, 1997).
3. For a description of cultural scripts, see Triandis, H. C., Marin, G., Lisansky, J., and Betancourt, H., *Simpatía* As a Cultural script of Hispanics, *Journal of Personality and Social Psychology*, 47(6), 1984: 1363–1375.
4. For more on the concept of mindfulness see Thich, N. H., *Peace Is Every Step: The Path of Mindfulness in Everyday Life*, (New York: Bantam Books, 1991) and Langer, E. J., *The Power of Mindful Learning*, (Reading, MA: Addison-Wesley, 1997).

5. For a more complete discussion see Ting-Toomey, S. (1999), *Communicating across Cultures*, New York: The Guilford Press.
6. The idea of using stereotypical behavior as a first best guess is presented in Adler, N. J. (1997), *International Dimensions of Organizational Behavior*, 3rd ed., Cincinnati: South-Western.
7. Many of the ideas about the influence of culture on communication presented in this section are drawn from Stella Ting-Toomey's excellent book, *Communicating across Cultures* (1999).
8. The idea of "conversational currency" was first presented by Brein, D., and David, K. H. (1971), "Intercultural Communication and the Adjustment of the Sojourner," *Psychological Bulletin*, 76(3): 215–230.
9. Empirical evidence of this idea is presented in Benson, P. G. (1978), "Measuring Cross-Cultural Adjustment: The Problem of Criteria," *International Journal of Intercultural Relations*, 2(1): 21–37.
10. For a more complete discussion of this point see Hui, H. C., and Cheng, I. W. M. (1987), "Effects of Second Language Proficiency of Speakers and Listeners on Person Perception and Behavioural intention: A Study of Chinese Bilinguals," *International Journal of Psychology*, 22: 421–30.
11. For more information on the relationship between intercultural communication and organizational learning, see Taylor, S., and Osland, J. S. (2002), "The Impact of Intercultural Communication on Global Organizational Learning, in M. Easterby-Smith and M. A. Lyles (eds.), *Handbook of Organizational Learning and Knowledge*, Oxford: Blackwell.
12. A more complete discussion of language accommodation can be found in Gallois, C., and Callan, V. (1997), *Communication and Culture: A Guide for Practice*, Chichester: John Wiley.
13. The high- and low-context communication style was first identified by Hall, E. T. (1976), *Beyond Culture*, New York: Doubleday. Also see Ting-Toomey (1999): 272.
14. This style consideration is well documented in Gudykunst, W. B., Ting-Toomey, S., and Chua, E. (1988), *Culture and Interpersonal Communication*, Newbury Park: CA: Sage.
15. For more information about the cultural use of this style see Giles, H., Coupland, N., and Wiemann, J. M. (1992), "Talk Is Cheap. . . but My word Is My Bond: Beliefs About Talk," in K. Bolton and H. Kwok (eds.), *Sociolinguistics Today: International Perspectives*, London: Routledge: 218–243.
16. For more information on this style difference see Ting-Toomey (1999).
17. Two empirical studies with regard to praise across cultures are Barnlund, D. C., and Araki, S. (1985), "Intercultural Encounters: The management of Compliments by Japanese and Americans," *Journal of Cross-Cultural Psychology*, 16: 9–26; and Loh, T. W. C. (1993), "Responses to Compliments Across Languages and Cultures: A Comparative Study of British and Hong Kong Chinese," research report no. 30, City University of Hong Kong.
18. Based on Noller, P. (1984), *Nonverbal Communication and Marital Interaction*, Oxford: Pergamon.
19. *Proxemics* is the term that has been coined to describe the study the way in which people use personal space in their interactions with others. See Hall, E. T. (1966), *The Hidden Dimension*, Garden City, NY: Doubleday.
20. Ting-Toomey (1999).
21. See Bennett, M. (1993), "Towards ethnorelativism: A Developmental Model of Intercultural Sensitivity," in R. M. Paige (ed.), *Education for the Intercultural Experience*, Yarmouth, ME: Intercultural Press: 21–71.
22. For a more complete discussion of social categorization see Wilder, D. A. (1986), "Social Categorization: Implications for Creation and Reduction of Intergroup Bias," in L. Berkowitz (ed.), *Advances in Experimental Social Psychology*, New York: Academic Press, Vol. 19: 291–355.
23. See E. Aronson (1976), *The Social Animal*, San Francisco: W. H. Freeman, for one of the original descriptions of stereotyping.
24. For more information on stereotypes see Ashmore, R. D., and Del Boca, F. K. (1981), "Conceptual Approaches to Stereotypes and Stereotyping," in D. L. Hamilton (ed.),

Cognitive Processes in Stereotyping and Intergroup Behavior, Hillsdale, NJ: Erlbaum: 1–35.

25. For example, see Katz, D., and Braly, K. W. (1933), "Verbal Stereotypes and Racial prejudice," *Journal of Abnormal and Social Psychology*, 28: 280–290.
26. See Sidanius, J. (1993), "The Psychology of group Conflict and the Dynamics of Oppression: A Social Dominance Perspective," in S. Iyenger and W. McGuire (eds.), *Explorations in Political Psychology*, Durham, NC: Duke University Press.
27. See Hannerz, U (1996), "Cosmopolitans and Locals in World Culture," in U. Hannerz, *Transnational Connections: Culture, People, Places*, London: Routledge: 102–111.
28. For more information on satisficing see Simon, H. A. (1955), "A Behavioral Model of Rational Choice, *Quarterly Journal of Economics*, 69: 129–138.
29. For a more complete discussion of satisficing in an intercultural context see Osland, J. S. (1995), *The Adventure of Working Abroad: Hero Tales from the Global Frontier*, San Francisco, CA: Jossey-Bass; and Osland, J., and Bird, A. (2000), "Beyond Sophisticated Stereotyping: Cultural Sensemaking in Context," *Academy of Management Executive*, 14(1), 65–87.
30. These findings are located in Ruben, B. D., and Kealey, D. J. (1979), "Behavioral Assessment of Communication Competency and the Prediction of Cross-Cultural Adaptation," *International Journal of Intercultural Relations*, 3: 15–48; Hammer, M. R. (1989), "Intercultural Communication Competence, in M. K. Asante and W. B. Gudykunst (eds.), *Handbook of International and Intercultural Communication*, Newbury Park, CA: Sage: 247–60; Hawes, F., and Kealey, D. J. (1981), "An Empirical Study of Canadian Technical assistance," *International Journal of Intercultural Relations*," 5(3): 239–58; and Clarke, C., and Hammer, M. R. (1995), "Predictors of Japanese and American Managers' Job success, Personal Adjustment, and Intercultural Interaction Effectiveness, *International Management Review*, 35(2): 153–70.
31. This list is compiled from the work of Kealey, D. J., and Ruben, B. D. (1983), "Cross-Cultural Personnel Selection Criteria, Issues, and Methods," in D. Landis and R. W. Brislin (eds.), *Handbook of Intercultural Training, Vol. 1: Issues in Training and Design*, New York: Pergamon; Kealey, D. J. (1996), "The challenge of International Personnel Selection," in D. Landis and R. S. Bhagat (eds.), *Handbook of Intercultural Training*, 2nd ed., Thousand Oaks, CA: Sage: 81–105; and Chen, G. M., and Starosta, W. J. (1996), "Intercultural Communication Competence: A Synthesis, *Communication Yearbook*, 19: 353–83.
32. See Kealey (1996).
33. Bhawuk, D. P. S., and Brislin, R. W. (2000), "Cross-Cultural Training: A Review," *Applied Psychology*, 49(1): 162–191; Hammer, M. R., and Martin, J. N. (1996), "The Effects of Cross-cultural Training on American Managers in a Japanese–American Joint Venture," *Journal of Applied Communication Research*, 20(2): 161–182; Black, J. S., and Mendenhall, M. (1990), Cross-Cultural Training Effectiveness: A Review and a Theoretical Framework for Future Research, *Academy of Management Review* 15(1): 113–136.
34. Hammer, M. R. (1995), "Making the Case with the Corporation: Tracking the Effects of an International Management Development Program," Presentation Given at the 21st annual congress of the Society for Intercultural Education, Training, and Research, Phoenix, AZ, May 14–17.

CHAPTER 9
PERCEPTION AND ATTRIBUTION

WHERE BIAS BEGINS: THE TRUTH ABOUT STEREOTYPES

Annie Murphy Paul

COMMUNICATING ACROSS CULTURES

Nancy J. Adler

This chapter deals with perception, the process by which we select, organize, and evaluate the stimuli in our environment to make it meaningful for ourselves. As a result, people can look at the same event or behavior and take away very different impressions and conclusions about what they "saw." People also make attributions, assigning causes to the behaviors they observe, in unique ways. Dealing with conflicting perceptions and attributions makes many aspects of organizational life more challenging—in particular, communication, teamwork, performance evaluation, and strategic decisions. One of the most common perception-related problems is stereotyping, which occurs when we attribute behavior or attitudes to people on the basis of the group or category to which they belong.

Annie Murphy Paul, senior editor at *Psychology Today*, argues that everyone uses stereotypes—not just bigots—in "Where Bias Begins: The Truth About Stereotypes." She reviews the research on the unconscious biases and automatic stereotyping of people who are different from us and discusses ways to reduce the negative aspect of stereotyping.

The potential for inaccurate perceptions, mistaken attributions, and stereotyping are very obvious in cross-cultural interactions. Nancy Adler, a well-known international scholar and consultant, describes the primary difficulties of "Communicating Across Cultures." She provides numerous examples of cultural errors in perception and a framework for understanding why they occur. Adler contends that stereotypes can be both helpful and harmful and provides advice on using them in a positive way.

WHERE BIAS BEGINS: THE TRUTH ABOUT STEREOTYPES*

Annie Murphy Paul

Psychologists once believed that only bigoted people used stereotypes. Now the study of unconscious bias is revealing the unsettling truth: We all use stereotypes, all the time, without knowing it. We have met the enemy of equality, and the enemy is us.

Mahzarin Banaji doesn't fit anybody's idea of a racist. A psychology professor at Yale University, she studies stereotypes for a living. And as a woman and a member of a minority ethnic group, she has felt firsthand the sting of discrimination. Yet when she took one of her own tests of unconscious bias, "I showed very strong prejudices," she says. "It was truly a disconcerting experience." And an illuminating one. When Banaji was in graduate school in the early 1980s, theories about stereotypes were concerned only with their explicit expression: outright and unabashed racism, sexism, anti-Semitism. But in the years since, a new approach to stereotypes has shattered that simple notion. The bias Banaji and her colleagues are studying is something far more subtle, and more insidious: what's known as automatic or implicit stereotyping, which, they find, we do all the time without knowing it. Though out-and-out bigotry may be on the decline, says Banaji, "if anything, stereotyping is a bigger problem than we ever imagined."

Previously, researchers who studied stereotyping had simply asked people to record their feelings about minority groups and had used their answers as an index of their attitudes. Psychologists now understand that these conscious replies are only half the story. How progressive a person seems to be on the surface bears little or no relation to how prejudiced he or she is on an unconscious level—so that a bleeding-heart liberal might harbor just as many biases as a neo-Nazi skinhead.

As surprising as these findings are, they confirmed the hunches of many students of human behavior. "Twenty years ago, we hypothesized that there were people who said they were not prejudiced but who really did have unconscious negative stereotypes and beliefs," says psychologist Jack Dovidio, Ph.D., of Colgate University. "It was like theorizing about the existence of a virus, and then one day seeing it under a microscope."

The test that exposed Banaji's hidden biases—and that this writer took as well, with equally dismaying results—is typical of the ones used by automatic stereotype researchers. It presents the subject with a series of positive or negative adjectives, each paired with a characteristically "white" or "black" name. As the name and word appear together on a computer screen, the person taking the test presses a key, indicating whether the word is good or bad. Meanwhile, the computer records the speed of each response.

A glance at subjects' response times reveals a startling phenomenon: Most people who participate in the experiment—even some African-Americans—respond more quickly when a positive word is paired with a white name or a negative word with a black name. Because our minds are more accustomed to making these associations, says Banaji, they process them more rapidly. Though the words and names aren't subliminal, they are presented so quickly that a subject's ability to make deliberate choices

*Reprinted with permission from *Psychology Today 31*, no. 3 (May-June 1998): 52–56.

is diminished—allowing his or her underlying assumptions to show through. The same technique can be used to measure stereotypes about many different social groups, such as homosexuals, women, and the elderly.

THE UNCONSCIOUS COMES INTO FOCUS

From these tiny differences in reaction speed—a matter of a few hundred milliseconds—the study of automatic stereotyping was born. Its immediate ancestor was the cognitive revolution of the 1970s, an explosion of psychological research into the way people think. After decades dominated by the study of observable behavior, scientists wanted a closer look at the more mysterious operation of the human brain. And the development of computers—which enabled scientists to display information very quickly and to measure minute discrepancies in reaction time—permitted a peek into the unconscious.

At the same time, the study of cognition was also illuminating the nature of stereotypes themselves. Research done after World War II—mostly by European emigrés struggling to understand how the Holocaust had happened—concluded that stereotypes were used only by a particular type of person: rigid, repressed, authoritarian. Borrowing from the psychoanalytic perspective then in vogue, these theorists suggested that biased behavior emerged out of internal conflicts caused by inadequate parenting.

The cognitive approach refused to let the rest of us off the hook. It made the simple but profound point that we all use categories—of people, places, things—to make sense of the world around us. "Our ability to categorize and evaluate is an important part of human intelligence," says Banaji. "Without it, we couldn't survive." But stereotypes are too much of a good thing. In the course of stereotyping, a useful category—say, woman—becomes freighted with additional associations, usually negative. "Stereotypes are categories that have gone too far," says John Bargh, Ph.D., of New York University. "When we use stereotypes, we take in the gender, the age, the color of the skin of the person before us, and our minds respond with messages that say hostile, stupid, slow, weak. Those qualities aren't out there in the environment. They don't reflect reality."

Bargh thinks that stereotypes may emerge from what social psychologists call in-group/out-group dynamics. Humans, like other species, need to feel that they are part of a group, and as villages, clans, and other traditional groupings have broken down, our identities have attached themselves to more ambiguous classifications, such as race and class. We want to feel good about the group we belong to—and one way of doing so is to denigrate all those who aren't in it. And while we tend to see members of our own group as individuals, we view those in out-groups as an undifferentiated—stereotyped—mass. The categories we use have changed, but it seems that stereotyping itself is bred in the bone.

Though a small minority of scientists argue that stereotypes are usually accurate and can be relied upon without reservations, most disagree—and vehemently. "Even if there is a kernel of truth in the stereotype, you're still applying a generalization about a group to an individual, which is always incorrect," says Bargh. Accuracy aside, some believe that the use of stereotypes is simply unjust. "In a democratic society, people should be judged as individuals and not as members of a group," Banaji argues. "Stereotyping flies in the face of that ideal."

PREDISPOSED TO PREJUDICE

The problem, as Banaji's own research shows, is that people can't seem to help it. A recent experiment provides a good illustration. Banaji and her colleague, Anthony Greenwald, Ph.D., showed people a list of names—some famous, some not. The next day, the subjects returned to the lab and were shown a second list, which mixed names from the first list with new ones. Asked to identify which were famous, they picked out the Margaret Meads and the Miles Davises—but they also chose some of the names on the first list, which retained a lingering familiarity that they mistook for fame. (Psychologists call this the "famous overnight-effect.") By a margin of two-to-one, these suddenly "famous" people were male.

Participants weren't aware that they were preferring male names to female names, Banaji stresses. They were simply drawing, on an unconscious stereotype of men as more important and influential than women. Something similar happened when she showed subjects a list of people who might be criminals: without knowing they were doing so, participants picked out an overwhelming number of African-American names. Banaji calls this kind of stereotyping implicit, because people know they are making a judgment—but just aren't aware of the basis upon which they are making it.

Even further below awareness is something that psychologists call *automatic processing*, in which stereotypes are triggered by the slightest interaction or encounter. An experiment conducted by Bargh required a group of white participants to perform a tedious computer task. While performing the task, some of the participants were subliminally exposed to pictures of African-Americans with neutral expressions. When the subjects were then asked to do the task over again, the ones who had been exposed to the faces reacted with more hostility to the request—because, Bargh believes, they were responding in kind to the hostility which is part of the African-American stereotype. Bargh calls this the "immediate hostile reaction," which he believes can have a real effect on race relations. When African-Americans accurately perceive the hostile expressions that their white counterparts are unaware of, they may respond with hostility of their own—thereby perpetuating the stereotype.

Of course, we aren't completely under the sway of our unconscious. Scientists think that the automatic activation of a stereotype is immediately followed by a conscious check on unacceptable thoughts—at least in people who think that they are not prejudiced. This internal censor successfully restrains overtly biased responses. But there's still the danger of leakage, which often shows up in non-verbal behavior: our expressions, our stance, how far away we stand, how much eye contact we make.

The gap between what we say and what we do can lead African-Americans and whites to come away with very different impressions of the same encounter, says Jack Dovidio. "If I'm a white person talking to an African-American, I'm probably monitoring my conscious beliefs very carefully and making sure everything I say agrees with all the positive things I want to express," he says. "And I usually believe I'm pretty successful because I hear the right words coming out of my mouth." The listener who is paying attention to non-verbal behavior, however, may be getting quite the opposite message. An African-American student of Dovidio's recently told him that when she was growing up, her mother had taught her to observe how white people moved to gauge their true feelings toward blacks. "Her mother was a very astute amateur psychologist—and about 20 years ahead of me," he remarks.

WHERE DOES BIAS BEGIN?

So where exactly do these stealth stereotypes come from? Though automatic-stereotype researchers often refer to the unconscious they don't mean the Freudian notion of a seething mass of thoughts and desires, only some of which are deemed presentable enough to be admitted to the conscious mind. In fact, the cognitive model holds that information flows in exactly the opposite direction: connections made often enough in the conscious mind eventually become unconscious. Says Bargh, "If conscious choice and decision making are not needed, they go away. Ideas recede from consciousness into the unconscious over time."

Much of what enters our consciousness, of course, comes from the culture around us. And like the culture, it seems that our minds are split on the subjects of race, gender, class, sexual orientation. "We not only mirror the ambivalence we see in society, but also mirror it in precisely the same way," says Dovidio. Our society talks out loud about justice, equality, and egalitarianism, and most Americans accept these values as their own. At the same time, such equality exists only as an ideal, and that fact is not lost on our unconscious. Images of women as sex objects, footage of African-American criminals on the six o'clock news—"this is knowledge we cannot escape," explains Banaji. "We didn't choose to know it, but it still affects our behavior."

We learn the subtext of our culture's messages early. By five years of age, says Margo Monteith, Ph.D., many children have definite and entrenched stereotypes about blacks, women, and other social groups. Adds Monteith, professor of psychology at the University of Kentucky "Children don't have a choice about accepting or rejecting these conceptions, since they're acquired well before they have the cognitive abilities or experiences to form their own beliefs." And no matter how progressive the parents, they must compete with all the forces that would promote and perpetuate these stereotypes: peer pressure, mass media, the actual balance of power in society. In fact, prejudice may be as much a result as a cause of this imbalance. We create stereotypes—African-Americans are lazy, women are emotional—to explain why things are the way they are. As Dovidio notes, "Stereotypes don't have to be true to serve a purpose."

WHY CAN'T WE ALL GET ALONG?

The idea of unconscious bias does clear up some nettlesome contradictions. "It accounts for a lot of people's ambivalence toward others who are different, a lot of their inconsistencies in behavior," says Dovidio. "It helps explain how good people can do bad things." But it also prompts some uncomfortable realizations. Because our conscious and unconscious beliefs may be very different—and because behavior often follows the lead of the latter—"good intentions aren't enough," as John Bargh puts it. In fact, he believes that they count for very little. "I don't think free will exists," he says, bluntly—because what feels like the exercise of free will may be only the application of unconscious assumptions.

Not only may we be unable to control our biased responses, we may not even be aware that we have them. "We have to rely on our memories and our awareness of what we're doing to have a connection to reality," says Bargh. "But when it comes to automatic processing, those cues can be deceptive." Likewise, we can't always be sure how biased others are. "We all have this belief that the important thing about prejudice is the external expression of it," says Banaji. "That's going to be hard to give up."

One thing is certain: We can't claim that we've eradicated prejudice just because its outright expression has waned. What's more, the strategies that were so effective in reducing that sort of bias won't work on unconscious beliefs. "What this research is saying is that we are going to have to change dramatically the way we think we can influence people's behaviors," says Banaji. "It would be naive to think that exhortation is enough." Exhortation, education, political protest—all of these hammer away at our conscious beliefs while leaving the bedrock below untouched. Banaji notes, however, that one traditional remedy for discrimination—affirmative action—may still be effective since it bypasses our unconsciously compromised judgment.

But some stereotype researchers think that the solution to automatic stereotyping lies in the process itself. Through practice, they say, people can weaken the mental links that connect minorities to negative stereotypes and strengthen the ones that connect them to positive conscious beliefs. Margo Monteith explains how it might work. "Suppose you're at a party and someone tells a racist joke—and you laugh," she says. "Then you realize that you shouldn't have laughed at the joke. You feel guilty and become focused on your thought processes. Also, all sorts of cues become associated with laughing at the racist joke: the person who told the joke, the act of telling jokes, being at a party, drinking." The next time you encounter these cues, "a warning signal of sorts should go off—'wait, didn't you mess up in this situation before?'—and your responses will be slowed and executed with greater restraint."

That slight pause in the processing of a stereotype gives conscious, unprejudiced beliefs a chance to take over. With time, the tendency to prevent automatic stereotyping may itself become automatic. Monteith's research suggests that, given enough motivation, people may be able to teach themselves to inhibit prejudice so well that even their tests of implicit bias come clean.

The success of this process of "de-automatization" comes with a few caveats, however. First, even its proponents concede that it works only for people disturbed by the discrepancy between their conscious and unconscious beliefs, since unapologetic racists or sexists have no motivation to change. Second, some studies have shown that attempts to suppress stereotypes may actually cause them to return later, stronger than ever. And finally, the results that Monteith and other researchers have achieved in the laboratory may not stick in the real world, where people must struggle to maintain their commitment to equality under less-than-ideal conditions.

Challenging though that task might be, it is not as daunting as the alternative researchers suggest: changing society itself. Bargh, who likens de-automatization to closing the barn door once the horses have escaped, says that "it's clear that the way to get rid of stereotypes is by the roots, by where they come from in the first place." The study of culture may someday tell us where the seeds of prejudice originated; for now, the study of the unconscious shows us just how deeply they're planted.

COMMUNICATING ACROSS CULTURES*

Nancy J. Adler

All business activity involves communication. Within the global business environment, activities such as leading, motivating, negotiating, decision making, and exchanging information and ideas are all based on the ability of managers and employees from one culture to communicate successfully with colleagues, clients, and suppliers from other cultures. Communicating effectively challenges managers worldwide even when the work force is culturally homogeneous, but when employees speak a variety of languages and come from an array of cultural backgrounds, effective communication becomes considerably more difficult (6:3–5, 121–128; 16:1).

CROSS-CULTURAL COMMUNICATION

Communication is the exchange of meaning: It is my attempt to let you know what I mean. Communication includes any behavior that another person perceives and interprets: It is your understanding of what I mean. Communication includes sending both verbal messages (words) and non-verbal messages (tone of voice, facial expression, behavior, and physical setting). It includes consciously sent messages as well as messages that the sender is totally unaware of having sent. Whatever I say and do, I cannot *not* communicate. Communication therefore involves a complex multilayered, dynamic process through which we exchange meaning.

Every communication has a message sender and a message receiver. The sent message is never identical to the received message. Why? Communication is not direct, but rather indirect; it is a symbolic behavior. I cannot communicate my ideas, feelings, or information directly; rather, I must externalize or symbolize them before they can be communicated. *Encoding* describes the producing of a symbol message. *Decoding* describes the receiving of a meaning from a symbol message. Message senders must encode their meaning into a form that the receiver will recognize—that is, into words and behavior. Receivers must then decode the words and behavior—the symbols—back into messages that have meaning for them.

For example, because the Cantonese word for *eight* sounds like *faat*, which means prosperity, a Hong Kong textile manufacturer, Mr. Lau Ting-Pong, paid $85 million in 1988 for car registration number 8. A year later, a European millionaire paid $4.8 million at Hong Kong's Lunar New Year auction for vehicle registration number 7, a decision that mystified the Chinese, since the number 7 has little significance in the Chinese calculation of fortune (12).

The process of translating meanings into words and behaviors—that is, into symbols—and back again into meanings is based on a person's cultural background and differs accordingly for each person. The greater the difference in background between senders and receivers, the greater the difference in meanings attached to particular words and behaviors.

---

*Excerpted with permission from *International Dimensions of Organizational Behavior* (Cincinnati, OH: South-Western: 2002): 73–102. Special thanks to John Szilagy.

CROSS-CULTURAL MISPERCEPTION

Do the French and the Chinese see the world in the same way? No. Do Venezuelans and Ghanaians see the world in the same way? Again, no. No two national groups see the world in exactly the same way. Perception is the process by which individuals select, organize, and evaluate stimuli from the external environment to provide meaningful experiences for themselves (1; 7; 8; 10). For example, when Mexican children simultaneously view tachistoscopic pictures of a bullfight and a baseball game, they only remember seeing the bullfight. Looking through the same tachistoscope, American children only remembered seeing the baseball game (2). Similarly, adult card players, when shown cards by researchers, fail to see black hearts and diamonds, or red clubs and spades.

Why didn't the children see both pictures? Why did the adults fail to see the unexpected playing card colors? The answer lies in the nature of perception. Perceptual patterns are neither innate nor absolute. They are selective, learned, culturally determined, consistent, and inaccurate.

- ***Perception is* selective.** At any one time there are too many stimuli in the environment for us to observe. Therefore, we screen out most of what we see, hear, taste, and feel. We screen out the overload and allow only selected information through our perceptual screen to our conscious mind (3).
- ***Perceptual patterns are* learned.** We are not born seeing the world in one particular way. Our experience teaches us to perceive the world in certain ways.
- ***Perception is culturally* determined.** We learn to see the world in a certain way based on our cultural background.
- ***Perception tends to remain* consistent.** Once we see something in a particular way, we continue to see it that way.
- ***Perception is* inaccurate.** We see things that do not exist and do not see things that do exist. Our background, values, interests, and culture act as filters and lead us to distort, block, and even create what we choose to see and to hear. We perceive what we expect to perceive. We perceive things according to what we have been trained to see, according to our cultural map.

For example, read the following sentence and quickly count the number of *F*'s in the sentence:

> *Finished Files Are the Result of Years of Scientific Study Combined with the Experience of Years.*

Most non-native English speakers see all six *F*'s. Many native English speakers only see three *F*'s, they do not see the *F*'s in the word *of* because *of* is not an important word in understanding the sentence's meaning. We selectively see those words that are important according to our cultural conditioning (in this case, our linguistic conditioning). Once we see a phenomenon in a particular way, we usually continue to see it in that way. Once we stop seeing *of*'s, we do not see them again (even when we look for them); we do not see things that do exist. One particularly astute manager at Canadian National Railways makes daily use of perceptual filters to her firm's advantage. She gives reports written in English to bilingual Francophones to proofread and those written in French to bilingual Anglophones. She uses the fact that the English

FIGURE 1 Perceptual Filters Change the Story

secretaries can "see" more errors—specially small errors—in French and that the French secretaries can "see" more errors in English.

"The distorting impact of perceptual filters causes us to see things that do not exist. In an executive development program, for example, U.S. executives were asked to study the picture shown in Figure 1 and then to describe it to a second colleague who had not seen the picture. The second colleague then attempted to describe the picture to a third colleague who had not seen the picture, and so on. Finally, the fifth colleague described his perception of the picture to the group of executives and compared it with the original picture. Among the numerous distortions, the executives, similar to other groups, consistently described the black and the white man as fighting; the knife as being in the hand of the black man; the white man as wearing a business suit; and the black man as wearing laborer's overalls. Clearly the inaccurate stereotype of blacks (as poorer, working class and more likely to commit crimes) and of whites (as richer, upper class, and less likely to perpetrate violent crime) altered the observers' perceptions, thus totally changing the meaning of the picture. The executives' personal and cultural experiences, and therefore their perceptual filters, allowed them to see things that did not exist and to miss seeing things that did exist."

CROSS-CULTURAL MISINTERPRETATION

Interpretation occurs when an individual gives meaning to observations and their relationships; it is the process of making sense out of perceptions. Interpretation organizes our experience to guide our behavior. Based on our experience, we make assumptions about our perceptions so we will not have to rediscover meanings each time we encounter similar situations. For example, we make assumptions about how doors work, based on our experience of entering and leaving rooms; thus we do not have to relearn how to open a door each time we encounter a new door. Our consistent patterns of interpretation help us to act appropriately and quickly within our day-to-day world.

CATEGORIES

Since we are constantly bombarded with more stimuli than we can absorb and more perceptions than we can keep distinct or interpret,we only perceive those images that may be meaningful to us. We group perceived images into familiar categories that help us to simplify our environment, become the basis for our interpretations, and allow us to function in an otherwise overly complex world. Categorization helps me to distinguish what is most important in my environment and to behave accordingly.

Categories of perceived images become ineffective when we place people and things in the wrong groups. Cross-cultural miscategorization occurs when I use my home country categories to make sense out of situations abroad. For example, a Korean businessman entered a client's office in Stockholm and encountered a woman sitting behind the desk. Assuming that she was a secretary, he announced that he wanted to see Mr. Silferbrand. The woman responded by saying that the secretary would be happy to help him. The Korean became confused. In assuming that most women are secretaries rather than managers, he had misinterpreted the situation and acted inappropriately. His categorization made sense because most women in Korean offices are secretaries, but it proved inaccurate and counterproductive here, since this particular Swedish woman was not a secretary.

STEREOTYPES

Stereotyping involves a form of categorization that organizes our experience and guides our behavior toward ethnic and national groups. Stereotypes never describe individual behavior; rather, they describe the behavioral norm for members of a particular group. Stereotypes, like other forms of categories, can be helpful or harmful depending on how we use them. Effective stereotyping allows people to understand and act appropriately in new situations. A stereotype becomes helpful when it is:

- ***Consciously held.*** People should be aware that they are describing a group norm rather than the characteristics of a specific individual.
- ***Descriptive rather than evaluative.*** The stereotype should describe what people from this group will probably be like and not evaluate those people as good or bad.
- ***Accurate.*** The stereotype should accurately describe the norm for the group to which the person belongs.
- ***The first best guess.*** about a group prior to having direct information about the specific person or persons involved.
- ***Modified.*** based on further observation and experience with the actual people and situations.

A subconsciously held stereotype is difficult to modify or discard even after we collect real information about a person, because it is often thought to reflect reality. If a subconscious stereotype also inaccurately evaluates a person or situation, we are likely to maintain an inappropriate, ineffective, and frequently harmful guide to reality. Indrei Ratiu (9), in his work with INSEAD, a leading international business school in

France, and the London Business School, found that managers identified as "most internationally effective" by their colleagues altered their stereotypes to fit the actual people involved, whereas managers identified as "least internationally effective" continued to maintain their stereotypes even in the face of contradictory information. Highly effective managers use the stereotype as a first best guess about the group's behavior prior to meeting any individuals from the group. As time goes on, they modify or discard the stereotype entirely; information about each individual supersedes the group stereotype. By contrast, the least internationally effective managers maintain their stereotypes. In drawing conclusions too quickly on the basis of insufficient information—premature closure (7)—their stereotypes become self-fulfilling (11). To be effective, global managers, therefore, become aware of their cultural stereotypes and learn to set them aside when faced with contradictory evidence. They do not *pretend* not to stereotype.

In conclusion, some people stereotype effectively and others do not. Stereotypes become counterproductive when we place people in the wrong group, when we incorrectly describe group norms, when we inappropriately evaluate the group or category, when we confuse the stereotype with the description of a particular individual, and when we fail to modify the stereotype based on our actual observations and experience.

SOURCES OF MISINTERPRETATION

Misinterpretation can be caused by inaccurate perceptions of a person or situation that arise when what actually exists is not seen. It can be caused by an inaccurate interpretation of what is seen; that is, by using my meanings to make sense out of your reality. Culture strongly influences, and in many situations determines, our interpretations. Both the categories and the meanings we attach to them are based on our cultural background. Sources of cross-cultural misinterpretation include subconscious cultural "blinders," a lack of cultural self-awareness, projected similarity, and parochialism.

SUBCONSCIOUS CULTURAL BLINDERS

Because most interpretation goes on at a subconscious level, we lack awareness of the assumptions we make and their cultural basis. Our home culture reality never forces us to examine our assumptions or the extent to which they are culturally based, because we share our cultural assumptions with most other citizens from our country. All we know is that things do not work as smoothly or logically when we work outside our own culture as when we work with people more similar to ourselves. For example:

> *Canadians conducting business in Kuwait became surprised when their meeting with a high-ranking official was not held in a closed office and was constantly interrupted. Using the Canadian-based cultural assumptions that important people have large private offices with secretaries to monitor the flow of people into the office, and that important business takes precedence over less important business and is therefore not interrupted, the Canadians interpreted the Kuwaiti's open office and constant interruptions to mean that the official was neither as high ranking nor as interested in conducting the business at hand as they had previously thought. The Canadians' interpretation of the office environment led them to lose interest in working with the Kuwaiti.*

The problem is that the Canadians' interpretation derives from their own North American norms, not from Middle Eastern cultural norms. The Kuwaiti may well have been a high-ranking official who was very interested in doing business. The Canadians will never know.

LACK OF CULTURAL SELF-AWARENESS

Although we may think that a major obstacle in conducting business around the world is in understanding foreigners, the greater difficulty involves becoming aware of our own cultural conditioning. As anthropologist Edward Hall explains, "What is known least well, and is therefore in the poorest position to be studied, is what is closest to oneself" (5:45). We are generally least aware of our own cultural characteristics and are quite surprised when we hear foreigners describe us. For example, many Americans are surprised to discover that foreigners see them as hurried, overly law-abiding, very hard working, extremely explicit, and overly inquisitive (see the box "Cross-Cultural Awareness: Americans As Others See Them"). Asking a foreign national to describe businesspeople from your country is a powerful way to see yourself as others see you.

CROSS-CULTURAL AWARENESS: AMERICANS AS OTHERS SEE THEM

People from other countries often become puzzled and intrigued by the intricacies and enigmas of American culture. Below is a selection of actual observations by people from around the world visiting the United States. As you read them, ask yourself in each case if the observer is accurate and how you would explain the trait in question.

India: "Americans seem to be in a perpetual hurry. Just watch the way they walk down the street. They never allow themselves the leisure to enjoy life; there are too many things to do."

Kenya: "Americans appear to us rather distant. They are not really as close to other people—even fellow Americans—as Americans overseas tend to portray. It's almost as if an American says, 'I won't let you get too close to me.' It's like building a wall."

Turkey: "Once we were out in a rural area in the middle of nowhere and saw an American come to a stop sign. Though he could see in both directions for miles and no traffic was coming, he still stopped!"

Colombia: "The tendency in the United States to think that life is only work hits you in the face. Work seems to be the one type of motivation."

Indonesia: "In the United States, everything has to be talked about and analyzed. Even the littlest thing has to be "Why, Why, Why? I get a headache from such persistent questions."

Ethiopia: "Americans are very explicit; [they] want a 'yes' or 'no.' If someone tries to speak figuratively, the American is confused."

Iran: "The first time my [American] professor told me, 'I don't know the answer; I will have to look it up,' I was shocked. I asked myself, 'Why is he teaching me?' In my country a professor would give the wrong answer rather than admit ignorance."[1]

To the extent that we can begin to see ourselves clearly through the eyes of people from other cultures, we can begin to modify our behavior, emphasizing our most appropriate and effective characteristics and minimizing those least helpful. To the extent that we are culturally self-aware, we can begin to predict the effect our behavior will have on others.

PROJECTED SIMILARITY

Projected similarity refers to the assumption that people are more similar to you than they actually are or that another person's situation is more similar to your own situation than it in fact is. Projecting similarity reflects both a natural and a common process. American professors asked managers from 14 countries to describe the work and life goals of a colleague in their work team from another country (4). In every case the managers assumed that their foreign colleagues were more like themselves than they actually were. Projected similarity involves assuming, imagining, and actually perceiving similarity when differences exist. Projected similarity particularly handicaps people in cross-cultural situations. As a South African, I assume that my Greek colleague is more South African than he actually is. As an Egyptian, I assume that my Chilean colleague is more similar to me than she actually is. When I act based on this assumed similarity, I often find that I have acted inappropriately and thus ineffectively.

At the base of projected similarity is a subconscious parochialism. I assume that there is only one way to be: my way. I assume that there is only one way to see the world: my way. I therefore view other people in reference to me and to my way of viewing the world. People may fall into an illusion of understanding while being unaware of [their] misunderstandings. "I understand you perfectly but you don't understand me" is an expression typical of such a situation. Or all communicating parties may fall into a collective illusion of mutual understanding. In such a situation, each party may wonder later why other parties do not live up to the "agreement" they had reached.

Most global managers do not see themselves as parochial. They believe that as world travelers they are able to see the foreigner's point of view. This is not always true. While it is important to understand and respect the other culture's point of view, it is not necessary to either accept or adopt it. Understanding and respect do not imply acceptance. However, a rigid adherence to our own belief system expresses a form of parochialism, and parochialism underlies projected similarity.

CROSS-CULTURAL MISEVALUATION

Even more than perception and interpretation, cultural conditioning strongly affects evaluation. Evaluation involves judging whether someone or something is good or bad. Cross-culturally, we use our own culture as a standard of measurement, judging that which is like our own culture as normal and good and that which is different as abnormal and bad. Our own culture becomes a self-reference criterion: Since no other culture is identical to our own, we tend to judge all other cultures as inferior. Evaluation rarely helps in trying to understand, communicate with, or do business with people from another culture. The following example highlights the consequences of misevaluation:

A Swiss executive waits more than an hour past the appointed time for his Spanish colleague to arrive and to sign a supply contract. In his impatience he concludes that Spaniards must be lazy and totally unconcerned about business. The Swiss executive has misevaluated his colleague by negatively comparing him to his own cultural standards for business punctuality. Implicitly, he has labeled his own culture's behavior as good ("The Swiss arrive on time and that is good") and the other culture's behavior as bad ("The Spanish do not arrive on time and that is bad").

COMMUNICATION: GETTING THEIR MEANING, NOT JUST THEIR WORDS

Effective cross-cultural communication is possible; however, global managers cannot approach communication in the same way as do domestic managers. First, effective global managers "know that they don't know." They assume difference until similarity is proven rather than assuming similarity until difference is proven.

Second, in attempting to understand their colleagues from other cultures, effective global managers emphasize description, by observing what is actually said and done, rather than interpreting or evaluating it. Describing a situation is the most accurate way to gather information about it. Interpretation and evaluation, unlike description, are based more on the observer's own culture and background than on the observed situation. My interpretations and evaluations therefore tell me more about myself than about the actual situation. Although managers, as decision makers, must evaluate people (e.g., performance appraisal) and situations (e.g., project assessment) in terms of organizational standards and objectives, effective global managers delay judgment until they have had sufficient time to observe and interpret the situation from the perspective of all cultures involved.

Third, when attempting to understand or interpret an international situation, effective global managers try to see it through the eyes of their international colleagues. This role reversal limits the myopia of viewing situations strictly from one's own perspective.

Fourth, once effective global managers develop an explanation for a situation, they treat the explanation as a guess (as a hypothesis to be tested) and not as a certainty. They systematically check with colleagues both from home and abroad to make certain that their guesses—their initial interpretations—are plausible. This checking process allows them to converge meanings—to delay accepting their interpretations of the situation until they have confirmed them with others.

UNDERSTANDING: CONVERGING MEANINGS

There are many ways to increase the chances for accurately understanding businesspeople from other cultures. Each technique is based on presenting the message through multiple channels (for example, stating your position and showing a graph to summarize the same position), paraphrasing to check that colleagues from other cultures have understood your meaning (and not just your words), and converging meanings (always double-checking with the other person to verify that you have communicated what you had intended to communicate).

Endnotes

1. Individual country quotes taken from J. P. Feig and G. Blair, *There Is a Difference*, 2nd ed. (Washington, D.C.: Meridian House International, 1980).

References

Asch, S. "Forming Impressions of Persons," *Journal of Abnormal and Social Psychology 40* (1946), 258–290.

Bagby, J. W. "Dominance in Binocular Rivalry in Mexico and the United States," in I. Al-Issa and W. Dennis, eds., *Cross-Cultural Studies of Behavior* (New York: Holt, Rinehart and Winston, 1970), 49–56. Originally in *Journal of Abnormal and Social Psychology 54* (1957): 331–334.

Berry, J.; Kalin, R.; and Taylor, D. *Multiculturalism and Ethnic Attitudes in Canada* (Ottawa: Minister of Supply and Services, 1977).

Burger, P., and Bass, B. M. *Assessment of Managers: An International Comparison* (New York: Free Press, 1979).

Hall, E. T. *Beyond Culture* (Garden City, NY: AnchorPress/Doubleday, 1976). Also see E. T. Hall's *The Silent Language* (Doubleday, 1959, and Anchor Books, 1973) and *The Hidden Dimension* (Doubleday, 1966, and Anchor Books, 1969).

Kanungo, R. N. *Biculturalism and Management* (Ontario: Butterworth, 1980).

Lau, J. B., and Jelinek, M. "Perception and Management," *Behavior in Organizations: An Experiential Approach* (Homewood, IL: Irwin, 1984), 213–220.

Prekel, T. "Multi-Cultural Communication: A Challenge to Managers," paper delivered at the International Convention of the American Business Communication Association, New York, November 21, 1983.

Ratui, I. "Thinking Internationally: A Comparison of How International Executives Learn," *International Studies of Management and Organization, 13*, no. 1–2 (1983): 139–150. Reprinted by permission of publisher, M. E. Sharpe, Inc., Armonk, N.Y.

Singer, M. "Culture: A Perceptual Approach," L. A. Samovar and R. E. Porter, eds., *Intercultural Communication: A Reader* (Belmont, Calif.: Wadsworth, 1976), 110–119.

Snyder, M. "Self-Fulfilling Stereotypes," *Psychology Today* (July 1982): 60–68.

South China Morning Post, "Mystery Man Gives a Fortune for Lucky '7'" (January 22, 1989): 3; and "Lucky '7' to Go on Sale" (January 4, 1989): 4.

CHAPTER 10
GROUP DYNAMICS AND WORK TEAMS

VIRTUALITY AND COLLABORATION IN TEAMS

Cristina Gibson

HOW TO LEAD A SELF-MANAGING TEAM

Vanessa Urch Druskat
Jane V. Wheeler

Understanding group dynamics has always been an important skill; the proliferation of teams in the workplace, however, has focused even more attention on this area. The development of technology that allows people to collaborate from almost any location has contributed to the increasing use of virtual teams—teams in which members work in different physical locations and communicate electronically. In our first article, Cristina Gibson, one of the foremost authorities on virtual teams, examines the factors that contribute to the effectiveness of these teams in "Virtuality and Collaboration in Teams." As she notes, virtual teams are first and foremost teams. And, like most teams, they require certain elements to be effective, including design factors, such as team structure, and enabling conditions, such as shared understanding and trust. Gibson goes on to highlight specific strategies for ensuring that virtual teams reach and sustain peak effectiveness.

More and more companies are relying on self-managed work teams. This trend has empowered employees and thinned the ranks of middle managers, whose tasks, in many cases, are now carried out by teams. Reporting the results of a study of 300 self-managing teams in "How to Lead a Self-Managing Team," researchers Vanessa Druskat and Jane Wheeler examine how superior leaders accomplish the delicate balance of providing direction and guidance for these types of teams without diminishing their often fragile autonomy.

VIRTUALITY AND COLLABORATION IN TEAMS*

Cristina Gibson

Imagine a team responsible for prototyping a new wireless device that will enable children and families to transmit pictures to one another. This team includes members of six organizations from four European countries. The team members rarely meet in the same room; rather, they communicate via a comprehensive intranet created for the project, an e-mail system, and teleconferences. What challenges might they face in doing their work? What makes this collaboration different than a typical project in a high-technology firm? What advantages do they have over traditional teams? What techniques should the team use to increase its effectiveness? These issues are addressed here.

This collaboration is an example of what many scholars and practitioners have referred to as a *virtual team*. Yet, the term "virtual" conjures up images of virtual reality video games or, even worse, mirages that don't really exist! So what is so special about this form of collaboration? *Virtual teams* are first and foremost teams—that is, collections of individuals who are interdependent in their tasks, who share responsibility for outcomes, and who see themselves and are viewed by others as a team (Hackman, 1987). There are four key factors that often make these teams unique: electronic dependence, geographic dispersion, diversity, and dynamic structure (Gibson and Gibbs, 2005).

ELECTRONIC DEPENDENCE

To be considered "virtual," a team must have some degree of electronic dependence. That is, highly virtual teams rely upon electronically mediated communication to stay in touch and get their work done. They use a variety of technologies including telephones, faxes, teleconferences, e-mail, videoconferences, collaborative design tools, and knowledge management systems. These teams may meet face-to-face from time to time, but they could not do their work and effectively coordinate their activities without technological support. Of course, teams that are co-located also use teleconferencing and e-mail, and just the use of technology does not make a team virtual. It is the degree of reliance on electronic communication that increases virtuality.

GEOGRAPHIC DISPERSION

Beyond technological features, perhaps the second most prominent feature of highly virtual teams that sets them apart from co-located teams is that members of virtual teams work from many different locations: They are often spread out over cities, continents, and time zones. Thus, members cannot take for granted that other members share their contextual knowledge or have a common frame of reference (Riopelle et al., 2003). In fact, the more contexts represented on a virtual team, the more information there is to be shared. In particular, members need to share more information about context and in much greater detail than they would if working in the same location (Cramton and Orvis, 2003).

*Written for *The Organizational Behavior Reader*.

CULTURAL DIVERSITY

Virtuality often brings together members that represent highly diverse groups, including different nations, regions, organizations, or professions (Gibson & Cohen, 2003). The co-mingled national, organizational, and professional cultures each have their own shared understanding, sensemaking, beliefs, expectations, and behaviors (Gibson & Manuel, 2003). On some virtual teams, members share many cultural characteristics; on others there is a high degree of cultural differences.

Thus, virtual teams are not just technological systems; they are sociotechnological systems: social systems completely intertwined with technology systems (Maznevski and Chuboda, 2000). Since different cultures are often involved, silence and lack of responses via technology can have multiple meanings for virtual team members, including indifference, technical failure, discomfort, or confusion (Cramton and Orvis, 2003). A fascinating and somewhat ironic finding is that when members of virtual teams share many cultural characteristics (e.g., all are Westernized, all share the same function, etc.), subtle cultural differences may go unnoticed but then cause real surprises as the team interacts (Elron and Vigoda, 2003). Cultural differences on virtual teams coincide with differences in the way in which people use language. These differences can be very subtle, yet profound. For example, across cultures, communication varies in the extent to which people use implicit versus explicit language (e.g., the use of qualifiers such as "maybe" "perhaps" or "somewhat"), the extent to which messages are context free or context specific, the degree to which messages contain emotional content or a serious tone, and the degree to which informal versus formal channels of communication are used (Gibson and Gibbs, 2005; Gibson and Manuel, 2003). In highly virtual teams, it is often necessary to create a "hybrid" culture, structure, and set of operating policies that represent a compromise among the various alternatives preferred by different team members (Riopelle et al., 2003).

DYNAMIC STRUCTURE

Finally, teams that are highly virtual often have a team structure that is dynamic and evolving (Gibson and Gibbs, 2005). In fact, even the participants may be unknown in advance; e.g., they may not be available due to other meetings, or they may choose not to attend based on other priorities. Therefore, a rigid sequence of activities cannot be imposed on the work, tools cannot be structured to assume the presence of any given participant (King and Majchzrak, 2003), and work structures must often emerge. Importantly, in highly virtual teams, the initial structure, start-up, and formation activities are potentially more critical than in co-located teams because they provide the common ground needed to bridge differences and develop basic operating structure (Riopelle et al., 2003). Further, team collaboration in a virtual environment is unique because it requires both synchronous (members working simultaneously) and asynchronous (members working sequentially or rotating) work.

In summary, teams range in their degree of virtuality, from slightly virtual to extremely virtual. A team that does all its work through e-mail, text exchanges, and teleconferences, never meeting face-to-face, is more virtual than a team that meets face-to-face monthly. A team that spans multiple continents and time zones is more virtual than one whose members are located in the same city. A team that has more cultural diversity is higher in virtuality, and teams that have very dynamic structures have greater virtuality. Increased virtuality adds complexity that must be managed. Yet, as we will see below, successfully managing that complexity has enormous benefits.

A FRAMEWORK FOR VIRTUAL COLLABORATION

Many factors work together to determine team effectiveness. What team members and leaders actually do is create the conditions that support effectiveness. They do not work using just one behavior or pulling one lever at a time; they use multiple techniques. As result, a comprehensive framework must include multiple design and implementation factors that help to create the conditions that support virtual collaboration in teams (Cohen and Gibson, 2003). One well-received framework for team effectiveness in virtual collaborations (see Figure 1) includes *design factors* that managers facilitate, which contribute to the establishment of *enabling conditions*, which in turn increase effectiveness *outcomes* (Cohen and Gibson, 2003). This framework also suggests that electronic dependence, geographic dispersion, diversity, and

FIGURE 1 Framework for Virtual Collaboration

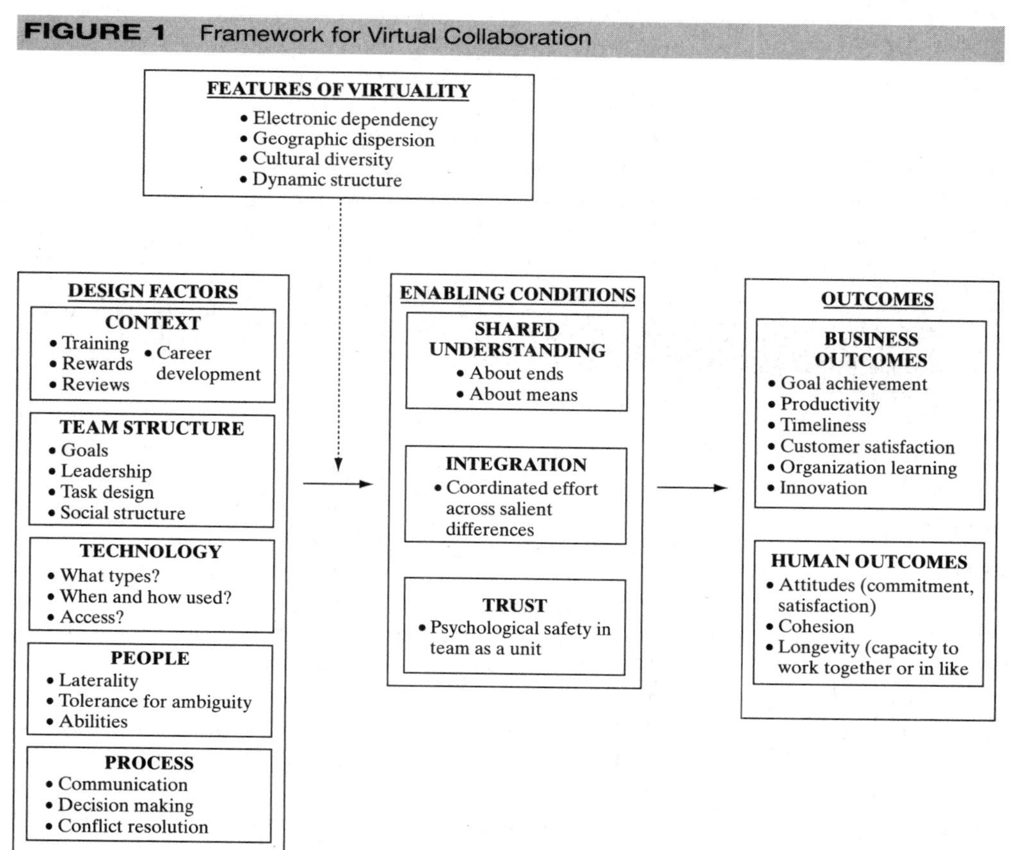

Adapted from Gibson and Cohen (2003).

dynamic structure amplify the effects of the design factors on the enabling conditions (Gibson and Gibbs, 2005; Gibson et al., 2005). Each component of the framework is addressed in the sections that follow.

DESIGN FACTORS

Design factors include features pertaining to the organization and team context, technology use, team member characteristics, and work and team processes (Cohen and Gibson, 2003). Several factors are embedded in each of these categories. For example, reward systems and decision-making policies are part of the organizational context. How an organization's reward system is structured, how its policies are designed, and how its practices are implemented may make it more likely (or less likely) that its teams will succeed when working virtually. Those who establish, lead, and support virtual teams can influence organizational systems, structures, policies, and practices. These are levers, discussed below, that can be pulled to promote enabling conditions and effectiveness.

Organization and Team Structure

The systems, structures, and policies that make up the organizational context and team context are important for virtual collaboration. There are often vast differences in job design and staffing patterns across participants and partners. Without common support systems, building competencies and expertise is difficult and this can hamper overall development, knowledge management, and sensemaking (Mohrman et al., 2003). Likewise, virtuality may make *individual-level* rewards (which are a common practice in many organizations) more precarious due to the increased needs for *team-level* cohesion, mutual accountability, and interdependence (Lawler, 2003). Finally, time is a critical resource that organizations must provide for virtual work. Virtual teaming typically lengthens the workday for virtual team members, and time zone dispersion narrows the window for real-time team interaction (Klein and Kleinhanns, 2003). Multitasking is a common strategy during meetings, which can distract members to such an extent that they miss an opportunity to provide valuable input. Likewise, the focus of members is often diluted by their local tasks and priorities (e.g., out of "site" is often out of mind). If local priorities override time team members had planned to devote to team assignments or meetings, process loss may result in teamwork requiring more time than planned (Klein and Kleinhanns, 2003). Virtual team members often complain that too much time is spent on merely sharing information in meetings rather than doing truly collaborative tasks such as decision making or problem solving (Klein and Kleinhanns, 2003).

However, in terms of decision-making policies, teams that operate across contexts have a strong potential advantage over co-located teams with respect to their ability to implement decisions, because of the strong ties distributed members can develop locally with clients, customers, and other external constituents (Maznevski and Athanassiou, 2003). In addition, similar to a decentralized organization structure, some forms of electronic media, such as text-based conferencing and discussion groups, have been found to facilitate a more equal and full representation of team member inputs (Tyran et al., 1992). Finally, it is less likely that a vocal and assertive member can dominate a group that relies primarily on text-based electronic media (Tyran et al., 2003), and virtuality often decreases power and hierarchy issues in teams (Elron and Vigoda, 2003) (see Table 1.)

TABLE 1 Tips for Addressing Organization and Team Structure in Virtual Collaboration

- Share measurement systems and metrics across sites—the more comprehensive, the more useful.
- Align incentive systems across subunits and recognize team-level efforts.
- Create knowledge management systems, such as team intranet, archives, index, and templates.
- Develop sponsors and champions who value virtual teaming.
- Provide a human link in the form of a facilitator.
- Develop a common training program across sites to strengthen necessary skills.

Information Technology

Tools for electronic communication provide the infrastructure for virtual collaboration. When implemented well, teammates are able to work around the clock without violating the personal time of any one member (Griffith et al., 2003). The technology needs to ensure team members from any location can effectively coordinate their work and should also support team development and work on tasks. Many commercialized products exist to support collaboration in virtual teams. The challenge for practitioners is to figure out which technologies are most appropriate for their teams.

Interestingly, research has demonstrated that use of advanced technologies (e.g., videoconferencing) is relatively uncommon in virtual teams, with most team members preferring to use email as the primary mode of communication (Kirkman et al., 2004; Raven, 2003). This may be because the use of technology is complicated by the composition of most virtual teams; that is, members have different access to and norms around use of technologies (Cramton and Orvis, 2003). Across members of teams operating virtually, the quality and capacity of the infrastructure for communication vary, limiting access and feasibility of high-bandwidth technologies such as videoconferencing. In addition, members often have different formats and protocols for storing knowledge (e.g., Lotus Notes databases versus Access or Outlook repositories) (King and Majchrzak, 2003). These variations in availability of advanced technology and resources to support them can cause major communication breakdowns (Klein and Kleinhanns, 2003). Some members may only have access to electronic communication during certain hours, and norms for how often members should check in for messages (e.g., email, voicemail, use of instant messaging) differ from context to context. These features are unique and surprisingly salient in teams that rely heavily on electronic communication. For example, research suggests that creative and reflective processes are often easier in synchronous mode (e.g., through teleconferences on webconferences); in fact, reflection will likely take longer if done asynchronously because responses may not be made with people in the same frame of mind, leading to a loss of "mind-share" between responses (Klein and Kleinhanns, 2003). (See Table 2.)

Team Members

Collaborating virtually often brings together representatives from numerous company locations and permits interaction among parties that might otherwise duplicate effort or even work at cross-purposes (Riopelle et al., 2003). Virtuality

TABLE 2 Tips for Addressing Technology Issues in Virtual Collaboration

- Simple is often ideal, but technology must match the task and structure
- Steps to include:
  - Identify options and preferences
  - Match technology to the task and people
  - Ensure access, connectivity, and compatibility
  - Train members to use tools and provide ongoing technical support
  - Develop guidelines and templates for use of different media
  - Conduct a limited number of critical face-to-face meetings
- Include explicit norms for team member interaction, such as:
  - How often to communicate
  - Expected response time
  - Determining which media to use
  - Prioritization of issues
- Confidentiality and legal clarity

Based on Gibson and Cohen (2003).

potentially increases the number of participants and overall contributions to meetings, and allows members to maintain access to their home computing environment and desktop tools, which facilitates knowledge capture and search (King and Majchrzak, 2003). By virtue of different locations, members can tap into multiple sources of information and knowledge, and this broad spectrum of knowledge can be leveraged on behalf of the team and the organization. The process of obtaining information is greatly facilitated by building relationships within and outside the team; members hear about what is important from other people they know, they are alerted to knowledge and information that is potentially useful, and they interpret meaning in part based on knowledge of its origins. Good relationships with the right people can help team members acquire knowledge and analysis that competitors cannot obtain (Maznevski and Athanssiou, 2003). Furthermore, if diverse intelligence is leveraged in virtual work, it allows better outcomes than the best individual team member could achieve (Klein and Kleinhanns, 2003).

The people who work in highly virtual teams should possess certain capabilities to work effectively with their teammates. First, they need sufficient task-related knowledge and skills. They also need to have the skills to work collaboratively in virtual space. For example, they need lateral skills to work with people quite different from themselves. Team members need to have a tolerance for ambiguity to deal with the unstructured communication that characterizes much of virtual teamwork. The personality dimensions and skills that team members possess will influence the establishment of enabling conditions. (See Table 3.)

Team and Work Processes

Internal team processes can help or hinder the creation of enabling conditions. In highly virtual teams, there is less opportunity to engage in informal and social interaction, communication is more formal, and there is less time allocated for nontask behavior (Hinds and Weisband, 2003). Further, involvement in the team is often less central than involvement with a member's local environment, so there is less emotional attachment, vested interest, and identification. In turn, this means lower familiarity and intimacy and

TABLE 3 Tips for Improving Team Member Skills in Virtual Collaboration

- Build "laterality" by becoming familiar with:
  - each other's competence and unique personal attributes
  - personal needs, concerns, interests, priorities, and fears of team members
  - using "round-robin sensemaking" where each member takes a turn telling what they know about a particular issue
  - being sensitive to cultural differences in intentions and interpretations
- Establish similarities across members (e.g., education, goals, etc.)
- Create a careful balance between specialization and generalization to take advantage of functional expertise
- Develop, recognize, and reward basic communication skills, including:
  - Surfacing differences
  - Testing for understanding
  - Active listening
- Mutual perspective taking

Based on Gibson and Cohen (2003).

less self-disclosure. English as a second language may exacerbate this and result in less depth and candor in exchanges, which increases psychological distance (Elron and Vigoda, 2003) and fears of misuse, miscommunication, and misinterpretation of knowledge (King and Majchrazk, 2003). As a result, there is often a higher perception of risk, which increases ambiguity and complexity of information exchanged. Even when English is designated as the official language of the collaborative effort and even when sophisticated technologies or translation procedures are used, language presents a key challenge to collective sensemaking processes in virtual teams (Mohrman et al., 2003).

In addition, communication through text-based media is more laborious so people tend not to type out details they would communicate verbally (Graetz et al., 1998). As a result, computer-mediated groups have lower communication efficiency than co-located groups (DeSanctis and Monge, 1999). The details, qualifications, social rituals, and cues that reveal meaning are often left out of text messages, and this may hinder interpretation, cohesion, and relationships in teams (Gibson and Zellmer-Bruhn, 2001). In the absence of rich auditory and visual cues such as voice intonation, understanding of complex messages is inhibited, and there is less feedback that information has not been understood (Hinds and Weisband, 2003). Receivers often fail to let a sender know their perception of the message that was sent (Gibson and Manuel, 2003). Adjustment to a shared norm of communication may be resented, particularly if that norm is more inclined toward a given culture (e.g., Israelis resent having to be more indirect due to the preferred style of U.S. participants) (Elron and Vigoda, 2003).

Finally, highly virtual teams may need more time to make sure all voices are adequately heard. Differences in phonics and syntax, unfamiliar accents, and inappropriate use of vocabulary can make it extremely hard or impossible to understand each other (Klein and Kleinhanns, 2003). Specifically, participants who are not physically located at or near headquarters or with the core of the team may be at a disadvantage because they do not have as many opportunities to participate in informal exchanges (Mohrman et al., 2003). All of these phenomena may hinder creativity and satisfaction, which are linked to team effectiveness.

In terms of conflict, relationship conflict (related to interpersonal or emotional issues), which has demonstrated dysfunctional impacts in teams, is more likely to be filtered out of computer-mediated communication (Griffith et al., 2003). Further, in teams that are highly virtual, conflict management is often more explicit and, therefore, may avoid the common problem of misunderstandings found in less explicit forms of communication. Similarly, highly involved virtual team members are often better able to notice conflict than less involved virtual team members (Griffith et al., 2003).

However, although teams do experience advantages related to conflict due to the virtual nature of their work, the flip side of these benefits may create challenges. For example, members of highly virtual teams often do not have the opportunity to serendipitously engage in sensemaking, and communication is often limited to short time episodes; this is efficient in some ways but may potentially increase opportunities for misunderstandings (Riopelle et al., 2003). Consensus is more difficult to reach in virtual teams, particularly in those teams working on complex, nontechnical issues (Hollingshead and McGrath, 1993). In addition, conflict is likely to be hidden longer in highly virtual teams, and there may be higher levels of process-based conflict (Griffith et al., 2003).

In terms of influence processes, rationality and sanction are used more frequently in highly virtual teams, and these tend to be the most functional forms of influence (Elron and Vigoda, 2003). On the other hand, the less popular and socially acceptable influence tactics, such as pressure, sanction, and legitimating, are typically used less frequently because lower familiarity and intimacy serve as gatekeepers to these tactics (Elron and Vigoda, 2003). Political behavior takes on a more careful and covert form in highly virtual teams because communication is more frequently documented. Cultural boundaries and differences restrain people from using extremely aggressive influence and politics (Elron, Shamir, and Ben Ari, 1999), and there are fewer stable political coalitions based on cultural subgroups in virtual teams (Elron and Vigoda, 2003). Members of highly virtual teams are often on "their best behavior" because they consider themselves as "ambassadors" of the groups they represent (Elron and Vigoda, 2003). Yet, ironically, in virtual teams, crisis and conflict are often the impetus that most clearly signals the need for integration and helps to bridge differences represented on the team (Riopelle et al., 2003). (See Table 4.)

ENABLING CONDITIONS

Careful management of the design factors helps to establish three enabling conditions in highly virtual team collaborations: (1) shared understanding about the team's goals, tasks, work processes, and member characteristics; (2) integration or coordination across key organizational systems and structures; and (3) mutual trust in the team (Cohen and Gibson, 2003). These are discussed next.

Shared Understanding

In most teams, it is important to establish commonalities in beliefs, expectations, and perceptions. Highly virtual teams need to develop this shared understanding about what they are trying to achieve (their goals), how they will achieve them (work and group processes), what they need to do (their tasks), and what each team member brings to the team task (member knowledge, skills, and abilities) (Cohen and Gibson, 2003). When teams involve people from different disciplines, business units, organizations, and cultures, their members will have different ways of perceiving their tasks and key issues, and of

TABLE 4 Tips for Addressing Work Process Issues in Virtual Collaborations

- Clearly delineate "who knows what" and member roles
- Explicitly address multiple team membership and "mind share"
- Responsibility lies with individuals to:
  - Make needed information available to others
  - Monitor relevant information
  - Tag information so people can quickly determine its relevance
- Meetings are designed to collectively *use* information
  - Follow good meeting management principles and teleconference etiquette
- Discuss conflict-resolution approaches
- Explicitly create cooperative norms
- Develop norms around pacing of divergence/convergence (when to let ideas flow openly and when to reach closure and move on)

Based on Gibson and Cohen (2003).

making sense of their situation (Earley and Gibson, 2002). Dougherty (1992) described new product development team members as inhabiting different "thought worlds" because of these differences. By developing shared understandings, virtual teams learn how to bridge the chasm between "thought worlds" (Hinds and Weisband, 2003). (See Table 5.)

Integration

A second key enabling condition captures the process of establishing ways in which the parts of an organization can work together to create value, develop products, or deliver services (Cohen and Gibson, 2003). The parts of the organization (or organizations) represented by team members who work virtually are likely to be highly differentiated in response to global competitive pressures and uncertain business environments. This differentiation across organizational units means that they are likely to have different policies, organizational structures, and systems. These differences can hinder effective collaboration in virtual teams both directly and indirectly. When organizational units have different information technology infrastructures, for example, connectivity can be a serious problem. At the most basic level, virtual team members may not be able to send e-mails to team members from other business units. In a more subtle way, business unit policies, structures, and systems influence employee behaviors. They provide incentives for certain behaviors and disincentives for others. Incentives for cross-unit

TABLE 5 Tips for Creating Shared Understanding in Virtual Collaborations

- Launch the team with face-to-face time and opportunities for both formal and informal interactions:
  - Establish clear leadership role(s)
  - Review broad organizational goals (often shared)
  - Review team mission
  - Identify collective work product(s)
  - Agree on objectives, measures, targets (less likely shared)
  - Establish integration mechanisms needed across teams
- Review with management and add processes for assessing the team
- As work continues, schedule time for informal team building ("scheduled informality")

Based on Gibson and Cohen (2003).

TABLE 6 Tips for Increasing Integration in Virtual Collaborations

- Carefully select members and partners (e.g., organizations) to be involved
- Build relationships by using a counterpart strategy of linking people in similar roles across sites
- Create social and structural integration mechanisms such as:
  - Periodic orientations
  - Informal gatherings
  - Social information exchange
  - "Round-robin" participation
  - "Buddy system" and "mirror image structures" (dyadic accountability)
- Clarification of formal and informal roles

Based on Gibson and Cohen (2003).

collaboration may be lacking. Policies, structures, and systems also shape employee perspectives and worldviews on what is and is not important. The greater the degree of differentiation in an organization, the greater the need for integration.

The type of relationships and linkages that are important in a virtual team depends on which task characteristics are dominant. Some virtual tasks relate primarily to integration (e.g., combining knowledge to develop a new product). Others require differentiation (e.g., customizing for different markets), and still others are learning tasks (e.g., benchmarking). Integration tasks require extensive internal networks of relationships. Differentiation tasks require extensive links external to the team, and ties can be weaker. Finally, learning tasks require a balance of the two types of networks (Maznevski and Athanassiou, 2003). Configurations of networks are often combined in virtual teams with varied tasks to achieve the best of all worlds.

In virtual teams, the flow of knowledge and information is related to the development of networks of relationships in the team, particularly the subgroups that often form. Interestingly, if subgroups tend to coincide with the different subtasks of the group (i.e., different types of expertise to apply to different client problems), then knowledge will flow more effectively; if the subgroups don't coincide with subtasks, then knowledge flows are often compromised (Maznevski and Athanassiou, 2003). (See Table 6.)

Trust

The third enabling condition is *mutual trust* in the team. Mutual or collective trust is a shared psychological state that is characterized by an acceptance of vulnerability based on expectations of intentions or behaviors of others within the team (Cummings and Bromiley, 1996; Rousseau, Sitkin, Burt and Camerer, 1998). Teams that have established mutual trust are safe environments for their members. Members are willing to take risks with one another and to let their vulnerabilities show. Given that many factors known to contribute to social control and coordination—such as geographical proximity, similarity in backgrounds, and experience with each other—are often absent in virtual teams, the development of collective trust is critical yet difficult to establish (Gibson and Manuel, 2003). People tend to trust those whom they perceive as similar to themselves. Further, electronically mediated communication lacks the interpersonal cues that are so important for building trust. Since nonverbal communication can be an important source of information when assessing the trustworthiness of a new teammate, the use of text-based electronic communication (e.g., e-mail), in particular, may impede the development of trust in virtual teams (Gibson and Manuel, 2003).

TABLE 7 Tips for Increasing Trust in Virtual Collaborations

- Assess and celebrate openness and psychological safety
- Acknowledge "risky" disclosures
- Celebrate supportive responses
- Continuously evaluate the trust climate and intervene when necessary
- Develop a supportive climate:
  - Active listening
  - Listening for ideas
  - Framing techniques
- Following-up techniques

Based on Gibson and Cohen (2003).

Further, text-based electronic communication makes it more difficult for team members to formulate impressions of their teammates and make inferences about one another's knowledge (Walther, 1993). Thus, members of highly virtual teams often err on the side of dispositional attributions (i.e., assuming behavior was caused by personality) because they lack situational information and are overloaded, and this may in turn make them less likely to try to modify problematic situations. Finally, geographic distance, different contexts, and reliance on technology lead to less similarities across members and greater possibility of divisive subgroups (Cramton and Orvis, 2003). Interdependence is often higher *within* subgroups (e.g., within a subset of members who are all from the same organization) than across subgroups (Gibson and Vermeulen, 2003). Without opportunities to demonstrate reliability and responsiveness across subgroups, collective trust cannot exist, and a negative cycle of divisive conflict will likely ensue (Gibson and Manuel, 2003). In sum, co-located teammates can often establish credibility with each other by a process that is not explicitly designed, but members of highly virtual teams must create much more explicit routines that will allow this to happen (Maznevski and Athanassiou, 2003). (See Table 7.)

OUTCOMES

A comprehensive framework for team effectiveness must include both business outcomes and human outcomes. Possible business outcomes are goal achievement, productivity, timeliness, customer satisfaction, organization learning, innovation, and cycle time. Possible human outcomes are team member attitudes, such as commitment and satisfaction, cohesion and longevity, the capacity to work together in the future.

CONCLUSION

As demonstrated, operating virtually can amplify the benefits of teamwork. The greater the degree of electronic dependence, geographic dispersion, diversity, and dynamic structure, the higher the potential benefit. Virtuality enables the best talent, irrespective of location, to be applied to solve business problems, create products, and deliver services. Problems can be framed in ways that allow for innovative solutions when people can apply knowledge from one domain to another. Thus, collaborating virtually has the potential of producing high-quality, innovative business solutions. Plus, face-to-face meetings can be scheduled when needed, but people can do most of the work from their primary, distant work settings. Thus, collaborating virtually offers efficiency benefits as well. The potential to produce high-quality, innovative solutions at lower costs offers organizations competitive advantage. The key is to harness this potential.

References

Alderfer, C. P. (1977). "Group and Intergroup Relations," in J. R. Hackman and J. L. Suttle (eds.), *Improving the Quality of Work Life*. Palisades, CA: Goodyear.

Cohen, S. G., and Gibson, C.B. (2003). "In the Beginning: Introduction and Framework," in C. B. Gibson and S. G. Cohen (eds.), *Virtual Teams That Work: Creating Conditions for Virtual Team Effectiveness* (pp. 1–19). San Francisco: Jossey-Bass.

Cramton, D. C., and Orvis, K. L. (2003). "Overcoming Barriers to Information Sharing in Virtual Teams," in C. B. Gibson and S. G. Cohen (eds.), *Virtual Teams That Work: Creating Conditions for Virtual Team Effectiveness* (pp. 214–230). San Francisco: Jossey-Bass.

Cummings, L. L., and Bromiley, P. (1996). "The Organizational Trust Inventory (OTI): Development and Validation," in R. M. Kramer and T. R. Tyler (eds.), *Trust in Organizations: Frontiers of Theory and Research*. Thousand Oaks, CA: Sage.

DeSanctis, G., and Monge, P. (1999). "Introduction to Special Issue: Communication Processes in Virtual Organizations," *Organization Science*, 19(6): 693–703.

Doughtery, D. (1992). "Interpretive Barriers to Successful Product Innovation in Large Firms," *Organization Science*, 13: 77–92.

Earley, P. C., and Gibson, C. B. (2002). *Multinational Teams: A New Perspective*. Mahwah, NJ: Lawrence Erlbaum Associates.

Elron, E., and Vigoda, E. (2003). "Influence and Political Processes in Virtual Teams," in C. B. Gibson and S. G. Cohen (eds.), *Virtual Teams That Work: Creating Conditions for Virtual Team Effectiveness* (pp. 317–334). San Francisco: Jossey-Bass.

Elron, E., Shamir, B., and Ben-Ari, E. (1999). "Why Don't They Fight Each Other? Cultural Diversity and Operational Unity in Multinational Forces," *Armed Forces and Society*, 26: 73–98.

Gibbs, J., and Gibson, C. B. (forthcoming). *Exploring the Role of Supportive Communication Climate in Mitigating Challenges of National Diversity for Team Innovation*. Chapter to appear in E. Mannix, and M. Neale, (eds.), Research in Managing Groups and Teams.

Gibson, C. B., and Gibbs, J. (2005). *Unpacking the Effects of Virtuality on Team Innovation*. Working Paper, University of California, Irvine.

Gibson, C. B., Cohen, S. G., Gibbs, J., Stanko, T. and Tesluk, P. (2005). *Is Everybody Out There? The Impact of Virtuality on Individual Psychological States and Work Team Enabling Conditions*. Work in Progress. Working Paper, University of California, Irvine.

Gibson, C. B., and Cohen, S. G. (2003). "The Last Word: Conclusions and Implications," in C. B. Gibson and S. G. Cohen (eds.), *Virtual Teams That Work: Creating Conditions for Virtual Team Effectiveness* (pp. 403–421). San Francisco: Jossey-Bass.

Gibson, C. B., and Manuel, J. A. (2003). "Building Trust: Effective Multicultural Communication Processes in Virtual Teams," in C. B. Gibson and S. G. Cohen (eds.), *Virtual Teams That Work: Creating Conditions for Virtual Team Effectiveness* (pp. 59–86). San Francisco: Jossey-Bass.

Gibson, C. B., and Vermeulen, F. (2003). "A Healthy Divide: Subgroups As a Stimulus for Team Learning," *Administrative Science Quarterly*, 48, 202–239.

Gibson, C. B., and Zellmer-Bruhn, M. (2001). "Metaphor and Meaning: An Intercultural Analysis of the Concept of Teamwork," *Administrative Science Quarterly*, 46: 274–303.

Graetz, K. A., et al. (1998). "Information Sharing in Face-to-Face, Teleconferencing, and Electronic Chat Teams," *Small Group Research*, 29(6): 714–743.

Griffith, T. L., Sawyer, J. E., and Neale, M. A. (2003). "Virtualness and Knowledge: Managing the Love Triangle of Organizations, Individuals, and Information Technology," *MIS Quarterly*, 27: 265–287.

Hackman, J. R. (1987). "The Design of Work Teams," in J. W. Lorsch (ed.), *Handbook of Organizational Behavior*. Upper Saddle River, NJ: Prentice Hall.

Hackman, J. R. and Oldham, G. R. (1980). *Work Redesign*. Reading, MA: Addison-Wesley.

Hinds, P. J., and Weisband, S. P. (2003). "Knowledge Sharing and Shared Understanding in Virtual Teams," in C. B. Gibson and S. G. Cohen (eds.), *Virtual Teams That Work: Creating Conditions for Virtual Team Effectiveness* (pp. 21–36). San Francisco: Jossey-Bass.

Hollingshead, A., and McGrath, J. (1995). "Computer-Assisted Groups: A Critical Review of the Empirical Research," in R. Guzzo and E. Salas (eds.). *Team Effectiveness and Decision Making in Organizations*. San Francisco: Jossey-Bass.

King, N., and Majchrzak, A. (2003). "Technology Alignment and Adaptation for Virtual Teams Involved in Unstructured Knowledge Work," in C. B. Gibson and S. G. Cohen (eds.), *Virtual Teams That Work: Creating Conditions for Virtual Team Effectiveness* (pp. 265–291). San Francisco: Jossey-Bass.

Kirkman, B. L., Rosen, B., Tesluk, P. E., and Gibson, C.B. (2004)."The Impact of Team Empowerment on Virtual Team Performance: The Moderating Role of Face-to-Face Interaction," *Academy of Management Journal*, 47: 175–192.

Klein, J. A., and Kleinhanns, A. (2003). "Closing the Time Gap in Virtual Teams," in C. B. Gibson and S. G. Cohen (eds.), *Virtual Teams That Work: Creating Conditions for Virtual Team Effectiveness* (pp. 381–400). San Francisco: Jossey-Bass.

Lawler, E. E. III (2003). "Pay Systems for Virtual Teams," in C.B. Gibson and S.G. Cohen (eds.), *Virtual Teams That Work: Creating Conditions for Virtual Team Effectiveness* (pp. 121–144). San Francisco: Jossey-Bass.

Maznevski, M. L., and Chudoba, K. M. (2000). "Bridging Space Over Time: Global Virtual-Team Dynamics and Effectiveness," *Organization Science*, 11: 473–492.

Maznevski, M. L., and Athanassiou, N. A. (2003). "Designing the Knowledge-Management Infrastructure in Virtual Teams: Building and Using Social Networks and Social Capital," in C. B. Gibson and S. G. Cohen (eds.), *Virtual Teams That Work: Creating Conditions for Virtual Team Effectiveness* (pp. 196–230). San Francisco: Jossey-Bass.

Mohrman, S. A., Klein, J. A., and Finegold, D. (2003). "Managing the Global New Product Development Network: A Sense-Making Perspective," in C. B. Gibson and S. G. Cohen (eds.), *Virtual Teams That Work: Creating Conditions for Virtual Team Effectiveness* (pp. 37–58). San Francisco: Jossey-Bass.

Raven, A. 2003. "Team or Community of Practice: Aligning Tasks, Structures, and Technologies," in C. B. Gibson and S. G. Cohen, eds. *Virtual Teams That Work: Creating Conditions for Virtual Team Effectiveness* (pp. 292–306). San Francisco: Jossey-Bass.

Rioppelle, K., Gluesing, J. C., Alcordo, T. C., Baba, M. L., Britt, D., McKether, W., Monplaisir, L., Ratner, H. H., and Wagner, K. H. (2003). "Context, Task, and The Evolution of Technology Use in Global Virtual Teams," in C. B. Gibson and S. G. Cohen, eds., *Virtual Teams That Work: Creating Conditions for Virtual Team Effectiveness* (pp. 239–264). San Francisco: Jossey-Bass.

Rousseau, D. M., Sitkin, S. B., Burt, R. S., and Camerer, C. (1998). "Not So Different After All: A Cross-Disciplinary View of Trust," *Academy of Management Review*, 23(3): 393–404.

Tyran, K. L., Dennis, A. R., Vogel D. R., and Nunamaker, J.F. (1992). "The Application of Electronic Meeting Technology to Support Strategic Management," *MIS Quarterly*, 16(3): 313–334.

Tyran, K. L., Tyran, C. K. and Shepherd, M. (2003). "Exploring Emergent Leadership in Virtual Teams," in C. B. Gibson and S. G. Cohen (eds.), *Virtual Teams That Work: Creating Conditions for Virtual Team Effectiveness* (pp. 183–195). San Francisco: Jossey-Bass.

Walther, J. B. (1993). "Impression Development in Computer-Mediated Interaction," *Western Journal of Communication*, 57: 381–398.

HOW TO LEAD A SELF-MANAGING TEAM*

Vanessa Urch Druskat
Jane V. Wheeler

To get work done, many companies organize employees into self-managing teams that are basically left to run themselves with some guidance from an external leader. In fact, comprehensive surveys report that 79 percent of companies in the *Fortune* 1,000 and 81 percent of manufacturing organizations currently deploy such "empowered,""self-directed" or "autonomous" teams.[1] Because of their widespread use, much research has been devoted to understanding how best to set up self-managing teams to maximize their productivity and effectiveness. Interestingly, though, relatively little attention has been paid to the leaders who must oversee such working groups.

At first, it seems contradictory: Why should a self-managing team require any leadership? After all, doesn't the group manage itself? In actuality, though, self-managing teams require a specific kind of leadership. Even a team that is autonomous in terms of its activities and decision making must still continually receive direction from higher levels in the organization. And it also must report to that hierarchy through a person who is ultimately held accountable for the group's performance. Many managers today are expected to fulfill the role of external leader, but most receive conflicting signals regarding how to go about it.[2] Should they, for instance, be involved in their team's decision-making process? If so, how should they participate without detracting from the group's autonomy?

To investigate such issues, we conducted a study of 300 self-managing teams at a large manufacturing plant of a *Fortune* 500 corporation. (See "About the Research.") We investigated both average- and superior-performing external leaders at that site to determine the behaviors that separated one group from the other. Our research has shown that, contrary to common perception, the best external leaders were not necessarily the ones who had adopted a hands-off approach, nor were they simply focused on encouraging team members in various ways.[3] Instead, the external leaders who had contributed most to their team's success excelled at one skill: managing the boundary between the team and the larger organization. That process required specific behaviors that can be grouped into four basic functions: relating, scouting, persuading, and empowering. (See Figure 1.) External leaders who excelled at those capabilities were able to drive their teams to superior performance.

MANAGING IN NO-MAN'S LAND

As recently as the 1960s, self-managing teams were practically unheard of. Indeed, an early experiment by General Foods Corp. to deploy self-managing teams on its Gaines dog-food production line more than 30 years ago was something of a sensation. Even

*Reprinted with permission from *MIT Sloan Management Review* (Summer 2004): 65–71.

FIGURE 1 The Work of the External Leader

External leaders must perform 11 behaviors that can be grouped into four categories: relating, scouting, persuading, and empowering. The behaviors are distinct but mutually reinforcing, and they require the external leader to continually cross the border between the team and the broader organization. In this model of external leadership, social and political awareness of the broader organization provides access to the individuals and groups that can help the leader best meet the team's needs; strong relationships allow the leader access to information in the team and the organization, which aids the leader in making sense of the needs of both parties; good information enables the leader to encourage or persuade the team to behave in ways that facilitate the organization's effectiveness: and the sense of control afforded by that influence allows the leader to empower the team more fully, resulting in greater team effectiveness.

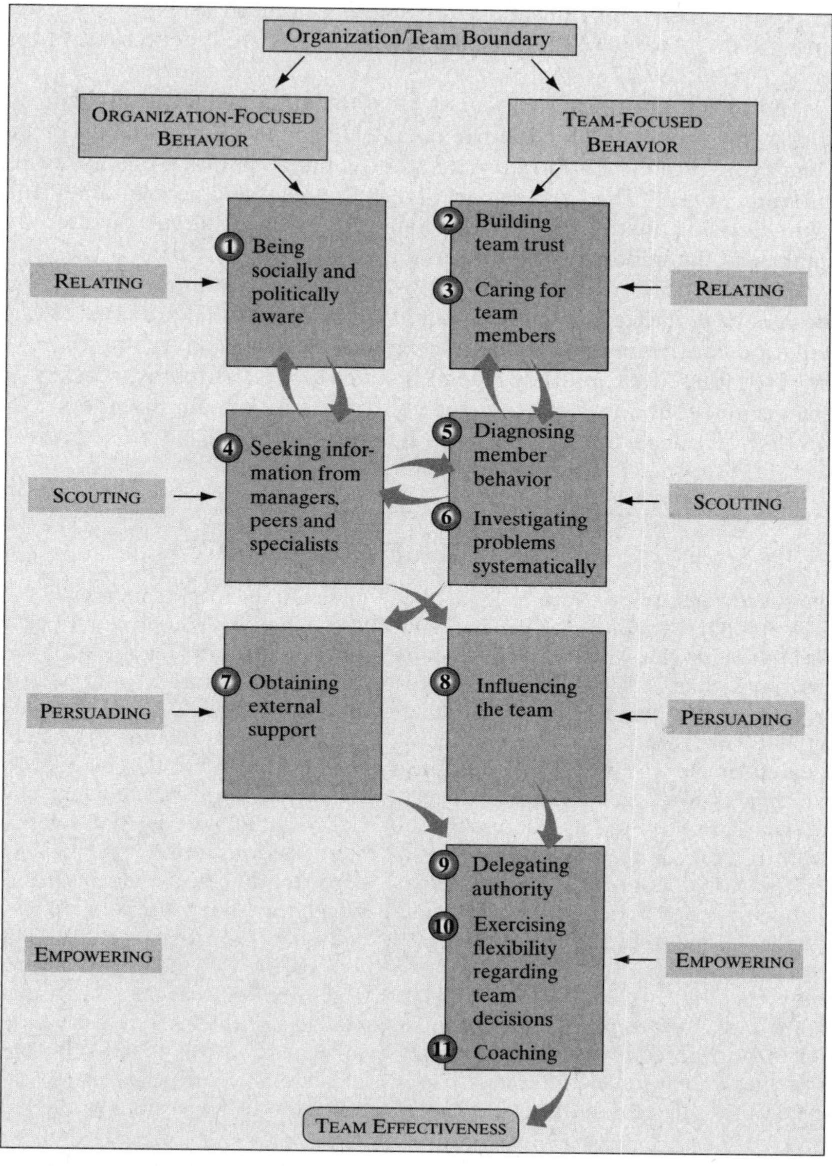

the company's own senior management expected the project to fail.[4] Since then, self-managing teams have become an increasingly popular way for companies to get work done. Even so, the role of the people in charge of those groups has remained somewhat of a mystery.

To be sure, leading a team that needs to manage itself is inherently tricky. The role is highly ambiguous by nature (and, on the face of it, oxymoronic). In general, self-managing teams tend to have well-defined job functions and are responsible for monitoring and managing their own performance. Instead of managers telling them what to do, these teams gather and synthesize information, make important decisions, and take collective responsibility for meeting their goals. What's left for the external leader to do? As one of the external leaders in our study remarked, "Maybe we're not needed, you know?"

But the reality is that the buck stops at the external leaders. Specifically, companies hold them responsible for their team's performance. If the quality or productivity of a team is substandard, its external leader is taken to task. As another team leader in our study noted, "The hardest part is that I'm also held accountable. If they make the wrong decision, it still comes back on me." In essence, the job of external leader exists squarely in the middle of a managerial no-man's land.

Back in 1977, a field study published about that early experiment at General Foods revealed external leaders caught in the middle: Their teams criticized them for being too controlling, while their own managers complained that they were being too lax.[5] Not long after, another research study looked at teams in other organizational settings and found that those three constituencies—team members, external leaders and their upper-level managers—all had different ideas about the role.[6]

ABOUT THE RESEARCH

We conducted a study of external leaders at a *Fortune* 500 durable-consumer-goods manufacturing plant in the Midwest. The facility employs more than 3,000 people and is the world's largest manufacturer of its particular product. We chose this site because it offered a rich research sample: The plant had transitioned to self-managing work teams almost five years prior to our data collection, and there were 300 such teams reporting up through 66 external leaders. This large pool of external leaders in one location provided a wide range of individuals in that role and allowed us to control for organizational context.

Our method was to select samples of high-performing and average external leaders and to discover through interviews how their behaviors, strategies and attitudes differed. We used three criteria for selecting our key participants: nominations from team members, nominations from managers and objective performance data for the leaders' teams. We then conducted intensive three-hour interviews with each of the 19 individuals selected, regarding critical incidents they recalled. The interviews were conducted blind to the "superior" or "average" status of the leaders. A content analysis of those interviews allowed us to develop an exhaustive list of actions and behaviors that were noted consistently by superior leaders but not by average ones. Initially, our exhaustive list contained approximately 30 behaviors that we hypothesized made a difference between the "superior" and "average" performers. Iterative readings of the interview transcripts helped us to winnow down that list to the 11 distinct behaviors reported in this article. Two expert coders, who were blind to the "superior" and average" status of the leaders, coded all transcripts for the presence of the 11 behaviors and determined the reliability of the codes. The mean reliability was 92 percent. Statistical analyses also revealed that 10 of the behaviors were demonstrated significantly more often by the superior-performing leaders. (The exception was "diagnosing member behavior," which was demonstrated often by both average and superior performers.)

To help interpret the findings and to develop our model of how these 11 behaviors emerge as the process of effective external leadership, we also spoke with a total of 90 team members: 52 in focus groups and 38 in one-on-one interviews. We supplemented that information with interviews of the 10 managers to whom the external leaders reported, and we also collected information via questionnaires from the broader group of senior managers and directors at the plant.

Furthermore, we later examined the applicability of our findings by interviewing external leaders at other organizations and in different industries, including those for product-development groups in a design organization and executive-level teams at a bank, a health-care organization and a manufacturing company. This subsequent work suggests that our results have broader applicability for any leader of an empowered team, regardless of the group's level or task.

Unfortunately, that lack of consensus generally remains today. Prior to and since our study, we have found confusion about the external-leader role in other companies and at all organizational levels. Consider the senior executive of a large Midwestern bank who desperately wanted to empower his team of high-level bank executives but was unsure how to go about that. When he attended meetings, he felt team members relied too heavily on his opinion, but when he stopped going to meetings, he felt stuck in an information black hole. Even with his many years of experience, he really did not know how to manage that group.

The problem is that a self-managing team requires leadership of a very different sort. Researchers agree that the external-leader role is more complex than the traditional manager role.[7] This is true partly because the typical external leader is in charge of several self-managing teams at any one time. (In our study, they were responsible for as many as eight.)

More important, the external leader absolutely must avoid any heavy-handed attempts at managing. Case studies have shown that external leaders who struggle with their role usually end up exerting too much control, which then undermines the self-managing team's ability to get work done.[8] Because of that and other issues, various researchers have labeled external leaders as the most common impediment to the success of self-managing teams.[9]

Confusion about the role of the external leader might be tolerable if that function weren't so crucial, but a variety of studies have shown that the success of a self-managing team greatly depends on its external leader.[10] A newly created group, for example, often needs both effective coaching and a champion who can represent its decisions to other executives in the organization. Teams also depend on external leaders for help in acquiring resources. That's why it's common to see an underperforming team successfully turn itself around with only the change of its external leader—or to see a once-great team suffer after its external leader departs.

FOUR FUNCTIONS, 11 BEHAVIORS

Although the essence of a self-managing team is autonomy, the quality of its link to the organization is pivotal to success. Some external leaders perform that role much better than others, with the superior ones tending to excel at relating, scouting, persuading, and empowering. Each function requires specific behaviors, of which there are a total of 11. In Figure 1 the relating activities are shown at the beginning of the process because, without the formation of those relationships, external leaders will find scouting difficult. Scouting, in turn, equips external leaders with the information they need to persuade. And various aspects of scouting and persuading help pave the way for greater empowerment of a team, which then contributes to the group's ultimate effectiveness.

The well-known key to making self-managing teams work is to delegate considerable authority to the group, granting it tremendous flexibility in making its own decisions.[11] What is less well-known are the kinds of leadership activities and behaviors that are needed to build the foundation for team empowerment. Relating, scouting and persuading are those critical building blocks.

Relating

External leaders must continually move back and forth between the team and the broader organization to build relationships. Success in this area requires three behaviors: being socially and politically aware, building team trust and caring for team members.

Being Socially and Politically Aware During our research study, we heard stories of both team triumphs and irritations. In one case, an external leader recounted the time he allowed one of his teams a freedom that was inconsistent with the company's informal policies. Later, he was taken aback by the backlash he experienced from his peers in the organization. Recalls the leader, "This person sends a note to my manager, to his manager and to my colleagues . . . saying, 'Since when did this policy change?' " The leader was also vehemently attacked by another team leader for his "ineffective supervision."

What happened? Clearly, the incident suggests a lack of political awareness: The leader simply didn't anticipate the impact of his decision on others. Nor did he perceive the need to build a broader consensus. Incidentally, in our study the performance of that leader had been categorized as average. By contrast, the superior external leaders had consistently demonstrated an understanding of the broader organization, including the individual concerns and decision-making criteria of important constituencies, such as the engineering and human resources groups. As one superior leader bluntly put it, "I've got a good rapport with all those groups, and most things I ask for get done. . . . You can get moved to the top of the list for things in a hurry if you're not [upsetting] people."

Building Team Trust Superior external leaders also consistently recognized the value of building good relationships with their teams, even to the point of achieving insider status. Given that the leaders had little time to spend with any one team, such acceptance was far from automatic. In fact, one leader in our study was impeached by her team members, who did not trust that she had their best interests in mind. Contrast that with the experience of another leader who, when his team complained of problems with new equipment, said, "Whatever it costs, if you guys aren't happy with it, we'll get another system in here . . . because you're the ones who are gonna have to work with it." The team was incredulous. One member pointed out that the new system had cost $23,000 to install.

Caring for Team Members In our study, average leaders were more likely to see the personal problems of the team members as impediments to getting work done, whereas superior leaders more often recognized them as opportunities to build relationships. One superior leader described an incident in which one of his employees had a problem with her disability leave. The leader took it upon himself to call the insurance department in the health center to clear the dispute, which had been an ongoing source of worry for the worker. "It was . . . instant relief for that person," recalls the leader. "It was not a big problem, but it was big to her."

Scouting

To scout effectively, external leaders must demonstrate three behaviors: seeking information from managers, peers and specialists; diagnosing member behavior; and investigating problems systematically.

Seeking Information from Managers, Peers, and Specialists Superior leaders appeared to be significantly more likely to seek information from others in the organization, whether as advice or simply in response to technical questions from the team. Sometimes the leaders used that information to influence team decision making, especially when they wanted to persuade people to take into account broader organizational considerations. For example, when a team wanted to hire a colleague who had filled in for absent members in the past, the group's external leader wisely decided to step in. The leader wanted his team members to be able to make their own choice, but he also sensed that their lack of knowledge and respect for a new hiring policy at the company could create problems with management. "I could tell this was going to be a sticky situation," he recalls, because the new policy was more formal and favored candidates with greater seniority. So the leader talked to HR as well as other external leaders as to how they filled their jobs. He then informed his boss about the situation and invited him to the team's next meeting. At the meeting, the team members were able to persuade the external leader's boss to delay implementing the new policy so that they could hire the person they wanted. By seeking and relaying all the pertinent information, the leader was able to enable his team to make its own decision (without disrupting the organization), which helped boost the team's morale.

Not surprisingly, external leaders who routinely sought information from the broader organization were able to advocate more effectively for their teams. They were able to help their teams gain valuable political awareness and build social capital for them—all of which would often pay off in less obvious, but no less important, ways. The team members themselves realized the importance of having an external leader who could get information faster than they could, had access to data they didn't have and could easily make contact with upper management. On the other hand, when team members felt that an external leader was not keeping them adequately informed, they tended to develop an "us against them" attitude. As one such member put it, "[They] don't want to give up information; it's their power."

Diagnosing Member Behavior Because external leaders are typically responsible for the performance of several teams, they are rarely on the scene when something critical occurs within a specific group. As a result, they must often gain insight after the fact. To do so, they frequently need to add to their incomplete information by analyzing and making sense of verbal and nonverbal cues from team members. One leader described an episode when his team had done months of benchmarking research to suggest a policy change to the directors of the organization. But the directors quickly shot down the proposal and instead told the team members that their time might be better spent improving their quality and productivity. When the leader heard the news he had mixed emotions. He was upset because he knew how much time his team had spent on the proposal, yet he also knew he had to support the directors' decision, because, after all, he was part of management. So he went to the team members and started to give them a pep talk but quickly stopped himself. "I could tell they thought I was full of you-know-what. You could see it in their eyes," he recalls. So, he instead offered people a sympathetic ear and acknowledged their well-intentioned efforts.

Interestingly, both the superior and the average leaders in our study talked about the need to read their team members accurately. In fact, it was the leadership capability they most commonly identified as important.

Investigating Problems Systematically When superior leaders got wind of a potential problem, they were significantly more likely to deploy an inquisitive and systematic approach to investigate the matter. They would begin by asking the team members myriad questions to collect data and identity the issues, after which they might visit an external constituent to collect additional information. "You've got to be down on the floor," one superior leader asserted. "When the line is down, I'm over there within a minute." By collecting firsthand information from the team members, superior leaders were able to fully understand their group's perspective, enabling them to make *informed* recommendations that would be acceptable to their teams as well as to external constituents. In contrast, average leaders were more likely to attempt problem solving with less data or input from the team members.

Persuading

With respect to external leadership, effective persuasion requires two behaviors: obtaining external support and influencing the team.

Obtaining External Support Teams often need support from the broader organization, and superior leaders are able to perform this advocacy role more effectively. One such leader remembered a time when his team members were having equipment problems. After talking with them, he used their ideas to sketch a new piece of machinery and came in during other shifts to gain additional input from other teams. He was then able to obtain management's authorization to build the new piece of equipment. In our study, team members agreed that leaders were most helpful when they were able to get the attention of important external constituents. Average leaders seemed to seek such external support less frequently, and when they did they were less successful in obtaining it. One average leader remembered an incident when he pleaded with the scheduling department to make a change for one of his teams. But because he had not built relationships with that department and had not expended the effort to obtain the information necessary to support his case, his request was denied.

Influencing the Team Effective external leaders were also adept at swaying their teams to decisions that best met the needs of the organization. Keep in mind that prior to doing so, these superior leaders had already established trust with their teams, had systematically investigated the problem at hand and had used their external contacts to obtain all necessary information. One superior leader, for example, collected statistics from the accounting department to persuade his struggling team to think of ways to improve its productivity. Using that data, the leader impressed upon his team how much the company lost in profits every minute a manufacturing line was down. "This is the money that we didn't make," the leader told the team. "If somebody is cutting the line off just to eat a sandwich, it is costing everybody." Three months later, the group's performance had improved markedly, and whenever the team was about to fall behind schedule, people would work a little longer to stay on track. Interestingly, those team members were going the extra distance without their leader having to ask (let alone demand) that they do so.

Empowering

External leaders of self-managing teams can empower those teams by demonstrating three behaviors: delegating authority, exercising flexibility regarding team decisions and coaching.

Delegating Authority External leaders typically have great discretion over the amount and type of authority that they delegate. In general, the superior leaders tended to empower their teams with more responsibility. For example, when one team was told by management that it had to move its assembly line, its leader left it up to the team to work out the details. "They very much had ownership," remembers the leader. "They knew what we needed to do and took it from there. This needed to be their baby." However, average leaders tended to be more fearful about delegating authority, and they would often make decisions for the team and solve its problems covertly. It is important to note that the average leaders' reluctance to delegate authority was not because they were leading the poorer-performing teams. In fact, many of the superior leaders in our study had been transferred to a problem team and had worked with it until they felt comfortable delegating authority. Eventually, as the team gained more and more ownership, its performance improved.

Exercising Flexibility Regarding Team Decisions Sometimes a team proposes something that is outlandish or that appears to reflect poorly on its leader. In such situations, average leaders were likely to express their reservations, whereas superior leaders frequently replied with comments such as, "It's not what I think; it's what you think." One of the teams in our study, for example, wanted to present its quarterly performance results at the department meeting by performing a skit. At first, the team's leader was a little hesitant because nothing like that had been done before and the meeting would be attended by all of the managers in the organization. "I thought,

'Oh, we could look so foolish on this,'" she recalls. But she gave the team her approval and, as it turned out, the skit went over well, which boosted the team's sense of cohesion and identity. Of course, teams don't always make good decisions, and a major responsibility of external leaders is to prevent serious mistakes. But even when a team has to be reined in, superior leaders did so only after considering the proposal as open-mindedly as possible.

Coaching Coaching involves a number of activities, including working one-on-one with employees, giving feedback to the team and demonstrating certain behaviors (such as effective meeting facilitation) for others to model. Past research has found that superior leaders tend to be active in educating and coaching others,[12] and our study confirmed that. In particular, superior leaders focused on strengthening a team's confidence, its ability to manage itself and its contributions from individual members. A common coaching behavior was for leaders to work with people who had just taken on roles of greater responsibility. For example, after a meeting in which people argued for 20 minutes about coffee, one superior leader helped the team member in charge to run more efficient meetings, first by developing an agenda and then by keeping the group focused on that agenda.

SELF-MANAGEMENT IN THE LONG RUN

For external leaders to relate, scout, persuade and empower, they must frequently—but quietly—cross the boundary between the team and the broader organization. The idea that a leader must manage this boundary is certainly not new; past research has linked it to the effectiveness of traditionally managed teams,[13] and several studies of empowered teams have proposed that it is the central focus of the external leader's role.[14] Our own research supports those findings. Specifically, the superior leaders in our study were able to develop strong relationships both inside the team and across the organization. In contrast, average performers tended to relate well to the team or to those in the broader organization, but not to both.

The four functions—relating, scouting, persuading, and empowering—are important for the leader of any group, but particularly so for those in charge of self-managing teams. (After all, if a team has not been empowered, how can it manage itself?) And the same process would be useful for leaders of geographically dispersed teams, given their similar challenge of having to rely on imperfect information to influence behavior from a remote location.

An important thing to remember about team autonomy is that self-management is not an either-or condition. Instead, it's a continuum, and external leaders should also be constantly guiding and developing their teams so that they become increasingly independent. In fact, the ultimate goal of the external leader should be the delegation of all 11 of the behaviors described. For example, external leaders should be developing their teams' relationships with relevant individuals and other groups in the broader organization, eventually relinquishing that primary activity to the teams themselves. And when teams do become less dependent on their external leaders, the leaders will theoretically be freer to assume the responsibility for an even larger number of groups.

The teams in our study had made the transition to self-management five years before our research commenced. At that time, the superior participants were already performing the 11 essential behaviors of external leadership. We would not be surprised to learn today that those individuals have since moved their teams further along the continuum of increased autonomy and independence. In fact, we would be greatly surprised if that were not the case.

Endnotes

1. E. E. Lawler III, "High Involvement Management" (San Francisco: Jossey-Bass, 1986); E. E. Lawler III, "Strategies for High Performance Organizations" (San Francisco: Jossey-Bass, 1998); and G. Taninecz, T. H. Lee, A. V. Feigenbaum, B. Nagle and P. Ward, "Best Practices and Performances: Manufacturers Tackling Leading-Edge Initiatives Generally Reap the Best Results," *Industry Week*, Dec. 1, 1997: 28–43.
2. M. M. Beyerlein, D. A. Johnson and S. T. Beyerlein, "Introduction," in M. M. Beyerlein, D. A. Johnson and S. T. Beyerlein, eds., *Advances in Interdisciplinary Studies of Work Teams*. vol. 3 (Greenwich, Connecticut: JAI Press, 1996): ix–xv; C. C. Manz and H. P. Sims Jr., "Searching for the 'Unleader': Organizational Member Views on Leading Self-Managed Groups," *Human Relations* 37 (1984): 409–424; and C.C. Manz and H.P. Sims Jr., "Leading Workers to Lead Themselves: The External Leadership of Self-Managed Work Teams," *Administrative Science Quarterly* 32 (1987): 106–128.
3. See C. C. Manz, "Leading Workers to Lead Themselves."
4. R. E. Walton, "The Topeka Work System: Optimistic Visions, Pessimistic Hypotheses and Reality," in R. Zager and M. P. Rosow, eds., *The Innovative Organization: Productivity Programs in Action* (Elmsford, New York: Pergamon Press, 1982): 260–287.
5. R. E. Walton, "Work Innovations at Topeka: After Six Years," *Journal of Applied Behavioral Science* 13 (1977): 422–433; and R.E. Walton, "The Topeka Work System."
6. C. C. Manz, "Searching for the 'Unleader.'"
7. M. M. Beyerlein, "Introduction" and J. R. Hackman, "The Psychology of Self-Management in Organizations," in M. S. Pallack and R. O. Perloff, eds., *Psychology and Work: Productivity, Change and Employment* (Washington, D.C.: American Psychological Association, 1986): 89–136.
8. See. for example, E. E. Lawler III, "High Involvement Management;" R. E. Walton, "Work Innovations at Topeka;" and R. E. Walton, "The Topeka Work System."
9. R. I. Beekun, "Assessing the Effectiveness of Sociotechnical Interventions: Antidote or Fad?" *Human Relations* 47 (1989): 877–897; and R. E. Walton and L. A. Schlesinger, "Do Supervisors Thrive in Participative Work Systems?" *Organizational Dynamics* 8 (Winter 1979): 24–39.
10. S.G. Cohen, L. Chang, and G. E. Ledford Jr., "A Hierarchical Construct of Self-Management Leadership and Its Relation-ship to Quality of Work Life and Perceived Work Group Effectiveness," *Personnel Psychology* 50, no. 2 (Summer 1997): 275–308; B. L. Kirkman and B. Rosen, "A Model of Work Team Empowerment," in R. W. Woodman and W. A. Pasmore, eds., *Research in Organizational Change and Development*, vol. 10 (Greenwich, Connecticut: JAI Press, 1997): 131–167; and B. L. Kirkman and B. Rosen, "Beyond Self-Management: Antecedents and Consequences of Team Empowerment," *Academy of Management Journal* 42 (1999): 58–74.
11. S. G. Cohen, G. E. Ledford Jr. and G. M. Spreitzer, "A Predictive Model of Self-Managing Work Team Effectiveness," *Human Relations* 49 (1996): 643–676; B. L. Kirkman, "Beyond Self-Management;" and R.E. Walton, "The Topeka Work System."
12. C. C. Manz, "Leading Workers To Lead Themselves"; R. Wageman, "Critical Success Factors for Creating Superb Self-Managing Teams," *Organizational Dynamics* 26 (Summer 1997): 49–61; and R. Wageman, "How Leaders Foster Self-Managing Team

Effectiveness: Design Choices Versus Hands-On Coaching," *Organization Science* 12. no. 5 (2001): 559–577.

13. D. G. Ancona and D. F. Caldwell, "Bridging the Boundary: External Activity and Performance in Organizational Teams," *Administrative Science Quarterly* 37, no. 4 (December 1992): 634–665.

14. See S. G. Cohen, "A Hierarchical Construct of Self-Management Leadership;" J. L. Cordery and T. D. Wall, "Work Design and Supervisory Practice: A Model," *Human Relations* 38. no. 5 (1985): 425–441; and J. R. Hackman, *Leading Teams: Setting the Stage for Great Performances* (Boston: Harvard Business School Press, 2002).

CHAPTER 11
PROBLEM SOLVING

PUTTING YOUR COMPANY'S WHOLE BRAIN TO WORK

Dorothy Leonard
Susaan Straus

WHY WORK-OUT WORKS: THE UNDERLYING PRINCIPLES

Dave Ulrich
Steve Kerr
Ron Ashkenas

A talent for problem solving has always been a requirement for managers and executives. With the advent of programs designed to increase organizational effectiveness, such as self-managed work teams, employee empowerment, total quality efforts, continuous improvement programs, reengineering, and organizational learning, problem-solving skills are needed by employees at all levels. Without problem-solving expertise, organizations cannot work as effectively and efficiently as they should, and their long-term survival and ability to adapt are threatened. The selections in this chapter reflect both a micro and macro approach to problem solving.

Myopia often keeps individuals, teams, and organizations from accurately seeing and defining problems; it also hinders their ability to come up with creative solutions. Therefore, one of the basic tenets of good problem solving is drawing on diverse perspectives. Dorothy Leonard, business professor, and Susaan Straus, consultant, tackle this issue in "Putting Your Company's Whole Brain to Work." Individuals do not approach problem solving in the same way, which can be a source of conflict in today's highly integrated ways of working. Leonard and Straus underscore the importance of understanding, appreciating, and working effectively with people who have different cognitive preferences and communication styles.

Many firms take a systemic approach to problem solving. For example, the total quality movement first gained popularity in Japan and is credited with transforming that country's reputation from a producer of low-quality to high-quality products. The original focus was to teach problem-solving skills to teams that tackled quality problems in the manufacturing process. This has evolved into a program called Six Sigma that is used to improve quality in various organizational processes, not just manufacturing. In addition to adopting Six Sigma, GE pioneered "Work-Out," another systemic process for addressing and solving problems quickly. "Why Work-Out Works" was written by people who helped design and roll out the program: Dave Ulrich, HR scholar and consultant; Steve Kerr, who was CLO at GE when Work-Out was introduced; and Ron Ashkenas, a management consultant with an OB background. This excerpt from their book, *The GE Work-Out*, explains the details of this program and shows why it succeeded in cutting through the bureaucracy and making fundamental changes in one of the world's most successful firms.

PUTTING YOUR COMPANY'S WHOLE BRAIN TO WORK*

Dorothy Leonard
Susaan Straus

Innovate or fall behind: The competitive imperative for virtually all businesses today is that simple. Achieving it is hard, however, because innovation takes place when different ideas, perceptions, and ways of processing and judging information collide. That, in turn, often requires collaboration among various players who see the world in inherently different ways. As a result, the conflict that should take place constructively among ideas all too often ends up taking place unproductively among people who do not innately understand one another. Disputes become personal, and the creative process breaks down.

Stakes are high enough. That said, we all tend to have one or two preferred habits of thought that influence our decision-making styles and our interactions with others—for good or for ill.

The most widely recognized cognitive distinction is between left-brained and right-brained ways of thinking. This categorization is more powerful metaphorically than it is accurate physiologically; not all the functions commonly associated with the left brain are located on the left side of the cortex and not all so-called right-brained functions are located on the right. Still, the simple description does usefully capture radically different ways of thinking. An analytical, logical, and sequential approach to problem framing and solving (left-brained thinking) clearly differs from an intuitive, values-based, and nonlinear one (right-brained thinking).

Cognitive preferences also reveal themselves in work styles and decision-making activities. Take collaboration as opposed to independence. Some people prefer to work together on solving problems, whereas others prefer to gather, absorb, and process information by themselves. Each type does its best work under different conditions. Or consider thinking as opposed to feeling. Some people evaluate evidence and make

*Reprinted with permission from *Harvard Business Review* (July-August 1997): 112–121.

decisions through a structured, logical process, whereas others rely on their values and emotions to guide them to the appropriate action.

The list goes on. Abstract thinkers, for instance, assimilate information from a variety of sources, such as books, reports, videos, and conversations. They prefer learning about something rather than experiencing it directly. Experiential people, in contrast, get information from interacting directly with people and things. Some people demand quick decisions no matter the issue, whereas others prefer to generate a lot of options no matter the urgency. One type focuses on details, whereas the other looks for the big picture: the relationships and patterns that the data form.

Not surprisingly, people tend to choose professions that reward their own combination of preferences. Their work experience, in turn, reinforces the original preferences and deepens the associated skills. Therefore, one sees very different problem-solving approaches among accountants, entrepreneurs, social workers, and artists. Proof to an engineer, for example, resides in the numbers. But show a page of numerical data to a playwright, and, more persuaded by his intuition, he may well toss it aside. Of course, assessing people's likely approaches to problem solving only by their discipline can be as misleading as using gender or ethnicity as a guide. Within any profession, there are always people whose thinking styles are at odds with the dominant approach.

The best way for managers to assess the thinking styles of the people they are responsible for is to use an established diagnostic instrument as an assessment tool. A well-tested tool is both more objective and more thorough than the impressions of even the most sensitive and observant of managers. Dozens of diagnostic tools and descriptive analyses of human personality have been developed to identify categories of cognitive approaches to problem solving and communication. All the instruments agree on the following basic points:

- Preferences are neither inherently good nor inherently bad. They are assets or liabilities depending on the situation. For example, politicians or CEOs who prefer to think out loud in public create expectations that they sometimes cannot meet; but the person who requires quiet reflection before acting can be a liability in a crisis.
- Distinguishing preferences emerge early in our lives, and strongly held ones tend to remain relatively stable through the years. Thus, for example, those of us who crave certainty are unlikely ever to have an equal love of ambiguity and paradox.
- We can learn to expand our repertoire of behaviors, to act outside our preferred styles. But that is difficult—like writing with the opposite hand.
- Understanding others' preferences helps people communicate and collaborate.

Managers who use instruments with the credibility of the Myers-Briggs Type Indicator (MBTI®) or the Herrmann Brain Dominance Instrument (HBDI) find that their employees accept the outcomes of the tests and use them to improve their processes and behaviors. (See the box "Identifying How We Think: The Myers-Briggs Type Indicator® and the Herrmann Brain Dominance Instrument.")

IDENTIFYING HOW WE THINK: THE MYERS-BRIGGS TYPE INDICATOR® AND THE HERRMANN BRAIN DOMINANCE INSTRUMENT

The Myers-Briggs Type Indicator (MBTI®) is the most widely used personality-assessment instrument in the world. Designed by a mother-and-daughter team, Isabel Myers and her mother Katherine Cook Briggs, the MBTI® is based on the work of Carl Jung. Myers and Briggs developed the instrument during World War II on the hypothesis that an understanding of personality preferences might aid those civilians who were entering the workforce for the first time to find the right job for the war effort. The instrument conforms to standard testing conventions and, at last count in 1994, had been taken by more than two-and-a-half million people around the world. The MBTI® is widely used in business, psychology, and education, as well as in career counseling.

The MBTI® uses four different pairs of attributes to create a matrix of 16 personality types:

- ***Introversion Versus Extraversion[1]*** The first pair measures the degree to which one is an introvert (I) or an extravert (E). These I/E descriptors focus on the source of someone's mental energy: extraverts draw energy from other people; introverts draw energy from themselves. Each finds the other's preferred operating conditions enervating.
- ***Sensing Versus "INtuiting"*** The second pair identifies how one absorbs information. "Sensors" (S) gather data through their five senses, whereas "iNtuitives" (N) rely on less direct perceptions, such as patterns, relationships, and hunches. For example, when asked to describe the same painting, a group of S's might comment on the brush strokes or the scar on the subject's left cheek, whereas a group of N's might imagine from the troubled look in the subject's eyes that he lived in difficult times or suffered from depression.
- ***Thinking Versus Feeling*** The third pair measures how one makes decisions once information is gathered. Feeling types (F) use their emotional intelligence to make decisions based on values—their internal sense of right and wrong. Thinking types (T) tend to make decisions based on logic and "objective" criteria—their assessment of truth and falsehood.
- ***Judging Versus Perceiving*** The fourth pair reflects how slowly or rapidly one comes to a decision. Judging types (J) have a high need for closure. They reach conclusions quickly based on available data and move on. Perceiving types (P) prefer to keep their options open. They wait until they have gathered what they consider to be enough information to decide. J's crave certainty, and P's love ambiguity.

To read descriptions of the personality types identified in the MBTI®, see the matrix in Table 1.

Ned Herrmann created and developed the Herrmann Brain Dominance Instrument (HBDI) while he was a manager at General Electric. Starting his research with large groups within GE, he expanded it over 20 years through tens of thousands of surveys and has validated the data with prominent psychometric research institutions, including the Educational Testing Service.

The HBDI measures a person's preference both for right-brained or left-brained thinking and for conceptual or experiential thinking. These preferences often correspond to specific professions. Engineers, for example, consistently describe themselves as analytical, mathematical, and logical, placing them on the left end of the continuum. Artists, in contrast, describe themselves as emotional, spatial, and aesthetic, placing them on the right end of the continuum.

Table 1 The MBTI®

		Sensing Types (S)		Intuitive Types (N)	
		Thinking (T)	Feeling (F)	Feeling (F)	Thinking (T)
Introverts (I)	Judging (J)	**ISTJ** Serious, quiet, earn success by concentration and thoroughness. Practical, orderly, matter-of-fact, logical, realistic, and dependable. Take responsibility.	**ISFJ** Quiet, friendly, responsible, and conscientious. Work devotedly to meet their obligations. Thorough painstaking, accurate. Loyal, considerate.	**INFJ** Succeed by perseverance, originality, and desire to do whatever is needed or wanted. Quietly forceful, conscientious, concerned for others. Respected for their firm principles.	**INTJ** Usually have original minds and great drive for their own ideas and purposes. Skeptical, critical, independent, determined, often stubborn.
Introverts (I)	Perceiving (P)	**ISTP** Cool onlookers-quiet, reserved, and analytical. Usually interested in impersonal principles, how and why mechanical things work. Flashes of original humor.	**ISFP** Retiring, quietly friendly, sensitive, kind, modest about their abilities. Shun disagreements. Loyal followers. Often relaxed about getting things done.	**INFP** Care about learning, ideas, language and independent projects of their own. Tend to undertake too much, then somehow get it done. Friendly, but often too absorbed.	**INTP** Quiet, reserved, impersonal. Enjoy theoretical or scientific subjects. Usually interested mainly in ideas, little liking for parties or small talk. Sharply defined interests.
Extraverts (E)	Perceiving (P)	**ESTP** Matter-of-fact, do not worry or hurry, enjoy whatever comes along. May be a bit blunt or insensitive. Best with real things that can be taken apart or put together.	**ESFP** Outgoing, easygoing, accepting, friendly, make things fun for others by their enjoyment. Like sports and making things. Find remembering facts easier than mastering theories.	**ENFP** Warmly enthusiastic, high-spirited, ingenious, imaginative. Able to do almost anything that interests them. Quick with a solution and to help with a problem.	**ENTP** Quick, ingenious, good at many things. May argue either side of a question for fun. Resourceful in solving challenging problems, but may neglect routine assignments.
Extraverts (E)	Judging (J)	**ESTJ** Practical, realistic, matter-of-fact, with a natural head for business or mechanics. Not interested in subject they see no use for. Like to organize and run activities.	**ESFJ** Warm-hearted, talkative, popular, conscientious, born cooperators. Need harmony. Work best with encouragement. Little interest in abstract thinking or technical subjects.	**ENFJ** Responsive and responsible. Generally feel real concern for what others think or want. Sociable, popular. Sensitive to praise and criticism.	**ENTJ** Hearty, frank, decisive, leaders. Usually good at anything that requires reasoning and intelligent talk. May sometimes be more positive than their experience in an area warrants.

Source: Modified and reproduced by special permission of the publisher, Consulting Psychologists Press, Palo Alto, CA 94303 from *Report Form from the Myers-Briggs Type Indicator* by Isabel Briggs Myers.

(*Continued*)

(Continued)

The charts below (Figure 1) show how the different preferences combine into four distinct quadrants and how one can use the chart to analyze teams with different cognitive preferences.

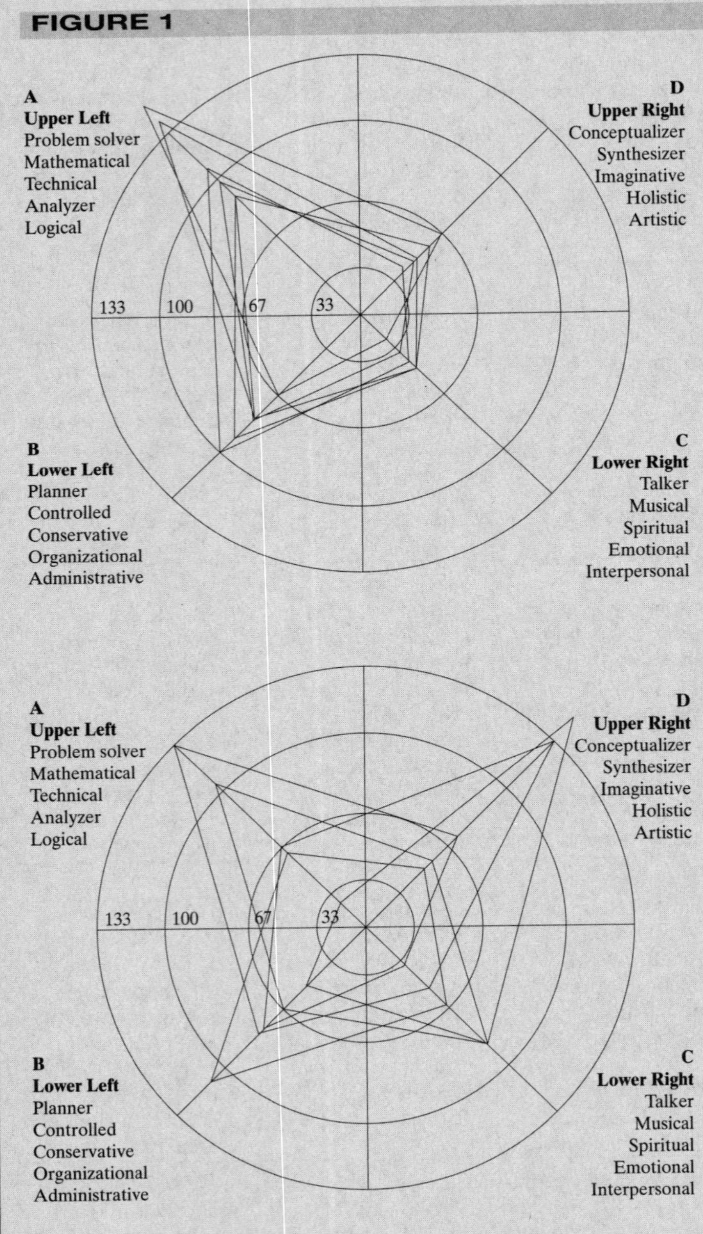

Composite One: The Homogeneous Team

The chart on the left shows that everyone in the group approaches problems and challenges with the same emphasis on correctness. As engineers, the members of the team know how to do things correctly. Although the quality of their work is excellent, the members are difficult to work with. They have their own ways of doing things, and they reject variations from set standards. As a corporate function, the team has long enjoyed a captive audience in the company. Recently, members found themselves in trouble when the company restructured and other functions in the organization were allowed to outsource engineering.

Composite Two: The Heterogeneous Team

The Management Services Group includes managers from information technology, the mail room, and the cafeteria. Although members share such goals as an orientation toward quality, they encounter a wide range of business problems. The manager's dominant thinking style is in the lower right quadrant: a natural facilitator, she develops people, listens empathetically, and fosters a spirit of respect among her reports. Her leadership unified what had been a fragmented, inefficient collection of functions. Members regard one another as resources, enjoy the group's diversity, and take great pride in their work.

HOW WE ACT

All the assessment in the world means nothing unless new understanding brings different actions. Instruments such as the MBTI® and the HBDI will help you understand yourself and will help others understand themselves. The managerial challenge is to use the insights that these instruments offer to create new processes and encourage new behaviors that will help innovation efforts succeed.

Understand Yourself

Start with yourself. When you identify your own style, you gain insight into the ways your preferences unconsciously shape your style of leadership and patterns of communication. You may be surprised to discover that your style can stifle the very creativity you seek from your employees. Consider the experiences of two managers of highly creative organizations. Each was at odds with his direct reports—but for very different reasons.

Jim Shaw, executive vice president of MTV Networks, is a left-brained guy in a right-brained organization. Said Shaw:

> *I have always characterized the creative, right-brained, visionary-type people here as dreamers. What I've realized is that when a dreamer expressed a vision, my gut reaction was to say, "Well, if you want to do that, what you've got to do is A, then B, then you have to work out C, and because you've got no people and you've got no satellite up-link, you'll have to do D and E." I've learned that saying that to a creative type is like throwing up on the dream. When I say that stuff too soon, the dreamer personalizes it as an attack. I've learned not to put all of the things that need to be done on the table initially. I can't just blurt it all out—it makes me look like a naysayer. What I've learned to do is to leak the information gradually, then the dreamer knows that I am meeting him halfway.*

Jerry Hirshberg, president of Nissan Design International, ran into precisely the opposite problem. Hirshberg discovered that some of his employees craved the very kind of structure that he personally abhorred. Before this epiphany, he inundated them with information and expected creativity in return. In short, he tried to manage his employees the way *he* would have wanted to be managed. Hirshberg found, however, that a few individuals reacted to every suggestion with a "Yes but. . . . " Initially, he interpreted such hesitancy as an anti-innovation bias. But he eventually realized that some of his employees preferred to have more time both to digest problems and to construct logical approaches to his intuitively derived ideas. Given a bit of extra time, they would return to the project with solid, helpful, and insightful plans for implementation. Ironically, it was their commitment to the success of the initiative that caused the employees to hesitate: They wanted the best possible result. Hirshberg recognized that their contributions were as critical as his own or those of any of the other "right-brainers" in the company.

Both Shaw and Hirshberg came to realize that their own cognitive preferences unconsciously shaped their leadership styles and communication patterns. In fact, their automatic reactions initially stifled the very creativity they sought from their employees. And note that it was just as important for the predominantly right-brained manager to recognize the contributions of the logicians as it was for the left-brained manager to acknowledge the organic approach of the visionaries. Except in theoretical models, creativity is not the exclusive province of one side or the other.

If you want an innovative organization, you need to hire, work with, and promote people who make you uncomfortable. You need to understand your own preferences so that you can complement your weaknesses and exploit your strengths. The biggest barrier to recognizing the contributions of people who are unlike you is your own ego. Suppose you are stalled on a difficult problem. To whom do you go for help? Usually to someone who is on the same wavelength or to someone whose opinion you respect. These people may give you soothing strokes, but they are unlikely to help spark a new idea. Suppose you were to take the problem instead to someone with whom you often find yourself at odds, someone who rarely validates your ideas or perspectives. It may take courage and tact to get constructive feedback, and the process may not be exactly pleasant. But that feedback will likely improve the quality of your solution. And when your adversary recovers from his amazement at your request, he may even get along with you better because the disagreement was clearly intellectual, not personal.

Forget the Golden Rule

Don't treat people the way you want to be treated. Tailor communications to the receiver instead of the sender. In a cognitively diverse environment, a message sent is not necessarily a message received. Some people respond well to facts, figures, and statistics. Others prefer anecdotes. Still others digest graphic presentations most easily. Information must be delivered in the preferred "language" of the recipient if it is to be received at all.

For example, say you want to persuade an organization to adopt an open office layout. Arguments appealing to the analytical mind would rely on statistics from well-documented research conducted by objective experts that prove that open architecture enhances the effectiveness of communication. Arguments geared toward the action-oriented type would answer specific questions about implementation: How long will the office conversion take? Exactly what kind of furniture is needed? What are the implications for acoustics? Arguments aimed at people-oriented individuals would focus on such questions as, How does an open office affect relationships? How would this setup affect morale? and Are people happy in this sort of setup? Arguments crafted for people with a future-oriented perspective would include graphics as well as artists' renderings of the proposed environment. In short, regardless of how you personally would prefer to deliver the message, you will be more persuasive and better understood if you formulate messages to appeal to the particular thinking style of your listener.

Create "Whole-Brained" Teams

Either over time or by initial design, company or group cultures can become dominated by one particular cognitive style. IBM, in the days when it was known as "Big Blue," presented a uniform face to the world; Digital Equipment prided itself on its engineering culture. Such homogeneity makes for efficient functioning—and limited approaches to problems or opportunities. Companies with strong cultures can indeed be very creative, but within predictable boundaries—say, clever marketing or imaginative engineering. When the market demands that such companies innovate in different ways, they have to learn new responses. Doing so requires adopting a variety of approaches to solving a problem—using not just the right brain or the left brain but the *whole* brain.

Consider the all-too-common error made by John, a rising star in a large, diversified instrument company: He forfeited an important career opportunity because he failed to see the need for a whole-brained team. Appointed manager of a new-product development group, John had a charter to bring in radically innovative ideas for products and services for launch in three to six years. "Surprise me," the CEO said.

Given a free hand in hiring, John lured in three of the brightest M.B.A.'s he could find. They immediately went to work conducting industry analyses and sorting through existing product possibilities, applying their recently acquired skills in financial analysis. To complete the team, John turned to the pile of résumés on his desk sent to him by human resources. All the applicants had especially strong quantitative skills, and a couple were engineers. John was pleased. Surely a group of such intelligent, well-trained, rigorous thinkers would be able to come up with some radical innovations for the company. Ignoring advice to hire some right-brained people to stimulate different ideas, he continued to populate his group with left-brained wizards. After 18 months, the team had rejected all the proposed new projects in the pipeline on the basis of well-argued and impressively documented financial and technical risk analysis. But the team's members had not come up with a single new idea. The CEO was neither surprised nor pleased, and the group was disbanded just short of its second anniversary.

In contrast, Bob, a successful entrepreneur embarking on his latest venture, resisted the strong temptation to tolerate only like-minded people. He knew from his prior ventures that his highly analytical style alienated some of his most creative people. Despite his unusual degree of self-awareness. Bob came within a hair's breadth of firing a strong and experienced manager, Wally, his director of human resources. According to Bob, after several months on board, Wally appeared to be "a quart and a half low." Why? Because Bob was inattentive in budget meetings and focused on what he perceived as trivia—day care, flextime, and benefits. Before taking action, however, Bob decided to look at the management team through the lens of thinking styles. He soon realized that Wally was exactly the kind of person he needed to help him grow his small company. Wally contributed a key element that was otherwise missing in the management team: a sensitivity to human needs that helped the company foresee and forestall problems with employees. So Bob learned to meet Wally halfway. Describing his success in learning to work with Wally, he told us, "You would have been proud of me. I started our meetings with five minutes of dogs, kids, and station wagons." Although the concern Wally demonstrated for the workers in the company did not eliminate union issues completely, it did minimize antagonism toward management and made disputes easier to resolve.

The list of whole-brained teams that continue to innovate successfully is long. At Xerox PARC, social scientists work alongside computer scientists. For instance, computer scientist Pavel Curtis, who is creating a virtual world in which people will meet and mingle, is working with an anthropologist who understands how communities form. As a result, Curtis's cyberspace meeting places have more human touches and are more welcoming than they would have been had they been designed only by scientists. Another example is the PARC PAIR (PARC Artist In Residence) program, which links computer scientists with artists so that each may influence the other's perceptions and representations of the world. At Interval Research, a California think tank dedicated to multimedia technologies, Director David Liddle invites leaders from various disciplines to visit for short "sabbaticals." The purpose is to stimulate a cross-fertilization of ideas and approaches to solving problems. The resulting exchanges have helped Interval Research create and spin off several highly innovative start-ups. And Jerry Hirshberg applies the whole-brain principle to hiring practices at Nissan Design by bringing designers into his organization in virtual pairs. That is, when he hires a designer who glories in the freedom of pure color and rhythm, he will next hire a very rational, Bauhaus-trained designer who favors analysis and focuses on function.

Complete homogeneity in an organization's cognitive approach can be very efficient. But as managers at Xerox PARC, Interval Research, and Nissan Design have learned, no matter how brilliant the group of individuals, their contributions to innovative problem solving are enhanced by coming up against totally different perspectives.

Look for the Ugly Duckling

Suppose you don't have the luxury of hiring new people yet and find your organization mired in a swamp of stale thinking patterns. Consider the experience of the CEO of the U.S. subsidiary of a tightly controlled and conservative European chemical company. Even though the company's business strategy had never worked well in the United States, headquarters pushed the CEO to do more of the same. He knew he needed to figure out a fresh approach because the U.S. company was struggling to compete in a rapidly changing marketplace. But his direct reports were as uniformly left-brained as his superiors in Europe and were disinclined to work with him to figure out new solutions.

Rather than give up, the CEO tested thinking preferences further down in the organization. He found the cognitive disparity that he needed in managers one layer below his direct reports—a small but dynamic set of individuals whose countercultural thinking patterns had constrained their advancement. In this company, people with right-brained preferences were seen as helpful but were not considered top management material. They were never promoted above a certain level.

The CEO changed that. He elevated three managers with right-brained proclivities to the roles of senior vice president and division head-lofty positions occupied until then exclusively by left-brained individuals. The new executives were strong supporters of the CEO's intentions to innovate and worked with him to develop new approaches to the business. They understood that their communication strategy with headquarters would be critical to their success. They deliberately packaged their new ideas in a way that appealed to the cognitive framework of their European owner. Instead of lecturing about the need to change and try new ideas as they had in the past, the Americans presented their ideas as ways of solving problems. They supported their positions with well-researched quantitative data and with calculated anticipated cost savings and ROI—and described how similar approaches had succeeded elsewhere. They detailed the specific steps they would follow to succeed. Within two years, the U.S. subsidiary embarked on a major organizational redesign effort that included such radical notions as permitting outside competition for internal services. The quality of internal services soared—as did the number of innovations generated by the company in the United States.

Manage the Creative Process

Abrasion is not creative unless managers make it so. Members of whole-brained teams don't naturally understand one another, and they can easily come to dislike one another. Successful managers of richly diverse groups spend time from the outset getting members to acknowledge their differences—often through a joint exploration of the results of a diagnostic analysis—and devise guidelines for working together before attempting to act on the problem at hand. Managers who find it awkward or difficult to lead their groups in identifying cognitive styles or in establishing guidelines can usually enlist the aid of someone who is trained in facilitation.

People often feel a bit foolish creating rules about how they will work together. Surely, the thinking goes, we are all adults and have years of experience in dealing with group dynamics. That, of course, is the problem. Everyone has practiced dysfunctional behavior for years. We learn to value politeness over truth at our mothers' knees. (Who hasn't mastered the art of the white lie by age 16?) We often discount an argument if it has an element of emotion or passion. We opt out if we feel ignored—people with unappreciated thinking styles learn to sit against the wall during meetings (the organizational back-of-the-bus). And we usually don't even notice those behaviors because they are so routine.

But the cost of allowing such behaviors to overtake a group is too high. Bob Meyers, senior vice president of interactive media at NBC, uses a sports analogy to make the point: "On a football team, for example, you have to use all kinds of people. Like the little, skinny guy who can only kick the ball. He may not even look as if he belongs on the team. This guy can't stand up to the refrigerator types that play in other positions. But as long as he does his job, he doesn't need to be big. He can just do what he does best. The catch is that the team needs to recognize what the little skinny guy can do—or they lose the benefit of his talent."

Managing the process of creative abrasion means making sure that everyone is at the front of the bus and talking. Some simple but powerful techniques can be helpful. First, clarify why you are working together by keeping the common goal in front of the group at all times. "If the goal is a real-world one with shared accountability and timetables attached," one manager observed, "then everyone understands the relevance of honoring one another's differences."

Second, make your operating guidelines explicit. Effective guidelines are always simple, clear, and concise. For example, one group set up the following principles about handling disagreements: "Anyone can disagree about anything with anyone, but no one can disagree without stating the reason," and "When someone states an objection, everyone else should listen to it, try to understand it, treat it as legitimate, and counter with their reasons if they don't agree with it." Some principles are as simple as "Discuss taboo subjects," "Verify assumptions," and "Arrive on time with your homework done."

Third, set up an agenda ahead of time that explicitly provides enough time for both divergent discussion to uncover imaginative alternatives and convergent discussion to select an option and plan its implementation. Innovation requires both types of discussion, but people who excel at different types can, as one manager observed, "drive each other nuts." Another manager said, "If you ask people comfortable with ambiguity whether they prefer A or B, they will ask, 'How about C?'" Meanwhile, the people who crave closure will be squirming in their seats at the seemingly pointless discussion. Moreover, if one approach dominates, the unbalanced group process can risk producing an unacceptable or unfeasible new product, service, or change. Clearly allocating time to the two different types of discussion will contain the frustrations of both the decisive types, who are constantly looking at their watches wanting the decision to be made now, and the ambiguous types, who want to be sure that all possible avenues for creativity have been explored. Otherwise, the decisive members generally will pound the others into silence by invoking time pressures and scheduling. They will grab the first viable option rather than the best one. Or if the less decisive dominate, the group may never reach a conclusion. Innovation requires both divergent and convergent thinking, both brainstorming and action plans.

Depersonalize Conflict

Diverse cognitive preferences can cause tremendous tensions in any group, yet innovation requires the cross-fertilization of ideas. And because many new products are systems rather than stand-alone pieces, many business projects cannot proceed without the cooperation of people who receive different messages from the same words and make different observations about the same incidents. The single most valuable contribution that understanding different thinking and communication styles brings to the process of innovation is taking the sting out of intellectual disagreements that turn personal.

Consider the experience of the product manager of a radically new product for a medical supplies company. Facing a strict deadline of just 14 months to design and deliver a new surgical instrument, the manager's team needed to pull together fast. Design felt misled by marketing, however, and manufacturing couldn't understand design's delay in choosing between two mechanical hinges. The disagreements turned personal, starting with "you always . . . " and ending with ". . . irresponsible ignorance." Two months into the project, the manager began to wonder whether he should disband the team and start over again. But he knew that his boss, the vice president of marketing, would not agree to extend the deadline. "I was desperate," he recalled. "I decided to make one last attempt at getting them to work together."

The manager decided to experiment with an offsite gathering of his staff, including sessions diagnosing cognitive preferences. When they returned to work, the team members used the new language they had learned to label their differences in opinion and style. "At first, using the terms was kind of a joke," the manager recalled. "They'd say things like, 'Well, of course I want the schedule right now. I'm a J!' Yet you could tell that people were really seeing one another in a different light, and they weren't getting angry." The team made its deadline; perhaps even more important, several members voluntarily joined forces to work on the next iteration of the product. This willingness to work together generated more value for the company than just "warm fuzzies." Critical technical knowledge was preserved in one small, colocated group—knowledge that would have been scattered had project members dispersed to different product lines. Moreover, keeping part of the team together resulted in a rapid development time for the derivative product.

People who do not understand cognitive preferences tend to personalize conflict or avoid it—or both. The realization that another person's approach is not wrong-headed and stubborn, but merely predictably different, diffuses anger. For example, at Viacom, a planning session involving two managers had ground to a halt. One manager simply wouldn't buy into the idea that the other was presenting. Suddenly, the presenter slapped his head and said, "Oooohhh! I get it! You're left-brained! Give me half an hour to switch gears, and I'll be right back. Let me try this one more time."

The left-brained manager laughingly agreed—he understood the paradigm—and the meeting resumed with the presenter armed with quantitative data and a much more cohesive and logical presentation. Establishing that kind of effective two-way communication led to a common understanding of the issues at hand and, ultimately, a solution.

Understanding that someone views a problem differently does not mean you will agree. But an important element in understanding thinking styles is recognizing that no one style is inherently better than another. Each style brings a uniquely valuable perspective to the process of innovation, just as each style has some negatives associated with it. Stereotypes of the cold-hearted logician, the absentminded, creative scientist, and the bleeding-heart liberal have some basis in reality. If people even partially internalize the inherent value of different perspectives, they will take disagreements less personally and will be better able to argue and reach a compromise or a consensus with less animosity. They will be open to the possibility that an alien view of the world might actually enhance their own. They will be better equipped to listen for the "a-ha" that occurs at the intersection of different planes of thought.

CAVEAT EMPTOR

Personality analysis of the type we describe is no more than a helpful tool, and it has many limitations. The diagnostic instruments measure only one aspect of personality: preferences in thinking styles and communication. They do not measure ability or intelligence, and they do not predict performance. Neither the MBTI® nor the HBDI measure other qualities that are critical to successful innovation such as courage, curiosity, integrity, empathy, or drive.

Preferences tend to be relatively stable, but life experiences can affect them. For example, repeated application of the MBTI® over a period of years has revealed a tendency for people to drift from a thinking style toward a feeling style when they have children. For the most part, however, studies done with both the MBTI® and the HBDI suggest that people retain their dominant preferences throughout a variety of work and social circumstances.

One critical warning label should be attached to any of these diagnostic instruments: only trained individuals should administer them. Not only can results be incorrectly interpreted (for instance, what are intended to be neutral descriptions of preferences might be labeled "right" or "wrong" behavior), but they can also be misused to invade people's privacy or to stereotype them. Of course, it is a human tendency to simplify in order to comprehend complexities; we stereotype people all the time on the basis of their language, dress, and behavior. Because these diagnostics have the weight of considerable psychological research behind them, however, they can be dangerous when misused. Without structured, reliable diagnoses, judgments are likely to be superficial and flawed. And without a substantial investment of time and resources, managers can't expect abrasion to be creative.

One of the paradoxes of modern management is that, in the midst of technical and social change so pervasive and rapid that it seems out of pace with the rhythms of nature, human personality has not altered throughout recorded history. People have always had distinct preferences in their approaches to problem solving. Why then is it only now becoming so necessary for managers to understand those differences? Because today's complex products demand integrating the expertise of individuals who do not innately understand one another. Today's pace of change demands that these individuals quickly develop the ability to work together. If abrasion is not managed into creativity, it will constrict the constructive impulses of individuals and organizations alike. Rightly harnessed, the energy released by the intersection of different thought processes will propel innovation.

WHY WORK-OUT WORKS: THE UNDERLYING PRINCIPLES*

Dave Ulrich

Steve Kerr

Ron Ashkenas

GE is one of the most successful companies on earth. Yet every day, thousands of people at GE face the very same set of problems and challenges that confront every other organization in the world, regardless of size, shape, or mission. What's the best way to deliver products and services to our customers? How can we improve our margins and our efficiency? How do we get everyone onto the same page? How do we stay ahead of the competition? How do we attract, develop, and retain the best talent? How can we make the best use of technology? How do we move quickly to new opportunities?

Does GE have answers to all these questions while other organizations do not? Of course not. But what GE does have that most organizations lack is a deeply engrained and internalized process for addressing and solving its problems—quickly, simply, and with the involvement of people who will ultimately carry out the decision. That process is called *Work-Out*.

No program—not even Work-Out—can transform your organization overnight. But in the short run, Work-Out will help you solve problems faster. And in the long run, it can help your organization develop the culture and the skills necessary to move more quickly, nimbly, and successfully in our complex, global world.

Consider the following example: SmithKline Beecham Pharmaceuticals (now GlaxoSmithKline) wanted to speed up the "back end" of the drug-development cycle, where data from clinical trials is analyzed and then prepared for submission to the Food and Drug Administration or other regulators. Traditional ideas such as adding more data analysts, increasing computing power, using outsourced analysis firms, and giving staff more training had already been tried, resulting in only modest gains. So a Work-Out was organized to see if a fresh approach could be developed and implemented quickly.

Participants in this Work-Out included professionals from a number of phases in the drug-development process—beyond just data analysis. These multiple perspectives immediately helped to make some of the previously rigid boundaries in the process

*Excepted with permission from *The GE Work-Out*. (New York: McGraw-Hill), 2002: XI–46.

more permeable. For instance, clinical researchers, biometric statisticians, data analysts, and experts in FDA requirements had never actually worked together—at the same time—to agree on a clinical-trial protocol. Instead, each of them worked on a number of drug candidates simultaneously, and tended to hand their work on to the next function sequentially, with lots of documents being passed back and forth "over the transom." By talking together, they came up with the idea of "reverse engineering" the process, starting with FDA requirements and then working backward. When they implemented this approach—starting with one drug—they were able to reduce the amount of data that was collected by almost 30 percent, which of course reduced the analysis time. Two other Work-Outs developed a series of ideas for improving the quality of data submissions from the trial sites so as to reduce the time needed to scrub and recheck the data.

Through this and a series of other Work-Outs, the company was able to take several months out of the overall clinical-submission process while substantially reducing the costs of data analysis. More importantly, it accelerated its evolution into a more flexible, fast-moving and high-performing firm. It effectively reshaped its culture while enhancing its business operations.

WORK-OUT AS A FORCE FOR GROWTH

The pharmaceutical company's gains were possible because while each Work-Out event addresses specific business issues, Work-Out also explicitly aims to help an organization grow along five key dimensions:

- Focus on "stretch"
- Development of "systems thinking"
- Encouragement of lateral thinking
- Creation of true empowerment and accountability
- Injection of rapid-cycle change and fast decision making

1. *Focus on "Stretch"*

Part of Work-Out's power is its ability to force an organization to rethink what it is doing. The impetus for that rethinking is the establishment of what GE eventually called "stretch"—a goal or challenge that is significantly beyond the organization's current performance level.[1] The idea is that if a goal is modest or incremental (say, a five-percent improvement), then people will just work harder or make a few minor changes in what they are doing. But if management lays down the gauntlet and challenges a group to achieve a 30-percent or 50-percent improvement, then they will need to step back and fundamentally rethink how they are working.

With this principle in mind, Work-Out almost always encourages stretch of some sort. Sometimes, stretch is built into the goals, as with these examples:

- Reduce breakage in key products by 50 percent in four months.
- Accelerate the product-development cycle by bringing out the next new product in half the usual time.
- Reduce the number of customer claims by 30 percent in the next year—which means putting new processes in place within 100 days.

- Improve the accuracy of data entered into the system by 50 percent within three months.
- Reduce overhead costs by $10 million in six months.

And sometimes stretch is built into the dialogue about recommendations. For example, when a plant team at GE Lighting proposed that overtime approvals be reduced to just one supervisor instead of two, the business leader asked the group why approvals were needed at all. And that led to a discussion of why time cards were needed at all.

Note that for stretch to be effective it should first be tied to the overall business strategy so that it turns that strategy into a specific issue that employees can accomplish. It should also have a relatively short time frame and a specific way to measure results. The time frames need to be short to help create the sense of urgency that is part of Work-Out's energy and excitement. If people know that they have a year to work on something, then they probably won't put it high on the priority list until the deadline is in sight. If results have to be achieved right away, then action starts tomorrow.

The results measure ensures that the stretch goal is not just focused on a "nice-to-do" activity—it addresses something that will truly make a difference in the business. People in organizations are always choosing different ways to spend their time, and, faced with more choices than time allows, will tend to do things that they are used to. To force change, people need to see that their actions will indeed lead to better results. Work-Out allows you to set things up so high-value activities drive out low-value "busyness."[2]

2. *Development of "Systems Thinking"*

The concept of *stretch* disrupts the organization; it breaks up old patterns and makes people realize that they cannot continue to work in the same ways as before. To give them a different view of how the stretch goal might be accomplished, Work-Out encourages and even forces people to take a systems perspective. That is, the Work-Out goal can only be achieved if people see it as the endpoint of a set of processes that cut across functions within the organization—and perhaps even includes groups outside of the firm, such as suppliers and customers. No one department or business unit can get there on its own. Changing one program may affect others and hurt overall performance. "Systems thinking" looks at how parts fit together. For example, if someone in a Work-Out recommends abolishing a report to save one unit time, others will speak up if that report is critical to another unit's decision making. In that case, it would not make sense to abolish the report, but to prepare it more effectively.

This novel systems perspective is introduced in the initial design phase of Work-Out, as part of organizing the Work-Out event. At this point, the design team creates a high-level map that describes the various steps, processes, and subprocesses that are involved in producing the current results the business is getting.

In many Work-Out sessions, facilitators also help the participants create more detailed process maps that teach and reinforce the systems perspective. For example, detailed process maps were developed by various teams in the SmithKline Beecham Work-Out described earlier. Through the joint creation of such maps, participants from different functions not only begin to understand the areas outside of their own, but also they begin to identify psychologically with the whole system instead of just with their own part. As this shift in allegiance starts to occur, participants are more willing and able to see possible changes in the overall process, and they feel less defensive about ideas for change that may affect their own function. In other words, they begin to realize that they are all in it together and that achieving the stretch goal can only be done through collective effort.

This does not mean that taking on a systems perspective by itself eliminates resistance to change. Claiming that would be naive. However, encouraging the systems perspective is one key factor that helps soften up the boundaries—to make participants more open to looking at alternatives to how things have always been done.

3. *Encouragement of Lateral Thinking*

Once participants feel the urgency to change and begin to see the whole picture of the current situation, they are then ready to focus on new ideas. How can the process be improved? What can be done differently to achieve the stretch goal?

Using the process map as a starting point, Work-Out asks participants to brainstorm ways of achieving the goal, and then provides a structure for quickly sorting through the ideas, selecting the best ones, and developing them into recommendations for change. As with any brainstorming process, Work-Out encourages people to toss out any idea, no matter how minor, how crazy, how seemingly impossible. And the process helps people learn how to build on each other's ideas, combine ideas, and think "out of the box." In fact, when the old Aetna Insurance Company implemented its version of Work-Out, the program's sponsors called it "Out of the Box."

Low-Hanging Fruit. While many change processes include brainstorming of some sort, Work-Out is unique in several ways. First, Work-Out begins by focusing on the "low-hanging fruit"—the easy, no-brainer fixes that can be made to virtually any process. Almost all operations, as they evolve over time, develop some amount of clutter or inefficiency—reports with unnecessary data that go to people who do not need them; requests for signoffs or approvals from people who may not be in the best position to decide; extra steps that take time but don't add value. Work-Out calls these inefficiencies "RAMMPP" activities, an acronym for *reports, approvals, meetings, measures, policies*, and *practices*. Work-Out acknowledges that these inefficiencies exist and encourages participants to root them out right away, using the RAMMPP matrix in Figure 1 as a framework for assessing and analyzing them. Going through this process gives people an immediate sense of accomplishment and quickly serves to clean up—and speed up—the process being addressed. When employees remove work that they don't find valuable, they feel empowered and in control of their work setting. As managers at an early Work-Out session at Wal-Mart said, this part of Work-Out is aimed at "getting the dumb" out of the system.

A Clean Sheet. The idea-development process for Work-Out, however, can go far beyond just process streamlining. Participants also are asked to do "clean-sheet" process thinking—to consider how they might redo the process from scratch so as to achieve the stretch goals. In this context, the Work-Out facilitators encourage the group to challenge assumptions and explore why things need to be done in certain

	CONTROL				
	Self	Department	Group	Company	External
Reports					
Approvals					
Meetings					
Measures					
Policies					
Practices					

Could it be:

1. Eliminated?
2. Partially eliminated?
3. Delegated downward?
4. Done less often?
5. Done in a less complicated/time-consuming manner?
6. Done with fewer people involved?
7. Done using a more productive technology?
8. Other?

FIGURE 1 The RAMMPP Matrix

ways, or at all. What might competitors do? What would someone else do to put you out of business by doing this differently?

Analysis. In addition to generating ideas, Work-Out also forces a quick but crucial analysis of the ideas so as to select those that are worth moving forward. In the process, it teaches participants not only how to generate ideas but also how to move quickly from ideas to action. Thus, following each brainstorming session in Work-Out, participants quickly sort the ideas that were developed into categories using a "Payoff Matrix" (see Figure 2). This tool forces people to think through both impact and achievability. The point is that an idea that might save millions of dollars is worth nothing if it cannot be implemented; often a more modest idea that can be put into play quickly can have more impact. The Work-Out culture, then, encourages a bias toward action—the notion first articulated by Kurt Lewin that the best way to change an organization is not to talk about it but to start to change it right now.

4. *Creation of True Empowerment and Accountability*

Work-Out is not just about generating ideas and recommendations. Part of its value is its ability to create a culture where ideas are translated into action and results. All too often people in organizations have great ideas about how to do things differently, but the ideas never go anywhere. The person with the idea can't get the time, permission, or resources to act, or faces outright resistance and gives up—or, more often, nobody picks up the ball on the idea. It is, in essence, a "disembodied idea," an idea without an owner.

One of the ground rules of most Work-Outs is "no complaining, no blaming." Often employees want to turn empowerment forums into gripe sessions. When Work-Out participants had complaints, they were pushed to turn them into suggestions . . . of a report, approval, meeting, measure, or policy to change. Chronic complainers were not helpful unless they could turn their concerns into recommendations. Blaming often occurs when employees seek a cause of their disenfranchisement—"management

	Easy to Implement	Tough to Implement
Small Pay-Off	Quick Win! (QW)	Time-Wasters (TW)
Big Pay-Off	Business Opportunities (BO)	Special Effort (SE)

FIGURE 2 Payoff Matrix

won't let me do this." Employees are encouraged not to blame others but to focus on what they could do to make a difference.

Create Ownership. One of the keys to creating an action-oriented culture is to make sure that every recommendation that comes out of a Work-Out session has someone who is accountable for making it happen, and has the power to drive it forward. The Work-Out ground rules state that each team can present a recommendation at the Town Meeting only if one team member is willing to be the "owner" of the idea—to take accountability for driving it through to a result—if it's approved. Accountability for a Work-Out idea, however, does not mean that the owner personally implements the idea. Instead, it means that the owner mobilizes the resources needed, puts together a plan that everyone agrees to, ensures that everyone does their part, and has public accountability to the senior management.

Do Whatever It Takes. When an idea is approved at the Town Meeting, the business leader tells the owner to do whatever is necessary to make it happen. Part of Work-Out's power is that this delegation of authority is genuine, not just lip service. If an idea is approved at a Town Meeting, then the owner has the authority to make sure it is implemented—even if that means going across functional lines or pushing people at higher levels to do something. For many participants in Work-Out, this is a very difficult concept to accept. Most people do not like to buck hierarchical or functional authority—to challenge organizational superiors. They are most comfortable within their own organizational boundaries and usually only make demands on people who work for them directly. Yet one of the ground rules of a Work-Out is that someone who is given the authority to implement a recommendation becomes a "virtual boss" with all the power and authority of the business leader in regard to that recommendation.

Review and Catch-Up. This empowerment and accountability is reinforced at the periodic reviews that occur 30, 60, and 90 days after the Work-Out event. At these sessions, each owner reports on progress in implementing the assigned Work-Out ideas, including whether there has been any resistance or difficulty. If the owner has encountered resistance—or people who have not done their part—the business leader is encouraged not to jump in, which would be the traditional (and easy) reaction, but to coach the idea owner about how to handle the resistance, what else to try, what to say. The business leader can of course step in as a final resort—but it is more powerful if the owner can learn how to influence people across functional and hierarchical lines. When an organization is open to this kind of influence, it is a sign that its boundaries are becoming more permeable and it is more capable of translating ideas into action.

5. *Injection of Rapid-Cycle Change and Fast Decision Making*

Like a chemical formula that needs a catalyst to create a reaction, the first four ingredients described in this section only become active when the last ingredient—speed—is added to the mix. Speed counts. Speed means decisions are made quickly. Speed means that action occurs. Speed engages people because they see progress. Thus, the fifth but perhaps most pervasive aspect of Work-Out is the constant drive for speed.

Most organizations talk a good game when it comes to speed in decision making, customer responsiveness, and other key processes. Yet the reality is that most organizations operate slowly. Processes tend to be sequential rather than simultaneous. Most people are not willing to make decisions right away. They would rather check with their boss, their colleagues, their subordinates. In this way, if the decision turns out to be wrong or to lead to undesired consequences, someone else can take the blame.

Senior managers who are supposed to be decision makers are often notorious for not making speedy decisions. To insulate themselves against failure, they tend to rely on staff experts and analysts to study issues for them and advise them. They also rely on hierarchy to help with decisions—making sure that all managers below them have signed off on something before they will make something official. For example, a number of years ago in the old AlliedSignal Automotive Sector, before Larry Bossidy became chairman, 26 signatures were required for capital expenditures above \$100,000. We found that, on average, every approval took 4 days, so the 26 signatures meant over 100 days (21 weeks) before the decision was made. When the so-called decision finally arrived on the sector head's desk, so much time had elapsed that the business reason for the request was at least partially out of date, and so many people had looked at it that there really was no decision to make. The only real question for the sector head at that point was where to find room on the document for one more signature! It was no wonder that the business was in trouble.

One of the original aims of Work-Out at GE was to force a pattern of faster decision making and a rapid-cycle change process. In the decades preceding Work-Out, GE had developed an analytical, control-oriented culture. Nobody made decisions without a thorough justification, often prepared by or with the help of the Audit staff or Finance function. Long papers and detailed presentations were common. Fast decisions—and decisions made "close to the action"—were rare. Jack Welch, realizing that the survival of the company in the 1990s and beyond would depend on being faster than the competition, wanted to foster the idea of "speed." And Work-Out was the vehicle to make that happen. As he said, "Faster, in almost every case, is better."

Although the injection of speed is apparent throughout the Work-Out process, it is most visible in the context of the Town Meeting. It is here that senior business leaders are challenged to make decisions on the spot, right away, without all the usual crutches of time, analysis, staff opinions, and deep consideration. Instead, the business leader needs to listen carefully to truly grasp the idea, ask questions to get a good understanding of the implications, solicit views from other people attending the Town

Meeting, and then make a decision—either yes or no. And for each Work-Out recommendation, this decision cycle needs to be a matter of minutes, rather than days, weeks, or months. But the idea of speed is not just a one-time phenomenon aimed at Town Meeting decisions. It is a pervasive concept that begins to shape the entire cycle of action, experimentation, and change in an organization.

Here we have described the underlying theory that makes Work-Out such a powerful tool for both performance improvement and cultural change. By giving people new ways to conduct dialogue, Work-Out creates an organization with more flexible, permeable boundaries—which is thus more capable of rapid innovation and change.

Endnotes

1. The concept of "stretch" has some similarity to what Collins and Porras call a BHAG, a "big hairy audacious goal." James C. Collins and Jerry I. Porras, *Built to Last: Successful Habits of Visionary Companies*, New York: HarperCollins, 1997.
2. See the article, "Managers Can Avoid Wasting Time," by Ronald N. Ashkenas and Robert H. Schaffer, *Harvard Business Review*, (May–June 1982).

CHAPTER 12
MANAGING CREATIVITY

WEIRD IDEAS THAT WORK—BUILDING COMPANIES WHERE INNOVATION IS A WAY OF LIFE

Robert I. Sutton

IMPROVING THE CREATIVITY OF ORGANIZATIONAL WORK GROUPS

Leigh Thompson

Managers face a dilemma when managing creativity. On the one hand, they need to stimulate new ideas, products, and services. On the other hand, they need to find ways to ensure enough stability so that products and services can be reliably produced. Robert Sutton, a Stanford University professor, examines this dilemma in the first article in this chapter. In "Weird Ideas That Work—Building Companies Where Innovation Is a Way of Life," he explicitly addresses the need to simultaneously control the organization yet still stimulate creativity. His "weird ideas" provide a road map for managers who are interested in understanding how to design effective innovative organizations.

As noted in the chapter on group dynamics, teams, as popular as they are, can either hinder or facilitate performance. The same is true with creativity. For example, teams often do more poorly than individuals when brainstorming new ideas, but they are better than individuals at developing more creative solutions to certain problems. Leigh Thompson, a Northwestern University professor who is an expert on teams and negotiation, discusses the barriers that keep teams from being creative and provides practical advice on how to significantly enhance creativity in "Improving the Creativity of Organizational Work Groups."

WEIRD IDEAS THAT WORK—BUILDING COMPANIES WHERE INNOVATION IS A WAY OF LIFE*

Robert I. Sutton

Most managers are quick to *say* that drastically different practices are needed for innovation, as opposed to routine work. You might even react to my weird ideas by saying, "Sure, they're not weird." Yet many managers don't act as if they mean it. They see practices that spark innovation as strange, even downright wrong. And they act as if practices suited only for routine work are generically good for running all businesses all the time. So they end up stifling innovation instinctively.

This happens to the best managers and companies. Start-ups are as vulnerable as established companies. A typical scenario is that a young company generates some great ideas. Once successful, the company reaches a point where it needs "discipline," or as some venture capitalists say, "It's time for some adult supervision." This means that part of the company—sometimes most of it—is organized for routine work. Tasks like accounting, sales, and human resource management can be done in innovative ways. But when "professional management" is brought into a start-up, routinization takes hold. After all, experimenting with unproven accounting practices can increase the chances a young company will stumble. The trouble starts, however, when the "adult" practices spread to innovative work. Although these managers have the best of intentions, they may unwittingly destroy what made the company vibrant in the first place.

Consider what happened at the Lotus Development Corporation in the mid-1980s. Lotus (which is now part of IBM) was founded in 1982 by Mitchell Kapor and Jonathan Sachs. The company's first product was Kapor and Sachs's Lotus 1-2-3, a business productivity tool. Industry observers give this "killer app" much credit for the success of the IBM personal computer in the mid-1980s. Lotus 1-2-3 sales grew from 53 million in 1982 to 156 million in 1984, which led to an urgent need for experienced professional managers. McKinsey consultant James Manzi was brought in as president in 1984 and became CEO in 1985. Manzi built enormously profitable marketing and sales operations, focusing on building operations modeled after *Fortune* 500 companies. The head of sales was from IBM, as was most of his sales force. Many early employees were resentful of the compensation and other perks granted to the sales force. They saw these salespeople as merely order-takers, because Lotus 1-2-3 was flying off the shelves.

Revenues continued to grow. But Lotus started having trouble developing successful new products. Part of the problem was that techniques suitable only for managing routine work were being used throughout the company. By 1985 or so, around the time the company had grown to over 1,000 employees, many original members felt they no longer fit in at Lotus. Some were simply not competent, but most were creative people who couldn't find a place in the company and found that their skills were no longer valued. Most of the new hires were cut out of the "big company mold," having worked for such firms as Coca-Cola and Procter & Gamble and then going on to get MBA degrees. One disenchanted early hire described them as "boring people who had never created a product or a company spirit."

---

*Adapted and reprinted with the author's permission from *Weird Ideas That Work* (New York: The Free Press, 2002): 177–199.

In 1985, Mitchell Kapor (then chairman of the board) and Freada Klein (then head of organizational development and training) tried an experiment. With Kapor's approval, Klein pulled together the résumés of the first 40 people to join the company. She changed each résumé slightly, usually just disguising the employee's name. Kapor's was changed a bit more because he was known for working as a disk jockey and teaching transcendental meditation. Some of these people had the right technical and managerial skills for the jobs they applied for, but they also had done a lot of "wacko and risky things." They had been community organizers, clinical psychologists, and transcendental meditation teachers (not just Kapor), and several had lived at an ashram.

Not one of the 40 applicants was called back for an interview. Kapor and Klein viewed this as a sign that Lotus was unwittingly screening out innovative people. All signs are that they were correct. The only hit product invented by the company after Lotus 1-2-3, Lotus Notes, was developed 20 miles from headquarters, as Klein put it, "so the team could work unfettered by the narrow Lotus culture." Lotus did need great marketing and sales organizations to cash in on its innovative ideas. The narrowness that came along with these changes, however, was a double-edged sword. It is hard to generate new ideas when practices are used that screen out (and drive out) people with varied ideas and who see things in disparate ways. Kapor and Klein's experiment shows that every company, even a great one like Lotus, needs to be mindful about what it takes to spark innovation. Otherwise, it will be filled with replicants who think alike and act as if the future will be a perfect imitation of the past.[1]

THE BEST MANAGEMENT IS SOMETIMES NO MANAGEMENT

Leading innovation can require a soft touch, or getting out of the way completely. We have seen how leaders of some of the most innovative companies expect and encourage their so-called subordinates to ignore and defy them. They institute policies like 3M's 15 percent rule or Corning's "Friday Afternoon Experiments" to make sure that employees can follow their hunches, even when their bosses believe those hunches are wrong.[2] Yet some managers still have a hard time bringing themselves to "manage by getting out of the way." After all, everything from Hollywood movies to an MBA education teaches us that management is about overseeing people, giving them orders, goading them on, and inspiring them to perform. As we have also seen, managers can have huge positive effects by creating self-fulfilling prophecies or allocating critical resources to a project. But managers can be oblivious to the harm they cause. Rather than following Pfeffer's advice that, like physicians, managers should "first, do no harm," they take ignorant actions that make things worse. William Coyne, former head of research and development at 3M, tells how a human resource manager once threatened to fire a scientist who was asleep under his bench. Coyne took the HR manager to 3M's "Wall of Patents" to show him that the sleeping scientist had developed some of 3M's most profitable products. Coyne advised, "Next time you see him asleep, get him a pillow."[3] Unfortunately, not all executives are so wise.

Why do so many managers delude themselves into believing they are helping their companies even though they have no effect, or are even hampering innovation?

This delusion, called the self-enhancement bias, helps explain why so many companies hesitate to delegate authority despite strong evidence that it enhances productivity and employee commitment. Yet when managers can bring themselves to get out of the way, good things can happen. Basketball coach Phil Jackson, who won numerous championships with the Chicago Bulls during the Michael Jordan era, and more recently with the Los Angeles Lakers, is a great example. Jackson is renowned for his light touch, for sitting quietly and not calling time-outs during slumps and crucial junctures in the game.[4] Most coaches shout out numerous plays during a game, but "Jackson almost never calls plays; he thinks play-calling makes players feel as if they are on a string (his)."[5] The key to Jackson's success, like David Kelley at IDEO and managers at Corning's lab, is that he has the humility to lead skilled people by giving them what they need to do their jobs and then to leave them alone. When Jackson arrived in Los Angeles, he was ballyhooed as the team's savior, the one person who could lead the underachieving Lakers to a championship. He responded, "I'm no savior. . . . They have to be the savior of themselves."[6] Ironically, he *was* the Laker's savior because he made it clear that winning was up to the players, not him.

INNOVATION MEANS SELLING, NOT JUST INVENTING, NEW IDEAS

Creativity is in the eye of the beholder. As cases from the Beatles' music to Ballard's fuel cell show, no matter how wonderful something new is, it will only be accepted if the right people can be persuaded of its value. Ralph Waldo Emerson was wrong when he said, "If you build a better mousetrap, the world will beat a path to your door." Too many innovations succeed because they are sold better, not because they are objectively superior to those of competitions.

The competition between gas and electric lighting in the 1880s is a good illustration.[7] Researchers Andrew Hargadon and Yellowless Douglas show there was little difference in the illumination provided by gas lamps and the 12-watt light bulbs Thomas Edison sold at the time. Early electric lighting was plagued by black-outs, unreliable lamps and light bulbs, and fires from short circuits and poor wiring. It was more expensive than gas, and "the Welsbach mantle, introduced in 1885 as a response to the incandescent bulb, provided a sixfold increase in the candlepower of gas lamps, changing the flickering of the faint, yellow glow into a clean, white light."[8] Even though electric lighting was not clearly superior, gas lighting was nearly extinct in the United States by 1903. Hargadon and Douglas show how this innovation triumphed largely through Edison's marketing skill and design decisions that, rather than making it as technologically advanced and inexpensive as possible, made electric lighting systems, lamps, and the language used to describe them as similar to gas lighting as possible. Remember, familiarity is comforting.

Selling a completed new product or service is crucial for cashing in on any idea. That is why Bob Metcalfe, who invented the Ethernet and founded 3Com, said, "Most engineers don't understand that selling matters. They think that on the food chain of life, salespeople are below green slime. They don't understand that nothing happens until *something gets sold.*"[9] As we have seen, selling starts inside companies long before an innovation is brought to market. Disney employees are invited to pitch ideas for new "attractions" at monthly open forums. At 3M, inventors write proposals for $50,000 "Genesis Grants" to develop prototypes and market tests. The innovation process in every big organization—from Ford, to NASA, to McDonald's, to Virgin Airlines, to Siemens—is punctuated with formal and informal gatherings where innovators try to sell their ideas to peers and bosses. A hallmark of successful innovations in big companies is that they are promoted by persistent and politically skilled champions.[10]

Similarly, all but the wealthiest entrepreneurs must convince investors to support their start-ups. Experienced entrepreneurs and investors Audrey McLean and Mike Lyons teach Stanford students how to do so with an "elevator pitch" exercise. Class that day is conducted *inside* two elevators in a five-story building. Aspiring entrepreneurs are graded on how well they sell their product, market opportunity, and management team to McLean and Lyons during a two-minute elevator ride.

I am writing about innovation, not persuasion. But if an innovator can't sell an idea, or find a representative to do it, then it rarely travels beyond the inventor's mind. This is why so many people practice selling their ideas, study how others do it, seek coaching, and read books such as Robert Cialdini's *Influence*.[11] Innovators especially need to know that judgments of them and their ideas are intertwined, perhaps inseparable. As Arthur Rock, the pioneer venture capitalist who funded Intel and Apple Computer, emphasizes, "I generally pay more attention to the people who prepare a business plan than to the proposal itself." When Rock meets entrepreneurs, he looks for those who "believe so firmly in the idea that everything else pales in comparison," and he claims, "I can usually tell the difference between people who have that fire in their stomachs and those who see their ideas primarily as a way to get rich."[12]

INNOVATION REQUIRES BOTH FLEXIBILITY AND RIGIDITY

Innovation requires flexibility. Generating different ideas and seeing old things in new ways can only be accomplished by people who can revise their beliefs easily. But recall how much rigidity, how much downright stubbornness, was required for Geoffrey Ballard to develop those fuel cells and for the team at Sun to develop the Java language. Some rigidity is necessary for developing successful innovations. It helps to define problems narrowly enough so they can be talked about in a constructive way, so people know what to focus attention on and what to ignore, and so ideas can be developed and tested in sufficient depth to see if they are any good.

A useful guideline for striking a healthy balance between rigidity and flexibility is to hold either the solution *or* the problem constant, and to let the other vary. The most common strategy is to find a problem and then to search for and evaluate alternative solutions, to *keep the problem rigid and the possible solutions flexible*. McDonald's has tried thousands of solutions to the problem of getting more people to visit their restaurants. Disney's Imagineers constantly tinker with solutions to the intertwined problems of making the long lines of "guests" in their parks *actually* move quickly and *seem* to move quickly. Gillette's research and development laboratory in Reading, England, will test virtually any material or design if it might lead to a fashionable product that works. The lab's ultimate goal is crystal clear: A closer and more comfortable shave, "The Holy Grail as far as shaving techies are concerned."[13]

The other way to balance rigidity and flexibility is to *hold the solution constant and let the problems vary*, or a "solution-driven search." This is what a two-year-old does with a hammer: hit everything in sight to see what happens. It happens when some new or old technology, product, theory, or service is treated as the possible solution to many as-yet-unknown problems. I mentioned earlier that 3M's Microreplication Technology Center used a three-dimensional surface composed of tiny pyramids to develop a display for laptop computers that used less power than conventional displays. Microreplication was developed in the 1950s to increase the brightness of overhead projectors. 3M managers believed that the microscopic pyramids could be used in many other applications, but did not know exactly how or where. They opened the center to find ways to put Microreplication in as many products as possible. It is now used in dozens of 3M products including recording tape, sandpaper, traffic lights, grinders, and mouse pads.

The Freeplay Group in Cape Town, South Africa, also innovates via a solution-driven search. They invent and sell "self-powered" devices that generate electricity when the user cranks the handle on a 2-inch-wide, 20-foot-long ribbon of carbonized steel flashlight. As the spring unwinds, it produces enough electricity to power a radio (the firm's first product) for 30 minutes. This radio is not just a cool gadget that attracted computer geeks at the Consumer Electronics Show in Las Vegas. It is changing the lives of the world's poorest people, who can now have working radios without using (unattainable) electricity or expensive batteries. Co-CEO Rory Stear says, "We are not just in the radio business. We are in the energy business. We always ask ourselves, what else can we do with this technology?" This solution-driven thinking has led them to develop, or start developing, self-powered products including a flashlight, global-positioning system, land-mine detector, water purifier, and a mechanism for a toy monster truck.[14]

INCITE AND UNCOVER DISCOMFORT

As should be obvious by now, discomfort is an inevitable and desirable part of innovation. The weird idea to hire people who make you uncomfortable makes this point directly. Discomfort can also be generated by hiring people you don't need, when employees defy bosses, when people imagine dumb things and try to do them, and when people argue over their precious ideas. Discomfort isn't much fun, but it helps people to avoid and break out of mindless action.

Unfamiliar ideas and things generate negative feelings like irritation, anxiety, and disapproval, as do interruptions of routine action and challenges to taken-for-granted assumptions. If everyone always likes your ideas, it probably means that you are not doing many original things. When Howard Schulz, founder of Starbucks, wanted to partner with former basketball star Magic Johnson to build seven coffee houses in low-income African-American neighborhoods in Los Angeles, other Starbucks executives objected because it was risky. They had built many Starbucks overseas but never in an inner-city neighborhood. These executives also reacted with discomfort when, to appeal to African-American tastes, Johnson wanted to sell food like sweet potato pie and play music like Miles Davis and Stevie Wonder. Schulz and other Starbucks executives ultimately decided to build these stores and to tailor them to the inner city. This decision to overcome their discomfort proved to be wise: The initial agreement with Johnson was expanded after the first stores posted spectacular sales and profits, and executives' fears that crime would be rampant in and around the stores proved unfounded.[15]

Discomfort plays another role. Many successful ideas were invented because someone got upset about something and then did something about it. Inventor David Levy uses "The Curse Method."[16] Levy says, "Whenever I hear someone curse, it's a sign to invent something."[17] Levy designed the Wedgie lock after he heard a coworker cursing because a thief had stolen his bicycle seat. Levy noticed that the streets near his lab in Cambridge, Massachusetts, were filled with abandoned bikes without seats, suggesting there was a market for a good bicycle seat lock. Being uncomfortable or downright unhappy isn't much fun, but it can be an innovator's inspiration. Says Levy, "When I lie in bed, I try to think of things that suck."[18]

TREAT EVERYTHING LIKE A TEMPORARY CONDITION

The organizing principles for routine work reflect the assumption that everything is a permanent condition; the organizing principles for innovative work reflect the opposite assumption. Both are useful fictions. After all, exploiting existing knowledge is only wise if what worked in the past will keep working. And bringing in varied ideas—seeing things in new ways, and, of course, breaking from the past—only makes sense when, even if old ways still work, they will soon be obsolete. Leaders of innovative companies constantly create alarm and warn that just because things are working well now does not mean that they will work later. Andrew Grove of Intel is famous for being paranoid that a "disruptive" change—a new technology that makes their technology or business model obsolete—will appear. John Chambers of Cisco does pretty much the same thing, as does Jorma Ollila, CEO of the Finnish telephone giant Nokia.

Sustaining innovation requires treating everything from procedures and product lines to teams and organizations as things that might be useful now but will need to be discontinued. It can also mean forming temporary companies, not just temporary projects and teams like AES and Lend Lease. The goal at birth would be a planned and graceful death, with disbanding done once the company had completed a project or intertwined set of projects. The argument for temporary organizations is that constant disbanding and reforming keeps variance and *vu ja de* high in a company, and makes it difficult for people to engage in mindless action. [*Vu ja de* is what happens when you feel and act as if an experience or object is brand new even if you have had it or seen it hundreds of times.]

This is why some traditional companies, including a team at General Motors Research and Development Center in Warren, Michigan, have examined the film industry to get ideas about sparking innovation. The "Hollywood model" is intriguing because these days a temporary production company is formed to make most films. After the film is completed, any money made by these single-project organizations is distributed, the team is disbanded, and the life-of-project workers go on to their next job. Hollywood was once dominated by large studios like MGM, Warner Brothers, and Paramount, which employed all workers, including directors, writers, and actors. In contrast, contemporary Hollywood producers rely on brokers to supply "packages" of people and to help build the temporary companies that make films. Talent agencies like William Morris and the Creative Artists Agency are among the enduring hubs in a complex network of formal and informal relationships, which explains why, although film production companies are temporary, there is much stability and predictability in the industry.

There are intriguing parallels between Hollywood and new-economy industries. There has been a great rise in contract work—especially by skilled professionals with technical skills—and an associated set of agencies to supply companies with temporary help to meet short-term demands in high-tech industries. Although there is much rhetoric about forming "built-to-last" companies in Silicon Valley, most start-ups in this region are temporary. Those that endure as freestanding firms are rare; far more are acquired by large firms, and demise is even more likely. Regardless of whether employees are classified as temporary or permanent, there is enormous turnover in Silicon Valley. This didn't start in the Internet age: Turnover has averaged over 20 percent per year in high-technology companies since the early 1980s. In both Hollywood and Silicon Valley, people constantly take new roles, work with an ever-changing cast of characters, and new companies are constantly formed with new combinations of existing talent.

MAKE THE PROCESS AS SIMPLE AS POSSIBLE

A hallmark of innovative companies and teams is that they follow the law of parsimony: Make everything as simple as possible (but no simpler). They use work practices that help people focus on what matters and ignore the rest. Needless complexity arises when companies consider every contingency and involve anyone who could possibly improve, support, or be opposed to an idea. These misguided efforts to inject order and control, and to achieve perfection, can tangle aspiring innovators in red tape and condemn them to meeting after meeting with people who barely understand their work (but don't hesitate to give them advice about how to do it). These complex and dysfunctional processes can also require innovators to devote too much time to selling ideas and playing organizational politics, and not enough to developing ideas.

Innovation is easier to sustain in companies that follow the law of parsimony. General Electric's Jack Welch says, "Bureaucracy hates simplicity. . . . Simple messages travel faster, simpler designs reach market faster, and the elimination of clutter allows faster decision making."[19]

Innovation can be simplified by reducing the number of products or services developed and sold. When Steve Jobs returned to Apple in July of 1997, the company was selling so many computer models that, as he put it, "we couldn't even tell our friends which ones to buy." By 1999, Apple had only four computer models: a laptop and desktop for home and educational markets, and a laptop and desktop for business markets. This simplification was crucial to Apple's return to profitability.

Finally, a simple philosophy about what an innovation will be—and will not be—reduces unnecessary distraction and effort. If everyone follows a simple vision, it speeds development, focuses effort, and results in simpler products or services (which will be easier to build or implement). Jeff Hawkins, inventor of the Palm Pilot, also led the development of the hugely successful Palm V, telling the design team, "This product is all about style, it's all about elegance." He said, "I gave examples of products. I said—when the first [StarTac] phone came out, it sold for $1,600, and people were lining up to buy it. Why? Because it was new and it was elegant. So I said—I want to do the StarTac of PDAs." The team pressed Hawkins to add features like more software and a microphone. But he said, "No, no. Palm V is all about elegance and style and I won't entertain anything else." This simple vision, and Hawkins's persistence in putting it into action, made crystal clear to the team where to focus their creative efforts.[20]

INNOVATION MEANS LIVING WITH SOME NASTY DRAWBACKS

The terms *creativity, innovation*, and *fun* are often used in the same breath. But before you rush ahead to build or join an innovative company, I feel obliged to warn you about the hazards. Working in an innovative place can be annoying and frustrating, or worse. James Adams at Stanford and Barry Staw from the University of California assert that many people *say* they want a creative workplace, but few would be happy if they actually worked in one. Indeed, a few years ago the Intel Corporation removed "Fun" from the list of core values that employees wear on their badges. A cynic might say that Intel has never been a fun place, so at least they are no longer hypocritical about it. After all, Intel is well known for encouraging conflict and internal competition. They even hold classes on how to use "constructive confrontation." Intel might be a bit nastier than absolutely necessary, but to build a company where innovation is a way of life, things need to be done that are unpleasant, or even downright frightening.

The 11 1/2 weird ideas here work, but that doesn't mean you will enjoy hiring people you don't like and who probably won't like you. It doesn't mean you will like being around people who are constantly fighting with you and one another. I don't know about you, but I get aggravated when I ask people who work for me to do something and they defy my request.

Think about the other weird ideas. If you like an orderly workplace, you won't be happy with the chaos that results when your organization is filled with people who have never been taught what they are supposed to do. There are some people who like working in a place where most things fail, are never finished, or reach dead ends. But not most people. When companies are too efficient, it is a warning sign that they are stifling innovation.

Beyond these annoying aspects of innovative places, you should also think hard about the risks that the evolutionary model implies for the average person or company with a new idea. The human tendency to be optimistic means that most of us believe we will be among the small percentage who succeed. But the most likely outcome is that you or your company will be among the many casualties required so that a few can survive and flourish.

I don't want to leave you with the impression that innovative companies are horrible places or that you are destined to lose all your money if you work in one. Many people love the mess and confusion. It is more satisfying to come up with new ideas than to repeat the same actions—and the same thoughts—again and again. It is exciting to work with people who are thrilled about some new idea. Even though many new ideas fail, these setbacks often occur where failure is tolerated, even rewarded. And there are large numbers of people who have become rich working in such places, even if the percentage is small. But you should know the hazards of innovation before devoting your days to it.

LEARN TO FAIL FASTER, NOT LESS OFTEN

If you believe this book, you will cringe when people talk about making innovation more efficient. It usually means they want to use the logic of routine work to manage innovative work. Once companies try to "reduce the number of screw-ups," innovation usually grinds to a halt. The key to more efficient innovation is failing faster, not less often. Consider what Audrey MacLean told me about failure. MacLean was CEO of Adaptive and is now a successful "angel" investor (she calls herself a "mentor capitalist") who has been featured in *Forbes* and *Red Herring* cover stories in recent years. She argues that one unrecognized reason people made so much money investing in

Internet firms during the late 1990s was that failure was inexpensive. MacLean notes, "Since it didn't take much time or money to put up a Web site, you could find out pretty quickly if it was going to fly or not. A lot of money was made very quickly when something worked, and not much money was lost on failed experiments."

Barry Staw and Jerry Ross have studied the problem of throwing good money after bad for over 25 years and have developed guidelines for avoiding such situations. The most important one is that people who are responsible for starting some project or company, and who have made public statements saying they are committed to it and it is destined to succeed, should not be involved in deciding its fate. Projects need to be structured so that separate groups make decisions about starting and stopping. This is why most banks use one group to sell loans and a different group to decide whether to pull the plug on troubled loans.

Irrational persistence can also be reduced by eliminating or softening the costs of failure. If people believe that their reputations will be ruined by failure, they may rightly believe that pulling the plug means certain ruin and that—no matter how slim the chances—their only hope is to find some way to succeed. Three of the companies I've talked about here—AES, Hewlett-Packard, and SAS Institute—are well known for such "soft landings." Staw and Ross also advise that "just knowing that one is under the sway of escalation can help." They suggest looking at situations from an outsider's perspective, routinely stopping and asking: "If I took the job for the first time today and found this project going on, would I support it or get rid of it?" This sort of question prompted Intel executives Gordon Moore and Andy Grove to get out of the unprofitable memory-chip business in 1985 and focus on microprocessors, a decision that made Intel billions. An even more aggressive way to avoid escalation situations is to sow the seeds for pulling the plug while a company, project, or product is still a success. Smart executives keep their people vigilant about ways that a current success can turn bad or be eclipsed by competitors.

OPEN IS GOOD, CLOSED IS BAD

Being open to ideas from other people and places brings in variance and different perspectives, which can help your company avoid getting stuck in the past. And by being open to outsiders, ideas that are old to them, but new to you, can be borrowed or blended with what you already know to invent new management practices, services, and products. The value of openness is perhaps the main lesson from AnnaLee Saxenian's book *Regional Advantage*, which shows why Silicon Valley companies like Hewlett-Packard, Intel, Sun Microsystems, and Cisco have been so innovative, while once-great companies on Boston's Route 128 like DEC, Wang, and Data General declined and died. She shows how Silicon Valley thrives because engineers share ideas so openly, both to get help with technical problems and to show off how much they know.[21] This doesn't happen just inside companies, it happens between engineers from different companies. Not only do engineers routinely violate their intellectual property agreements, several CEOs have admitted to me that being a bit "leaky" in the right conversations is expected and desirable, because everyone understands that it makes innovation happen.

There are, of course, limits to how open a company can and should be about ideas. Concerns about protecting intellectual property are legitimate, and companies that are careful to guard their ideas can make a fortune, at least for a while. Kevin Rivette and David Kline show, for example, that many companies are sitting on unused patents that are worth millions.[22] IBM licensed its unused patents in 1990 and saw its royalties jump from $30 million a year to more than $1 billion in 1999, providing over one-ninth of its annual profits. Intellectual property constraints can also lead to innovation because, if one company owns a solution to some problem, it can spur people in other companies to invent an alternative solution.

Nonetheless, companies that are paranoid about their precious ideas being stolen can kill innovation because, when people from the company get a reputation for listening to other companies' ideas but not talking about their own, the lack of reciprocity may lead others to clam up. Or if people from such companies realize they can't engage in two-way exchanges, they may avoid talking with outsiders who can give them useful advice.

Among the most extreme and impressive illustrations of openness is the development of open source or free software. This includes Linux, currently the only serious challenge to Microsoft Windows. The main benefit of open source development is what is called Linus's Law, that "with more eyes, all bugs are shallow."[23] As the development community grows, each new release grows more resilient and bug free because more people find and fix bugs. The open source community has developed a method of licensing that protects their openness. Open source software is protected by what they call "copylefting" work—not copyrighting it. Open source licenses that follow the copyleft principle add "distribution terms, which are a legal instrument that gives everyone the rights to use, modify, and redistribute the program's code or any program derived from it but only if the distribution terms are unchanged. Thus, the code and the freedoms become legally inseparable."[24]

These restrictions allow the code to stay open. Anyone has access to the source code and is free to modify it, but modifications must be returned to the code base. This causes odd situations in companies and other organizations like universities where a programmer improves some code that their employer wants to copyright and profit from, but the copyleft agreement makes that leverage impossible. An open source Web site points out: "When we explain to the employer that it is illegal to distribute the improved version except as free software, the employer usually decides to release it as free software rather than throw it away."[25] There are philosophical reasons for developing free software, but much of the recent enthusiasm for the open source principle is pragmatic: By being open to diverse people and their ideas, the product keeps getting better and better.

THE ATTITUDES OF INNOVATION

I hope that you use the weird ideas in this book to make your company more innovative. These ideas work. But after a decade of tinkering with them, I've realized that the exact methods used to innovate are less important than building a company where people have the right attitudes toward their work and each other. Psychologists tell us that emotions are the engine that propels human action. Feelings—not cold cognitions—drive people to turn good ideas and intentions into reality. So people who have the right attitudes will not only have an easier time implementing the weird ideas here, their worldview will also drive them to invent and use their own ideas about spurring innovation.

Every innovative company I know of is filled with people who are passionate about solving problems. When I talk to founder and chairman Jeff Hawkins and director of product design engineering Peter Skillman at Handspring about hand-held computers, they bounce up and down like my children do when they play with a wonderful new toy. I see the same spirit in Joey Reiman of BrightHouse, the "ideation company" that charges clients like Coca-Cola, Hardee's, and Georgia Pacific $500,000 to $1 million for a single idea. I can see Reiman in my mind's eye, roller skating around a circular stage in Berlin, bellowing to an audience from the advertising firm McCann-Erickson, "We do heartstorming, not brainstorming; creativity is much more about what people feel than what they think." The passion is more subtle in other innovative companies, but you can always find it.

Playfulness and curiosity are related attitudes of innovation. When Kay Zufall started cutting little shapes out of the wallpaper cleaner made at her brother-in-law's factory, she wasn't thinking about trying to develop a new product; she did it because she loves to tinker with ideas and things. Zufall is always trying to make things better and to have some fun along the way. I saw the same spirit in the IDEO engineers who grabbed my new digital camera (one of the first sold) and took it apart on the spot. They couldn't help themselves. They had never seen one before and *had* to see how it was put together. This persistent curiosity leads to odd moments, such as when a waiter asked some IDEO designers why they were taking the napkin holder apart. The answer—"because we wanted to look at how the springs work"—was not treated as credible. But it was true, and it is one of the main reasons IDEO has developed a renowned culture of innovation.

My last attitude of innovation is really a pair of attitudes: the ability to switch emotional gears between cynicism and belief, or between deep doubt and unshakable confidence. These emotions are the tag-team partners of the innovation process. If your company is dominated by only one, you are in trouble. Every innovative company we examined closely here makes use of this blend of emotions, from Disney, to 3M, to Handspring, to Sottsass Associates. People in these places believe that everything is wonderful, that all is possible when generating ideas, but they become cynics—or bring in some cynics—when deciding which to develop and which to stop. Once they pick an idea to develop and implement, belief rises again.

A blend of belief and cynicism can also help you get the most out of this book. As I said at the outset, when you think about my weird ideas, try to suspend disbelief, just for a while. Ask yourself: *What if these ideas are true*? How might I help organize or manage my company differently? How should I act differently to make myself more creative? Play with these ideas in your mind and experiment with them in your company. These weird ideas have firm grounding and have helped other companies develop useful new ideas, but they are not immutable truths. Some cynicism is needed to make the best use of them. Treat them like toys you might buy to mess around with: Try to break them, take apart the pieces to see how they work, try to improve them, and mix them with your other toys. You might develop some of your own counterintuitive ideas along the way. Ultimately, anything that brings in new knowledge, helps people see old things in new ways, or helps a company break from the past will do the trick.

Endnotes

1. This experiment was described to me in a telephone interview I conducted with Freada Klein on October 12, 2000.
2. Fishman, C., "Creative Tension," *Fast Company* (November 2000): 358–88.
3. From a speech that William E. Coyne gave at Motorola University in Schaumburg, IL, July 11, 2000.
4. Shields, D., "The Good Father," *The New York Times Magazine* (April 23, 2000): 58–61.
5. Ibid., 60.
6. Ibid.
7. Hargadon, A., and Y. Douglas, "When Innovations Meet Institutions: Edison and the Design of the Electric Light," working paper, Warrington College of Business Administration, September 2000. University of Florida Gainesville.
8. Ibid., 19.
9. Metcalfe, B., "Invention Is a Flower, Innovation Is a Weed," *MIT Technology Review* (November/December 1999): 56.
10. See, for example, Burgelman, R. A., "A Process Model of Internal Corporate Venturing in the Diversified Firm," *Administrative Science Quarterly* 28 (1983): 223–44.
11. Cialdini, R. B., *Influence: The New Psychology of Modern Persuasion* (New York: Quill, 1984).
12. Rock, A., "Strategy vs. Tactics from a Venture Capitalist," *Harvard Business Review* (November–December 1987).
13. Surowiecki, J., "The Billion-Dollar Blade," *The New Yorker* (June 15, 1998): 43–49.
14. Dahle, C., "The Agenda—Social Justice," *Fast Company* (April 1999): 166–82.
15. Platt, L., "Magic Johnson Builds an Empire," *The New York Times Magazine* (December 10, 2000): 118–21.
16. MacFarquhar, L., "Looking for Trouble," *The New Yorker* (December 6, 1999).
17. Ibid., 80.
18. Ibid., 78.
19. Slater, R., *Jack Welch and the GE Way* (New York: McGraw-Hill, 1999), 135.
20. From an interview Robert Sutton conducted with Jeff Hawkins on August 2, 2000.
21. Saxenian, A., *Regional Advantage: Culture and Competition in Silicon Valley and Route 128* (Cambridge: Harvard University Press, 1996).
22. Rivette, K., and D. Kline, *Rembrandt's in the Attic* (Boston: Harvard Business School Press, 1999).
23. Raymond, E. S., *The Cathedral & the Bazaar, Musings on Linux and Open Source by an Accidental Revolutionary* (O'Reilly: Sebastopol, CA, 1999), 27.
24. www.gnu.org/copyleft/copyleft.html.
25. Ibid.

IMPROVING THE CREATIVITY OF ORGANIZATIONAL WORK GROUPS*

Leigh Thompson

Creativity—how to ignite it and how to regenerate it—is a key question that managers and executives pose to management educators and consultants. Several organizational changes and developments make creativity a valuable necessity for the new economy and the organizations that inhabit it. First, flatter organizational structures require companies, divisions, and managers to act in a more entrepreneurial and inventive fashion. The absence of hierarchy and bureaucracy creates fertile opportunity for creative knowledge and action. Second, by nearly all counts, businesses are growing more competitive. Strictly speaking, this means that companies continually need to

*Reprinted with permission from *Academy of Management Executive*, 17(1), 2003: 96–109, via the Copyright Clearance Center.

reinvent themselves. Frank and Cook's book *The Winner-Take-All Society* provides compelling data on how companies are becoming more competitive, resulting in "winners" who gain more and more market share.[1] Third, blurred lines between traditional notions of who's "inside" and who's "outside" the company allow teams to form new relationships with suppliers, complementary businesses, and shadow industries. In *Co-opetition*, Brandenburger and Nalebuff argue that cooperation and competition can co-exist in business relationships.[2] Finally, the focus on customer service is more important than ever, and the quest to satisfy and delight the customer or client requires creativity.

Just because the challenges facing a team call for creativity, however, is no guarantee that the team members will be creative. In fact, several factors that seem to foster creativity might actually thwart it.

CREATIVE REALISM

Most people think that creative ideas are wild ideas; on the contrary, creativity is the production of novel and useful ideas. Creativity is important for innovation. If creativity pertains to ideas, then innovation pertains to the services and products that result from creative ideas. According to the famous psychologist James Guilford, creative thinking occurs when a problem solver invents a novel solution to a problem.[3] Creative ideas and creative acts are original and valuable. Figure 1 shows a 2 × 2 grid defining, on the horizontal continuum, creative and conservative ideas.[4] According to the model, teams should strive to achieve creative ideas, which represent highly original and novel ideas, as opposed to conservative, traditional ideas.

The vertical continuum is the one that is too often overlooked. It distinguishes new ideas that are *realistic* (connected to current ideas and knowledge) from ideas that are

FIGURE 1 Four General, Conceptual Domains into Which New Ideas Can Be Classified

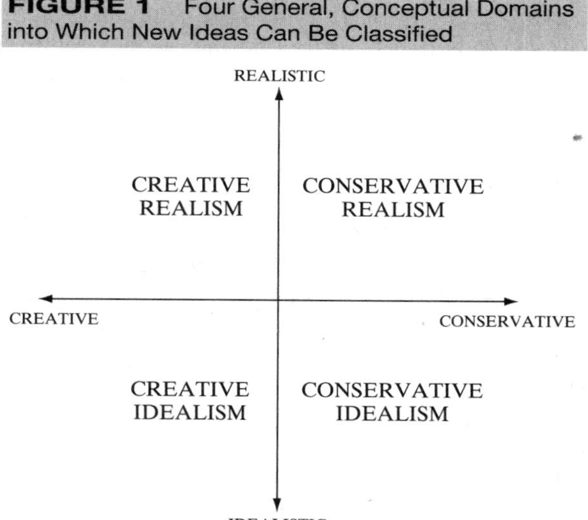

Source: Finke, R. A. "Creative realism" in S. M. Smith, T. B. Ward, and R. A. Finke (Eds.), *The Creative Cognition Approach*, Cambridge, MA: MIT Press, 1995, 303–326. Used with permission.

idealistic (disconnected from current knowledge). If new ideas are not connected to current ideas and knowledge, they are often unimplementable.

The best of all possible worlds is to get ideas in the upper left quadrant. This domain is called *Creative Realism* because these ideas are highly imaginative and highly connected to current structures and ideas. *Conservative Realism* represents ideas that are highly traditional and highly connected to current knowledge and practices. This realm contains little ambiguity and little uncertainty. *Conservative Idealism* is perhaps the worst type of thinking for a company: an extension of a common idea that is unrealistic to begin with. Such ideas exhibit little or no imagination and are not connected to existing knowledge. *Creative Idealism* represents highly original, yet highly unrealistic, ideas.

The key question is how teams can maximize the probability of landing in the upper left (Creative Realism) quadrant. The ideas that flow from this type of thinking are highly original and very useful. An excellent example of Creative Realism was Edison's development of the electric light system.[5] After Edison invented the incandescent light, his next project was to develop an entire system whereby the invention could be made commercially successful. At the time, there were two in-place lighting systems (neither developed by Edison): gas lights and electrical arc lights. Gas lights could be directly controlled for brightness; gas fuel was produced off-site and sent through buried gas mains. Arc lighting was produced by an electrical spark between carbon rods, was very hot, and produced fumes. The generating plant was located at the user's site. Edison's electric lighting system was based on the principles of gas lighting. Edison wrote in his workbooks that he completely imitated the gas system, replacing the gas with electricity. In Edison's electric system, the source of power was remote from the user, and the wires that brought the power were underground. Further, the individual lights were turned on and off by the user. The light bulb in Edison's system was called a burner and was designed to produce the same amount of light as a gas burner.

As we shall see, the efforts that people make to generate ideas in the Creative Realism quadrant sometimes ensure that they won't end up there. As it turns out, the route to creative, useful ideas is often indirect and non-obvious.

MEASURING CREATIVITY

In my MBA and executive education courses, I challenge participants to assess their own creativity using a standard creativity measure: Guilford's cardboard-box task.[6] The procedure is very simple: all participants spend ten minutes writing down all of the uses that they can think of for a cardboard box. (The same can be done for a brick, etc.) I am always surprised by the variation in the number, originality, and quality of ideas within the class.

The next step is to instruct participants in how to evaluate creativity, using this very simple task as a model. To do so, I introduce Guilford's three-factor model of creativity: fluency, flexibility, and originality.[7] *Fluency* is simply a measure of *how many* different ideas a person is able to generate. As we will see, Alex Osborn (the father of modern brainstorming) was right: Quantity often does breed quality.[8] The typical range that I get in my MBA and executive classes is 5–40.

Flexibility is a measure of *how many different types* of ideas a person generates. For example, suppose that one person who completes this exercise, Sandy, generates three ideas: using the box as a cage for a hamster, a container for a turtle, and a kennel for a dog. Sandy would receive three points for fluency, because there are three different ideas, but only one point for flexibility, because the ideas are of the same category (i.e., homes for animals). Conversely, Pat suggests using the cardboard box as a god, a telephone (via two boxes and some string), and trading it as currency.[9] Pat would receive a score of three points for fluency (same as Sandy), but score three points for flexibility, because there are three separate categories of ideas—one involving religion, another communication, and the third economics. Clearly, some of Pat's ideas do not meet the requirements for structural connectedness, but as we will see, Pat and her team are in a much better position to set the stage for creative realism than Sandy. Think of flexibility as a kind of mental gymnastics—the ability to entertain different types of ideas, all in a short amount of time. Most people, and in particular most teams, tend to get stuck in one or two types of categories of thought, a kind of cognitive arthritis. The typical range that I get in my MBA and executive classes is 4–17 categories.

Originality is a measure of the uniqueness or originality of the idea. (This is what is meant by creativity on the conservative–creative continuum in Figure 1.) Statistically, original ideas are ideas that are generated by less than 5 percent of a given sample. Thus, in my investigations, if there are 50 executives in a given class, an originality point is given to an idea only if two or fewer people come up with that particular idea. The typical range that I get for originality scores in my MBA and executive classes is 0–14.

There is always a striking correlation among the three measures, such that the people who get the highest scores on originality also get high scores on flexibility and fluency. Thus, there is a strong association between quantity, diversity, and novelty of ideas. According to Guilford, flexibility is the driver. This runs counter to most business notions of creativity, in which diversity of ideas is often not rewarded, quantity is not valued, and *quality* is viewed as the single most important goal. If flexibility is indeed the driver, how do we set the stage for it?

CONVERGENT VERSUS DIVERGENT THINKING

Convergent thinking is thinking that proceeds toward or converges on a single answer. For example, consider a gambling problem: The EV, or expected value, of a 70 percent chance of earning $1,000 is obtained through a simple algorithm, such that $1,000 is multiplied by .7 to obtain $700. In contrast, divergent thinking moves outwards from a problem in many directions and involves thinking without boundaries. Divergent thinking is somewhat like Janusian thinking. Janus was the Roman deity who had two faces looking in opposite directions. In this context, Janusian thinking refers to the ability to cope with conflicting ideas, paradoxes, ambiguity, and doubt. To stimulate Janusian thinking, Tom Verberne suggests asking, "What if the world turned into your worst nightmare or your nicest dream?"[10] Open-ended questions stimulate divergent thinking. After participants answer such questions, have them identify factors that influence the opposing scenarios. This kind of thinking can prevent people from jumping to the most obvious (and often the most expensive) solution. Verberne gives the example of hotel guests complaining to a hotel manager that they have to wait too long for the elevators. The manager refers the problem to an engineer, who suggests installing another elevator. The manager is not convinced to adopt the costly solution, so she asks a psychologist for advice. The psychologist recommends giving people something to do while they wait—e.g., putting mirrors and a magazine rack near the elevators. The manager chooses the low-cost option, and the complaints stop. Verberne also suggests role switching, where participants ask what important opportunity or problem faces their organization, take each other's roles within the organization, and ask what's important from the perspective of their new, assumed roles.

Impossibilities can also stimulate divergent thinking. Participants think of ideas that are at present impossible to execute (e.g., living on the moon, traveling by satellite, etc.) and then identify conditions that might lead to the idea's fruition.

Many of the factors that make up creative problem solving are related to divergent thinking. Most teams do require some convergent thinking. As we shall see, however, teams tend to focus on convergent thinking at the expense of divergent thinking. Thus, one paradox for teams, when it comes to creativity, is that teams excel at convergent thinking, but individuals excel at divergent thinking. This is paradoxical because intuitively, most people strongly believe that teams are more creative than individuals, when in fact they aren't.

A large body of research in social and organizational psychology reveals that when teams are pitted against individuals, it is teams who excel at tasks requiring convergent thinking. For example, in a classic decision-making game that has a proven best answer, groups of people generate superior decisions with greater frequency than do individuals. Moreover, business and social institutions seem to know this and capitalize on it. Presumably, one reason for having a jury of 12 peers is that the resulting judgment will be more balanced and accurate than if only one person weighs the evidence.

The most difficult task for most teams is divergent thinking, often referred to as "Thinking Outside the Box." As a general observation, the ideas that groups and teams come up with are more clichéd and traditional than the ideas that individuals generate when working on their own. It is as if teams act as a norming device, thereby making group members more likely to conform to one another. In several organizational situations, this is highly desirable, such as when teams want to build cohesion and identity. However, by its very definition, creativity requires diversity of thought and ideas. Marshall Fisher, a co-founder of Century 21 Real Estate, realized that most people, left to their own devices, engage in conformist, convergent thinking. The idea behind his IdeaFisher program is that alternatives need to be freed up. The IdeaFisher program uses keywords and phrases and cross-references them with other like words and phrases to put together diverse and different ideas that normally don't come together in a highly organized fashion.[11] Diversity also means conflict, among other things; and most teams want to avoid conflict at any cost. Conflict avoidance can actually cost a lot.

BRAINSTORMING

Alex Osborn, an advertising executive in the 1950s, wanted to increase the creativity of teams in organizations. He believed that one of the main blocks to organizational creativity was the premature evaluation of ideas. He was convinced that two heads were better than one when it came to generating ideas, but only if people could be trained to *defer judgment* of their own and others' ideas during the idea generation process.

TABLE 1 Rules for Brainstorming

No Criticism:	Do not criticize ideas. Group members should not evaluate ideas in any way during the generation phase; all ideas should be considered valuable.
Freewheeling Welcome:	Group members should express any idea that comes to mind, no matter how strange, weird, or fanciful. Group members are encouraged not to be constrained nor timid. They should freewheel whenever possible.
Quantity Desired:	Group members should generate as many ideas as possible. Groups should strive for quantity, as the more ideas, the better. A high quantity of ideas increases the probability of finding excellent solutions.
Combining/Improving Ideas Encouraged:	Because all of the ideas belong to the group, members should try to modify and extend the ideas suggested by other members whenever possible.

Source: Adapted from A. F. Osborn. *Applied Imagination* (revised edition). New York: Scribner, 1957.

Osborn then developed the most widespread business practice used by companies to encourage creative thinking: brainstorming.

In his influential book *Applied Imagination*, Osborn suggested that brainstorming could considerably increase the quality and quantity of ideas produced by group members.[12] Osborn therefore believed that the group product could be greater than the sum of the individual parts if certain conditions were met. Hence, he developed rules to govern the conduct of brainstorming. Contrary to popular corporate lore that brainstorming sessions are wild and crazy free-for-alls where anything goes, Osborn's rules were specific: (1) criticism is ruled out; (2) freewheeling is welcome; (3) quantity is desired; and (4) combination and improvement of ideas are encouraged (see Table 1).

Osborn aptly noted that quantity is a good catalyst for quality: A team is more likely to discover a really good idea if it has a lot of ideas to choose from. But there is even more to brainstorming than mere quantity. Osborn believed that the ideas generated by one person in a team could stimulate ideas in other people in a synergistic fashion.

Many companies still use the original brainstorming rules suggested by Osborn over 40 years ago. Silicon Valley's IDEO design firm lives by these rules. Douglas Dayton of IDEO says that five rules govern every brainstorming session at IDEO: "Have one conversation at a time. Build upon the ideas of others. Defer judgment. Encourage wild ideas (not wild behavior). Stay focused on the subject."[13]

Osborn claimed to have (but did not provide) research evidence that a team which adopted these rules could generate twice as many ideas as similar numbers of individuals working alone. Thus, the comparison Osborn had in mind was a real group working face-to-face and a control group of sorts, known in the literature as a nominal group.

DOES IT WORK?

This is the question organizational theorists asked about the brainstorming technique. Nearly all laboratory studies have found that group brainstorming leads to the generation of fewer ideas than comparable numbers of solitary brainstormers in both laboratory and organizational settings (i.e., nominal groups).[14] Thus, 40 or so

TABLE 2 Performance Data of Group and Solitary Brainstorming

	Face-to-face brainstorming group	*The same number of people working independently (solitary brainstorming)*
Quantity: The number of ideas generated	28	74.5
Quality: Percentage of "good ideas" (judged anonymously by independent experts)	8.9%	12.7%

Source: Adapted from Diehl, M., and Stroebe, W. "Productivity Loss in Brainstorming Groups: Toward a Solution of a Riddle" *Journal of Personality and Social Psychology*, 53 (1987) : 497–509.

years of research on brainstorming has found that brainstorming is significantly *worse* in terms of fostering creativity than just having the same number of individuals work independently. In fact, virtually all of the empirical investigations of group brainstorming are strongly (not just mildly) negative about its effectiveness compared to solitary brainstorming.

As a typical example, look at the statistics in Table 2, which are actual performance data of brainstorming groups and solitary groups in terms of quantity and quality of ideas. On the basis of these results, which have been replicated several hundred times with a variety of teams brainstorming about all kinds of things, the same pattern emerges again and again. According to Mullen, et al., "It appears particularly difficult to justify brainstorming techniques in terms of any performance outcomes, and the long-lived popularity of brainstorming techniques is unequivocally and substantially misguided."[15]

However, companies who use brainstorming don't like to hear this. Despite the empirical evidence for its ineffectiveness, group brainstorming remains popular in business and industry.[16]

MAJOR THREATS TO TEAM CREATIVITY

Four major problems stifle the effectiveness of brainstorming in teams. The basic problem is not teamwork itself, but rather the social-cognitive processes that operate in teamwork and how teams are managed. I refer to these problems as social loafing, conformity, production blocking, and downward norm setting.

SOCIAL LOAFING

Social loafing is the tendency for people in a group to slack off—i.e., not work as hard either mentally or physically in a group as they would alone. Indeed, when organizational members perceive their own contributions to be unidentifiable and dispensable, they are likely to loaf.[17] If loafing is extreme disinterest in a task, then "flow" is extreme involvement and interest. According to psychologist Mihaly Csikszentmihalyi, people who really enjoy a task often experience a state of "flow." The idea of flow is that an activity is challenging enough to be interesting and rewarding, but not so challenging that the player is threatened or inhibited. Flow is the experience of enjoying an activity so much that it becomes worth doing even though it may have no consequences beyond its own context.[18] Thus, the process is more important than the outcome for people in a flow state.

CONFORMITY

A basic human principle is the desire to be liked and accepted by others, particularly others in one's groups. Several theories of social behavior (e.g., social identity theory) provide compelling evidence that people seek to identify with groups and sometimes will engage in bizarre behaviors to ensure their acceptance by a group.[19] In brainstorming teams this means, for example, that managers may be cautious about their presentation of ideas and suggestions because they fear that others may negatively evaluate the ideas.[20] This, of course, will lead members to respond with "appropriate," traditional, conservative, and highly similar ideas—exactly the kind of behavior that most organizations would like to avoid. For example, word association studies reveal that people make more conventional and clichéd responses when they are in a group than when they are alone. Some companies have liberated teams by using free-association exercises. For example, at Campbell's Soup Company, a group of product developers began brainstorming by randomly selecting the word "handle" from a dictionary. Through free association, someone suggested the word "utensil." This led to "fork." One participant joked about a soup that could be eaten with a fork. The group reasoned (in a convergent fashion) that soup could not be eaten with a fork unless it was thick with vegetables and meat—and Campbell's Chunky Soups, an extraordinarily successful product line, were born.[21]

Conformity can occur when group members are concerned that others in the group will be critical of their suggestions, despite instructions designed to minimize such concerns.[22] Many social conventions in companies suggest that people should stay "on topic" and not present ideas that diverge greatly from those being discussed. This type of conformity is usually not a good idea when it comes to creative thinking.

PRODUCTION BLOCKING

A person working alone on a problem can enjoy an uninterrupted flow of thought. In contrast, brainstorming group members cannot speak at the same time; they have to wait for their turns to speak. Consequently, people may forget their ideas or decide during the waiting period not to present them.[23] Their idea production is blocked. Waiting can certainly be frustrating, especially if the meeting is not managed well. Production blocking works both ways too: It is difficult for group members to listen to and process ideas generated by other group members while they are generating their own ideas.

DOWNWARD NORM SETTING

It is commonly observed that the performance of people working within a group tends to converge over time. For example, at CDW (Computer Discount Warehouse), salespeople working in the same area in the building report monthly sales figures more similar to one another than to those working in other buildings and areas.[24] So far, no problem. However, there is a pervasive tendency for the lowest performers in a group to pull down the average. Indeed, individuals working in brainstorming groups tend to match their performance to that of the least productive member, also known as downward norm setting.[25] It is most likely to occur when there are no strong internal or external incentives for high performance in teams.[26] This low performance level may set the benchmark for the team, in that it is seen as an appropriate or typical level of performance. For example, participants in interactive dyads or groups of four tend to be more similar in their rate of idea generation than non-interacting groups.[27] Unfortunately, the least productive members of the team are often more influential in determining overall team performance than the high performers.

WHAT GOES ON DURING A TYPICAL BRAINSTORMING SESSION?

What exactly might we expect to observe in a typical company brainstorming session? Video- and tape-recorded interactions reveal an interesting set of events. The four problems noted above combine to cause people in most brainstorming groups to:

- Experience inhibitions, anxiety, and self-presentational concerns
- Reduce their production
- Participate in social rituals, such as telling stories, repeating ideas, and giving positive feedback (a natural pattern of conversation that works well at cocktail parties but kills creativity)
- Set their performance benchmarks too low
- Conform in terms of ideas
- Conform in terms of rate of idea generation

THE FAULTY-PERFORMANCE ILLUSION

Most brainstorming teams have no idea that these behaviors are occurring; most interactive brainstorming teams feel quite confident about their productivity. Thus, though the group's esteem has been soothed via the social rituals, the esteem has a faulty basis. Brainstorming groups, and the companies who use them, are their own worst enemy: They fall prey to the illusion that they function very effectively. They suffer from illusions of invulnerability, collective rationalization, belief in the morality of the group, and stereotyping of outgroups. In fact, the illusion of performance is so self-serving that people often take credit for the ideas generated by others.[28]

BUILDING TEAM CREATIVITY

Fortunately, teams can take actions to ward off the typical problems that brainstorming produces. The ten strategies outlined below all have a strong scientific research basis, are practical, and are reasonable in cost.

1. DIVERSIFY THE TEAM

Team members that have different backgrounds, training, and perspectives are naturally going to offer different categories of thought and ways of looking at a problem compared to homogenous teams. The more heterogeneous a team is, the more likely that the team will excel in all measures of creativity. Indeed, teams in which members are diverse with regard to background and perspective outperform teams with homogeneous members on tasks requiring creative problem solving and innovation.[29] Teams with heterogeneous members generate more arguments, apply a greater number of strategies, detect more novel solutions, and are better at integrating multiple perspectives than teams without conflicting perspectives. For example, IDEO design firm deliberately hires people with diverse backgrounds.

A wonderful working illustration of the diverse-team concept is in place at some microbiology labs. Dunbar undertook a massive and exhaustive study of microbiology laboratories over an extended period of time.[30] He attended all meetings and painstakingly recorded all interactions, both formal and informal, in his search for the conditions that might generate creativity. Over time, some labs distinguished themselves in terms of having more breakthrough discoveries, as evidenced by the number of patents. These successful laboratories did not have larger staff, nor were their scientists better paid or smarter. The key difference involved diversity in training within the lab groups. Lab teams that were more heterogeneous in composition were more likely to engage in divergent thinking, learned from their failures, and freely drew from other domains to address their problems.

2. ANALOGICAL REASONING

Analogical reasoning is the act of applying a concept or idea from a particular domain to another domain. The simplest analogy might be something like this: Green is to go as red is to stop. A much more complex analogy is Kepler's application of concepts from light to develop a theory of orbital motion of planets.[31] Similarly, chemist Friedrich Kekulé discovered the closed hexagonal structure of the benzene ring by imagining a snake biting its own tail. To the extent that teams can recognize when a particular known concept might be useful for solving a new problem, creativity can be enhanced. The problem is that it is not easy to transfer relevant information from one domain to another; people almost always tend to solve problems based on their surface-level similarity to other situations, rather than on their deep, or structural, similarity.

This tendency points to a serious problem with creative teamwork: People usually have the knowledge they need to solve problems, but they fail to access it because it comes from a different context. For example, when people are given the "tumor problem" (concerning how to use a ray to destroy a patient's tumor, the problem being that a ray of sufficient strength will destroy healthy tissue en route to the tumor), an elegant (but not obvious) solution involves using a series of low-intensity rays from different angles that all converge on the tumor spot as their destination.[32] Only about 10 percent of people solve this problem. Gick and Holyoak asked whether performance would improve if the participants were given an analogous problem beforehand involving a general who is trying to capture a fortress but is prevented from making a frontal attack with his entire army. An elegant (and analogous) solution is to divide the army into small groups of ground troops that each approach the fortress from a different road at the same time. Even when the tumor problem was presented immediately after the fortress problem, only 41 percent of people spontaneously transferred the "first divide and then converge" solution. In the research done in our laboratory, we have demonstrated similar lack of transfer with managers and executives.[33] Thus, applying previously learned knowledge to new situations is surprisingly difficult for most managers. This is known as the "inert knowledge" problem.

Many companies are recognizing the box-breaking potential of analogical reasoning as a way of using ideas that people have about other, seemingly unrelated things to solve pressing business problems. Alan Heeks, a Harvard MBA who worked at Procter & Gamble, uses an organic farm as a model for business life. Heeks goes so far as to run workshops at a 132-acre farm where analogies run rampant—participants think about harvesting for their future development, recycling, fertility, and sustainability. Heeks helps participants draw analogies between soil and a company's staff.[34]

The Pennsylvania Chamber of Business in downtown Harrisburg is a broad-based business association representing more than 6,500 companies in Pennsylvania that make use of the private work force. The organization chose the novel *River Horse* by William Least Heat-Moon as an analogy for the changes and transformation their organization is going through.[35] Chamber president Floyd Warner selected the book for his group to read and discuss on a regular basis.

Another use of analogy: When NASA found it necessary to design a satellite that would be tethered to a space station by a thin wire 60 miles long, designers realized that the motion of reeling in the satellite would cause it to act like a pendulum with an ever-widening arc. Stanford scientist Thomas Kane, using the analogy of a yo-yo, determined that a small electric motor on the satellite would allow it to crawl back up the tether to the space station.[36]

As another example, a manufacturer of potato chips faced a frequently encountered problem: Potato chips took up too much shelf space when they were packed loosely, but they crumbled when packed in smaller packages. The manufacturer found a solution by using a direct analogy: Dried leaves are highly similar to potato chips. They crumble very easily and they are bulky. Pressed leaves are flat. Could potato chips be shipped flat? As it turned out, they could not. However, the team realized that leaves are not pressed when they are dry but when they are moist. So, they packed potato chips in stacks, moist enough not to crumble, but dry enough to be nearly flat. The result was Pringles™.[37]

Prem Kamath, head of management resources for Hindustan Lever, described how his firm uses analogies from the movie *Tora! Tora! Tora!* to guard itself against complacency.[38] And Barry Schuler, Marriott International's senior vice president of strategy and planning for information resources, has helped to technically season Marriott's executives by speaking in analogies. Schuler, a former race car driver, sold a new network with the following analogy: "Bill Marriott, Jr. (CEO and chairman of the board) owns several exotic cars. He loves talking about cars. I tell him that the infrastructure—the hardware and system software connecting the network—[is] like the road. Then I ask him, 'Why would you want a thousand roads coming to the same place, when you can have one?' I compare our applications to trucks and cars driving on the road. And Information Resources people are the pit crew."[39] Analogical reasoning involves the application of diverse categories to a company's present problem or challenge. Another example: The D'Arcy advertising firm often holds "kidnappings" in which employees are suddenly whisked away to museums and then asked to think about a certain artist or exhibit as an analogy to their current product or service.[40]

3. BRAINWRITING

Brainwriting works like this: At various key points in time during a brainstorming session, group members will cease all talking and write down their own ideas silently.[41] Writing ideas instead of speaking them eliminates the problem of production blocking, since group members don't have to wait their turn to generate ideas. It may also reduce conformity, since the written format eliminates the need for public speaking and is typically more anonymous than oral brainstorming. The written ideas can be subsequently shared by the group in a round-robin fashion and summarized on a blackboard or flipchart. For example, investigations of brainstorming groups of four people revealed that brainwriting, followed by a round-robin exchange, eliminated production blocking and social loafing as compared to standard brainwriting.[42] I personally have employed this technique in the executive classroom and have gotten strange reactions: Managers feel uncomfortable sitting in silence; they claim that it breaks their rhythm. But the proof is in the pudding: Brainwriting groups consistently generate more and better ideas than groups who follow their natural instincts. It is worthwhile noting that even if the facilitator does not use brainwriting per se, merely taking breaks can be almost as effective. Even if group members don't write anything down, taking brief breaks can serve a function similar to brainwriting.[43] The more silences and pauses that occur, the more likely it is that a divergent cycle can be created.

4. NOMINAL GROUP TECHNIQUE

The nominal group technique, or NGT, is a variation of the standard brainwriting technique.[44] It begins with a session of brainwriting (independent writing of ideas). These ideas are subsequently shared by the group in a round-robin fashion and summarized on a blackboard. Then the group discusses the ideas for clarification and evaluation. Finally, each person rank-orders the ideas. This technique was compared with an interactive brainstorming process, and the NGT technique overwhelmingly outperformed the standard brainstorming group.[45] Also, nominal groups that perform in the same room generate more ideas than those in separate rooms.[46] One variant of the NGT is the anonymous nominal group technique. Members first write down their ideas on individual sheets of paper or note cards. The meeting facilitator (or a group member) then collects the note cards, shuffles them, and redistributes them randomly to individuals, who read the cards aloud or discuss them in small groups. This variation creates greater acceptance of others' ideas because the ideas are semi-anonymous and prevents individual members from championing only their own ideas.

Another variant of the nominal group technique is the Delphi technique. In this technique, group members do not interact in a face-to-face fashion at any point. This technique is ideally suited for groups whose members are geographically dispersed, making meetings difficult to attend, and for teams whose members experience such great conflict that it is difficult to get through a meeting. This technique requires a leader or facilitator who is trusted by team members. The entire process proceeds through questionnaires followed by feedback, which can be computerized. The leader distributes a topic or question to members and asks for responses from each team member. The leader then aggregates the responses, sends them back out to the team, and solicits feedback. This process is repeated until the issue in question is resolved.

The Delphi technique provides maximum structure, ensures equal input, and avoids production blocking; it is pretty easy to avoid coordination loss when team members never interact directly! The technique is a good alternative for teams who are physically separated but nevertheless need to make decisions. Because members respond independently, conformity pressures and evaluation apprehension are limited. One problem associated with this technique, but not associated with regular or nominal brainstorming, is that it can be quite time-consuming. "Sessions" can last several days, even weeks.

5. CREATING AN ORGANIZATIONAL MEMORY

Among the biggest drains on group performance are the repetition of ideas and the forgetting of ideas. Groups can create an organizational memory by recording ideas in full view. Group members more often waste time by repeating ideas when ideas are not physically indexed. Recording all ideas improves brainstorming sessions greatly. For example, Buckman Laboratories Inc., a manufacturer of specialty chemicals for aqueous industrial systems based in Memphis, Tennessee, connects all of its associates worldwide with a proprietary knowledge network, K'Netix.[47] Also, Sun Microsystems' Java migration team created a shared-code library, which serves as a central communication hub from which they can check out whole pieces of software codes rather than recreate them every time.[48]

6. TRAINED FACILITATORS

A trained facilitator can better follow the rules of brainstorming, help to create an organizational memory, and keep teams on track, in terms of making sure that downward norming does not occur. Indeed, trained facilitators can bring the level of team performance up to that of nominal groups.[49] Furthermore, there can be long-term benefits to this investment: Teams guided by facilitators in several sessions of productive idea generation demonstrate high levels of productivity in subsequent sessions without facilitators.[50] Facilitators can teach teams to share ideas without extensive social interaction or "filler" talk. At IDEO design firm, group leaders are used to facilitate all brainstorming sessions. According to IDEO managers, the key qualification of the facilitators is that they are "good with groups," not that they are experts in the particular product area.

7. HIGH BENCHMARKS

Brainstorming groups often underperform because they don't have relevant benchmarks. Information about other members' activity levels may increase performance as long as the benchmark is not too high.[51] Providing brainstormers with high performance standards greatly increases the number of ideas generated.[52] Even when members are working independently, announcing to others how many ideas they are generating every five minutes increases the number of ideas generated by the team.[53] Similarly, a facilitator can periodically call the attention of brainstormers to a graph on the computer screen indicating how the team's performance compares with that of other teams. This feedback significantly enhances the number of ideas generated by the group.[54] Simply forewarning teams that they will see a display of all ideas at the end of the session also increases the number of unique ideas generated.[55] It is also helpful for members to record their own ideas after the brainstorm.

8. MEMBERSHIP CHANGE

Groups do not usually remain completely intact; rather, members enter and exit most groups.[56] My colleague, Hoon-Seok Choi, and I have extensively examined small groups that remain perfectly intact (no turnover) versus groups that experience at least one membership change (holding the total number of group members constant). We find dramatic evidence that groups who experience membership change (i.e., an exit of an old member and the entry of a new member) generate more ideas (higher fluency) and more different kinds of ideas (higher flexibility) than do groups who remain intact.

Here is what we think happens: Groups that stay together without any change in membership develop a sort of cognitive arthritis; they get stuck in their same old ruts when it comes to idea generation. In contrast, groups that experience a change in membership are naturally exposed to more ideas due to greater member diversity in task-relevant skills and information. Moreover, when a group experiences a membership change, old members are in a unique position to look at themselves more thoughtfully. That is, the presence of a newcomer can motivate old-timers to revisit their task strategies and develop new and improved methods for performing group tasks.[57] At that point, we think the group is in a better position not only to think about their working style but also to learn from others. Finally, groups that experience membership change are more task-oriented than are groups that keep the same members, due to the transitory nature of interaction among members of groups whose membership changes.[58]

The stepladder technique is a variant of the membership-change technique. In this technique, members are added one by one to a team.[59] Step 1 of the technique involves the creation of a two-person subgroup (the core) that begins preliminary discussion of the group task. After a fixed time interval, another member joins the core group and presents ideas concerning the task. The three-person group then discusses the task in a preliminary manner. The process continues in steps until all members have systematically joined the core group. The complete group then arrives at a final solution. Each group member must have sufficient time to think about the problem before entering into the core group. More important, the entering members must present their preliminary solutions before hearing the core group's preliminary solutions. Self-pacing stepladder groups (which proceed through group activities at a self-determined pace) produce significantly higher quality group decisions than conventional groups.[60] Members with the best individual decisions exert more influence in stepladder groups than in free interaction groups.

9. ELECTRONIC BRAINSTORMING

Also known as EBS, electronic brainstorming makes use of computers to interact and exchange ideas. In a typical EBS session, members are seated around a table that contains individual computer stations. A large screen projects all ideas generated by members. Because members don't have to compete for floor time, production blocking is virtually eliminated. And because ideas are anonymously posted, conformity is virtually eliminated.

Mattel Media uses an interesting variation of electronic brainstorming in their team meetings. A self-proclaimed "technographer" records team members' new-product ideas on a laptop, the entries appearing before the group either on a 35-inch color monitor or on the wall. Bernie DeKoven, whose title at Mattel was "Doctor Fun/Staff Design," did not allow anyone to write, in an attempt to minimize production blocking (based on the belief that if you are writing, you are not thinking). Thus, the note-taker recorded everyone's ideas in front of the group. These ideas could be rated, evaluated, and eventually accepted or dumped. Furthermore, everyone left the meeting with a hard copy of the notes in hand, thus providing the organizational memory.

In addition, DeKoven kept a "boneyard"—a file of ideas that were rejected in the meeting. Some of those dismissed notions became valuable later on in the context of other projects. For example, when Andy Rifkin, senior vice president of creative development for Mattel Media, was touring with toy buyers, he got repeated requests for activity-based toys for boys. Picking through the boneyard of a year-old meeting, he found a Hot Wheels CD-ROM concept for designing and decorating cars and printing licenses and tickets. The Hot Wheels Custom Car Designer became a bestselling item in stores.[61]

10. BUILD A PLAYGROUND

One of the most popular approaches for stimulating creativity in the short term, as well as instilling long-term passion and motivation, is the creation of the work playground. There is no single recipe for the playground. The basic idea is to break with old ideas about what it means to be at work. In the playground, beige walls turn into tent-shaped fabric sails; "chat-zapping" elevators are replaced with conversation-instigating escalators; and the brainstorming areas (called "chill-out zones" at one office) are painted in funky Technicolor hues.[62] Most importantly, functionality guides the fun playground.

Spaces that are designed to foster creativity involve a lot of fun elements. For example, Southern California's Foote, Cone & Belding advertising agency has reinvented the traditional workspace with 156 surfboards on the walls of its boardroom, removal of all doors from offices, and the use of basketball and Italian bocce ball courts for creative brainstorming.[63] In St. Louis, employees at the D'Arcy Masius Benton & Bowles advertising agency rock climb, visit art museums, and go to the movies on company time, and executives at Aurora Foods encourage employees to write on the walls with markers and experiment with Play-Doh and Slinkies.[64]

Whereas there is little or no research on whether bocce ball courts increase creativity, a powerful body of research suggests that positive affect—whether it comes from reading a funny cartoon or seeing puppies play—increases creativity.[65] The business of space is serious enough that some companies, like Steelcase, have pioneered the workspaces of the future. "Innovation spaces," custom designed by Steelcase, have transformed the way that British Petroleum searches for oil and the way that ultra high-end fashion designer Prada sells clothes to its customers.[66]

CREATIVITY AS PART OF THE CULTURE

Teams can be much more creative than they often are. Traditional management practices—such as asking for suggestions, only one person speaking at a time, and evaluating options before exhausting them—hurt rather than facilitate creative teamwork. The ten strategies we have reviewed can be applied to a wide range of groups, from intact, long-term, intensive work teams to ad hoc groups and meetings. Table 3 summarizes the strategies and indicates the particular threat to creativity that each addresses.

TABLE 3 How the Key Strategies Deal with the Major Threats to Creative Teamwork

	Threats to Creativity			
Strategy	*Social loafing*	*Conformity*	*Production blocking*	*Downward norm setting*
Diversify the team		Diverse teams less likely to have common group norms		
Analogical reasoning		Can lead teams to think about different, nontraditional ideas		
Brainwriting	Especially helpful if the individual group members are accountable	Members are not influenced by others	Everyone can be productive at the same time	Individuals are not aware of others' performance
Nominal group technique	Individuals feel accountable	Members are not influenced by others	Everyone can be productive at the same time	Members less inclined to adjust performance
Creating organizational memory			Group members less likely to repeat ideas	
Trained facilitators	Trained facilitator can keep motivation high	Trained facilitator can use strategies to avoid conformity	Trained facilitator can use strategies to avoid production blocking	
High benchmarks	Clear and high goals reduce loafing			Each member will be reminded of benchmark, which serves as key goal
Membership change	Individuals may be less likely to loaf when newcomers are present	Group norms may be more scrutinized (less conformity)		Teams have exposure to different and potentially higher benchmarks
Electronic brainstorming		Removal of group pressure because of greater (perceived) anonymity	Everyone can be productive at the same time	
Create a playground	If people are motivated and intrigued, they are less likely to loaf	Non-conformist spaces lead to non-conformist behavior		

Creative teamwork is not only good for the bottom line; it can also be an intensely rewarding experience. The paradox is that most of our instincts about creativity are wrong. Tapping into ideas that are creatively realistic requires that companies support teams that do seemingly purposeless and senseless things, such as striving for quantity rather than quality (at least initially), suggesting deliberately impossible-to-realize ideas, and creating havens for individual thinking. Groups and teams can click creatively, but the four threats to creativity—social loafing, conformity, production blocking, and downward norm setting—can kill a naïve attempt at creativity. The ten strategies for enhancing creativity do not carry high price tags; the main challenge will be to make them part of the creative team's culture.

Endnotes

1. See Frank, R. H., and Cook, P. J. 1996. *The Winner-Take-All Society: Why the Few at the Top Get So Much More Than the Rest of Us* (Reprint edition). New York: Penguin.
2. See Brandenburger, A. M., and Nalebuff, B. J. 1996. *Co-opetition*. New York: Doubleday.
3. See Guilford, J. P. 1950. Creativity. *American Psychologist*, 5: 444–454.
4. See Finke, R. A. 1995. Creative realism. In S. M. Smith, T. B. Ward, and R. A. Finke (Eds.), *The Creative Cognition Approach*: 303–326. Cambridge, MA: MIT Press.
5. Contrary to popular belief, Edison's idea was not out of the blue. His lighting system was an extension of current lighting systems. For a description of how he developed the ideas, see Basalla. G. 1988. *The Evolution of Technology*. New York: Cambridge University Press. Also Weisberg, R. W. 1997. "Case Studies of Creative Thinking," in S. M. Smith, T. B. Ward, and R. A. Finke (Eds.), *The Creative Cognition Approach*: 53–72. Cambridge, MA: MIT Press.
6. See Guilford, J. P. 1959. *Personality*. New York: McGraw-Hill; also Guilford, J. P., 1967. *The Nature of Human Intelligence*. New York: McGraw-Hill.
7. Ibid.
8. One of the most often overlooked contributions of Osborn's pioneering work on brainstorming is his intuition about the positive relationship between quantity and quality. Osborn correctly noted that demands for "great ideas" will often stifle the creative process. However, it is easy for people to strive for quantity. The probability of having one truly excellent idea can be directly predicted from the number of ideas generated. Moreover, the likelihood of building and integrating ideas can be facilitated with quantity as well.
9. This example was suggested by Professor Terri Kurtzberg, whose dissertation focuses on creativity. She has extensively used the cardboard box task.
10. See Verberne, T. "Creative Fitness," *Training and Development*, 1 August 1997: 68–71.
11. See Camm, M. "Learn How to Clap with One Hand," *Sydney Morning Herald* (Sydney), 24 March 1994: 15.
12. See Osborn, A. F. 1957. *Applied Imagination* (rev. ed.). New York: Scribner.
13. See Gendron, G. "FYI: Growing by Design," *Inc.*, May 1998: 9.
14. Meta-analytic reviews of brainstorming provide compelling data on how individuals outperform groups. A strong example is Mullen, B., Johnson, C., and Salas, E. 1991. "Productivity Loss in Brainstorming Groups: A Meta-Analytic Integration," *Basic and Applied Social Psychology*, 12(1): 3–23. Other papers that address this apparent enigma include Diehl, M., and Stroebe, W. 1987. "Productivity Loss in Brainstorming Groups: Toward a Solution of a Riddle," *Journal of Personality and Social Psychology*, 53(3): 497–509; also Paulus, P. B., and Dzindolet, M. T. 1993. "Social Influence Processes in Group Brainstorming," *Journal of Personality and Social Psychology*, 64(4): 575–586; Jablin, F. M. 1981. "Cultivating Imagination: Factors That Enhance and Inhibit Creativity in Brainstorming Groups," *Human Communication Research*, 7(3): 245–258;

Paulus, P. B., Larey, T. S., and Ortega, A. H. 1995. "Performance and Perceptions of Brainstormers in an Organizational Setting," *Basic and Applied Social Psychology*, 17(1–2): 249–265; and Taylor, D. W., Berry, P. C., and Block, C. H. 1958. "Does Group Participation When Using Brainstorming Facilitate or Inhibit Creative Thinking?" *Administrative Science Quarterly*, 3: 23–47.

15. See Mullen, Johnson, & Salas, op. cit., 18.
16. Several scholars who have worked directly with teams in companies report that most companies claim to use brainstorming. However, the question of whether it is used effectively is a matter of debate. For examples of how companies use brainstorming, see Hackman, J. R. 1990. "Work Teams in Organizations: An Oriented Framework," in J. Hackman (Ed.), *Groups That Work and Those That Don't*. San Francisco: Jossey-Bass; also Sutton, R. I., and Hargadon, A. 1996. "Brainstorming Groups in Context: Effectiveness in a Product Design Firm," *Administrative Science Quarterly*, 41(4): 685–718; Swezey, R. W., and Salas, E. (Eds.) 1992. *Teams: Their Training and Performance*. Norwood, NJ: Ablex Publishing Corp.; and Woodman, R. W., Sawyer, J. E., and Griffin, R. W. 1993. "Toward a Theory of Organizational Creativity," *Academy of Management Review*, 18(2): 293–321.
17. A large research literature has examined several factors that might mitigate the powerful social loafing effect. For examples of these methods, see Bouchard. T. J. 1972. "Training, Motivation, and Personality as Determinants of the Effectiveness of Brainstorming Groups and Individuals," *Journal of Applied Psychology*, 56(4): 324–331; also Diehl and Stroebe, op. cit.; Harkins, S. G., and Petty. R. E. 1982. "Effects of Task Difficulty and Task Uniqueness on Social Loafing," *Journal of Personality and Social Psychology*, 43(6): 1214–1229; and Shepperd, J. A. 1993. "Productivity Loss in Performance Groups: A Motivation Analysis," *Psychological Bulletin*, 113(1): 67–81.
18. See Csikszentmihaly, M. 1997. *Finding Flow: The Psychology of Engagement with Everyday Life*. New York: Basicbooks.
19. See Tajfel's work on social identity theory; specifically: Tajfel, H. 1978. *Differentiation Between Social Groups: Studies in the Social Psychology of Intergroup Relations*. New York: Academic Press.
20. See Camacho, L. M., and Paulus, P. B. 1995. "The Role of Social Anxiousness in Group brainstorming," *Journal of Personality and Social Psychology*, 68(6): 1071–1080.
21. See Higgins, J. 1994. "Creating Creativity," *Training and Development*, 48(11): 11–15.
22. People pay attention to status cues in a group and, as a general principle, lower-status members conform to what they perceive to be the views of high-status members. For examinations of the conformity effect, see Collaros. P. A., and Anderson, L. R. 1969. "Effect of Perceived Expertness Upon Creativity of Members of Brainstorming Groups," *Journal of Applied Psychology*, 53(2, Pt. 1): 159–163; also Diehl and Stroebe, op. cit.; and Harari, O., and Graham, W. K. 1975. "Tasks and Task Consequences as Factors in Individual and Group Brainstorming," *Journal of Social Psychology*, 95(1): 61–65.
23. Production blocking refers to both the difficulty in speaking and processing information simultaneously as well as the difficulty in several people competing for the floor. Diehl and Stroebe, op. cit., offer a direct examination of production blocking; see also Diehl, M., and Stroebe, W. 1991. "Productivity Loss in Idea-Generating Groups: Tracking Down the Blocking Effect," *Journal of Personality and Social Psychology*, 61(3): 392–403; and Stroebe, W., and Diehl, M. 1994. "Why Are Groups Less Effective Than Their members? On Productivity Losses in Idea Generating Groups," *European Review of Social Psychology*, 5: 271–301.
24. This observation was shared by a high-level manager in the company.
25. See Camacho and Paulus, op. cit.; and Paulus and Dzindolet, op. cit.
26. See Shepperd, op. cit.
27. See Camacho and Paulus, op. cit.; Paulus and Dzindolet, op. cit.
28. See Stroebe, W., Diehl, M., and Abakoumkin, G. 1992. "The Illusion of Group Effectivity," *Personality and Social Psychology Bulletin*, 18(5): 643–650.
29. See Jackson, S. E. 1992. "Team Composition in Organizational Settings: Issues in Managing

an Increasingly Diverse Workforce," in S. Worchel, W. Wood, & J. A. Simpson (Eds.), *Group process and Productivity*: 138–173. Newbury Park: Sage.

30. See Dunbar. K. 1997. "How Scientists Think: Online Creativity and Conceptual Change in Science," in T. B. Ward, S. M. Smith, and J. Vaid (Eds.), *Creative Thought: An Investigation of Conceptual Structures and Processes*: 461–493. Washington, D.C.: American Psychological Association.
31. See Gentner, D., Brem, S., Ferguson, R., and Wolff, P. 1997. "Analogy and Creativity in the Works of Johannes Kepler," in T. B. Ward and S. M. Smith (Eds.), *Creative Thought: An Investigation of Conceptual Structures and Processes:* 403–459. Washington, DC: American Psychological Association.
32. This example, first experimentally used by Gick and Holyoak in 1980, points to the vexing problem concerning the general inability of people to transfer knowledge learned in one domain to another.
33. See Thompson, L., Loewenstein, J., and Gentner, D. 2000. "Avoiding Missed Opportunities in Managerial Life: "Analogical Training More Powerful Than Individual Case Training," *Organizational Behavior and Human Decision Processes*, 82(1): 60–75. This paper provides data from managers indicating that analogical reasoning is more powerful than the simple case method. Another article by Loewenstein and Thompson provides our view on how managers should be taught; see Loewenstein, J., and Thompson, L. 2000. "The Challenge of Learning," *Negotiation Journal*, October: 399–408.
34. See Cox, A. "Where There's Muck There's Brass: Can a Few Days on the Farm Really Improve Your Performance at Work?" *The Guardian* (London), 2 August 2000.
35. See Jaffe, A. Chamber gleans words of wisdom from novel's plot. *The Sunday Patriot News* (Harrisburg, PA), November 2000, D01.
36. See Higgins, op. cit.
37. Ibid.
38. See *The Economic Times*. The Human Touch. 7 November 2000.
39. See Radcliff, D. Marriott: "Want to See the Benefits of IT and Business Alignment?" *Computer World*, 10 April 2000, 58.
40. See Lee, T. "Get Those Creative Juices Flowing," Business Plus section. *St. Louis Post-Dispatch*, 7 January 2002, 8B.
41. Brainwriting has proved to be an effective technique in enhancing the performance of real groups. For direct, empirical examinations, see Geschka, H., Schaude, G. R., and Schlicksupp, H. 1973. "Modern Techniques for Solving Problems," *Chemical Engineering*, August: 91–97; also Paulus, P. B., and Yang, H. 2000. "Idea Generation in Groups: A Basis for Creativity in Organizations," *Organizational Behavior and Human Decision Processes*, 82(1): 76–87.
42. See Paulus and Yang, op. cit.
43. See Horn, E. M. 1993. "The Influence of Modality Order and Break Period on a Brainstorming Task." Honors thesis. University of Texas at Arlington.
44. See Van de Ven, A. H., and Delbecq. A. L. 1974. "The Effectiveness of Nominal, Delphi, and Interacting Group Decision Making Processes," *Academy of Management Journal*, 17(4): 605–621.
45. For a clear demonstration of how NGT is more effective than traditional brainstorming, see Gustafson, D. H., Shukla, R., Delbecq, A., and Walster, W. 1973. "A Comparative Study in Subjective Likelihood Estimates made by Individuals, Interacting Groups, Delphi Groups, and Nominal Groups," *Organizational Behavior and Human Performance*, 9(2): 280–291.
46. See Mullen, Johnson, and Salas, op. cit.
47. See Wah, L. "Making Knowledge Stick," *Management Review*, 1 May 1999, 24–29.
48. Ibid.
49. Trained facilitators are able to address many of the process-loss problems encountered by brainstorming groups. For studies that have empirically examined the effectiveness of trained facilitators, see Offner, A. K., Kramer, T. J., and Winter, J. P. 1996. "The Effects of Facilitation, Recording, and Pauses on Group Brainstorming," *Small Group Research*, 27(2): 283–298; also Oxley, N. L., Dzindolet, M. T., and Paulus, P. B. 1996. "The Effects of Facilitators on the Performance of Brainstorming Groups," *Journal of Social Behavior and Personality*, 11(4): 633–646.

50. See Paulus, P. B., Putman, V. L., Coskun, H., Leggett, K. L., and Roland, E. J. 1996. "Training Groups for Effective Brainstorming." Paper presented at the Fourth Annual Advanced Concepts Conference on Work Teams—Team Implementation Issues, Dallas, TX.
51. See Seta, J. J. 1982. "The Impact of Comparison Processes on Co-actors' Task Performance," *Journal of Personality and Social Psychology*, 42(2): 281–291.
52. See Paulus and Dzindolet, op. cit.
53. See Paulus, P. B., Larey, T. S., Putman, V. L., Leggett, K. L., and Roland, E. J. 1996. "Social Influence Processes in Computer Brainstorming," *Basic and Applied Social Psychology*, 18(1): 3–14.
54. See Shepherd, M. M., Briggs, R. O., Reinig, B. A., Yen, J., and Nunamaker, J. F. Jr. 1995–1996. "Invoking Social Comparison to Improve Electronic Brainstorming: Beyond Anonymity," *Journal of Management Information Systems*, 12(3): 155–170.
55. See Roy, M. C., Gauvin, S., and Limayem, M. 1996. "Electronic Group Brainstorming: The Role of Feedback on Productivity," *Small Group Research*, 27(2): 215–247.
56. This is based on research by Hoon-Seok Choi and myself conducted over the past year. A paper that reviews our research can be obtained from either myself or Professor Hoon-Seok Choi, Management & Organizations Department, Kellogg School of Management, Northwestern University, Evanston, IL 60208.
57. See Sutton, R. L., and Louis, M. R. 1987. "How Selecting and Socializing Newcomers Influences Insiders," *Human Resource Management*, 26(3): 347–361.
58. See Ziller, R. C. 1965. "Toward a Theory of Open and Closed Groups," *Psychological Bulletin*, 64(3): 164–182.
59. See Rogelberg, S. G., Barnes-Farrell, J. L., and Lowe, C. A. 1992. "The Stepladder Technique: An Alternative Group Structure Facilitating Effective Group Decision Making," *Journal of Applied Psychology*, 77(5): 730–737.
60. See Rogelberg, S. G., and O'Connor, M. S. 1998. "Extending the Stepladder Technique: An Examination of Self-Paced Stepladder Groups," *Group Dynamics: Theory, Research, and Practice*, 2(2): 82–91.
61. See Grossmann, J. "We've Got to Start Meeting Like This," *Inc.*, 1 April 1998.
62. See Long, S. "This CEO Handles Complaints Himself," *The Straits Times*, 12 April 2002.
63. See *P. R. Newswire*, "Surfboards in the BoardRoom and Bocce Ball Out Back," 25 September 2001.
64. See Lee, op. cit.
65. For an extensive review of the effects of positive affect on creativity, see Isen, A. M., Daubman, K. A., and Nowicki, G. P. 1987. "Positive Affect Facilitates Creative Problem Solving," *Journal of Personality and Social Psychology*, 52(6): 1122–1131.
66. For a look at how the fashion company Prada is rethinking creativity, see Brown, J. "Prada Gets Personal," *BusinessWeek*, 18 March 2002, EB8. For an in-depth treatment of how BP is searching for oil in the depths of the sea, see Verrengia, J. B. "Finding Footprints Under Arctic Ice," *Associated Press*, 8 April 2002, via www.msnbc.com.

CHAPTER 13
CONFLICT AND NEGOTIATION

Learning to manage conflict, an essential skill for both managers and employees, can be a challenging and sometimes uncomfortable process. The negative results of poorly managed conflict are readily observed in many organizations. When there is too much conflict, we find people consumed by negative feelings who fail to perceive common goals they may share with their adversaries. Valuable time, energy, and resources are devoted to competitive actions and counteractions that simply escalate the hostilities. The absence of conflict, however, is not the answer. A recurring theme in organizational behavior, as evidenced in this book, is the benefit of surfacing and listening to diverse opinions. Fighting for ideas in a constructive manner creates a healthy, moderate level of conflict that is far preferable to either too much or too little conflict.

One characteristic of effective teams is the ability to challenge ideas and disagree constructively. In the first article, Kathleen Eisenhardt, Jean Kahwajy, and L. J. Bourgeois III, business professors, focus on constructive conflict in teams. Their decade-long research program on the relationship among conflict, politics, and speed in strategic decision making in top-management teams made it possible for them to follow and observe several teams in action. In "How Management Teams Can Have a Good Fight," they contrast teams in which conflict produced healthy disagreement with teams in which conflict ended up in interpersonal hostility. The outcome is six tactics teams can use for managing interpersonal conflict.

The second article also includes lessons that can be learned from contrasting effective and ineffective practice. In "World-Class Negotiating Strategies," Frank Acuff explains how highly skilled negotiators differ from average negotiators. This chapter from Acuff's book, *How to Negotiate with Anyone from Anywhere*, draws primarily on his extensive experience and observations as an international businessman and negotiator. Acuff relates anecdotes from all over the world and spells out numerous practical tips on negotiating and getting along with people from other cultures.

HOW MANAGEMENT TEAMS CAN HAVE A GOOD FIGHT*

Kathleen M. Eisenhardt
Jean L. Kahwajy
L. J. Bourgeois III

Top managers are often stymied by the difficulties of managing conflict. They know that conflict over issues is natural and even necessary. Reasonable people, making decisions under conditions of uncertainty, are likely to have honest disagreements over the best path for their company's future. Management teams whose members challenge one another's thinking develop a more complete understanding of the choices, create a richer range of options, and ultimately make the kinds of effective decisions necessary in today's competitive environments.

But, unfortunately, healthy conflict can quickly turn unproductive. A comment meant as a substantive remark can be interpreted as a personal attack. Anxiety and frustration over difficult choices can evolve into anger directed at colleagues. Personalities frequently become intertwined with issues. Because most executives pride themselves on being rational decision makers, they find it difficult even to acknowledge—let alone manage—this emotional, irrational dimension of their behavior.

The challenge—familiar to anyone who has ever been part of a management team—is to keep constructive conflict over issues from degenerating into dysfunctional interpersonal conflict, to encourage managers to argue without destroying their ability to work as a team.

We have been researching the interplay of conflict, politics, and speed in strategic decision making by top-management teams for the past 10 years. In one study, we had the opportunity to observe closely the work of a dozen top-management teams in technology-based companies. All the companies competed in fast changing, competitive global markets. Thus all the teams had to make high-stakes decisions in the face of considerable uncertainty and under pressure to move quickly. Each team consisted of between five and nine executives; we were allowed to question them individually and also to observe their interactions firsthand as we tracked specific strategic decisions in the making. The study's design gives us a window on conflict as top-management teams actually experience it and highlights the role of emotion in business decision making.

In 4 of the 12 companies, there was little or no substantive disagreement over major issues and therefore little conflict to observe. But the other 8 companies experienced considerable conflict. In 4 of them, the top-management teams handled conflict in a way that avoided interpersonal hostility or discord. We've called those companies Bravo Microsystems, Premier Technologies, Star Electronics, and Triumph Computers. Executives in those companies referred to their colleagues as *smart, team player*, and *best in the business.* They described the way they work as a team as *open, fun*, and *productive.* The executives vigorously debated the issues, but they wasted little time on politicking and posturing. As one put it, "I really don't have time." Another said, "We don't gloss over the issues; we hit them straight on. But we're not political." Still

*Reprinted with permission from *Harvard Business Review* (July–August 1997): 77–85.

another observed of her company's management team, "We scream a lot, then laugh, and then resolve the issue."

The other four companies in which issues were contested were less successful at avoiding interpersonal conflict. We've called those companies Andromeda Processing, Mega Software, Mercury Microdevices, and Solo Systems. Their top teams were plagued by intense animosity. Executives often failed to cooperate, rarely talking with one another, tending to fragment into cliques, and openly displaying their frustration and anger. When executives described their colleagues to us, they used words such as *manipulative, secretive, burned out*, and *political.*

The teams with minimal interpersonal conflict were able to separate substantive issues from those based on personalities. They managed to disagree over questions of strategic significance and still get along with one another. How did they do that? After analyzing our observations of the teams' behavior, we found that their companies used the same six tactics for managing interpersonal conflict. Team members:

- worked with more, rather than less, information and debated on the basis of facts;
- developed multiple alternatives to enrich the level of debate;
- shared commonly agreed-upon goals;
- injected humor into the decision process;
- maintained a balanced power structure; and
- resolved issues without forcing consensus.

Those tactics were usually more implicit than explicit in the decision-making work of the management teams, and if the tactics were given names, the names varied from one organization to the next. Nonetheless, the consistency with which all four companies employed all six tactics is testimony to their effectiveness. Perhaps most surprising was the fact that the tactics did not delay—and often accelerated—the pace at which the teams were able to make decisions.

FOCUS ON THE FACTS

Some managers believe that working with too much data will increase interpersonal conflict by expanding the range of issues for debate. We found that more information is better—if the data are objective and up-to-date—because it encourages people to focus on issues, not personalities. At Star Electronics, for example, the members of the top-management team typically examined a wide variety of operating measures on a monthly, weekly, and even daily basis. They claimed to "measure everything." In particular, every week they fixed their attention on indicators such as bookings, backlogs, margins, engineering milestones, cash, scrap, and work-in-process. Every month, they reviewed an even more comprehensive set of measures that gave them extensive knowledge of what was actually happening in the corporation. As one executive noted, "We have very strong controls."

Star's team also relied on facts about the external environment. One senior executive was charged with tracking such moves by competitors as product introductions, price changes, and ad campaigns. A second followed the latest technical developments through his network of contacts in universities and other companies. "We over-M.B.A. it," said the CEO, characterizing Star's zealous pursuit of data. Armed with the facts, Star's executives had an extraordinary grasp of the details of their business, allowing them to focus debate on critical issues and avoid useless arguments rooted in ignorance.

At Triumph Computer, we found a similar dedication to current facts. The first person the new CEO hired was an individual to track the progress of engineering-development projects, the new-product lifeblood of the company. Such knowledge allowed the top-management team to work from a common base of facts.

In the absence of good data, executives waste time in pointless debate over opinions. Some resort to self-aggrandizement and ill-formed guesses about how the world might be. People—and not issues—become the focus of disagreement. The result is interpersonal conflict. In such companies, top managers are often poorly informed both about internal operations, such as bookings and engineering milestones, and about external issues, such as competing products. They collect data narrowly and infrequently. In these companies, the vice presidents of finance, who oversee internal data collection, are usually weak. They were often described by people in the companies we studied as "inexperienced" or "detached." In contrast, the vice president of finance at Premier Technologies, a company with little interpersonal conflict, was described as being central to taking "the constant pulse of how the firm is doing."

Management teams troubled by interpersonal conflict rely more on hunches and guesses than on current data. When they consider facts, they are more likely to examine a past measure, such as profitability, which is both historical and highly refined. These teams favor planning based on extrapolation and intuitive attempts to predict the future, neither of which yields current or factual results. Their conversations are more subjective. The CEO of one of the four high-conflict teams told us his interest in operating numbers was "minimal," and he described his goals as "subjective." At another such company, senior managers saw the CEO as "visionary" and "a little detached from the day-to-day operations." Compare those executives with the CEO of Bravo Microsystems, who had a reputation for being a "pragmatic numbers guy."

There is a direct link between reliance on facts and low levels of interpersonal conflict. Facts let people move quickly to the central issues surrounding a strategic choice. Decision makers don't become bogged down in arguments over what the facts *might* be. More important, reliance on current data grounds strategic discussions in reality. Facts (such as current sales, market share, R&D expenses, competitors' behavior, and manufacturing yields) depersonalize the discussion because they are not someone's fantasies, guesses, or self-serving desires. In the absence of facts, individuals' motives are likely to become suspect. Building decisions on facts creates a culture that emphasizes issues instead of personalities.

MULTIPLY THE ALTERNATIVES

Some managers believe that they can reduce conflict by focusing on only one or two alternatives, thus minimizing the dimensions over which people can disagree. But, in fact, teams with low incidences of interpersonal conflict do just the opposite. They deliberately develop multiple alternatives, often considering four or five options at once. To promote debate, managers will even introduce options they do not support.

For example, Triumph's new CEO was determined to improve the company's lackluster performance. When he arrived, new products were stuck in development, and investors were getting anxious. He launched a fact-gathering exercise and asked senior executives to develop alternatives. In less than two months, they developed four. The first was to sell some of the company's technology. The second was to undertake a major strategic redirection, using the base technology to enter a new market. The third was to redeploy engineering resources and adjust the marketing approach. The final option was to sell the company.

Working together to shape those options enhanced the group's sense of teamwork while promoting a more creative view of Triumph's competitive situation and its technical competencies. As a result, the team ended up combining elements of several options in a way that was more robust than any of the options were individually.

The other teams we observed with low levels of interpersonal conflict also tended to develop multiple options to make major decisions. Star, for example, faced a cash flow crisis caused by explosive growth. Its executives considered, among other choices, arranging for lines of credit from banks, selling additional stock, and forming strategic alliances with several partners. At Bravo, managers explicitly relied on three kinds of alternatives: sincere proposals that the proponent actually backed; support for someone else's proposal, even if only for the sake of argument; and insincere alternatives proposed just to expand the number of options.

There are several reasons why considering multiple alternatives may lower interpersonal conflict. For one, it diffuses conflict: Choices become less black and white, and individuals gain more room to vary the degree of their support over a range of choices. Managers can more easily shift positions without losing face.

Generating options is also a way to bring managers together in a common and inherently stimulating task. It concentrates their energy on solving problems, and it increases the likelihood of obtaining integrative solutions—alternatives that incorporate the views of a greater number of the decision makers. In generating multiple alternatives, managers do not stop at obvious solutions; rather, they continue generating further—usually more original—options. The process in itself is creative and fun, setting a positive tone for substantive, instead of interpersonal, conflict.

By contrast, in teams that vigorously debate just one or two options, conflict often does turn personal. At Solo Systems, for instance, the top-management team considered entering a new business area as a way to boost the company's performance. They debated this alternative versus the status quo but failed to consider other options. Individual executives became increasingly entrenched on one side of the debate or the other. As positions hardened, the conflict became more pointed and personal. The animosity grew so great that a major proponent of change quit the company in disgust while the rest of the team either disengaged or slipped into intense and dysfunctional politicking.

CREATE COMMON GOALS

A third tactic for minimizing destructive conflict involves framing strategic choices as collaborative, rather than competitive, exercises. Elements of collaboration and competition coexist within any management team: executives share a stake in the company's performance, yet their personal ambitions may make them rivals for power. The successful groups we studied consistently framed their decisions as collaborations in which it was in everyone's interest to achieve the best possible solution for the collective.

They did so by creating a common goal around which the team could rally. Such goals do not imply homogeneous thinking, but they do require everyone to share a vision. As Steve Jobs, who is associated with three high-profile Silicon Valley companies—Apple, NeXT, and Pixar—has advised, "It's okay to spend a lot of time arguing about which route to take to San Francisco when everyone wants to end up there, but a lot of time gets wasted in such arguments if one person wants to go to San Francisco and another secretly wants to go to San Diego."

Teams hobbled by conflict lack common goals. Team members perceive themselves to be in competition with one another and, surprisingly, tend to frame decisions negatively, as reactions to threats. At Andromeda Processing, for instance, the team focused on responding to a particular instance of poor performance, and team members tried to pin the blame on one another. That negative framing contrasts with the positive approach taken by Star Electronics executives, who, sharing a common goal, viewed a cash crisis not as a threat but as an opportunity to "build the biggest war chest" for an impending competitive battle. At a broad level, Star's executives shared the goal of creating "the computer firm of the decade." As one Star executive told us, "We take a corporate, not a functional, viewpoint most of the time."

Likewise, all the management team members we interviewed at Premier Technologies agreed that their common goal—their rallying cry—was to build "the best damn machine on the market." Thus in their debates they could disagree about critical technical alternatives—in-house versus offshore manufacturing options, for example, or alternative distribution channels—without letting the conflict turn personal.

Many studies of group decision making and intergroup conflict demonstrate that common goals build team cohesion by stressing the shared interest of all team members in the outcome of the debate. When team members are working toward a common goal, they are less likely to see themselves as individual winners and losers and are far more likely to perceive the opinions of others correctly and to learn from them. We observed that when executives lacked common goals, they tended to be closed-minded and more likely to misinterpret and blame one another.

USE HUMOR

Teams that handle conflict well make explicit—and often even contrived—attempts to relieve tension and at the same time promote a collaborative esprit by making their business fun. They emphasize the excitement of fast-paced competition, not the stress of competing in brutally tough and uncertain markets.

All the teams with low interpersonal conflict described ways in which they used humor on the job. Executives at Bravo Microsystems enjoyed playing gags around the office. For example, pink plastic flamingos—souvenirs from a customer—graced Bravo's otherwise impeccably decorated headquarters. Similarly, Triumph Computers' top managers held a monthly "dessert pig-out," followed by group weight watching. Those seemingly trivial activities were part of the CEO's deliberate plan to make work more fun, despite the pressures of the industry. At Star Electronics, making the company "a fun place" was an explicit goal for the top-management team. Laughter was common during management meetings. Practical jokes were popular at Star, where executives—along with other employees—always celebrated Halloween and April Fools' Day.

At each of these companies, executives acknowledged that at least some of the attempts at humor were contrived—even forced. Even so, they helped to release tension and promote collaboration.

Humor was strikingly absent in the teams marked by high interpersonal conflict. Although pairs of individuals were sometimes friends, team members shared no group social activities beyond a standard holiday party or two, and there were no conscious attempts to create humor. Indeed, the climate in which decisions were made was often just the opposite—hostile and stressful.

Humor works as a defense mechanism to protect people from the stressful and threatening situations that commonly arise in the course of making strategic decisions. It helps people distance themselves psychologically by putting those situations into a broader life context, often through the use of irony. Humor—with its ambiguity—can also blunt the threatening edge of negative information. Speakers can say in jest things that might otherwise give offense because the message is simultaneously serious and not serious. The recipient is allowed to save face by receiving the serious message while appearing not to do so. The result is communication of difficult information in a more tactful and less personally threatening way.

Humor can also move decision making into a collaborative rather than competitive frame through its powerful effect on mood. According to a large body of research, people in a positive mood tend to be not only more optimistic but also more forgiving of others and creative in seeking solutions. A positive mood triggers a more accurate perception of others' arguments because people in a good mood tend to relax their defensive barriers and so can listen more effectively.

How Teams Argue but Still Get Along

Tactic	*Strategy*
Base discussion on current, factual information Develop multiple alternatives to enrich the debate	Focus on issues, not personalities
Rally around goals Inject humor into the decision-making process	Frame decisions as collaborations aimed at achieving the best possible solution for the company
Maintain balanced power structure Resolve issues without forcing consensus	Establish a sense of fairness and equity in the process

BALANCE THE POWER STRUCTURE

We found that managers who believe that their team's decision-making process is fair are more likely to accept decisions without resentment, even when they do not agree with them. But when they believe the process is unfair, ill will easily grows into interpersonal conflict. A fifth tactic for taming interpersonal conflict, then, is to create a sense of fairness by balancing power within the management team.

Our research suggests that autocratic leaders who manage through highly centralized power structures often generate high levels of interpersonal friction. At the other extreme, weak leaders also engender interpersonal conflict because the power vacuum at the top encourages managers to jockey for position. Interpersonal conflict is lowest in what we call *balanced power structures*, those in which the CEO is more powerful than the other members of the top-management team, but the members do wield substantial power, especially in their own well-defined areas of responsibility. In balanced power structures, all executives participate in strategic decisions.

At Premier Technologies, for example, the CEO—described by others as a "team player"—was definitely the most powerful figure. But each executive was the most powerful decision maker in some clearly defined area. In addition, the entire team participated in all significant decisions. The CEO, one executive observed, "depends on picking good people and letting them operate."

The CEO of Bravo Microsystems, another company with a balanced power structure, summarized his philosophy as "making quick decisions involving as many people as possible." We watched the Bravo team over several months as it grappled with a major strategic redirection. After many group discussions, the final decision was made at a multiday retreat involving the whole team.

In contrast, the leaders of the teams marked by extensive interpersonal conflict were either highly autocratic or weak. The CEO at Mercury Microdevices, for example, was the principal decision maker. There was a substantial gap in power between him and the rest of the team. In the decision we tracked, the CEO dominated the process from start to finish, identifying the problem, defining the analysis, and making the choice. Team members described the CEO as "strong" and "dogmatic." As one of them put it, "When Bruce makes a decision, it's like God!"

At Andromeda, the CEO exercised only modest power, and areas of responsibility were blurred within the top-management team, where power was diffuse and ambiguous. Senior executives had to politick amongst themselves to get anything accomplished, and they reported intense frustration with the confusion that existed at the top.

Most executives expected to control some significant aspect of their business but not the entirety. When they lacked power—because of either an autocrat or a power vacuum—they became frustrated by their inability to make significant decisions. Instead of team members, they became politicians. As one executive explained, "We're all jockeying for our spot in the pecking order." Another described "maneuvering for the CEO's ear."

The situations we observed are consistent with classic social-psychology studies of leadership. For example, in a study from the 1960s, Ralph White and Ronald Lippitt examined the effects of different leadership styles on boys in social clubs. They found that boys with democratic leaders—the situation closest to our balanced power structure—showed spontaneous interest in their activities. The boys were highly satisfied, and within their groups there were many friendly remarks, much praise, and significant collaboration. Under weak leaders, the boys were disorganized, inefficient, and dissatisfied. But the worst case was autocratic rule, under which the boys were hostile and aggressive, occasionally directing physical violence against innocent scapegoats. In imbalanced power situations, we observed adult displays of verbal aggression that colleagues described as violent. One executive talked about being "caught in the cross fire." Another described a colleague as "a gun about to go off." A third spoke about "being beat up" by the CEO.

SEEK CONSENSUS WITH QUALIFICATION

Balancing power is one tactic for building a sense of fairness. Finding an appropriate way to resolve conflict over issues is another—and, perhaps, the more crucial. In our research, the teams that managed conflict effectively all used the same approach to resolving substantive conflict. It is a two-step process that some executives call *consensus with qualification.* It works like this: executives talk over an issue and try to reach consensus. If they can, the decision is made. If they can't, the most relevant senior manager makes the decision, guided by input from the rest of the group.

When a competitor launched a new product attacking Premier Technologies in its biggest market, for example, there was sharp disagreement about how to respond. Some executives wanted to shift R&D resources to counter this competitive move, even at the risk of diverting engineering talent from a more innovative product then in design. Others argued that Premier should simply repackage an existing product, adding a few novel features. A third group felt that the threat was not serious enough to warrant a major response.

After a series of meetings over several weeks, the group failed to reach consensus. So the CEO and his marketing vice president made the decision. As the CEO explained, "The functional heads do the talking. I pull the trigger." Premier's executives were comfortable with this arrangement—even those who did not agree with the outcome—because everyone had had a voice in the process.

People usually associate consensus with harmony, but we found the opposite: teams that insisted on resolving substantive conflict by forcing consensus tended to display the most interpersonal conflict. Executives sometimes have the unrealistic view that consensus is always possible, but such a naive insistence on consensus can lead to endless haggling. As the vice president of engineering at Mega Software put it, "Consensus means that everyone has veto power. Our products were too late, and they were too expensive." At Andromeda, the CEO wanted his executives to reach consensus, but persistent differences of opinion remained. The debate dragged on for months, and the frustration mounted until some top managers simply gave up. They just wanted a decision, any decision. One was finally made when several executives who favored one point of view left the company. The price of consensus was a decimated team.

In a team that insists on consensus, deadlines can cause executives to sacrifice fairness and thus weaken the team's support for the final decision. At Andromeda, executives spent months analyzing their industry and developing a shared perspective on important trends for the future, but they could never focus on making the decision. The decision-making process dragged on. Finally, as the deadline of a board meeting drew imminent, the CEO formulated and announced a choice—one that had never even been mentioned in the earlier discussions. Not surprisingly, his team was angry and upset. Had he been less insistent on reaching a consensus, the CEO would not have felt forced by the deadline to act so arbitrarily.

BUILDING A FIGHTING TEAM

How can managers encourage the kind of substantive debate over issues that leads to better decision making? We found five approaches that help generate constructive disagreement within a team:

1. ***Assemble a heterogeneous team, including diverse ages, genders, functional backgrounds, and industry experience.*** If everyone in the executive meetings looks alike and sounds alike, then the chances are excellent that they probably think alike, too.
2. ***Meet together as a team regularly and often.*** Team members that don't know one another well don't know one another's positions on issues, impairing their ability to argue effectively. Frequent interaction builds the mutual confidence and familiarity team members require to express dissent.
3. ***Encourage team members to assume roles beyond their obvious product, geographic, or functional responsibilities.*** Devil's advocates, sky-gazing visionaries, and action-oriented executives can work together to ensure that all sides of an issue are considered.
4. ***Apply multiple mind-sets to any issue.*** Try role-playing, putting yourself in your competitors' shoes or conducting war games. Such techniques create fresh perspectives and engage team members, spurring interest in problem solving.
5. ***Actively manage conflict.*** Don't let the team acquiesce too soon or too easily. Identify and treat apathy early, and don't confuse a lack of conflict with agreement. Often, what passes for consensus is really disengagement.

How does consensus with qualification create a sense of fairness? A body of research on procedural justice shows that process fairness, which involves significant participation and influence by all concerned, is enormously important to most people. Individuals are willing to accept outcomes they dislike if they believe that the process by which those results came about was fair. Most people want their opinions to be considered seriously but are willing to accept that those opinions cannot always prevail. That is precisely what occurs in consensus with qualification. As one executive at Star said, "I'm happy just to bring up my opinions."

Apart from fairness, there are several other reasons why consensus with qualification is an important deterrent to interpersonal conflict. It assumes that conflict is natural and not a sign of interpersonal dysfunction. It gives managers added influence when the decision affects their part of the organization in particular, thus balancing managers' desires to be heard with the need to make a choice. It is an equitable and egalitarian process of decision making that encourages everyone to bring ideas to the table but clearly delineates how the decision will be made.

Finally, consensus with qualification is fast. Processes that require consensus tend to drag on endlessly, frustrating managers with what they see as time-consuming and useless debate. It's not surprising that the managers end up blaming their frustration on the shortcomings of their colleagues and not on the poor conflict-resolution process.

LINKING CONFLICT, SPEED, AND PERFORMANCE

A considerable body of academic research has demonstrated that conflict over issues is not only likely within top-management teams but also valuable. Such conflict provides executives with a more inclusive range of information, a deeper understanding of the issues, and a richer set of possible solutions. That was certainly the case in the companies we studied. The evidence also overwhelmingly indicates that where there is little conflict over issues, there is also likely to be poor decision making. "Groupthink" has been a primary cause of major corporate- and public-policy debacles. And although it may seem counterintuitive, we found that the teams that engaged in healthy conflict over issues not only made better decisions but moved more quickly as well.

Without conflict, groups lose their effectiveness. Managers often become withdrawn and only superficially harmonious. Indeed, we found that the alternative to conflict is usually not agreement but apathy and disengagement. Teams unable to foster substantive conflict ultimately achieve, on average, lower performance. Among the companies that we observed, low-conflict teams tended to forget to consider key issues or were simply unaware of important aspects of their strategic situation. They missed opportunities to question falsely limiting assumptions or to generate significantly different alternatives. Not surprisingly, their actions were often easy for competitors to anticipate.

In fast-paced markets, successful strategic decisions are most likely to be made by teams that promote active and broad conflict over issues without sacrificing speed. The key to doing so is to mitigate interpersonal conflict.

WORLD-CLASS NEGOTIATING STRATEGIES*

Frank L. Acuff

If I listen, I have the advantage; if I speak, others have it.

FROM THE ARABIC

There are many negotiating strategies that tend to work very well in one culture but are ineffective in other cultures. A case in point is the Miami-based project manager who put together a very detailed, thorough, research-oriented proposal and presentation for his Brazilian client. "I felt good that we had done our homework," he later noted. "I was very disappointed, however, to find that the Brazilian representatives were flatly uninterested in the details I was prepared to explain. A similar approach worked extremely well in Germany only four months earlier."

In spite of the many different negotiating approaches required among cultures, there are 10 strategies that tend to be effective anywhere in the world. While there may be local variations in how these strategies are applied, their basic premises remain viable.

TEN NEGOTIATING STRATEGIES THAT WILL WORK ANYWHERE

The 10 strategies that tend to be effective in negotiations throughout the world are as follows:

1. Plan the negotiation.
2. Adopt a win-win approach.
3. Maintain high aspirations.

*Reprinted with permission of AMACOM from *How to Negotiate Anything with Anyone Anywhere Around the World* (New York: Amacom, 1997): 68–94, via Copyright Clearance Center.

4. Use language that is simple and accessible.
5. Ask lots of questions, then listen with your eyes and ears.
6. Build solid relationships.
7. Maintain personal integrity.
8. Conserve concessions.
9. Make patience an obsession.
10. Be culturally literate and adapt negotiating strategies to the host country environment.

STRATEGY 1: PLAN THE NEGOTIATION

Everybody wants to get a good deal, to get a sizable share of the pie, and to feel good about the negotiation. Everybody wants to be a winner. Yet not everyone is willing to do the homework necessary to achieve these ends. The essential steps necessary to plan your negotiation are as follows: (1) identify all the issues (2) prioritize the issues (3) establish a settlement range and (4) develop strategies and tactics. Make this preparation a habit and you will set the stage for getting what you want.

There are other factors to consider prior to global negotiations. You can use the Tune-Up Checklist to ensure that you put yourself in the strongest possible position before the negotiation.

The Tune-Up Checklist: Prior to the Negotiation

This is the data-gathering stage where you should get background information related to The Other Side (TOS), to his or her culture and its effects on the negotiating process, to TOS's organization and other potential players in the negotiation, and to the history of any past negotiations. What do you know about:

TOS

- Family status (e.g., married, single, children)?
- Leisure or recreational activities?
- Work habits (e.g., long hours, early to work)?
- Behavior style (e.g., perfectionist, "big picture"-oriented, task-oriented, people-oriented)?
- Number of years with current organization?
- Stability in current position?
- Overall reputation as a negotiator?
- What special-interest groups might affect the negotiator?

TOS's Culture and Its Effects on Negotiations

- Are meetings likely to be punctual?
- What can you expect the pace of the negotiations to be?
- How important is "saving face" likely to be?
- Are differences of opinion likely to be emotional or argumentative?
- Will TOS bring a large team?
- Will you need an agent or interpreter?
- Should you prepare a formal agenda?

TOS's Organization

- What is the organization's main product or service?
- What is its past, present, and projected financial status?
- What organizational problems exist (e.g., downsizing, tough competition)?
- Who is TOS's boss, and what do you know about him or her?
- Is the organization under any time pressures?

Past Negotiations

- What were the subjects of past negotiations?
- What were the main obstacles and outcomes of the negotiations?
- What objections were raised?
- What strategies and tactics were used by TOS?
- How high were the initial offers compared with the eventual settlement?
- How was the outcome achieved, and over what period of time?

There are many ways to plan negotiations. One study identified five approaches skilled negotiators share when planning their negotiations:

1. They consider twice as wide a range of action options and outcomes as do less skilled negotiators.
2. They spend over three times as much attention on trying to find common ground with TOS.
3. They spend more than twice as much time on long-term issues.
4. They set range objectives (such as a target price of $50 to $60 per unit), rather than single-point objectives (e.g., $55). Ranges give negotiators flexibility.
5. They use "issue planning" rather than "sequence planning." That is, skilled negotiators discuss each issue independently rather than in a predetermined sequence or order of issues.[1]

STRATEGY 2: ADOPT A WIN-WIN APPROACH

We don't adopt the win-win approach simply because we are wonderful human beings. It helps us get what we want. There is a difference between how skilled and unskilled negotiators prepare for the win-win approach. Skilled negotiators, for example, tend to spend less time on defense/attack behavior and in disagreement. They also tend to give more information about their feelings and have fewer arguments to back up their position.[2] This last point may seem odd. It might seem that the more arguments one has for one's position, the better. Skilled negotiators know, however, that having only a few strong arguments is more effective than having too many arguments. With too many arguments, weak arguments tend to dilute strong arguments, and TOS often feels pressured or manipulated into settlement.

To achieve a win-win situation, you must tune in to the frequency with which TOS can identify: WIIFT ("What's In It For Them"). This means different things in different cultures. For example, in Saudi Arabia a certain amount of haggling back and forth on terms may indicate your sincerity about striking a deal.

To refuse a somewhat expressive give-and-take would be an insult to many Saudi negotiators. A Dallas-based commercial building contractor now experienced in Saudi Arabia discovered this on his first trip there. "I really got off-base in our early discussions in Riyadh. I felt we were being extremely polite as we patiently explained the reasonableness of our proposal. We fell flat on our faces. The Saudis felt we were inflexible and not serious about doing business. The next project we bid had a lot of fat built into it. We haggled back and forth for four meetings, and they ended up loving us. That's what they wanted—someone to bargain with back and forth. It showed them we cared." This negotiator adds, "I still get a knot in my stomach sometimes when I go through a Saudi negotiation, but at least I know what works now."

Fortunately for this negotiator, he quickly learned the win-win approach for his Saudi client. Yet the very idea of haggling would be a sure win-lose proposition in many parts of the world. In England, for example, it would be hard to come up with a worse idea than to engage TOS in an emotional afternoon of haggling back and forth. The British idea of win-win is a somewhat formal, procedural, and detailed discussion of the facts.

Achieving a win-win result also requires careful scrutiny of both parties' overall goals. You may be seeking short-term profit and cash flow, while your Japanese counterparts may be more interested in long-term viability. In many cases, different goals can lead to overall win-win results. Consider the company president negotiating a joint venture in Hungary in order to take advantage of a skilled, inexpensive workforce, while her TOS is motivated to find business linkages outside Eastern Europe.

Wherever you negotiate, focusing on win-win results sharply increases your chances for success, particularly in the long term.

STRATEGY 3: MAINTAIN HIGH ASPIRATIONS

In the spring of 1978, the International Air Transport Association (IATA) discontinued its policy of airline ticket price compliance. IATA had been for many years a powerful enforcer that had maintained a firm grip on the airline ticket prices of the world's domestic and international airlines. Immediately after this announcement was made, Leroy Black, my boss, suggested I contact the airlines to determine what, if any, ticket price concessions we might extract as a result of this policy change. The Middle East Division where we worked was located in Dubai, United Arab Emirates, a small oil sheikdom adjoining Saudi Arabia. Our 3,500 workers and many of their family members collectively logged millions of air miles per year.

"That's a good idea," I remember telling Leroy. Shaving 5 or 10 percent—perhaps even 15 percent—would amount to substantial savings on our $4 million annual airline expenses. I was stunned, though, when Leroy suggested we ask for a 50 percent price decrease in ticket costs.

"Are you kidding?" I asked, quite shocked.

"I think that 50 percent is about right," Leroy said serenely.

Our first appointment was with representatives from British Airways. They told us, in a reserved, nice kind of way, to take a hike.

Then KLM, in a not particularly nice kind of way, suggested the same recourse as British Airways. The same with Lufthansa. "We really are being a bit chintzy on this thing," I thought to myself.

"Leroy, let's try asking for a little less and see what happens," I suggested.

"I don't know. Let's hang in there awhile longer," Leroy insisted.

Next was Alitalia. As in our appointments with the other airlines, I went through a short prologue explaining the company's position, and assertively put forth that we would like to see a 50 percent reduction in future fares. This caused quite a commotion with the Alitalia representatives, who waved their arms and with great conviction gave us several reasons why this was not possible.

"This is really a little embarrassing," I thought.

They then asked if they could privately telephone their regional headquarters staff. They returned in about 10 minutes in a solemn mood.

"Mr. Acuff," one of the representatives said with a grave look on his face. "What you ask is quite impossible. The very most we can offer you is a 40 percent reduction," he said apologetically.

"Excuse me?" I asked. He repeated his offer.

"Unbelievable," I thought to myself. "Give us some time to think about it," I replied.

As soon as they were out of earshot, Leroy and I almost jumped for joy. As it turned out, this was the first of several key concessions we received from the various airlines, ranging from 15 to 45 percent discounts. British Airways, KLM, Sabena, and Lufthansa all soon after reduced their rates well beyond my initial expectations.

This situation was a valuable lesson with regard to aspiration levels in negotiations. What at first seemed like a brash, overbearing approach to business turned out to be very positive. But was it win-win?, you ask. Didn't you just bleed the airlines at a time when they were vulnerable? Not at all. We later found out that the airlines were quite pleased with the new arrangements. They thought discounts might be greater than they were, and, of course, some of the airlines were delighted that they had negotiated better terms than their competitors.

We have all kinds of negative fantasies about high initial demands (HIDs):

"They won't like me anymore. I'll make them really mad and it will hurt the relationship."

"I'll price myself out of the market."

"Maybe we aren't being reasonable."

"This is embarrassing."

In spite of these concerns, there are compelling reasons to go for it, which are summarized in the following World-Class Tips.

WORLD-CLASS TIPS: SEVEN REASONS WHY YOU SHOULD HAVE HIGH INITIAL DEMANDS

1. Don't take away your own power. TOS may do it to you, but don't do it to yourself.
2. HIDs teach people how to treat you.
3. They lower the expectations of TOS.
4. HIDs demonstrate your persistence and conviction.

5. You can always reduce your asking offer or demand. HIDs give you room to make concessions.
6. Remember that time is on your side. Making HIDs gives you more time to learn about your counterpart, and time heals many wounds.
7. There is an emotional imperative for TOS to beat you down. It's important for TOS to feel that they've "won."[3]

World-Class Tip 7 is especially important. Many negotiators find it hard to accept that there is an emotional imperative for TOS to beat you down. To illustrate this point, let's get in the other person's shoes to see how the TOS might feel. You are in Germany to negotiate the purchase of the Drillenzebit, a precision tool-making machine from a Munich-based firm. You say to yourself, "This time won't be like the other times. This time I'm going to do my homework—I will read appropriate industry periodicals and talk to consultants, clients, suppliers, and others who know a lot about the Germans, the German business environment, and the competitive market for precision tool-making machines." So you do your homework and begin to negotiate with the Germans for the Drillenzebit machine. When the subject of price arises, you are ready. You've got the facts, figures, and some savoir-faire about German negotiating practices. So you say, "Mr. Dietrich, today I'm going to offer you one price and one price only for this fine Drillenzebit machine. That final price is $74,000—that's U.S. dollars."

Dietrich looks at you for a moment and says, "Let me see if I have this right. That's $74,000—in U.S. dollars?"

"That's right," you repeat, proud that you're sticking by your guns.

"Seventy-four thousand dollars. You've got it. The machine is yours!" he beams.

How would you feel in this situation? Wonderful? Exuberant? If you are like most people, you would have a morbid, sinking feeling that you had just been taken. Your first thought would probably be, "Damn. I should have offered less." Is this reaction logical? No. You did, after all, get what you asked for. You reacted as you did because only part of your needs were met—the logical part—while the emotional part was not.

There are cultural differences as to how high our aspiration level should be with our foreign counterparts, but as a rule of thumb, go for it! If you really want $30,000 for your widget machine, don't ask for $30,500. Ask for $60,000. Put TOS in the position of saying to his or her boss, "You know, this woman came in asking $60,000. This price was completely off-the-wall. Excellent negotiator that I am, I got her down to $38,000. I saved us $22,000." And if you are in a competitive bidding situation, stress the quality, service, and other aspects that make your price an excellent value.

STRATEGY 4: USE LANGUAGE THAT IS SIMPLE AND ACCESSIBLE

American English is filled with thousands of clichés and colloquialisms that make it very hard for others to understand. Phrases such as "getting down to brass tacks," "getting down to the nitty-gritty," wanting to "zero in on problems," or "finding out where the rubber meets the road" only clog communication channels.

Don't assume that because your foreign counterpart speaks English, he or she fully understands it. This individual may know English as it was taught in school but may not be able to speak it or understand it in conversation with an American. An American executive who regularly travels to Taiwan makes this point. "When I first asked my Taiwanese client if he spoke English, he told me yes. I found out the hard way that his understanding was very elementary and that I used way too many slang expressions. We still do business together, but now I speak more slowly and simply, and I'm learning some Chinese."

This doesn't apply only to slang. Make sure you use the simplest, most basic words possible. Exhibit 1 provides examples of simplified words and terms you should use, even if you're speaking English.

This reliance on slang makes it very difficult for TOS to grasp our meaning, even if TOS speaks English. By using simple, straightforward language, we can help ourselves by helping others understand us.

EXHIBIT 1 Simplifying English Words and Terms

Don't use this . . .	*when this will do.*
annual premium	annual payment
accrued interest	unpaid interest
maturity date	final payment date
commence	start
utilize	use
acquaint	tell
demonstrate	show
endeavor	try
modification	change
proceed	go
per diem	daily

Phrases	*Typical Meanings*	*Sport*
"What's your game plan?"	"What's your approach to this negotiation?"	American football, basketball, etc.
"We're not going to throw in the towel."	"We're not going to give up."	Boxing, American football, etc.
"They're trying an end run."	"They are going around normal organizational channels."	American football
"You threw us a curve."	"We didn't do well in this situation."	Baseball
"You're batting a thousand."	"You've had all your demands met."	Baseball
"Have we covered all the bases?"	"Have we considered all the options?"	Baseball
"That's the way the ball bounces."	"It was unpredictable but it is over now and there is no use to worrying about it."	American football, basketball, etc.

TEENAGE WHAT?

The session had been interesting, with a good exchange of ideas. About thirty top Russian managers were learning about "How to Negotiate with Americans." Each of the participants was wired so that we could communicate with each other through an interpreter. I would say a few words and wait four or five seconds for the translation from English to Russian to be completed, listening through my earphones to the translator's crisp, confident tone.

All this was working fine until we began discussing Americans' need for achievement and how this affected the competitive approach of many American negotiators. One of the participants asked about what heroes represented this achievement orientation, and whether this achievement orientation impacted American children. I made a few observations about various American heroes and then made my big mistake. I noted that, yes, American children have their achievement-oriented heroes too, and I mentioned the Teenage Mutant Ninja Turtles as an example. Suddenly there was silence from the translator. I looked to the back of the room where he was sitting in a booth. The participants looked around nervously at him. He had a blank look on his face. Finally, after about 15 seconds, some tentative, awkward sounds came forth.

Then I realized how impossible a job I had given him. What would his translation possibly be. . . something like, "Turtles in their teenage years . . . who have physical deformities . . . and practice Far Eastern martial arts?"

STRATEGY 5: ASK LOTS OF QUESTIONS, THEN LISTEN WITH YOUR EYES AND EARS

Asking good questions is vital throughout the negotiation, but particularly in the early stages. Your main goal is receiving information. Making a brilliant speech to TOS about your proposal may make you feel good, but it does far less in helping you achieve your ends than asking questions that give you data about content and the emotional needs of TOS.

Exhibit 2 illustrates the importance of asking questions. Skilled negotiators ask more than twice the number of questions as unskilled negotiators. They also engage in much more active listening than those who are less skilled.

EXHIBIT 2 Questioning and Listening in Skilled and Average Negotiators

Negotiating Behavior	*Skilled Negotiators*	*Average Negotiators*
Questions, as a percentage of all negotiating behavior	21.3%	9.6%
Active listening		
• Testing for understanding	9.7	4.1
• Summarizing	7.5	4.2

Source: Neil Rackham, "The Behavior of Successful Negotiators" (Reston, VA.: Huth-waite Research Group, 1976), as reported in Ellen Raider International, Inc. (Brooklyn, N.Y.) and *Situation Management Systems*, Inc. (Plymouth, MA.), *International Negotiations: A Training Program for Corporate Executives and Diplomats* (1982).

There is one important consideration when asking questions: Don't do anything that would embarrass your international counterpart. Questions can be much more direct and open in cultures such as the United States, Canada, Australia, Switzerland, Sweden, and Germany than in Japan, Taiwan, Brazil, or Colombia, where indirectness is prized.

Judge a man by his questions rather than by his answers.
VOLTAIRE

Effective listening is especially challenging when different cultures are involved. This can be the case even when English is the first language of TOS. Mike Apple, an American engineering and construction executive, found this to be the case in England and Scotland. Apple notes that even though English is spoken, one must listen very carefully to English and Scottish negotiators because of their dialects. "When I first got to Scotland, I wondered if some kind of challenge was in the making when a union negotiator told me he was going to 'mark my card.' I asked a colleague about it. As it turned out, the term is one used by Scottish golfers to explain the best approach to the course for those who haven't played there before. The union negotiator was only trying to be helpful," Apple notes. "The lesson learned here? When in doubt, ask for clarification."

If the communication pattern is from high-context countries, such as Japan, China, Saudi Arabia, Greece, or Spain, listening is even more challenging for Americans. In these cultures the message is embedded in the context of what is being said. Mike McMahon, a former managing director for National Semiconductor's Singapore plant, found Singaporeans reluctant to respond directly to questions. He notes, "I had to listen very carefully to figure out what was really on their minds."[4]

Here are some additional tips for effective listening:

- Limit your own talking.
- Concentrate on what TOS is saying.
- Maintain eye contact (but don't stare).
- Paraphrase and summarize TOS's remarks.
- Avoid jumping to conclusions. Be postjudicial, not prejudicial, regarding what TOS is saying.
- Watch for non-verbal cues.
- Listen for emotions.
- Ask for clarification: Assume differences, not similarities, if you are unsure of meaning.
- Don't interrupt.
- Pause for understanding; don't immediately fill the voids of silence.

Some of the rituals of international negotiating serve dual purposes of entertainment and information gathering. Foster Lin, director of the Taiwanese Far East Trade Service Office in Chicago, considers formal Taiwanese banquets and other entertainment as a prime opportunity to gain information on one's negotiating counterpart. Says Lin, "Entertainment demonstrates courtesy toward our foreign guests. It also helps us find out more about the individual person. Is this someone we can trust and want to do business with?" Such occasions can help you as well. Careful listening in this "offstage" time, away from the formal negotiating sessions, can give you another side to the negotiators. Use this time to gather additional data on your counterpart.

A key part of listening relates to body language. TOS may encode messages, making sophisticated, cogent arguments. However, one thing almost always happens during a moment of insecurity or deception: body movements change (e.g., the person literally squirms in his or her seat or blinks more rapidly). Also, be aware of the impact of your own nonverbal behavior. For example, if your gestures are quite expressive and TOS is from Sweden and quite reserved, tone it down a bit. Alternatively, if your facial and arm gestures are unexpressive and you are meeting a Brazilian who is very expressive, loosen up a bit—smile and use expressive hand and arm gestures.

WORLD-CLASS TIPS: FIVE POSITIVE THINGS YOU CAN DO WITHOUT SAYING A WORD

1. ***Smile!*** It's a universal lubricant that can help you open the content of the negotiation. A genuine smile says very loudly, "I'd appreciate doing business with you."
2. ***Dress appropriately and groom well.*** Shined shoes, combed hair, clean nails, and clothes appropriate for the occasion show that you respect yourself and your counterpart. It also communicates that you are worthy of your counterpart's business.
3. ***Lean forward.*** This communicates interest and attention in almost every culture.
4. ***Use open gestures.*** Crossed arms in front of your chest may be viewed as disinterest or resistance on your part. More open gestures send a signal that you are open to your counterpart's ideas.
5. ***Take every opportunity to nod your head.*** Don't you like it when people agree with you? Let TOS know that you are listening by this simple action.

STRATEGY 6: BUILD SOLID RELATIONSHIPS

Stay away from value issues, which are full of potential land mines. When is the last time you won an argument on politics? On religion? That's right; you never have and you never will. Discussion of subjects such as politics, religion, race, and the role of women in the workplace will not help build a relationship with your negotiating counterpart, even if the other person brings up the subject or there is potential agreement. No matter what our particular view on these subjects, we tend to think that we have God, truth, and light on our side.

The personal relationship you develop with your counterpart provides the basis, or context, for the content portion of the negotiation. In many cultures it is the quality of the relationship more than the work accomplished that counts. There is more emphasis on building a solid personal relationship in some cultures than others. In Brazil, Japan, Greece, Spain, and the Czech Republic, for example, a strong personal relationship almost surely precedes any deal. In other countries, such as Germany and Switzerland, the content portion of the negotiation usually precedes any substantial relationship building. In most cases, a strong relationship is critical to even short-term success. In all cases, it is critical to long-term success.

Be a pleasure to do business with. Even if you don't agree on the content part of the negotiation, you want TOS to have a positive view of you when they see you coming.

WORLD-CLASS TIPS: FIFTEEN STATEMENTS THAT WILL HELP BUILD SOLID RELATIONSHIPS (OR AT LEAST KEEP YOU OUT OF DEEP SOUP)

1. "I'm very pleased to meet you."
2. "Could you tell me more about your proposal?"

3. "I have a few more questions I'd like to ask you."
4. "We might be able to consider X if you could consider Y."
5. "Let me try to summarize where we stand now in our discussion."
6. "I'm very happy to see you again."
7. "Could you tell me more about your concerns?"
8. "Let me tell you where I have a concern."
9. "I feel disappointed that we haven't made more progress."
10. "I really appreciate the progress that we've made."
11. "Thank you."
12. "Can I answer any more questions about our organization or proposal?"
13. "What would it take for us to close this deal?"
14. "I've enjoyed doing business with you."
15. "I haven't talked to you since we signed the contract. I just wanted to follow up with you to see how things are working out."

Even when you mean well, there are some terms and phrases that carry negative overtones. One study found that skilled negotiators used only 2.3 irritating words and phrases per hour in face-to-face negotiations, compared with 10.8 "irritators" per hour for average negotiators. Irritators included such phrases as "generous offer," "fair price," and "reasonable arrangement."[5] Exhibit 3 is a "dirty-word list" that details other phrases that tend to upset others, regardless of the culture involved.

EXHIBIT 3 Words and Phrases to Avoid

These Words:	*May Provoke These Reactions:*
You always/You never . . .	I always, I never? Perhaps I often or seldom behave in that way, but not always or never.
What you need to understand . . .	I'll let you know if I need to understand it.
Be reasonable . . .	I didn't think I was being unreasonable. (Have you ever met anyone in your whole life who told you, "I don't tend to be very reasonable, and I just thought I'd let you know?")
Calm down!	If they were calm, they won't be after you tell them this!
Needless to say . . .	Then why are you saying it?
Obviously . . .	You've somehow cornered the market on what is and is not obvious?
The fact of the matter is . . .	You know what is factual and I don't?
You can't tell me . . .	You bet I can tell you—that is, if you'll just listen!
Listen . . .	I may choose to listen, but I don't want to be directed to do so.
As you know . . .	Maybe I do and maybe I don't.
Most people would . . .	Are you suggesting that I'm some kind of oddball if I don't happen to agree with you?

There's another word that should be taken out of your business vocabulary: negotiate. Yes, we use it when discussing the subject, but in real-life situations, all kinds of images come to mind when you tell someone, "Let's negotiate this deal." There's the feeling that something manipulative is about to happen. Instead, say something like, "Let's work out something that is good for both of us" or "Let's discuss the concerns you have."

Reaching a deadlock or impasse is a common and often frustrating experience. This can happen even when both parties are bargaining in good faith and are trying hard to reach an agreement. When you reach an impasse with TOS, take steps to break the deadlock and yet keep the relationship strong. The following list of World-Class Tips provides some helpful methods.

WORLD-CLASS TIPS: SEVENTEEN WAYS TO BREAK DEADLOCKS AND YET KEEP THE RELATIONSHIPS

1. Recap the discussion to ensure there really is a deadlock.
2. Emphasize mutual interests.
3. Stress the cost of not agreeing and situations you want to avoid.
4. Reach an agreement in principle, postponing difficult parts of the agreement.
5. Try to find out if the problem is based on something TOS isn't telling you.
6. Change the type of contract.
7. Change contract specifications or terms.
8. Add options to the contract.
9. Hold informal discussions in a different setting.
10. Make concessions that are contingent upon settling all of the issues.
11. Form a joint study committee.
12. Change a team member or team leader.
13. Discuss how both you and TOS might respond to a hypothetical solution, without committing either party to a course of action.
14. Tell a funny story.
15. Take a recess.
16. Consider setting a deadline for resolution. Deadlines create a sense of urgency and encourage action.
17. Be patient.

Keep in mind that both the tone and the content of the current negotiation will impact future negotiations with TOS. This is true even if you don't successfully conclude the current negotiation; sometimes you are really setting the stage for the next one. It's like arguing with the umpire in American baseball. Why do baseball managers do it? They never prevail. Aside from pleasing the crowd, the manager argues with the umpire for one simple reason—not for this call, but for the next call! So, too, in your negotiations, put markers in TOS's mind for the next time you sit down to do business. Leave him or her with two thoughts: (1) you're a good person for TOS to do business with and (2) here are some expectations to keep in mind.

STRATEGY 7: MAINTAIN PERSONAL INTEGRITY

A few years ago a businessman came up to me before I was about to make a speech on negotiations. He said that he was a good Christian and, as such, didn't know if he should stay for the speech since he assumed I'd be talking about scheming ways to manipulate other people. I told him that while I didn't know whether or not he should stay, negotiators who use manipulative, scheming, hidden agendas do not do very well in negotiations. He seemed somewhat shocked but **relieved** by my response.

Personal integrity is absolutely critical for your effectiveness as a world-class negotiator. My conviction on this point is not related to religion but to pragmatism. There are two reasons why personal integrity and trust are vital. The first reason has to do with information. No one tells you anything of importance if he or she doesn't trust you.* If you are not viewed as trustworthy, people will tell you only what they must tell you because of your position or title. For example, if you are trusted, after a negotiating session TOS may ask for some confidential "whisper time." She may confide in you as follows:

TOS: Look, I know we've been pressing for A, B, C, and D in there. But, off the record, what we're really interested in is only C and D.
YOU: But you've been really pushing hard for A and B.
TOS: I know. But if you can find a way to give us C and D, we've got a deal.

This is a rich disclosure. This is the stuff that will make you successful, not because you are technically brilliant, but because you are trusted. Risky, key data are shared with you only if your personal integrity is unquestioned.

Personal integrity is vital to building your negotiating strength for a second reason: *Issues of trust are the most difficult relationship problems to repair.* In fact, these are often irreparable. With some hard work, some skill, and a little luck, other types of relationship problems can be healed, but the trust issue hardly ever gets fixed. Think of the people you really don't trust in your professional or personal life. Is there *anything* they can do to repair the relationship and get back in your good graces? If you are like most people, the answer is "nothing."

American negotiators sometimes try to resolve issues of trust by formalizing the intent of the parties in an ironclad contract. We then hold TOS to the contract, regardless of how much we trust them. In many cultures, however, it is the person or the relationship that your counterpart trusts, not a piece of paper. Making and keeping contractual commitments is not a high priority for many of your international counterparts. Much of this view relates to the relative uncertainty felt by those from other cultures compared with Americans. Malaysians, for example, prefer to have exit clauses in their contracts in case things don't work out. They feel little control over future business events or even their country as a whole and want provisions for a respectable withdrawal should future circumstances make their compliance impossible.[6] In much of the Arab world, negotiators stress mutual trust and see themselves doing business with "the man" rather than a company or a contract.[7] In Britain, there are strong legal precedents but less reliance on formalized contracts than in the United States. Tom Wilson, a British management consultant, observes, "Detailed legal contracts are seldom the order of the day. The British feel aggrieved when outsmarted by clever contract language. Besides," he adds, "a legal decision will not enforce that for which there is no will to perform."

*Herb Cohen talks about this effectively in his video *Persuasive Negotiating.*

Building trust can be a long process, particularly in global negotiating, and it can be harmed in subtle ways. This is why you should avoid excessive use of phrases such as "to be honest with you . . ." (are you not normally honest?), "to tell you the truth . . . " (are you not normally truthful?), and "frankly . . ." (are you not usually candid?). Though TOS may not be conscious of why he or she doesn't trust you, too many of these phrases lead to a conclusion that you are not trustworthy, even if you are honest.

If you are viewed as trustworthy by TOS, protect this aspect of the negotiation at all costs. Remember, *lose the deal if you must, but keep the trust.* This will be vital for your next negotiation with TOS.

STRATEGY 8: CONSERVE CONCESSIONS

Concessions give valuable information about you, your style, and your resolve. How you use them sets the tone, not only for a current negotiation, but for future negotiations as well. Your current concession pattern teaches TOS how to treat you in the future.

Let's say you're in Budapest, involved in a tough negotiation with the Hungarians. You have traded data with them and made logical defenses of your negotiating position for five long meetings. The negotiation seems to be going nowhere. This particular negotiation is price-sensitive, and in the first meeting, you quoted $80 per unit for your product. The Hungarians have offered you $20. You know that building a good relationship is important in any negotiation. They haven't budged from the $20 since the first meeting.

In order to break the logjam, you show your good faith in working out this negotiation by making a counteroffer of $45. This, you think, shows that you mean business in resolving this issue and that you are acting in good faith. Besides, your "really asking" price is $40, and you will certainly have gone more than halfway. The Hungarians will surely do the same, and you can all conclude the session, have some vodka, and go home.

It may not work out this way. In fact, in the case related above, you can bet you are about to get clobbered. Like many negotiators, you might feel that making a concession will create goodwill or soften up TOS. Unfortunately, a much more likely scenario is that such a concession will suggest weakness on your part, make your counterpart greedy, or even make your counterpart suspicious. You must therefore be extremely careful in making concessions.

WORLD-CLASS TIPS: TEN GUIDELINES ON MAKING CONCESSIONS

1. Don't be the first to make a concession on an important issue.
2. Never accept the first offer.
3. Make TOS reduce a high initial demand; don't honor a high demand by making a counteroffer.
4. Make small concessions. Lower the expectation of TOS.
5. When you make concessions, make them slowly (like wine, they improve with time).
6. Make TOS feel good by making concessions of low value to you but of perceived high value to TOS.
7. Defer concessions on matters that are important to you.
8. Make contingent concessions (i.e., get something in return, or concede only on the condition that all issues be settled).

9. Celebrate the concessions you get. Don't feel guilty.
10. Don't feel that you must reciprocate every concession made to you.

The number of initial concessions differs among cultures. One study found that Japanese negotiators made fewer initial concessions per half-hour bargaining session (6.5) than did negotiators from the United States (7.1) or Brazil (9.4).[8] As a rule, the fewer the concessions, the better.

Also, beware when TOS asks for a concession on the grounds of "fairness." Whenever your counterparts tell you that they want you to make a concession because their offer to you has been very "fair" or "reasonable," don't believe them. More often than not, this is a manipulative tactic to make you feel guilty.

STRATEGY 9: MAKE PATIENCE AN OBSESSION

Since almost every stage of a global negotiation tends to take longer than the domestic, patience is not only a virtue, but a necessity. Patience serves three vital functions: (1) It facilitates getting information from TOS, (2) it builds the relationship by sending out signals of courtesy, and (3) it increases your chances of effective concession making. Patience is linked to concession behavior because impatient negotiators tend to make both more counterproposals and more concessions. Skilled negotiators make fewer counterproposals than do less skilled negotiators.[9]

Patience may also be one of TOS's negotiating tactics, since TOS tries to wear you down with their patience. They are counting on your becoming anxious and making concessions that you otherwise wouldn't make. Don't be a victim. Take these countermeasures:

- Give yourself plenty of time.
- Relax and make yourself comfortable.
- Prepare your own people back home for a long negotiation.
- Recognize that it may be tougher on TOS than on you.
- Consider setting a deadline.

JUST-IN-TIME MANAGEMENT

I was in the small Central American country of Belize to address a management conference. I was scheduled to speak at 9:00 A.M., so I was ready to go about 8:00 A.M., waiting for my hosts in the hotel lobby. They weren't there. 8:15—no one. 8:30—nobody. 8:45—nope. I checked with the front desk to make sure I had set my watch to the correct time zone. 9:00—9:15—still no one. Now I'm getting out my letter of invitation, thinking, "Could this be my worst nightmare? Could I be in the wrong country on the wrong date? At about 9:20 my hosts showed up, and we drove to the hotel where the conference was being held. After a short discussion about my flight, the weather, and related items, I said, "It's about 9:30. Wasn't I on the agenda for 9:00 A.M.?"

No response.

"I'm just curious, but if it's about 9:35, aren't we late for the conference?" I persisted.

"Oh no, Mr. Acuff," one of my hosts said jovially. "Nothing here in Belize starts at the time on the agenda. We'll be quite early. The conference won't start for another hour or so."

"Thank you," I said, relieved. My life was good again.

Patience, as important as it is, can be hard work. One manager from an American oil company illustrates this point in the Pacific Rim: "Negotiating in Indonesia is like drinking a thousand cups of tea—very challenging and very slow." Ted Cline, who has negotiated many large contracts in the Middle East, stresses the importance of persistence. "I tell my people: If you beat your head on the wall, it will get bloody. But if you keep constant pressure on the wall, some day it will fall down."

STRATEGY 10: BE CULTURALLY LITERATE AND ADAPT THE NEGOTIATING PROCESS TO THE HOST COUNTRY ENVIRONMENT

By acquiring insight into the culture of TOS, as well as into your own cultural predispositions, you can bridge the cultural gap to become a more effective negotiator. You can be empathetic with TOS only if you understand the culture and environment in which TOS operates. Every step of the negotiating process must be seen through the lens of the host-country culture. Increasing your cultural IQ pays off in every step of the negotiating process, from the initial planning and greeting TOS right down to setting the stage for future business.

Cultural savvy takes many forms. Witness, for example, a supplier of oilfield technology that sent a program administrator to resolve the snags associated with a Russian joint venture. Despite the progress on technical details, the Russians continued to be very standoffish. Only later did the firm learn that sending a midlevel manager with the title of program administrator was an insult to the Russians, who felt that anyone with such a lowly title was unlikely to have the authority to negotiate a substantial deal, and that sending a midlevel manager was disrespectful of them. Such title and rank considerations are important to Russian negotiators. In this particular case, the firm's vice-president of international projects relates that now, when the program administrator travels to Russia, his title is revised to "managing director of special projects." The vice-president notes, "The title change makes the Russians feel like they are dealing with the right level of person, and all it costs us are new business cards."

Moira Crean, manager of contracts administration for MasterCard International, finds that cultural savvy takes the form of sensitivity to age in mainland China. "Age," she explains, "can be a key aspect in a big negotiation. Our Chinese partners have been known to dismiss a young person—let's say, a 35-year-old vice president—and say, 'Send over the old guy.'"

Even concession making must be seen through a cultural perspective. Exhibit 4 illustrates different perceptions of your good intentions. The reaction to a large concession may range from pleasure (a U.S. negotiator) to dismay (a Swiss negotiator).

EXHIBIT 4 How a Large Concession from You Might Be Perceived by Negotiators from Different Countries

Negotiators From	*Likely Reaction*
United States	"I gotcha."
Netherlands	"I cannot trust you."
Japan	"This has hurt the harmony."
Switzerland	"This person did not prepare well."
Saudi Arabia	"This is how business is done."

If you just remember the following two guidelines, you will not only be culturally literate, but you will be a superb global negotiator.

1. Adopt the Platinum Rule

Most of us grew up with the Golden Rule or something similar: "Do unto others as *you* would that they do unto you." This works well when we are surrounded by people like us—whoever "us" might be. We know how to treat the other person because of shared backgrounds and traits. With our international counterparts, the Golden Rule is no longer very helpful, because how you want to be treated may indeed be very different from how Chin, Suresh, Ivan, Miguel, Mohanuned, Isobella, or Isa wants to be treated. Instead, adopt what I call the Platinum Rule: "Do unto others as *they* would have done unto them." You might be comfortable with a firm handshake, with being direct and open, and with getting right down to business. But if the culture of TOS encourages other behaviors and your cultural savvy enables you to engage in them, you will be ahead of the competition. As you increase your comfort zone with others, so too will you increase your negotiating effectiveness.

Is there a place for common courtesy? You bet, as long as such courtesy isn't defined only on your terms. If common courtesy means a smile upon greeting or not interrupting others, this works almost anywhere. If it means inviting TOS to lunch, picking up the tab, complimenting TOS about his or her office, extending a firm handshake, or providing a gift as a token of your appreciation, then your courtesy may be another person's idea of irritating behavior. Tact has been called intelligence of the heart. In global business affairs, tact includes knowledge of the host-country culture.

2. Conduct Yourself as an Effective Foreigner

The idea is not to go native,[10] but to be culturally savvy while remaining a foreigner. Don't worry about minor gaffes in the many rituals and customs associated with every culture. If your handshake is a little too firm in Rio de Janeiro, or you can't remember that phrase you learned in Polish, it is not the end of the world. TOS will normally give you an A for effort even if the details of the execution need a little work. Be culturally savvy, but also be authentic. If the sight of fish eyes makes you squeamish in Singapore, if it means you're going to spend an hour being sick in the bathroom, don't eat the fish eyes.

MIDDLE EAST BUSINESS PRACTICES 101: WHEN COMPLIMENTS ARE COSTLY

The Labour Minister for the United Arab Emirates was in my office to help negotiate an end to a work stoppage by the local Dubai construction workers. The meeting went well until we finished our discussions. While walking with His Highness to the door of my office, I mentioned that he had a beautiful briefcase (mine was in a general state of disrepair). As I reached the door I noticed that he was no longer walking with me. I turned around to see His Highness emptying the contents of his briefcase on my desk.

"Did you lose something?" I asked, trying to be helpful.

"No, no," he replied. "I want you to have," he added, as he presented his briefcase to me. "This is for you. You are my friend."

After profusely apologizing, I convinced him that I really couldn't accept the briefcase.

The lesson learned? In that part of the world, don't go around complimenting people on their possessions. You just might end up with them.

Notes

1. N. Rackham, "The Behavior of Successful Negotiators" (Reston, VA: Huthwaite Research Group, 1976), as reported in Ellen Raider International, Inc. (Brooklyn, NY) and Situation Management Systems, Inc. (Plymouth, MA), *International Negotiations: A Training Program for Corporate Executives and Diplomats* (1982).
2. Ibid.
3. See P. Sperber, *Fail-Safe Business Negotiating: Strategies and Tactics for Success* (Upper Saddle River, NJ: Prentice Hall, 1983), 40–41; and R. J. Lewicki and J. A. Litterer, *Negotiation* (Homewood, IL: Richard D. Irwin, 1985), 75–79.
4. F. L. Acuff, "What It Takes to Succeed in Overseas Assignment," *National Business Employment Weekly* (August 25, 1991): 17–18.
5. Rackham, "The Behavior of Successful Negotiators."
6. N. J. Adler, *International Dimensions of Organizational Behavior* (Cincinnati: South-West, 1997), 209.
7. P. R. Harris and R. T. Moran, *Managing Cultural Differences*, 2nd ed. (Houston: Gulf Publishing, 1987), 474.
8. John Graham, "The Influence of Culture on Negotiations," *Journal of International Business Studies, XVI*, no. 1 (Spring 1985): 81–96.
9. Rackham, "The Behavior of Successful Negotiators," 180.
10. Adler, *International Dimensions*, 187.

CHAPTER 14
MANAGING DIVERSITY

GENERATIONS: BOOMERS AND ECHOS AND NEXTERS—OH MY!

Harriet Hankin

THE GLASS CEILING: DOMESTIC AND INTERNATIONAL PERSPECTIVES

Nancy Lockwood

Workplace diversity is another issue that requires careful management and attention in organizations. On the individual and team levels, there is more emphasis on understanding the differences people bring to work and the need to incorporate an appreciation of these differences into the way we manage and work with others. Globalization and labor migration have resulted in more work contact with people from other cultures. The definition of diversity, however, extends beyond cultural background to include differences resulting from thinking styles, working styles, age, functional disciplines, years of service, religious beliefs, sexual orientation, marital status, physical appearance/abilities, education, and gender. This chapter deals with generational diversity and gender diversity.

Harriet Hankin, a consultant, examines the first issue in "Generations: Boomers and Echos and Nexters—Oh My!" Hankin argues that understanding generations is a useful tool for recognizing what motivates individuals because members of a generation share some of the same experiences that influence their perceptions and priorities. Managers can benefit from understanding the forces and influences that shaped each generation so they can design workplaces in which every individual can do his or her best work.

Nancy Lockwood, a researcher at the Society for Human Resource Management, examines the status of women in the global workplace in "The Glass Ceiling: Domestic and International Perspectives." Although women have made gains, discrepancies in employment status and pay still exist. Lockwood discusses the barriers to women's advancement and tells managers how they can design organizations that are gender friendly.

GENERATIONS: BOOMERS AND ECHOS AND NEXTERS—OH MY!*

Harriet Hankin

When I got married more than twenty-five years ago, I was shocked by the number of socks my husband brought with him. He cleared out two or three drawers and filled them with socks. Some of them had never been opened and still had tags on them; others had tremendous holes. Being the new and doting wife, I sorted the socks—matched sizes and colors, tossed the "holey" ones, unwrapped the new ones. Big mistake! Bob loved his socks—ALL of them—and I wasn't to throw out a single one. Over the years, Bob's socks have become a running family joke, but the root of the attachment is quite clear. Raised during the depression, he had to wash out his socks each night and keep wearing them over and over again. This was the first time the differences in generations hit home for me—we are shaped by the experiences we live through. Separated by nearly sixteen years, my husband and I are from two different generations. He was eight years old when America was stunned by the attack on Pearl Harbor, December 7, 1941. It was a day that had a tremendous impact on him and has shaped his values and priorities even today.

I, on the other hand, am a Baby Boomer, a label I've always hated. Still, it meant that I always had enough socks and never kept or attempted to darn a "holey" one. Pearl Harbor was a chapter in my history book. I did, however, grow up with the belief that holding a textbook over my head while I crouched under my desk at school would keep me safe from the Russian threat of a nuclear bomb. The assassinations of John F. Kennedy, Martin Luther King, Jr., and Robert Kennedy were life-shaping historic moments for me.

For my daughter's generation, socks are important only as a fashion statement and they probably never heard of the word "darn" in reference to a sock. At twenty-one, my daughter is part of a new generation that seems to care very deeply about the future of our world. Their historical markers include the explosion of the space shuttle *Columbia* (though they don't remember the 1986 *Challenger* explosion), the war in Iraq, and most significantly, the terrorist attacks on the World Trade Center and Pentagon on September 11, 2001.

So, using my little family as a springboard, I can readily identify the significance and potential of three generations. At the same time, I realize that we are not only a product of our home environment and heredity but also of the historical context of our upbringing.

In the future, successful organizations will find the different generations more relevant than ever. Why? In short, because they are all working and will continue to do so. For the first time in our history, four generations are active in the workforce at one time. They are, in fact, working together, interacting in the workplace. It's not just old man Jones sitting up in the executive suite and young Billy down in the mailroom, never to cross paths. Billy is probably up in Mr. Jones's office, helping him set up his computer to retrieve specific data he needs every day. As I am finding in so many areas, old paradigms of thinking are just that: old—and outdated. They will not work in the future.

---

*Excerpted with permission of AMACOM from *The New WorkForce* (New York: AMACOM, 2004):45–63, via the Copyright Clearance Center.

In the past, companies could put generations into three tidy little groups, each with its own area of focus:

- ***The Older Generation:*** retired or getting ready to retire and concerned with their pensions
- ***The Middle Generation:*** the bulk of the workforce focused primarily on benefits and compensation
- ***The Younger Generation:*** the workforce of future, in need of training and education

Think about it. Many companies solved most of their workforce issues within these three silos. Need to shake things up? Save some money? Get rid of the "dead wood" and have an early retirement drive. Want to motivate your workers? Give them "family friendly" benefits and an annual picnic. Want to whip those up-and-comers into shape and attract the best and the brightest at the same time? Put together a management training program, complete with lectures, guest speakers, and job rotations. It was so easy, wasn't it? Now look! People are working who are 20, 40, 60, and even 80. It's all getting so complicated—or is it?

In the future, companies will face many generations active in the workforce simultaneously, thanks mainly to increased longevity and people looking to remain on the job years past what used to be considered retirement age. How will companies need to adjust their human resource functions—from recruiting and training to benefits and compensation—based on the different needs and expectations of the different generations? If they are looking to develop satisfied, productive workforces blending a wide variety of skills and experiences—which, of course, they should be—companies will start answering these questions today.

In this chapter, I will define the generations, delve a little deeper into what makes them tick, and then look at the implications for employers of these generations all working together. According to the book *Generations at Work* by Ron Zemke, Claire Raines, and Bob Filipczak:

> *The three generations that occupy today's workplace and the fourth generation that is entering it are clearly distinguishable by all these criteria—their demographics, their early life experiences, the headlines that defined their times, their heroes, music, and sociology, and their early days in the workplace. Their differences can be a source of creative strength and a source of opportunity, or a source of stifling stress and unrelenting conflict. Understanding generational differences is critical to making them work for the organization and not against it. It is critical to creating harmony, mutual respect, and joint effort where today there is suspicion, mistrust, and isolation.*[1]

DEFINING THE GENERATIONS

Here is a thumbnail sketch of each of the major generations of today. I found some differences in birth years attributed to each, so I took the most common or that used by the Census Bureau. All the names, nicknames, birth years, and overlap became confusing. Laying it out this way was helpful to me. Consider it as a vertical timeline.

The Silent Generation

- Born 1922 to 1945.
- Key Influences: The Great Depression and the New Deal; World War II; Holocaust; Hiroshima; radio and movies.
- Other Names: The Veterans; Seniors; The Greatest Generation.

The Baby Boomers

- Born 1946 to 1964.
- Key Influences: Vietnam War; assassinations of JFK, Martin Luther King, Jr., and Robert Kennedy; putting a man on the Moon; Watergate; Cold War and bomb shelters; television; women's liberation, sexual revolution; environmental concerns (Green Party, Exxon *Valdez*).
- Other Names: Boomers; "Me" Generation.

Generation X

- Born 1965 to 1976.
- Key Influences: Demolition of the Berlin Wall; *Challenger* disaster; Clinton sex scandal; the skyrocketing growth of the stock market and the abundant economy in the 1980s and 1990s; 24-hour live, remote news coverage; the dot-com economy; hi-tech start-ups.
- Other Names: Baby Bust; Xers.

Baby Boom Echo

- Born 1977 to 2000.
- Key Influences: Oklahoma City bombing; Rodney King beating; O.J. Simpson trial; Columbine High School massacre; Y2K; Internet; September 11, 2001, terrorist attacks; corporate scandals (Enron); video games; instant messaging.
- Other Names: Generation Y; Nexters; Internet Generation; Millennials (for those born in the 1980s and 1990s).

Millennium Generation

- Born Since 2000.
- Key Influences: Yet to be determined.
- Other Names: I call this generation the Millennials. I feel that twenty years is a large span for one generation and I want to make the point that children who are just coming into the world with the new century will have their own set of influences. These babies will be the ones living the trends we are predicting now. This generation, and the one yet to come, will be the workforce that picks up where the Boomers leave off.

HOW GENERATIONS ENHANCE UNDERSTANDING

There are varying views about whether understanding the generations is a useful tool for understanding what motivates an individual. Both sides of the argument make relevant points. On the one hand is the argument that factors other than birth year have a major impact on who one is: upbringing, education, affluence or lack of it, and even geography, just to name a few. I agree. On the other hand, members of a generation do share a history that reflects the news, views, politics, and entertainment that shaped their youth. I think both influences are relevant.

For employers, however, generations are perhaps the most consistent indicator of work needs. While a person can move, get an education, or change financial circumstances, a birth date never changes. It is a useful and dependable benchmark for certain information and is critical for longitudinal studies and trends. Companies and coworkers alike benefit from an understanding of the characteristics of the generations.

People born in the same generation have shared experiences that influence their perceptions and priorities and that shape who they are. They share the historic events, economics, and culture of their time. For example, members of the Silent Generation may remember going to bed hungry, or, similarly to my husband, not having enough socks.

They remember the attack on Pearl Harbor as a cataclysmic event beyond anything they could imagine. They also grew up in a time when holding hands on a date was a really big deal. As a result, they bring a certain set of principles and priorities to work. We call them the Silent Generation because they pretty much would "put up and shut up." They could remember things much worse than anything they were facing in the workplace. They were duty bound and loyal to their employers because people generally worked in one place for life.

Recognizing these key commonalities for a given generation helps guide employers as they seek to attract, retain, and support them as employees. This does not mean buying into and reinforcing stereotypes about the different age groups; it does mean having a basic understanding of the forces and influences that helped shape each generation and being aware of the needs and concerns of each group. As always, each employee is an individual and should be treated as such.

DELVING A LITTLE DEEPER INTO THE GENERATIONS

In order to understand this trend and what it will mean for employers, we have to take a closer look at each of the generations outlined above:

THE SILENT GENERATION: BORN 1922 TO 1945

Let's put the country's most mature generation in perspective. According to Louis Pol, demographer and associate dean of the College of Business Administration at the University of Nebraska at Omaha, the birthrate was fairly stable early in the 20th century. Then, during the Great Depression and World War II, the birthrate declined. At the same time, though, we had massive migrations from Europe to the United States. During these times, people knew greater economic turmoil and hardship than any American generation before or since. They survived through self-discipline, sacrifice, and pure hard work. The New Deal made construction workers out of many who had previously held jobs in other professions. The war led women to join the assembly lines of American factories. After the war, this generation enjoyed, albeit conservatively, a life of steadily increasing affluence and luxury.

The Silent Generation is the most traditional: working fathers, nuclear families, and traditional work ethics. They tend to be highly disciplined, hardworking, and loyal employees who play by the rules. They are the wisdom-keepers of America. They have so much to offer all of the generations—where America came from and what our elders endured to give us all that we take for granted today.

Even if they do not hold managerial positions, many of these senior employees are natural workplace leaders. They know how things are done—and why. They can assist younger workers in finding information they need or in determining who is the right person to go to in a given situation. Much of this type of knowledge is not written down in employee handbooks and job descriptions—it is simply woven into the fabric of a workplace. Still, it is vital in maintaining a thriving team atmosphere.

A natural affinity is developing between this generation and the Baby Boom Echo Generation. The indication for employers is that a mentor relationship between a Senior and an Echo would be a good match. While the Silent Generation has felt undervalued for quite a while, it seems that the tide is turning and that they are becoming open to remaining at work (or coming back to the workplace after they reach retirement age) if given adequate flexibility.

THE BABY BOOMERS: BORN 1946 TO 1964

At the end of the World War II, we enjoyed an economic boom. It was a time of optimism and industry and growth. Spurred on by returning veterans, the large influx of immigrants, and the general sense of optimism pervading the country, we made babies like crazy. In her article "Generational Divide," Alison Stein Wellner says that America was "in the mood" to make babies after World War II.[2] (If you get the reference to Glenn Miller, give yourself an extra credit point.) During the Baby Boom years, there were more than 75 million births. What's more, each year the birthrate increased over the preceding year until 1964. From 1946 to 1964, there were over 4 million births per year in the United States—that is the definition of the Baby Boom.

The Baby Boom Generation took the steadily increasing affluence that their parents were enjoying after World War II and ran with it. That was their parents' plan—to create the opportunity for their children to have more than they did. Education became a top priority. Many of the Boomers were raised in homes enjoying economic prosperity and a strong nuclear family. Most of their mothers were homemakers; most of their fathers were the family breadwinners.

The Boomers are an interesting group. The sheer size of the group means that society goes where they go. Perhaps the "Silent" Generation just can't be heard above the roar of the Boomers.

The Boomers gave us hippies, communes, and free love. They also gave us the 80-hour workweek. Although generally seen as self-absorbed, Boomers are active in social issues, civil rights, and politics. They are an optimistic, competitive group that focuses deeply on personal accomplishment.

THREE IN ONE: DISSECTING THE BABY BOOM

The Baby Boom is often viewed as three generations in one. The leading edge of the Baby Boom, the first six years, came after a much lower birth generation, but in big-growth, high-optimism years. That group was able to study whatever they wanted in college, or even to get good jobs without attending college. They were able to burn their bras, burn the flag, burn their draft cards, burn their brains on drugs, take a couple of years off to find themselves and come back to get a good job.

The next seven years make up the middle of the Baby Boom. These middle Boomers had a very different situation—they could not get good jobs as easily because the older Boomers had clogged the pipeline. They had to have strong, clean transcripts and not take a lot of chances if they wanted to get the same good jobs that the leading edge of the Baby Boom had coasted into.

The tail end, the last five years of the Baby Boom, had a completely different set of circumstances. These late Boomers were at a disadvantage. They had a huge number of Boomers ahead of them in the workforce moving up into middle management. There was no place for the tail end to go. They had to settle for jobs that people previously started right out of high school, except now they needed a college degree to land these jobs. Also prices had greatly escalated for basics, such as housing. The Late Boomers did not have the same sense of entitlement. They had to have an MBA to get that same job that the leading edge of the Boom could have gotten right out of college or maybe even high school. As futurist Edie Weiner puts it, "If you think that the Baby Boom is one generation from beginning to end, then you think Peter, Paul, and Mary, and Metallica are cut from the same cloth, and they clearly aren't, right?"[3]

A recent book by Jonathan Pontell sought to break out the last piece of the Baby Boom into a distinct segment he coined "Generation Jones." He defines this generation as those born from 1954 to 1965. In his view, this generation is too young for the Baby Boom and too old for the Baby Bust/Generation Xers. While some are agreeing with him, others say that his views are just typical of the Baby Boom—self-focused, wanting special recognition.

BOUND BY VALUES

Ken Dychtwald, president of Age Wave, is one of the nation's leading authorities on the Baby Boom. While acknowledging differences among the Boomers, he likens them to a forest of trees sharing the same root system. "Boomers are an extremely diverse generation, an extraordinarily complex yet individualistic collection of men and women," he says. "But under the surface, we're a generation with many, many common values and experiences. We're bound together by deeply rooted values." According to Dychtwald, these values include a belief in meritocracy, a respect for knowledge, and a lack of respect for authority.[4]

BOOMERS AND FINANCES

An interesting debate rages over the amount of money that will be passed down to the Boomers from their Silent Generation parents. One school of thought is that this will determine how long the Boomers will stay working. There are some 50 million Silent Generation Americans, and they are the wealthiest group of seniors in U.S. history. Estimates are that they control as much as two-thirds of the country's financial assets—including 40 percent of the mutual funds, 60 percent of the annuities, and 48 percent of luxury cars. Still, with all this wealth, the amount earmarked for inheritance is dwindling on a couple of fronts. First, the Silent Generation is facing unprecedented health-care costs and other expenses. Second, as they live longer and better, the Silent Generation is less willing to sock it away for their children. In the early 1990s, 56 percent of those over age 65 felt it was important to leave an inheritance. By 2000, that figure had dropped to less than half, 47 percent. This is credited not only to increased life expectancy and rising expenses, but also to a realization that their children are doing even better than they did.

At the same time, Boomers are notoriously poor savers. The Me Generation spends, spends, spends. They buy more products and services than any other generation. They may need that inheritance when it's all said and done.

They have time to start saving, though. Boomers are entering their Golden Age according to sociologists. The positions they hold, the money they make, and the achievements they can attain are just reaching their peak.

HOW LONG WILL THE BOOMERS WORK?

Boomers will continue to work far beyond what was traditionally considered retirement age. In spite of the fact that many people attribute this to the Boomers' lack of savings, I believe that, in large part, they will continue to work because they want to work. Boomers are so driven to succeed that I cannot imagine that they will settle down and do nothing for the last twenty-five or thirty years of their life. They would get too bored.

I do see them working at something they enjoy, however. After driving themselves to tension headaches and high blood pressure for the first half of their career, the Boomers will seek employment that better aligns with their dreams and aspirations. In addition, the Baby Boom includes the first generation of professional career businesswomen, many of whom will just be hitting their stride in their fifties and beyond. I believe a large number of smart, skillful businesswomen will be rejoining the workforce once their own children have grown. While as many as one in three Boomers say they would stop working if they could afford it, I'm not sure that this will be the reality.

At the same time, the Boomers will move toward better balance between work and home. Many are willing to trade higher pay for more time for themselves and their families. This is a trend we are seeing across the generations, a trend that is gaining support and momentum. Boomers, given their propensity to spend and self-focus, are expected to increase their travel and recreational activities as a means to enhance their work–life balance. They will be less stressed, hopefully, and bring a more balanced, patient perspective to their jobs. In addition, they will gain insight, appreciation, and a broader view as a result of seeing places other than their office and doing things other than their work. After all, this is the group that gave us the term "workaholic," and most "-aholics" need the help of a twelve-step program to get control.

BOOKEND BOOMERS

Sometimes called the Bookend or Sandwich generation, Boomers are surrounded by issues from elder parents on one end and children in their twenties on the other. Young adult offspring continue to put demands on their time and energy, demands that the Boomers themselves never would have thought to make of their own parents. At the same time, more and more Boomers are being put in the position of needing to parent their parents, who are elderly and in declining health. This will be relevant to employers whose Boomer employees face stresses, time demands, and money constraints, all of which require company support and understanding.

GENERATION X: BORN 1965 TO 1976

Douglas Coupland first coined this label in his book *Generation X.* When the book was written in 1992, Generation Xers were " twenty-something." Now many of them are well into their thirties. Generation X is fascinating. On one hand, it is considered a generation raised with even more of a silver spoon and a sense of entitlement and much less political interest than the Baby Boomers. As a result, they are often viewed as slackers with less involvement in, and more pessimistic views about, politics and other issues. On the other hand, some Xers are hard-core traditionalists—optimistic and hardworking. Some are like a second wave of hippies and some are narrow-minded believers in gender roles and stereotypes. Generation X, more than any other generation I studied, is the one that is most elusive because the differences among its members can be so extreme. In many cases, the labels ascribed to them are not only too general, they are outright wrong.

Generation X is also the group most attached to (or blamed for) the dot-com fury and the stock market boom days of the 1980s and 1990s. According to Benjamin Soskis, this is largely a misperception. Fewer than 5 percent of Gen Xers are employed in computer-related industries. Moreover, a 1998 investor study by the Investment Company Institute found that the median stockholding of Xers was $20,000 and the median age for investors was 47, i.e., more Boom than Bust.

Fifty-one million Americans are considered members of Generation X. Just like those generations that came before them, Xers grew up in a different world. The divorce of their parents has often been cited as the event having the single greatest impact upon them. The high rate of divorce and increased number of working mothers led to Xers being the first generation of latch-key kids. As a result, traits of independence, resilience, and adaptability are often among their attributes.

Generation X feels strongly that they do not need someone looking over their shoulders. They also desire immediate and ongoing feedback and are equally comfortable giving feedback to others. Other traits of this group include working well in multicultural settings, desire for some fun in the workplace, and a pragmatic approach for getting things done.

Generation X also saw their parents get laid off and face job insecurity in a way that previous generations never did. They have redefined loyalty. Instead of remaining loyal to their employer, they have a commitment to the work—to the teams with whom they work and to the bosses for whom they work.

BABY BOOM ECHO: BORN 1977 TO 2000

By 1977, many Boomers decided to have children, and the birthrate began to climb again. This created a surge in the population and a generation called the Baby Boom Echo. I found many different starting and ending years attributed to the Baby Boom Echo—beginning anywhere from 1976 to 1982 and ending around 1994 to 2001.

The Baby Boom Echo is entering the workforce now and will be coming on in force through the first quarter of the 21st century. Nearly 75 million strong, this generation is coming of age as powerful and positive. Their parents, the Boomers, are seen as the most child-centered caregivers in American history. This brings us to another label—the Soccer Mom. Parents of the Echo are shuttling their children everywhere—soccer, softball, karate, dance, tutors, singing, and piano—and that's just one child! With the taxi service come high expectations of achievement, as the highly competitive Boomer parents see their children as both an extension and a reflection of themselves. It seems that even when it comes to parenting, the Boomers are all about "me." At any rate, the Baby Boom Echo is seen as a largely self-confident group, sometimes even cocky. They like to set goals and go for them. Since they have had to be good at time management since day one, Echos are multitaskers and team players. In fact, they typically prefer to work in groups rather than alone. They also tend to socialize in groups rather than as couples.

High-tech is second nature to them. Many of the Echos have never seen a dial phone and cannot imagine that we saw *The Wizard of Oz* only once a year. In spite of the showers of attention they received, they do expect to work hard. They desire structure and direction in the workplace. Perhaps as a result of years of having coaches and headstrong parents, the Echos are respectful of positions and titles and desire a relationship with their boss. This may not always sit well with Generation X, who are largely hands-off, independent workers. On the other hand, the Echo is the group, as I mentioned before, that is expected to work very well with the Seniors.

One reason for this affinity may be the hardships witnessed by the Baby Boom Echo. In between soccer and softball, this generation saw parents lose their jobs in record numbers due to layoffs and "right-sizing." The Echos saw retirees struggling to get by, and seniors taking jobs at McDonald's to make ends meet. The recession of the late 1990s and into the 2000s brought an abrupt end to the Roaring '80s and '90s, similar to the abrupt end of the Roaring '20s. Another interesting commonality between the World War II generation and the Baby Boom Echo is their faith in the military. A poll for the Harvard Institute of Politics finds that 75 percent of 1,200 undergraduates surveyed report trusting the military "to do the right thing" all or most of the time.[5]

ENCOURAGING THE CONNECTION

Hewlett-Packard (HP) is one company that is taking advantage of the natural affinity between the Silent Generation and the Baby Boom Echo. In 1995, the company began a mentoring program pairing HP employees with thousands of middle- and high-school students. Primarily through the use of e-mail communication, the program is credited with having a tremendous positive impact on the students.

Employers are already looking forward to getting the rest of the Baby Boom Echo into the workforce, expecting this large and positive group to change society for the better and increase productivity. Echos are generally found to be more favorable about their work situation and to feel that management has a clearly communicated vision. They are looking for guidance, and 75 percent report that their managers are available when needed.[6] They are also expected to be fiercely loyal to managers whom they trust to teach and nurture them—much as they trusted their coaches.

According to the book *Generations at Work*, by Ron Zemke, Claire Raines, and Bob Filipczak, seven attributes characterize the Baby Boom Echo:

1. Their supervisory style is not fixed. How closely they monitor and manage, for instance, is a product of each individual's track record and personal preferences. Control and autonomy are a continuum, not solitary options.
2. Their leadership style is situationally varied. Some decisions are consensually made; others are made by the manager, but with input and consultation.
3. They depend less on positional than on personal power.
4. They know when and how to make personal policy exceptions, without causing a team riot.
5. They are thoughtful when matching individuals to a team, or matching a team or individual to an assignment.
6. They balance concern for tasks and concern for people. They are neither slave drivers nor country club managers.
7. They understand the elements of trust and work to gain it from their employees. They are perceived as fair, inclusive, good communicators, and competent in their own right.[7]

While some sources anticipate that this will be the next generation of workaholics, I don't agree. According to Mercer Human Resources Consulting, 64 percent of Baby Boom Echo employees reported reaching a balance between home and work. Only about 40 percent of the other generations reported finding such a balance. In addition, other trends, such as spirituality in the workplace, are at play that will continue to reinforce balance as a priority.

At the same time, however, this generation is not afraid of hard work. They will be more efficient, working smarter instead of longer. A 2001 study found that 88 percent of the Echos surveyed had specific goals for the next five years and were confident about reaching them.[8] This type of goal-oriented optimism would not be expected from either Boomers or Xers. Echos reflect their parents' priority around education. Not only are they well educated in the traditional sense, but also most hit the workforce with relevant work experience or internships to their credit. In addition, Echos are expected to continue their education throughout adulthood, consistently seeking out job-related and other types of training.

WHAT ECHOS WANT

While companies are eager for the hardworking Echos to join the workforce, they will find that this generation has strong demands for their employers—demands that they will expect to be met. In their book *Managing Generation Y*, Bruce Tulgan and Carolyn A. Martin cite Echo expectations of the workplace including challenging work that matters, clearly delegated assignments balanced with freedom and flexibility, increased responsibility as a reward for accomplishment, ongoing training/learning opportunities, and mentor relationships. In another book, *Generations*, authors William Strauss and Neil Howe predict that the Baby Boom Echos, who are also expected to become politically active, will require even more dramatic employment adjustments, such as:

- Pay equity among all workers
- Fewer job definitions
- A reestablished middle class
- Downgraded salaries for CEOs and other executives
- Trade barriers
- Government regulation of labor standards
- Revitalized unions[9]

Not only demanding, the Echos may also be needy and harder to please. They are expected to require more direction and supervision than the Boomers or Xers. Companies will need strong team leaders to manage them. Training, orientation, and consistent feedback will also be important to their success. A majority (67 percent) expressed an interest in the opportunity to take time away for training—compared to 52 percent or less for the other generations. Echos also reported being less satisfied at work—significantly less satisfied than the other generations—with both their job and their companies. Less than half of Echos said they feel fairly treated at work, compared to 64 percent of all generations. In addition, while 75 percent of Xers feel that they are being challenged with interesting work, only 64 percent of Echos do. One reason for this may be that they feel they are ready to move to the next rung of the corporate ladder, but haven't yet done so.[10]

Company loyalty and motivation of the Baby Boom Echos is influenced by factors other than pay, especially when compared to the other generations. As mentioned above, Echos are very loyal to their managers, whom they view as caring coaches. When asked about factors that affect their commitment and motivation to work, 82 percent cited flexible working arrangements, a figure much higher than that for the other generations. While the other generations most often cited base pay as the primary work factor, fewer Echos did. Still, more than half of the Echos said they would be willing to leave their current employer for another offering better benefits.

THE MILLENNIUM GENERATION: BORN SINCE 2000

As I mentioned in the thumbnail sketches of the generations at the beginning of this chapter, I am breaking out a fifth, new generation that I call the Millennium Generation, or the Millennials, to describe babies being born since the turn of the 21st century.* As interesting as all this generational information is, it is only part of the picture. New babies are being born every day, and historical, political, and even entertainment events will influence them in ways that I cannot even dare to imagine. With my futurist hat firmly in place, I see young people entering the workplace who will be comfortable with diversity, who will expect equal pay as an everyday occurrence, and who will be flexible and

*Many writers use the term *millennials* to refer to people born in the late 1980s and 1990s. Again, the terminology can be confusing. I prefer my usage; it was, after all, in 2000 that we celebrated in "millennium."

interested in carving out their own niche both at home and at work. Technology will be so advanced that the time-clock-punching mentality will be a thing of the past. Results will rule. Recognition and reward will follow naturally and without angst or struggle.

One thing is for sure. Millennials will live a long time. By 2020, we may have five generations working side by side. Surveys and studies will continue to pour out of established and prestigious sources as each generation enters each phase of their lives. Companies will have instant access to all of this information. More importantly, though, companies will have a front-row seat for the interactions, associations, and priorities of the four or five generations working side by side. This firsthand information will prove the most valuable in determining how to best manage the generations for maximum employee satisfaction and productivity.

MANY GENERATIONS: ONE WORKFORCE

Insight into the differences among the generations is beneficial to employers seeking to create a workplace where people can do their best work. Generalizations aside, every one in every generation is a person. At the end of the day, each individual wants to be recognized as such: an individual, not a number or statistic or label. This is not preaching, this is priority insight #1.

What generation are you in? As I already mentioned, I am considered a Baby Boomer. In researching the generations, I found characteristics I shared with my Boomer brethren, and ones I did not. No big surprise! I bet you would say the same thing. More importantly, though, I found a common thread throughout all of the generations—as individuals, regardless of their age, they share a desire for individual dignity. In the workplace this translates into:

- Respect
- Fair treatment
- Equality
- Balance
- Flexibility
- Appropriate feedback
- Job enhancement and advancement opportunities

GENERATIONAL DIVERSITY

First off, it's inevitable that the generations will all be present in the workforce at the same time. Smart businesses, however, will proactively seek generational diversity in their employee base for a number of reasons, including:

- ***Wisdom and Experience:*** A new appreciation for the corporate wisdom, but also the life wisdom, of the older workers is renewing their role as a valuable asset.
- ***Fresh Ideas and Fearlessness:*** Younger workers bring a value in their "why not" ways that have come as a result of their fresh approach and independence.
- ***Individual Wisdom and Skills:*** Regardless of their age, each individual brings a unique skill and experience set. Finding just the right blend for a given position requires that we open up opportunities across the generations and reach out for the diverse and wonderful things they each can offer.

- ***The Need for More Workers:*** Many sources predict worker shortages in the millions in the first half of the 21st century.
- ***Reflection of the Marketplace:*** All these vital and active generations will be the vital and active marketplace from which your customers will come. An employee base that mirrors the marketplace is largely accepted and expected to be more effective.

CONCLUSION

What we are seeing today, early in the 21st century, is just the tip of the iceberg. We can find examples of four generations active in the workplace scattered here and there. At this point, they are novel enough even to be newsworthy. By 2050, though, four or even five generations will be working together in full force. It won't just be Seniors working at Burger King or serving as ex-officio board members, and it won't just be young people, still wet behind the ears, needing to learn to fit in and earn their stripes. Many generations of workers—all strong, all valuable, and all side-by-side—will provide unprecedented opportunities for development and profitability. Combining the wisdom and experience of the older worker with the energy and stamina of the young, the workplace of the future stands to gain considerably.

Finding and keeping the best and the brightest from all the generations will be the challenge of the future. Management, compensation, scheduling, and training will all be affected by the multigenerational workforce.

Notes

1. Ron Zemke, Claire Raines, and Bob Filipczak, *Generations at Work: Managing the Clash of Veterans, Boomers, Xers, and Nexters in Your Workplace* (New York: AMACOM, 2000).
2. Alison Stein Wellner, "Generational Divide," *American Demographics*, October 2000: 52–56, 58.
3. Edie Weiner, interview, August 2003.
4. Quoted in Wellner, "Generational Divide", 545.
5. Robin Toner, "Trust in the Military Heightens Among Baby Boomers' Children," *The New York Times*, May 27, 2003: A1.
6. Eric Hazard, "Mercer (HR Consulting): Gen Y Positive About Career but Not Satisfied," www.PlanSponsor.com, July 16, 2003.
7. Zemke, Raines, and Filipczak, *Generations at Work.*
8. Ibid, 144.
9. William Strauss and Neil Howe, *Generations: The History of America's Future, 1584 to 2069* (New York: William Morrow, 1992).
10. Hazard, "Mercer (HR Consulting): Gen Y Positive About Career."

THE GLASS CEILING: DOMESTIC AND INTERNATIONAL PERSPECTIVES*

Nancy Lockwood

Worldwide, individual women have been breaking through the glass ceiling. Since the year 2000, New Zealand has appointed its first woman prime minister; the first woman became president of Central Bank in Finland; the former president of Ireland became

*Reprinted with Permission of *SHRM Research Quarterly*, The Society for Human Resource Management, Alexandria, VA (2004): 2–10, via the Copyright Clearance Center.

the first woman Commissioner of Human Rights in the United Nations; and the World Health Organization has its first woman Director-General, the former prime minister of Norway.[1]

> *"Women advance in the workplace but still trail men."*
>
> THE JOURNALNEWS.COM, MARCH 28, 2004

Yet, newspaper headlines today highlight the glass ceiling which continues to affect women in the workplace. This chapter explores facets of the glass ceiling focusing on domestic and international research regarding personal, institutional and societal barriers that affect women's advancement—and how human resource professionals and organizations can address these issues.

DEFINITION OF THE GLASS CEILING

The term "glass ceiling" was coined in a 1986 *Wall Street Journal* report on corporate women by Hymowitz and Schellhardt.[2] The glass ceiling is a concept that most frequently refers to barriers faced by women who attempt, or aspire, to attain senior positions (as well as higher salary levels) in corporations, government, education and nonprofit organizations. It can also refer to racial and ethnic minorities and men when they experience barriers to advancement. For the purpose of this article, the glass ceiling is discussed regarding women in business with a focus on advancement to senior positions.

WHY HR PROFESSIONALS NEED TO UNDERSTAND THE CONCEPT OF THE GLASS CEILING

Human resource professionals are often in leadership positions that allow them to have a broad impact on organizations. As a result, it is important that they are knowledgeable about how the glass ceiling phenomenon may directly or indirectly impact an organization's reputation, customer loyalty, diversity of skill sets, growth potential and even its bottom line. Oftentimes, the CEO or president of an organization may tap HR professionals for their advice and expertise on the strategic organizational changes that are necessary to reduce the existence of a glass ceiling in order to maximize an organization's performance and reputation.

HR professionals are also required to be knowledgeable of employment laws, programs and practices for their organization. Because the law provides protection for certain demographic groups, such as women, in the labor market, HR professionals need to understand the potential impact of glass-ceiling barriers (e.g., discrimination) on women—including women of color—regarding advancement in the workplace.

In the United States, discrimination in the workplace is illegal (see Figure 1). Yet discrimination exists in many forms. For women, for example, discrimination can result in lower pay and fewer advances in salary when compared with men. It may also manifest in hiring practices, training and development, and promotional opportunities that are disproportionately in favor of men.

Workplace changes that are facilitated and implemented by HR professionals—such as hiring, transfers, training and development, promotions, succession planning, and terminations—have the potential to either positively or negatively impact glass-ceiling

- Title VII of the Civil Rights Act—1964
- Age Discrimination in Employment Act (ADEA)—1967
- Americans With Disabilities Act (ADA)—1990
- Equal Employment Opportunity (EEO)
- Affirmative action policies

FIGURE 1 United States Employment Laws and Policies That Affect Women in the Workplace

Source: Adapted from SHRM Learning System (2003). Alexandria, VA: Society for Human Resource Management.

barriers. For example, many organizations are required to develop affirmative action plans (AAP), complete EEO reports and undergo audits. A critical section of the AAP is the utilization analysis, which compares the number of women and minorities available in the labor market to those employed in the organization. Corporate management reviews, sometimes called glass-ceiling audits, are another compliance requirement, usually conducted during the overall AAP audit and focused primarily on the decision-making process of senior executives and CEOs. For AAP noncompliance, companies can be severely fined. Further, companies who do not comply with Title VII of the Civil Rights Act of 1964 and other U.S. employment laws risk large court-imposed fines and unfavorable publicity.

At the end of this article, recommendations are presented for HR professionals to help prevent and/or eliminate glass-ceiling barriers.

SIGNS OF THE GLASS CEILING IN THE WORKPLACE

Evidence of the glass ceiling has been described as invisible, covert and overt. At the root of the glass ceiling are gender-based barriers, commonly cited in the literature and noted anecdotally. These barriers run the gamut from gender stereotypes to preferred leadership styles to tokenism in the high managerial ranks (see Figure 2).

FIGURE 2 Gender-Based Barriers

- Corporate policies and practices
- Training and career development
- Promotion policies
- Compensation practices
- Behavioral and cultural explanations
- Behavioral double binds
- Communication styles
- Stereotypes
- Preferred leadership styles
- Power in corporate culture
- Maintaining the status quo ("old boy" networks)
- Tokenism in top management circles

Source: Adapted from Oakley, J. G. (2000, October). "Gender-based Barriers to Senior Management Positions: Understanding the Scarcity of Female CEOs," *Journal of Business Ethics*, 27, 4: 321–335.

A major sign of the effect of the glass ceiling is gender-biased compensation. Countless studies and anecdotal reports have shown huge discrepancies in salary in favor of men, even for similar positions in similar organizations. For example, in 2002 the median total compensation of male CEOs in nonprofit organizations was $147,085, approximately 50% higher than the median total of female CEOs ($98,108) in similar settings.[3] Discrepancies in favor of men still existed even when organizational revenue sizes were compared. Also, women who do not have opportunities to gain additional competencies are not likely to have the skills, such as specific managerial experience, required to compete for and be awarded equal positions as men and close the pay gap.

Another indicator of the glass ceiling is when women's advancement is hampered by well-ingrained corporate cultures. For example, corporate policies and practices can subtly maintain the status quo by keeping men in positions of corporate power. Boards of directors, which are mostly comprised of men, sometimes perpetuate the status quo by selecting CEOs who look like them. Other gender-based barriers include behavioral and communication styles that differ vastly from the company's norms and women's lack of opportunity to gain general management/line experience.[4]

Work/life balance challenges can impact women's advancement and, if not dealt with, may contribute to the glass-ceiling phenomenon. Women are typically the primary family caregivers for children and/or the elderly. Assumptions are often made regarding women's availability to do a job without interference from family responsibilities. Further, some organizations may not offer work/life programs that support outside commitments, particularly for senior-level positions. Therefore, many women are at a disadvantage to take steps that would increase the likelihood of advancing up the corporate ladder.

Finally, opportunities for promotion often favor men due to developmental prospects, such as mentoring and networks. Women may not have full access to informal networks men use to develop work relationships in the company, and these networks often tend to exclude women due to the nature of their activities or the perception that these are "male activities" (e.g., golf), thus contributing to gender barriers in the workplace.

STUDIES ABOUT THE GLASS CEILING IN THE UNITED STATES

Several groundbreaking studies address the glass ceiling on the domestic front:

- In the early 1990s, the Center for Creative Leadership conducted studies on the glass ceiling. Their 1995 study surveyed human resource managers from 304 large industrial and service firms from *Fortune* 1000, 500 and 50 companies. Two key findings that create and perpetuate the glass ceiling were revealed:

  1. The discomfort of white male managers with those unlike themselves (e.g. women and women of color).
  2. The lack of accountability or incentives in organizations to develop diversity.[5]

- In 1996 Catalyst, one of the leading nonprofit research organizations for women in business, conducted a pioneering study to examine perceptions and experiences of the *Fortune* 1000's most senior-level women and CEOs. (However, the study did not indicate the gender of the CEOs.) Comparison of this study with their 2003 study on women in corporate leadership roles reveals valuable information regarding the state of the workplace for executive women, as well as CEOs' perspectives on the glass ceiling. Overall, women's views about advancement opportunities indicate that the glass ceiling remains well intact.

1. Compared with 23 percent of women in 1996, in 2003 only 30 percent of women believed the opportunities for senior positions in their own organizations have greatly improved in the past five years.
2. Only 11 percent of women believed opportunities in the United States have improved in general.[6]

- CEOs' views regarding women's advancement are critical to supporting women's talents in high-ranking positions. In 2003 Catalyst surveyed CEOs (who were not identified by gender) from the Fortune 1000 companies and compared their views with those of senior-level female employees:

1. Women and CEOs agreed that the lack of general management or line experience was the top barrier to women's advancement to senior leadership roles.
2. Nearly two-thirds (64 percent) of CEOs believed it was the organization's responsibility to change to meet the needs of women in management.
3. Forty-seven percent of women said that exclusion from informal networks was a barrier to advancement, in contrast to 18 percent of CEOs.
4. Lack of mentoring was noted by 16 percent of women, in comparison with 21 percent of CEOs.[7]

- The glass-ceiling literature discusses differences in management/leadership styles between men and women. For example, communication styles of management and leadership in the corporate world that are typically most valued are those often used by men (e.g., being direct and factual), rather than the interpersonal style women often use.
  Therefore, women who use the more direct communication style may be more likely to advance in the corporate world than women who do not. However, a recent study shows that women tend to be more flexible in their leadership styles than men and engage different styles and approaches. This report compared highly successful women executives in senior leadership positions with successful men executives and less successful women from large *Fortune* 400 companies, including PepsiCo, IBM, Unilever and Prudential.

1. The key findings note that successful women executives are twice as likely to use a more interpersonal style than men.
2. Women also use leadership styles that men typically use, such as directive and authoritative.
3. The study suggests that the best leaders—men or women—do not use the style they are most comfortable with, but rather use the style best suited to the situation/people.[8]

- A 2004 study shows that those companies that have managed to "break through" the glass-ceiling have prospered financially. Of 353 *Fortune* 500 companies, those with the highest representation of women on their top management teams had better financial performance than did the group with the lowest women's representation: the Return on Equity (ROE) was 35 percent higher and the Total Return to Shareholders (TRS) was 34 percent higher.[9]

STATISTICS DON'T EXPLAIN EARNINGS DIFFERENCES

The number of women in the labor force is growing. In the United States in 1998, women represented 45 percent of the labor force and men 55 percent. It is predicted that by 2008 women will comprise 48 percent of the labor force and men 52 percent.[10] Yet in spite of women's large share in the labor force, pay inequities continue to exist. In the discussion of the glass ceiling, one of the foremost topics is pay equality. Title VII of the Civil Rights Act of 1964 mandates pay equality between men and women.

Based on a U.S. General Accounting Office (GAO) report, research on equal pay and career advancement does not explain the magnitude of earnings differences between men and women, nor why these differences exist. The GAO investigated factors that contribute to earnings differences. Taking into account differences between work patterns of men and women, as well as other key factors, women earned, on average, 80 percent of men's earnings in 2000. However, the GAO earnings model cannot account for the remaining earnings difference. The report suggests that pay differences may be the result of managing work and family responsibilities differently.[11]

According to the Institute for Women's Policy Research (IWPR), factors that explain these differences include work experience, education and lack of opportunities. Historically, women's wages lag behind men's.[12] In addition, the gap between women's and men's earnings increases with age. The U.S. Bureau of Labor Statistics shows that in 2002 the difference between women's and men's earnings was much greater among workers aged 45 to 54: women in this age range earned 75 percent as much as men. In contrast, women aged 16 to 24 earned 93 percent of men's wages.[13] Young women are closing the wage gap; in 2000 they earned 82 percent of young men's earnings, compared with 68 percent in 1979.[14] HR professionals can play a large role in closing the salary gender gap.

WOMEN OF COLOR

Women of color often face additional challenges in regard to the impact of the glass ceiling. Not only do they have to contend with gender-based barriers, but they sometimes have to overcome racial and ethnic obstacles to move up the corporate ladder.

A 2004 research report of African-American women notes exclusion from informal networks and even conflicting relationships with white women. Although 75 percent of Fortune 500 companies have formal diversity programs, 37 percent of African-American women state that opportunities to advance to senior positions are declining. The primary barriers for African-American women are:

1. Negative race-based stereotypes.
2. Lack of institutional support.
3. Frequent questioning of African-American women's authority and credibility.

To combat these barriers, African-American women recommend three proactive success factors: communicating effectively, exceeding performance expectations, and building positive relationships with managers and colleagues.[15]

Catalyst conducted research on women of color and the glass ceiling that yielded slightly more optimistic findings. Overall, they found that women of color experienced positive career growth—for example, 57% were promoted at least once (data consistent with other studies of white women and women of color). While this research shows women of color employ several strategies for advancement and place great emphasis on networking and mentoring, it also reports that women of color are less hopeful about their career prospects since the same barriers from the past remain today.[16]

THE GLASS CEILING AND INTERNATIONAL IMPLICATIONS FOR HR PROFESSIONALS

The glass ceiling is not a U.S. phenomenon. Glass-ceiling barriers are evidenced worldwide, often compounded by cultural values and traditional gender roles. With the expansion of globalization, HR professionals who work in the United States or abroad—in U.S.-owned or foreign-owned operations—must be educated regarding the U.S. and international employment laws that affect their organizations (see below).

Extraterritorial laws that apply to U.S. firms conducting business outside the United States:

- Title VII of the Civil Rights Act of 1964
- Age Discrimination in Employment Act (ADEA)
- Americans with Disabilities Act (ADA)

International laws that require nondiscrimination in employment:

- European Union (EU)—Equal Pay Directive
- International Labour Organization (ILO)—Equal Remuneration Convention No. 100
- Organization for Economic Cooperation and Development (OECD)—Guidelines for Multinational Enterprises
- United Nations—Global Compact

An emerging issue of the aging workforce is the lack of global talent. Where will HR professionals find the right people for their organizations as the baby-boomer generation retires? One of the missing key ingredients is female global managers. Women employees offer a wide range of talent and potential but are largely underdeveloped in the global managerial ranks (see Figure 3). Developing global leaders requires experience outside the home country, and, increasingly, international experience is a requirement for global senior leadership positions.

FIGURE 3 Top Three Barriers for Women to Gaining Global Business Experience

- Getting selected—the biggest hurdle to enter the global business arena
- Being perceived as less internationally mobile than men due to work and personal responsibilities
- Lack of mentors and networks on international assignments

Source: Adapted from *Passport to Opportunity: U.S. Women in Global Business* (2000). New York: Catalyst.

INTERNATIONAL STUDIES ON THE GLASS CEILING

A number of studies regarding the glass ceiling point to issues in the international arena:

- A 2002 report documents the top barriers to women in international leadership roles as stereotypes and preconceptions of women's roles and abilities, and the lack of mentors and visible successful female role models.[17]
  1. Many of the respondents—men and women in senior positions at large corporations across 20 European countries—noted that the opportunities for women's advancement have greatly improved in the past five years.
  2. Nearly 25 percent of women stated there has been no change; 9 percent of men agreed.
  3. For women who want to advance in the global arena, the barriers of tokenism, exclusion and isolation remain unchanged.
- A study of women expatriate managers representing a wide range of industry and service sectors in Europe found that they are disadvantaged due to the lack of organizational support which is readily available to their male counterparts. These findings suggest that few organizations have developed career models for women expatriates.
  1. All women managers in the study stated they hit the glass ceiling in their organizations early in their careers and affirmed the glass ceiling is very real in Europe.
  2. Only 25 percent believed they could make it to the top of their professions.
  3. Lifestyle choices are even more difficult for women expatriate managers than for domestic women managers, primarily due to the strain on personal relationships and poor quality of life resulting from commuter marriages.
  4. Career success is still based on a male career model that ignores factors of marriage, pregnancy, children and household duties. In the early stages of women's careers, gender stereotypes remain a major obstacle.[18]
- To determine why so few women have international opportunities, catalyst interviewed and surveyed over 1,000 employees from U.S. based global companies, including 522 human resource executives. Key findings revealed the following:[19]
  1. It is often assumed that only men are interested in expatriate positions. Forty-two percent of women said that stating their interest was an important factor to being offered a global assignment, compared with 29 percent of men.
  2. Women are perceived to be disadvantaged, compared with men, regarding international mobility, balancing work and personal responsibilities, and building business relationships outside the United States.
  3. There is a shortage of experienced international talent for the traditional three to five-year international assignment, due, in large part, to dual-career marriages. This demographic places a larger burden on women. Of the married expatriates in this study, 91 percent of women were in dual-career marriages, compared with 50 percent of men.
  4. Women in international assignments tend to be more isolated than their male counterparts, often lacking formal support, such as mentors and networks, from their organizations.

WOMEN IN SENIOR POSITIONS IN THE UNITED STATES AND ABROAD

According to research, the advancement of women to senior positions is paradoxical at best. While there has been some movement, much remains unchanged. Advancement continues to be a challenge due to the lack of support at the organizational level from organizational culture, policies and practices, insufficient training opportunities to develop new competencies, lack of role models and mentors, and few opportunities for advancement abroad, often due to cultural values and norms. With many barriers remaining in place, women are not gaining the required experience to compete with men (see Figure 4). For example, in 2002 women held only 10 percent of the 6,428 total line corporate officer positions in the *Fortune* 50.[20] Women who have successfully attained senior positions recommend a number of career strategies, such as consistently exceeding performance expectations (see Figure 5). One of the critical measures of women in senior positions is the number of women who hold corporate directorships. For example, in the United States in 1995, women represented 10 percent of board directors, increasing to 16 percent in 2002.[21] In Canada, women held about 11 percent of board positions in 2001 and 2003.[22] In the United Kingdom in 2003, women passed a milestone with 101 directorships on FTSE 100 boards when the number of companies with female directors increased from 61 to 68.[23] However, in other high-ranking positions, women representation is much lower than in directorships. In 1995, the Fortune 500 had one woman CEO. Today, there are seven female CEOs (an increase from 0.2 percent to 1.4 percent).[24]

FIGURE 4 Overt and Covert Barriers for Women to Domestic and International Senior Positions

- Balancing home life and career
- Isolation and loneliness
- Constant awareness of being a woman in a man's world
- Lack of access to male networks
- Having to prove oneself to others
- Having to work harder and be better than male counterparts
- Having to ask for promotions
- Having to ask for international assignments
- Less time available for networking due to domestic commitments

Source: Adapted from Linehan, M., & Scullion, H. (2001). "European Female Expatriate Careers: Critical Success Factors," *Journal of European Industrial Training, 25*, 8: 392–419.

FIGURE 5 Critical Career Strategies for Women to Attain Senior Positions

1. Consistently exceed performance expectations
2. Develop a style with which male managers feel comfortable
3. Seek out challenging and visible assignments
4. Obtain the support of an influential mentor

Source: Ragins, B. R., Townsend, B., & Mattis, M. (February 1998), Gender Gap in the Executive Suite: CEOs and Female Executives Report on Breaking the Glass Ceiling, "*The Academy of Management Executive*", *12*, 1: 28–43.

- Increased compensation
- Opportunity to develop new skills/competencies
- Greater advancement opportunities
- Increased intellectual stimulation
- Different type of work
- More authority to make decisions
- Organizational values compatible with their own

FIGURE 6 Reasons for Women Leaving Current Organization

Source: Adapted form *Women in U.S. Corporate Leadership: 2003.* (2003). New York: Catalyst.

WOMEN ENTREPRENEURS

As a path around the glass ceiling, there is a movement of women toward entrepreneurship. Key factors in business ownership are leadership recognition and the authority to make decisions. Women's decisions to leave corporations include a mix of personal and professional reasons—from lack of work/life balance to gender discrimination to the opportunity to pursue new challenges (see Figure 6).

In the United States the growing number of women-owned or majority women-owned businesses demonstrates that women entrepreneurs are breaking through the glass ceiling. According to the U.S. Department of Labor, the Census Bureau's latest Survey of Women-Owned Business Enterprises reported that women owned 51 percent or more of 5,417,034 firms in 1997. The four industries with the largest total revenues for women-owned businesses were wholesale trade, service, retail trade and manufacturing.[25]

Women of color are also making significant inroads as entrepreneurs. Between 1997 and 2002, the number of minority women-owned firms increased by 32 percent. In terms of the *proportion*, in 2002 one in five women-owned businesses in the United States was owned by a woman of color.[26]

Increasingly, women entrepreneurs are being recognized for their work and for their growing companies. For example, according to a new study, a number of women entrepreneurs own million-dollar firms.[27] In addition, the Veuve Clicquot Business Woman of the Year Award acknowledges women at the leading edge of entrepreneurship.[28]

THE OTHER SIDE OF THE COIN—IS THERE REALLY A GLASS CEILING?

To complete the discussion of the glass ceiling, it is essential to mention three primary divergent views against the glass-ceiling concept. The first argument is that women can get to senior-level positions on their own merit, through hard work, ambition and adding value to the bottom line—if they want to. That is, some women choose not to pursue more ambitious career goals.[29]

The second argument states that it is work/family challenges that get in the way of women's advancement, as opposed to obstacles within the organization or those set by top management.[30] As they climb the corporate ladder or earn the corner office, many women discover that family is more important to them, and they risk missing out on special moments in their children's lives. *Fast Company* recently interviewed a number of high-level women who had chosen to step down from their positions. As a woman who had been a vice president of an international bank commented, "There's a different quality of what men give up versus what women give up." She explained, "The sacrifices for women are deeper, and you must weigh them very consciously if you want to continue."[31]

Finally, the third viewpoint is that glass-ceiling literature tends to ignore smaller companies, and women's entrepreneurial success in smaller companies appears to carry less value in comparison with senior roles in traditional and larger corporate settings.[32]

RECOMMENDATIONS: WHAT HR CAN DO TO HELP BREAK THE GLASS CEILING

HR professionals should take a proactive role to identify whether the glass-ceiling phenomenon is operating within their organization and should lead the way to find solutions to overcome it. Below are a number of actions that HR professionals can take to break the glass-ceiling barriers. By no means is this an exhaustive list, but instead it serves as a starting place. Understanding the organization's culture, values and norms is the first step. Change, however, will only successfully occur with the commitment of the organization's top management. Key to organizational change is education—of management, women and the overall workforce. Finally, measurement is critical to map the path for change and chart the results.

Examine the Organizational Culture

- Review HR policies and practices to determine if they are fair and inclusive (e.g., pay differences, hiring practices, history of promotions to senior positions, affirmative action plans).
- Examine the organization's informal culture: Look at subtle behaviors, traditions and norms that may work against women.
- Through surveys and focus groups, discover men's and women's perceptions about the organization's culture, their career expectations and what drives their intentions to stay or leave.
- Identify the organization's best practices that support women's advancement.
- Map the strengths and weaknesses of policies and programs.

Drive Change Through Management Commitment

- Support top-management commitment to talent management, including women in senior positions.
- Ensure that diversity (including women in senior positions) is a key business measurement for success that is communicated to all employees by top management.
- Require line management accountability for advancement of women by incorporating it in performance goals.
- Train line managers to raise awareness and understand barriers to women's advancement.

Foster Inclusion

- Establish and lead a change-management diversity program for managers and employees.
- Affirm diversity inclusion in all employment brand communications.

- Develop a list of women for succession planning.
- Develop and implement retention programs for women.

Educate and Support Women in Career Development

- Emphasize the importance of women acquiring line management experience.
- Encourage mentoring via informal and formal programs.
- Acknowledge successful senior-level women as role models.
- Support the development and utilization of women's networks inside and outside the organization.
- Create and implement leadership development programs for women, including international assignments, if applicable.

Measure for Change

- Monitor the impact of recruiting strategies designed to attract women to senior levels of the organization.
- Track women's advancement in the organization (hiring, job rotation, transfers, international assignments, promotions).
- Determine who gets access to leadership and management training and development opportunities.
- Evaluate differences between salary of men and women at parallel levels within the organization.
- Measure women's turnover against men's.
- Explore reasons why women leave the organization.

CONCLUSION

Both domestically and globally, women represent a relatively untapped source of talent for leadership in the workplace. While progress has been made across the globe, barriers to women's advancement continue to exist, including cultural norms, stereotypes, and employer policies and practices. As the renowned economist Lester Thurow, Lemelson Professor of Management and Economics at the Massachusetts Institute of Technology, recently said, "Great challenges lay ahead and our economic future is at stake. Organizations cannot compete in a global environment without using women."[33] Human resource professionals have a significant part to play—through organizational culture, workplace policies and practices, change management and workforce education—to develop women leaders at home and abroad.

Below are resources and tools that human resource professionals may use in their role to help shatter the impact of the glass ceiling.

RESOURCES

Catalyst: www.catalystwomen.org

Center for Advanced Human Resource Studies (CAHRS): www.ilr.cornell.edu/depts/cahrs/aboutcahrs.html

Center for Women's Business Research: www.nfwbo.org/

Cranfield School of Management – Centre for Developing Women Business Leaders: www.som.cranfield.ac.uk/som/research/centres/cdwbl

Eurostat: http://europa.eu.int/comm/eurostat/

Institute for Women's Policy Research: www.iwpr.org

International Labour Organization: www.ilo.org

OECD: Guidelines for Multinational Enterprises: www.oecd.org/department/0.2688.en_2649_34889_1_1_1_1_1,00.html

Online Women's Business Center: www.onlinewbc.gov/

Promotion of Women Entrepreneurship: http://newcome.de/prowomen/english/ index.php

Recommendations of the Federal Glass Ceiling Commission: www.ilr.cornell.edu/library/downloads/keyWorkplaceDocuments/GlassCeilingRecommendations.pdf

United Nations – Division for the Advancement of Women: www.un.org/womenwatch/daw/

United Nations – The Global Compact: www.unglobalcompact.org/Portal/ Default.asp

Women & Equality Unit – EU and International Work: www.womenandequalityunit.gov.uk/eu_int/index.htm

U.S. Department of Labor – Women's Bureau: www.dol.gov/wb/

Women's Research and Education Institute: www.wrei.org

Bibliography

"*Advancing African-American Women in the Workplace: What Managers Need to know,*" (February 18, 2004). Catalyst: News Release. Retrieved March 8, 2004, from www.catalystwomen.org/2004afri_woc.htm

American Society of Association Executives. (2003). *Association Executive Compensation and Benefits Study, 14th Ed.* Washington, D.C.

Bureau of Labor Statistics. (September 2003). *Highlights of Women's Earnings in 2002.* Washington, D.C.: U.S. Department of Labor.

Bureau of Labor Statistics. (February 2000). *Women's share of labor force to edge higher by 2008.* Retrieved February 11, 2004, from www.bls.gov/opub/ted/2000/feb/wk3/art01.htm

Caiazza, A.B. (2003). *The Status of Women in the States.* Retrieved February 4, 2004, from www.iwpr.org/states2002/pdfs/US.pdf. Washington, D.C.: Institute for Women's Policy Research.

Cutler, M. M., and Jackson, A. L. (2002, Fall). "A 'Glass Ceiling' or Work/Family Conflict?" *The Journal of Business and Economics Studies* 8, 2: 73–85.

DiNatala, M., and Boraas, S. (2002, March). "The Labor Force Experience of Women from 'Generation X,' " *Monthly Labor Review*, 3–15.

Facts on Working Women: Women Business Owners. (November 2002). Retrieved April 14, 2004, from www.dol.gov/wb/factsheets/wbo02.htm

Fransson. S., Johansson, L., and Svenaeus, L. (2000). *Highlighting Pay Differentials Between Women And Men.* Sweden: Eu2001, SE.

HayGroup. (2003). *Style Matters: Why Women Executives Shouldn't Ignore Their "Feminine Side."* Boston, MA: The McClelland Center.

Hymowitz. C., and Schellhardt. T. D. (1986, March 24). "The Glass Ceiling" *Wall Street Journal*, Special Report on the Corporate Woman.

International Labour Organization. (2003). *Time for Equality at Work.* Geneva, Switzerland: International Labour Office.

Linehan, M., and Scullion, H. (2001). "European Female Expatriate Careers: Critical Success Factors," *Journal of European Industrial Training, 25*, 8: 392–419.

Minority Women-Owned Businesses in the United States, 2002: A Fact Sheet, (2001). Center for Women's Business Research, www.nfwbo.org

Morrison, A. M., Schreiber, C. T., and Price, K. F. (1995). *A Glass Ceiling Survey: Benchmarking Barriers and Practices.* Greensboro, NC: Center for Creative Leadership.

OECD: Guidelines for Multinational EnterPrises. Retrieved March 31, 2004, from www.oecd.org/department/0.2688, en_2649_34, 889_1_1_1_1_1,00.html

One in 9 Corporate Directors of FP500 Are Women in Latest Count. (2004, February 19). Catalyst: News Release. Retrieved March 8, 2004, from www.catalystwomen.org/ 2004can_wbd.htm"

"Passport to Opportunity: U.S. Women in Global Business" (executive summary). (2000). New York: Catalyst.

Pipes, S. C. (1996, April). "Glass Ceiling? So What?" *Chief Executive, 112*, 16.

Singh, V. (2002). *Managing Diversity for Strategic Advantage.* Crown Copyright: Council for Excellence in Management and Leadership.

Singh, V., and Vinnicombe, S. (2003). *Women Pass a Milestone: 101 Directorships on the FTSE 100 Boards.* Retrieved February 9, 2004, from www.som.cranfield.ac.uk/som/research/centre/ cdwbl/projects.asp

The Bottom Line: Connecting Corporate Performance and Gender Diversity. (2004). New York: Catalyst.

Thurow, L. C. (2003). *Fortune Favors the Bold: What We Must Do to Build a New and Lasting Global Prosperity.* New York: HarperCollins Publishers, Inc.

Tischler, L. (2004, February). "Where Are the Women?" *Fast Company, 79*, 52–60.

"United Nations: The global compact," Retrieved March 31, 2004, from www.unglobalcompact.org/Portal/ Default.asp

Vinnicombe, S., and Bank, J. (2003). *Women with Attitude: Lessons for Career Management.* London: Routledge.

Wirth, L. (1998). "Women in Management: Closer to Breaking Through the Glass Ceiling?" *International Labour Review, 137*, 1: 93–103.

Women Demonstrate They Have What It Takes to Build Million-Dollar Firms. Retrieved February 18, 2004, from www.womens-businessresearch.org/milliondollar/

Women in Leadership: A European Business Imperative. (2002). New York: Catalyst.

Women in U.S. Corporate Leadership: 2003. (2003). New York: Catalyst.

Women of Color in Corporate Management: Three Years Later. (2002). New York: Catalyst.

Women's Earnings: Work Patterns Partially Explain Difference Between Men's and Women's Earnings (2003, October). Washington, D.C.: U.S. General Accounting Office.

Endnotes

1. Wirth, L. (1998). "Women in Management: Closer to Breaking Through the Glass Ceiling?" *International Labour Review. 137,* 1, 93–103.
2. Hymowitz. C., and Schelinardt, T.D. (1986, March 24). "The Glass Ceiling". *The Wall Street Journal*, Special Report on the Corporate Woman.
3. American Society of Association Executives. (2003). *Association Executive Compensation & Benefits Study, 14th Ed.* Washington. D.C.
4. *Women in U.S. Corporate Leadership: 2003.* (2003). New York: Catalyst.
5. Morrison, A. M., Schreiber, C. T., and Price, K.F. (1995). *A Glass Ceiling Survey: Benchmarking Barriers and Practices*. Greensboro, NC: Center for Creative Leadership.
6. *Women in U.S. Corporate Leadership: 2003.* (2003). New York: Catalyst.
7. Ibid.
8. HayGroup. (2003). *Style Matters: Why Women Executives Shouldn't Ignore Their 'Feminine Side.'* Boston, MA: The McClelland Center.
9. The Bottom Line: Connecting Corporate Performance and Gender Diversity (2004). New York: Catalyst.

10. Bureau of Labor Statistics. (2000, February). "Women's Share of Labor Force to Edge Higher by 2008." Retrieved February 11, 2004, from www.bls.gov/opub/ted/2000/teb/wk3/art01. htm
11. *Women's Earnings: Work Patterns Partially Explain Difference Between Men's and Women's Earnings*. (2003, October). Washington, D.C.: U.S. General Accounting Office.
12. Caiazza, A.B. (2003). *The Status of Women in the States.* Retrieved February 4, 2004, from www.iwpr.org/states2002/pdfs/US.pdf. Washington, D. C.: Institute for Women's Policy Research.
13. Bureau of Labor Statistics (2003, September). *Highlights of Women's Earnings in 2002.* Washington, D.C.: U.S. Department of Labor.
14. DiNatala, M., and Boraas, S. (2002, March). "The Labor Force Experience of Women from 'Generation X,'" *Monthly Labor Review,* 3–15.
15. Advancing African American Women in the Workplace: What Managers Need to Know" (2004, February 18). Catalyst: News Release. Retrieved March 8, 2004, from www.catalystwomen.org/2004afri_woc_htm.
16. Women of Color in Corporate Management: Three Years Later. (2002). New York: Catalyst.
17. *Women in leadership: A European business imperative.* (2002). New York: Catalyst.
18. Linenan, M., and Scullion. H. (2001). European Female Expatriate Careers: Critical Success Factors," *Journal of European Industrial Training* 25, 392–419.
19. Passport to Opportunity: U.S. Women in Global Business (executive summary). (2000). New York: Catalyst.
20. *Women in U.S. Corporate Leadership: 2003.* (2003) New York: Catalyst.
21. Ibid.
22. One in Nine corporate Directors of FP500 Are Women in Latest Count" (2004, February 19). Catalyst: News Release. Retrieved March 8, 2004, from www.catalystwomen.org/2004can_wbd.htm
23. Singh, V., and Vinnicombe, S. (2003), Women Pass a Milestone: 101 Directorships on the FTSE 100 Boards. Retrieved February 9, 2004 from www.som.cranfield.ac.uk/som/research/centers/cdwbl/projects.asp
24. Women in U.S. Corporate Leadership: 2003. (2003). New York: Catalyst.
25. Facts on Working Women: Women Business Owners (2002, November). U.S. Department of Labor. http://www.dol.gov/wb/factsheets/wbo02.htm
26. Minority Women–owned Business in the United States, 2002: A Fact Sheet. (2001). Center for Women's Business Research, www.ntwbo.org
27. Women Demonstrate They Have What It Takes to Build Million-Dollar Firms." Retrieved February 18, 2004, from www.womensbusinessresearch.org/milliondollar.
28. Vinnicombe, S., and Bank, J. (2003). Women with Attitude: Lessons for Career Management. London: Routledge.
29. Pipes, S.C. (1996, April). "Glass Ceiling? So What?" *Chief Executive 112*, 16.
30. Cutler, M. M., and Jackson, A. L. (2002, Fall). "A 'Glass Ceiling,' or Work/family Conflict?" *The Journal Business and Economics Studies 8*, 2: 73–85
31. Tischler, L. (2004, February) Where Are the Women? *Fast Company 79*: 52–60
32. Pipes. S.C. (1996. April). Glass Ceiling? So What? *Chief Executive 112*, 16.
33. Thurow, L.C. (2003). *Fortune Favors the Bold: What We Must Do to Build a New and Lasting Global Prosperity.* New York: HarperCollins Publishers, Inc.

PART III

LEADERSHIP AND MANAGEMENT

This section of the Reader focuses on the knowledge and essential skills required of effective leaders, managers, team leaders, and self-leaders.

CHAPTER 15
LEADERSHIP

WHY DOES VISION MATTER?

Burt Nanus

CREATING AND BUILDING TRUST

Ellen Whitener
Günter K. Stahl

LEVEL 5 LEADERSHIP

Jim Collins

Leadership is one of the most frequently researched topics in organizational behavior, which makes it difficult to choose among the thousands of articles written on this subject. Our conceptions or schemas of what constitutes a good leader vary from culture to culture and can also change over time within the same culture.

The first article is a classic by Burt Nanus, an educator, author, and consultant who has written widely on leadership. In "Why Does Vision Matter?" Nanus explains the role of vision and its effect on organizations. He compares organizations with visions to those without visions.

Our second choice was "Creating and Building Trust," by Ellen Whitener, a U.S. scholar, and Günter Stahl, a German scholar who works out of Singapore. Many people implicitly recognize that trust is a crucial factor in all types of business relationships, but, somewhat surprisingly, this is a topic that has only recently begun to garner more attention and find its way into organizational behavior textbooks. Whitener and Stahl summarize what scholars know about trust and walk us through real-life cases of business crises in which leaders either created or destroyed trust. Their chapter highlights the challenge global leaders face in building and maintaining trust across numerous cultural boundaries, where trust has different meanings and operationalizations.

Our final choice came from Jim Collins's best-selling book, *Good to Great*, which compared pairs of firms in the same industry whose performance was similar and "good" at one point. He and his researchers examined in depth why some firms went on to become "great" and sustained that level of performance, beating the general stock market by an average of seven times over a fifteen-year period. One of the reasons they identified was a type of leadership they call "Level 5 Leadership." Countries have implicit theories of leadership—an ideal profile for leaders—that influence how leaders are selected, groomed, and evaluated by others. Collins' description of B effective leaders who achieve greatness adds a new wrinkle to the U.S. CEO leader profile.

WHY DOES VISION MATTER?*

Burt Nanus

Max DePree, CEO of the brilliantly successful Herman Miller Company, says, "The first responsibility of a leader is to define reality."[1] The reality of an organization has many dimensions:

- How it grew to its current size. The challenges it faced and overcome. The decisions that proved right and those that proved costly.
- Its character and culture. Its traditions and rituals. The way it conducts its business. Its organizational structure.
- The challenges and prospects facing it. Product obsolescence. Emerging opportunities. New production processes.
- Its competitive advantages and limitations. Its distinctive competence. Its resource base. Competitive threats.
- The skills and knowledge of its workers and managers. Its capacity for training and development.
- The trends in the outside world that affect it. New technologies. Possible government regulations. Changes in the needs and wants of customers.

All these factors converge to help an effective leader define a sense of direction or vision. A vision is "a realistic, credible, attractive future for the organization."[2] A vision is a beckoning symbol of all that is possible for the organization—a shining destination, a distinctive path that no other organization is likely to have, even one that may be in the very same business.

LEADERS AND VISIONS

As the main person setting direction, the leader points the way. He or she champions a particular image of what is possible, desirable, and intended for the future of the enterprise. "Let's go this way," says the leader. "Together we'll be able to realize our own deepest desires for meaning, accomplishment, and self-fulfillment. Here's where the action is. Here's where we can make our unique contributions. On this path lie the glittering prizes. Follow me."

Such an image has great power. As deBono said, "The sense of direction urges action. The sense of direction shapes the action. The sense of direction allows the value of the action to be satisfied: Has it got me nearer my goal? The sense of direction allows all judgments and decisions to be made more easily: Does this help me toward my goal or hinder me?"[3]

---

*Excerpted with permission from *Leading the Way to Organizational Renewal* (Portland, OR: Productivity Press, 1996).

Think of some of the great leaders of history: Jefferson, Lincoln, Gandhi, Henry Ford. We see them as great mainly because their unique visions powered great efforts and accomplishments. These leaders were captivated by their dreams. They were obsessed with the need to turn dreams into reality. They were able to infect others with enthusiasm and commitment to their visions. Eventually, a critical mass shared the dream, and the visions became a reality that motivated behavior. It became a target and plans were made for achieving it. Actions followed plans, and people were able to live the dream.

THE POWER OF A VISION

Why is vision so powerful? The key reason is that it grabs attention. It provides focus. Every organization has lots of ways to go. The outside world pulls it in every direction. Each has its own attractions. Yet, no organization can be all things to all people—not General Motors, not IBM, not even the United States of America. So amidst all the chaos and conflicting pressures, the vision compels an organization to remember what's really important and where it intends to go. With focus, other benefits follow:

- ***Vision creates meaning for everyone in the organization.*** It cuts through confusion and makes the world understandable. It helps explain why things are being done the way they are, why some things are considered good and rewarded while others are not. Once they see the big picture, people can see how their own jobs relate to it. They can look at their own skills and interests and see if there's a future for them in the organization.
- ***Vision provides a worthwhile challenge.*** It stretches people by showing them a joint accomplishment that they can be a part of. It generates pride in being part of a team with a useful goal. It makes people feel important. It goads them on to higher levels of commitment and performance.
- ***Vision is energizing.*** It provides something to believe in. It is exhilarating and exciting. Shared aspirations lead to commitment, which energizes people. It provides the spark that ignites the engine of change. It encourages risk-taking, experimentation. It inspires new ways to think, behave, act, and learn.
- ***Vision brings the future into the present.*** When one imagines what can be and gives it a name, it becomes real right now. Real enough to become a beacon. Real enough to change today's decisions. Real enough to define what is essential and filter out distractions. Real enough to concentrate resources and decisions where they truly matter.
- ***Vision creates a common identity.*** People work together with a sense of common ownership and common destiny. A common identity fosters cooperation and promotes synergy. It aligns people's energies in a common direction.

In short, vision is the main tool leaders use to lead from the front. Effective leaders don't push or pressure their followers. They don't boss them around or manipulate them. They are out front showing the way. The vision allows leaders to inspire, attract, align, and energize their followers—to empower them by encouraging them to become part of a common enterprise dedicated to achieving the vision.

Contrast all this with organizations that lack vision (see Figure 1).

If they're well managed, they may still operate reasonably well, at least in the short run. They may have a certain momentum. The products may get out the door on time.

	Organization Without Vision	*Organizations With Shared Vision*
Primary thrust	Problem-driven	Opportunity-driven
Worldview	Stability	Change
Information systems based on:	Past performance	Progress toward goals
Decision making	Tactical	Strategic
Performance measures	Short-term results	Long-term results
Control mechanism	Habit, fear	Peer group pressure
Planning style	Reactive	Proactive

FIGURE 1 Organizations With and Without Vision

The bills get paid. Orders continue to come in. But there's no energy. No excitement. No sense of going somewhere. No sense of progress or renewal. None of the extra effort that people will invest only if they are committed to something challenging and worthwhile.

In the worst situations, organizations without a shared vision begin to stagnate. Managers can't agree on priorities. They are less willing to take risks. Forces for the status quo, always strong, may be unopposed. The initiative for innovation slowly erodes. Workers worry about their prospects for the future. Conflicts become difficult to resolve. Schedules begin to slip.

Eventually, the organization is less able to serve its customers or clients. Revenues erode. Staff may be laid off, further weakening morale and the ability to serve customers. The downward spiral may end up in total failure unless a new leader can be found who can give the organization a new sense of direction.

Notes

1. M. DePree, *Leadership Is an Art* (New York: Doubleday, 1989): 9.
2. B. Nanus, *Visionary Leadership* (San Francisco: Jossey-Bass, 1992): 8.
3. L. deBono, *Tactics—The Art and Science of Success* (Boston: Little, Brown, 1984): 4.

CREATING AND BUILDING TRUST*

Ellen Whitener

Günter K. Stahl

THE IMPORTANCE OF TRUST IN LEADING GLOBAL ORGANIZATIONS: THE EXAMPLE OF FORD–FIRESTONE

Trust may be taken for granted until a crisis occurs. Ford and Firestone provide an interesting example of the importance of trust in leading global organizations—and the consequences of not appreciating the impact of cultural differences on

*Adapted and reprinted with permission from *The Blackwell Handbook of Global Management: A Guide to Managing Complexity* (Oxford, UK: Blackwell, 2004): 109–120.

building and maintaining trust. The comparison of the actions of the CEOs of Ford and Firestone provides some lessons about creating and building trust as global leaders.

Ford and Firestone faced serious challenges in restoring the trust that customers, suppliers, employees, and even the country, had in the companies in the wake of the Ford Explorer accidents and Firestone tire failures:

> When reports began to surface that the treads of Firestone tires on Ford Explorer sport utilities and Ranger pickup trucks were peeling off under pressure and causing fatal accidents, [Ford CEO Jacques Nasser] seized on the crisis as an opportunity to show that Ford was, in his words, not "just another car company." The tires are now related to over 1,400 accidents and other mishaps in the United States involving 88 deaths, and the federal government has launched an investigation. . . . Though the problems are not of Nasser's making, they are his responsibility. Says a Ford insider: "This is a test of character for Jac. He's been saying we're a consumer-focused company, and the way he handles this will determine his credibility going forward—both internally and externally."[1]

Indeed, trust in both Ford and Firestone would depend on how their leaders responded to the crisis.

After the giant Japanese tire manufacturer Bridgestone acquired U.S.-based Firestone in 1988, it retained the American CEO, John Nevin. But it soon became clear that his straightforward and assertive leadership style didn't fit with the polite and reserved style of his Japanese bosses. In 1989, he was succeeded by a Japanese executive, who in 1993 was followed, as part of a regular rotation, by Masatoshi Ono. Ono had spent his whole career with Bridgestone, starting in 1959 as an engineer and working his way into management. His style sharply contrasted with Nevin's. In an interview with *Modern Tire Dealer,* he described his style of management: "See—Think—Plan—Do. I believe in getting a first-hand, on-site understanding of the actual situation—seeing and thinking about conditions. . . before making a decision or taking action."[2]

Nasser became CEO of Ford in 1998 after 30 years working for the company—all but six outside of Detroit in Australia, Thailand, the Philippines, Venezuela, Mexico, Argentina, Brazil, and Europe. Born in Lebanon, raised in Australia, he speaks five languages. He is "as close to zero percent American as you can get. . . but [he] has one distinctly American characteristic. . . a highly entrepreneurial, impatient, can-do mentality."[3]

Ford, with Nasser at the helm, became aware of problems with tire separations in 1997 and 1998 when reports of failures of Firestone tires on Ford vehicles began to filter through to the company from Saudi Arabia, Qatar, Kuwait, and Venezuela. Firestone blamed these incidents on customer misuse and refused to act. Taking its cue from Firestone, Ford did not explore the problems thoroughly. But at the instigation of its national affiliates, Ford replaced or upgraded tens of thousands of Firestone tires on its sport utility vehicles. Firestone did not participate in the replacement program in the Middle East, allegedly because it didn't want regulatory officials in the United States to find out.[4]

Neither company initiated further action until mid-2000, when evidence of similar problems started to accumulate in the United States. Despite a media and public outcry and an inquiry from the National Highway Traffic Safety Administration, Ford responded quietly, focusing on gathering information and waiting for its tire supplier, Firestone, to respond. Nasser did get the company organized to find out more about the problem, setting up a "war room" and designating a crisis management team, but avoided direct interaction with the public. He turned down invitations to testify before congressional committees and instructed Ford's researchers to study tire failure and separations at the company's test tracks, instead of gathering information in the field, directly from customers. Problems continued, pressure mounted, and Ford's credibility declined. So Nasser decided to quit waiting on Firestone and reach out directly to the public, participating in Internet chat rooms and starring in a series of print and TV advertisements in which he apologized for the problems.

Ono and his boss, Yoichiro Kaisaki, CEO of parent Bridgestone, practiced *fugenjikko*—no words, only action.[5] After stalling for several weeks, the company joined Ford in authorizing a recall of 6.5 million tires in August 2000. In addition, they initiated an advertising campaign focused, according to a Firestone spokesperson, on helping consumers get accurate information about which tires were involved in the recall.[6] Ono and Kaisaki stayed behind the scenes, pushing John Lampe, Corporate Executive Vice-President and President of the tire sales division, more visibly into the fray. He appeared in advertisements asserting Firestone's commitment to safety and product quality. Otherwise, Firestone's spokespeople denied knowing of any pattern of problems until early August 2000. Then they pointed fingers at Ford for recommending low tire pressures and at customers for poor maintenance and did not apologize.

Although Nasser and Ono responded differently, both personally lost the trust of their customers, their employees, their suppliers, and their investors. Indeed, by fall 2001, both had been replaced (Nasser by a Ford grandson; Ono by American John Lampe). But more questions remain about whether Firestone can regain the trust of the public than Ford: "It takes a long time to build consumer trust in a brand, but a fraction of the time to destroy that trust. . . . It is possible to rebuild the brand, but it will be expensive. They [Firestone] may have done too little too late."[7] Indeed, numerous experts in crisis management allege that Firestone may not recover from its basic failure to accept responsibility and apologize: "America is a forgive-and-forget country. What America doesn't like is someone who doesn't own up;"[8] "The public is very forgiving for those institutions that will admit their shortcomings and really level with them all the way."[9]

The Ford–Firestone example illustrates the qualities global leaders need to possess and the managerial actions they need to take in order to avoid the mistakes made by Nasser and Ono and to create and build trust globally. What theory tells us about trust and trust building across cultures, found in the next section, provides a framework for identifying those qualities and actions in the third section.

BUILDING TRUST WITHIN GLOBAL ORGANIZATIONS: THE THEORY

Evidence of the importance of trust in leading global organizations comes from a large body of research on intra- and inter-organizational trust. Trust can be defined as "a psychological state comprising the intention to accept vulnerability based upon positive expectations of the intentions or behavior of another."[10]

Research on trust within organizations has suggested that trust is important in a number of ways: it can improve the quality of employee work performance, problem-solving, and communication, and can enhance employee commitment and citizenship behavior. Trust can also improve manager—subordinate working relationships, implementation of self-managed work groups, and the firm's ability to adapt to complexity and change.[11]

Trust also plays a central role in the formation and implementation of cooperative alliances between firms, such as joint ventures, R&D collaborations, or marketing partnerships.[12] For example, joint ventures or supplier—buyer relationships, communication and information exchange, task coordination, informal agreements, and low extents of surveillance and monitoring all require a willingness to be vulnerable, and, hence, trust, on the part of the parties.[13]

Third, trust is important in customer–organization relationships.[14] Customer trust in the service provider, the manufacturer, or the brand seems to be rooted in the actions of the organization or its representatives—such as the listening behavior of sales representatives[15] or the manner in which mistakes or complaints are handled.[16] Trust affects the level of customer loyalty, future intentions, mutual disclosure, and cooperative intentions.[17]

Finally, trust is of critical importance to the success of mergers and acquisitions, by overcoming employee anxiety and resistance, enhancing employee commitment and work performance, and increasing the quality of communication and cooperation between the members of merging or acquired organizations.[18]

THE IMPORTANCE OF PERSONAL RELATIONSHIPS

Though represented as employees', suppliers', customers', joint venture partners' or merger partners' trust in the organization, trust is essentially rooted in the personal relationships among individuals (for example, the customer service representative, sales person, joint venture manager). Roger Mayer and his colleagues developed a framework representing the psychological process associated with building trust in relationships.[19] They proposed that individuals' trust in others is based on their propensity to trust and their perceptions of others' trustworthiness, rooted in their interpretation of the attributes and behavior of others. First, individuals vary in their general willingness to trust. Their propensity to trust is a stable within-person, dispositional factor of the trustor that affects the likelihood that they will trust others. At the most global and abstract level, this approach to trust relies on a process by which people develop generalized expectations about how others will treat them.[20] The expectations reflect the extent to which individuals have deep faith in themselves, others, systems, culture, or society,[21] possess an attitude that people are basically trustworthy, moral, responsible, and cooperative,[22] and can rely on the words, promises, and written or verbal statements of others.[23]

Second, the trust individuals have in others also depends on their perceptions of the attributes of the trustee. Many attributes have been proposed to be part of the assessment of trustworthiness (for example, competence, discreetness, integrity, openness, and receptivity);[24] they can be parsimoniously organized into three categories: perceptions of another's ability or competence, benevolence, and integrity.[25] These factors of perceived trustworthiness likely combine multiplicatively in determining the overall degree of trust that one party has with respect to another party.[26] That is, a very low level of trust in terms of any of the dimensions can undermine trust, and greater trust exists in a given referent when high levels of trust along several dimensions are present. For example, greater trust exists in a manager when that person is perceived to be both competent and concerned for the welfare of his or her subordinates. A manager who is either incompetent or does not care for his or her subordinates will likely not be trusted at all.

DOES TRUST DIFFER ACROSS CULTURES?

The question arises, then, whether individuals from different cultures see trust differently. Evidence exists through the World Values Survey that individuals from different cultures have different propensities to trust. In this survey, an international, cross-disciplinary team of researchers studied the basic values and beliefs of individuals in over sixty countries. In the 1990–3 survey, subjects in 43 countries indicated whether they agreed with the statement that "most people can be trusted." The differences in the responses across the 43 countries were significant. For example, almost 70 percent of respondents in the Scandinavian countries of Finland, Norway, and Sweden, approximately 50 percent of those surveyed in China, the United States, and Canada, 42 percent in Japan, and less than 20 percent in Latvia, Slovenia, Romania, Turkey, and Brazil agreed with the statement that most people can be trusted.[27]

These results provide rough evidence that individuals from different cultures have different generalized propensities to trust others; however, the results of comparative research using more sophisticated measures offer additional support. For example, using a survey instrument of trust versus suspiciousness that they carefully crafted and extensively pretested, a team of researchers found that managers in the United States had higher trust than managers from a cluster of regions (Scandinavia, central Europe, Thailand, Spain, South Africa, and Japan) and substantially higher trust than managers from Greece.[28]

People from different cultures therefore seem to start with different levels of generalized trust in others. The question then becomes whether individuals from different cultures view the factors of perceived trustworthiness as universally effective in facilitating trust in interpersonal relationships. One study specifically designed to explore this question found that the answer is yes, and no. After taking into consideration their different propensities to trust, managers in Norway, the United States, and the People's Republic of China all indicated that their trust in their managers was associated with two-way communication and benevolence/demonstration of concern. Integrity was related to trust only for managers in the United States; and delegation of control was related to trust only for managers in China.[29]

In a study of leadership, Bob House led a large team of researchers[30] in exploring implicit leadership theories in 62 countries. The team found that many of the elements of leader trustworthiness were seen universally as contributing to outstanding leadership. Specifically, different facets of leader integrity (justice, honesty, trustworthiness), competence (administratively skilled, win-win problem solver, communicative), and benevolence were found to be universal positive leader characteristics and attributes such as egocentricity, irritableness, or lack of cooperation were universally viewed as impediments to effective leadership. However, a common preference for a certain type of leadership does not preclude cultural differences in actual leader behavior. A shared preference for what has been described in the trust literature as attributes of managerial trustworthiness[31] does not mean these attributes will be enacted in exactly the same way across cultures or that similar meaning would be attached to all exhibited behavior across all cultures.

Indeed, members of international cross-cultural teams find that building trust is problematic.[32] Differing orientations toward trust and other values, rooted in cultural differences, may create conflict among the members, polarizing them into cultural subgroups and reinforcing ethnographic or cultural stereotypes. As discussed below, however, leaders who understand and address the tensions that cultural differences in propensity to trust and perceptions of trust-building behavior can create in building trust should bridge the differences and build trusting, cooperative, and high-performance relationships among management, staff, customers, and suppliers.[33]

CREATING AND BUILDING TRUST GLOBALLY

The Ford–Firestone example illustrates the qualities global leaders need to possess (or should not possess) and what managerial actions they need to take (or should avoid) in order to build and sustain trust globally. As shown in Figure 1, global leaders need to accurately diagnose situations, identify effective managerial action, and act

FIGURE 1 Building and Sustaining Trust Globally

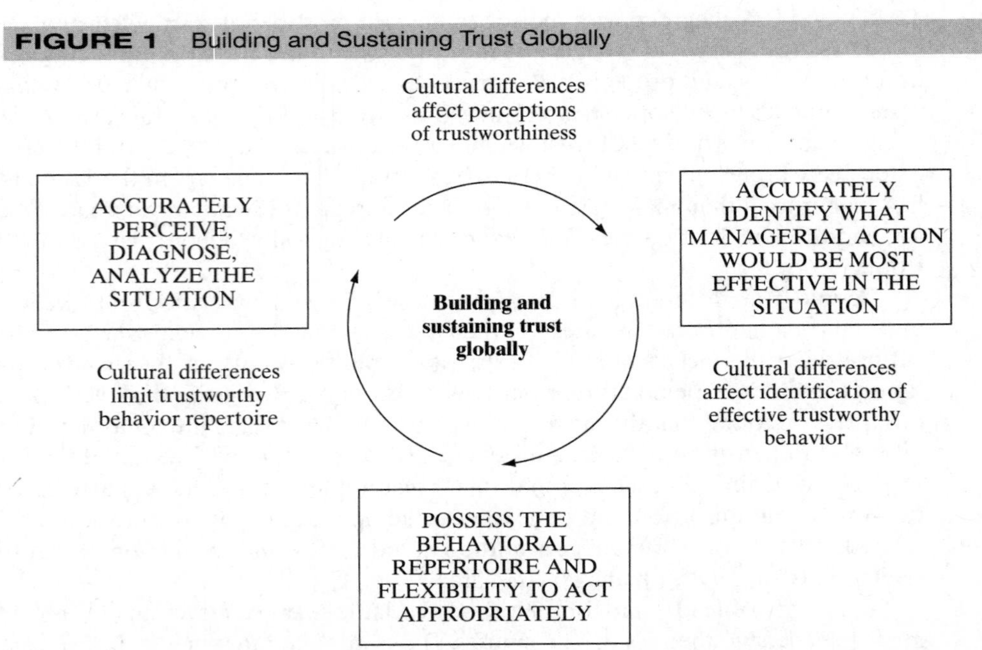

appropriately. With regard to trust building, they need to recognize that cultural differences frame their own and others' perceptions of trustworthiness, affect determination of effective action, and limit their behavioral repertoire. A comparison of Nasser's and Ono's perceptions and actions illustrates the role of cultural differences in developing trust and suggests ways that leaders can understand and act to effectively build trust across cultures. We use the effectiveness cycle for our analysis.

ACCURATE DIAGNOSIS OF THE SITUATION

Both Nasser and Ono made mistakes in handling the crisis that ultimately led to their dismissal, but Ono seems to have had more difficulty in diagnosing the issue, deciding to act, and then acting effectively. First, Nasser seems to have understood historical, legal, and cultural aspects of the crisis that facilitated his diagnosis of the situation. He recognized the power of historical precedent in framing others' interpretation of his response. He knew that customers and government regulators believed that car companies, including Ford, had blundered in previous crises (for example, exploding gas tanks in the Pinto, instability in the Corvair, rollovers with the Bronco). He appreciated the dilemma that this created—on the one hand, customers expected Ford to take responsibility and respond quickly to what they believed was a serious problem, and on the other, they expected Ford to stonewall and dodge, like it and other companies had done in the past—and vowed to respond more swiftly and responsibly.[34] Nasser realized the situation encompassed more than the current crisis—and people's interpretation of Ford's response would be compared against historical responses.

Firestone also has a history. In the 1970s, customers started to complain about tread separation on steel-belted radial tires. Firestone blamed the problem on inadequate maintenance and argued with the government for months before recalling over 13 million tires. At the time, Ono was not CEO and Bridgestone did not own the company; but because they responded in exactly the same way as Firestone had responded before, it appears that they did not understand that the situation was bigger than the current incident.

Nasser also understood that although the customer orientation in the United States has significant legal support when safety is threatened, Americans see the problem in ethical–moral terms. Interest groups and government agencies actively protect the safety and rights of consumers; and the legal system abounds with product liability lawsuits, primarily to ensure that companies respond ethically. Early on Nasser realized the moral and ethical tone of the crisis. When asked in an interview in *Fortune* how he felt about the crisis, he replied, "Well, the first one is sorrow about the defective tires and the fact that we have had deaths attributed to these faulty tires. I think whenever there is a break in trust it pulls at our heartstrings. We don't want to let anyone down. And when something unintended like this happens, it really doesn't matter whose fault it is. We feel morally and emotionally connected to the people who buy our vehicles."[35] Ono was really not available for comment, suggesting he may not have fully appreciated the legal or moral context. Consumers in Japan have few rights and product liability lawsuits are almost nonexistent.[36]

Finally, Nasser realized that Americans expect action and contrition. Americans tend to have a high propensity to trust. They are likely, therefore, to have high and significant expectations of others and a willingness to take risks and make themselves vulnerable to others. Yet they may also be quick to lower those expectations and abandon trust if they believe they are being taken advantage of: "Fool me once, shame on you; fool me twice, shame on me." The American public was wary of Ford and Firestone, because they had been "fooled" before. Yet Nasser seemed more aware of this than Ono and acted quickly to try to fulfill rather than disappoint their positive expectations. After pressuring Firestone to respond and getting the brush-off, first in Saudi Arabia and then in the United States, Ford started to act on its own. Ford replaced tires themselves in the Middle East, and when the crisis spread to American shores, they initiated an advertising campaign in which Nasser himself apologized to the people for the problem. He also took the very visible action of temporarily closing three automobile assembly plants and using their tires for the recall. Ono's management style of See-Think-Plan-Do, coupled with a Japanese discomfort with public disclosure and repentance, led to delays and denials.

Interestingly, at the time the crisis started to unfold, Nasser had lived and worked in the United States for less time than Ono; perhaps, however, his experiences in many different cultures over the course of his career with Ford sensitized him to looking for the nuances in a culture's perceptions.

IDENTIFICATION AND INITIATION OF EFFECTIVE MANAGERIAL ACTION

With their long history of corporate crises, Americans have come to expect specific responses from corporate leaders: a crisis mentality, full disclosure, resources backing up the rhetoric, and top leader visibility. Nasser's mindful communication skills helped him recognize the list of responses that Americans expected, and he gave them most of these. If Ono recognized the list, he did not perform the responses, suggesting that he underappreciated their role in maintaining his credibility and their trust and confidence in him and his company.

Once he realized that Firestone was not going to take the lead on the tire problem, Nasser acted swiftly. He created an organizational structure to manage the company's interaction with the problem, designating a crisis management team and assigning two executives as chairs. He set in motion several mechanisms for gathering more information, directing research engineers to study tire separations on their test tracks and, when that was inconclusive, sending them to the field to get data directly from customers. He also gathered information himself by logging onto chat rooms and interacting with concerned customers. He committed significant resources to replacing the tires, authorizing Ford to spend its own money (ultimately $3 billion) to replace Firestone tires and closing three automobile assembly plants to poach the tires originally destined for new cars. And he shared information with the public, meeting with members of the press and appearing in advertisements to explain what they were doing and to express his regret for the situation.

Ono went to his public relations firm, Fleishman-Hillard, to handle the crisis. But the agency resigned from the account when Firestone ignored its counsel to take "positive, dramatic steps to address the crisis."[37] Ono replaced them with another firm (Ketchum) with strong ties to Washington. In addition, Firestone said it didn't keep track of consumer tire failures and didn't describe any attempts to gather that information once the reports started to emerge. It did respond to specific consumer complaints by pointing out that most tire failures are a result of improper inflation at high temperatures. When finally pressured into the recall, Ono did get Bridgestone to fly more tires from Japan and to increase production. He also offered consumers up to $100 per tire if they wanted to purchase a competitor's tire. Finally, Ono assigned the job of spokesperson to Corporate Executive Vice-President John Lampe. Lampe appeared in several advertisements expressing Firestone's commitment to quality and safety. Firestone complemented this approach with a website and dedicated customer service hotline to provide consumers with recall information.

Finally, when congressional hearings convened in late 2000, both Nasser and Ono blamed each other. Observers described Nasser as poised and comfortable in the hearings and Ono as rattled, inconsistent, and uncomfortable. One senator reacted to Ono's performance: "What does it take to put a company on notice that perhaps they've got a defective product out there?"[38]

BEHAVIORAL REPERTOIRE AND FLEXIBILITY TO ACT APPROPRIATELY

Finally, global leaders need to recognize that cultural differences limit their behavioral repertoire and flexibility to act appropriately. The demonstration of integrity, for example, may differ significantly across cultures. Several analysts of the Ford and Firestone crisis indicated that Americans are forgiving if an offending official accepts responsibility and tells the truth. Nasser fairly quickly hit the advertising and print channels with that message. However, Japanese norms of integrity may differ; indeed, in October 2000, Ono followed a practice common in Japan, resigning from his position, symbolically accepting the responsibility for the company's problems.[39] Americans' assumptions that leaders with integrity would immediately and publicly accept responsibility clashed with the Japanese assumption that leaders with integrity try to fix the problem and then resign quietly. It may have been just as improbable for Ono to do what Nasser did as it seems to have been for Americans to trust Ono when he didn't apologize.

CONCLUSION

The example of the CEOs of Ford and Firestone in the tire separation crisis combined with research on trust provides a framework to guide global leaders in building and sustaining trust in their cross-cultural organizational relationships. Generally, global leaders need to recognize that individuals from different cultures vary in their propensity to trust. They also need to ascertain the historical, legal/moral/ethical, and cultural differences underpinning perceptions of interactions and situations, identify the expectations of interaction partners with diverse cultural backgrounds, and modify their behavior to fit those expectations.

Individuals differ greatly in their perceptions of situations, preferences for certain behaviors, and predilections to act. Individuals with the same experiences and cultural backgrounds often share tendencies to understand situations and behaviors in similar ways. In contrast, individuals who don't share those experiences and backgrounds can struggle to connect with them. Therefore, leaders must figure out how to bridge the cultural and individual differences in perceptions, preferences, and predilections to build and sustain trust. Leaders with a global mindset, perhaps rooted as is Nasser in a wide array of cross-cultural experiences, and with mindful communication skills, will be better equipped to successfully build and maintain trust in their cross-cultural organizational relationships.

Endnotes

1. Taylor (2000): 123.
2. Stoyer (1993): 24.
3. Zesiger (1998): 80.
4. O'Rourke (2001).
5. Eisenberg (2000).
6. Cardona (2000).
7. Robert Kahn, director of a branding company as quoted in Lucas (2001): 22.
8. Bill Lyddan, CEO of an advertising company, quoted in Cardona (2000): 54.
9. Harold Burson, CEO of a public relations firm, quoted in Eisenberg (2000): 40.
10. Rousseau et al. (1998): 395.
11. For recent reviews see Kramer (1999); Mayer, Davis, and Schoorman (1995); Rousseau et al. (1998); Whitener et al. (1998).
12. Das and Teng (1998); Ring and Van de Ven (1992); Zaheer, McEvily, and Perrone (1998).
13. Doney and Cannon (1997); Inkpen and Currall (1998).
14. Berry (1995); Ganesan (1994); Garbarino and Johnson (1999).
15. Ramsey and Sohi (1997).
16. Tax, Brown, and Chandrashekaran (1998).
17. Crosby, Evans, and Cowles (1990); Singh and Sirdeshmukh (2000); Sirdeshmukh, Sing, and Sabol (2002); Swan, Bowers, and Richardson (1999).
18. E.g., Nikandrou, Papalexandris, and Bourantas (2000); Stahl and Sitkin (2001).
19. Mayer, Davis, and Schoorman (1995).
20. Stack (1978).
21. Erikson (1963).
22. Wrightsman (1992).
23. Rotter (1967; 1971).
24. Butler (1991).
25. Mayer, Davis, and Schoorman (1995).
26. Mishra (1996).
27. Inglehart (1997); Inglehart, Basanez, and Moreno (1998).
28. Harnett and Cummings (1980).
29. Whitener et al. (1999).
30. Den Hartog et al. (1999); House et al. (1999).
31. E.g., Mayer, Davis, and Schoorman (1995); Whitener et al. (1998).
32. Moosmüller, Spieβ, and Podsiadlowski (2001); Smith and Noakes (1996).
33. Moosmüller et al. (2001).
34. Taylor (2000).
35. Taylor (2000): 128.
36. Eisenberg (2000).
37. O'Rourke (2001): 261.
38. Eisenberg (2000).
39. Griffin and Pustay (2002).

References

Berry, Leonard L. (1995). "Relationship Marketing of Services—Growing Interest, Emerging Perspectives," *Journal of the Academy of Marketing Science*, 23: 236–245.

Butler, John K., Jr. (1991). "Towards Under-Standing and Measuring Conditions of Trust: Evolution of a Conditions of Trust Inventory," *Journal of Management*, 17: 643–663.

Cardona, M. M. (2000). "CEOs' Summer Fashion—The Hair Shirt;" "Corporate Contrition Means Execs Must Go Beyond Apologies: Pundits," *Advertising Age*, 71(37): 54.

Crosby, L. A., Evans, K. R., and Cowles, D. (1990). "Relationship Quality in Services Selling: An Interpersonal Influence Perspective," *Journal of Marketing*, 54: 68–81.

Das, T. K., and Teng, B-S. (1998). "Between Trust and Control: Developing Confidence in Partner Cooperation in Alliances," *Academy of Management Review*, 23(3): 491–512.

Den Hartog, D. N., House, R. J., Hanges, P. J., Ruiz-Quintanilla, S. A., Dorfman, P. W., et al. (1999). "Culture-Specific and cross-Culturally Generalizable Implicit Leadership Theories: Are Attributes of Charismatic/Transformational Leadership Universally Endorsed?" *Leadership Quarterly*, 10: 219–256.

Doney, P. M., and Cannon, J. R. (1997). "An Examination of the Nature of Trust in Buyer–Seller Relationships," *Journal of Marketing*, 61: 35–51.

Eisenberg, D. (2000), September 18. "Firestone's rough road: Facing the wrath of Congress and the public, Can the tiremaker survive?" *TIME*, 156(12): 38–40.

Erikson, E. H. (1963). *Childhood and Society.* 2nd ed., New York: Norton.

Ganesan, S. (1994). "Determinants of Long-Term Orientation in Buyer–Seller Relationships," *Journal of Marketing*, 58: 1–19.

Garbarino, E., and Johnson, M. S. (1999). "The Different Roles of Satisfaction, Trust, and Commitment in Customer Relationships," *Journal of Marketing*, 63: 70–87.

Griffin, R. W., and Pustay, M. W. (2002). *International Business: A Managerial Perspective.* 3rd ed., Upper Saddle River, NJ: Prentice Hall.

Harnett, D. L., and Cummings, L. L. (1980). *Bargaining Behavior: An International Study.* Houston: Dame Publications.

House, R., Hanges, P. J., Quintanilla, A., Dorfman, P. W., Dickson, M. W., Javidan, M., et al. (1999). "Cultural Influences on Leadership and Organizations: Project Globe," in W. H. Mobley, M. J. Gessner, and V. Arnold (eds.), *Advances in Global Leadership*, vol. 1, Greenwich, CT: JAI Press.

Inglehart, R. (1997). *Modernization and Postmodernization: Cultural, Economic, and Political Change in 43 Societies.* Princeton, NJ: Princeton University Press.

Inglehart, R., Basanez, M., and Moreno, A. (1998). *Human Values and Beliefs: A Cross-Cultural Sourcebook.* Ann Arbor: University of Michigan Press.

Inkpen, A., and Currall, S. C. (1998). "The Nature, Antecedents, and Consequences of Joint Venture Trust," *Journal of International Management*, 4: 1–20.

Kramer, R. M. (1999). "Trust and Distrust in Organizations: Emerging Perspectives, Enduring Questions," *Annual Review of Psychology*, 50: 569–598.

Lucas, P. (2001). Is It the End of the Road for Firestone?" *Journal of Business Strategy*, 22(5): 21–22.

Mayer, R. C., Davis, J. H., and Schoorman, F. D. (1995). "An Integrative Model of Organizational Trust," *Academy of Management Review*, 20: 709–734.

Mishra, A. K. (1996). "Organizational Responses to Crisis: The Centrality of Trust," in R. M. Kramer and T. R. Tyler (eds.), *Trust in Organizations: Frontiers of Theory and Research*: 261–287. Thousand Oaks, CA: Sage.

Moosmüller, A., Spieβ, E., and Podsiadlowski, A. (2001). "International Team Building," in M. E. Mendenhall, T. M. Kühlmann, and G. K. Stahl (eds.), *Developing Global Business Leaders: Policies, Processes, and Innovations*: 211–224. Westport: Quorum.

Nikandrou, I., Papalexandris, N., and Bourantas, D. (2000). "Gaining Employee Trust After Acquisition: Implications for Managerial Action," *Employee Relations*, 22(4): 334–355.

O'Rourke, J. (2001). Bridgestone/Firestone, Inc. and Ford Motor Company: How a product Safety Crisis Ended a Hundred-Year Relationship," *Corporate Reputation Review*, 4(3): 255–264.

Ramsey, R. P., and Sohi, R. S. (1997). "Listening to Your Customers: The Impact of Perceived Salesperson Listening Behavior on Relationship Outcomes," *Journal of the Academy of Marketing Science*, 25(2): 127–137.

Ring, P. S., and Van de Ven, A. H. (1992). "Structuring Cooperative Relationships Between Organizations," *Strategic Management Journal*, 13: 483–498.

Rotter, J. B. (1967). "A New Scale for the Measurement of Interpersonal Trust," *Journal of Personality*, 35: 615–665.

Rotter, J. B. (1971). "Generalized Expectancies for Interpersonal trust," *American Psychologist*, 26: 443–452.

Rousseau, D. M., Sitkin, S. B., Burt, R. S., and Camerer, C. (1998). "Not So Different

After All: "A Cross-Discipline View of Trust," *Academy of Management Review*, 23: 393–404.

Singh, J., and Sirdeshmukh, D. (2000). "Agency and Trust Mechanisms in Consumer Satisfaction and Loyalty Judgments," *Journal of the Academy of Marketing Science*, 28(1): 150–167.

Sirdeshmukh, D., Singh, J., and Sabol, B. (2002). "Consumer Trust, Value, and Loyalty in Relational Exchanges," *Journal of Marketing*, 66: 15–37.

Smith, P. B., and Noakes, J. (1996). "Cultural Differences in Group Processes," in A. West (ed.), *Handbook of Work Group Psychology.* Chichester: John Wiley: 479–501.

Stack, L. C. (1978). "Trust," in H. London and J. E. Exner, Jr. (eds.), *Dimensions of Personality.* New York: John Wiley: 561–599.

Stahl, G. K., and Sitkin, S. (2001). "Trust in Mergers and Acquisitions," paper presented at the Academy of Management Conference, Washington, D.C., August 3–8.

Stoyer, L. (1993). "Masatoshi Ono: Finally Off to the Races?" *Modern Tire Dealer*, 74(9): 22–25.

Swan, J. E., Bowers, M. R., and Richardson, L. D. (1999). "Customer Trust in the Salesperson: An Integrative Review and Meta-Analysis of the Empirical Literature," *Journal of Business Research*, 44(2): 93–107.

Tax, S. S., Brown, S. W., and Chandrashekaran, M. (1998). "Customer Evaluations of Service Complaint Experiences: Implications for Relationship Marketing," *Journal of Marketing*, 62: 60–76.

Taylor, Alex, III (2000). "Jac Nasser's biggest test," *Fortune*, 142(6): 123–124, 126, 128.

Whitener, E. M., Brodt, S. E., Korsgaard, M. A., and Werner, J. M. (1998). "Managers as Initiators of Trust: An Exchange Relationship Framework for Understanding Managerial Trustworthy Behavior," *Academy of Management Review*, 23: 513–530.

Whitener, E. M., Maznevski, M. L., Hua, W., Saebo, S., and Ekelund, B. (1999). "Testing the Cultural Boundaries of a Model of Trust: Subordinate–Manager Relationships in China, Norway and the United States," paper presented at the 59th Annual Meeting of the Academy of Management, Chicago, August.

Wrightsman, L. W. (1992). *Assumptions about Human Nature: Implications for Researchers and Practitioners*, 2nd ed., Newbury Park, CA: Sage.

Zaheer, A., McEvily, B., and Perrone, V. (1998). "Does Trust Matter? Exploring the Effects of Interorganizational and Interpersonal Trust on Performance," *Organization Science*, 9: 141–159.

Zesiger, S. (1998). "Jac Nasser Is Car Crazy," *Fortune*, 137(12): 80–82.

LEVEL 5 LEADERSHIP*

Jim Collins

> *You can accomplish anything in life, provided that you do not mind who gets the credit.*
>
> HARRY S. TRUMAN[1]

In 1971, a seemingly ordinary man named Darwin E. Smith became chief executive of Kimberly-Clark, a stodgy old paper company whose stock had fallen 36 percent behind the general market over the previous twenty years.

Smith, the company's mild-mannered in-house lawyer, wasn't so sure the board had made the right choice—a feeling further reinforced when a director pulled Smith aside and reminded him that he lacked some of the qualifications for the position.[2] But CEO he was, and CEO he remained for 20 years.

---

*Reprinted with the author's permission from *Good to Great: Why Some Companies Make the Leap . . . and Others Don't.* (New York: HarperCollins Publishers, 2001): 17–40. Jim Collins is also co-author of *Built to Last: Successful Habits of Visionary Companies*. A recipient of the Distinguished Teaching Award while a faculty member at the Stanford University Graduate School of Business, Jim now works from his management-research laboratory in Boulder, Colorado. More of Jim Collins' work can be found at www.jimcollins.com.

What a twenty years it was. In that period, Smith created a stunning transformation, turning Kimberly-Clark into the leading paper-based consumer products company in the world. Under his stewardship, Kimberly-Clark generated cumulative stock returns 4.1 times the general market, handily beating its direct rivals Scott Paper and Procter & Gamble and outperforming such venerable companies as Coca-Cola, Hewlett-Packard, 3M, and General Electric. (See Figure 1.)

It was an impressive performance, one of the best examples in the twentieth century of taking a good company and making it great. Yet few people—even ardent students of management and corporate history—know anything about Darwin Smith. He probably would have liked it that way. A man who carried no airs of self-importance, Smith found his favorite companionship among plumbers and electricians and spent his vacations rumbling around his Wisconsin farm in the cab of a backhoe, digging holes and moving rocks.[3] He never cultivated hero status or executive celebrity status.[4] When a journalist asked him to describe his management style, Smith, dressed unfashionably like a farm boy wearing his first suit bought at J. C. Penney, just stared back from the other side of his nerdy-looking black-rimmed glasses. After a long, uncomfortable silence, he said simply: "Eccentric."[5] The *Wall Street Journal* did not write a splashy feature on Darwin Smith.

But if you were to think of Darwin Smith as somehow meek or soft, you would be terribly mistaken. His awkward shyness and lack of pretense was coupled with a fierce, even stoic, resolve toward life. Smith grew up as a poor Indiana farm-town boy, putting himself through college by working the day shift at International Harvester and attending Indiana University at night. One day, he lost part of a finger on the job. The story goes that he went to class that evening and returned to work the next day. While that might be a bit of an exaggeration, he clearly did not let a lost finger slow down his progress toward graduation. He kept working full-time, he kept going to class at night, and he earned admission to Harvard Law School.[6] Later in life, two months after becoming CEO, doctors diagnosed Smith with nose and throat cancer, predicting he had less than a year to live. He informed the board but made it clear that he was not dead yet and had no plans to die anytime soon. Smith held fully to his demanding work schedule while commuting weekly from Wisconsin to Houston for radiation therapy and lived twenty-five more years, most of them as CEO.[7]

Smith brought that same ferocious resolve to rebuilding Kimberly-Clark, especially when he made the most dramatic decision in the company's history: Sell the mills.[8] Shortly after he became CEO, Smith and his team had concluded that the traditional core business—coated paper—was doomed to mediocrity. Its economics were bad and the competition weak.[9] But, they reasoned, if Kimberly-Clark thrust itself into the fire of the *consumer* paper-products industry, world-class competition like Procter & Gamble would force it to achieve greatness or perish.

So, like the general who burned the boats upon landing, leaving only one option (succeed or die), Smith announced the decision to sell the mills, in what one board member called the gutsiest move he'd ever seen a CEO make. Sell even the mill in Kimberly, Wisconsin, and throw all the proceeds into the consumer business, investing in brands like Huggies and Kleenex.[10]

The business media called the move stupid and Wall Street analysts downgraded the stock.[11] Smith never wavered. Twenty-five years later, Kimberly-Clark owned Scott Paper outright and beat Procter & Gamble in six of eight product categories.[12] In retirement, Smith reflected on his exceptional performance, saying simply, "I never stopped trying to become qualified for the job."[13]

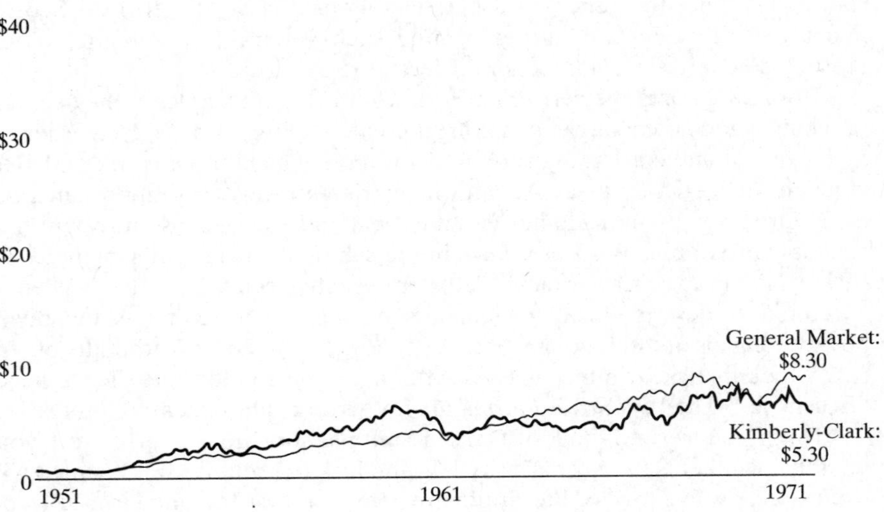

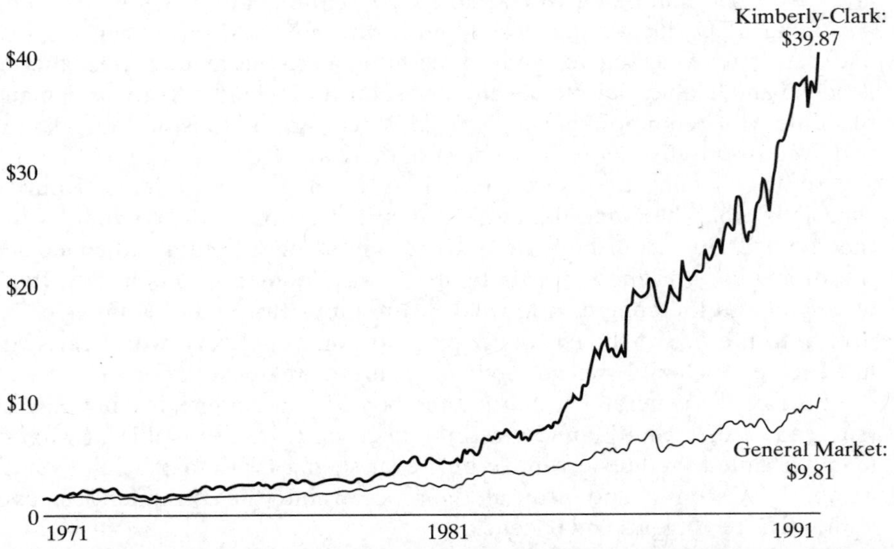

FIGURE 1 Kimberly-Clark Before and During Darwin Smith's Tenure

NOT WHAT WE EXPECTED

Darwin Smith stands as a classic example of what we came to call a Level 5 leader—an individual who blends extreme personal humility with intense professional will. We found leaders of this type at the helm of every good-to-great company during the transition era. Like Smith, they were self-effacing individuals who displayed the fierce resolve to do whatever needed to be done to make the company great.

> ***Level 5 leaders channel their ego needs away from themselves and into the larger goal of building a great company. It's not that Level 5 leaders have no ego or self-interest. Indeed, they are incredibly ambitious—but their ambition is first and foremost for the institution, not themselves.***

The term *Level 5* refers to the highest level in a hierarchy of executive capabilities that we identified in our research. (See Figure 2.) While you don't need to move in sequence from Level 1 to Level 5—it might be possible to fill in some of the lower levels later—fully developed Level 5 leaders embody all five layers of the pyramid. I am not going to belabor all five levels here, as Levels 1 through 4 are somewhat self-explanatory and are discussed extensively by other authors. This chapter will focus instead on the distinguishing traits of the good-to-great leaders—namely Level 5 traits—in contrast to the comparison leaders in our study [in matched firms that were not able to make the leap from good to great].

But first, please permit a brief digression to set an important context. We were not looking for Level 5 leadership or anything like it. In fact, I gave the research team

FIGURE 2 Level 5 Hierarchy

LEVEL 5
LEVEL 5 EXECUTIVE
Builds enduring greatness through a paradoxical blend of personal humility and professional will.
LEVEL 4
EFFECTIVE LEADER
Catalyzes commitment to and vigorous pursuit of a clear and compelling vision, stimulating higher performance standards.
LEVEL 3
COMPETENT MANAGER
Organizes people and resources toward the effective and efficient pursuit of predetermined objectives.
LEVEL 2
CONTRIBUTING TEAM MEMBER
Contributes individual capabilities to the achievement of group objectives and works effectively with others in a group setting.
LEVEL 1
HIGHLY CAPABLE INDIVIDUAL
Makes productive contributions through talent, knowledge, skills, and good work habits.

explicit instructions to *downplay* the role of top executives so that we could avoid the simplistic "credit the leader" or "blame the leader" thinking common today.

To use an analogy, the "Leadership is the answer to everything" perspective is the modern equivalent of the "God is the answer to everything" perspective that held back our scientific understanding of the physical world in the Dark Ages. In the 1500s, people ascribed all events they didn't understand to God. Why did the crops fail? God did it. Why did we have an earthquake? God did it. What holds the planets in place? God. But with the Enlightenment, we began the search for a more scientific understanding—physics, chemistry, biology, and so forth. Not that we became atheists, but we gained deeper understanding about how the universe ticks.

Similarly, every time we attribute everything to "Leadership," we're no different from people in the 1500s. We're simply admitting our ignorance. Not that we should become leadership atheists (leadership *does* matter), but every time we throw our hands up in frustration—reverting back to "Well, the answer must be Leadership!"—we prevent ourselves from gaining deeper, more scientific understanding about what makes great companies tick.

So, early in the project, I kept insisting, "Ignore the executives." But the research team kept pushing back, "No! There is something consistently unusual about them. We can't ignore them." And I'd respond, "But the comparison companies also had leaders, even some great leaders. So, what's different?" Back and forth the debate raged.

Finally—as should always be the case—the data won.

The good-to-great executives were all cut from the same cloth. It didn't matter whether the company was consumer or industrial, in crisis or steady state, offered services or products. It didn't matter when the transition took place or how big the company. All the good-to-great companies had Level 5 leadership at the time of transition. Furthermore, the absence of Level 5 leadership showed up as a consistent pattern in the comparison companies. Given that Level 5 leadership cuts against the grain of conventional wisdom, especially the belief that we need larger-than-life saviors with big personalities to transform companies, it is important to note that Level 5 is an empirical finding, not an ideological one.

HUMILITY + WILL = LEVEL 5

Level 5 leaders are a study in duality: modest and willful, humble and fearless. To quickly grasp this concept, think of United States President Abraham Lincoln (one of the few Level 5 presidents in United States history), who never let his ego get in the way of his primary ambition for the larger cause of an enduring great nation. Yet those who mistook Mr. Lincoln's personal modesty, shy nature, and awkward manner as signs of weakness found themselves terribly mistaken, to the scale of 250,000 Confederate and 360,000 Union lives, including Lincoln's own.[14]

While it might be a bit of a stretch to compare the good-to-great CEOs to Abraham Lincoln, they did display the same duality. Consider the case of Colman Mockler, CEO of Gillette from 1975 to 1991. During Mockler's tenure, Gillette faced three attacks that threatened to destroy the company's opportunity for greatness. Two attacks came as hostile takeover bids from Revlon, led by Ronald Perelman, a cigar-chomping raider with a reputation for breaking apart companies to pay down junk bonds and finance more hostile raids.[15] The third attack came from Coniston

Partners, an investment group that bought 5.9 percent of Gillette stock and initiated a proxy battle to seize control of the board, hoping to sell the company to the highest bidder and pocket a quick gain on their shares.[16] Had Gillette been flipped to Perelman at the price he offered, shareowners would have reaped an instantaneous 44 percent gain on their stock.[17] Looking at a $2.3 billion short-term stock profit across 116 million shares, most executives would have capitulated, pocketing millions from flipping their own stock and cashing in on generous golden parachutes.[18]

Colman Mockler did not capitulate, choosing instead to fight for the future greatness of Gillette, even though he himself would have pocketed a substantial sum on his own shares. A quiet and reserved man, always courteous, Mockler had the reputation of a gracious, almost patrician gentleman. Yet those who mistook Mockler's reserved nature for weakness found themselves beaten in the end. In the proxy fight, senior Gillette executives reached out to thousands of individual investors—person by person, phone call by phone call—and won the battle.

Now, you might be thinking, "But that just sounds like self-serving entrenched management fighting for their interests at the expense of shareholder interests." On the surface, it might look that way, but consider two key facts.

First, Mockler and his team staked the company's future on huge investments in radically new and technologically advanced systems (later known as Sensor and Mach 3). Had the takeover been successful, these projects would almost certainly have been curtailed or eliminated, and none of us would be shaving with Sensor, Sensor for Women, or the Mach 3—leaving hundreds of millions of people to a more painful daily battle with stubble.[19]

Second, at the time of the takeover battle, Sensor promised significant future profits that were not reflected in the stock price because it was in secret development. With Sensor in mind, the board and Mockler believed that the future value of the shares far exceeded the current price, even with the price premium offered by the raiders. To sell out would have made short-term shareflippers happy but would have been utterly irresponsible to long-term shareholders.

In the end, Mockler and the board were proved right, stunningly so. If a shareflipper had accepted the 44 percent price premium offered by Ronald Perelman on October 31, 1986, and then invested the full amount in the general market for ten years, through the end of 1996, he would have come out three times *worse* off than a shareholder who had stayed with Mockler and Gillette.[20] Indeed, the company, its customers, and the shareholders would have been ill served had Mockler capitulated to the raiders, pocketed his millions, and retired to a life of leisure. (See Figure 3.)

Sadly, Mockler was never able to enjoy the full fruits of his effort. On January 25, 1991, the Gillette team received an advance copy of the cover of *Forbes* magazine, which featured an artist's rendition of Mockler standing atop a mountain holding a giant razor above his head in a triumphal pose, while the vanquished languish on the hillsides below. The other executives razzed the publicity-shy Mockler, who had likely declined requests to be photographed for the cover in the first place, amused at seeing him portrayed as a corporate version of Conan the Triumphant. Walking back to his office, minutes after seeing this public acknowledgment of his sixteen years of struggle, Mockler crumpled to the floor, struck dead by a massive heart attack.[21]

I do not know whether Mockler would have chosen to die in harness, but I am quite confident that he would not have changed his approach as chief executive. His placid persona hid an inner intensity, a dedication to making anything he touched the

Cumulative Value of $1 Invested, 1976 – 1996
Gillette versus Takeover Bid and Market

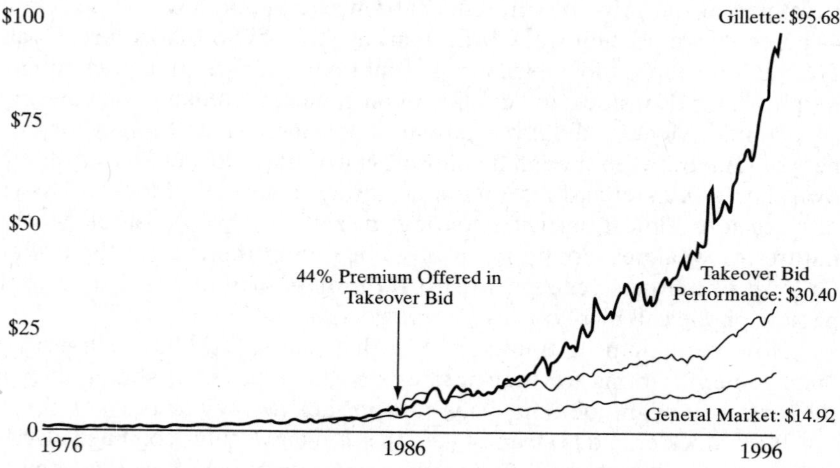

This chart shows how an investor would have fared under the following scenarios:
1. $1 invested in Gillette, held from December 31, 1976 through December 31, 1996.
2. $1 invested in Gillette, held from December 31, 1976 *but then sold* to Ronald Perelman for a 44.44% premium on October 31, 1986, the proceeds then invested in the general stock market.
3. $1 invested in General Market held from December 31, 1976 through December 31, 1996.

FIGURE 3 Colman Mockler's Triumph

best it could possibly be—not just because of what he would get, but because he simply couldn't imagine doing it any other way. It wouldn't have been an option within Colman Mockler's value system to take the easy path and turn the company over to those who would milk it like a cow, destroying its potential to become great, any more than it would have been an option for Lincoln to sue for peace and lose forever the chance of an enduring great nation.

AMBITION FOR THE COMPANY: SETTING UP SUCCESSORS FOR SUCCESS

When David Maxwell became CEO of Fannie Mae in 1981, the company was losing $1 million every single business day. Over the next nine years, Maxwell transformed Fannie Mae into a high-performance culture that rivaled the best Wall Street firms, earning $4 million every business day and beating the general stock market 3.8 to 1. Maxwell retired while still at the top of his game, feeling that the company would be ill served if he stayed on too long, and turned the company over to an equally capable successor, Jim Johnson. Shortly thereafter, Maxwell's retirement package, which had grown to be worth $20 million based on Fannie Mae's spectacular performance, became a point of controversy in Congress (Fannie Mae operates under a government charter). Maxwell responded by writing a letter to his successor, in which he expressed concern that the controversy would trigger an adverse reaction in Washington that could jeopardize the future of the company. He then instructed Johnson not to pay him the remaining balance—$5.5 million—and asked that the entire amount be contributed to the Fannie Mae foundation for low-income housing.[22]

David Maxwell, like Darwin Smith and Colman Mockler, exemplified a key trait of Level 5 leaders: ambition first and foremost for the company and concern for *its* success rather than for one's own riches and personal renown. Level 5 leaders want to see the company even more successful in the next generation, comfortable with the idea that most people won't even know that the roots of that success trace back to their efforts. As one Level 5 leader said, "I want to look out from my porch at one of the great companies in the world someday and be able to say, 'I used to work there.'"

In contrast, the comparison leaders, concerned more with their own reputation for personal greatness, often failed to set the company up for success in the next generation. After all, what better testament to your own personal greatness than that the place falls apart after you leave?

In over three quarters of the comparison companies, we found executives who set their successors up for failure or chose weak successors, or both.

Some had the "biggest dog" syndrome—they didn't mind other dogs in the kennel, as long as they remained the biggest one. One comparison CEO was said to have treated successor candidates "the way Henry the VIII treated wives."[23]

Consider the case of Rubbermaid, an unsustained comparison company that grew from obscurity to number one on *Fortune's* annual list of America's Most Admired Companies and then, just as quickly, disintegrated into such sorry shape that it had to be acquired by Newell to save itself. The architect of this remarkable story, a charismatic and brilliant leader named Stanley Gault, became synonymous in the late 1980s with the success of the company. In 312 articles collected on Rubbermaid, Gault comes through as a hard-driving, egocentric executive. In one article, he responds to the accusation of being a tyrant with the statement, "Yes, but I'm a sincere tyrant."[24] In another, drawn directly from his own comments on leading change, the word *I* appears forty-four times ("I could lead the charge"; "I wrote the twelve objectives"; "I presented and explained the objectives"), whereas the word *we* appears just sixteen times.[25] Gault had every reason to be proud of his executive success. Rubbermaid generated forty consecutive quarters of earnings growth under his leadership—an impressive performance, and one that deserves respect.

But—and this is the key point—Gault did not leave behind a company that would be great without *him.* His chosen successor lasted only one year on the job and the next in line faced a management team so shallow that he had to temporarily shoulder four jobs while scrambling to identify a new number two executive.[26] Gault's successors found themselves struggling not only with a management void, but also with strategic voids that would eventually bring the company to its knees.[27]

Of course, you might say, "Yes, Rubbermaid fell apart after Gault, but that just proves his personal greatness as a leader." Exactly! Gault was indeed a tremendous Level 4 leader, perhaps one of the best in the last fifty years. But he was not a Level 5 leader, and that is one key reason why Rubbermaid went from good to great for a brief shining moment and then, just as quickly, went from great to irrelevant.

A COMPELLING MODESTY

In contrast to the very *I*-centric style of the comparison leaders, we were struck by how the good-to-great leaders *didn't* talk about themselves. During interviews with the good-to-great leaders, they'd talk about the company and the contributions of other executives as long as we'd like but would deflect discussion about their own contributions. When pressed to talk about themselves, they'd say things like, "I hope I'm not sounding like a big shot." Or, "If the board hadn't picked such great successors, you probably wouldn't be talking with me today." Or, "Did I have a lot to do with it? Oh, that sounds so self-serving. I don't think I can take much credit. We were blessed with marvelous people." Or, "There are plenty of people in this company who could do my job better than I do."

It wasn't just false modesty. Those who worked with or wrote about the good-to-great leaders continually used words like *quiet, humble, modest, reserved, shy, gracious, mild-mannered, self-effacing, understated, did not believe his own clippings*; and so forth. Board member Jim Hlavacek described Ken Iverson, the CEO who oversaw Nucor's transformation from near bankruptcy to one of the most successful steel companies in the world:

> *Ken is a very modest and humble man. I've never known a person as successful in doing what he's done that's as modest. And, I work for a lot of CEOs of large companies. And that's true in his private life as well. The simplicity of him. I mean little things like he always gets his dogs at the local pound. He has a simple house that's he's lived in for ages. He only has a carport and he complained to me one day about how he had to use his credit card to scrape the frost off his windows and he broke the credit card. "You know, Ken, there's a solution for it; enclose your carport." And he said, "Ah, heck, it isn't that big of a deal. . . ." He's that humble and simple.*[28]

The eleven good-to-great CEOs are some of the most remarkable CEOs of the century, given that only eleven companies from the *Fortune* 500 met the exacting standards for entry into this study. Yet, despite their remarkable results, almost no one ever remarked about them! George Cain, Alan Wurtzel, David Maxwell, Colman Mockler, Darwin Smith, Jim Herring, Lyle Everingham, Joe Cullman, Fred Allen, Cork Walgreen, Carl Reichardt—how many of these extraordinary executives had you heard of?

> ***When we systematically tabulated all 5,979 articles in the study, we found fewer articles surrounding the transition date for the good-to-great companies than for the comparisons, by a factor of two.[29] Furthermore, we rarely found articles that focused on the good-to-great CEOs.***

The good-to-great leaders never wanted to become larger-than-life heroes. They never aspired to be put on a pedestal or become unreachable icons. They were seemingly ordinary people quietly producing extraordinary results.

Some of the comparison leaders provide a striking contrast. Scott Paper, the comparison company to Kimberly-Clark, hired a CEO named Al Dunlap, a man cut from a very different cloth than Darwin Smith. Dunlap loudly beat on his own chest, telling anyone who would listen (and many who would prefer not to) about what he had accomplished. Quoted in *Business Week* about his nineteen months atop Scott Paper, he boasted, "The Scott story will go down in the annals of American business history as one of the most successful, quickest turnarounds ever, [making] other turnarounds pale by comparison."[30]

According to *Business Week*, Dunlap personally accrued $100 million for 603 days of work at Scott Paper (that's $165,000 *per day*), largely by slashing the workforce, cutting the R&D budget in half, and putting the company on growth steroids in preparation for sale.[31] After selling off the company and pocketing his quick millions, Dunlap wrote a book about himself, in which he trumpeted his nickname Rambo in Pinstripes. "I love the Rambo movies," he wrote. "Here's a guy who has zero chance of success and always wins. Rambo goes into situations against all odds, expecting to get his brains blown out. But he doesn't. At the end of the day he succeeds, he gets rid of the bad guys. He creates peace out of war. That's what I do, too."[32] Darwin Smith may have enjoyed the mindless Rambo movies as well, but I suspect he never walked out of a theater and said to his wife, "You know, I really relate to this Rambo character; he reminds me of me."

Granted, the Scott Paper story is one of the more dramatic in our study, but it's not an isolated case. In over two thirds of the comparison cases, we noted the presence of a gargantuan personal ego that contributed to the demise or continued mediocrity of the company.[33]

We found this pattern particularly strong in the unsustained comparisons—cases where the company would show a leap in performance under a talented yet egocentric leader, only to decline in later years. Lee Iacocca, for example, saved Chrysler from the brink of catastrophe, performing one of the most celebrated (and deservedly so) turnarounds in American business history. Chrysler rose to a height of 2.9 times the market at a point about halfway through his tenure. Then, however, he diverted his attention to making himself one of the most celebrated CEOs in American business history. *Investor's Business Daily* and the *Wall Street Journal* chronicled how Iacocca appeared regularly on talk shows like the *Today* show and *Larry King Live*, personally starred in over eighty commercials, entertained the idea of running for president of the United States (quoted at one point, "Running Chrysler has been a bigger job than running the country. . . . I could handle the national economy in six months"), and widely promoted his autobiography. The book, *Iacocca*, sold seven million copies and elevated him to rock star status, leading him to be mobbed by thousands of cheering fans upon his arrival in Japan.[34] Iacocca's personal stock soared, but in the second half of his tenure, Chrysler's stock fell 31 percent behind the general market.

Sadly, Iacocca had trouble leaving center stage and letting go of the perks of executive kingship. He postponed his retirement so many times that insiders at Chrysler began to joke that Iacocca stood for "I Am Chairman of Chrysler Corporation Always."[35] And when he did finally retire, he demanded that the board continue to provide a private jet and stock options.[36] Later, he joined forces with noted takeover artist Kirk Kerkorian to launch a hostile takeover bid for Chrysler.[37]

Chrysler experienced a brief return to glory in the five years after Iacocca's retirement, but the company's underlying weaknesses eventually led to a buyout by German carmaker Daimler-Benz.[38] Certainly, the demise of Chrysler as a stand-alone company does not rest entirely on Iacocca's shoulders (the next generation of management made the fateful decision to sell the company to the Germans), but the fact remains: Iacocca's brilliant turnaround in the early 1980s did not prove to be sustained and Chrysler failed to become an enduring great company.

UNWAVERING RESOLVE . . . TO DO WHAT MUST BE DONE

It is very important to grasp that Level 5 leadership is not just about humility and modesty. It is equally about ferocious resolve, an almost stoic determination to do whatever needs to be done to make the company great.

Indeed, we debated for a long time on the research team about how to describe the good-to-great leaders. Initially, we penciled in terms like "selfless executive" and "servant leader." But members of the team violently objected to these characterizations.

"Those labels don't ring true," said Anthony Chirikos. "It makes them sound weak or meek, but that's not at all the way I think of Darwin Smith or Colman Mockler. They would do almost anything to make the company great."

Then Eve Li suggested, "Why don't we just call them Level 5 leaders? If we put a label like 'selfless' or 'servant' on them, people will get entirely the wrong idea. We need to get people to engage with the whole concept, to see *both* sides of the coin. If you only get the humility side, you miss the whole idea."

Level 5 leaders are fanatically driven, infected with an incurable need to produce *results.* They will sell the mills or fire their brother, if that's what it takes to make the company great.

When George Cain became CEO of Abbott Laboratories, it sat in the bottom quartile of the pharmaceutical industry, a drowsy enterprise that had lived for years off its cash cow, erythromycin. Cain didn't have an inspiring personality to galvanize the company, but he had something much more powerful: inspired standards. He could not stand mediocrity in any form and was utterly intolerant of anyone who would accept the idea that good is good enough. Cain then set out to destroy one of the key causes of Abbott's mediocrity: nepotism. Systematically rebuilding both the board and the executive team with the best people he could find, Cain made it clear that neither family ties nor length of tenure would have anything to do with whether you held a key position in the company. If you didn't have the capacity to become the best executive in the industry in your span of responsibility, then you would lose your paycheck.[39]

Such rigorous rebuilding might be expected from an outsider brought in to turn the company around, but Cain was an eighteen-year veteran insider *and* a family member, the son of a previous Abbott president. Holiday gatherings were probably tense for a few years in the Cain clan. ("Sorry I had to fire you. Want another slice of turkey?") In the end, though, family members were quite pleased with the performance of their stock, for Cain set in motion a profitable growth machine that, from its transition date in 1974 to 2000, created shareholder returns that beat the market 4.5 to 1, handily outperforming industry superstars Merck and Pfizer.

Upjohn, the direct comparison company to Abbott, also had family leadership during the same era as George Cain. Unlike George Cain, Upjohn's CEO never showed the same resolve to break the mediocrity of nepotism. By the time Abbott had filled all key seats with the best people, regardless of family background, Upjohn still had B level family members holding key positions.[40] Virtually identical companies with identical stock charts up to the point of transition, Upjohn then fell 89 percent behind Abbott over the next twenty-one years before capitulating in a merger to Pharmacia in 1995.

As an interesting aside, Darwin Smith, Colman Mockler, and George Cain came from inside the company. Stanley Gault, Al Dunlap, and Lee Iacocca rode in as saviors from the outside, trumpets blaring. This reflects a more systematic finding from our study. The evidence does not support the idea that you need an outside leader to come in and shake up the place to go from good to great. In fact, going for a high-profile outside change agent is *negatively correlated* with a sustained transformation from good to great.

Ten out of eleven good-to-great CEOs came from inside the company, three of them by family inheritance. The comparison companies turned to outsiders with six times greater frequency—yet they failed to produce sustained great results.[41]

A superb example of insider-driven change comes from Charles R. "Cork" Walgreen 3rd, who transformed dowdy Walgreens into a company that outperformed the stock market by over fifteen times from the end of 1975 to January 1, 2000.[42] After years of dialogue and debate within his executive team about Walgreens' food-service operations, Cork sensed that the team had finally reached a watershed point of clarity and understanding: Walgreens' brightest future lay in convenient drugstores, not food service. Dan Jorndt, who succeeded Walgreen as CEO in 1998, described what happened next:

> *Cork said at one of our planning committee meetings, "Okay, now I am going to draw the line in the sand. We are going to be out of the restaurant business completely in five years." At the time, we had over five hundred restaurants. You could have heard a pin drop. He said, "I want to let everybody know the clock is ticking. . . ." Six months later, we were at our next planning committee meeting and someone mentioned just in passing that we only had five years to be out of the restaurant business. Cork was not a real vociferous fellow. He sort of tapped on the table and said, "Listen, you have four and a half years. I said you had five years six months ago. Now you've got four and a half years." Well, that next day, things really clicked into gear to winding down our restaurant business. He never wavered. He never doubted; he never second-guessed.*[43]

Like Darwin Smith selling the mills at Kimberly-Clark, Cork Walgreen's decision required stoic resolve. Not that food service was the largest part of the business (although it did add substantial profits to the bottom line). The real problem was more emotional. Walgreens had, after all, invented the malted milkshake and food service was a long-standing family tradition dating back to his grandfather. Some food-service outlets were even named after the CEO himself—a restaurant chain named Corky's. But no matter, if Walgreens had to fly in the face of long-standing family tradition in order to focus its resources where it could be the best in the world (convenient drugstores), Cork would do it. Quietly, doggedly, simply.[44]

The quiet, dogged nature of Level 5 leaders showed up not only in big decisions, like selling off the food-service operations or fighting corporate raiders, but also in a personal style of sheer workmanlike diligence. Alan Wurtzel, a second-generation family member who took over his family's small company and turned it into Circuit City, perfectly captured the gestalt of this trait. When asked about differences between himself and his counterpart CEO at Circuit City's comparison company, Wurtzel summed up: "The show horse and the plow horse—he was more of a show horse, whereas I was more of a plow horse."[45]

THE WINDOW AND THE MIRROR

Alan Wurtzel's plow horse comment is fascinating in light of two other facts. First, he holds a doctor of jurisprudence degree from Yale—clearly, his plow horse nature had nothing to do with a lack of intelligence. Second, his plow horse approach set the stage for truly *best in show* results. Let me put it this way: If you had to choose between $1 invested in Circuit City or $1 invested in General Electric on the day that the legendary Jack Welch took over GE in 1981 and held to January 1, 2000, you would have been better off with Circuit City—by six times.[46] Not a bad performance, for a plow horse.

You might expect that extraordinary results like these would lead Alan Wurtzel to discuss the brilliant decisions he made. But when we asked him to list the top five factors in his company's transformation, ranked by importance, Wurtzel gave a surprising answer: The number one factor was *luck*. "We were in a great industry, with the wind at our backs."

We pushed back, pointing out that we selected the good-to-great companies based on performance that surpassed their industry's average. Furthermore, the comparison company (Silo) was in the same industry, with the same wind and probably bigger sails! We debated the point for a few minutes, with Wurtzel continuing his preference for attributing much of his success to just being in the right place at the right time. Later, when asked to discuss the factors behind the enduring nature of the transformation, he said, "The first thing that comes to mind is luck. . . . I was lucky to find the right successor."[47]

Luck. What an odd factor to talk about. Yet the good-to-great executives talked a lot about luck in our interviews. In one interview with a Nucor executive, we asked why the company had such a remarkable track record of good decisions; he responded: "I guess we were just lucky."[48] Joseph F. Cullman 3rd, the Level 5 transition CEO of Philip Morris, flat-out refused to take credit for his company's success, attributing his good fortune to having great colleagues, successors, and predecessors.[49] Even the book he wrote—a book he undertook at the urging of his colleagues, which he never intended to distribute widely outside the company—had the unusual title *I'm a Lucky Guy*. The opening paragraph reads: "I was a very lucky guy from the very beginning of my life: marvelous parents, good genes, lucky in love, lucky in business, and lucky when a Yale classmate had my orders changed to report to Washington, D.C., in early 1941, instead of to a ship that was sunk with all hands lost in the North Atlantic, lucky to be in the Navy, and lucky to be alive at eighty-five."[50]

We were at first puzzled by this emphasis on good luck. After all, we found no evidence that the good-to-great companies were blessed with more good luck (or more bad luck, for that matter) than the comparison companies. Then we began to notice a contrasting pattern in the comparison executives: They credited substantial blame to *bad* luck, frequently bemoaning the difficulties of the environment they faced.

Compare Bethlehem Steel to Nucor. Both companies operated in the steel industry and produced hard-to-differentiate products. Both companies faced the competitive challenge of cheap imported steel. Yet executives at the two companies had completely different views of the same environment. Bethlehem Steel's CEO summed up the company's problems in 1983 by blaming imports: "Our first, second, and third problems are imports."[51] Ken Iverson and his crew at Nucor considered the same challenge from imports a *blessing*, a stroke of good fortune ("Aren't we lucky; steel is heavy, and they have to ship it all the way across the ocean, giving us a huge advantage!"). Iverson saw the first, second, and third problems facing the American steel industry not to be imports, but *management.*[52] He even went so far as to speak out publicly against government protection against imports, telling a stunned gathering of fellow steel executives in 1977 that the real problems facing the American steel industry lay in the fact that management had failed to keep pace with innovation.[53]

The emphasis on luck turns out to be part of a pattern that we came to call *the window and the mirror.*

> ***Level 5 leaders look out the window to apportion credit to factors outside themselves when things go well (and if they cannot find a specific person or event to give credit to, they credit good luck). At the same time, they look in the mirror to apportion responsibility, never blaming bad luck when things go poorly.***

The comparison leaders did just the opposite. They'd look out the window for something or someone outside themselves to blame for poor results, but would preen in front of the mirror and credit themselves when things went well. Strangely, the window and the mirror do not reflect objective reality. Everyone outside the window points inside, directly at the Level 5 leader, saying, "He was the key; without his guidance and leadership, we would not have become a great company." And the Level 5 leader points right back out the window and says, "Look at all the great people and good fortune that made this possible; I'm a lucky guy." They're both right, of course. But the Level 5s would never admit that fact.

CULTIVATING LEVEL 5 LEADERSHIP

Not long ago, I shared the Level 5 finding with a gathering of senior executives. A woman who had recently become chief executive of her company raised her hand and said, "I believe what you say about the good-to-great leaders. But I'm disturbed because when I look in the mirror, I know that I'm not Level 5, not yet anyway. Part of the reason I got this job is because of my ego drives. Are you telling me that I can't make this a great company if I'm not Level 5?"

"I don't know for certain that you absolutely must be a Level 5 leader to make your company great," I replied. "I will simply point back to the data: Of 1,435 companies that appeared on the *Fortune* 500 in our initial candidate list, only eleven made the very tough cut into our study. In those eleven, all of them had Level 5 leadership in key positions, including the CEO, at the pivotal time of transition."

She sat there, quiet for moment, and you could tell everyone in the room was mentally urging her to ask *the question.* Finally, she said, "Can you learn to become Level 5?"

SUMMARY: THE TWO SIDES OF LEVEL 5 LEADERSHIP

Professional Will	Personal Humility
Creates superb results, a clear catalyst in the transition from good to great.	Demonstrates a compelling modesty, shunning public adulation; never boastful.
Demonstrates an unwavering resolve to do whatever must be done to produce the best long-term results, no matter how difficult.	Acts with quiet, calm determination; relies principally on inspired standards, not inspiring charisma, to motivate.
Sets the standard of building an enduring great company; will settle for nothing less.	Channels ambition into the company, not the self; sets up successors for even greater success in the next generation.
Looks in the mirror, not out the window, to apportion responsibility for poor results, never blaming other people, external factors, or bad luck.	Looks out the window, not in the mirror, to apportion credit for the success of the company—to other people, external factors, and good luck.

My hypothesis is that there are two categories of people: Those who do not have the seed of Level 5 and those who do. The first category consists of people who could never in a million years bring themselves to subjugate their egoistic needs to the greater ambition of building something larger and more lasting than themselves. For these people, work will always be first and foremost about what they *get*—fame, fortune, adulation, power, whatever—not what they *build*, create, and contribute.

The great irony is that the animus and personal ambition that often drive people to positions of power stand at odds with the humility required for Level 5 leadership. When you combine that irony with the fact that boards of directors frequently operate under the false belief that they need to hire a larger-than-life, egocentric leader to make an organization great, you can quickly see why Level 5 leaders rarely appear at the top of our institutions.

The second category of people—and I suspect the larger group—consists of those who have the potential to evolve to Level 5; the capability resides within them, perhaps buried or ignored, but there nonetheless. And under the right circumstances—self-reflection, conscious personal development, a mentor, a great teacher, loving parents, a significant life experience, a Level 5 boss, or any number of other factors—they begin to develop.

In looking at the data, we noticed that some of the leaders in our study had significant life experiences that might have sparked or furthered their maturation. Darwin Smith fully blossomed after his experience with cancer. Joe Cullman was profoundly affected by his World War II experiences, particularly the last-minute change of orders that took him off a doomed ship on which he surely would have died.[54] A strong religious belief or conversion might also nurture development of Level 5 traits. Colman Mockler, for example, converted to evangelical Christianity while getting his MBA at Harvard, and later, according to the book *Cutting Edge,* became a prime mover in a group of Boston business executives who met frequently over breakfast to discuss the carryover of religious values to corporate life.[55] Other leaders in our study, however, had no obvious catalytic event; they just led normal lives and somehow ended up atop the Level 5 hierarchy.

I believe—although I cannot prove—that potential Level 5 leaders are highly prevalent in our society. *The problem is not, in my estimation, a dearth of potential Level 5 leaders. They exist all around us, if we just know what to look for.* And what is that? Look for situations where extraordinary results exist but where no individual steps forth to claim excess credit. You will likely find a potential Level 5 leader at work.

For your own development, I would love to be able to give you a list of steps for becoming Level 5, but we have no solid research data that would support a credible list. Our research exposed Level 5 as a key component inside the black box of what it takes to shift a *company* from good to great. Yet inside that black box is yet another black box—namely, the inner development of a *person* to Level 5. We could speculate on what might be inside that inner black box, but it would mostly be just that—speculation. So, in short, Level 5 is a very satisfying idea, a powerful idea, and, to produce the best transitions from good to great, perhaps an essential idea. A "Ten-Step List to Level 5" would trivialize the concept.

My best advice, based on the research, is to begin practicing the other good-to-great disciplines we discovered. We found a symbiotic relationship between Level 5 and the remaining findings. On the one hand, Level 5 traits enable you to implement the other findings; on the other hand, practicing the other findings helps you to become Level 5. Think of it this way: This chapter is about what Level 5s *are*; the rest of the book describes what they *do.* Leading with the other disciplines can help you move in the right direction. There is no guarantee that doing so will turn you into a full-fledged Level 5, but it gives you a tangible place to begin.

We cannot say for sure what percentage of people have the seed within, or how many of those can nurture it. Even those of us who discovered Level 5 on the research team do not know for ourselves whether we will succeed in fully evolving to Level 5. And yet, all of us who worked on the finding have been deeply affected and inspired by the idea. Darwin Smith, Colman Mockler, Alan Wurtzel, and all the other Level 5s we learned about have become models for us, something worthy to aspire toward. Whether or not we make it all the way to Level 5, it is worth the effort. For like all basic truths about what is best in human beings, when we catch a glimpse of that truth, we know that our own lives and all that we touch will be the better for the effort.

LEVEL 5 LEADERSHIP

Key Points

- Every good-to-great company had Level 5 leadership during the pivotal transition years.
- "Level 5" refers to a five-level hierarchy of executive capabilities, with Level 5 at the top. Level 5 leaders embody a paradoxical mix of personal humility and professional will. They are ambitious, to be sure, but ambitious first and foremost for the company, not themselves.
- Level 5 leaders set up their successors for even greater success in the next generation, whereas egocentric Level 4 leaders often set up their successors for failure.
- Level 5 leaders display a compelling modesty, are self-effacing and understated. In contrast, two thirds of the comparison companies had leaders with gargantuan personal egos that contributed to the demise or continued mediocrity of the company.
- Level 5 leaders are fanatically driven, infected with an incurable need to produce sustained *results.* They are resolved to do whatever it takes to make the company great, no matter how big or hard the decisions.
- Level 5 leaders display a workmanlike diligence—more plow horse than show horse.
- Level 5 leaders look out the window to attribute success to factors other than themselves. When things go poorly, however, they look in the mirror and blame themselves, taking full responsibility. The comparison CEOs often did just the opposite—they looked in the mirror to take credit for success, but out the window to assign blame for disappointing results.
- One of the most damaging trends in recent history is the tendency (especially by boards of directors) to select dazzling, celebrity leaders and to de-select potential Level 5 leaders.
- I believe that potential Level 5 leaders exist all around us, if we just know what to look for, and that many people have the potential to evolve into Level 5.

Unexpected Findings

- Larger-than-life, celebrity leaders who ride in from the outside are negatively correlated with going from good to great. Ten of 11 good-to-great CEOs came from *inside* the company, whereas the comparison companies tried outside CEOs six times more often.
- Level 5 leaders attribute much of their success to good luck, rather than personal greatness.
- We were not looking for Level 5 leadership in our research, or anything like it, but the data was overwhelming and convincing. It is an empirical, not an ideological, finding.

Endnotes

1. David McCullough, *Truman* (New York: Simon and Schuster, 1992): 564.
2. Robert Spector, based on research and a manuscript by William W. Wicks, *Shared Values: A History of Kimberly-Clark* (Connecticut: Greenwich Publishing Group, 1997): 101.
3. "Darwin Smith May Have Done Too Good a Job," *Business Week*, August 1, 1988, 57; "Rae Takes On the Paper Industry's Tough Lone Wolf," *Globe and Mail*, July 20, 1991; "Former CEO of K-C Dies," *Dallas Morning News*, December 27, 1995, 1D.
4. Research Interview #5-E, page 26.
5. Research Interview #5-E, page 26.
6. "Darwin Smith May Have Done Too Good a Job," *Business Week*, August 1, 1988: 57.

7. "Darwin Smith May Have Done Too Good a Job," *Business Week*, August 1, 1988: 57; "Kimberly-Clark Bets, Wins on Innovation," *Wall Street Journal*, November 22, 1991: A5; "Darwin E. Smith, 69, Executive Who Remade a Paper Company," *New York Times*, December 28, 1995: B9; Robert Spector, based on research and a manuscript by William W. Wicks, *Shared Values: A History of Kimberly-Clark* (Connecticut: Greenwich Publishing Group, 1997): 101.
8. Robert Spector, based on research and a manuscript by William W. Wicks, *Shared Values: A History of Kimberly-Clark* (Connecticut: Greenwich Publishing Group, 1997): 112.
9. *International Directory of Company Histories*, Vol. 3 (Chicago: St. James Press, 1991): 40; "Kimberly-Clark—Aiming for the Consumer," *Financial World*, April 1, 1970: 15.
10. Robert Spector, based on research and a manuscript by William W. Wicks, *Shared Values: A History of Kimberly-Clark* (Connecticut: Greenwich Publishing Group, 1997): 106, 112; "Darwin E. Smith, 69, Executive Who Remade a Paper Company," *New York Times*, December 28, 1995: B9; "Former CEO of K-C Dies," *Dallas Morning News*, December 27, 1995: 1D; Research Interview #5-E, page 6; "Paper Tiger: How Kimberly-Clark Wraps Its Bottom Line in Disposable Huggies," *Wall Street Journal*, July 23, 1987: 1.
11. "The Battle of the Bottoms," *Forbes*, March 24, 1997: 98.
12. "The Battle of the Bottoms," *Forbes*, March 24, 1997: 98.
13. Robert Spector, based on research and a manuscript by William W. Wicks, *Shared Values: A History of Kimberly-Clark* (Connecticut: Greenwich Publishing Group, 1997): 10.
14. Shelby Foote, *The Civil War: A Narrative: Red River to Appomattox* (New York: Random House, 1975): 1040; James M. McPherson, *Battle Cry of Freedom: The Civil War Era* (New York: Ballantine Books, 1989): 854.
15. Gordon McKibben, *Cutting Edge: Gillette's Journey to Global Leadership* (Boston: Harvard Business School Press, 1998): 14.
16. Company "Chronology," Gillette corporate typescript, 1995; Gordon McKibben, *Cutting Edge: Gillette's Journey to Global Leadership* (Boston: Harvard Business School Press, 1998): 198, 199; Rita Ricardo-Campbell, *Resisting Hostile Takeovers: The Case of Gillette* (Connecticut: Praeger Publishers, 1997): 153.
17. Gordon McKibben, *Cutting Edge: Gillette's Journey to Global Leadership* (Boston: Harvard Business School Press, 1998): 159.
18. Rita Ricardo-Campbell, *Resisting Hostile Takeovers: The Case of Gillette* (Connecticut: Praeger Publishers, 1997).
19. Author conversation with Gillette CEO, summer 2000. "We invested almost $1.5 billion in Sensor and Mach 3. We believed that these projects would have been scrapped had the takeover happened."
20. Gordon McKibben, *Cutting Edge: Gillette's Journey to Global Leadership* (Boston: Harvard Business School Press, 1998): 158. Calculations run using CRSP data.
21. Gordon McKibben, *Cutting Edge: Gillette's Journey to Global Leadership* (Boston: Harvard Business School Press, 1998): 254.
22. "Maxwell Relinquishes Rights to $5.5 Million Final Retirement Payment," *PR Newswire*, January 21, 1992; "$5.5 Million Declined by Ex-Official," *Washington Post*, January 22; 1992: F1.
23. "Iacocca's Last Stand," *Fortune*, April 20, 1992: 63.
24. "Sincere Tyranny," *Forbes*, January 28, 1985: 54.
25. "Managing: Leaders of Corporate Change," *Fortune*, December 14, 1992: 104.
26. "Chairman Quits Post," *New York Times*, November 17, 1992, D5; "Rubbermaid's Sad Succession Tale," *New York Times*, July 5, 1987: C1.
27. "Is Rubbermaid Reacting Too Late?" *New York Times*, December 22, 1996: A1.
28. Research Interview #7-D, page 17.
29. Chris Jones and Duane Duffy, "Media Hype Analysis" (unpublished), *Good to Great* research project, summers 1998: 1999.
30. "Did CEO Dunlap Save Scott Paper—or Just Pretty It Up? The Shredder," *Business Week*, January 15, 1996.

31. "Did CEO Dunlap Save Scott Paper—or Just Pretty It Up? The Shredder," *Business Week*, January 15, 1996; "Chain Saw Al to the Rescue?" *Forbes*, August 26, 1996; "After the Fall," *Across the Board*, April 1996: 28–33; "Only the Paranoid Survive," *Worth Online*, October 1996; Albert J. Dunlap with Bob Andelman, *Mean Business: How I Save Bad Companies and Make Good Companies Great* (New York: Fireside, 1997): 20.
32. Albert J. Dunlap with Bob Andelman, *Mean Business: How I Save Bad Companies and Make Good Companies Great* (New York: Fireside, 1997): 132.
33. The cases where a charismatic CEO eventually became a liability for the company were Great Western, Warner-Lambert, Scott Paper, Bethlehem Steel, R. J Reynolds, Addressograph-Multigraph, Eckerd, Bank of America, Burroughs, Chrysler, Rubbermaid, and Teledyne.
34. "President Iacocca," *Wall Street Journal*, July 28, 1982: 1; "Iacocca Hands Over the Keys to Chrysler," *Investor's Business Daily*, January 4, 1993: 1.
35. "Iacocca Hands Over the Keys to Chrysler," *Investor's Business Daily*, January 4, 1993: 1.
36. "How Chrysler Filled Detroit's Biggest Shoes," *Wall Street Journal*, September 7, 1994: B1.
37. "Why Certain Stocks Appear To Be Worth More Than Their Price," *Wall Street Journal*, April 13, 1995, A1; "Chrysler's New Plan: Sell Cars," *Fortune*, June 26, 1995: 19.
38. "Will Success Spoil Chrysler?" *Fortune*, January 10, 1994; "Company of the Year: Chrysler Has the Hot Cars. More Important, It Has a Smart, Disciplined Management Team," *Forbes*, January 13, 1997: 82; "Daimler-Benz Will Acquire Chrysler in $36 Billion Deal That Will Reshape Industry," *New York Times*, May 7, 1998: A6.
39. Research Interview #1-A, page 3; Research Interview #1-G, page 35; "A Drugmaker's Return to Health," *Business Week*, April 26, 1976: 38; Herman Kogan, *The Long White Line: The Story of Abbott Laboratories* (New York: Random House, 1963): 249.
40. The Upjohn Company, *International Directory of Company Histories*, 707; "The Medicine Men of Kalamazoo," *Fortune*, July 1959: 106.
41. Leigh Wilbanks, "CEO Analysis Unit" (unpublished), *Good to Great* research project, summer 1998.
42. University of Chicago Center for Research in Securities Prices data, all dividends reinvested and adjusted for stock splits.
43. Research Interview #10-D, pages 9–10.
44. Herman Kogan and Rick Kogan, *Pharmacist to the Nation* (Deerfield, Ill.: Walgreens Company, 1989), 236; Research Interview #10-F, page 3.
45. Research Interview #2-G, page 10.
46. University of Chicago Center for Research in Securities Prices data, all dividends reinvested and adjusted for stock splits.
47. Research Interview #2-G, page 16.
48. Research Interview #7-H, page 12.
49. Research Interview #8-A, pages 4–5, 9, 10.
50. Joseph F. Cullman 3rd, *I'm a Lucky Guy* (Joseph F. Cullman 3rd, 1998): 1.
51. "Searching for Profits at Bethlehem," *New York Times*, December 25, 1983: C1.
52. "Steel Man Ken Iverson," *Inc.*, April 1, 1986: 40.
53. Jeffrey L. Rodengen, *The Legend of the Nucor Corporation* (Fort Lauderdale, Fla.: Write Stuff Enterprises, 1997): 71.
54. Joseph F. Cullman 3rd, *I'm a Lucky Guy* (Joseph F. Cullman 3rd, 1998).
55. Gordon McKibben, *Cutting Edge: Gillette's Journey to Global Leadership* (Boston: Harvard Business School Press, 1998): 78–79.

CHAPTER 16
ORGANIZATIONAL CULTURE

UNCOVERING THE LEVELS OF CULTURE

Edgar H. Schein

EVOLUTION AND REVOLUTION AS ORGANIZATIONS GROW

Larry E. Greiner

Organizational culture greatly influences the way people behave at work. Ever since this discovery was made, scholars and managers alike have been interested in learning how to create, manage, and maintain productive and healthy organizational cultures. Organizational culture can play either a positive or negative role in attracting and retaining employees. When leaders understand the role of organizational culture and manage it effectively, it can serve as the glue that holds organizations together and helps them succeed.

Edgar Schein, management professor emeritus, has contributed much of our current knowledge about organizational culture. The first selection, "Uncovering the Levels of Culture," is a chapter from his book *Organizational Culture and Leadership*, which is considered a classic in its field. Schein defines organizational culture and explains how it works.

Our second article is an updated classic by Larry Greiner, management and organization professor. In "Evolution and Revolution as Organizations Grow," Greiner outlines five developmental phases that organizations traverse as they grow. Within each stage, organizations gradually evolve until they reach a crisis that necessitates serious change—a revolution. The resulting solution is eventually outgrown, when the organization has to move on to the next stage. According to Greiner, leaders should understand where their organization is in this developmental scheme, in part because each phase requires a different type of leadership and organizational emphasis. Learning to "grow" the organization can help leaders avoid the pitfalls that derail so many firms.

UNCOVERING THE LEVELS OF CULTURE*

Edgar H. Schein

The culture of a group can now be defined as

> *A pattern of shared basic assumptions that the group learned as it solved its problems of external adaptation and internal integration, that has worked well enough to be considered valid and, therefore, to be taught to new members as the correct way to perceive, think, and feel in relation to those problems.*

The purpose of this chapter is to show that culture can be analyzed at several different levels, where the term *level* refers to the degree to which the cultural phenomenon is visible to the observer. Some of the confusion of definition of what culture really is results from not differentiating the levels at which it manifests itself. These levels range from the very tangible overt manifestations that one can see and feel to the deeply embedded, unconscious basic assumptions that I am defining as the essence of culture. In between we have various espoused values, norms, and rules of behavior that members of the culture use as a way of depicting the culture to themselves and others.

Many other culture researchers prefer the concept of "basic values" for describing the deepest levels. As I will try to show with later examples, my preference is for "basic assumptions" because these tend to be taken for granted and are treated as nonnegotiable. Values can be and are discussed, and people can agree to disagree about them. Basic assumptions are so taken for granted that someone who does not hold them is viewed as crazy and automatically dismissed. The levels at which culture can be analyzed are shown in Figure 1.

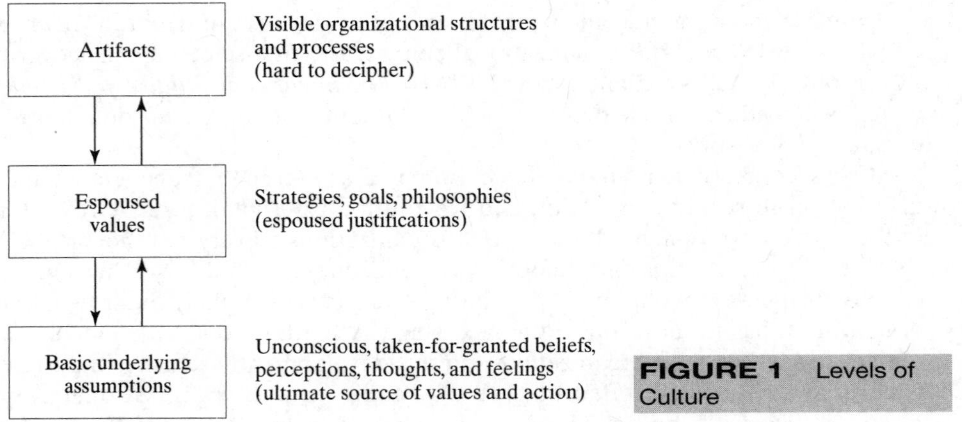

FIGURE 1 Levels of Culture

*Excerpted with permission from *Organizational Culture and Leadership*, Copyright © 1997: 16–27. Reprinted by permission of Jossey-Bass, Inc., a subsidiary of John Wiley & Sons, Inc.

ARTIFACTS

At the surface we have the level of *artifacts*, which includes all the phenomena that one sees, hears, and feels when one encounters a new group with an unfamiliar culture. Artifacts would include the visible products of the group such as the architecture of its physical environment, its language, its technology and products, its artistic creations, and its style as embodied in clothing, manners of address, emotional displays, myths and stories told about the organization, published lists of values, observable rituals and ceremonies, and so on. For purposes of cultural analysis this level also includes the visible behavior of the group and the organizational processes into which such behavior is made routine.

The most important point about this level of the culture is that it is easy to observe and very difficult to decipher. The Egyptians and the Maya both built highly visible pyramids, but the meaning of pyramids in each culture was very different—tombs in one and temples as well as tombs in the other. In other words, the observer can describe what she sees and feels but cannot reconstruct from that alone what those things mean in the given group, or whether they even reflect important underlying assumptions.

On the other hand, one school of thought argues that one's own response to physical artifacts such as buildings and office layouts can lead to the identification of major images and root metaphors that reflect the deepest level of the culture (Gagliardi, 1990). This would be especially true if the organization one is deciphering is in the same larger culture as the researcher. The problem is that symbols are ambiguous, and one can only test one's insight into what something might mean if one has also experienced the culture at the level of its values and the level of its basic assumptions.

It is especially dangerous to try to infer the deeper assumptions from artifacts alone because one's interpretations will inevitably be projections of one's own feelings and reactions. For example, when one sees a very informal, loose organization, one may interpret that as inefficient if one's own background is based on the assumption that informality means playing around and not working. Alternatively, if one sees a very formal organization, one may interpret that to be a sign of lack of innovative capacity if one's own experience is based on the assumption that formality means bureaucracy and formalization.

Every facet of a group's life produces artifacts, creating the problem of classification. In reading cultural descriptions, one often notes that different observers choose to report on different sorts of artifacts, leading to noncomparable descriptions. Anthropologists have developed classification systems, but these tend to be so vast and detailed that cultural essence becomes difficult to discern.

If the observer lives in the group long enough, the meanings of artifacts gradually become clear. If, however, one wants to achieve this level of understanding more quickly, one can attempt to analyze the espoused values, norms, and rules that provide the day-to-day operating principles by which the members of the group guide their behavior. This kind of inquiry takes us to the next level of cultural analysis.

ESPOUSED VALUES

All group learning ultimately reflects someone's original values, someone's sense of what ought to be as distinct from what is. When a group is first created or when it faces a new task, issue, or problem, the first solution proposed to deal with it reflects some individual's own assumptions about what is right or wrong, what will work or not work.

Those individuals who prevail, who can influence the group to adopt a certain approach to the problem, will later be identified as "leaders" or founders, but the group as a group does not yet have any shared knowledge because it has not yet taken a common action in response to the new problem. Therefore, whatever is proposed can only have the status of a value from the point of view of the group, no matter how strongly the proponent may believe that he or she is uttering absolute proven truth. Until the group has taken some joint action and its members have together observed the outcome of that action, there is not as yet a shared basis for determining what is factual and real.

For example, in a young business if sales begin to decline, a manager may say, "We must increase advertising" because of her belief that advertising always increases sales. The group, never having experienced this situation before, will hear that assertion as a statement of that manager's values: "She believes that when one is in trouble it is a *good* thing to increase advertising." What the leader initially proposes, therefore, cannot have any status other than a value to be questioned, debated, challenged, and tested.

If the manager convinces the group to act on her belief and if the solution works and if the group has a shared perception of that success, then the perceived value that advertising is "good" gradually starts a process of *cognitive transformation.* First, it will be transformed into a *shared value or belief* and, ultimately, into a *shared assumption* (if action based on it continues to be successful). If this transformation process occurs—and it will occur only if the proposed solution continues to work, thus implying that it is in some larger sense "correct" and must reflect an accurate picture of reality—group members will tend to forget that originally they were not sure and that the proposed course of action was at an earlier time debated and confronted.

Not all values undergo such transformation. First of all, the solution based on a given value may not work reliably. Only values that are susceptible to physical or social validation and that continue to work reliably in solving the group's problems will become transformed into assumptions. Second, value domains dealing with the less controllable elements of the environment or with aesthetic or moral matters may not be testable at all. In such cases consensus through social validation is still possible, but it is not automatic.

By social validation I mean that certain values are confirmed only by the shared social experience of a group. Such values typically involve the group's internal relations, where the test of whether they work or not is how comfortable and anxiety-free members are when they abide by them. Social validation also applies to those broader values that involve relationships to the environment but in a nontestable fashion, such as religion, ethics, and aesthetics.

In these realms the group learns that certain such values, as initially promulgated by prophets, founders, and leaders, work in the sense of reducing uncertainty in critical areas of the group's functioning. And as they continue to work, they gradually become transformed into nondiscussable assumptions supported by articulated sets of beliefs, norms, and operational rules of behavior. The derived beliefs and moral/ethical rules remain conscious and are explicitly articulated because they serve the normative or moral function of guiding members of the group in how to deal with certain key situations and in training new members in how to behave. A set of values that becomes embodied in an ideology or organizational philosophy thus can serve as a guide and as a way of dealing with the uncertainty of intrinsically uncontrollable or difficult events.

Values at this conscious level will predict much of the behavior that can be observed at the artifactual level. But if those values are not based on prior learning, they may also reflect only what Argyris and Schön (1978) have called *espoused values*, which predict well enough what people will say in a variety of situations but which may be out of line with what they will actually *do* in situations where those values should, in fact, be operating. Thus, a company may say that it values people and has high quality standards for its products, but its record in that regard may contradict what it says.

If the espoused values are reasonably congruent with the underlying assumptions, then the articulation of those values into a philosophy of operating can be helpful in bringing the group together, serving as a source of identity and core mission. But in analyzing values one must discriminate carefully between those that are congruent with underlying assumptions and those that are, in effect, either rationalizations or only aspirations for the future. Often such lists of values are not patterned, sometimes they are even mutually contradictory, and often they are inconsistent with observed behavior. Large areas of behavior are often left unexplained, leaving us with a feeling that we understand a piece of the culture but still do not have the culture as such in hand. To get at that deeper level of understanding, to decipher the pattern, and to predict future behavior correctly, we have to understand more fully the category of basic assumptions.

BASIC ASSUMPTIONS

When a solution to a problem works repeatedly, it comes to be taken for granted. What was once a hypothesis, supported only by a hunch or a value, comes gradually to be treated as a reality. We come to believe that nature really works this way. Basic assumptions, in this sense, are different from what some anthropologists call dominant value orientations in that such dominant orientations reflect the preferred solution among several basic alternatives, but all the alternatives are still visible in the culture, and any given member of the culture could, from time to time, behave according to variant as well as dominant orientations (Kluckhohn and Strodtbeck, 1961).

Basic assumptions, in the sense in which I want to define the concept, have become so taken for granted that one finds little variation within a cultural unit. In fact, if a basic assumption is strongly held in a group, members will find behavior based on any other premise inconceivable. For example, a group whose basic assumption is that the individual's rights supersede those of the group members will find it inconceivable that members would commit suicide or in some other way sacrifice themselves to the group even if they had dishonored the group. In a capitalist country, it is inconceivable that one might design a company to operate consistently at a financial loss or that it does not matter whether or not a product works. Basic assumptions, in this sense, are similar to what Argyris has identified as *theories-in-use*, the implicit assumptions that actually guide behavior, that tell group members how to perceive, think about, and feel about things (Argyris, 1976; Argyris and Schön, 1974).

Basic assumptions, like theories-in-use, tend to be those we neither confront nor debate and hence are extremely difficult to change. To learn something new in this realm requires us to resurrect, reexamine, and possibly change some of the more stable portions of our cognitive structure, a process that Argyris and others have called double-loop learning or frame breaking (for example, Argyris, Putnam, and Smith, 1985; Bartunek and Moch, 1987). Such learning is intrinsically difficult because the reexamination of basic assumptions temporarily destabilizes our cognitive and interpersonal world, releasing large quantities of basic anxiety.

Rather than tolerating such anxiety levels we tend to want to perceive the events around us as congruent with our assumptions, even if that means distorting, denying, projecting, or in other ways falsifying to ourselves what may be going on around us. It is in this psychological process that culture has its ultimate power. Culture as a set of basic assumptions defines for us what to pay attention to, what things mean, how to react emotionally to what is going on, and what actions to take in various kinds of situations. Once we have developed an integrated set of such assumptions, which might be called a thought world or mental map, we will be maximally comfortable with others who share the same set of assumptions and very uncomfortable and vulnerable in situations where different assumptions operate either because we will not understand what is going on, or, worse, misperceive and misinterpret the actions of others (Douglas, 1986).

The human mind needs cognitive stability. Therefore, any challenge to or questioning of a basic assumption will release anxiety and defensiveness. In this sense, the shared basic assumptions that make up the culture of a group can be thought of at both the individual and group levels as psychological cognitive *defense mechanisms* that permit the group to continue to function. Recognizing this connection is important when one thinks about changing aspects of a group's culture, for it is no easier to do that than to change an individual's pattern of defense mechanisms. In either case the key is the management of the large amounts of anxiety that accompany any relearning at this level.

To understand how unconscious assumptions can distort data, consider the following example. If we assume, on the basis of past experience or education, that other people will take advantage of us whenever they have an opportunity, we expect to be taken advantage of and then interpret the behavior of others in a way that coincides with those expectations. We observe people sitting in a seemingly idle posture at their desks and interpret their behavior as loafing rather than thinking out an important problem. We perceive absence from work as shirking rather than doing work at home.

If this is not only a personal assumption but one that is shared and thus part of the organization's culture, we will discuss with others what to do about our "lazy" work force and institute tight controls to ensure that people are at their desks and busy. If employees suggest that they do some of their work at home, we will be uncomfortable and probably deny the request because we will assume that at home they would loaf (Bailyn, 1992; Perin, 1991).

In contrast, if we assume that everyone is highly motivated and competent, we will act in accordance with that assumption by encouraging people to work at their own pace and in their own way. If someone is discovered to be unproductive in the organization, we will assume that there is a mismatch between the person and the job assignment, not that the person is lazy or incompetent. If the employee wants to work at home, we will perceive that as evidence of wanting to be productive even if circumstances require him to be at home.

In both cases there is the potential for distortion. The cynical manager will not perceive how highly motivated some of the subordinates really are, and the idealistic manager will not perceive that there are subordinates who are lazy and who are taking advantage of the situation. As McGregor (1960) noted several decades ago, such assumption sets in the human area become the basis of whole management and control systems that perpetuate themselves because if people are treated consistently in terms of certain basic assumptions, they come eventually to behave according to those assumptions in order to make their world stable and predictable.

Unconscious assumptions sometimes lead to ridiculously tragic situations, as illustrated by a common problem experienced by American supervisors in some Asian countries. A manager who comes from an American pragmatic tradition takes it for granted that solving a problem always has the highest priority. When that manager encounters a subordinate who comes from a different cultural tradition, in which good relationships and protecting the superior's "face" are assumed to have top priority, the following scenario can easily result.

The manager proposes a solution to a given problem. The subordinate knows that the solution will not work, but his unconscious assumption requires that he remain silent because to tell the boss that the proposed solution is wrong is a threat to the boss's face. It would not even occur to the subordinate to do anything other than remain silent or even reassure the boss that they should go ahead and take the action if the boss were to inquire what the subordinate thought.

The action is taken, the results are negative, and the boss, somewhat surprised and puzzled, asks the subordinate what he would have done. When the subordinate reports that he would have done something different, the boss quite legitimately asks why the subordinate did not speak up sooner. This question puts the subordinate in an impossible bind because the answer itself is a threat to the boss's face. He cannot possibly explain his behavior without committing the very sin he is trying to avoid in the first place—namely, embarrassing the boss. He might even lie at this point and argue that what the boss did was right and only "bad luck" or uncontrollable circumstances prevented it from succeeding.

From the point of view of the subordinate, the boss's behavior is incomprehensible because it shows lack of self-pride, possibly causing the subordinate to lose respect for that boss. To the boss the subordinate's behavior is equally incomprehensible. The boss cannot develop any sensible explanation of the subordinate's behavior that is not cynically colored by the assumption that the subordinate at some level just does not care about effective performance and therefore must be gotten rid of. It never occurs to the boss that another assumption such as "one never embarrasses a superior" is operating and that to the subordinate that assumption is even more powerful than "one gets the job done."

If assumptions such as these operate only in an individual and represent her idiosyncratic experience, they can be corrected more easily because the person will detect that she is alone in holding a given assumption. The power of culture comes about through the fact that the assumptions are shared and therefore mutually reinforced. In these instances probably only a third party or some cross-cultural education could help to find common ground whereby both parties could bring their implicit assumptions to the surface. And even after they have surfaced, such assumptions would still operate, forcing the boss and the subordinate to invent a whole new communication mechanism that would permit each to remain congruent with her or his culture—for example, agreeing that before any decision is made and before the boss has stuck her neck out, the subordinate will be asked for suggestions and for factual data that will not be face threatening. Note that the solution must keep each cultural assumption intact. One cannot in these instances simply declare one or the other cultural assumption "wrong." One has to find a third assumption to allow them both to retain their integrity.

I have dwelled on this example to illustrate the potency of implicit, unconscious assumptions and to show that such assumptions often deal with fundamental aspects of life—the nature of time and space; human nature and human activities; the nature of truth and how one discovers it; the correct way for the individual and the group to relate to each other; the relative importance of work, family, and self-development; the proper role of men and women; and the nature of the family.

We do not develop new assumptions about each of these areas in every group or organization we join. Each member of a new group will bring her or his own cultural learning from prior groups, but as the new group develops its own shared history, it will develop modified or brand-new assumptions in critical areas of its experience. Those new assumptions make up the culture of that particular group.

Any group's culture can be studied at these three levels—the level of its artifacts, the level of its values, and the level of its basic assumptions. If one does not decipher the pattern of basic assumptions that may be operating, one will not know how to interpret the artifacts correctly or how much credence to give to the articulated values. In other words, the essence of a culture lies in the pattern of basic underlying assumptions, and once one understands those, one can easily understand the other more surface levels and deal appropriately with them.

SUMMARY AND CONCLUSIONS

Though the essence of a group's culture is its pattern of shared, taken-for-granted basic assumptions, the culture will manifest itself at the levels of observable artifacts and shared espoused values, norms, and rules of behavior. It is important to recognize in analyzing cultures that artifacts are easy to observe but difficult to decipher and that values may only reflect rationalizations or aspirations. To understand a group's culture, one must attempt to get at its shared basic assumptions and one must understand the learning process by which such basic assumptions come to be.

Leadership is originally the source of the beliefs and values that get a group moving in dealing with its internal and external problems. If what a leader proposes works and continues to work, what once was only the leader's assumption gradually comes to be a shared assumption. Once a set of shared basic assumptions is formed by this process, it can function as a cognitive defense mechanism both for the individual members and for the group as a whole. In other words, individuals and groups seek stability and meaning. Once these are achieved, it is easier to distort new data by denial, projection, rationalization, or various other defense mechanisms than to change the basic assumption. As we will see, culture change, in the sense of changing basic assumptions is, therefore, difficult, time consuming, and highly anxiety provoking. This point is especially relevant for the leader who sets out to change the culture of the organization.

The most central issue for leaders, therefore, is how to get at the deeper levels of a culture, how to assess the functionality of the assumptions made at each level, and how to deal with the anxiety that is unleashed when those levels are challenged.

References

Argyris, C. *Integrating the Individual and the Organization* (New York: Wiley, 1976).

Argyris, C. and D. A. Schön, *Theory in Practice: Increasing Professional Effectiveness* (San Francisco: Jossey-Bass, 1974).

Argyris, C. and D. A. Schön, *Organizational Learning* (Reading, MA: Addison-Wesley, 1978).

Argyris, C., R. Putnam, and D. M. Smith, *Action Science* (San Francisco: Jossey-Bass, 1985).

Bailyn, L., "Changing the Conditions of Work: Implications for Career Development," *Career Development in the 1990's: Theory and Practice*, D. H. Montross and C. J. Shinkman (Springfield, IL: Thomas, 1992).

Bartunek, J., and M. K. Moch, "First Order, Second Order, and Third Order Change and Organization Development Interventions: A Cognitive Approach," *Journal of Applied Behavioral Science 23* (1987): 483–500.

Douglas, M., *How Institutions Think* (Syracuse, NY: Syracuse University Press, 1986).

Gagliardi, P. (ed.), *Symbols and Artifacts: Views of the Corporate Landscape* (New York: de Gruyter, 1990).

Kluckhohn, F. R., and F. L. Strodtbeck, *Variations in Value Orientations* (New York: Harper & Row, 1961).

McGregor, D. M., *The Human Side of Enterprise* (New York: McGraw-Hill, 1960).

Perin, C., "The Moral Fabric of the Office," S. Bacharach, S. R. Barley, and P. S. Tolbert (eds.), *Research in the Sociology of Organizations* (special volume on the professions) (Greenwich, CT: JAI Press, 1991).

EVOLUTION AND REVOLUTION AS ORGANIZATIONS GROW*

Larry E. Greiner

Key executives of a retail store chain hold on to an organizational structure long after it has served its purpose because the structure is the source of their power. The company eventually goes into bankruptcy.

A large bank disciplines a "rebellious" manager who is blamed for current control problems, when the underlying causes are centralized procedures that are holding back expansion into new markets. Many young managers subsequently leave the bank, competition moves in, and profits decline.

The problems at these companies are rooted more in past decisions than in present events or market dynamics. Yet management, in its haste to grow, often overlooks such critical developmental questions as, Where has our organization been? Where is it now? and What do the answers to these questions mean for where it is going? Instead, management fixes its gaze outward on the environment and toward the future, as if more precise market projections will provide the organization with a new identity.

In stressing the force of history on an organization, I have drawn from the legacies of European psychologists who argue that the behavior of individuals is determined primarily by past events and experiences, rather than by what lies ahead. Extending that thesis to problems of organizational development, we can identify a series of developmental phases through which companies tend to pass as they grow. Each phase begins with a period of evolution, with steady growth and stability, and ends with a revolutionary period of substantial organizational turmoil and change—for

*Reprinted by permission from *Harvard Business Review* (May-June 1998): 55–65.

instance, when centralized practices eventually lead to demands for decentralization. The resolution of each revolutionary period determines whether or not a company will move forward into its next stage of evolutionary growth.

A MODEL OF HOW ORGANIZATIONS DEVELOP

To date, research on organizational development has been largely empirical, and scholars have not attempted to create a model of the overall process. When we analyze the research, however, five key dimensions emerge: an organization's age and size, its stages of evolution and revolution, and the growth rate of its industry. The graph "How Companies Grow" shows how these elements interact to shape an organization's development.

Age of the Organization

The most obvious and essential dimension for any model of development is the life span of an organization (represented on the graph as the horizontal axis). History shows that the same organizational practices are not maintained throughout a long life span. This demonstrates a most basic point: management problems and principles are rooted in time. The concept of decentralization, for example, can describe corporate practices at one period but can lose its descriptive power at another.

FIGURE 1 How Companies Grow

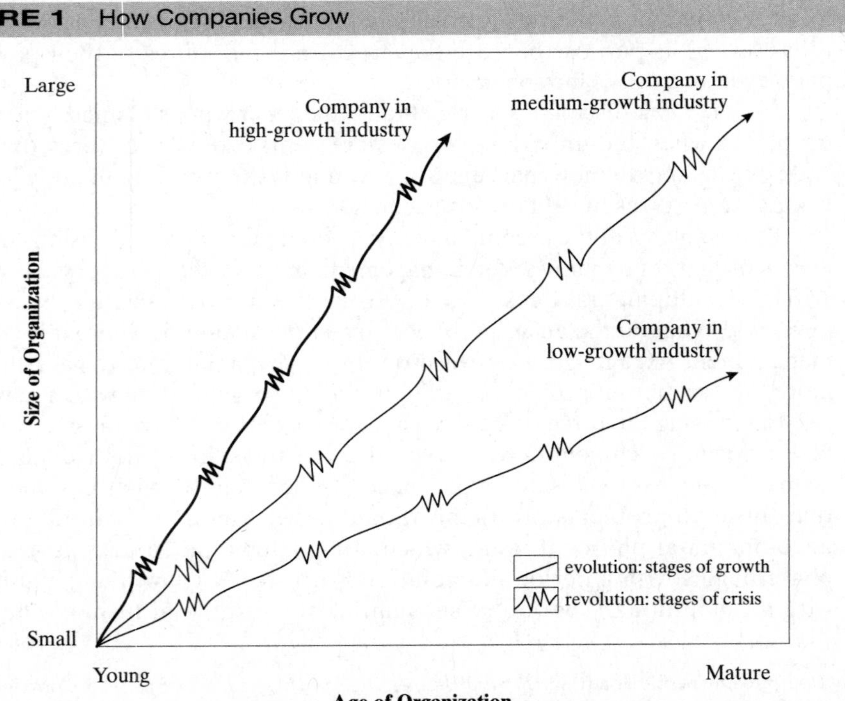

The passage of time also contributes to the institutionalization of managerial attitudes. As these attitudes become rigid and eventually outdated, the behavior of employees becomes not only more predictable but also more difficult to change.

Size of the Organization

This dimension is depicted on the chart as the vertical axis. A company's problems and solutions tend to change markedly as the number of its employees and its sales volume increase. Problems of coordination and communication magnify, new functions emerge, levels in the management hierarchy multiply, and jobs become more interrelated. Thus, time is not the only determinant of structure; in fact, organizations that do not become larger can retain many of the same management issues and practices over long periods.

Stages of Evolution

As organizations age and grow, another phenomenon emerges: prolonged growth that we can term the *evolutionary period.* Most growing organizations do not expand for two years and then contract for one; rather, those that survive a crisis usually enjoy four to eight years of continuous growth without a major economic setback or severe internal disruption. The term *evolution* seems appropriate for describing these quiet periods because only modest adjustments appear to be necessary for maintaining growth under the same overall pattern of management.

Stages of Revolution

Smooth evolution is not inevitable or indefinitely sustainable; it cannot be assumed that organizational growth is linear. *Fortune*'s "500" list, for example, has had considerable turnover during the last 50 years. In fact, evidence from numerous case histories reveals periods of substantial turbulence interspersed between smoother periods of evolution.

We can term the turbulent times *periods of revolution* because they typically exhibit a serious upheaval of management practices. Traditional management practices that were appropriate for a smaller size and earlier time no longer work and are brought under scrutiny by frustrated top-level managers and disillusioned lower-level managers. During such periods of crisis, a number of companies fall short. Those that are unable to abandon past practices and effect major organizational changes are likely either to fold or to level off in their growth rates.

The critical task for management in each revolutionary period is to find a new set of organizational practices that will become the basis for managing the next period of evolutionary growth. Interestingly enough, those new practices eventually sow the seeds of their own decay and lead to another period of revolution. Managers therefore experience the irony of seeing a major solution in one period become a major problem in a later period.

Growth Rate of the Industry

The speed at which an organization experiences phases of evolution and revolution is closely related to the market environment of its industry. For example, a company in a rapidly expanding market will have to add employees quickly; hence, the need for new organizational structures to accommodate large staff increases is accelerated. Whereas evolutionary periods tend to be relatively short in fast-growing industries, much longer evolutionary periods occur in mature or slow-growing industries.

Evolution can also be prolonged, and revolutions delayed, when profits come easily. For instance, companies that make grievous errors in a prosperous industry can still look good on their profit-and-loss statements; thus, they can buy time before a crisis forces changes in management practices. The aerospace industry in its highly profitable infancy is an example. Yet revolutionary periods still occur, as one did in aerospace when profit opportunities began to dry up. By contrast, when the market environment is poor, revolutions seem to be much more severe and difficult to resolve.

PHASES OF GROWTH

With the foregoing framework in mind, we can now examine in depth the five specific phases of evolution and revolution. As shown in the graph "The Five Phases of Growth," each evolutionary period is characterized by the dominant management style used to achieve growth; each revolutionary period is characterized by the dominant management problem that must be solved before growth can continue. The pattern presented in the chart seems to be typical for companies in industries with moderate growth over a long period; companies in faster-growing industries tend to experience all five phases more rapidly, whereas those in slower-growing industries encounter only two or three phases over many years.

FIGURE 2 The Five Phases of Growth

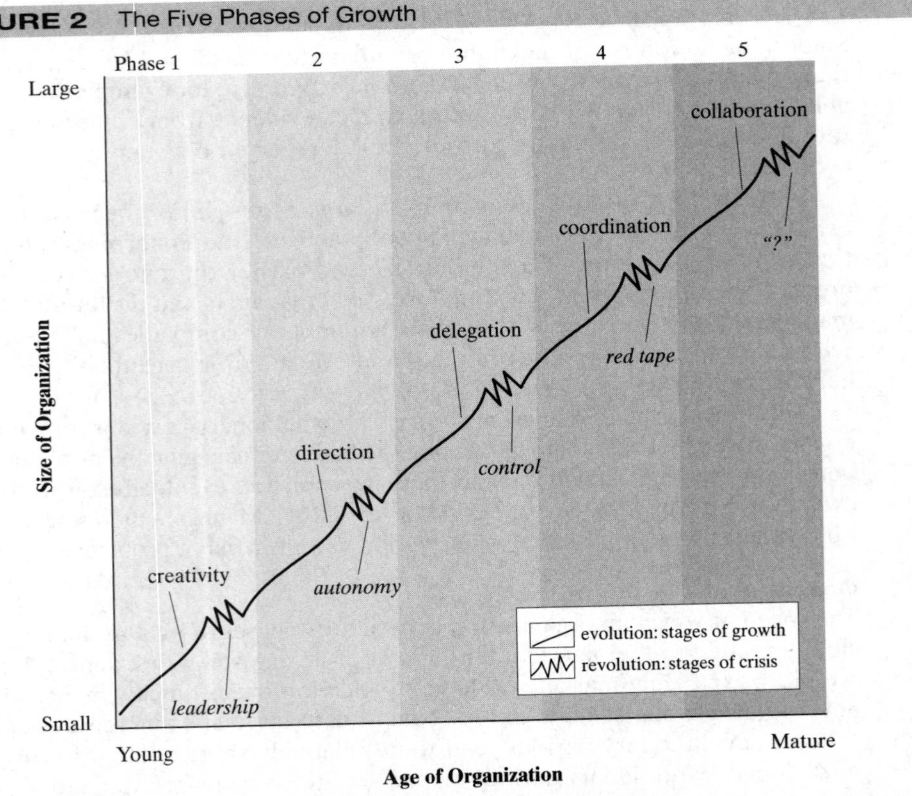

It is important to note that each phase is at once a result of the previous phase and a cause for the next phase. For example, the evolutionary management style in Phase 3 is delegation, which grows out of and becomes the solution to demands for greater autonomy in the preceding Phase 2 revolution. The style of delegation used in Phase 3, however, eventually provokes a revolutionary crisis that is characterized by attempts to regain control over the diversity created through increased delegation.

For each phase, managers are limited in what they can do if growth is to occur. For example, a company experiencing an autonomy crisis in Phase 2 cannot return to directive management for a solution; it must adopt a new style—delegation—in order to move forward.

Phase 1: Creativity

In the birth stage of an organization, the emphasis is on creating both a product and a market. The following are the characteristics of the period of creative evolution:

- The founders of the company are usually technically or entrepreneurially oriented, and they generally disdain management activities; their physical and mental energies are absorbed entirely by making and selling a new product.
- Communication among employees is frequent and informal.
- Long hours of work are rewarded by modest salaries and the promise of ownership benefits.
- Decisions and motivation are highly sensitive to marketplace feedback; management acts as customers react.

All the foregoing individualistic and creative activities are essential for a company to get off the ground. But as the company grows, those very activities become the problem. Larger production runs require knowledge about the efficiencies of manufacturing. Increased numbers of employees cannot be managed exclusively through informal communication, and new employees are not motivated by an intense dedication to the product or organization. Additional capital must be secured, and new accounting procedures are needed for financial control. The company's founders find themselves burdened with unwanted management responsibilities. They long for the "good old days" and try to act as they did in the past. Conflicts among harried leaders emerge and grow more intense.

At this point, a *crisis of leadership* occurs, which is the onset of the first revolution. Who will lead the company out of confusion and solve the managerial problems confronting it? Obviously, a strong manager is needed—one who has the necessary knowledge and skills to introduce new business techniques. But finding that manager is easier said than done. The founders often resist stepping aside, even though they are probably temperamentally unsuited to the job. So here is the first critical choice in an organization's development: to locate and install a strong business manager who is acceptable to the founders and who can pull the organization together.

Phase 2: Direction

Those companies that survive the first phase by installing a capable business manager usually embark on a period of sustained growth under able, directive leadership. Here are the characteristics of this evolutionary period:

- A functional organizational structure is introduced to separate manufacturing from marketing activities, and job assignments become increasingly specialized.
- Accounting systems for inventory and purchasing are introduced.
- Incentives, budgets, and work standards are adopted.
- Communication becomes more formal and impersonal as a hierarchy of titles and positions grows.
- The new manager and his or her key supervisors assume most of the responsibility for instituting direction; lower-level supervisors are treated more as functional specialists than as autonomous decision-making managers.

Although the new directive techniques channel employees' energy more efficiently into growth, they eventually become inappropriate for controlling a more diverse and complex organization. Lower-level employees find themselves restricted by a cumbersome and centralized hierarchy. They have come to possess more direct knowledge about markets and machinery than do their leaders at the top; consequently, they feel torn between following procedures and taking initiative on their own.

Thus, the second revolution emerges from a *crisis of autonomy.* The solution adopted by most companies is to move toward more delegation. Yet it is difficult for top-level managers who previously were successful at being directive to give up responsibility to lower-level managers. Moreover, the lower-level managers are not accustomed to making decisions for themselves. As a result, numerous companies flounder during this revolutionary period by adhering to centralized methods, while lower-level employees become disenchanted and leave the organization.

Phase 3: Delegation

The next era of growth evolves from the successful application of a decentralized organizational structure. It exhibits these characteristics:

- Much greater responsibility is given to the managers of plants and market territories.
- Profit centers and bonuses are used to motivate employees.
- Top-level executives at headquarters limit themselves to managing by exception based on periodic reports from the field.
- Management often concentrates on acquiring outside enterprises that can be lined up with other decentralized units.
- Communication from the top is infrequent and usually occurs by correspondence, telephone, or brief visits to field locations.

The delegation phase allows companies to expand by means of the heightened motivation of managers at lower levels. Managers in decentralized organizations, who have greater authority and incentives, are able to penetrate larger markets, respond faster to customers, and develop new products.

A serious problem eventually emerges, however, as top-level executives sense that they are losing control over a highly diversified field operation. Autonomous field managers prefer to run their own shows without coordinating plans, money, technology, and personnel with the rest of the organization. Freedom breeds a parochial attitude.

Soon, the organization falls into a *crisis of control.* The Phase 3 revolution is under way when top management seeks to regain control over the company as a whole. Some top-management teams attempt a return to centralized management, which usually fails because of the organization's newly vast scope of operations. Those companies that move ahead find a new solution in the use of special coordination techniques.

Phase 4: Coordination

The evolutionary period of the coordination phase is characterized by the use of formal systems for achieving greater coordination and by top-level executives taking responsibility for the initiation and administration of these new systems. For example:

- Decentralized units are merged into product groups.
- Formal planning procedures are established and intensively reviewed.
- Numerous staff members are hired and located at headquarters to initiate companywide programs of control and review for line managers.
- Capital expenditures are carefully weighed and parceled out across the organization.
- Each product group is treated as an investment center where return on invested capital is an important criterion used in allocating funds.
- Certain technical functions, such as data processing, are centralized at headquarters, while daily operating decisions remain decentralized.
- Stock options and company wide profit sharing are used to encourage employees to identify with the organization as a whole.

All these new coordination systems prove useful for achieving growth through the more efficient allocation of a company's limited resources. The systems prompt field managers to look beyond the needs of their local units. Although these managers still have a great deal of decision-making responsibility, they learn to justify their actions more carefully to a watchdog audience at headquarters.

A lack of confidence, however, gradually builds between line and staff, and between headquarters and the field. The many systems and programs introduced begin to exceed their usefulness. A *red-tape crisis* is in full swing. Line managers, for example, increasingly resent direction from those who are not familiar with local conditions. And staff people, for their part, complain about uncooperative and uninformed line managers. Together, both groups criticize the bureaucratic system that has evolved. Procedures take precedence over problem solving, and innovation dims. In short, the organization has become too large and complex to be managed through formal programs and rigid systems. The Phase 4 revolution is under way.

Phase 5: Collaboration

The last observable phase emphasizes strong interpersonal collaboration in an attempt to overcome the red-tape crisis. Where Phase 4 was managed through formal systems and procedures, Phase 5 emphasizes spontaneity in management action through teams and the skillful confrontation of interpersonal differences. Social control and self-discipline replace formal control. This transition is especially difficult for the experts who created the coordination systems as well as for the line managers who relied on formal methods for answers.

The Phase 5 evolution, then, builds around a more flexible and behavioral approach to management. Here are its characteristics:

- The focus is on solving problems quickly through team action.
- Teams are combined across functions to handle specific tasks.
- Staff experts at headquarters are reduced in number, reassigned, and combined into interdisciplinary teams that consult with, not direct, field units.
- A matrix-type structure is frequently used to assemble the right teams for the appropriate problems.
- Formal control systems are simplified and combined into single multipurpose systems.
- Conferences of key managers are held frequently to focus on major problems.
- Educational programs are used to train managers in behavioral skills for achieving better teamwork and conflict resolution.
- Real-time information systems are integrated into daily decision-making processes.
- Economic rewards are geared more to team performance than to individual achievement.
- Experimenting with new practices is encouraged throughout the organization.

What will be the revolution in response to this stage of evolution? Many large U.S. companies are now in the Phase 5 evolutionary stage, so the answer is critical. Although there is little clear evidence regarding the outcome, I imagine that the revolution arising from the "?" crisis will center around the psychological saturation of employees who grow emotionally and physically exhausted from the intensity of teamwork and the heavy pressure for innovative solutions.

My hunch is that the Phase 5 revolution will be solved through new structures and programs that allow employees to periodically rest, reflect, and revitalize themselves. We may even see companies with dual organizational structures: a habit structure for getting the daily work done and a reflective structure for stimulating new perspective and personal enrichment. Employees could move back and forth between the two structures as their energies dissipate and are refueled.

One European organization has implemented just such a structure. Five reflective groups have been established outside the company's usual structure for the purpose of continuously evaluating five task activities basic to the organization. The groups report directly to the managing director, although their findings are made public throughout the organization. Membership in each group includes all levels and functions in the company, and employees are rotated through the groups every six months.

Other concrete examples now in practice include providing sabbaticals for employees, moving managers in and out of hot-spot jobs, establishing a four-day workweek, ensuring job security, building physical facilities for relaxation during the workday, making jobs more interchangeable, creating an extra team on the assembly line so that one team is always off for reeducation, and switching to longer vacations and more flexible work hours.

The Chinese practice of requiring executives to spend time periodically on lower-level jobs may also be worth a nonideological evaluation. For too long, U.S. management has assumed that career progress should be equated with an upward path toward title, salary, and power. Could it be that some vice presidents of marketing might just long for, and even benefit from, temporary duty in field sales?

IMPLICATIONS OF HISTORY

Let me now summarize some important implications for practicing managers. The main features of this discussion are depicted in the table "Organizational Practices in the Five Phases of Growth," which shows the specific management actions that characterize each growth phase. These actions are also the solutions that ended each preceding revolutionary period.

In one sense, I hope that many readers will react to my model by seeing it as obvious and natural for depicting the growth of an organization. To me, this type of reaction is a useful test of the model's validity.

But at a more reflective level, I imagine some of these reactions come more from hindsight than from foresight. Experienced managers who have been through a developmental sequence can identify that sequence now, but how did they react when in the midst of a stage of evolution or revolution? They can probably recall the limits of their own developmental understanding at that time. Perhaps they resisted desirable changes or were even swept emotionally into a revolution without being able to propose constructive solutions. So let me offer some explicit guidelines for managers of growing organizations to keep in mind.

Organizational Practices in the Five Phases of Growth

Category	*Phase 1*	*Phase 2*	*Phase 3*	*Phase 4*	*Phase 5*
Management Focus	Make and sell	Efficiency of operations	Expansion of market	Consolidation of organization	Problem solving and innovation
Organizational Structure	Informal	Centralized and functional	Decentralized and geographical	Line staff and product groups	Matrix of teams
Top-Management Style	Individualistic and entrepreneurial	Directive	Delegative	Watchdog	Participative
Control System	Market results	Standards and cost centers	Reports and profit centers	Plans and investment centers	Mutual goal setting
Management Reward Emphasis	Ownership	Salary and merit increases	Individual bonus	Profit sharing and stock options	Team bonus

Know where you are in the developmental sequence Every organization and its component parts are at different stages of development. The task of top management is to be aware of the stages; otherwise, it may not recognize when the time for change has come, or it may act to impose the wrong solution.

Leaders at the top should be ready to work with the flow of the tide rather than against it; yet they should be cautious because it is tempting to skip phases out of impatience. Each phase produces certain strengths and learning experiences in the organization that will be essential for success in subsequent phases. A child prodigy, for example, may be able to read like a teenager, but he cannot behave like one until he matures through a sequence of experiences.

I also doubt that managers can or should act to avoid revolutions. Rather, these periods of tension provide the pressure, ideas, and awareness that afford a platform for change and the introduction of new practices.

Recognize the limited range of solutions In each revolutionary stage, it becomes evident that the stage can come to a close only by means of certain specific solutions; moreover, these solutions are different from those that were applied to the problems of the preceding revolution. Too often, it is tempting to choose solutions that were tried before but that actually make it impossible for the new phase of growth to evolve.

Management must be prepared to dismantle current structures before the revolutionary stage becomes too turbulent. Top-level managers, realizing that their own managerial styles are no longer appropriate, may even have to take themselves out of leadership positions. A good Phase 2 manager facing Phase 3 might be wise to find a position at another Phase 2 organization that better fits his or her talents, either outside the company or with one of its newer subsidiaries.

Finally, evolution is not an automatic affair; it is a contest for survival. To move ahead, companies must consciously introduce planned structures that not only solve a current crisis but also fit the next phase of growth. That requires considerable self-awareness on the part of top management as well as great interpersonal skills in persuading other managers that change is needed.

Realize that solutions breed new problems Managers often fail to recognize that organizational solutions create problems for the future, such as when a decision to delegate eventually causes a problem of control. Actions in the past determine much of what will happen to a company in the future.

An awareness of this effect should help managers evaluate company problems with a historical understanding instead of pinning the blame on a current development. Better yet, it should place managers in a position to predict problems and thereby to prepare solutions and coping strategies before a revolution gets out of hand.

Top management that is aware of the problems ahead could well decide not to expand the organization. Managers may, for instance, prefer to retain the informal practices of a small company, knowing that this way of life is inherent in the organization's limited size, not in their congenial personalities. If they choose to grow, they may actually grow themselves out of a job and a way of life they enjoy.

And what about very large organizations? Can they find new solutions for continued evolution? Or are they reaching a stage when the government will act to break them up because they are too large?

Clearly, there is still much to learn about processes of development in organizations. The phases outlined here are merely five in number and are still only approximations. Researchers are just beginning to study the specific developmental problems of structure, control, rewards, and management style in different industries and in a variety of cultures.

One should not, however, wait for conclusive evidence before educating managers to think and act from a developmental perspective. The critical dimension of time has been missing for too long from our management theories and practices. The intriguing paradox is that by learning more about history, we may do a better job in the future.

REVOLUTION IS STILL INEVITABLE

I wrote the first draft of this article while I was felled by a bad leg during a ski vacation in Switzerland. At the time, the business world was buzzing with numerous faddish techniques. Perhaps it was the size and height of the mountains that made me feel that there were deeper and more powerful forces at work in organizations.

Four basic points still seem valid about the model. First, we continue to observe major phases of development in the life of growing companies, lasting anywhere from 3 to 15 years each. Although scholars debate the precise length and nature of these phases, everyone agrees that each phase contains its own unique structure, systems, and leadership. The growth rate of the industry seems to determine the phases length.

Second, transitions between developmental phases still do not occur naturally or smoothly, regardless of the strength of top management. All organizations appear to experience revolutionary difficulty and upheaval, and many of these organizations falter, plateau, fail, or get acquired rather than grow further. IBM before Lou Gerstner and General Electric before Jack Welch both suffered badly at the end of the fourth phase of coordination, when sophisticated management systems evolved into rigid bureaucracies.

Third, the logic of paradox underlying the model continues to ring true, although it often haunts and confuses the managerial psyche. Managers have difficulty in understanding that an organizational solution introduced by them personally in one phase eventually sows the seeds of revolution.

Fourth, the greatest resistance to change appears at the top because revolution often means that units under each senior executive will be eliminated or transformed. That is why we so often see new chief executives recruited from the outside and why senior managers frequently leave companies. Executives depart not because they are "bad" managers but because they just don't fit with where the company needs to go.

As for the differences that I have observed since the article's original publication, there is obviously much more "death" in the life of organizations today. Few organizations make it through all the phases of growth. If they don't fail, as most do in the initial phase of creativity and entrepreneurship, they often get acquired by companies that are in a later phase.

The phases are not as cleanly marked off as I depicted them. The vestiges of one phase remain as new approaches are introduced. Such overlaps are most notable in the case of the first phase entrepreneur hanging on when professional management is added in the second phase of direction.

There are also miniphases within each evolutionary stage. The delegation phase, for example, does not typically begin with the complete decentralization of the entire organization into multiple product units, as the article implies. Usually one product group is launched, and then others are added over time. Also, as delegation—or *decentralization*, as I now prefer to call this phase—advances, senior managers at the corporate office are not as hands-off as I depicted them. The addition of multiple product or geographic units over time requires a sophisticated level of involvement by senior management to review strategies, evaluate results, and communicate the organization's values—but not to micro-manage the units under them.

I would change some of the things I said about the fifth phase of collaboration. My original description of this phase suggests that the entire organization is turned into a matrix of teams. I now see the matrix as confined largely to senior management, where the heads of geographic areas, product lines, and functional disciplines collaborate as a team in order to ensure that their decisions are coordinated and implemented across global markets. The most significant change in this phase occurs when the previously bureaucratic Phase 4 control-oriented staff and systems are replaced by a

(*Continued*)

(*Continued*)

smaller number of consulting staff experts who help facilitate, rather than control, decisions.

My speculation that "psychological saturation" is the crisis ending Phase 5 now seems wrong. Instead, I think the crisis is one of realizing that there is no internal solution, such as new products, for stimulating further growth. Rather, the organization begins to look outside for partners or for opportunities to sell itself to a bigger company.

A sixth phase may be evolving in which growth depends on the design of extra-organizational solutions, such as creating a holding company or a network organization composed of alliances and cross-ownership. GE may have developed a similar model in which a periphery of companies is built around a core "money" company or bank (GE Capital) that attracts capital, earns high returns, and feeds the growth of other units.

I doubt that the advancement of information technology has made much of a difference in the basic aspects of the model. Information technology appears useful as a tool that evolves in different forms to fit each phase. For example, the Phase 2 functional organizational structure requires data that reflect revenue and cost centers, whereas Phase 3 decentralization needs data that measure profit center performance.

I wrote the article mainly about industrial and consumer goods companies, not about knowledge organizations or service businesses, which had yet to come into prominence. After recently studying a number of consulting, law, and investment firms, our research team found that those organizations also experience evolution and revolution as they grow.

In the first, entrepreneurial phase, the professional service firm pursues and tests a variety of market paths. The phase ends with the partners arguing about whether or not to stay together to concentrate on one partner's vision for the future. In the second phase, the firm focuses on one major service and eventually finds itself with a debate among the partners about whether to continue focusing on the current practice or to open another office or add additional services. A third phase of geographic or service expansion typically ends with a struggle over ownership: How much equity are the original partners willing to share with the younger partners who led the expansion and brought in new clients? The fourth phase involves institutionalizing the firm's name, reputation, and its standard way of operating, and ends in a crisis of cultural conformity in the face of which the firm must restore innovation and flexibility.

Finally, as a strong caveat, I always remind myself and others that the "ev and rev" model depicted in this article provides only a simple outline of the broad challenges facing a management concerned with growth. It is not a cookie-cutter solution or panacea. The rate of growth, the effective resolution of revolutions, and the performance of the company within phases still depend on the fundamentals of good management: skillful leadership, a winning strategy, the heightened motivation of employees, and a deep concern for customers.

CHAPTER 17
DECISION MAKING

LEADERSHIP AND THE DECISION-MAKING PROCESS

Victor H. Vroom

HOW PEOPLE REALLY MAKE DECISIONS

Gary Klein

TOUGH CALLS IN A SPEED-DRIVEN WORLD

J. Keith Murnighan
John Mowen

Decision making is more than coming up with a good judgment; managing the process of making the decision is equally important. Most supervisors and managers can point to at least one decision-making debacle in their early career caused by failing to include key players or seek out all the relevant information from the right sources. Managers and leaders also seem to struggle with the question of who should make decisions.

Victor Vroom, management professor and consultant, has devoted many years to answering this question. He and his colleagues developed a contingency theory called the leadership-participation model, which is summarized in the first article, "Leadership and the Decision-Making Process." This updated model assumes that different decision situations require different types of leadership. As with so many contingency theories, the profile of an effective leader or manager is one who is capable of analyzing the context and choosing from various styles the one that is most appropriate.

The rational decision-making process has always been popular among businesspeople, especially in the United States where rationality is highly valued. Intuitive decision making has traditionally received less respect and attention. There is a growing trend, however, toward acknowledging the contributions of intuitive decision making and acknowledging that rational decision making and intuitive decision making are complementary. In our opinion, the most important contribution to understanding intuitive decision making in recent years is Gary Klein's book,

Sources of Power: How People Make Decisions. Klein, chief scientist at Klein Associates, and his colleagues studied and observed decision makers in action in order to discover "How People Really Make Decisions." This excerpt explains the recognition-primed decision model, which takes most of the mystery out of intuitive decision making and frames it as a form of expert thinking.

In "Tough Calls in a Speed-Driven World," business professors Keith Murnighan and John Mowen provide a framework to help managers make difficult choices that are timely, confident, and accurate. Their seven-step model is based on extensive research on the differences between excellent and flawed decisions. They explain how and when to use the model effectively and walk us through a case study of a difficult business decision.

LEADERSHIP AND THE DECISION-MAKING PROCESS*

Victor H. Vroom

THE JIM BURNS DECISION

Jim Burns is an emergency response manager in a large company, specializing in ecological control systems. His work runs the gamut from removal and disposal of toxic waste to cleaning up spills of oil and other contaminants. Typically, his firm works on contracts with organizations both public and private, but occasionally Jim is called upon to deal with situations not covered by existing contracts.

This morning Jim received a phone call from the police in a nearby town. They asked for his firm's assistance in dealing with an oil spill that threatened a nearby river. Jim drove to the site with four of his associates, and within an hour the team of five had obtained the following picture of what happened.

While filling an oil tanker, the driver had gone into the cab and had fallen asleep. Before it was noticed, 10,000 gallons of crude oil had escaped and begun making its way five miles downstream and was within four hours of reaching a wildlife sanctuary.

Although the potential for environmental damage is clear, the liability is not. The driver was an employee of a small subcontractor who was uninsured and who would be forced into bankruptcy, if deemed liable. The oil company contacted its insurance company, which denied any responsibility for claims that might be made against it. Representatives of the State Environmental Protection Agency and Department of Fish and Game were contacted, and they offered their moral support, but neither had the half million dollars Jim estimated would be necessary to contain and clean up the spill.

A decision must be made soon about whether to risk the company's money in a matter in which reimbursement, if any, may have to be decided by the courts. The decision is Jim's to make, and he is experienced in making the difficult judgments that are called for. Although conscientious, the members of his team lack this experience

*Reprinted with permission of Elsevier from *Organizational Dynamics*, 28 (4) (2000): 82–94.

and are likely to look to him for direction. Nonetheless, they will have to carry out any action, and Jim has found that their involvement in decisions helps them to work together as a team.

Jim Burns' challenge raises two general issues relevant to solving problems and making decisions in organizations. The first issue involves determining what solution or decision should be adopted. In this case should Jim begin the cleanup or defer any action pending resolution of the liability issues? It is this facet of decision making that is the focus of most business school curricula and of the optimization models developed by management scientists. (To be sure, the nature of this particular problem complicates matters further by the introduction of a potential conflict between organizational goals and broader social concerns.)

The second issue revolves around not *what* should be decided but *how* and with *whom* it should be decided. Should Jim decide himself, or should he involve the team in some way in determining what decision would be made? In this second issue, theories of decision making intersect with theories of leadership style.

LEADERSHIP STYLE

It is the latter perspective that has interested my colleagues and me and has become the focus of a large-scale program of research at Yale. We are interested in what happens between a leader and the leader's associates in decision-making situations. Our interest was inspired by an article by Bob Tannenbaum and Warren Schmidt. Their work distinguished seven different styles, varying in influence by the manager and the size of the area of freedom afforded subordinates.

Being a believer in parsimony, I have collapsed some of their alternatives, resulting in five styles that are labeled Decide, Consult Individually, Consult Group, Facilitate and Delegate. Definitions of each of these styles were given to forty specialists in the field of organization development. The specialists were then asked to locate the styles on a 10-point scale, corresponding to the relative opportunities for influencing the decision that they were likely to provide to group or team members. The definitions of these five processes, adapted from Tannenbaum and Schmidt, and the mean-scale values assigned by the OD professionals, are shown in Exhibit 1.

This language for describing leadership styles can be used in two distinctly different ways. It can be the starting point for the development of a *normative* model that would help managers or leaders to select the style that best fits a given situation. Like our predecessors, we are convinced that each of the styles is appropriate to certain kinds of situations, and that an effective leader is one who explicitly tailors his or her style to demands of the immediate problem at hand.

The taxonomy of leadership styles in Exhibit 1 can also be used to describe what people do. A common vocabulary, independent of its normative uses, may be helpful in communication and setting of expectations between leaders and their colleagues. Furthermore, these concepts can be used by social scientists in developing a descriptive model aimed at understanding how managers actually decide whether and when to share their decision-making power.

Over the last two decades, my colleagues and I at Yale have conducted a program of research designed to provide us with a normative model that can be used by

EXHIBIT 1 Vroom's Adaption of Tannenbaum and Schmidt's Taxonomy

Influence by Leader

Area of Freedom for Group

0	3	5	7	10
Decide	**Consult Individually**	**Consult Group**	**Facilitate**	**Delegate**
You make the decision alone and either announce or "sell" it to the group. You may use your expertise in collecting information that you deem relevant to the problem from the group or others.	You present the problem to the group members individually, get their suggestions, and then make the decision.	You present the problem to the group members in a meeting, get their suggestions, and then make the decision.	You present the problem to the group in a meeting. You act as facilitator, defining the problem to be solved and the boundaries within which the decision must be made. Your objective is to get concurrence on a decision. Above all, you take care to ensure that your ideas are not given any greater weight than those of others simply because of your position.	You permit the group to make the decision within prescribed limits. The group undertakes the identification and diagnosis of the problem, developing alternative procedures for solving it, and deciding on one or more alternative solutions. While you play no direct role in the group's deliberations unless explicitly asked, your role is an important one behind the scenes, providing needed resources and encouragement.

managers in evaluating specific decisions that they face and in selecting the most effective leadership style for each. The result has been the development of an "expert system" that shows substantial promise in helping managers through the myriad of factors that need attention in deciding when and how to involve associates in making decisions. In addition, we have made progress in developing a descriptive model of what managers' decision-making practices actually do. Our studies, which now involve over 100,000 managers, have been aimed at understanding the factors that actually influence what managers do. Specifically, we have looked at such factors as organizational level, cultural influences, and the role of gender in leadership style. This article outlines the normative model first and then examines our progress in understanding its similarities to, and differences from, what managers actually do.

TOWARD A NORMATIVE MODEL

DECISION QUALITY

Let us first examine what is at stake in the choice of how much and in what way to involve others in solving problems and making decisions. The first, and undoubtedly the most important, is the quality of the decision. Above all we want wise, well reasoned, and analytically sound decisions that are consistent with the goals to be achieved and with potentially available information about the consequences of alternative means of achieving them.

What happens to decision quality as one moves from the autocratic process to more participative processes? Undoubtedly the nature of the decision and its quality will change as we move across the scale. But will decision quality increase or decrease? A conservative answer, and one that we believe to be consistent with the available research evidence, is that the effects of participation on decision quality depend on certain observable features of the decision-making situation. It depends on where the relevant knowledge or expertise resides, that is, in the leader, in the group, or both. It depends on the goals of the potential participants, particularly on the extent to which group or team members support the organizational objectives embedded in the problem. Finally, the amount of synergy exhibited in team-based processes depends on the skills and abilities of team members in working together effectively in solving problems.

DECISION IMPLEMENTATION

Although the quality of the decision may be the most important component of its effectiveness, it is not the only component. Many high-quality decisions have been ineffective because they were not effectively implemented. The effectiveness with which a group or team implements a decision can be shown to depend on the extent to which they are committed to its success. Here the evidence is clearer and less equivocal. People do support what they help to build. Under a wide range of conditions, increasing participation leads to greater "buy-in," commitment to decisions, and motivation to implement them effectively. To be sure, there are some situations in which the motivational benefits of greater commitment are nonexistent or irrelevant to implementation. Sometimes the team may not be playing a role in implementation; in other situations, the team may view the leader as the expert or as a person with the legitimate right to make the decision and, as a result, may fully support whatever decision the leader might make.

COSTS OF DECISION MAKING

Apart from considerations of decision quality and implementation, which determine the effectiveness of the decision, there are considerations of efficiency relevant to the decision process. Use of any decision-making process consumes resources. At the same time it can add to resources, albeit of a different kind. The resources consumed are costs and principally involve the time "used up" in the decision-making process. Increasing the amount of participation will increase the elapsed time to make the decision and, to an even greater degree, increase the number of hours consumed by the process. Both of these meanings of time constitute liabilities of participative leadership styles. Seeking consensus slows down the process and consumes substantially more hours than the directive or even consultative methods of decision making. The first of these costs, increasing the time interval between the occurrence of a problem and obtaining a solution, is most relevant in emergencies where a quick or immediate response is necessary. The second consideration, the hours consumed, is more generally relevant.

DEVELOPMENT

Potentially offsetting these costs are developmental benefits of increased participation. Moving from the autocratic to highly participative styles increases the potential value of the group or team to the organization in three ways: (1) It develops the knowledge and competence of individual members by providing them with opportunities to work through problems and decisions typically occurring at higher organizational levels. (2) It increases teamwork and collaboration by providing opportunities to solve problems as part of a team. (3) It increases identification with organizational goals by giving people "a voice" in making significant decisions in *their* organizations. These developmental benefits may be negligible when the decision lacks significance, that is, when the issue being decided is trivial and lacks consequences to the organization. Furthermore, the development benefits may be of negligible value if the group or team members have a nonexistent or tenuous future within the broader organization.

We term a style inefficient when it wastes time without a commensurate return in development. Conversely, it is efficient when it is used judiciously in precisely those situations in which sufficient developmental benefits are realized. It is interesting to note that costs (time) and development, the two components of efficiency, are realized at different points in time. The time costs are immediately realizable. The slowness of response and the number of hours consumed in a group meeting have immediate effects. In contrast, the growth and development of individuals and teams may not pay off for a substantial period of time.

PUTTING IT ALL TOGETHER

So far our inquiry has led us to identify four outcomes of participation, each of which is contingent on one or more situational factors. To be useful to leaders, we must supplement our analysis with a suitable tool for synthesizing the effects that we have postulated. Exhibits 2 and 3 depict decision matrices that constitute such a tool. In Exhibit 2 we show the Time-Driven Model. It is short-term in its orientation, being concerned with making effective decisions with minimum cost. No value is placed on employee development.

In contrast, Exhibit 3 shows the Development-Driven Model. It may be thought of as a long-term model, because it is concerned with making effective decisions with maximum developmental consequences. No value is placed on time.

To use one of these two models, you must have a decision problem in mind that has two properties. First, it must fall within your area of freedom or discretion, that is, it must be up to you to decide. Second, there must be some identifiable group of others who are potential participants in the decision.

EXHIBIT 2 Time-Driven Model

TIME-DRIVEN MODEL

Instruction: The matrix operates like a funnel. You start at the left with a specific decision problem in mind. The column headings denote situational factors which may or may not be present in that problem. You progress by selecting High or Low (H or L) for each relevant situational factor. Proceed down from the funnel, judging only those situational factors for which a judgement is called for, until you reach the recommended process.

	Decision Significance	Importance of Commitment	Leader Expertise	Likelihood of Commitment	Group Support	Group Expertise	Team Competence	
PROBLEM STATEMENT	H	H	H	H	-	-	-	Decide
				L	H	H	H	Delegate
							L	Consult (Group)
						L	-	
					L	-	-	
			L	H	H	H	H	Facilitate
							L	Consult (Individually)
						L	-	
					L	-	-	
				L	H	H	H	Facilitate
							L	Consult (Group)
						L	-	
					L	-	-	
		L	H	-	-	-	-	Decide
			L	-	H	H	H	Facilitate
							L	Consult (Individually)
						L	-	
					L	-	-	
	L	H	-	H	-	-	-	Decide
				L	-	-	H	Delegate
							L	Facilitate
		L	-	-	-	-	-	Decide

(Reprinted from A Model of Leadership Style by Victor Vroom) 1999.

EXHIBIT 3 Development-Driven Model

DEVELOPMENT-DRIVEN MODEL

PROBLEM STATEMENT	Decision Significance	Importance of Commitment	Leader Expertise	Likelihood of Commitment	Group Support	Group Expertise	Team Competence	
	H	H	-	H	H	H	H	Delegate
							L	Facilitate
						L	-	Consult (Group)
					L	-	-	
				L	H	H	H	Delegate
							L	Facilitate
						L	-	
					L	-	-	Consult (Group)
		L	-	-	H	H	H	Delegate
							L	Facilitate
						L	-	Consult (Group)
					L	-	-	
	L	H	-	H	-	-	-	Decide
				L	-	-	-	Delegate
		L	-	-	-	-	-	Decide

(Reprinted from A Model of Leadership Style by Victor Vroom) 1999.

One enters the matrix at the left-hand side, at "Problem Statement." Arranged along the top of the matrix are seven situational factors, each of which may be present (H for high) or absent (L for low) in that problem. To obtain the recommended process, you first ascertain whether the decision to be made is a significant one. If so, you select H and answer the second question, concerning the importance of gaining commitment from the group. Continuing this procedure (avoiding the crossing of any horizontal line) will bring you to a recommended process. Sometimes a conclusive

EXHIBIT 4 Situational Factors in the Normative Model

DECISION SIGNIFICANCE:	The significance of the decision to the success of the project or organization.
IMPORTANCE OF COMMITMENT:	The importance of team members' commitment to the decision.
LEADER'S EXPERTISE:	Your knowledge or expertise in relation to this problem.
LIKELIHOOD OF COMMITMENT:	The likelihood that the team would commit itself to a decision that you might make on your own.
GROUP SUPPORT FOR OBJECTIVES:	The degree to which the team supports the organization's objectives at stake in this problem.
GROUP EXPERTISE:	Team members' knowledge or expertise in relation to this problem.
TEAM COMPETENCE:	The ability of team members to work together in solving problems.

determination can be made based on as few as two factors (e.g., L,L); others require three (e.g., L,H,H), four (e.g., H,H,H,H,), or as many as seven factors (e.g., H,H,L,L,H,H,H).

Submitting the same problem to both the Time-Driven and Development-Driven Model can be instructive. Sometimes the two models yield identical recommendations. Where they differ, the Development-Driven Model recommends a higher level of participation. Occasionally, the difference may be greater than one position on the participation scale. For example, in the Jim Burns case with which this article began, the Time-Driven Model recommends Decide (H,H,H,H) and the Development-Driven Model recommends Consultation with the Group (H,H,H,H,L).

Although the situational factors that identify the columns in Exhibits 2 and 3 are sufficient for the experienced user of these matrices, a less experienced user may wish to refer to explanations of the situational factors in Exhibit 4. To practice using the models, read each of the four cases in Exhibit 5. Underneath each case, we have shown the recommended actions made by the two models, along with the path by which these recommendations are obtained.

WHERE DID THE MODEL COME FROM?

The model is an outgrowth of 25 years of research on leadership and decision-making processes. We began by collecting cases from managers of successful and unsuccessful decisions and ascertaining which decision process they used on each. If the decisions were unsuccessful, we wanted to find out why, whether it could have been avoided, and if so, how. Our goal was to build a model that would maximize the frequency of successful decisions, while avoiding as many of the unsuccessful ones as possible. Early on, we were joined by social scientists operating in various parts of the world, which helped us to test our concepts. We were somewhat encouraged by the findings

EXHIBIT 5 Applying the Matrices to the Sample Cases

Setting: Banking;
Your Position: President & Chief Executive Officer

The bank examiners have just left, insisting that many of your commercial real estate loans be written off, thereby depleting already low capital. Along with many other banks in your region, your bank is in serious danger of being closed by the regulators. As the financial problems surfaced, many of the top executives left to pursue other interests, but fortunately, you were able to replace them with three highly competent younger managers. While they had no prior acquaintance with one another, each is a product of fine training program with one of the money center banks in which they rotated through position in each of the banking functions.

Your extensive experience is the industry leads you to the inevitable conclusion that the only hope is a two-pronged approach involving reduction of all but the most critical expenses and the sale of assets to other banks. The task must be accomplished quickly since further deterioration of the quality of the loan portfolio could result in a negative capital position forcing regulators to close the bank.

The strategy is clear to you, but you have many details that will need to be worked out. You believe that you know what information will be needed in order to get the bank on a course for future prosperity. You are fortunate in having three young executives to help you out. While they have had little or no experience in working together you know that each is dedicated to the survival of the bank. Like you, they know what needs to be done and how to do it.

ANALYSIS
TIME DRIVEN:
H H H L H H L-CONSULT GROUP
DEVELOPMENT DRIVEN:
H H L H H L-FACILITATE

Setting: Repertory Theater;
Your Position: Executive Director

You are the executive director of a repertory theater affiliated with a majority university. You are responsible for both financial and artistic direction of the theater. While you recognize that both of these responsibilities are important, you have focused your efforts where your own talents lie—on insuring the highest level of artistic quality to the theater's productions. Reporting to you is a group of four department heads responsible for production, marketing, development, and administration, along with an assistant dean who is responsible for the actors who are also students in the university. They are a talented set of individuals, and each is deeply committed to the theater and experienced in working together as a team.

Last week you received a comprehensive report from an independent consulting firm commissioned to examine the financial health of the theater. You were shocked by the major conclusion of the report. *"The expenses of operating the theater have been growing much more rapidly than income, and by year's end the theater will be operating in the red. Unless expenses can be reduced, the surplus will be consumed, and within five years the theater might have to be closed."*

You have distributed the report to your staff and are surprised at the variety of reactions that it has produced. Some dispute the report's conclusions criticizing its assumptions or methods. Others are more shaken, but even they seem divided about what steps ought to be taken and when. None of them or, in fact, anyone connected with the theater would want it to close. It has a long and important tradition both in the university and in its surrounding community.

ANALYSIS
TIME DRIVEN:
H H L L H H H-FACILITATE
DEVELOPMENT DRIVEN:
H H L H H H-DELEGATE

Setting: Auto Parts Manufacturer;
Your Position: Country Manager

Your firm has just acquired a small manufacturer of spare auto parts in Southeast Asia. The recent collapse in the economies in this region made values very attractive. Your senior management decided to acquire a foothold in this region. It was less interested in the particular acquired firm, which produces parts for the local market, than it was in using it as a base from which to produce parts at reduced cost for the worldwide market.

When you arrived at your new assignment two weeks ago, you were somewhat surprised by the less than enthusiastic reception that you received from the current management. You attribute the obvious strain in working relations not only to linguistic and cultural differences but also to a deep-seated resentment to their new foreign owners. Your top management team seem to get along very well with one another, but the atmosphere changes when you step into the room.

Nonetheless, you will need their help in navigating your way through this unfamiliar environment. Your immediate need is to develop a plan for land acquisition on which to construct new manufacturing and warehouse facilities. You and your administrative assistant, who accompanied you from your previous assignment, should be able to carry out the plan, but its development would be hazardous without local knowledge.

ANALYSIS
TIME DRIVEN:
H L L L –CONSULT INDIVIDUALLY
DEVELOPMENT DRIVEN:
H L L – CONSULT GROUP

Setting: Manufacturer of Internal Combustion Engines;
Your Position: Project Manager

Your firm has received a contract from one of the world's largest automobile manufacturers to produce an engine to power their "flagship" sports car. The engine is of Japanese design and is very complex not only by American but by world standards. As project manager, you have been involved in this venture from the outset, and you and your team of engineers have taken pride at the rave reviews the engine has received in the automotive press. Your firm had previously been known as a producer of outboard engines for marine use, and its image is now greatly enhanced as the manufacturer of the power plant of one of the world's fastest sports cars.

Your excitement at being a part of this project was dashed by a report of serious engine problems in cars delivered to customers. Seventeen owners of cars produced in the first month have experienced engine seizures—a circumstance which has caused the manufacturer to suspend sales, to put a halt to current production, and to notify owners of this year's production not to drive the cars! Needless to say, this situation is a disaster and unless solved immediately could expose your firm to extended litigation as well as terminate what had been a mutually beneficial relationship. As the person most informed about the engine, you have spent the last two weeks on the road inspecting several of the seized engines, the plant in which they are installed, and reviewing the practices in your own company's plant in which the engine is manufactured. As a result of this research, you have become convinced that the problem is due to operation of the engine at very high RPM's before it has warmed up to develop sufficient oil pressure. The solution would be to install an electronic control limiting engine RPM's until the engine has reached normal operating temperature.

ANALYSIS
TIME DRIVEN:
H H H H –DECIDE
DEVELOPMENT DRIVEN:
H H H H L– CONSULT GROUP

(based on six separate studies conducted in three different countries): decisions made in accordance with a decision tree on which we were working at the time were almost twice as likely to be successful as were decisions that were inconsistent with the model.

But these investigations also made it clear that we had a long way to go, so we continued our efforts to extend and refine our early work. Now we have developed a complex set of equations that show great promise in forecasting the consequences of participation on quality, implementation, cost, and development. The decision matrices shown in Exhibits 2 and 3 are derived from the use of these equations and are the simplest way in which the implications of the model can be shown *on paper.* However, the full power of the model is better revealed in a computer program that allows much more complexity and precision whereas, at the same time, is easier to use. Contained on a CD-ROM, the program has a number of features not possible in a decision matrix. These include: (1) using eleven situational factors, rather than the seven shown in the matrices, (2) permitting five possible responses, corresponding to the degree to which situational factors are present, (3) incorporating the Value of Time and Value of Development as situational factors, rather than portraying them as separate matrices, and (4) guiding managers through the process of analyzing the situations they face with definitions, examples, and other sources of help.

We have found by observing managers' use of the model on problems they are currently facing on their jobs that the model's recommendations can be affected by the way in which the problem is framed. For example, if the problem is seen as a deficiency within the team, efforts to find a solution are less likely to be affected than if the problem is located in the situation. Accordingly, we have provided a help screen for "testing" a manager's framing of the problem, to make sure that it has been defined in a way that is likely to be productive. In addition, we have found in this rapidly changing world that groups defined by a common manager may not be the most effective for solution of organizational problems. Thus, the software provides a help screen called Team Formation, which provides advice on making up a group to solve a particular problem or make a particular decision.

WHAT DETERMINES MANAGERS' STYLES?

TOWARD A DESCRIPTIVE MODEL

To study managerial styles (as they are, rather than how our models say they should be), we have developed an innovative measuring device that we term a problem set. It consists of a set of 30 cases, each depicting a manager faced with a decision to make. Exhibit 5 gives examples of some of the shorter cases from a typical set. Cases are based on real situations. Each has been condensed to fit on a single page, providing information on the manager's role, the organizational context, the decision that has to be made, the group of persons that the manager is considering involving, and so on.

The set of cases covers the whole gamut of managerial decisions. Titles include "Saving a Savings Bank," "Trimming Expense Accounts," "Relocating the Head Office," and so forth. However, the cases are not randomly selected. Rather, they vary with respect to the critical factors that the model deems highly relevant to choice of leadership style. Each of the factors contained in the decision matrices shown in Exhibits 2 and 3 is varied across the set of cases, and each is varied independently of each other factor. This latter feature, which statisticians refer to as a multifactorial experimental design, is most important, because it permits determining which of the relevant factors influences each individual manager, in what way, and to what degree. Thus, the problem set becomes a powerful diagnostic tool capable of revealing "the manager's model," that is, the way in which each individual manager responds to decision-making situations.

Although we originally developed the problem set as a research tool, we discovered early on that managers enjoyed and benefited from the experience of thinking through how they would deal with highly different situations, and attempting to make sense out of the different choices they made. To aid in the learning that was resulting from this measuring instrument, we have developed a Java-based computer program that could quickly analyze a manager's choices and produce a five-page individualized report comparing him or her with peers and with the models, both time-driven and development-driven. Furthermore, due to the power of the statistical design underlying the problem set, we are able to show each manager how his or her choices were influenced by each of the situational factors used in the decision matrices. Each manager's individualized analysis also shows how well his or her choices are likely to result in decisions that are (1) of high quality, (2) would be effectively implemented, (3) were economical in use of time, and (4) would have favorable developmental consequences on their team.

Here we will focus not on what *managers have learned* from having a mirror held up to them but rather what *we have learned from managers* about how they go about deciding when and where to share their decision-making power. In a world in which it is common to label managers with terms like autocratic or participative or theory X or Theory Y, it was instructive to see that managers make different choices in different situations. In fact, it makes somewhat more sense to talk about autocratic and participative situations than autocratic or participative managers do. The differences in behavior among managers are about one-third of the size of the differences among situations.

Managers behave situationally. They adapt their behavior to the situations they face. Furthermore, the kinds of situations that evoke autocratic and participative styles are very similar to those in which the normative model would recommend such styles. Each of the seven situational factors shown at the top of Exhibits 2 and 3 affects the average manager in roughly the same way as they affect the behavior of the model. Managers make more participative choices on highly significant decisions, when they need the commitment of the group, when they lack the expertise, when the likelihood of commitment to *their* decision is low, when the group's expertise is high and when the group has a history of working together effectively.

But not all managers behave that way! Some are influenced by only one or two of these factors and seem to ignore the rest. Still others are affected by one of these factors, but in what we believe to be the wrong way. For example, one fifth of the U.S. managers that we have studied (and three quarters of all managers from Poland) are more likely to involve others in insignificant, trivial decisions.

One of the most important functions of the feedback is to draw each individual's attention to those aspects of the situation that they are overlooking. We should make it clear that the model not only responds to the seven situational factors, but also does so configurally. Thus, the effects of one factor depend on the level of certain other factors. For example, where the knowledge resides (in the leader or in the group or both or neither) has more effect on leadership style in highly significant decisions than in those of lesser significance.

Of great interest to us is the fact that managers also behave configurally. There is evidence in our data that managers attend to combinations of factors rather than being influenced by each factor separately. However, these effects are less strong among managers than in the model, suggesting that only a small number of managers behave that way or that, in the typical manager, the configural effects are small in relation to those that are linear.

We said earlier that the situational effects dwarfed the differences among individual managers. Although that statement is true, it does not imply that differences among managers in their typical or overall behavior are insignificant or inconsequential. If one averages the choices of a manager on the 30 cases, one obtains a mean score that reflects, on average, where he or she stands on the scale shown in Exhibit 1. We turn now to consider some of the things that we have found to correlate with differences in where people stand on our 10-point scale of participation.

The first factor is *when* people took the test! Our data have been collected over a 25-year period, and throughout most of that period we have observed an increase in the use of the more participative processes on that scale. Something seems to be producing a move toward higher involvement, more participation, greater empowerment, and more frequent use of teams over time. We do not know precisely what is producing this, but we suspect that it reflects changes in (1) the external environment of organizations (greater rates of change, greater complexity), (2) the flattening of the pyramid (greater spans of control resulting in difficulties in hierarchical control), (3) the growth of information technology, making it easier to get information closer to the occurrence of problems, and (4) the changing nature of the labor force (higher education, higher needs for independence, etc.). Of the demographic factors, the culture in which the organization functions accounts for the greatest variance. High involvement managers are more likely to be found in countries with high per capita GNP, with a strong democratic tradition and with a highly educated work force.

We have also investigated gender differences and have found women managers to be significantly more participative than their male counterparts. Supporting this conclusion, we have found sizeable differences in the reactions to autocratic men and autocratic women managers. In general, being participative is valued by direct reports, but this is truer for women than for men. Participative men and women are equally valued, but autocratic males are strongly preferred to autocratic women.

A third demographic factor that correlates with leadership style as measured by our problem sets is level in the organization. In each organization that we have studied in depth, the higher the level in the organizational ladder, the more participative the manager. To be sure, we have never carried our investigation up to the level of the CEO, where we cannot rely on sample size and the law of large numbers to cancel out chance factors due to personality or to measurement.

We should point out that our findings are restricted to what managers say they would do on a standardized set of cases. Although managers have no incentive to lie (because it will only decrease the accuracy of the computer feedback that they alone will receive), we have no guard against self-deception. As a possible check on such tendencies, we have given the same problem sets to both the managers and to his or her direct reports. The latter are asked to describe how their manager would respond to each case. The result is striking. Virtually all managers are seen by their direct reports as closer to the left side of that scale than they see themselves. We have referred to this difference as the autocratic shift. We do not know whether the biases are in managers' conceptions of themselves, the perceptions of them held by their direct reports, or both.

CONCLUSION

Historically, the people dimension of management has been viewed as basically intuitive, clinical, and "touchy-feely." The kinds of analytical approaches that are customary in finance, operations, and to a lesser degree, strategy, have not been applied, or even viewed as applicable to issues of behavior. We have violated that norm and have sought to apply analytical methods to the development of better normative and descriptive tools for understanding leadership style. We will be the first to admit that our model is far from perfect. We ignore deliberately what style managers are "good at," what they are accustomed to practicing, and what they are encouraged to use in their "organizational culture." We do this because we believe that what worked in the past is no guarantee of success in the future. We believe that leadership styles deserve a fresh look.

At Yale and in other environments, when I teach the model presented in this paper and provide people with computer feedback on their own leadership style, I stress that both are intended to stimulate reflection and self-examination. They are not tools to be slavishly embraced and used in all decisions. I believe that much of the behavior that is currently driven by habits needs to be converted back into choices. The changing demands of today demand that we reexamine the styles we used in the past and reassess their appropriateness to today's environment.

Selected Bibliography

The original inspiration for this body of work may be found in an article written in the *Harvard Business Review* by Bob Tannenbaum and Warren Schmidt ("How to Choose a Leadership Pattern," *Harvard Business Review,* 1958: 99–101).

My initial work on leadership was done with Philip Yetton (*Leadership and Decision Making,* University of Pittsburgh Press: 1973). Subsequently I collaborated with Arthur G. Jago in writing *The New Leadership* (Prentice Hall: 1988).

HOW PEOPLE REALLY MAKE DECISIONS*

Gary Klein

During the past 25 years, the field of decision making has concentrated on showing the limitations of decision makers—that is, that they are not very rational or competent. Books have been written documenting human limitations and suggesting remedies: training methods to help us think clearly, decision support systems to monitor and guide us, and expert systems that enable computers to make the decisions and avoid altogether the fallible humans.

This book was written to balance the others and takes a different perspective. Here I document human strengths and capabilities that typically have been downplayed or even ignored.

In 1985, I did my first study of how firefighters make life-and-death decisions under extreme time pressure. That project led to others—with pilots, nurses, military leaders, nuclear power plant operators, chess masters, and experts in a range of other domains. A growing number of researchers have moved out of the laboratory, to work in the area of naturalistic decision making—that is, the study of how people use their experience to make decisions in field settings. We try to understand how people handle all of the typical confusions and pressures of their environments, such as missing information, time constraints, vague goals, and changing conditions. In doing these studies, my research team and I have slept in fire stations, observed intensive care units, and ridden in M-1 tanks, U.S. Navy AEGIS cruisers, Blackhawk helicopters, and AWACS aircraft. We have learned a lot about doing field research.

Instead of trying to show how people do not measure up to ideal strategies for performing tasks, we have been motivated by curiosity about how people do so well under difficult conditions. We all have areas in which we can use our experience to make rapid and effective decisions, from the mundane level of shopping to the high-stakes level of fire-fighting. Shopping in a supermarket does not seem like an impressive skill until you contrast an experienced American shopper to a recent immigrant from Russia. Moving to the other extreme of high-stakes decisions, an example is a fireground commander working under severe time pressure while in charge of a crew at a multiple-alarm fire at a four-story apartment building. Our research concentrated on this high-stakes world. The fireground commanders seemed to be making effective decisions. See "The Torn Artery" description in Example 1.

Example 1 shows decision making at a very high level. Lieutenant M handled many decision points yet spent little time on any one of them. He drew on his experience to know just what to do. Yet merely saying that he used his experience is not an answer. The challenge is to identify how that experience came into play.

We have found that people draw on a large set of abilities that are sources of power. The conventional sources of power include deductive logical thinking, analysis of probabilities, and statistical methods. Yet the sources of power that are needed in natural settings are usually not analytical at all—the power of intuition, mental simulation, metaphor, and storytelling. The power of intuition enables us to size up a situation quickly. The power of mental simulation lets us imagine how a course of action might

*Excerpted with permission from *Sources of Power: How People Make Decisions* (Cambridge, MA: MIT Press, 1998): 1–35.

EXAMPLE 1

THE TORN ARTERY

My research assistant, Chris Brezovic, and I are sitting in a fire station in Cleveland on a Saturday afternoon in the summer of 1985. We slept only a few hours in the station the night before since we had been up late interviewing the commander during that shift. He was going to stay up all night catching up on his work. We were assigned beds on the second floor. I was told to be ready to get down the stairs and onto the truck no more than 25 seconds after an alarm sounded. (No, we did not slide down the pole, although the station still had one. Too many firefighters had broken ankles that way, so they no longer used the pole.) I even slept with my eyeglasses on, not wanting to waste precious seconds fumbling with them. There was only one call, at around 3:00 in the morning. The horn suddenly began blaring, we all jumped out of bed, ran down the flight of stairs, pulled on our coats and boots, and climbed onto the trucks within the time limit. The fire was pretty small—a blaze in a one-car garage.

Chris and I are feeling a little sleepy that next afternoon when the alarm comes in at 3:21 P.M. for the emergency rescue team. Three minutes later, the truck is driving up to a typical house in a residential neighborhood. It is summer, and young women in bikinis who had been tanning themselves on their lawns are running over to their neighbor's yard.

When we pull to a stop, we see a man laying face down in a pool of blood, his wife crouching over him. As the emergency rescue team goes to work, the woman quickly explains that her husband had been standing on a ladder doing some home repair. He slipped, and his arm went through a pane of glass. He reacted foolishly by pulling his arm out and, in doing so, sliced open an artery. The head of the rescue team, Lieutenant M, later told us that the man had lost two units of blood. If he lost four units, he would be dead. Watching his life leak out of his arm, the man is going into shock.

The first decision facing Lieutenant M is to diagnose the problem. As he ran to the man, even before listening to the wife, he made his diagnosis. He can see from the amount of blood that the man has cut open an artery, and from the dishcloths held against the man's arm he can tell which artery. Next comes the decision of how to treat the wound. In fact, there is nothing to deliberate over. As quickly as possible, Lieutenant M applies firm pressure. Next, he might examine whether there are other injuries, maybe neck injuries, which might prevent him from moving the victim. But he doesn't bother with any more examination. He can see the man is minutes from death, so there is no time to worry about anything else.

Lieutenant M has stopped the bleeding and directs his crew to move the man on a stretcher and to the truck. He assigns the strongest of his crew to the hardest stretcher work, even though the crew member has relatively little experience. Lieutenant M decides that the man's strength is important for quick movement and thinks the crew member has enough training that he will not drop the stretcher as it is maneuvered in through the back of the rescue truck.

On the way to the hospital, the crew puts inflatable pants on the victim. These exert pressure on the man's legs to stabilize his blood pressure. Had the crew put the pants on the man before driving, they would have wasted valuable time. When we reach the hospital I look down at my watch: 3:31 P.M. Only 10 minutes has elapsed since the original alarm.

be carried out. The power of metaphor lets us draw on our experience by suggesting parallels between the current situation and something else we have come across. The power of storytelling helps us consolidate our experiences to make them available in the future, either to ourselves or to others. These areas have not been well studied by decision researchers.

This book examines some recent findings that have emerged from the field of naturalistic decision making. It also describes how research can be done outside the laboratory setting by studying realistic tasks and experienced people working under typical conditions. Features that help define a naturalistic decision-making setting are time pressure, high stakes, experienced decision makers, inadequate information (information that is missing, ambiguous, or erroneous), ill-defined goals, poorly defined procedures, cue learning, context (e.g., higher-level goals, stress), dynamic conditions, and team coordination (Orasanu and Connolly 1993).

Soelberg's course on decision making at the MIT Sloan School of Management taught students how to perform the classical decision analysis method we can call the rational choice strategy. The decision maker:

1. Identifies the set of options.
2. Identifies the ways of evaluating these options.
3. Weights each evaluation dimension.
4. Does the rating.
5. Picks the option with the highest score.

For his Ph.D. dissertation, Soelberg studied the decision strategies his students used to perform a natural task: selecting their jobs as they finished their degrees. He assumed that they would rely on the rational choice strategy. He was wrong. His students showed little inclination toward systematic thinking. Instead, they would make a gut choice. By interviewing his students, Soelberg found he could identify their favorite job choice and predict their ultimate choice with 87 percent accuracy—up to three weeks before the students themselves announced their choice.

Soelberg had trained his students to use rational methods, yet when it was time for them to make a rational and important choice, they would not do it. Soelberg was also a good observer, and he tried to capture the students' actual decision strategies.

What did the students do during this time? If asked, they would deny that they had made a decision yet. For them, a decision was just what Soelberg had taught: a deliberated choice between two or more options. To feel that they had made such a decision, they had to go through a systematic process of evaluation. They selected one other candidate as a comparison, and then tried to show that their favorite was as good as or better than the comparison candidate on each evaluation dimension. Once they had shown this to their satisfaction (even if it meant fudging a little or finding ways to beef up their favorite), then they would announce as their decision the gut favorite that Soelberg had identified much earlier. They were not actually making a decision; they were constructing a justification.

We hypothesized that the fireground commanders would behave in the same way. We thought this hypothesis—that instead of considering lots of options they would consider only two—was daring. Actually, it was conservative. The commanders did not consider two. In fact, they did not seem to be comparing any options at all. This was disconcerting, and we discovered it at the first background discussion we had with a fireground commander, even before the real interviews. We asked the commander to tell us about some difficult decisions he had made.

"I don't make decisions," he announced to his startled listeners. "I don't remember when I've ever made a decision."

For researchers starting a study of decision making, this was unhappy news. Even worse, he insisted that fireground commanders never make decisions. We pressed him further. Surely there are decisions during a fire—decisions about whether to call a second alarm, where to send his crews, how to contain the fire.

He agreed that there were options, yet it was usually obvious what to do in any given situation. We soon realized that he was defining the making of a decision in the same way as Soelberg's students—generating a set of options and evaluating them to find the best one. We call this strategy of examining two or more options at the same time, usually by comparing the strengths and weaknesses of each, *comparative evaluation.* He insisted that he never did it. There just was no time. The structure would burn down by the time he finished listing all the options, let alone evaluating them.

We sought to explain two puzzles: how the commanders could reliably identify good options and how they could evaluate an option without comparing it to any others.

Our results turned out to be fairly clear. It was not that the commanders were *refusing* to compare options; rather, they did not have to compare options. I had been so fixated on what they were not doing that I had missed the real finding: that the commanders could come up with a good course of action from the start. That was what the stories were telling us. Even when faced with a complex situation, the commanders could see it as familiar and know how to react.

The commanders' secret was that their experience let them see a situation, even a nonroutine one, as an example of a prototype, so they knew the typical course of action right away. Their experience let them identify a reasonable reaction as the first one they considered, so they did not bother thinking of others. They were not being perverse. They were being skillful. We now call this strategy *recognition-primed decision making.*

EXAMPLE 2

THE OVERPASS RESCUE

A lieutenant is called out to rescue a woman who either fell or jumped off a highway overpass. She is drunk or on drugs and is probably trying to kill herself. Instead of falling to her death, she lands on the metal supports of a highway sign and is dangling there when the rescue team arrives.

The lieutenant recognizes the danger of the situation. The woman is semiconscious and lying bent over one of the metal struts. At any moment, she could fall to her death on the pavement below. If he orders any of his team out to help her, they will be endangered because there is no way to get a good brace against the struts, so he issues an order not to climb out to secure her.

Two of his crew ignore his order and climb out anyway. One holds onto her shoulders and the other to her legs.

A hook-and-ladder truck arrives. The lieutenant doesn't need their help in making the rescue, so tells them to drive down to the highway below and block traffic in case the woman does fall. He does not want to chance that the young woman will fall on a moving car.

Now the question is how to pull the woman to safety.

First, the lieutenant considers using a rescue harness, the standard way of raising victims. It snaps onto a person's shoulders and thighs. In imagining its use, he realizes that it requires the person to be in a sitting position or face up.

(*Continued*)

(Continued)

He thinks about how they would shift her to sit up and realizes that she might slide off the support.

Second, he considers attaching the rescue harness from the back. However, he imagines that by lifting the woman, they would create a large pressure on her back, almost bending her double. He does not want to risk hurting her.

Third, the lieutenant considers using a rescue strap—another way to secure victims, but making use of a strap rather than a snap-on harness. However, it creates the same problems as the rescue harness, requiring that she be sitting up or that it be attached from behind. He rejects this too.

Now he comes up with a novel idea: using a ladder belt—a strong belt that firefighters buckle on over their coats when they climb up ladders to rescue people. When they get to the top, they can snap an attachment on the belt to the top rung of the ladder. If they lose their footing during the rescue, they are still attached to the ladder so they won't plunge to their death.

The lieutenant's idea is to get a ladder belt, slide it under the woman, buckle it from behind (it needs only one buckle), tie a rope to the snap, and lift her up to the overpass. He thinks it through again and likes the idea, so he orders one of his crew to fetch the ladder belt and rope, and they tie it onto her.

In the meantime, the hook-and-ladder truck has moved to the highway below the overpass, and the truck's crew members raise the ladder. The firefighter on the platform at the top of the ladder is directly under the woman shouting, "I've got her. I've got her." The lieutenant ignores him and orders his men to lift her up.

At this time, he makes an unwanted discovery: ladder belts are built for sturdy firefighters, to be worn over their coats. This is a slender woman wearing a thin sweater. In addition, she is essentially unconscious. When they lift her up, they realize the problem. As the lieutenant put it, "She slithered through the belt like a slippery strand of spaghetti."

Fortunately, the hook-and-ladder man is right below her. He catches her and makes the rescue. There is a happy ending.

Now the lieutenant and his crew go back to their station to figure our what had gone wrong. They try the rescue harness and find that the lieutenant's instincts were right: neither is usable.

Eventually they discover how they should have made the rescue. They should have used the rope they had tied to the ladder belt. They could have tied it to the woman and lifted her up. With all the technology available to them, they had forgotten that you can use a rope to pull someone up.

This rescue helped us see several important aspects of decision making. First, the lieutenant's deliberations about options took him only about a minute. That may seem too short, but if you imagine going through it in your mind, a minute is about right.

Second, the decision maker looked at several options yet never compared any two of them. He thought of the options one at a time, evaluated each in turn, rejected it, and turned to the next most typical rescue technique. We can call this strategy a *singular evaluation approach*, to distinguish it from comparative evaluation. Singular evaluation means evaluating each option on its own merits, even if we cycle through several possibilities.

Distinguishing between comparative and singular evaluation strategies is not difficult. When you order from a menu, you probably compare the different items to find the one you want the most. You are performing a comparative evaluation because you are trying to see if one item seems tastier than the others. In contrast, if you are in an unfamiliar neighborhood and you notice your car is low on gasoline, you start searching for service stations and stop at the first reasonable place you find. You do not need the best service station in town.

The difference between singular and comparative evaluation is linked to the research of Herbert Simon, who won a Nobel Prize for economics. Simon (1957) identified a decision strategy he calls *satisficing*: selecting the first option that works. Satisficing is different from optimizing, which means trying to come up with the best strategy. Optimizing is hard, and it takes a long time. Satisficing is more efficient. The singular evaluation strategy is based on satisficing. Simon used the concept of satisficing to describe the decision behavior of businesspeople. The strategy makes even more sense for fireground commanders because of their immense time pressure.

Our model of recognitional decision making was starting to fit together. The experienced fireground commanders could judge a situation as prototypical and know what to do. If their first choice did not work out, they might consider others—not to find the best but to find the first one that works.

But there was still the second puzzle. If they did not compare one course of action to another, how did they evaluate the options? All of the evaluation procedures we knew about required contrast: looking at the degree to which each option satisfies each criterion, weighing the importance of the criteria, tabulating the results, and finding the best option. If the commanders did not compare options, how did they know that a course of action was any good?

The answer lies in the overpass rescue story. To evaluate a single course of action, the lieutenant imagined himself carrying it out. Fireground commanders use the power of mental simulation, running the action through in their minds. If they spot a potential problem, like the rescue harness not working well, they move on to the next option, and the next, until they find one that seems to work. Then they carry it out. As the example shows, this is not a foolproof strategy. The advantage is that it is usually better than anything else they can do.

Before we did this study, we believed that novices impulsively jumped at the first option they could think of, whereas experts carefully deliberated about the merits of different courses of action. Now it seemed that it was the experts who could generate a single course of action, while novices needed to compare different approaches.

In one case we studied commanders who had no experience with the type of incident they faced. This helped us to see better what is required for proficient decision making.

EXAMPLE 3

THE CHRISTMAS FIRE

Dotted around the Midwest are oil tank farms: large complexes of storage tanks filled with oil piped in from the Texas and Oklahoma fields and held at these farms before being pumped to specific points in the Midwest. This incident took place at a tank farm. The pipeline field at this farm had 20 tanks, each 45 feet high and 100 feet in diameter and each with a capacity of more than 60,000 barrels of oil.

On Christmas night in the middle of a bitterly cold winter, one of the tanks bursts open. The oil comes pouring out—a bad enough situation—and then ignites. A large oil tank instantly turns into a giant torch and sets fire to another tank. Most of the big power lines of the tanks are down and burning. The telephone lines are also on fire. Burning oil has spilled into a ditch, and fierce winds push the fire along.

(*Continued*)

(Continued)

The setting is a rural farm community crisscrossed with underground oil pipes. If the flames spread, they can conceivably set the whole town on fire.

The fire departments of the surrounding townships report to the call. These departments are staffed by volunteer firefighters who are used to putting out barn fires and garage fires, and maybe a house fire or two in a year. Now they are looking at a wall of flames 50 to 100 feet high. They have never seen anything like it before in their lives. As one commander described it to us, "Our heads turned to stone."

As they watch, one of the two burning tanks ruptures. A wave of crude oil rides over the highway and engulfs a new tank, number 91, which is filled with oil. A man from the pipeline company tells the fireground commanders that if the fire comes any farther south, it will reach a 20-inch propane gas line. The oil is following gravity northward, "creepin' like a little monster" toward a large chemical plant.

Because of the cold, everyone is bundled up, many wearing face masks. The crews have trouble recognizing if someone is from their own district. It is hard to tell who the commanders are. Worse, there is no source of water in the area. Foam is needed to put out oil fires, but the commanders can locate only a thousand gallons.

In short, they have no resources for fighting the fire and no understanding of what to do. They are afraid the fire will spread to the other tanks. They wonder if they should evacuate the town. They are bewildered.

For two days, they remain uncertain about how to proceed. A commander of one of the fire departments orders a trench to be built to contain the oil. A different commander's idea is to pipe the oil out of tank 91. But no one can tell if the lines are still working, and no one wants to take a chance of leaking oil into a field where the fire might spread. A third commander calls the power company to turn off the electricity to the downed power lines, but the power company does not comply right away. Each department goes off in a different direction.

Eventually the power company turns off power in the early morning of the second day. Crews can approach tank 91. The plan is to spray foam down onto the fire, if they can get enough foam. It is freezing cold and windy. Where should they position the ladder truck? Should a firefighter, carrying a hose, climb up a ladder to the rim of tank 91? The dikes around the tank make it hard to get close, and the field around the dikes has dangerous ravines. Eventually a ladder truck gets near tank 91, and firefighters spray foam onto the rim of the oil tank. The wind just blows the foam away, and suddenly the origination point fire, in a nearby tank, starts to boil up menacingly. Fearing an eruption, the commander evacuates his men.

Sometime during the second day, one of the chiefs asks a person working at the oil company if all the pipes leading into the complex have been turned off. The reply is that no one knows, since the tangle of pipelines is so confusing. Spurred on by the question, the plant personnel start tracing all the incoming pipelines and find a source of fuel: a large 22-inch pipe that has been pumping new oil directly into one of the burning tanks. During the second day, they get all the pipes turned off.

On the third day, the volunteer fire chiefs finally take organized action: they choose not to try to do anything. They let the fire burn while they devote all their energies to planning. One of the fireground commanders later told us that this was their first effective decision.

Here is how they go about planning. They ask themselves what their options are, and what the advantages and disadvantages are of each. Finally, in the confusion of a runaway oil fire, we find the strongest example of deliberative decision making—by chiefs who are essentially baffled about what is happening: They try rising up a tower to get a man above the rim of a tank to spray foam down onto the fire. Near the rim, he sees cracks with crude oil coming through. The pumps start spraying foam, and the command is given to start the water truck cycle. Because of earlier delays, the water truck freezes up before it can be used. Then the foam pump starts to malfunction, so they give up and call the firefighter down.

Next they try rigging up a nozzle to spray the foam down, but the high winds sweep it away, and the heat cooks it off. They order more foam from a nearby U.S. Air Force base, but the different foams that arrive are incompatible. Finally, they give up, abandon their pride, and call in some consultants. They call in the team of "Boots and Coots," former colleagues of Red Adair, a world-famous fighter of oil well fires.

Boots and Coots arrive, look briefly at the scene, and say that they will need a great deal more foam. "We don't have that much foam," the volunteer fireground commanders argue. "Of course not," Boots and Coots answer. "We've already ordered it. It will be here tomorrow."

From that point on, under the direction of the experts, the fire operations go smoothly. The entire fire is extinguished within the next two days. Although no one is seriously injured, the cost of the fire is estimated at $10 to $15 million.

From this episode we learn that there are times for deliberating about options. Usually these are times when experience is inadequate and logical thinking is a substitute for recognizing a situation as typical. Although the commanders in this case study had been firefighters for a long time, they had no experience with a fire this large. Deliberating about options makes a lot of sense for novices, who have to think their way through the decision. It is what I do when I have to buy a house or a car. I have to start from scratch, identifying features I might want, looking at the choices.

DEFINING THE RECOGNITION-PRIMED DECISION MODEL

The recognition-primed decision (RPD) model fuses two processes: the way decision makers size up the situation to recognize which course of action makes sense, and the way they evaluate that course of action by imagining it.

Figure 1 shows the basic strategy, as variation 1. Decision makers recognize the situation as typical and familiar—a typical garage fire, or apartment building fire, or factory fire, or search-and-rescue job—and proceed to take action. They understand what types of *goals* make sense (so the priorities are set), which cues are important (so there is not an overload of information), what to expect next (so they can prepare themselves and notice surprises), and the *typical ways of responding* in a given situation. By recognizing a situation as typical, they also recognize a *course of action* likely to succeed. The recognition of goals, cues, expectancies, and actions is part of what it means to recognize a situation.

Some situations are more complex, as shown by variations 2 and 3 in Figure 1. Variation 2 occurs when the decision maker may have to devote more attention *to diagnosing* the situation, since the information may not clearly match a typical case or may map onto more than one typical case. The decision maker may need to gather more information in order to make a diagnosis. Another complication is that the decision maker may have misinterpreted the situation but does not realize it

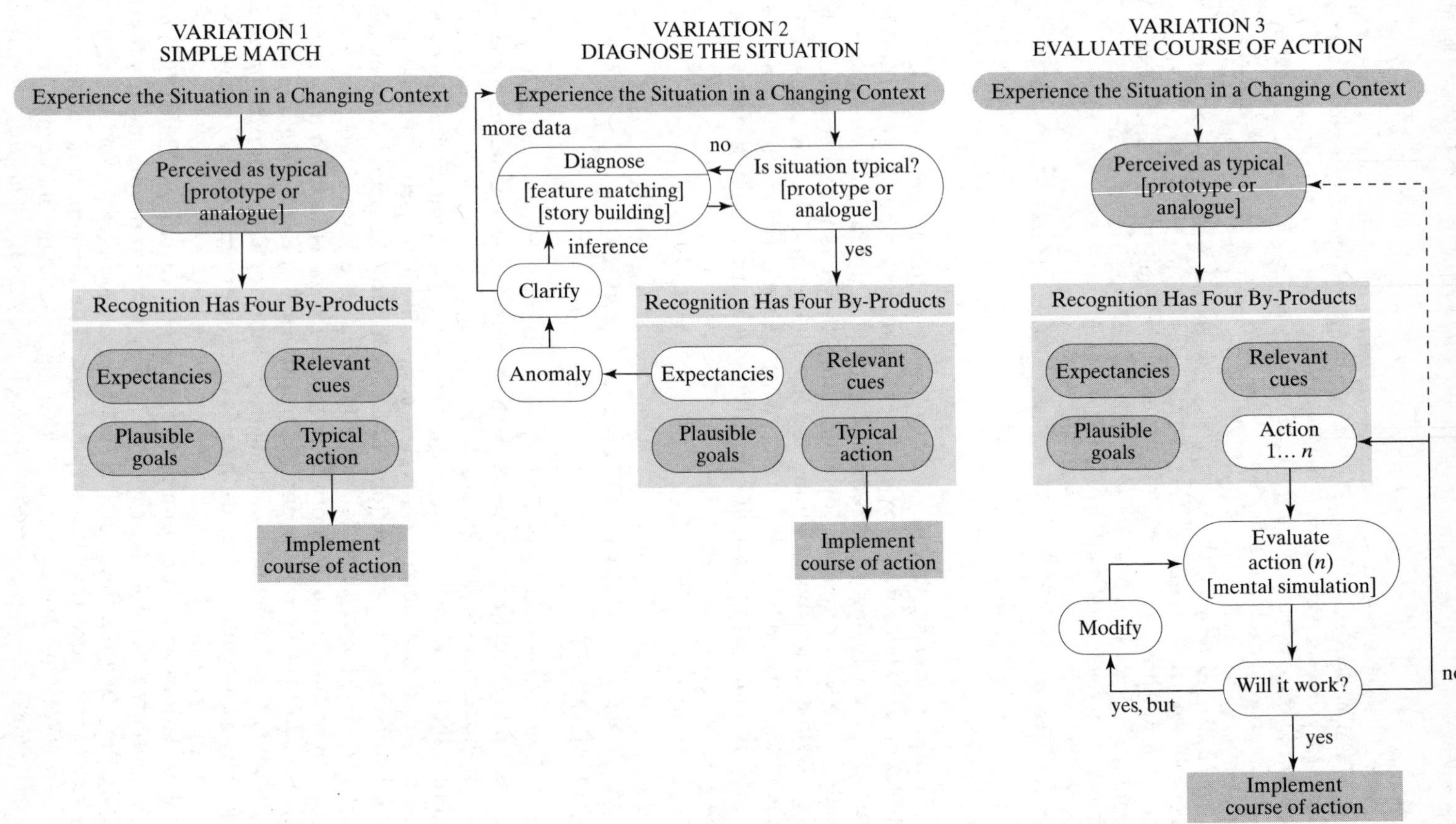

FIGURE 1 Integrated Version of Recognition-Primed Decision Model

until some *expectancies* have been violated. At these times, decision makers will respond to the anomaly or ambiguity by checking which interpretation best matches the features of the situation. They may try to build a story to account for some of the inconsistencies.

Variation 3 explains how decision makers evaluate single options by imagining how the course of action will play out. A decision maker who anticipates difficulties may need to *adjust* the course of action, or maybe *reject* it and look for another option.

One way to think about these three variations is that variation 1 is basically an "if . . . then" reaction, an antecedent followed by the rule-based response. The expertise is in being able to recognize when the antecedent condition has been met. Variation 2 takes the form "if (???). . . then," with the decision maker deliberating about the nature of the situation. Variation 3 takes the form if. . . then (???), as the decision maker ponders the outcome of a reaction. Figure 2 shows an integrated version of all three variations.

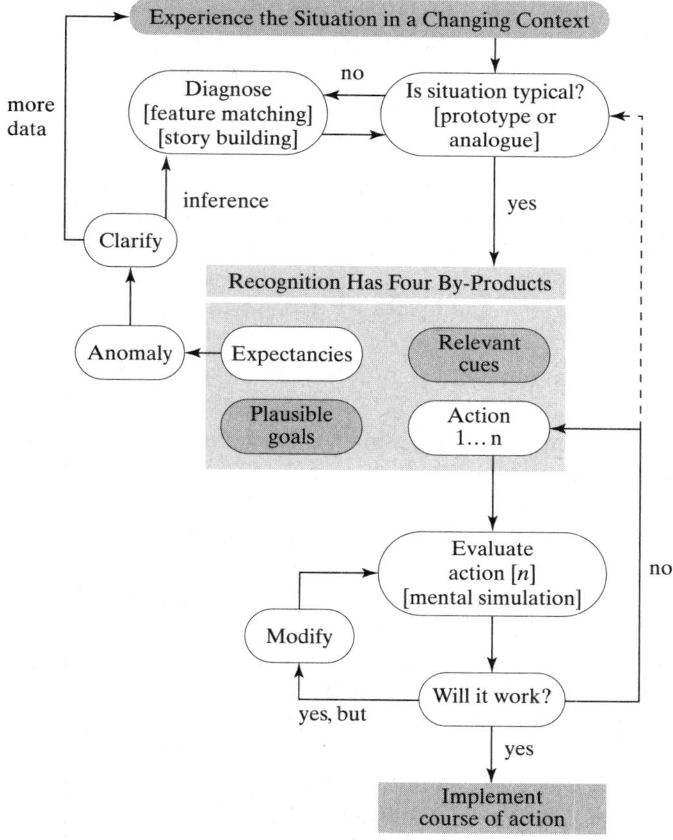

FIGURE 2 Recognition-Primed Decision Model

THE THEORETICAL IMPORTANCE OF THE RPD MODEL

Recognitional decision making can be contrasted with the more classical approaches. Perhaps the most widely known of these models stems from the work of Janis and Mann (1977), who warned that people try to avoid making decisions because of the stress of carrying out the analysis. Janis and Mann offered these prescriptions for making better decisions:

- Thoroughly canvas a wide range of options.
- Survey a full range of objectives.
- Carefully weigh the costs, risk, and benefits of each option.
- Intensively search for new information in evaluating options.
- Assimilate all new information.
- Reexamine the positive and negative consequences of each option.
- Carefully plan to include contingencies if various risks occur.

Janis and Mann probably did not intend this advice for time-pressured situations, but the RPD model predominates even when time is sufficient for comparative evaluations. Yet in one form or another, Janis and Mann's prescriptive advice is held up as an ideal of rationality and finds its way into most courses on cognitive development. The advice is more helpful for beginners than for experienced decision makers. In most applied settings, beginners are not going to be put in a position to make critical decisions.

The prescriptions of Janis and Mann are an example of the rational choice strategy that we had encountered: define the evaluation dimensions, weight each one, rate each option on each dimension, multiply the weightings, total up the scores, and determine the best option—that is, unless you do not have all the data you need, or are not sure how to do the ratings, or disagree with the weights, or run out of time before you have finished.

There are advantages to the rational choice strategy:

- It should result in reliable decisions (that is, the same result each time for the same analysis).
- It is quantitative.
- It helps novices determine what they do not know.
- It is rigorous; it does not leave anything out.
- It is a general strategy, which could apply in all sorts of situations.

The problem is that the assumptions of the rational choice strategy are usually too restrictive. Rarely is there the time or the information needed to make this type of strategy work. Furthermore, if we cannot trust someone to make a big judgment, such as which option is best, why would we trust all of the little judgments that go into the rational choice strategy. Clearly this method is not going to ensure that novices make good choices, and it usually is not helpful for experienced decision makers. It can be useful in working with teams, to calibrate everyone's grasp of the strengths and weaknesses of different options.

THE POWER OF INTUITION

Intuition depends on the use of experience to recognize key patterns that indicate the dynamics of the situation. Because patterns can be subtle, people often cannot describe what they noticed, or how they judged a situation as typical or atypical. Therefore, intuition has a strange reputation. Skilled decision makers know that they can depend on their intuition, but at the same time they may feel uncomfortable trusting a source of power that seems so accidental.

Bechara, Damasio, Tranet, and Damasio (1997) found that intuition has a basis in biology. They compared patients who were brain damaged to a group of normal subjects. The brain-damaged subjects lacked intuition, an emotional reaction to anticipated consequences of good and bad decisions. In the normal subjects, this system seemed to be activated long before they were consciously aware that they had made a decision.

For the first formal interview that I did in our first research project with firefighters, I was trying to find some difficult incident where my interviewee, a fireground commander, had to make a tough decision. He could think of only one case, years ago, where he said his extrasensory perception (ESP) had saved the day. I tried to get him to think of a different incident because the one he had in mind was too old, because he was only a lieutenant then, not a commander, and because I do not have much interest in ESP. But he was determined to describe this case, so I finally gave up and let him tell his story.

EXAMPLE 4

THE SIXTH SENSE

It is a simple house fire in a one-story house in a residential neighborhood. The fire is in the back, in the kitchen area. The lieutenant leads his hose crew into the building, to the back, to spray water on the fire, but the fire just roars back at them.

"Odd," he thinks. The water should have more of an impact. They try dousing it again, and get the same results. They retreat a few steps to regroup.

Then the lieutenant starts to feel as if something is not right. He doesn't have any clues; he just doesn't feel right about being in that house, so he orders his men out of the building—a perfectly standard building with nothing out of the ordinary.

As soon as his men leave the building, the floor where they had been standing collapses. Had they still been inside, they would have plunged into the fire below.

"A sixth sense," he assured us, and part of the makeup of every skilled commander. Some close questioning revealed the following facts:

- He had no suspicion that there was a basement in the house.
- He did not suspect that the seat of the fire was in the basement, directly underneath the living room where he and his men were standing when he gave his order to evacuate.
- But he was already wondering why the fire did not react as expected.
- The living room was hotter than he would have expected for a small fire in the kitchen of a single-family home.
- It was very quiet. Fires are noisy, and for a fire with this much heat, he would have expected a great deal of noise.

The whole pattern did not fit right. His expectations were violated, and he realized he did not quite know what was going on. That was why he ordered his men out of the building. With hindsight, the reasons for the mismatch were clear. Because the fire was under him and not in the kitchen, it was not affected by his crew's attack, the rising heat was much greater than he had expected, and the floor acted like a baffle to muffle the noise, resulting in a hot but quiet environment.

This incident helped us understand how commanders make decisions by recognizing when a typical situation is developing. In this case, the events were not typical, and his reaction was to pull back, regroup, and try to get a better sense of what was going on. By showing us what happens when the cues do not fit together, this case clarified how much firefighters rely on a recognition of familiarity and prototypicality. By the end of the interview, the commander could see how he had used the available information to make his judgment. (I think he was proud to realize how his experience had come into play. Even so, he was a little shaken since he had come to depend on his sixth sense to get him through difficult situations, and it was unnerving for him to realize that he might never have had ESP.)

This is one basis for what we call *intuition*: recognizing things without knowing how we do the recognizing. In the simple version of the RPD model, we size the situation up and immediately know how to proceed: which goals to pursue, what to expect, how to respond. We are drawn to certain cues and not others because of our situation awareness. (This must happen all the time. Try to imagine going through a day without making these automatic responses.)

There may be other aspects of intuition than the one I have been describing. I do know that the firefighters' experience enables them to recognize situations quickly.

Many people think of intuition as an inborn trait—something we are born with. I am not aware of any evidence showing that some people are blessed with intuition, and others are not. My claim is that intuition grows out of experience.

We should not be surprised that the commander in this case was not aware of the way he used his experience. Rather than giving him specific facts from memory, the experience affected the way he saw the situation. Another reason that he could not describe his use of experience was that he was reacting to things that were not happening rather than to things that were. A third reason that he was unaware of his use of experience was that he was not drawing on his memory for any specific previous experience. A large set of similar incidents had all blended together.

Described in this way, intuition does not sound very mysterious. In fact, the simple version of the RPD model is a model of intuition.

Intuition is an important source of power for all of us. Nevertheless, we have trouble observing ourselves use experience in this way, and we definitely have trouble explaining the basis of our judgments when someone else asks us to defend them. Therefore, intuition has a bad reputation compared with a judgment that comes from careful analysis of all the relevant factors and shows each inference drawn and traces the conclusion in a clear line to all of the antecedent conditions. In fact, research by Wilson and Schooler (1991) shows that people do worse at some decision tasks when they are asked to perform analyses of the reasons for their preferences or to evaluate all the attributes of the choices.

Intuition is not infallible. Our experience will sometimes mislead us, and we will make mistakes that add to our experience base. Imagine that you are driving around in an unfamiliar city, and you see some landmark, perhaps a gas station, and you say, "Oh, now I know where we are," and (despite the protests of your spouse, who has the map) make a fateful turn and wind up on an unescapable entrance ramp to the highway you had been trying to avoid. As you face the prospect of being sent miles out of your way, you may lamely offer that the gas station you remembered must have been a different one: "I thought I recognized it, but I guess I was wrong."

PRACTICAL IMPLICATIONS

- Be sensitive to when you need to compare options and when you do not. For many tasks, we are novices, and the rational choice method helps us when we lack the expertise to recognize situations. Sometimes we may need to use formal methods to look at wide array of alternatives. Other times we may judge that we should rely on our expertise to look in greater depth at a smaller set of alternatives—maybe the first one considered.
- The part of intuition that involves pattern matching and recognition of familiar and typical cases can be trained. The ideas set forth in this chapter imply that we do not make someone an expert through training in formal methods of analysis. Quite the contrary is true, in fact: We run the risk of slowing the development of skills. If the purpose is to train people in time-pressured decision making, we might require that the trainee make rapid responses rather than ponder all the implications. If we can present many situations an hour, several hours a day, for days or weeks, we should be able to improve the trainee's ability to detect familiar patterns. The design of the scenarios is critical, since the goal is to show many common cases to facilitate a recognition of typicality along with different types of rare cases so trainees will be prepared for these as well.

We can summarize the key features of the RPD model in comparison to the standard advice given to decision makers. The RPD model claims that with experienced decision makers:

- The focus is on the way they assess the situation and judge it familiar, not on comparing options.
- Courses of action can be quickly evaluated by imagining how they will be carried out, not by formal analysis and comparison.
- Decision makers usually look for the first workable option they can find, not the best option.
- Since the first option they consider is usually workable, they do not have to generate a large set of options to be sure they get a good one.
- They generate and evaluate options one at a time and do not bother comparing the advantages and disadvantages of alternatives.
- By imagining the option being carried out, they can spot weaknesses and find ways to avoid these, thereby making the option stronger. Conventional models just select the best, without seeing how it can be improved.
- The emphasis is on being poised to act rather than being paralyzed until all the evaluations have been completed.

References

A. Bechara, H. Damasio, D. Tranel, and A. R. Damasio, "Deciding Advantageously Before Knowing the Advantageous Strategy," *Science 275* (1997): 1293–1295.

I. L. Janis and L. Mann, *Decision Making: A Psychological Analysis of Conflict, Choice, and Commitment* (New York: Free Press, 1977).

J. Orasann and T. Connolly, "The Reinvention of Decision Making," *Decision Making in Action: Models and Methods*, eds. G. Klein, J. Orasanu, R. Calderwood, and C. E. Zsambok (Norwood, NJ: Ablex, 1993): 3–20.

H. A. Simon, *Models of Man: Social and Rational* (New York: Wiley 1957).

P. O. Soelberg, "Unprogrammed Decision Making," *Industrial Management Review 8* (1967): 19–29.

T. D. Wilson and J. W. Schooler, "Thinking Too Much: Introspection Can Reduce the Quality of Preferences and Decisions," *Journal of Personality and Social Psychology 60* (1991): 181–192.

TOUGH CALLS IN A SPEED-DRIVEN WORLD*

J. Keith Murnighan

John Mowen

The value of art is not beauty, but right action.
W. SOMERSET MAUGHAM

Put yourself in the shoes of Jim Bronson. You are 36 years old and have just received the national entrepreneur-of-the-year award. You and your partner have successfully opened 27 Chicago Brew Pubs in the last nine years. It is 1995, and investment bankers are at your door, wanting you to take your company public so that they can make you rich.

In 1986, you left a position as a senior analyst on Wall Street to pursue your dream of successfully developing a restaurant chain. You and your partner, Paul Springfield, make a great team. You favor a conservative approach to growth, whereas Paul, a natural marketer, constantly pushes you to grow faster. Your decisions so far have been phenomenally successful. Your strategy of carefully growing by three pubs a year has really paid off.

Now that you have won this big award, however, the competitive environment in the brewing industry is changing. Investment bankers are interested in other brew pubs, including L. A. Brew Pub, Big Apple, California Brew Pub, Big City Brew Pub, and Simpsons. There is a chance that each company may announce public offerings this year. You realize that within a one-year period, there may be 300 million to 400 million investment dollars flowing into brew pubs.

You now face a classic tough call. Do you continue your strategy of avoiding serious debt and slowly growing your company, or do you go public and exponentially grow your company as the investment bankers propose? You face a soon-to-close window of threat and opportunity. If you continue your present strategy of slow growth, your more highly capitalized competitors could invade your territory and potentially drive you out of business. If you follow the investment bankers' advice and double the number of Chicago Brew Pubs each year for four consecutive years, you could potentially make several million dollars, but it will also place extreme demands on your managerial ability. Either

*Reprinted and adapted with permission from J. Keith Murnighan and John C. Mowen. *The Art of High-Stakes Decision-Making: Tough Calls in a Speed-Driven World* (New York: John Wiley & Sons, 2002): 3–22.

choice could mean great success or dismal failure. You only have a short time to decide. Once your competitors go public, you may not get a second chance.

Jim Bronson and his partner had only a few weeks to make their decision. They worried that if they failed to act, they would fall behind the power curve; that is, their competitors would become so well capitalized that no matter how hard they tried, or how well they made their future decisions, they would be unable to compete effectively. To stay ahead of the curve, they would be unable to compete effectively. To stay ahead of the curve, they would have to make the investment. Yet there was an incredible downside to the high-growth strategy. They faced a tremendously tough call, a true decision dilemma. If you were Jim Bronson, what would you do?

A CRASHING PLANE

Now change the situation and the time to December 20, 1995. American Airlines flight 965 is running smoothly. You are the pilot. Suddenly, the crash avoidance system barks, "Terrain, terrain. . . pull up, pull up." You pull up the nose of the Boeing 757 to gain lift. At the same time, you shove the throttle forward to increase air speed. The plane climbs, but not sharply enough. It clips some trees and slams into the side of a mountain ridge in Colombia, South America. Amazingly, 4 of the 163 passengers survive.

Like any airplane crash, it was a tremendous tragedy. In many ways, the aftermath made things even worse, when investigations revealed that any of three different choices could have led to no crash at all. First, analysis of the data by investigators suggested that the cause of the crash was pilot error. Apparently, the pilot had punched the wrong coordinates into the airplane's computer, making its readouts inaccurate and confusing. Subsequent choices that depended on these inaccurate readings placed the plane in great danger. Second, the accident occurred during the early stages of landing when the pilot followed standard operating procedures to extend small spoilers (called speed breaks) from the top of the plane's wings to reduce life. When the alarm sounded and a steep climb was necessary, the pilot failed to retract the spoilers. As a result, the plane could not climb steeply enough to clear the mountain. The pilot had fallen behind the power curve, and he did not respond quickly enough when his actions determined the fate of everyone on board his plane.

A third factor also contributed to the tragedy. According to *The Wall Street Journal*, executives at Boeing faced a tough call when they designed the plane, and their choice contributed to the tragedy. Unlike Airbus, Boeing actively decided *not* to build a system into the plane that would automatically retract the spoilers when an emergency climb was necessary. As one retired pilot lamented, "They only needed another two hundred feet to make it, and if that plane had automatically retracting spoilers, they would have made it."

TOUGH CALLS DEFINED

Tough calls are high-stakes decisions that must be made when information is ambiguous, values conflict, and experts disagree. By their nature, they never offer a clear-cut, obvious choice. Due to the high risk that accompanies such hard choices, they may result in tremendous coups or dreadful blunders. Some people have jobs that require them to make tough calls all the time. Those who are successful and who can handle the pressure become the leaders of their fields. In today's society, they become the chief executive officers (CEOs), the eminent scientists, the pilots, the entrepreneurs, and the national leaders whose decisions impact the lives of thousands, if not millions, of people every year.

Over time, the quality of our decisions determines our future. Each day we make dozens of decisions. Do I wear a seatbelt? Do I have five servings of fruits and vegetables? Do I get an hour of physical activity? We call these habitual decisions "multiplay decisions" because over the course of a few years, we make these routine choices thousands of times. Because their effects accumulate, they can have an enormous impact on our lives. If we choose to develop poor habits, we pay the consequences. Hundreds of books have been written on this type of routine decision making.

We focus on the tough calls that occur less often, but with surprising frequency, in either our personal or our professional lives. Do I sell my company? Do I change my career? Do I report the unethical behavior of my boss? Do I fire an employee? How do I approach the need for increased care for my elderly parents? The answers to these questions have one commonality: The results of these decisions will seriously affect your future as well as the lives of other people.

Our goal is to provide you with a structure and a set of guidelines for making tough calls. Peter Volanakis, the executive vice president of Corning Glass Corporation, argued that managers within an organization should share a common decision-making process for making fast, effective judgments. A sound decision-making process will give you the courage to take responsible high-stakes risks. Volanakis argued that this process will both improve and increase risk taking because managers "have no trouble defending their decision when they know they have taken all the important factors into consideration and used an objective, rational system to evaluate the available information."

We present a process called SCRIPTS for making tough calls. SCRIPTS identifies seven parameters that will ensure that your high-stakes decisions will stand the test of time. The seven parameters are: **s**earch for signals of threats and opportunities, find the **c**auses, evaluate the **r**isks, apply **i**ntuition and emotion, take different **p**erspectives, consider the **t**ime frame, and **s**olve the problem. Just as Somerset Maugham suggested in the quote introducing this chapter, the benefit of following a tested procedure is not in its elegance or beauty. Rather, it is in the positive outcomes that result.

Our high-stakes decisions determine our long-term happiness and success. Indeed, research tells us that we most frequently second-guess the hard choices that we have *not* made. It is not a lack of motivation that prevents success. Rather, it is the fear of making high-stakes decisions. By developing an in-depth understanding of the SCRIPTS process, you will be able to identify high-stakes decisions and how you can make them with the courage that comes from developing the essential ability to make hard choices. You will also learn how to make tough calls with the velocity that our speed-driven world requires.

ILLUSTRATING THE FOUR CHARACTERISTICS OF TOUGH CALLS

The Chicago Brew Pub case illustrates the four key characteristics of tough calls. First, the stakes were high—the fate of an organization and the jobs of five hundred employees were at stake. Second, the available information was ambiguous. No one could tell with any certainty, in advance, which course of action would result in the most favorable outcome. Third, basic values were in conflict. On the one hand, Jim Bronson wanted to follow his conservative instincts and build the company slowly and prudently. On the other hand, he knew that a failure to grow the company at this critical time could create difficulties that he might not be able to handle. Fourth, experts disagreed as to the most appropriate choice. The investment bankers urged him to act before the window of opportunity closed. In contrast, traditional bankers counseled him to be extremely wary of the siren song of quick riches.

The fate of American Airlines flight 965 also illustrates the characteristics of tough calls. The pilot faced a crisis situation in which many lives were in his hands. He had to react quickly based on his training, intelligence, and ability to handle stress. The case also identifies two additional aspects of tough calls. First, it illustrates the idea that tough calls can be made by both organizations and individuals. At the individual level, the pilot had to react quickly and skillfully to the crisis. At the organizational level, a team of executives had to decide whether to install a software system that automatically retracted the spoilers.

The flight 965 case also shows that decisions made at one time may impact outcomes many years later. Years prior to the crash, aeronautical engineers and company managers made the decision to leave it to pilots to determine whether to retract the spoilers in an emergency. In the design philosophy of building an airplane, managers must decide whether to maximize a pilot's or a computer's control of the plane and its many systems and safety features. Needless to say, computers can malfunction and cause accidents just like pilots can. The two giant airplane manufacturers, Boeing and Airbus, took alternative routes. Airbus installed software that instructed the computer system to retract the spoilers; Boeing relied on pilots.

The experts at Boeing and the experts at Airbus disagreed in part because of their different organizational value systems. At Boeing, the value system emphasizes allowing pilots to have maximum control of the airplane. At Airbus, the value system focuses to a larger extent on using technology to fly an airplane. Thus experts in each company examined exactly the same data and came to opposite conclusions.

When choices are tough, no absolutely right answer exists. You can consult the most outstanding experts, but they will disagree on what to do. You can use complex computer programs, but they may only add to the confusion when subtle changes of an assumption or estimates of key variables lead to completely different answers. Even though no one "right" answer exists, you must make the decision and you must bear the consequences.

TYPES OF TOUGH CALLS

We have developed a simple matrix that identifies the types of tough calls that individuals and organizations face. As shown in Figure 1, the two dimensions of the matrix are (1) the time available to make the decision and (2) whether the decision is repeated. The time available to make the decision can range from instantaneous (like the pilot on flight 965) to having months to work out a solution. We must make short-fuse decisions quickly and decisively. Long-fuse decisions give us time to think, bring in experts, and even employ computer simulations.

The second dimension of the matrix represents the frequency with which the same decision is repeated. In our terminology, choices that occur infrequently and are rarely replayed are single-play decisions. At an organizational level, the decision by Boeing not to install automatic retracting spoilers was a single-play decision. Once made, it

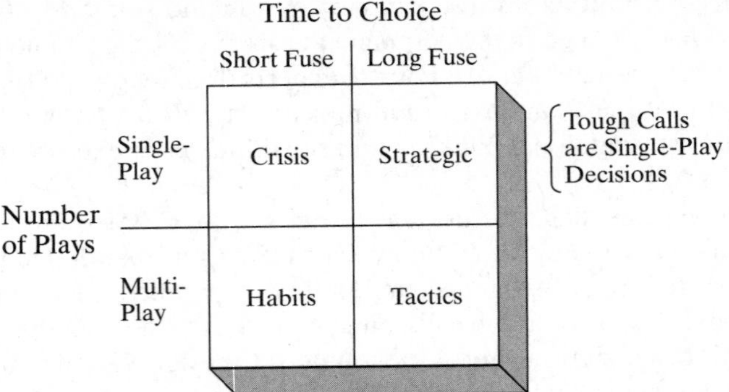

FIGURE 1 A Matrix of Decision Types

would be very hard to change. In contrast, banks replay thousands of times the decision concerning the financial criteria to give credit cards to consumers. The decisions that identify these criteria are strategic decisions. Replaying them over and over again illustrates the tactical application of the tough call. On a personal level, getting married, building a home, and undertaking major elective surgery are all examples of single-play decisions (at least for most people). In contrast, having dessert after dinner, selecting the right outfit to wear, and choosing to drive or use mass transit to get to work are all multiplay decisions.

Tough choices are almost always single-play decisions—whether they have a short or long time fuse. American Airlines flight 965 illustrates both types of single-play decisions. The few seconds that the pilot had to respond to the emergency represent the ultimate in crisis decision-making. Thus, **crisis choices** are single-play decisions with a short time fuse, and **strategic decisions** are single-play decisions with a long time fuse. The design decision by Boeing to give pilots maximum control over the plane's functions represents a strategic decision. The decision faced by Jim Bronson represents a strategic decision. The selection of a career represents a strategic decision. Similarly, within organizations, the decision to enter an entirely new market represents a strategic choice. Each of these examples is a single-play decision with an outcome that has the potential of being a horrible blunder. By their very nature, then, tough choices entail considerable risk.

Multiplay decisions, in contrast, involve the execution of many smaller decisions, often over a long time period. Thus, when multiplay decisions have a short time fuse, we think of them as **habitual**. Habitual choices tend to involve low stakes—if only because we get so used to making them. Some personal examples include choosing whether to wear a seat belt in a car, the mechanics of monthly bill paying, and how we choose which phone calls to return. Examples of habitual decisions in corporations include choices to highlight or ignore small defects in a product and the choice of internal e-mail for ordinary announcements.

Any single execution of a multiplay decision is unlikely to cause major problems. Thus, not wearing a seat belt on one trip to the grocery store is unlikely to cause any problems. When repeated many times over a long time period, however, multiplay decisions can have enormous consequences.

When time is available to make a multiplay decision, what would otherwise become habitual decisions can now be made tactically. **Tactical decisions** result from the development of a plan of action that fits within a broader, strategic decision. When acting rationally, we make our strategic decisions first and then move on to the nitty-gritty of tactics; strategic decisions provide the umbrella under which we make our tactical decisions. When we make strategic decisions, we focus on grand goals and big objectives and expect to achieve them over the long haul. We use tactics to implement our strategies. Like habitual choices, we make many tactical decisions. When we have time, we can make them deliberately.

THE LAW OF LARGE NUMBERS AND MULTIPLAY DECISIONS

We have known people who scoff at the importance of habitual and tactical decisions in their personal and professional lives. They are completely correct in suggesting that the outcome of any single tactical habitual decision is unlikely to have much of an impact on their organization. Two facts, however, make multiplay decisions extremely important. First, they occur very frequently; one researcher recently estimated that 95 percent of our decisions are not just habitual but automatic. Second, multiplay decisions playing out over time have an inexorable quality: If you get them right, you will invariably win; but if you get them wrong, you will invariably lose. The law of large numbers explains why.

The law of large numbers is simple. If you do the same thing over and over again, the chances of failure and the chances of success will reveal themselves much more clearly than if you did that thing only once. Stated differently, if you replay a bet many times, your outcome will probably be very close to the bet's underlying expected value. Thus, if the odds are 60–40 for you, placing the bet a thousand times means that you will win very close to six hundred and you will lose very close to four hundred of the bets.

The law of large numbers explains why casinos are so incredibly profitable. The house has a small probability advantage on every single bet, whether made at the craps table, at roulette, or at blackjack. It also has a small probability advantage on every pull of every slot machine. (It's no wonder that they call them one-armed bandits.) Because they have this small advantage over many, many bets, the house's profits almost precisely match its edge in the odds. And the more bets that people make in any one casino, the higher the profits and the more certain they are to occur. This is why casinos treat big winners so well (e.g., offering free rooms and liquor). They know that if they can keep people betting, the law of large numbers will ensure that the house will increase its winnings. The law also explains why polling services can give such good estimates of election outcomes. By randomly sampling voters as they leave voting booths on election day, polling services can project with tremendous accuracy what the outcome of the election will be, long before all of the votes are in. (In fact, getting data from about 2,400 people provides a prediction of the total population's view within about three percentage points.) The law of large numbers is very powerful.

We can see the implications of the law of large numbers for decision-making by considering two different gambles. First, imagine that we have asked you to flip a fair coin. Before you see the result, you must choose heads or tails. If you are right, we will give you $10,000. If you are wrong, you give us $5,000. When we do this with managerial and executive groups, most people choose not to make the bet—even though the expected value is positive and considerable. Indeed, the mathematical calculation gives an expected value of $2,500. Suppose, however, that we change the bet. This time we will toss the coin one hundred times. For each bet that you win, we give you $100; for each bet that you lose, you pay us $50. The expected value of these hundred bets is exactly the same as the expected value of our one big bet—$2,500. When we offer this bet to managers and executives, they all choose to play.

The first bet is a large, single-play decision. The second is a series of smaller, identical multiplay decisions. The law of large numbers operates in the second case but not the first. Over the course of a hundred rounds of the multiplay bet, you will almost certainly win about $2,500. When we do the single-play bet, however, you will either win $10,000 or lose $5,000. The fear of losing $5,000 makes taking the bet too risky for most people, even though the prize for winning is twice as big.

It is critical to remember, however, that the underlying odds of multiplay decisions are what determine their final, cumulative outcome. When you make many choices, you will win in the long run only *if* the overall expected value of your choices is positive. If the expected value is negative, the law of large numbers will lead you to a terrible final outcome.

*SCRIPT*ING TOUGH CALLS

By considering each of seven SCRIPTS parameters, you will improve your odds of successfully navigating your own tough calls in a timely and confident way.

1. **S**earch for signals of threats and opportunities.
2. Find the **c**auses.
3. Evaluate the **r**isks.
4. Apply **i**ntuition and emotion.
5. Take different **p**erspectives.
6. Consider the **t**ime frame.
7. **S**olve the problem.

SEARCH FOR SIGNALS OF THREATS AND OPPORTUNITIES

The first step in making tough calls is to identify signals of threats and opportunities. Unless threats are identified early, they can compound, sometimes rapidly. According to the law of the power curve, the longer we wait to address a problem, the more severe it will become. Master decision makers employ situation analysis to monitor their environment and detect problem signals. To perform effective situation analysis, we must know our goals, have outstanding information systems, and have the expertise necessary to interpret the data and recognize the presence of problem signals.

Signal-detection analysis can help us determine whether to respond to a possible problem. In this approach, the decision maker determines the strength of the signal for action and compares it to a trigger for how much evidence is required before taking action. The trigger for action is based on the relative costs of making the two types of possible errors—a needless blunder or a missed opportunity. As exemplified by the

USS *Vincennes*, [which shot down an Iran Air passenger plane it mistook for combat aircraft], a needless blunder occurs when an action is taken when it should not have been. As exemplified by the USS *Stark*, [which was bombed by an Iraqi combat plane that was not perceived as a threat], a missed opportunity occurs when an action is not taken when it should have been. If a missed opportunity will be more negative than a needless blunder, we should set a hair trigger for action. If a needless blunder will be more negative, we should set a sticky trigger for action.

Decision-makers must be aware of the various biases that impact their detection of signals. In particular, the overconfidence bias may cause a person to set a hair trigger when charting an initial course of action. A hair trigger, however, increases the likelihood of a needless blunder. On the other hand, a previous choice of action allows overconfidence to lead to a sticky trigger. As a result, the decision-maker may have difficulty abandoning a losing course of action.

If we identify a signal of a threat or opportunity, it is critical to determine whether the situation has a short or a long fuse. For short-fuse crises, we truncate the SCRIPTS process and employ guided intuition to solve the problem. For long-fuse problems, we can activate the entire SCRIPTS process. Prior to moving to the second stage of the SCRIPTS process, we summarize the seven principles of signal detection.

THE SIGNAL-DETECTION PRINCIPLES

1. Employ situation analysis to identify signals of threats and opportunities.
2. Avoid the zone of false hope by identifying problem signals early.
3. Set your trigger so that a mistake will lead to the least-negative outcome.
4. Strive for accuracy in detecting signals by creating outstanding systems for gathering and interpreting data.
5. Recognize that the overconfidence bias can decrease accuracy and influence trigger setting.
6. If you are facing a short-fuse situation, truncate the SCRIPTS process by going directly to guided intuition.
7. Be realistic when making a decision, and be confident when implementing it.

FIND THE CAUSES

The causes of a threat or opportunity can range dramatically in complexity. On the one hand, a threat or opportunity may arise from a single factor. Usually, however, when high-stakes decisions are involved, multiple factors converge to create the quandary. As a result, it is critical to take a systems approach to understanding causation.

The use of a systems approach often reveals that the cause of a serious incident is overdetermined; that is, a number of factors have come together to produce the problem. Reality is extremely complex because it is marked by multiple factors coming together to cause threats and opportunities.

Root-Cause Analysis

To this point, we have shown that catastrophes are often overdetermined. We have not, however, described how to find the causes. If you are an engineer or work for a hospital, you will know the answer—root-cause analysis. There are many definitions of root-cause analysis. One of our favorites was developed at Cisco Systems. Managers at this high-tech company define root-cause analysis as the "process of analyzing cause–effect relationships between events in complex systems." We think of root-cause analysis as a structured process for assessing the cause–effect relationships in a system and identifying which component, or components, are responsible for an event. A number of principles apply, including the following:

1. Begin by determining the sequence of events that has led to the incident.
2. Constantly seek answers to the "why" question.
3. Carefully examine human decision making as well as physical systems.
4. Recognize that a single cause can generate many symptoms and may share symptoms with other causes.
5. Understand that there may be more than one root cause.

After the basic problem or problems have been identified, we then seek to find a set of alternative solutions. We recognize that it is important to identify as many solutions as possible. The most frequent error in this phase is to truncate the solution-identification process too early. Other sources of error include the overconfidence bias (overconfidence leads to underestimating threats and failing to collect necessary information), hindsight bias (retrospectively overestimating how well a problem or outcome could have been anticipated), and availability bias (weighting more heavily accessible information in decision making).

CAUSAL PRINCIPLES

1. Use root-cause analysis to identify the cause or causes of the threat or opportunity.
2. Analyze causes from a systems perspective, and recognize that failures are often overdetermined.
3. Avoid causal illusions by acknowledging that neither you nor mysterious outside forces can influence events governed by chance.
4. Avoid the availability bias by knowing that the cause of an outcome may not be the most available factor that comes to mind.
5. Defensive, ego-driven attributions can lead to a failure to identify causes. Learn more by realizing (a) that the situation is not always the cause of our poor outcomes and (b) that we are not always completely responsible for our good outcomes.
6. Avoid the fundamental attribution error by recognizing that situational factors (e.g., good/bad luck or the difficulty of the task) may be a serious influence in the performance of others.
7. Avoid the hindsight bias; that is, don't exaggerate in hindsight what you could not have anticipated in foresight.

EVALUATE THE RISKS

Six risk factors are important when we evaluate the negative consequences (i.e., the risks) of a missed opportunity or a needless blunder. Each is concerned with anticipating the regret that we would experience following the ultimate outcome. We use the acronym SMILES to identify the six factors:

The Six Risk Dimensions

Social risk: How will others view me? What will it do to my reputation?
Monetary risk: How will the outcome impact my financial and material resources?
Information risk: How much will I learn from the experience?
Life/health risk: Will the outcome threaten my life or health?
Experience risk: How much will I enjoy or hate the experience?
Sink-the-boat risk: Does a false action create the potential for a catastrophic, irretrievable loss?

To assess the consequences of a needless blunder or a missed opportunity, we try to anticipate potential regret for each of the SMILES dimensions.

A critical problem, of course, is determining the actual value of the risks of the different choices available in high-stakes decisions. There is no true "reality" as to what the actual risks and benefits are because they are based on perceptions, not objective reality. The problem is even more difficult because several perceptual and motivational factors often bias our estimates and perceptions. These include the anchoring and insufficient adjustment bias (the tendency to make estimates by starting from an initial point or anchor and then adjusting from that value to generate a prediction), the law of decreasing marginal effect (the positive or negative reaction to each additional unit of something—money, praise, losses, etc.—decreases as the amount increases), entrapment in decisions (not ending a failing project or "throwing good money after bad"), and failing to carry through a course of action (quitting too soon).

One quite effective approach to managing risk involves developing rules of thumb for action. These are easily followed rules that typically result in satisfactory but not always optimal decisions. Heuristics have several advantages: They are quick to implement, they tend to be simple, and they are frequently based on years of experience. One of the most basic is the principle of diversification—or not putting all your eggs in one basket. Another is the use of milestones or objectives that must be met in order for a project to be continued.

APPLY INTUITION AND EMOTION

Reason, intuition, and emotion all play an important role in high-stakes decision-making. The tough call is *when* to use reason, *when* to employ intuition, and *when* to allow your emotions to influence your actions. We recommend that when a strategic decision must be made, the decision-maker should use reason and guided intuition. The reasoning process involves moving through the seven SCRIPTS steps prior to taking action. The decision-maker then compares the conclusion derived from the SCRIPTS procedure to the solution that emerges from employing guided intuition.

Whether we are employing the full SCRIPTS procedure or using intuition, emotion can get in the way to bias how we estimate probabilities and how we value outcomes. For example, in crisis situations, the emotions of anger and fear can activate flight or fight responses that are highly dysfunctional. Taking the time to think through the situation and develop options can be critical. Once a decision has been made, however, emotions can add that extra spark to get the decision implemented and to provide the energy to perform the work quickly and efficiently.

Finally, we propose that decision-makers employ a guided-intuition process whether making crisis or strategic decisions. We define guided intuition as the instantaneous use of the SCRIPTS procedure to make experienced-based intuitive decisions. Thoroughly practicing the SCRIPTS procedure on many problems allows the steps to become ingrained and reflexive. When a crisis situation occurs, the decision-maker can then automatically engage this intuitive process, in which causes are sought, risks are identified, alternative perspectives are taken, and time is considered in a matter of seconds or minutes. Thus, the SCRIPTS procedure guides the use of both reason and intuition in high-stakes decision-making. While using intuition or moving through the SCRIPTS procedure, turn down the flames of emotions and avoid letting anger, fear, or greed hijack you. When you identify a solution, however, allow your emotions to provide explosive force to implement the course of action with overwhelming energy and drive.

PRINCIPLES OF INTUITION AND EMOTION

1. Guided-intuition is best employed by experts when time is short and/or when a rational analysis has resulted in two or more essentially equivalent options.
2. Emotions are required to move a decision-maker to action and to implement solutions energetically.
3. When time is available, use rational decision analysis to identify alternative courses of action, the probability of success of the options, and the positive and negative outcomes that may occur.
4. Emotions exaggerate and bias perceptions of the probability of outcomes and the perceptions of positive and negative values.
5. Fear increases the belief that negative outcomes will happen and causes people to view bad outcomes more negatively.
6. Optimism increases the belief that good things will happen and increases the perceived value of positive outcomes.

TAKE DIFFERENT PERSPECTIVES

The perspective that we employ provides a set of values and salient issues that influence the factors that we consider in our decision-making processes. As a result, it influences our final choice. By explicitly viewing decision problems from divergent perspectives, master decision-makers ensure that they develop a full understanding of the situation. Clear-headed decision-makers know that if they do not plainly evaluate the decision from alternative frames of reference, their decision will almost invariably be misconstrued.

Our perspectives act as lenses that focus our attention on particular decision elements and personal values. In the next section, we discuss eight divergent perspectives that are prevalent in U.S. corporations. We describe how each perspective can have both positive and negative effects on decision making. We then show how the perspectives have influenced decision-makers in a variety of high-stakes contexts. After discussing the critical importance of viewing decisions from an ethical perspective, we conclude the chapter with a discussion of the principle of multiframe superiority.

Eight Professional Perspectives

The eight professional perspectives we identify here are engineering/technology, sales/marketing, production, political, legal, accounting/finance, competitive, and ethical. At the risk of overloading on acronyms, note that the eight perspectives can be remembered via the phrase ESP-PLACE.

Engineering/Technology Frame The first important frame of reference in organizations is the engineering/technology perspective. This frame is at its best when it causes executives to focus on producing innovative, high-quality products in an efficient and timely manner. On the downside, the engineering/technology frame can result in look-alike, cost-ineffective products designed for the engineer rather than the customer. At its worst, the needs and wants of consumers are ignored. This can result in the creation of products that are easy to use for the engineers. For consumers, however, the products may be so complicated as to be nearly incomprehensible and useless.

The Sales/Marketing Frame The sales/marketing frame represents another lens that many professionals use to view the world. At its best, the sales frame causes managers to take a customer perspective in which they focus on increasing customer satisfaction and developing innovative products that fulfill the needs and wants of consumers. Unfortunately, the sales viewpoint can result in a P. T. Barnum–like focus on hype and gimmicky sales-promotion efforts. At its worst, the sales perspective results in the use of misrepresentation and deceit to foist inferior products onto unsuspecting consumers.

The Production Frame A production focus represents a third lens that managers use to view the world. At its best, it emphasizes efficiency and productivity. The goal is to optimize output by having long production runs with a similar design and minimal changes to reduce costs. When overdone, however, a production mentality results in a loss of focus on the customer's needs and wants. If the market changes and product innovation fails to keep pace, everyone loses. A production focus can also cause managers to search out and use the latest production technology and then find themselves saddled with dramatic overcapacity. Matching production to the market can be overlooked when a production frame dominates a person's view.

The Political Frame Another important frame of reference for decision-making is a political focus. On the positive side, a political perspective allows a manager to use a combination of relationships, compromise, power, and persuasion to bring disparate sides together to get things done. When a person views the world with a political lens, the goal also becomes one of staying in power and building alliances with and rewarding those who either contributed to the process or are likely to contribute in the future. On the negative side, a political perspective can lead to decisions that are based on ideology and favoritism rather than on a focus on getting the job done most effectively.

The Legal Frame A legal frame is another important perspective for managers. At its best, a legal perspective causes executives to carefully consider the relationship of high-stakes decisions to appropriate laws and regulations. Because the U.S. legal system is adversarial in nature, a legal perspective can inculcate a high degree of competitiveness in decision-makers and negotiators. Like the other perspectives, however, an overuse of the legal frame can cause problems. It can lead managers to focus solely on whether a particular action is legal and forget about the effects of the action on consumers and suppliers. As a result, an action can be taken that is legal but that also has extremely negative consequences for public relations. In addition, as we have already seen, the legal frame can result in an extreme competitiveness that alienates potential partners.

The Accounting/Finance Frame When appropriately used, the accounting/finance perspective keeps costs under control and a company on solid financial footing. When improperly used, it focuses attention on achieving short-term profits and stifles innovation. For example, during the 1990s reengineering craze, U.S. corporations dramatically cut personnel. The short-term result was a dramatic increase in productivity and profitability. Unfortunately, over the longer term, the remaining employees were over-worked. As a result, they could not attend to their customers or to research and development. The net effect was a decrease in consumer satisfaction and new product innovations. These effects were particularly strong in the banking industry; as the headline in the November 2000 issue of the American Banking Association's *Banking Journal* stated, "Put Away the Axe: You Can't Cut Your Way to Profitability Anymore."

The Competitive Frame Those who employ a competitive perspective think in terms of military campaigns or sports contests. Managers frequently use military and sports terminology in the hallways of giant corporations, start-ups, and small retailers. On the military side, managers will employ phrases that come directly from the jargon of war: an advertising campaign, launching a new product blitz, battling competitors, biting the bullet, identifying the flagship brand, being under the gun. On the sports side, the phrases and metaphors are almost as numerous. We often hear managers describe themselves or others as running a two-minute drill, dropping the ball, running interference, quarterbacking the team, being a team player, punting on an issue, and scoring a touchdown.

Employing a competitive perspective in the language that we use to communicate our ideas influences how we actually perceive the situation. At its best, a competitive perspective emphasizes the values of teamwork, achievement, and winning victories. Each of these values can make a positive contribution to making high-stakes decisions. At its worst, a competitive orientation can result in a cutthroat mentality that emphasizes secrecy and winning at any cost.

The Ethical Frame The last of our perspectives is an ethical frame of reference. Increasingly, major corporations include a position called the ethics officer. When used appropriately, viewing the world from an ethical perspective will result in long-term benefits. By asking what the "right" thing to do is, managers can avoid talking themselves into taking actions that can lead to short-term profits but long-term disaster. When used improperly, however, the constant questioning of choices that can result from an ethics perspective can slow the decision-making process to a crawl.

Using a multiframe approach is exactly the opposite of our normal tendencies. Most of us recognize that we can't see all aspects of every big decision that we confront and that other sources of information and other perspectives might help us to make better decisions. But as human beings, we love to hear that our opinions are sound, that our inclinations are correct, and that the decisions we are considering are on track. In a word, we yearn for support. Thus, we tend to ask our friends for their opinions when we make big decisions—and our friends tend to be like us. In many instances, they may have exactly the same perspectives that we do. So they are most likely to be convinced by our logic.

We are biased not to ask people who are different from us to evaluate our potential decisions but only to ask people who are similar to us. But different kinds of people are exactly the people whom we should seek out. First, they can help us see things differently and give us some foresight about our potentially disastrous blunders. Second, if they do agree with our decisions, from a totally different perspective, we can be much more confident that we are making the right decision. Thus, the idea of using multiple perspectives means that we must go against our natural tendencies and consciously seek out people with different kinds of insights that can better inform our decision making.

CONSIDER THE TIME FRAME

High-stakes decisions require us to accept trade-offs. It is a rare but wonderful occasion when we can have our cake and eat it, too. We have already discussed one trade-off that managers frequently make—that of freedom versus control. For example, Boeing executives exchanged computerized control of the 757 for giving pilots the freedom to make critical decisions in flight.

The difficulty of present-future trade-offs is compounded by the fact that any single decision can have both good and bad outcomes. These outcomes can occur together or separately, in the present or in the future. This juxtaposition of positive and negative outcomes over time strongly influences both business and personal decisions. Present-future trade-offs can lead to decision myopia, which results from our natural tendency to overweight the present and underweight the future.

SOLVE THE PROBLEM

A Three-Step Process for Solving the Problem

Our approach to solving the problem is to take our philosophy of structured analysis to its logical conclusion. We do this in three steps. The first step is to set our trigger, that is, determine how sticky or how quick it should be. Second, we assess how the evidence that we have been able to accumulate contributes to the probability of success if we act. Finally, we compare our evidence to our trigger setting. If our estimate of the probability of success surpasses the trigger setting, we act; if not, we remain in a status quo position. Through this three-step process, we provide a simple, but powerful, means for making high-stakes decisions. In the sections below, we discuss each step in the solve-the-problem process.

Step 1: Set the Trigger The trigger identifies the amount of evidence that we will require for action. We discussed what it means to set a sticky, a neutral, or a hair trigger, settings based on which type of error is more costly. Thus, we set a sticky trigger when the risk of a needless blunder is substantially higher than the risk of a missed opportunity. An example is the criterion for guilt employed in the criminal justice system in the United States. The instruction that the defendant must be found guilty "beyond a reasonable doubt" means that we have set a sticky trigger because we believe that it is worse to convict an innocent person (a needless blunder) than to let a guilty person go free (a missed opportunity). In contrast, the instructions in civil trials represent a neutral trigger; the jury (the set of decision-makers) is told that a verdict for the plaintiff can be based on a "preponderance of the evidence," which implicitly indicates that the risk of a needless blunder is no greater than the risk of a missed opportunity.

Thus far, we have described the trigger setting in terms of a process of balancing the risk of a missed opportunity versus the risk of a needless blunder. There is a simple way to quantify this balancing process. We recommend the creation of a risk ratio. We produce a risk ratio by dividing the value of the needless blunder by the sum of the values of the missed opportunity and the needless blunder. The risk ratio will range from zero to one because the value of the denominator (the sum of the value of the needless blunder and the value of the missed opportunity) will always be larger than the value of the numerator (the value of the needless blunder). The denominator represents the range of possible outcomes, from the worst to the best. The numerator represents the downside risk if you take the action and are wrong:

$$\text{Risk Ratio} = \frac{\text{the value of a needless blunder}}{\text{the value of a needless blunder} \div \text{the value of a missed opportunity}}$$

Step 2: Assess the Evidence for Acting After setting the trigger, a decision-maker needs to assess the strength of the evidence that the project will succeed. We begin by identifying the milestones that must be achieved for the endeavor to be successful. Then, we multiply the probabilities of each milestone together.

Just as we adjusted the risk ratio when we set the trigger, we must also adjust this probability estimate of success. To do so, we list all of the reasons why action should work and all of the reasons why it may not. This approach borrows ideas that go back at least to Benjamin Franklin when he described how to make complex choices. He suggested beginning the process by taking a sheet of paper and listing the pros and cons of engaging in an action. He next advocated, after contemplation and thought, striking out comparable pros and cons until the process simplified itself and an obvious choice emerged. Our process for solving the problem builds on Franklin's intuitive approach.

Step 3: Compare the Likelihood of Success to the Risk Ratio With the calculations of the risk ratio and the probability of success, we are now in position to make a high-stakes decision. This straightforward step simply entails comparing the two figures. If the likelihood of success is greater than the risk ratio, the evidence points toward action. In contrast, if the likelihood of success is less than the risk ratio, there is a strong indication to not act.

We conclude with a strong suggestion, an admonition, to always identify as many options as possible. One of the most frequent mistakes of high-stakes decision-makers is to focus quickly on a single solution and then act to justify its selection. Once we identify the possible causes of a problem, we should identify as many solutions as possible. By the time we have moved through the SCRIPTS process and have reached the stage of solving the problem, we will quickly eliminate most options.

As master decision-makers, we should strive to employ the three-step process on several alternatives, not just two. In this way, we can be more confident that we haven't eliminated any better solutions.

PRINCIPLES FOR SOLVING THE PROBLEM

1. Move through a three-step sequence to calculate a risk ratio, estimate the probability of success if you act, and choose action if your probability-of-success estimate exceeds your risk ratio.
2. When faced with multiple options for action, select the option that has the largest confidence margin.
3. When monetary considerations dominate, use them first in calculating your risk ratio. Then adjust on the basis of the other SMILES risk dimensions.
4. When nonmonetary considerations dominate, start with a risk ratio of .50. Then use the six SMILES dimensions to adjust it.
5. Calculate the likelihood of success by (1) estimating the probability of achieving each milestone necessary for an action to succeed and by multiplying the probabilities together and (2) adjusting your result by considering the effects of intuition, emotions, perspective, and time.

*SCRIPT*ING THE BREW PUB CASE

The Chicago Brew Pub case provides examples for each of the seven SCRIPTS parameters. First, Jim Bronson and his partner had to **s**earch for signals of threats and opportunities. They recognized that the competitive environment was about to become much more difficult. But Jim also realized that going public would create its own set of problems.

Jim and Chicago Brew Pub did decide to go public. The days just before their initial public offering, however, provided a clear signal of impending difficulties. For 11 days, Jim traveled to 24 states and appeared at 73 meetings. He recognized that this exhausting experience was a harbinger of the difficulties of doubling the number of restaurants for four consecutive years.

The second parameter of tough calls is to find the **c**auses of threats and opportunities. Jim certainly knew what would cause his opportunities to vanish: Only so much money was available to open brew pubs, and unless he acted quickly, the money would dry up. What he failed to ask, however, was why the opportunities appeared in the first place. He knew that the Chicago Brew Pub was the only profitable brew pub chain at the time. Another key question that needed an answer involved whether the market would support a dramatic increase in the number of brew pubs.

Interestingly, Jim told us that neither he nor his partner took any formal steps to evaluate the **r**isks—the third parameter in the SCRIPTS process. One risk factor, however, did impact his decision. He recognized that by going public, they could immediately pay off the $3 million debt that they had taken on to begin a process of franchising restaurants. Thus, on one dimension that was immediately obvious to them, going public would decrease risk.

Next, Jim Bronson and his partner needed to apply **i**ntuition and emotion—the fourth SCRIPTS parameter—when they considered their options. When we turn to intuition, it is critical to control the effects of our emotions on our decisions. Emotions such as greed and fear can short-circuit an otherwise effective process employing intuition. Emotions do have a role, however, in high-stakes decision making. They are always present because of the stress that inevitably accompanies the decision process. The key is to employ the energy that emotions create to help implement the decision.

For the fifth parameter of tough calls, take different **p**erspectives, the two partners took different viewpoints. Paul Springfield took a marketing approach and focused on the issue of how to please customers and grow the business. Jim Bronson took a finance perspective that focused on how to hold down costs and make a profit. Their perspectives for making decisions influenced their interpretation of the evidence and the values that they brought to the decision-making process. As in many successful partnerships, the interplay of individuals taking divergent perspectives resulted in a winning strategy for many years.

Professional training provides people with a particular perspective. The best decision-makers recognize the biases that their own frame of reference creates, so they try to increase the number of perspectives that they use to analyze a problem. By viewing a problem through multiple perceptual lenses, they can select the optimum approach (or approaches) for making tough choices.

The sixth SCRIPTS parameter, consider the **t**ime frame, also applies here. Of particular importance is the question of how long the window of opportunity will remain open. In the brew pub case, it appeared that the chance to go public would disappear in less than six months. As a result, the partners needed to make a major strategic decision relatively quickly—but not immediately. Time pressure can dramatically affect the quality of our decisions. Master decision-makers can still function extremely well even in such stressful situations. In addition, they recognize that even in our fast-paced world, not all of their decisions need to be made quickly. Indeed, some of the worst disasters result from taking a "ready, fire, aim" approach to making tough choices and acting more quickly than is really necessary.

After considering the first six SCRIPTS parameters, decision makers have the information that they need to take the final step, **s**olve the problem, and make the tough call. We provide a three-step procedure for making the final decision. When time is available, the procedure can be more formal and employ explicit calculations. When time is short, the procedure will need to be less formal and seriously abbreviated. Having more time will allow you to make better decisions, but the SCRIPTS process will still facilitate quick decisions in important ways.

The SCRIPTS process can handle both long- and short-fuse decision situations. By first identifying and understanding the problem, you will immediately know whether your problem is a crisis or a strategic decision. If you are in a crisis, you must truncate lengthier procedures and use your experience, training, and intuition to make the tough call. If your problem is strategic, you can afford to use the more formal three-step procedure. By practicing the three-step procedure on numerous problems, you will begin to equip yourself to make crisis decisions. The rational decision-making procedures that we provide can thus be hard-wired so that your reactions become almost reflexive. In essence, you will begin to develop the kind of experienced intuition that will allow you to cope with crises quickly and effectively.

THE CONCLUSION

You may be wondering what happened to Jim Bronson and his partner and Chicago Brew Pub. After making a small public offering of stock, they paid the investment bankers and retired their debt of $3 million, leaving them with $15 million for expansion. They began opening pubs but quickly realized that it was extremely difficult to find suitable properties in the fast-growing industry. Over the next three years, they opened as many pubs as their experience and sound judgment indicated. By 1998, they had 67 locations.

Early in 1999, however, the industry started collapsing as competitor after competitor entered the market. In Dallas, for example, the number of brew pubs increased from 3 to 40 in two-and-a-half years.

We interviewed Janice Kline, who was the chief financial officer (CFO) for a company that owned 80 restaurant franchises. Beginning in 1996, she carefully watched the explosion of brew pubs because they were competitors of her firm. For her, the growth of the brew pub industry also represented an opportunity. As the competing brew pub companies sought to spend the $400 million in new capital that they had to expand, they needed to purchase existing properties. Janice was more than happy to sell her company's worst properties for inflated prices. Big Apple, for instance, paid handsomely for properties because of their investment bankers' requirement to grow. Janice told us that she simply waited for the inevitable collapse.

It didn't take long. Every analyst employed by the investment bankers failed the tough call as each company that had gone public lost money. In the end, every publicly traded brew pub company either went bankrupt or was purchased at distressed prices by another firm, resulting in almost complete devastation for what was an emerging brew pub industry. In early 1999, there were about eight thousand brew pubs. By 2000, the number had been cut in half. Unfortunately, Chicago Brew Pub was caught in the carnage. In 2000, the company went bankrupt.

The experience of Jim Bronson, Paul Springfield, and Chicago Brew Pub illustrates two additional features of tough calls, First, because hard choices are made under conditions of great risk and uncertainty, even the best decision can have bad consequences. Only through the 20–20 vision of hindsight can we criticize the decision of these two young entrepreneurs to go public.

Second, the need to make decisions on fast time can be illusory. After being approached to take his company public, Jim Bronson recognized that he had to take sufficient time to formulate an effective strategy. Because of the pressure of the investment bankers, however, he perceived that his window of opportunity for making the decision would remain open for only a few weeks. In hindsight, however, had he waited longer, his outcomes would have been much better. Indeed, had he waited a couple of years to take his company public, he may have been able to buy up the other failed brew pubs at a fraction of their true value. Considering the time frame is a critical step in making tough calls. It's all too easy to get caught up with the idea that "I need to make a decision NOW!"

Master decision-makers follow a tested process (such as SCRIPTS) for making decisions, they do much of their own research (or have trusted advisors help them with it), they first gain and then learn from experience, they have fun and experiment, and they implement their decisions with precision. When making tough choices, master decision-makers recognize that even the best decisions can turn out poorly. As a result, they focus on the process rather than the outcome. They recognize that whether the outcome turns out well or badly, they must learn from it and then put it behind them. With a top-notch process, the odds are increased that the outcome of the next tough call will be successful.

CHAPTER 18
POWER AND INFLUENCE

THE SCIENCE OF PERSUASION

Robert Cialdini

INFLUENCE WITHOUT AUTHORITY: THE USE OF ALLIANCES, RECIPROCITY, AND EXCHANGE TO ACCOMPLISH WORK

Allan R. Cohen
David L. Bradford

The command-and-control management style, which was more prevalent in the past, went hand in hand with an autocratic approach to using power and influence. In the current work environment, however, people in positions of authority are expected to earn the respect of their subordinates, explain the rationale for their decisions and orders, and focus on commitment rather than control with their employees. Furthermore, many employees work in cross-disciplinary teams—their influence efforts are more often directed horizontally at peers rather than vertically up or down a hierarchy. These changes have resulted in the need for a broader range of skills relating to power and influence. Power is defined as the capacity to influence the behavior of others, whereas influence is the process by which people successfully persuade others to follow their advice, suggestions, or orders.

In "The Science of Persuasion," Robert Cialdini, professor of psychology, examines six pervasive influence tactics that we use to persuade one another and discusses how to resist unwanted persuasion. He documents his extensive research on these tactics, providing numerous examples. Cialdini also considers how culture impacts the use and effectiveness of various tactics.

Allan Cohen and David Bradford, management professors and consultants, perceived early on that many employees have to influence people whom they do not supervise. Their classic article, "Influence Without Authority: The Use of Alliances, Reciprocity, and Exchange to Accomplish Work," explains the different "currencies" we can use to influence others and the reciprocal nature of mutual influence.

THE SCIENCE OF PERSUASION*

Robert Cialdini

SOCIAL PSYCHOLOGY HAS DETERMINED THE BASIC PRINCIPLES THAT GOVERN GETTING TO "YES"

I'd like to let you in on something of great importance to you personally. Have you ever been tricked into saying yes? Ever felt trapped into buying something you didn't really want or contributing to some suspicious-sounding cause? And have you ever wished you understood why you acted in this way so that you could withstand these clever ploys in the future?

Yes? Then clearly this article is just right for you. It contains valuable information on the most powerful psychological pressures that get you to say yes to requests. And it's chock-full of NEW, IMPROVED research showing exactly how and why these techniques work. So don't delay, just settle in and get the information that, after all, you've already agreed you want.

The scientific study of the process of social influence has been under way for well over half a century, beginning in earnest with the propaganda, public information and persuasion programs of World War II. Since that time, numerous social scientists have investigated the ways in which one individual can influence another's attitudes and actions. For the past 30 years, I have participated in that endeavor, concentrating primarily on the major factors that bring about a specific form of behavior change—compliance with a request. Six basic tendencies of human behavior come into play in generating a positive response: reciprocation, consistency, social validation, liking, authority and scarcity. As these six tendencies help to govern our business dealings, our societal involvements and our personal relationships, knowledge of the rules of persuasion can truly be thought of as empowerment.

RECIPROCATION

When the Disabled American Veterans organization mails out requests for contributions, the appeal succeeds only about 18 percent of the time. But when the mailing includes a set of free personalized address labels, the success rate almost doubles, to 35 percent. To understand the effect of the unsolicited gift, we must recognize the reach and power of an essential rule of human conduct: the code of reciprocity.

All societies subscribe to a norm that obligates individuals to repay in kind what they have received. Evolutionary selection pressure has probably entrenched the behavior in social animals such as ourselves. The demands of reciprocity begin to explain the boost in donations to the veterans group. Receiving a gift—unsolicited and perhaps even unwanted—convinced significant numbers of potential donors to return the favor.

---

*Reprinted with permission from *Scientific American*, 14(1) 2004: 76–81. This article was first published by *Scientific American* in February, 2001.

Charitable organizations are far from alone in taking this approach: food stores offer free samples, exterminators offer free in-home inspections, health clubs offer free workouts. Customers are thus exposed to the product or service, but they are also indebted. Consumers are not the only ones who fall under the sway of reciprocity. Pharmaceutical companies spend millions of dollars every year to support medical researchers and to provide gifts to individual physicians—activities that may subtly influence investigators' findings and physicians' recommendations. A 1998 study in the *New England Journal of Medicine* found that only 37 percent of researchers who published conclusions critical of the safety of calcium channel blockers had previously received drug company support. Among those whose conclusions attested to the drugs' safety, however, the number of those who had received free trips, research funding or employment skyrocketed—to 100 percent.

Reciprocity includes more than gifts and favors; it also applies to concessions that people make to one another. For example, assume that you reject my large request, and I then make a concession to you by retreating to a smaller request. You may very well then reciprocate with a concession of your own: agreement with my lesser request. In the mid-1970s my colleagues and I conducted an experiment that clearly illustrates the dynamics of reciprocal concessions. We stopped a random sample of passersby on public walkways and asked them if they would volunteer to chaperone juvenile detention center inmates on a day trip to the zoo. As expected, very few complied, only 17 percent.

For another random sample of passersby, however, we began with an even larger request: to serve as an unpaid counselor at the center for two hours per week for the next two years. Everyone in this second sampling rejected the extreme appeal. At that point we offered them a concession. "If you can't do that," we asked, "would you chaperone a group of juvenile detention center inmates on a day trip to the zoo?" Our concession powerfully stimulated return concessions. The compliance rate nearly tripled, to 50 percent, compared with the straightforward zoo-trip request.

CONSISTENCY

In 1998 Gordon Sinclair, the owner of a well-known Chicago restaurant, was struggling with a problem that afflicts all restaurateurs. Patrons frequently reserve a table but, without notice, fail to appear. Sinclair solved the problem by asking his receptionist to change two words of what she said to callers requesting reservations. The change dropped his no-call, no-show rate from 30 to 10 percent immediately.

The two words were effective because they commissioned the force of another potent human motivation: the desire to be, and to appear, consistent. The receptionist merely modified her request from "Please call if you have to change your plans" to "Will you please call if you have to change your plans?" At that point, she politely paused and waited for a response. The wait was pivotal because it induced customers to fill the pause with a public commitment. And public commitments, even seemingly minor ones, direct future action.

In another example, Joseph Schwarzwald of Bar-Ilan University in Israel and his co-workers nearly doubled monetary contributions for the handicapped in certain neighborhoods. The key factor: Two weeks before asking for contributions, they got residents to sign a petition supporting the handicapped, thus making a public commitment to that same cause.

SOCIAL VALIDATION

On a wintry morning in the late 1960s, a man stopped on a busy New York City sidewalk and gazed skyward for 60 seconds, at nothing in particular. He did so as part of an experiment by City University of New York social psychologists Stanley Milgram, Leonard Bickman, and Lawrence Berkowitz that was designed to find out what effect this action would have on passersby. Most simply detoured or brushed by; 4 percent joined the man in looking up. The experiment was then repeated with a slight change. With the modification, large numbers of pedestrians were induced to come to a halt, crowd together, and peer upward.

The single alteration in the experiment incorporated the phenomenon of social validation. One fundamental way that we decide what to do in a situation is to look to what others are doing or have done there. If many individuals have decided in favor of a particular idea, we are more likely to follow, because we perceive the idea to be more correct, more valid.

Milgram, Bickman, and Berkowitz introduced the influence of social validation into their street experiment simply by having five men rather than one look up at nothing. With the larger initial set of upward gazers, the percentage of New Yorkers who followed suit more than quadrupled, to 18 percent. Bigger initial sets of planted up-lookers generated an even greater response: a starter group of 15 led 40 percent of passersby to join in, nearly stopping traffic within one minute.

Taking advantage of social validation, requesters can stimulate our compliance by demonstrating (or merely implying) that others just like us have already complied. For example, a study found that a fund raiser who showed homeowners a list of neighbors who had donated to a local charity significantly increased the frequency of contributions; the longer the list, the greater the effect. Marketers, therefore, go out of their way to inform us when their product is the largest-selling or fastest-growing of its kind, and television commercials regularly depict crowds rushing to stores to acquire the advertised item.

Less obvious, however, are the circumstances under which social validation can backfire to produce the opposite of what a requester intends. An example is the understandable but potentially misguided tendency of health educators to call attention to a problem by depicting it as regrettably frequent. Information campaigns stress that alcohol and drug use is intolerably high, that adolescent suicide rates are alarming, and that polluters are spoiling the environment. Although the claims are both true and well intentioned, the creators of these campaigns have missed something basic about the compliance process. Within the statement "Look at all the people who are doing this undesirable thing" lurks the powerful and undercutting message "Look at all the people who are doing this undesirable thing." Research shows that, as a consequence, many such programs boomerang, generating even more of the undesirable behavior.

For instance, a suicide intervention program administered to New Jersey teenagers informed them of the high number of teenage suicides. Health researcher David

Shaffer and his colleagues at Columbia University found that participants became significantly more likely to see suicide as a potential solution to their problems. Of greater effectiveness are campaigns that honestly depict the unwanted activity as damaging despite the fact that relatively few individuals engage in it.

LIKING

"Affinity," "rapport," and "affection" all describe a feeling of connection between people. But the simple word "liking" most faithfully captures the concept and has become the standard designation in the social science literature. People prefer to say yes to those they like. Consider the worldwide success of the Tupperware Corporation and its "home party" program. Through the in-home demonstration get-together, the company arranges for its customers to buy from a liked friend, the host, rather than from an unknown salesperson. So favorable has been the effect on proceeds that, according to company literature, a Tupperware party begins somewhere in the world every two seconds. In fact, 75 percent of all Tupperware parties today occur outside the individualistic U.S., in countries where group social bonding is even more important than it is here.

Of course, most commercial transactions take place beyond the homes of friends. Under these much more typical circumstances, those who wish to commission the power of liking employ tactics clustered around certain factors that research has shown to work.

Physical attractiveness can be such a tool. In a 1993 study conducted by Peter H. Reingen of Arizona State University and Jerome B. Kernan, now at George Mason University, good-looking fundraisers for the American Heart Association generated nearly twice as many donations (42 versus 23 percent) as did other requesters. In the 1970s researchers Michael G. Efran and E.W.J. Patterson of the University of Toronto found that voters in Canadian federal elections gave physically attractive candidates several times as many votes as unattractive ones. Yet such voters insisted that their choices would never be influenced by something as superficial as appearance.

Similarity also can expedite the development of rapport. Salespeople often search for, or outright fabricate, a connection between themselves and their customers: "Well, no kidding, you're from Minneapolis? I went to school in Minnesota!" Fund raisers do the same, with good results. In 1994 psychologists R. Kelly Aune of the University of Hawaii at Manoa and Michael D. Basil of the University of Denver reported research in which solicitors canvassed a college campus asking for contributions to a charity. When the phrase "I'm a student, too" was added to the requests, the amount of the donations more than doubled.

Compliments also stimulate liking, and direct salespeople are trained in the use of praise. Indeed, even inaccurate praise may be effective. Research at the University of North Carolina at Chapel Hill found that compliments produced just as much liking for the flatterer when they were untrue as when they were genuine.

Cooperation is another factor that has been shown to enhance positive feelings and behavior. Salespeople, for example, often strive to be perceived by their prospects as cooperating partners. Automobile sales managers frequently cast themselves as "villains" so the salesperson can "do battle" on the customer's behalf. The gambit naturally leads to a desirable form of liking by the customer for the salesperson, which promotes sales.

AUTHORITY

Recall the man who used social validation to get large numbers of passersby to stop and stare at the sky. He might achieve the opposite effect and spur stationary strangers into motion by assuming the mantle of authority. In 1955, University of Texas at Austin researchers Monroe Lefkowitz, Robert R. Blake, and Jane S. Mouton discovered that a man could increase by 350 percent the number of pedestrians who would follow him across the street against the light by changing one simple thing. Instead of casual dress, he donned markers of authority: a suit and tie.

Those touting their experience, expertise or scientific credentials may be trying to harness the power of authority: "Babies are our business, our only business," "Four out of five doctors recommend," and so on. There is nothing wrong with such claims when they are real, because we usually want the opinions of true authorities. Their insights help us choose quickly and well.

The problem comes when we are subjected to phony claims. If we fail to think, as is often the case when confronted by authority symbols, we can easily be steered in the wrong direction by ersatz experts—those who merely present the aura of legitimacy. That Texas jaywalker in a suit and tie was no more an authority on crossing the street than the rest of the pedestrians who nonetheless followed him. A highly successful ad campaign in the 1970s featured actor Robert Young proclaiming the health benefits of decaffeinated coffee. Young seems to have been able to dispense this medical opinion effectively because he represented, at the time, the nation's most famous physician. That Marcus Welby, M.D., was only a character on a TV show was less important than the appearance of authority.

SCARCITY

While at Florida State University in the 1970s, psychologist Stephen West noted an odd occurrence after surveying students about the campus cafeteria cuisine: ratings of the food rose significantly from the week before, even though there had been no change in the menu, food quality, or preparation. Instead the shift resulted from an announcement that because of a fire, cafeteria meals would not be available for several weeks.

This account highlights the effect of perceived scarcity on human judgment. A great deal of evidence shows that items and opportunities become more desirable to us as they become less available. For this reason, marketers trumpet the unique benefits or the one-of-a-kind character of their offerings. It is also for this reason that they consistently engage in "limited time only" promotions or put us into competition with one another using sales campaigns based on "limited supply."

Less widely recognized is that scarcity affects the value not only of commodities but of information as well. Information that is exclusive is more persuasive. Take as evidence the dissertation data of a former student of mine, Amram Knishinsky, who owned a company that imported beef into the United States and sold it to supermarkets. To examine the effects of scarcity and exclusivity on compliance, he instructed his telephone salespeople to call a randomly selected sample of customers and to make a standard request of them to purchase beef. He also instructed the salespeople to do the same with a second random sample of customers but to add that a shortage of

Australian beef was anticipated, which was true, because of certain weather conditions there. The added information that Australian beef was soon to be scarce more than doubled purchases.

Finally, he had his staff call a third sample of customers, to tell them (1) about the impending shortage of Australian beef and (2) that this information came from his company's exclusive sources in the Australian national weather service. These customers increased their orders by more than 600 percent. They were influenced by a scarcity double-whammy: not only was the beef scarce, but the information that the beef was scarce was itself scarce.

INFLUENCE ACROSS CULTURES

Do the six key factors in the social influence process operate similarly across national boundaries? Yes, but with a wrinkle. The citizens of the world are human, after all, and susceptible to the fundamental tendencies that characterize all members of our species. Cultural norms, traditions and experiences can, however, modify the weight that is brought to bear by each factor.

Consider the results of a report published in 2000 by Stanford University's Michael W. Morris, Joel M. Podolny and Sheira Ariel, who studied employees of Citibank, a multinational financial corporation. The researchers selected four societies for examination: the United States, China, Spain and Germany. They surveyed Citibank branches within each country and measured employees' willingness to comply voluntarily with a request from a co-worker for assistance with a task. Although multiple key factors could come into play, the main reason employees felt obligated to comply differed in the four nations. Each of these reasons incorporated a different fundamental principle of social influence.

Employees in the United States took a reciprocation-based approach to the decision to comply. They asked the question, "What has this person done for me recently?" and felt obligated to volunteer if they owed the requester a favor. Chinese employees responded primarily to authority, in the form of loyalties to those of high status within their small group. They asked, "Is this requester connected to someone in my unit, especially someone who is high ranking?" If the answer was yes, they felt required to yield.

Spanish Citibank personnel based the decision to comply mostly on liking/friendship. They were willing to help on the basis of friendship norms that encourage faithfulness to one's friends, regardless of position or status. They asked, "Is this requester connected to my friends?" If the answer was yes, they were especially likely to want to comply.

German employees were most compelled by consistency, offering assistance in order to be consistent with the rules of the organization. They decided whether to comply by asking, "According to official regulations and categories, am I supposed to assist this requester?" If the answer was yes, they felt a strong obligation to grant the request.

In sum, although all human societies seem to play by the same set of influence rules, the weights assigned to the various rules can differ across cultures. Persuasive appeals to audiences in distinct cultures need to take such differences into account.

KNOWLEDGE IS POWER

I think it noteworthy that many of the data presented in this article have come from studies of the practices of persuasion professionals—the marketers, advertisers, salespeople, fund raisers and their comrades whose financial well-being depends on their ability to get others to say yes. A kind of natural selection operates on these people, as those who use unsuccessful tactics soon go out of business. In contrast, those using procedures that work well will survive, flourish and pass on these successful strategies. Thus, over time, the most effective principles of social influence will appear in the repertoires of long-standing persuasion professions. My own work indicates that those principles embody the six fundamental human tendencies examined in this article: reciprocation, consistency, social validation, liking, authority, and scarcity.

From an evolutionary point of view, each of the behaviors presented would appear to have been selected for in animals, such as ourselves, that must find the best ways to survive while living in social groups. And in the vast majority of cases, these principles counsel us correctly. It usually makes great sense to repay favors, behave consistently, follow the lead of similar others, favor the requests of those we like, heed legitimate authorities and value scarce resources. Consequently, influence agents who use these principles honestly do us a favor. If an advertising agency, for instance, focused an ad campaign on the genuine weight of authoritative, scientific evidence favoring its client's headache product, all the right people would profit—the agency, the manufacturer and the audience. Not so, however, if the agency, finding no particular scientific merit in the pain reliever, "smuggles" the authority principle into the situation through ads featuring actors wearing white lab coats.

Are we then doomed to be helplessly manipulated by these principles? No. By understanding persuasion techniques, we can begin to recognize strategies and thus truly analyze requests and offerings. Our task must be to hold persuasion professionals accountable for the use of the six powerful motivators and to purchase their products and services, support their political proposals or donate to their causes only when they have acted truthfully in the process.

If we make this vital distinction in our dealings with practitioners of the persuasive arts, we will rarely allow ourselves to be tricked into assent. Instead we will give ourselves a much better option: To be informed into saying yes. Moreover, as long as we apply the same distinction to our own attempts to influence others, we can legitimately commission the six principles. In seeking to persuade by pointing to the presence of genuine expertise, growing social validation, pertinent commitments or real opportunities for cooperation, and so on, we serve the interests of both parties and enhance the quality of the social fabric in the bargain.

Surely, someone with your splendid intellect can see the unique benefits of this article. And because you look like a helpful person who would want to share such useful information, let me make a request. Would you buy this [book] for 10 of your friends? Well, if you can't do that, would you show it to just one friend? Wait, don't answer yet. Because I genuinely like you, I'm going to throw in—at absolutely no extra cost—a set of references that you can consult to learn more about this little-known topic.

Now, will you voice your commitment to help? . . . Please recognize that I am pausing politely here. But while I'm waiting, I want you to feel totally assured that many others just like you will certainly consent. And I love that shirt you're wearing.

PERSUASIVE TECHNIQUES

FAST FACTS

1. Six basic tendencies of human behavior come into play in generating a positive response to a request: reciprocation, consistency, social validation, liking, authority, and scarcity.
2. The six key factors are at work in various areas around the world as well, but cultural norms and traditions can modify the weight brought to bear by each factor.
3. Knowledge of these tendencies can empower consumers and citizens to make better-informed decisions about, for example, whether to purchase a product or vote for legislation.

Further Reading

G. Richard Shell. *Bargaining for Advantage.* Viking, 1999

A. J. Pratkanis and E. Aronson. *Age of Propaganda: The Everyday Use and Abuse of Persuasion.* Revised edition. W. H. Freeman and Company, 2001.

Influence: Science and Practice. Fourth edition. Robert B. Cialdini. Allyn & Bacon, 2001.

Robert Levine. *The Power of Persuasion: How We're Bought and Sold.* John Wiley & Sons, 2003.

For regularly updated information about the social influence process, visit http://www. influenceatwork.com

INFLUENCE WITHOUT AUTHORITY: THE USE OF ALLIANCES, RECIPROCITY, AND EXCHANGE TO ACCOMPLISH WORK*

Allan R. Cohen
David L. Bradford

Bill Heatton is the director of research at a $250 million division of a large west coast company. The division manufactures exotic telecommunications components and has many technical advancements to its credit. During the past several years, however, the division's performance has been spotty at best; multimillion dollar losses have been experienced in some years despite many efforts to make the division more profitable. Several large contracts have resulted in major financial losses, and in each instance the various parts of the division blamed the others for the problems. Listen to Bill's frustration as he talks about his efforts to influence Ted, a colleague who is marketing director, and Roland, the program manager who reports to Ted.

*Reprinted with permission of Elsevier, from *Organizational Dynamics*, 17(3), Winter 1989: 5–17.

Another program is about to come through. Roland is a nice guy, but he knows nothing and never will. He was responsible for our last big loss, and now he's in charge of this one. I've tried to convince Ted, his boss, to get Roland off the program, but I get nowhere. Although Ted doesn't argue that Roland is capable, he doesn't act to find someone else. Instead, he comes to me with worries about my area.

I decided to respond by changing my staffing plan, assigning to Roland's program the people they wanted. I had to override my staff's best judgment about who should be assigned. Yet I'm not getting needed progress reports from Roland, and he's never available for planning. I get little argument from him, but there's no action to correct the problem. That's bad because I'm responding but not getting any response.

There's no way to resolve this. If they disagree, that's it. I could go to a tit-for-tat strategy, saying that if they don't do what I want, we'll get even with them next time. But I don't know how to do that without hurting the organization, which would feel worse than getting even!

Ted, Roland's boss, is so much better than his predecessor that I hate to ask that he be removed. We could go together to our boss, the general manager, but I'm very reluctant to do that. You've failed in a matrix organization if you have to go to your boss. I have to try hard because I'd look bad if I had to throw it in his lap.

Meanwhile, I'm being forceful, but I'm afraid it's in a destructive way. I don't want to wait until the program has failed to be told it was all my fault.

Bill is clearly angry and frustrated, leading him to behave in ways that he does not feel good about. Like other managers who very much want to influence an uncooperative co-worker whom they cannot control, Bill has begun to think of the intransigent employee as the enemy. Bill's anger is narrowing his sense of what is possible; he fantasizes revenge but is too dedicated to the organization to actually harm it. He is genuinely stuck.

Organizational members who want to make things happen often find themselves in this position. Irrespective of whether they are staff or line employees, professionals or managers, they find it increasingly necessary to influence colleagues and superiors. These critical others control needed resources, possess required information, set priorities on important activities, and have to agree and cooperate if plans are to be implemented. They cannot be ordered around because they are under another area's control and can legitimately say no because they have many other valid priorities. They respond only when they choose to. Despite the clear need and appropriateness of what is being asked for (certainly as seen by the person who is making the request), compliance may not be forthcoming.

All of this places a large burden on organizational members, who are expected not only to take initiatives but also to respond intelligently to requests made of them by others. Judgment is needed to sort out the value of the many requests made of anyone who has valuable resources to contribute. As Robert Kaplan argued in his article "Trade Routes: The Manager's Network of Relationships" (*Organizational Dynamics,* Spring 1984), managers must now develop the organizational equivalent of "trade routes" to get things done. Informal networks of mutual influence are needed. In her book, *The Change Masters* (Simon & Schuster, 1983), Rosabeth Moss Kanter showed that developing and implementing all kinds of innovations require coalitions to be built to shape and support new ways of doing business.

A key current problem, then, is finding ways to develop mutual influence without the formal authority to command. A peer cannot "order" a colleague to change priorities, modify an approach, or implement a grand new idea. A staff member cannot "command" his or her supervisor to back a proposal, fight top management for greater resources, or allow more autonomy. Even Bill Heatton, in dealing with Roland (who was a level below him in the hierarchy but in another department), could not dictate that Roland provide the progress reports that Bill so desperately wanted.

EXCHANGE AND THE LAW OF RECIPROCITY

The way influence is acquired without formal authority is through the "law of reciprocity"—the almost universal belief that people should be paid back for what they do, that one good (or bad) deed deserves another. This belief is held by people in primitive and not-so-primitive societies all around the world, and it serves as the grease that allows the organizational wheel to turn smoothly. Because people expect that their actions will be paid back in one form or another, influence is possible.

In the case of Bill Heatton, his inability to get what he wanted from Roland and Ted stemmed from his failure to understand fully how reciprocity works in organizations. He therefore was unable to set up mutually beneficial exchanges. Bill believed that he had gone out of his way to help the marketing department by changing his staffing patterns, and he expected Roland to reciprocate by providing regular progress reports. When Roland failed to provide the reports, Bill believed that Ted was obligated to remove Roland from the project. When Ted did not respond, Bill became angry and wanted to retaliate. Thus, Bill recognized the appropriateness of exchange in making organizations work. However, he did not understand how exchange operates.

Before exploring in detail how exchange can work in dealing with colleagues and superiors, it is important to recognize that reciprocity is the basic principle behind all organizational transactions. For example, the basic employment contract is an exchange ("an honest day's work for an honest day's pay"). Even work that is above and beyond what is formally required involves exchange. The person who helps out may not necessarily get (or expect) immediate payment for the extra effort requested, but some eventual compensation is expected.

Think of the likely irritation an employee would feel if his or her boss asked him or her to work through several weekends, never so much as said thanks, and then claimed credit for the extra work. The employee might not say anything the first time this happened, expecting or hoping that the boss would make it up somehow. However, if the effort were never acknowledged in any way, the employee, like most people, would feel that something important had been violated.

Exchanges enable people to handle the give-and-take of working together without strong feelings of injustice arising. They are especially important during periods of rapid change because the number of requests that go far beyond the routine tends to escalate. In those situations, exchanges become less predictable, more free-floating, and spontaneous. Nevertheless, people still expect that somehow or other, sooner or later, they will be (roughly) equally compensated for the acts they do above and beyond those that are covered by the formal exchange agreements in their job. Consequently, some kind of "currency" equivalent needs to be worked out, implicitly if not explicitly, to keep the parties in the exchange feeling fairly treated.

CURRENCIES: THE SOURCE OF INFLUENCE

If the basis of organizational influence depends on mutually satisfactory exchanges, then people are influential only insofar as they can offer something that others need. Thus, power comes from the ability to meet others' needs.

A useful way to think of how the process of exchange actually works in organizations is to use the metaphor of "currencies." This metaphor provides a powerful way to conceptualize what is important to the influencer and the person to be influenced. Just as many types of currencies are traded in the world financial market, many types are "traded" in organizational life. Too often people think only of money or promotion and status. Those "currencies," however, usually are available only to a manager in dealing with his or her employees. Peers who want to influence colleagues or employees who want to influence their supervisors often feel helpless. They need to recognize that many types of payments exist, broadening the range of what can be exchanged.

Some major currencies that are commonly valued and traded in organizations are listed in Exhibit 1. Although not exhaustive, the list makes evident that a person does not have to be at the top of an organization or have hands on the formal levers of power to command multiple resources that others may value.

Part of the usefulness of currencies comes from their flexibility. For example, there are many ways to express gratitude and to give assistance. A manager who most values the currency of appreciation could be paid through verbal thanks, praise, a public statement at a meeting, informal comments to his peers, and/or a note to her boss. However, the same note of thanks seen by one person as a sign of appreciation may be seen by another person as an attempt to brownnose or by a third person as a cheap way to try to repay extensive favors and service. Thus, currencies have value not in some abstract sense but as defined by the receiver.

Although we have stressed the interactive nature of exchange, "payments" do not always have to be made by the other person. They can be self-generated to fit beliefs about being virtuous, benevolent, or committed to the organization's welfare. Someone may respond to another person's request because it reinforces cherished values, a sense of identity, or feelings of self-worth. The exchange is interpersonally stimulated because the one who wants influence has set up conditions that allow this kind of self-payment to occur by asking for cooperation to accomplish organizational goals. However, the person who responds because "it is the right thing to do" and who feels good about being the "kind of person who does not act out of narrow self-interest" is printing currency (virtue) that is self-satisfying.

Of course, the five categories of currencies listed in Exhibit 1 are not mutually exclusive. When the demand from the other person is high, people are likely to pay in several currencies across several categories. They may, for example, stress the organizational value of their request, promise to return the favor at a later time, imply that it will increase the other's prestige in the organization, and express their appreciation.

EXHIBIT 1 Commonly Traded Organizational Currencies

Inspiration-related Currencies	
Vision	Being involved in a task that has larger significance for the unit, organization, customers, or society.
Excellence	Having a chance to do important things really well.
Moral/Ethical Correctness	Doing what is "right" by a higher standard than efficiency.
Task-related Currencies	
Resources	Lending or giving money, budget increases, personnel, space, and so forth.
Assistance	Helping with existing projects or undertaking unwanted tasks.
Cooperation	Giving task support, providing quicker response time, approving a project, or aiding implementation.
Information	Providing organizational as well as technical knowledge.
Position-related Currencies	
Advancement	Giving a task or assignment that can aid in promotion.
Recognition	Acknowledging effort, accomplishment, or abilities.
Visibility	Providing a chance to be known by higher-ups or significant others in the organization.
Reputation	Enhancing the way a person is seen.
Importance/Insiderness	Offering a sense of importance, of "belonging."
Network/Contacts	Providing opportunities for linking with others.
Relationship-related Currencies	
Acceptance/Inclusion	Providing closeness and friendship.
Personal support	Giving personal and emotional backing.
Understanding	Listening to others' concerns and issues.
Personal-related Currencies	
Self-Concept	Affirming one's values, self-esteem, and identity.
Challenge/Learning	Sharing tasks that increase skills and abilities.
Ownership/Involvement	Letting others have ownership and influence.
Gratitude	Expressing appreciation or indebtedness.

ESTABLISHING EXCHANGE RATES

What does it take to pay back in a currency that the other party in an exchange will perceive as equivalent? In impersonal markets, because everything is translated into a common monetary currency, it generally is easy to say what a fair payment is. Does a ton of steel equal a case of golfclubs? By translating both into dollar equivalents, a satisfactory deal can be worked out.

In interpersonal exchanges, however, the process becomes a bit more complicated. Just how does someone repay another person's willingness to help finish a report? Is a simple thank-you enough? Does it also require the recipient to say something nice about the helper to his or her boss? Whose standard of fairness should be used? What if one person's idea of fair repayment is very different from the other's?

Because of the natural differences in the way two parties can interpret the same activity, establishing exchanges that both parties will perceive as equitable can be problematic. Thus, it is critical to understand what is important to the person to be influenced. Without a clear understanding of what that person experiences and values, it will be extremely difficult for anyone to thread a path through the minefield of creating mutually satisfactory exchanges.

Fortunately, the calibration of equivalent exchanges in the interpersonal and organizational worlds is facilitated by the fact that approximations will do in most cases. Occasionally, organizational members know exactly what they want in return for favors of help, but more often they will settle for very rough equivalents (providing that there is reasonable goodwill).

THE PROCESS OF EXCHANGE

To make the exchange process effective, the influencer needs to (1) think about the person to be influenced as a potential ally, not an adversary; (2) know the world of the potential ally, including the pressures as well as the person's needs and goals; (3) be aware of key goals and available resources that may be valued by the potential ally; and (4) understand the exchange transaction itself so that win-win outcomes are achieved. Each of these factors is discussed below.

POTENTIAL ALLY, NOT ADVERSARY

A key to influence is thinking of the other person as a potential ally. Just as many contemporary organizations have discovered the importance of creating strategic alliances with suppliers and customers, employees who want influence within the organization need to create internal allies. Even though each party in an alliance continues to have freedom to pursue its own interests, the goal is to find areas of mutual benefit and develop trusting, sustainable relationships. Similarly, each person whose cooperation is needed inside the organization is a potential ally. Each still has self-interests to pursue, but those self-interests do not preclude searching for and building areas of mutual benefit.

Seeing other organizational members as potential allies decreases the chance that adversarial relationships will develop—an all-too-frequent result (as in the case of Bill Heatton) when the eager influencer does not quickly get the assistance of cooperation needed. Assuming that even a difficult person is a potential ally makes it easier to understand that person's world and thereby discover what that person values and needs.

THE POTENTIAL ALLY'S WORLD

We have stressed the importance of knowing the world of the potential ally. Without awareness of what the ally needs (what currencies are valued), attempts to influence that person can only be haphazard. Although this conclusion may seem self-evident, it is remarkable how often people attempt to influence without adequate information about what is important to the potential ally. Instead, they are driven by their own definition of "what should be" and "what is right" when they should be seeing the world from the other person's perspective.

For example, Bill Heatton never thought about the costs to Ted of removing Roland from the project. Did Ted believe he could coach Roland to perform better on this project? Did Ted even agree that Roland had done a poor job on the previous project, or did Ted think Roland had been hampered by other departments' shortcomings? Bill just did not know.

Several factors can keep the influencer from seeing the potential ally clearly. As with Bill Heatton, the frustration of meeting resistance from a potential ally can get in the way of really understanding the other person's world. The desire to influence is so strong that only the need for cooperation is visible to the influencer. As a result of not being understood, the potential ally digs in, making the influencer repeat an inappropriate strategy or back off in frustration.

When a potential ally's behavior is not understandable ("Why won't Roland send the needed progress reports?"), the influencer tends to stereotype that person. If early attempts to influence do not work, the influencer is tempted to write the person off as negative, stubborn, selfish, or "just another bean counter/whiz kid/sales-type" or whatever pejorative label is used in that organizational culture to dismiss those organizational members who are different.

Although some stereotypes may have a grain of truth, they generally conceal more than they reveal. The actuary who understands that judgment, not just numbers, is needed to make decisions disappears as an individual when the stereotype of "impersonal, detached number machine" is the filter through which he or she is seen. Once the stereotype is applied, the frustrated influencer is no longer likely to see what currencies that particular potential ally actually values.

Sometimes, the lack of clear understanding about a potential ally stems from the influencer's failure to appreciate the organizational forces acting on the potential ally. To a great extent, a person's behavior is a result of the situation in which that person works (and not just his or her personality). Potential allies are embedded in an organizational culture that shapes their interests and responses. For example, one of the key determinants of anyone's behavior is likely to be the way the person's performance is measured and rewarded. In many instances, what is mistaken for personal orneriness is merely the result of the person's doing something that will be seen as good performance in his or her function.

The salesperson who is furious because the plant manager resists changing priorities for a rush order may not realize that part of the plant manager's bonus depends on holding unit costs down—a task made easier with long production runs. The plant manager's resistance does not necessarily reflect his or her inability to be flexible or lack of concern about pleasing customers or about the company's overall success.

Other organizational forces that can affect the potential ally's behavior include the daily time demands on that person's position; the amount of contact the person has with customers, suppliers, and other outsiders; the organization's information flow (or lack of it); the style of the potential ally's boss; the belief and assumptions held by that person's co-workers; and so forth. Although some of these factors cannot be changed by the influencer, understanding them can be useful in figuring out how to frame and time requests. It also helps the influencer resist the temptation to stereotype the noncooperator.

SELF-AWARENESS OF THE INFLUENCER

Unfortunately, people desiring influence are not always aware of precisely what they want. Often their requests contain a cluster of needs (a certain product, arranged in a certain way, delivered at a specified time). They fail to think through which aspects are more important and which can be jettisoned if necessary. Did Bill Heatton want Roland removed, or did he want the project effectively managed? Did he want overt concessions from Ted, or did he want better progress reports?

Further, there is a tendency to confuse and intermingle the desired end goal with the means of accomplishing it, leading to too many battles over the wrong things. In *The Change Masters*, Kanter reported that successful influencers in organizations were those who never lost sight of the ultimate objective but were willing to be flexible about means.

Sometimes influencers underestimate the range of currencies available for use. They may assume, for example, that just because they are low in the organization they have nothing that others want. Employees who want to influence their boss are especially likely not to realize all of the supervisor's needs that they can fulfill. They become so caught up with their feelings of powerlessness that they fail to see the many ways they can generate valuable currencies.

In other instances, influencers fail to be aware of their preferred style of interaction and its fit with the potential ally's preferred style. Everyone has a way of relating to others to get work done. However, like the fish who is unaware of the water, many people are oblivious of their own style of interaction or see it as the only way to be. Yet interaction style can cause problems with potential allies who are different.

For example, does the influencer tend to socialize first and work later? If so, that style of interaction will distress a potential ally who likes to dig right in to solve the problem at hand and only afterward chat about sports, family, or office politics. Does the potential ally want to be approached with answers, not problems? If so, a tendency to start influence attempts with open-ended, exploratory problem solving can lead to rejection despite good intentions.

NATURE OF THE EXCHANGE TRANSACTION

Many of the problems that occur in the actual exchange negotiation have their roots in the failure to deal adequately with the first three factors outlined above. Failure to treat other people as potential allies, to understand a potential ally's world, and to be self-aware are all factors that interfere with successful exchange. In addition, some special problems commonly arise when both parties are in the process of working out a mutually satisfactory exchange agreement.

- ***Not knowing how to use reciprocity.*** Using reciprocity requires stating needs clearly without "crying wolf," being aware of the needs of an ally without being manipulative, and seeking mutual gain rather than playing "winner takes all." One trap that Bill Heatton fell into was not being able to "close on the exchange." That is, he assumed that if he acted in good faith and did his part, others would automatically reciprocate. Part of his failure was not understanding the other party's world; another part was not being able to negotiate cleanly with Ted about what each of them wanted. It is not even clear that Ted realized Bill was altering his organization as per Ted's requests, that Ted got what he wanted, or that Ted knew Bill intended an exchange of responses.
- ***Preferring to be right rather than effective.*** This problem is especially endemic to professionals of all kinds. Because of their dedication to the "truth" (as their profession defines it), they stubbornly stick to their one right way when trying to

line up potential allies instead of thinking about what will work given the audience and conditions. Organizational members with strong technical backgrounds often chorus the equivalent of "I'll be damned if I'm going to sell out and become a phone salesman, trying to get by on a shoeshine and smile." The failure to accommodate to the potential ally's needs and desires often kills otherwise sound ideas.

- ***Overusing what has been successful.*** When people find that a certain approach is effective in many situations, they often begin to use it in places where it does not fit. By overusing the approach, they block more appropriate methods. Just as a weight lifter becomes muscle-bound from overdeveloping particular muscles at the expense of others, people who have been reasonably successful at influencing other people can diminish that ability by overusing the same technique.

For example, John Brucker, the human resources director at a medium-size company, often cultivated support for new programs by taking people out to fancy restaurants for an evening of fine food and wine. He genuinely derived pleasure from entertaining, but at the same time he created subtle obligations. One time, a new program he wanted to introduce required the agreement of William Adams, head of engineering. Adams, an old-timer, perceived Brucker's proposal as an unnecessary frill, mainly because he did not perceive the real benefits to the overall organization. Brucker responded to Adams's negative comments as he always did in such cases—by becoming more friendly and insisting that they get together for dinner soon. After several of these invitations, Adams became furious. Insulted by what he considered to be Brucker's attempts to buy him off, he fought even harder to kill the proposal. Not only did the program die, but Brucker lost all possibility of influencing Adams in the future. Adams saw Brucker's attempts at socializing as a sleazy and crude way of trying to soften him up. For his part, Brucker was totally puzzled by Adams's frostiness and assumed that he was against all progress. He never realized that Adams had a deep sense of integrity and a real commitment to the good of the organization. Thus, Brucker lost his opportunity to sell a program that, ironically, Adams would have found valuable had it been implemented.

As the case above illustrates, a broad repertoire of influence approaches is needed in modern organizations. Johnny-one-notes soon fall flat.

THE ROLE OF RELATIONSHIPS

All of the preceding discussion needs to be conditioned by one important variable: the nature of the relationship between both parties. The greater the extent to which the influencer has worked with the potential ally and created trust, the easier the exchange process will be. Each party will know the other's desired currencies and situational pressures, and each will have developed a mutually productive interaction style. With trust, less energy will be spent on figuring out the intentions of the ally, and there will be less suspicion about when and how the payback will occur.

A poor relationship (based on previous interactions, on the reputation each party has in the organization, and/or on stereotypes and animosities between the functions or departments that each party represents) will impede an otherwise easy exchange. Distrust of the goodwill, veracity, or reliability of the influencer can lead to the demand for "no credit; cash up front," which constrains the flexibility of both parties.

The nature of the interaction during the influencer process also affects the nature of the relationship between the influencer and the other party. The way that John Brucker attempted to relate to William Adams not only did not work but also irreparably damaged any future exchanges between them.

Few transactions within organizations are one-time deals. (Who knows when the other person may be needed again or even who may be working for him or her in the future?) Thus, in most exchange situations two outcomes matter: success in achieving task goals and success in improving the relationship so that the next interaction will be even more productive. Too often, people who want to be influential focus only on the task and act as if there is no tomorrow. Although both task accomplishment and an improved relationship cannot always be realized at the same time, on some occasions the latter can be more important than the former. Winning the battle but losing the war is an expensive outcome.

INCONVERTIBLE CURRENCIES

We have spelled out ways organizational members operate to gain influence for achieving organizational goals. By effectively using exchange, organizational members can achieve their goals and at the same time help others achieve theirs. Exchange permits organizational members to be assertive without being antagonistic by keeping mutual benefit a central outcome.

In many cases, organizational members fail to acquire desired influence because they do not use all of their potential power. However, they sometimes fail because not all situations are amenable to even the best efforts at influencing. Not everything can be translated into compatible currencies. If there are fundamental differences in what is valued by two parties, it may not be possible to find common ground, as illustrated in the example below.

The founder and chairman of a high-technology company and the president he had hired five years previously were constantly displeased with one another. The president was committed to creating maximum shareholder value, the currency he valued most as a result of his MBA training, his position, and his temperament. Accordingly, he had concluded that the company was in a perfect position to cash in by squeezing expenses to maximize profits and going public. He could see that the company's product line of exotic components was within a few years of saturating its market and would require massive, risky investment to move to sophisticated end-user products.

The president could not influence the chairman to adopt this direction, however, because the chairman valued a totally different currency, the fun of technological challenge. An independently wealthy man, the chairman had no interest in realizing the $10 million or so he would get if the company maximized profits by cutting research and selling out. He wanted a place to test his intuitive, creative research hunches, not a source of income.

Thus, the president's and chairman's currencies were not convertible into one another at an acceptable exchange rate. After they explored various possibilities but failed to find common ground, they mutually agreed that the president should leave—on good terms and only after a more compatible replacement could be found. Although this example acknowledges that influence through alliance, currency conversion, and exchange is not always possible, it is hard to be certain that any situation is hopeless until the person desiring influence has fully applied all of the diagnostic and interpersonal skills we have described.

Influence is enhanced by using the model of strategic alliances to engage in mutually beneficial exchanges with potential allies. Even though it is not always possible to be successful, the chances of achieving success can be greatly increased. In a period of rapid competitive, technological, regulative, and consumer change, individuals and their organizations need all the help they can get.

CHAPTER 19
EMPOWERMENT AND COACHING

WHY TREATING PEOPLE RIGHT PAYS OFF

Edward E. Lawler III

MANAGEMENT DIALOGUES: TURNING ON THE MARGINAL PERFORMER

John R. Schermerhorn, Jr.
William L. Gardner
Thomas N. Martin

By this point, you have read several references in different articles about the growing obsolescence of the command-and-control management style. Managers with this mentality conceive of their jobs as making decisions, giving orders, and ensuring that subordinates obey. A more effective approach is high involvement (high performance or high commitment) management, which focuses on employee commitment and empowerment. Empowerment is defined as granting employees the autonomy to assume more responsibility within an organization and strengthening their sense of effectiveness. Managers empower employees by sharing power, information, and the responsibility to manage their own work as much as possible.

Renowned management professor, scholar, and consultant Edward Lawler contends in "Why Treating People Right Pays Off" that achieving competitive advantage requires both hiring and retaining great people and maintaining great organizational practices. He suggests that treating people right is about identifying and implementing things that are good for both organizational performance and individuals, including leaders who create commitment and reward systems that reinforce core values.

Whereas the first article in this chapter focuses on system-level management practices, the second article returns us to the perennial micro-level problem of how to handle and coach poorly performing employees. "Management Dialogues: Turning on the Marginal Performer," written by management professors John Schermerhorn, Jr., William Gardner, and Thomas Martin, provides blow-by-blow advice for dealing with performance problems. Reading this article will prepare you for the inevitable job interview question, "What would you do if you had an employee who wasn't doing an acceptable job?" Don't miss the reference to the attribution errors that were introduced in Chapter 9.

WHY TREATING PEOPLE RIGHT PAYS OFF*

Edward E. Lawler III

We are entering a new era in the relationship between organizations and their employees. The world of work is sharply altering most of the century-old understandings between employers and employees. No longer can organizations think of people as either loyal "family members" or as easily replaceable resources when it comes to accomplishing their business objectives.

In this new era, people need to be respected and treated as precious human capital, more essential to an organization's effectiveness than its financial capital. People can now be the primary source of a company's competitive advantage in most businesses. To put it bluntly, how people are treated increasingly determines whether a company will prosper and even survive.

In the past, arguments about the importance of how people are treated have largely fallen on deaf ears in the executive offices and boardrooms of most organizations. Yes, there are many companies that claim that their people are their most important asset, and they even put pictures of them (always smiling) in their annual reports. But most of these companies do not behave like their people are their number one priority. All too often, they treat them as replaceable parts that add little value.

But today, a number of powerful and compelling factors are coalescing into a new reality: to be effective, organizations must excel in organizing and managing their people. In the twenty-first century, treating people right is not an option; it is a necessity.

THE COMPELLING FORCES OF CHANGE

Every reader of this book knows that the business environment of the twenty-first century is different from what it was twenty or thirty years ago. In fact, the business world today is vastly different from what it was just five years ago. There can be no doubt that the world is changing more rapidly and has become more chaotic, demanding, and competitive than ever before.

But let's get specific about how the world is now different. Let me invite you to take a step back for a moment and consider the business environment throughout most of the second half of the twentieth century.

For organizations, the business environment was relatively stable and predictable and offered numerous opportunities for growth. An organization was assured of at least a degree of success and profitability as long as it produced moderately good products or services and made productive use of its employees. It could gain competitive advantage with relative ease by controlling its sources of raw materials or by obtaining low-cost financial capital and physical assets. Some organizations also gained competitive advantage because they had government-created protection from competition.

For people, too, the old environment was also relatively stable and secure. Most employees who worked for governments or large corporations lived under a "loyalty contract," a tacit agreement with their employers that if they were loyal, they could

*Adapted and reprinted with permission from *Treat People Right!* (San Francisco, CA: Jossey-Bass, 2003): 3–21.

have a comfortable life with that organization. They had not just a job but a career that included the security of a regular paycheck, benefits, and retirement income. Even for employees not covered under a loyalty contract, the growth and power of the union movement provided many of them with benefits and protections that guaranteed a good quality of life.

Now contrast that with today's business environment.

For most organizations today, the sense of stability and assured success is in question. It is no longer easy to find competitive advantage and, once found, to maintain it for very long. New threats seem to come from everywhere: start-ups, international competitors, legal changes, new technologies. Most organizations must fight tooth and nail to secure their profits and continue their growth. Most also regularly struggle to find qualified people for their leadership and knowledge work jobs. As a result, the past decades have seen the downfall of many venerable companies, as well as the overnight birth and death of many seemingly smart start-ups—witness the many failed dot-coms that originally seemed destined for success.

For most people, the new environment is equally insecure. The promise of a steady job has all but disappeared, with millions of workers downsized, furloughed, laid off, or voluntarily choosing to move from company to company. Many people have found that they simply don't have the skills needed to compete in the marketplace, having lost their personal competitive advantage and their value as human captial. Many of today's workers are finding that although they still have jobs, they are falling behind the business, scientific, and technical needs that organizations have.

These starkly contrasting sketches of the business environment are the result of four major changes:

- The globalization of competition
- The rapid development of scientific and technical knowledge
- The death of the loyalty contract
- The scarcity of skilled employees

Of course, not all of these have affected or will affect every organization in the same way, but most organization have felt or will feel the impact of at least several of them. Most people, too, will feel the impact of several of them at some point during their careers.

Let's explore these forces in greater detail so that you can understand how each affects orgnizations and people.

GLOBALIZATION OF COMPETITION

The old days of limited competition are over. With the diappearance of communist and totalitarian regimes in many parts of the world, more and more countries are opening up to foreign business and trade. While this increasing globalization has created new markets and growth opportunities for many existing organizations, it has also dramatically elevated the level of competition in nearly all industries.

Many new competitors exist. Over just the past decade, we have seen the emergence of a coalition of Western European countries into a major new economic power, the emergence of India as a global competitor in software and technology, the entrance of the formerly socialist or communist Eastern European bloc countries into the world market, the awakening of the Chinese and Southeast Asian dragons, and the adoption of the North American Free Trade Agreement. Each of these developments has created competitors searching for profits, dominance, and new markets. Many of these newer competitors have distinct advantages in areas ranging from geographical proximity to important markets to high-skilled, relatively low-wage workforces to large storehouses of financial capital with which to buy new plants and equipment as well as to acquire other companies.

While some organizations have found expanded profits in the new global markets, many others have struggled due to increased competition and the complexities involved in operating on the global stage. Globalization has also had a negative impact on millions of people whose jobs have been transferred to foreign countries where the labor is cheaper. They have been forced either to find new jobs, often at lower pay, or to retrain themselves to compete in new industries. If it hasn't already, at some time in the future, globalization is likely to dramatically affect your career, and you will face some important choices about how to manage your career in this new era of global competition.

GREATER SCIENTIFIC AND TECHNICAL KNOWLEDGE

In the past several decades, the bar has been significantly raised with respect to the level of scientific and technological knowledge that organizations need in order to compete. And there is every reason to believe that the growth of new knowledge will continue to accelerate.

The amount of knowledge now required to be competitive has altered the core of what organizations do, the types of products they produce, and how they operate, as well as where they can find competitive advantage. Entire industries, including communications, entertainment, consulting, housing, banking, finance, retailing, and manufacturing, have been forced to rethink their strategies and how they go about their business.

Changes in technology have also caused many of the world's most venerable companies to completely change their direction or invest large amounts of capital to develop new products or to acquire new technologies. And like dinosaurs, a few historic companies (Polaroid and Westinghouse, for example) have been vanquished by faster, smarter competitors who were able to invent or adopt new technologies.

Perhaps the most vivid example of the rapid evolution of technology and its impact on organizations is the Internet. In the blink of an eye, the Internet created a host of new competitors that served customers in new and different ways. While many Internet companies accomplished little other than the expenditure of huge amounts of investment capital, many others truly succeeded in changing the world (think of Amazon.com and eBay), creating the need for competitors to adopt new business models.

Meanwhile, the demand for increased scientific and technical knowledge has put significant pressure on workers everywhere. Increasingly, today's employees in developed countries must have highly sophisticated skills with respect to managing information, developing knowledge, and dealing in abstract concepts. They need to have the ability to think, analyze, and problem-solve. Fewer workers are needed to do the mind-numbing, repetitive manual tasks that formerly dominated the work scene. These are being done by machines or sent to low-wage economies. Needless to say, it has become absolutely clear that people who cannot keep pace with scientific and technological change are quickly losing their value as employees.

DEATH OF THE LOYALTY CONTRACT

Throughout most of the twentieth century, organizations maintained a tacit agreement with their workers that as long as they were generally productive, their jobs and a reasonable pension plan were guaranteed. This was often referred to as the "loyalty contract."

However, globalized competition, the rise of technology, and the increasing demand for knowledge workers with state-of-the-art skills has made maintaining the loyalty contract unrealistic in the case of most companies. More and more organizations have realized that buying their workers' long-term loyalty is simply not a good investment.

Despite its honorable tradition, today the loyalty contract is in many ways counterproductive. By providing employees with a relatively secure and comfortable lifestyle, it serves to attract and retain only those people who want secure, predictable employment situations. It does not attract or retain those who want to be part of an entrepreneurial organization or who want to be part of a rapidly changing, technologically advanced, or knowledge-intensive organization. A loyalty relationship also does little to encourage individuals to learn new skills, keep up with technology changes, and keep the company financially competitive.

Beginning in the 1980s, more and more companies ended their loyalty contracts. Such revered organizations as General Electric, IBM, and AT&T shattered their contracts by laying off thousands of employees. In retrospect, it is clear that most of these organizations had no choice. At that time, laying off their workers was the best way these firms could adapt to the dramatic changes in their businesses. To have done otherwise would have been fatal for them.

The death of the loyalty contract has had enormous repercussions in today's business environment. One of its major effects has been on the cost, availability, and attitudes of good labor. Most people, especially younger workers, understand and accept that loyalty to their organization is largely a losing proposition. As a result, many of them are no longer willing to be dependent on their employers or amenable to accepting practices and decisions that are not advantageous to them. Without the benefits of the old loyalty contract, today's employees are demanding substitutes such as challenging work, opportunities for learning, and substantive rewards. And when they do not get what they want, today's workers are quick to move on to more attractive employment situations.

The change is significant: Organizations can no longer count on their members' loyalty, so they must continuously compete for talent. They have to focus on attracting and hiring the most talented people and retaining their existing talent. Because of the increased mobility of individuals, organizations need to change the fundamental way they think about their employees. They need to look for approaches to managing them that are advantageous to both themselves and their employees.

SCARCITY OF SKILLED EMPLOYEES

Two powerful forces are contributing to an increasing shortage of knowledgeable skilled employees: workforce demographics and education.

First, many industrialized countries are facing the burden of an aging population.[1] Increasingly in the United States, Europe, and Japan, a high percentage of the workforce is approaching or has attained the traditional age of retirement. This demographic shift is a result of a combination of relatively low birth rates, especially in countries like Japan, Italy, and Germany, as well as longer life expectancies. Although many potential retirees can remain in the workforce, they have to be sold on the idea of continuing to work. They also may not be able to meet the needs that organizations have for employees with knowledge.

The other force behind the growing scarcity of skilled labor in the United States is an underperforming educational system. It is accepted in the business world that our schools simply do not produce enough well-educated students who are capable of doing the type of complex knowledge work that is increasingly needed in today's world. Fewer and fewer new graduates leave school ready to handle the challenges and intricacies of today's competitive jobs. Particularly lacking are people who can problem-solve and do cutting-edge technical and engineering work.

When it comes to human capital, you must not underestimate the importance of a highly skilled workforce. As tasks become more complicated, the difference between an average performer and a good performer rises dramatically. If you examine a simple, repetitive assembly line job, the difference between the best performer and the worst may only be a few percentage points in productivity. However, the difference between an outstanding knowledge worker and an average one can be 1,000 percent or more.

In the old competitive environment, many jobs did not require highly effective performance for an organization to be successful, so the demand for highly talented people was relatively limited. Many organizations simply did not need to make it a priority to fill jobs with highly talented individuals, other than at the very senior levels of management and in a few key technical areas. In most cases, organizations were satisfied to fill jobs with people who could perform at a "good enough" level because the work was not particularly challenging or difficult and how well it was done did not have a significant impact on the organization's overall performance.

But in the new competitive environment, the situation is radically different. There is now an undeniable need for highly knowledgeable, skilled people, and many corporations are having trouble finding enough of them. With more and more technically difficult and personally demanding jobs, creating an extraordinary workforce is a constant challenge, while the payoff from staffing with top performers can be tremendous.

You may be wondering if the shortage of skilled human capital is just a temporary phenomenon; after all, it did ease after the dot-com bust. I am convinced that the problem is here to stay. While the ups and downs of birth rates and economic cycles will affect the labor market over short time spans, the shortage of highly qualified human capital is likely to remain a reality for decades. The reason is simple: The growth of knowledge and technology continuously creates higher demands for an educated workforce.

THE NEW COMPETITIVE ADVANTAGE

The four major changes we have just reviewed show every sign of continuing. There is little question that we will experience a further globalization of business and even more competition. The demand for scientific and technical knowledge workers will continue to grow as organizations need to commit more resources to developing and delivering new and more complex products and services. And there is no stopping the increasing need for skilled people to handle more and more complex business management issues, products, and decision making. In light of the increasing demand for talent, people are more and more likely to see themselves as free agents.

In the future, organizations will undoubtedly need to meet new challenges if they are to survive and thrive. To do this, organizations must learn how to attract, retain, motivate, organize, and manage talented individuals. People are the key to helping organizations stay ahead of change and to having a competitive advantage. This calls for a new type of relationship between organizations and people, one that recognizes the true importance of *human capital.*

How should organizations recognize the importance of human capital? History has some important lessons to teach us about what not to do. One thing not to do is to put the human assets on the corporate balance sheet. If human assets truly matter, the argument goes, they should be valued and accounted for. Yet efforts at human asset accounting have failed, largely because they are based on flawed thinking—people are not comparable to the assets already appearing in corporate accounting statements. Assets are owned and can be bought, sold, and manipulated. But people cannot be owned; they make their own decisions, and they have their own unique competencies and capabilities that make managing and organizing them far more complex and challenging than managing buildings, equipment, and other corporate assets. In short, it is a serious mistake to think of people as assets.

However, from an organizational point of view, it is valid to consider people as human *capital* and at least as important as an organization's financial capital. Like financial capital, people need to be treated with care, respect, and commitment if the organization expects them to stay invested. It must also provide them with the returns they need. Just as in managing financial capital, organizations cannot afford to waste their human capital or risk having it go to places where it can get a better return. Like financial capital, human capital needs to be carefully allocated, utilized, and managed.

I recently heard a radio ad that illustrates the erroneous thinking behind the traditional approach to the role of human capital in organizations. The ad was for a company that specializes in outsourcing human resource management for corporations, and the ad ended with the jingle, "We take care of your people so you can take care of your business." This sounds great, but it actually is the opposite of how a company should think about its people. A more appropriate slogan would be something like, "We take care of your people so *they* can take care of your business." As my revision of this slogan indicates, it is the people who must deal with the business in today's world, because they are the business and the best source of competitive advantage.

TALENTED PEOPLE AND WELL-DESIGNED ORGANIZATIONS

Let me clarify one point about treating people right and the importance of human capital. I am not suggesting that having the right people alone will make organizations effective. Treating people right is not just about talented people; it is also about strategies, practices, designs, and policies that make organizations into places where people want to perform well and can work effectively. Extraordinary results can be obtained only by having talented people *and* well-designed organizations with the best management systems.

In fact, opinions differ regarding the importance of talent. Some academics such as Charles O'Reilly and Jeffrey Pfeffer argue that companies can gain competitive advantage and achieve extraordinary results with ordinary people.[2] In their view, if you have the right systems, you don't have to worry about having the best people.

Others have argued that talent is all that counts. For example, Secretary of State Colin Powell, in many of his speeches on leadership, has argued that "organization does not really accomplish anything. Only by attracting the best people will you accomplish great deeds."

My position is that both are wrong. Achieving the competitive advantage needed today requires *both* great people and great organizational practices. It is misleading to claim that organizations can get extraordinary results with ordinary people, just as it is misleading to argue that organizations can get extraordinary results with ordinary management practices. To be effective, organizations need both outstanding people and outstanding management systems, because that is what produces world-class results for both individuals and organizations.

Outstanding individuals and organizational practices tend to reinforce each other and seek each other out because of the momentum they create. Effective organizational practices attract outstanding people, and outstanding people create effective structures and practices. Treating people right is all about identifying and implementing the things organizations can do that are good for organizational performance and individuals.

THE ULTIMATE GOAL: A VIRTUOUS SPIRAL

Treating people right leads to powerful win-win virtuous spirals of success. Virtuous spirals occur when organizations treat people right by implementing the effective practices needed to motivate them and enable them to perform well. Virtuous spirals are actually the ultimate competitive advantage—powerful and hard-to-duplicate sources of positive momentum and higher levels of performance.

A virtuous spiral begins when an organization takes intelligent, strategy-driven, conscious actions to attract, retain, motivate, develop, and effectively organize committed, high-performance individuals. This generates a high-performance organization. It boosts the rewards for employees, which increases their motivation and commitment. The more challenging and rewarding environment that results further reinforces the organization's ability to attract, retain, and develop effective employees, who further positively affect performance. Thus a virtuous spiral forms and expands, carrying the organization and its members to greater heights. Figure 1 captures this in graphic form.

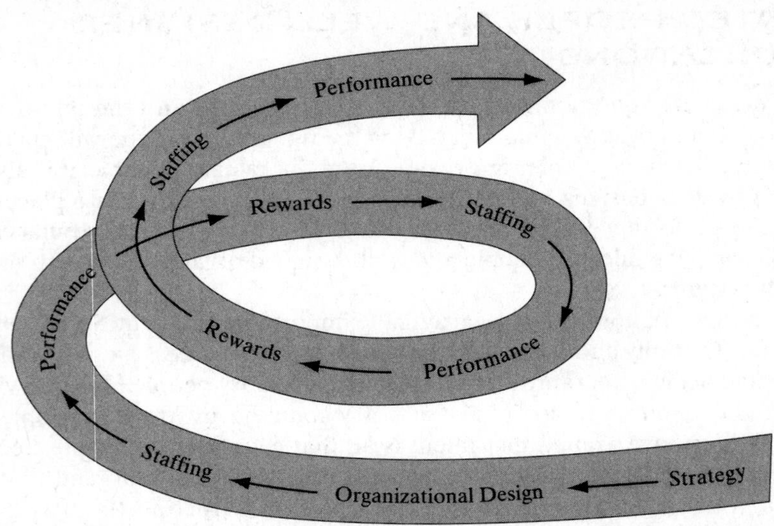

FIGURE 1 Virtuous Spiral

To successfully develop a virtuous spiral, organizations need to emphasize ever-increasing levels of performance, higher rewards for individuals, and increasingly competent employees. As they achieve these goals, a positive performance momentum develops that feeds on itself and provides a powerful competitive advantage.

VIRTUOUS SPIRAL ORGANIZATIONS

Let me present a few examples of organizations that have achieved impressive results due to their dedication to treating people right. Because I have studied and consulted with these organizations, I can state with considerable confidence that their success is very much due to their ability to create and sustain virtuous spirals.

Microsoft is one of the most impressive examples of a company that has profited from a virtuous spiral relationship with its people for decades. Since the early 1980s, the company has had an environment in which its employees have done well and the company has done well. The employees have had challenging work and of course, one of the most highly rewarding stock plans around. Microsoft has been an enormously attractive place to work, especially for high performers. As a result, it has attracted some of the country's top software engineers and marketing executives.

Because of its relationship with its human capital. Microsoft has been able to generate a powerful dynamic in which success begets success, which begets more success. The company's seemingly unstoppable growth began to slow down only in the late 1990s, when it faced a rapidly changing competitive environment along with government challenges to its growing power. But even in the market downturn of the early years of the new century. Microsoft has continued on a virtuous spiral of increasing growth and success.

Another organization that has clearly enjoyed a virtuous spiral of success for decades is General Electric. Even before Jack Welch became CEO in the early 1980s, GE had already established an environment where highly talented individuals wanted to work because of the opportunities the company offered for career development and financial rewards. Able to attract and retain highly talented individuals, GE has enjoyed decades of enviable growth in profits and as a result has attracted more and more talented individuals. GE is a clear example of a cycle of successful performance leading to successful recruitment and motivation of individuals, which in turn produce even more successful performance.

Southwest Airlines is a third example of an organization that has managed to maintain a virtuous spiral for decades. From its very beginning, Southwest was a human capital–focused organization that sought a high-quality relationship with its employees. Its founder, Herb Kelleher, stressed from day one that the company's competitive advantage is its people. The result has been excellent customer service and an absence of the hostile labor relationship characteristic of every other major airline. Despite being highly unionized, Southwest has never had a strike and is frequently mentioned as one of the best places to work.

Like many other organizations that have created virtuous spirals, there is no one secret to Southwest's success. The company has emphasized the careful selection of employees, building an employee-friendly work environment, giving employees freedom to control their jobs and work environment, profit sharing and stock ownership for all employees, and the opportunity for employees to grow, develop, and advance in the company.

Procter & Gamble is yet another example. Though the company is over one hundred years old, the past forty years of its existence have been marked by many forward-thinking efforts to establish a virtuous spiral relationship with its employees based on employee involvement and the development of leaders throughout the company. P&G was an early adopter of employee involvement practices in its manufacturing plants. It also has a stock ownership plan that has placed over 30 percent of its stock into the hands of its employees.

Other examples of virtuous spiral organizations are worth noting quickly:

- Johnson & Johnson has had a long-term virtuous spiral relationship with its employees. Key to its success are numerous separate business units that allow for a high level of autonomy and a clear mission vision and statement of ethical standards. It, like Procter & Gamble, also has a high level of stock ownership by its employees and has done an outstanding job of instituting employee involvement practices in many of its manufacturing locations.
- Capital One, the financial services firm, is a relatively new firm that has had a virtuous spiral relationship with its employees since its founding. Its human resource management system focuses on the development of people, and most employees own Capital One stock.
- Harley-Davidson recovered from near extinction in the 1970s by building a strong cooperative relationship with its unions and using employee involvement to improve quality and productivity. It continues to be a market leader both in its business sector and in the way it treats its people.
- Medtronic is a leading manufacturer of medical equipment that has grown rapidly by creating innovative lifesaving products. It goes out of its way to involve

all employees in the mission of the company, which is to improve the quality and length of people's lives. As a result, employees profit both financially and intrinsically as a result of working there.

- Applied Materials is the world's leading producer of semiconductor manufacturing equipment. It is frequently listed as one of the best places to work despite the fact that it is in a highly cyclical business. It deals with this by using slowdowns to train and develop people, and it uses stock to be sure that everyone wins when the business is strong.

WHEN ORGANIZATIONS DON'T TREAT PEOPLE RIGHT

Organizations that do not attempt to treat people right and to initiate a virtuous spiral are susceptible to the opposite result, the *death spiral.*

Death spirals occur when organizations mistreat their human capital, and as a result, their performance declines, causing repercussions that lead to further declines and in many cases death. When organizations experience declining performance, they are perceived to be in trouble. As a result, they cannot attract the right human capital to fix their situation or the financial assets and the customers they need to reverse their decline. They soon become a place no one wants to be associated with. They become less and less of a competitor and ultimately die. Death spirals can last decades or just a few days.

Perhaps the most recent dramatic example of a death spiral is the complete collapse of Arthur Andersen. In a very short period of time, it went from being one of the world's five premier accounting firms to oblivion. In essence, it lost the reputation of its brand and its attractiveness as an employer. Both customers and employees began leaving the company, and in just a matter of months, its ability to function ended.

The collapse of Arthur Andersen illustrates an important point about death spirals. Organizations like Andersen whose market worth is in its intangible assets, such as its reputation, brand, and human capital, are extremely vulnerable to sudden death spirals. Many knowledge work firms, like consulting firms and publishers, have intangible assets that represent more than 75 percent of their market value; only a small portion of their assets are in their plant, equipment, and financial assets. When such organizations lose their attractiveness as an employer or their reputation as a good place to do business, they can plunge, much like an airplane that has lost its forward momentum. Their performance decreases so quickly that almost overnight they go out of business.

Rapid death spirals rarely happen to old-economy companies in industries like steel, automobiles, and energy because they have more tangible assets. As a result, it usually takes longer for them to fail. They can even defy gravity and exist in a zero-momentum condition if they have significant tangible assets and operate in a forgiving environment. For example, most public utilities have been able to maintain a steady-state existence because of their monopoly power. But when they have been deregulated, they rarely do well: Witness the declines of AT&T, Nortel, and Lucent.

Several major organizations today are in a slow death spiral. General Motors has been for decades and has had great difficulty reversing its downward momentum, losing market share year after year. Two of the great retailers in American history, Montgomery Ward and Sears, have both declined, although at different rates. Montgomery Ward has already gone into bankruptcy, while Sears continues to lose market share. It has new, fierce competitors—namely Wal-Mart, Target, Lowe's, and Home Depot—that continue to take market share away from it in part because they have developed virtuous spirals.

Without exception, organizations that are in death spirals have failed to fully recognize and respond to the compelling forces of change in the world today. None has adequately altered its strategy and management practices to fit the new world or changed its relationship with employees in ways that can reverse the death spirals. These companies are no longer seen as good places to work and have increasing difficulty attracting the kind of human talent that they need in order to be effective.

The world of professional sports provides an excellent juxtaposition between actions that create a virtuous spiral and those that lead to a death spiral. In the 1980s, one of my consulting clients, the NFL, reached an agreement with its players' union that effectively created a virtuous spiral relationship. In essence, it assured labor and management that each would share in any revenue improvements that took place in the business. This resulted in a virtuous spiral relationship that has enriched both the owners and the players. Strikes became a thing of the past, and the game of professional football has grown in popularity and revenue; today it is the most popular spectator sport in the United States.

Just the opposite has happened in professional baseball. Labor and management have never been able to agree on an acceptable revenue-sharing relationship. Instead of creating the kind of virtuous spiral relationship that pro football enjoys, it has created a death spiral. Contract negotiations with the union have been highly acrimonious. There have been eight work stoppages since 1972, one of which led to the cancellation of the World Series. In 2002, after months of hostile negotiations, a contract was reached without a strike, but it did little to forge a cooperative labor-management relationship. TV ratings for the 2002 World Series reached an all-time low, in part because fans were turned off by the threat of a strike. Instead of both sides winning, both management and labor have ended up losing relative to what might have been.

THE SEVEN PRINCIPLES FOR TREATING PEOPLE RIGHT AND CREATING A VIRTUOUS SPIRAL

By now, I hope that the rationale for treating people right and creating a virtuous spiral is clear. The only question that remains is how to do it. What steps do organizations need to take to treat people right and potentially launch a virtuous spiral?

To be competitive in this new world, an organization must attract and retain highly talented, high-performing individuals. It needs to encourage people to develop the skills and knowledge that the organization needs in order for them to perform effectively. It needs to motivate them to perform their work well and to commit themselves to the success of the organization. Finally, it needs to create an organization design and a leadership capability that lead to effective organizational performance.

Creating a virtuous spiral is something most organizations can do. Through my research and study of many leading organizations, I have identified seven principles that are key to organizations' developing virtuous spirals. These seven principles guide a wide assortment of specific practices that I have seen implemented in exemplary organizations with positive results.

These seven principles are summarized in Exhibit 1.

EXHIBIT 1 Seven Principles for Treating People Right and Creating a Virtuous Spiral

1. *Attraction and Retention*
   Organizations must create a value proposition that defines the type of workplace they want to be so that they can attract and retain the right people.
2. *Hiring Practices*
   Organizations must hire people who fit with their values, core competencies, and strategic goals.
3. *Training and Development*
   Organizations must continuously train employees to do their jobs and offer them opportunities to grow and develop.
4. *Work Design*
   Organizations must design work so that it is meaningful for people and provides them with feedback, responsibility, and autonomy.
5. *Mission, Strategies, and Goals*
   Organizations must develop and adhere to a specific organizational mission, with strategies, goals, and values that employees can understand, support, and believe in.
6. *Reward Systems*
   Organizations must devise and implement reward systems that reinforce their design, core values, and strategy.
7. *Leadership*
   Organizations must hire and develop leaders who can create commitment, trust, success, and a motivating work environment.

YOUR OWN VIRTUOUS SPIRAL

Let me point out that there are a number of important implications of treating people right that you need to consider if you work with or for an organization.

On the positive side, just as organizations need to view you as human capital, you need to begin seeing yourself as human capital, not an asset. Consider your time, energy, intelligence, and skills. You have the opportunity to invest your knowledge and skills in any organization you want, and you can choose to withdraw it from one organization and invest it elsewhere if better returns are offered. In today's highly competitive world, you are a valuable resource for organizations. If you manage your career right, you will be in demand, and organizations will vie for your services more than they vie for investment dollars. In fact, the more you improve your skills and knowledge and invest in your personal development, the more you can build your own personal virtuous spiral of career success. Figure 2 depicts the type of virtuous spiral that you can create. It shows that increased skills and performance can lead to better jobs and higher rewards.

For you to have the best opportunity to develop a virtuous career spiral, your organization needs to be in a virtuous spiral. Organizations cannot thrive unless their people prosper, but at the same time, people cannot thrive unless their organizations prosper. Although Figures 1 and 2 show separate spirals for organizations and individuals, in practice they are intertwined. They depend on each other and feed off each other.

This suggests that you too need to continuously increase your commitment, dedication, and value to any organization you work for. With the death of the loyalty contract, however, you must also behave and think as a free agent, because no matter

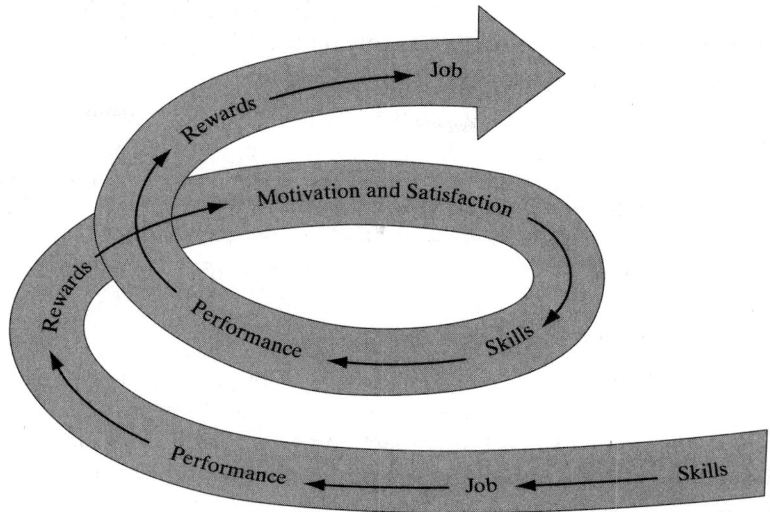

FIGURE 2 Virtuous Career Spiral

where you work, your organization may not be able to keep you employed indefinitely. You need to learn how to negotiate for what you want while getting it because of what you can offer.

Endnotes

1. K. Dychtwald, *Age Power: How the 21st Century Will Be Ruled by the New Old.* New York: Tarcher/Putnam, 1999.
2. C. A. O'Reilly III and J. Pfeffer, *Hidden Value: How Great Companies Achieve Extraordinary Results with Ordinary People.* Boston: Harvard Business School Press, 2000.

MANAGEMENT DIALOGUES: TURNING ON THE MARGINAL PERFORMER*

John R. Schermerhorn, Jr.
William L. Gardner
Thomas N. Martin

Bob is an employee in the R&D laboratory of a large high-technology firm. He was hired by the lab supervisor, Fred, after a thorough recruitment and selection process. Both men were enthusiastic about the appointment. Bob had excellent technical credentials, was glad to be hired by the lab, and really liked Fred. Fred was confident in

*Reprinted, with permission of Elsevier from *Organizational Dynamics*, 18, (Spring 1990): 47–59.

Bob's abilities and sure that Bob was just the person the lab needed. He passed by Bob's work station during Bob's first day on the job. Here's the way things started off:

FRED: Hi, Bob. First full day on the job, I see?
BOB: Yes, and I'm ready to go to work.
FRED: Good. I just thought I'd stop by first thing to say hi and remind you we're expecting good results. You'll be pretty much on your own here, so it will be your responsibility to stay on top of things.
BOB: Well, that shouldn't be a problem.
FRED: I hope not. But if you hit any snags, don't be afraid to call me.
BOB: All right.
FRED: Good enough, Bob. See you later.

Everything seemed in order with this brief but positive exchange between a manager and his new employee. The two men talked easily with each other. Fred quite specifically reminded Bob of his expectations and pledged his support. Bob expressed confidence in his ability to fulfill Fred's expectations, and he acknowledged the offer of support.

But six months later, things had changed dramatically. For example, consider one of Bob's typical workdays. He arrived late for work and looked at the clock, which read 8:55. "Little late this morning," he thought to himself. "Oh well, no big deal. Fred's not around anyway." Later in the day he noted that he had "come up short again" in his work. "But not too bad," he said. "This ought to be enough to keep Fred off my back." Finally, just before quitting time he considered getting a jump on the next day's schedule. But after thinking just a moment, he concluded, "Ah, why sweat it? I'll do it tomorrow."

People like Bob show up in most work sites. Although they initially seem capable and highly motivated, they become marginal performers—workers who do just enough to get by. Many frustrated managers simply consider these people unfortunate employment mistakes that must be tolerated. By contrast, we believe managers can "turn around" many marginal performers and thereby produce large productivity gains for their organization. Such *high-performance management* gets the best from each and every individual contributor.

Let's go back to the opening vignette to determine what went wrong in Fred and Bob's relationship and what could have been done about it. Why did Bob, a capable and motivated person, become a marginal performer? What could Fred have done to turn the situation around so that Bob's high-performance potential would have been realized?

A COMPREHENSIVE APPROACH TO INDIVIDUAL PERFORMANCE

The answers can be found in a management framework based on what we call the *individual performance equation: Performance = Ability × Support × Effort.* Central to the equation is the principle that high levels of work performance result from the combination of a person's job-related abilities, various forms of organizational support, and individual work efforts. The multiplication signs indicate that all three factors must exist for high performance to occur. Take any one or more away, and performance will be compromised. High-performance management starts with the following implications of the individual performance equation.

1. Performance Begins with Ability

Individual abilities are the skills and other personal characteristics we use in a job. For someone to perform well, he or she must have the skills and abilities required to complete the work. If the person lacks the requisite baseline abilities, it will be very difficult for even extraordinary effort and support to produce high performance.

Because ability is a prerequisite for performance, it is the first factor to consider when searching for explanations of marginal work. Initially, managers must determine whether employees have the skills and aptitudes necessary to succeed. The best way to ensure that they do is to develop selection procedures that properly match individual talents and job demands. In cases where employees lack essential skills, managers should use training and development programs to help them acquire these skills. The manager may also consider replacing or reassigning personnel to achieve a better match of individual abilities with job requirements.

In addition, as Victor Vroom's expectancy theory of motivation points out, individuals must believe in their abilities if they are to exhibit high performance. A person may have the right abilities but may fail to develop the expectation that by using these skills, he or she will achieve the desired performance levels. Thus part of a manager's job is to help build self-confidence among the individual contributors—to help them realize that they have the abilities required to meet high-performance expectations.

2. Performance Requires Support

The second but frequently overlooked high-performance factor is support. Even the most hard-working and highly capable individuals will be unable to maximize their performance if they do not have the necessary support.

In searching for the causes of marginal performance, managers need to examine two major dimensions of support. First, they must ask if they have done their part to create a physical work setting that supplies employees with broad opportunities to fully use their abilities. A supportive work environment provides appropriate technologies, tools, facilities, and equipment; offers adequate budgets; includes clearly defined task goals; gives autonomy without the burden of too much red tape and other performance obstacles; and pays a market-competitive base wage or salary. Deficiencies in these areas impose situational constraints that too often frustrate employees' performance efforts.

Second, managers must give proper attention to the social aspects of the work environment. Recent research into job stress, for example, suggests that social support is critical for sustained high performance. Emotional support from a person's supervisor and co-workers, as well as from non-job sources (i.e., spouse, family, and friends), can have long-term positive effects on job performance. Indeed, empathy can help a worker better handle such work stresses as skill underutilization, high workloads, and role ambiguity.

A manager's responsibility thus includes providing every individual contributor with the maximum opportunity to perform at a high level. This advice echoes Robert House's path-goal theory of leadership. Path-goal theory suggests that effective managers use various management styles—directive, supportive, achievement oriented, and participative—as necessary to ensure that employees have clear "paths" as they seek to accomplish their goals. That is, good managers use leadership behaviors that maximize the amount of situational support available to others.

3. Performance Involves Effort

Effort is the final, and perhaps most commonly emphasized, individual performance factor. Here, effort refers to the amount of energy (physical and/or mental) a person applies to perform a task. In other words, it represents someone's willingness to work hard.

Effort is necessary to achieve high-performance results. Capable, well-supported, but uninspired employees are no more likely to succeed than are hard-working persons who lack ability and/or support. Yet unlike the other performance factors, which are subject to direct managerial control, the decision to exert or withhold one's effort rests solely with the individual contributor. To understand why employees sometimes decide *not* to work as hard as possible, it is again useful to consider Vroom's expectancy theory of motivation. According to this perspective, the motivation to work is the product of expectancy, instrumentality, and valence: *Expectancy* is the individual's assessment of the likelihood that his or her work effort will lead to task performance; *instrumentality* is the individual's belief that a given level of performance will lead to certain work outcomes; and *valence* is the value the person attaches to these outcomes. If the level of any one of these factors is low, motivation is likely to suffer. To avoid motivational deficits, managers are advised to make sure individual contributors see clear linkages between how hard they work, their performance results, and their rewards.

BOB, THE MARGINAL PERFORMER

Let's return to the opening vignette and begin to apply the individual performance equation. All three elements of the equation—ability, support, and effort—appear to exist. Fred set the stage for Bob's high performance by (1) hiring a technically competent person, (2) indicating his intention to provide support, and (3) encouraging Bob to work hard and use his ability to good advantage. Our first clues as to what went wrong are found in a conversation that took place after Bob had been on the job about a month.

Fred happened to pass by Bob's area and noticed Bob was working hard. He thought to himself how fortunate he was to have a dependable go-getter like Bob in his department. Bob noticed Fred approaching and wondered whether Fred would mention his good performance from the past week.

FRED: Hi, Bob. It sure is good weather, wouldn't you say?

BOB: Yes, it sure is.

FRED: I was just passing through the building on another matter. While I'm here, I thought I'd show you some new schedule changes.

BOB: Oh yes, Darlene (the project manager) told me all about them. Say, how'd we end up last week anyway?

FRED: Pretty good, pretty good. If you have any questions about those schedule changes, just call the project manager. Well, I've got to run. See you later, Bob.

In this interaction Bob obviously wanted Fred's praise. What he got was a lukewarm "Pretty good, pretty good" followed by "I've got to run." Fred passed up a perfect opportunity to recognize directly Bob's accomplishments. From an expectancy theory perspective, this oversight could prove costly. Bob's expectation was probably quite high—he had already shown he could do the job when he wanted to. The valence he attached to possible work outcomes, such as praise, also was probably high. But Bob's instrumentality may have become low because he sensed little or no relationship between performing well and receiving the desired supervisory recognition. The positive reinforcement he both desired and needed was just not there. As a result, his motivation to work hard was reduced.

Things could have gotten better if the motivational dynamics had improved in later interactions between Fred and Bob. Unfortunately, as we'll now see, they didn't. Several weeks later while reading the weekly lab reports, Fred noticed a decline in Bob's performance. This was a serious problem, so Fred decided to chat with Bob right away. Bob had met high performance standards in the past and should still have been able to reach them. When Fred stopped by Bob's work station, they engaged in the following conversation.

FRED: Hi, Bob, how's it going?
BOB: Pretty good.
FRED: Say, I wanted to check with you about your performance figures for the past couple of weeks. They've been down a little, you know.
BOB: Well, I got stuck on a couple of things that threw me off. But I think I'm back on track now.
FRED: The only reason I'm bringing it up is that you've busted the charts in the past. I know you can do it when you put your mind to it. You're one of our top performers. I figured if you were off on the numbers there must be a reason.
BOB: Well, I'm sure my performance results will be back up this week.
FRED: Okay, good, Bob, Take care now.

Reviewing this interaction, Fred thought it had been right to let Bob know he wasn't happy with his performance. But in this developing scheme, we have an indication that the only time Bob got the desired personal attention from Fred was when he did poorly. As social-learning theorists will tell us, Bob was essentially "learning" through reinforcement to work below his actual performance potential. By giving attention only when Bob turned in marginal, rather than high, performance, Fred was positively reinforcing the wrong behaviors and neglecting critical opportunities to positively reinforce the right ones. As long as this pattern continued, Bob was likely to remain a marginal performer. And, as we will see, a manager's frustrations with this situation can all too easily lead him or her to adopt ever more punitive approaches.

A few weeks later Fred noted that Bob's performance still wasn't back up to standard. While he was not the worst performer in the lab, he surely could have been doing a lot better; Bob's past record was proof positive. Being even more concerned now, Fred went to Bob's work area to discuss things with him.

FRED: Bob, I want to talk to you.
BOB: Hi, Fred, what's on your mind?

FRED: Your lousy performance, that's what! Your output has been down again for the past two weeks. Look, Bob, I know you can hit the numbers, but you're just not putting out. I need someone in here who can get the job done. If it is not you, I'll get someone else. I hope I won't have to do that. Now let's get to it?

BOB: (No response.)

Theorists advise us that Fred's threats reveal a number of shortcomings. For example, behaviors targeted for punishment frequently receive positive reinforcement from another source—like peers and co-workers or even the supervisor's inadvertent actions. For another, managers who use punishment often come to be viewed negatively by the recipients of the punishment. At the very least, then, we can expect that Fred had set the stage for potentially irreparable damage to his working relationship with Bob! It is not clear what Fred really gained as a result of his punitive managerial posture.

One thing is clear from the above episode. Fred was telling Bob that it was *Bob's* responsibility to find out what had gone wrong over the past couple of weeks, then take steps to correct it. Implicitly he was also attributing Bob's marginal performance to one or more things that might be wrong—with Bob! Unfortunately, Fred made a common mistake: He focused only on what the employee might have been doing wrong while overlooking other possible causes for the marginal performance.

ATTRIBUTION ERRORS IN PERFORMANCE MANAGEMENT

Take a look at the data in Exhibit 1. It summarizes how managers from the health care and banking industries responded to two questions: (1) "What is the most frequent cause of poor performance by your employees?" and (2) "What is the most frequent cause of poor performance by yourself?" The exhibit shows quite different patterns of responses: When employees' performance deficiencies were at issue, the managers tended to attribute the problem to employees' lack of ability and/or effort; when the manager's own performance deficiencies were at issue, the problem was overwhelmingly viewed as a lack of outside support. But, we must ask, if managers need better support to achieve higher performance, doesn't the same hold true for their employees?

Responses such as these are of no great surprise to those familiar with an area of management research known as attribution theory. When dealing with marginal performers like Bob, the theory predicts that managers like Fred are more likely to "attribute" any performance problems to some deficiency within the individual—that is, to a lack of ability or lack of effort—rather than to a deficiency in the work situation, like a lack of organizational or managerial support. Given that Bob was considered technically competent when he was hired (thus satisfying the ability factor), Fred probably assumed that Bob's reduced performance resulted from a lack of motivation (a problem with the effort factor).

Managers who view performance problems in such a manner will spend valuable time and money trying to find ways to increase their employees" motivation directly and immediately. When these initial efforts fail, the threatening and punitive approach that Fred used in the last episode is likely to follow.

EXHIBIT 1 Marginal Performance: Attributions Given by Managers and by Employees Themselves

Number of Responses to the Question: Most common cause of poor performance by your employees?	*Attribution*	*Number of Responses to the Question: Most common cause of poor performance by yourself?*
22	Lack of Ability	2
15	Lack of Support	66
36	Lack of Effort	6

The fact that employees tend to attribute deficiencies in their performance to external causes, such as inadequate support, rather than to the internal causes their managers favor further complicates such situations. Bob, for example, is more likely to attribute his mediocre performance to a lack of supervisory recognition (an external cause) than to his own laziness (an internal cause)—which Fred seems to assume is the case. When such gaps between attributions exist, employees like Bob typically resent the harsh and punitive responses their managers use. On the other hand, managers get increasingly frustrated because they cannot understand the employee's failure to perform.

If this cycle of mismatched manager-employee attributions is allowed to continue, a worst-case scenario, in the form of what social psychologists call "learned helplessness," may occur. This term refers to the tendency for people who are exposed to repeated punishment or failure to believe they do not possess the skills needed to succeed at their job. As a result they become passive in their work, and they tend to remain so even after situational changes occur that make success once again possible. A feeling that outcomes are beyond one's control, when in fact they are not, is the essence of learned helplessness. People become convinced that they are doomed to fail no matter what they do. As a consequence, employees who experience learned helplessness will usually continue to exhibit passive and maladaptive behavior long after changes (such as increased support or the arrival of a new manager) occur that make success possible.

In Bob's case, learned helplessness resulting from Fred's punitive responses may cause Bob eventually to doubt the very abilities that led to his hiring and early successes. While learned helplessness is a worst-case scenario, it exemplifies the serious complications that can arise if managers fail to address marginal performance in a constructive way. The approach that we recommend for dealing more positively with the marginal performer is outlined below.

DEALING WITH BOB—A BETTER WAY

Many marginal performers, like Bob, are aware that they are not working up to their potential—and they know why. Given a positive environment for dialogue, they are often willing and able to pinpoint the causes—both personal and situational—of their performance problems. They are also willing to assume their share of the responsibility for correcting them. Toward this end, we suggest the following managerial strategy for "turning around" a marginal performer.

- Bring the performance gap to the marginal performer's attention.
- Ask in a nonthreatening manner for an explanation.
- Describe the implications of the marginal performer's substandard work.
- Restate the original and still-desirable performance objectives.
- Offer the external support necessary for the marginal performer to improve his or her performance.
- Express confidence that the marginal performer will respond as expected.
- Agree on an appropriate time frame for jointly evaluating future performance in terms of the agreed-upon standards.
- Continue the process until it succeeds or the individual admits to an employment mismatch that can be reconciled only by a job change.

To illustrate how these steps can be followed, let's go back in time and pick up our vignette at the point where Fred first noticed that Bob's performance had dropped off. We'll assume he was prepared to adopt this more positive approach to the situation. As Fred's dialogue with Bob develops, we'll occasionally interject some discussion of his actions and Bob's responses. This will help illustrate the steps and potential benefits of the recommended approach.

Fred noticed that Bob's performance had been down for two weeks. After thinking it over, he realized that a capable person like Bob should have been consistently performing at a higher level—but he may have needed some help. Fred decided to walk to Bob's work station and talk to him about the matter at once.

FRED: Bob? I'd like to talk with you a bit. This last production report shows you came in below standard again the past week.

BOB: Yeah, I guess I was a bit behind.

Immediately, Fred brought the performance gap to Bob's attention. He did this politely, but specifically and face-to-face. Bob readily admitted he had fallen behind.

FRED: How do you feel about falling behind?

BOB: Well, every time I get rolling I get hit with a schedule change. Sometimes they make sense, sometimes they don't. I'm not always clear about what to do. I didn't want to say much. So I just tried to struggle through on my own.

In the above exchange, Fred gave Bob a chance to express his feelings without putting him on the defensive. His next step was to try to identify the causes for Bob's substandard performance. To do this, Fred asked in a non-threatening manner for an explanation.

FRED: There certainly have been a lot of schedule changes lately. Which ones are giving you the most problems?

BOB: Mostly the changes with the Series J designs. I'm just not clear on how to handle them.

FRED: Yeah, they can be tricky. Have you asked anyone about them?

BOB: Well, I realize the project manager has a lot on her mind. I just didn't want to bother her with my own problems. And . . .

FRED: And?

BOB: Uh . . . I just didn't want her to think I couldn't do the job.

This back-and-forth talk revealed Bob's belief that his performance suffered from unclear schedule changes, something beyond his control. Fred listened to the content of Bob's message and tried to understand his feelings. He also asked Bob to clarify certain points, such as the types of schedule changes he had the most problems with and the reasons why he didn't ask for help. By remaining open-minded and avoiding common attribution errors, Fred learned a lot about the possible causes of Bob's poor performance. In fact, his active listening revealed that Bob feared he would look incompetent if he brought his problems with the design changes to the project manager's attention. Next, Fred provided Bob with some immediate support to reassure him that he was viewed as a capable and trustworthy worker.

FRED: You shouldn't worry about it, Bob. She thinks highly of you. In fact, she said having you here is really going to make things a lot easier. And your part of the process really counts. The project manager needs your help to meet the deadlines.

BOB: Well, I thought I could work it out, even if it took extra time.

FRED: I'm sure you could, Bob, with your technical skills. But on this project time counts, and there are other people here to help you when needed. It's important that you understand completely what happens when you don't make your numbers because of confusion over the schedule changes. You slow down the next process, and that compounds the schedule changes down the line. Then our standards fall off, and we risk missing the target dates. So you see, your work directly affects the overall performance of the unit.

BOB: Yes, I can see where it would.

After reassuring Bob that he was viewed as a highly capable and dependable worker, Fred made sure Bob understood the implications of his substandard work. Fred explained to Bob what happened when he slowed down on the job and stressed that his performance affected the entire project. This reminded Bob that others depended on his work being done well and on time so they could meet their performance objectives. It highlighted not only the significance of his job in general, but also the significance of high performance in that job. From the perspective of House's path-goal theory, Fred clarified the path Bob needed to follow to achieve the desired goal of high performance. But Fred wasn't finished yet.

FRED: Bob, before going further, let's review the performance objectives we established for you. They are. . . . (Fred and Bob review objectives.)

BOB: Yes, Fred, they're clear to me.

FRED: Well look, Bob, the next schedule change you get hit with, I want you to talk to the project manager or to me before it throws you behind. In the meantime, let's discuss ways of dealing with schedule changes for the Series J designs so that you know how to handle them. Then I'm sure your performance will be back up to the standard level where it belongs. Okay?

BOB: Okay, I'll sure feel better when things are back on track.

During this exchange Fred once again stated Bob's original and still-desired performance objectives. By doing this face-to-face, Fred reinforced the personal dimensions of their relationship, further heightened Bob's commitment to improve, and increased Bob's sense of accountability to Fred. In addition, Fred offered the support necessary for Bob to improve his performance. He urged Bob to ask for help when he ran into problems, something Bob had previously considered an unwelcome intrusion on the project manager. He further suggested that the two of them discuss how to deal with the Series J schedule changes. This was an offer of immediate help for dealing with a perceived job constraint. Finally, Fred expressed confidence that Bob would respond as expected. Bob readily agreed that he would be able to do so.

Following this discussion, Bob probably felt pretty good. Fred then made one more effort to ensure that Bob would get back on and stay on the high-performance track.

FRED: I feel real good about our conversation, Bob. You're a capable guy, and I know you'll be right back on top soon. Just to make sure things go okay, though, let's talk again after next week's reports are in. What do you think?

BOB: I'll look forward to it. It'll give us a chance to touch base.

Fred established an appropriate time frame and standards for evaluating Bob's future performance. By adding this control, he helped ensure that the promised improvements in productivity would become a reality. Bob was assured that Fred was interested in his ongoing performance and that productivity gains would receive attention. He also saw that a failure to obtain the desired results would require an explanation. By formally scheduling further meetings with Bob, Fred assured himself of opportunities to recognize performance improvements. If such improvements did not occur, the meetings would ensure that Bob's marginal performance would receive further attention before too much time had elapsed. At that point Fred could continue the process with Bob or, if he believed the job was a true mismatch, work with Bob to develop an alternative solution. Thus, the stage seemed set once again for Bob to become the high performer everyone expected him to be.

BROAD-BASED HIGH-PERFORMANCE MANAGEMENT

Our continuing example offers managers a starting point for developing personal and situation-specific strategies for dealing with marginal performers. Of course the exact nature of the marginal performance will vary from one person to the next. Our example has dealt with only one type—the capable individual whose work efforts have declined over time. From the individual performance equation, however, we know that marginal performance can arise from a lack of ability, effort, or support, or from some combination of these factors. To deal with the uniqueness of each situation, we suggest asking the diagnostic questions listed in Exhibit 2. The following guidelines also highlight useful actions.

TO MAXIMIZE ABILITY

The manager's task is to achieve and maintain an appropriate match between the capabilities of the marginal performer and the job he or she is asked to do. Depending on the nature of the job and the person, one of several options may be selected. In some cases the individual's abilities can be developed through training; in other cases the job may have to be changed so it better fits the individual; and in still others, individuals may have to be replaced with more capable workers. In all cases a job vacancy must be

EXHIBIT 2 Questions Managers Can Ask When Dealing with a Marginal Performer

Questions to Ask About Ability
Has the individual performed at a higher level in the past?
Is the performance deficiency total, or is it confined to particular tasks?
How well do the individual's capabilities match the job's selection criteria?
Has the individual been properly trained for current task requirements?

Questions to Ask About Support
Have clear and challenging task goals been set?
Are other employees having difficulty with the same tasks?
Is the job properly designed to achieve a "best fit" with the individual's capabilities?
Do any policies and/or procedures inhibit task performance?
Is the manager providing adequate feedback?
Is the individual being fairly compensated?
Is the work environment comfortable?
Is the manager providing sufficient empathy and emotional support?
Are the individual's co-workers providing sufficient emotional support?
Has the manager actually encouraged high performance?

Questions to Ask About Effort
Does the individual lack enthusiasm for work in general? For the assigned tasks in particular?
Are individuals with similar abilities performing at higher levels?
Has the individual been properly recognized for past accomplishments?
Are rewards and incentives provided on a performance-contingent basis?
Is the individual aware of possible rewards and incentives?
Does the individual have an appropriate role model?

recognized for what it is—perhaps the manager's greatest opportunity to build high-performance potential into a system by hiring a person whose talents and interests match the job's requirements.

Earlier we noted that repeated exposure to failure and punishment can lead to learned helplessness. Because the ability deficits are more imagined than real, however, individuals suffering from learned helplessness will need help in refocusing their concerns toward other performance factors. Take, for example, the case of a newly appointed manager who inherits a team of marginal performers who had received little or no support from their previous supervisor. To restore their feelings of competence, the manager must first help them understand that any past performance problems were not due to a lack of ability. This is the first step of a "turnaround" strategy.

TO MAXIMIZE SUPPORT

The manager's task here is to (1) help marginal performers secure the resources they need to achieve high levels of job performance, and (2) help remove any and all obstacles that inhibit high performance. Success with this factor sometimes requires a dramatic change in the way managers view their responsibilities. Rather than simply being the person who directs and controls the work of others, an effective manager always acts to facilitate their accomplishments. This involves doing much more than telling employees what to do and then following up on them. The truly effective manager creates a supportive work environment by clarifying performance expectations, changing job designs, providing immediate feedback, fostering better interpersonal relations, and eliminating unnecessary rules, procedures, and other job constraints.

Consider again the case of the newly appointed supervisor. Support is an especially critical component of an effort to alleviate learned helplessness. Once marginal performers are convinced through attributional training that they do have the ability required to perform, they must be further persuaded that they will receive the support required to excel. The manager should engage marginal performers in dialogues that identify the types of external support needed to help them apply their abilities to best advantage. Ideally initial task assignments will then be created to produce successful experiences that further bolster employees' newfound self-confidence.

TO MAXIMIZE EFFORT

Basic principles of motivation and positive reinforcement should be applied whenever managers deal with marginal performers. First, the marginal performer should be made aware whenever his or her performance falls below standard. He or she should also be told how substandard performance adversely impacts other workers, subunits, and the organization as a whole. Immediate positive reinforcement should follow performance improvements and all above-standard achievements. Punishment should be avoided. By serving as an enthusiastic role model, a supervisor can further help marginal performers become high achievers.

For the new supervisor dealing with a group of marginal performers, strategies to correct ability and support deficits must be accompanied by assurances that high performance will lead to desired outcomes. The most powerful means of persuasion are successful experiences clearly followed by positive reinforcement—praise, recognition, and other valued rewards. It is also helpful to provide positive role models who obtain desired rewards through skilled utilization and task accomplishment.

Finally, it is important to note that managers' motivational attempts gain leverage from ability and support efforts. The key is what psychologists call the *effectance motive,* a natural motivation that occurs from feelings of self-efficacy. When people feel competent in their work, the argument goes, they can be expected to work harder at it. Competence, in turn, comes from ability and the feeling that one's skills and aptitudes are equal to the tasks at hand. Competence also comes from support and the feeling that one's work environment helps, rather than hinders, task accomplishment.

It is said that the very best motivation is that which comes from within. Thus, managers can gain additional motivational impact by investing in ability and support factors. To the extent that greater perceived ability and support enhance one's sense of competence, internal motivation is a likely consequence. Rather than concentrating only on motivational strategies designed to encourage more work effort externally, managers should make sure they take full advantage of the improved internal motivation that may be derived when ability and support factors are addressed.

A VAST POOL OF RESOURCES

Marginal performers present significant challenges to their managers—but they also represent a vast pool of human resources with the potential to offer major productivity gains to their organizations. To capitalize on this potential, managers must be committed to working with marginal performers to identify the causes of their problems and take positive actions to move them toward greater accomplishments. The individual performance equation can provide managers with the insight they need to tap the true potential of the marginal performer. Specifically, it directs a manager's attention toward three major factors that influence individual performance—the often neglected support factor as well as the more commonly recognized ability and effort factors. Guided by this action framework, managers can take advantage of every interaction and every conversation with marginal performers to pursue their turnaround strategies. In the final analysis, the foundations for high-performance management rest with the managers themselves. To achieve the desired results, managers must:

- **Recognize that marginal performers are potential sources of major productivity gains for organizations.** At the very least, they must be considered just as important as any other human resource within the organization.
- **Recognize the need to implement positive turnaround strategies for dealing with marginal performers.** Systematic and well-considered attention, rather than outright neglect and even punishment, is the order of the day—every day of a manager's workweek.
- **Be ready to accept at least partial responsibility for the fact that a subordinate has become a marginal performer.** Many workers learn to be marginal performers from the way they are treated in the workplace—they don't start out to be that way. Bob, for one, sure didn't.

ACKNOWLEDGMENT

The case setting for this article was developed from a vignette presented in Wilson Learning Corporation's instructional video "Dealing with the Marginal Performer" (*Building Leadership Skills,* New York: Wiley, 1986) and examined in William L. Gardner's accompanying instructor's guide. The initial four dialogues reported here are loosely adapted from the video. We are indebted to Wilson Learning Corporation and John Wiley & Sons for allowing us to build upon this case framework.

CHAPTER 20
PERFORMANCE MANAGEMENT

ON THE FOLLY OF REWARDING A, WHILE HOPING FOR B

Steven Kerr

PERFORMANCE MANAGEMENT IN GLOBAL TEAMS

Bradley L. Kirkman
Deanne N. Den Hartog

Developing employees to have the skills needed to accomplish an organization's strategic goals, reinforcing good performance, providing feedback, and following up on unacceptable performance are all components of high-involvement management and performance management systems. Leaders and managers, in partnership with human resources, have the overall responsibility for ensuring that their organization's performance management system accomplishes its purpose. The responsibility for evaluating employee performance, however, is more likely to be shared with people throughout the organizational hierarchy. Due to the use of peer evaluations, reverse evaluations (subordinates evaluating bosses), and multirater evaluations (by subordinates, colleagues, supervisors, and sometimes customers and suppliers), companies that are serious about doing performance management well focus on developing the necessary skill set in a wide range of employees.

Leaders and managers should analyze the impact of their organization's performance management system and avoid the design flaws that Steven Kerr describes in an updated version of his classic article "On the Folly of Rewarding A, While Hoping for B." Kerr, Chief Learning Officer at Goldman Sachs, contends that many systems foster the wrong behavior by using rewards incorrectly. A failure to understand social reinforcement theory invariably results in dysfunctional behavior at work. Kerr notes that a common management folly is hoping for teamwork but rewarding individual behavior.

This problem is addressed in "Performance Management in Global Teams," written by Bradley Kirkman, a U.S. scholar who focuses on teams, and Deanne Den Hartog, a Dutch scholar who worked on the GLOBE project studying international leadership. They discuss how performance management should be carried out and explain how cultural dilemmas can be avoided.

ON THE FOLLY OF REWARDING A, WHILE HOPING FOR B*

Steven Kerr

Whether dealing with monkeys, rats, or human beings, it is hardly controversial to state that most organisms seek information concerning what activities are rewarded, and then seek to do (or at least pretend to do) those things, often to the virtual exclusion of activities not rewarded. The extent to which this occurs of course will depend on the perceived attractiveness of the rewards offered, but neither operant nor expectancy theorists would quarrel with the essence of this notion.

Nevertheless, numerous examples exist of reward systems that are fouled up in that the types of behavior rewarded are those which the rewarder is trying to discourage, while the behavior desired is not being rewarded at all.

FOULED-UP SYSTEMS

IN POLITICS

Official goals are "purposely vague and general and do not indicate . . . the host of decisions that must be made among alternative ways of achieving official goals and the priority of multiple goals . . ."[1] They usually may be relied on to offend absolutely no one, and in this sense can be considered high acceptance, low quality goals. An example might be "All Americans are entitled to health care." Operative goals are higher in quality but lower in acceptance, since they specify where the money will come from, and what alternative goals will be ignored.

The American citizenry supposedly wants its candidates for public office to set forth operative goals, making their proposed programs clear, and specifying sources and uses of funds. However, since operative goals are lower in acceptance, and since aspirants to public office need acceptance (from at least 50.1 percent of the people), most politicians prefer to speak only of official goals, at least until after the election. They of course would agree to speak at the operative level if "punished" for not doing so. The electorate could do this by refusing to support candidates who do not speak at the operative level. Instead, however, the American voter typically punishes (withholds support from) candidates who frankly discuss where the money will come from, rewards politicians who speak only of official goals, but hopes that candidates (despite the reward system) will discuss the issues operatively.

IN WAR

If some oversimplification may be permitted, let it be assumed that the primary goal of the organization (Pentagon, Luftwaffe, or whatever) is to win. Let it be assumed further that the primary goal of most individuals on the front lines is to get home alive. Then there appears to be an important conflict in goals—personally rational behavior by those at the bottom will endanger goal attainment by those at the top.

---

*Reprinted with permission from the *Academy of Management Executive 9*, no. 1 (February 1995): 7–14, via Copyright Clearance Center.

But not necessarily! It depends on how the reward system is set up. The Vietnam War was indeed a study of disobedience and rebellion, with terms such as *fragging* (killing one's own commanding officer) and *search and evade* becoming part of the military vocabulary. The difference in subordinates' acceptance of authority between World War II and Vietnam is reported to be considerable, and veterans of the Second World War were often quoted as being outraged at the mutinous actions of many American soldiers in Vietnam.

Consider, however, some critical differences in the reward system in use during the two conflicts. What did the GI in World War II want? To go home. And when did he get to go home? When the war was won! If he disobeyed the orders to clean out the trenches and take the hills, the war would not be won and he would not go home. Furthermore, what were his chances of attaining his goal (getting home alive) if he obeyed the orders compared to his chances if he did not? What is being suggested is that the rational soldier in World War II, whether patriotic or not, probably found it expedient to obey.

Consider the reward system in use in Vietnam. What did the soldier at the bottom want? To go home. And when did he get to go home? When his tour of duty was over! This was the case whether or not the war was won. Furthermore, concerning the relative chance of getting home alive by obeying orders compared to the chance if they were disobeyed, it is worth noting that a mutineer in Vietnam was far more likely to be assigned rest and rehabilitation (on the assumption that fatigue was the cause) than he was to suffer any negative consequence.

In his description of the "zone of indifference," Barnard stated that "a person can and will accept a communication as authoritative only when . . . at the time of his decision, he believes it to be compatible with his personal interests as a whole."[2] In light of the reward system used in Vietnam, wouldn't it have been personally irrational for some orders to have been obeyed? Was not the military implementing a system which rewarded disobedience, while hoping that soldiers (despite the reward system) would obey orders?

IN MEDICINE

Theoretically, physicians can make either of two types of error, and intuitively one seems as bad as the other. Doctors can pronounce patients sick when they are actually well (a type 1 error), thus causing them needless anxiety and expense, curtailment of enjoyable foods and activities, and even physical danger by subjecting them to needless medication and surgery. Alternately, a doctor can label a sick person well (a type 2 error), and thus avoid treating what may be a serious, even fatal ailment. It might he natural to conclude that physicians seek to minimize both types of error.

Such a conclusion would be wrong. It has been estimated that numerous Americans have been afflicted with iatrogenic (physician caused) illnesses.[3] This occurs when the doctor is approached by someone complaining of a few stray symptoms. The doctor classifies and organizes these symptoms, gives them a name, and obligingly tells the patient what further symptoms may be expected. This information often acts as a self-fulfilling prophecy, with the result that from that day on the patient for all practical purposes is sick.

Why does this happen? Why are physicians so reluctant to sustain a type 2 error (pronouncing a sick person well) that they will tolerate many type 1 errors? Again, a look at the reward system is needed. The punishments for a type 1 error are real: guilt, embarrassment, and the threat of a malpractice suit. On the other hand, a type 1 error (labeling a well person sick) is a much safer and conservative approach to medicine in today's litigious society. Type 1 errors also are likely to generate increased income and a stream of steady customers who, being well in a limited physiological sense, will not embarrass the doctor by dying abruptly. Fellow physicians and the general public therefore are really rewarding type 1 errors while hoping fervently that doctors will try not to make them.

A current example of rewarding type 1 errors is provided by Broward County, Florida, where an elderly or disabled person facing a competency hearing is evaluated by three court-appointed experts who get paid much more *for the same examination* if the person is ruled to be incompetent. For example, psychiatrists are paid $325 if they judge someone to be incapacitated, but earn only $125 if the person is judged competent. Court-appointed attorneys in Broward also earn more—$325 as opposed to $175—if their clients lose than if they win. Are you surprised to learn that, of 598 incapacity proceedings initiated and completed in the county in 1993, 570 ended with a verdict of incapacitation?[4]

IN UNIVERSITIES

Society hopes that professors will not neglect their teaching responsibilities but rewards them almost entirely for research and publications. This is most true at the large and prestigious universities. Clichés such as "good research and good teaching go together" notwithstanding, professors often find that they must choose between teaching and research-oriented activities when allocating their time. Rewards for good teaching are usually limited to outstanding teacher awards, which are given to only a small percentage of good teachers and usually bestow little money and fleeting prestige. Punishments for poor teaching are also rare.

Rewards for research and publications, on the other hand, and punishments for failure to accomplish these, are common. Furthermore, publication-oriented résumés usually will be well-received at other universities, whereas teaching credentials, harder to document and quantify, are much less transferable. Consequently it is rational for university professors to concentrate on research, even to the detriment of teaching and at the expense of their students.

By the same token, it is rational for students to act based upon the goal displacement[5] which has occurred within universities concerning what they are rewarded for. If it is assumed that a primary goal of a university is to transfer knowledge from teacher to student, then grades become identifiable as a means toward that goal, serving as motivational, control, and feedback devices to expedite the knowledge transfer. Instead, however, the grades themselves have become much more important for entrance to graduate school, successful employment, tuition refunds, and parental respect, than the knowledge or lack of knowledge they are supposed to signify.

It therefore should come as no surprise that we find fraternity files for examinations, term paper writing services, and plagiarism. Such activities constitute a personally rational response to a reward system which pays off for grades rather than knowledge. These days, reward systems—specifically, the growing threat of lawsuits—encourage teachers to award students high grades, even if they aren't earned. For example:

> *When Andy Hansen brought home a report card with a disappointing C in math, his parents . . . sued his teacher . . . . After a year and six different appeals within the school district, another year's worth of court proceedings, $4,000 in legal fees paid by the Hansens, and another $8,500 by the district . . . the C stands. Now the student's father, auto dealer Mike Hansen, says he plans to take the case to the State Court of Appeals. "We went in and tried to make a deal: They wanted a C, we wanted an A, so why not compromise on a B?" Mike Hansen said. "But they dug in their heels, and here we are."*[6]

IN CONSULTING

It is axiomatic that those who care about a firm's well-being should insist that the organization get fair value for its expenditures. Yet it is commonly known that firms seldom bother to evaluate a new TQM, employee empowerment program, or whatever, to see if the company is getting its money's worth. Why? Certainly it is not because people have not pointed out that this situation exists; numerous practitioner-oriented articles are written each year on just this point.

One major reason is that the individuals (in human resources, or organization development) who would normally be responsible for conducting such evaluations are the same ones often charged with introducing the change effort in the first place. Having convinced top management to spend money, say, on outside consultants, they usually are quite animated afterwards in collecting rigorous vignettes and anecdotes about how successful the program was. The last thing many desire is a formal, revealing evaluation. Although members of top management may actually hope for such systematic evaluation, their reward systems continue to reward ignorance in this area. And if the HR department abdicates its responsibility, who is to step into the breach? The consultants themselves? Hardly! They are likely to be too busy collecting anecdotal "evidence" of their own, for use on their next client.

IN SPORTS

Most coaches disdain to discuss individual accomplishments, preferring to speak of teamwork, proper attitude, and one-for-all spirit. Usually, however, rewards are distributed according to individual performance. The college basketball player who passes the ball to teammates instead of shooting will not compile impressive scoring statistics and is less likely to be drafted by the pros. The ballplayer who hits to right field to advance the runners will win neither the batting nor home run titles, and will be offered smaller raises. It therefore is rational for players to think of themselves first, and the team second.

IN GOVERNMENT

Consider the cost-plus contract or its next of kin, the allocation of next year's budget as a direct function of this year's expenditures—a clear-cut example of a fouled-up reward system. It probably is conceivable that those who award such budgets and contracts really hope for economy and prudence in spending. It is obvious, however, that adopting the proverb "to those who spend shall more be given" rewards not economy, but spending itself.

IN BUSINESS

The past reward practices of a group health claims division of a large eastern insurance company provides another rich illustration. Attempting to measure and reward accuracy in paying surgical claims, the firm systematically kept track of the number of returned checks and letters of complaint received from policyholders. However, underpayments were likely to provoke cries of outrage from the insured, while overpayments often were accepted in courteous silence. Since it was often impossible to tell from the physician's statement which of two surgical procedures, with different allowable benefits, was performed, and since writing for clarifications would have interfered with other standards used by the firm concerning percentage of claims paid within two days of receipt, the new hire in more than one claims section was soon acquainted with the informal norm: "When in doubt, pay it out!"

This situation was made even worse by the firm's reward system. The reward system called for annual merit increases to be given to all employees, in one of the following three amounts:

1. If the worker was "outstanding" (a select category, into which no more than two employees per section could be placed): 5 percent
2. If the worker was "above average" (normally all workers not "outstanding" were so rated): 4 percent
3. If the worker committed gross acts of negligence and irresponsibility for which he or she might be discharged in many other companies: 3 percent.

Now, since the difference between the five percent theoretically attainable through hard work and the four percent attainable merely by living until the review date is small, many employees were rather indifferent to the possibility of obtaining the extra one percent reward. In addition, since the penalty for error was a loss of only one percent, employees tended to ignore the norm concerning indiscriminant payments.

However, most employees were not indifferent to a rule which stated that, should absences or latenesses total three or more in any six-month period, the entire four or five percent due at the next merit review must be forfeited. In this sense, the firm was *hoping* for performance, while *rewarding* attendance. What it got, of course, was attendance. (If the absence/lateness rule appears to the reader to be stringent, it really wasn't. The company counted "times" rather than "days" absent, and a ten-day absence therefore counted the same as one lasting two days. A worker in danger of accumulating a third absence within six months merely had to remain ill—away from work—during a second absence until the first absence was more than six months old. The limiting factor was that at some point salary ceases, and sickness benefits take over. This was usually sufficient to get the younger workers to return, but for those with 20 or more years' service, the company provided sickness benefits of 90 percent of normal salary, tax-free! Therefore . . .)

Thanks to the U.S. government, even the reporting of wrongdoing has been corrupted by an incredibly incompetent reward system that calls for whistleblowing employees to collect up to 30 percent *of the amount of a fraud* without a stated limit. Thus prospective whistleblowers are encouraged to delay reporting a fraud, even to actively participate in its continuance, in order to run up the total and, thus, their percentage of the take.

TABLE 1 Common Management Reward Follies

We hope for . . .	*But we often reward . . .*
• Long-term growth; environmental responsibility	• Quarterly earnings
• Teamwork	• Individual effort
• Setting challenging "stretch" objectives	• Achieving goals; "making the numbers"
• Downsizing; rightsizing; delayering; restructuring	• Adding staff; adding budget; adding Hay points
• Commitment to total quality	• Shipping on schedule, even with defects
• Candor; surfacing bad news early	• Reporting good news, whether it's true or not; agreeing with the boss, whether or not (s)he's right

I'm quite sure that by now the reader has thought of numerous examples in his or her own experience which qualify as "folly." However, just in case, Table 1 presents some additional examples well worth pondering.

CAUSES

Extremely diverse instances of systems which reward behavior A although the rewarder apparently hopes for behavior B have been given. These are useful to illustrate the breadth and magnitude of the phenomenon, but the diversity increases the difficulty of determining commonalities and establishing causes. However, the following four general factors may be pertinent to an explanation of why fouled-up reward systems seem to be so prevalent.

1. ***Fascination with an "Objective" Criterion.*** Many managers seek to establish simple, quantifiable standards against which to measure and reward performance. Such efforts may be successful in highly predictable areas within an organization, but are likely to cause goal displacement when applied anywhere else.
2. ***Overemphasis on Highly Visible Behaviors.*** Difficulties often stem from the fact that some parts of the task are highly visible while other parts are not. For example, publications are easier to demonstrate than teaching, and scoring baskets and hitting home runs are more readily observable than feeding teammates and advancing base runners. Similarly, the adverse consequences of pronouncing a sick person well are more visible than those sustained by labeling a well person sick. Team-building and creativity are other examples of behaviors which may not be rewarded simply because they are hard to observe.
3. ***Hypocrisy.*** In some of the instances described, the rewarder may have been getting the desired behavior, notwithstanding claims that the behavior was not desired. For example, in many jurisdictions within the United States, judges' campaigns are funded largely by defense attorneys, while prosecutors are legally barred from making contributions. This doesn't do a whole lot to help judges to be "tough on crime" though, ironically, that's what their campaigns inevitably promise.
4. ***Emphasis on Morality or Equity Rather Than Efficiency.*** Sometimes consideration of other factors prevents the establishment of a system which rewards behavior desired by the rewarder. The felt obligation of many Americans to vote for one

candidate or another, for example, may impair their ability to withhold support from politicians who refuse to discuss the issues. Similarly, the concern for spreading the risks and costs of wartime military service may outweigh the advantage to be obtained by committing personnel to combat until the war is over. The 1994 Clinton health plan, the Americans with Disabilities Act, and many other instances of proposed or recent governmental intervention provide outstanding examples of systems that reward inefficiency, presumably in support of some higher objective.

ALTERING THE REWARD SYSTEM

Managers who complain about lack of motivation in their workers might do well to consider the possibility that the reward systems they have installed are paying off for behavior other than what they are seeking. This, in part, is what happened in Vietnam, and this is what regularly frustrates societal efforts to bring about honest politicians and civic-minded managers.

A first step for such managers might be to explore what types of behavior are currently being rewarded. Chances are excellent that these managers will be surprised by what they find—that their firms are not rewarding what they assume they are. In fact, such undesirable behavior by organizational members as they have observed may be explained largely by the reward systems in use.

This is not to say that all organizational behavior is determined by formal rewards and punishments. Certainly it is true that in the absence of formal reinforcement some soldiers will be patriotic, some players will be team oriented, and some employees will care about doing their job well. The point, however, is that in such cases the rewarder is not causing the behavior desired but is only a fortunate bystander. For an organization to act upon its members, the formal reward system should positively reinforce desired behavior, not constitute an obstacle to be overcome.

POSTSCRIPT

An irony about this article's being designated a management classic is that numerous people claim to have read and enjoyed it, but I wonder whether there was much in it that they didn't know. I believe that most readers already know, and act on in their non-work lives, the principles that underlie this article. For example, when we tell our daughter (who is about to cut her birthday cake) that her brother will select the first piece, or inform our friends before a meal that separate checks will be brought at the end, or tell the neighbor's boy that he will be paid five dollars for cutting the lawn after we inspect the lawn, we are making use of prospective rewards and punishments to cause other people to care about our own objectives. Organizational life may seem to be more complex, but the principles are the same.

Another irony attached to this "classic" is that it almost didn't see the light of day. It was rejected for presentation at the Eastern Academy of Management and was only published in the *Academy of Management Journal* because Jack Miner, its editor at the time, broke a tie between two reviewers. Nobody denied the relevance of the content, but reviewers were quite disturbed by the tone of the manuscript, and therefore its appropriateness for an academic audience. A compromise was reached whereby I added a bit of the great academic cure-all, data (Table 1 in the original article, condensed and summarized in this update), and a copy editor strangled some of the life from my writing style. In this respect, I would like to acknowledge the extremely competent editorial work performed on this update by John Veiga and his editorial staff. I am grateful to have had the opportunity to revisit the article, and hope the reader has enjoyed it also.

Endnotes

1. C. Perrow, "The Analysis of Goals in Complex Organizations," *Readings on Modern Organizations*, ed. A. Etzioni (Upper Saddle River, NJ: Prentice Hall, 1969). 66.
2. C. I. Barnard, *The Functions of the Executive* (Cambridge, MA: Harvard University Press, 1964). 165.
3. L. H. Garland, "Studies of the Accuracy of Diagnostic Procedures," *American Journal Roentgenological, Radium Therapy Nuclear Medicine 82* (1959): 25–38; and T. J. Scheff, "Decision Rules, Types of Error, and Their Consequences in Medical Diagnosis," *Mathematical Explorations in Behavioral Science*, eds. F. Massarik and P. Ratoosh (Homewood, IL: Irwin, 1965).
4. *Miami Herald*, May 8, 1994. 1a, 10a.
5. Goal displacement results when means become ends in themselves and displace the original goals. See P. M. Blau and W. R. Scott, *Formal Organizations* (San Francisco, CA: Chandler, 1962).
6. "San Francisco Examiner," reported in *Fortune*, February 7, 1994. 161.

PERFORMANCE MANAGEMENT IN GLOBAL TEAMS*

Bradley L. Kirkman
Deanne N. Den Hartog

When organizations globalize, most of the work dedicated to this effort gets done through the collaboration and coordination of many people located in different nations. Often this collaboration takes the form of global work teams. In fact, teams form the basic building blocks of most global organizations. Globalization rarely occurs without teamwork. The "global" aspect of teamwork in organizations adds another layer of complexity to the complicated overall globalization process. Thus, there is a pressing need to understand the role of teamwork in globalization and what factors account for successful global teams.

The purpose of this chapter is to discuss the performance management of teams in an international context. Performance management is problematic in teams of this type because members are likely to bring widely disparate viewpoints about appropriate ways to reward, recognize, evaluate, and train and develop global team members. In this chapter, we first discuss the issue of global team-based rewards and recognition. Second, we highlight the difficult task of evaluating contributors in global teams. Finally, we discuss the importance of training and development in global teams. We also note that many of the issues we discuss in this chapter could be applied to other

*Reprinted with permission from *The Blackwell Handbook of Global Management: A Guide to Managing Complexity* (Oxford, UK: Blackwell, 2004): 250–272.

organizational units in addition to teams, such as work units, departments, divisions, whole organizations, or even one-on-one manager–employee relationships. We focus specifically on teams here due to their wide-spread use in global organizing.

REWARDS AND RECOGNITION IN GLOBAL TEAMS

If the many failures of implementing global teams and other organizational forms world wide could be traced to one single factor, that factor would most likely be inappropriate reward and recognition strategies. Key management decisions related to reward and recognition include:

- Should rewards be based on individual performance, team performance, or both?
- What are the important factors to consider when using team-based pay?
- How can recognition be used in addition to, or instead of, monetary rewards?

REWARDING GLOBAL TEAMS

Managers have many choices for rewarding global teams, but generally the issue comes back to two major strategies: rewarding team members based on individual performance and rewarding team members based on team performance as a whole. Whether organizations are team-based or individual-based, most U.S. managers continue to reward organizational contributions individually. Managers and employees set individual goals and develop individual action plans, and individuals are held accountable for their progress toward their goals. This approach becomes problematic in a team setting because often tasks are accomplished by people working together, interdependently, and individual contributions cannot be identified or, in some cases, are non-existent. Consider the example of a software design team whose members frequently exchange the latest versions of a software program. Software may undergo hundreds or even thousands of iterations; and keeping track of specific, individual contributions neither makes sense in their context nor is feasible. This effect may be exacerbated in many global teams because of their reliance on electronic rather than face-to-face communication, which makes assessing individual contributions even more problematic. As Charles Handy stated when discussing virtual organizations. "How do you manage people whom you do not see?"[1]

INDIVIDUAL-BASED REWARDS

Individual rewards, in most cases, do just what they are designed to do. They elicit behaviors that are consistent with an individual's focus and persistence toward his or her own goals, not those of a team, especially in individualist contexts. For example, the piece-rate pay system, so often used in manufacturing settings worldwide, compensates individuals for the number of units they produce daily. The more an individual produces, the more he or she gets paid. Consider what happens, however, when a team-based work system is implemented in such an environment. Imagine the reaction of a piece-rate-compensated worker being asked to step away from his or her work area for an hour or two to help a new team member learn a task. While helping a new team member, the piece-rate worker produces nothing that will be counted and monetarily rewarded. The new team member who needs the help might as well be reaching into the person's wallet or purse and removing money while being helped! Simply put, individual-based pay motivates individual-based behavior. Unless there is an incentive for teamwork, most human beings won't react positively to simply being told to "act like a team."

TEAM-BASED REWARDS

At the other end of the spectrum are team-based rewards. Incentives are not based on individual output, but on the output or performance of the team as a whole. Such plans might range from 100 percent team-based pay to as little as 5 to 10 percent, but the intent is the same: to reward team members for performing well as a team. As with individual pay, team members receiving team-based pay will likely be motivated consistent with the manner in which they are paid. Unfortunately, what looks good on paper often does not translate well in the workplace. Some companies that have transitioned to team-based pay systems, such as the apparel maker Levi Strauss in the United States, have fared no better, and in some cases, worse than companies retaining their individual-based pay systems. The underlying reason for much of the failure may be social loafing.[2]

Social loafing is a phenomenon best described by the "tug-of-war" example. Tug-of-war usually involves two groups of individuals pulling in opposite directions on a rope, sometimes across an unpleasant middle ground such as a mud pit or pool of water. One team wins when it successfully pulls the other team into or across the unpleasant middle ground. Studies have shown, however, that as more and more individuals are added to either side of the rope, individual pulling efforts decrease.[3] That is, team members who initially used 100 percent of their pulling strength reduce their efforts to, say, 80 or 90 percent, once new team members are added. Team members simply see no reason to continue exerting maximum effort once their comrades have joined the fray. Social loafing effects have been found in a variety of countries.[4]

The same phenomenon can and does occur in the workplace, and team-based pay can be the culprit. When Levi Strauss abandoned their piece-rate pay system and transitioned to 100 percent team-based pay in the United States, chaos erupted.[5] Slower workers and those who took long lunch breaks or slacked off on the job were verbally assaulted and threatened with physical violence. To maintain order, law-enforcement officers were stationed at one Levi Docker's trouser-producing plant in Powell, Tennessee. Higher-performing team members reacted very negatively to fellow members whom they held responsible for reducing the overall compensation of the team. What's worse, the workers who were most negatively affected by team-based pay were the highest performing under the old piece-rate system. Many saw their take-home pay decrease as rewards were tied to team, not individual, performance. Levi's lost many of these high-performing workers to rival factories before abandoning team-based pay.

COMBINING INDIVIDUAL AND TEAM-BASED REWARDS

So, if the lesson above is not to use either purely individual-based pay or purely team-based pay in global teams, then the answer must lie somewhere in between. Indeed, most team researchers and compensation specialists argue that a combination of individual- and team-based rewards provides a better solution (even though some research has not supported this claim).[6] Companies can use global team-based pay to encourage teamwork, and individual-based pay to stimulate individual accountability and decrease social loafing. However, such a solution raises another question. What is the best combination of individual- and team-based rewards? Should companies strive for a fifty-fifty balance or lean more heavily in one direction or the other? And, if the latter, how does one decide the direction of emphasis? There is no easy answer here, but part of the answer lies in at least five distinct areas: the nature of the task, the stability of team membership, the national culture of the team members, the national and local labor laws affecting employee compensation, and reward options.

NATURE OF THE TASK

By nature of the task, we refer specifically to how *interdependent* the tasks are that the team performs. As defined earlier, task or workflow interdependence is defined as the degree of communication and coordination required between team members to get their jobs done.[7] Low task interdependence might occur in a group of project managers who perform their tasks relatively autonomously in different regions of the world, rarely interacting or exchanging information. High task interdependence would be characteristics of a surgical team or a globally distributed team of software design engineers who constantly exchange information and materials to accomplish tasks. A rule of thumb would be the more interdependent the task, the higher the level of team-based rewards relative to individual-based rewards. This rule of thumb also applies to larger work units as in the case of unit-based pay, such as departments or divisions.

MEMBERSHIP STABILITY

The stability of team membership is another important factor affecting the proportion of team-based rewards used. If there are frequent composition changes in a global team, it will be difficult to accurately assess the contributions of various members and, in turn, reward based on global team performance. For example, Eastman Chemical (Kodak) abandoned team-based rewards because the company found it impossible to draw indisputable lines around "the team."[8] Managers will likely have to move to a higher level of rewards such as unit-level or organization-level rather than team-based rewards to ensure fair compensation when firm team boundaries cannot be drawn. Perhaps team members themselves can be a part of the design and administration of a rewards and recognition program, especially in countries in which employee participation is commonly used and valued.

NATIONAL CULTURE OF TEAM MEMBERS

One of the strongest points we can make is that the whole concept of performance management will vary across different countries and cultures. For example, reward and recognition systems are often designed based on Western-oriented notions of goal- and task-oriented conceptualizations of work. These work concepts are unlikely to hold up in Eastern cultures or those cultures in which work is not considered a central life interest.[9] It should come as no surprise that in countries like the United States, Great

Britain, and Australia, cultural individualism pervades rewards and recognition programs based on individual performance. The notion of "sharing" rewards or credit for an accomplishment is as foreign a notion in individualistic countries as, say, an "employee of the month" award would be in collectivistic countries like Japan, China, or Malaysia.

Should the managers at Levi Strauss have been surprised at the reaction of their U.S. workers when the company tried to implement team-based rewards? Perhaps hindsight is a luxury here, but not only were Levi's operating in what many consider to be the most individualistic country in the world,[10] they hired workers who assumed they would be working in a piece-rate system. It doesn't take a lot of imagination to guess what type of worker is attracted and selected into this compensation system: individualistic workers who like to work autonomously and be responsible solely for their outcomes. Simply put, a piece-rate system rewards the fastest individual workers. So, not only did Levi's try to implement team-based pay in a highly individualistic country, they tried to implement it in a facility in which they had hired individualistic workers from the most individualist country in the world.[11]

The impact of individualism–collectivism on team and other unit-based reward strategies can also be seen in more collectivist-oriented countries such as China. In China, harmony is seen as a key element in relationships among workers. Maintaining such harmony ensures smoothly running work processes. A research study on human resource management in China showed that few companies in China implement individual-based rewards, as these types of rewards could lead to so-called "red-eye disease" among workers, an expression commonly used in China to refer to jealousy.[12] Jealousy emanating from individual-based pay could constitute a disruption of harmony and, as such, have a negative impact on working relationships and performance.[13] Such interpersonal dynamics in the workplace may undergo some changes in the coming years owing to China's fast paced economic development and increased openness to Western organizations and management styles. However, paying attention to the different meanings and effects that recognition and reward for performance may have in different cultures is important.

Thus, where global teams are concerned, in addition to looking at tasks, managers need to take into account the heterogeneity level or diversity of individualism–collectivism of the team members. That is, if a global team or work unit comprises primarily members from individualist countries such as those in North America, Western Europe, and Australia (all the members are basically the same on the individualism–collectivism dimension), rewards should be based more on individual performance rather than on team or unit performance.[14] Similarly, if a global team or work unit comprises mostly members from collectivist countries such as those in Asia, Latin America, and Africa (again, the members are basically the same on the individualism–collectivism dimension), managers can use a higher proportion of team- or unit-based rewards compared to individual-based rewards. Reinforcing this strategy, there is evidence that supports the link between one's degree of collectivism and a preference for team-based rewards[15] and between individualism and resistance to team-based work systems in general.[16] One could argue, however, that using a large proportion of team-based rewards might again lead to higher levels of social loafing in collectivistic countries. Research does not support this contention, however. In fact, in an experiment designed to compare social loafing between U.S. and Chinese managers, Americans performed less effectively when working in groups compared to working alone.[17] Chinese managers, on the other hand, never demonstrated a social loafing effect and, in fact, performed better in a group than working alone. These results suggest that the lack of a social loafing effect in collectivistic countries provides additional support for using a high proportion of team- or unit-based rewards.

Perhaps the trickiest reward scenario is for a global team that is characterized by a high level of cultural value heterogeneity on the individualism–collectivism dimension. For example, team members comprising a global team from countries such as those in Asia, Europe, Latin America, and North America would likely bring completely different assumptions and beliefs about the appropriateness of team-based rewards. Team leaders should seek the input of heterogeneous teams before designing and implementing a team-based reward system. It is likely that the parameters of such a system will have to be negotiated among team members with such diverse viewpoints on reward appropriateness. The greater the cultural diversity on a global team, the more likely will be the need for team leaders and members to think through the design and implementation of team- or unit-based reward systems. Taking action quickly on these issues may lead to problems.[18]

LABOR LAWS

Local labor laws on compensation issues must be considered when deciding between individual-based and higher-level rewards. For example. Genencor International, the second largest biotechnology company in the world and a joint venture between Eastman Chemical and Finland's Cultor, has operations in Argentina, Belgium, Finland, and the United States with headquarters in Rochester, New York. In an attempt to streamline their human resource practices worldwide, managers at Genencor wanted to implement team-based pay at all of their facilities. They were not successful in Finland, however, because of local labor laws and active union involvement at the facilities.[19] Finnish labor unions control and regulate salaries by job levels. Managers found that they were required to conform to national and state labor laws and the industry union-based collective bargaining agreements. While some companies, such as General Electric, have been very successful in dealing with unions, especially in Europe, managers should keep in mind that their ability to manipulate compensation to stimulate teamwork and to establish other performance-related pay plans might be constrained by national labor laws.

REWARD OPTIONS

A final key point is the role of recognition as it relates to team performance. Employees often value gestures of recognition more than pure financial rewards. For example, when asked what is important in a job, most U.S. workers ranked a "full appreciation of work done" and a "feeling of being in on things" much higher than good wages.[20] Many managers all over the world often overlook recognition as a relatively inexpensive way in which to reinforce desired team-related behaviors. Guidelines for using recognition should be similar to those for designing reward systems for teams.

Richard Daft tells the story of an American executive in Japan who offered a holiday trip to the top salesperson, but employees showed no interest. After changing the individual recognition program to group recognition in accordance with the collectivist values of the Japanese employees, the entire group reached the sales target.[21] Thus, recognizing teams or units when the members have, on the whole, collectivist values and recognizing individuals when the members have individualist values are good rules of thumb.

In summary, when designing and implementing global team-based reward systems, managers should be certain to:

- use a combination of individual- and team-based rewards to motivate team-related behavior but avoid social loafing (the balance of this combination will vary by culture);
- use a higher level of team-based relative to individual-based rewards the higher the level of task interdependence in a global team;
- use a higher level of individual-based relative to team-based rewards as the instability of global team membership increases;
- use a higher level of team-based rewards the more collectivistic the global team; use a higher level of individual-based rewards the more individualistic the global team; and when the heterogeneity level of individualism–collectivism in the team is high, reward systems will be best negotiated among team members with such diverse viewpoints on reward appropriateness;
- pay attention to national and state labor laws and the collective bargaining agreements established with industry unions when designing and implementing reward systems for global teams;
- take into account the importance of recognition to supplement or complement tangible reward systems for global teams, tailoring recognition to the cultural values of each global team member.

PERFORMANCE EVALUATION AND APPRAISAL IN GLOBAL TEAMS

As with the reward and recognition of global teams and work units, evaluation of individual global team members and teams as a whole has presented many challenges to those who lead global teams. In most organizations, evaluations are often tied to important rewards such as promotions or highly visible assignments. Thus, there is a clear link between performance evaluation and rewards: in order to be able to design effective performance-related pay systems, one must first be able to measure performance. This holds for both global team and individual-based systems. One of the most frequently observed reasons why performance-related pay systems fail to reach the desired results is that the criteria for performance evaluation are unclear or unfair.[22] Key decisions in global team-based performance appraisal include:

- On what additional knowledge, skills, and abilities (KSAs) should workers be evaluated when they are working in a global team versus individually?
- Who should have input into global team member evaluations (supervisor, peers, customers)?

- How can managers ensure the perceived fairness of the performance evaluation process in multicultural global teams?

APPRAISALS

Taking the knowledge, skills, and abilities decision first, evaluating global team members on team-relevant KSAs is another way to reinforce and motivate teamwork in organizations in addition to monetary rewards and recognition. There is a link between good reward systems and appraisals; timely and appropriate rewards require an appraisal system that ensures performance is measured adequately. As such, appraisal acts as a basis for the reward.

Effective appraisal systems enable the assessment of task performance and monitor whether people are good team players whose behavior is conducive to the effectiveness of the entire team. Effective appraisal systems should both reward good team players and discourage behaviors that are not conducive to global team effectiveness.[23] Each organization is responsible for conducting job analyses to determine the specific KSAs needed for each global team. Beyond task-specific KSAs are the more general, process-oriented ones, such as conflict resolution, collaborative problem-solving, communication, decision-making, and team member support. In most studies of team effectiveness, these KSAs have been found to be critical to team success.[24] Such processes vary by culture and country.

U.S. researchers have found that conflict about task-related issues (rather than interpersonal-related issues) enhances team performance, especially the quality of team decision-making.[25] Thus, for teams composed predominantly of U.S. and other Western members, managers would be encouraged to stimulate and encourage this type of conflict to increase team performance. There are cultural differences, however, that might make this advice problematic for non-Western global team members. For example, the concept of "face-saving" is related to group harmony and conversational indirectness. In Eastern cultures such as China, Japan, and the Philippines, the loss of face, or public humiliation, can result from receiving negative feedback.[26] Thus, while team members in the United States might openly confront one another in meetings and question the rationale behind decisions in order to enhance decisionmaking, such behaviors in cultures that value face might be cause for extreme shame, ending in retaliation or possibly physical violence such as the Indonesian ship-worker who chased his boss into his quarters with an axe after being publicly berated in front of other crew members.[27]

EVALUATION INPUT

Another key decision in global team-based performance appraisals is who should have input into the evaluation process. Accompanying the increase in the use of 360° feedback, or getting evaluation input from one's boss, peers, and subordinates, in the United States has been the use of peer evaluations in teams.[28] The logic for their use is, who can better assess the performance of team members than the people who work with each other on a daily basis?

Rather than relying solely on just one source of feedback for team member evaluations, many companies integrate multiple sources similar to a 360°-feedback program. Nancy Kurland and Diane Bailey, researchers who study telecommuting, or workers who do their jobs from remote locations and communicate electronically, stated:

> *A major challenge for [global team] managers is their inability to physically observe their employees' performance. They question, "How do you measure productivity, build trust, and manage people who are physically out of sight?" If a manager can't see her subordinates in action, then she can't note where the employee is struggling and where he is strong . . . monitoring and measuring [employee] performance remain problematic and a source of concern.*[29]

Clearly, assessing the performance of global team members who are geographically dispersed is a challenge. One company on the cutting edge of global virtual team performance evaluation and assessment is Sabre, Inc., the Dallas/Fort Worth, Texas-based reservation company.[30] Sabre provides computer reservation systems for American Airlines, United Airlines, and over 60,000 travel agents in 114 countries. Sabre is also a majority owner of Travelocity.com, the on-line reservation service, and uses global virtual teams in part of its North American Canadian and U.S. operations. Sabre has built comprehensive performance review system, which uses actual customer satisfaction ratings as part of an overall "balanced scorecard"[31] measure, or a measure that includes both financial and non-financial performance indicators, of global team effectiveness. Managers assess individual contributions to team effectiveness by monitoring electronic communications and by systematically collecting data from peers and direct reports using the 360° format. Performance data provide a solid foundation for recognizing and rewarding team and individual performance, developing new training programs to assist virtual teams, and identifying individual team members who could benefit from off-line mentoring and coaching. As one manager at Sabre stated, "Most everyone's work is measured in the results they produce and through statistics, and it can all be pulled out systematically for each individual."[32] For global teams at Sabre, U.S. and Canadian team members can be judged more on what they actually do rather than on what they appear to be doing.

ASSESSMENT ACROSS CULTURES

Cultural values that would be likely to affect how global team members in different countries give each other feedback are the individualism–collectivism, power distance, and uncertainty avoidance dimensions and the concepts of harmony, assertiveness, and face. Research has shown that collectivists give more generous evaluations to fellow team members than do individualists, and this is especially true if the team member is an in-group rather than an out-group member.[33] In-group members are similar others such as family and close friends while out-group members lie outside these preferred groups. Thus, fair and unbiased peer evaluations may be more difficult to obtain when collectivistic global team members have to rate members of their in-group, especially in face-to-face, rather than virtual teams in which the pressures for conformity may be higher.

Power distance is the second cultural value likely to affect peer evaluations in global teams. Power distance refers to the extent to which power differences and status inequalities in a society are tolerated. In high power-distance countries such as China,

Mexico, and the Philippines, subordinates are typically more reluctant to challenge their supervisors than are employees in low power-distance countries such as Finland, Israel, and the United States. In line with this, employees in high power-distance cultures were shown to be more fearful in expressing disagreement with their managers.[34] If global teams are composed of members of different status levels, and lower-status team members are asked to evaluate the performance of higher-status members, evaluations are likely to be positively skewed, especially for face-to-face teams. People in high power-distance cultures are likely to be reluctant to provide negative feedback to superiors, and the acceptability of the idea that subordinates would be allowed to provide such ratings is likely to be less in high power-distance cultures, as this may be perceived to threaten status positions.

Uncertainty avoidance refers to cultures in which members shun ambiguity.[35] People in such cultures want things to be predictable and easy to interpret, and rituals such as elaborate planning and control systems are put into place to ensure this. The concept of lifelong employment in Japan is a good example of how organizations can reduce uncertainty. Looking at performance appraisal, one would expect a much higher degree of formalization in high uncertainty avoidance cultures. The performance appraisal system is likely to be spelled out in more detail, and there are more regulations and procedures in place, ensuring that complaints or grievances are handled through a predesigned structure. For example, German culture ranks high on uncertainty avoidance and research has shown that German employees typically prefer formalized performance evaluations such as clear goals, time frames, and exact measurements.[36]

The emphasis on maintaining harmony found in several Eastern cultures may lead to skewed peer and subordinate ratings in a positive direction, since global team members would be reluctant to jeopardize their relationships with fellow members. Similarly, team members from cultures that are typically highly assertive, aggressive, and dominant in social relationships are more likely to provide negative feedback than those in less assertive cultures.[37] People in highly assertive cultures such as the United States prefer direct feedback and communication and have a "tell it like it is" mentality. For example, at General Electric, all employees are ranked from the top to the bottom of the organization. The bottom 10 percent may be given either an opportunity to improve, or outplacement services. Former CEO Jack Welch argues that such a system is appropriate because softening feedback for under-performing workers is unfair to them and akin to outright lying because it might prevent them from finding opportunities that are more suitable. In contrast, in many Asian cultures the subtleties of conversational indirectness are preferred.[38] We do not want to give the impression that directness is the one best way to provide feedback in order to enhance performance in global teams. The real issue here is maintaining harmony and how that may affect peer and subordinate ratings in global teams. Directness may not be as appropriate in Eastern cultures, but subtle approaches may be just as effective because the elaborate networks that exist in these cultures will ensure that everyone will already know relevant performance feedback.

Similar to the effect it has on open conflict, saving face will likely prevent open discussion of individual global team member performance by fellow members, especially in face-to-face teams. However, this does not mean that peer feedback cannot be used on teams that have members that value saving face. At Motorola in the Philippines, for example, issues regarding team performance are raised in more general form in team meetings.[39] No one is singled out personally, but often this is enough to motivate the under-performing team members to step up their efforts. When performance appraisal data must be collected from global team members, it can be collected anonymously and presented in summary form to mask authorship. Such a strategy has worked very effectively for Motorola's teams in the Philippines and in other countries that value face-saving.

FAIRNESS ACROSS CULTURES

The third and final issue for performance evaluation and appraisal in global teams is ensuring perceptions of fairness or justice in the performance appraisal process. In Western management thought, justice in organizations has generally been conceived of as having three dimensions:

- *Distributive justice*—the perceived fairness of the distribution of outcomes. This type of justice emanated from equity theory.[40]
- *Procedural justice*—the perceived fairness of the criteria used to make decisions regarding the distribution of outcomes, including voice, or the opportunity for the employee to have a say in decisions.[41]
- *Interactional justice*—the perceived fairness of how decisions are communicated, including adequate explanations and consideration of employee welfare by managers.[42]

While the perceived fairness of evaluation procedures has received considerable attention in dyadic manager–employee settings,[43] there has been considerably less attention paid to the perceived fairness of *team-based* evaluation settings.[44] One recent study did examine general employee justice concerns during an implementation of self-managing work teams in two U.S. *Fortune* 50 organizations.[45] Many employee concerns centered on issues of the fairness of team-based performance appraisals. Open-ended comments from the study included: "Will peer reviews be fair and objective?"; "Who will fairly judge my contribution to the business?"; and "I hate peer ratings because it is a personality contest and not a question of merit." Clearly, employees in the United States were very concerned about the fairness of team-based performance appraisals. In additon, these employees expressed the desire to have voice in the performance appraisal process. This finding was echoed at the dyadic level by Jerald Greenberg who found that U.S. employee perceptions of procedural justice in the appraisal decision were based on, among other elements, the ability to rebut or challenge a supervisor's appraisal.[46]

Owing to cultural differences, there are reasons to believe that global team members may have different mental models regarding what constitutes a fair team-based performance appraisal. In other cultural contexts, employees may not conceive of distributive, procedural, and interactional justice in the same manner.[47] For example, while Western conceptualizations of procedural justice include the ability to challenge or rebut decisions, research has shown that in China, procedural justice does not include this component.[48]

The most likely explanation for this difference is the cultural value of power distance.[49] While power distance was originally conceived of as a country- or nation-level phenomenon,[50] like many of the other cultural values, reseachers have adopted this dimension to explain variations in individual behavior. For example, Joel Brockner and his colleagues found that when employees did not have a say in managerial decisions, they were less committed to their organizations. However, this effect was much more pronounced in lower power-distance cultures such as the United States and Germany than in high power-distance cultures such as China, Mexico, and Hong Kong.[51] It has also been shown that the relationships between procedural justice and trust in supervisors and between distributive justice and psychological (implied) contract fulfillment were stronger for those lower, rather than higher, in power distance.[52] Simon Lam and his colleagues found similar results with justice–work outcome relationships, with the effects of fairness stronger for those lower, rather than higher, in power distance.[53]

These findings suggest that managers should pay attention to cultural value differences especially power distance, when designing and implementing global team-based performance appraisal systems if team members are to perceive them as fair. This is important because a number of studies have shown that employees who perceive managerial decisions as unjust will react unfavorably.[54] Unfortunately, at times there may be very little managers can do to ensure fairness in employee work assignments in global teams. For example, at ItemField, a New York-based business-to-business software developer, new-hire Israeli team members located in Israel who typically do not work on Friday were told that they had to be on call on Fridays to support the U.S. sales force.[55] Even though Israeli employees were alerted in advance, business demands limited the actions that U.S. managers took to enhance fairness perceptions among their Israeli global team members.

There is also evidence that the performance evaluation process may be fairer (less biased) in globally distributed teams versus face-to-face teams. Differences in such demographic factors as race, gender, and age can lower performance ratings for employees who differ in these aspects from their bosses,[56] and for team members who are different from team leaders.[57] However, when team leaders do not see team members on a daily basis, the opportunities for bias to enter the performance appraisal process may be fewer. In addition, contamination of evaluations by perceptual biases is less likely when team leaders have extensive objective data at their disposal.[58]

When designing and implementing global team-based performance evaluation and appraisal systems, managers should be certain to:

- reward good team players but also discourage behaviors that are not conducive to global team effectiveness;
- in addition to determining task-specific KSAs, include evaluations of global team processes such as conflict resolution, collaborative problem-solving, communication, decision-making, and team member support;
- use multidimensional, balanced performance evaluation systems that include a mixture of objective and subjective ratings such as 360º feedback and altering peer feedback systems based on cultural differences, along with technology-based measures to document global team member achievements such as e-mail and electronic team meeting archives; customer surveys and team member input;
- enhance the fairness of global team peer evaluations by: (1) attempting to broaden team member in-groups by stressing value similarity among members; (2) standardizing the appraisal system by training peer raters and using job-relevant rating scales; (3) enhancing the fairness of peer evaluations by informing employees of

when and how ratings will be collected; (4) rewarding team members on their ability and willingness to provide accurate ratings that differentiate between low and high performers; and (5) assessing team members on the individualism-collectivism dimension in order to anticipate potential bias in peer ratings.[59]

TRAINING AND DEVELOPMENT IN GLOBAL TEAMS

One of the most important facets of effective global team implementation is the effective use of team training and development. Working in global teams can be a very foreign concept to many employees, and if managers decide that teams are appropriate, they need guidance in order to effectively shape appropriate global team behaviors. One facet that is often missing from global team training is the inclusion of the whole team in hands-on capability development.[60] Global teams should be treated as a whole unit and training should be applied as the team performs actual job-related tasks.[61] As a result, the value of the training is established in the context of the work that the team does. Key questions to consider with regard to training and development include:

- What are the best methods for training and development in global team-based organizations?
- What should global team members be trained to do?
- How can training be leveraged to increase the amount of global team learning and flexibility?

BEST METHODS

Regarding methods or techniques for global team training and development, there are at least three general techniques used by training specialists to enhance team member abilities. First, there is the cognitive style, which normally involves traditional classroom instruction in which a trainer covers basic principles of team operation such as forming a team charter, setting ground rules for teams, or managing conflict. Second, there is the behavioral style, or experiential learning, which can involve immersing team members in situations similar to those they are likely to face in their actual jobs. Such simulations might include performing a complex task in a limited amount of time, purposefully engaging in conflict over a valued resource, or role-playing a key event in a team's life cycle. Finally, there is the affective style, which typically involves some level of emotional involvement on the part of team members. This may take the form of heart-to-heart talks between team members such as intimate self-disclosure, or intense personal feedback between global team members guided by experienced facilitators.

With at least three possible methods of training and development, the question still remains: What is the best method to use? The answer is, not surprisingly, all three. Since human beings differ in the manner in which they learn most effectively, that is, some are classroom learners, some have to experience it before they understand, and still others need to be moved emotionally to internalize key learnings, most training and development specialists advocate a combination of these three techniques to enhance the transfer of training for all global team members.

As stated, people differ in the way they learn most effectively. An individual's learning strategy can be seen as a predisposition to use certain types of learning behavior.[62] For example, one can distinguish between *surface* (instruction-oriented) and *deep* (meaning-oriented) learning strategies, the latter fostering managers' career success.[63] The different ways in which people learn reflect different existing modes of thought or cognitive styles. The most widely recognized distinction in this area is between *analytical*, that is, logical, sequential information processing, and *intuitive*, in other words, more integrative and nonlinear thinking styles.[64] There are also cross-cultural differences to be considered in the way people think and prefer to learn; however, the evidence regarding cross-cultural differences in these cognitive styles is somewhat mixed. Whereas some propose a contrast between the "analytic West" and the "intuitive East," many studies find different pattern. In a six-nation study among managers from organizations in both the public and private sectors and management students, the most integrative and nonlinear thinking was seen among managers from the most developed countries (U.K., Australia, Hong Kong, Singapore), whereas an emphasis on logical and sequential thinking was seen in the developing and Arab countries (Jordan, Nepal).[65] The explanation for the differences may lie in the increasing complexity of management problems in many organizations in highly developed countries. Such high complexity may call for integrative, non-linear thinking.

What about cross-cultural differences in learning preferences? According to Hofstede, people in uncertainty avoidant cultures have been programmed from childhood to feel comfortable in structured environments.[66] Such differences in the need for structure are also reflected in the learning environment. In cultures high on uncertainty avoidance (Germany) one thus often finds structured learning situations with precise objectives, detailed arrangements, and strict timetables. People prefer tasks with a correct answer that they can find and like to be rewarded for accuracy. On the other hand, those from cultures low on uncertainty avoidance (United Kingdom) are more likely to prefer less structure. They prefer open-ended questions, vague objectives and no timetables. They do not believe that there should be a single correct answer and expect to be rewarded for originality.[67] Similar patterns may be expected in a training situation, where people from cultures high on uncertainty avoidance are likely to prefer much more structured processes and assignments compared with people from cultures low on uncertainty avoidance.

Another cultural dimension to consider is power distance. In cultures high on power distance, the role and status of the teacher or trainer are likely to be different from such a role in cultures low on power distance. In cultures high on power distance, the teacher-student relationship is essentially an unequal relationship, in which the more powerful party (teacher) is treated with respect and hardly ever openly receives uninvited criticism from the less powerful party (students). The process is likely to be teacher-centered, with the teacher initiating conversation and deciding on what is to be taught. In contrast, in cultures low on power distance, teachers and students have a more equal relationship. The process is more student-centered: students take more initiative and decide on and pursue what they want to learn. Open communication, questioning teachers, and arguing their opinion is the rule rather than the exception.[68] Again, similar patterns may be expected in a training situation.

TRAINING CONTENT

Beyond the methods and techniques used for training and the learning styles of trainees, the second key issue is the actual content of the training for team members. As discussed in our section on evaluation (performance appraisal), team-relevant knowledge, skills, and abilities (KSAs) must be identified by each organization for each job, so that global team members will know and can be trained for the most job-relevant KSAs. Also relevant are interpersonal processes such as communication, decision-making, and conflict resolution, all critical for global team success. In addition to KSAs and global team processes, development of self-management skills among global team members is important. Since the purpose of many global teams is to be proactive and take on the many responsibilities traditionally reserved for management, starting team members down the path of self-management to increase global team effectiveness is critically important.

The main question then becomes: How much autonomy is appropriate for most global teams? There are several contingency factors that are crucial to consider here. First is the type of global team. Research has shown that autonomy is highly effective for line-level work teams but can have detrimental effects on cross-functional project teams that have a high level of complexity and rich information-processing requirements.[69] In these types of teams strong leadership is needed to help team members manage complexity.

Second, there is the level of task interdependence, defined earlier in this chapter as the degree of coordination and communication needed between members to perform a task. Granting teams high autonomy when tasks are interdependent results in higher levels of team effectiveness; in contrast, for tasks low in interdependence, giving autonomy to a team can actually result in lower team effectiveness.[70]

Third, there are several cultural values that are likely to affect initial acceptance of training on self-management. Global team members from high power-distance countries such as Mexico, China, and the Philippines may have difficulty engaging in self-management-related activities such as setting their own goals or taking initiative without asking for supervisory permission. Also, management in such countries may be less likely to allow the global team members a high level of autonomy. A being orientation refers to the extent to which people in a society focus on non-work activities. People in high being-oriented societies work only as much as they need in order to live and would likely resist taking on the additional responsibilities associated with a high degree of self-management. Determinism refers to the extent to which people in a society believe that their outcomes are determined by forces outside of their control such as luck, fate, or a deity. Because self-management requires that employees set their own goals and take actions to bring them closer to achieving their goals, employees high in determinism would likely resist self-management in teams.[71]

Recent research has supported a link between these cultural values and employee resistance to self-management in teams in different countries.[72] So, does this mean that managers should not try to train employees on self-management in countries that are high in power distance, being orientation, and/or determinism? The answer is not so much whether employees are trained on self-management or not, but *how* such training occurs and gets carried out.[73] For example, employees in high power-distance countries are likely to need more reinforcement that organizational authorities support their taking on more self-management in their global teams. Perhaps having high-level keynote speakers during training sessions would encourage high power-distance employees to internalize the self-management training. Training modules could be designed around more routine tasks that would become self-managing, rather than higher-level tasks such as hiring and firing fellow team members or initiating management-level decisions. Self-management training and development need to be adapted to fit the cultural values of team members in different countries.[74]

LEVERAGING GLOBAL TEAM TRAINING

A final key issue for training and development involves leveraging global team training and development for maximum team learning and flexibility. In a true team-based organization, learning is required across functions, levels, and even organizations.[75] Such learning requires norms that are very different to those present in traditional organizations. For example, true team learning requires that organizations encourage team members to surface bad news and act on it.[76] However, if the organizational *status quo* maintains the typical reaction of negatively evaluating the messenger of bad news, organizational learning will not take place. Only organizations that encourage experimentation and innovation and set up mechanisms for shared team reflection, or what Amy Edmondson calls a climate of psychological safety,[77] will be likely to be able to successfully captialize on this learning.[78]

In this respect, differences among people as they deal with errors are of interest. In organizational life, errors are unavoidable. Even with the best checks and procedures there is almost always some margin for error. Focusing too much on error prevention, through bureaucratic procedures and checks, and having a negative approach to errors, by punishment of those responsible, may lead global team members to low levels of risk-taking and exploration.[79] In such circumstances, people may cover up errors or blame others rather than take responsibility for their errors and share their experiences so others can learn from them. In describing his role in the Barings Bank disaster in 1993, for instance, Nick Leeson noted that a major reason he started an unauthorized shadow account was that he was afraid to admit errors.[80] Leeson found a way to hide errors and their negative consequences and make up for them without having to admit to them. Barings had a very punishing culture, quickly firing those that made mistakes or were not successful enough, which apparently reinforced covering up mistakes.[81]

As Peter Senge notes, a learning organization needs to have a positive attitude toward exploration and errors.[82] Thus, an important management issue becomes "the design and nurture of work environments in which it is possible to learn from mistakes and to collectively avoid making the same ones in the future."[83] In order to be able to learn from errors, it is necessary to use active rather than passive approaches.[84] Thus, a strategy that ensures negative consequences of errors such as loss of time, accidents, and faulty products are minimized (a control goal) and at the same time fosters the potential positive side of errors (learning, innovation, resilience—a learning goal), seems optimal.[85] Error orientations are shared within teams and even organizations. The above example of the punishing culture at Barings that resulted in Leeson's trying to cover up errors illustrates the reinforcement outcomes of covering up errors. In a Dutch study, error aversion (feeling strained by and covering up errors) was negatively related to team performance; and a mastery orientation (taking on the challenges of error occurrences) was positively related to organizational performance.[86] A link between dealing with errors and uncertainty avoidance seems likely.[87] Cultures high on uncertainty avoidance are likely to be low on risk-taking and probably have a more negative view of errors. In line with this, these cultures may then be high on error strain and covering up errors and low on learning from them.[88] The concept of saving face is critical for how global team members handle the discussion of errors. If team members are concerned about admitting mistakes to avoid humiliation, this could severely hamper global team learning. On the other hand, if the global team members knew how to decode and design for this dynamic, conceivably they might understand what was going on, take appropriate actions, save face, and promote team learning.

As stated above, to reflect on one's actions and surroundings is crucial to organizational learning. For example, reflection can be important for recognizing how certain present ways of operating can be obsolete, owing to environmental changes.[89] Teams often use "habitual routines" to guide team behavior. Habitual routines exist when groups repeatedly exhibit a functionally similar pattern of behavior in similar situations without explicitly selecting this pattern over alternative ways of behaving.[90] Although having some "ground rules" on what to do in certain circumstances seems helpful to smooth interactions and effective functioning, groups tend to stick to the patterns of interactions that are set early in their life, even when circumstances have changed and these patterns are no longer adequate. Reflexive behavior in teams seems important to counteract the tendency to rely on routines that may be no longer effective.

At the team level, reflexivity is defined as the extent to which group members overtly reflect on and communicate about the group's objectives, strategies (decision-making) and processes (communication), and adapt these to current or anticipated circumstances.[91] Differences between people in reflexivity are also important. As was seen above, teams need to reflect on errors, but also analyze their success, think about whether current group composition is adequate to meet objectives, talk about their use of time and resources, and decide how to deal with changes in the environment.[92] Besides reflecting on such issues, teams also need to engage in action planning to ensure that envisioned changes are acted upon. Reflexivity can thus be seen as an iterative three-stage process of reflection, planning, and taking action. Reflexivity is especially important for the effective functioning of teams involved in complex decision-making. Such teams have high autonomy and work in highly uncertain and unpredictable environments.[93] Research has found reflexivity to be positively related to subjective as well as objective measures of team performance in the United Kingdom as well as in the Netherlands.[94]

A trusting and open team climate and non-authoritarian leadership styles are conducive to reflexivity in teams. However, only few teams actually take the time to reflect on their strategies and actions on a regular basis.[95] Given the fact that in many organizations global teams are increasingly autonomous and need to make increasingly complex decisions, more attention to the creation of work environments that are conducive to reflexivity and learning seems relevant to help improve global team functioning.[96] For example, the United States, Brazilian, and Italian team members on Whirlpool Corporation's North American Appliance Group developed a chlorofluorocarbon-free refrigerator using a global team. To enhance team learning, the team met face to face every four months to discuss the project and the ground rules necessary to stimulate creative, out-of-bounds thinking. A key to the project's success was the informal social gathering that took place, allowing team members to build relationships and develop a climate for freedom of expression.[97] Similarly, Mobil Corporation has its global team members huddle in one location at the launch of a new product so the members can build the relationships necessary for true learning to take place.[98] Beyond anecdotal evidence, to date levels of team reflexivity have not been thoroughly compared across different cultures. However, reflexivity seems most likely to occur in cultures that are relatively low on power distance. In high power-distance cultures, team members are less likely to speak up or disagree with team leaders or other higher-status members. This may hamper reflexivity and global team learning in general.

The planning aspect of reflexivity is likely to be linked to uncertainty avoidance. For example, Rauch and colleagues compared German and Irish small enterprises.[99] Germany and Ireland are similar on all but one of Hofstede's culture dimensions. Where the German culture is high on uncertainty avoidance, Ireland ranks as one of Europe's lowest on uncertainty avoidance. Thus, Germany has a culture in which one would expect business owners to plan more and in greater detail. Customers will expect such planning and doing things "right," and meeting customer expectations in such an environment should be linked to careful and detailed planning. In contrast, in Ireland planning is seen as less necessary. Customers will have less respect for plans, show unplanned behavior themselves, and expect high flexibility. Planning too much will render small business owners inflexible. Thus, Rauch and colleagues expected and found that planning had a positive influence on small business success in Germany and a negative influence on small business success in Ireland. The cultural appropriateness of planning will influence its success.

Training and development systems aimed to maximize global team learning and success need to take cultural values such as those ensuing from power distance and uncertainty avoidance into account. Culture differences will lead to different expectations of the role of the trainer or teacher, differences in the likelihood of people "speaking up" during the learning process, different preferences in structure and planning approaches, and different approaches to errors—all variables that may play a role in designing effective learning environments for global teams. When designing and implementing global team-based training and development systems, managers should be certain to:

- use a combination of training techniques to enhance the transfer of training for all the members of a global team (cognitive, behavioral, and affective styles);
- use structured learning situations with precise objectives, detailed arrangements, and strict timetables for team members high in uncertainty avoidance cultural contexts; and open-ended questions, vague objectives, and few timetables for team members low in certainty avoidance contexts: use teacher-centered training for team members in cultures high in power distance and student-centered training for team members with cultures low in power distance;
- train global team members to be self-managing when appropriate (as with work teams versus project teams, highly interdependent versus highly independent teams that have relatively low levels of power distance, being orientation, and determinism);
- leverage global team training and development for maximum team learning and flexibility (increase global team psychological safety, avoid a focus on error prevention, and increase team reflexivity).

CONCLUSION

We have discussed global team performance management in the areas of rewards and recognition, performance evaluation and appraisal and training and development. In each of these areas, we have seen how the cultural values of those belonging to global teams had important implications for the design and administration of global team performance management. Clearly, there is not one ideal way to manage global team performance or the performance of other work units, such as departments or divisions. Implementing a best practice without regard for culture would likely result in a high level of employee resistance to such initiatives.[100] To increase the chances for effective global teams and work units, managers should take into account the complexity of the cultural differences represented on the team. Only then will organizations be able to realize the true global team effectiveness.

Notes

1. Handy, C. (1995). "Trust and the Virtual Organization," *Hardward Business Review, 73:* 40–48.
2. Latane, B., Williams. K. D., and Harkins, S. (1979). "Many Hands Make Light the Work: The Causes and Consequences of Social Loafing," *Journal of Personality and Social Psychology, 37,* 822–832.
3. Moede, W. (1927). "Die Richtlinien Der Leistungs-Psychologic," *Industrielle Psychotechnik," 4,* 193–207; Ringelmann, M. (1913). *Aménagement des fumeriers et des purins*, Paris: Librarie agricole de la Maison rustique.
4. Thompson, L. 2000. *Making the Team: A Guide for Managers.* Upper Saddle River, NJ: Prentice Hall.
5. King, R. T., Jr. 1998. "Jeans Therapy: Levi's Factory Workers are Assigned to Teams, and Morale Takes a Hit," *Wall Street Journal*, 232: Al, A6.
6. Wageman, R. 1998. "Interdependence and Group Effectiveness," *Administrative Science Quarterly,* 40: 145–180.
7. Shea, G. P., and Guzzo, R. A. (1987). "Groups as Human Resources," in G. Ferris and K. Rowland (eds.). *Research in Personnel and Human Resources Management*, Greenwich. CT: JAI Press, Vol. 5: 323–356.
8. Lipnack, J., and Stamps; J. (2000). *Virtual Teams: People Working Across Boundaries with Technology*, 2nd edn. New York: Wiley.
9. Trompenaars. F. (1993). *Riding the Waves of Culture: Understanding Diversity in Global Business*, Chicago: Irwin.
10. Hofstede, G. (1980). *Culture's Consequences: International Differences in Work-Related Values.* Beverly Hills, CA: Sage.
11. *Ibid.;* Au, K. Y. (1999). "Intra-Cultural Variation: Evidence and Implications for International Business," *Journal of International Business Studies*, 30: 799–812.
12. Verburg. R. M. (1996). "Developing HRM in Foreign-Chinese Joint Ventures," *European Management Journal,* 14(5), 518–525.
13. Verburg, R. M, Drenth, P. J. D., Koopman, P. L. Van Muijen, J. J., and Wang, Z. M. (1999), "Managing Human Resources Across Cultures: A Comparative Analysis of Practices in Enterpreneurial Organizations in China and the Netherlands," *International Journal of Human Resource Management,* 10(3): 391–410.
14. Kirkman, B. L., Gibson, C. B., and Shapiro, D. L. (2001). "Exporting Teams: Enhancing the Implementation and Effectiveness of Work Teams in Global Affiliates," *Organizational Dynamics,* 30(1), 12–29.
15. Cable, D. M., and Judge, T. A. 1994. "Pay Preferences and Job Search Decisions: A Person-Environment Fit Perspective," *Personnel Psychology*, 47: 317–348. Kirkman, B. L., and Shapiro, D. L. (2000). "Understanding Why Team Members Won't Share: An Examination of Factors Related to Employee Receptivity to Team-Based Rewards," *Small Group Research*, 31: 175–209.
16. Kirkman, B. L., and Shapiro, D. L. (2001a). "The Impact of Employee Cultural Values on

Productivity, Cooperation, and Empowerment in Self-Managing Work Teams," *Journal of Cross-Cultural Psychology*, 32(5): 597–617; Kirkman. B. L., and Shapiro, D. L., (2001b), "The Impact of Cultural Values on Job Satisfaction and Organizational Commitment in Self-Managing Work Teams: The Mediating Role of Employee Resistance," *Academy of Management Journal*, 44(3): 557–569.

17. Earley, P. C. (1989). "Social Loafing and Collectivism: A Comparison of the United States and the People's Republic of China," *Administrative Science Quarterly*, 34: 565–581.
18. Maznevski, M. L., and Chudoba, K. M. (2001). "Bridging Space Over Time: Global Virtual Team Dynamics and Effectiveness," *Organization Science*, 11(5): 473–492.
19. Kirkman et al. (2001).
20. Kovach, K. A. (1987). "What Motivates Employees? Workers and Supervisors Give Different Answers," *Business Horizons* 30: 61.
21. Daft, R. L., (1987). *Management*. Chicago: Dryden Press.
22. Richardson. R. (2001). "Performance-Related Pay: Another Management Fad?," *Inaugural Addresses Series in Research in Management*, EIA-2001-01-ORG. Rotterdam: Erasmus Research Institute of Management, Erasmus University.
23. Gibson, C. B., and Kirkman, B. L. (1999). "Our Past, Present, and Future in Teams: The Role of Human Resources Professionals in Managing Team Performance," in A. I. Kraut and A. K. Korman (eds.). *Evolving Practices in Human Resources Management: Responses to a Changing World of Work,* San Francisco: Jossey-Bass, 90–117.
24. Campion, M. A., Medsker, G. J., and Higgs, A. C. (1993). "Relations Between Work Group Characteristics and Effectiveness: Implications for Designing Effective Work Groups," *Personnel Psychology*, 46: 823–850; Campion, M. A., Papper, E. M., and Medsker, G. J. (1996). "Relations Between Work Group Characteristics and Effectiveness: A Replication and Extension," *Personnel Psychology*, 49: 429–452; Hyatt, D. E., and Ruddy, T. M. (1997). "An Examination of the Relationship Between Work Group Characteristics and Performance: Once More into the Breech," *Personnel Psychology*, 50: 553–585.
25. Pelled, L. H., Eisenhardt, K. M., and Xin, K. R. (1999). "Exploring the Black Box: An Analysis of Work Group Diversity, Conflict, and Performance," *Administrative Science Quarterly*, 44: 1–28.
26. Earley, P. C. (1997). *Face, Harmony, and Social Structure: An Analysis of Organizational Behavior across Cultures.* New York: Oxford University Press.
27. Daft (1987).
28. Saavedra, R., and Kwun, S. K. (1993). "Peer Evaluation in Self-Managing Work Groups," *Journal of Applied Psychology*, 78: 450–462.
29. Kurland, N. B., and Bailey, D. E., (1999). "Telework: The Advantages and Challenges of Working Here, There, Anywhere, and Anytime," *Organizational Dynamics*, 28(2): 53–67.
30. Kirkman, B. L., Rosen, B., Gibson, C. B., Tesluk, P. E., and McPherson, S. O. (2003), "Five Challenges to Virtual Team Performance: Lessons from Sabre, Inc.," *Academy of Management Executive*, 16(3): 67–79.
31. Kaplan, R. S., and Norton, D. P. (1996). "Using the Balanced Scorecard as a Strategic Management System," *Harvard Business Review*, 74: 75–85.
32. *Ibid.*
33. Gomez, C. B., Kirkman, B. L., and Shapiro, D. L. (2000). "The Impact of Collectivism and Ingroup/Outgroup Membership on the Evaluation Generosity of Team Members," *Academy of Management Journal*, 43(6): 1097–1106.
34. Adsit, D. J., London. M., Crom, S., and Jones, D. (1997). "Cross-Cultural Differences in Upward Ratings in a Multinational Company," *International Journal of Human Resource Management*, 8(4): 385–401.
35. Hofstede (1980); Hofstede, G. (2001). *Culture's Consequences: Comparing Values, Behaviors, Institutions, and Organizations across Nations.* Thousand Oaks, CA: Sage.
36. Lindholm, N. (1999). "National Culture and Performance Management in MNC Subsidiaries," *International Studies of Management and Organization*, 29(4): 45–66.
37. Den Hartog, D. N. (2003). "Assertiveness," in R. J. House, P. J. Hanges, M. Javidan, P. W. Dorfman, V. Gupta. and GLOBE Associates (eds.). *Cultures, Leadership, and*

Organization: A 62 Nation GLOBE Study. Thousand Oaks, CA: Sage, vol. 1.

38. *Ibid.*; Holtgraves, T. (1997). "Styles of Language Use: Individual and Cultural Variability in Conversational Indirectness," *Journal of Personality and Social Psychology,* 73: 624–637.
39. Kirkman et al. (2001).
40. Adams, J. S. (1965). "Inequity in Social Exchange," in L. Berkowitz (ed.), *Advances in Experimental Social Psychology.* New York: Academic Press, vol. 2, 267–299.
41. Lind, E. A., and Tyler, T. R. (1988). *The Social Psychology of Procedural Justice*. New York: Plenum.
42. Bies, R. J., and Moag, J. S. (1986). "International Justice: Communication Criteria of Fairness," in R. Lewicki, M. Bazerman, and B. Sheppard (eds.). *Research on Negotiation in Organizations*, Greenwich, CT: JAI Press. vol. 1, 43–55.
43. Cropanzano, R., and Greenberg, J. (1997). "Progress in Organizational Justice: Tunneling Through the Maze," in C. L. Cooper and I. T. Robertson (eds.). *International Review of Industrial and Organizational Psychology*, New York: John Wiley, vol. 2, 317–372; Greenberg, J. (1986). "Determinants of Perceived Fairness of Performance Evaluations," *Journal of Applied Psychology*, 71(2): 310–342; Greenberg, J. (1990). "Organizational Justice: Yesterday, Today, and Tomorrow," *Journal of Management*, 16: 399–432; Korsgaard, M. A. and Roberson, L. (1995). "Procedural Justice in Performance Evaluation: The Role of Instrumental and Non-Instrumental Voice in Performance Appraisal Discussion," *Journal of Management*, 21: 657–669.
44. Colquitt, J. A., Noe, R. A., and Jackson, C. L., 2002. "Justice in Teams: Antecedents and Consequences of Procedural Justice Climate," *Personnel Psychology,* 55(1): 83–109.
45. Kirkman, B. L., Shapiro, D. L., Novelli, L., Jr., and Brett. J. M. 1996. "Employee Concerns Regarding Self-Managing Work Teams: A Multidimensional Justice Perspective," *Social Justice Research,* 9(1): 47–67.
46. Greenberg, (1986).
47. Lind, E. A., and Earley, P. C. 1992. "Procedural Justice and Culture," *International Journal of Psychology*, 27(2): 227–242; Greenberg. J. A. (2001). "Studying Organizational Justice Cross-Culturally: Fundamental Challenges," *International Journal of Conflict Management*, 12(4), 365–375.
48. Kirkman, B. L., Lowe, K. B., and Peng, D. (2000). "The Role of Procedural Justice, Perceived Organizational Support, and Individualism-Collectivism in Motivating Organizational Citizenship Behavior of Employees in the People's Republic of China," paper presented at the annual meeting of the Academy of Management, Toronto, Canada, August.
49. Pillai, R., Scandura. T. A., and Williams, E. A. (1999). "Leadership and Organizational Justice: Similarities and Differences Across Cultures," *Journal of International Business Studies*, 30(4): 763–779.
50. Hofstede, (1980).
51. Brockner. J., Ackerman. G., Greenberg, J., Gelfand, M. J., Francesco, A. M., Chen, Z. X., Leung, K., Bierbrauer, G., Gomez, C., Kirkman, B. L., and Shapiro, D. L. (2001). "Culture and Procedural Justice: The Moderating Influence of Power Distance on Reactions to Voice," *Journal of Experimental Social Psychology*, 37(4): 300–315.
52. Lee, C., Pillutla, M., and Law, K. S., 2000. "Power-Distance, Gender, and Organizational Justice," *Journal of Management*, 26, 685–704.
53. Lam, S. S. K., Schaubroeck, J., and Aryee. S. (2002). "Relationship Between Organizational Justice and Employee Work Outcomes: A Cross-National Study," *Journal of Organizational Behavior*, 23: 1–18.
54. Cropanzano and Greenberg, (1997).
55. Alexander, S. (2000). "Virtual Teams Going Global," *Infoworld*, 22(46), 55–56.
56. See, e.g., Kraiger, K., and Ford, J. K. (1985). "A Meta-Analysis of Rater Race Effects in Performance Ratings," *Journal of Applied Psychology*, 70(1): 56–65. See also Pulakos, E. D., Oppler, S. H., White, L. A., and Borman, W. C., (1989). "Examination of Race and Sex Effects on Performance Ratings," *Journal of Applied Psychology*, 74(5): 70–78.
57. Baugh, S. G., and Graen. G. B. (1997). "Effects of Team Gender and Racial Composition on

Perceptions of Team Performance in Cross-Functional Teams," *Group &Organization Management*, 22(3): 366–383. See also Kirkman. B. L., Tesluk. P. E., and Rosen, B. (in press), "The Impact of Demographic Heterogeneity and Team Leader-Team Member Demographic Fit on Team Empowerment and Effectiveness," *Group and Organization Management.*

58. Kirkman et al. (in press).
59. Gomez et al. (2000).
60. Gibson and Kirkman, (1999).
61. Mohrman, S. A., Cohen, S. G., and Mohrman, A. M., Jr. (1995), *Designing Team-Based Organizations: New Forms for Knowledge Work.* San Francisco: Jossey-Bass.
62. Biggs, J. B. (1993). "What Do Inventories of Students' Learning Processes Really Measure? A Theoretical Review and Clarification," *British Journal of Educational Psychology*, 63: 3–19.
63. Hoeksema, L. H., Van de Vliert, E., and Williams, A. R. T. (1996). "The Interplay Between Learning Strategy and Organizational Structure in Predicting Career Success," *International Journal of Human Resource Management*, 8: 307–327.
64. Allinson, C. W., and Hayes, J. 2000. "Cross-National Differences in Cognitive Style Implications for Management," *International Journal of Human Resource Management*, 11(1): 161–170.
65. *Ibid.*
66. Hofstede, G. (1991). *Cultures and Organizations: Software of the Mind*, London: McGraw-Hill.
67. *Ibid.*
68. *Ibid.*
69. Cohen, S. G., and Bailey, D. E., (1997). "What Makes Teams Work: Group Effectiveness Research from the Shop Floor to the Executive Suite," *Journal of Management*, 23, 239–290.
70. Langfred, C. W. (2000). "Work-Group Design and Autonomy: A Field Study of the Interaction between Task Interdependence and Group Autonomy," *Small Group Research*, 31: 54–70.
71. Kirkman, B. L., and Shapiro, D. L., (1997). "The Impact of Cultural Values on Employee Resistance to Teams: Toward a Model of Globalized Self-Managing Work Team Effectiveness," *Academy of Management Review*, 22(3): 730–757.
72. Kirkman and Shapiro (2001a, 2001b).
73. Elenkov, D. S. (1998). "Can American Management Concepts Work in Russia? A Cross-Cultural Comparative Study," *California Management Review*, 40: 133–156; Kirkman and Shapiro (2001b); Nicholls, C. E., Lane, H. W., and Brechu, M. B. (1999). "Taking Self-Managed Teams to Mexico," *Academy of Management Executive*, 13: 15–27.
74. Kirkman, B. L., Lowe, K. B., and Gibson. C. B. (2002). "Two Decades of *Culture's Consequences:* A Review of the Empirical Research on Hofstede's Cultural Value Dimensions," working paper. Georgia Institute of Technology.
75. Mohrman et al. (1995).
76. Edmondson, A. (1999). "Psychological Safety and Learning Behavior in Work Teams," *Administrative Science Quarterly*, 44: 350–383; Kasl, E., Marsick, V. J., and Dechant. K. (1997). "Teams as Learners: A Research-Based Model of Team Learning," *Journal of Applied Behavioral Science*, 33(2): 227–246.
77. Edmondson (1999).
78. Gibson and Kirkman (1999); Mohrman et al. (1995).
79. Edmondson (1999).
80. Leeson, N. (1996). *Rogue Trader*, London: Little, Brown.
81. Rawnsley, J. (1995). *Total Risk: Nick Leeson and the Fall of Barings Bank.* New York: Harper; Van Dyck. C. (2000). *Putting Errors to Good Use: Error Management Culture in Organizations.* Amsterdam: KLI Dissertation series. 2000–3.
82. Senge, P. M. (1990). *The Fifth Discipline: The Art and Practice of the Learning Organization*, New York: Currency Doubleday.
83. Edomondson (1999), p. 25.
84. Frese, M. (1995). "Error Managment in Training: Conceptual and Empirical Results," in C. Zucchermaglio, S. Bandura, and S. U. Stucky (eds.), *Organizational Learning and Technological Change,* New York: Springer.
85. Van Dyck (2000).
86. *Ibid.*
87. Hofstede (1991).

88. Rybowiak, V., Garst, H., Frese, M., and Baltinic. B. (1999). "Error Orientation Questionnaire (E.O.Q): Reliability, Validity, and Different Language Equivalence," *Journal of Organizational Behavior.* 20: 527–547.
89. Tjosvold. D. (1991). *Team Organization: An Enduring Competitive Advantage.* New York: John Wiley.
90. Gersick, C. J., and Hackman, J. R. (1990). "Habitual Routines in Task-Performing Groups," *Organizational Behavior and Human Decision Processes*, 17: 65–97.
91. West, M. A., Garrod, S., and Carletta. J. (1997). "Group Decision-Making and Effectiveness. Unexplored Boundaries," in C. L. Cooper and S. E. Jackson, (eds.), *Creating Tomorrow's Organizations: A Handbook for Future Research in Organizational Behavior.* Chichester: John Wiley, 293–316.
92. West, M. A. (1996), "Reflexivity and Work Group Effectiveness: A Conceptual Intergration," in M. A. West (ed.), *Handbook of Work Group Psychology,* Chichester: John Wiley, 555–579.
93. *Ibid.*
94. Carter. S. M., and West, M. A. (1998). "Reflexivity, Effectiveness, and Mental Health in BBC-TV Production Teams," *Small Group Research*, 29: 583–601; Schippers. M. C., Den Hartog, D. N., and Koopman, P. (2001). "Reflexivity in Teams: The Development of a Questionnaire and the Relationship with Trust, Leadership, and Performance of Work Teams," manuscript submitted for publication.
95. West (1996).
96. Maznevski and Chudoba (2001).
97. Geber. B. (1995). "Virtual teams," *Training*, 32(4): 36–40.
98. Solomon. C. M. (1998). "Building Teams Across Borders," *Global Workforce*, November: 12–17.
99. Rauch A., Frese. M., and Sonnentag, S. (2000). "Cultural Differences in Planning/Success Relationships: A Comparison of Small Enterprises in Ireland, West Germany, and East Germany," *Journal of Small Business Management*, 38(4): 28–41.
100. Kirkman and Shapiro (1997).

PART IV

MANAGING EFFECTIVE ORGANIZATIONS

In this section of the book, we're going to make a more obvious transition from micro-level topics in organizational behavior dealing with individuals and groups to macro-level issues that affect the entire organization. In addition to a thorough grounding in the topics we have already covered, organization design and managing change are heavily dependent on systems thinking and analytical skills.

CHAPTER 21
ORGANIZATION DESIGN

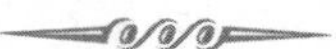

THE ORGANIZATION OF THE FUTURE: STRATEGIC IMPERATIVES AND CORE COMPETENCIES FOR THE TWENTY-FIRST CENTURY

David A. Nadler
Michael L. Tushman

MAKING MERGERS AND ACQUISITIONS WORK: STRATEGIC AND PSYCHOLOGICAL PREPARATION

Mitchell Lee Marks
Philip H. Mirvis

STRATEGIES FOR RESPONSIBLE RESTRUCTURING

Wayne F. Cascio

Organizations cannot function at peak capacity if they are not well designed. Managers have various "building blocks" at their disposal (such as strategy, structure, systems, type of staff, competencies, managerial style, rewards, and so forth). Most design experts assume that a good, complementary "fit" among these various components is necessary to organizational success—with some exceptions that allow for evolution and adaptation to change.

The end of the millennium produced numerous writings and predictions about the next century. In our opinion, the best attempt at taking stock of where we are and where business needs to go is David Nadler and Michael Tushman's "The Organization of the Future: Strategic Imperatives and Core Competencies for the Twenty-first Century." Based on the changes they see in the environment, Nadler, chairman and CEO of the Delta Consulting Group Inc., and Tushman, professor and consultant, list six strategies essential for organizations of the future. Next, they identify the organizational competencies and architecture needed to carry out these strategies.

The second article, "Making Mergers and Acquisitions Work: Strategic and Psychological Preparation," notes that three out of four mergers and acquisitions fail to achieve their financial and strategic objectives. Mitchell Marks and Philip Mirvis, internationally recognized consultants on mergers and acquisitions, discuss the managerial actions that lead to successful combinations.

Employment downsizing and restructuring continue to be major tactics used in hopes of enhancing organizational competitiveness and performance. As with mergers and acquisitions, downsizing and restructuring efforts frequently fail to produce long-term payoffs. In "Strategies for Responsible Restructuring," business professor Wayne Cascio examines the common mistakes companies make in downsizing and details proactive steps for wisely developing and using a firm's human assets.

THE ORGANIZATION OF THE FUTURE: STRATEGIC IMPERATIVES AND CORE COMPETENCIES FOR THE 21ST CENTURY*

David A. Nadler

Michael L. Tushman

Poised on the eve of the next century, we are witnessing a profound transformation in the very nature of our business organizations. Historic forces have converged to fundamentally reshape the scope, strategies, and structures of large, multi-business enterprises.

Driven by new competitive demands and fueled by an abundance of capital, companies have massively rearranged their portfolios, adding and discarding businesses to sharpen their strategic focus. Those discreet and dramatic portfolio plays, characterized by the high-profile mergers and acquisitions of the past three years, have provided a constant flow of front page news. But beyond the headlines lies a more subtle story, one with greater long-term significance than the acquisitive appetites of auto makers and telecom giants. Heading into the new century, the most important business development is the pursuit of competitive advantage in an uncertain world through new approaches to organization design.

These new approaches should lead those of us concerned with the theory and practice of organizational design to reconsider those ideas still grounded in the post-War, pre-Internet world that lasted through the 1980s. As this remarkable decade draws to a close, it's appropriate to reflect on the state of organization design and to distill those timeless ideas that will guide us in designing the effective organization of the future.

Our purpose here is first to present our perspectives on the most relevant lessons of organization design. We'll then examine the challenges of the new environment and their implications for tomorrow's organizations. Next, we'll identify six new strategic imperatives that flow from this reshaped environment. We'll conclude by proposing a set of organizational challenges that encompass the most critical design issues for the organization of the future.

A PERSPECTIVE ON ORGANIZATION DESIGN

What we think of today as "organization design" began to evolve in the aftermath of World War II. Building on the research of the 1920s and 1930s and the experience of the 1940s, the notion of the "organization as machine" gave way to a more subtle perspective

*Reprinted with permission of Elsevier from *Organizational Dynamics, 28* (Summer 1999): 45–59.

on the social and technical aspects of the organization. Much of our contemporary thinking can be traced to the landmark work *Organization and Environment* by Lawrence and Lorsch (1969), which introduced several profound ideas. The first was "contingency theory"—the notion that organizations are most effective when their design characteristics match their environment. The second major idea flowed from the first; if two units of the same organization operate in different environments, each should take on different characteristics. That creates a dual demand for both "differentiation" and "integration," or the capacity to link different units within the same organization.

The twin principles of "integration and differentiation" are more relevant than ever, given the complexity of modern organizations. The new challenge is to effectively manage dramatically different businesses that overlap or even compete against one another within a single, strategically focused enterprise. What's more, there will be a growing need for integration patterns—joint ventures, alliances, etc.—that extend beyond traditional corporate boundaries.

We believe there are four core lessons of organization design that will retain their relevance in the coming decade:

1. The environment drives the strategic architecture of the enterprise, either through anticipation of, or reaction to, major changes in the marketplace. Every industry evolves through cycles of incremental change punctuated by turbulent periods of disequilibrium that call for radical or discontinuous change. The organization's capacity to understand its environment and to make the right kinds of strategic changes at the appropriate point in the cycle will determine its competitive strength.
2. Strategy drives organizational architecture, a term that describes the variety of ways in which the enterprise structures, coordinates, and manages the work of its people in pursuit of strategic objectives. Over the years, we have described this concept as the congruence model of organizational behavior (Figure 1). This

FIGURE 1 Congruence Model of Organizational Behavior

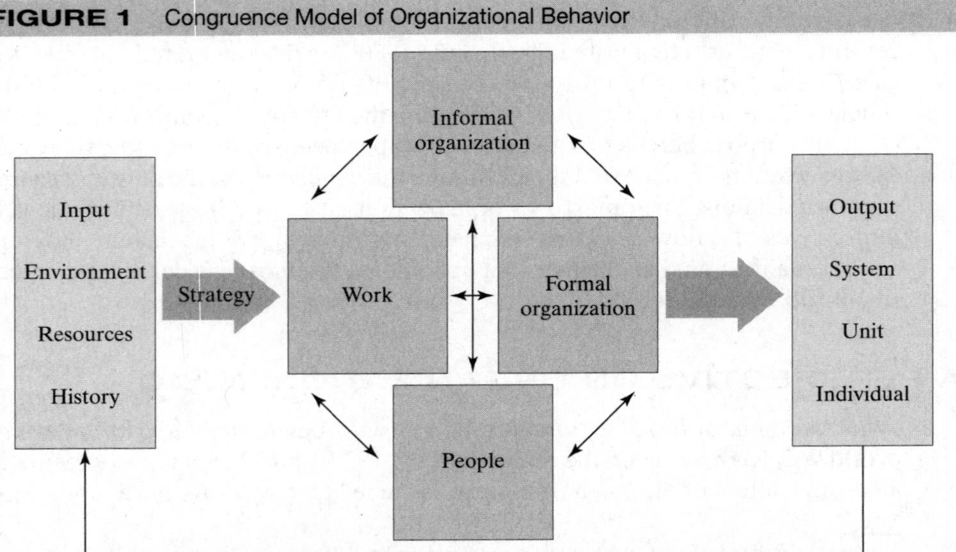

model views the organization as an open system that transforms input from the external environment into output of various types. The organization, consisting of the formal and informal arrangements, the people, and the core work, is driven by an articulated strategy. The more closely each component of the organization is aligned with the others—and with the strategy—the more effective the overall performance. Consequently, effective organizations design patterns of formal and informal structures and processes best suited to their strategic objectives.

3. The relationship between strategy and organization design is reciprocal. How an enterprise is organized will influence its focus and time horizons, either encouraging or restricting its people's ability to develop creative strategies.
4. The basic dilemma of organizational design remains unchanged. This raises several questions: How do we design and manage both differentiation and integration? How do we group people, processes, and operating units in ways appropriate to their unique competitive environments and strategic requirements, while maintaining their link to the larger organization? How do we encourage both divergence and cohesion? The key to effective design requires an appreciation of the underlying duality of this challenge.

Assuming these are the relevant lessons that should continue to guide us, our task in the remainder of this paper is to address three key issues:

1. What are the key characteristics of the changing business environment? What are the critical changes that will drive new thinking in strategic and organizational architecture?
2. What are the strategic imperatives that flow from the environmental changes we've identified?
3. What organizational challenges will be created by the new strategic imperatives? How will effective organizations translate strategic imperatives into new organizational architectures and new leadership priorities?

To answer these questions, we begin by considering the historic trends that have already begun to reshape the competitive environment.

THE NEW BUSINESS ENVIRONMENT

In many ways, today's business environment has changed qualitatively since the late 1980s. The end of the Cold War radically altered the very nature of global politics and economics. In just a few short years, the triumph of capitalism has spawned a variety of trends with profound consequences: the opening of markets, true global competition, widespread industry deregulation, and an abundance of accessible capital. We have experienced both the benefits and perils of a truly global economy, with both Wall Street and Main Street feeling the pangs of economic dislocation half a world away.

At the same time, we have fully entered the information age. Startling breakthroughs in information technology have irreversibly altered the ability to conduct business unconstrained by the traditional limitations of time or space. Today, it's almost impossible to imagine a world devoid of intranets, e-mail, and laptops. With stunning speed, the Internet is profoundly changing the way we work, shop, do business, and communicate.

In less than 10 years, the changes wrought by new information technology have been phenomenal.

As a consequence, we have truly entered the post-industrial economy. We are rapidly shifting from an economy based on manufacturing and commodities to one that places the greatest value on information, services, support, and distribution. That shift, in turn, places an unprecedented premium on "knowledge workers," a new class of affluent, educated, and mobile people who view themselves as free agents in a seller's market.

Beyond the realm of information technology, the accelerated pace of technological change in virtually every industry has created entirely new businesses, wiped out others, and produced a pervasive demand for continuous innovation. New product, process, and distribution technologies provide powerful levers for creating competitive value. More companies are learning the importance of destructive technologies—innovations that hold the potential to make a product line, or even an entire business segment, virtually obsolete.

Another major trend has been the fragmentation of consumer and business markets. There's a growing appreciation that superficially similar groups of customers may have very different preferences in terms of what they want to buy and how they want to buy it. Now, new technology makes it easier, faster, and cheaper to identify and serve targeted micromarkets in ways that were physically impossible or prohibitively expensive in the past. Moreover, the trend feeds on itself, a business's ability to serve sub-markets fuels customers' appetites for more and more specialized offerings.

IMPLICATIONS OF ENVIRONMENTAL CHANGE

We all know that change has become an inherent part of business. What's more significant is the rapidly accelerating velocity of change. More specifically, the lifespan of product, process, and distribution technologies has contracted with breathtaking speed.

The critical issue is time. The rapidly increasing velocity of change warps organizational time and space, bending the very shape of the enterprise. It's not just simply a matter of doing the same things, only faster; it's more like the difference between checkers and three-dimensional chess. The massive demands imposed by time compression will force organizations to:

- Compete and innovate simultaneously in multiple venues and in overlapping time frames; and
- Find creative ways to design and implement new organizational architectures in half the time required by current processes without sacrificing the benefits traditionally associated with deliberate planning and appropriate participation.

Together, these changes in the business environment challenge our fundamental assumptions of organizational design. Historically, the purpose of organizational structures was to institutionalize stability; in the organization of the future, the goal of design will be to institutionalize change. In that sense, we stand in the midst of a profound shift in the design and purpose of organizational design.

THE NEW STRATEGIC IMPERATIVES

We believe that the changing environment we've just described creates six strategic imperatives for the organization of the future. It will be required to: increase strategic clock speed; focus portfolios, with various business models; abbreviate strategic life cycles; create "go-to-market" flexibility; enhance competitive innovation; and manage intra-enterprise cannibalism. We will describe each in turn.

1. Increase Strategic Clock Speed

From a strategic standpoint, speed is quickly becoming a critical success factor. In a strategic context, speed involves an organizational capacity to understand, anticipate, and respond appropriately to those external changes that fundamentally alter the rules of engagement and the sources of value in a given industry or business segment. Examples abound: the deregulation of telecommunications and other utilities, the emergence of new technologies such as wireless communication, the development of e-commerce, and the rise of "category killer" outlets in consumer segments such as home improvement (Home Depot) and toys (Toys "R" Us). Virtually every industry has seen vast changes in the way it designs, produces, or reaches the market with its offerings.

Timing is everything. During periods of radical, discontinuous change, the first movers enjoy significant advantages. Those who perceive the early signs of discontinuity in the environment and then rapidly fashion an appropriate new strategy are infinitely more successful than those who miss the warning signs or delay their response. Those who move slowly find they must react to competitors; those who wait too long find themselves struggling for survival.

2. Focus Portfolios, with Various Business Models

Over the past 40 years, there's been significant change in the underlying strategies that defined our large and complex business enterprises. Through the mid-1960s, the classical form or organizational architecture consisted of companies with a single dominant business design that was largely duplicated down through the pyramid of divisions and operating companies. These shared designs allowed for tight linkages and a sense of consistency.

The mid-1960s saw the rise of the conglomerate. Driven by a thirst for growth, a fundamental belief that "bigger is better," and a desire to offset the cyclical downturns in specific industries, companies diversified their portfolios in unprecedented ways. Within each corporation, there might be dozens of companies with wholly unrelated strategies and entirely different business designs. The holding company model involved only the most minimal linkages across the enterprise, with each business operating essentially as an independent agent in pursuit of financial goals dictated from above.

Now we're witnessing the emergence of the new "strategic enterprise." The changing marketplace no longer rewards unfocused growth and gross market share. Instead, companies are reshaping their portfolios in the pursuit of strategic focus, concentrating on those businesses where they can create sustainable value by applying their core competencies to provide competitive advantage. They are spinning off or selling businesses that either dilute focus, in terms of resources and managerial energy, or whose potential value cannot be leveraged within the larger enterprise. In effect, companies are breaking up and reassembling the traditional value chain.

This sharpened focus is leading companies to seek new ways to compete within a given competitive space, operating simultaneously in mature, emerging, and future segments of the same markets. Consequently, we're going to see more and more variations in business design within a single enterprise. In this context, we use the term *business design* as defined by Slywotzky and Morrison as encompassing four dimensions: which customers to pursue, how to capture value (i.e., profit), how to maintain a unique value proposition, and what scope of activities to pursue.

For example, consider the case of Lucent Technologies, a spinoff created by AT&T in 1995 from four of its businesses and much of Bell Labs. As part of AT&T, those businesses were locked in a strategic dilemma created by deregulation: In order to realize their full value, they would have to do business with AT&T's widening array of direct competitors. That created major conflicts for everyone concerned. Once Lucent became independent from AT&T, its value as a manufacturer and supplier of telecommunications equipment and systems skyrocketed; its profits more than quadrupled between 1995 and 1998, and its stock price rose from $13.50 a share in 1996 to nearly $120, adjusted for splits.

But it wasn't long before Lucent realized that it, too, would have to reshape its business design. Just a few years after the spinoff, Lucent exited the consumer business, where it lacked the front-end linkages—sales, distribution, customer base—to sufficiently leverage its back-end technology and production strengths. Instead, Lucent chose to focus exclusively on business communications. In early 1999, it acquired Ascend Communications Inc., a move that represented a $20 billion bet on data networking—a business involving substantially different technology than Lucent's traditional circuit switching. Now, the challenge for Lucent is figuring out how to manage these two different—and, in some ways, directly competing—business designs.

3. Abbreviated Strategic Life Cycles

Each industry progresses through a fairly predictable life cycle. There may be huge differences in the duration of that cycle depending upon the industry segment, but the pattern of cycles is consistent. Understanding those cycles is essential for leaders. Different stages in the cycle of industry evolution—the well-known "S-curve"—demand different strategies at various points along the curve.

But waves of change in industry leadership suggest that firms must engage in both incremental and discontinuous technical change, as well as architectural innovation—taking the same product and taking it to different markets. Thus in photolithography for disk drives, leading firms were unable to take known technologies and move to new customers. Dynamic capabilities seem to be rooted in shaping streams of different types of innovation in a given product class.

The consequences of the sweeping and rapid changes in the environment discussed earlier have had the effect of substantially shortening those evolutionary cycles for every industry. In the past, companies large and small, including AT&T, General Motors, and even IBM, could get along for a decade, and sometimes longer, without any fundamental changes in strategy. Those days are gone. Rather than thinking in terms of decades, the pace of change in the environment will require the organization of the future to significantly change its underlying strategy on a regular basis of between 18 months and 5 years, depending upon the industry. Indeed, it's not uncommon to hear executives, as they talk about strategic cycles, talk in terms of "Web years," signifying a compressed timeframe of 3 months rather than 12.

4. Create "Go-to-Market" Flexibility

The fragmentation of markets, one of the significant changes in the environment, has enormous strategic implications for organizations. In order to reach each market segment in the most effective way, companies have begun focusing more intensely than ever before on the rising demand for "go-to-market" variability. Various market segments offer widely divergent demands for the same core product or service in terms of pricing options, sales and service support, speed of delivery, customization, and so forth. Today, no organization can succeed with a "one size fits all" approach to the marketplace.

The most highly publicized changes, of course, have involved the Internet and the emergence of so-called "e-commerce"; by some accounts, sales of goods over the Internet rose from being barely measurable in 1996 to more than $4 billion during the 1998 Christmas season. Waves of change in distribution channels are coming faster all the time. It was only a few years ago that independent booksellers were wilting under the pressure of the book superstores, such as Barnes & Noble and Borders. Then, practically overnight, Amazon.com reshaped the industry, putting the leading competitors on the defensive and forcing them to follow the upstart onto the Web, despite their enormous investments in brick-and-mortar outlets.

Implicit in the notion of "go-to-market" variability is the potential it creates for conflicting internal priorities. Consider the auto industry. By some estimates, we are quickly approaching the point when more than half of all new car buyers in the United States start out by searching the Internet for information, comparing models, options, prices, and financing alternatives before they ever set foot in a showroom. What many shoppers are looking for is a vehicle's factory invoice price, the essential number that equips them to bargain knowledgeably with the local dealer. That's not good news for the dealer; but at this point, the auto companies have no choice but to cater to the demands of sophisticated customers for more and better information. At the same time, reeling from assaults by Car-Max and other high-volume used-car chains, the auto companies have to think seriously about starting their own used-car outlets—an historic shift in distribution that would put a further squeeze on profits of their own franchised dealerships.

5. Enhance Competitive Innovation

It has practically become an article of faith that innovation provides a critical source of competitive advantage. But the accepted definition of *innovation* is too narrow; we would argue that the scope of innovation must be expanded to include the full range of an organization's capabilities.

Innovation traditionally focused on products and processes. More recently, distribution has attracted attention as an area where significant innovation can lead to dramatic gains. But the combination of product, process, and distribution still fails to capture the full potential for organizational innovation.

We believe the successful organization of the future will also develop exceptional skills to innovate in two other areas: strategy development and organization design. If the most critical characteristic of the new business environment is the accelerating pace of change, then the ability to quickly and creatively develop and implement new strategies and the organization designs required to make them work will become a major source of competitive differentiation.

6. Manage Intra-Enterprise Cannibalism

What we call *purposeful cannibalism*—the need to develop and support new strategies, product lines, and distribution channels that might eventually dry up existing revenue streams—is not a new idea. Visionary business leaders have done it for years. But two elements of intra-enterprise cannibalism are new.

The first change is that cannibalism has been rare. Business historians praise Tom Watson Jr. for his foresight in developing the IBM 360, which held the potential to wipe out many of the company's best-selling product lines. His willingness to put a major revenue stream at risk was remarkable in large part because it was so uncommon. In the successful organization of the future, the idea of cannibalism will become routine, an accepted part of each company's strategy.

The other change relates, once again, to speed. In the future, it won't suffice to make one big bet each decade. The pace of innovation and the abbreviated strategic cycles will force companies to place multiple bets on an ongoing basis, acknowledging that a new product may be well on its way to obsolescence by the time it reaches the market.

Lucent Technologies' $20 billion acquisition of Ascend, which we mentioned earlier, involved more than a strategy of multiple bets on alternative technologies. There's a good chance that the newly acquired data networking strategy based on packet switching may actually displace the circuit switching technology that now provides the bulk of Lucent's profits. And before long, it's entirely possible that Lucent will have to invest in alternative packet switching strategies as new technologies come along and require new business designs.

ORGANIZATIONAL CHALLENGES

The six strategic imperatives described above create a compelling need for some new and unconventional organizational architectures. As we said earlier, organizational architecture throughout much of this century was generally viewed as a way to institutionalize and manage stability. But today, the challenge is to design organizational architectures that are flexible and adaptive, that enable the organization to perform effectively in the face of uncertainty—not just day-to-day, but in the broader context of profound discontinuous change.

In our view, the new strategic imperatives create a corresponding set of challenges for the organization of the future; to succeed, organizations will be forced to become proficient in eight core competencies (Figure 2).

1. Increase Organizational Clock Speed

The strategic imperative of timely anticipation and speedy response to change will require the design of organizations with the capacity to do everything faster. The ability to configure the organization in ways that ensure a constant and acute awareness of impending changes in the marketplace will become an essential capability that will separate the leaders from the laggards.

Beyond that, organizations will have to find creative ways to achieve unprecedented speed in all their operating and support processes. They'll want to significantly reduce their time to market and time to volume. They'll want to accelerate decision-making up and down the line. They'll need to substantially cut the time it takes to design

Strategic Imperatives
• Increase strategic clock speed
• Focus portfolios with various business models
• Abbreviate strategic life cycles
• Create "go-to-market" flexibility
• Enhance competitive innovation
• Manage intra-enterprise cannibalism
Organizational Challenges
• Increase organizational clock speed
• Design structural divergence
• Promote organizational modularity
• Structure hybrid distribution channels
• Design asymmetrical research and development
• Construct conflict management processes
• Maintain organizational coherence
• Develop executive teams

FIGURE 2 Strategic Imperatives and Organizational Challenges

and implement strategic and organizational changes. Enlightened leaders already understand that speed doesn't mean operating the same way as in the past, only faster; they know that radical improvements in speed involve doing things differently. In order to increase strategic clock speed, organizations will face three challenges.

First, senior leaders will need a much deeper understanding of the quickening cycle times in their industries. They will have to alter their assumptions about large-scale change, both in terms of the frequency and speed of major change initiatives. Once upon a time, CEOs were expected to be the stewards of stability. Through the 1980s, a CEO might expect to lead one or, in extreme cases, two episodes of radical change. Today, and in the coming decades, leaders of complex organizations should enter their jobs with the expectation that they might well be required to reinvent their organizations three, four, or even more times over the course of their tenure. That will require a fundamentally different attitude about the role of the CEO as an agent of change.

Second, successful enterprises will need to develop sensitive organizational antennae—the roles, structures, and processes that will significantly enhance their ability to detect the early warning signs of value migration. In particular, they will have to keep close watch on minor players and industry outliers, the frequent sources of major innovation. They are the ones to monitor most carefully; they are the ones most likely to employ new technologies and distribution patterns to nullify the dominant conventional business designs.

Finally, companies will need to redesign their organizational architectures in ways that encourage the "capacity to act" in response to indications of environmental change. In too many organizations, managers lack clear accountabilities, support from above, adequate resources, and sufficient information; faced with major opportunities or challenges, they freeze in their tracks. The growing demand for speed in every facet of the business will require organizations to fashion the formal structures, processes, and roles as well as the informal operating environment necessary to encourage managers throughout the enterprise to act swiftly and independently.

2. Design Structural Divergence

The changing environment is requiring enterprises to employ a variety of business designs as they develop multiple ways to achieve value within a defined competitive space. The organizational challenge will be to master the art of designed divergence—the ability to create, support, and link, where necessary, a wide variety of related businesses that use dramatically different architectures to pursue varying and sometimes conflicting strategies.

In recent years, we have argued the case for ambidextrous management—the ability to maintain superior performance in established businesses while managing innovation in targeted areas. The organization of the future will have to be more than just ambidextrous; in a sense, it will have to become polydextrous. Rather than operating, in essence, in both the present and the future, polydextrous leadership will also require an ability to coordinate businesses that are both complementary and competitive in the current marketplace (Figure 3). That will require a fundamental rethinking of the form and purpose of organizational architecture. The framework we have developed over the

FIGURE 3 Designed Structural Divergence

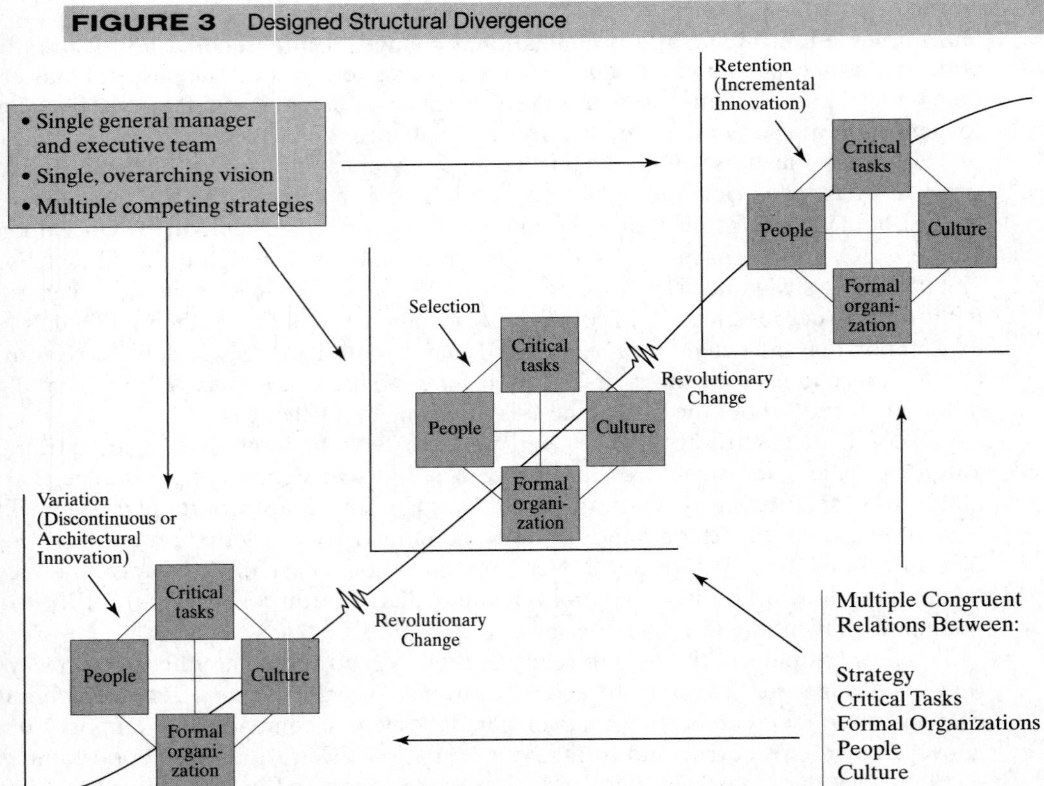

past 20 years, the Congruence Model, is generally synonymous with consistency. It implies that effective organizations maintain a consistent architecture with minor variations, throughout the enterprise. We now believe that the organization of the future will seek congruence at the enterprise level, providing an effective framework that successfully melds a broad array of different architectures at the business unit level and beyond. Rather than seeking blanket consistency, leaders will come to perceive internal architectural divergence as a powerful source of evolutionary strength.

The most critical issue will be to figure out the appropriate linkages across a broad range of very different businesses. The challenge involves an inherent balancing act: minimizing linkages in order to maximize the focus of independent business units while, at the same time, capitalizing on potential sources of leverage to create value from the joint ownership and management of multiple businesses. In other words, leaders will have to learn when it's best to encourage autonomy and differentiation, and how to create value through the selective use of linking structures and integrative processes.

In reality, the choices are somewhat limited. Businesses can be linked on the back end, through common technology architectures. They can be linked in the middle through infrastructure—manufacturing processes, supply chains, etc. And they can be linked on the front end, through shared customer relationships, distribution channels, sales and service operations, and so on (Figure 4). The more points of linkage, the more diffused the focus. So the issue is to start with a clean slate, to weigh the marginal costs and benefits of each potential linkage, and to arrive at the correct scope and intensity of linkage at each point in the value chain. Corning Inc., for example, has come to the conclusion that its various businesses—photonic devices for telecommunications, stepper lenses for photolithography (for creating chips), ceramic substrates for catalytic converters—offer no leverage on the front end, minimal leverage in the middle, and considerable leverage on the back end, where common technologies provide innovations with applications across its businesses.

3. Promote Organizational Modularity

The growing prevalence of abbreviated strategic life cycles will require ever-faster development and implementation of appropriate organizational designs. That requirement clearly calls for both product and process innovation in the domain of organizational design. The implications may be far-reaching, indeed.

FIGURE 4 Linkage Points

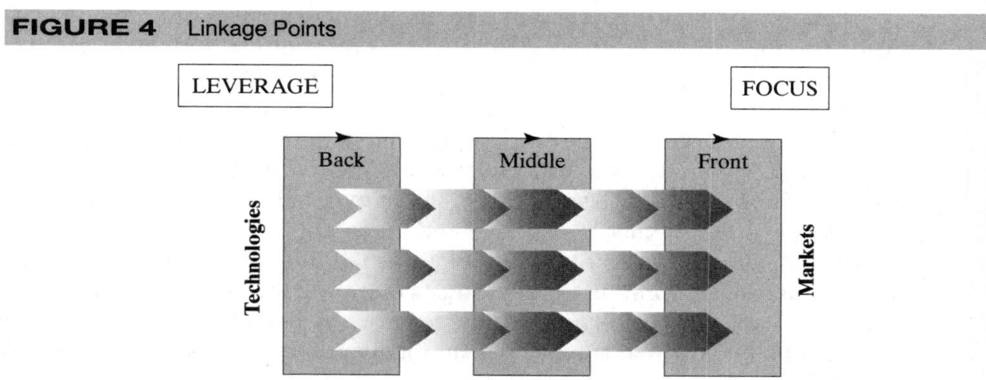

In recent decades, we have rejected the notion of "off-the-rack" organization designs. We have steadfastly argued in favor of "custom designs." Our thinking was based on two fundamental beliefs; first, that each design should be suited to the unique demands of the organization—its environment, its strategy, its people, and its culture; and second, that the very process of designing the appropriate structures, processes, systems, and roles held inherent long-term value for the organization and the individuals who took part in the process.

As valuable as it has been, it may well be time to rethink that approach. The transforming requirements of speed might well dictate situations in which there is simply not enough time to engage in a conventional organization design process. We may be approaching a time when theorists and practitioners ought to develop a set of design principles that will allow organizations to quickly select an appropriate architecture for a given strategy.

Many organizations will no longer be able to afford the luxury of spending six or nine months creating and implementing a new design; few companies will be able to wait that long to address the imminent changes in their environment. So the notion of starting each design process with a blank slate will soon become obsolete. The challenge will be to devise a streamlined process, employing modular design, that still retains some of the important benefits—the learning, insight, team-building and ownership—that we attempt to create through the customized design approach.

4. Structure Hybrid Distribution Channels

The strategic imperative for go-to-market variability will require organizations to develop different kinds of structures that will enable them to simultaneously manage different channels of distribution in order to serve highly fragmented markets. Xerox Corp.'s early 1999 restructuring—its third in less than a decade—illustrates the kind of new, creative designs that will be required by the organization of the future.

For years, Xerox basically sold a range of generic products through a sales force that called on companies, built relationships, and helped customers to learn about the features and benefits of those products. But changes in the environment battered the business design that had served Xerox so well. Early in the 1990s, Xerox reorganized into business units that focused on selling particular products to corresponding segments of the office market. But after just a few years, that design, and its later refinements, failed to keep pace with the continued fragmentation of the market. The digital office, the proliferation of small businesses and home offices, the demand for new ways to purchase and service equipment, the unique document requirements of specific industries—they all served to fragment the market for office equipment and solutions.

In many cases, companies were no longer satisfied with just "the box," a freestanding copier sitting in a side office. As the digital office became a reality, more customers demanded a networked, multi-function machine to help them solve production, distribution, and archiving problems; others wanted the software and systems design to make the whole set-up work seamlessly. And in extreme cases, they wanted Xerox not only to supply the system, but to design and operate it as well. At the other end of the spectrum was the so-called SOHO market (Small Office/Home Office), whose customers were primarily interested in products that were inexpensive, high quality, easily installed and operated, and quickly ordered, often by phone or over the Internet. And in the middle was still a substantial conventional market, businesses that were happy to keep dealing with the traditional sales force.

Early in 1999, Xerox reconfigured the front end of the organization to focus on customer segments (Figure 5). These segments recognized the geographic distinctions markets in varying stages of economic development and the specific needs of customers in various industries. Facing these customer segments were an array of targeted operations and business groups. General Markets Operations, for example, was aimed at the lower end of the market, and consequently required the structures, processes, culture, and clock speed needed to meet the demands of the small customer. On the other hand, Industry and Solutions Operations focused on solutions rather than products, and was further segmented by industry on the principle that systems solutions in financial services and pharmaceuticals, for example, must be unique and custom-tailored.

The Xerox organization design leverages the back end of the value chain, the common technologies. It involves an uncommonly complex design on the front end, however, one that recognizes that Xerox must provide immense variety in the ways it goes to market if it is to compete successfully in a marketplace characterized by the fragmentation of sub-markets.

5. Design Metrical Research and Development

The strategic imperative of competitive innovation will require the organization of the future to design the structures and processes that guide research and development in some new and creative ways.

Today, different companies design their R&D processes in different configurations, but in the end, there tends to be a single innovation model patterned around the basic business model. That model is entirely inconsistent with the notion of design divergence. Within the same enterprise, businesses and operations with very different

FIGURE 5 Xerox Organizational Design

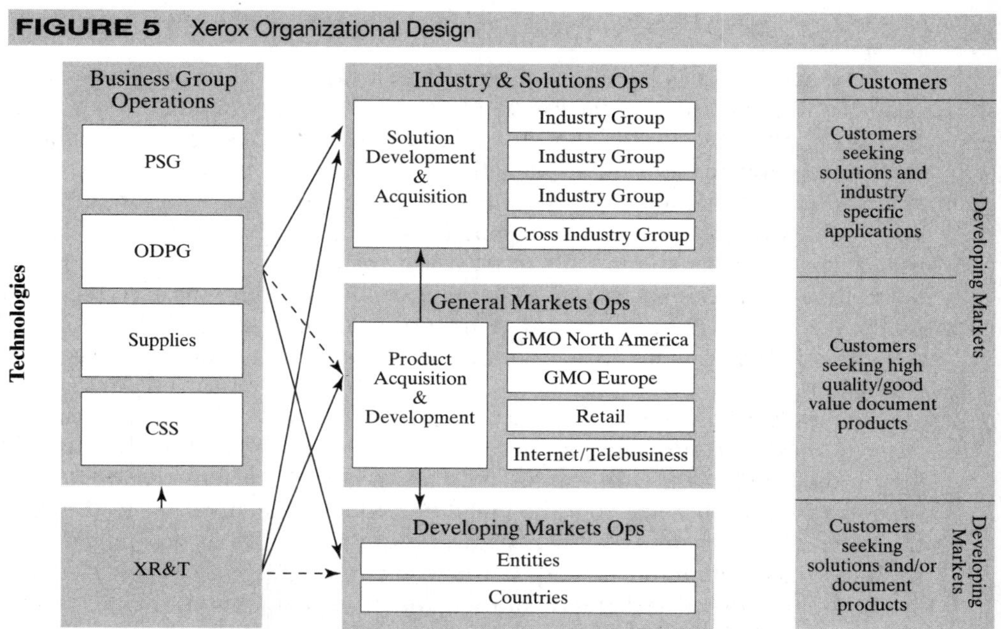

strategies will require dramatically different innovation streams, or processes for turning ideas into marketable products. Organizations that insist on applying a single innovation process symmetrically across the enterprise will inevitably run into trouble.

The problem is that competing simultaneously in both the present and the future requires a range of R&D processes, structures, priorities, and behavior. In a mature business, the emphasis in innovation is on the right solution—the absolutely right solution. The marketplace will accept nothing less. Particularly if you're among the market leaders, you can follow a highly structured process with strictly enforced priorities, deadlines and resource allocations.

The picture is entirely different in emerging markets. There, the priorities are speed and flexibility. If you can be first to market, a roughly right solution is better than none; in the extra time it might take to find the absolutely perfect solution, the market could well pass you by. And in those early stages of product life cycle, the customer calls the shots; R&D operations need the flexibility to respond swiftly to unexpected opportunities and challenges.

Consequently, companies whose strategy requires a range of business designs cannot employ symmetrical innovation processes and hope to succeed. There will still be value in a core R&D function; allocating all R&D to the business units eliminates an important potential source of leverage. But the processes by which R&D operates in relation to each business unit—goal setting, funding mechanisms, conflict resolution, etc.—need to be customized and asymmetrical.

6. Construct Conflict Management Processes

In the past, as we've mentioned, an important role of organization design was to preserve consistancy, stability, and perhaps even a degree of harmony within the organization. But as we look to the future, organizations that use design to impose an artificial sense of stability in the face of sweeping environmental change will become their own worst enemy.

Instead, effective leaders will actually use organization design to import the conflict and competition of the marketplace into the very structure of their companies. But as the proliferation of internally competitive strategies becomes commonplace, what are the implications for organizations and their leaders?

In short, conflict management will become an essential organizational capability. Today, an extremely short list of companies—Intel usually tops the list—have established reputations for their ability to creatively manage internal conflict. What is a rare talent today will become a standard requirement before long. The successful organization of the future will need to develop the processes, cultures, and behaviors capable of accommodating and resolving conflict in ways that benefit the customer and strengthen the value proposition.

So far, we've been describing organizational challenges that directly correspond with the new strategic imperatives. There are two additional organizational challenges that apply to the full range of strategic imperatives: the changing nature of organizational coherence, and the magnified role of executive teams. Both address the issue of how to manage the organization of the future as it changes to address the growing demands of speed, variable business design, abbreviated strategic cycles, greater go-to-market variability, competitive innovation, and intra-enterprise cannibalism.

7. Organizational Coherence

In recent years, we've witnessed a growing recognition that values, culture, and shared goals are replacing formal structures as the glue that holds organizations together. That trend will rapidly accelerate as the result of the strategic and organizational changes we've discussed here.

As business units and operating companies become increasingly autonomous, to the point of becoming outright competitors with one another, the very nature of organizational coherence will undergo a radical transformation. Job titles, formal structures, and bureaucratic procedures will have less and less importance to people whose primary loyalty will be to their own business group and, even more narrowly, to their own professional discipline. Organizational coherence at the enterprise level will become increasingly difficult to maintain, and will rest almost entirely on a common goal and a small number of shared values—not the formal rhetorical flourishes that are the organization's espoused values, but those few values that truly embody the way people think of themselves and their enterprise.

In that context, the notions of "brand" and identity will assume growing importance within the enterprise. The dominant cultural norms—the HP Way, the feistiness of Sun Microsystems, the insistence on winning at Lucent Technologies, Intel's creative conflict, or Microsoft's self-image as the best and the brightest—these will be the understood, though not always explicit, values that will hold divergent enterprises together. The so-called "soft stuff" will, over time, become the essential stuff.

8. Executive Teams

Where will the leadership come from to generate this intangible coherence while managing the tangible hardware of the enterprise? The answer will be in the executive team.

Consider the degree of complexity we're envisioning for the organization of the future. In a sense, what we're talking about is the capacity to manage paradoxes. Large organizations will have to be managed as if they were small; they'll have to be both global and local; they'll need to promote both internal conflict and overall coherence. It's virtually impossible to imagine how a single person, in the form of the CEO, could possess the staggering combination of leadership skills, managerial talent, and technical knowledge required to meet these assorted strategic and organizational challenges. It's absurd to expect that of one person.

Instead, it will fall more and more to the executive team to become the key mechanism for managing the organization of the future. That does not diminish the role of the CEO; to the contrary, the effective CEO will have to become a deft leader of the executive team, a major job in itself. It will require the combined efforts of the CEO and the executive team, working together, to truly understand and anticipate the changes in the environment. It will be up to them to make the critical strategic decision. It will require their combined efforts to understand the timing and guide the implementation of the constant refinement and tuning the complex organization will demand—redesigning the structure to add focus here or to provide more leverage there.

These sophisticated tasks will require the combined intellect of senior people who share a commitment to the common good of the enterprise. Indeed, the enormity of the challenge suggests that senior leadership will need to be expanded for certain types of work, drawing upon the skills, knowledge, and insights of people who haven't traditionally been viewed as members of the senior-level inner circle. One of the challenges for top leaders will be to determine when, how, and in what situations to make the top team more inclusive rather than less.

What is clear is that the organization of the future, in order to succeed, will become less dependent on the independent actions of disaggregated individuals. To succeed, organizations will have to develop a competency in the design and leadership of executive teams, a collective skill that will be just as important as the ability to design innovative strategies and organizational architectures.

MAKING MERGERS AND ACQUISITIONS WORK: STRATEGIC AND PSYCHOLOGICAL PREPARATION*

Mitchell Lee Marks
Philip H. Mirvis

Fewer than one quarter of mergers and acquisitions achieve their financial objectives, as measured in ways including share value, return on investment, and postcombination profitability. Many factors account for this dismal track record: buying the wrong company, paying the wrong price, making the deal at the wrong time. Another factor, however, seems to be at the core of many failed combinations—the process through which the deal is conceived and executed.[1]

Corporate combinations—the merger of separate entities into a new firm or the acquisition of one firm by another—have become a regular component of the managerial repertoire. Many motives prompt executives to acquire or merge with another organization. Perhaps a combination can help a company pursue a strategy that would otherwise be too costly, risky, or technologically advanced to achieve independently. Other deals are opportunistic, as when a troubled competitor seeks a savior or when a bidding war ensues after a firm is put into play. Still other acquisitions or mergers can be defensive moves to protect market share in a declining or consolidating industry.

The overarching reason for combining with another organization is that the union will provide for the attainment of strategic goals more quickly and inexpensively than if the company acted on its own.[2] In this era of intense and turbulent change, involving rapid technological advances and ever increasing globalization, combinations also enable organizations to gain flexibility, leverage competencies, share resources, and create opportunities that otherwise would be inconceivable.

Despite their frequency, corporate combinations have proven difficult events for organizational researchers to assess. The nature of doing a deal runs counter to the requirements of sound research. For both legal and competitive reasons, merger negotiations are shrouded in secrecy. This hinders data collection, but also means that researchers cannot anticipate and identify research sites before the combination occurs. Even after the announcement of a deal, more questions than answers remain.

---

*Reprinted with permission from *Academy of Management Executive,* 15(2) 2001: 80–92, via Copyright Clearance Center.

Executives are harried and employees anxious; no one has the time or the inclination to cooperate with a research program. And combinations pose some substantial methodological dilemmas. For example, when does a merger begin—as it is conceived, when it is announced, or when it receives legal approval? Similarly, there is no discrete ending to a merger.

As a result, most research investigations of the process through which combinations have been managed tend to be retrospective. A typical research design asks senior executives to assess the relative influence of various factors on the outcomes of their past combination activities. With 20/20 hindsight, executives acknowledge the human, organizational, and cultural aspects of the combination-management process. However, the lessons learned from past combinations are not being applied in a systematic manner to the management of current combinations.

COMBINATION PHASES

For more than 20 years, we have been involved in an action research program investigating and addressing human, cultural, and organizational aspects of corporate combinations.[3] During this time, we have participated as researchers or consultants in over 70 mergers and acquisitions. These combinations have involved large, medium, and small companies, have been friendly and unfriendly, and have spanned a broad range of industry sectors—including financial services, telecom, high tech, health care, pharmaceuticals, manufacturing, professional services, consumer products, entertainment, and government.

Early in our research program, we collaborated with Management Analysis Center of Cambridge, MA, in a study of combinations in banking and finance.[4] This research showed that significant differences could be identified between typical and successful cases by separating the distinct phases organizations go through in the transition from independent to integrated entities:

- precombination phase, as the deal is conceived and negotiated by executives and then legally approved by shareholders and regulators;
- combination phase, as integration planning ensues and implementation decisions are made;
- postcombination phase, as the combined entity and its people regroup from initial implementation and the new organization settles in.

To be sure, these are not clear-cut phases. Integration planning increasingly occurs in the precombination phase, before the deal receives legal approval. Pfizer and Warner-Lambert launched integration planning teams before their deal closed in June 2000, and AOL's President Robert Pittman moved into an office at Time-Warner's New York City headquarters even as federal regulators were reviewing that corporate marriage. Still, some distinct emphases emerged during the earliest months as a deal was being conceived and negotiated that distinguished the combinations that did and did not meet their strategic and financial objectives.

In the precombination phase, a financial tunnel vision predominated in the typical disappointing cases. Buyers concentrated on the numbers: what the target was worth; what price premium, if any, to pay; what the tax implications were; and how to structure the transaction. The decision to do a deal was typically framed in terms of the combined balance sheet of the companies, projected cash flows, and hoped-for return on investment.

Two interrelated human factors added to this financial bias. First, members of the buy team in most instances came from financial positions or backgrounds. They brought a financial mindset to their study of a partner and their judgments about synergies were mostly informed by financial models and ratios. They often did not know very much about, say, manufacturing or marketing; nor did they bring an experienced eye to assessments of a partner's capabilities in these regards. There was also a tendency for hard criteria to drive out soft matters in these cases. If the numbers looked good, any doubts about organizational or cultural differences tended to be scoffed at and dismissed.

In the successful cases, by contrast, buyers brought a strategic mindset to the deal. They positioned financial analyses in a context of an overarching aim and intent. Successful buyers also had a clear definition of specific synergies they sought in a combination and concentrated on testing them well before momentum built and any negotiations commenced. Here, too, human factors played a part. Members of the buy team in successful cases came from technical and operational, as well as financial, positions. And during the scouting phase, they dug deep into the operations and markets of a candidate when gauging its fit. Sensible buyers considered carefully the risks and problems that might turn a strategically sound deal sour. This does not mean that the financial analyses were neglected or that they were any less important to success. To the contrary, what put combinations on the road toward success was both an in-depth financial understanding of a proposed combination, and a serious examination of what it would take to produce desired financial results.

PUTTING A COMBINATION ON THE PATH TOWARD SUCCESS

Steering a combination toward the successful path begins in the precombination phase. Many observers liken organizational combinations to organ transplants. The surgery must be well thought out and planned, and the surgical team and patient prepped, prior to the operation, to allow for rapid execution and minimize the likelihood of rejection. We urge clients to be proactive in the precombination phase: planning and preparation are integral to success when companies join forces.

Preparation in a combination covers strategic and psychological matters. The strategic challenges concern key analyses that clarify and bring into focus the sources of synergy in a combination. This involves reality testing potential synergies in light of the two sides' structures and cultures and establishing the desired relationship between the two companies. The psychological challenges cover the actions required to understand the mindsets that people bring with them and develop over the course of a combination. This means raising people's awareness of and capacities to respond to the normal and to-be-expected stresses and strains of living through a combination.

PURPOSE, PARTNER, PARAMETERS, AND PEOPLE

The journey toward a successful combination begins well before dealings commence. As strategic intent and selection criteria are set, as a deal is being conceived, and as potential partners are screened, assessed, and negotiated with, executives, staff specialists, and advisors need to continuously address at least four different aspects of their potential combination: purpose, partner, parameters, and people.

PURPOSE: PUTTING STRATEGY TO WORK

The strategic synergies in a combination should lead to a set of decisions in the precombination phase on the intentions, rationale, and criteria for the deal. They guide eventual action for excavating sources of productive combination.

STRATEGIC INTENT

Strategy setting begins with scrutiny of an organization's own competitive and market status, its strengths and weaknesses, its top management's aspirations and goals. The results define a direction for increased growth, profitability, or market penetration in existing businesses, for diversification into new areas, or simply for cash investment—which may or may not involve combination activity.

In successful acquisition programs, the CEO, relevant corporate and division management, and various advisors translate these objectives into specific strategic and investment criteria. Most buying companies have standard metrics for evaluating a candidate that include its earnings, discounted cash flow, and annual return on investment. They also have objectives about the impact of a combination on profitability, the combined organization's earnings per share, and future funding requirements.

Here the typical and successful combination roads part ways. In so many cases, financial fit receives a disproportionate amount of attention and priority in the search for a partner. In successful cases, financial criteria are respected and adhered to, but are balanced by careful consideration of each of the synergies sought in a combination and what it will take to realize them. Knowledge gained from this careful look at synergies not only sharpens the parties' assessment of their potential acquisitions, it also enables leadership to put forward a clear and convincing rationale for the combination that goes beyond the numbers. Most combinations involve expense-reduction. Executives who seek to create value have to be able to demonstrate to staff on both sides that there is more to the deal than cost-cutting—and that involves a crisp statement of how synergies will be realized and what that means for the people involved. Two recent oil industry mergers illustrate how early intentions influence subsequent integration. BP selected Amoco and ARCO as integration partners because both provided good fits with BP's retail operations and oil reserves. Exxon Mobil was a copy-cat merger. Rather than highlight strategic intent, these firms were motivated by a need to catch up with the scale of the new market leader and relied purely on financial analyses. With no strategic intent guiding integration, the result was a political free-for-all in which integration decisions were based on empire building and turf protection rather than strategy.

If the true motives underlying a combination have less to do with strategy and more to do with non-rational forces—for example, the desire to run the largest company in an industry or the fear of being swallowed up by competitors—then a successful combination is unlikely because there are no true benefits to reap by joining forces. Yet combinations based on such motives are not infrequent. A blue-ribbon panel of financial experts concluded 20 years ago that CEO ego was the primary force driving mergers and acquisitions in the United States.[5] More recently, a Columbia University business school study found that the bigger the ego of the acquiring company's CEO, the higher the premium the company is likely to pay for a target.[6]

CLEAR CRITERIA

When they have a voice in and can agree on the merits of a strategy, top executives, corporate planners, and line managers operate from a common interest and perspective. To enforce this consensus, corporate leaders assert strategic criteria and make sure the acquisition team searches for candidates that fit them.

A firm first needs to know what it is looking for in an acquisition candidate or merger partner. Having a full and open review of these criteria allows for debate and consensus building between staff and line executives. If conflicts or confusion about these criteria are not fully addressed up front, they will persist down the road. Applying these criteria religiously greatly increases the likelihood of selecting a partner that will bring true productive value to the combination, rather than one that will just be an acquisition for the sake of doing a deal. Understanding precisely what synergies are sought sets the stage for subsequently mining opportunities through the combination planning and implementation phases. The more unified both sides are—within and between themselves—about what is being sought, the more focused they can be in realizing their objectives.

Two sets of criteria help here. One is a generic set of criteria that guide a firm's overall combination program and strategy. These are characteristics of organizations that must be present in any combination partner. At Emerson Electronic, a few factors guide search and selection of all alliance partners, such as not going into business with firms in turnaround situations and not straying beyond its core competency in manufacturing.[7]

The second set of criteria guide the assessment and selection of a specific of a specific partner. In its effort to acquire other healthcare providers, a southern California hospital established criteria for what it was looking for in this particular search. These included "maintain/enhance quality of care—bring a continually improving level of quality care to the community served by the hospital" and "geographic distribution—enhance the geographic reach of the hospital across Los Angeles county and throughout southern California." Some selection criteria were at odds with one another, such as finding a partner that both is the "low-cost provider" and "adds prestige." The hospital's executive team prioritized the relative importance of each criterion prior to the selection process. When it came time to evaluate choices, the team then assessed the multiple candidates and weighted the high priority criteria accordingly.

PARTNER: SEARCH AND SELECTION

Successful acquirers know what they are looking for and conduct a thorough due diligence to ensure that they get what they want. Their screening of candidates covers the obvious strategic and financial criteria, but extends also to include assessments of the human and cultural elements that can undermine an otherwise sound deal. How deep is the management talent in the target? What labor relations issues lurk around the corner? How does the company go about doing its business? Is their culture a good enough fit with ours?

THOROUGH SCREENING

The value-creating acquisition of Benham Capital Management Group by Twentieth Century Advisors began with a screening process that integrated human and cultural issues with strategic and operational criteria. Both firms meshed along operational lines in offering only no-load mutual funds and treating small shareholders well; but one senior executive told us that an exchange of corporate values statements during due diligence was among the data indicating that cultural compatibility existed as well; "Their 'Guiding Principles' and our 'Statement of Beliefs' were very similar. Both companies stated honesty as a fundamental belief and you don't too often see that both stated and acted out in the financial-services industry."

A thorough assessment of combination candidates also covers less tangible matters. First, it reveals the motives of the sellers in an acquisition or partners in a merger. Why does leadership of the target want to sell? Are they responding to a business opportunity or are they driven by more personal motives, like wanting to cash out their investment? Does senior leadership want to stay on board after the sale? Do the buyers want the seller's leadership to stay? If so, will there be good chemistry between the leaders of the two sides?

Second, thorough screening gets below the top leadership and considers the mindsets of the two management teams. How do the target's people feel about working with or for the buyer's people? Are they looking for a company with deep pockets to fund them to glory, or are they likely to fight hard to fend off any threats to their autonomy after the deal closes? Does the buyer's management team buy into this deal or do factions exist? Where does the target's team stand? Are the technical and professional staff—who are outside the inner circle, but are needed to make the combination work—involved in the process? Are they apt to depart after a combination is announced? Even if answers to these questions are not deal killers, they indicate what has to be done to win people over during courtship phase.

A thorough precombination screening comes only from speaking directly with a good cross-section of the management team from the potential partner. Automated Data Processing CEO Art Weinbach is clear on the value of face-to-face due diligence with an array of managers from potential partners: "The greater surprises have come to us in the people and the people relationships. We have to spend more time on the people side of the equation in the due-diligence period. That is not as simple as looking at organizational charts; it requires speaking and listening to people both for the formal business issues as well as the less formal how does it really work issues. You learn a lot by listening."[8]

DILIGENT DUE DILIGENCE

In most combination programs, true diligence needs to be put back into due diligence. Typically, the financial people who dominate due-diligence teams get a sense of the partner they want and build a case for combination going forward. It is important to get people on the team who will probe deeply and thoroughly enough to work backward and identify faulty assumptions and what might hinder eventual success.

Take information technology as an example. Proper due diligence ascertains first the extent to which the candidate's system has the capacity to meet its own current and future business needs, and then considers the compatibility between the two sides' systems right now and following anticipated growth. If the capacity and compatibility are not there, then the cost for getting there—and the impact of that cost on the financials of the deal—needs to be determined through a realistic (as opposed to an overly optimistic) evaluation.

Broadening the membership of the team also enhances organizational due diligence. Membership can be expanded to include staff professionals from areas like human resources and information technology, and operating managers who will be working with new partners if the combination is carried out. A functional specialist provides a breadth of analysis that simply cannot be conducted by a corporate generalist. Operations managers have a particularly important role on due-diligence teams. They can find many reasons why a deal that looks good on paper would crash on takeoff. In addition to reviewing operational issues, they can also assess the chemistry between themselves and their counterparts. If it is not there early on, it is not likely to be developed later. Differing viewpoints and preferences for how to conduct business are not in and of themselves reasons to negate a deal, but incongruent values, genuine distrust, and outright animosity should be noted as red flags.

Some organizations we have worked with place up to 20 people on their due-diligence teams. This may be bulky in terms of scheduling logistics and organizing findings, but it pays off when a potential showstopper gets unearthed. One organization convenes two diligence teams to assess candidates and overcome the deal fever that frequently afflicts due diligence. Knowing that a poor partner can exact a huge financial toll and be a tremendous burden on management time and energy, this company goes forward only with combinations that pass muster with both teams.

Due diligence is also a time to size up the breadth and depth of managerial talent in the potential partner. A study of large combinations found that 65 percent of successful acquirers reported managerial talent to be the single most important instrument for creating value in a deal.[9] Smart buyers not only evaluate current executives but also look closely at managers not yet in leadership positions.

PARAMETERS: DEFINING THE COMBINATION

There is a tendency for buyer and seller to get mired in the details of their transaction and lose sight of the big picture. Studies of the acquisition process have found that a fragmentation of financial, strategic, organizational, and cultural analyses leaves the executives involved with different, and often competing, perspectives on how to put their organizations together.[10] In addition, each company has its own way of doing business, its own preferences and power structure, and a history of past decisions, forsaken options, and financial and physical investments. What appears to yield strong financial and strategic synergy between, say, two manufacturing groups may not be realizable because of incompatible structures and systems or sharp differences in cultures.

DEFINING THE END STATE

Partners in successful combinations share a commonality of purpose and recognize and accept the terms of their relationship. People are able to focus their energy on a common goal and let go of any wishful thinking that may run counter to the realities of the combination. Yet in so many cases, corporate marriage contracts, like those between individuals, tend to be implicit rather than explicit, and are open to interpretation and misunderstanding. Carefully defining the end state of a deal can bring the pleasantries and promises of the precombination courtship to a quick halt. Failing to do so can lead to an even more unpleasant divorce.

While the work of achieving the desired end state will involve many people, the initial step is the responsibility of senior executives involved in doing the deal. In the best cases, the senior executive from the buying side puts his or her cards on the table regarding expectations and assumptions for the combining organizations. The senior executive needs to think through and come to the precombination discussions with a clear sense of which aspects of this desired end state are open to negotiation and which are not during precombination discussions and subsequent planning.

With this in mind, executives who hope to combine their companies are well advised to consider and share their hopes, expectations, and biases for how the postcombination organization will be structured. These intentions are largely determined by the degree of integration anticipated for the combined organization. We use a grid of different types of postcombination change to help executives think through their options and clarify their intentions. (See Figure 1.)

PRESERVATION

This end state where the acquired company faces a modest degree of integration and retains its ways of doing business is typically found in diversified firms that promote cultural pluralism among business units. To succeed, corporate management has to

FIGURE 1 Defining the Integration End State

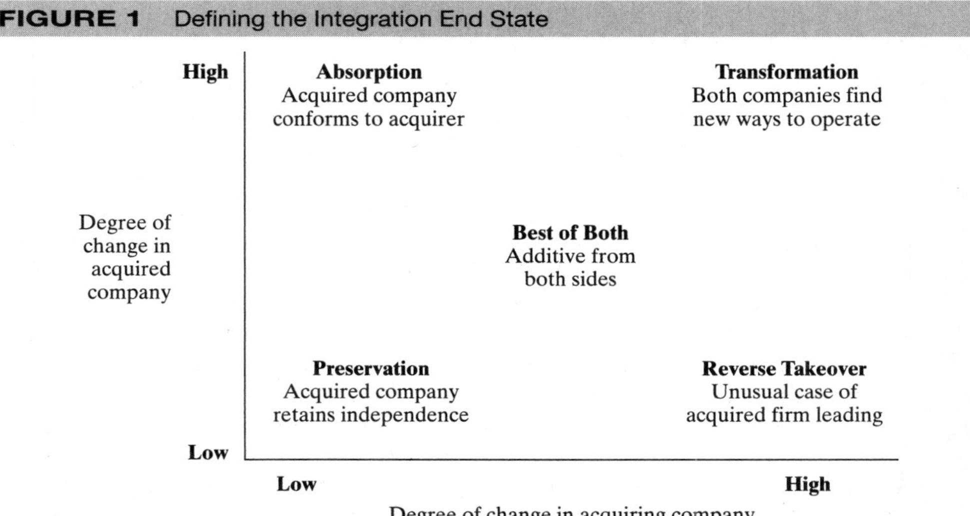

protect the boundary of the subsidiary, limiting intrusions by its corporate staff and minimizing conformance to its rules and systems. Strategic synergies generated in a preservative combination come from the cross-pollination of people and work on joint programs.

ABSORPTION

When the acquired company is absorbed by a parent and assimilated into its culture, the lead companies generally bring in new management and conform the target to corporate reporting relationships and regimens. Acquisitions in the airline industry, such as American's absorption of Air California, Delta's of Western, and USAir's of PSA, are classic examples.

REVERSE TAKEOVER

In the mirror image of the absorption combination, the acquired company dictates the terms of the combination and effects cultural change in the lead company. When this unusual type of combination occurs, it typically involves the absorption by an acquired business unit or division of a parallel unit in an acquirer. For example, Marriott Corporation acquired Saga and folded its own contract food-services business into it.

BEST OF BOTH

Studies find the achieving of synergy between companies through their partial to full integration to be more successful than others—and most fraught with risk. It can also be the bloodiest. Financial and operational synergies are achieved by consolidation. This means crunching functions together and often leads to reductions in force. The optimal result is full cultural integration—the blending of both companies' policies and practices. The merger of equals between Chemical Bank and Manufacturers Hanover and the combination of Canada's Molson Breweries with Carling O'Keefe are examples.

TRANSFORMATION

When both companies undergo fundamental change following their combination, synergies come not simply from reorganizing the businesses, but from reinventing the company. This is the trickiest of all the combination types and requires a significant investment and inventive management. Transformation poses a sharp break from the past. Existing practices and routines must be abandoned and new ones discovered and developed. In the integration of Pfizer Animal Health and SmithKline Beecham's animal pharmaceutical business in Europe, president Pedro Lichtinger took two orthodox operations and transformed them into a new organization geared toward the emerging realities of the European Community. In doing so, he broke down traditional country-specific structures and cultures and forged a pan-European strategy, structure, team, and identify as the precombination parties merged.

A senior executive will frequently enter a combination with ideas for differing functions to end up at various points on the grid. In Pfizer's acquisition of Warner-Lambert, financial reporting systems clearly were mandated by the buyer. A reverse acquisition occurred in the consumer-products area, however, where Warner-Lambert's business was much larger. John Niblack, head of Pfizer's R&D function, used the merger to transform that organization. An executive has a picture of where he or she wants combination to end, and makes those intentions clear to all parties. Certainly this end state may change as the partners learn more about each other, and about opportunities and challenges that arise during the combination-planning and implementation phases, but both sides enter into the combination with a shared sense of the desired end state.

CARDS ON THE TABLE

One of the worst moves any buyer can make is to talk merger and act acquisition. Sometimes buyers think they are doing the right thing by softening their messages and welcoming target personnel as partners. Other times, they are being outright manipulative by wooing the other side with pledges of a merger of equals when their true intention is to dominate. When postcombination parameters do not mesh with precombination promises, the result can only be disenchantment and distrust.

Whatever the intentions of the lead organization, false expectations abound in the target. Sometimes, people innocently misinterpret what they hear because of the inconsistent use of language across partners. Other times, being in a state of psychological denial interferes with partners' truly hearing what is being stated. Still other times, a partner knows quite well what is being said, but presumes that its own political skills will reign and change the situation as the organizations come together.

Announcing the desired end state provides an early opportunity to clear the air of any misperceptions or fantasies about how the two sides will coexist in the combined organization. Beyond checking misperceptions, a well articulated desired end state communicates to the work force that their leadership has a solid sense of where it wants to take the combination. This breeds employee confidence that leadership is managing the combination well. It also gives people something tangible to talk about, rather than turn to the worst-case scenarios, rumors, and naysaying that predominate in most combinations. Finally, a clear and understood desired end state guides combination planning and implementation. With the parameters established, integration planning teams and busy executives can study options and make recommendations within a realistic context rather than worry about having plans shot down by a senior executive because they did not fit preconceived expectations.

PEOPLE: MANAGING THE DEALINGS

Combination partners typically enter a deal with distinct mindsets. In an acquisition, the buyer and seller usually have very different psychological perspectives on the deal. Often they bring a one-up versus one-down outlook into their dealings, particularly when the acquiree is strapped for cash and has had a downturn in business performance. In cases where the roles of lead and target are not so well delineated, psychological factors can also influence the relationship. Members of one side may see themselves—or be seen by the other side—as more worldly, technically sophisticated, financially strong, or savvy in the marketplace. Yet the very premise for the merger—that the partners will gain access to or leverage each other's technology, patents, customers, or some other capability that they do not already possess—calls for a true meeting of the minds. The AOL-Netscape integration, for example, was

TABLE 1 Precombination Mindsets of Buyers and Sellers

Party	*Mindset*	*What to expect*
Buyer	Air of superiority	Headiness
	Drive to consolidate gains	Urgency
	Urge to dominate the action	Power moves
Seller	State of shock	Anxiety and anger
	Defensive retreat	Resistance
	Sense of fatalism	Hostility and defeatism

slowed by Netscape's self-perceptions of technical superiority; the people who believed they had invented the Internet were dismayed at combining with a firm they considered the McDonald's of the Internet.

Psychological mindsets certainly influence early dealings and can dominate the critical months of transition planning and implementation. (See Table 1.) And they often carry over into the combined organization. Awareness of these mindsets—both one's own and one's partner's—helps both sides prepare for a successful combination.

MINDSET OF THE BUYER

To the victors go the spoils. Bidding wars and hostile takeovers are certainly exhilarating for the winners. And even for executives involved in a friendly deal, there are few moments in a career that equal the intensity and satisfaction of buying another company.

Acquiring another organization, or assuming the role of lead party in a merger, translates into a strong air of superiority. This attitude frequently carries over into assumptions that the buying company's business acumen—and policies, procedures, people, and systems—are superior to those of the purchased firm. Being the dominant party contributes to condescending attitudes about the other side: On more than one occasion, we heard executives from buying companies crow: "They are still battling the problems we solved five years ago. Wait until we show them how to do things." Thus AOLers themselves felt superior to their counterparts from Netscape.

As the combination begins, lead companies are impelled to move fast and consolidate their gains. A sense of urgency prevails in the lead organization as it wants to put its plans into motion fast. There is always something uncertain about precisely what has been bought—who they are, what they do, whether they really know how to run their business. Corporate staffers pounce on the target to get their hands on things in a hurry.

This fuels managers' momentum in the lead company to dominate the action. They have studied the situation longer and have more detailed plans and priorities. Top management may have promised to go slow and honor traditions during the precombination negotiations, but vice presidents, corporate staffers, and managers get the taste of power and have their own designs. Moreover, they are rewarded for meeting budgets and producing results, not for how fairly or smoothly they manage the combination. As a result, lead managers often unilaterally dominate the action and impose their own integration plans. Prior promises mean nothing.

MINDSET OF THE SELLER

Why is being acquired so debilitating to an organization? In a hostile deal or one imposed by the board, there is from the start a sense of violation: Executives we have interviewed have likened it to a rape and described their buyer as an attacker or barbarian. Even in friendly deals, acquired managers often describe themselves as being seduced by promises that changes will be minimal, and as being taken advantage of once they are forced to accommodate to the new owner's demands.

A state of shock permeates a company following an acquisition announcement. Executives wander the halls after a combination is announced, unprepared to assume new duties and responsibilities. Executive recruiter John Handy found that 90 percent of nearly one thousand senior and middle executives he studied were psychologically unprepared for the changes in status and organizational structure they would encounter following their company's acquisition.[11] Seeing and sensing the anxiety in their superiors, other employees grow anxious about the combination, how it will be managed, and their personal fate in it.

One way executives cope with their shock is by a defensive retreat. This allows acquired executives to regroup and reformulate a battle plan for countering the enemy. At one acquired manufacturing firm, this led to a strategy of noncompliance and various tactics to resist the overtures of the lead company. Even in mergers of equals, perceived fears of losing status or ways of doing things lead executives to dig in and protect their turf.

Acquirees often feel powerless to defend their interests or control their fate. Even when the deal is friendly or when a company is rescued from a hostile deal by a sympathetic third party, the consequences are frequently out of the acquirees' control. Sellers sometimes respond with passive or aggressive hostility; other times, they withdraw with a sense of defeatism.

Many managers use Elisabeth Kübler-Ross's stages of reactions to death and loss to illustrate their personal reactions to being acquired.[12] Initially, there is denial and disbelief. Upon learning they are up for sale, executives go into a state of shock, denying the reality and their own vulnerability. The work force can both under- and overreact, predicting that nothing will happen or that everything will change. People in the target company then experience anger. They will be angry at their leadership for selling out and then for cashing in. Later they will be angry with the buyer. While expressions of anger allow people to vent their emotions, many become stuck at this stage and are never able to move on to accommodate to the new situation.

For those who can psychologically move forward, next comes bargaining. People's natural tendency is to look out for themselves. Some will leave what they consider to be a sinking ship. Others will try to make themselves indispensable. Some will cozy up to new management and pitch their importance and value to the organization. Others will guard data or customer relationships as leverage for survival.

Only after time will people accept the reality of the new situation and be ready to work with counterparts in a genuine and committed way. For some, this may be a matter of weeks or months. Others take years. Some individuals never reach the stage of acceptance.

PSYCHOLOGICAL PREPARATION

An executive we worked with suggested that preparing for a combination was like "preparing to be hit by a Mack truck." Maybe so, but at least it helps to know that others have gotten up off the pavement and gone on with their lives. Psychological preparation for a combination means raising awareness of the normal and to-be-expected mindsets of combination partners. Preparation alerts executives on both sides to the mindsets of the buyer and the seller, and holds up the mindset of partnership as the standard to achieve.

In many combinations in which we have been involved, employees from both sides have participated in sensitization seminars to foster dialogue about their respective mindsets. Individuals hear about combination mindsets, express their hopes and concerns going forward, and learn tactics for coping with their mindset and that of their counterparts.

Another way to raise awareness of combination mindsets is by educating people through readings, presentations, or discussions of the human realities of a combination. Many organizations distribute books and articles describing the mindsets of buyer and seller, sponsor workshops in which outside experts describe the dynamics of combining, and engage executives in discussing expectations or experiences in going through combinations. In organizations with experience in combinations, veterans of previous mergers and acquisitions can share their first-hand experiences with novices. Central to Cisco's fine reputation as a successful acquirer is its use of a buddy system to link veteran acquirees with newly acquired executives.

COMBINATION PREPARATION WORKSHOPS

A more dynamic approach to raise awareness of these mindsets is through an experiential activity that helps people develop a true feeling of what it is like to acquire or be acquired. This proved to be a powerful intervention when two CEOs of high-technology companies shook hands on what they jointly termed "a merger of equals." Little did they know that they held quite different interpretations of that phrase. The target company CEO assumed this meant that both sides would have equal say in combination decisions. The lead company CEO, however, intended it to mean that his side would have the final say, but would engage its counterparts to determine how to best implement those decisions. Both CEOs prepared their terms according to their personal interpretations and ultimately destroyed the goodwill between them.

The target CEO convened his board and asked it to negate the deal. The target company was in a weak financial condition, however, and the board could not justify that course of action. The deal remained, but so did the bad blood between the two sides.

One of us engaged executives from both sides in a two-day meeting that combined educational with experiential activities. The morning of the first day began with a discussion of human, cultural, and organizational issues in combinations, including the mindsets of buyers and sellers. After a lunch break, the two teams went to work on a business simulation. Acquired executives played the Green Widget Company and lead company executives the Red Widget Company. Being competitive business people, they threw themselves into the simulation and established strategies and tactics for maximizing their returns. Just five minutes before the close of the first day's session, however, the facilitator announced that the Green company intended to acquire the Red company, reversing their roles in the actual deal. Nothing further was said about the details of the acquisition, though more information was promised for the next morning. Day one adjourned and all were invited to cocktails and dinner.

In the lounge, it was as if the simulation were still on. Red Company executives huddled in one corner, wondering out loud what their fate might be at the hands of their new owners and plotting ways to resist any changes in control. Green Company executives, at the other end of the bar, began planning how they would establish authority in their new acquisition.

The next morning, the two groups identified their negotiating teams and readied their combination strategies. The Red team was determined to protect its independence despite the change in ownership. The Green team aimed toward consolidating operations quickly. Neither team was coached to develop these mindsets; they developed naturally based on their roles. It was then announced that the two sides would participate in a series of negotiating sessions, with time allotted for the teams to report back to their colleagues. After three rounds of negotiations, no progress had been made target executives were obstinate in their resistance and lead executives grew increasingly disenchanted with the lack of progress in negotiations and planning. In a fit of frustration at the next negotiating session, the Green team head fired the executive who headed the Red team. The facilitators then called an end to the simulation and the two sides were brought together to discuss what they had experienced.

Green Company executives began by asserting how uncooperative and unrealistic their acquired counterparts had been. Red Company executives, in turn, complained that the Greens never intended to listen to any input from their side, were disrespectful to them and their way of doing things, and were not willing to negotiate alternative courses for approaching the combination. Red executives acknowledged that what they saw the Green team doing in the simulation reflected their own tendencies in the real acquisition: They were eager to move ahead with consolidation and assumed things would go their way. More than this, however, the Reds gained a deep understanding of what it is like to have one's organization suddenly taken away in a combination. They became more sympathetic and empathetic toward the plight of their real-life acquired counterparts. The Greens, for their part, came to see how easy it was to slip into the mindset of the buyer and dominate the action. The awareness of self and others raised in the experiential activity led to the creation of formal ground rules for combination planning.

As the combination became legal and integration planning hit full stride, no one expected a complete turnaround in people's behaviors. Yet both sides saw enough movement from their counterparts and give-and-take in their relationships to build confidence in their ability to move forward together.

COMMITMENT FROM TOP LEADERSHIP

Another way to rein in the controlling behaviors of the lead company is to have the proper outlook modeled and managed at the top. In the merger of paper producers Abitibi-Price and Stone-Consolidated, we got senior team executives to meet early in the precombination phase, well before the deal became legal. Working with internal human, resources professionals, one of us designed an offsite meeting agenda that included frank discussion about the role of the group in leading the combination and the ground rules that would guide its leadership. One ground rule directed executives to reach out to the other side as they proceeded to make staffing and integration decisions. Only if they practiced partnership and overcame the tendency to favor people and practices familiar from their side, the executives acknowledged, could middle-level managers be expected to do the same.

Middle managers who must make the deal work also manifest the mindsets of buyer and seller. Some headiness on the part of lead company managers down the line is inevitable. It is imperative, then, that senior executives set the proper tone, articulate the principles of integration, and bring those principles to life in their own actions. Senior executives must also be prepared to act accordingly when the principles are not followed. A top executive form the lead company in an entertainment merger one of us worked on recalled: "Despite all of the urgings for partnership from our CEO, a sense of 'when in doubt, go with our way' prevailed among middle-level managers from our company. It is very difficult to get people to put aside their way of doing things." In this case, lead company executives listened and responded to complaints from acquired counterparts and spent time coaching their own middle managers. Realistically, acts of domination were not overturned, but the acquired team recognized that a genuine effort was made to counter excessive domination.

PRECOMBINATION PLANNING

Some firms are beginning to complement preparation for a specific deal with a more generic approach to precombination planning, particularly in industries, like telecom and healthcare, where combinations have become recurring events. Their aim is to have their act together when a combination opportunity arises.

As these organizations survey their competitive environments and deliberate strategic responses, they see that combinations are increasingly important for getting them where they want to go. Knowing that acquisitions and mergers are essential to meeting their strategic objectives—and in some cases necessary for their basic survival—executives take the opportunity to prepare to meet the organizational challenges in combining entities. A small but growing number of companies have either learned from their own failed combinations or taken seriously the feeble track record of other organizations and recognized the need to beef up their readiness for combining successfully.

Kaiser Permanente, the large health-maintenance organization, determined through its strategic-planning process that multiple acquisitions and strategic alliances would be essential for its long-term growth and survival in the volatile healthcare industry. Kaiser's leadership recognized that it did not have the internal competence to identify and implement combination opportunities. Advice from external consultants, coupled with the urging of an executive with considerable combination experience who had just joined Kaiser's senior team, led to the formation of an internal Acquisitions and Alliances SWAT Team. Middle-level managers from a broad array of functions and geographical units were asked to contribute their perspectives in the full combination process, from target selection to integration. Team members received a crash course in everything from valuation to culture clash. Nearly fifty managers graduated into roles to complement staff professionals and external advisors in targeting and integrating acquisition targets and alliance partners.

At Weyerhauser, the forestry and paper-products giant, consolidation among other industry players and the recognition that new ventures were likely to be pursued through acquisitions and alliances prompted senior executives to enhance their awareness of combination pitfalls and success factors and their readiness to manage a combination. Finance, strategy, and human resources executives joined with operations executives who had managed previous acquisitions in the company for an earnest assessment of their acquisition performance. The open discussion of what had and had not worked in previous combinations, both inside and outside the company, led to a more thorough and rigorous regard for the full set of organizational challenges in a combination.

At both Kaiser and Weyerhauser, organizational preparation began well in advance of combination activity. Even when organizations have not been this foresightful, there is still time to act after the initial combination announcement. In some large acquisitions, several months can pass awaiting legal approval. Most organizations waste this time. Others use it. At Pfizer, even before the Warner-Lambert acquisition received legal approval, merger-management training programs raised awareness of combination mindsets and alerted executives to the realities of the integration process. Internal facilitators participated in a day-long integration-team launch meeting that described pitfalls common to other firms' integration-team efforts and guided team members building effective teamwork in their planning groups.

A particularly in-depth precombination planning session was coordinated by internal organization development professional Ronny Versteenskitse of Seagram Spirits and Wine Group (SSWG). Soon after acquiring Seagram, French entertainment conglomerate Vivendi announced its intention to retain the target's film and music holdings, but divest its liquor and wine businesses. Employees in SSWG were in limbo as their unit was put on the auction block. Rather than wait and see what the buyer would do, Versteenskitse convened a four-day meeting of senior human-resources professionals. The meeting featured discussions of the status of major HR initiatives in the company in *light of the eventual change in ownership,* the fate of employees who would not be retained after the sale, success factors in mergers and acquisitions, and the human and cultural realities of joining forces. On the closing day, executives from BP and Amoco and Chemical Bank and Chase discussed their successful integrations. The meeting concluded with a discussion of strategies for actively dealing with the buyer by sharing the output produced at the meeting and reaching out to form a collaborative relationship with counterparts in the lead organization. There was no assurance that the buyer would be receptive to this outreach, but HR professionals left the conference feeling confident that they were doing the best job possible to prepare themselves, their organization, and their new colleagues for the rigors of integrating previously separate organizations.

PREPARING TO MOVE FORWARD

Actions taken—and not taken—in the precombination phase as a deal is being conceived and negotiated set a direction whereby a merger or acquisition heads down a successful path or veers off toward failure. In this phase, leadership sets its growth objectives and business strategy, and determines what kind of firm it wants to partner with, how, and why. It conducts a search, selects a partner, and negotiates a deal. To enhance the likelihood of a successful combination, leadership uses this period to prepare to join forces strategically and psychologically.

Successful combinations begin with self-scrutiny and analyses that yield a conclusion that a company can realize strategic goals more realistically, rapidly, and/or cost-efficiently through a combination than by acting on its own. This creates the basic rationale for scouting the marketplace with the intention of merging or acquiring. Fleshed out further, it also informs search criteria and is applied in screening candidates. As a partner is identified, strategy comes to life in preparing a business case for how the two parties will create value and in thoroughly analyzing potential costs and risks in putting the two together.

Companies have to organize themselves to buy and sell. On both sides, this means putting together a team that includes not only corporate staff and the CEO but also the executives who ultimately have to lead the combination. In addition to its obvious part in determining strategic and financial fit, thorough screening explores a partner's motivation for doing a deal, its culture, and the makeup of its people. Diligent due diligence, in turn, digs deep to understand if the values of the potential partner are compatible; if the bench strength exists to manage the combination while running the core business; if all parties are on the same wavelength on synergies and what it takes to combine; and if there is enough trust and chemistry to propel the combined organization into becoming more than the sum of its parts. Such diligence counters momentum and the rush to close, giving the parties a chance to get better acquainted and—when warranted—to back out gracefully.

Good strategies do not necessarily produce good combinations. Psychological preparation educates people about the mindsets of winners and losers and readies them to meet and work with their counterparts. Seminars and simulations help employees contend with the concerns that arise early on and increase once integration starts.

In the period between the announcement of a sale and its legal close, executives can begin to identify the optimal points of integration between firms, define a desired cultural end state, and prepare for the grueling work of forming transition teams. They also need to think through how to allocate executive time and talent to the combination process. Meanwhile, preparations can be made to ramp up communications, conduct training, and develop and implement retention and layoff policies.

Strategic and psychological challenges afflict all combinations, even the friendliest and most soundly conceived ones. The more these issue are raised and worked through during the precombination period, the more prepared people will be to take on the challenges of integration and contribute to mining the strategic synergies in a combination. Precombination planning readies people to move forward in their personal and organizational transitions, and establishes the dynamics that endure as the combining teams come together to manage the transition to a unified postcombination organization.

Endnotes

1. For studies of postcombination financial results, see Wright, M. Hoskisson, R. E. and Businetz. L. W. 2001. Firm rebirth: Buyouts as facilitators of strategic growth and entrepreneurship. *The Academy of Management Executive*, 15(1): 111–125; Davidson. K. M. 1991: Why acquisitions may not be the best route to innovation. *Journal of Business Strategy*, 12(3): 50–52; Elsass. P. M. and Veiga, J. F. 1994. Acculturation in acquired organizations: A force-field perspective. *Human Relations*, 47(4): 431–453; Hitt, M. A., Hoskisson. R. E., Ireland, R. D., and Harrison, J. S. 1991. Effects of acquisitions on

R&D inputs and outputs. *Academy of management Journal*, 34(4): 693–706; and Lubatkin, M. H. 1983. Mergers and the performance of the acquiring firm. *Academy of Management Review*, 8(2): 218–225.
2. The strategic role of combinations is discussed in Haspeslagh. P. and Jemison, D. B. 1991. *Managing Acquisitions: Creating Value Through Corporate Renewal.* New York: The Free Press.
3. Marks, M. L. and Mirvis, P. H. 1998. *Joining forces: Making One Plus One Equal Three in Mergers, Acquisitions, and Alliances.* San Francisco: Jossey-Bass.
4. Management Analysis Center. 1985. A study of the performance of mergers and acquisitions in the financial services sector. Cambridge, MA.
5. Boucher, W. L. 1980. The process of conglomerate merger. Washington, DC: Bureau of Competition, Federal Trade Commission.
6. Sirower, M. L. 1997. *The Synergy Trap.* New York The Free Press.
7. Conference Board. 1994. *Change Management: Strategic Alliances*. New York.
8. McCreight and Company. 1996. *Ensuring Success with Mergers and Acquisitions.* Wiltion, CT.
9. Anslinger, P. L. and Copeland, T. E. 1996. Growth through acquisitions: A fresh look. *Harvard Business Review*, January-February.
10. Jemison, D. B. and Sitkin, S. B. 1986. Acquisitions: The process can be a problem. *Harvard Business Review,* March-April.
11. Handy, J. 1969. How to face being taken over. *Harvard Business Review*, November-December.
12. Kubler-Ross, E. 1969. *On Death and Dying.* New York: Simon and Schuster.

STRATEGIES FOR RESPONSIBLE RESTRUCTURING*

Wayne F. Cascio

EMPLOYMENT DOWNSIZING: THE JUGGERNAUT CONTINUES

The job churning in the labor market that characterized the 1990s has not let up. If anything, its pace has accelerated. However, the free-agent mentality of the late 1990s that motivated some people to leave one employer so that they could make 5 percent more at another, a strategy that benefited men more than women[1] is over. Layoffs are back—and with a vengeance. Thus, in 2001, companies in the United States announced layoffs of almost two million workers, with firms such as American Express, Lucent, Hewlett-Packard, and Dell conducting multiple rounds in the same year. Corporations announced 999,000 job cuts between September 11, 2001 and February 1, 2002 alone![2] Indeed, the 443,134 job cuts announced in the first quarter of 2002 exceeded those announced in the first quarter of 2001 by nine percent.[3] Medium- and large-sized companies announced most layoffs, and they involved *all* levels of employees, top to bottom. A study by Bain & Company's Worldwide Strategy Practice reported that in 2000, for example, 22 percent of the CEOs of the largest publicly traded companies

*Reprinted with permission of *Academy of Management Executive*, 16 (3) 2002: 80–91, via Copyright Clearance Center.

either lost their jobs or retired, as opposed to just 13 percent in 1999.[4] Morgan Stanley estimates that about 80 percent of the U. S. layoffs involved white-collar, well-educated employees. According to Morgan Stanley's chief economist, that's because 75 percent of the 12.3 million new jobs created between 1994 and 2000 were white-collar jobs. What the companies created, they are now taking away.

Are there gender differences in the likelihood of layoffs and in their consequences? A longitudinal data set of more than 4,000 large Australian firms covering the period 1990–1998 found that men were more likely than women to experience employment downsizing, but that women's re-employment rates after downsizing were lower than men's.[5] Evidence indicates that such career disruptions have particularly negative consequences on the future earnings of women.[6]

THE ECONOMIC LOGIC THAT DRIVES DOWNSIZING

What makes downsizing such a compelling strategy to firms worldwide? The economic rationale is straightforward. It begins with the premise that there really are only two ways to make money in business: either you cut costs or you increase revenues. Which is more predictable, future costs or future revenues? Anyone who makes monthly mortgage payments knows that future costs are far more predictable than future revenues. Payroll expenses represent fixed costs, so by cutting payroll, other things remaining equal, one should reduce overall expenses. Reduced expenses translate into increased earnings, and earnings drive stock prices. Higher stock prices make investors and analysts happy. The key phrase is "other things remaining equal." As we shall see, other things often do not remain equal, and therefore the anticipated benefits of employment downsizing do not always materialize.

WHAT DOES RESEARCH ON THE ECONOMIC CONSEQUENCES OF EMPLOYMENT DOWNSIZING TELL US?

In a series of studies that included data from 1982–1994, 1995–2000, and 1982–2000, my colleagues and I examined financial and employement data from companies in the Standard & Poor's 500. The S&P 500 is one of the most widely used benchmarks of the performance of U. S. equities. It represents leading companies in leading industries and consists of 500 stocks chosen for their market size, liquidity, and industry-group representation. Our purpose was to examine the relationships between changes in employment and financial performance. We assigned companies to one of seven mutually exclusive categories based upon their level of change in employment and their level of change in plant and equipment (assets). We then observed the firms' financial performance (profitability and total return on common stock) from one year before to two years after the employment-change events. We examined results for firms in each category on an independent as well as on an industry-adjusted basis.[7]

In our most recent study, we observed a total of 6,418 occurrences of changes in employment for S&P 500 companies over the 18-year period from 1982 through 2000. As in our earlier studies, we found no significant, consistent evidence that employment downsizing led to improved financial performance, as measured by return on assets or industry-adjusted return on assets. Downsizing strategies, either employment downsizing or asset downsizing, did not yield long-term payoffs that were significantly larger than those generated by Stable Employers—those companies in which the complement of employees did not fluctuate by more than ±5 percent.

This conclusion differs from that in our earlier analysis of the data from 1982 to 1994.[8] In that study we concluded that some types of downsizing, e.g., Asset Downsizing, do yield higher ROAs than either Stable Employers or their industries. However, when the data from 1995–2000 are added to the original 1982–1994 data, a different picture emerges. That picture suggests clearly that, at least during the time period of our study, it was not possible for firms to "save" or "shrink" their way to prosperity. Rather, it was only by growing their businesses (Asset Upsizing) that firms outperformed Stable Employers as well as their own industries in terms of profitablity and total returns on common stock. With respect to such returns, Asset Upsizers generated returns that were 41 percent higher than those of Employment Downsizers and 43 percent higher than those of Stable Employers, by the end of Year 2.

This is not to say that firms should not downsize. In fact, many firms have downsized and restructured successfully to improve their productivity. They have done so by using layoffs as part of a broader business plan. As examples, consider Sears Roebuck & Company and Praxair. Inc. In January 2001 Sears cut 2,400 jobs as part of a restructuring that included closing 89 stores and several smaller businesses. Shares rose 30 percent in six months. Praxair, Inc., a $5 billion supplier of specialty gases and coatings, cut 900 jobs in September 2001 in response to the economic slowdown. At the same time, however, it also announced initiatives designed to pull it out of the slump, including two new plants for products where demand was on the rise. The result? The value of its shares rose 30 percent in three months.

In the aggregate, the productivity and competitiveness of many firms have increased in recent years. However, the lesson from our analysis is that firms cannot simply *assume* that layoffs are a quick fix that will necessarily lead to productivity improvements and increased financial performance. The fact is that layoffs alone will not fix a business strategy that is fundamentally flawed. Thus when Palm, Inc. trimmed 250 jobs in an effort to cut costs after a delayed product launch slowed demand, shares lost nearly half their value in one day and never recovered. In response, Palm's chief financial officer, Judy Bruner, noted, "There were a lot of questions about the viability of the business."[9]

In short, employment downsizing may not necessarily generate the benefits sought by management. Managers must be very cautious in implementing a strategy that can impose such traumatic costs on employees, both on those who leave as well as on those who stay.[10] Management needs to be sure about the sources of future savings and carefully weigh those against *all* of the costs, including the increased costs associated with subsequent employment expansions when economic conditions improve.

WHAT'S DIFFERENT ABOUT CURRENT LAYOFFS IN THE UNITED STATES

In some important ways, the cuts that firms in the United States are making now differ from those they made in the 1990s.

PREEMPTIVE LAYOFFS BY LARGE FIRMS

Today's job cuts are not solely about large, sick companies trying to save themselves, as was often the case in the early 1990s (e.g., IBM, Sears). They are also about healthy companies hoping to reduce costs and boost earnings by reducing head count (e.g., Goldman Sachs and AOL). They are about trying to preempt tough times instead of simply reacting to them. These layoffs are radical, preventive first aid.[11] On the other hand, small companies, especially small manufacturers, tend to resist layoffs because they are trying to protect the substantial investment they made in finding and training workers.[12]

TAILORING THE COMPLEMENT OF SKILLS

At the same time that firms are firing some people, they are hiring others, presumably people with the skills to execute new strategies. According to the American Management Association's annual survey of its member companies, which employ one quarter of the American workforce, 36 percent of firms that eliminated jobs in the previous 12 months said they had also created new positions. That's up from 31 percent in 1996.[13] As companies lose workers in one department, they are adding people with different skills in another, continually tailoring their workforces to fit the available work and adjusting quickly to swings in demand for products and services. What makes this flexibility possible is the rise in temporary and contract workers.[14] On a typical day, they allow companies to meet 12 percent of their staffing needs. On peak days that figure may reach 20 percent.[15]

SYMPATHY TOWARD AN EMPLOYER'S REASONS FOR LAYOFFS, AND A REFUSAL TO PERSONALIZE THE EXPERIENCE

From the perspective of employees, layoffs have a new character. More managers are briefing employees regularly about the economic status of their companies. This information raises awareness and actually prepares employees for what might happen to them. To many, the layoffs seem justified because of the slowdown in economic growth, the plunge in corporate profits, and the dive in stock prices. While being laid off even once used to be traumatic, some employees can now expect to go through that experience twice or even three times before they reach 50.[16]

OUTPLACEMENT CENTERS AS HIRING HALLS

Outplacement centers have become America's new hiring halls—gathering places for those between assignments. As the managing principal of the New York office of outplacement firm Right Associates put it, "These people are not ashamed, but they do feel dislocated, and there is anger. They were on track, and now they are trying to get back on track." Right has redesigned its offices to accommodate the new matter-of-factness about downsizing. Instead of enclosed offices and cubicles, where the downsized of the 1990s kept to themselves they pursued jobs, there are many more glass walls and open gathering places where the downsized of the 21st century get to know each other. They socialize, and they even re-create office buzz. Said the managing principal, "It took us awhile to recognize that this had become important."

LAYOFFS IN OTHER COUNTRIES

The phenomenon of layoffs is not limited to the United States. Asia and Europe have been hard hit as well. Japan's chip and electronics conglomerates have shed tens of thousands of jobs in the past year as the worldwide information-technology slump and fierce competition from foreign rivals have battered their bottom lines. High-profile firms such as Hitachi, Fujitsu, NEC, Toshiba, Matsushita Electric Industrial, and Sony have cut deeply, as has Mazda in automobile production.[17] In Hong Kong, fully 43 percent of firms in a recent survey expect to lay off workers in 2002, and in mainland China, more than 25.5 million people were laid off from state-owned firms between 1998 and 2001. Another 20 million are expected to be laid off from traditional state-owned firms by 2006.[18]

The incidence of layoffs varies among countries in Western Europe. Labor laws in countries such as Italy, France, Germany, and Spain make it difficult and expensive for companies to dismiss workers. In Germany, for example, all "redundancies" must by law be negotiated in detail by a workers' council, which is a compulsory part of any big German company and often has a say in which workers can be fired. Moreover, setting the terms of severance is tricky, because the law is vague and German courts often award compensation if workers claim that they received inadequate settlements. In France, layoffs are rare. As an example, consider that now-bankrupt apppliance maker Moulinex, once considered an icon of French industry, repeatedly tried to restructure in 2001 but was blocked by the French Socialist government because its cost-cutting plans included layoffs. At present, even if companies offer generous severance settlements to French workers, as both Michelin and Marks & Spencer did in 2001, the very announcement of layoffs triggers a political firestorm.[19]

Multinational companies are dealing with this problem in several different ways. One strategy is to turn to other locations within the 15-nation European Union where labor laws are more flexible. Thus Britain has attracted car assembly plants from Nissan Motor Company and PSA Peugeot Citroen, while Ireland hosts EU-wide operations for such technology companies as Microsoft and Intel. A second strategy, practiced by multinationals such as General Motors and Ford, is to move production to Eastern Europe, Turkey, and other lower-cost areas.[20]

U.S.-style layoffs are more common among some European multinationals. Thus London-based EMI Recorded Music, facing a declining global market and growing threat from Internet piracy, recently announced cuts affecting 18 percent of its workforce. Stockholm-based LM Ericsson, the world's largest manufacturer of equipment for cell-phone networks, with operations in 140 countries, had 107,000 employees in April 2001. By January 2002 it was down to 85,000, and in April 2002 it announced an additional 17,000 job cuts.[21] Such massive corporate and personal disruption one again raises important questions about the long-term benefits of strategies that emphasize reductions in the workforce. To put that issue into perspective, let us consider a key driver of business success in the new millennium: business concept innovation.

BUSINESS CONCEPT INNOVATION

As Gary Hamel notes in his book *Leading the Revolution* (2000), the age of incremental progress is over. Its mantra—faster, better, cheaper—is true of fewer and fewer companies. Today change has changed. No longer is it additive. No longer does it move in a straight line. In many industries it is now discontinuous, abrupt, and distinctly nonlinear, as radically different ideas and commercial developments render established products and services obsolete.[22] Perhaps the most far-reaching change of all is the Internet, which has rendered geography meaningless.

In the age of incremental progress, companies practiced rigorous planning, continuous improvement, statistical process control, six sigma quality-enhancement programs, reengineering, and enterprise resource planning.[23] If companies missed something that was changing in the environment—for example in TVs, stereos, and other consumer electronics, as in the 1970s and 1980s—there was plenty of time to catch up.

Today, if a company misses a critical new development—for example in digital phones, Internet auctions, or corporate extranets (networks that connect firms to their suppliers or customers, that is, the entire value chain)—it may never catch up. As an example of the latter, consider enterprise resources planning (ERP). Firms employed armies of consultants to help them use ERP to integrate internal operations like purchasing, manufacturing, and accounting. Such activities are important and useful, but now many companies use the Web to link up with suppliers and customers. Many ERP consultants (and their firms) are not players in this area, and the Web is the wave of the future.

Industrial-age management is a liability in a post-industrial world. Never before has there been such an incredible need for visionary leadership and the capacity to manage change effectively. Today the challenge is to think differently—to move beyond scientific management and kaizen (continuous improvement). As Hamel points out, the focus today is not on the slow accretion of scientific knowledge but on leaps of human imagination. In a non-linear world, only non-linear ideas will create new wealth and lead to radical improvement in human welfare.

The starting point today is not a product or a service. It's the entire business concept. Here are just a few examples:

- Internet telephony (the use of Internet facilities, where voice transmission is one form of communication) versus dedicated voice networks (e.g., telephones, allowing only voice transmission)
- Buying insurance over the Internet versus going to a physical agency
- Searching for a job at Monster.com versus help-wanted ads in a local newspaper

- Downloading music via MP3 files versus purchasing CDs at a music store
- Instant buyer co-operatives (Mercata.com) versus shopping at a mall

The list goes on and on. Now let's consider what business concept innovation is not.

WHAT BUSINESS CONCEPT INNOVATION IS NOT

Some popular strategies today are spin-offs of noncore businesses, stock buy-backs, tracking stocks, and efficiency programs. All of these *release* wealth but they do not *create* wealth.[24] This is financial engineering, not business concept innovation. Strategies like these do not create new customers, markets, or revenue streams. Their only purpose is to wring a bit more wealth out of yesterday's strategies. Sure, money talks, but it doesn't think. Machines work efficiently, but they don't invent. Thinking and inventing are done by the only true, long-term source of innovation and renewal that organizations possess: smart, well-trained people.

How do you increase the probability that radical, new, wealth-creating ideas will emerge in your organization? Certainly not by indiscriminate downsizing of your workforce or by trying to imitate the best practices of other companies. Rather, a key task for leaders is to create an environment in which the creativity and imagination of employees at *all* levels can flourish. In many cases doing so requires a radical shift in the mindset of managers at all levels. That new mindset is called *responsible restructuring.*

RESPONIBLE RESTRUCTURING—WHAT IS IT?

In 1995 I wrote a publication for the U.S. Department of Labor entitled *Guide to Responsible Restructuring.*[25] As I investigated the approaches that various companies, large and small, public and private, adopted in their efforts to restructure, what became obvious to me was that companies differed in terms of how they viewed their employees. Indeed, they almost seemed to separate themselves logically into two groups. One group of firms, by far the larger of the two, saw employees as *costs to be cut.* The other, much smaller group of firms, saw employees as *assets to be developed.* Therein lay a major difference in the approaches they took to restructure their organizations.

- **Employees as costs to be cut**—these are the downsizers. They constantly ask themselves: What is the minimum number of employees that we need to run this company? What is the irreducible core number of employees that the business requires?
- **Employees as assets to be developed**—these are the responsible restructurers. They constantly ask themselves: How can we change the way we do business, so that we can use the people we currently have more effectively?

The downsizers see employees as commodities—like paper clips or light bulbs, interchangeable and substitutable one for another. This is a "plugin" mentality: plug them in when you need them; pull the plug when you no longer need them. In contrast, responsible restructurers see employees as sources of innovation and renewal. They see in employees the potential to grow their businesses.

DOWNSIZING'S HIDDEN RISK TO LEARNING ORGANIZATIONS

Learning organizations, from high-technology firms to the financial services industry, depend heavily on their employees—their stock of human capital—to innovate and grow. Learning organizations are collections of networks in which interrelationships among individuals, that is, social networks, generate learning and knowledge. This knowledge based constitutes a firm's "memory." Because a single individual has multiple relationships in such an organization, indiscriminate, non-selective downsizing has the potential to inflict considerable damage on the learning and memory capacity of organizations.[26] That damage is far greater than might be implied by a simple tally of individuals.

When one considers the multiple relationships generated by one individual, it is clear that restructuring which involves significant reductions in employees can inflict damage and create the loss of significant "chunks" of organizational memory. Such a loss damages ongoing processes and operations, forfeits current contacts, and may lead to foregone business opportunities. Which kinds of organizations are at greatest risk? Those that operate in rapidly evolving industries, such as biotechnology, pharmaceuticals, and software, where survival depends on a firm's ability to innovate constantly.

TEN MISTAKES TO AVOID WHEN RESTRUCTURING

Downsizing a learning organization is not the only mistake that some companies make. Here are ten others to ponder and learn from.[27]

1. ***Failure to be clear about long- and short-term goals.*** Always ask: What do our customers expect from us, and how will restructuring affect our ability to meet those expectations?[28]
2. ***Use of downsizing as a first resort, rather than as a last resort.*** In some cases, firms downsize because they see competitors doing it. This is a "cloning" response, in which executives in different firms follow one another's actions under conditions of uncertainty,[29] but it fails to consider alternative approaches to reducing costs. Such alternatives include delaying new-hire start dates, reducing perks, revoking job offers, freezing salaries and promotions, and asking employees to take unpaid vacations.[30]
3. ***Use of non-selective downsizing.*** Across-the-board job cuts miss the mark. So also do cuts based on criteria such as last-in-first-out (because then firms lose all their bright young people), removing everyone below a certain level in the hierarchy (because top-heavy firms become even top heavier), or weeding out all middle managers (because firms lose a wealth of experience and connections).[31] Are all departments and all employees equally valuable to the firm? Probably not. With respect to employees, think about performance and replaceability.[32] Employees who are top performers and who are difficult to replace are most valuable. They are the "stars" that firms will depend on to innovate, to create new markets and new customers. Do everything you can to retain them.
4. ***Failure to change the ways work is done.*** Some firms mistakenly believe that they can keep making products or delivering services the same way as before downsizing.

They fail even to consider changing from an old way to a new way of working. The same amount of work is simply loaded on the backs of fewer workers. Such a "pure-employment downsizing" approach does not lead to long-term improvements either in profitability or in total returns on common stock.[33]

5. ***Failure to involve workers in the restructuring process.*** It is a truism that employees are more likely to support what they helped to create. Yet many restructuring efforts fail to involve employees in any decisions either about the process or the desired outcome. As a result, employees feel powerless and helpless, and there is massive uncertainty in the organization. Conversely, when employees were asked to rate various factors that affect attracting, motivating, and retaining superior employees, one of the most important factors was "opportunities to participate in decisions."[34]
6. ***Failure to communicate openly and honestly.*** Failure to provide regular, ongoing updates not only contributes to the atmosphere of uncertainty; it also does nothing to dispel rumors. Open, honest communication is crucial if employees are to trust what management says, and trust is crucial to successful restructuring.[35] People trust leaders who make themselves known and make their positions clear.[36]
7. ***Inept handling of those who lose their jobs.*** Failure to treat departing employees with dignity and respect (e.g., having security guards escort them off company property), failure to provide training to supervisors in how to handle emotional factors, and failure to provide assistance to departing employees (financial, counseling, redeployment, training, outplacement) is another crucial mistake.[37]
8. ***Failure to manage survivors effectively.*** Employee morale is often the first casualty of downsizing, as survivors become narrow-minded, self-absorbed, and risk averse.[38] Many firms underestimate the emotional damage that survivors suffer by watching others lose their jobs. In fact, a great deal of research shows that survivors often suffer from heightened levels of stress, burnout, uncertainty about their own roles in the new organization, and an overall sense of betrayal.[39] In unionized environments, downsizing may be related to increased grievances, higher absenteeism rates, workplace conflict, and poorer supervisor–union member relations.[40] In fact, survivors are looking for signals such as the following: Were departing employees treated fairly, and with dignity and respect? Why should I stay? What new opportunities will be available to me if I choose to do so? Is there a new business strategy to help us do a better job of competing in the marketplace?
9. ***Ignoring the effects on other stakeholders.*** In addition to survivors and victims, it is important to think through the potential consequences of restructuring on customers, suppliers, shareholders, and the local community. A comprehensive program addresses and manages consequences for each of these groups.
10. ***Failure to evaluate results and learn from mistakes.*** Restructuring is not a one-time event for most firms. I have found in my research that unless firms are brutally honest about the processes and outcomes of their restructuring efforts, they are doomed to repeat the same mistakes over and over again. Don't be afraid to ask employees and managers at all levels, "What did you like most and like least about our restructuring effort?" Don't be afraid to ask customers if the firm is now meeting their needs more effectively, and for suggestions on how it might do so.

THREE DOWNSIZING STRATEGIES FOR RESPONSIBLE RESTRUCTURING

Now that we have seen what so many firms do wrong, let's examine three responsible restructuring strategies that some firms are doing right. These examples are by no means exhaustive, but they do represent the strategies of firms in several different industries (financial services, management consulting, high technology, telecommunications, manufacturing) and countries (the United States and Singapore).

CHARLES SCHWAB & COMPANY: USE DOWNSIZING AS A LAST RESORT; AT THE SAME TIME REINVENT YOUR BUSINESS

At the end of the second quarter of 2001, Schwab's commission revenues were off 57 percent from their peak 15 months earlier. Overall revenue was down 38 percent, losses totaled $19 million, and the stock had dropped 75 percent from its high. Something had to give. How did the company respond? It took five steps *before* finally cutting staff.[41]

- When Schwab first saw business begin to deteriorate the year before, it put projects on hold and cut back on such expenses as catered staff lunches, travel, and entertainment. Management went out of its way to explain to employees the short-term nature of these cuts.[42]
- As it became clear that more savings were needed, top executives all took pay cuts: 50 percent each for the company's two CEOs, 20 percent for executive vice presidents, 10 percent for senior vice presidents, and 5 percent for vice presidents.
- It encouraged employees to take unused vacation and to take unpaid leaves of up to 20 days.
- Management designated certain Fridays as voluntary days off without pay for employees who didn't have clients to deal with.
- Only after the outlook darkened again, at the end of the first quarter of 2001, did the firm announce layoffs: 2,000 out of a workforce of 25,000. Even then the severance package included a $7,500 "hire-back" bonus for any employee rehired within 18 months. It also included between 500 and 1,000 stock options, cash payments to offset the increased costs of healthcare insurance for laid-off employees, and a full range of outplacement services.[43] Further, everyone being laid off, nearly 5,000 people by the end of September 2001, was eligible for a $20,000 tuition voucher paid for by the founder himself. That could cost him as much as $10 million.

Over the past decade or so, Schwab & Company has had a lengthy record of product innovation. Perhaps its greatest innovation was one of the gutsiest moves of the 1990s: offering online trading in a bigger and better way than anyone else, even though it meant cutting commission rates by more than half. The result? In early 2000 Schwab could boast of having generated a better 10-year return for investors than Microsoft!

Today, however, the company is reinventing its business model. Sure, it is cutting costs by making its website easier to use, thus cutting down on expensive phone traffic, and it is raising fees for customers who don't trade very often and are unprofitable for the firm. But its biggest bet—where it thinks the bulk of its future revenue will come from—will be a radical new approach to winning and keeping business. The firm that was founded on the principle that it would never tell customers what stocks to buy is about to do just that—but with an ingenious twist.

The plan is to have computers analyze customers' portfolios, compare them with a computer-generated list of Schwab-recommended stocks for that investor's risk profile, and then convey that message to the client. When the objective analysis is supplemented with research reports from partner Goldman Sachs, plus occasional access to a salaried investment specialist, the company feels that these steps will fill in the final gap in what will be a complete set of services for virtually every investor.[44]

Schwab is practicing responsible restructuring. How? At the same time that it is demonstrating by its actions that it sees its employees as assets to be developed, it is developing business concept innovations that will allow it to generate new customers and new streams of revenue in order to grow its business.

CISCO SYSTEMS, ACCENTURE, MOTOROLA: "PARK" THE BEST; RESPECT THE REST

A second downsizing strategy is to retain top employees, while generating good will, even loyalty, among those departing. The United States has just sailed through five years of labor shortfalls on a scale not seen in more than three decades. What's more, the unemployment rate, while still rising, remains at historically low levels. Indeed, the unemployment rate for white-collar workers remains at just 2.2 percent.[45] Many employers are cautious about laying off too many workers, only to find themselves scrambling to refill the positions when demand picks up. To avoid that scenario, some are developing ingenious plans to "park" their most highly skilled employees until the economy recovers, and to promote good will, even loyalty, among those they have to let go.

Cisco Systems, which is shrinking its staff to 30,500 from 38,000 and paying six-months' salary to those who sign severance agreements, is also trying a 21st-century version of the old industrial furlough. In a pilot program, it is paying 70 employees one-third of their salaries while lending them to non-profit organizations for a year. In effect Cisco is warehousing them until they might be needed.[46]

Accenture, a large management consulting firm, did cut 600 support staff last June. But to retain skilled employees, it developed the idea of partially paid sabbaticals. The firm pays 20 percent of each employee's salary for six to twelve months, plus benefits, and it lets the employee keep a work phone number, laptop, and email. About 1,000 employees took the offer. Said Accenture's managing partner for internal operations "This is a way to cut costs that gives us the ability to hang onto people we spent so much time recruiting and training."[47]

Motorola has been hard hit by the global slowdown in telecommunications. As a result it is eliminating 30,000 jobs of the 147,000 that existed in January 2001, but at the same time it does not want to waste the results of its assiduous recruiting during the late 1990s. Every laid-off employee in the United States is getting a minimum of eight-weeks' pay as severance, a benefit that until the late 1990s was not so broadly available to lower-ranking employees.

Motorola has also become more active in sponsoring job fairs and outplacement clinics where those leaving the company can receive help in writing resumes, honing interviewing skills, and making contacts.[48] Why is Motorola going to such lengths to generate goodwill among departing employees? It views these initiatives as subtle tools for future recruiting, once the economy revives and hiring resumes.

PHILIPS ELECTRONICS SINGAPORE: OFFER TRAINING, COUNSELING, AND JOB-FINDING ASSISTANCE TO DISPLACED WORKERS

A third downsizing strategy for responsible restructuring is to help displaced workers find new jobs. Philips has operations in more than 60 countries in the areas of lighting, consumer electronics, domestic appliances, components, semiconductors, medical systems, business electronics, and information technology services. It began manufacturing operations in Singapore in 1969.[49]

Since the 1980s, manufacturing companies operating in Singapore have been following the global trend of relocating low-end production to lower-cost countries in the region. More recently, the trend has been to relocate to China and newly emerging economies with large supplies of low-cost labor and growing markets. In 1999 Philips Singapore took advantage of this opportunity to relocate part of its consumer electronics and domestic appliances business to China, Eastern Europe, and Mexico, thus lowering its operating costs while remaining based in Singapore. This restructuring exercise resulted in about 750 excess production operators, technicians, and related support staff.

In an effort to maintain a lean and flexible workforce in its low-end production in anticipation of an eventual relocation out of Singapore, Philips adopted the following human resource management strategies:

- Managers were required to assess long-term workforce projections carefully before recruiting new employees.
- Vacancies had to filled from within the organization unless present staff could not meet the requirements.
- Philips recruited contract workers rather than full-time workers to meet increased demand and to provide flexibility when demand fluctuates.

When it became clear that the relocation would result in 750 excess employees, management informed the union, a branch of the Union of Workers in Electronics and Electrical Industries (UWEEI), of the situation. They worked together to ensure that the retrenched workers were given as much support and help as possible in finding alternative work.

Philips puts a high priority on employee self-development, with the belief that people are its most valuable resources. It has earned a reputation for being an enlightened and caring employer having won several prestigious awards from the National Trade Union Congress (NTUC) and from the government. Its demonstrated commitment to its employees, as stated in its philosophy of management, is that employees should be respected, challenged, encouraged, and given equal opportunities.

KEY INITIATIVES AT PHILIPS

Skills upgrading and training for employability. Together with the UWEEI and the NTUC, Philips encouraged all of the affected workers to take advantage of a program that had been initiated by the NTUC: the Skills Redevelopment Program. That program provides attractive training grants to companies. Its objective is to help workers, especially those who are older and lower skilled, to become more employable through skills upgrading. Philips encouraged the 750 affected workers to enroll in the

Certificate of Competence in Electronic Maintenance program under the Skills Redevelopment Program.

Counseling and Employment Assistance

On the day that the retrenchments were announced in December 1999, the company made sure that all affected workers were registered with the NTUC Employment Assistance Program, and company and union representatives were available to answer questions. Later, a job fair was organized by the Ministry of Manpower and union representatives to assist affected workers in their job search.

Job Matching

The first priority was to help workers secure alternative employment, by trying to match them with vacancies in job data banks kept by the NTUC Employment Assistance Program and the government-sponsored Employment Services Department. In an initial effort in December 1999, more than 30 retrenched workers were identified as having the necessary qualifications to pursue further training for a higher skills job such as wafer fabrication. The union approached ST Microelectronics, which had vacancies in this area, and got its agreement to interview interested workers. The union encouraged other workers who were qualified or interested to undergo training in order to qualify for higher-paying employment opportunities.

Financial Assistance

To minimize financial hardship, retrenchment benefits were paid according to the collective bargaining agreement: one month's pay for every year of service, for those with three or more years of service, and one week's pay for every year for those with fewer than three years' service. In addition, workers received one month's pay in lieu of notice of retrenchment, and those retrenched in December still received the one-month annual wage supplement normally paid at the end of the year.

OUTCOMES

Many of the laid-off workers had worked for Philips for more than 20 years, and this had been their first job. They understood the company's need to reduce operating costs and to remain competitive. At the same time, they appreciated the support provided both by the management and by the union in helping them to adjust to the sad reality. Such support also boosted the morale and confidence of those who continued to work in the plants.

RESTRUCTURING RESPONSIBLY: WHAT TO DO

At this point you are probably wondering how to proceed. We have highlighted some things not to do and have provided examples of how to use downsizing as part of a strategy for responsible restructuring. We believe it can all be put together by following these suggestions.

1. ***Carefully consider the rationale behind restructuring.*** Invest in analysis and consider the impact on those who stay, those who leave, and the ability of the organization to serve its customers.[50] Do you have a long-term strategic plan that identifies the future mission and vision of the organization, as well as its core competencies?

Does the plan consider factors such as changes in the firm's external environment and industry, the business cycle, the stage of internationalization of the firm, market segments, and life cycles of products in the various segments? Does the plan consider how processes can be redesigned while retaining the high performers who will be crucial to the firm's future success? Is there a plan to sell off unprofitable assets? Is employment downsizing part of a plan or is it *the* plan? All of these factors could impact the need for and extent of restructuring.

2. ***Consider the virtues of stability.*** In many cases, companies can maintain their special efficiencies only if they can give their workers a unique set of skills and a feeling that they belong together. Teams work best if the team members get to know and trust each other and if each team member masters a broad enough range of skills to be able to fill in for absent colleagues. Moreover, profit sharing as a reward system makes sense only if the employees are around when profits are disbursed. Sometimes the virtues of stability outweigh the potential benefits of change.[51]
3. ***Before making any final decisions about restructuring, managers should make their concerns known to employees and seek their input.*** Some times workers have insightful ideas that may make layoffs unnecessary. However, even if lay-offs are necessary, seeking employee input will foster a sense of participation, belonging, and personal control. Make special efforts to secure the input of "star" employees or opinion leaders, for they can help communicate the rationale and strategy of restructuring to their fellow employees and can also help to promote trust in the restructuring effort.[52]
4. ***Don't use downsizing as a "quick fix" to achieve short-term goals in the face of long-term problems.*** Consider other alternatives first, and ensure that management at all levels shares the pain and participates in any sacrifices employees are asked to beat. Make downsizing truly a last resort, not a first resort.
5. ***If layoffs are necessary, be sure that employees perceive the process of selecting excess positions as fair, and make decisions in a consistent manner.***[53] Make special efforts to retain the best and the brightest, and provide maximum advance notice to terminated employees.
6. ***Communicate regularly and in a variety of ways in order to keep everyone abreast of new developments and information.*** Use newsletters, emails, videos, and employee meetings for this purpose. Sharing confidential financial and competitive information with employees establishes a climate of trust and honesty. High-level managers should be visible, active participants in this process. Be sure that lower-level managers are trained to address the concerns of victims as well as survivors.[54]
7. ***Give survivors a reason to stay, and prospective new hires a reason to join.*** As one set of authors noted, "People need to believe in the organization to make it work, but they need to see that it works to believe in it."[55] Recognize that surviving employees ultimately are the people you will depend on to provide the innovation, superior service to customers, and healthy corporate culture that will attract and retain top talent. Do everything you can to ensure their commitment and their trust.
8. ***Train employees and their managers in the new ways of operating.*** Restructuring means change, and employees at all levels need help in coping with changes in

areas such as reporting relationships, new organizational arrangements, and reengineered business processes. Evidence indicates clearly that firms whose training budgets increase following a restructuring are more likely to realize improved productivity, profits, and quality.[56]

9. ***Examine all HR systems carefully in light of the change of strategy or environment facing the firm.***[57] Training employees in the new ways of operating is important, but so also are other HR systems. These include workforce planning based on changes in business strategy, markets, customers, and expected economic conditions; recruitment and selection, based on the need to change both the number and skills mix of new hires; performance appraisal, based on changes in the work to be done; compensation, based on changes in skill requirements or responsibilities; and labor relations, based on the need to involve employees and their unions in the restructuring process.

Above all, if you do choose to restructure, do it responsibly, and use it as an opportunity to focus ever more sharply on those areas of the business where your firm enjoys its greatest competitive strengths. By restructuring responsibly through the use of effective downsizing strategies, your organization will be better able to achieve the 3C's of organizational success: Care of customers, Constant innovation, and Committed people.[58]

Endnotes

1. Brett, J. M., and Stroh. L. K. 1997. Jumping ship: Who benefits from an external labor market career strategy? *Journal of Applied Psychology,* 82(3): 331–341.
2. Shadow of recession. 9 February 2002. *http://www.cbsmarketwatch.com.*
3. Planned job cuts continue fall. 3 April 2002. *http://www.cbsmarketwatch.com.*
4. Morris, B. White-collar blues. *Fortune.* 23 July 2001, 98–110.
5. Dawkins, P., and Littler, C. R. (Eds.). July 2001. *Downsizing: Is it working for Australia? http://www.ceda.com.au.*
6. See, for example, Blau, F. D., and Ferber, M. A. 1987. *The Economics of Women, Men, and Work.* Upper Saddle River, NJ: Prentice Hall; Schneer, J. A., and Reitman. F. 1997. The interrupted managerial career path: A longitudinal study of MBAs. *Journal of Vocational Behavior,* 51(3): 411–434; and Schneer, J. A., and Reitman, F. 1995. The impact of gender as managerial careers unfold. *Journal of Vocational Behavior,* 47(3): 290–315.
7. Cascio, W. F., and Young, C. E. 2001. Financial consequences of employment-change decisions in major U.S. corporations: 1982–2000. In K. P. De Meuse and M. L. Marks (Eds.). *Resizing the Organization.* In press, San Francisco: Jossey-Bass. See also Cascio, W. F., Young, C. E., and Morris, J. R. 1997. Financial consequences of employment-change decisions in major U.S. corporations. *Academy of Management Journal,* 40(5): 1175–1189; and Morris, J. R., Cascio, W. F., and Young, C. E. 1999. Have employment downsizings been successful? *Organizational Dynamics,* 27(3): 78–87.
8. Cascio, et al., op. cit.
9. Brunet, J., quoted in Lavelle, L. Swing that ax with care. *BusinessWeek,* 11 February 2002. 78.
10. Cascio. W. F. 1993. Downsizing: What do we know? What have we learned? *The Academy of Management Executive,* 7(1): 95–104. See also Cascio. W. F. Strategies for responsible restructuring. Keynote address presented at the National Manpower Summit, Singapore, 18 October 2001.
11. Morris, op. cit.
12. Ansberry, C. Private resources: By resisting layoffs, small manufacturers help protect economy. *Wall Street Journal,* 6 July 2001, A1, A2.
13. American Management Association. 2000. *2000 American Management Association survey: Stafting and Structure.* New York: Author.

14. Eig, J. Shrinking week: Do part-time workers hold the key to when the recession breaks? *Wall Street Journal,* 3 January 2002, A1, A2.
15. Uchitelle, L. Pink slip? Now, it's all in a day's work. *New York Times,* 5 August 2001. *http://www.NYTimes.com.*
16. Ibid.
17. Hitachi decides another 4,000 workers in Japan must go, *South China Morning Post,* 31 January 2002, 1; Kunii, I. Under the knife. *BusinessWeek,* 10 September 2001, 62; and Larimer, T. Worst-case scenario. *Time*, 26 March 2001, 54–56. See also Shirouzu. N. Leaner and meaner: Driven by necessity—and by Ford–Mazda downsizes, U.S.-style, *Wall Street Journal,* 5 January 2000, A1, A10. See also Sony's shake up. *BusinessWeek,* 22 March 1999, 52, 53.
18. 43pc of firms plan to cut staff, says poll. *South China Morning Post,* 26 February 2002, 1; and China warns of 20 million urban jobless. *South China Morning Post, 30 April 2002,* 1.
19. Winestock, G. A reticent European right balks on labor. *Wall Street Journal,* 21 June 2002, A6, A7; and Matlack. C. The high cost of France's aversion to layoffs. *BusinessWeek,* 5 November 2001, 56.
20. Winestock, op. cit.
21. Larsen, K. EMI plans job cuts, large cost savings. *Asian Wall Street Journal,* 21 March 2002, M6; Pritchard, S. Deregulation and debt serve to hasten inevitable. *South China Morning Post,* 26 March 2002, 2; and Gamel, K. Ericsson to cut 17,000 jobs. 22 April 2002. *http://www.cbsmarketwatch.com.*
22. Hamel, G. 2000. *Leading the Revolution.* Boston: Harvard Business School Press.
23. Statistical process control (SPC) is a quality-control technique that is based on statistical theory. Its objective is to study the variation in the output of production processes. Six sigma is a standard in SPC where almost all variability in product or service output has been eliminated. In a six-sigma system, one expects only 3.4 defects per million units of output. Enterprise resource planning is a computer-based software system that integrates all departments and functions into a single information database.
24. Norris, F. Financial magic looked good, but left companies weak. *New York Times,* 28 September 2001. *http://www.NYTimes.com.*
25. U.S. Department of Labor, 1995. *Guide to Responsible Restructuring.* Washington, DC: U.S. Government Printing Office.
26. Fisher, S. R., and White, M. A. 2000. Downsizing in a learning organization: Are there hidden costs? *Academy of Management Review,* 25(1): 244–251.
27. The sources of these recommendations, unless otherwise noted, are my own research, as described in *Guide to Responsible Restructuring,* op. cit., as well as the following: Cravotta, R., and Kleiner, B. H. 2001. New developments concerning reductions in force. *Management Research News,* 24(3/4): 90–93. See also Moravec, M. The right way to rightsize. *Industry Week*, 5 September 1994. 46.
28. For more on this topic, see Seiders, K., and Berry, L. L. 1998. Service fairness: What it is and why it matters. *The Academy of Management Executive.* 12(2): 8–20.
29. McKinley, W., Zhao, J., and Rust, K. G. 2000. A sociocognitive interpretation of organizational downsizing. *Academy of Management Review,* 25(1): 227–243.
30. Lavelle, L. Thinking beyond the one-size-fits-all pay cut. *BusinessWeek,* 3 December 2001, 45.
31. Ibid, See also The year downsizing grew up. *The Economist,* 21 December 1996, 97–99.
32. Martin, D. C., and Bartol, K. M. 1985. Managing turnover strategically. *Personnel Administrator,* 30(11): 63–73. See also Cascio, W. F. 2000. *Costing Human Resources: The Financial Impact of Behavior in Organizations.* 4th ed. Cincinnati, OH: South-Western College Publishing.
33. Cascio and Young, op. cit.
34. Mirvis, P. H. 1997. Human resource management: Leaders, laggards, and followers. *The Academy of Management Executive.* 11(2): 43–56.
35. Mishra, K. E., Spreitzer, G. M., and Mishra, A. K. 1998. Preserving employee morale during downsizing. *Sloan Management Review,* 39(2): 83–95. See also Gray. R. Internal communication: Its critical role during business reorganizations. Presentation to the Australian Human Resources Institute, Sydney, 1 November 2001.

36. Darling. J., and Nurmi, R. 1995. Downsizing the multinational firm: Key variables for excellence. *Leadership & Organization Development Journal*, 16(5): 22–28.
37. As one example of this, see Barrionuevo, A. Jobless in a flash. Enron's ex-employees are stunned, bitter, ashamed. *Wall Street Journal,* 11 December 2001, B1, B12.
38. Cascio, W. F. Downsizing: What do we know? op. cit.
39. Appelbaum, S. H., Everard, A. and Hung, L. T. S. 1999. Strategic downsizing: Critical success factors. *Management Decision,* 37(7): 535–552.
40. Wagar. T. H. 2001. Consequences of work force reduction: Some employer and union evidence. *Journal of Labor Research,* 22(4): 851–862.
41. Vogelstein, F. Can Schwab get its mojo back? *Fortune,* 17 September 2001, 93–98. See also Bernstein, A. America's future: The human factor. *BusinessWeek,* 27 August 2001. 118–122.
42. Boyle, M. How to cut perks without killing morale. *Fortune,* 19 February 2001, 241, 242, 244.
43. Jossi, F. Laying off well. *HRMagazine,* July 2001. 48.
44. Schwab versus Wall Street. *BusinessWeek*, 3 June 2002, 64–70.
45. Bernstein, op. cit.
46. Uchitelle, op. cit.
47. Bernstein, op. cit.
48. Uchitelle, op. cit.
49. Source: Singapore Ministry of Manpower, February 2001. *Managing excess manpower, case study series*, Singapore: Author.
50. *Guide to responsible restructuring,* op. cit.
51. Cascio & Young, op. cit. See also Conlin, M. Where layoffs are a last resort. 8 October 2001. *http://www.businessweek.com*.
52. See Roth, D. How to cut pay, lay off 8,000 people, and still have workers who love you. *Fortune,* 4 February 2002, 62–68.
53. Colquitt, J. A., Conlon, D. E., Wesson, M. J., Porter, C. O. L. H., and Ng. K. Y. 2001. Justice at the millennium: A meta-analytic review of 25 years of organizational justice research. *Journal of Applied Psychology,* 86(3): 425–445.
54. Feldmen, M., and Spratt, M. 1999, *Five Frogs on a Log: A CEO's Field Guide to Accelerating the Transition in Mergers, Acquisitions, and Gut-wrenching Change.* New York: Harper.
55. De Vries, M., and Balazs, K. 1997. The downside of downsizing. *Human Relations,* 50(1): 11–50.
56. Appelbaum, S. H., Lavigne-Schmidt, S., Peytchev, M., and Shapiro, B. 1999. Downsizing: Measuring the costs of failure. *Journal of Management Development,* 18(5): 436–463.
57. Becker, B. E., Huselid, M. A., and Ulrich, D. 2001. *The HR Scorecard: Linking People, Strategy, and Performance.* Boston: Harvard Business School Press. See also Delery, J. E., and Doty, D. H. 1996. Modes of theorizing in strategic human resource management: Tests of universalistic, contingency, and configurational performance predictions. *Academy of Management Journal,* 39(4): 802–835.
58. Darling & Nurmi, op. cit.

CHAPTER 22
MANAGING CHANGE

THE HEART OF CHANGE

John P. Kotter
Dan S. Cohen

SURFING THE EDGE OF CHAOS

Richard T. Pascale

RULES OF THUMB FOR CHANGE AGENTS

Herbert A. Shepard

A turbulent business environment and a global economy demand swift adaptation, which has made it necessary to master our final topic, managing change. Change management is an art as well as a skill. Making a difference at work often boils down to helping your organization or department change, regardless of your position in the hierarchy. Successfully applying the knowledge and skills acquired in your study of organizational behavior requires a good understanding of how the change process works. Change efforts generally fail due to implementation problems rather than the lack of good ideas for change. The art of organizational change involves many of the competencies mentioned throughout the *Reader:* the ability to perceive different mental maps and question their validity, the ability to understand why people and groups behave as they do and appreciate the differences among them, the ability to analyze what's really going on in organizations (including the political and informal aspects), and a thorough understanding of what distinguishes effective and ineffective employees, teams, managers, and organizations. Furthermore, successful change agents, like successful managers, have a great deal of self-awareness.

The importance of emotional intelligence has spread to the change field. John Kotter and Dan Cohen, in "The Heart of Change," contend that unsuccessful changes often result from relying solely on data analysis and rational persuasion. In contrast, they suggest that successful change efforts rely on an orchestrated, choreographed sequence of steps that tangibly demonstrates the need for change, makes people emotionally feel committed to the change, and then removes barriers to change and reinforces behavior consistent with the change.

In recent years, organizational scholars have borrowed theories from natural science and applied, for example, the lessons of chaos theory and complexity theory to human organisms. Richard Pascale, in "Surfing the Edge of Chaos," has written a fascinating treatise on the relationship between complex adaptive systems (bee colonies, amoebae, etc.) and organizational strategy and change. Pascale, a consultant and business professor, uses the change efforts of Royal Dutch/Shell, one of his clients, to test the validity of his argument that complexity theory has lessons for human organizations. We have included his article as an example of cutting-edge thinking that has the potential to take the field of organizational behavior in new directions.

One of the first writers to capture the art of organizational change was Herb Shepard. He was an early practitioner of organizational development (OD), a specialized area of organizational behavior focused on planned change. Shepard's "Rules of Thumb for Change Agents" is a classic that contains a great deal of wisdom for both OD consultants and anyone who wants to make changes in his or her organization.

THE HEART OF CHANGE*

John P. Kotter
Dan S. Cohen

The single most important message in this book is very simple. People change what they do less because they are given *analysis* that shifts their *thinking* than because they are *shown* a truth that influences their *feelings*. This is especially so in large-scale organizational change, where you are dealing with new technologies, mergers and acquisitions, restructurings, new strategies, cultural transformation, globalization, and e-business—whether in an entire organization, an office, a department, or a work group. In an age of turbulence, when you handle this reality well, you win. Handle it poorly, and it can drive you crazy, cost a great deal of money, and cause a lot of pain.

The lessons here come from two sets of interviews, the first completed seven years ago, the second within the last two years. About 400 people from 130 organizations answered our questions. We found, in brief, that

- Highly successful organizations know how to overcome antibodies that reject anything new. They know how to grab opportunities and avoid hazards. They see that *bigger leaps* are increasingly associated with winning big. They see that continuous gradual improvement, by itself, is no longer enough.
- Successful large-scale change is a complex affair that happens in *eight stages*. The flow is this: Push urgency up, put together a guiding team, create the vision and strategies, effectively communicate the vision and strategies, remove barriers to action, accomplish short-term wins, keep pushing for wave after wave of change until the work is done, and, finally, create a new culture to make new behavior stick.
- The central challenge in all eight stages is *changing people's behavior*. The central challenge is not strategy, not systems, not culture. These elements and many others can be very important, but the core problem without question is behavior—what people do, and the need for significant shifts in what people do.

---

*Excerpted and reprinted by permission of Harvard Business School Press. From *The Heart of Change: Real-Life Stories of How People Change Their Organizations* by John P. Kotter and Dan S. Cohen. Boston, MA, 2002.

- Changing behavior is less a matter of giving people analysis to influence their thoughts than helping them to see a truth to influence their feelings. Both thinking and feeling are essential, and both are found in successful organizations, but the heart of change is in the emotions. The flow of see-feel-change is more powerful than that of analysis-think-change. These distinctions between seeing and analyzing, between feeling and thinking, are critical because, for the most part, we use the latter much more frequently, competently, and comfortably than the former.

When we are frustrated, we sometimes try to convince ourselves there is a decreasing need for large-scale change. But powerful and unceasing forces are driving the turbulence. When frustrated, we sometimes think that problems are inevitable and out of our control. Yet some people handle large-scale change remarkably well. We can all learn from these people. CEOs can learn. First-line supervisors can learn. Nearly anyone caught up in a big change can learn.

THE EIGHT STAGES OF SUCCESSFUL LARGE-SCALE CHANGE

To understand why some organizations are leaping into the future more successfully than others, you need first to see the flow of effective large-scale change efforts. In almost all cases, there is a flow, a set of eight steps that few people handle well.

The process of change involves subtle points regarding overlapping stages, guiding teams at multiple levels in the organization, handling multiple cycles of change, and more. Because the world is complex, some cases do not rigidly follow the eight-step flow. But the eight steps, summarized in Table 1, are the basic pattern associated with significant useful change—all possible *despite* an inherent organizational inclination not to leap successfully into a better future.

The stories that accompany some of the steps show what can be done to enable this process and appeal to the heart to overcome the obstacles to change.

STEP ONE: INCREASE URGENCY

Whether at the top of a large private enterprise or in small groups at the bottom of a nonprofit, those who are most successful at significant change begin their work by creating a sense of *urgency* among relevant people. In smaller organizations, the "relevant" are more likely to number 100 than 5, in larger organizations 1,000 rather than 50. The less successful change leaders aim at 5 or 50 or 0, allowing what is common nearly everywhere—too much complacency, fear, or anger, all three of which can undermine change. A sense of urgency, sometimes developed by very creative means, gets people off the couch, out of a bunker, and ready to move.

First, people are shocked, then the gut-level sense of complacency shrinks and urgency grows. It's not just a matter of the data saying that changes are necessary in the purchasing process so people alter their behavior. Instead, it's subtler and deeper. It's a loud sound that catches attention in a day filled with thousands of words and dozens of events. It's an image, hard to shake, that evokes a feeling that we must *do* something.

TABLE 1 The Eight Steps for Successful Large-Scale Change

Step	*Action*	*New Behavior*	*What Works*	*What Does Not Work*
1	Increase urgency	People start telling each other, "Let's go, we need to change things!"	• Showing others the need for change with a compelling object that they can actually, see, touch, and feel • Showing people valid and dramatic evidence from outside the organization that demonstrates that change is required • Looking constantly for cheap and easy ways to reduce complacency • Never underestimating how much complacency, fear, and anger exists, even in good organizations	• Focusing exclusively on building a "rational" business case, getting top management approval, and racing ahead while mostly ignoring all the feelings that are blocking change • Ignoring a lack of urgency and jumping immediately to creating a vision and strategy • Believing that without a crisis or burning platform you can go nowhere • Thinking that you can do little if you're not the head person
2	Build the guiding team	A group powerful enough to guide a big change is formed and they start to work together well.	• Showing enthusiasm and commitment (or helping someone do so) to help draw the right people into the group • Modeling the trust and teamwork needed in the group (or helping someone to do that) • Structuring meeting formats for the guiding team so as to minimize frustration and increase trust • Putting your energy into step 1 (raising urgency) if you cannot take on the step 2 challenge and if the right people will not	• Guiding change with weak task forces, single individuals, complex governance structures, or fragmented top teams • Not confronting the situation when momentum and entrenched power centers undermine the creation of the right group • Trying to leave out or work around the head of the unit to be changed because he or she is "hopeless"
3	Get the vision right	The guiding team develops the right vision and strategy for the change effort.	• Trying to see, literally, possible futures • Visions that are so clear that they can be articulated in one minute or written up on one page • Visions that are moving—such as a commitment to serving people	• Assuming that linear or logical plans and budgets alone adequately guide behavior when you're trying to leap into the future • Overly analytic, financially based vision exercises

(*Continued*)

(Continued)

			• Strategies that are bold enough to make bold visions a reality • Paying careful attention to the strategic question of how quickly to introduce change	• Visions of slashing costs, which can be emotionally depressing and anxiety creating • Giving people fifty-four logical reasons why they need to create strategies that are bolder than they have ever created before
4	Communicate for buy-in	People begin to buy into the change, and this shows in their behavior.	• Keeping communication simple and heartfelt, not complex and technocratic • Doing your homework before communicating, especially to understand what people are *feeling* • Speaking to anxieties, confusion, anger, and distrust • Ridding communication channels of junk so that important messages can go through • Using new technologies to help people see the vision (intranet, satellites, etc.)	• Undercommunicating, which happens all the time • Speaking as though you are only transferring information • Accidentally fostering cynicism by not walking the talk
5	Empower action	More people feel able to act, and do act, on the vision.	• Finding individuals with change experience who can bolster people's self-confidence with we-won-you-can-too anecdotes • Recognition and reward systems that inspire, promote optimism, and build self-confidence • Feedback that can help people make better vision-related decisions • "Retooling" disempowering managers by giving them new jobs that clearly show the need for change	• Ignoring bosses who seriously disempower their subordinates • Solving the boss problem by taking away their power (making them mad and scared) and giving it to their subordinates • Trying to remove all the barriers at once • Giving in to your own pessimism and fears

6	Create short-term wins	Momentum builds as people try to fulfill the vision, while fewer and fewer resist change.	• Early wins that come fast • Wins that are as visible as possible to as many people as possible • Wins that penetrate emotional defenses by being unambiguous • Wins that are meaningful to others—the more deeply meaningful the better • Early wins that speak to the powerful players whose support you need and do not yet have • Wins that can be achieved cheaply and easily, even if they seem small compared with the grand vision	• Launching fifty projects all at once • Providing the first win too slowly • Stretching the truth
7	Don't let up	People make wave after wave of changes until the vision is fulfilled.	• Aggressively ridding yourself of work that wears you down—tasks that were relevant in the past but not now, tasks that can be delegated • Looking constantly for ways to keep the urgency up • Using new situations opportunistically to launch the next wave of change • As always—show 'em, show 'em, show 'em	• Developing a rigid four-year plan (be more opportunistic) • Convincing yourself that you're done when you aren't • Convincing yourself that you can get the job done without confronting some of the more embedded bureaucratic and political behaviors • Working so hard you physically and emotionally collapse (or sacrifice your off-the-job life)
8	Make change stick	New and winning behavior continues despite the pull of tradition, turnover of change leaders, etc.	• Not stopping at step 7—it isn't over until the changes have roots • Using new employee orientation to compellingly show recruits what the organization really cares about • Using the promotions process to place people who act according to the new norms into influential and visible positions • Telling vivid stories over and over about the new organization, what it does, and why it succeeds • Making absolutely sure you have the continuity of behavior and results that help a new culture grow	• Relying on a boss or compensation scheme, or anything but culture, to hold a big change in place • Trying to change culture as the first step in the transformation process

INCREASE URGENCY—GLOVES ON THE BOARDROOM TABLE

FROM JON STEGNER

We had a problem with our whole purchasing process. I was convinced that a great deal of money was being wasted and would continue to be wasted into the future, and that we didn't even know how much money was being thrown away. I thought we had an opportunity to drive down purchasing costs not by 2 percent but by something in the order of $1 billion over the next five years. A change this big meant a big shift in the process. This would not be possible, however, unless many people, especially in top management, saw the opportunity, which for the most part they did not. So nothing was happening.

To get a sense of the magnitude of the problem, I asked one of our summer students to do a small study of how much we pay for the different kinds of gloves used in our factories and how many different gloves we buy. I chose one item to keep it simple, something all the plants use and something we can all easily relate to.

When the student completed the project, she reported that our factories were purchasing 424 different kinds of gloves! *Four hundred and twenty four.* Every factory had their own supplier and their own negotiated price. The same glove could cost $5 at one factory and $17 at another. Five dollars or even $17 may not seem like much money, but we buy a *lot* of gloves, and this was just one example of our purchasing problem. When I examined what she had found, even I couldn't believe how bad it was.

The student was able to collect a sample of every one of the 424 gloves. She tagged each one with the price on it and the factory it was used in. Then she sorted the bags by division in the firm and type of glove.

We gathered them all up and put them in our boardroom one day. Then we invited all the division presidents to come visit the room. What they saw was a large, expensive table, normally clean or with a few papers, now stacked high with gloves. Each of our executives stared at this display for a minute. Then each said something like, "We buy all these different kinds of gloves?" Well, as a matter of fact, yes we do. "Really?" Yes, really. Then they walked around the table. Most, I think, were looking for the gloves that their factories were using. They could see the prices. They looked at two gloves that seemed exactly alike, yet one was marked $3.22 and the other $10.55.

It's a rare event when these people don't have anything to say. But that day, they just stood with their mouths gaping.

This demonstration quickly gained notoriety. The gloves became part of a traveling road show. They went to every division. They went to dozens of plants. Many, many people had the opportunity to look at the stacks of gloves. The road show reinforced at every level of the organization a sense of "this is how bad it is."

Through more research, again done quickly and inexpensively by one of our students, we discovered what some of our competitors were doing. The "competitive benchmarking" was added to the road show. As a result, we were given a mandate for change. People would say "We must act now," which of course we did, and saved a great deal of money that could be used in much more sensible ways.

Even today, people still talk about the glove story.

STEP TWO: BUILD THE GUIDING TEAM

With urgency turned up, the more successful change agents pull together a *guiding team* with the credibility, skills, connections, reputations, and formal authority required to provide change leadership. This group learns to operate as do all good teams, with trust and emotional commitment. The less successful rely on a single person or no one, weak task forces and committees, or complex governance structures, all without the stature and skills and power to do the job. The landscape is littered with task forces ill equipped to produce needed change.

A feeling of urgency helps greatly in putting together the right group to guide change and in creating essential teamwork within the group. When there is urgency, more people want to help provide leadership, even if there are personal risks. But additional effort is necessary to get the right people in place with the trust, emotional commitment, and teamwork to do the job. That's the step 2 challenge.

For example, the army officer doesn't pull together his new change team with a rational argument. Instead, he shocks them by taking a risk for the greater good with his comments in a meeting. He then helps them begin to tell emotion-packed stories around a campfire. More positive feelings and trust grow making them act as an effective team.

STEP THREE: GET THE VISION RIGHT

In the best cases, the guiding team creates sensible, clear, simple, uplifting *visions* and sets of strategies. In the less successful cases, there are only detailed plans and budgets that, although necessary, are insufficient, or a vision that is not very sensible in light of what is happening in the world and in the enterprise, or a vision that is created by others and largely ignored by the guiding team. In unsuccessful cases, strategies are often too slow and cautious for a faster-moving world.

In successful large-scale change, a well-functioning guiding team answers the questions required to produce a clear sense of direction. What change is needed? What is our vision of the new organization? What should not be altered? What is the best way to make the vision a reality? What change strategies are unacceptably dangerous? Good answers to these questions position an organization to leap into a better future.

Far too often, guiding teams either set no clear direction or embrace visions that are not sensible. The consequences can be catastrophic for organizations and painful for employees—just ask anyone who has suffered through a useless fad forced on them from above.

GET THE VISION RIGHT—THE PLANE WILL NOT MOVE!

FROM DEBBIE COLLARD

A C-17 is a huge aircraft. Its tail rises four stories. Watching it being built is an incredible thing.

Aircraft are typically assembled in a series of locations within one manufacturing facility, locations we call "positions." You start work in one place, then when a set of tasks are completed, you move the plane to a second, and then another until you're done. In the case of the C-17, the main fuselage might be assembled in position A, the tail attached over in position B, the wings attached in position C, the cockpit electronics installed in position D, and so on. For this you have to have a hangar that's large enough for two or three 747-sized aircraft to be in production, along with the equipment. This is a huge amount of square footage. Fifteen hundred of our employees would be in this giant hangar. They would be dealing with many, many thousands of parts. It's an incredible production process that requires complex scheduling and coordination.

The speed with which an airplane moves through the different positions is driven by the schedule. If work is not complete at one position when the schedule says it should move, or if needed parts don't arrive in time, the plane

(*Continued*)

(Continued)

moves anyway and the unfinished work is done at the end. As you can imagine, taking apart a plane at the end of the line, adding parts, and then reassembling leads to quality problems and delays. But this was the way the whole industry did things. No one questioned it. I suppose it was like third-grade children going to school from 8:00 to 3:00 and sitting in rooms with teachers. Of course you do it that way.

As soon as Koz arrived, he made it clear that the priorities for the C-17 program were to excel in terms of quality, schedule, and cost, in that order. He really raised the bar, setting a clear vision of the significantly improved performance we needed. I bet he talked to everyone about this and got much head-nodding. "Sure, boss." And I bet most people wanted that vision and did try a little harder. But many accepted the existing basic production system as the only way to do things, and with that they accepted certain problems as inevitable. The mind-set was, "Yeah, it would be nice if we were never out of needed parts, but that's impossible in this industry." So while people made small adjustments, the overall production strategy did not come close to achieving Koz's raised-bar vision.

Then one day he stood up in a management meeting and made an announcement. "We are not going to move an airplane until it is complete in position. Quality is number one, so that's what we are going to focus on. Until the plane is done and done right, no movement. Period."

Everyone thought he was off his rocker. You didn't do things this way. I think some of his direct reports, in particular, thought he was crazy. They were convinced that we would never be able to deliver on time if we did it this way. Never. Wouldn't happen, anybody knows that. Something would always bring everything to a halt. You'd have employees twiddling their thumbs at great expense to the company. You might as well expect cars to be made by secretaries on the fifty-ninth floor of the Sears building in Chicago.

We had all heard the quality speech before, but here was a guy telling us that nothing goes anywhere unless it's properly done. Koz showed complete conviction that this radical idea was right. And if his words didn't win us over, all day long we had to look at a plane that was not moving until it was complete in a position. All day long, there it was, not moving. Nope. Sitting there.

After Koz made his proclamation, things began to change faster. The fact that out-of-position work would not be tolerated meant that suddenly having parts arrive on time was critical. Our procurement guys got motivated like I'd never seen before. They started coming up with all kinds of new change strategies for their operation. And—incredible since this couldn't be done—they started succeeding in getting our suppliers to operate in new ways. So we began getting the right parts at the right time! Overall, people just didn't want to be the reason that a plane was held in position for longer than it was supposed to. They didn't want to be embarrassed, they didn't want to hurt the company, they didn't want to hurt their careers, and they didn't want to let Koz down. So they started breaking through walls. As evidence began to accumulate that this nutty idea might actually be working, more people got with the program. More started finding ways to punch through walls. When they couldn't do it by themselves, they would come to Koz with specific ideas, sometimes very clever ideas, for what was needed and for how problems could be solved. Koz would then work with them to remove the obstacles. So if it helped for Koz to talk to the president of a parts company, he'd do it.

Holding the planes in place eliminated all sorts of bad habits. No longer could we say, "Of course some percentage of parts won't arrive on time. That's just life." No, that's not life. That's life as we knew it.

To make a long story short, we transformed the place, and, as a result, quality has gone up and all of our aircraft have not only been on time, they've been early!

To this day people still tell this story, from the shop floor to the executive offices. "He said the plane would not move. Period."

STEP FOUR: COMMUNICATE FOR BUY-IN

Communication of the vision and strategies comes next—simple heartfelt messages sent through many unclogged channels. The goal is to induce understanding, develop a gut-level commitment, and liberate more energy from a critical mass of people. Here, deeds are often more important than words. Symbols speak loudly. Repetition is key. In the less successful cases, there is too little effective communication, or people hear words but don't accept them. Remarkably, smart people undercommunicate or poorly communicate all the time without recognizing their error.

In successful change efforts, the vision and strategies are not locked in a room with the guiding team. The direction of change is widely communicated, and communicated for both understanding and gut-level buy-in. The goal: to get as many people as possible acting to make the vision a reality.

When we communicate about a large-scale change, common responses are: "I don't see why we need to change that much," "They don't know what they're doing," "We'll never be able to pull this off," "Are these guys serious or is this a part of some more complicated game I don't understand?" "Are they just trying to line their pockets at my expense?" and "Good heavens, what will happen to me?" In successful change efforts, a guiding team doesn't argue with this reality, declaring it unfair or illogical. They simply find ways to deal with it. The key is one basic insight: Good communication is not just data transfer. You need to show people something that addresses their anxieties, that accepts their anger, that is credible in a very gut-level sense, and that evokes faith in the vision. Great leaders do this well almost effortlessly. The rest of us usually need to do homework before we open our mouths.

Matching Words and Deeds

People in change-successful enterprises do a much better job than most in eliminating the destructive gap between words and deeds. Deeds speak volumes. When you say one thing and then do another, cynical feelings can grow exponentially. Conversely, walking the talk can be most powerful. You say that the whole culture is going to change to be more participatory, and then for the first time ever you change the annual management meeting so that participants have real conversations, not endless talking heads with short, trivial Q&A periods. You speak of a vision of innovation, and then turn the people who come up with good new ideas into heroes. You talk globalization and immediately appoint two foreigners to senior management. You emphasize cost cutting and start with eliminating the extravagance surrounding the executive staff.

STEP FIVE: EMPOWER ACTION

In the best situations, you find a heavy dose of *empowerment.* Key obstacles that stop people from acting on the vision are removed. Change leaders focus on bosses who disempower, on inadequate information and information systems, and on self-confidence barriers in people's minds. The issue here is removing obstacles, not "giving power." You can't hand out power in a bag. In less successful situations, people are often left to fend for themselves despite impediments all around. So frustration grows, and change is undermined.

In highly successful change efforts, when people begin to understand and act on a change vision, you remove barriers in their paths. You take away the tattered sails and give them better ones. You take a wind in their faces and create a wind at their backs. You take away a pessimistic skipper and give the crew an optimistic boss.

The word "empowerment" comes with so much baggage, you might be tempted to abandon it. We won't. As we use the term, empowerment is not about giving people new authority and new responsibilities. It is all about removing barriers.

Removing the "Boss" Barrier

Often the single biggest obstacle is a boss—an immediate manager or someone higher in the hierarchy, a first-line supervisor or an executive vice president. Subordinates see the vision and want to help, but are effectively shut down. The supervisor's words, actions, or even subtle vibrations say "This change is stupid." The underlings, not being fools, either give up or spend an inordinate amount of time trying to maneuver around the barrier.

The "boss barrier" is typically handled in one of three ways. We ignore the issue, we send the obstacle to a short training course, or (rarely) we try to fire, demote, or transfer the person. None of these are great solutions, the first for obvious reasons, the second because it usually has little effect, and the third because, if not handled well, fear will escalate and become a disempowering force itself.

In cases of highly successful change, people begin by confronting the issue. In order to be fair, they explain the situation to the individual creating the problem. When explaining fails, as it often does, they try more creative solutions.

EMPOWER ACTION—RETOOLING THE BOSS

FROM TIM WALLACE

There was one superintendent in our company, Joe, who was considered so "old school" that people had warned me he would never change his ways. He had been with the company for over twenty years and he was very proud of our products. Whenever a customer would want a change in the product or how we made it, this man would get bent out of shape. He felt we were giving people a great product and that they were too picky. When someone would suggest something, he would respond in one of two ways: We tried it and it didn't work, or we thought about it and decided not to try it. It seemed to me he was basically a good man, a talented man, and a man with a lot of valuable experience who was stuck in an old paradigm. He just couldn't see anything from the customer's point of view.

Once, it became so tense that one of our best customers said that we needed to replace Joe. I didn't like the idea of terminating an employee who probably thought he was protecting the company. So I thought about it and then said to the customer, "Let's do something different which might help both of us."

We asked them if Joe could go to work for their company for six months at our expense. He would work at a different place and have a different boss. To help make this happen, we agreed to keep paying his salary. We further said that after six months we would bring him back into our company as a customer representative, inspecting our products specifically for that customer. This would be a different job than he had before, but an important job. The idea was to convert the guy from being an obstacle for others into someone who would actively help us.

Joe's boss thought the plan wouldn't work—may have even thought it was nuts—but he agreed to go along with it. Joe was at first also very reluctant to accept the idea. "I have my own job to do and I don't want to do something else." I told him we really needed his expertise so that he could tell us what was going on when our tankers arrived at the customer's facility. But he was a real hard rock. He didn't want any part of this plan. So we had his boss tell him that he couldn't have his existing job anymore, that he could take our offer or leave.

Off he went into a different world. His new job was to be a quality inspector at the customer's plant. I don't know how difficult it was on him at first, but he had to change to survive. He had to learn a new job, a new company, and how to look at our products from that customer's point of view. If he didn't, he failed.

Well, he didn't want to fall, so he tried to do the new job. And when he started really looking, he found that an old product of ours, which he thought was very good, didn't meet the customer's needs. He found that they bought this product because they didn't have an alternative and switching would be costly. He found that another product, which he also thought was very high-quality, was not seen by the customer that way because of how they needed to use it. And he found that our delivery on another product created additional problems.

So then he came back to us saying "This is no good. You don't understand that by doing this, you are hurting the customer. We've got to change or we risk losing their business."

Joe ended up being the best inspector the customer had ever had. They loved him. When he came back to us he was a new man. The "old school" barrier, the change resistor, became one of our best managers.

I suppose there are many people that you can't do much with, or people that you can't afford the expense of doing much with. But I think you need to be very careful when you hear people saying that so-and-so is hopeless. It might be true, or it might not.

STEP SIX: CREATE SHORT-TERM WINS

With empowered people working on the vision, in cases of great success those people are helped to produce *short-term wins.* The wins are critical. They provide credibility, resources, and momentum to the overall effort. In other cases, the wins come more slowly, less visibly, speak less to what people value, and have more ambiguity as to whether they really are successes. Without a well-managed process, careful selection of initial projects, and fast enough successes, the cynics and skeptics can sink any effort.

In successful change efforts, empowered people create short-term wins—victories that nourish faith in the change effort, emotionally reward the hard workers, keep the critics at bay, and build momentum. Without sufficient wins that are visible, timely, unambiguous, and meaningful to others, change efforts inevitably run into serious problems.

In the following Bulletin Board story, four priorities instead of 150 means focus. Focus means more is achieved quickly. Quick achievements provide so much: a feeling of accomplishment, a sense of optimism. With this, behavior changes. Those who have worked so hard to create the wins are reenergized. Those who have been pessimistically or skeptically sitting on the sidelines begin to help. Cynics make less disruptive noise. So momentum grows.

Bulletin boards are misused all the time. Put them off to the side where people do not congregate. Clutter the boards with fifty pieces of paper. Put up propaganda ("We're all committed to the vision!"). Make vague statements ("We're making progress"). Not in this story.

CREATE SHORT-TERM WINS—THE LIST ON THE BULLETIN BOARDS

FROM ROSS KAO

We have learned that when an organization has a great many things to do to correct its course, those leading the change are tempted to put 150 balls in the air all at one time. There is so much to do, you certainly can find 150 balls to put into play. Everyone can come up with a long list of things. But with so much going on at once, you run the danger of getting nothing finished very fast. This creates problems. It leads to frustration. People wonder where you're leading them—and whether or not you're taking the right approach.

To avoid that, we created something called "the Big Four." We knew what our priorities were. We could have listed the top twenty, but we didn't. Instead, we went public with just four goals. In essence, we said to the entire organization. "These are the top four things that we're working on. And until we get one substantially completed, we're not adding number five."

We literally published: "Here are the top four." At every work site we located large bulletin boards that everyone frequented and posted these top four items. In a factory, the board was in the canteen. It quickly became a device for saying, "Look! We're going to go do something. We're going to get it done. And guess what? Everybody look! It's done. And look, we just added another one to the list. And oh, by the way, this one is going to be done in another two weeks." The next thing you know, people are saying, "You know what? Things are happening. Things *are* getting done."

I remember I was out in the factory and I happened to be standing beside the Big Four list. This guy from the line came by and looked at the list with me. After about half a minute he turns to me and he says, "We're really knocking 'em down." People knew it. They felt the energy.

Now, granted, there were some people running around the organization saying, "You mean what I've been doing isn't important?" "No," we'd say, "that isn't what we mean. We're just telling you that that's not what we're working on right now. You need to know that what we're going to do is get something done with lightning speed. We're going to get it completed, and we're going to make sure we've got enough energy and collective participation to get this thing implemented before we move on to the next item."

For an organization that had been treading water, creating and communicating our quick wins really helped us begin to gather momentum.

STEP SEVEN: DON'T LET UP

After the first set of short-term wins, a change effort will have direction and momentum. In successful situations, people build on this momentum make a vision a reality by keeping urgency up and a feeling of false pride down; by eliminating unnecessary, exhausting, and demoralizing work; and by not declaring victory prematurely.

In the best cases, change leaders *don't let up.* Momentum builds after the first wins. Early changes are consolidated. People shrewdly choose what to tackle next, then create wave after wave of change until the vision is a reality. In less successful cases, people try to do too much at once. They unwittingly quit too soon. They let momentum slip to the point where they find themselves hopelessly bogged down.

STEP EIGHT: MAKE CHANGE STICK

Tradition is a powerful force. Leaps into the future can slide back into the past. We keep a change in place by helping to create a new, supportive, and sufficiently strong organizational culture. A supportive culture provides roots for the new ways of operating. It keeps the revolutionary technology, the globalized organization, the innovative strategy, or the more efficient processes working to make you a winner.

In the best cases, change leaders throughout organizations *make change stick* by nurturing a new culture. A new culture—group norms of behavior and shared values—develops through consistency of successful action over a sufficient period of time. Here, appropriate promotions, skillful new employee orientation, and events that engage the emotions can make a big difference. In other cases, changes float fragile on the surface. A great deal of work can be blown away by the winds of tradition in a remarkably short period of time.

In one organization, staff write a good speech about the values the firm has created and needs to strengthen and retain if their transformation is to be firmly entrenched. But the real power comes when they present a real customer to employees. He tells an inspirational story showing the consequences of living those values.

See, Feel, Change

Significantly changing the behavior of a single person can be exceptionally difficult work. Changing 101 or 10,001 people can be a Herculean task. Yet organizations that are leaping into the future succeed at doing just that. Look carefully at how they act and you'll find another pattern. They succeed, regardless of the stage in the overall process, because their most central activity does not center on formal data gathering, analysis, report writing, and presentations—the sorts of actions typically aimed at changing thinking in order to change behavior. Instead, they compellingly *show* people what the problems are and how to resolve the problems. They provoke responses that reduce feelings that slow and stifle needed change, and they enhance feelings that motivate useful action. The emotional reaction then provides the energy that propels people to push along the change process, no matter how great the difficulties.

A core pattern is associated with successful change.

1. SEE. People find a problem in some stage of the change process—too many of their colleagues are behaving complacently, no one is developing a sensible strategy, too many are letting up before the strategy has been achieved. They then create dramatic, eye-catching, compelling situations that help others visualize the problem or a solution to the problem.
2. FEEL. The visualizations awaken feelings that facilitate useful change or ease feelings that are getting in the way. Urgency, optimism, or faith may go up. Anger, complacency, cynicism, or fear may go down.
3. CHANGE. The new feelings change or reinforce new behavior, sometimes very different behavior. People act much less complacently. They try much harder to make a good vision a reality. They don't stop before the work is done, even if the road seems long.

Successful see-feel-change tactics tend to be clever, nor clumsy, and never cynically manipulative. They often have an afterglow, where the story of the event is told again and again or where there is a remaining visible sign of the event that influences additional people over time. When done well over all eight stages of a change process, the results can be breathtaking. Mature (old-fashioned, clunky, or heavy) organizations take a leap into the future. Laggards start to become leaders. Leaders jump farther ahead.

TABLE 2 Achieving a Change of Behavior within Each of the Eight Steps

Almost Always the Core Method Is: SEE-FEEL-CHANGE	***Rarely the Core Method Is: ANALYSIS-THINK-CHANGE***
1. *HELP PEOPLE SEE.* Compelling, eye-catching, dramatic situations are created to help others visualize problems, solutions, or progress in solving complacency, strategy, empowerment, or other key problems within the eight steps.	1. *GIVE PEOPLE ANALYSIS.* Information is gathered and analyzed, reports are written, and presentations are made about problems, solutions, or progress in solving urgency, teamwork, communication, momentum slippage, or other key problems within the eight steps.
As a result	*As a result*
2. *SEEING SOMETHING NEW HITS THE EMOTIONS.* The visualizations provide useful ideas that hit people at a deeper level than surface thinking. They evoke a visceral response that reduces emotions that block change and enhances those that support it.	2. *DATA AND ANALYSIS INFLUENCE HOW WE THINK.* The information and analysis change people's thinking. Ideas inconsistent with the needed change are dropped or modified.
3. *EMOTIONALLY CHARGED IDEAS CHANGE BEHAVIOR OR REINFORCE CHANGED BEHAVIOR.*	3. *NEW THOUGHTS CHANGE BEHAVIOR OR REINFORCE CHANGED BEHAVIOR.*

The point is not that careful data gathering, analysis, and presentation are unimportant. They are important. Sometimes it is behavior changed by analysis that sends people into a see-feel-change process. Sometimes change launched through feelings creates a radically better approach to analysis. Often small changes are a necessary part of a larger change effort, and the small changes are driven by analysis. Occasionally, careful analysis is required to get show-me-the-numbers finance people or engineers in the mood to see.

But analysis has at least three major limitations. First, in a remarkable number of cases, you don't need it to find the big truths. You may not need to do much work to find that the old strategy isn't working and that a new one isn't being embraced. You don't need a fifty-page report to see there is insufficient new product development and that a number of factors make it impossible for the engineers to do what is necessary. You don't need reams of financial data to learn that you cannot stay out of e-business and that the first step is simply to take the first step. It isn't necessary for a team of psychologists to study Fred and his team to find out they are failing and must be replaced. Yes, there are many exceptions—deciding on which $100 million IT system to buy, for example—but the general point is valid.

Second, analytical tools have their limitations in a turbulent world. These tools work best when parameters are known, assumptions are minimal, and the future is not fuzzy.

Third, good analysis rarely motivates people in a big way. It changes thought, but how often does it send people running out the door to act in significantly new ways? And motivation is not a thinking word; it's a feeling word.

We fail at change efforts not because we are stupid, overcontrolled, and unemotional beings, although it can seem that way at times. We fail because we haven't sufficiently experienced highly successful change. Without that experience, we are too often left pessimistic, fearful, or without enough faith to act. So we not only behave in less effective ways, we don't even try.

Consider the implications of this pattern in an age of accelerating change, at a time when we are making a mind-boggling transition from an industrial to an information/knowledge economy. Consider the implications in light of how managers, management educators, and others today deal with large-scale change.

Of course there are many difficulties here, but being uninformed and pessimistic does not help. We need more leaps into the future. And although we are becoming better at this, there is no reason that we cannot learn to become much better still.

In light of the stakes, we must become better still.

SURFING THE EDGE OF CHAOS*

Richard T. Pascale

Treating organizations as complex adaptive systems provides powerful insights into the nature of strategic work.

Every decade or two during the past one hundred years, a point of inflection has occurred in management thinking. These breakthroughs are akin to the S-curves of technology that characterize the life cycle of many industrial and consumer products: Introduction → Acceleration → Acceptance → Maturity. Each big idea catches hold slowly. Yet, within a relatively short time, the new approach becomes so widely accepted that it is difficult even for old-timers to reconstruct how the world looked before.

The decade following World War II gave birth to the "strategic era." While the tenets of military strategy had been evolving for centuries, the link to commercial enterprise was tenuous. Before the late 1940s, most companies adhered to the tenet "make a little, sell a little, make a little more." After the war, faculty at the Harvard Business School (soon joined by swelling ranks of consultants) began to take the discipline of strategy seriously. By the late 1970s, the array of strategic concepts (SWOT analysis, the five forces framework, experience curves, strategic portfolios, the concept of competitive advantage) had become standard ordnance in the management arsenal. Today, a mere twenty years later, a grasp of these concepts is presumed as a threshold of management literacy. They have become so familiar that it is hard to imagine a world without them.

It is useful to step back and reflect on the scientific underpinnings to this legacy. Eric Beinhocker writes:

> *The early micro-economists copied the mathematics of mid-nineteenth century physics equation by equation. ['Atoms'] became the individual, 'force' became the economists' notion of 'marginal utility' (or demand), 'kinetic energy' became total expenditure. All of this was synthesized into a coherent theory by Alfred Marshall—known as the theory of industrial organization.*[1]

Marshall's work and its underpinnings in nineteenth-century physics exert a huge influence on strategic thinking to this day. From our concept of strategy to our efforts at

*Reprinted with permission from *Sloan Management Review 40* (Spring 1999): 83–94.

organizational renewal, the deep logic is based on assumptions of deterministic cause and effect (i.e., a billiard ball model of how competitors will respond to a strategic challenge or how employees will behave under a new incentive scheme). And all of this, consistent with Newton's initial conceptions, is assumed to take place in a world where time, space (i.e., a particular industry structure or definition of a market), and dynamic equilibrium are accepted as reasonable underpinnings for the formulation of executive action. That's where the trouble begins. Marshall's equilibrium model offered appropriate approximations for the dominant sectors of agriculture and manufacturing of his era and are still useful in many situations. But these constructs run into difficulty in the far from equilibrium conditions found in today's service, technology, or communications-intensive businesses. When new entrants such as Nokia, Amazon.com, Dell Computer, or CNN invade a market, they succeed despite what traditional strategic thinkers would write off as a long shot.

During the 1980s and 1990s, performance improvement (e.g., total quality management, kaizen, just-in-time, reengineering) succeeded the strategic era. It, too, has followed the S-curve trajectory. Now, as it trails off, an uneasiness is stirring, a feeling that "something more" is required. In particular, disquiet has arisen over the rapidly rising fatality rates of major companies. Organizations cannot win by cost reduction alone and cannot invent appropriate strategic responses fast enough to stay abreast of nimble rivals. Many are exhausted by the pace of change, and their harried attempts to execute new initiatives fall short of expectations.

The next point of inflection is about to unfold. To succeed, the next big idea must address the biggest challenge facing corporations today—namely, to dramatically improve the hit rate of strategic initiatives and attain the level of renewal necessary for successful execution. As in the previous eras, we can expect that the next big idea will at first seem strange and inaccessible.

Here's the good news. For well over a decade, the hard sciences have made enormous strides in understanding and describing how the living world works. Scientists use the term "complex adaptive systems" ("complexity" for short) to label these theories. To be sure, the new theories do not explain everything. But the work has identified principles that apply to many living things—amoebae and ant colonies, beehives and bond traders, ecologies and economies, you and me.

For an entity to qualify as a complex adaptive system, it must meet four tests. First, it must be comprised of many agents acting in parallel. It is not hierarchically controlled. Second, it continuously shuffles these building blocks and generates multiple levels of organization and structure. Third, it is subject to the second law of thermodynamics, exhibiting entropy and winding down over time unless replenished with energy. In this sense, complex adaptive systems are vulnerable to death. Fourth, a distinguishing characteristic, all complex adaptive systems exhibit a capacity for pattern recognition and employ this to anticipate the future and learn to recognize the anticipation of seasonal change.

Many systems are complex but not adaptive (i.e., they meet some of the above conditions, but not all). If sand is gradually piled on a table, it will slide off in patterns. If a wave in a stream is disturbed, it will repair itself once the obstruction is removed. But neither of these complex systems anticipates and learns. Only living systems cope with their environment with a predictive model that anticipates and pro-acts. Thus, when the worldwide community of strep bacteria mutates to circumvent the threat of the latest antibiotic (as it does rather reliably within three years), it is reaffirming its membership in the club of complexity.

Work on complexity originated during the mid-1980s at New Mexico's Santa Fe Institute. A group of distinguished scientists with backgrounds in particle physics, microbiology, archaeology, astrophysics, paleontology, zoology, botany, and economics were drawn together by similar questions.[2] A series of symposia, underwritten by the Carnegie Foundation, revealed that all the assembled disciplines shared, at their core, building blocks composed of many agents. These might be molecules, neurons, a species, customers, members of a social system, or networks of corporations. Further, these fundamental systems were continually organizing and reorganizing themselves, all flourishing in a boundary between rigidity and randomness and all occasionally forming larger structures through the clash of natural accommodation and competition. Molecules form cells; neurons cluster into neural networks (or brains); species form ecosystems; individuals form tribes or societies; consumers and corporations form economies. These self-organizing structures give rise to emergent behavior (an example of which is the process whereby pre-biotic chemicals combined to form the extraordinary diversity of life on earth). Complexity science informs us about organization, stability, and change in social and natural systems. "Unlike the earlier advances in hard science," writes economist Alex Trosiglio, "complexity deals with a world that is far from equilibrium, and is creative and evolving in ways that we cannot hope to predict. It points to fundamental limits to our ability to understand, control, and manage the world, and the need for us to accept unpredictability and change."[3]

The science of complexity has yielded four bedrock principles relevant to the new strategic work:

1. Complex adaptive systems are at risk when in equilibrium. Equilibrium is a precursor to death.[4]
2. Complex adaptive systems exhibit the capacity of self-organization and emergent complexity.[5] Self-organization arises from intelligence in the remote clusters (or nodes) within a network. Emergent complexity is generated by the propensity of simple structures to generate novel patterns, infinite variety, and often, a sum that is greater than the parts. (Again, the escalating complexity of life on earth is an example.)
3. Complex adaptive systems tend to move toward the edge of chaos when provoked by a complex task.[6] Bounded instability is more conducive to evolution than either stable equilibrium or explosive instability. (For example, fire has been found to be a critical factor in regenerating healthy forests and prairies.) One important corollary to this principle is that a complex adaptive system, once having reached a temporary "peak" in its fitness landscape (e.g., a company during a golden era), must then "go down to go up" (i.e., moving from one peak to a still higher peak requires it to traverse the valleys of the fitness landscape). In cybernetic terms, the organism must be pulled by competitive pressures far enough out of its usual arrangements before it can create substantially different forms and arrive at a more evolved basin of attraction.
4. One cannot direct a living system, only disturb it.[7] Complex adaptive systems are characterized by weak cause-and-effect linkages. Phase transitions occur in the realm where one relatively small and isolated variation can produce huge effects. Alternatively, large changes may have little effect. (This phenomenon is common in the information industry. Massive efforts to promote a superior operating

system may come to naught, whereas a series of serendipitous events may establish an inferior operating system—such as MS-DOS—as the industry standard.)

Is complexity just interesting science, or does it represent something of great importance in thinking about strategic work? As these illustrations suggest, treating organizations as complex adaptive systems provides useful insight into the nature of strategic work. In the following pages, I will (1) briefly describe how the four bedrock principles of complexity occur in nature, and (2) demonstrate how they can be applied in a managerial context. In particular, I use the efforts underway at Royal Dutch/Shell to describe an extensive and pragmatic test of these ideas.

The successes at Shell and other companies described here might be achieved with a more traditional mind-set (in much the same way as Newton's laws can be used to explain the mechanics of matter on earth with sufficient accuracy so as to not require the General Theory of Relativity). But the contribution of scientific insight is much more than descriptions of increasing accuracy. Deep theories reveal previously unsuspected aspects of reality that we don't see (the curvature of space-time in the case of relativity theory) and thereby alter the fabric of reality. This is the context for an article on complexity science and strategy. Complexity makes the strategic challenge more understandable and the task of strategic renewal more accessible. In short, this is not a polemic against the traditional strategic approach, but an argument for broadening it.

STABLE EQUILIBRIUM EQUALS DEATH

An obscure but important law of cybernetics, the law of requisite variety, states: For any system to survive, it must cultivate variety in its internal controls. If it fails to do so internally, it will fail to cope with variety successfully when it comes from an external source.[8] Here, in the mundane prose of a cybernetic axiom, is the rationale for bounded instability.

A perverse example of this axiom in action was driven home by the devastating fires that wiped out 25 percent of Yellowstone National Park in 1992. For decades, the National Park Service had imposed equilibrium on the forest by extinguishing fires whenever they appeared. Gradually, the forest floor became littered with a thick layer of debris. When a lightening strike and ill-timed winds created a conflagration that could not be contained, this carpet of dry material burned longer and hotter than normal. By suppressing natural fires for close to 100 years, the park service had prevented the forest floor from being cleansed in a natural rhythm. Now a century's accumulation of deadfall generated extreme temperatures. The fire incinerated large trees and the living components of top soil that would otherwise have survived. This is the price of enforced equilibrium.

The seductive pull of equilibrium poses a constant danger to successful established companies. Jim Cannavino, a former IBM senior executive, provides an anecdote that speaks to the hazards of resisting change. In 1993, Cannavino was asked by IBM's new CEO, Lou Gerstner, to take a hard look at the strategic planning process. Why had IBM so badly missed the mark? Cannavino dutifully examined the work product—library shelves filled with blue binders containing 20 years of forecasts, trends, and strategic analysis.

"It all could be distilled down to one sentence," he recounts. " 'We saw it coming'—PC open architecture, networking intelligence in microprocessors, higher margins in software and services than hardware; it was all there. So I looked at the operating plans. How did they reflect the shifts the strategists had projected? These blue volumes (three times as voluminous as the strategic plans) could also be summarized in one sentence: 'Nothing changed.' And the final dose of arsenic to this diet of cyanide was the year-end financial reconciliation process. When we rolled up the sector submissions into totals for the corporation, the growth opportunities never quite covered the erosion of market share. This shortfall, of course, was the tip of an iceberg that would one day upend our strategy and our primary product—the IBM 360 mainframe. But facing these fundamental trends would have precipitated a great deal of turmoil and instability. Instead, year after year, a few of our most senior leaders went behind closed doors and raised prices."[9]

While equilibrium endangers living systems, it often wears the disguise of an attribute. Equilibrium is concealed inside strong values or a coherent, close-knit social system, or within a company's well-synchronized operating system (often referred to as "organizational fit"). Vision, values, and organizational fit are double-edged swords.

Species are inherently drawn toward the seeming oasis of stability and equilibrium—and the further they drift toward this destination, the less likely they are to adapt successfully when change is necessary. So why don't all species drift into the thrall of equilibrium and die off? Two forces thwart equilibrium and promote instability: (1) the threat of death and (2) the promise of sex.

The Darwinian process, called "selection pressures" by natural scientists, imposes harsh consequences on species entrapped in equilibrium. Most species, when challenged to adapt too far from their origins, are unable to do so and gradually disappear. But from the vantage point of the larger ecological community, selection pressures enforce an ecological upgrade, insofar as mutations that survive offer a better fit with the new environment. Natural selection exerts itself most aggressively during periods of radical change. Few readers will have difficulty identifying, these forces at work in industry today. There are no safe havens. From toothpaste to camcorders, pharmaceuticals to office supplies, bookstores to booster rockets for space payloads, soap to software, it's a Darwinian jungle out there, and it's not getting easier.

As a rule, a species becomes more vulnerable as it becomes more genetically homogeneous. Nature hedges against this condition through the reproductive process. Of the several means of reproduction that have evolved on the planet, sex is best. It is decisively superior to parthenogenesis (the process by which most plants, worms, and a few mammals conceive offspring through self-induced combination of identical genetic material).

Sexual reproduction maximizes diversity. Chromosome combinations are randomly matched in variant pairings, thereby generating more permutations and variety in offspring. Oxford's evolutionary theorist, William Hamilton, explains why this benefits a species. Enemies (i.e., harmful diseases and parasites) find it harder to adapt to the diverse attributes of a population generated by sexual reproduction than to the comparative uniformity of one produced by parthenogenesis.[10]

How does this relate to organizations? In organizations, people are the chromosomes, the genetic material that can create variety. When management thinker Gary Hamel was asked if he thought IBM had a chance of leading the next stage of the information revolution, he replied: "I'd need to know how many of IBM's top 100 executives had grown up on the west coast of America where the future of the computer industry is being created and how many were 40 years of age. If a quarter or a third of the senior group were both under 40 and possessed a west coast perspective, IBM has a chance."[11]

Here's the rub: The "exchanges of DNA" attempted within social systems are not nearly as reliable as those driven by the mechanics of reproductive chemistry. True, organizations can hire from the outside, bring seniors into frequent contact with iconoclasts from the ranks, or confront engineers and designers with disgruntled customers. But the enemy of these methods is, of course, the existing, social order, which, like the body's immune defense system, seeks to neutralize, isolate, or destroy foreign invaders. "Antibodies" in the form of social norms, corporate values, and orthodox beliefs nullify the advantages of diversity. An executive team may include divergent interests, only to engage in stereotyped listening (e.g., "There goes Techie again") or freeze iconoclasts out of important informal discussions. If authentic diversity is sought, all executives, in particular the seniors, must be more seeker than guru.

DISTURBING EQUILIBRIUM AT SHELL

In 1996, Steve Miller, age 51, became a member of Shell's committee of managing directors—the five senior leaders who develop objectives and long-term plans for Royal Dutch/Shell.[12] The group found itself captive to its hundred-year-old history. The numbing effects of tradition—a staggering $130 billion in annual revenues, 105,000 predominantly long-tenured employees, and global operations—left Shell vulnerable. While profits continued to flow, fissures were forming beneath the surface.

Miller was appointed group managing director of Shell's worldwide oil products business (known as "Downstream"), which accounts for $40 billion of revenues within the Shell Group. During the previous two years, the company had been engaged in a program to "transform" the organization. Yet the regimen of massive reorganization, traumatic downsizing, and senior management workshops accomplished little. Shell's earnings, while solid, were disappointing to financial analysts who expected more from the industry's largest competitor. Employees registered widespread resignation and cynicism. And the operating units at the "coal face" (Shell's term for its front-line activities within the 130 countries where Downstream does business) saw little more than business as usual.

For Steve Miller, Shell's impenetrable culture was worrisome. The Downstream business accounted for 37 percent of Shell's assets. Among the businesses in the Shell Group's portfolio, Downstream faced the gravest competitive threats. From 1992 to 1995, a full 50 percent of Shell's retail revenues in France fell victim to the onslaught of the European hypermarkets; a similar pattern was emerging in the United Kingdom. Elsewhere in the world, new competitors, global customers, and more savvy national oil companies were demanding a radically different approach to the marketplace. Having observed Shell's previous transformation efforts, Miller was convinced that it was essential to reach around the resistant bureaucracy and involve the front lines of the organization, a formidable task given the sheer size of the operation. In addition to Downstream's 61,000 full-time employees, Shell's 47,000 filling stations employed hundreds of thousands, mostly part-time, attendants and catered to more than 10 million customers every day. In the language of complexity, Miller believed it necessary to tap the emergent properties of Shell's enormous distribution system and shift the locus of strategic initiative to the front lines. He saw this system as a fertile organism that needed encouragement to, in his words, "send green shoots forth."

In an effort to gain the organization's attention (i.e., disturb equilibrium), beginning in mid-1996, Miller reallocated more than 50 percent of his calendar to work directly with front-line personnel. Miller states:

> *Our Downstream business transformation program had bogged down largely because of the impasse between headquarters and the operating companies, Shell's term for its highly independent country operations. The balance of power between headquarters and field, honed during a period of relative equilibrium, had ground to a stalemate. But the forces for continuing in the old way were enormous and extended throughout the organization. We were overseeing the most decentralized operation in the world with country chief executives that had, since the 1950s, enjoyed enormous autonomy. This had been part of our success formula. Yet we were encountering a set of daunting, competitive threats that transcended national boundaries. Global customers—like British Airways or Daimler Benz—wanted to deal with one Shell contact, not with a different Shell representative in every country in which they operate. We had huge overcapacity in refining, but each country CEO (motivated to maximize his own P&L) resisted the consolidation of refining capacity. These problems begged for a new strategic approach in which the task at the top was to provide the framework and then unleash the regional and local levels to find a path that was best for their market and the corporation as a whole.*

Shell had tried to rationalize its assets through a well-engineered strategic response: directives were issued by the top and driven through the organization. But country heads successfully thwarted consolidation under the banner of host-country objections to the threatened closing of their dedicated refining capacity. Miller continues: "We were equally unsuccessful at igniting a more imaginative approach toward the marketplace. It was like the old game of telephone that we used to play when we were kids: you'd whisper a message to the person next to you, and it goes around the circle. By the time you get to the last person, it bears almost no resemblance to the message you started with. Apply that to the 61,000 people in the Downstream business across the globe, and I knew our strategic aspirations could never penetrate through to the marketplace. The linkages between directives given and actions taken are too problematic." What made sense to Miller was to fundamentally alter the conversation and unleash the emergent possibilities. Midway through the process, Miller became acquainted with core principles of living systems and adopted them as a framework to provide his organization with a context for renewal.

Miller's reports in the operating companies were saying, "Centralization will only bog us down." "They were partly right," he acknowledges. "These are big companies. Some earn several hundreds of millions a year in net income. But the alternative wasn't centralization—it was a radical change in the responsiveness of the Downstream business to the dynamics of the marketplace—from top to bottom such that we could come together in appropriate groups, solve problems, and operate in a manner which transcended the old headquarters versus field schism. What initially seemed like a huge conflict has gradually melted away, I believe, because we stopped treating the Downstream business like a machine to be driven and began to regard it as a living system that needed to evolve."

Miller's solution was to cut through the organization's layers and barriers, put senior management in direct contact with the people at the grassroots level, foster strategic initiatives, create a new sense of urgency, and overwhelm the old order. The first wave of initiatives spawned other initiatives. In Malaysia, for example, Miller's pilot efforts with 4 initiative teams (called "action labs") have proliferated to 40. "It worked," he states, "because the people at the coal face usually know what's going on. They see the competitive threats and our inadequate response every day. Once you give them the context, they can do a better job of spotting opportunities and stepping up to decisions. In less than two years, we've seen astonishing progress in our retail business in some 25 countries. This represents around 85 percent of our retail sales volume, and we have now begun to use this approach in our service organizations and lubricant business. Results? By the end of 1997, Shell's operations in France had regained initiative and achieved double-digit growth and double-digit return on capital. Market share was increasing after years of decline." Austria went from a probable exit candidate to a highly profitable operation. Overall, Shell gained in brand-share preference throughout Europe and ranked first in share among other major oil companies. By the close of 1998, approximately 10,000 Downstream employees have been involved in this effort with audited results (directly attributed to the program) exceeding a $300 million contribution to Shell's bottom line.

SELF-ORGANIZATION AND EMERGENT COMPLEXITY

Santa Fe Institute's Stuart Kauffman is a geneticist. His lifetime fascination has been with the ordered process by which a fertilized egg unfolds into a newborn infant and later into an adult. Earlier Nobel Prize-winning work on genetic circuits had shown that every cell contains a number of "regulatory" genes that act as switches to turn one another on and off. Modern computers use sequential instructions, whereas the genetic system exercises most of its instructions simultaneously. For decades, scientists have sought to discover the governing mechanism that causes this simultaneous, non-linear system to settle down and replicate a species.[13]

Kauffman built a simple simulation of a genetic system. His array of 100 light bulbs looked like a Las Vegas marquee. Since regulatory genes cause the cells (like bulbs) to turn on or off, Kauffman arranged for his bulbs to do just that, each independently of the other. His hypothesis was that no governing mechanism existed; rather, random and independent behavior would settle into patterns—a view that was far from self-evident. The possible combinations in Kauffman's arrangement of blinking lights was two (i.e., on and off), multiplied by itself 100 times (i.e., almost one million, trillion, trillion possibilities!).

When Kauffman switched the system on, the result was astonishing. Instead of patterns of infinite variety, the system always settled down within a few minutes to a few more or less orderly states. The implications of Kauffman's work are far-reaching. Theorists had been searching for the sequence of primordial events that could have produced the first DNA—the building block of life. Kauffman asked instead, "What if life was not just standing around and waiting until DNA happened? What if all those amino acids and sugars and gasses and solar energy were each just doing their thing like the billboard of lights?" If the conditions in primordial soup were right, it wouldn't take a miracle (like a million decks of cards falling from a balcony and all coming up aces) for DNA to randomly turn up. Rather, the compounds in the soup could have formed a coherent, self-reinforcing web of reactions and these, in turn, generated the more complex patterns of DNA.[14]

Emergent complexity is driven by a few simple patterns that combine to generate infinite variety. For example, simulations have shown that a three-pronged "crow's foot" pattern, if combined in various ways, perfectly replicates the foliage patterns of every fern on earth. Similar phenomena hold true in business. John Kao, a specialist in creativity, has observed how one simple creative breakthrough can evoke a cascade of increasing complexity.[15] "Simple" inventions such as the wheel, printing press, or transistor lead to "complex" offshoots such as automobiles, cellular phones, electronic publishing, and computing.

The phenomenon of emergence arises from the way simple patterns combine. Mathematics has coined the term *fractals* to describe a set of simple equations that combine to form endless diversity.[16] Fractal mathematics has given us valuable insight into how nature creates the shapes we observe. Mountains, rivers, coastline vegetation, lungs, and circulatory systems are fractal, replicating a dominant pattern at several smaller levels of scale. Fractals, in effect, act like genetic algorithms enabling a species to efficiently replicate essential functions.

One consequence of emerging complexity is that you cannot see the end from the beginning. While many can readily acknowledge nature's propensity to self-organize and generate more complex levels, it is less comforting to put oneself at the mercy of this process with the foreknowledge that we cannot predict the shape that the future will take. Emerging complexity creates not one future but many.

SELF-ORGANIZATION AND EMERGENCE AT SHELL

Building on (1) the principles of complexity, (2) the fractal-like properties of a business model developed by Columbia University's Larry Seldon,[17] and (3) a second fractal-like process, the action labs, Steve Miller and his colleagues at Shell tapped into the intelligence in the trenches and channeled it into a tailored marketplace response.[18]

Miller states:

> *We needed a vehicle to give us an energy transfusion and remind us that we could play at a far more competitive level. The properties of self-organization and emergence make intuitive sense to me. The question was how to release them. Seldon's model gave us a sharp-edged tool to identify customer needs and markets and to develop our value proposition. This, in effect, gave our troops the 'ammunition' to shoot with—analytical distinctions to make the business case. Shell has always been a wholesaler. Yet the forecourt of every service station is an artery for commerce that any retailer would envy. Our task was to tap the potential of that real estate, and we needed both the insight and the initiatives of our front-line troops to pull it off. For a company as large as Shell, leadership can't drive these answers down from the top. We needed to tap into ideas that were out there in the ranks—latent but ready to bear fruit if given encouragement.*

At first glance, Shell's methods look pedestrian. Miller began bringing six- to eight-person teams from a half-dozen operating companies from around the world into "retailing boot camps." The first five-day workshop introduced tools for identifying and exploiting market opportunities. It also included a dose of the leadership skills necessary to enroll others back home. Participants returned ready to apply the tools to achieve breakthroughs such as doubling net income in filling stations on the major north-south highways of Malaysia or tripling market share of bottled gas in South Africa. As part of the discipline of the model, every intention (e.g., "to lower fuel delivery costs") was translated into "key business activities" (or KBAs). As the first group went home, six more teams would rotate in. During the next 60 days, the first group of teams used the analytical tools to sample customers, identify segments, and develop a value proposition. The group would then return to the workshop for a "peer challenge"—tough give-and-take exchanges with other teams. Then it would go back again for another 60 days to perfect a business plan. At the close of the third workshop, each action lab spent three hours in the "fishbowl" with Miller and several of his direct reports, reviewing business plans, while the other teams observed the proceedings. At the close of each session, plans were approved, rejected, amended. Financial commitments were made in exchange for promised results. (The latter were incorporated in the country's operating goals for the year.) Then the teams went back to the field for another 60 days to put their ideas into action and returned for a follow-up session.

Miller continues:

> *Week after week, team after team, my six direct reports and I and our internal coaches reached out and worked directly with a diverse cross-section of customers, dealers, shop stewards, and young and mid-level professionals. And it worked. Operating company CEOs, historically leery of any 'help' from headquarters, saw their people return energized and armed with solid plans to beat the competition. The grassroots employees who participated in the program got to touch and feel the new Shell—a far more informal, give-and-take culture. The conversation down in the ranks of the organization began to change. Guerrilla leaders, historically resigned to Shell's conventional way of doing things, stepped forward to champion ingenious marketplace innovations (such as the Coca-Cola Challenge in Malaysia—a free Coke to any service-station customer who is not offered the full menu of forecourt services. It sounds trivial, but it increased volume by 15 percent). Many, if not most, of the ideas come from the lower ranks of our company who are in direct contact with the customer. Best of all, we learned together. I can't overstate how infectious the optimism and energy of these committed employees was for the many managers above them. In a curious way, these front-line employees taught us to believe in ourselves again.*

As executives move up in organizations, they become removed from the work that goes on in the fields. Directives from the top become increasingly abstract as executives tend to rely on mechanical cause-and-effect linkages to drive the business: strategic guidelines, head-count controls, operational expense targets, pay-for-performance incentives, and so forth. These are the tie rods and pistons of "social engineering"—the old model of change. Complexity theory does not discard these useful devices but it starts from a different place. The living-systems approach begins with a focus on the intelligence in the nodes. It seeks to ferret out what this network sees, what stresses it is undergoing, and what is needed to unleash its potential. Other support elements (e.g., controls and rewards) are orchestrated to draw on this potential rather than to drive down solutions from above.

Miller was pioneering a very different model from what had always prevailed at Shell. His "design for emergence" generated hundreds of informal connections between headquarters and the field, resembling the parallel networks of the nervous system to the brain. It contrasted with the historical model of mechanical linkages analogous to those that transfer the energy from the engine in a car through a drive train to the tires that perform the "work."

EDGE OF CHAOS

Nothing novel can emerge from systems with high degrees of order and stability—for example, crystals, incestuous communities, or regulated industries. On the other hand, complete chaotic systems, such as stampedes, riots, rage, or the early years of the French Revolution, are too formless to coalesce. Generative complexity takes place in the boundary between rigidity and randomness.

Historically,[19] science viewed "change" as moving from one equilibrium state (water) to another (ice). Newtonian understandings could not cope with the random, near-chaotic messiness of the actual transition itself. Ecologists and economists similarly favored equilibrium conditions because neither observation nor modeling techniques could handle transition states. The relatively inexpensive computational power of modern computers has changed all that. Non-equilibrium and non-linear simulations are now possible. These developments, along, with the study of complexity, have enabled us to better understand the dynamics of "messiness."

Phase transitions occur in the realm near chaos where a relatively small and isolated variation can produce huge effects. Consider the example of lasers: While only a complex system and not an adaptive one, the infusion of energy into plasma excites a jumble of photons. The more the energy, the more jumbled they become. Still more and the seething mass is transformed into the coherent light of a laser beam. What drives this transition, and how can we orchestrate it? Two determinants—(1) a precise tension between amplifying and damping feedback, and (2) (unique to mankind) the application of mindfulness and intention—are akin to rudder and sail when surfing near the edge of chaos.

Two factors determine the level of excitation in a system. In cybernetics, they are known as amplifying (positive) and damping (negative) feedback.[20] Damping feedback operates like a thermostat, which keeps temperatures within boundaries with a thermocouple that continually says "too hot, too cold." Amplifying feedback happens when a microphone gets too close to a loudspeaker. The signal is amplified until it oscillates to a piercing shriek. Living systems thrive when these mechanisms are in tension.

Getting the tension right is the hard part. Business obituaries abound with examples of one or the other of these feedback systems gone amok. IT&T trader Harold Geneen or Sunbeam under "Chainsaw" Al Dunlap thrive briefly under stringent damping controls, then fade away owing to the loss of imagination and creative energy. At the opposite end, Value Jet thrives in an amplifying phase, adds more planes, departures, and staff without corresponding attention to the damping loop (operational controls, safety, reliability, and service standards).

Psychologists tell us that pain can cause us to change, and this is most likely to occur when we recontextualize pain as the means by which significant learning occurs. When the great Austro-American economist Joseph Schumpeter described the essence of free-market economies as "creative destruction," it could be interpreted as a characterization of the hazards near the edge of chaos. Enduring competitive advantage entails disrupting what has been done in the past and creating a new future.

Hewlett-Packard's printer business was one of the most successful in its portfolio. Observing a downward spiral of margins as many "me too" printers entered the market, HP reinvented its offering. Today, HP's printers are the "free razor blade"—the loss leader in a very different strategy. To maintain scale, HP abandoned its high-cost distribution system with a dedicated sales force, opting instead for mass channels, partnering, and outsourcing to lower manufacturing costs. To protect margins, it targeted its 40 biggest corporate customers and formed a partnership to deliver global business printing solutions—whether through low-cost, on-premise equipment, or networked technology. States Tim Mannon, president of HP's printer division: "The biggest single threat to our business today is staying with a previously successful business model one year too long."[21]

SHAPING THE EDGE OF CHAOS AT SHELL

Shell moved to the edge of chaos with a multipronged design that intensified stress on all members of the Shell system.[22] First, as noted, Miller and his top team performed major surgery on their calendars and reallocated approximately half their time to teaching and coaching wave after wave of country teams. When the lowest levels of an organization were being trained, coached, and evaluated by those at the very top, it both inspired—and stressed—everyone in the system (including mid-level bosses who were not present). Second, the design, as we have seen, sent teams back to collect real data for three periods of 60 days (interspersed with additional workshop sessions). Pressure to succeed and long hours both during the workshops and back in the country (where these individuals continued to carry their regular duties along with project work) achieved the cultural "unfreezing" effects. Participants were resocialized into a more direct, informal, and less hierarchical way of working.

Miller states:

> *One of the most important innovations in changing all of us was the fishbowl. The name describes what it is: I and a number of my management team sit in the middle of a room with one action lab in the center with us. The other team members listen from the outer circle. Everyone is watching as the group in the hot seat talks about what they're going to do and what they need from me and my colleagues to be able to do it. That may not sound revolutionary—but in our culture, it was very unusual for anyone lower in the organization to talk this directly to a managing director and his reports.*
>
> *In the fishbowl, the pressure is on to measure up. The truth is, the pressure is on me and my colleagues. The first time we're not consistent, we're dead meat. If a team brings in a plan that's really a bunch of crap, we've got to be able to call it a bunch of crap. If we cover for people or praise everyone, what do we say when someone brings in an excellent plan? That kind of straight talk is another big culture change for Shell.*
>
> *The whole process creates complete transparency between the people at the coal face and me and my top management team. At the end, these folks go back home and say, 'I just cut a deal with the managing director and his team*

to do these things.' It creates a personal connection, and it changes how we talk with each other and how we work with each other. After that, I can call up those folks anywhere in the world and talk in a very direct way because of this personal connectedness. It has completely changed the dynamics of our operations.

DISTURBING A LIVING SYSTEM

An important and distinct property of living systems is the tenuous connection between cause and effect. As most seasoned managers know, the best-laid plans are often perverted through self-interest, misinterpretation, or lack of necessary skills to reach the intended goal.

Consider the war of attrition waged by ranchers and the U.S. Fish and Wildlife Service to "control" the coyote. A cumulative total of $3 billion (in 1997 dollars) has been spent during the past 100 years to underwrite bounty hunters, field a sophisticated array of traps, introduce novel morsels of poisoned bait, and interject genetic technology (to limit fertility of females)—all with the aim of protecting sheep and cattle ranchers from these wily predators. Result? When white men first appeared in significant numbers west of the Mississippi in the early 1800s, coyotes were found in twelve western states and never seen east of the Mississippi. However, as a direct result of the aggressive programs to eliminate the coyote, the modern day coyote is 20 percent larger and significantly smarter than his predecessor. The coyote is now found in 49 of the 50 states—including suburbs of New York City and Los Angeles. How could this occur? Human intervention so threatened the coyote's survival that a significant number fled into Canada where they bred with the larger Canadian wolf. Still later, these visitors migrated south (and further north to Alaska) and, over the decades, bred with (and increased the size of) the U.S. population. The same threats to survival that had driven some coyotes into Canada drove others to adapt to climates as varied as Florida and New Hampshire. Finally, the persistent efforts to trap or hunt or poison the coyote heightened selection pressures. The survivors were extremely streetwise and wary of human contact. Once alerted by a few fatalities among their brethren, coyotes are usually able to sniff out man's latest stratagem to do them harm.

As the tale of the coyote suggests, living systems are difficult to direct because of these weak cause-and-effect linkages. The best laid efforts by man to intervene in a system, to do it harm, or even to replicate it artificially almost always miss the mark. The strategic intentions of governments in Japan, Taiwan, and Germany to replicate Silicon Valley provide one example. The cause-and-effect formula seemed simple: (1) identify a region with major universities with strong departments in such fields as microelectronics, genetics, and nuclear medicine and having a geography with climate and amenities suitable to attract professionals, and (2) invest to stimulate a self-reinforcing community of interests. But these and many similar efforts have never quite reached a critical mass. The cause-and-effect relationships proved unclear.[23] A lot depends on chance. One is wiser to acknowledge the broad possibilities that flow from weak cause-and-effect linkages and the need to consider the second- and third-order effects of any bold intervention one is about to undertake.

DISTURBING A COMPLEX SYSTEM AT SHELL

In today's fast-changing environment, Shell's Steve Miller dismisses the company's old traditional approach as mechanistic. "Top-down strategies don't win ballgames," he states. "Experimentation, rapid learning, and seizing the momentum of success is the better approach."[24]

Miller observes:

We need a different definition of strategy and a different approach to generating it. In the past, strategy was the exclusive domain of top management. Today, if you're going to have a successful company, you have to recognize that the top can't possibly have all the answers. The leaders provide the vision and are the context setters. But the actual solutions about how best to meet the challenges of the moment, those thousands of strategic challenges encountered every day, have to be made by the people closest to the action—the people at the coal face.

Change your approach to strategy, and you change the way a company runs. The leader becomes a context setter, the designer of a learning experience—not an authority figure with solutions. Once the folks at the grassroots realize they own the problem, they also discover that they can help create and own the answers, and they get after it very quickly, very aggressively, and very creatively, with a lot more ideas than the old-style strategic direction could ever have prescribed from headquarters.

A program like this is a high-risk proposition, because it goes counter to the way most senior executives spend their time. I spend 50 percent to 60 percent of my time at this, and there is no direct guarantee that what I'm doing is going to make something happen down the line. It's like becoming the helmsman of a big ship when you've grown up behind the steering wheel of a car. This approach isn't about me. It's about rigorous, well-taught marketing concepts combined with a strong process design, that enable front-line employees to think like businesspeople. Top executives and front-line employees learn to work together in partnership.

People want to evaluate this against the old way, which gives you the illusion of 'making things happen.' I encountered lots of thinly veiled skepticism: 'Did your net income change from last quarter because of this change process?' These challenges create anxiety. The temptation, of course, is to reimpose your directives and controls even though we had an abundance of proof that this would not work. Instead, top executives and lower-level employees learn to work together in partnership. The grassroots approach to strategy development and implementation doesn't happen overnight. But it does happen. People always want results yesterday. But the process and behavior that drive authentic strategic change aren't like that.

There's another kind of risk to the leaders of a strategic inquiry of this kind—the risk of exposure. You're working very closely and intensely with all levels of staff, and they get to assess and evaluate you directly. Before, you were remote from them; now, you're very accessible. If that evaluation comes up negative, you've got a big-time problem.

Finally, the scariest part is letting go. You don't have the same kind of control that traditional leadership is used to. What you don't realize until you do it is that you may, in fact, have more controls but in a different fashion. You get more feedback than before, you learn more than before, you know more through your own people about what's going on in the marketplace and with customers than before. But you still have to let go of the old sense of control.

Miller's words testify to his reconciliation with the weak cause-and-effect linkages that exist in a living system. When strategic work is accomplished through a "design for emergence," it never assumes that a particular input will produce a particular output. It is more akin to the study of subatomic particles in a bubble chamber. The experimenter's design creates probabilistic occurrences that take place within the domain of focus. Period. Greater precision is neither sought nor possible.

Endnotes

This article is drawn from R. Pascale, M. Millemann, and L. Gioja, *Surfing the Edge of Chaos: How the Smartest Companies Use the New Science to Stay Ahead* (New York: Crown, 2000).

1. E. Beinhocker, "Strategy at the Edge of Chaos," *McKinsey Quarterly,* no. 1 (1997): 25.
2. For an entertaining treatment of this inquiry, see: M. M. Waldrop, *Complexity* (New York: Simon & Schuster, 1992).
3. A. Trosiglio, "Managing Complexity" (unpublished working paper, June 1995): 3; and D. Deutsch, *The Fabric of Reality* (New York: Penguin, 1997): 3–21.
4. See S. Kauffman, *At Home in the Universe* (New York: Oxford University Press, 1995): 21; and G. Hamel and C. K. Prahalad, "Strategic Intent," *Harvard Business Review 67* (May-June 1989): 63–76.
5. See Kauffman (1995): 205; and J. H. Holland, *Hidden Order* (Reading, MA: Addison-Wesley, 1995): 3.
6. See Kauffman (1995): 230; and M. Gell-Mann, *The Quark and the Jaguar* (New York: Freeman, 1994): 249.
7. See Gell-Mann (1994): 238–239; and Holland (1995): 5 and 38–39.
8. W. Ashby, *An Introduction to Cybernetics* (New York: Wiley, 1956).
9. R. Pascale, interviews with James Cannavino, May 1996.
10. See Gell-Mann (1994): 64, 253; and S. J. Gould, *Full House* (New York: Crown, 1996): 138.
11. G. Hamel, "Strategy as Revolution," *Harvard Business Review 74* (July-August 1996): 69–82.
12. Information and quotations in this section are drawn from: R. Pascale, interviews with Steve Miller, London, The Hague, and Houston, October 1997 through February 1998.
13. Kauffman (1995): 80–86.
14. Waldrop (1992): 110.
15. J. Kao, *Jamming: The Art and Discipline of Business Creativity* (New York: HarperCollins, 1997).
16. I. Marshall and D. Zohar, *Who's Afraid of Schrodinger's Cat?* (New York: Morrow, 1997): 16, 19, 153–158.
17. Seldon's work is unpublished. He considers it proprietary and solely for consulting purposes.
18. Information and quotations in this section are drawn from: R. Pascale, interviews with Steve Miller, London, The Hague, and Houston, October 1997 through February 1998.
19. Gell-Mann (1994): 228–230.
20. Waldrop (1992): 138–139.
21. R. Hof, "Hewlett Packard," *Business Week,* February 13, 1995: 67.
22. Information and quotations in this section are drawn from: R. Pascale, interviews with Steve Miller, London, The Hague, and Houston, October 1997 through February 1998.
23. A Saxenian, "Lessons from Silicon Valley," *Technology Review 97,* no. 5, July 1994: 42–45.
24. Information and quotations in this section are drawn from: R. Pascale, interviews with Steve Miller, London, The Hague, and Houston, October 1997 through February 1998.

RULES OF THUMB FOR CHANGE AGENTS*

Herbert A. Shepard

The following aphorisms are not so much bits of advice (although they are stated that way) as things to think about when you are being a change agent, a consultant, an organization or community development practitioner—or when you are just being yourself trying to bring about something that involves other people.

RULE I: STAY ALIVE

This rule counsels against self-sacrifice on behalf of a cause that you do not wish to be your last.

Two exceptionally talented doctoral students came to the conclusion that the routines they had to go through to get their degrees were absurd, and decided they would be untrue to themselves to conform to an absurd system. That sort of reasoning is almost always self-destructive. Besides, their noble gesture in quitting would be unlikely to have any impact whatever on the system they were taking a stand against.

This is not to say that one should never take a stand or a survival risk. But such risks should be taken as part of a purposeful strategy of change and appropriately timed and targeted. When they are taken under such circumstances, one is very much alive.

But Rule I is much more than a survival rule. The rule means that you should let your whole being be involved in the undertaking. Since most of us have never been in touch with our whole beings, it means a lot of putting together of parts that have been divided, of using internal communications channels that have been closed or were never opened.

Staying alive means loving yourself. Self-disparagement leads to the suppression of potentials, to a win-lose formulation of the world, and to wasting life in defensive maneuvering.

Staying alive means staying in touch with your purpose. It means using your skills, your emotions, your labels and positions, rather than being used by them. It means not being trapped in other people's games. It means turning yourself on and off, rather than being dependent on the situation. It means choosing with a view to the consequences as well as the impulse. It means going with the flow even while swimming against it. It means living in several worlds without being swallowed up in any. It means seeing dilemmas as opportunities for creativity. It means greeting absurdity with laughter while trying to unscramble it. It means capturing the moment in the light of the future. It means seeing the environment through the eyes of your purpose.

RULE II: START WHERE THE SYSTEM IS

This is such ancient wisdom that one might expect its meaning had been fully explored and apprehended. Yet in practice the rule—and the system—are often violated.

The rule implies that one should begin by diagnosing the system. But systems do not necessarily *like* being diagnosed. Even the term *diagnosis* may be offensive. And the system may be even less ready for someone who calls himself or herself a "change

*Reprinted by permission of the author from the *OD Practitioner*, December 1984. Organization Development Network, Portland, Oregon.

agent!" It is easy for the practitioner to forget that the use of jargon which prevents laypeople from understanding the professional mysteries is a hostile act.

Starting where the system is can be called the Empathy Rule. To communicate effectively, to obtain a basis for building sound strategy, the change agent needs to understand how clients see themselves and their situation, and needs to understand the culture of the system. Establishing the required rapport does not mean that the change agent who wants to work in a traditional industrial setting should refrain from growing a beard. It does mean that, if he has a beard, the beard is likely to determine where the client is when they first meet, and the client's curiosity needs to be dealt with. Similarly, the rule does not mean that a female change agent in a male organization should try to act like one of the boys, or that a young change agent should try to act like a senior executive. One thing it does mean is that sometimes where the client is, is wondering where the change agent is.

Rarely is the client in any one place at any one time. That is, she or he may be ready to pursue any of several paths. The task is to walk together on the most promising path.

Even unwitting or accidental violations of the Empathy Rule can destroy the situation. I lost a client through two violations in one morning. The client group spent a consulting day at my home. They arrived early in the morning, before I had my empathy on. The senior member, seeing a picture of my son in the living room said, "What do you do with boys with long hair?" I replied thoughtlessly, "I think he's handsome that way." The small chasm thus created between my client and me was widened and deepened later that morning when one of the family tortoises walked through the butter dish.

Sometimes starting where the client is, which sounds both ethically and technically virtuous, can lead to some ethically puzzling situations. Robert Frost* described a situation in which a consultant was so empathetic with a king who was unfit to rule that the king discovered his own unfitness and had himself shot, whereupon the consultant became king.

Empathy permits the development of a mutual attachment between client and consultant. The resulting relationship may be one in which their creativities are joined, a mutual growth relationship. But it can also become one in which the client becomes dependent and is manipulated by the consultant. The ethical issues are not associated with starting where the system is, but with how one moves with it.

RULE III: NEVER WORK UPHILL

This is a comprehensive rule, and a number of other rules are corollaries or examples of it. It is an appeal for an organic rather than a mechanistic approach to change, for a collaborative approach to change, for building strength and building on strength. It has a number of implications that bear on the choices the change agent makes about how to use him/herself, and it says something about life.

COROLLARY 1: DON'T BUILD HILLS AS YOU GO

This corollary cautions against working in a way that builds resistance to movement in the direction you have chosen as desirable. For example, a program which has a favorable effect on one portion of a population may have the opposite effect on other portions of the population. Perhaps the commonest error of this kind has been in the

*Robert Frost, "How Hard It Is to Keep from Being King When It's in You and in the Situation." *In the Clearing* (New York: Holt, Rinehart and Winston, 1962) 74–84.

employment of T-group training in organizations: turning on the participants and turning off the people who didn't attend, in one easy lesson.

COROLLARY 2: WORK IN THE MOST PROMISING ARENA

The physician–patient relationship is often regarded as analogous to the consultant-client relationship. The results for system change of this analogy can be unfortunate. For example, the organization development consultant is likely to be greeted with delight by executives who see in his specialty the solution to a hopeless situation in an outlying plant. Some organization development consultants have disappeared for years because of the irresistibility of such challenges. Others have wiled away their time trying to counteract the Peter Principle by shoring up incompetent managers.

COROLLARY 3: BUILD RESOURCES

Don't do anything alone that could be accomplished more easily or more certainly by a team. Don Quixote is not the only change agent whose effectiveness was handicapped by ignoring this rule. The change agent's task is an heroic one, but the need to be a hero does not facilitate team building. As a result, many change agents lose effectiveness by becoming spread too thin. Effectiveness can be enhanced by investing in the development of partners.

COROLLARY 4: DON'T OVERORGANIZE

The democratic ideology and theories of participative management that many change agents possess can sometimes interfere with common sense. A year or two ago I offered a course to be taught by graduate students. The course was oversubscribed. It seemed that a data-based process for deciding whom to admit would be desirable, and that participation of the graduate students in the decision would also be desirable. So I sought data from the candidates about themselves, and xeroxed their responses for the graduate students. Then the graduate students and I held a series of meetings. Then the candidates were informed of the decision. In this way we wasted a great deal of time and everyone felt a little worse than if we had used an arbitrary decision rule.

COROLLARY 5: DON'T ARGUE IF YOU CAN'T WIN

Win-lose strategies are to be avoided because they deepen conflict instead of resolving it. But the change agent should build her or his support constituency as large and deep and strong as possible so that she or he can continue to risk.

COROLLARY 6: PLAY GOD A LITTLE

If the change agent doesn't make the critical value decisions, someone else will be happy to do so. Will a given situation contribute to your fulfillment? Are you creating a better world for yourself and others. Or are you keeping a system in operation that should be allowed to die? For example, the public education system is a mess. Does that mean that the change agent is morally obligated to try to improve it, destroy it, or develop a substitute for it? No, not even if he or she knows how. But the change agent does need a value perspective for making choices like that.

RULE IV: INNOVATION REQUIRES A GOOD IDEA, INITIATIVE, AND A FEW FRIENDS

Little can be accomplished alone, and the effects of social and cultural forces on individual perception are so distorting that the change agent needs a partner, if only to maintain perspective and purpose.

The quality of the partner is as important as the quality of the idea. Like the change agent, partners must be relatively autonomous people. Persons who are authority-oriented—who need to rebel or need to submit—are not reliable partners: The rebels take the wrong risks and the good soldiers don't take any. And rarely do they command the respect and trust from others that is needed if an innovation is to be supported.

The partners need not be numerous. For example, the engineering staff of a chemical company designed a new process plant using edge-of-the-art technology. The design departed radically from the experience of top management, and they were about to reject it. The engineering chief suggested that the design be reviewed by a distinguished engineering professor. The principal designers were in fact former students of the professor. For this reason he accepted the assignment, charged the company a large fee for reviewing the design (which he did not trouble to examine) and told the management that it was brilliantly conceived and executed. By this means the engineers not only implemented their innovations, but also grew in the esteem of their management.

A change agent experienced in the Washington environment reports that he knows of only one case of successful interdepartmental collaboration in mutually designing funding and managing a joint project. It was accomplished through the collaboration of himself and three similarly-minded young men, one from each of four agencies. They were friends and met weekly for lunch. They conceived the project and planned strategies for implementing it. Each person undertook to interest and influence the relevant key people in his own agency. The four served one another as consultants and helped in influencing opinion and bringing the decision-makers together.

An alternative statement of Rule IV is as follows: Find the people who are ready and able to work, introduce them to one another, and work with them. Perhaps because many change agents have been trained in the helping professions, perhaps because we have all been trained to think bureaucratically, concepts like organization position, representatives or need are likely to guide the change agent's selection of those he or she works with.

A more powerful beginning can sometimes be made by finding those persons in the system whose values are congruent with those of the change agent, who possess vitality and imagination, who are willing to work overtime, and who are eager to learn. Such people are usually glad to have someone like the change agent join in getting something important accomplished, and a careful search is likely to turn up quite a few. In fact, there may be enough of them to accomplish general system change, if they can team up in appropriate ways.

In building such teamwork the change agent's abilities will be fully challenged, as he joins them in establishing conditions for trust and creativity; dealing with their anxieties about being seen as subversive; enhancing their leadership, consulting, problem-solving, diagnosing and innovating skills; and developing appropriate group norms and policies.

RULE V: LOAD EXPERIMENTS FOR SUCCESS

This sounds like counsel to avoid risk taking. But the decision to experiment always entails risk. After that decision has been made, take all precautions.

The rule also sounds scientifically immoral. But whether an experiment produces the expected results depends upon the experimenter's depth of insight into the conditions and processes involved. Of course, what is experimental is what is new to the system: it may or may not be new to the change agent.

Build an umbrella over the experiment. A chemical process plant which was to be shut down because of the inefficiency of its operations undertook a union management cooperation project to improve efficiency. which involved a modified form of profit-sharing. Such plans were contrary to company policy, but the regional vice president was interested in the experiment, and successfully concealed it from his associates. The experiment was successful; the plant became profitable. But in this case, the umbrella turned out not to be big enough. The plant was shut down anyway.

Use the Hawthorne effect. Even poorly conceived experiments are often made to succeed when the participants feel ownership. And conversely, one of the obstacles to the spread of useful innovations is that the groups to which they are offered do not feel ownership of them.

For example, if the change agent hopes to use experience-based learning as part of his/her strategy, the first persons to be invited should be those who consistently turn all their experiences into constructive learning. Similarly, in introducing team development processes into a system, begin with the best functioning team.

Maintain voluntarism. This is not easy to do in systems where invitations are understood to be commands, but nothing vital can be built on such motives as duty, obedience, security-seeking, or responsiveness to social pressure.

RULE VI: LIGHT MANY FIRES

Not only does a large monolithic development or change program have high visibility and other qualities of a good target, it also tends to prevent subsystems from feeling ownership of, and consequent commitment to the program.

The meaning of this rule is more orderly than the random prescription—light many fires—suggests. Any part of a system is the way it is partly because of the way the rest of the system is. To work towards change in one subsystem is to become one more determinant of its performance. Not only is the change agent working uphill, but as soon as he turns his back, other forces in the system will press the subsystem back towards its previous performance mode.

If many interdependent subsystems are catalyzed, and the change agent brings them together to facilitate one another's efforts, the entire system can begin to move.

Understanding patterns of interdependency among subsystems can lead to a strategy of fire-setting. For example, in public school systems, it requires collaboration among politicians, administrators, teachers, parents, and students to bring about significant innovation, and active opposition on the part of only one of these groups to prevent it. In parochial school systems, on the other hand, collaboration between the administration and the church can provide a powerful impetus for change in the other groups.

RULE VII: KEEP AN OPTIMISTIC BIAS

Our society grinds along with much polarization and cruelty, and even the helping professions compose their world of grim problems to be "worked through." The change agent is usually flooded with the destructive aspects of the situations he enters. People in most systems are impressed by one another's weaknesses, and stereotype each other with such incompetencies as they can discover.

This rule does not advise ignoring destructive forces. But its positive prescription is that the change agent be especially alert to the constructive forces which are often masked and suppressed in a problem-oriented, envious culture.

People have as great an innate capacity for joy as for resentment, but resentment causes them to overlook opportunities for joy. In a workshop for married couples, a husband and wife were discussing their sexual problem and how hard they were working to solve it. They were not making much progress, since they didn't realize that sex is not a problem, but an opportunity.

Individuals and groups locked in destructive kinds of conflict focus on their differences. The change agent's job is to help them discover and build on their commonalities, so that they will have a foundation of respect and trust which will permit them to use their differences as a source of creativity. The unhappy partners focus on past hurts, and continue to destroy the present and future with them. The change agent's job is to help them change the present so that they will have a new past on which to create a better future.

RULE VIII: CAPTURE THE MOMENT

A good sense of relevance and timing is often treated as though it were a "gift" or "intuition" rather than something that can be learned, something spontaneous rather than something planned. The opposite is nearer the truth. One is more likely to "capture the moment" when everything one has learned is readily available.

Some years ago my wife and I were having a very destructive fight. Our nine-year-old daughter decided to intervene. She put her arms around her mother and asked: "What does Daddy do that bugs you?" She was an attentive audience for the next few minutes while my wife told her, ending in tears. She then put her arms around me: "What does Mommy do that bugs you?" and listened attentively to my response, which also ended in tears. She then went to the record player and put on a favorite love song ("If Ever I Should Leave You"), and left us alone to make up.

The elements of my daughter's intervention had all been learned. They were available to her, and she combined them in a way that could make the moment better.

Perhaps it's our training in linear cause-and-effect thinking and the neglect of our capacities for imagery that makes us so often unable to see the multiple potential of the moment. Entering the situation "blank" is not the answer. One needs to have as many frameworks for seeing and strategies for acting available as possible. But it's not enough to involve only one's head in the situation; one's heart has to get involved too. Cornelia Otis Skinner once said that the first law of the stage is to love your audience. You can love your audience only if you love yourself. If you have relatively full access to your organized experience, to yourself and to the situation, you will capture the moment more often.